T0210485

Lecture Notes in Computer Science 9194

Jia Zhou · Gavriel Salvendy (Eds.)

Human Aspects of IT for the Aged Population

Design for Everyday Life

First International Conference, ITAP 2015
Held as Part of HCI International 2015
Los Angeles, CA, USA, August 2–7, 2015
Proceedings, Part II

Editors
Jia Zhou
Chongqing University
Chongqing
P.R. China

Gavriel Salvendy
Purdue University
West Lafayette, IN
USA

and

Tsinghua University
Beijing
P.R. China

ISSN 0302-9743 ISSN 1611-3349 (electronic)
Lecture Notes in Computer Science
ISBN 978-3-319-20912-8 ISBN 978-3-319-20913-5 (eBook)
DOI 10.1007/978-3-319-20913-5

Library of Congress Control Number: 2015942800

LNCS Sublibrary: SL3 – Information Systems and Applications, incl. Internet/Web, and HCI

Springer Cham Heidelberg New York Dordrecht London

Printed on acid-free paper

Springer International Publishing AG Switzerland is part of Springer Science+Business Media
(www.springer.com)

Foreword

The 17th International Conference on Human-Computer Interaction, HCI International 2015, was held in Los Angeles, CA, USA, during 2–7 August 2015. The event incorporated the 15 conferences/thematic areas listed on the following page.

A total of 4843 individuals from academia, research institutes, industry, and governmental agencies from 73 countries submitted contributions, and 1462 papers and 246 posters have been included in the proceedings. These papers address the latest research and development efforts and highlight the human aspects of design and use of computing systems. The papers thoroughly cover the entire field of Human-Computer Interaction, addressing major advances in knowledge and effective use of computers in a variety of application areas. The volumes constituting the full 28-volume set of the conference proceedings are listed on pages VII and VIII.

I would like to thank the Program Board Chairs and the members of the Program Boards of all thematic areas and affiliated conferences for their contribution to the highest scientific quality and the overall success of the HCI International 2015 conference.

This conference could not have been possible without the continuous and unwavering support and advice of the founder, Conference General Chair Emeritus and Conference Scientific Advisor, Prof. Gavriel Salvendy. For their outstanding efforts, I would like to express my appreciation to the Communications Chair and Editor of HCI International News, Dr. Abbas Moallem, and the Student Volunteer Chair, Prof. Kim-Phuong L. Vu. Finally, for their dedicated contribution towards the smooth organization of HCI International 2015, I would like to express my gratitude to Maria Pitsoulaki and George Paparoulis, General Chair Assistants.

May 2015

Constantine Stephanidis
General Chair, HCI International 2015

HCI International 2015 Thematic Areas and Affiliated Conferences

Thematic areas:

- Human-Computer Interaction (HCI 2015)
- Human Interface and the Management of Information (HIMI 2015)

Affiliated conferences:

- 12th International Conference on Engineering Psychology and Cognitive Ergonomics (EPCE 2015)
- 9th International Conference on Universal Access in Human-Computer Interaction (UAHCI 2015)
- 7th International Conference on Virtual, Augmented and Mixed Reality (VAMR 2015)
- 7th International Conference on Cross-Cultural Design (CCD 2015)
- 7th International Conference on Social Computing and Social Media (SCSM 2015)
- 9th International Conference on Augmented Cognition (AC 2015)
- 6th International Conference on Digital Human Modeling and Applications in Health, Safety, Ergonomics and Risk Management (DHM 2015)
- 4th International Conference on Design, User Experience and Usability (DUXU 2015)
- 3rd International Conference on Distributed, Ambient and Pervasive Interactions (DAPI 2015)
- 3rd International Conference on Human Aspects of Information Security, Privacy and Trust (HAS 2015)
- 2nd International Conference on HCI in Business (HCIB 2015)
- 2nd International Conference on Learning and Collaboration Technologies (LCT 2015)
- 1st International Conference on Human Aspects of IT for the Aged Population (ITAP 2015)

Conference Proceedings Volumes Full List

1. LNCS 9169, Human-Computer Interaction: Design and Evaluation (Part I), edited by Masaaki Kurosu
2. LNCS 9170, Human-Computer Interaction: Interaction Technologies (Part II), edited by Masaaki Kurosu
3. LNCS 9171, Human-Computer Interaction: Users and Contexts (Part III), edited by Masaaki Kurosu
4. LNCS 9172, Human Interface and the Management of Information: Information and Knowledge Design (Part I), edited by Sakae Yamamoto
5. LNCS 9173, Human Interface and the Management of Information: Information and Knowledge in Context (Part II), edited by Sakae Yamamoto
6. LNAI 9174, Engineering Psychology and Cognitive Ergonomics, edited by Don Harris
7. LNCS 9175, Universal Access in Human-Computer Interaction: Access to Today's Technologies (Part I), edited by Margherita Antona and Constantine Stephanidis
8. LNCS 9176, Universal Access in Human-Computer Interaction: Access to Interaction (Part II), edited by Margherita Antona and Constantine Stephanidis
9. LNCS 9177, Universal Access in Human-Computer Interaction: Access to Learning, Health and Well-Being (Part III), edited by Margherita Antona and Constantine Stephanidis
10. LNCS 9178, Universal Access in Human-Computer Interaction: Access to the Human Environment and Culture (Part IV), edited by Margherita Antona and Constantine Stephanidis
11. LNCS 9179, Virtual, Augmented and Mixed Reality, edited by Randall Shumaker and Stephanie Lackey
12. LNCS 9180, Cross-Cultural Design: Methods, Practice and Impact (Part I), edited by P.L. Patrick Rau
13. LNCS 9181, Cross-Cultural Design: Applications in Mobile Interaction, Education, Health, Transport and Cultural Heritage (Part II), edited by P.L. Patrick Rau
14. LNCS 9182, Social Computing and Social Media, edited by Gabriele Meiselwitz
15. LNAI 9183, Foundations of Augmented Cognition, edited by Dylan D. Schmorrow and Cali M. Fidopiastis
16. LNCS 9184, Digital Human Modeling and Applications in Health, Safety, Ergonomics and Risk Management: Human Modeling (Part I), edited by Vincent G. Duffy
17. LNCS 9185, Digital Human Modeling and Applications in Health, Safety, Ergonomics and Risk Management: Ergonomics and Health (Part II), edited by Vincent G. Duffy
18. LNCS 9186, Design, User Experience, and Usability: Design Discourse (Part I), edited by Aaron Marcus
19. LNCS 9187, Design, User Experience, and Usability: Users and Interactions (Part II), edited by Aaron Marcus
20. LNCS 9188, Design, User Experience, and Usability: Interactive Experience Design (Part III), edited by Aaron Marcus

21. LNCS 9189, Distributed, Ambient and Pervasive Interactions, edited by Norbert Streitz and Panos Markopoulos
22. LNCS 9190, Human Aspects of Information Security, Privacy and Trust, edited by Theo Tryfonas and Ioannis Askoxylakis
23. LNCS 9191, HCI in Business, edited by Fiona Fui-Hoon Nah and Chuan-Hoo Tan
24. LNCS 9192, Learning and Collaboration Technologies, edited by Panayiotis Zaphiris and Andri Ioannou
25. LNCS 9193, Human Aspects of IT for the Aged Population: Design for Aging (Part I), edited by Jia Zhou and Gavriel Salvendy
26. LNCS 9194, Human Aspects of IT for the Aged Population: Design for Everyday Life (Part II), edited by Jia Zhou and Gavriel Salvendy
27. CCIS 528, HCI International 2015 Posters' Extended Abstracts (Part I), edited by Constantine Stephanidis
28. CCIS 529, HCI International 2015 Posters' Extended Abstracts (Part II), edited by Constantine Stephanidis

Human Aspects of IT for the Aged Population

Program Board Chairs: Gavriel Salvendy, USA & P.R. China, and Jia Zhou, P.R. China

- Jenay Beer, USA
- Marc-Eric Bobillier Chaumon, France
- Alan H.S. Chan, Hong Kong
- Veena Chattaraman, USA
- George Demiris, USA
- Jesús Favela, Mexico
- Tova Gamliel, Israel
- Mohammad Anwar Hossain, Saudi Arabia
- Sri Kurniawan, USA
- Jiunn-Woei (Allen) Lian, Taiwan
- Eugene Loos, The Netherlands

- Jean-Claude Marquie, France
- Tracy L. Mitzner, USA
- Lisa J. Molnar, USA
- Karen Renaud, UK
- Marie Sjölinder, Sweden
- António J.S. Teixeira, Portugal
- Patrice Terrier, France
- Gregg Vanderheiden, USA
- Ying Wang, R.P. China
- Wan Chul Yoon, Korea
- Martina Ziefle, Germany

The full list with the Program Board Chairs and the members of the Program Boards of all thematic areas and affiliated conferences is available online at:

http://www.hci.international/2015/

HCI International 2016

The 18th International Conference on Human-Computer Interaction, HCI International 2016, will be held jointly with the affiliated conferences in Toronto, Canada, at the Westin Harbour Castle Hotel, 17–22 July 2016. It will cover a broad spectrum of themes related to Human-Computer Interaction, including theoretical issues, methods, tools, processes, and case studies in HCI design, as well as novel interaction techniques, interfaces, and applications. The proceedings will be published by Springer. More information will be available on the conference website: http://2016.hci.international/.

General Chair
Prof. Constantine Stephanidis
University of Crete and ICS-FORTH
Heraklion, Crete, Greece
Email: general_chair@hcii2016.org

http://2016.hci.international/

Contents – Part II

Health Care Technologies and Services for the Elderly

Home and Work Support

Smart Environments and AAL

Contents – Part I

HCI Design and Evaluation Methods for the Elderly

Aging, the Web and Social Media

The Elderly and Mobile Devices

Health Care Technologies and Services for the Elderly

The Role of Health Status in Older Adults' Perceptions of the Usefulness of eHealth Technology

Ryan Best[1(✉)], Dustin J. Souders[1], Neil Charness[1], Tracy L. Mitzner[2], and Wendy A. Rogers[2]

[1] Florida State University, Tallahassee, FL, USA
{best, souders, charness}@psy.fsu.edu
[2] Georgia Institute of Technology, Atlanta, GA, USA
{tracy, wendy}@gatech.edu

Abstract. Objectives: To investigate the relationship between an older individual's self-reported health and the perceived usefulness of computers in assisting with health-related tasks. Methods: A total of 210 older adults (age ≥ 60) completed questionnaire items pertaining to demographics, general health, perception of importance of daily activities, technology experience and use, and perceived usefulness of computers and the Internet. Results were obtained using a factor analysis and multiple regression. Results: Self-reported health was found to have a significant negative relationship with the importance of health-related activities to daily living (Beta = -0.210) but a significant positive relationship with the perceived usefulness of computers in assisting with the same health-related activities (Beta = 0.151). Discussion: Results indicate that adoption of health-supporting technologies could be facilitated by user-centered designs that better accommodate older adults in poor health. Alternatively, adoption may be facilitated by making the potential usefulness of computers more salient to older adults.

Keywords: Self-reported health · eHealth technology · Technology adoption

1 Introduction

eHealth technologies are a potentially valuable tool for addressing the rising health care needs of the aging American population [1]. These technologies have the potential to facilitate health interventions by both increasing the availability and efficiency of existing health care activities as well as providing additional services. For example, computers and the Internet can be useful in assisting patients with contacting physicians, scheduling appointments, tracking health metrics, maintaining schedules (e.g., for medications or appointments), and searching for health-related information. eHealth alternatives to traditional physician visits have the potential to reduce associated costs of health care by increasing efficiency of patient interaction without sacrificing quality of care [2].

However, subjective attitudes toward the use of eHealth technologies are a potential barrier to adoption. In general, older adults are less likely to use technology than their

J. Zhou and G. Salvendy (Eds.): ITAP 2015, Part II, LNCS 9194, pp. 3–14, 2015.
DOI: 10.1007/978-3-319-20913-5_1

younger counterparts [3, 4]. However, the relationship between attitudes toward the usefulness of eHealth technology and health status is not well-specified. In this study we assess whether those in poorer health, who potentially stand to benefit the most from eHealth interventions, perceive technology as less useful in the health domain.

1.1 Aging and Self-reported Health Status

Health status is often measured by self-report. As a measure, self-rated health is meant to convey an individual's overall sense of physical well-being [5]. Self-rated health has been found to be associated with functional status and objective measures of health [6, 7], mortality [8], and the use of health care services [9]. With regard to functional health, Pinquart [10] found stronger associations between perceived health and basic competence (activities of daily living) than with expanded competence (instrumental activities of daily living and leisure activities). That is, people's perceptions about their health and their competence in basic daily living skills (e.g., bathing, dressing) was more related to their functional health than their competence in activities such as cooking, cleaning, financial management, and medication adherence. Specifically related to technology, self-rated health has been found to display a significant positive relationship with general computer use [11].

Compared to young and middle age adults, older adults are more likely to self-report their health as being fair or poor (23.3 % of 65 + year old adults) and make more visits to the offices of doctors or other health care professionals. Nearly 60 % of 65 + year old adults make more than four office visits per year [12] and perceived health status likely underlies the decision to seek health care.

Critical to interpreting self-reported health ratings, how individuals gauge their subjective health may change over the life span. Older adults may be more likely than younger adults to attribute lower levels of function to the aging process, rather than to poor or deteriorating health [13–15]. Pinquart [10] observed an age-associated decrease in the relationship between perceived health and actual physical and functional health, and concluded that older adults mitigated the aging process's (presumed) negative effect on their global health perception by adapting the objective criteria that they used to judge their perceived health to account for the growing number of age-associated objective health problems. This flexibility in older individuals' definition of perceived health deteriorates in the old-old though, shown by stronger ratings of decline in absolute health in this group. For a more in-depth review of the correlates of subjective health ratings in older adults, and what factors older adults consider when making these ratings, see [9, 16]. Thus, although health status declines with age, perceived health ratings may provide a conservative view of actual health status and potentially mask relationships between health status and other variables.

1.2 Aging and Technology

Older adults may particularly benefit from eHealth technologies due to their disproportionately greater health care needs compared to younger cohorts. An important prerequisite for the adoption of eHealth technologies is that the intended user must be comfortable using computers, the Internet, and other related communications technologies [17]. Unfortunately, age is negatively related to perceived ease of use and perceived usefulness of the Internet [18], two significant predictors of technology acceptance [19], which could represent a barrier for eHealth adoption. Although an age bias against older adults using computer technology has been documented [20], recent Pew reports show that the number of older adults using the Internet grew from 40 % of those polled in 2010 [21] to 57 % in 2014 [4]. Additionally, when provided with training and an opportunity to use the Internet, older adults seem willing to adopt Internet use into their repertoire. In a randomized controlled trial, White et al. [22] taught a group of older adults how to use the Internet in a total of nine hours of small group training over two weeks and found that five months after the end of the trial, 60 % of those in the trained group still used the Internet on a weekly basis. Moreover, older adult Internet users are reportedly comfortable with using the Internet for health-related tasks [23]. Therefore, there is reason to believe that eHealth adoption by older adults has the potential to increase in the future.

1.3 Self-reported Health and eHealth Adoption

Like age, health status could serve as a barrier for eHealth adoption, but the evidence of a relationship between the two variables is mixed. White et al. [22] reported no significant effect of self-reported health status on general Internet use in a convenience sample of 48 older adults in their intervention group (being trained to use a computer system), finding that 65 % of those reporting good to excellent health used the Internet compared to 53 % of those who reported fair to poor health. But, lower self-reported health may be negatively related to using the Internet specifically for health-related activities. In fact, a cross-sectional survey of a representative Parisian sample (n = 3023) investigating the use of the Internet for seeking health information found that after adjusting for socioeconomic characteristics, all ages of individuals reporting lower levels of health used the Internet less for health-related purposes than healthy individuals [24]. Similarly, a study of seven European countries' use of eHealth services found that those individuals who described their health status as poor were less likely to use the Internet for health information, *but* being diagnosed with a long-term illness or disability and a high number of visits to a general practitioner were related to more use of the Internet to access health information [25]. It seems, from the evidence provided in this 2007 study, that those who suffer from illness but who nevertheless feel healthy use the Internet the most for health purposes.

Although previous studies have reported on the relationship between self-reported health and Internet use for health-related purposes, the factors driving those relationships are unclear. Additionally, many of the aforementioned studies investigated a general population, with potential confounds between age and technology use. Among older adult populations, we propose that perceptions about the usefulness of computers for health-related activities may be a contributing factor in the relationship between self-reported health and use of computers and the Internet for health-related purposes. In a focus group study with older adults [26], the perceived benefit of technology was more indicative of technology acceptance than perceived cost. For the individuals who have less computer and Internet experience [20], the perception of usefulness of computers for health-related tasks may be a more appropriate dependent variable than current use of the Internet for health-related tasks. The current study specifically investigated the relationship between older adults' self-reported health status, the importance of health-related activities, and perceived usefulness of computers for health-related activities while controlling for age, income, education, computer use, and frequency of computer use. The control variables were included to account for variance not described by the primary variables.

2 Methods

2.1 Participants

Three hundred and twenty-one older adults (57 % female) between the ages of 60 and 93 (M = 74.62; SD = 5.98) completed and returned the Computer Preferences and Usage questionnaire. Questionnaires were distributed by mail to individuals drawn from databases of older adults in the Tallahassee, FL and Atlanta, GA metro areas. Participants were not compensated for their participation. Further information about the total sample is available in [27].

Only individuals who completed all of the target items (described below under the heading "measures & descriptive statistics") were included in the final analysis, resulting in total sample of 210 older adults (53.5 % female) between the ages of 60 and 89 (M = 74.1; SD = 5.75). An additional 16 respondents completed the questions necessary for computation of the dependent variable but did not provide their age, resulting in a final sample size of 194 older adults for the analysis including age as a variable.

2.2 Materials

The 381-item Computer Preferences and Usage questionnaire comprised five sections. The first two sections of the questionnaire collected information on demographics and technology experience, respectively. The third addressed the individual's perceptions of the importance of various tasks in their daily life. The fourth section addressed the perceived usefulness of computers in assisting with the tasks described in the third section. The fifth section of the questionnaire, which was not used in the current analysis, collected data on preferences for design and features for a hypothetical computer system. Preference and importance-related items were answered on a 5 point Likert scale with "1" indicating strong disagreement, "3" indicating a neutral response, and "5" indicating strong agreement. More information on the measure can be found in [27].

2.3 Measures

The current analysis focuses on only a subset of the overall questionnaire data. The goal was to assess the degree to which self-reported general health was predictive of the perceived importance of health care/maintenance tasks to daily life and the perceived usefulness of computers in assisting with these tasks.

Demographics. In addition to self-reported general health rating, data pertaining to potentially confounding variables (education, income, computer use, and frequency of computer use) were included.

Table 1. Demographics of Participants (total n = 210)

	Sample n	%
General Health		
Poor	2	1
Fair	26	12.3
Good	76	36.2
Very good	79	37.6
Excellent	27	12.9
Education		
Less than high school graduate	1	0.5
High school graduate/GED	25	11.9
Vocational training	3	1.4
Some college/Associate's degree	55	26.2
Bachelor's degree	65	31.0
Master's degree (or other post-graduate training)	50	23.8
Doctoral degree (PhD, MD, EdD, DDS, JD, etc.)	11	5.2
Income		
Less than $10,000	3	1.4
$10,000-$19,999	16	7.6
$20,000-$39,999	42	20.0
$40,000-$59,999	52	24.8
$60,000-$79,999	22	10.5
$80,000 or more	44	21.0
Do not know /Do not wish to answer	31	14.8
Computer Use		
Yes	208	99.0
No	2	1.0
Frequency of Computer/Internet Use		
Less than 1 h per week	13	6.2
Between 1-5 h per week	44	20.9
More than 5, but less than 10 h per week	65	31.0
10 or more hours per week	88	41.9

Importance of Health-Related Tasks. A subset of questions asked participants to rate the importance of 9 different health-related tasks in their daily life. The tasks included communicating with doctors and health professionals, creating appointment reminders, creating medication reminders, managing illnesses, researching health-related issues, researching symptoms, researching health insurance, researching medications, and scheduling appointments.

Usefulness of Computers in Health-Related Tasks. A separate subset of questions asked participants to rate the perceived usefulness of computers in assisting with the same 9 tasks described above.

3 Results

3.1 Demographic Data

The demographic data is presented in Table 1. Out of the 210 participants included in the current analysis, response rate for the demographics questions was 100 % with the exception of the questions pertaining to yearly household income to which 31 individuals indicated either that they did "not know for certain" or did "not wish to answer" and age to which 16 individuals did not respond.

Overall, respondents rated their health positively with a median of "very good". Median values for education (Bachelor's degree; national average: Completed high school), income ($40,000-$59,999; national average: $25,704 for males and $15,072 for females), computer/Internet use (99 %, national average: 53 %), and frequency of computer use (> 5 but < 10 h per week) indicated a rather well educated [28] and technology experienced [21] sample when compared to the national average.

3.2 Factor Analysis

The questionnaire items of interest to the present analysis (importance of health-related tasks and usefulness of computers in health-related tasks) were presented in separate sections of the questionnaire. Even though the two groups of questions were conceptually separated during the questionnaire design, the lack of a priori hypotheses concerning the relationship between self-reported health and the dependent variables led us to conduct an exploratory factor analysis as a method of reducing the health-related task questionnaire items to a set of factor scores. The exploratory factor analysis was conducted on the 18 items covering perceptions of importance to daily life and usefulness of computers for the 9 health-related tasks using principal components extraction and varimax rotation. The initial factor analysis discovered multicollinearity. An investigation of the individual item correlations uncovered that the item "researching symptoms" in both the importance and usefulness subsets was highly correlated (> 0.8) with the other "researching" related items. This item was removed in both subsets, resulting in a final group of 16 items.

The factor analysis on the remaining 16 items used principal components extraction with varimax rotation. Three factors emerged explaining 68.09 % of the variance and were labeled: "usefulness of technology for functional support of health", "importance of functional support of health", and "health-related information gathering". Items and factor loadings are presented in Table 2.

Table 2. Factor loading by questionnaire item. Responses on a scale of 1 to 5, where 1 indicates strong disagreement, 3 indicates a neutral position, and 5 indicates strong agreement

Factor /Items (sorted from highest to lowest mean)	Factor Loading	Mean (SD)
1. Usefulness of Technology for Functional Support of Health		
Computers/Internet are useful…		
Communicating with doctors or other health care professionals	.71	2.75 (1.40)
Creating appointment reminders	.87	2.63 (1.46)
Managing Illnesses	.74	2.63 (1.38)
Scheduling appointments	.86	2.49 (1.50)
Creating medication reminders	.88	2.37 (1.35)
2. Importance of Functional support of health		
Health activity important to my daily life…		
Communication with doctors and health professionals	.74	4.55 (.80)
Managing Illnesses	.77	4.37 (.97)
Scheduling appointments	.80	4.30 (.95)
Creating appointment reminders	.75	4.25 (.90)
Creating medication reminders	.76	3.76(1.19)
3. Health-Related Information Gathering		
Health activity important to my daily life…		
Researching general health issues	.72	3.79 (1.04)
Researching medications	.76	3.72 (1.10)
Computers/Internet are useful…		
Researching general health issues	.74	3.58 (1.36)
Health activity important to my daily life…		
Researching health insurance	.73	3.46 (1.16)
Computers/Internet are useful…		
Researching health insurance	.63	2.80 (1.45)
Researching medications	.77	3.33 (1.44)

3.3 General Health X Health-Related Factors

We examined the unique contribution of health to attitudes by conducting regression analyses predicting each of the three factor scores from general health rating (n = 210). As seen in Table 1, only 2 participants (< 1 % of the total sample) reported their general health as "poor". For purposes of the regression analyses, general health was recoded to combine individuals who reported either "poor" or "fair" health into one group, resulting in four distinct health classifications. A significant positive relationship was found between general health rating and Factor 1 (Usefulness of technology for functional support of health) (Beta = 0.146, p = .044), whereas a significant negative relationship was found between general health rating and Factor 2 (Importance of functional support of health) (Beta = -0.197, p = .006). No significant relationship between general health rating and Factor 3 (Health-related information gathering) was found (Beta = 0.092, p = .202).

To control for the effects of potentially confounding variables, a second regression analysis was conducted with the inclusion of age, education, income, gender, and frequency of computer use (n = 194). The control variables were added in an attempt to isolate the relationship between general health and the health-related factor scores. Overall, in this second model the relationships between general health rating and health-related factor scores were unchanged. A significant positive relationship was found between general health rating and Factor 1 (Usefulness of technology for functional support of health; Beta = 0.151, p = .040), whereas a significant negative relationship was found between general health rating and Factor 2 (Importance of functional support of health; Beta = -0.210, p = .003). No significant relationship between general health rating and Factor 3 (Health-related information gathering) was found (Beta = 0.084, p = .243). Along with the effect of general health rating in these expanded models, age was found to have a positive relationship with Factor 2 (Beta = 0.225, p = .002) and frequency of computer use (Beta = 0.191, p = .008) and being female (Beta = 0.222, p = .005) were found to have a positive relationship with Factor 3.

4 Discussion

In the current study, we investigated the relationship between self-reported health and perceptions of the importance of health-related activities and the usefulness of computers in supporting health-related activities. As a method of reducing the questionnaire data into factor scores, an exploratory factor analysis uncovered three factors among the health-related questionnaire items. The factors were characterized by items pertaining to the functional support of health (Factor 2: Importance of functional support of health), the usefulness of computers in assisting with the same aforementioned support-related activities items (Factor 1: Usefulness of technology for functional support of health), and items related to both the importance of- and usefulness of computers in searching for health-related information (Factor 3: Health-related information gathering).

Self-reported health significantly predicted factor scores for the first two factors; those containing items pertaining to the importance of health-supporting activities and the usefulness of computers in assisting with the same activities. As might be expected, self-reported health had a negative relationship with the importance of health-related activities to daily living (i.e., increasing self-reported health was related to decreasing ratings of importance for health-related activities). On the other hand, self-reported health had a positive relationship with the perceived usefulness of computers in assisting with health-related activities (i.e., increasing self-reported health is related to increasing ratings of perceived usefulness of computers for health-related activities). Even though health management activities were reported to be increasingly important as self-reported health decreased, computers were perceived as being decreasingly useful in assisting with these tasks along the same self-reported health trend.

Unfortunately, the design of the study did not allow us to investigate why individuals reporting lower levels of health perceive computers as being less useful in assisting with health-related tasks that they find important to their daily lives. Two potential reasons can be postulated. First, these individuals may have attempted to use computers to assist with their health management activities but found that computers were too difficult to use or provided no benefit over other methods. Second, these individuals may not have experience with computers being used in the capacities identified in the questionnaire items. Perceptions of computers being less useful for assisting in these activities may be driven by preconceived notions of a computer's ability to assist with a health management activity or a general technology aversion. To better understand these findings, future studies should separate preconceived perceptions and those resulting from experience.

Individuals who have experience with computers in assisting with health-related activities may find them less useful when compared to low-tech aids with which they are familiar. For example, one of the items that loaded onto the "Usefulness of technology for functional support of health" factor asked individuals about their perceptions of the usefulness of computers in assisting with creating medication reminders. Park et al. [29] found that older adults (who were allowed to use external aids to promote medication adherence) were actually more likely than younger adults to adhere to a medication schedule. Participants were able to adhere to the medication schedule at a high level without the use of computer-based reminders. Another item queried perceptions of the usefulness of computers in creating appointments and communicating with doctors. Leong et al. [30] found that patients were satisfied with email communication with physicians, finding it convenient. But, response time for email correspondence was slower compared to traditional telephone contact (i.e., 83.5 % of phone messages were addressed the same day compared to only 38 % of emails being answered the same day). Individuals in poorer health might prefer the low-tech option because they may have more time sensitive health-related issues for which they need to promptly reach their physician. Computers would be less useful in this instance compared to telephone communication.

Our results indicate that self-reported health status was not related to items pertaining to searching for health-related information. Searching for health-related information is the third most frequently reported activity of individuals using the Internet, with 80 % of all Internet users reporting looking for health information online [20]. Of the 40 % of 65 + aged adults who reported using the Internet in 2010, nearly three quarters have looked online for health information. More recent data report 53 % of 65 + aged adults now go online [21], likely resulting in an increase in the population of seniors searching for health information online. But, personal health status may not always act as the catalyst for health information searching online. Seniors reported that their last search for health information was on their own behalf only 48 % of the time [31]. An individual's health status as well as the health status of friends and family could result in an individual searching for health information online.

When dealing with older adults' subjective health measures it is important to note that the number of health problems and general frailty increase in old age. More critically, this one-item rating scale may not provide factorial invariance with age, that is, it may measure different health constructs at different ages. Thus, the relationships observed between this one-item measure of health status and perceptions of the importance of health to everyday activities and the usefulness of computers for supporting health care activities needs further replication. Nonetheless, health status held different relationships with other variables (positive, negative, zero) suggesting that it is a promising predictor.

5 Conclusion

eHealth technologies have the potential as health care aids to increase the availability, efficiency, and effectiveness of health care interventions. In order to facilitate the adoption of these technologies, it is necessary to identify and address potential barriers within the target user base. The current study highlights the importance of educating potential older users about such technologies given current negative perceptions about their utility in supporting health care activities. Individuals reporting lower levels of health, who may receive the most potential benefit from health-related technologies, may be resistant to technology adoption due to a lower perception of usefulness of computers in assisting with health-related activities. Models of technology adoption, such as UTAUT2 [32], indicate that perceived usefulness and perceived ease of use are robust predictors of acceptance and adoption. Melenhorst et al. [26] found that perceived benefit was more related to technology acceptance than perceived cost. The potential benefits provided by the integration of technology in health care interventions should be clearly communicated to potential users to increase the likelihood of adoption. Alternatively, low-health seniors who have found computers less useful than low-tech solutions for supporting health can be specifically included in participatory design. The addition of these individuals in the design process could provide designers with information needed to improve usability and functionality of health technology as well as lower the costs associated with learning to use eHealth technology in the target population.

References

1. Charness, N., Demiris, G., Krupinski, E.A.: Designing TeleHealth for an Aging Population: A human Factors Perspective. CRC Press, Boca Raton (2011)
2. Rohrer, J.E., Angstman, K.B., Adamson, S.C., Bernard, M.E., Bachman, J.W., Morgan, M.E.: Impact of online primary care visits on standard costs: a pilot study. Popul. Health Mnag. **13**(2), 59–63 (2010)
3. Czaja, S.J., Charness, N., Fisk, A.D., Hertzog, C., Nair, S.N., Rogers, W.A., Sharit, J.: Factors predicting the use of technology: findings from the center for research and education on aging and technology enhancement (CREATE). Psychol. Aging. **21**, 333–352 (2006)
4. Fox, S., Rainie, L.: The web at 25 in the U.S. Pew Research Center. http://www.pewinternet.org/files/2014/02/PIP_25th-anniversary-of-the-Web_0227141.pdf

5. George, L.K., Bearon, L.: Quality of life in older persons. Human Sciences Press, New York (1980)
6. Cutler, S.J., Grams, A.E.: Correlates of self-reported everyday memory problems. J. Gerontol. **43**, 82–90 (1988)
7. Menec, V.H., Chipperfield, J.G.: The interactive effect of perceived control and functional status on health and mortality among young-old and old-old adults. J. Gerontol. **52B**, 118–126 (1997)
8. Idler, E.L., Kasl, S.V.: Self-ratings of health: do they also predict change in functional ability? J. Gerontol. B-Psychol. **50**, 244–353 (1995)
9. Strain, L.A.: Good health: what does it mean in later life? J. Aging Health. **5**, 338–364 (1993)
10. Pinquart, M.: Correlates of subjective health in older adults: a meta-analysis. Psychol. Aging **16**(3), 414–426 (2001)
11. Tun, P.A., Lachman, M.E.: The association between computer use and cognition across adulthood: use it so you won't lose it? Psychol. Aging **25**, 560–568 (2010)
12. Centers for Disease Control and Prevention. U.S. Department of Health and Human Services. Summary Health Statistics for U.S. Adults: National Health Interview Survey (2011). http://www.cdc.gov/nchs/data/series/sr_10/sr10_256.pdf
13. Idler, E.L.: Age differences in self-assessments of health: age changes, cohort differences, or survivorship? J. Gerontol. B-Psychol. **48B**, 289–300 (1993)
14. Koval, M., Dobie, S.: Why do the elderly seek or avoid care? Qual. Anal. Fam. Med. **28**, 352–357 (1996)
15. Leventhal, E.A., Prohaska, T.R.: Age, symptom interpretation, and health behavior. J. Am. Geriatr. Soc. **34**, 185–191 (1986)
16. Benyamini, Y., Leventhal, E.A., Leventhal, H.: Elderly people's ratings of the importance of health-related factors to their self-assessments of health. Soc. Sci. Med. **56**, 1661–1667 (2003)
17. Redford, L.J., Whitten, P.: Ensuring access to care in rural areas: the role of communications technology. Generations. **21**(3), 19–23 (1997)
18. Porter, C.E., Donthu, N.: Using the technology acceptance model to explain how attitudes determine internet useage: the role of perceived access barriers and demographics. J. Bus. Res. **59**, 999–1007 (2006)
19. Davis, F.D.: Perceived usefulness, perceived ease of use, and user acceptance of information technology. MIS Quart. **13**, 319–340 (1989)
20. Ryan, E.B., Szechtman, B., Bodkin, J.: Attitudes toward younger and older adults learning to use computers. J. Gerontol. **47**(2), 96–101 (1992)
21. Fox, S.: Health topics: 80 % of internet users look for health information online. Pew Research Center's Internet & American Life Project. http://www.pewinternet.org/~/media//Files/Reports/2011/PIP_Health_Topics.pdf
22. White, H., McConnell, E., Clipp, E., Branch, L.G., Sloane, R., Pieper, C., Box, T.L.: A randomized controlled trial of the psychosocial impact of providing internet training and access to older adults. Aging Ment. Health. **6**, 213–221 (2002)
23. Taha, J., Czaja, S.J., Sharit, J.: Use of and satisfaction with sources of health information among older internet users and non-users. Gerontologist. **49**, 663–673 (2009)
24. Renahy, E., Parizot, I., Chauvin, P.: Health information seeking on the internet: a double divide? results from a representative survey in the Paris metropolitan area, France, 2005-2006. BMC Public Health. **8**, 69 (2008)
25. Andreassen, H.K., Bujnowska-Fedak, M.M., Chronaki, C.E., Dumitru, R.C., Pudule, I., Santana, S., Voss, H., Wynn, R.: European citizens' use of E-health services: a study of seven countries. BMC Public Health. **7**, 53 (2007)

26. Melenhorst, A.S., Rogers, W.A., Bouwhuis, D.G.: Older adults' motivated choice for technological innovation: evidence for benefit-driven selectivity. Psychol. Aging **21**, 190–195 (2006)
27. Mitzner, T.L., Burnett, J., Trexler, E.J., Rogers, W.A., Charness, N.: Guiding the development of PRISM-C: results from the computer preferences and usage questionnaire (HFA-TR-1003). Institute of Technology, School of Psychology, Human Factors and Aging Laboratory, Atlanta, GA (2010)
28. Administration on Aging. U.S. Department of Health and Human Services. A Profile of Older Americans (2011). http://www.aoa.gov/AoARoot/Aging_Statistics/Profile/2011/docs/2011profile.pdf
29. Park, D.C., Hertzog, C., Leventhal, H., Morrell, R.W., Leventhal, E., Birchmore, D., Martin, M., Bennett, J.: Medication adherence in rheumatoid arthritis patients: older is wiser. J. Am. Geriatrics. Society. **47**, 172–183 (1999)
30. Leong, S.L., Gingrich, D., Lewis, P.R., Mauger, D.T., George, J.H.: Enhancing doctor-patient communication using email: a pilot study. J. Am. Board Fam. Pract. **18**, 180–188 (2005)
31. Pew Research Center's Internet and American Life Project. Health online 2013: 35 % of U.S. adults have gone online to figure out a medical condition; Of these, half followed up with a visit to a medical professional. http://pewinternet.org/~/media//Files/Reports/PIP_HealthOnline.pdf
32. Venkatesh, V., Thong, J.Y.L., Xu, X.: Extending the unified theory of acceptance and use of technology. MIS Quart. **36**, 157–178 (2012)

The Use of Smartwatches for Health Monitoring in Home-Based Dementia Care

Costas Boletsis[1(✉)], Simon McCallum[1], and Brynjar Fowels Landmark[2]

[1] Gjøvik University College, Teknologivegen 22, 2815 Gjovik, Norway
{konstantinos.boletsis,simon.mccallum}@hig.no
[2] Inland Hospital Trust Mental Health Division, 2320 Hamar, Norway
BrynjarL@online.no

Abstract. A large number of dementia patients receive home-based care, in order to maintain their independence and improve quality of life and health status. The current formal home-based care model presents certain limitations related to the monitoring of the patients and the reporting of the progression of physical and cognitive decline. In recent years, novel care models and assistive technologies have been proposed in order to improve the quality of care and assistance services. In this paper, we test the assumption that the use of smartwatches for monitoring physical health aspects of dementia patients can benefit formal home-based care, by providing formal caregivers with additional, important information about significant, health-related events that may have happened during the non-visit home care hours. We perform a qualitative feasibility study - consisted of a small-scale usability study with one dementia patient, and an expert (physician) review - in order to test and evaluate the efficacy of a smartwatch intervention in home-based dementia care, as well as to examine its potential for a subsequent, larger-scale study. The smartwatch documented participant's health-related issues regarding night sleep disturbances, potentially frequent toilet visits, daytime snoozing, low sleep quality and early waking up times. Those issues were verified by the project's physician and, subsequently, measures can be taken to ensure the patient's good health, safety, and quality of life.

Keywords: Cognitive impairment · Dementia · Home-Based care · Smartwatch · Wearable computing

1 Introduction

Dementia is one of the most significant problems facing social welfare systems [10,11]. There are an estimated 35.6 million people with dementia worldwide. This number will nearly double every 20 years, to an estimated 65.7 million in 2030, and 115.4 million in 2050 [1].

People with dementia experience progressive cognitive impairments that typically commence with short term memory problems, but can encompass language deficits, difficulties initiating tasks, planning, monitoring and regulating

J. Zhou and G. Salvendy (Eds.): ITAP 2015, Part II, LNCS 9194, pp. 15–26, 2015.
DOI: 10.1007/978-3-319-20913-5_2

behaviour, visuospatial difficulties, agnosia and apraxia [5,11]. Dementia, being a syndrome of a chronic or progressive nature, presents its symptoms in diverse forms and time ranges, gradually leading to serious memory loss. (Fig. 1) [17,23].

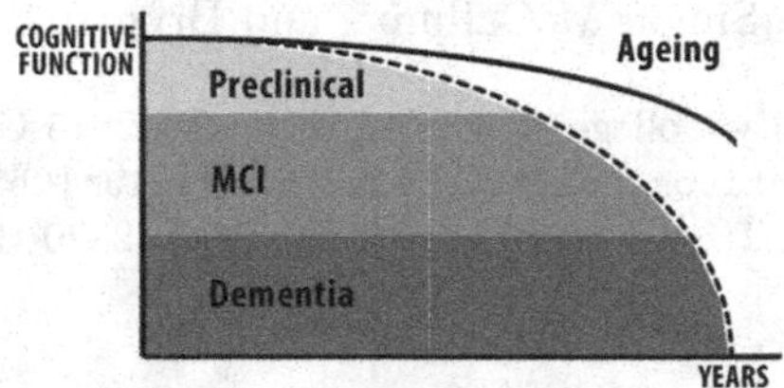

Fig. 1. The continuum of normal ageing and Alzheimer's cognitive decline [19].

A large number of dementia patients receive *home-based care*, in order to maintain their independence and improve quality of life and health status. The home-based care models place point-of-care at patients home and need an organized care system ("care network"), based on the active role and cooperation of the several heterogeneous actors such as: patients, family members, clinicians, general practitioners and social community members [12].

The current *formal home-based care* model, i.e. the monitoring of the patients and the reporting of the progression of physical and cognitive decline, depends on health operators (clinicians, general practitioners, nurses) visits. This presents certain limitations.

Firstly, *the home visits are scheduled based on the passage of time, rather than the physical and cognitive function of the patients over time* [4]. The progressing and chronic nature of dementia creates different screening needs for the patients, thus some patients may require more frequent visits than others, depending on their physical and cognitive function.

Moreover, the health operators of home-based care rely on self reporting and changing symptoms to reconstruct health events and changes, that took place during their absence, therefore the patients' physical and cognitive status during the home visits is merely a sample of ongoing behaviour. As a result of this, *the physical/cognitive home-based screening of dementia patients often follows a holistic and untargeted approach*, which *takes time out of the visits social aspect* (leading to limited quality time with the patients) [5], *it may not produce reliable or valid results* (since the self-report method is utilised in patients with impaired memory) [18] and *increases formal healthcare costs* [6,8,21].

In recent years, novel care models have been proposed in order to improve the quality of care and assistance services [5,12]. Assistive technologies offer much potential and can make a very significant difference to the lives of people with dementia and to their formal caregivers [5]. Indeed, it has been noted that technologies should be part of a formal home-based care package and should be provided in a thoughtful, sensitive, and ethical way [5,22]. The physical health monitoring of dementia patients while performing daily activities, using portable and wearable devices could be a promising option to support formal caregivers in their work, by improving the access to patient information, as well as to support independent well-being of the person with dementia (at home). Various sensor technologies are currently used to monitor emergency situations (e.g. fall detection [3,15,16], wandering [3,15,17]), however the monitoring of physical health during daily activities requires a constant, non-intrusive, comfortable, and reliable mechanism [5,17].

1.1 Contribution and Paper Organisation

In this paper, we test the assumption that the use of smartwatches (i.e. computerised wristwatches) for monitoring physical health aspects of dementia patients can benefit formal home-based care, by providing the physician with additional, important information about significant events that may have happened during the day, and which may not be recollected by the dementia patient in a later session, or witnessed by the visiting nurse. The contribution of this work is summarised as follows:

- perform a small-scale usability study in a real-life scenario, to examine the smartwatch's feasibility for providing additional physical health information of the dementia patient,
- perform an expert review, where the project's physician analyses and interprets the smartwatch's measurements, in order to evaluate their value in supplementing the patient health profile and home-based care, and
- present and suggest the methodology of a qualitative study for examining the effect of a smartwatch health monitoring device on home-based dementia care, potentially utilised for future larger-scale studies of the same - or similar - scope.

The rest of the paper is organised as follows. Section 2 describes background and related work and Sect. 3 presents the study and its details. Next, Sect. 4 discusses the experimentation and results obtained, while the paper is concluded in Sect. 5.

2 Related Work

Cahill et al. [5] provide an overview of the dementia care and the effect of technology on the dementia treatment. This study provides a detailed report of the dementia's clinical aspects and stresses the need for further technological advances. It also documents the user requirements and user needs that the new technological systems and devices should fulfil, in order to support formal caregivers, promote patients' independence and maximise quality of life.

In the same context, Topo [20] maps out the academic space to document the relationship between technology and dementia, by performing a literature review of studies which focus on technology supporting people with dementia and their caregivers. The review analyses 46 studies with original data, as to their goals, the technology used, the treatment environment and the experimental designs. The review of Topo documents the academic work in the researched field and, at the same time, acts as a source of valuable methodological information and issues, which can be of great significance for future related projects.

Through the studies of Cahill et al. [5] and Topo [20], valuable information about the technical, financial, social, and design features of a future dementia-related technological system can be obtained. The basic user requirements, user needs, as well as experimental and formal health-care logistics are satisfied by the technology of the smartwatch, as supported in the studies of Raghunath & Narayanaswami [14] and Shin et al. [17]. The study of Raghunath & Narayanaswami [14] is an early exploration of the smartwatch's technical features, revealing its potential as a promising interface paradigm. Shin et al. [17] put the previous knowledge into practice, by utilising a smartwatch device for monitoring the location of dementia patients (in case of wandering) and for detecting the user' steps, in order to further analyse the patients' activities. The step detection algorithm of the smartwatch showed a promising 94 % accuracy, highlighting the need for the extraction of more physical data from the smartwatch use and for "a more comprehensive analysis of a patient's activities..." [17]. Basis B1 (developed by Basis Science Inc.) is a smartwatch that can track accurately several activity states (i.e. sleeping, walking, being active). The Basis B1 smartwatch was used in a sleep-related study of Patel et al. [13], where it was shown that the sleep analysis algorithm of the smartwatch demonstrated excellent agreement with polysomnography data for sleep duration and sleep staging.

3 The Smartwatch Study

3.1 Motivation and Goal

The motivation for this study comes from the need for better formal home-based health care. The current formal home-based care model presents certain limitations (as described in Sect. 1), which do not allow formal caregivers to have a representative image of the dementia patients' physical health status, during the non-visit hours.

The ultimate goal of this study is: by optimising the current care model and by improving the access to significant patient health information, to support formal caregivers in their work, thus further supporting independent living and well-being of the person with dementia (at home) [20]. The current study can be seen as a first step towards the acceptance of a future, medical smartwatch device, both from the patient's and the doctor's perspectives.

3.2 Technology and User Requirements

The overall opportunities technology can create for people with dementia have to date not been fully utilised, since choosing the appropriate assistive technology is not always easy [5,9]. Today, there is a wide range of different technologies that can be adapted and used for people with dementia, to help them maintain their independence and improve their health status and quality of life. People react differently to different assistive technologies and there are no quick fix solutions in dementia care, nor do solutions necessarily have to be highly technical [5].

The nature of dementia may make people cautious and suspicious of trying new devices [5]. Therefore certain user requirements should be taken into consideration, according to Cahill et al. [5]:

- the new device/product should fulfil the individual and formal caregiver needs,
- the design of the product is important, focusing on its familiarity and the fact that no new learning should be required on the part of the person with a dementia,
- a comprehensive assessment of needs should take place ideally at home with a health service professional fully trained in dementia care,
- pre-testing is critical to ensure that the chosen device/product is reliable and effective, and
- it is important to find a product that suits the individual and is not complex or stigmatising.

In this study, we propose the use of smartwaches for monitoring the physical functions of dementia patients. A smartwatch has many attractive features as a form factor for a wearable computer. It has the advantage of always being with the user, having a ubiquitous and non-intrusive presence, its design - being a wristwatch - is quite familiar, and its use is not complex or stigmatising [14].

3.3 The Device: Basis B1 Smartwatch

The smartwatch chosen for this study is the Basis B1 band (Fig. 2), based on the the fullfilment of the requirements described in Sect. 3.2. Its choice over several competitors was based on the several metrics captured by the sensors, as well as the simple user interaction required.

The charging and uploading-data process of the Basis B1 is straight-forward (by just connecting it to an external device, e.g. laptop or mobile), while it is able to automatically recognise the user's activity state (e.g. sleeping) without the user pressing any button to mark the start or end time of the activity (which is the case with many similar smartwatches). Therefore, the Basis B1 is a simple, plug-n-play device, which does not require new learning from the user's side and whose full functionality does not require any interaction, apart from charging it, once every 3 days.

The Basis B1 band is a new class of health and wellness device that is a sophisticated convergence of five sensor technologies and advanced data aggregation and analysis. Through sophisticated algorithms, the Basis B1 band translates the user's biosignals into metrics on how everyday activities affect the body. These daily activities (sleeping, walking, and being active) offer information that can help provide an objective overview of daily behaviour [2].

Fig. 2. The back side (*left*) and the front side (*right*) of Basis B1.

The Basis B1 band is built around five sensors that act in concert and simultaneously in real time to provide a view of a persons health immediately and over extended periods of time: optical blood flow sensor, 3D accelerometer, body temperature, ambient temperature reading, and galvanic skin response [2]. Rather than make assumptions from limited metrics, Basis uses all five of its sensors and its analysis to estimate the current state of the user [2].

Since the Basis is not a medical device, there is the issue of the validity and accuracy of the physical health data. In this study, we do not deal with the correlation between the "gold standard" medical devices and the Basis B1; we examine the smartwatch's feasibility for providing additional, potentially useful physical information about the dementia patient.

3.4 Design Study

Feasibility studies of potential therapies are useful and important, not only to test and evaluate the potential effectiveness of an intervention, but also to refine and improve it prior to a subsequent study [7]. Although data from qualitative evaluation are less often considered as a means to assist investigators to develop and refine research interventions, it has been shown that such data provide useful information to capture and describe processes, explore individual differences between experiences and outcomes, evaluate an evolving intervention, and understand the meaning of an intervention for its participants [7]. As stated before, dementia presents its symptoms in diverse forms and time ranges, making the qualitative evaluation of a health intervention on dementia patients a difficult task. In this feasibility study, we are using a qualitative approach to test and evaluate the efficacy of a complementary technological (smartwatch) intervention in home-based dementia care, as well as to examine its potential for a subsequent, larger-scale study.

The study follows a two-conditioned (C1: patient receiving home-based care and not wearing the smartwatch, C2: patient receiving home-based care and wearing the smartwatch), within-subject design with one late-stage dementia patient in home based-care as participant. The within-subjects study design is chosen for addressing the problem of individual variability, since it would be nearly impossible to maintain sample homogeneity across several dementia patients. The sample size, even though cannot produce statistically significant results, can lead to clear and safe indications. The choice of only one participant is based, firstly, on practicality reasons, since "building" and maintaining a long, medical relationship with a patient is a resource-demanding and time-consuming process. The second reason is that we want to avoid the generalisation of the study's results. Even if we have tried to select subjects of the same age, gender, background, and cognitive status, we could not then extrapolate the results to encompass wider groups, because of dementia's various manifestations. The cost-benefit analysis of the feasibility study's elements led us to the chosen sample size.

The utilised feasibility study can be divided in two stages. At first, we conduct a *small-scale usability study* of the Basis B1 smartwatch use with a dementia patient in home-based care. At this stage, we focus on the smartwatch as an artifact, evaluating its functionality and its usefulness. The evaluation process is based on observational reports and informal open interviews conducted by the assigned physician Dr. Brynjar Landmark. The usability part of the study took place from mid-October to early November 2014 with one advanced dementia patient in home-based care using the Basis device. The participant has mobility aids (walking frame, stair elevator), gets four home nurse visits/day, needs assistance for nearly all daily chores and has no ability to communicate about recent events since all short term memory is lost (MMSE score$<$10). During the usability stage of the study, the quality/social time with the participant was increased, in order for the project's physician to be able to document all the necessary elements for the usability study and the following expert review.

An *expert review* takes place at the next stage, where the project's physician evaluates the usability results of the first stage and interprets the smartwatch's measurements. The interpretation of the measurements are validated by observational means, repetitive behavioural patterns over the study duration and reporting sessions with the participant and the visiting nurse. The expert/project's physician has accumulated a vast expertise in treating dementia and cognitive impaired patients and has spent a considerable amount of time with the participant prior to the study, getting accustomed to the sleeping, eating and, generally, daily habits.

3.5 Results

The usability study gave us valuable insight on the smartwatch's use by frail elderly.

- The smartwatch did not cause any discomfort or anxiety to the participant, as it acquired the role of a regular watch. Consequently, the smartwatch was used only as a time indicator and the participant was able to read the numericals on the display. The charging of the device was taking place during the doctor's or nurse's visit and the smartwatch was removed during the process.
- A discovered issue was that almost no walking steps and activity were recorded, due to the use of the walking frame by the participant. Furthermore, for

short periods of time there were disruptions in the smartwatch's functionality (Figs. 3 and 5). Apart from those minor issues - which did not affect the final measurements - the sensors were functioning properly, getting the additional measurements, i.e. heart rate, skin temperature, and perspiration.

The project's physician was able to extract useful information regarding the participant's daily activities and physical state from the devices measurements. The analysis of the measurements is patient-specific and the patient's medical background plays an important part in the process. However, the range of information (direct or indirect) that can be obtained from the smartwatch are indicative of its potential for use with dementia patients. The main observations from the Basis' use are presented hereafter.

- The patient was up many times in the night, which the advanced dementia patient cannot recall the next morning. Night disturbances are part of the behavioural disturbances of dementia and are difficult to quantify (Fig. 3).
- Steps are not registered when using a walking frame, however the patients heart rate increased at any effort, revealing patterns of activities, such as toilet visits (Fig. 3). This is a common problem in patients with this degree of disability, who are not able to notify their surroundings; it is all up to the caretakers to recognise the change in behaviour or frequency. Changes in this pattern, together with temperature/perspiration, may alert caretakers to e.g. recognise a urine infection and take a urine sample to the physician.
- The total registered sleeping time for the participant was 12-16 hours (Fig. 4); the registered data sums up naps and total daytime snoozing in a manner the caretakers are not able to evaluate accurately. The majority of the smartwatch's sleeping-related measurements revealed that there is not much difference between day and night sleep, registering almost the same sleeping pattern in the afternoon as in the night. This situation could be addressed by adding activities or daytime stimulation.
- When the home care nurse arrives for morning assistance (around 10:00-11:00 am), the Basis monitor can indicate when the patient woke up. In many instances, the patient had been awake for three hours before assistance arrived (Fig. 5). The arrival hours may be adjusted to the patients need.

4 Discussion

It is true that home-based care cannot be provided to the patient on a 24/7 basis. However, a smartwatch monitoring device, like the Basis B1, can provide formal care with user's health information, for those hours that are not covered by the caretakers' visit. Especially for cognitive impaired, elderly patients - where the self-reporting method can be unreliable or even impossible - such devices can provide an estimation of the patient's daily activities. Naturally, the measurements of the device can lead to several interpretations, depending on the user's health profile/background and daily habits.

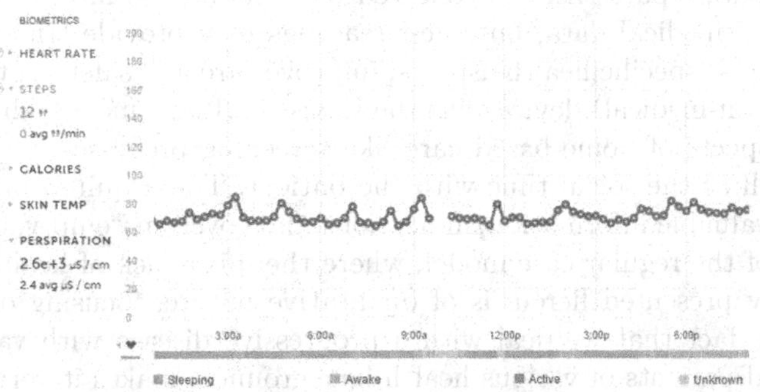

Fig. 3. An indicative day's measurements, showing the disrupted sleep pattern and the heart rate increases of the participant.

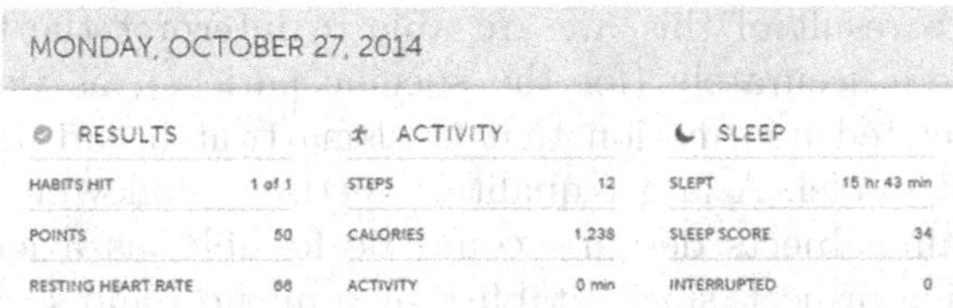

MONDAY, OCTOBER 27, 2014

RESULTS		ACTIVITY		SLEEP	
HABITS HIT	1 of 1	STEPS	12	SLEPT	15 hr 43 min
POINTS	50	CALORIES	1,238	SLEEP SCORE	34
RESTING HEART RATE	66	ACTIVITY	0 min	INTERRUPTED	0

Fig. 4. A day's measurements, presenting the total sleeping time in a 24-hour period.

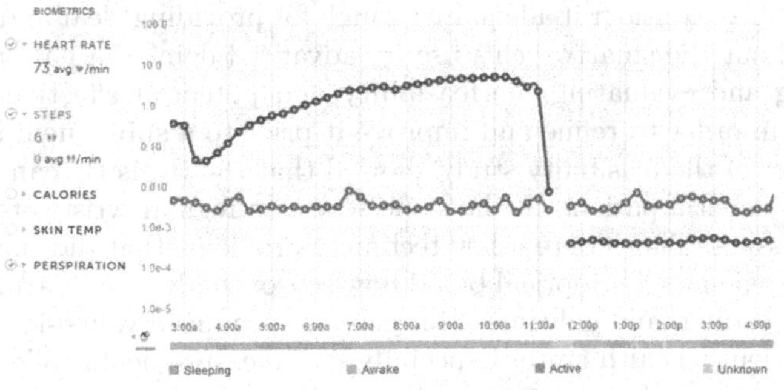

Fig. 5. An instance of the participant waking up at 7:00 am, but getting out of bed at 11:00 am (perspiration drops), when the home care nurse arrives.

In our case, even though the Basis B1 smartwatch provided new insight in the patient's daily patterns, the collected data cannot be interpreted as accurate, validated medical data, but their readings may provide triggers for caretakers to address specific health aspects, improve care and safety of the patients. Well-being (non-medical) devices like the Basis B1, by no means, should replace important aspects of home-based care like screening processes, physical monitoring, as well as the social time with the patient. The acquired measurements can provide valuable information/indications and cover an "empty space" inside the context of the regular care model, where there is a lack of health data.

The study presented herein is of qualitative nature, focusing on a real-life scenario. The fact that we deal with a progressive disease with various manifestations and patients of various health backgrounds, makes it very difficult to study the effectiveness of a smartwatch monitoring device in a quantitative way, on a large sample and under realistic conditions, without facing generalisation and assignment bias issues. The focus on one participant allows us to detect the changes that the Basis B1 smartwatch brings into the regular patient care, since, in fact, we utilise a two-conditioned, within-subject study. Prior to the Basis B1 experimental process, there is an extensive treatment period of the dementia patient and a deep knowledge of the patient's medical background and daily habits. As a result of this, we are able to interpret the following Basis measurements more accurately (for the specific patient), as well as recognise the new health-related information that the smartwatch can introduce to the current treatment model. A larger qualitative study - following the same two-conditioned, within-subjects design - could be feasible, as a longitudinal and resource-demanding project, since establishing a medical and social relationship with each patient is a challenging, time-consuming, yet necessary task. The small sample size of the study ensured that the observational evaluation method, the extra social time, and all the safety/ethical cautions would take place in an unobtrusive, focused manner, setting the groundwork for a robust, qualitative methodology which could serve a large-scale project of the same or similar scope. Even though, it is clear that such a sample size cannot produce statistically significant results, we consider it adequate enough for providing clear and significant indications about the smartwatch's use by advanced dementia patients, as well as for testing and evaluating the feasibility and potential effectiveness of the intervention, in order to refine and improve it prior to a subsequent study.

The results of the feasibility study showed that the Basis B1 can be used by a late stage dementia patient, in the same way as a regular wristwatch, without causing any issues. There were a few technical problems that did not affect the overall measurements. The optical blood flow sensor, body temperature, ambient temperature reading, and galvanic skin response produced valuable information about the patient's health state. Especially, the measurements collected during the non-visit hours, when the patient was not physically monitored, managed to provide a representative image of the patient's health-related actions during those hours. As presented in Sect. 3.5, the Basis B1 documented health-related issues regarding night sleep disturbances, potentially frequent toilet visits, daytime snoozing, low sleep quality and early waking up times. Those issues were verified by the project's physician and, subsequently, measures can be taken to ensure the patient's good health, safety, and quality of life.

5 Conclusion

The study - even though constrained by certain limitations - assisted in acquiring meaningful data that would be difficult or even impossible to otherwise acquire. The ultimate outcome of the study is the promising potential that a smartwatch device can have for dementia patients in home-based care. Additional features like an alert notification system (setting patient-personalised measurements' "thresholds"), GPS functionality (addressing the wandering problem), and a local database with limited access (for secure access and storing of sensitive health information) could be implemented as part of a future certified, medical, smartwatch device.

References

1. Alzheimer's Disease International: Dementia statistics (2014). http://www.alz.co.uk/research/statistics. Accessed 26 December 2014
2. Basis Science Inc.: Basis B1 Band Presents the Whole Picture - in Real Time, All the Time (2011). http://www.mybasis.com/wpcontent/uploads/2012/01/BasisTechnologyOverview1014111.pdf. Accessed 22 December 2014
3. Beauvais, B.S., Rialle, V., Sablier, J.: Myvigi: an android application to detect fall and wandering. In: The Sixth International Conference on Mobile Ubiquitous Computing, Systems, Services and Technologies, UBICOMM 2012, pp. 156–160 (2012)
4. Boletsis, C., McCallum, S.: Connecting the player to the doctor: utilising serious games for cognitive training & screening. In: NordiCHI 2014 Workshop on Designing Self-Care for Everyday Life (2014). https://designingselfcareforeverydaylife.files.wordpress.com/2014/10/connecting-the-player-to-the-doctor.pdfx. Accessed 28 January 2015
5. Cahill, S., Macijauskiene, J., Nygrd, A., Faulkner, J., Hagen, I.: Technology in dementia care. Technol. Disabil. **19**(2), 55–60 (2007)
6. Comas-Herrera, A., Northey, S., Wittenberg, R., Knapp, M., Bhattacharyya, S., Burns, A.: Future costs of dementia-related long-term care: exploring future scenarios. Int. Psychogeriatr. **23**, 20–30 (2011)
7. Fonteyn, M., Bauer-Wu, S.: Using qualitative evaluation in a feasibility study to improve and refine a complementary therapy intervention prior to subsequent research. Complement. Ther. Clin. Pract. **11**(4), 247–252 (2005)
8. Jönsson, L., Eriksdotter-Jönhagen, M., Kilander, L., Soininen, H., Hallikainen, M., Waldemar, G., Nygaard, H., Andreasen, N., Winblad, B., Wimo, A.: Determinants of costs of care for patients with Alzheimer's disease. Int. J. Geriatr. Psychiatry **21**(5), 449–459 (2006)
9. Marshall, M.: ASTRID: A Social and Technological Response to Meeting the Needs of Individuals with Dementia and Their Carers. Hawker Publications, London (2000)
10. McCallum, S.: Gamification and serious games for personalized health. Stud. Health Technol. Inform. **177**, 85–96 (2012)

11. Norwegian Ministry of Health and Care Services: Dementia Plan 2015: making the most of good days. Norwegian Ministry of Health and Care Services (2007)
12. Paganelli, F., Giuli, D.: An ontology-based system for context-aware and configurable services to support home-based continuous care. IEEE Trans. Inf Technol. Biomed. **15**(2), 324–333 (2011)
13. Patel, S., Ahmed, T., Lee, J., Ruoff, L., Unadkat, T.: Validation of Basis Science Advanced Sleep Analysis: Estimation of Sleep Stages and Sleep Duration (2014). http://www.mybasis.com/wp-content/uploads/2014/04/Validation-of-Basis-Science-Advanced-Sleep-Analysis.pdf. Accessed 22 December 2014
14. Raghunath, M.T., Narayanaswami, C.: User interfaces for applications on a wrist watch. Pers. Ubiquit. Comput. **6**(1), 17–30 (2002)
15. Schwarzmeier, A., Besser, J., Weigel, R., Fischer, G., Kissinger, D.: A compact back-plaster sensor node for dementia and Alzheimer patient care. In: Sensors Applications Symposium (SAS), 2014, pp. 75–78. IEEE (2014)
16. Schwenk, M., Hauer, K., Dutzi, I., Mohler, J., Najafi, B.: Predicting in-hospital falls in geriatric patients with dementia using one body-worn sensor. J. Am. Geriatr. Soc. **62**, S146–S147 (2014)
17. Shin, D.-M., Shin, D.I., Shin, D.: Smart watch and monitoring system for dementia patients. In: Park, J.J., Arabnia, H.R., Kim, C., Shi, W., Gil, J.-M. (eds.) GPC 2013. LNCS, vol. 7861, pp. 577–584. Springer, Heidelberg (2013)
18. Smith, S., Lamping, D., Banerjee, S., Harwood, R., Foley, B., Smith, P., Cook, J., Murray, J., Prince, M., Levin, E., Mann, A., Knapp, M.: Measurement of health-related quality of life for people with dementia: development of a new instrument (DEMQOL) and an evaluation of current methodology. Health Technol. Assess. **9**(10), 1–93 (2005)
19. Sperling, R.A., Aisen, P.S., Beckett, L.A., Bennett, D.A., Craft, S., Fagan, A.M., Iwatsubo, T., Jack, C.R., Kaye, J., Montine, T.J., Park, D.C., Reiman, E.M., Rowe, C.C., Siemers, E., Stern, Y., Yaffe, K., Carrillo, M.C., Thies, B., Morrison-Bogorad, M., Wagster, M.V., Phelps, C.H.: Toward defining the preclinical stages of Alzheimer's disease: recommendations from the National Institute on Aging-Alzheimer's Association workgroups on diagnostic guidelines for Alzheimer's disease. Alzheimer's & Dementia **7**(3), 280–292 (2011)
20. Topo, P.: Technology studies to meet the needs of people with dementia and their caregivers: a literature review. J. Appl. Gerontol. **28**(1), 5–37 (2009)
21. Wimo, A., Jnsson, L., Gustavsson, A., McDaid, D., Ersek, K., Georges, J., Gulcsi, L., Karpati, K., Kenigsberg, P., Valtonen, H.: The economic impact of dementia in europe in 2008 - cost estimates from the eurocode project. Int. J. Geriatr. Psychiatry **26**(8), 825–832 (2011)
22. Woolham, J.: Assistive Technology in Dementia Care: Developing the Role of Technology in the Care and Rehabilitation of People with Dementia - Current Trends and Perspectives. Hawker Publications, London (2006)
23. World Health Organization: Dementia - a public health priority (2014). http://www.who.int/mental_health/neurology/dementia/en/. Accessed 27 December 2014

Lack of Development and Usability Descriptions in Evaluation Reports on Online Health Information Tools for Older Patients

Sifra Bolle[1(✉)], Julia C.M. van Weert[1], Ellen. M.A. Smets[2], and Eugène F. Loos[1]

[1] Amsterdam School of Communication Research/ASCoR, University of Amsterdam, Amsterdam, The Netherlands
{s.bolle,j.c.m.vanweert,e.f.loos}@uva.nl

[2] Department of Medical Psychology, Academic Medical Centre, University of Amsterdam, Amsterdam, The Netherlands
e.m.smets@amc.uva.nl

Abstract. New media play an increasing role in the everyday life of older individuals. They extensively use the Internet to search for health-related information. In our systematic review we found that online health information tools have been proven to be effective in improving self-efficacy and several clinical outcomes in older (≥ 65 years) patients. The aim of this study was to evaluate the development and usability of the effective online health information tools. The reporting of the development of the online health information tools turned out to be too succinct. Moreover, we were unable to evaluate the usability of online health information tools as none of them were publicly available. We argue the need to report more detailed information about the development and usability of online health information tools in evaluation studies in order to replicate findings and to develop new evidence-based online health information tools for older patients.

Keywords: Older adults · eHealth · Website usability · Online health information tools

1 Introduction

To provide patients with information, a wide variety of online health information tools, such as websites, patient portals, and mobile phone applications have been developed. As common diseases such as cancer, diabetes and hypertension are often diseases of older people [1], they are also increasingly confronted with online health information tools. These tools therefore play an increasing role in the everyday life of older patients. To illustrate, research dating back to 2002 showed that only 22 % of Europeans that were over 50 years of age had access to the Internet and only 38 % had interest in retrieving health information online [2]. More than a decade later, 85 % of the Dutch population between 65 and 75 years of age has access to the Internet in 2013. Of this group, 57 % uses the Internet to search for health information [3]. These numbers indicate that the medical digital divide is narrowing down.

J. Zhou and G. Salvendy (Eds.): ITAP 2015, Part II, LNCS 9194, pp. 27–37, 2015.
DOI: 10.1007/978-3-319-20913-5_3

In a recent systematic review we found evidence for the effectiveness of online health information tools for older patients (≥ 65 years) on self-efficacy as well as clinical outcomes (i.e., blood pressure, hemoglobin levels, and cholesterol levels) in four online health information tools [4]. These four online health information tools have in common that they consist out of multiple functions. Online health information tools for patients can have several functions, such as information provision, enhancing information exchange, and promoting self-management [5]. Online health information tools that were able to improve self-efficacy, clinical outcomes, or both, had in common that they had a 'promoting self-management' function, and additionally had a 'providing information' and/or an 'enhancing information exchange' function.

Now that we know that these tools can lead to positive outcomes in older patients, it is important to investigate how we can develop evidence-based online health information tools for this age group. Although we found that four online health information tools were effective, it is still unclear how the interventions were developed and how they were used by the participants. By distinguishing the useful, useable and used components of the interventions we can build a base for the systematical development of evidence-based online health information tools for older patients.

The first step in this process is to take a closer look at the development of the online health information tools that have been proven to be effective. More specifically, an important step that needs to be considered in the development of online health information tools is its usability as its benefits can only be realized if older adults can use them. Usability is an important issue to consider for this age group in particular, as older individuals have more problems using computer technologies [6]. The aim of this paper is therefore to give a more qualitative and in-depth overview of the effective online health information tools by evaluating the development process and the usability of these tools.

1.1 The Development of Online Health Information Tools

We evaluated the development of the online health information tools using the Medical Research Council's (MRC) framework and the Spiral Technology Action Research (STAR). The Medical Research Council's framework is a framework for the development of health-related interventions in general [7]. This framework distinguishes four key elements of intervention development.

- The first element considers the development of the intervention by identifying existing evidence, identifying and developing theory, and modelling the process and outcomes;
- The second element relates to the assessment of the feasibility of the intervention by examining the key uncertainties that have been identified during the development;
- The third element exists of the implementation of the intervention;
- The fourth element considers the evaluation of the effectiveness of the intervention.

Additionally, there are frameworks specifically designed for the development of web-based interventions. One example is the Spiral Technology Action Research (STAR) model [8]. This model describes the steps that need to be taken during the development of web-based health education and behavior change promotion. The model consists of five cycles.

- The first cycle considers listening to the intended users of the intervention. For example, by understanding how users interact with existing systems;
- The second cycle concerns the development of a plan for addressing the users' needs and to identify the technical and organizational requirements of the intervention;
- During the third cycle, the online health information tool will be developed. These three cycles relate to the first element of the MRC framework. At the end of this cycle, the first prototype will be developed;
- During the fourth cycle, the prototype will be evaluated. This cycle can be compared with the second element of the MRC framework, in which the feasibility of the intervention is tested;
- In the fifth and last cycle, the online health information tool will be launched and implemented. This cycle relates to the third element of the MRC framework.

These frameworks have in common that developing interventions is a holistic cyclical process. Van Gemert-Pijnen et al. [9] also argue for a holistic framework which takes the complexity of healthcare and the involvement of a wide variety of stakeholders into account. Also, both models have in common that interventions need to be theory-based. Using these frameworks, we will evaluate the development of the online health information tools that have proven to be effective in our systematic review.

In this study we will describe the development, the evaluation of the feasibility, and the implementation of the online health information tools, which corresponds to the first three elements of the MRC framework and the first four cycles of the STAR model. The last element of the MRC framework (the evaluation of the effectiveness of the online health information tools) is reported in our systematic review [4].

1.2 The Usability of Online Health Information Tools

As is mentioned before, in the development of online health information tools, their usability is an important issue to consider. Online health information tools that are easy to use for younger individuals might not be easy to use for older individuals, for instance because older individuals are less experienced with new media. To evaluate the usability of the online health information tools for older individuals we will use the guidelines that Pernice and Nielsen [10] have proposed to develop easy to use websites for this age group. They identify seven usability categories, of which four are specifically relevant for the development of online health information tools: (1) presenting information and text, (2) presenting navigational elements and links, (3) search, (4) and web address and home page. The other three categories are not relevant for the evaluation of the usability of online health information tools as they relate to webshops and the operating system or browser of the user.

2 Method

In our systematic review [4], we assessed the methodological quality of studies evaluating the effectiveness of online health information tools. We rated the studies that used a Randomized Controlled Clinical Trial (RCT) design as high or low quality. Next we performed a 'Best Evidence Synthesis' by attributing levels of evidence to the outcomes of the online health information tools (i.e., evidence, limited evidence, indicative findings, no/insufficient evidence). The level of evidence was attributed to outcomes of online health information tools for which significant improvements were found in two or more high quality RCTs. For four online health information tools we found evidence for the outcomes self-efficacy, blood pressure, hemoglobin levels, and/or cholesterol levels. To describe the development of the online health information tools we used articles that reported on the effectiveness of the four online health information tools from our systematic review. From the articles, we extracted the information about the content and development of the online health information tool. Next, we searched the literature for articles in which the development of the online health information tools was reported. To evaluate the usability of the online health information tools, we tried to obtain the online health information tools online. We created a codebook using the above mentioned four website design guidelines that were proposed by Pernice and Nielsen [10], see Table 1. However, the online health information tools were not publicly available (anymore) and no screenshots were reported that allowed us to evaluate the usability. We sent emails to the corresponding authors of the articles of the evaluation studies. Only one author responded and pointed out that their online health information tool no longer existed and had closed at the end

Table 1. Codebook te evaluate usability of online health information tools for older patients

Category	Number of items	Example items
Presenting information and text	9	• The text size is at least 12 point by default
Presenting navigational elements and links	10	• The website contains static navigational elements (e.g., no moving menus) • A link's color changes after a user visits it
Search	7	• The user's query is repeated in the search results • The search field is precisely labeled. The word *search* is revered for open fields where users can type in actual search queries
Web address and home page	5	• A homepage link is added to all website pages, except the homepage. The homepage link only links to the homepage and not to secondary homepages • If an unregistered user tries to log-in erroneously, a message will be given telling what parts of the website can be used without logging in, and how to use them. Also the benefits of logging in are briefly outlined

of the evaluation study. Hence, we were not able to evaluate the usability of the online health information tools. Therefore, we will only report the evaluation results of the development of the four online health information tools for older patients which we found to be effective in our review.

3 Results

3.1 Description of the Online Health Information Tools

Of the four online health information tools, two were developed for patients with diabetes and two for patients with hypertension. One of the online health information tools for diabetes patients concerned a website where patients could enter their blood glucose readings, exercise programs, weight changes, blood pressure, and medication data [11, 12]. In case of changes, nurses could contact their patients via e-mail or instant-messaging/chat. The website also offered weekly online educational group discussion via MSN Messenger software. This online health information tool significantly improved self-efficacy, blood pressure, hemoglobin levels and cholesterol levels. The second intervention for diabetes patients concerned an online health information tool consisting of four functions: (1) videoconferencing with nurse case managers, (2) remote monitoring of glucose and blood pressure, (3) a web-portal providing access to patients' own clinical data and secure web-based messaging with nurse case managers, and (4) access to an educational web site [13–17]. The use of this online health information tool also significantly improved self-efficacy, blood pressure, hemoglobin levels and cholesterol levels. One of the online health information tools for patients with hypertension concerned a home monitoring system where patients could send their self-measured blood pressure readings for review by their attending nurse or doctor, who in turn had the possibility to give automated patient decision support by text or email. Patients had the possibility to view their blood pressure readings on a website [18]. Patients that used this online health information tool had significantly improved blood pressure. The other online health information tool for patients with hypertension concerned a personal education program on a wireless tablet computer [19]. Patients received immediate individually tailored feedback on their medication use. Also, corrective strategies were printed and sent to nurses prior to the patient's primary care visit. The use of this online health information tool significantly improved self-efficacy.

The development of these online health information tools will be described in the following paragraphs following the first three elements of the MRC framework and the first three development cycles of the STAR model.

3.2 Phase 1: Identifying Existing Evidence

All authors report that the online health information tools had been developed using existing empirical findings on how online health information tools can improve health-related outcomes. However, as there is little evidence, the empirical evidence that is used is very general or of low quality [18], making it difficult to predict whether the results will maintain for the specific older patient groups.

Moreover, a strong theoretical basis of the online health information tool has not been reported, with the exception of Neafsey et al. [19]. Based on the Social Cognitive Theory, they expected that their online health information tool could 'enhance self-efficacy in patients to motivate them to adopt safe self-medication practices and modify adverse self-medication behaviors' [19, p. 161]. The authors argue that animations form mental pictures in the patients mind and give meaning to their own self-medication experiences and will therefore guide their future self-medication behavior. In addition, the animations in the intervention have related multiple choice questions, which allow observational learning. Tailored interactive questions with feedback about self-efficacy will help patients gain confidence in self-medication. In line with the principle of 'reciprocal determinism', the learning is expected to continue during the visit with the nurse.

3.3 Phase 2: Assessing the Feasibility of the Online Health Information Tools

To the best of our knowledge, the feasibility of three of the four online health information tools has been reported. Bond [20] discusses the lessons learned from the development and the implementation of the online health information tool. During its development, the online health information tool was tested on its usability by focus groups, heuristic evaluations and think aloud sessions. First, a focus group session with 22 older patients with diabetes was held. They gave suggestions about the lay-out, the content and the design of the website. The prototype of the website was adapted according to participants' suggestions. However, the author did not report which suggestions from the participants were retrieved and which elements of the prototype were adapted. Next, during the heuristic evaluation, experts identified usability problems using criteria and guidelines based on the W3C's Web Accessibility guidelines [see 21]. Bond reports some examples of the feedback from the experts, such as the provision of a 'contact us' link and/or FAQ, prominent 'how to use the site' information, a 'site tour', a 'forgot your password mechanism', and a second navigation bar at the bottom of each page. Finally, the usability of the online health information tool was tested using think aloud sessions with five older participants that were recruited from assisted living facilities. Although the author reports that several problems were indicated by the participants, she does not mention which specific problems were mentioned and targeted. Moreover, the author does not mention the age of the participants or whether the five participants that participated in the think aloud session were patients with diabetes.

Starren et al. [22] describe the development objectives of one online health information tool. The first design objective relates to the usability of the technology. However, we found no literature concerning any usability tests with (potential) users of the system. The authors only mentioned one measure that was taken to make the system easy to use, namely a customized mousepad with four buttons that allows patient to answer video calls, to access the Internet, and to submit glucose and blood pressure.

Lin, Neafsey, and Strickler [23] reported on the usability testing of the PEP-NG eHealth intervention among older (≥ 60 years) patients with hypertension. The PEP-NG intervention was developed in four stages. In the first stage, the usability of the first pilot version of the prototype was assessed by five focus group participants. The second version of the prototype was adapted according to the results of the focus group. The results of the focus group interviews were, however, not reported. During the second stage, the second pilot version of the prototype was again tested using a focus group with new participants. Also, two participants were involved in a think aloud session. Using the results of the focus group and the think aloud observations, the first version of the prototype was developed for the formal usability testing. In stage three, this version was tested using a think aloud protocol and two focus groups. The second version of the prototype was adapted on the basis of the first formal usability tests. During the fourth stage, the second version of the prototype with a new sample of ten participants in a think aloud session. On the basis of these results, the beta-version of the PEP-NG was built. However, the authors have not reported the outcomes of the usability tests that they have performed.

3.4 Phase 3: The Implementation and Usage of the Online Health Information Tools

To our knowledge, the implementation of two of the four online health information tools was reported. For the implementation of one online health information tool [20], computers were installed in the homes of the study participants. The researchers faced some problems with the installation of the computers, such as viruses, a failing modem, memory board or printer, which was caused by a lack of software testing and damages to the computer during transportation. Next, the study participants received a training manual and one-on-one training to learn how to use the online health information tool. The training was based on computer classes for older adults. After the online health information tool was implemented, its performance was tested during the evaluation study. At that time some problems occurred. First, the website of the online health information tool had been hacked. However, the author did not report how this problem was solved. Second, there were problems with the hosting service. Participants received error messages and were not always able to submit their data. To resolve this issue, participants could sent the error messages to technical support personnel that resolved the problems and improved the online health information tool. The study lost one subject that was not able to enter data. For another online health information tool, the technical implementation has been described in detail [see 22]. The authors make the recommendation that the human component must not be eliminated during the implementation of the online health information tool. Adequate interaction between evaluation staff, implementation staff, and the telecommunication vendor is very important.

Some data on the usage have been reported, to our knowledge, for three out of the four online health information tools. For one online health information tool it was reported that the use varied widely under study participants [12]. However, the authors did not report if this influenced the outcomes of the study. With regard to the use of another online health information tool, the authors report a high compliance with the blood monitoring system, where participants submitted their blood pressure readings. However, the authors did not report whether the participants used the decision support information they received or whether they looked up their blood pressure readings on the website [18]. One online health information tool was used at the office of the healthcare provider. Participants were assisted in using the online health information tools where needed. The online health information tool was used before every visit to the nurse [19]. It is, however, not clear whether patients could use the online health information tool at home.

4 Conclusion and Discussion

The aim of this study was to evaluate the development and the usability of online health information tools for older patients, that have been proven to be effective. Following the MRC framework and the STAR model, the first step in intervention development is to identify existing evidence to create a theoretical and empirical basis. Most online health information tools were based on a scarce amount of literature and only for one online health information tool [19] the theoretical basis was reported. The next step in the development of online health information tools is testing its feasibility and more specifically its usability. Only usability tests of two online health information tools were reported. However, only the methods and not the results of these tests were reported. Hence, we were not able to identify the specific usability issues of the online health information tools. This information would be very useful in the development of new online health information tools for older patients. For two online health information tools, the implementation was described. Lessons learned from the implementation of existing online health information tools provide us with useful information for the implementation of new online health information tools for older patients. With regard to the usage of the online health information tools, the authors did not report any information about the use of the separate components. As a result we cannot be sure what the active ingredients of the interventions were.

It is important to consider that the evaluation of online health information tools is part of the development cycle and reporting about the evaluation is as important as the other parts of the development cycle. Therefore, we stress that authors adhere to existing guidelines to report on the development and usability of online health information tools in detail. Specifically, we recommend using the CONSORT EHEALTH guidlines [24]. According to these guidelines, eleven points are highly recommended or are essential to report on the development and content of the online health information tools. Authors should report (1) the names, credentials, and affiliations of the developers, sponsors and owners, (2) the development process (i.e., usability testing), (3) revisions and updating, (4) the source code and/or screenshots/screen-capture video, and/or flowcharts of the algorithms used to ensure replicability, (5) the URL of the application and/or details of where the intervention is archived, (6) how participants accessed the online health information tool, (7) the mode of delivery, features/functionalities/components of the intervention and comparator, and the theoretical framework, (8) use parameters, (9) the level of human involvement, (10) any prompts/reminders (e.g., letters, emails, phone calls, SMS) to use the online health information tool, (11) any co-interventions. According to these guidelines, the four interventions were described too succinct.

Regarding the usability, we were not able to evaluate the online health information tools, as they were not publicly available. Not reporting the online health information tool itself by reporting the URL, the place where the intervention is archived, or screenshots of the interventions, poses a threat for the replicability, which is essential in scientific reporting. Moreover, replication and synthesizesation of the results is important as this can help in the development of new evidence-based interventions. Because the development of online health information tools can be a complex process and a lot of different choices have to be made, we emphasize the importance of reporting the content of the online health information tool as detailed as possible.

The fact that we found that online health information tools were not available anymore also has an important implication for practice. Online health information tools are often developed with the help of (large) grants. When these tools have been proven to be effective in improving health-related outcomes, it is important that more patients can benefit from these tools. We therefore suggest that researchers put more effort in the dissemination and long term implementation of effective online health information tools for older patients.

To conclude, evidence exists that online health information tools can be effective in improving self-efficacy and clinical outcomes in older patients. Researchers are increasingly evaluating the outcomes of online health information tools [25], even for older patients [4]. However, it is still difficult to replicate the studies and synthesize results, as the online health information tools are not reported in detail. We therefore recommend to systematically develop online health information tools, which have a strong theoretical basis and which have been extensively tested on usability. Also, we argue that it is essential to report the content of the online health information tool in detail in a way that other researchers should be able to replicate the study. The CONSORT-EHEALTH is a useful tool to follow when reporting studies on online health information tools. Following these guidelines allows for the replicability of studies and the synthesizing of research results, and consequently a strong evidence base for the development of online health information tools for older patients.

References

1. Barnett, K., Mercer, S., Norbury, M., Watt, G., Guthrie, B.: Epidemiology of multimorbidity and implications for health care, research, and medical education: a cross-sectional study. Lancet **380**, 37–43 (2012)
2. Stroetmann, V.N., Husing, T., Kubitschke, L., Stroetmann, K.A.: The attitudes, expectations and needs of elderly people in relation to e-health appllications: results from a european survey. J. Telemed. Telecare **8**(S2), 82–84 (2002)
3. Statistics Netherlands. ICT Gebruik van Personen naar Persoonskenmerken. (ICT Use by Persons Subject to Personal Characteristics). http://statline.cbs.nl/StatWeb/publication/?VW=T&DM=SLNL&PA=71098NED&D1=33-133&D2=0,13&D3=a&HD=111219-1122&HDR=G1,G2&STB=T

4. Bolle, S., Van Weert, J.C.M., Daams, J.G., Loos, E.F., De Haes, J.C.J.M., Smets, E.M.A.: Online Health Information Tool Effectiveness for Older Patients: A Systematic Review of the Literature. Journal of Health Communication (2014) (in Press)
5. Bol, N., Scholz, C., Smets, E.M.A., Loos, E.F., de Haes, J.C.J.M., van Weert, J.C.M.: Senior patients online: Which functions should a good patient website offer? In: Stephanidis, C., Antona, M. (eds.) HCII 2013. LNCS, vol. 8010, pp. 32–41. Springer, Heidelberg (2013)
6. Craig, P., Dieppe, P., Macintyre, S., Michie, S., Nazareth, I., Petticrew, M.: Developing and evaluating complex interventions: the new medical research council guidance. Bri. Med. J. **337**, a1655 (2008)
7. Becker, S.A.: A study of web usability for older adults seeking online health sources. ACM Trans. Comput.-Hum. Interact. (TOCHI) **11**, 387–406 (2004)
8. Skinner, H.A., Maley, O., Norman, C.D.: Developing internet-based ehealth promotion programs: the spiral technology action research (STAR) model. Health Promot. Pract. **7**, 406–417 (2006)
9. Van Gemert-Pijnen, J.E.W.C., Nijland, N., Van Limburg, M., Ossebaard, H.C., Kelders, S.M., Eysenbach, G., Seydel, E.R.: A holistic framework to improve the uptake and impact of eHealth technologies. J. Med. Internet Res. **13**, e111 (2011)
10. Pernice, K., Nielsen, J.: Web Usability for Senior Citizens. Design Guidelines Based on Usability Studies with People Age 65 and Older. Nielsen Norman Group, Fremont (2002)
11. Bond, G.E., Burr, R., Wolf, F., Price, M., McCurry, S.M., Teri, L.: The effects of a web-based intervention on the physical outcomes associated with diabetes among adults age 60 and older: A randomized trial. Diabetes Educ. **9**, 52–59 (2007)
12. Bond, G.E., Burr, R.L., Wolff, F.M., Feldt, K.: The effects of a web-based intervention on psychosocial well-being among adults age 60 and older: A randomized trial. The Diabetes Educator **36** (2010)
13. Shea, S., Weinstock, R.S., Starren, J., Teresi, J., Palmas, W., Field, L.: Lantigua, R.A.: A randomized trial comparing telemedicine case management with usual care in older, ethnically diverse, medically underserved patients with diabetes mellitus. J. Am. Med. Inf. Assoc. **13**, 40–51 (2006)
14. Shea, S., Weinstock, R.S., Teresi, J.A., Palmas, W., Starren, J., Cimino, J.J., Eimicke, J.P.: A randomized trial comparing telemedicine case management with usual care in older, ethnically diverse, medically underserved patients with diabetes mellitus: 5 year results of the IDEATel study. J. Am. Med. Inf. Ass. **16**, 446–456
15. Trief, P.M., Teresi, J.A., Izquierdo, R., Morin, P.C., Goland, R., Field, L., Weinstock, R.S.: Psychosocial outcomes of telemedicine case management for elderly patients with diabetes: the randomized IDEATel trial. Diabetes Care **30**, 1266–1268 (2007)
16. Trief, P.M., Teresi, J.A., Eimicke, J.P., Shea, S., Weinstock, R.S.: Improvement in diabetes self-efficacy and glycaemic control using telemedicine in a sample of older, ethnically diverse individuals who have diabetes: the IDEATel project. Age Ageing **38**, 219–255 (2009)
17. Trief, P.M., Izquierdo, R., Eimicke, J.P., Teresi, J.A., Goland, R., Palmas, W., Weinstock, R.S.: Adherence to diabetes self care for white, african-american and hispanic american telemedicine participants: 5 year results from the IDEATel project. Ethn. Health **18**, 83–96 (2013)
18. McKinstry, B., Wild, S., Pagliari, C., Lewis, S., Stoddart, A., Padfield. P.: Telemonitoring based service redesign for the management of uncontrolled hypertension: multicenter randomized controlled trial. Br. Med. J. **346** (2013)
19. Neafsey, P.J., M'Ian, C.E., Ge, M., Walsh, S.J., Lin, C.A., Anderson, E.: Reducing adverse self-medication behaviors in older adults with hypertension: results of an e-Health clinical efficacy trial. Ageing Int. **36**, 159–191 (2011)

20. Bond, G.E.: Lessons learned from the implementation of a web-based nursing intervention. Comput. Inf. Nursing **24**, 66–74 (2006)
21. Berners, T.L.: W3C Web Accessibility Initiative Web site. Guidelines from the World Wide Web Consortium for a more Accessible Web Site (2005). http://www.w3.org/WAI
22. Starren, J., Hripcsak, G., Sengupta, S., Abbruscato, C.R., Knudson, P.E., Weinstock, R.S., Shea, S.: Columbia university's informatics for diabetes education and telemedicine (IDEATel) project: technical implementation. J. Am. Med. Inf. Ass. **9**, 25–36 (2002)
23. Lin, C.A., Neafsey, P.J., Strickler, Z.: Usability testing by older adults of a computer-mediated health communication program. J. Health Commun. **14**, 102–118 (2009)
24. Eysenbach, G.: CONSORT-EHEALTH: improving and standardizing evaluation reports of web-based and mobile health interventions. J. Med. Internet Res. **13**, e126 (2011)
25. Kreps, G.L., Neuhauser, L.: New directions in eHealth communication: opportunities and challenges. Patient Edu. Couns. **78**, 329–336 (2010)

Older Users' Rejection of Mobile Health Apps a Case for a Stand-Alone Device?

André Calero Valdez(✉) and Martina Ziefle

Human-Computer Interaction Center, RWTH Aachen University, Campus-Boulevard 57, Aachen, Germany
{calero-valdez,ziefle}@comm.rwth-aachen.de

Abstract. Mobile health apps make up an enormous market in mobile phone app stores. These apps allow automatic measurement of vital parameters and transmission of data to the doctor. Older users often reject mobile health apps for various reasons. We investigate the influence of several user factors on the willingness to use a health app integrated in a mobile phone vs. a stand-alone device. Furthermore we look into the modality for data transmission and its influence on the overall acceptance. In a questionnaire study (n=245) we ask both healthy and chronically ill (heart disease and diabetes) for their preferences. Using multiple linear regression analysis we found that the motives to use such a device influence the preference for an integrated device four times more strongly than the participants age. Still, the older the users are the more they prefer a stand-alone device.

Keywords: Diabetes · Heart disease · User diversity · Mobile phones · Aging · Technology acceptance

1 Introduction

The size and structure of the global demography has changed drastically. Life expectancy has increased over 30 years and projections claim that within the next 40 years another two billion people will be added to the world population of already seven billion. This increase comes mostly from people over 50 years of age. And as a complication the amount of people with an age of 60 and older will quadruple by the year 2050 [1]. According to the Statisches Bundesamt [2], Germany will have at least 22 million seniors older than 65 years in 2060.

The increase of life expectancy comes with a price tag. In regard to chronic diseases, a larger proportion of older citizens means a higher prevalence. Currently there are 285 million people diagnosed with diabetes worldwide [3]. A conservative projection goes as far as to assume 438 million diabetes patients in 2030, which would mean a doubling of total prevalence in comparison to 2000 [4]. Similar projections can be made for heart disease [5]. In an effort to treat the chronically ill and prevent further surge in prevalence, mobile health applications are often used [6] in treatment and prevention [7]. Whether these approaches are

J. Zhou and G. Salvendy (Eds.): ITAP 2015, Part II, LNCS 9194, pp. 38–49, 2015.
DOI: 10.1007/978-3-319-20913-5_4

feasible is still largely a question [8]. Very few studies go further than pilot studies when using mobile phones for health applications. Yet, we don't know whether using the mobile phone at all is the best approach for all users.

2 Related Work

Technical requirements for a mobile health device may be derived from literature [9] and interviews with medical experts, but when personal data is stored on the Web further considerations must be made.

Kollmann et al. [10] successfully tested a mobile application for type 1 Diabetes patients with ten patients of a mean age of 36 years. Data transmission of recorded data was still done manually in their study. Similar to an approach suggested by Tani et al. [11] who evaluated their solution positively with twenty patients. Their approach also needed manual transmission of data. With the discontinuation of Google Health in 2012, online patient records must be investigated again to find out whether application acceptance or privacy requirements triumph when storing vital parameters of patients in the cloud.

Using mobile phones or mobile applications for health applications has been tried several times, yet acceptance of these devices, critical to their success, is not fully understood. Lv et al. [12] investigated the application of a mobile phone health application with 492 participants. Yielding only self-efficacy as the major factor in acceptance for the elderly. Hung et al. [13] using the TAM model investigated acceptance of a mobile health application and confirmed the model, adding the notion that younger users are more likely to use mobile health applications. The TAM model based on the factors *ease of use* and *usefulness* also shifts the acceptance to more general questions: Why do I need it? Can I use it?

Self-efficacy in using a device stems from performance in using a device [14]. Performance itself requires domain knowledge [15] and an expertise with the technological framework (i.e. mobile phones). Suitable user interfaces may guide in constructing adequate mental models [16], but inexperienced users will revert to other models, insufficient to explain the behavior of the application, thus leading to poor performance. This is particularly true for elderly users. A device with no prior mental model, and thus not dependent on mobile phone UI frameworks, could theoretically appeal to these mobile phone "refuseniks".

The overall acceptance though may depend on further aspects than self-efficacy and mobile phone integration. The cultural context [17], the hedonic aspects of the design [18], the adequacy of the technological framework [19] and infrastructure [6] all influence acceptance of health technology. In some cases going "mobile" is not always the best option [20]. Maybe using a dedicated device harmonized with users privacy needs could bridge the gap of mobile health application acceptance.

3 Method

In this article we investigate the influence of user diversity on the preference to have a health application integrated into a mobile phone vs. a stand-alone device. We did this using two independent questionnaires, one for patients with diabetes and one for heart disease patients.

Here the applied methodology of the study is presented. This includes used scales as well as independent and dependent variables. The questionnaires were designed with SurveyMonkey.com[1] as an online survey. Half of the answers were assessed paper-based to reach a non-online audience as well. The target-audience for the diabetes survey was diabetics or people with a diabetes-precursor who might need to use a diabetes management assistant. A similar target group was selected for the heart patient survey.

3.1 Variables

As independent variables we assessed a persons age, gender, and health status. As dependent variables we assessed the following concepts using six- and four-point Likert scales. We assessed the decrease in vision using three items (PVD, see Table 1) under the assumption that small screens pose a barrier to people with hampered vision. We also assessed the perceived ease of use of mobile phones, by measuring the perceived ease of use of eight features of mobile phones (MPEoU, see Table 2). As the target variable we measured the desire for an integrated device using three items (MPI, see Table 3).

Table 1. Perceived Vision Disability scale (PVD). Scale Reliability: $\alpha_1 = .777$, $\alpha_2 = .728$, $\alpha = .738$. Explained variance: 67 %

I am able to read letters on a mobile phone without my glasses.
I am able to read books easily without my glasses.
I am able to read writing on bill-boards without my glasses.

In order to get common scales, all items were z-transformed before generating additive scales. Subscripts indicate the sample (1=Diabetes, 2=Heart Disease). Using no subscript indicates the joint sample. In addition we measured items on how an integration might look like in a mobile phone in regard to automatic data transfer (see Fig. 2). These items measure the modality of how automatic data transfer should be conducted. Should the user be notified, asked for permission or be responsible for data transmission?

We also measured five additional motives and four possible barriers for a mobile phone integration to get further information for the reasons of user preferences (see Table 5 at the end of the article). These were derived from previous qualitative research (i.e. interview studies) are now being tested for their influence.

[1] http://www.surveymonkey.com.

Table 2. Mobile Phone Ease of Use scale (MPEoU). Scale Reliability: $\alpha_1 = .850$, $\alpha_2 = .889$, $\alpha = .874$. Explained variance: 70 %

On my mobile phone I find the following feature easy to use ...	
... making a call.	... sending/reading a text message.
... using the address book.	... using the calendar.
... using the integrated camera.	... using the GPS.
... surfing the Internet	... setting an alarm

Table 3. Mobile Phone Integration scale (MPI). Scale Reliability: $\alpha_1 = .806$, $\alpha_2 = .709$, $\alpha = .729$. Explained variance: 65 %. *=inverted item

The device should ...
... be a separate device (in contrast to integrated into a mobile phone)*
... integrate various features (e.g. health and calendar).
... be integrated into a mobile phone.

3.2 Hypotheses

Because of the results from previous studies and from related work we derive the following hypotheses (see also Fig.1). Older participants should have a stronger perceived disability in vision (H_1). They should also perceive mobile phones to be less easy to use (H_2) in accordance with previous results. Gender does often show a strong influence on technical self-efficacy and thus on perceived ease of use (H_3). The health status should influence the preference for data transfer modality (H_8) as diabetics have drastically more experience in dealing with data (i.e. diary keeping). This should also influence the motives and barriers for a possible mobile phone integration (H_4).

Furthermore we expect the users expertise with a mobile phone to influence the willingness to have a health app integrated into their mobile phone. Thus PVD (H_5) and MPEoU (H_6) should influence the MPI. Also the motives and barriers should influence the MPI (H_7).

4 Results

Both surveys are evaluated descriptively on their own while common results are derived after z-transformation of the same variables. We report the descriptive statistics for both surveys separately and jointly, when applicable. Here, central tendency (means and standard errors) are reported in figures (error bars denote the standard error). We then report bi-variate correlations for the hypotheses that we investigate. For normally distributed data we use Pearson's r in all other cases we use Spearman's rank coefficient ρ. We assume a level of significance of .95 and .99 for the α-error probability. This means that there is a 1/20 chance

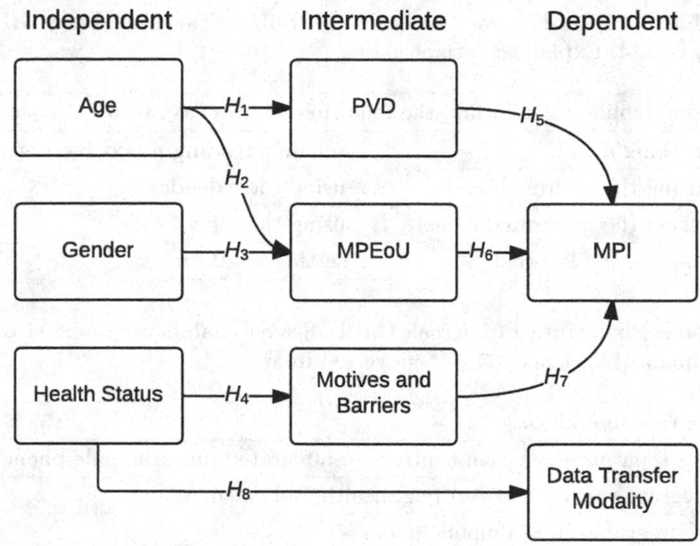

Fig. 1. Hypotheses between independent, intermediate and dependent variables.

of significant findings being caused by chance and a 1/100 chance for highly significant findings.

In order to understand the strength of prediction, multiple linear regression analyses for MPI is used. The Remove-Method was chosen. Reported are the model and its predictors. The increase of explained variance over the scale mean is reported for the assumed underlying population (adj. R^2). Furthermore the F-Value with its degrees of freedoms for the model are reported along with its significance ($F(df1, df2)$, p). Additionally the parameter estimates and their standard errors (B, SEB) are reported, as well as non-standardized and standardized slope (β). When a single predictor does not increase the explained variance significantly, it is excluded from the model.

For effect sizes the r (correlation, student's t-test) or adjusted R^2 (MLR) values are reported.

4.1 Description of the Sample

A total of $N = 310$ participants took part in our study ($n_1 = 120$,$n_2 = 190$) from which $N = 245$ completed the questionnaire fully ($n_1 = 59$,$n_2 = 186$). Out of the participants completing the survey 134 were men (54 %) and 111 were women. We had 56 diabetics, 80 heart disease patients and 109 healthy participants. The latter were all showing precursors for either disease nonetheless. The age of the sample ranged from $16 - 87$ ($r_1 = 16 - 87$,$r_2 = 19 - 85$), with a mean age of $M = 51.2$ years ($SD = 16$). Both samples showed a similar age distribution ($M_1 = 43.4$, $M_2 = 53.6$, $SD_1 = 16$, $SD_2 = 15.7$).

4.2 Descriptive Results

In general when looking at the modality preferences for automatic data transfer, healthy and heart disease patients show a similar picture (see Fig. 2). Both groups agree with data transmission in general, although they prefer to be informed, asked for permission or want to trigger the transfer themselves. Diabetes patients on the other hand show a stronger preference for not transmitting data automatically. Their preferences can be seen to be inverse to both healthy and heart disease patients. Diabetics mostly prefer to trigger the data transfer themselves (see Fig. 2).

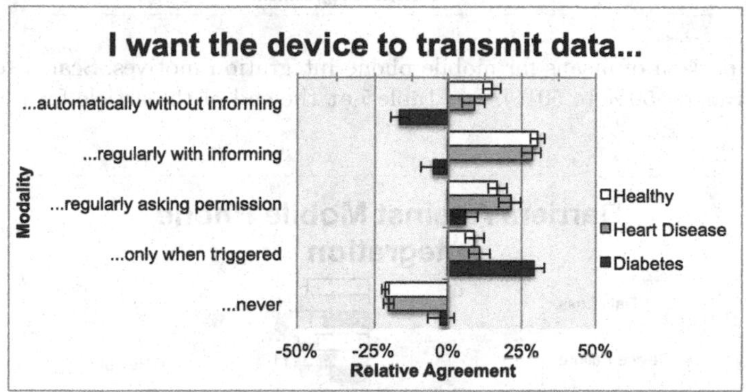

Fig. 2. Comparison of means for data transfer modality. Data transfer means transfer to the personal doctor in this case. Scaled to relative agreement (range: -50 % to 50 %)

When looking at what would get a participant to argue in favor of mobile phone integration the five investigated motives show very similar behavior as the data transfer modality. Healthy and heart disease patients show similarly high agreement with the motives *practicality* and *familiarity*, indicating that they assume the integration would benefit from their prior mobile phone experience. Diabetics on the other hand are not so convinced about *practicality* but almost agree on *familiarity* (see Fig. 3). The motive *usage frequency* seems irrelevant for diabetics (they have to use their glucose meter anyways) while healthy and heart disease participants do see a benefit. A very similar pattern can be seen for the motive *enjoyment*. The highest agreement between the three groups can be seen in the *inconspicuousness* motive. All agree that having a health app integrated into a phone is a benefit because it is inconspicuous (see Fig. 3).

The barriers to use a mobile health app when integrated into a mobile phone are perceived less strongly than the motives. Here, the three groups show relatively similar behavior. *Data loss* and *device failure* are seen as the most important barriers for a mobile health application. The general tendency to reject mobile phones is not pronounced and the *ease of use* is also not seen as a barrier. Diabetics in particular disagree that a lack of *ease of use* would pose a barrier for mobile health applications (see Fig. 4).

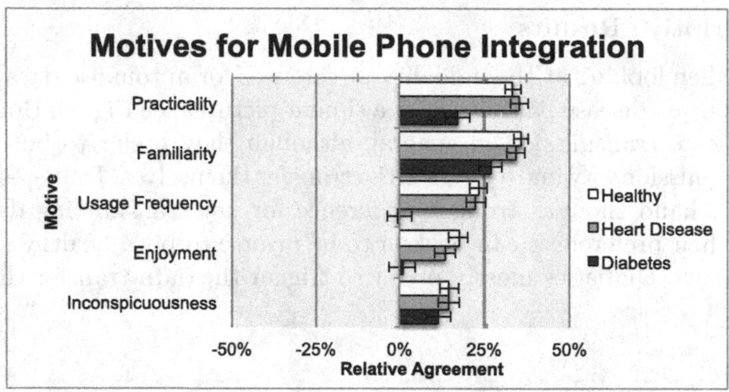

Fig. 3. Comparison of means for mobile phone integration motives. Scaled to relative agreement (range: -50 % to 50 %). See Table 5 at the end of the article for items.

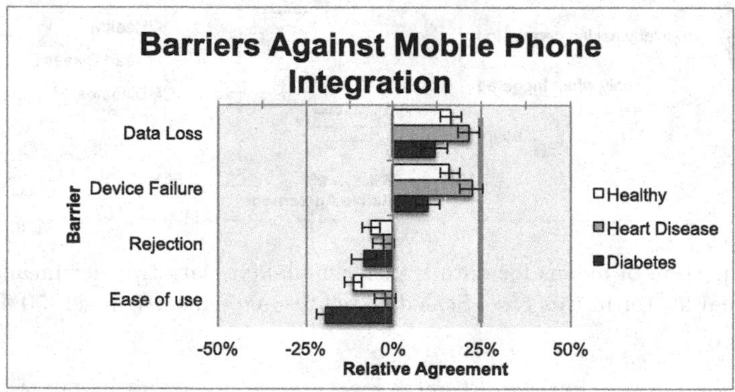

Fig. 4. Comparison of means for mobile phone integration barriers. Scaled to relative agreement (range: -50 % to 50 %). See Table 5 at the end of the article for items.

Both motives and barriers can be used as a additive scale and will be used in correlation analyses. Here motives showed a good reliability (Cronbach's $\alpha = .818$) where the barriers only showed a questionable to acceptable reliability (Cronbach's $\alpha = .699$).

4.3 Interaction Analysis

In order to verify our hypotheses we look at various correlations between independent, intermediate and dependent variables (see Fig. 5). We were able to verify a correlation between age and all intermediate variables, the strongest for the perceived ease of use of mobile phones ($r = .464$, $p < .01$). The older a participant was, the less they perceived a mobile phone to be easy to use (H_2 ✓). Even an association with both barriers and motives were found ($r = -.210$, $p < .05$), albeit a small one. Older participants show stronger agreement with barriers and less agreement with motives. Also as expected (H_1 ✓), older users were more disabled in regard to their vision capabilities ($r = .291$, $p < .01$).

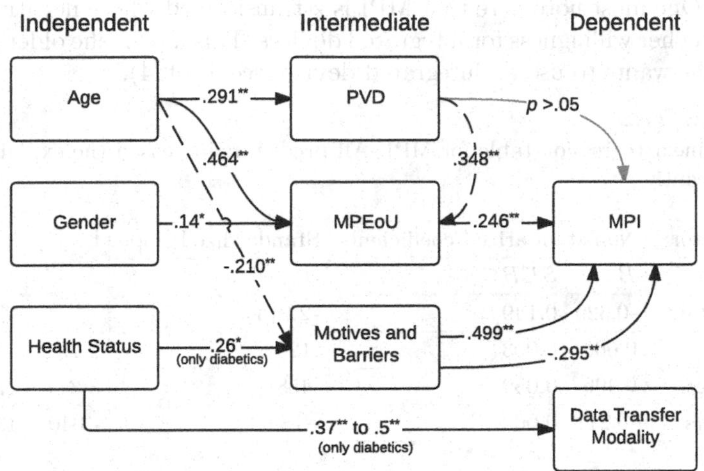

Fig. 5. Bi-variate correlations between variables. Numbers denote Pearson's r or Spearman ρ depending on scale level. Dashed lines indicate correlations that were not hypothesized.

Gender did influence MPEoU as expected (H_3 ✓). The difference between means was $\Delta M = -.199$ ($t(235) = -2.134$, $p < .05$, $r = .14$) and variances were equal (Levene's $F = .141$, $p > 0.5$).

Health did influence automatic data transmission (H_8 ✓) but only for diabetics (see also Figs. 3 and 4). Diabetics agreed less to having uninformed automatic data transmission ($t(160) = -5.052, < .01, r = .37$), uniformed data transmission ($t(159) = -6.016$, $p < .01$, $r = .43$) and agreed more with self triggered transmission ($t(163) = 5.884$, $p < 0.1$, $r = .42$) and in their rejection of transmission overall ($t(157) = 7.212$, $p < .01$, $r = .5$). Furthermore being a diabetic influences the motive of *usage frequency* ($t(163) = -3.44$, $p < .01$, $r = .26$), making the motive highly significantly less important to diabetics (H_4 ✓).

When looking at the interactions of intermediate and dependent variables, no interaction of PVD and MPI was found (H_5✗, $p > 0.5$) and only a small correlation was found for MPEoU (H_6 ✓, $r = .226$, $p < .01$). Motives ($r = .499$, $p < .01$) and barriers ($r = .-295$, $p < .01$) both correlated with MPI (H_7 ✓). In order to clarify the determination of MPI multiple linear regression analysis will be performed.

4.4 Linear Regression Analysis

Using all factors that correlate with MPI and removing predictors that fail to reach significance, we derive a model of MPI consisting of only three predictors

($F(3, 238) = 35.878$, $p < .01$, see Fig. 6). This model was able to explain 30 % more variance than the scales mean alone (adj. $R^2 = .303$).

Interestingly, the general agreement with motives for the integration was about two times more influential in predicting MPI than both age and barriers combined. One must note here that MPI is z-transformed where negative values indicate a higher willingness for integrated devices. This means the older a person is the less he wants to use an integrated device (see Table 4).

Table 4. Linear regression table for MPI. All predictors increased the explained variance significantly.

Predictor	Non-standarized coefficients		Standardized slope	t	VIF
	B	SEB	β		
(Constant)	-0.329	0.149	-2.213		
Age	0.006	0.003	.126	2.291	1.042
Motives	0.496	0.059	.458	8.377	1.035
Barriers	-0.211	0.062	-.189	-3.403	1.069

Astonishingly, neither gender nor ease of use of mobile phones remained in the model. This indicates that not the expertise with mobile phones was determining the readiness to integrate into a mobile phone, but truly the factor age itself. Health status was removed as the last predictor, failing to reach significance ever so slightly (but nonetheless so).

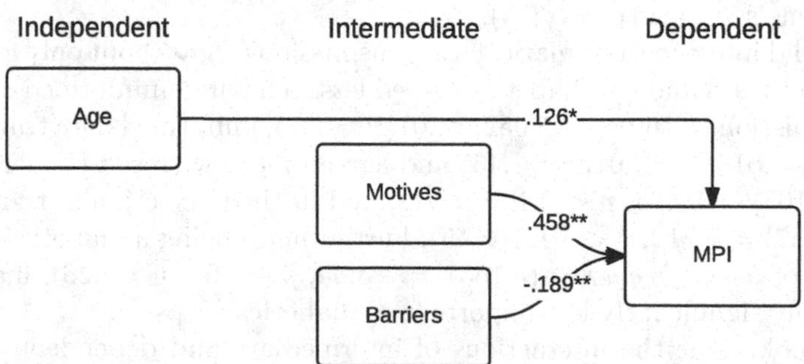

Fig. 6. Visual linear regression results. Numbers denote standardized beta values from the final model.

5 Discussion

Overall when looking at our results, we can see that the willingness to have a health application integrated into a mobile phone is dependent on the users age.

Furthermore whether the user sees motives to use a device (often based in previous experience) is important, as are perceived barriers (often fear of data loss).

Whether these factors are optimized in a stand-alone device must be investigated in the individual case. A case can be made for a standalone devices that do not require a mobile phone, particularly for the oldest user group.

The question of data privacy can not be fully answered in this article. Yet, a striking difference between diabetics and healthy/heart disease patients becomes clear. This might be due to the diabetes stricken patients' experience with constant diary keeping, device failures, stronger experience in diabetes applications, and higher domain knowledge in both theoretical (information about the disease as such) and also the practical experience.

The vital data recorded for heart disease patients and diabetics is also different in nature. Heart disease patients often only report few numeric parameters (e.g. weight, blood pressure, blood coagulation), while diabetics report more lifestyle related parameters (e.g. food intake, physical activity). A mobile application would get a deeper insight into the private life of a diabetic when automatically recording data. This might explain the reluctance of diabetics to uninformed or even non permitted data transfer. Diabetes also degenerates over a far longer period of time than heart disease, which can immediately become life-threatening in a cardiac arrest situation. The heart disease patients on the other hand might perceive the vital parameters by far more life-saving in the hands of a doctor than in their own hands.

In regard to motives in the discrepancy in *ease of use* perception can be explained by the sheer amount of data input by diabetics. Diabetics record data multiple times daily, while heart disease patients often only do so once per day.

Table 5. Items for motives and barriers for mobile phone integration and the measured concepts.

Motive or Barrier	Item
Practicality	I find it more practical to use only one device.
Familiarity	I am already comfortable using my phone.
Usage Frequency	I would use the device more often.
Enjoyment	I would have more fun using the device.
Inconspicuousness	The device would be less conspicuous.
Data loss	I fear that my data could get lost.
Device Failure	I fear that the device would not work properly.
Rejection	I don't want to use a mobile phone.
Ease of Use	I find mobile phones hard to use

6 Outlook and Future Work

In this research we looked at age as a numerical value. The model is able to predict only a small portion of the variance in mobile phone integration acceptance.

Research on aging shows that age is not a mere numerical number, as people age differently. Age solely intensifies the strength of diversity in different capabilities. When the numerical age still is a dominant factor in acceptance prediction, the question on generational differences arises. This must be investigated.

A general case for a stand-alone device could be derived from this research. Yet, when designing a product series it is helpful to keep the user diversity in mind. Market segmentation will lead to both stand-alone and mobile phone integrated solutions — in best case scenarios integrating seamlessly.

Limitations. The healthy subgroup of this research was mostly addressed in the heart disease questionnaire. Although both surveys used the same wording, by sending the survey to a heart disease aware healthy person, similar responses as to a heart disease patient are to be expected.

Acknowledgments. We would like to thank the anonymous reviewers for their constructive comments on an earlier version of this manuscript. Thank you also to Firat Alagöz for his valuable research input. This work was funded by the RWTH Aachen University Graduate Scholarships.

References

1. Bloom, D.E., Canning, D.: Global demographic change: Dimensions and economic significance. Working Paper 10817, National Bureau of Economic Research. October 2004
2. Statistisches Bundesamt: Datenreport Deutschland 2011. Retrieved February 8th 2012, (2011). https://www.destatis.de/DE/Publikationen/Datenreport/Downloads/Datenreport2011.pdf?__blob=publicationFile
3. International Diabetes Federation (IDF): Annual report 2010. Technical report (2010)
4. Wild, S., Roglic, G., Green, A., Sicree, R., King, H.: Global prevalence of diabetes. Diabetes Care **27**(5), 1047–1053 (2004)
5. Roger, V.L., Go, A.S., Lloyd-Jones, D.M., et al.: Heart disease and stroke statistics-2011 update: a report from the american heart association. Circulation **123**(4), e18–e19 (2011)
6. Alagöz, F., Valdez, A.C, Wilkowska, W., Ziefle, M., Dorner, S., Holzinger, A.: From cloud computing to mobile internet, from user focus to culture and hedonism: the crucible of mobile health care and wellness applications. In: 2010 5th International Conference on Pervasive Computing and Applications (ICPCA), pp. 38–45, IEEE (2010)
7. Holzinger, A., Dorner, S., Födinger, M., Valdez, A.C., Ziefle, M.: Chances of increasing youth health awareness through mobile wellness applications. In: Leitner, G., Hitz, M., Holzinger, A. (eds.) USAB 2010. LNCS, vol. 6389, pp. 71–81. Springer, Heidelberg (2010)
8. Joe, J., Demiris, G.: Older adults and mobile phones for health: a review. J. Biomed. Inform. **46**(5), 947–954 (2013)
9. Ramachandran, A., Pai, V.: Patient-centered mobile apps for chronic disease management, pp. 948–952 (2014)

10. Kollmann, A., Riedl, M., Kastner, P., Schreier, G., Ludvik, B.: Feasibility of a mobile phone-based data service for functional insulin treatment of type 1 diabetes mellitus patients. J. Med. Internet Res. **9**(5) (2007)
11. Tani, S., Marukami, T., Matsuda, A., Shindo, A., Takemoto, K., Inada, H.: Development of a health management support system for patients with diabetes mellitus at home. J. Med. Syst. **34**(3), 223–228 (2010)
12. Lv, X., Guo, X., Xu, Y., Yuan, J., Yu, X.: Explaining the mobile health services acceptance from different age groups: a protection motivation theory perspective. Int. J. Advancements Comput. Technol. **4**(3), 1–9 (2012)
13. Hung, M.C., Jen, W.Y.: The adoption of mobile health management services: an empirical study. J. Med. Syst. **36**(3), 1381–1388 (2012)
14. Valdez, A.C., Ziefle, M., Horstmann, A., Herding, D., Schroeder, U.: Task performance in mobile and ambient interfaces. does size matter for usability of electronic diabetes assistants? In: 2010 International Conference on Information Society (i-Society), pp. 514–521. IEEE (2010)
15. Calero Valdez, A., Ziefle, M., Horstmann, A., Herding, D., Schroeder, U.: Effects of aging and domain knowledge on usability in small screen devices for diabetes patients. In: Holzinger, A., Miesenberger, K. (eds.) USAB 2009. LNCS, vol. 5889, pp. 366–386. Springer, Heidelberg (2009)
16. Calero Valdez, A., Ziefle, M., Alagöz, F., Holzinger, A.: Mental models of menu structures in diabetes assistants. In: Miesenberger, K., Klaus, J., Zagler, W., Karshmer, A. (eds.) ICCHP 2010, Part II. LNCS, vol. 6180, pp. 584–591. Springer, Heidelberg (2010)
17. Alagöz, F., Ziefle, M., Wilkowska, W., Valdez, A.C.: Openness to accept medical technology - a cultural view. In: Holzinger, A., Simonic, K.-M. (eds.) USAB 2011. LNCS, vol. 7058, pp. 151–170. Springer, Heidelberg (2011)
18. Holzinger, A., Dorner, S., Födinger, M., Ziefle, M., Valdez, A.C.: Motivational features of a mobile web application promoting a healthy lifestyle. In: 24th BCS Conference on Human Computer Interaction, University of Abertay, Dundee, Scotland (2010)
19. Rashvand, H., Traver Salcedo, V., Montn Snchez, E., Iliescu, D.: Ubiquitous wireless telemedicine. IET Commun. **2**(2), 237–254 (2008)
20. Holzinger, A., Sommerauer, B., Spitzer, P., Juric, S., Zalik, B., Debevc, M., Lidynia, C., Valdez, A.C., Roecker, C., Ziefle, M.: Mobile computing is not always advantageous: lessons learned from a real-world case study in a hospital. In: Teufel, S., Min, T.A., You, I., Weippl, E. (eds.) CD-ARES 2014. LNCS, vol. 8708, pp. 110–123. Springer, Heidelberg (2014)

Delivering Telemonitoring Care to Digitally Disadvantaged Older Adults: Human-Computer Interaction (HCI) Design Recommendations

Hongtu Chen[1(✉)] and Sue E. Levkoff[2]

[1] Department of Psychiatry, Harvard Medical School, 1280 Massachusetts Ave, Suite 505, Cambridge, MA 02138, USA
hongtuchen@hotmail.com

[2] SmartHOME, University of South Carolina, Columbia, USA

Abstract. Although telemonitoring has promise in improving care delivery and reducing unnecessary health care costs, the recent years have witnessed growing interest in identifying and resolving barriers to engagement, participation, and spreading of telemonitoring service programs among digitally disadvantaged populations. Based on a review of three key conceptual perspectives relevant to the problem of the digital divide, specific issues concerning technological acceptance, human resources development, and collaboration with service systems are described. Major strategies and policy implications are discussed with regard to HCI design considerations for telemonitoring of medical and aging conditions of the target population, integration of the telemonitoring service into the existing clinical and social context, and development of reimbursement policy that supports not only service use but also access to technology services and additional training for effective use of the technology.

Keywords: Digital divide · Telemonitoring · Older adults · Policy

1 Introduction

Telemonitoring or remote monitoring between a health care provider and a patient in a home setting is a promising technological innovation to enable older persons with disabling disease such as chronic heart failure to remain at home while receiving improved care and reducing health care costs1. During the past decade, numerous randomized trials have demonstrated the efficacy of telemonitoring interventions in reducing hospital readmission rates and emergency department visits, and therefore health care costs, along with lower numbers of deaths and increased quality of life [1–6]. Telemonitoring care also comes with other benefits valued by patients. Telemonitoring has the ability to minimize the barriers to care among individuals with common co-morbid conditions—like arthritis, vision impairment, and cognitive decline—that makes transportation to doctor's appointments difficult without extensive support from formal or informal caregivers. Telemonitoring also offers the opportunity to provide patients with frequent and timely advice and instructions without the need for

J. Zhou and G. Salvendy (Eds.): ITAP 2015, Part II, LNCS 9194, pp. 50–60, 2015.
DOI: 10.1007/978-3-319-20913-5_5

face-to-face, in-person interaction, thus supporting patients' capacity of self care and needs for autonomy in their home environments [7]. Telemonitoring may even be preferable for some older adults, who would choose the familiar, low pressure home setting to direct communication with healthcare providers in their busy offices [8]. Telemonitoring, in theory, encourages more widespread, equalized access to more frail and less mobile individuals, as well as those living in rural areas, by allowing them the same access to providers as their urban counterparts.

The problem of concern here is about the other side of the coin – those elderly persons who cannot benefit from telemonitoring opportunities. Evidence has begun to emerge, indicating an alarming phenomenon of digital divide—i.e., the inequality of access to, participation in, and benefit from the telemonitoring care programs for older adults, as shown below:

Older adults with high income levels are more likely to have access to equipment, such as computers and internet access that can be used for telemonitoring and telecommunication [9].

Older adults with higher levels of education are more likely to accept telemonitoring, adhere to medication regimes and taking responsibility for healthcare, due to generally increased levels of health literacy and better access to care [10].

When access to telecommunication equipment is not an issue, refusal to participating in a telemonitoring intervention program can be based on a combination of any of the following reasons, including: (a) feeling overly burdened to acquire the skills to engage in new tasks such as registration and routine data entry (low digital literacy); (b) feeling uncomfortable to take on responsibility for one's own health, given they have grown up being a part of a cohort that was brought up to believe that health problems should be taken care by health care professionals (lower self-efficacy in self care); and/or (c) fear that telemonitoring will leave their medical data unsecure (technological phobia and distrust) [11–13].

Some refuse to adopt or terminate the telemonitoring service not because of the complexity of the medical condition itself, but because of co-morbidities—such as cognitive or sensory impairments—that could inhibit the use of telemonitoring technologies [14].

Those rural elders and their caregivers who originally accepted and participated in a telemonitoring program for heart failure terminated prematurely, often because the burden experienced by caregivers, heightened by the worsening or complications of the health problem of the elder patient, led caregivers to stop collecting and entering and monitoring the data [15].

The above problems are by no means easy to solve. As a result, a large number of older adults may not be able to participate in telemonitoring care. The exiting literature seems to point us to at least three different conceptual frameworks or perspectives about key factors contributing to the phenomena of digital divide. Below we briefly summarize these perspectives in order to provide a basic analysis of the problem of unequal access to, use of, and benefit from the telemonitoring care for elders.

2 Understanding Psychological Factors in Technological Acceptance

One of the most influential lines of research seeking to elucidate specific barriers to the acceptance and use of technology has to do with the Technology Acceptance Model (TAM) and its use in health care. TAM was originally developed in 1980's and gained increasing recognition in the health care field during the last decade [16, 17]. By emphasizing the key constructs such as perceived usefulness and perceived ease of use, subjective social norm, and behavioral intention, TAM reveals the cognitive processes through which the psychological, social, and behavioral factors contribute to the decision or choice of acceptance or adaption of new technology.

The key limitations of the TAM approach are two fold: one is its overall trend of expansion of the model by adding more variables into the original TAM in order to accommodate the complexity of issues facing the constantly changing IT world. Various independent attempts to expand TAM have been made [18–20], with repeatedly adding new variables that some critiques regard as causing "a state of theoretical chaos and confusion" [21]. The other limitation is the TAM's focus on the inner psychological process while relatively neglecting external contextual factors. Although newer versions of TAM-like modeling are able to incorporate contextual or moderating variables as shown in the Unified Theory of Acceptance and Use of Technology (UTAUT) that includes "facilitating conditions" [22] as a determinant of behavioral intention to accept technology, the critiques of TAM believe that this approach ignores the critical processes or stages of health information technology (HIT) development and implementation, and is not able to advise which technology is better for a particular social group and clinical setting, and what kind of social and financial consequences of HIT use might be [23].

According to the TAM perspective, the success of a telecommunication program, particularly in terms of reaching and engaging digitally disadvantaged groups, will very much depend on the thoughtful design of the telemonitoring device that should be not only affordable to the target population but also able to take into account the possible differences in their ways of perceiving whether the equipment is useful and easy to operate. An elderly patient with a higher level of health literacy, for instance, may agree to enroll in a telemonitoring program primarily based on her own perception of usefulness when she sees a diagram showing how the relevant symptoms can be recorded by the equipment and transmitted to her doctor for central monitoring, whereas her counterpart with a lower level of health literacy, at least some of them, may be more likely to be persuaded by the endorsement of her familiar doctor than the explanation of how the equipment is able to pick up a list of clinical indicators.

Also, we can expect those with higher digital literacy to take a more active part in the telemonitoring process (e.g., manually entering some of the monitoring data, in addition to those that can be automatically collected via blue-tooth technology) as they may not view a task like data entry as difficult, but for those who are less familiar with digital devices, an automated data recording scheme may become a necessity for a successful telemonitoring program. In general, the TAM perspective, with its focus on user perception and acceptance of technological design's functional characteristics, tends to guide us towards a more client-centered or user-sensitive design, which is critical for a successful telemonitoring program.

3 Understanding Sociological Determinants of Digital Divide

In contrast to the TAM model that focuses on the inner psychological processes of technology adoption, another emerging approach is primarily derived from the digital divide phenomena and related literature that points towards the importance of the broad contextual perspective.

The digital divide literature emerged from the observation of a broad variation or gap among large groups, populations, or geographical regions. The gap reveals the inequality of substantial social consequences in terms of access to, knowledge about, and use of the information and communication technology [24, 25]. If HIT is believed to be a promising solution to modern health care delivery to general population, the digital divide phenomenon suggests a profound challenge to the above belief, that is, the population-based heterogeneity as revealed in digital divide indicates the possibility that a large group of digitally disadvantaged people may not be able to access, use, and benefit from the HIT-based heath care, while the digitally advantaged group can. If the digital divide is a proxy reflection of the social-economic status, education level, age, and/or geographic region such as rurality, as many digital divide researchers are concerned, then advance of HIT may expand the persisting health disparities in our society rather than reducing them.

The notion of digital divide has evolved and broadened, mainly in the past decade, to become a multi-layered concept that includes at least three waves of conceptualization. Prior to the term of digital divide was ever coined, there was discussion in 1980 s about differences between those who had computers and those who did not [26]. In the late 1990 s, the initial concept of "digital divide" first merged and was primarily centered on the inequality in access to digital hardware of equipment and infrastructure, such as computer, internet, and mobile technology, that are necessary for enabling information and communication technology. Despite the increased availability of ICT products, which seems to reduce the general technological divide across age, gender, and income levels, [25] inequality persists particularly in terms of access to latest or most advanced technological products.

The second wave of the digital divide concept had more to do with human resource development than technological access. What Hargittai [27] called "Second-Level Digital Divide" focused on skills or what was later referred to as digital literacy (i.e., knowledge and familiarity with ICT), and further e-health literacy (e.g., able to use HIT to address health needs), as barriers to the use of digital technologies. The digital divide discourse at this second level turned the access concern about "Haves and Have-Nots" to a deeper inquiry of those "don't-want-tos" (i.e., when the computing device is a convenient social setting, at no cost, some people would still choose not to use) [28]. Furthermore, the digital divide at the literacy level also entails how leaders or "early adopters" play a role in facilitating training and other community activities that improve related literacy and skills of community members to use and engage with HIT. For the older population, such enabling efforts may also need to take into account the disability conditions or physical limitations such as visual deficits, arthritis and joint pain that often reduce one's confidence in learning new ways of managing one's health, thus limiting the adoption of technology for healthcare purposes [29, 30]. In addition to physical impairments like decreased dexterity and vision loss, older adults' restrictions also include cognitive decline such as decreased concentration, which, even as a result of normal aging rather than disease, may contribute to perceived difficulty in use of technology [31].

The third wave of the digital divide conceptualization further extended the notion of the human resource development to its context, with a focus particularly on building an organizational or community culture that is committed to promoting the pro-technology, pro-health, and pro-responsibility values, and to integrating these values with institutional and policy support for use of digital technology. Those who live in a community without such a culture may witness and experience technology phobia or distrust, concerns about cost or low return of investment of money and effort, and over-dependence on external authority such as doctors to make decision on care management, thus prohibiting behavioral digital engagement, including initial use, subsequent use, and/or sustained use of health information technology [7].

Different from TAM, which takes a micro-analytic approach to the problem of variation in adopting or using digital technologies and tends to psychologize all relevant determinants of technology acceptance, the trajectory of the conceptual evolution of the digital divide is heading towards an increasingly macro-contextual approach, representing a rather intuitive realism and providing a broad framework to allow actual technological entities such as equipment and software as well as social processes including training on digital literacy and community activities to promote pro-health and pro-technology values and culture. Such a framework makes it easier to link an intervention design to its implementation setting. Based on this broadened digital divide perspective, efforts aiming to improve a digitally disadvantaged group's access to and engagement with telemonitoring programs should include not only educational interventions to improve digital and ehealth literacy, but also social and community interventions for promoting values of self care and active participation in technology-based care improvement schemes.

4 Finding Technology Accelerators for Older Adults

Consistent with, but independent of the above digital divide literature and TAM discussions, researchers from the Center for Technology and Aging proposed a model for Accelerating Diffusion of Proven Technologies (ADOPT) [32]. Their ADOPT model suggests that in addition to technology developers, external collaborators (organizations and individuals who work directly with older adults) could play an important role in facilitating technology diffusion. These collaborators include but are not limited to aging service organizations, formal/informal caregivers, family members, medical providers, and health plans. The presence of collaborators is especially important for older adults, as this population often has a lower level of familiarity/awareness of technology, cognitive or physical limitations that make it difficult to use technology, and limited resource to access technology. Without collaborators, technology access and user education can be difficult, if not impossible. Besides collaborators, Wang et al. also pointed out that the wider context in which older adults live could also impact their intention and ability to use technology. Two key context factors that they indentified are policy (including reimbursement, privacy considerations, and interoperability) and resources/access relating to technology. For example, reimbursement and policies that either reimburse technologies directly or incentivize health outcomes could likely increase diffusion of beneficial technologies.

According to the ADOPT model, in order to successfully promote a telemonitoring program among digitally disadvantaged people, it would be critical to form partnerships with "collaborators" including not only caregivers and family members but also those associated with a service organization such as aging service agency, medical center, and health insurance company, instead of promoting it alone by e-health developers or health care innovators. These collaborators can help accelerate the diffusion of technologies through adjusting incentivizing mechanisms and service arrangements to encourage and enable at-risk older adults to enroll in, engage with, and continually use and benefit from the telemonitoring care services as well as incentivizing their providers for participation in the service program. The notion of using a group of members of a community to help another group of people to accelerate diffusion or adoption of technology can be traced back to original writing of Everett Rogers [33] who explained the importance of innovation champions and opinion leaders in the technology diffusion process.

5 HCI Design Recommendations

These three conceptual frameworks lead to different emphases and directions—i.e., centering on technological design, human resource development, and service system collaboration, respectively—in finding possible solutions to the problem of designing telemonitoring care services for technologically, socially, and clinically disadvantaged groups.

As summarized in Table 1, from the TAM perspective, the key strategy to improve patient engagement and adherence is through careful product design that aims to enhance usability (e.g., "perceived usefulness") and lower usage barriers (i.e., "perceived ease of use"), so that those who already have access to the monitoring device will feel motivated to use the telemonitoring services. From the broadened digital divide perspective, effective designs of telemonitoring intervention for digitally disadvantaged users, who typically are low-income, low-literacy, home-bound older adults, should focus on supporting, strengthening, and enabling digitally disadvantaged individuals and communities at various levels. From the technology accelerator perspective, the technology-based intervention design efforts should focus on integration of telemonitoring programs with the social, clinical, and financial environments.

Table 1. HCI design recommendations for effective delivery of telemmonitoring care to digitally disadvantaged users: based on three conceptual perspectives

Perspective	Key emphasis	HCI design recommendations
1. Technology acceptance model	Enhance "perceived usefulness"	(1) Individual tailoring to a user's needs (e.g., adjusting brightness levels for those with light sensitivity, personalized feedback, to culturally sensitive content and user interface designs);
		(2) Increasing functionality and flexibility to accommodate changing health conditions over time;
		(3) Including the add-on functionality for common co-morbidities like heart failure, chronic obstructive pulmonary disease, and diabetes.
	Increase "ease of use"	(1) Making product compatible with existing hardware, thus reducing the burden of learning new behaviors;
		(2) Simplifying the design of the technology and user interface to accommodate physical and cognitive disabilities that often impede older adults from performing technology-related tasks;
		(3) Increasing automation in data collection and transmission thus lowering data entry burden as much as possible;
		(4) Using audio, video or graphical displays along with the text to minimize the literacy level required of users;
		(5) Using customized alerts to remind elderly patients;
		(6) providing clear instructions.
2. Digital divide	Support digitally disadvantaged individuals and communities	(1) Designing the product either based on existing device commonly available to the users, or using a new device but making sure that the additional financial and training costs are not burdensome to the user;

(*Continued*)

Table 1. (*Continued*)

Perspective	Key emphasis	HCI design recommendations
		(2) Addressing digital literacy and specific health literacy by increasing exposure to ehealth services, reducing technology phobia and distrust, and increasing overall recognition of the value of the HIT as a general health care solution;
		(3) Training elders and their caregivers to improve not only general digital literacy but also familiarity and fluency in using telemonitoring devices and procedures;
		(4) Coordinating professional and peer support through online and off-line mechanisms;
		(5) Promoting a culture and value of self care particularly through enhancing self-efficacy in taking responsibility for one's own health care, obtaining knowledge and skills for managing illness, and actively using digital technology-based services.
3. Technology accelerator	Integrate telemonitoring programs with social, clinical, and financial environments	(1) Designing telemonitoring care interventions that are not only patient-centered, but also caregiver-centered, to fully mobilize the collaborative care resources;
		(2) Integrating telemonotoring care with clinical workflow of disease management and care coordination;
		(3) developing policy for reimbursing not only use of telemonitoring services but also the training needed for operating telemonitoring device.

6 Limitations and Under-Addressed Issues

These theory-based recommendations are consistent with the emerging literature on factors contributing to differential technology and information use in general and adoption of telemonitoring technology among older adults in particular [8, 34–40].

Nevertheless, several issues, which may be regarded as beyond the scope of the aforementioned conceptual frameworks, remain under-addressed by the research community interested in delivering telemonitoring care to digitally disadvantaged older adults. One, most of the measures used for analyzing the digital divide assume a quantitative difference (e.g., ehealth literacy) between digitally high-access and low-access groups, while less attention is paid to possible qualitative differences between these two groups. For instance, if values, priority of goals, meanings of usefulness, exposure to health care systems and HIT services, types of digital literacy, and disability conditions of the target users are all different from general population, it would argue for the need of more qualitative inquiry, such as ethnographic research to deepen our understanding of the profile of various digitally disadvantaged groups, before quantitative research is planned. Two, most of the discussion focuses on initial behavioral acceptance, use, engagement, or adoption of telemonitoring technology, with much less attention paid to retention, or temporal variation in user intention and usage behavior. While recognizing that the barriers to sustained usage or adherence are of critical clinical significance, we know very little about how to model or analyze the temporal variation of these barriers and their complex inter-relations, while taking into account normal age-related physical and cognitive changes in late life, as well as disease related decline, fatigue of engagement over time, and psychological adaptation to and habituation of routine activities. Three, although for many older, frail adults, the decision of using or continuing to use a telemonitoring care service is made by, or in collaboration with, informal and formal caregivers, very limited research effort and intervention designs are centered on caregivers to elders in need of telemonitoring services.

The future success of telemonitoring care will depend on whether we can effectively spread the technology-based service across the digital divide that has prevented a large population from access to, adoption of, and benefit from telemonitoring care programs. Much work, including perhaps both qualitative policy research and quantitative intervention research, is still ahead of us to develop better and more aging friendly devices and programs, to strengthen and build the user community, and to integrate the telemonitoring program within existing clinical, financial, and social contexts.

Acknowledgement. Preparation of this manuscript was supported by National Institute on Aging of the National Institutes of Health under award number R43AG038210, and R43MD008661.

References

1. Klersy, C., De Silvestri, A., Gabutti, G., Regoli, F., Auricchio, A.: A meta-analysis of remote monitoring of heart failure patients. J. Am. Coll. Cardiol. **54**(18), 1683–1694 (2009)
2. Goldberg, L.R., Piette, J.D., Walsh, M.N., et al.: Randomized trial of a daily electronic home monitoring system in patients with advanced heart failure: the weight monitoring in heart failure (WHARF) trial. Am. Heart J. **146**(4), 705–712 (2003)

3. Cleland, J.G., Louis, A.A., Rigby, A.S., Janssens, U., Balk, A.H.: TEN-HMS investigators. noninvasive home telemonitoring for patients with heart failure at high risk of recurrent admission and death: the trans-european network-home-care management system (TEN-HMS) study. J. Am. Coll. Cardiol. **45**(10), 1654–1664 (2005)
4. Myers, S., Grant, R., Lugn, N., Holbert, B., Kvedar, J.: Impact of home-based monitoring on the care of patients with congestive heart failure. Home Health Care Manage. Pract. **18**(6), 444–451 (2006)
5. Chaudhry, S.I., Mattera, J.A., Curtis, J.P., et al.: Telemonitoring in patients with heart failure. N. Engl. J. Med. **363**(24), 2301–2309 (2010)
6. Inglis, S.C., Clark, R.A., McAlister, F.A., et al.: Structured telephone support or telemonitoring programmes for patients with chronic heart failure. Cochrane Database Syst. Rev., CD007228 (2010)
7. Boyne, J.J., Vrijhoef, H.J.: Implementing telemonitoring in heart failure care: barriers from the perspectives of patients, healthcare professionals and healthcare organizations. Curr. Heart Fail Rep. **10**(3), 254–261 (2013)
8. Bickmore, T.W., Paasche-Orlow, M.K.: The role of information technology in health literacy research. J. Health Commun. **17**(Suppl. 3), 23–29 (2012)
9. Peacock, S.E., Kunemund, H.: Senior citizens and internet technology: reasons and correlates of access versus non-access in a european comparative perspective. Eur. J. Ageing **4**(4), 191–200 (2007)
10. Or, C.K., Karsh, B.T.: A systematic review of patient acceptance of consumer health information technology. J. Am. Med. Inform. Assoc. **16**(4), 550–560 (2009)
11. Gruber, H.-G., Wolf, B., Reiher, M.: Innovation barriers for telemonitoring. In: IFMBE Proccedings, vol. 25, pp. 48–50 (2009)
12. Jimison, H., Gorman, P., Woods, S., et al.: Barriers and drivers of health information technology use for the elderly, chronically ill, and underserved. Evidence Report/Technology Assessment No. 175 (Prepared by the Oregon Evidence-based Practice Center under Contract No. 290-02-0024). AHRQ Publication No. 09-E004. Agency for Healthcare Research and Quality, Rockville, MD, November 2008
13. Ellis, R.D., Allaire, J.C.: Modeling computer interest in older adults: the role of age, education, Computer knowledge, and computer anxiety. Hum. Factors **41**, 345–355 (1999)
14. Clarke, M., Shah, A., Sharma, U.: Systematic review of studies on telemonitoring of patients with congestive heart failure: a meta-analysis. J. Telemed. Telecare **17**(1), 7–14 (2011)
15. Azhar, G., Chen, H., Lu, X., Levkoff, S.: Access to telecommunication technologies among rural elders. Paper presented at GSA Annual Conference (2012)
16. Holden, R.J., Karsh, B.T.: The technology acceptance model: its past and its future in health care. J. Biomed. Inform. **43**(1), 159–172 (2010)
17. Yarbrough, A.K., Smith, T.B.: Technology acceptance among physicians: a new take on TAM. Med. Care Res. Rev. **64**(6), 650–672 (2007)
18. Venkatesh, V., Davis, F.D.: A theoretical extension of the technology acceptance model: Four longitudinal field studies. Manage. Sci. **46**(2), 186–204 (2000)
19. Venkatesh, V., Bala, H.: Technology acceptance model 3 and a research agenda on interventions. Decis. Sci. **39**(2), 273–315 (2008)
20. Kim, J., Park, H.A.: Development of a health information technology acceptance model using consumers' health behavior intention. J. Med. Internet Res. **14**(5), e133 (2012)
21. Izak, B., Barki, H.: Quo vadis TAM? J. AIS **8**(3), 211–218 (2007)
22. Venkatesh, V., Morris, M.G., Davis, G.B., Davis, F.D.: User acceptance of information technology: toward a unified view. MIS Quart. **27**(3), 425–478 (2003)
23. Bagozzi, R.P.: The legacy of the technology acceptance model and a proposal for a paradigm shift. J. Assoc. Inf. Syst. **8**(4), 243–255 (2007)

24. Pippa Norris's superb Digital Divide: Civic Engagement, Information Poverty & the Internet Worldwide. Cambridge Uni. Press, Cambridge (2001)
25. Zickuhr, K., Smith, A.: Digital Differences. Pew Research Center, Washington, DC (2012)
26. Compaine, B.M.: The Digital Divide: Facing a Crisis or Creating a Myth?. MIT Press, Cambridge (2001)
27. Hargittai, E.: Second-level digital divide: differences in people's online skills. First Monday **7**(4) (2002)
28. Crump, B., McIlroy, A.: The digital divide: why the "don't-wants-tos" won't compute: lessons from a New Zealand ICT project. First Monday **8**(12) (2003)
29. Gatto, S.L., Tak, S.H.: Computer, internet, and e-mail use among older adults: benefits and barriers. Educ. Gerontol. **34**(9), 800–811 (2008)
30. Pedone, C., Incalzi, R.: Telemonitoring in older adults: does one size fit all? Arch. Intern. Med. **172**(20), 1611 (2012)
31. Czaja, S.J., Lee, C.C.: The impact of aging on access to technology. Univ. Access. Inf. Soc. **5**(4), 341–349 (2006)
32. Wang, A., Redington, L., Steinmetz, V., Lindeman, D.: The ADOPT model: accelerating diffusion of proven technologies for older adults. Ageing Int. **36**(1), 29–45 (2011)
33. Rogers, E.M.: Diffusion of Innovations. Free Press, New York (1962)
34. Eichner, J., Dullabh, P.: Accessible health information technology (Health IT) for populations with limited literacy: a guide for developers and purchasers of health IT. (Prepared by the National Opinion Research Center for the National Resources Center for Health IT). AHRQ Publication No. 08-0010-EF. Agency for Healthcare Research and Quality, Rockville, MD (2007)
35. Workman, M.: Advancements in technology: new opportunities to investigate factors contributing to differential technology and information use. Int. J. Manage. Decis. Making **8** (2), 318–342 (2007)
36. Hardiker, N.R., Grant, M.J.: Barriers and facilitators that affect public engagement with eHealth services. Stud. Health Technol. Inform. **160**(Pt. 1), 13–17 (2010)
37. Mahoney, D.F.: An evidence-based adoption of technology model for remote monitoring of elders' daily activities. Ageing Int. **36**(1), 66–81 (2010)
38. Xie, B.: Effects of an eHealth literacy intervention for older adults. J. Med. Internet Res. **13** (4), e90 (2011)
39. Desai, A.S.: Does home monitoring heart failure care improve patient outcomes? Home monitoring heart failure care does not improve patient outcomes: looking beyond telephone-based disease management. Circulation **125**, 828–836 (2012)
40. Choi, N.G., DiNitto, D.M.: The digital divide among low-income homebound older adults: internet use patterns, ehealth literacy, and attitudes toward computer/internet use. J. Med. Internet Res. **15**(5), e93 (2013)

Accessibility in Serious Games for Adults Aging with Disability

Keiko Gomez-Gurley[1], Anne Collins McLaughlin[1(✉)], Maribeth Gandy Coleman[2], and Jason C. Allaire[1]

[1] Department of Psychology, North Carolina State University, Raleigh, NC, USA
{kegomezg, anne_mcLaughlin, jason_allaire}@ncsu.edu
[2] Georgia Institute of Technology, Interactive Media and Technology Center, Atlanta, GA, USA
maribeth.gandy@imtc.gatech.edu

Abstract. As serious games rise in number and popularity, particularly for therapeutic purposes, so rises the importance of making these games accessible to those with disabilities. We discuss the state of accessibility for commercial and research-based serious games, common age-related considerations for accessible designs, and recommendations for usability testing protocols. We close with a case study of a visual accessibility investigation of a research-based cognitive training game, *Food for Thought*.

Keywords: Aging · Design · Accessibility · Age-related change · Cognition · Perception · Movement · Displays · Serious games · Cognitive training games

1 Introduction

Zyda (2005) defined a serious game as "a mental contest, played with a computer in accordance with specific rules, that uses entertainment to further government or corporate training, education, health, public policy, and strategic communication objectives." We extend that definition to include any game with a purpose other than entertainment, not necessarily involving a computer, and that purpose may be educational, for skill development, job training, rehabilitation, or improvements in health and well-being. What constitutes a game can also be defined as any task with a goal, rules for achieving that goal, feedback, and voluntary participation (McGonigal, 2011). In this paper, we first review a handful of examples of serious games and their applications. We take a look at the portion of the population who might benefit from accessible games, then discuss age related changes that should be taken into consideration when designing for older adults. We explore accessibility concerns using a case study of a current serious game project. We close with final thoughts and suggestions for developing accessible serious games in the future.

Some serious games are intended for older adults, and their benefits have been studied in experimental settings. For example, persons recovering from a stroke often have the most difficulty fully extending their arm. Physical therapy encourages such movement, but it has been found that a serious game can provide a level of motivation,

J. Zhou and G. Salvendy (Eds.): ITAP 2015, Part II, LNCS 9194, pp. 61–71, 2015.
DOI: 10.1007/978-3-319-20913-5_6

feedback, and reward difficult to achieve in traditional physical therapy (Harley et al. 2011). In this pinball-type game, the more the patient extended their arm, the more "power" behind the ball and the further it bounced through the obstacles. Game sounds and visuals gave feedback and a feeling of accomplishment for this difficult task. In another therapeutic application Imbeault et al. (2011) created a game to improve memory, planning skills, initiative and perseverance in older persons with progressing dementia. Players performed cooking tasks in multi-step sequences (e.g., toast a piece of bread and then butter it) and were shown their progress throughout the task via a percentage value. Multi-tasking was encouraged by the game (e.g., toast your bread while making coffee), and a timer provided the rules and feedback motivating play. Even commercial games can be "serious": *Rise of Nations*, a real time strategy game, was successfully used as a cognitive training intervention for older adults. The game required complex planning and task execution, with the motivating rewards, visuals, and audio typical of a high-budget commercial game. Participants in the study showed improvements in executive control functions after play (Basak et al. 2008). Unfortunately, there is a growing audience of potential players for whom these games are difficult or impossible to use: those with a disability. Persons at older ages reported higher levels of disability, (Ferrucci et al. 1996), however there are a large number of persons at younger ages aging with a disability (USCB, 2012).

Perhaps due to their focused goals and populations, both commercial and research-based serious games have not made accessibility a priority. However, with the aging of the baby boomer generation, more adults with disability than ever before will be aging with their disability. The combination of disability and age-related changes in perception, cognition, and movement control is challenging, and we discuss the importance of considering potential disability and age-related interactions in serious game design, iteration, and testing. As the goal of many serious games is to support older persons in recovery or in living independently, those in most need of the games are likely those with a disability.

A small number of commercially available games for entertainment consider accessibility issues and there are resources available to designers interested in accessibility (e.g., Atkinson et al. 2006). Some have made progress such as in the game *Final Fantasy XIV: A Realm Reborn*, which was selected by the AbleGamer Foundation as the most accessible mainstream game of 2013 (Ablegamers, 2013). Much of the accessibility was due to the allowed choice and customization of interface and controls and the time allowed to use the controls during gameplay. The creators of *Final Fantasy* admitted this was no easy task, and they incorporated feedback into iterations of the design to achieve high accessibility (Ablegamers, 2013). In recent news, the company who produces the game *World of Warcraft* has introduced settings that will aid color-blind users, allowing them to customize filters (BBC News). This will help distinguish between characters, a good step toward leveling the playing field between normal-sighted and color-blind users. However, success stories such as *Final Fantasy* and *World of Warcraft* demonstrate that accessibility in mainstream games is possible, not that it is common (Bierre et al. 2005; Yuan et al. 2010).

Creating accessible serious games is unlike creating other accessible interfaces, or even other games. Serious games have a purpose, and often that purpose is tied directly to the gameplay, interface, goals, rules, and feedback of the game. As a simple example, imagine the game *Rise of Nations* made more accessible by removing time constraints and the need to juggle multiple demands. Though these changes would make it playable by a variety of older persons, particularly those who need cognitive accessibility changes, it would likely no longer have a therapeutic effect. These challenges are over and above "pure" accessibility. However, we believe there are heuristics and processes that can make games more accessible without changing the nature of the therapeutic gameplay.

As a last challenge, many serious games are research projects, with the understandably narrow initial focus on a particular sub-population expected to benefit from the game. For example, we created the game *Food for Thought* to teach multi-tasking skill for older adults as a cognitive training game. In recruiting participants for testing the efficacy of the game, older adults with dementia or other cognitive disabilities were excluded to reduce uncontrolled variability. However, those older adults would be key toward understanding how to make the game more accessible. In sum, serious games have emerged as an important focus for society and it is time to design and test them for accessibility, particularly those targeting older players (Gamberini et al. 2006).

2 Age-Related Change

When discussing the needs of older persons aging with a disability, it is useful to understand what age-related changes in ability tend to occur in all persons and how those may interact with an existing disability. First, the signifier "age-related" is important: persons differ greatly in their abilities across the lifespan. Second, it is important to remember that older age is not only a time of decline - forms of cognition and ability are maintained or even increase until late in the lifespan. If designers only consider declines, they miss taking advantage of the knowledge and skills possessed by many older persons and how those attributes may compensate.

In many areas, older persons perform more highly than younger. These include tests of crystallized knowledge (called declarative knowledge), in emotional regulation, in social tasks, and in domains where they achieved high skill over time. Examples of declarative knowledge include vocabulary, factual knowledge, and political knowledge. Examples of emotional regulation would be that older persons report more positive emotions in general and focus on positive emotional stimuli, going against the stereotype of the depressed older adult (Carstensen and Mikels, 2005). Examples of social expertise include a more nuanced judgment of the disposition and actions of other people when given information about a person's behavior (Blanchard-Fields et al. 2007). Last, skills built over a lifetime, such as the skills of a pilot or architect, are well-maintained into older age (Hardy and Parasuraman, 1997). These capabilities can be leveraged in design and in accessibility accommodations. For example, logins or identifiers can be made memorable by connecting them to a piece of declarative knowledge and feedback can focus on accomplishments that resonate with the selection of positive emotional states.

The abilities that do tend to decline with age generally fall under the category of fluid abilities, such as spatial ability, response time, and executive function. However, even as age-related declines are discussed, many of the skills that are composed of these fluid abilities are maintained, provided they were well learned and practiced (to the point of automatization) across the lifespan. Age-related change is typically divided into the categories of perceptual change, cognitive change, and motor change.

Physical changes drive the changes in perception. For example, the aging of the lens in the eye tends to result in yellowing of the lens and general muscle weakening extends to the ciliary muscles that flex the lens in the eye. Most recommendations for aiding older vision include increasing the visual angle of text or icons, but colors and the time needed to focus must also be considered. In hearing, older ears tend to lose the highest and lowest frequencies. Fortunately, most human speech occurs in the middle frequencies, but the feedback or auditory rewards in a game may not. Pathological hearing loss at older ages tends to be due to lifetime exposure to extreme or long-term sound, and thus is age-related but only because an older person has had more time for exposure. Skin on the fingers tends to thicken with age, with the result of less tactile acuity. The fingers also tend to sweat less and be less conductive, meaning that some touch technologies that depend on capacitance work poorly or not at all for older persons.

Age-related changes in cognition relevant to serious games include changes in attention, visual search, and working memory capacity. For attention, it can be difficult to selectively attend to game elements while ignoring irrelevant elements. In our work, we found that entertaining background characters and movement, while stimulating to younger participants, were distracting to our older participants, who were not always able to separate the interaction elements from the decorative ones. Although pre-attentive search ability is preserved with age, visual search that requires the combination of attributes can become more difficult due to the need for working memory. For example, finding the red dot among blue is not slowed or more difficult, but there can be increased difficulty for finding the red, left-facing icon in a field of red and blue right and left facing icons. This is an effortful search at all ages, but the combination of attributes can make a task impossible for an older player.

Age-related changes in motor skills include changes in response time, reaction time, precision, and skill acquisition time. Response time can be thought of as having two parts: the time it takes to perceive a stimulus plus the time to initiate a response. In general, response time increases with age, but this increase is attributed to a delayed physical response rather than a slowed RT. Precision also can become more difficult, but older persons can activate small targets quickly when they are physically separated from other targets (Rogers et al. 2005).

Last there are other age-related individual differences that can affect an older person's experience in a serious game. For example, game-specific displays and input devices may be unfamiliar, although many older adults have computer experience. It is common to claim that the current cohort of older adults will be the last that is unfamiliar with computers, but we believe that there will always be novel technologies unfamiliar to older persons, even those who are currently young and consider themselves technologically savvy.

3 Case Study: *Food for Thought*

We use a serious game, *Food for Thought* (FFT), as an example of how *visual* accessibility concerns may be measured and addressed, particularly for the sub population of older adults aging with a disability. The purpose of FFT is cognitive training, particularly for multi-tasking skill. Thus, the game requires the player to shift priority for different tasks co-occurring in time. Any accessibility integration must preserve the core mechanic of multi-tasking with varying priorities for the tasks, but we have discovered numerous ways of maintaining the multi-tasking core while taking into account varying perceptual, cognitive, and movement needs.

The game itself was based around multi-tasking during cooking. The display for the game was designed with older players in mind - all clickable targets were large (at least 1" × 1") and drawn in a high-contrast style with bright colors (Fig. 1). The left side of the screen was divided into four "stations," a cooking station, a chopping station, a mixing station, and a spicing station. Each of these stations could have 1–4 sub-stations that would hold and process ingredients. The right side of the screen contained the "counter" where ingredients were stored and the processing steps required for each ingredient were displayed. Multi-tasking was induced by time limits that required ingredients to be processed at the same time, moving back and forth between counter and processing station while avoiding being left on a station until they were over processed (burned, over spiced, over chopped, or over mixed).

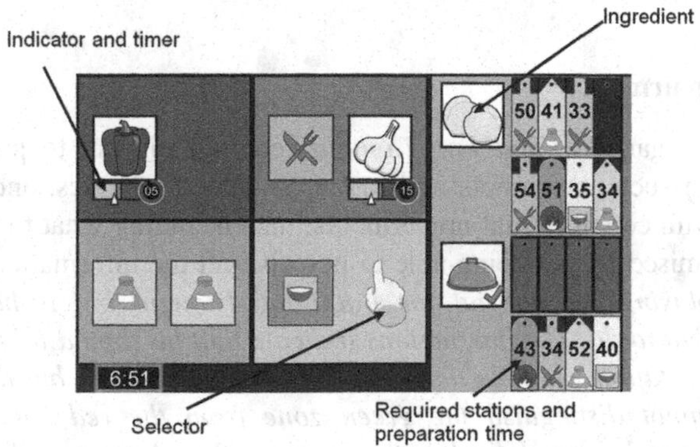

Fig. 1. The *Food for Thought* interface, displaying a simple version of the game used in a early tutorial. The ingredients and steps are on the right side of the screen and the food preparation occurs on the left.

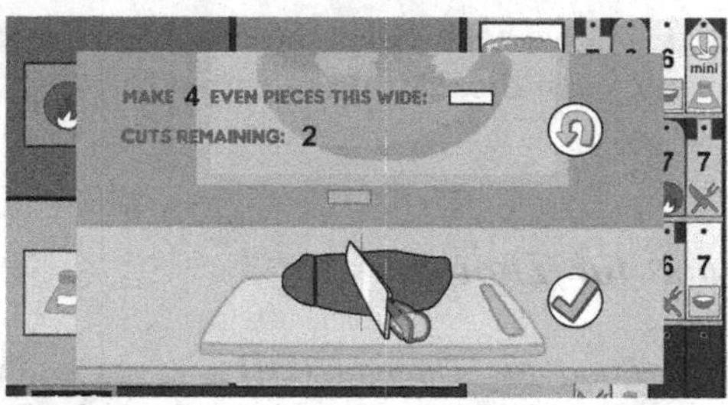

Fig. 2. A minigame in *Food for Thought* that requires the player to "cut" even slices in a loaf of bread (by clicking) with a specific number of cuts. This task requires ability to spatially judge how wide each slice should be.

Additionally, the game contained "minigames" within the main game to add multitasking and difficulty (Fig. 2). These mini games included such tasks as cutting a loaf of bread into even slices, stirring vegetables in a pan to keep them from burning, and sorting colored apples into groups of the same color. These mini games had varying levels of difficulty, with the most difficult requiring multiple steps and coordinated movements (e.g., click and drag). They were introduced one by one, beginning with the simplest, as the player progressed through the game. Players played the minigame while simultaneously monitoring the ingredients occupying their stations. All of the minigames required higher levels of vision, cognition, and motor control than the main game, however they were optional and could be excluded during level design.

In testing the game we discovered several areas in which the gameplay was not accessible to those with a visual disability or those experiencing age-related changes in visual ability. These discoveries were made via multiple stages of user testing, including a formal human factors analysis for users with visual impairments utilizing "aging suit" methodologies (McClellan and Williams, 2014).

3.1 Visual Impairment

Like most serious games, *Food For Thought* required players to process complex visual information such as symbols, indicators, animated graphics, and color coding. For individuals with certain visual impairments, understanding what to do in the game could be compromised by not being able to perceive all the information of the screen.

Jim began playing the tutorial for Food for Thought but is having difficulty understanding what to do. The instructions indicate that he should take the ingredient out of its cooking station when its timer reaches the green zone, but due to his color blindness, he cannot distinguish the green zone from the red zone. To him, the ingredient appears to be "ready" when the timer reaches the very end of the indicator bar, but when he receives feedback at the end of the level, he finds out that all of his ingredients were over processed.

In this example, we highlight the limitation that occurred when the game interface required players to interpret meanings based on one sensory modality (Figs. 3 and 4). Jim could not perceive the colors of the indicator bars, therefore he failed the task.

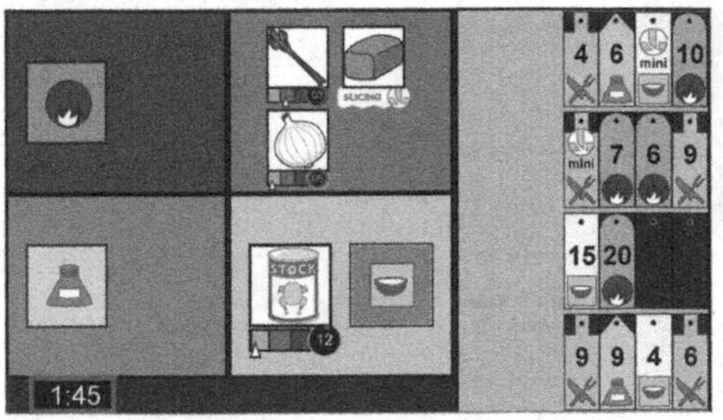

Fig. 3. *Food For Thought* interface as seen by a person with normal color vision. There are indicator bars for how "done" the ingredient is that use the colors yellow, green, and red to represent underdone, done and overdone.

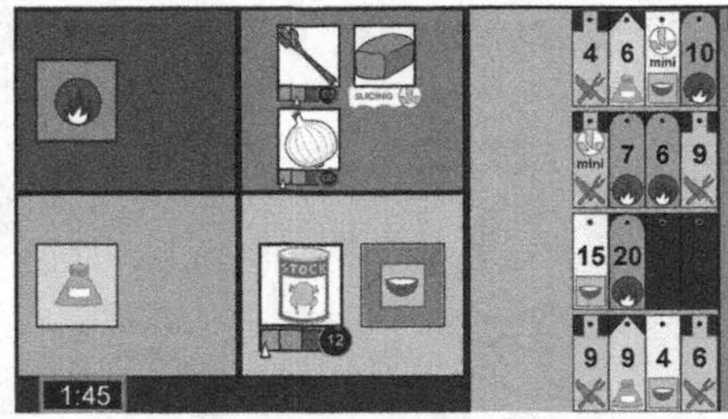

Fig. 4. *Food for Thought* interface as seen by a person with deuteranopia, which causes lowered sensitivity to green and red. Indicator bars cannot be interpreted correctly.

Jimmight not be able to distinguish the colors of the indicator bars, but he could detect motion. One solution to this problem might involve adding a blinking element to the interface to signal that an ingredient is "ready." Color blind users would also benefit from auditory information, such as a rising tone that changed as the indicator moves between color-coded zones. Although not technically color blindness, age-related changes in color perception also created problems in differentiation, typically issues with blue hues, which could be addressed using the same solutions as for color blindness.

Individuals with visual impairments such as glaucoma and macular degeneration experience occlusion in their field of view (Figs. 7 and 8). Macular degeneration typically begins in the fovea. Frustratingly, if the user moves his or her eyes toward an attention grabbing stimulus in the periphery, that area becomes foveal and therefore occluded. However, visual focus and attentional focus can be dissociated, meaning that a user may focus on the center of the screen, but direct attention to different parts of their periphery. In some games it is possible to move important elements to the periphery and changing their size according to established peripheral acuity guidelines (Anstis, 1974). When this is possible, games may retain their challenge and therapeutic value.

Popular game mechanisms can be included in the design of the game to retain playability for those with glaucoma as well. One standard mechanism is the "spotlight," usually visualized as a flashlight controlled by an input device that reveals only portions of a screen at a time. This is opposite to the symptoms of macular degeneration, where the fovea is lost - with issues such as glaucoma the fovea is retained as the periphery becomes more difficult. The flashlight mechanism operates at two levels: it can make competitive or cooperative play more possible by limiting the field of view of the fully sighted player and it can also be a way to ensure the game is designed so that a spot-lit display, whether via the game or due to the player's vision, is playable and enjoyable.

McClellan and Williams (2014) initiated an analysis plan (Fig. 5) centered on visual accessibility for older players. Through heuristic analyses and initial testing with

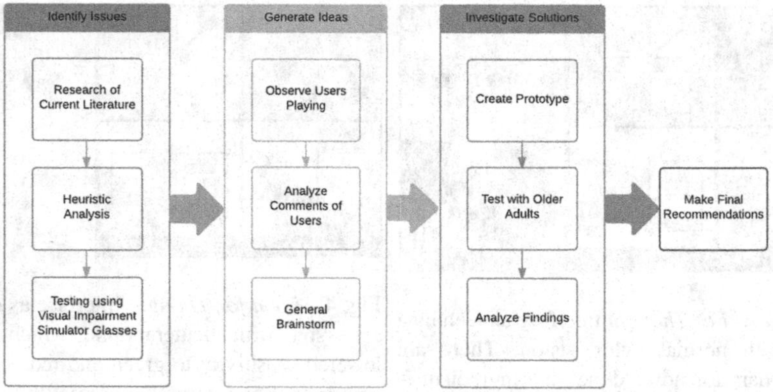

Fig. 5. Human factors methods for testing visual accessibility in a cognitive training game for older adults chosen by McClellan & Williams (2014).

glasses to simulate visual impairment, they found that several game elements were imperceptible: small moving objects such as the white triangle to indicate "doneness" and the cursor. An iterative re-design with larger fonts, indicators and greater contrast between figure and ground was tested on older users. Results found that the indicators were more easily followed and that the new designs were preferred.

3.2 User Testing

One of the biggest challenges in the design and development of therapeutic games is access to a population for usability testing throughout the process. Ideally, representative users are included in formative as well as evaluative assessments, engaging in some portion of participatory design throughout the development cycle. Large companies with resources dedicated to human factors may be able to achieve such participation and iterative design (although many choose not to), but smaller operations and research labs will need to creatively approximate the ideal methods.

To quickly test iterative designs, a "suit" may be employed that mimics the accessibility needs of the target users. Such suits can be, literally, suits: for example, automotive designers have successfully used suits that mimic age-related perceptual, movement, and flexibility issues. Glasses with different lenses can be used to mimic the symptoms of myopia/presbyopia, macular degeneration, glaucoma, and other visual disabilities (Figs. 6 and 7). Although true performance data are difficult to gather from younger or abled users wearing these suits, their subjective experience with the therapeutic game in the suit is of value. Such suits have been widely used on the designers themselves, allowing more insight into the issues their users will face and influencing their designs. Thus far, these suits have mimicked perceptual and physical disabilities. However, the concept of the suit can be extended into the cognitive realm. For example, as mentioned earlier, older users tend to have more difficulty inhibiting irrelevant stimuli. With the large visual field in most games and the tendency to use attention grabbing visuals and sound, the first step would be to pare down the

Fig. 6. *Food for Thought* interface as seen by a person with macular degeneration. This disorder is caused by the deterioration the center of the retina, which causes the center of the field of view to be obscured.

Fig. 7. *Food for Thought* interface as seen by a person with advanced vision loss from glaucoma. Increased pressure in the eye causes damage to the optic nerve, and peripheral vision decreases.

experience so that users can dedicate their resources to the portions of the game with therapeutic value. A cognitive suit might simply be a dual-task that requires the same sensory modalities as the primary task, with instruction to play the game while maintaining high performance on the secondary task. Specific to inhibition, an auditory or visual stimulus with much higher salience than the game could be displayed, with instruction to ignore its presence. We have found that young designers still tend to err on the side of more stimulation and demands rather than less. A cognitive aging suit could be a way to produce empathy and understanding.

Despite the benefits for early testing and promoting understanding and empathy in designers, accessibility "suits" are not sufficient for all user testing. Designs should still be tested with the target population, in representative tasks, and across a variety of accessibility needs. When such testing is done early it can often promote flexibility in the game design before the game mechanisms, inputs, and displays are too far advanced for changes. Advice specific to running usability analyses with older adults can be found in Pak and McLaughlin (2010).

4 Conclusion and Future Directions

It is clear that one of the biggest challenges in accessibility is to influence early game design, inputs, and mechanisms. Designers have an idea for a game mechanism, with its goals, rules, and feedback, and this tends to lock in certain interface elements. A sheet of heuristics should be developed to support a formative planning system for designers to consider at the earliest discussion of the game. Questions should include: "What are alternate ways to display the information gamers need for this part of the gameplay? Can visual be made auditory or tactile (or any reversal of these senses)? Would that affect the gameplay? How can it be revised to support the goal of the game through alternate means? Plan ahead for the interface to allow both." As concepts and prototypes develop, we recommend testing with representative users when possible but to also take advantage of simulations, including physical suits such as glasses that mimic vision problems, both for testing and to allow the designers themselves to experience the game as their players might.

Second, there is a need for the development of a taxonomy of symptoms and possibly their interactions paired with evidence-based ways of making serious games more accessible. The taxonomy does not need to address specific diseases or conditions, only their symptoms. In formulating the taxonomy, it will be important to include frequently comorbid symptoms (i.e., expect all age-related changes to be in combination with some other symptom of disability). Though a preliminary list, we have made several suggestions to address certain accessibility issues in serious games. More research is needed to expand and test these suggestions. These changes should only be considered if they do not interfere with the therapeutic nature of the game. For serious games in particular, we must promote performance that makes the serious game effective. This is an accessibility challenge beyond that faced by commercial games designed for entertainment. Serious games may be less flexible in their accessibility options to maintain the challenges required for effectiveness, but changes can still be made. For example, a game that trains multi-tasking requires multi-tasking, but it could have more easy levels early in training.

Last, though we recommend initial and rapid prototypes be tested with abled-users using techniques such as simulation suits and glasses, there must be testing with older adults and older adults aging with disability. It is time we codified and standardized user testing and accessibility testing for serious games, as they leave the world of research and become established therapies for older adults.

Acknowledgements. This research was partially supported in part by a grant from the National Institute on Disability and Rehabilitation Research (Department of Education) Grant H133E130037 under the auspices of the Rehabilitation and Engineering Research Center on Technologies to Support Successful Aging with Disability (TechSAge; www.techsage.gatech.edu). The contents of this paper were developed under a grant from the Department of Education. However, those contents do not necessarily represent the policy of the Department of Education, and you should not assume endorsement by the Federal Government. We thank Alexis McClellan and Chris Williams for their contribution to determining accessibility issues in *Food for Thought* and sharing their results.

References

Ablegamers. Accessibility awards for 2013 including mainstream accessible game of the year (2013). http://www.ablegamers.com/tag/accessible-game

Anstis, S.M.: A chart demonstrating variations in acuity with retinal position. Vision. Res. **14**(7), 589–592 (1974)

Atkinson, M.T., Gucukoglu, S., Machin, C.H.C., Lawrence, A.E.: Making the mainstream accessible: redefining the game. In: Sandbox 2006: Proceedings of the 2006 ACM SIGGRAPH Symposium on Videogames, pp. 21–28 (2006)

Basak, C., Boot, W.R., Voss, M.W., Kramer, A.F.: Can training in a real-time strategy video game attenuate cognitive decline in older adults? Psychol. Aging **23**, 765–777 (2008)

BBC News. Colour-blind aid for World of Warcraft game (2015). http://www.bbc.com/news/technology-31502904. Accessed 12 February 2015

Bierre, K., Ellis, B., Hinn, M., Ludi, S., Westin, T.: Game not over: accessibility issues in video games. In: Proceedings of the 3rd International Conference on Universal Access in Human-Computer Interaction (HCI International 2005), pp. 22–27 (2005)

Blanchard-Fields, F., Mienaltowski, A., Seay, R.B.: Age differences in everyday problem-solving effectiveness: older adults select more effective strategies for interpersonal problems. J. Gerontol. B Psychol. Soc. Sci. **62**(1), 61–64 (2007)

Carstensen, L.L., Mikels, J.A.: At the intersection of emotion and cognition aging and the positivity effect. Curr. Dir. Psychol. Sci. **14**(3), 117–121 (2005)

Ferrucci, L., Guralnik, J.M., Simonsick, E., Salive, M.E., Corti, C., Langlois, J.: Progressive versus catastrophic disability: a longitudinal view of the disablement process. J. Gerontol. **51** (3), 123–130 (1996)

Gamberini, L., Raya, M.A., Barresi, G., Fabregat, M., Ibanez, F., Prontu, L.: Cognition, technology and games for the elderly: an introduction to ELDERGAMES Project. PsychNology J. **4**(3), 285–308 (2006)

Hardy, D.J., Parasuraman, R.: Cognition and flight performance in older pilots. J. Exp. Psychol. Appl. **3**(4), 313–348 (1997)

Harley, L., Robertson, S., Gandy, M., Harbert, S., Britton, D.: The design of an interactive stroke rehabilitation gaming system. In: Jacko, J.A. (ed.) Human-Computer Interaction, Part IV, HCII 2011. LNCS, vol. 6764, pp. 167–173. Springer, Heidelberg (2011)

Imbeault, F., Bouchard, B., Bouzouane, A.: Serious games in cognitive training for Alzheimer's patients. In: IEEE 1st International Conference on Serious Games and Applications for Health (SeGAH), pp. 1–8 (2011)

McClellan, A., Williams, C.: Visual accessibility analysis of food for thought. Technical report. North Carolina State University, Raleigh, NC (2014)

McGonigal, J.: Reality Is Broken: Why Games Make Us Better and How They Can Change the World. Penguin, London (2011)

Pak, R., McLaughlin, A.C.: Designing Displays for Older Adults. CRC Press, Boca Raton (2010)

Rogers, W.A., Fisk, A.D., McLaughlin, A.C., Pak, R.: Touch a screen or turn a knob: choosing the best device for the job. Hum. Factors **2**(18), 271–288 (2005)

United States Census Bureau. Nearly 1 in 5 people have a disability in the U.S., Census Bureau Reports (2012). http://www.census.gov/newsroom/releases/archives/miscellaneous/cb12-134.html

Zyda, M.: From visual simulation to virtual reality to games. Computer **38**(9), 25–31 (2005)

How Measuring an Older Person's Walking Pattern Can Help Keep Them Mobile

'Personalised Healthcare for Mobility'

Diana Hodgins[1(✉)] and Ian McCarthy[2]

[1] School of Engineering and Technology, University of Hertfordshire, Hatfield, UK
dmh@etb.co.uk

[2] Pedestrian Accessibility and Movement Environment Laboratory, University College London, London, UK
i.mccarthy@ucl.ac.uk

Abstract. One of the common causes of falls is gait deficiency, and the first aim of the study was to ascertain how specific gait parameters of elderly people with gait and balance issues compare to those of the healthy elderly population. Eleven 'at risk' elderly people were compared with eighteen healthy people.

The second aim was to explore the potential of using objective data to support personalised exercise over a two year period to help prevent falls. The 'at risk' group attended a weekly balance class and were monitored regularly.

The results indicate that gait can be adapted by instruction and exercises. Regular monitoring provided the participants with the incentive to continue with the exercises. No participant fell during the monitoring period and all remained active. These results indicate that it is possible to personalise exercises and provide motivation using gait data and this could potentially reduce falls in the elderly.

Keywords: Mobility · Gait · Monitoring · Sensors · Elderly · Falls

1 Statement of the Objective and Significance of the Work

Mobility of the elderly relates directly to the number of falls, with one of the common causes of falls in the elderly related to gait deficiencies [1]. Currently, gait is monitored visually and hence provides no objective data which can be shared between groups, either locally, nationally or internationally. Classic assessments of gait such as the Berg Balance test [2], the Timed up and Go test [3] assess balance rather than gait and provide scores for the different activities which are themselves subjective. Simple speed tests, using distance and time measurements provide objective data for speed but do not ascertain the corresponding gait parameters. Without gait data it is impossible to identify the cause of the gait deficiency and hence objective advice on how to improve cannot be provided. For example one person with a slow gait may have a knee problem, another a problem with medial-lateral movement of the thigh and another an ankle problem. Early stage Parkinson's Disease, dementia and a stroke also affect a person's gait pattern. All of these conditions would reduce speed, yet their management

J. Zhou and G. Salvendy (Eds.): ITAP 2015, Part II, LNCS 9194, pp. 72–81, 2015.
DOI: 10.1007/978-3-319-20913-5_7

would be entirely different. Hence it is essential to understand the underlying gait parameters for each individual. To date studies have not specifically focused on gait parameters or investigated any correlation between gait parameters that define angular movement of the limbs and falls in the elderly.

The risk of falling increases with age and one in three adults over 65 falls each year [4]. It is recognised that many of these falls relate to the individual's health and are preventable. However, falls can cause distress, pain, injury and most importantly loss in confidence and after a fall nearly 50% have a fear of falling again. There are numerous references that show correlation of falling with speed, including one where speed was correlated with survival rate [5]. However, there are others that state speed is not age dependent but medial-lateral movement is and it is this that affects the likeliness of falling [6]. Unfortunately the cohort of subjects is not consistent between studies and some studies are done overland and others on a treadmill, which introduces additional variables. Another study found a correlation between quadriceps strength and gait speed in older people [7]. All of these studies provide further support that there are a wide variety of reasons why older people have problems with walking.

Gait parameters for healthy people of all ages have already been published [8] and it was found that there was little change in gait with age up to 80 years old.

The aims of the study were twofold; (i) to ascertain how specific gait parameters of elderly people with gait and balance issues compare to those of the healthy elderly population, (ii) to explore the potential of using objective gait data to support personalised exercise over a two year period to help prevent falls. This was to be achieved using a sensor based gait analysis system (GaitSmart, ETB, UK).

GaitSmart provides information on the orientation of each segment in the sagittal and coronal plane and also the joint angle between two segments. Up to six sensors can be used, mounted on the pelvis, thigh and tibia, often referred to as the calf. The system has been used to monitor the rehabilitation phase of people recovering from hip and knee replacement [9, 10] and to identify gait changes due to early stage knee osteoarthritis [11].

It was decided that for the purpose of this study, the range of motion (ROM) of the knee and the symmetry between the left and right knee ROM would be analysed, requiring just four sensors. This provides a good indication of stride length plus how well the individual picks their feet up, reducing the risk of tripping. Older people may reduce their thigh range of motion and this reduces their knee angle and stride length [8, 12]. The symmetry indicates whether the individual is balanced. This minimises the amount of data that the individual needs to understand so that they can act upon the information.

2 Methods

Two groups were monitored using the sensor-based gait analysis system, and for both groups the process of measuring gait was the same. Four elastic straps with pockets were applied to each thigh and shank. Thigh straps were attached to a belt fitted around the waist with a further Velcro strap. They were attached so as to lie approximately 10 cm above the knee joint/ lateral condyle of the femur. The shanks straps were applied around the widest part of the calf, rather than a set distance from the knee joint as this varied with people of different heights with regards to calf musculature. Four IMUs, which each contain three orthogonal gyroscopes and three orthogonal accelerometers were inserted into the pockets in the elastic straps. The thigh IMUs were orientated along an imaginary line from the greater trochanter to the lateral condyle of the femur; tibia IMUs were orientated along an imaginary line drawn between the head of the fibula and the lateral malleolus. All straps were applied over the participants' clothing, as shown in Fig. 1.

Participants were asked to walk at their self-selected speed for 10 m along a corridor unaided. Each person took no more than 5 min to test. At the end of the test the sensors were removed and attached to the laptop to download and analyse the data.

The first group comprised eighteen healthy elderly people, mean age 70, range 62 to 83, were used to obtain reference gait parameters for healthy people of the older age group. Participants were excluded if they had had previous surgery on their lower limbs, had a neuromuscular condition that might affect gait (e.g. stroke, Parkinson's disease), had current back pain, were not able to walk 10 m without a walking aid, or if they could not give informed consent. Ethical approval for the study was given by UCL Research Ethics Committee, and all participants gave informed consent. These individuals were monitored once [8].

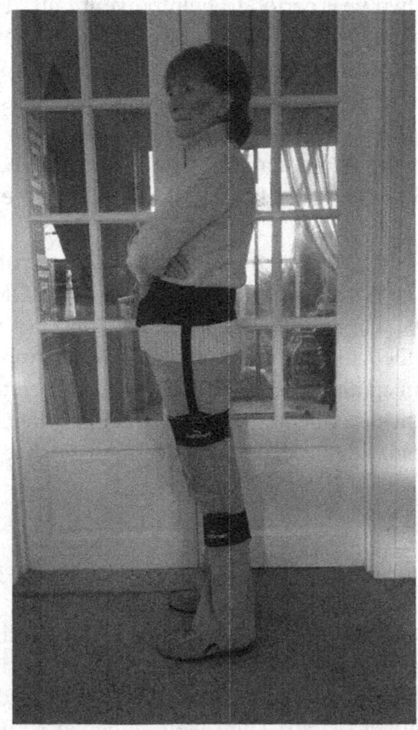

Fig. 1. Healthy older person with the straps and sensors attached

The second group comprised eleven older people with walking and balance problems who were monitored in the longitudinal study. These individuals attended a balance class open to the public at a council run day centre. At the chosen centre the class runs for 45 min and includes a range of gentle exercises done whilst sitting down. All the attendees were provided with information of the study and all participants gave informed consent. As the individuals joined at various times during the study, the monitoring period varied between 8 to 130 weeks, with seven over 50 weeks.

The group included:

- Person who had suffered a stroke
- Person who had had a brain tumour
- Person with lower limb prosthesis
- Person with emphysema

The age ranged from 68 to 91 with the mean age of 78. The individuals were monitored approximately every 10 weeks during this period.

For each individual their gait pattern was measured and a report produced at each session and their medical data noted. From this a summary report was provided for each individual, which identified how their knee angle and symmetry between left and right differed from the healthy reference and from their previous tests. At the end of the class anyone that was noticeably away from their previous values had further discussions with the balance class teacher who then suggested specific exercises to address the specific problem area. The aim was to help the individual maintain or even improve their knee ROM and reduce their asymmetry by developing a personalised treatment plan for the individuals. This was done with the balance class teacher and the individual, referring to the knee angle gait data. Each individual was left for approximately 10 weeks to follow their personalised plan with weekly input from the balance class teacher. At the next session their results were compared to their previous history and their results added to their personal report.

Knee range of motion (ROM) provides a good indication as to how well the person lifts their feet during walking. Asymmetry in the knee ROM indicates how stable they are when walking.

3 Results

Knee ROM and knee asymmetry are plotted against age in Figs. 2a and b for the healthy reference group.

Average knee ROM was 61° with a spread of 22°. Average asymmetry was 0.9% with a spread of from -14% to 22%. Neither parameter was age dependent.

The balance class group were then compared to the healthy reference group and the results summarised in Table 1. For the healthy group this is the average for the 18 subjects. For the balance class group it is the overall average of the eleven subjects, where for each subject it is their average over time. The results show that the stride duration is longer for the balance class group, the average knee ROM is lower and the asymmetry greater.

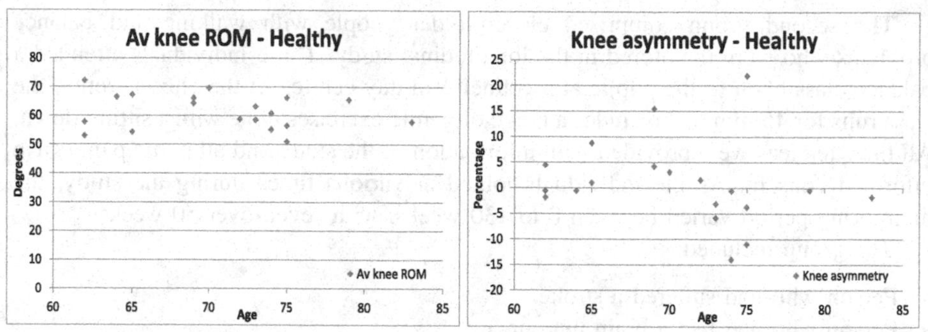

Fig. 2. (a) Knee ROM for healthy group and (b) Knee asymmetry for the healthy group

Table 1. Mean and SD for healthy elderly and balance class group

	Age	Knee ROM	Knee % asymmetry	Stride duration
Balance class				
Av ±SD	78.3±7.7	52. 6 ±12.7	−3.3±4.4	1.24±0.17
Healthy				
Av ±SD	70.6±6.0	61.3±6.0	0.9±8.2	1.05±0.11

For the balance class group an example of the report that was provided to the individuals is provided in Table 2. A hard copy was also provided, which many took home to discuss with their family.

The lower limit data was 1 SD from the healthy elderly data, and the numbers were highlighted in red if outside the lower limits.

The changes in knee flexion and asymmetry over time for the 11 participants are shown in Fig. 3. Three of the individuals were consistently below the −2 SD level for knee flexion, and could be considered as in a danger region, in that the low knee flexion means that the foot is at risk of catching objects on the ground. Four people were consistently above the −1 SD and the other four varied between normal and −2 SD.

One person that was below −2 SD for knee ROM had reduced muscle strength at 91 years old. He did however have a symmetric gait and maintained his walking for nearly a year at a fairly constant level, see Fig. 4. He did this knowing he was in the warning area and keeping up with the exercises suggested from the exercise teacher.

The second person in the danger zone was an 83 year old lady who had very weak muscles. Again she was advised to try and keep moving as much as possible and she did not deteriorate.

The third was a lady fitted with a prosthesis below the knee (subject 11). She was aware that she needed to ensure that her gait did not deteriorate, and only once did knee flexion go below 30°. This was a warning to her and she worked harder at the exercises. The result was that two years after starting monitoring her gait was better than when she started: 35° of knee flexion after 110 weeks compared to 30° at the start (see Fig. 5).

Table 2. Example report provided to the balance class attendee

Week from start	Walking aid	Medical condition	Stride duration (s)	Left knee ROM (°)	Right knee ROM (°)	Left/ right Asymmetry (%)
Lower limit		*healthy*	*>1.2*	*55*	*55*	*(-8 to 9)*
0	None	Healthy	1.3	63	54	-15
10	None	Healthy	1.1	61	57	-7
20	None	Healthy	1.1	61	51	-17
28	None	Healthy	1.1	65	57	-13
38	None	Healthy	1.1	60	59	-2
43	None	Healthy but new shoes	1.1	65	51	-24
52	None	Healthy	1.1	64	56	-13
66	None	Healthy	1.1	62	57	-8
76	None	Healthy	1.1	63	58	-8
82	None	Healthy	1.1	59	55	-7
88	None	Slight back ache	1.1	61	52	-16
125	None	Slight leg aches	1.2	62	55	-12

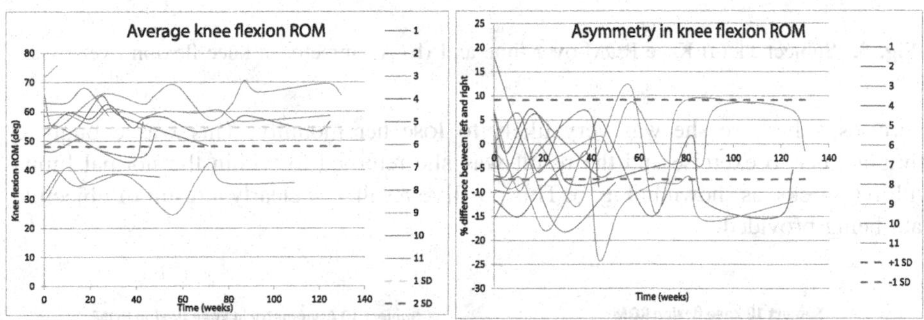

Fig. 3. (a) Average knee flexion over time (dotted lines show 1 and 2 SD from healthy ref) (b) Asymmetry in knee flexion over time (dotted lines show ±1SD)

One person dropped in to the warning zone once in a 40 week period (subject 10). This 76 year old lady stumbled after 6 weeks of monitoring and then had a fear of falling. She continued to go to the balance classes but did not work hard at the exercises, despite being advised of the problem getting worse from the balance class teacher. A request was made for a special monitoring session and the results showed the person in question that her gait had deteriorated significantly (week 38). She was advised that at this age she needed to start using the muscles properly and do the

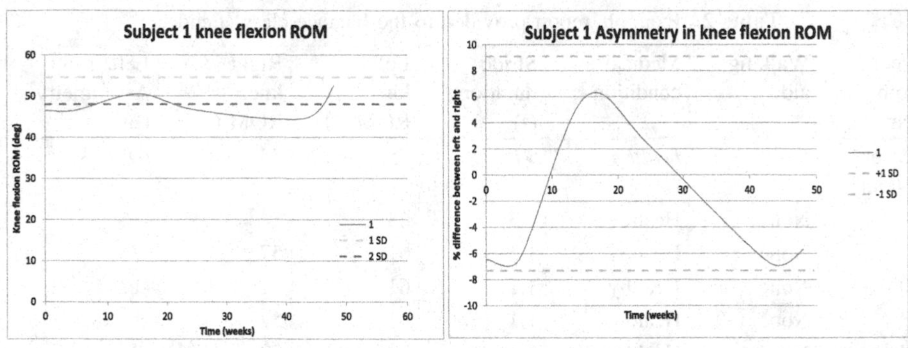

Fig. 4. Subject 1 (a) Knee ROM over time and (b) Asymmetry in knee flexion over time

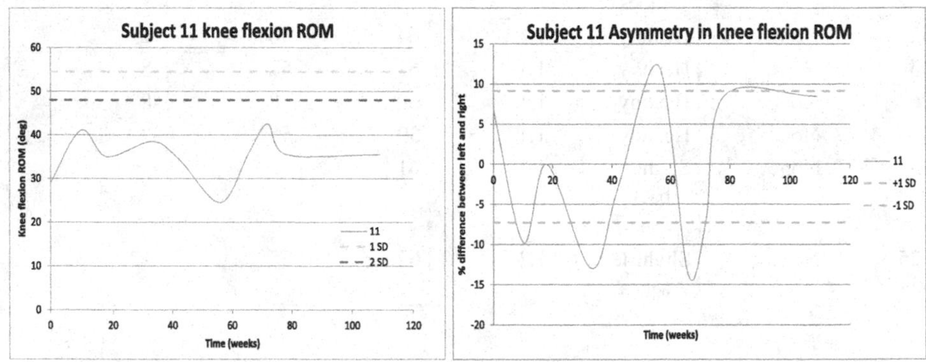

Fig. 5. Subject 11 (a) Knee ROM over time and (b) Asymmetry in knee flexion over time

exercises, otherwise she was very likely to lose her mobility. This was enough to stimulate her to exercise and the result was she returned to within the normal limits within 6 weeks, as shown in Fig. 6. This positive result was clearly a result of objective data being provided.

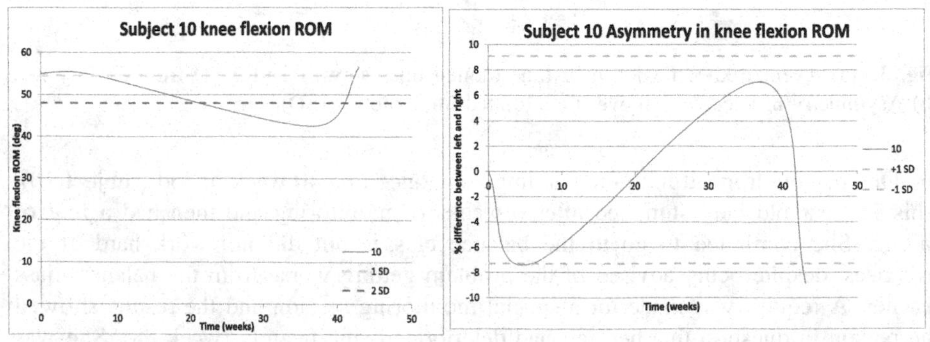

Fig. 6. Subject 10 (a) Knee ROM over time and (b) Asymmetry in knee flexion over time

Regarding knee symmetry, the majority were close to the –1 SD value, and where they were outside these limits, corrective action was taken by the individual to improve. There was only one 80 year old lady that moved outside the limits on a few occasions (subject 6). This lady had good knee ROM but had suffered a stroke that affected one side. When she was advised that the asymmetry was getting worse she worked hard on the required exercises to bring it back to normal. 120 weeks after starting the monitoring she was better than when she started, as shown in Fig. 7.

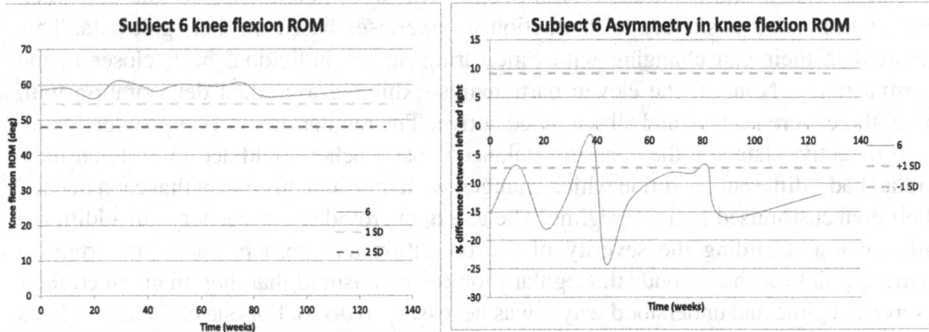

Fig. 7. Subject 6 (a) Knee ROM over time and (b) Asymmetry in knee flexion over time

When considering the average values for each of the balance class attendees, shown in Fig. 8 it can be seen that for the knee ROM three were above the average value for healthy older people, three were above –1 SD, two were above –2 SD and three below the –2SD. These three were the ones most at risk of falling.

When referring to the average knee asymmetry in Fig. 8 the majority were very close to symmetric and only two of the eleven people were outside +/–1 SD, the worst of whom was the lady who had suffered a stroke.

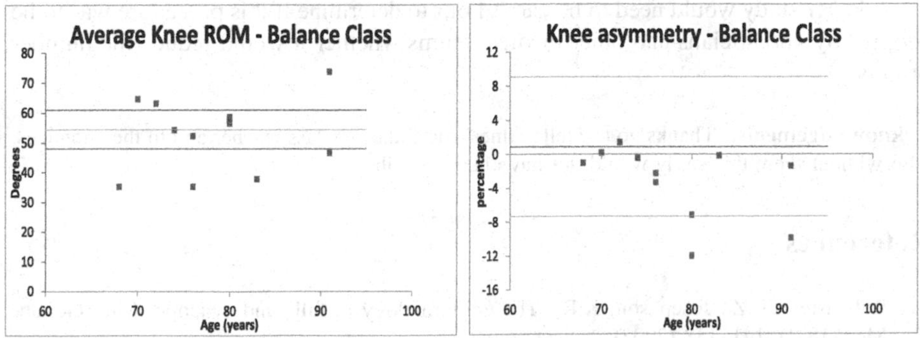

Fig. 8. (a) Average knee ROM for balance class and (b) average knee asymmetry for balance class

4 Discussion of Results

The gait data for the healthy older subjects is knee ROM 61.3° (6°), knee symmetry of 0.9 % (8.2 %) and stride duration 1.05 s (0.11 s), with an average age of 70.6. For the Balance Class group, the average knee ROM reduced to 52.6° (12.7°), significantly below average for their age group. The knee asymmetry was –3.3 % (4.4 %) which is within the 1SD of the healthy group. The stride duration was significantly slower at 1.24 s (0.17 s), which is typical for a person who has a trouble walking.

These results show that the eleven people who were monitored over the 130 week period responded positively to instruction on exercises based on their gait data. This resulted in their gait changing with time, bringing the individual back closer to the normal range. None of the eleven participants exhibited a gradual deterioration with time, there were no falls and all remained active. The regular monitoring provided them with objective data that they and the Balance Class teacher could act upon. Each individual had a different condition which changed with time and this meant that each needed their own customised exercise regime. The gait data provided the teacher with additional information regarding the severity of the condition and perhaps more important, a starting point for the individual. Regular monitoring ensured that they maintained their exercise regime and understood why it was necessary to do so. For one of the individuals with a worsening gait, it was only once she understood the severity the problem through the objective data that she responded and followed the guidance of the teacher.

5 Conclusions

All of the 'at risk' older people who attended the balance class responded well to instruction on exercises from the teacher, which was based on the evidence from the gait test. In all cases the gait parameters did not worsen over the two years and in many cases it improved. All of the individuals remained active over the 130 week trial period.

Whilst this is only a small sample size it provides evidence that gait does not have to deteriorate with age, even when the person suffers from a disability or illness that can affect it. Acting on instructions from a professional in terms of suitable exercises provided motivation to the individuals.

A larger study would need to be carried out to determine if this procedure was to be adopted by geriatricians and other medical teams whether it would reduce the number of falls.

Acknowledgements. Thanks go to Stella Hines, the Balance Class teacher and to the attendees, who without them this study would not have been possible.

References

1. Rubenstein, L.Z., Josephson, K.R.: The epidemiology of falls and syncope. Clin. Geriatr. Med. **18**(2), 141–158 (2002)
2. Langley, F., Mackintosh, S.F.: Functional balance assessment of older community dwelling adults: a systematic review of the literature. Internet J. Allied Health Sci. Pract. **5**(4) (2007)

3. Herman, T., Giladi, N., Hausdorff, J.M.: Properties of the 'Timed Up and Go' test: more than meets the eye. Gerontology **57**(3), 203–210 (2011). PMC. Web, 11 December 2014
4. National conference of state legislators (NCSL). Elderly Falls Prevention Legislation and Statutes, 28 July 2014
5. Studenski, S., Perera, S., Patel, K., Rosano, C., Faulkner, K., Inzitari, M., Brach, J., Chandler, J., Cawthon, P., Connor, E.B., Nevitt, M., Visser, M., Kritchesvsky, S., Badinelli, S., Harris, T., Newman, A.B., Cauley, J., Ferrucci, L., Guralnik, J.: Gait speed and survival in older adults. JAMA : J. Am. Med. Assoc. **305**(1) (2011)
6. Terrier, P., Reynard, F.: Effect of age on the variability and stability of gait: a cross-sectional treadmill study in healthy individuals between 20 and 69 years of age. Gait Posture, **41**(1) (2015)
7. Brown, M., Sinacore, D.R., Host, H.H.: The relationship of strength to function in the older adult. J. Gerontol. Biol. Sci. Med. Sci. **50**(Spec No.), 55–59 (1995)
8. Monda, M., et al.: Use of inertial measurement units to assess age-related changes in gait kinematics in an active population. J. Aging Phys. Act. **23**, 18–23 (2015)
9. McCarthy, I., et al.: Gait assessment as a functional outcome measure in total knee arthroplasty: a cross-sectional study. BMC Musculoskelet. Disord. (under review)
10. Doyle, F.J., Timperley, A.J., Hodgins, D.: Assessment of hip range of motion in the sagittal plane post total hip arthroplasty using a novel six sensor inertial measurement unit system Br. Hip Soc. Annu. Conf. (2014)
11. McCarthy, I., Hodgins, D., Mor, A., Elbaz, A., Segal, G.: Analysis of knee flexion characteristics and how they alter with the onset of knee osteoarthritis: a case control study. BMC Musculoskelet. Disord. **14**, 169 (2013)
12. Kerrigan, D.C., Lee, L.W., Collins, J.J., Riley, P.O., Lipsitz, L.A.: Reduced hip extension during walking: healthy elderly and fallers versus young adults. Arch. Phys. Med. Rehabil. **82**(1), 26–30 (2001)

Opportunities for Technology: Translating an Efficacious Intervention to Improve Medication Adherence Among Older Adults

Kathie Insel[1(✉)], Jeannie K. Lee[2], Gilles O. Einstein[3], and Daniel G. Morrow[4]

[1] College of Nursing, University of Arizona, Tucson, AZ 85721, USA
insel@email.arizona.edu
[2] College of Pharmacy, University of Arizona, Tucson, AZ 85721, USA
jlee@pharmacy.arizona.edu
[3] Department of Psychology, Furman University, Greenville, SC 29613, USA
gil.einstein@furman.edu
[4] Beckman Institute, University of Illinois, Urbana, IL 61801, USA
dgm@illinois.edu

Abstract. We developed and tested the Multifaceted Prospective Memory Intervention (MPMI) to improve medication adherence among older adults (≥ 65 years of age) who were prescribed at least one daily medication for the control of high blood pressure. Blood pressure control is important because high blood pressure is a leading cause of stroke, heart failure, retinopathy, renal disease as well as pathology in other end organs including the brain. The MPMI resulted in improvement from 57 % at baseline to 78 % adherence to the inter-dose interval post intervention, but most of these gains were lost after 5 months. The control condition started at 68 %, was stable during the intervention, but dropped to 62 % after 5 months of additional monitoring. The intervention was successful, but the effects were not sustained. Continued investigation to find ways to enhance self-management among older adults using technology is needed in order to maintain health and function.

Keywords: Medication adherence · Aging

1 Introduction

Nonadherence is an important barrier to the treatment of hypertension [1–3]. Our previous work [e.g., 4, 5] demonstrated strong initial, but not sustained, benefits on adherence of the Multifaceted Prospective Memory Intervention (MPMI). We believe that incorporating the MPMI strategies into mobile devices, such as smartphones or tablets and/or incorporation of the strategies into web-based programs to reinforce the strategies; will help people maintain the benefits of the intervention.

The control of hypertension among older adults is a significant problem. The prevalence of hypertension in 2009-2010 was estimated at 66.7 % for people ≥ 60 years and 73 % for people ≥ 80 years of age [6]. The effects of poor blood pressure control in older adults are devastating and associated with cerebrovascular disease, coronary artery disease, aortic and peripheral arterial disease, and chronic kidney

J. Zhou and G. Salvendy (Eds.): ITAP 2015, Part II, LNCS 9194, pp. 82–88, 2015.
DOI: 10.1007/978-3-319-20913-5_8

disease, and these chronic conditions affect quality of life [7]. Hypertension is the single most important risk factor for stroke [8–10] and a primary risk factor for myocardial infarction, heart failure, and end organ damage to the kidneys, retina, and brain [11–14]. Older individuals with a history of uncontrolled hypertension are at risk for cognitive decline, and this further compromises the capacity to self-manage chronic illness [15]. Given the prevalence and deleterious outcomes of uncontrolled hypertension among older adults, it is unfortunate that adherence to treatment is only 50 % [e.g., 1, 3].

We focused the medication adherence intervention on supporting the necessary cognitive processes for remembering to take medications as prescribed. Prospective memory is remembering to complete an intended action sometime in the future. Medication taking is a prospective memory activity since the taking of medication is planned for some time in the future and often, in the face of delays and distractions, it can be forgotten. There is good evidence associating cognitive function and medication adherence [15, 16 for a review see 17]. The most common reasons for nonadherence are cited as forgetfulness, changing medication schedules or busy lifestyles [17]. Each of these reasons is potentially cognitive in nature. Forgetfulness is failing to remember to take medications at the designated times, changing schedules is likely to interfere with memory strategies that are based on routine and on associated environmental cues in one's routine context, and busy lifestyles contribute to nonadherence by adding cognitive distractions that challenge limited working memory capacity. Adherence may particularly depend on executive function and working memory [15] because past research demonstrates only small effects of interventions that address education [e.g., 18] or the design of medication instructions (and therefore patient understanding) [see for example 19]. Therefore, adherence may be improved by interventions that target executive function and working memory. We used the following model to create the MPMI and will use this model to augment the MPMI by using technology with the goal of sustaining the effectiveness of the intervention strategies.

2 Model of Cognitive Factors in Self-Management Among Older Adults

As shown, nonadherence to treatment increases the severity of hypertension leading to declines in cognitive function [20, 21], and cognitive function is related to medication adherence in real-world settings [15] and to poorer prospective memory performance in laboratory settings on tasks that do not have easily identifiable external cues [22].

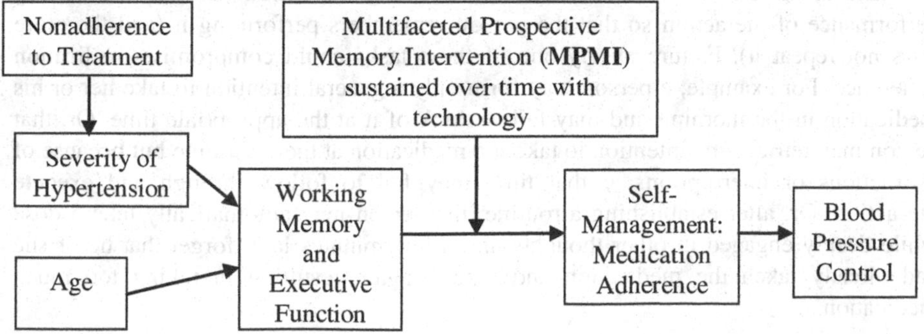

Two conclusions from the prospective memory and aging literatures suggest that strategies that target memory processes will be successful. First, there is remarkable variability in age effects on laboratory tests of prospective memory, with some studies showing minimal or no age differences [23, 24] and others showing striking age differences [e.g., 25–27]. Second, there is evidence that normal aging has more pronounced disruptive effects on cognitive functioning mediated by the frontal lobes (e.g., working memory and executive attention) [28–30] than it does on cognitive functioning mediated by the medial temporal areas (e.g., relatively automatic associative retrieval processes). Consistent with reviews of the aging and prospective memory literature [24, 30, 31], the emerging pattern is that older adults show substantial deficits when they rely on working memory and executive resources for prospective remembering, but minimal deficits when they rely on mostly preserved and relatively automatic associative retrieval processes. For example, age differences are robust on prospective memory tasks that require strategic monitoring for the correct opportunity to perform an intended action or when the retrieved action must be delayed (thus placing a demand on working memory and attentional resources for keeping the retrieved intention activated over the delay). In contrast, age differences are minimal when there are good external or environmental cues that support relatively automatic retrieval of the intended action (cues that have been associated with intended actions) and when the action can be performed immediately [32]. Thus, the focus of technology can be to encourage older adults' use of environmentally supported associative retrieval processes (thought to be relatively spared with age) in place of prospective memory processes that heavily rely on working memory and executive resources (thought to be compromised with age). Indeed, findings from our prior MPMI study suggest that older adults who scored lower on a composite measure of working memory/executive function benefitted more from the intervention, presumably because the intervention allowed them to use associative retrieval more than executive control processes in order to take their medications.

The intervention, supported by technology, needs to target all of the memory and attentional processes thought to be critical for successful prospective memory performance in everyday tasks such as medication taking [33, 34]. These include (1) forming a good encoding of the intended action and the condition(s) that is appropriate for initiating the action, (2) remembering the intention over the retention interval, (3) retrieving the intention at the appropriate point in time, (4) inhibiting other ongoing activities at the critical time and actually executing the action, and (5) monitoring performance of the action so that the person remembers performing it (and therefore does not repeat it). Failure at any one of these tasks could compromise medication adherence. For example, a person may form only a general intention to take her or his medication in the morning and may fail to think of it at the appropriate time. Or, that person may retrieve the intention to take the medication at the right time but because of distractions or interruptions at that time may fail to follow through and execute the action. Or, after establishing a routine, the person may automatically take a dose while deeply engaged in other thoughts and a few minutes later forget that he or she had already taken the medication and take it again resulting in taking too much medication.

3 The MPMI Strategies

We used a variety of strategies to facilitate medication taking. The training protocol for the interventionists included establishing a relationship and identifying individual goals that involved active listening to promote collaboration in medication taking. Using Leventhal's Common-Sense Model of Self-Regulation [35], we sought comprehension of the patient's illness representation. That is, what is the patient's timeline (chronic or acute), what is the patient's view of the causes, controllability and consequences of hypertension. If hypertension cannot be controlled because it is "God's will," it is important to understand that this is the patient's perspective. We also examined how the individual talked about hypertension. What words were used to label hypertension and its causes, controllability and consequences? We then addressed beliefs through education and attention. Importantly, in the test of the MPMI both control condition and intervention groups received education and attention, the later which was accomplished by equating time spent with the participant. We then focused the intervention group on the strategies used for enhancing successful prospective remembering to take medications as intended. We helped the participant identify his/her routine, with the goal of taking medications at the same time and in the same place. If they got up at 4:00 a.m., we discussed medication taking strategies within the routine and honored that his/her day started at 4:00 a.m. We did not try to change the routine. Then, we asked how can plans for medication taking be linked to his/her routine? We asked that they use a diary to record when the routine changed and why and if this explained missing doses of medications. We discussed external strategies and worked with participants to place cues in the home environment that would facilitate remembering. All of the strategies mentioned were covered in an initial meeting with the participant. We also taught them to "do it now," not to delay taking medications when they thought of them because we explained even a short delay of five seconds could lead to failure to take the medication as planned [36, 37]. We encouraged participants to elaborate the action of taking medications to make the action more memorable and to convert a medication taking event that was scheduled or time-based to a daily event, like eating breakfast or watching a particular television program [38]. We had them use organizers to enhance monitoring that the medication was taken as intended since habitual activities are repetitious and accurate completion of the activity can be confused [39].

Technology used to support medication taking must be designed to sustain the interaction with the intervention perhaps through ongoing coaching and/or by continuing the strategies even after the nurse leaves the home or the patient leaves the clinic. The technological support delivered by mobile devices or web based programs, would need, at minimum, to remind participants at the correct time and request that they indicate that the medication was taken. Individuals need some choice, for example, how reminders appear and how often they are reminded until the action is completed. If technology can be used to continue the strategies in the intervention, then theoretically the effects of the intervention can be sustained over time.

4 Technological Challenges

The tested in-home intervention, the MPMI, used several strategies [5]. Translation of these strategies to a mobile application or other technological support system is going to require creativity. Standard reminding devices are unlikely to result in the positive benefit found with the tested intervention. Also, there are many reminding devices and applications currently on the market, many of which are too complex for older and younger users alike and have no empirical testing and hence, no evidence based support. Older adults also represent a unique and evolving group in relationship to use of technology. A recent study examining baby boomers' adoption of health technologies found that baby boomers were similar to younger age groups in readiness to use some technologies (websites, email, automated call centers, medical video conferencing and texting), but not others (smartphones, podcasts, kiosks, blogs and wikis) [40]. There is increasing evidence that older adults want to remain independent and find hope in the possibility of technology to allow them to do so [41]. Therefore, the challenges of developing support for self-management are outweighed by the opportunities involved. As baby boomers move into older years, they will take with them greater familiarity with technology and use of smartphones and tablets to improve quality of life and maintain function. They are also more likely to seek health information on the internet and could use internet based programs to reinforce learned strategies. Translating efficacious interventions to technologically supported interventions is challenging and presents opportunities for continued health and function in later years.

References

1. Osterberg, L., Blacschke, T.: Adherence to medications. N. Engl. J. Med. **353**(5), 487–497 (2005)
2. Viswanathan, M., et al.: Interventions to improve adherence to self-administered medications for chronic diseases in the United States: a systematic review. Ann. Intern. Med. **157**(11), 785–795 (2012)
3. Vrijens, B., et al.: Adherence to prescribed antihypertensive drug treatments: longitudinal study of electronically compiled dosing histories. BMJ **336**(7653), 1114–1117 (2008)
4. Insel, K.C.: Close out report multifaceted prospective memory intervention to improve medication adherence. National Institutes of Health: National Institutes of Health era commons (2013)
5. Insel, K.C., et al.: A multifaceted prospective memory intervention to improve medication adherence: design of a randomized control trial. Contemp. Clin. Trials **34**(1), 45–52 (2013)
6. Guo, F., et al.: Trends in prevalence, awareness, management, and control of hypertension among United States adults, 1999 to 2010. J. Am. Coll. Cardiol. **60**(7), 599–606 (2012)
7. Aronow, W.S., et al.: ACCF/AHA 2011 expert consensus document on hypertension in the elderly: a report of the american college of cardiology foundation task force on clinical expert consensus documents developed in collaboration with the american academy of neurology, american geriatrics society, american society for preventive cardiology, american society of hypertension, american society of nephrology, association of black cardiologists, and european society of hypertension. J. Am. Soc. Hypertens. **5**(4), 259–352 (2011)

8. Dahlof, B.: Prospects for the prevention of stroke. J. Hypertens. Suppl. **24**(2), 3–9 (2006)
9. Fields, L.E., et al.: The burden of adult hypertension in the United States 1999 to 2000: a rising tide. Hypertens. **44**(4), 398–404 (2004)
10. Lloyd-Jones, D., et al.: Heart disease and stroke statistics–2010 update: a report from the american heart association. Circulation **121**(7), e46–e215 (2010)
11. Flack, J.M., et al.: Prevention of hypertension and its complications: theoretical basis and guidelines for treatment. J. Am. Soc. Nephrol. **14**(7 Suppl 2), S92–S98 (2003)
12. de Leeuw, F.E., et al.: Endothelial cell activation is associated with cerebral white matter lesions in patients with cerebrovascular disease. Ann. NY Acad. Sci. **977**, 306–314 (2002)
13. Raz, N., Rodrigue, K.M., Acker, J.D.: Hypertension and the brain : vulnerability of the prefrontal regions and executive functions. Behav. Neurosci. **117**(6), 1169–1180 (2003)
14. Bohm, M., et al.: Effects of nonpersistence with medication on outcomes in high-risk patients with cardiovascular disease. Am. Heart J. **166**(2), 306–314 (2013). e7
15. Insel, K., et al.: Executive function, working memory, and medication adherence among older adults. J. Gerontol. B Psychol. Sci. Soc. Sci. **61**(2), 102–107 (2006)
16. Hayes, T.L., et al.: Medication adherence in healthy elders: small cognitive changes make a big difference. J. Aging Health **21**(4), 567–580 (2009)
17. Stone, V.E.: Strategies for optimizing adherence to highly active antiretroviral therapy: lessons from research and clinical practice. Clin. Infect. Dis. **33**(6), 865–872 (2001)
18. Burge, S., et al.: Correlates of medication knowledge and adherence: findings from the residency research network of South Texas. Fam. Med. **37**(10), 712–718 (2005)
19. Shrank, W.H., et al.: Can improved prescription medication labeling influence adherence to chronic medications? an evaluation of the target pharmacy label. J. Gen. Intern. Med. **24**(5), 570–578 (2009)
20. Raz, N., et al.: Vascular health and longitudinal changes in brain and cognition in middle-aged and older adults. Neuropsychology **21**(2), 149–157 (2007)
21. Novak, V., Hajjar, I.: The relationship between blood pressure and cognitive function. Nat. Rev. Cardiol. **7**(12), 686–698 (2010)
22. Scullin, M.K., et al.: Evidence for a detrimental relationship between hypertension history, prospective memory, and prefrontal cortex white matter in cognitively normal older adults. Cogn. Affect. Behav. Neurosci. **13**(2), 405–416 (2013)
23. Kvavilashvili, L., et al.: Differential effects of age on prospective and retrospective memory tasks in young, young-old, and old-old adults. Memory **17**(2), 180–196 (2009)
24. Einstein, G.O., McDaniel, M.A., Scullin, M.: Prospective memory and aging: understanding the variability. In: Ohta, N., Naveh-Benjamin, M., (eds.) Memory and Aging, pp. 153–179. Psychology Press, New York (2012)
25. Maylor, E.A.: Aging and forgetting in prospective and retrospective memory tasks. Psychol. Aging **8**(3), 420–428 (1993)
26. Maylor, E.A.: Age-related impairment in an event-based prospective-memory task. Psychol. Aging **11**(1), 74–78 (1996)
27. West, R., Herndon, R.W., Covell, E.: Neural correlates of age-related declines in the formation and realization of delayed intentions. Psychol. Aging **18**(3), 461–473 (2003)
28. Raz, N.: The aging brain observed in vivo: differential changes and their modifiers. In: Cabeza, R., Nyberg, L., Park, D., (eds.) Cognitive Neuroscience of Aging: Linking Cognitive and Cerebral Aging, pp. 19–57. Oxford University Press, Oxford (2005)
29. West, R.L.: An application of prefrontal cortex function theory to cognitive aging. Psychol. Bull. **120**(2), 272–292 (1996)
30. McDaniel, M.A., Einstein, G.O.: The neuropsychology of prospective memory in normal aging: a componential approach. Neuropsychologia **49**(8), 2147–2155 (2011). Epub 28 Dec 2010

31. McDaniel, M.A., Einstein, G.O., Jacoby, L.L.: New considerations in aging and memory: the glass may be half full. In: Craik, F.I.M., Salthouse, T.A., (eds.) The Handbook of Aging and Cognition (3rd edn.), pp. 251–310. Psychology Press, New York (2008)
32. Mullet, H.G., et al.: Prospective memory and aging: evidence for preserved spontaneous retrieval with exact but not related cues. Psychol. Aging **28**(4), 910–922 (2013)
33. Ellis, J.: Prospective memory or the realization of delayed intentions: a conceptual framework for research. In: Brandimonte, M., Einstein, G.O., McDaniel, M.A., (eds.) Prospective Memory Theory and Applications, pp. 1–22. Lawrence Erlbaum Associates Mahwah, NJ (1996)
34. McDaniel, M.A., Einstein, G.O.: Prospective Memory: An Overview and Synthesis of an Emerging Field. Sage Publications Inc., Thousand Oaks (2007)
35. Leventhal, H., Brissette, I., Leventhal, E.A.: The common-sense model of self-regulation of health and illness. In: Cameron, L.D., Leventhal, H., (eds.) Self-Regulation of Health and Illness Behaviour, pp. 42–65. Routledge, New York (2003)
36. McDaniel, M.A., Einstein, G.O.: Prospective memory components most at risk for older adults and implications for medication adherence. In: Park, D.C., Liu, L.L.,(eds.) Medical Adherence and Aging: Social and Cognitive Perspectives, pp. 49–75, American Psychological Association, Washington DC (2007)
37. McDaniel, M.A., et al.: Delaying execution of intentions: overcoming the costs of interruptions. Appl. Cogn. Psychol. **18**(5), 533–547 (2004)
38. Einstein, G.O., et al.: Aging and prospective memory: examining the influences of self-initiated retrieval processes. J. Exp. Psychol. Learn. Mem. Cogn. **21**(4), 996–1007 (1995)
39. Repetition errors in habitual prospective memory: Elimination of age differences via complex actions or appropriate resource allocation. Neuropsychol. Dev. Cogn. B Aging Neuropsychol. Cogn. **16**(5), 563–588 (2009). Epub 28 May 2009
40. LeRouge, C., et al.: Baby boomers' adoption of consumer health technologies: survey on readiness and barriers. J. Med. Internet Res. **16**(9), e200 (2014)
41. Long, S.O.: Bodies, technologies, and aging in Japan: thinking about old people and their silver products. J. Cross Cult. Gerontol. **27**(2), 119–137 (2012)

Taiwanese Middle-Aged and Elderly Patients' Acceptance and Resistance Toward the Health Cloud

Wen-Tsung Ku[1] and Pi-Jung Hsieh[2(✉)]

[1] Department of Physical Medicine and Rehabilitation, St. Martin de Porres Hospital, Chiayi City, Taiwan, Republic of China
kib56265@gmail.com

[2] Department of Hospital and Health Care Administration, Chia Nan University of Pharmacy and Science, Tainan, Taiwan, Republic of China
beerun@seed.net.tw

Abstract. As the Taiwanese society ages, the demand for cloud services is rising, particularly among middle-aged and elderly patients, since it enables people to live independently and access health care easily. Despite cloud services great potential, there are gaps in our understanding of how patients evaluate change related to the health cloud and why they resist it. In keeping with the technology acceptance and status quo bias perspectives, this study develops an integrated model to explain middle-aged and elderly patients' intention to use and resistance to health cloud services. A field survey was conducted in Taiwan to collect data from middle-aged and elderly patients. The structural equation model was used to examine the data. The results showed that patients' resistance to use health cloud services was caused by sunk costs, inertia, and transition costs. Attitude, subjective norm, and perceived behavior control have positive and direct effects on behavioral intention to use. The results also indicate a significant negative effect in the relationship between middle-aged and elderly patients' intention and resistance to using the health cloud. Our research illustrates the importance of incorporating user resistance into technology acceptance studies in general and health technology usage studies in particular. There are grounds for a resistance model that can serve as the starting point for future studies in this relatively unexplored, yet potentially fertile, area of research.

Keywords: Health cloud · Middle-aged and elderly patients · User resistance · Technology acceptance · Status quo bias

1 Introduction

Since 1995, the National Health Insurance program has been providing comprehensive health-care coverage for the majority of Taiwan's 23 million inhabitants. The majority of patients tend to visit several hospitals throughout their lives, and "hospital shopping" has become a relatively common occurrence in Taiwan. Furthermore, due to falling birth rates and a longer average life expectancy, Taiwanese society is aging [1]. Thus,

J. Zhou and G. Salvendy (Eds.): ITAP 2015, Part II, LNCS 9194, pp. 89–100, 2015.
DOI: 10.1007/978-3-319-20913-5_9

the accelerated growth of the middle-aged and elderly population makes health promotion and disease prevention imperative for these citizens. Given this fact, the Ministry of Health and Welfare intends to build a health platform by storing every citizen's health-care information in the health cloud. The health cloud program consists of the following: (a) a medical cloud for sharing electronic medical records across facilities in different hospitals; (b) a care cloud enabling wireless devices that allow for the monitoring of a patient's blood pressure, heart rate, and glucose level, among other functions, and enable a patient's health data to be transmitted between different locations; and (c) a wellness cloud that uses open data and cloud platforms to encourage value-added service providers to develop various innovative applications, thereby allowing people to obtain health-related information at any time to enhance self-health management. In the future, it will be possible for patients to access these health cloud services at home without the need for hospitalization, thereby reducing the cost and emotional stress endured, and the effort invested, by middle-aged and elderly patients and their families. The health cloud services are personalized and pervasive, making them especially critical for middle-aged and elderly patients. Therefore, these patients' acceptance of, and support for, the health cloud is particularly critical in Taiwan. However, user resistance is unavoidable and may cause performance of the system to be lower than expected. User resistance demonstrates asymmetric behaviors that are typical of inhibitors because the presence of resistance hurts information system (IS) usage; however, a lack of resistance does not necessarily enhance IS usage [2]. Thus, there is a need to investigate the critical factors that stimulate technology acceptance and resistance and to examine the relationship between intention to use the health cloud and resistance against using it. From a practical standpoint, understanding why middle-aged and elderly patients resist and use the health cloud and how such resistance is manifested in their subsequent behavior can help government agencies and health-care administrators to devise appropriate intervention strategies for minimizing patient resistance and any adverse effects on health-care policy. In keeping with the technology acceptance and status quo bias perspectives, this study develops an integrated model to explain middle-aged and elderly patients' intention to use and resistance against health cloud services.

2 Background

Despite the emerging interest in the field of medical informatics and studies that have identified the application of the merits of the health cloud [3–7], only a limited understanding of middle-aged and elderly patients' behavior exists concerning the health cloud. Thus, the problem may be rooted in the absence of a generalized theory of user resistance and the lack of grounding within an established stream of research. In the next section, we attempt to develop such a research framework while grounding it in the literature related to IS acceptance and resistance.

2.1 Technology Acceptance and Resistance

When an innovative technology is implemented, users may decide to adopt or resist it based on their evaluation of the change associated with the new system [8]. In particular, health information technology (IT) has great potential to improve quality of care and patient safety [9]; however, this benefit is not always realized because many health IT efforts encounter difficulties or fail. Many of these failures and problems can be traced back to user resistance [10]. Resistance is not quite equivalent to non-usage, because non-usage may imply that potential adopters are simply unaware of a new system or are still evaluating it prior to its adoption, while resistance implies that the new system has been considered and rejected by these users [11]. Resistance is often marked by open hostility toward the change agents or covert behaviors to stall or undermine change, while non-usage does not generally engender such outcomes. Accordingly, this study defines user resistance as the opposition of users to the change associated with the implementation of a new technology. However, technology acceptance and resistance must be examined jointly within a common theoretical model because user resistance is clearly a barrier to IS usage [2]. Thus, health IT leaders and administrative leaders face the problem of how to address user resistance.

2.2 Theory of Planned Behavior

Among social cognition theories, the theory of reasoned action (TRA) [12] and the theory of planned behavior (TPB) [13] have been tested across a variety of populations, behaviors, and contexts. The TRA suggests that a person's behavior is determined by his or her intention to perform the behavior and that this intention is consequently a function of the person's attitude and his or her subjective norm toward that behavior [12]. Although the TRA has been evaluated and supported in numerous contexts, it offers a weak explanation of the essence of behavior. Ajzen [13] asserted that the TPB eliminated the TRA's limitations regarding managing behavior over which people have incomplete volitional control. Ajzen [13] showed that attitude and subjective norm determine a person's intention to use, and he further proposed that the person's perceived behavioral control (PBC) reflects the degree to which he or she feels that successfully engaging in that behavior is completely under his or her control. Behavioral intention (BI) measures the strength of a person's willingness to exert effort when performing certain behavioral activities. Attitude (A) explains the assessment of a favorable behavior for the person, which directly influences the strength of that behavior, as well as the beliefs regarding the anticipated outcome. Subjective norm (SN) expresses the perceived social pressure of a person who intends to perform a behavior, and it is related to normative beliefs regarding the expectations of other people. PBC is composed of human beliefs concerning capability and the controllability of performing the behavior. There are several examples of using the TPB to explain patients' behavior, and a number of studies have applied the TPB to guideline implementations [14–16]. TPB has focused on users' enabling perceptions related to IS usage [2]. Thus, we propose that middle-aged and elderly patients' intention to use a new IS, such as the health cloud, is based on three enablers of IS usage: their attitude, SN, and PBC of IS usage.

2.3 The Status Quo Bias Theory

Status quo bias (SQB) theory aims to explain people's preference for maintaining their current status or situation [17]. Thus, SQB theory provides a set of useful theoretical explanations for understanding the impact of incumbent system use as an inhibitor of new system acceptance [18]. Samuelson and Zeckhauser [17] separated SQB explanations into three main categories: (a) psychological commitment stemming from misperceived value costs, (b) cognitive misperceptions in the presence of inertia, and (c) rational decision making in the presence of transition costs. The first SQB explanation is based on psychological commitment. Psychological commitment may be due to incorrectly factoring in sunk costs, striving for cognitive consistency in decision making, attempting to maintain one's social position, attempting to avoid regret that might result from making a bad decision, and desiring to maintain a feeling of being in control [18, 19]. SQB may also be the result of cognitive misperceptions due to inertia. Polites and Kankanhalli [19] defined inertia in an IS context as user attachment to, and persistence in using, an incumbent IS even if there are better alternatives or incentives to change. Thus, an individual's inertia contributes to cognitive misperceptions of loss aversion. From the rational decision-making viewpoint, transition costs are the costs incurred in adapting to the new situation. In the IS context, the SQB theory is relevant because it can provide theoretically driven explanations of new IS-related change evaluation and the reasons for user resistance. Thus, the SQB perspective provides a set of useful theoretical explanations for understanding the impact of maintaining their current status as inhibitors (e.g., sunk costs, inertia, and transition costs).

3 Research Model

Based on the preceding discussion, we propose that middle-aged and elderly patients' intention to use the health cloud is based on two opposing forces: enabling and inhibiting perceptions. In regard to enabling perceptions, we propose that patients' intention to use the health cloud is based on the traditional enablers of IS usage: their attitude, SN, and PBC of IS usage [13]. In regard to the inhibiting perceptions, in keeping with the SQB perspective, we extended the causes of user resistance to include sunk costs, inertia, and transition costs into three inhibitors to improve their explanatory power and arrive at a more precise understanding of user resistance antecedents. Similar to e-commerce, the health cloud is a platform for delivering services, and activities are performed online and processed virtually. Personal contact is absent and can raise doubts as to whether the requested information exchanges were correctly processed. Thus, the introduction of the health cloud often engenders significant changes in a patient's existing health-care process. If such change is of a sufficiently significant magnitude, given the natural human proclivity to oppose change, many middle-aged and elderly patients will tend to resist the health cloud, resulting in lower intention to use. Thus, we also examine the relationship between intention to use and resistance to use. Figure 1 is a diagram of the proposed research model, which details the various dimensions and the development of the theoretical arguments.

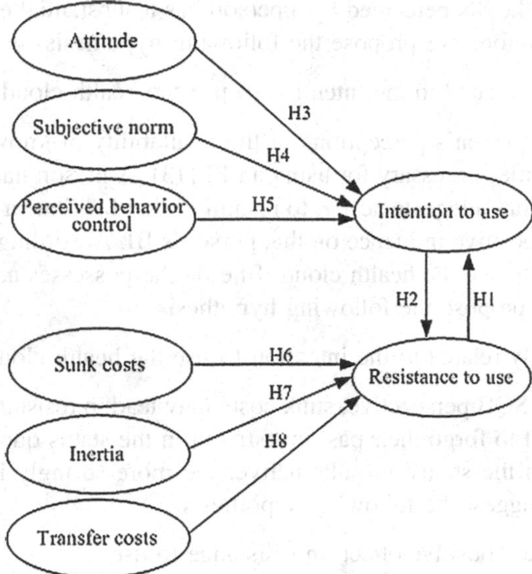

Fig. 1. Research framework

Norzaidi et al. [20] proposed an examination of the relationship between user resistance and usage. When usage is mandatory, the patients who initially refused to use the health cloud may finally do so because they have no alternative way to accomplish their health-care tasks. Moreover, there are circumstances in which patients may use the system voluntarily, but they will stop using it after a while. Another factor that is likely to cause user resistance to the health cloud is a prior negative experience. Previous studies have provided support for the negative effect of resistance on IS usage [11, 21]. Thus, we suggest the following hypotheses:

H1. Middle-aged and elderly patients' resistance to use is negatively related to their intention to use the health cloud.

H2. Middle-aged and elderly patients' intention to use is negatively related to their resistance to use the health cloud.

According to the TPB model, attitude influences behavioral intentions, and this relationship has received substantial empirical support [13]. People who form positive attitudes toward the health cloud have a stronger intention to adopt it; therefore, they are more likely to employ it. Prior studies on users' acceptance of health IT have also supported the attitude–BI correlation [22, 23]. Thus, we propose the following hypothesis on the relationship between attitude and intention to use:

H3. Attitude is positively related to the intention to use the health cloud.

SN is the extent to which a person feels that other people want him or her to perform a behavior [13]. The more people perceive that others think that they should engage in a behavior, the greater their motivation to comply. Prior studies have shown that the SN perceived by a person has a substantial effect on his or her BI [22, 23]. Therefore, we propose the following hypothesis:

H4. SN is positively related to the intention to use the health cloud.

PBC describes a person's perceptions of the availability of knowledge, resources, and the opportunities necessary for using an IS [13]. A person has a higher level of PBC if he or she has adequate access to resources that facilitate a specific behavior; thus, PBC has a positive influence on that person's BI. Accordingly, a patient has a greater intention to use the health cloud if he or she possesses adequate resources. Accordingly, we propose the following hypothesis:

H5. PBC is positively related to the intention to use the health cloud.

According to the SQB perspective, sunk costs may lead to resistance to use because users do not want to forgo their past investment in the status quo [18]. The greater the investment in the status quo alternative, the more strongly it will be retained [17]. Thus, we suggest the following hypothesis:

H6. Sunk costs have a positive effect on resistance to use.

Users persist in using an incumbent system either because this is what they have always done or because it may be too stressful or emotionally taxing to change [19]. Therefore, we suggest the following hypothesis:

H7. Inertia has a positive effect on resistance to use.

As the transient expenses and permanent losses increase, users are more likely to be resistant to the implementation of the new technology because they are motivated to cut their losses [24]. Hence, we propose the following hypothesis:

H8. Transition costs have a positive effect on resistance to use.

4 Research Method

4.1 Questionnaire Development

The construct measures shown in Fig. 1 were all adopted from previous studies and were rated using a 7-point Likert scale; the anchors ranged from "strongly agree" to "strongly disagree." Although previous studies have validated the questionnaire items, we conducted pretests by requesting several health-care professionals and information management professors to evaluate each item. To ensure validity and reliability, we conducted a pilot test with a sample that was representative of the actual respondents. We conducted structural equation modeling using partial least squares (PLS) estimations for the data analysis because the PLS method requires a minimal sample size and has few residual distribution requirements for model validation [25].

4.2 Sample and Data Collection

The target participants were middle-aged and elderly patients in Taiwan. Three medical institutions were successfully contacted to secure their collaboration. A total of 150 questionnaires were distributed through an administrator of the hospital, and 110 questionnaires were returned. We collected questionnaires from one medical center, one regional hospital, and one local hospital; after discarding five incomplete questionnaires, 105 were available for analysis. We assessed nonresponse bias by comparing early and late respondents (e.g., those who replied during the first three days and the last three days). We found no significant difference between the two respondent groups based on the sample attributes (e.g., gender and age).

5 Research Results

The resulting 105 valid questionnaires constituted a response rate of 70 %. The majority of the questionnaire respondents were men (57 %) between the ages of 51 and 60 years (60 %). We tested the reliability and validity of the proposed model. Reliability was assessed based on a construct reliability greater than 0.8 [26]. Convergent validity was assessed based on the following three criteria: (a) item loading greater than 0.7 and statistically significant, (b) composite construct reliability (CR) greater than 0.80, and (c) average variance extracted (AVE) greater than 0.5 [27]. The discriminant validity between the constructs was assessed based on the criterion that the square root of the AVE for each construct should be greater than the corresponding correlations with all other constructs [26]. In this study, the construct reliabilities are all greater than 0.9. For the convergent validity, the item loadings are all greater than 0.7, and the AVEs range from 0.77 to 0.97. For the discriminant validity, the square root of the AVE for a construct is greater than its corresponding correlations with other constructs. Table 1 shows the descriptive statistics of the principal constructs and the correlation

Table 1. Reliability and validity of the scale

Construct	Item loading	CR	AVE	Correlation							
				AT	SN	PBC	SC	IN	TC	IU	RU
AT	.78– .94	.94	.81	**.90**							
SN	.85– .90	.90	.77	.20	**.88**						
PBC	.87– .96	.96	.85	.45	.14	**.92**					
SC	.94– .97	.96	.92	−.07	−.07	.09	**.96**				
IN	.86– .94	.94	.83	−.37	−.07	−.03	.54	**.89**			
TC	.84– .91	.92	.78	−.29	−.13	−.04	.10	.24	**.88**		
IU	.98– .99	.99	.97	.55	.30	.09	−.21	−.60	−.45	**.98**	
RU	.95– .97	.98	.93	−.51	−.07	−.22	.22	.48	.54	−.65	**.96**

Note: Leading diagonal shows the square root of AVE of each construct Attitude (AT), Subjective norm (SN), Perceived behavior control (PBC), Sunk costs (SC), Inertia (IN), Transition costs (TC), Intention to use (IU), and Resistance to use (RU)

matrix, respectively. These results indicate acceptable reliability, convergent validity, and discriminant validity.

The testing results in the structural model are indicated in Fig. 2. In general, the statistical testing conclusions all support this research model. Intention to use in this study was jointly predicted by attitude (β = 0.214, standardized path coefficient, $p < 0.001$), SN (β = 0.205, $p < 0.001$), PBC (β = 0.106, $p < 0.001$), and resistance to use (β = -0.34, $p < 0.001$), and these variables together explained 54 % of the variance of intention to use. As a result, hypotheses 1, 3, 4, and 5 were all supported. In this study, resistance to using the health cloud was predicted by sunk costs (β = 0.128, $p < 0.001$), inertia (β = 0.573, $p < 0.001$), transfer costs (β = 0.411, $p < 0.001$), and intention to use (β = -0.51, $p < 0.001$). Together, these variables explained 53.8 % of the total variance. These findings validated hypotheses 2, 6, 7, and, 8 respectively.

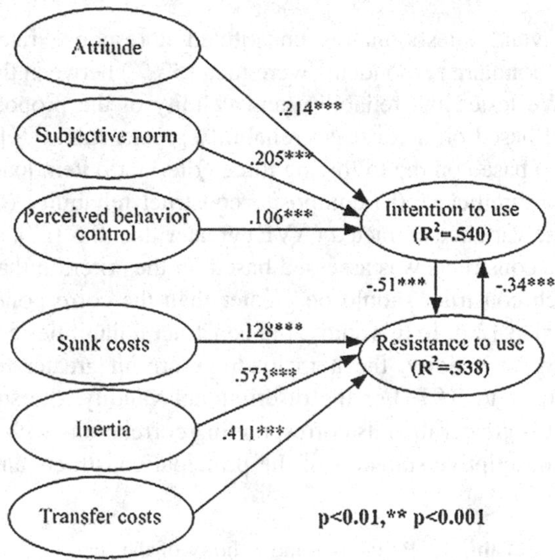

Fig. 2. Results of the structural model

6 Discussion

In this empirical study, we analyzed middle-aged and elderly patients' acceptance of and resistance to the health cloud. First, we analyzed the relationship between the three enablers (attitude, SN, and PBC) and intention to use. Second, we analyzed the three inhibitors (sunk costs, inertia, and transition costs) and resistance to use. Third, we analyzed the relationship between intention to use and resistance to use health cloud services. In the proposed models, the explained variance (R^2 = 0.54) appeared to be superior to the results of prior studies [1, 28] in explaining user intention or resistance to use the health IT. This implies that the proposed model could be a robust research model for predicting middle-aged and elderly patients' intention to use similar health IT.

Our study confirmed that the relationship between intention to use and resistance to use had a significant negative effect. This result coincided with the findings of previous studies on health IT adoption [11, 21]. As such, higher resistance will reduce middle-aged and elderly patients' intention to use the health cloud. Among the enablers under study, attitude is the most influential regarding the decision to use the health cloud. This implies that middle-aged and elderly patients' intention to accept the health cloud was directly influenced by their attitude toward using it. These findings are in accordance with the results of previous research [29, 30]. In other words, the effects of these enablers were significant in explaining middle-aged and elderly patients' acceptance behavior, which is in keeping with the work of Ajzen [13] (1985), who maintained that the relative importance of attitude, SN, and PBC in predicting usage intention varies across behaviors and situations.

Among the inhibitors under analysis, our study confirmed that middle-aged and elderly patients' resistance to use was caused by sunk costs, inertia, and transition costs. Inertia has a direct positive effect on user resistance to health care, meaning that higher inertia results in higher resistance to using the health cloud. This result coincided with the findings of previous studies on IS adoption [19]. In the absence of inertia, it is possible that a habitual patient of an incumbent system may readily recognize the advantages of switching to the health cloud and may form genuine intentions to do so. High perceptions of sunk costs have a direct positive effect on user resistance to health care, meaning that higher sunk costs lead to user resistance because people do not want to forgo their past investment in the traditional (face-to-face) health-care services. One possibility is that patients had either a formal or abstract awareness of the sunk cost effect, and once alerted to the past investment of resources, they consciously or subconsciously attempted to circumvent this bias and make a treatment decision based solely on the available clinical evidence. Further, perceived transition costs increase patients' resistance to using the health cloud. These findings are in accordance with previous findings [18]. This rationalization of the costs of transition from the incumbent system can, even in the absence of a known alternative, lead to resistance. Thus, the SQB perspective represents a comprehensive set of theoretical explanations that account for status quo bias, and these explanations are present in a health-care context.

This study has several implications for, and makes numerous contributions to, other research. A primary contribution is that technology acceptance and resistance theories are combined to examine how users assess overall change related to a new health IT. By making use of TPB to integrate and add to relevant concepts from SQB theory, the study contributes by operationalizing and testing the developed model through a survey methodology, which has little precedence in the user resistance literature. Hence, we provide theoretical insights for researchers that may assist in encouraging middle-aged and elderly patients to use a new health IT. Second, enablers and inhibitors have not been clearly defined or measured in prior research. Thus, we contribute to both IS research and the dual factor theoretical perspective by explicitly conceptualizing and measuring individual-level enablers and inhibitors. Our study confirms that attitude, SN, and PBC are critical factors for facilitating intention to use the system. While the role of inhibitors (e.g., sunk costs, inertia, and transition costs) is important, the driving forces would have a positive effect on the middle-aged and elderly patients' resistance to using the health cloud. This finding could interest and encourage researchers who are developing an IS acceptance and resistance model. Future research should aim to identify additional incumbent system constructs and theorize on the interplay between incumbent system and new system cognition and behaviors. This study has a third key theoretical implication in terms of SQB theory. This theory was developed for planning bias toward maintaining the status quo in human decision making and behavior. Since then, it has been applied to explain human decision making in the IS field [18, 19]. As an extension of previous research, this study has demonstrated how SQB theory can be applied in health IT research to explain middle-aged and elderly patients' resistance to new health IT-related change. Thus, this reliable and valid instrument provides an effective tool for researchers to measure user behavior, as well as to explain, justify, and compare the differences in study results.

The results of this study offer suggestions to management regarding how to alleviate user resistance in health cloud implementation. First, the results of the study show that attitude, SN, and PBC have a significant influence on usage intention. Thus, the health cloud should be designed in a more user-friendly manner that is consistent with current needs. Middle-aged and elderly patients who are able to use the health cloud with ease, as well those who can retrieve health-care data, are more likely to develop a positive attitude toward the system, thereby encouraging them to use the health cloud. Hospital managers should focus more on the following: (a) creating an environment that ensures middle-aged and elderly patients have a positive attitude toward the system; and (b) developing a system that meets the subjective norms of patients, and; and (c) providing adequate resources for patients who use the health cloud. Second, management should be aware of the critical effect of inhibitors on user resistance. Management can attempt to reduce sunk costs, inertia, and transition costs by enhancing middle-aged and elderly patients' favorable opinions toward new IS-related change. Third, management should aim to increase the perceived value of change to reduce middle-aged and elderly patients' resistance. To increase the perceived value of using the health cloud, the advantages should be emphasized from the viewpoints of middle-aged and elderly patients. The benefits, therefore, need to be communicated clearly to middle-aged and elderly patients before the health cloud implementation. Furthermore, most health IT designs tend to focus on system considerations, such as new functionalities and connectivity, rather than on user considerations, such as the system's impact on users' health-care behaviors and potential user resistance. A better understanding of users' resistance to health IT may help design better systems that are both functionally good and acceptable to their targeted user populations.

The limitations of our findings should be acknowledged. The first limitation is our choice of constructs, which was based on prior literature and our own observation of the behavior of middle-aged and elderly patients at our study site. There may be other enablers or inhibitors of health cloud usage that were not included in this study and that can be the subject of future research. Further, there may be additional predictors of resistance, beyond sunk costs, inertia, and transition costs, that should be examined in future research. The identification and validation of such constructs will also help advance our preliminary model of health cloud resistance. Second, the relevance of this study is confined to the health cloud behavior of a specific population: middle-aged and elderly patients. The findings and implications drawn from this study cannot be readily generalized to other groups, such as medical personnel. A study targeting medical personnel, who might have varying information needs and different levels of computing support and abilities, could obtain different results. Future research should focus on accumulating further empirical evidence and data to overcome the limitations of this study.

References

1. Lai, J.Y., Wang, J.: Switching attitudes of taiwanese middle-aged and elderly patients toward cloud healthcare services: an exploratory study. Technol. Forecast. Soc. Change (2014). doi:10.1016/j.techfore.2014.06.004
2. Cenfetelli, R.T.: Inhibitors and enablers and dual factor concepts in technology usage. J. Assoc. Inf. Syst. **5**(11–12), 472–492 (2004)
3. Kim, T.W., Kim, H.C.: A healthcare system as a service in the context of vital signs: proposing a framework for realizing a model. Comput. Math. Appl. **64**(5), 1324–1332 (2012)
4. Nur, F.N., Moon, N.N.: Health care system based on cloud computing. Asian Trans. Comput. **2**(5), 9–11 (2012)
5. Mathew, S.: Cloud computing: a new foundation towards health care. Int. J. Innovative Technol. Exploring Eng. **3**(2), 118–121 (2013)
6. Jaswanth, N., Durga, J., Kumar, D.K.: Migrating health care by analysing MYTHS in cloud technology. Orient. J. Comput. Sci. Technol. **6**(1), 49–54 (2013)
7. Kaur, P.D., Chana, I.: Cloud based intelligent system for delivering health care as a service. Int. J. Inf. Manage. **113**(1), 346–359 (2013)
8. Joshi, K.: Understanding user resistance and acceptance during the implementation of an order management system: a case study using the equity implementation model. J. Inf. Technol. Case Appl. Res. **7**(1), 6–20 (2005)
9. Wu, I.L., Hsieh, P.J.: Hospital innovation and its impact on customer-perceived quality of care: a process-based evaluation approach. Total Qual. Manage. Bus. Excellence **18**, 1–15 (2013)
10. Bartos, C.E., Butler, B.S., Crowley, R.S.: Ranked levels of influence model: selecting influence techniques to minimize IT resistance. J. Biomed. Inform. **44**, 497–504 (2011)
11. Bhattacherjee, A., Hikmet, N.: Physicians' resistance toward healthcare information technology: a theoretical model and empirical test. Eur. J. Inf. Syst. **16**(6), 725–737 (2007)
12. Fishbein, M., Ajzen, I.: Belief, Attitude, Intention, and Behavior: An Introduction to Theory and Research. Addison-Wesley, Reading (1975)
13. Ajzen, I.: From intentions to actions: a theory of planned behaviour. In: Kuhl, J., Beckmann, J. (eds.) Action-Control: From Cognition to Behavior, pp. 11–39. Springer, Heidelberg (1985)
14. Chapman, K.M., Ham, J.O., Liesen, P., Winter, L.: Applying behavioral models to dietary education of elderly diabetic patients. J. Nutr. Educ. **27**(2), 75–79 (1995)
15. Gupchup, G.V., Abhyankar, U.L., Worley, M.M., Raisch, D.W., Marfatia, A.A., Namdar, R.: Relationships between hispanic ethnicity and attitudes and beliefs toward herbal medicine use among older adults. Res. Soci. Adm. Pharm. **2**(2), 266–279 (2006)
16. Sivell, S., Edwards, A., Manstead, A.S.R., Reed, M.W.R., Caldon, L., Collins, K., Clements, A., Elwyn, G.: Increasing readiness to decide and strengthening behavioral intentions: evaluating the impact of a web-based patient decision aid for breast cancer treatment options (BresDex: www.bresdex.com). Patient Educ. Couns. **88**(2), 209–217 (2012)

17. Samuelson, W., Zeckhauser, R.: Status quo bias in decision making. J. Risk Uncertain. **1**, 7–59 (1988)
18. Kim, H.W., Kankanhalli, A.: Investigating user resistance to information systems implementation: a status quo bias perspective. MIS Q. **33**(3), 567–582 (2009)
19. Polites, G.L., Karahanna, E.: Shackled to the status quo: the inhibiting effects of incumbent system habit, switching costs, and inertia on new system acceptance. MIS Q. **36**(1), 21–42 (2012)
20. Norzaidi, M.D., Chong, S.C., Salwani, M.I., Rafidahl, K.: A study of intranet usage and resistance in malaysia's port industry. J. Comput. Inform. Syst. **49**(1), 37–47 (2008)
21. Poon, E.G., Blumenthal, D., Jaggi, T., Honour, M.M., Bates, D.W., Kaushal, R.: Overcoming barriers to adopting and implementing computerized physician order entry systems in U.S. hospitals. Health Aff. **24**(4), 184–190 (2004)
22. Presseau, J., Francis, J.J., Campbell, N.C., Sniehotta, F.F.: Goal conflict, goal facilitation, and health professionals' provision of physical activity advice in primary care: an exploratory prospective study. Implement Sci. **6**(1), 73–81 (2011)
23. Hsieh, P.J.: Physicians' acceptance of electronic medical records exchange: an extension of the decomposed TPB model with institutional trust and perceived risk. Int. J. Med. Inform. **84**(1), 1–14 (2015)
24. Kahneman, D., Tversky, A.: Prospect theory: an analysis of decision under risk. Econometrica **47**, 263–281 (1979)
25. Chin, W.W., Marcolin, B.L., Newsted, P.R.: A partial least squares latent variable modeling approach for measuring interaction effects: results from a monte carlo simulation study and an electronic-mail emotion/adoption study. Inform. Syst. Res. **14**(2), 189–217 (2003)
26. Chin, W.W.: Issues and opinion on structural equation modelling. MIS Q. **22**(1), 7–16 (1998)
27. Fornell, C., Larcker, D.: Structural equation models with unobservable variables and measurement error: algebra and statistics. J. Mark. Res. **18**(3), 382–388 (1981)
28. Yu, P., Li, H., Gagnon, M.P.: Health IT acceptance factors in long-term care facilities: a cross-sectional survey. Int. J. Med. Inform. **78**(4), 219–229 (2009)
29. Hung, S.Y., Ku, Y.C., Chien, J.C.: Understanding physicians' acceptance of the medline system for practicing evidence-based medicine: a decomposed TPB model. Int. J. Med. Inform. **81**(2), 130–142 (2010)
30. Chau, P.Y.K., Hu, P.J.H.: Investigating healthcare professionals' decisions to accept telemedicine technology: an empirical test of competing theories. Inform. Manage. **39**(4), 297–311 (2002)

Multi-disciplinary Design and In-Home Evaluation of Kinect-Based Exercise Coaching System for Elderly

Gregorij Kurillo[1(✉)], Ferda Ofli[1], Jennifer Marcoe[2], Paul Gorman[2], Holly Jimison[3], Misha Pavel[3], and Ruzena Bajcsy[1]

[1] University of California at Berkeley, Berkeley, CA, USA
{gregorij, fofli, bajcsy}@eecs.berkeley.edu

[2] Oregon Health and Science University, Portland, OR, USA
{marcoej, gormanp}@ohsu.edu

[3] Northeastern University, Boston, MA, USA
{h.jimison, m.pavel}@neu.edu

Abstract. Physical activity is recognized as one of the most effective measures to reduce risk of injury and to improve the quality of life in elderly. Many of the elderly however lack the motivation, confidence and skills to engage in regular exercise activity. One of the promising approaches is semi-automated coaching that combines exercise monitoring and interaction with a health coach. To gain a better understanding of the needs and challenges faced by the elderly when using such systems, we developed Kinect-based interactive exercise system to encourage healthy behavior and increase motivation to exercise. We present the multi-disciplinary design process and evaluation of the developed system in a home environment where various real-world challenges had to be overcome.

Keywords: Gerontechnology · Interactive exercise · Kinect · Health coaching

1 Introduction

Growing ageing population in the United States is having significant implications on the current healthcare system as the elderly face neurodegenerative conditions which may reduce the level of independence and increase the risk of falls and injury. There are currently almost 40 million persons aged 65 years or older living in the US, while the number is expected to increase to 72.1 million by 2030 [1]. By improving the quality of independent living through increased physical activity these challenges can be partially mitigated [2]. Many elderly, however, lack access to exercise facilities, or the skills and motivation to perform exercise at home.

To improve the health behavior and to overcome the lack of motivation in the general population, various forms of computer-assisted coaching and "gamification" of activity monitoring have been investigated; initially in the academic space and later on,

F. Ofli is now with Qatar Computing Research Institute (QCRI), Doha, Qatar.

J. Zhou and G. Salvendy (Eds.): ITAP 2015, Part II, LNCS 9194, pp. 101–113, 2015.
DOI: 10.1007/978-3-319-20913-5_10

with the introduction of affordable motion sensing, also in the commercial space. The success of interactive exercise products, as pointed out by Sinclair et al. [3], by and large depends on two interrelated dimensions: (1) *effectiveness*, which relates to achieving exercise goals, and (2) *attractiveness*, which refers to the level of engagement for the user to retain required duration and level of exercise. Many of the commercial products have focused on the attractiveness aspect, while the academic field has tried to examine the effectiveness of these technologies in exercise training and rehabilitation. Many of the commercially available systems, however, are targeting different demographics, such as younger users, and are as such less applicable for most older adults as they do not offer appropriate type and level of exercise and fail to provide appropriate safety considerations. Furthermore, the feedback provided by such systems may be overly-engaging. In addition, the interaction modality may entail of complex user interfaces, which may not be easy to use for elderly with reduced sensory and cognitive functions [4]. Although several interactive systems for exercise in elderly have been presented in research (e.g., [5, 6]), majority of the works focused on short-term and controlled in-laboratory evaluations. A comprehensive review of the research literature on interactive exercise in older adults can be found in [7, 8].

2 Background

The goal of this research was to develop an interactive exercise coaching system for elderly that would be integrated with the semi-automated coaching framework at the Oregon Center for Aging & Technology (ORCATECH) Living Lab,[1] which is focused on exploring technologies to support independent living of elderly. The coaching platform comprises of unobtrusive sensing of participant's behaviors in combination with artificial intelligence tools that aid the coach to send individualized messages to the participants [9]. Originally, the participants were encouraged to exercise alongside YouTube videos, however the system was not able to track individual's exercise habits or provide feedback on the performance that could be used to close the loop of the health-coaching support. To achieve the interactive component for the health coaching, we considered several different solutions, including wearable devices and 2D cameras. After the release of Kinect for Xbox 360 (Microsoft, Redmond, WA) and accompanying Kinect SDK, we decided to use the Kinect as it offered unobtrusive, low-cost and relatively reliable way of measuring human motion kinematics. Although several commercial applications for exercise have been developed to date, one of the challenges is how this technology can be introduced in homes of elderly.

3 Methods

3.1 Design Process

The design of the Kinect-based exercise system architecture followed participatory design concepts by engaging the computer scientists and researchers with the health

[1] http://www.orcatech.org.

coaches and caregivers during the interactive software development process over the last three years. We also took into account user feedback at several stages of the project. The interactions among the members of the team included the following:

- Identifying the requirements and objectives of the architecture;
- Researching the needs and expectations of the targeted population;
- Defining basic functionality of the exercise system;
- Determining what data should be collected by the system;
- Determining accuracy of the Kinect measurements;
- Determining the conditions for home deployment;
- Defining general user interaction flow with the system;
- Selecting exercises appropriate for elderly users and the Kinect;
- Recording exercise videos and defining movement features related to exercises;
- Testing and modifying the prototype system at several stages;
- Collecting and integrating user feedback;
- Resolving various technical issues related to the deployment and maintenance;
- Running in-home pilot studies with health-coaching support;
- Discussing and evaluating various forms of data analysis.

We have approached the goals of this project in two stages. Our first prototype deployment was primarily focused on understanding better the user needs and technical challenges related to the exercise monitoring, user interfaces, and the use of Kinect technology in homes of elderly users. We therefore installed the prototype exercise system with 12 basic exercises into the homes of six independently-living elderly individuals for an informal evaluation study. The system and results are described in details in our prior publication [10]. The lessons learned from this study were then used to make considerable improvements to the exercise system and evaluate it in an 18-week long deployment in 7 homes of elderly users. In this paper, we thus focus on the second stage of the design and evaluation. For completeness, we briefly describe some of the findings from the first stage of the project while further details can be found in our referred publications [10, 11].

3.2 Design Objectives

The primary goal of this research was to integrate an automated exercise coaching with semi-automated health coaching of elderly in order to improve their fitness level in terms of standard measures of fitness, such as flexibility, strength, balance, and endurance [12]. Table 1 summarizes the design objectives for the development of the exercise system and provides brief overview of identified issues from Phase 1 (described in [10]) and how they were addressed in Phase 2.

3.3 Implementation

In this section we describe the design, implementation, and setup of the Kinect-based exercise system. For completeness we briefly refer to some of the findings and lessons learned from Phase 1 while providing more details on the final version of the system used in the last pilot study.

Software. The exercise software was implemented in C++ with support from open source 3D library Ogre (ogre3d.org) for graphics, MyGUI (mygui.info) for UI, Microsoft Kinect SDK for data acquisition, and MySQL for database management.

Table 1. Design objectives for the Kinect-based exercise coaching system

Objective	*Phase 1* [10]	*Identified issues*	*Phase 2*
Unobtrusive, low-maintenance, and low-cost sensor	Microsoft Kinect 1	Space required for the camera	Microsoft Kinect 1; camera installed in living room
Standalone, turn-key system, minimum maintenance	All-in-one computer	Large footprint; complex interaction	Small footprint PC connected to TV
Age-appropriate UI	Basic UI	Information clutter; difficult to see text on buttons	UI design based on recommendations for elderly users
Easy interaction with UI	Wireless mouse & keyboard	Difficult to use at large distance	Use of wireless PowerPoint remote
Ability to record interaction with UI	None	Need to understand interaction issues	Timings of screens interactions
Inclusion of age-appropriate exercises	12 exercises	Users desired more exercises for variety	40 + exercises
Exercises grouping based on fitness level	None	Some find existing exercises too easy	3 groups with up to 3 difficulty levels
Ability to record raw kinematic measurements	Yes	None	Yes
Real-time in-exercise feedback to encourage and correct users' performance	Video feedback, audio & text cues	Users could not see what Kinect was recording	Video feedback, 3D Kinect feedback, audio & text cues
Summary of exercises to inform users of their overall performance	Performance measures	Difficult to understand the meaning	Repetition counts, summary statistics
Collection of subject-reported data on health status	None	Collected only during phone contact with the coach	Integration of pre- and post-exercise survey
Integration of the system with the health-coaching	None	Health coach did not have access to data	Health coaching database integration

Kinect System. Our exercise system is based on Microsoft Kinect camera [13] which was originally developed for the gaming console Xbox 360. The Kinect is a depth-sensing system (combining RGB and infrared cameras) that provides 3D reconstruction of the scene and segmentation of human blobs with real-time estimation of the 3D location of 20 joints. The accuracy of the pose reconstruction depends on various factors including orientation of the body, self-occlusions, interference with other objects, etc. During the planning stages, we examined the accuracy of the Kinect tracking alongside a motion capture system to identify the exercises where the tracking was robust and to determine the accuracy of joint estimation [11]. One of the challenges of using the Kinect camera was its limited field of view which requires users to be positioned between 1.8 m and 4 m. This can be particular challenging in smaller and cluttered homes. In addition, the pose estimation becomes less reliable when users are seated or turned sideways. These limitations posed several constraints on the system setup and exercise selection.

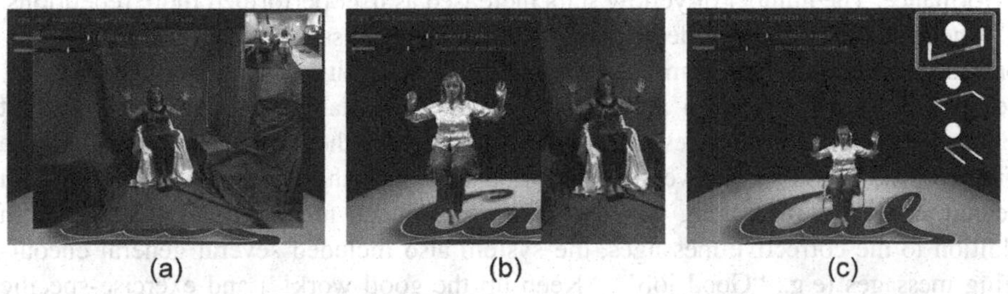

Fig. 1. Different in-exercise feedback options that were considered in early design stages.

Movement Analysis. The real-time movement analysis during the exercise was performed by first extracting *measurement primitives* from the skeletal data, such as joint angles, relative angles to the vertical/horizontal plane, distances, absolute positions, etc. These features were chosen manually based on the goals of specific exercise. The goals were defined in consultation with the health coach. The selected measurement primitives were then used to evaluate the performance of the exercise (e.g. how high person can reach), to support repetition counting, and to trigger feedback alerts. More details on the implementation can be found in [10].

Feedback and Visualization. During the development and testing phase, we examined different options on how to provide effective feedback during exercise. The possible feedback modalities included video, skeletal data, 3D graphics, 2D overlays, textual messages, and auditory feedback. During initial in-laboratory testing, we examined three different options as shown in Fig. 1. Informal usability assessment with coaches and several elderly users suggested a preference for full-screen video mode (Fig. 1a) which was further refined as shown in Fig. 2 (left). After the first pilot study [10], the feedback collected from six users indicated that although the participants liked the video guidance they were confused about what the camera sees and they were not always able to relate their movement to the movement of the coach. Therefore, we decided to include a mirrored human figure as captured by the Kinect depth sensor next to the video of the coach as shown in Fig. 2 (right). This element provided more intuitive way for a subject to relate their movement to the exercise performance. Additionally, we replaced all the videos with high definition recordings of the coach that were integrated into the 3D environment for more attractive overall appearance.

The visual feedback in the exercise software also included several informational elements that were displayed as 2D overlaid graphics and text. In the first version, we included *performance bars* which indicated how well the user is performing a particular exercise based on the measurement primitives. The users, however, found the performance bars difficult to understand and map to their own movements. In the second version, we instead decided to report the performance in terms of the number of accomplished repetitions. The current repetition count was indicated by a large numerical counter and corresponding number of yellow stars on the bottom of the screen. When the user first started the exercise, gray stars were shown while their number corresponded to the number of repetitions of the previous session. This information was intended to encourage the user to try to reach or exceed previous performance. The number of yellow stars increased as user performed more repetitions.

The feedback also included auditory and textual messages triggered by the performance evaluation. For example, if the subject were to sit tall in a particular exercise, the system would trigger an alert whenever the user started slouching. In the first version of the system, the messages were shown under the performance bar measure (Fig. 2, left). In the second version, we tried to reduce the clutter on the screen and created a separate messaging panel to display feedback messages (Fig. 2, right). In addition to the corrective messages, the system also included several general encouraging messages (e.g., “Good job!”, “Keep up the good work!”) and exercise-specific messages that would remind the users for correct performance (e.g. in Leg Lifts exercise: “Kick one foot up, then the other.”). These messages were displayed randomly. The main exercise screen also included a countdown clock with a graphical display and a numerical counter. As opposed to the first version, where the exercise would finish after completing 10 repetitions, we limited the exercise duration to 45 s as recommended by the health coach.

User Interface (UI) and Navigation. Since the initial pilot study was primarily focused on testing the feasibility of collecting exercise data at home, the user interface

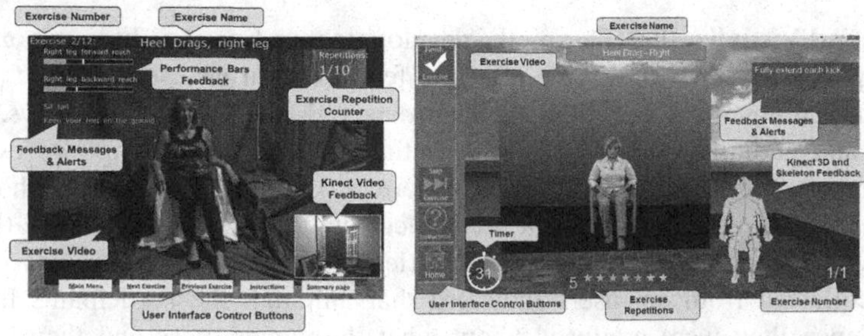

Fig. 2. Comparison of the in-exercise feedback screen between the initial [10] and the final version of the exercise software.

was relatively simple. Although we considered several different modalities to control the software (e.g., speech, gestures, presenter remote), we decided to use a wireless mouse and keyboard since the participants were familiar with these devices. In general the users found the software to be easy to use, however some participants reported that they were not able to read the text on the screen from the distance and had difficulty controlling the application in Windows environment.

Our focus in the second phase was to improve the user experience, especially since the system was intended to be used over a much longer time period. As recommended by guidelines for design of software for elderly users [4], we implemented the following improvements to the original interface:

- Large fonts for text messages and button labels;
- Familiar icons on buttons (e.g., video controls used icons similar to VCR);
- Consistent positioning of buttons with similar functions;
- Simple graphical elements;
- Color scheme with good contrast;
- Improved text-to speech (offered by the new Windows 8 platform);
- Minimal textual information on each screen;
- Overall reduction of screen clutter; information organized into display panels;
- Linear screen interaction flow;

Figure 3 shows several example screenshots from the updated software with the following interaction flow. From the main screen (Fig. 3a), the user is able to view help and safety videos, start a new session or complete unfinished session. Next, the user is presented with a survey of five questions about their general health and goals for the day (Fig. 3b). The user is able to skip a specific question if they prefer not to answer it. On the exercise selection screen users can select between three different exercise groups with various difficulty levels (Fig. 3c). Once the exercise group and level are selected, the user is prompted to perform optional warm-up which includes only the video playback of the coach without any feedback on the performance. Next, depending on selected preference, the full instructional video on benefits of the exercise or a short 10-second preview is displayed (Fig. 3d). Afterwards, the user performs the exercise for

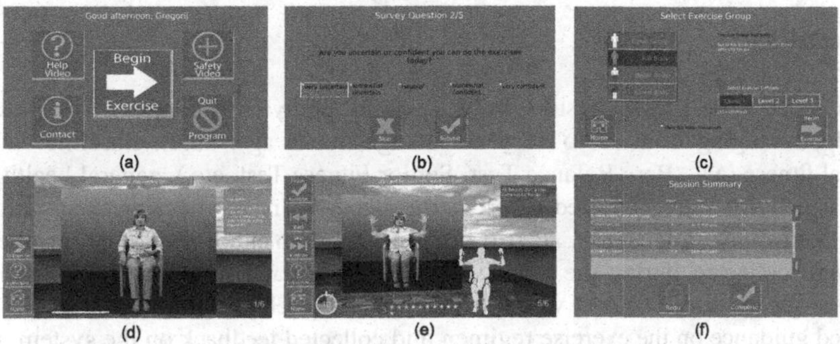

Fig. 3. Software interaction flow: (a) home screen, (b) daily survey, (c) exercise selection, (d) exercise preview/instructions, (e) in-exercise feedback, (f) session summary.

45 s with the real-time feedback and accompanying video (Fig. 3e). At any time, the user can review instructions, skip to the next exercise, or exit the session. Once the exercise is completed, a bar chart showing current and past repetition counts is displayed. After completing all the exercises, the session summary screen is shown, displaying the summary statistics of the particular exercise session compared to the past performance (Fig. 3f). Demo video can be viewed at: http://tinyurl.com/KinectExercise.

To simplify the navigation, we implemented support for a 3-button wireless PowerPoint remote with large buttons (Kensington, K72441AM). Two buttons on the remote were used to change the selection on the screen (which was highlighted) back and forth while the third button was used to confirm the current selection.

Exercises. The original system included 12 exercises (e.g., *Heel Drags*, *Lateral Stepping*, *Leg Extensions*, *Cops and Robbers*, *Buddha's Prayer*, etc. [10]) focused on improving balance, flexibility, and strength. Based on the feedback collected from the first pilot study, we included several variations of these exercises to provide variety for users of different capabilities. The final system included about 40 exercises which were grouped into three groups (i.e., full body, upper body with core & lower body) and arranged into three difficulty levels, each containing between 6 to 15 exercises.

System Setup. In the first pilot study, we used all-in-one computer with large screen which provided easy setup and portability. We found, however, that in some homes it was difficult to find sufficient space; therefore, the physical setup often had to be improvised to achieve the required distance for the Kinect. For easy interaction, we configured the system as a 'turn-key' system. A small desktop PC running Windows 8.1 was connected to participant's existing TV set using HDMI connection to transmit video and audio signals from the computer. To simplify the process of switching between the regular channels and PC input, we installed an HDMI switch. The PC was configured to be always on and to boot into the desktop without requiring users to log in. Remote connection to the PC was enabled via TeamViewer software (teamviewer.com) for administration of the system. For protection of privacy all the data saved on the PC were stored in temporary MySQL tables which were copied nightly to the external server. This process however turned out to cause occasional data loss as some of the homes experienced outages of network and power due to weather and construction.

4 Results

In this section we present results from 18-week study in the homes of 7 elderly individuals ranging from 77 to 96 years of age (mean age: 83.2). Baseline data on physical fitness (e.g., Berg Balance Test, Senior Fitness Test, etc.), general health, and physical activity were collected prior to the deployment of the Kinect system and subsequently every four weeks. As part of the Living Lab enrollment other quantitative data were collected during the study, such as sleep data, in-home motion sensors, cognitive games, etc. Subjects were also in contact weekly with a health coach who provided guidance on the exercise regimen and collected feedback on the system usage and any technical issues. The study protocols were approved by the Oregon Health and Science University IRB.

Figure 4 shows the exercise program adherence over the course of 18 weeks. The subjects were instructed to exercise 3–5 times a week. From the 7 subjects who were enrolled, four subjects performed the exercises somewhat regularly. Subject #1 got ill early on and never returned to the exercise. Subject #2 exercised regularly, however due to the internet connectivity issues, we were unable to recover the data of the second portion of the study. Subjects #3, #4, and #5 completed most of the exercise sessions. Subject #6 performed exercises intermittently but later on stopped using the system due to holidays and travel. Subject #7 initially used the system but found it was not as useful to him as he was already involved regularly in Tai Chi and riding exercise bike. Figure 4 also shows the type of exercise sessions the subjects performed. Most of the subjects performed full body exercise sessions. Subjects #2 and #4 were both able to increase the exercise level after a few weeks. Subject #3 was on the other hand alternating between the different exercise groups, which was also the general recommendation.

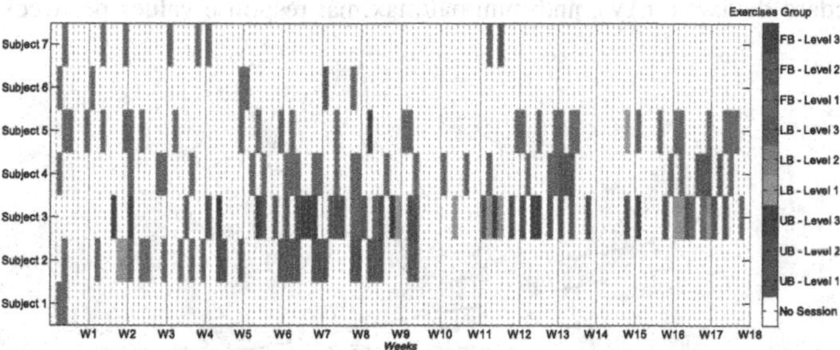

Fig. 4. Daily exercise adherence during the eighteen-week study. The color of the patches denotes the type and level of exercise (UB – Upper Body, LB – Lower Body, FB –Full Body).

Figure 5 shows the results of the post-exercise survey compared between subjects #3 and #5 who had the most completed sessions. The subjects' response data reflect their exercise habits. Subject #3 reported to be pain free most of the time and very motivated to exercise. On the other hand, subject #5 reported pain and low motivation, in particular in weeks 9 and 10 after which the subject took a break from the exercise. Daily survey responses could be in general used by the health coach or an automated system to provide appropriate intervention to increase the motivation of the user.

Figure 6 shows the raw Kinect skeleton output for six sample frames captured during the exercise *Shallow Squats*. The skeleton configurations are shown for every 30 frames corresponding to the time interval of 1 s. As mentioned previously, the skeletal data were used to extract the measurement primitives for repetition counting and feedback. Figure 7 shows the number of completed repetitions for the same exercise over the course of the study for subjects, #4 and #5, who had performed this exercise in majority of their sessions. Note that this exercise was included only in the Full Body - Level 1 and Lower Body – Level 2 exercise groups. For both subjects we can see the trend of an overall increase in the number of repetitions over time which is likely due to improved endurance.

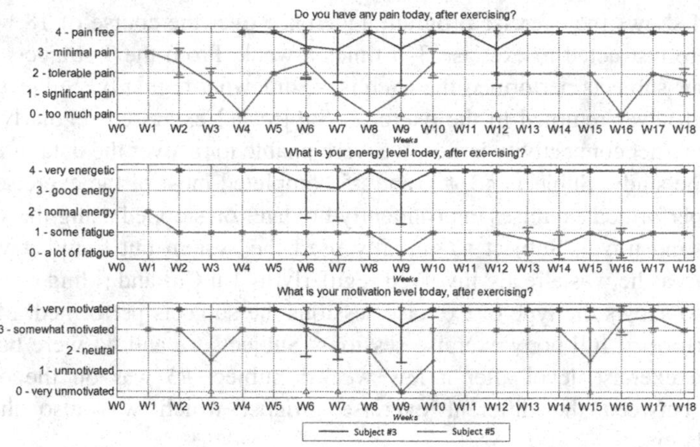

Fig. 5. Comparison of post-exercise survey replies for subjects #3 and #5. The charts show mean (*), standard deviation (ΔV), and minimal/maximal response values per week.

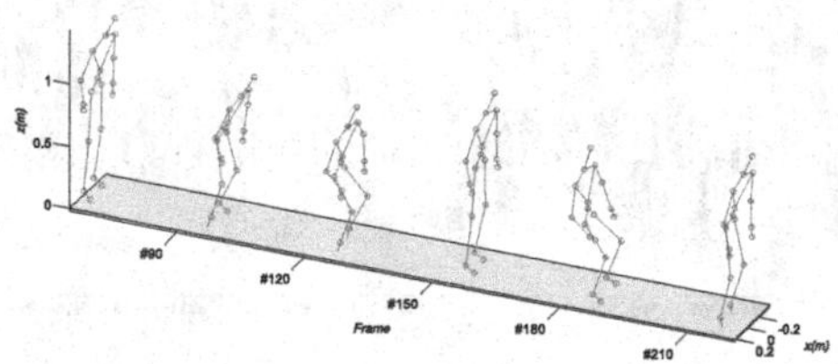

Fig. 6. Raw skeleton sequence recorded for the exercise Shallow Squats (Subject #3).

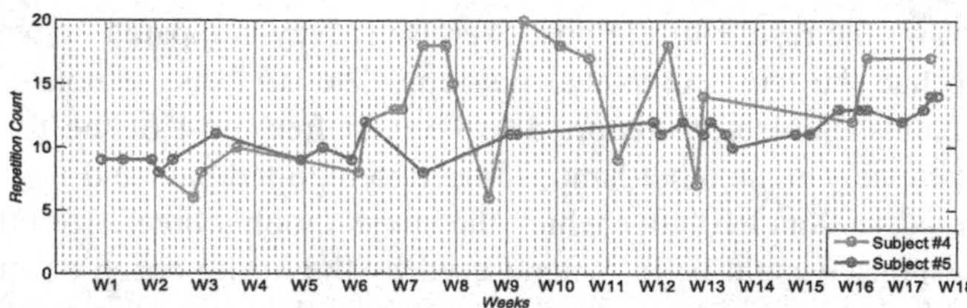

Fig. 7. Number of completed repetitions for the exercise *Shallow Squats* for subjects #4 and #5.

5 Discussion and Conclusion

Based on the findings from our Phase 1 study we have successfully improved the exercise system to achieve the objectives for long-term use that were summarized in Table 1. Majority of the changes in the design, additional exercises, and overall system performance were well-accepted by the participants. There were several minor technical issues that were identified and corrected during the first two weeks after the installation. These included changes to the scripts that suppressed various system pop-ups and always put the exercise software in the foreground of the desktop. We also noticed that some users were either double clicking or holding the button on the remote for a longer time period which sometimes resulted in multiple confirmations. These navigation issues were resolved by a subsequent software update. Overall, the wireless remote was easy to use for the participants after the initial issues were resolved. Only one user experienced a failure of the remote during the course of the study.

Since the users only had the wireless remote to control the system, we were not able to use the login mechanisms that would allow for the encryption of the hard drive in order to protect the privacy of the data in case the computer was stolen. Instead, all the data were stored in memory tables and subsequently copied to the remote server each night. This arrangement however created another technical challenge because some of the homes experienced internet and power outages that were not anticipated to happen at such frequency. Although the implementation worked for most users, several sessions from one of the users were lost in the process. For the future studies, we plan to investigate other mechanisms to ensure data privacy and security while providing a robust data collection regardless of the internet connectivity.

From the users' perspective, the biggest challenge was switching the TV setting from their regular cable channel to the PC input. Initially the users were instructed how to do that via their TV remote; however, some were not able to remember the steps. To resolve this issue, we installed for some users a physical HDMI switch that would allow them to more easily switch the inputs at their convenience.

On the software side, one of the common issues reported by the participants was the lack of or incorrect repetition counting in some of the more complex exercises. As reported previously [10], the real-time analysis is sensitive to various factors, which include camera position, inclusion of other objects in the scene, orientation of the user with respect to the camera, type of chair, etc. We are currently working on more robust methods to perform the analysis and repetition counting while using the collected dataset for benchmarking.

The feedback collected from the interviews with the participants revealed that lack of exercising was primarily due to reasons unrelated to the system itself, such as illness, scheduling, low motivation, etc. The subjects did express hope that any technical issues would be resolved in the future, such as more reliable exercise recognition and issues with the TV setup. Overall, the subjects who did use the system on regular basis provided mostly positive impressions, such as:

- *"I was excited to exercise, but should stick with every other day, I did it 2 days in a row and was sore."*
- *"I don't exercise that much, but try to complete the video 4x/week."*
- *"I exercise right before bed, I have seen that it helps me sleep better."*
- *"Coach very encouraging and that makes me want to do it."*
- *"Good program. Instructions well done; I like the bar chart, makes me feel better to exercise and helps me see what I need to work on... Feedback could be better, feels canned. Delays and technical issues would be great if not there."*

Due to the limited space, we have shown only a small subset of the results collected during the time the participants used the exercise system. Future analyses will include comparison of the exercise performance with the clinical measures that were collected before and during the study. Since the dataset also includes raw skeletal data, we are planning to further investigate how to quantify the exercise performance in terms of standard fitness measures, such as flexibility, balance, strength, and endurance [12]. Furthermore, we will analyze the strategies that the participants used to exercise by comparing their data to the data of the coach in the video. Such temporal analysis could quantify how closely the participants were following the movement of the coach or if they have developed their own strategy for each exercise. The results of the analysis will be important for implementing a more effective feedback in the future. Furthermore, we will investigate how the exercise system could be used in a closed-loop semi-automated coaching.

Acknowledgements. The authors would like to thank Štěpán Obdržálek, Alex Triana, and Kavan Sikand for contributions to software development; Sue Scott of Renewable Fitness for providing the exercises and her assistance in designing the exercise program; and Edmund Seto for contributions to the study design. This research was supported by the National Science Foundation (NSF) under Grant No. 1111965.

References

1. Department of Health & Human Services, Administration on Aging. http://www.aoa.gov. Accessed 1 February 2015
2. Sun, F., Norman, I., While, A.: Physical activity in older people: a systematic review. BMC Public Health **13**(1), 17 (2013)
3. Sinclair, J., Hingston, P., Masek, M.: Considerations for the design of exergames. In: Proceedings of the 5th International Conference on Computer Graphics and Interactive Techniques in Australia and Southeast Asia (GRAPHITE 2007), Perth, Australia (2007)
4. Doyle, J., Kelly, D., Caulfield, B.: Design considerations in therapeutic exergaming. In: Proceedings of 5th International Conference on Pervasive Computing Technologies for Healthcare (PervasiveHealth) and Workshops (2011)
5. Ganesan, S., Anthony, L.: Using the Kinect to encourage older adults to exercise: a prototype. In: CHI 2012 Extended Abstracts on Human Factors in Computing Systems (2012)
6. Pisan, Y., Marin, J.G., Navarro, K.F.: Improving lives: using Microsoft Kinect to predict the loss of balance for elderly users under cognitive load. In: Proceedings of the 9th Australasian Conference on Interactive Entertainment: Matters of Life and Death (2013)
7. Larsen, L.H., Schou, L., Lund, H.H., Langberg, H.: The physical effect of exergames in healthy elderly – a systematic review. Games Health J. **2**(4), 205–212 (2013)
8. Miller, K.J., Adair, B.S., Pearce, A.J., Said, C.M., Ozanne, E., Morris, M.M.: Effectiveness and feasibility of virtual reality and gaming system use at home by older adults for enabling physical activity to improve health-related domains: a systematic review. Age Ageing **43**(2), 188–195 (2013)
9. Jimison, H.B., Pavel, M.: Integrating computer-based health coaching into elder home care. In: Technology and Aging. Assistive Technology Research Series, vol. 21, pp. 122–129. IOS Press (2008)

10. Ofli, F., Kurillo, G., Obdrzalek, S., Bajcsy, R., Jimison, H., Pavel, M.: Design and evaluation of an interactive exercise coaching system for older adults: lessons learned. IEEE J. Biomed. Health Inform. (2015, accepted)
11. Obdržálek, Š., Kurillo, G., Ofli, F., Bajcsy, R., Seto, E., Jimison, H., Pavel, M.: Accuracy and robustness of Kinect pose estimation in the context of coaching of elderly population. In: Proceedings of 34th International Conference of the IEEE Engineering in Medicine and Biology Society (EMBEC), San Diego, CA (2012)
12. Caspersen, C.J., Powell, K.E., Christenson, G.M.: Physical activity, exercise and physical fitness: definitions and distinctions for health-related research. Public Health Rep. **100**(2), 126–131 (1985)
13. Zhang, Z.: Microsoft Kinect sensor and its effect. IEEE Multimedia **19**(2), 4–10 (2012)

Considerations in Evaluating Technologies in Memory Care Units

Amanda Lazar(✉), Hilaire J. Thompson, and George Demiris

University of Washington, Seattle, USA
{Alaz,Hilairet,gdemiris}@uw.edu

Abstract. As the population ages worldwide, dementia is becoming increasingly prevalent. There is a pressing need to investigate non-pharmacological interventions to meet the needs of people with dementia. Technology may be one tool to enhance the lives of people with dementia without the use of medication. However, conducting studies with people with dementia in memory care units (MCUs) has unique challenges. In this paper, we discuss methodological and logistical considerations in designing, recruiting for, and conducting technology evaluations in memory care units. These considerations are based on a six-month study evaluating a technology system designed to encourage people with dementia to participate in recreational activities. Findings will assist researchers in conducting studies deploying technology tools for people with dementia in memory care units and assisted living facilities.

Keywords: Dementia · Study planning · Computers · Multimedia

1 Introduction

As the population ages worldwide, dementia is becoming increasingly prevalent. In the United States, 14.7 % of adults over the age of 70 were estimated to have dementia in 2010, and the range of dementia care cost for each person was estimated to cost between 41,689 and 56,290 US dollars [1]. In addition to financial cost, dementia can have tremendous psychosocial costs for people with dementia as well as their family members and friends.

1.1 Dementia and Activities

Activities are one non-pharmacological approach to improving the health and quality of life of people with dementia. In one study, Schreiner et al. found that residents expressed happiness more than seven times as often during structured recreation time as opposed to during 'ordinary time' [2]. In another study, participants with dementia were observed during three activities: unstructured time, group activities, and group reminiscence therapy (during which memories of the past are revisited). Individuals demonstrated greater levels of wellbeing during both sets of structured activities [3]. Activities have benefits for people other than the individual with dementia: in a study in which staff at a day care center for people with Alzheimer's disease were interviewed,

J. Zhou and G. Salvendy (Eds.): ITAP 2015, Part II, LNCS 9194, pp. 114–122, 2015.
DOI: 10.1007/978-3-319-20913-5_11

Hasselkus found that facilitating activities served as a source of satisfaction and meaningful purpose for staff [4]. Despite the myriad benefits of engaging in leisure and recreational activities, there are barriers to doing so for people with dementia.

Dementia affects people's abilities to take part in activities of daily living through impairments in memory, language, judgment, and problem solving [5]. Dementia also affects people's abilities to take part in leisure and recreational activities: increased impairment from dementia has been found to be associated with lower participation in staff-led activities in a variety of care settings [6]. In addition, several studies have established that people with dementia in nursing homes and memory care units may lack sufficient activities. In one study, Wood et al. observed residents over several days and found that residents spent the majority of their time unengaged in activities [7]. In another study, 238 people with dementia from various care homes were assessed for unmet needs. The researchers found that while environmental and physical needs were often met, social needs such as company and activities were not sufficiently met [8].

1.2 Technology for Activity Engagement for People with Dementia

Technology has the capability to address some of the needs of people with dementia. Cited in Topo et al. [9], Marshall described nine technology uses for people with dementia: reminders, safety, surveillance, control, service coordination, assistance to relatives, compensation, and stimulation and relaxation [10]. To Marshall's list, Topo adds the use of technology for communication [9]. Wey further suggests five uses for assistive technology in dementia rehabilitation, including supporting cognitive abilities essential for everyday activities, enabling people to carry out difficult tasks, providing access to meaningful occupation, ensuring safety, and supporting caregivers [11]. Newell et al. recommend additional areas for technologies to potentially enhance the lives of older adults with cognitive impairments, including allowing people to retain independence and control, providing monitoring capabilities, keeping people active physically and intellectually, and facilitating communication [12].

Despite the inclusion of needs specific to people with dementia in many of the above lists, Topo points out that the majority of studies focus on the needs of the caregivers of people with dementia rather than the needs of people with dementia themselves. Additionally, Topo stresses the importance of include people with dementia in the evaluation of technologies [9]. Thus, there is a need for studies that involve people with dementia in the design and evaluation of technologies intended for use by or with them, particularly for technologies that support the activity needs of people with dementia.

In a recent six-month study, we evaluated a commercially available multi-functional computer system designed to facilitate access to recreational activities for people with dementia. This system was evaluated in a memory care unit (MCU) and in an activity group for people with early signs of memory impairment. Findings relating to the effect of the system are not discussed here: in this paper, we outline important issues researchers should consider when planning studies that evaluate technologies in MCUs.

2 Related Work

Other researchers have addressed methodological issues in conducting research with people with dementia.

2.1 Considerations in Conducting Studies with People with Dementia

In their study, Hall and colleagues describe the challenges of conducting qualitative interviews with older people living in nursing homes to obtain views on how to preserve dignity. Though the authors do not limit their study to people with dementia, many of the issues they discuss are pertinent in a dementia care setting, such as administering informed consent to residents who forgot they had signed up to participate in the study and difficulty scheduling sessions due to frequent activities and barriers such as residents not feeling well and having unexpected visitors [13].

In a systematic review, Lawrence et al. discuss conditions required for and challenges to successful implementations of psychosocial (as opposed to pharmacological) interventions with people with dementia. Conditions required for successful implementation include staff willing to provide access to and encourage use of interventions, the involvement of family members in notifying staff of likes and dislikes of residents, flexibility of the intervention to accommodate different ability levels of residents, and having an intervention long enough for residents to become comfortable with its use. Challenges to implementation include that psychosocial interventions often placed a burden on staff in terms of time and workload and that staff felt uncomfortable implementing the intervention. In the discussion, the authors emphasize the importance of gaining staff commitment before the intervention is implemented and the importance of collaborating with family members [14]. Despite the pertinence of some of these issues, the projects described above did not deploy a technology tool. Therefore, there are a wide range of issues specific to working with people with dementia and technology deployment that are left unaddressed.

2.2 Considerations in Conducting Technology Deployment Studies with People with Dementia

Several papers discuss methodological and logistical considerations in studies that utilize technology with people with dementia. Andersson et al. describe the importance of setting up a technical help desk, creating user manuals, and checking in periodically to identify issues that were not reported to the help desk. These findings are some of the lessons learned from the deployment of CogKnow, an information and communication technology tool for people with mild dementia [15].

Astell et al. discuss a broad range of findings from seven years of working with people with dementia, family members, and staff to design and evaluate CIRCA (Computer Interactive Reminiscence and Conversation Aid), a computer system designed to facilitate communication between people with dementia and others. The researchers discuss the importance of involving different stakeholders (such as spouses and staff), the particularities of navigating consent with people with dementia, and techniques to evaluate the engagement of people with dementia using verbal and nonverbal behaviors [16].

We build on these previous works by providing additional areas to consider, such as appropriate study time periods, recruitment of staff, and alternate ways to manage technical issues that emerge when using technology systems.

3 Considerations

Below we outline some of the issues researchers should consider when implementing technology studies in MCUs based on our experience.

3.1 Designing the Study

Time Period of Study. Though shorter studies require vastly fewer resources, a longer, six-month study was essential for us to see the ways staff incorporated the system into their activity routine. This was due to a long period during which staff became familiar and comfortable with the system and during which technical issues were resolved. Though the longer time resulted in a more positive view of the system, it is easy to imagine a system that is initially appreciated and then discarded after novelty wears off. We suggest at least three months for technology evaluation studies that involve staff. For the evaluation of systems with people with dementia, the length of a study can be shorter as residents may not be able to remember much from session to session (though they may become more comfortable due to growing relationships with the research team as well as recognizing the system).

We also found it very beneficial to have monthly interviews with staff in order to identify shifting attitudes and capture anecdotal experiences that could have been forgotten over a period of months. Monthly interviews were also beneficial given rapid staff turnover; if a staff member left the facility before the study was completed, we were still able to have more than one interview with them.

Involving Family Members. We found the inclusion of family members to be extremely valuable for several reasons. First, family members have the ability to assist the researcher in evaluating the technology by providing another angle that differs from the observations of the researcher and staff. Second, the family member may be very helpful in figuring out the kinds of applications the residents may like, which is especially useful for residents who have difficulty communicating their interests or appear apathetic. However, family members do not necessarily know residents' current interests; many family members ruled out certain types of application that their relatives actually did enjoy using. Additionally, family members may project their own feelings of fear and failure onto residents and attempt to protect them from experiences where they might fail.

We build on Lawrence et al.'s suggestion to involve family members and take into account their perspectives and advice for interacting with residents [14]. However, we add that it is essential for the researcher to interact with participants with dementia in a manner that is open to additional possibilities, respecting their current status, interests and opinions.

3.2 Recruiting Participants

Though recruitment may be an issue for many studies, studies taking place in MCUs have particular issues such as ensuring informed consent, the need to utilize legally authorized representatives for informed consent, and dealing with staff who are often overwhelmed by responsibilities and may be hesitant to take on the additional burden of participating in a study.

Navigating the Enrollment of People with Dementia Through Others. There are no universally accepted guidelines for what constitutes informed consent for someone with dementia. However, informed consent is a requirement of research involving human participants and necessitates that participants are competent enough to understand the implications of their decisions [17]. To address the lack of ability for people with dementia in middle and later stages to provide informed consent, legally authorized representatives (LARs) are often utilized as proxies for authorizing individuals with dementia to take part in research.

We navigated enrollment in a manner similar to what was described in [16]; however, we did not send recruitment letters to residents due to the level of their cognitive impairment which would make responding to or recalling the contents of the letter impossible. For our study, we sent letters to the people recorded as LARs in resident files asking them to contact us to enroll their relatives if they were interested. Once they signed a consent form, we were able to approach their relative in the MCU to gauge willingness to participate in the study and obtain 'assent'. Due to us having to go through LARs, some MCU residents who verbally expressed interest in taking part in the study after seeing us use the system with other residents could not take part in the study because their family members did not respond to our letters. In one instance, a resident told the first author she had wanted to use the system but thought that nobody would let her. We felt torn in situations such as these, when residents showed interest in the system yet due to lack of consent from LARs, we were not able to invite them to take part in the study. Unlike studies with the general population, where a person who is interested and meets criteria can take part, people in this population who are interested and would benefit from the study may be excluded due to whether or not their LAR chooses to have them participate.

We caution that the use of technology may make family members more hesitant to enroll their relatives with dementia: one family member wrote to us that he did not think his family member should be in the study as she may be "beyond using any type of technology." However all participants with the exception of one who had very severe dementia (MMSE score of 2) and was unable to respond to or follow instruction, were able to use the system. As noted by Hellström et al., having a family member serve as a gatekeeper to conduct (non-invasive) research with people with dementia is not optimal, but it is difficult to come up with another way to ensure that people with dementia are not manipulated or treated unethically [18]. Thus, it is important to come up with ways to introduce technology studies to family members so that participants who could benefit are not excluded. As mentioned above, family members often doubted that their relatives would be able to complete the study or interact with the technology, even when this was not the case. Recruitment materials should emphasize that people with all levels of dementia severity may be able to contribute to the study and that researchers will be present to instruct the participant in the use of the technology.

Staff presented another barrier to wide enrollment of residents. After the initial enrollment, during which letters were sent to all LARs, as new residents moved into the MCU, staff would only notify us about residents they saw as cognitively able to take part in studies. It may help to reinforce to staff that the researchers have methods of screening out residents who are unable to take part in research.

Enrolling Staff. It was difficult for us to find a time to speak to staff about the study. During one information session, staff were actively taking care of residents and were not able to fully focus on details of the study and did not express interest in signing up for the study. The staff who did sign up for the study had come to a separate, much smaller session that took place in another area of the facility, away from the residents. Though we believe that the distance from residents helped, the greater participation from this group may also be attributable to the staff members who attended that session having been more interested in the study to begin with. In general, we found that the staff members most likely to be involved were the ones already engaged in conducting and planning activities with residents (whether formally or informally). We suggest targeting these individuals in recruitment as 'champions' who may be motivate other staff members to take part in the study.

Staff in MCUs may be extremely busy and unlikely to want to take part in studies that do not have clear benefit to their workflow or practice. In our study, once the tool was in the MCU for several months, staff were much more open to taking part in the study and using the tool. If possible within the study methodology, we suggest letting staff become familiar with the system and its benefits over several weeks before recruiting for the study, as staff commitment before the intervention begins is essential [14]. If this is not possible, another option is to continue recruiting throughout the study. Additionally, some staff members may be willing to do an exit or one-off interview discussing their experience using the system even if they are not willing to be enrolled for the entire duration of the study.

3.3 Conducting the Study

Using the Technology System. Although many products are marketed as ready for deployment with older adults or people with dementia, in our experience, we have found that many have significant usability and technical issues despite being available for purchase. Many issues with the system used for the study were exacerbated by conditions in the memory care unit. For example, staff felt an intense sense of time pressure while conducting activities. They described situations where they would attempt to use an application with residents and it wouldn't immediately work or they would not know how to use it without multiple attempts, and residents would quickly lose interest and get up and leave the room. One staff member described how she never felt like she had enough time, as she prioritized spending time with the residents over other tasks (including learning to use the system deployed in the study). Although in the long run, learning to use the system might result in more opportunities for beneficial interactions with residents, it could be hard for staff to justify taking time away from interacting with residents to learn to use the system.

To address technical and usability issues, we attempted several solutions. We provided resources to help staff learn to use the system, such as pocket card instruction manuals (attached to the system and given to staff participating in the study) and created web resources, such as videos, to help staff learn how to use certain features. The system manufacturers had technical support staff available, and we left the technical support telephone number in several locations so staff could access them. Additionally, we conducted information sessions where we taught all staff how to use the system. Finally, research staff were on site several times a week to conduct sessions and to address any issues. We also asked staff during monthly interviews if they were having issues with the system.

Unlike Andersson et al. [15], we did not find that technical support staff or instruction manuals were useful for staff members at the MCU. Of all the solutions we attempted, staff mainly utilized on-site researchers as resources for addressing issues. This was useful for staff to notify us about issues that could be addressed, such as broken cables. It was also useful for staff to tell us about processes they found confusing. Based on in-person feedback from staff that this was a very confusing process, we placed a sticky note on the monitor that described how to plug in the system to the monitor. This small change was mentioned as very useful and as leading to greatly increased use. We suggest having researchers on site periodically to resolve issues, as staff did not contact us through email or the system's technical support team through phone.

Another way staff were able to learn to navigate some usability issues was through identifying a staff member that was comfortable using the system and asking them for assistance in the moment. It may be helpful to identify a 'champion' staff member who is willing to spend time with the researchers to learn to use the system and then serve as a person to answer questions from other staff members.

Scheduling. While all studies may experience variability in scheduling weekly sessions, we ran into issues particular to a memory care unit setting. These issues included unpredictable activity scheduling and periodic confusion on the part of residents. In one case, we spent some time with the activity director finding a time to schedule a session with a resident who was especially engaged in activities. Even after this scheduling, some days, staff members would not follow the activity schedule and spontaneously decide to conduct a favorite activity of the resident. Another issue in scheduling sessions occurred with fluctuating cognitive states and disorientation of residents.

In other types of studies, scheduling issues may be resolved through phone calls to avoid having a researcher show up without need. For residents in the MCU, this would not be possible. One solution to dealing with fluctuating cognitive states is identifying best times of the day for residents through talking to staff or family members. Many of the residents were most alert in the morning and experienced some form of "sundowning syndrome" (confusion and agitation which affects some people with dementia as the sun goes down). It was also helpful to be in contact with family members who visited frequently who could let us know if a resident was not feeling well or was experiencing more confusion than usual. We recommend speaking to family members and staff members to minimize scheduling issues.

4 Conclusion

Technology systems have the potential to benefit people with dementia and those that care for them by expanding the types of activities that are available. However, conducting research in memory care units and with people with dementia introduce challenges that are not present in other settings. We present methodological and logistical considerations in deploying technology tools with people with dementia that will assist researchers in conducting similar studies. We address various stages of the research process, such as designing, recruiting for, and conducting studies with this population.

Acknowledgements. We thank the participants who gave their time and effort to take part in this study. This work was supported by the National Science Foundation Graduate Research Fellowship [Grant DGE-1256082] and the National Library of Medicine Biomedical and Health Informatics Training Grant Program [Grant T15LM007442].

References

1. Hurd, M.D., Martorell, P., Delavande, A., Mullen, K.J., Langa, K.M.: Monetary Costs of Dementia in the United States. N. Engl. J. Med. **368**, 1326–1334 (2013)
2. Schreiner, A.S., Yamamoto, E., Shiotani, H.: Positive affect among nursing home residents with Alzheimer's dementia: the effect of recreational activity. Aging Ment. Health. **9**, 129–134 (2005)
3. Brooker, D., Duce, L.: Wellbeing and activity in dementia: a comparison of group reminiscence therapy, structured goal-directed group activity and unstructured time. Aging Ment. Health. **4**, 354–358 (2000)
4. Hasselkus, B.R.: The meaning of activity: day care for persons with Alzheimer disease. Am. J. Occup. Ther. **46**, 199–206 (1992)
5. Bird, T.D., Miller, B.L.: Alzheimer's disease and other dementias. In: Hauser, S., Josephson, S. (eds.) Harrison's Neurology in Clinical Medicine, pp. 298–319. McGraw Hill Professional, China (2010)
6. Kuhn, D., Fulton, B., Edelman, P.: Factors influencing participation in activities in dementia care settings. Alzheimers. care today. **1**, 144–152 (2004)
7. Wood, W., Harris, S., Snider, M., Patchel, S.A.: Activity situations on an Alzheimer's disease special care unit and resident environmental interaction, time use, and affect. Am. J. Alzheimers. Dis. Other Demen. **20**, 105–118 (2005)
8. Hancock, G.A., Woods, B., Challis, D., Orrell, M.: The needs of older people with dementia in residential care. Int. J. Geriatr. Psychiatry **21**, 43–49 (2006)
9. Topo, P.: Technology studies to meet the needs of people with dementia and their caregivers: a literature review. J. Appl. Gerontol. **28**, 5–37 (2008)

10. Marshall, M.: Dementia and technology: Some ethical considerations. In: Mollenkopf, H. (ed.) Elderly people in industrialised societies. Social integration in old age by or despite technology?, pp. 207–215. Edition Sigma, Rainer Bohn Verlag, Berlin (1996)
11. Wey, S.: One size does not fit all: person-centred approaches to the use of assistive technology. In: Marshall, M. (ed.) Perspectives on Rehabilitation and Dementia, pp. 202–208. Jessica Kingsley Publishers, London (2005)
12. Newell, A.F., Carmichael, A., Gregor, P., Alm, N.: Information technology for cognitive support. Hum. Comput. Interact. Handb. **2**, 464–481 (2002)
13. Hall, S., Longhurst, S., Higginson, I.J.: Challenges to conducting research with older people living in nursing homes. BMC Geriatr. **9**, 38 (2009)
14. Lawrence, V., Fossey, J., Ballard, C., Moniz-Cook, E., Murray, J.: Improving quality of life for people with dementia in care homes: making psychosocial interventions work. Br. J. Psychiatry **201**, 344–351 (2012)
15. Andersson, S., Andersson, A.-L.: Practical issues when planning for field trials. In: Mulvenna, M.D., Nugent, C.D. (eds.) Supporting People with Dementia Using Pervasive Health Technologies, pp. 191–195. Springer-Verlag, London Limited (2010)
16. Astell, A., Alm, N., Gowans, G., Ellis, M., Dye, R., Vaughan, P.: Involving older people with dementia and their carers in designing computer based support systems: some methodological considerations. Univers. Access Inf. Soc. **8**, 49–58 (2008)
17. Slaughter, S., Cole, D., Jennings, E., Reimer, M.A.: Consent and Assent to Participate in Research from People with Dementia. Nurs. Ethics. **14**, 27–40 (2007)
18. Hellström, I., Nolan, M., Nordenfelt, L., Lundh, U.: Ethical and methodological issues in interviewing persons with dementia. Nurs. Ethics. **14**(5), 608–619 (2007)

Influence of Mobile ICT on the Adherence of Elderly People with Chronic Diseases

Alexander Mertens[1(✉)], Peter Rasche[1], Sabine Theis[1], Matthias Wille[1], Christopher Schlick[1], and Stefan Becker[2]

[1] Research Group: Human Factors Engineering and Ergonomics in Healthcare, Institute of Industrial Engineering and Ergonomics of RWTH Aachen University, Aachen, Germany
{a.mertens,p.rasche,s.theis,m.wille, c.schlick}@iaw.rwth-aachen.de

[2] Department of Nephrology, University Duisburg-Essen, Essen, Germany
Stefan.Becker@uk-essen.de

Abstract. A great variety of applications for mobile devices are designed to support users during medical intake. One of these applications is 'Medication Plan' which aims at supporting regular and correct intake of medication and documentation of vital parameters. The purpose of this study is to examine the influence of demographic and health-related factors on user behavior and patterns of use. The application was available free of charge between 2010 and 2012 in the Apple™-App-Store™. The study is based on data collected via an online questionnaire. In total 1799 participants generated 1708 complete data sets. 69 % of the users (74 % male) with a median age of 45 applied 'Medication Plan' for more than one day. The mean duration of application increased substantially with age (< 21 years = 23.3 days; > 60 years = 103.9 days). However, other demographic factors (sex, educational status etc.) had no effect on usage intensity. Users with complicated medical treatment or aged > 60 years applied the application for 3 month on average. This is a promising trend towards the support treatment of chronic conditions with mobile applications.

Keywords: Adherence · Elderly patients · Ergonomics · HCI · ICT · Telemedicine

1 Introduction

Patients with chronic illnesses such as hypertension and chronic kidney disease are often burdened by high comorbidity and reduced awareness of their medical conditions, which creates a challenging environment in which to promote medication compliance [1]. Complexities of daily life, shifting priorities, and frequent poly-pharmacy likely contribute to patients' inability to deal adequately with their medical conditions. Frequent encounters with the medical system, which result in dosage adjustments, add to the problems with medication compliance in these patients [2]. For the individual, non-adherence is associated with a number a safety issues such as increased risk of

J. Zhou and G. Salvendy (Eds.): ITAP 2015, Part II, LNCS 9194, pp. 123–133, 2015.
DOI: 10.1007/978-3-319-20913-5_12

toxicity or more severe relapses [3]. For the health system in Germany alone, direct and indirect costs of non-adherence amount to approximately 7.5 to 10 billion Euros every year [4, 5]. Therefore novel strategies are required to address the needs of chronically ill patients and reduce. Mobile information technology may offer new system solutions to better meet these requirements. With more than 1 billion users having access to mobile broadband internet and a rapidly growing mobile app market, all stakeholders involved have high hopes that this technology may improve health care [6, 7]. Expectations range from overcoming structural barriers to access in low-income countries to more effective, interactive treatment of chronic conditions. Yet previous work suggests that even when sophisticated technology is available, older users (e.g., age 50 and above) find their initial experiences with medication applications frustrating [8]. The iNephro study introduced a "native" smartphone application ("Medication Plan"), which allowed users to maintain and alter personal drug therapy plans and document vital signs on their personal device [9]. Initial findings showed that the regular use of the application decreased considerably within the first 2 months. This paper presents a further analysis to better understand what is generally referred to as "attrition of app usage".

Pre-specified endpoints were used to identify user data with regards to demographic- and health-related factors associated with "duration of usage" and "intensity of usage per day" of the mobile application "Medication Plan".

2 Materials and Methods

The Department of Nephrology of the University Hospital Essen, Germany, developed and provided the "Medication Plan" application for the iOS platform in 2010 [10]. This native smartphone application allowed users to maintain and alter a drug therapy plan on their personal device (Fig. 1). Between December 2010 and January 2012 it was available free of charge for download in the German-language App Store™ by Apple™. Users were able to specify intake requirements according to the medication regimen issued by the prescribing physician and the patients' own personal needs (see tutorial at http://www.youtube.com/watch?v=nui78JqwMHE). A reminder function and local push-notification alerts reminded users to take their medications at a pre-specified time. No permanent internet connection was necessary and all data were stored locally on the device itself, reducing the possibility of erroneous transmission of personal health information. Users could enter vital sign data, and trends were presented graphically. Prior to using the application, users had to give their consent to a disclaimer as well as an agreement for a subsequent anonymous analysis of user data and this was done via activation of a hyperlink (implementation by QUEST objects GmbH, Tübingen). Additionally, users were invited to voluntarily and anonymously complete an online questionnaire, which had to be actively accessed via an additional hyperlink. The unique identifier numbers (UDID) of the respective iPhones™ were irreversibly encrypted by a MD5 message-digest algorithm (MD5-Hash).

The activity of the encrypted UDID was then tracked ("creation", "modification", or "deletion" of drug information, as well as the "confirmation" of drug adherence

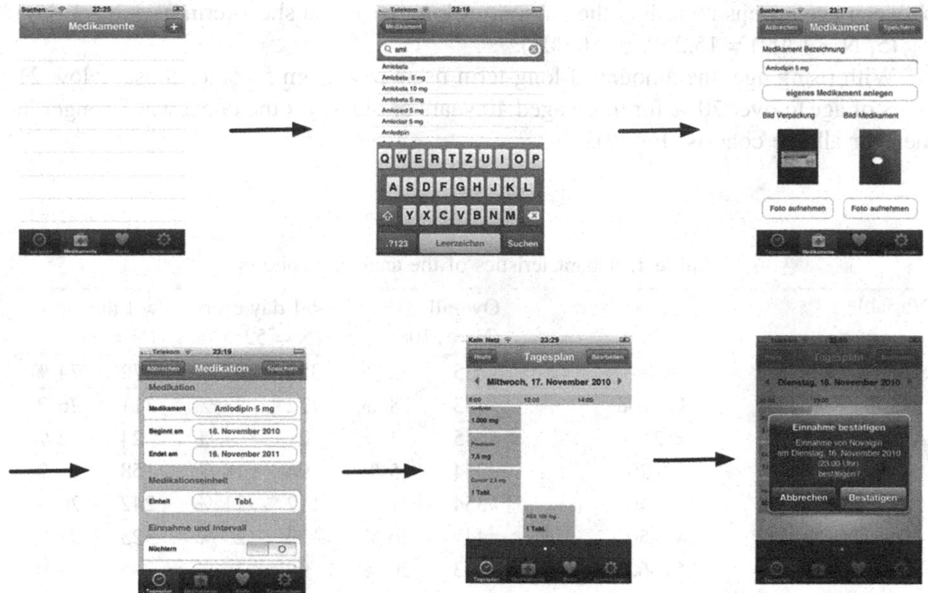

Fig. 1. Generating a medication plan on the smartphone ([9])

within the application "Medication Plan"). Activity of the respective, encrypted UDID addresses and if available, associated demographic information, were analyzed using self-implemented software of Fraunhofer ISST, Dortmund, Germany. Further statistical analysis was performed using *SPSS*® 21.0 (IBM®, U.S.A.): A multi-factorial analysis of variance (ANOVA) and chi-square test for the response variables with a significance level of 0.05 was conducted. The distributions of the groups were normal and the homogeneity of variances for the data analyzed was confirmed.

Following the APA guidelines the exact error probability p was specified for each analysis [11]. Dependent variables were "duration of long-term usage" (defined as use of > 1 per day; if no activity was recorded for > 10 days, this was rated as end of use) and "mean intensity of usage per day" during time of active usage.

Ethics: The Ethics Committee of the Medical Faculty of Essen University was consulted and a formal written waiver for the need of ethics approval was issued (13-5373-BO).

3 Results

Overall, activity of 1799 (1708 complete data sets) users was recorded between December 2010 and April 2012 (Table 1). More than two thirds of users (1183/1708) used "Medication Plan" for more than a day. There was a significant association between gender and amount of long-term and short-term users (χ^2 (1, N = 1761) = 6.715, $p < 0.010$). Looking at the different age cohorts, there was a significant difference between age groups regarding the amount of long-term and short-term users (> 1 day) (χ^2 (5, N = 1799) = 15.255, p < 0.001).

With rising age, the amount of long-term users rose from 50 % of those below 21 years of age to over 70 % for those aged 40 years or older, yet the effect was stronger in men for all age cohorts (Fig. 2).

Table 1. Characteristics of the analyzed cohorts

Variable		Overall (N = 1708)		< 1 day users (N = 525)		> 1 day users (N = 1183)	
Sex	Male	1225	72 %	353	67 %	872	74 %
	Female	483	28 %	172	33 %	311	26 %
Age (years)	< 21	45	3 %	21	4 %	24	2 %
	21–30	254	15 %	96	18 %	158	13 %
	31–40	354	21 %	112	21 %	242	20 %
	41–50	447	26 %	122	23 %	325	27 %
	51–60	343	20 %	98	19 %	245	21 %
	> 60	265	16 %	76	14 %	189	16 %
Highest educational qualification	Secondary school	904	53 %	274	52 %	630	53 %
	Qualif. for university	328	19 %	113	22 %	215	18 %
	University degree	476	28 %	138	26 %	338	29 %
Disease	Cardiovascular	894	52 %	243	46 %	651	55 %
	Transplantation	243	14 %	74	14 %	169	14 %
	Diabetes mellitus	125	7 %	46	9 %	79	7 %
	Lung disease	86	5 %	22	4 %	64	5 %
	Liver disease	90	5 %	32	6 %	58	5 %
Number of chronic conditions	0	495	29 %	174	33 %	321	27 %
	1	806	47 %	230	44 %	576	49 %
	2	280	16 %	83	16 %	197	17 %
	3	95	6 %	27	5 %	68	6 %
	4	24	1 %	7	1 %	17	1 %
	5 and more	8	0 %	4	1 %	4	0 %
Number of daily taken drugs	0	212	12 %	90	17 %	122	10 %
	1	397	23 %	121	23 %	276	23 %
	2	330	19 %	85	16 %	245	21 %
	3	257	15 %	74	14 %	183	15 %
	4	165	10 %	39	7 %	126	11 %
	5	149	9 %	54	10 %	95	8 %
	6	91	5 %	31	6 %	60	5 %
	7 and more	107	6 %	31	6 %	76	6 %

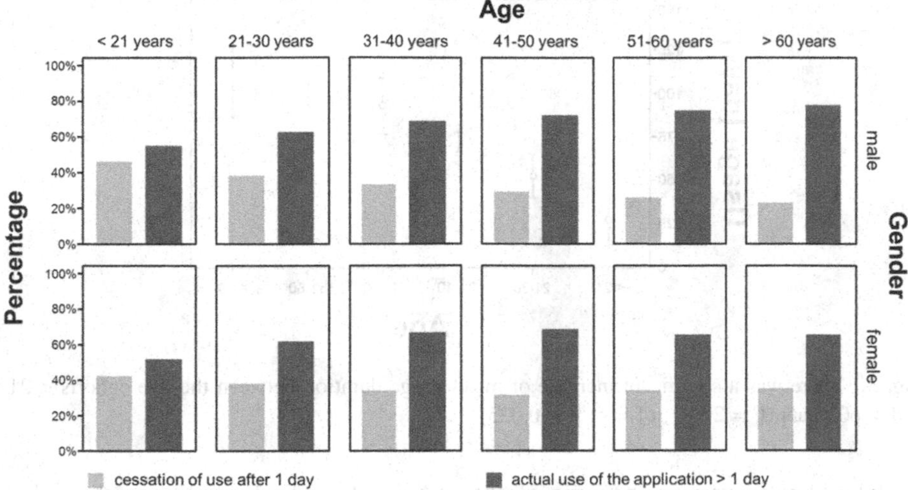

Fig. 2. Distribution of user behavior: actual use of the application > 1 day and cessation of use after 1 day by age and sex.

The number of diseases for each user significantly affected duration of usage (χ^2 (5, N = 1799) = 12.144, p = 0.030). While the proportion of individuals who stopped using the app after one day was 42 % for those that did not have to take any drugs, it was between 25 and 30 %, for those who were on regular medication. Similarly, the number of drugs significantly affected the duration of usage (χ^2 (7, N = 1799) = 30.612, p < 0.001). This effect is not surprising, as for users without any medical condition or the need to take drugs on a regular schedule, only a fraction of the available functionality was still useful (e.g. keeping track of weight and vital parameters).

Variance analysis presented the following effects with respect to duration of usage: With a mean duration of usage of 23.3 days (SD = 36.9) by users < 21 years, there was a substantial increase over all age cohorts up to users of 60 years and above using the application for 103.9 days on average (SD = 20.7) (F = 2.581; df = 5; p = 0.025). For users aged 50 and older, the usage duration remained static.

A post hoc pairwise analysis with Bonferroni correction showed significant differences between all age groups concerning usage duration with a minimum age difference of 20 years. I.e. users aged 50 used the app substantially more than those aged 30. Mean duration of usage, for users who did not abandon the application within the first day, was 85.4 days (SD 138.6) (Fig. 3). Sex (F = 1.084; df = 1; p = 0.298) and educational attainment (F = 0.656; df = 2; p = 0.519) had no effect for those that did not cease to use the application after one day.

The number of medical conditions (F = 0.403; df = 5; p = 0.847) as well as the number of drugs taken per day on a regular schedule (F = 0.967; df = 7; p = 0.259) did not affect the duration of usage significantly.

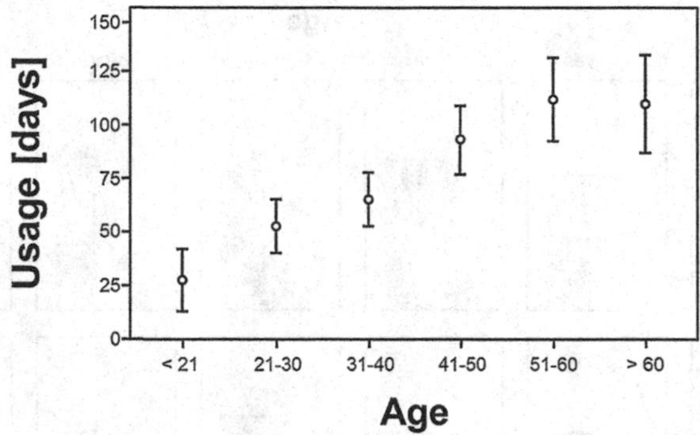

Fig. 3. There was a significant increase of mean usage duration between the age cohorts < 21 and > 60 years (F = 2.581; df = 5; p = 0.025).

Interestingly, variance-analysis of the individual medical conditions showed a significant effect on duration of usage if the user suffered from cardiovascular disease (F = 14.098; df = 1; p < 0.001) or had received a transplant (F = 12.503; df = 1; p < 0.001) (Fig. 4).

In either case, people with these a diseases used the system on average about 50 % longer compared to people not suffering from the same condition. Diabetes (F = 2.699; df = 1; p = 0.101), lung disease (F = 0.411; df = 1; p = 0.522) and liver disease had no significant impact on duration of usage (F = 2.221; df = 1; p = 0.136).

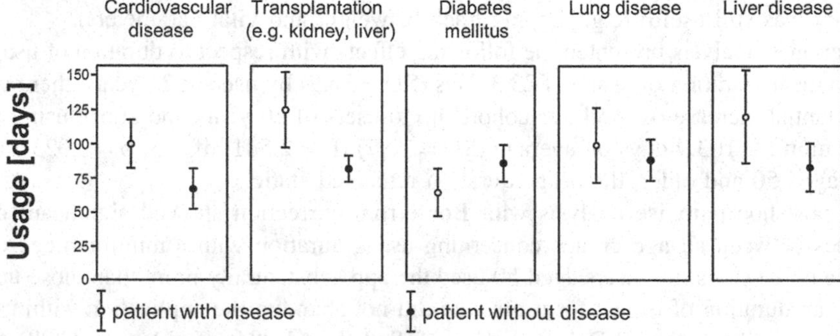

Fig. 4. Specific diseases are associated with a longer usage of the application

With regard to usage intensity, the number of diseases tended to affect usage intensity (F = 1.974; df = 5; p = 0.080). The number of regularly taken drugs had significant impact on usage intensity (F = 4.017; df = 7; p < 0.001) and increased with the number of drugs taken per day (Fig. 5).

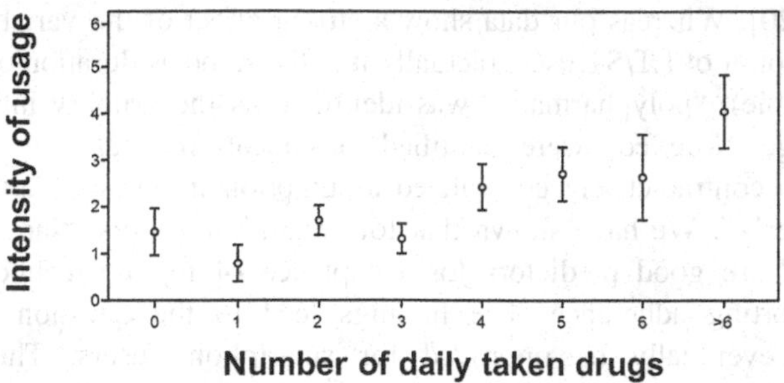

Fig. 5. The number of regularly taken drugs had significant impact on usage intensity ($F = 4.017$; $df = 7$; $p < 0.001$).

Demographic predictors such as sex ($F = 0.874$; $df = 1$; $p = 0.350$), age ($F = 0.646$; $df = 5$; $p = 0.665$) and educational attainment ($F = 0.905$; $df = 2$; $p = 0.405$) showed no significant effect.

4 Discussion

As far as we know our presented study is the first to describe the usage of a medication adherence-tool in a representative sample. More than 2/3 of users continued using "Medication Plan" after the first day. Over the entire study population, use of the application for more than one day grew with increasing age, yet the effect was greater in men over all age cohorts.

Once a user decided to log into the application, further factors (disease and associated medication) had an effect on the usage-duration and -intensity. Such findings may provide useful insights into behavioral-patterns of designated patient groups and assist in the design of effective interventions.

4.1 Brief Review of Findings and Comparison to Prior Studies

Thus far, most users of publicly available, health related, mobile communication services seem to have been "early adopters": middle-aged, male, well-educated and comparatively healthy [9, 12–14]. Furthermore, high attrition rates for internet interventions were reported, which may reflect deficits in usability or an early interest in the novelty of the application, with a declining eagerness as the newness of the intervention wears off [9, 15, 16].

The question that arises is whether mobile technology to support drug adherence is indeed an appropriate tool to support elderly patients with polypharmacy. So far, this issue has mostly been assessed indirectly via questionnaires [17–19]. Direct assessment of user activity can offer objective and more accurate data on the usefulness of a mobile application. Our findings offer new insights into what has been termed the "digital divide" [13, 14], a term coined by developers, which implies, that compared with the younger generation, older individuals are less likely to make extensive use of digital technology [8, 20]. Whereas our data show a strong effect of the variables "age" and "disease" on amount of LT/ST users (actually it is the same as duration only in form of an ordinal variable), "polypharmacy" was identified as the primary influence for the intensity of usage. No effects were identified for educational status.

Our findings contradict any generalized assumption implying "digital disengagement of the elderly". We have shown that for smartphone users, "increasing age" or "polypharmacy" are good predictors for acceptance of mobile technology when it comes to supporting adherence. The findings lead to the question whether drug adherence can eventually be improved for smartphone users. The Technology Acceptance Model suggests that acceptance depends on a user's perception of the usefulness and ease of use of a system [21]. Similarly, the diffusion of innovation model emphasizes that a new technology needs to offer a "relative advantage" over the status quo [22].

Together with previous findings suggesting that increasing age [23–25] and polypharmacy [26] negatively affect adherence, one may assume that the use of applications like "Medication Plan" will eventually improve drug adherence. In our investigation the lack of perceived usefulness or relative advantage likely was the reason for relative early cessation of app usage by patients stating to be suffering from diabetes is a point in proof [27]. "Medication Plan" did not offer many of these users the required added value such as a combined documentation of blood sugar, bread units consumed or administered doses of insulin. This finding demonstrates how important it is to bear in mind specific needs of users to achieve acceptance [28].

Furthermore, the success of "Medication Plan" with its very practical aspects of drug regimen management supports the concept of 'small data' [29], suggesting that people mainly need technology to help them make sense of their health condition, and to offer actionable steps. On another note, even though the three main drivers of adherence to chronic disease medication were identified as perceived concerns about medications, perceived need for medications, and perceived affordability of medications [30], it appears that practical support and reminders, while not directly targeting those issues, can still go a long way toward self-reported drug adherence.

Lastly it seems that the focus of iNephro on practicality and its main purpose to help users overcome the current barriers to health literacy were recognized and are mirrored by our results [31].

4.2 Strengths and Limitations

Despite evidence from pilot studies, most mHealth interventions can be seen as the equivalent of black boxes [19]. The problem of these studies is that a particular style of a black box application is compared to a situation without any black box application. This study presents a novel approach to directly assess usage and acceptance of mobile technology in the context of drug adherence.

Our elderly iPhone™ users can be seen as technologically savvy in the first place and findings may not apply across the entire population [32]. Age-related changes in hearing, vision, cognition, and mobility require special consideration and application designers need to take this into account.

Elderly patients tend to be more reserved towards the use of technology since they usually feel barriers to start using it [33]. Unless they see a clear benefit for themselves, older adults are less likely to adopt new technology [28].

5 Conclusion

The famous statement by Dr. Everett Koop, former U.S. Surgeon General, "Drugs don't work in patients who don't take them" may also be true for mobile medication management applications [8]. We were able to show that elderly, technologically savvy users, requiring polypharmacy, relied on a mobile application to support drug adherence and that the degree of engagement depended on disease/therapy-related as well as demographic factors.

With this knowledge, similar tools could be valuable in the drug management of these patients. However, particularly in elderly patients, drug adherence is a complex problem, requiring not only a trust based doctor-patient relationship but rather multi-dimensional approaches. These range from simplified therapy-regimes and sustained understanding of the disease on the patients' side to technological support including companion pillbox and communication devices.

Applications will have to be tailored closely to the specific demands of sick individuals to be accepted as part of their often complicated day-to day routines [34, 35]. Hence, interdisciplinary approaches and a profound understanding of the context and patients' needs are vital for successful realization of technological solutions and investments in the field [7, 36].

References

1. Vrijens, B., Vincze, G., Kristanto, P., Urquhart, J., Burinier, M.: Adherence to prescribed antihypertensive drug treatments: longitudinal study of electronically compiled dosing histories. BMJ **336**, 1114–1117 (2008)
2. Osterberg, L., Blaschke, T.: Adherence to medication. N. Engl. J. Med. **353**, 487–497 (2005)
3. De Geest, S., Sabaté, E.: Adherence to long-term therapies: evidence for action. Eur. J. Cardiovasc. Nurs. **2**(4), 323 (2003)
4. Volmer, T., Kielhorn, A.: Kosten der non-compliance. Gesundheitsökonomisches Qualitätsmanagement **4**, 55–61 (1999)
5. Gräf, M.: Die volkswirtschaftlichen Kosten der Non-Compliance: Eine entscheidungsorientierte Analyse. P.C.O.-Verlag, Bayreuth (2007)
6. Diamantidis, C.J., Becker, S.: Health information technology (IT) to improve the care of patients with chronic kidney disease (CKD). BMC Nephrol. **15**(1), 7 (2014)
7. Becker, S., Miron-Shatz, T., Schumacher, N., Krocza, J., Diamantidis, C.J., Albrecht, U.-V.: mHealth 2.0: experiences, possibilities, and perspectives. JMIR mHealth uHealth **2**(2), e24 (2014)
8. Grindrod, K.A., Li, M., Gates, A.: Evaluating user perceptions of mobile medication management applications with older adults: a usability study. JMIR mHealth uHealth **2**(1), e11 (2014)

9. Becker, S., Kribben, A., Meister, S., Diamantidis, C.J., Unger, N., Mitchell, A.: User profiles of a smartphone application to support drug adherence-experiences from the iNephro project. PLoS ONE **8**(10), e78547 (2013)
10. Charland, A., Leroux, B.: Mobile application development: web vs. native. Commun. ACM **54**(5), 49–53 (2014)
11. APA - American Psychological Association: Publication Manual of the American Psychological Association, 6. Edition. American Psychological Association, Washington (2009)
12. Smith, A.: http://pewinternet.org/~/media/Files/Reports/2012/Smartphone%ownership%202012.pdf
13. Sarkar, U., Karter, A.J., Liu, J.Y., Adler, N.E., Nguyen, R., Lopez, A., Schillinger, D.: Social disparities in internet patient portal use in diabetes: evidence that the digital divide extends beyond access. J. Am. Med. Inform. Assoc. **18**(3), 318–321 (2011)
14. Lorence, D.P., Park, H., Fox, S.: Racial disparities in health information access: resilience of the digital divide. J. Med. Syst. **30**(4), 241–249 (2006)
15. Boulos, M.N., Wheeler, S., Tavares, C., Jones, R.: How smartphones are changing the face of mobile and participatory healthcare: an overview, with example from eCAALYX. Biomed. Eng. Online **10**, 24 (2011)
16. Consumer Health Information Corporation. http://www.consumerhealth.com/press/2008/NewsReleaseSmartPhoneApps.php
17. Free, C., Phillips, G., Galli, L., Watson, L., Felix, L., Edwards, P., Patel, V., Haines, A.: The effectiveness of mobile-health technology-based health behavior change or disease management interventions for health care consumers: a systematic review. PLoS Med. **10**(1), e1001362 (2013)
18. Tomlinson, M., Rotheram-Borus, M.J., Swartz, L., Tsai, A.C.: Scaling up mHealth: where is the evidence? PLoS Med. **10**(2), e1001382 (2013)
19. Lester, R.T., Ritvo, P., Mills, E.J., Kariri, A., Karanja, S., Chung, M.H., Jack, W., Habyari, J., Habyarimana, J., Sadatsafavi, M., Najafzadeh, M., Marra, C.A., Estambale, B., Ngugi, E., Ball, T.B., Thabane, L., Gelmon, L.J., Kimani, J., Ackers, M., Plummer, F.A.: Effects of a mobile phone short message service on antiretroviral treatment adherence in Kenya: a randomised trial. Lancet **376**(9755), 1807–1808 (2010)
20. Olphert, W., Damodaran, L.: Older people and digital disengagement: a fourth digital divide? Gerontology **59**(6), 564–570 (2013)
21. Davis, F.D., Bagozzi, R.P., Warshaw, P.R.: User acceptance of computer technology: a comparison of two theoretical models. Manage. Sci. **35**(8), 982–1003 (1989)
22. Rogers, E.M.: Diffusion of Innovations, 5th edn. Free Press, New York (2003)
23. Morris, A.B., Li, J., Kroenke, K., Bruner-England, T.E., Young, J.M., Murray, M.D.: Factors associated with drug adherence and blood pressure control in patients with hypertension. Pharmacotherapy **26**(4), 483–492 (2006)
24. Pechère, J.C., Hughes, D., Kardas, P., Cornaglia, G.: Noncompliance with antibiotic therapy for acute community infections: a global survey. Int. J. Antimicrob. Agents **29**(3), 245–253 (2007)
25. Siegel, D., Lopez, J., Meier, J.: Antihypertensive medication adherence in the department of veterans affairs. Am. J. Med. **120**(1), 26–32 (2007)
26. Bjerrum, L., Søgaard, J., Hallas, J., Kragstrup, J.: Polypharmacy: correlations with sex, age and druge regimen. a prescription database study. Euro. J. Clin. Pharmacol. **54**(3), 197–202 (1998)
27. Heinz, M., Martin, P., Margrett, J.A., Yearns, M., Franke, W., Yang, H.-I., Wong, J., Chang, C.K.: Perceptions of technology among older adults. J. Geront. Nurs. **39**(1), 42–51 (2013)

28. Or, C.K., Karsh, B.-T., Severtson, D.J., Burke, L.J., Brown, R.L., Brennan, P.F.: Factors affecting home care patients' acceptance of a web-based interactive self-management technology. J. Am. Med. Inform. Assoc. **18**(1), 51–59 (2010)
29. Hansen, M.M., Miron-Shatz, T., Lau, A.Y.S., Paton, C.: Big data in science and healthcare: a review of recent literature and perspectives. In: Contribution of the IMIA Social Media Working Group. IMIA (International Medical Informatics Association) Yearbook of Medical Informatics. Yearb Med Inform (2014)
30. McHorney, C.A.: The adherence estimator: a brief, proximal screener for patient propensity to adhere to prescription medications for chronic disease. Curr. Med. Res. Opin.® **25**(1), 215–238 (2009)
31. Miron-Shatz, T., Elwyn, G.: To serve and protect? Electronic health records pose challenges for privacy, autonomy and person-centered medicine. Int. J. Patient Centered Med. **1**, 405–409 (2011)
32. Hixon, T.: http://www.forbes.com/sites/toddhixon/2014/04/10/what-kind-of-person-prefers-aniphone
33. Tacken, M., Marcellini, F., Mollenkopf, H., Ruoppila, I., Szeman, Z.: Use and acceptance of new technology by older people. Findings of the international MOBILATE survey: 'Enhancing mobility in later life'. Gerontechnology **3**(3), 126–137 (2005)
34. Diamantidis, C.J., Zuckerman, M., Fink, W., Aggarwal, S., Prakash, D.: Usability testing and acceptance of an electronic medication inquiry system for CKD patients. Am. J. Kidney Dis. Official J. Nat. Kidney Found. **61**(4), 644–646 (2013)
35. Diamantidis, C.J., Zuckerman, M., Fink, W., Hu, P., Yang, S., Fink, J.C.: Usability of a CKD educational website targeted to patients and their family members. Clin. J. Am. Soc. Nep. **7**(10), 1553–1560 (2012)
36. Miron-Shatz, T., Shatz, I., Becker, S., Patel, J., Eysenbach, G.: Promoting business and entrepreneurial awareness in healthcare professionals: lessons from venture capital panels in medicine 2.0 conferences. J. Med. Internet Res. **16**(8), e184 (2014)

Principles for Developing Digital Health Interventions for Prostate Cancer: A Community-Based Design Approach with African American Men

Otis L. Owens[1,2(✉)]

[1] College of Social Work, University of South Carolina, Columbia, SC 29208, USA
sowens06@gmail.com

[2] Statewide Cancer Prevention and Control Program, Arnold School of Public Health, University of South Carolina, Columbia, SC 29208, USA

Abstract. To reduce disparities related to prostate cancer among African American men, the American Cancer Society recommends that men make an informed decision with their healthcare provider about whether prostate cancer screening is right for them. The informed decision-making process can be facilitated through technology by teaching men about prostate cancer and providing them with activities to build their self-efficacy. However, these tools may be most effective when they are developed using a set of validated design principles, such as the Usability Engineering Lifecycle, in conjunction with a community-based participatory research (CBPR) process. Using CBPR can be especially useful in designing tools for minority communities, where men have the highest prostate cancer incidence and mortality. This paper describes the author's process for using CBPR principles to develop a prostate cancer education program for African American men and also discusses the value of using these principles within an existing usability framework.

Keywords: Usability · Community based participatory research · Health disparities · Prostate cancer · Minority health

1 Background

With the pronounced burden of prostate cancer (PrCA) among men of all races and the disparity of incidence and mortality between African American (AA) and European American (EA) men [1, 2], there is a critical need to develop technological interventions that can assist men with informed decision making [3]. In 2015, 220,800 men were diagnosed with PrCA and 27,540 are expected die from the disease [2]. However, PrCA incidence is 60 % higher in AAs and this racial group is two and a half times more likely to die from PrCA [2]. Informed decision making is described by the CDC as: when an individual understands the disease, is familiar with the risks, benefits, and uncertainties of a screening or treatment, actively participates in the decision-making

J. Zhou and G. Salvendy (Eds.): ITAP 2015, Part II, LNCS 9194, pp. 134–145, 2015.
DOI: 10.1007/978-3-319-20913-5_13

process at the level he or she desires, and makes a decision at the time of service or defers the decision to a later date [4]. Informed decision making is recommended by the American Cancer Society as a solution for reducing the PrCA mortality rate because of the unclear findings regarding the efficacy of prostate specific antigen screening, a blood test used to detect PrCA [3, 5, 6]. The two most recent, longitudinal studies on PrCA screening, titled "The European Randomized Study of Screening for PrCA" and "Prostate, Lung, Colorectal, and Ovarian (PLCO) Cancer Screening Trial on Prostate Cancer Mortality," (which included few African American men), concluded that the prostate specific antigen test was either not effective or led to over-detection of PrCA [5, 6]. Over-detection is a serious concern because it can lead to the treatment of indolent forms of PrCA and in some cases treatment can lead to life-long side effects such as incontinence and/or impotence [7].

In addition to possessing a thorough knowledge of PrCA and its screenings/ treatments, an individual must also believe that he possesses the capacity to engage in the informed decision-making process (i.e., self-efficacy) with a doctor or other healthcare provider [8, 9]. Multiple past studies have demonstrated that preparation for the informed decision-making process can be facilitated by computer-based education programs [10–12], but most of these and other studies on technology design do not report on the involvement of the target population in the intervention/technology design process. Applying community-based participatory research (CBPR) principles (primarily used in public health) to systems design can potentially enhance the impact of interventions by identifying the specific needs of the user and any foreseeable barriers to implementation [13–15]. This paper uses the Nielsen's Usability Engineering Lifecycle [16] as a framework for discussing the design of a computer-based PrCA education program, but focuses on how CBPR principles can enhance this framework. CBPR strategies are a promising way to address cancer disparities because they leverage community involvement in each phase of the research process to assist with making the most optimal decisions regarding everything from conceptualization to intervention [17–19]. Through the development of authentic partnerships with the target audience and stakeholders, cultural and contextual relevance of interventions is increased [18, 20]. Thus, the likelihood of improvement in knowledge and preventive behavior through an intervention is maximized, resulting in better health outcomes [18, 21, 22].

1.1 Community-Based Participatory Research Principles

There are eight CBPR principles [14, 15, 23–25]. These principles, created by Israel et al., (1998) include:

CBPR approaches emerge as a critical strategy to engage stakeholders and identify culturally and geographically appropriate methods to overcome health and cancer disparities [17, 18, 26]. The key to the success of designing a PrCA education program was operationalization of the CBPR principles in our research. We were able to operationalize all of the principles with the exception of principle 7 and only partial operationalization of principle 3. This success stemmed from the multiple interactive and iterative forums where AA men in the targeted community were provided with an opportunity to actively collaborate with researchers to develop a resource for enhancing their ability to make informed decisions about PrCA screening.

1. • Recognizing the community as a unit of identity (e.g. culture, social networks, shared needs)

2. • Building on the strengths and resources within the community (e.g., physical assets, social capital)

3 • Facilitating collaborative partnerships in all phases of the research (e.g., forming community advisory board)

4. • Integrating knowledge and action for mutual benefit of all partners (e.g., using research findings for promotion of social justice)

5. • Promoting a co-learning and empowering process that attends to social inequalities (e.g., teaching new skills to community members or partners)

6. • Implementing a cyclical and iterative process

7. • Addresses health from both positive and ecological perspectives (e.g., developing a systems-based approach for behavior change)

8. • Disseminating findings and knowledge gained to all partners (e.g., sponsoring community forum to share study findings)

1.2 Usability Engineering Lifecycle

The Usability Engineering Lifecycle (UEL) is an approach to systems design that emphasizes nine core principles that, when followed chronologically, can lead to an interface that has maximum usabilty [16]. Usability is defined by Nielsen as learnability, efficiency of use once the system has been learned, ability of frequent users to return to the system without having to relearn the system, frequency of error, and subjective user satsifaction [16]. The UEL (see Fig. 1) has been applied to projects such as desigining systems to allow gesture controlled interaction with virtual 3D content [27]. Some of the UEL's principles are similar in nature (e.g., iterative design) to CBPR principles, but do not emphasize the importance of community involvement throughout the entire design process. However, when the aforementioned CBPR principles are employed within the UEL, the conjunctional use of these principles may lead to a more optimal interface for any community-specific, digital interventions such as a computer-based PrCA education program. The discussion below is structured using UEL design principles as a chrononlogical framework while highlighting how CBPR principles can be employed within a UEL guided intervention development process.

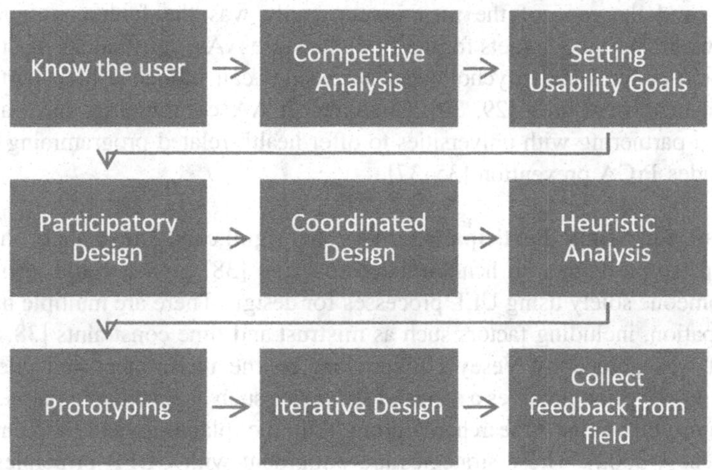

Fig. 1. Usability engineering lifecycle

2 Design Process

2.1 Know the User

Within the UEL, Nielsen suggests that the developers should study the users to assess their individual characteristics (e.g., age) and the environment in which the product will be used [16]. He also describes the process for implementing a competitive analysis where current products that are similar to a potential future product are empirically tested among members of the target population [16]. In CBPR it is customary, following an in-depth literature review of a problem, to recognize the target community for an intervention as a unit of identity. (1) **Recognizing the community as a unit of identity** extends beyond the demographics suggested by Nielsen and can be characterized by norms, values, customs, language, sexual orientation, etc. [14]. For example, our literature review on PrCA revealed that South Carolina has one of highest PrCA mortality disparity rates between AA and EA men in the country [28]. In addition, American Cancer Society recommends that men make an informed decision about PrCA screening beginning at the age of 45 for high risk groups (40 + for AA men with a family history) [3]. Therefore, a developer seeking to create an ideal computer-based education program for preparing AA men to make an informed PrCA screening decision must identify a defined community or subset of AA men who can help determine the best inclusions for the system and the environment in which the system should be housed. In a CBPR process, the researcher will investigate those cultural practices, shared needs, and self-constructed and social representations of identity. Becoming familiar with the community's identity, which can be separated into multiple social and geographic subgroups, can contribute to an end-product systems design that is customized to meet the needs of the target community. In addition, the formative nature of a CBPR approach essentially allows the community to have more involvement in and control over the product development. The prominent community of identity beyond the race of the men in our study was the faith community (i.e., churches). Churches were targets for the study because AAs' spiritual needs in addition to other socio-cultural and psychological necessities can influence their participation and trust in health research [29, 30]. Churches in AA communities have also been influential in partnering with universities to offer health-related programming [31–34], which includes PrCA prevention [35–37].

Recruitment for Study Participation. AAs are significantly less likely than other racial groups to participate in health-related research [38], which could also pose an issue for someone solely using UEL processes for design. There are multiple barriers to AA participation, including factors such as mistrust and time constraints [38, 39]. Our recruitment was guided by Vesey's framework on the recruitment and retention of minority groups, which involves a series of strategies such as leveraging partnerships in the community to assist researchers throughout the planning and implementation process (Vesey, 2002). These strategies are congruent with CBPR principles, particularly principle 3 which involves **facilitating collaborative partnerships in all phases of the research**. The specific strategies from Vesey's framework used for this study were: (1) conceptualization, planning, and development of the recruitment plan and promotional materials in collaboration with community partners (i.e., leaders in churches), (2) recruitment of study sample with partners/stakeholders, and (3) reporting findings to the community at various stages in the research process. Furthermore, knowing someone who has established relationships in the community of interest and allowing some flexibility in your recruitment/research implementation plan can be paramount to reaching a recruitment goal.

Knowing Someone Who Knows Someone. Reaching out to a colleague or an existing community partner can be effective for recruiting in minority communities. For example, churches connected to your academic colleagues have a higher likelihood of being open to working with researchers than a church that doesn't have a history of partnering with university researchers. In the course of recruitment for our study to develop a computer-based PrCA education program, there were three academic colleagues who provided the research team with names of churches with whom they had relationships. These churches not only helped to recruit their members for our research study (in conjunction with the research team), but also scheduled dates and times (e.g., after their midweek Bible study) when focus groups could be conducted. Recruitment efforts lasted two months in duration and resulted in 39 of the 40 men desired for the study. Almost all of these men were recruited through word of mouth within churches. Many of these churches were recommended by colleagues.

Other Important Things to Know When Approaching Communities of Identity With Your Research. During the process of approaching communities of identity (particularly churches) to gain support for your research, it should be noted that (1) the timeliness and relevance of the research or system aren't always consistent with the priorities of the community. For example, our research team approached a church that questioned the impact of the proposed PrCA education program and elected to forgo participation in our study. In addition, some communities are already conscious about a specific problem such as PrCA/informed decision making and are capable of providing their members with solutions (e.g., health education/decision support). Therefore, they may underestimate the benefit of your research to enhance their current goals. In this scenario you must make the decision whether to sell the importance of your research and how it can further enhance their current efforts or simply make contact with another community. (2) Be flexible and prepared to work around the community's schedule (e.g., they may invite you to implement your research prior to or at the beginning of an event and you may be asked to shorten your intended implementation time).

2.2 Competitive Analysis

Competitive analysis is not a key component of CBPR, but it is necessary to determine if there are products that exist that may be appropriate for your user. In our study, an analysis of competing products was accomplished (as suggested by Nielsen) through an Internet search and literature review for computer-based PrCA education programs, but most available products had either not been empirically tested among AA men or were not available for customization based on our formative research findings. These findings revealed specific PrCA information necessary for AA men in the study population to make an informed decision about prostate cancer screening and the essential functions/aesthetics of an ideal computer-based PrCA program. Therefore, it was decided by the research team to develop an original PrCA intervention.

2.3 Setting Usability Goals, Participatory/Coordinated Design

Nielsen recommends setting usability goals based on five constructs: learnability, efficiency of use once the system has been learned, ability of frequent users to return to the system without having to relearn the system, frequency of error, and subjective user satisfaction. He also explains that the priority of each usability goal and additional important attributes of the system will be dependent upon the targeted user. He then recommends a participatory design process where users have input on a specific prototype and that all aspects associated with the interface (e.g., documentation, tutorials, future releases) contain consistent elements (i.e., coordinated design). In CBPR the product usability goals are partly determined by the community because the community **is considered a collaborative partner in all phases of the research.** These usability goals should also **build on the strengths and resources within the community.** For example, men in our study attend church often, so considering how the product could fit into the church environment could be advantageous because the church could be a place where the system could be more accessible than the home environment. Furthermore, the support of the system by social networks within churches (e.g., clergy, men's ministry) may lead to a higher likelihood of system use [40].

In our formative approach, the research team examined the literature relevant to PrCA, informed decision-making behavior among AAs, and technology use/acceptance (in general and for health decision making). We then convened multiple focus groups to determine AA men's (1) current PrCA risk and screening knowledge, (2) decision-making processes for PrCA screening, (3) usage of, attitudes toward, and access to interactive communication technologies (e.g., computers, ATMs, kiosks), and (4) preferences for and characteristics of a computer-based PrCA education program. These discussions helped the research team determine what information should be included in a PrCA education program based on knowledge and decision-making needs such as facts about PrCA screening. Also, gaining information about technologies that AA men currently use on a frequent basis and what aspects of these technologies made them easy to use, helped the research team identify usability elements that could be incorporated into a digital PrCA education program. Finally, we were able to gain any additional input specifically on their openness to using a computer for PrCA decision making and create goals for designing a PrCA education program. All of the input gained through these groups was used to create a paper prototype (i.e., storyboard) in PowerPoint and a short animated clip displaying an avatar that could potentially be used in the program. A more detailed description of results can be found elsewhere [41].

The community was invited to participate in a second phase of focus groups to conduct a thorough review of the storyboard, the accompanying character script, and the clip of the AA male avatar who would be providing users with PrCA information throughout the course of the 12-minute education module. Prior to the focus group and consistent with CBPR principle 8, **findings and knowledge gained through the first focus groups were disseminated to study participants**. It was also explained how these findings had informed the development of a storyboard/script that captured the intended content and functionality of the future intervention. The community was then invited to ask questions prior to participating in our second phase focus groups. In the second phase of focus groups, participants were specifically asked to critique the content of the script to ensure that it was appropriate for users with diverse literacy levels and provide their thoughts on navigation elements for users who may have lower levels of computer fluency. Participants also provided input on the appearance and expected acceptance of the use of the AA male avatar. The focus groups provided a forum **for co-learning and empowerment** because the participants and the researchers' exchange led to both parties leaving the focus groups with useful information. For example, while the participants gained additional knowledge about PrCA and the development process, the research team gained knowledge about decision-making behavior among AA men. In addition, the research team learned about participants' specific technology needs, while the participants learned more about what was technologically possible. Ultimately, the feedback received was then used to revise the storyboard/script and develop a full prototype of a PrCA education program. The design of this prototype (based on significant community input) represented the integration of knowledge and action for the **mutual benefit of our partners** (i.e., the AA faith-based community).

2.4 Prototyping/Heuristic Analysis

In the UEL, prototyping is suggested after a heuristic analysis is performed, but our research team developed a prototype prior to the heuristic analysis using a series of usability guidelines [42] and significant community feedback. Developing the prototype prior to the heuristic analysis allowed us to receive optimal expert feedback early in the process. Waiting until after the heuristic analysis could be more costly in circumstances where the product is difficult to develop or modify.

The research team solicited assistance from an animator to help translate the storyboard (created in PowerPoint) into a full prototype. Co-learning and empowerment was also applicable to the relationship between the developer and the research team because both parties were actively involved in the development process, which translated into an exchange of information and skills (e.g., PI learned basic animation skills; Animator learned about PrCA). The prototyping process consisted of using software that facilitated motion capture through a Microsoft Kinect camera, which could be applied to a custom designed avatar. These rendered video clips were then uploaded to a learning software that was capable of playing clips based on user decision and administering quizzes throughout the user's educational experience. The resulting PrCA prototype was designed to be operated on any computer, but the preference of the community was that the final product be administered on a large touch screen monitor to accommodate aging users who may also have lower levels of computer fluency.

The PrCA education program was then mailed along with a heuristic evaluation instrument to six experts with experience and knowledge of digital health intervention design. The evaluation instrument was based on Nielsen's 10 usability heuristics for interface design [43]. Most of the changes recommended focused on aesthetics as opposed to issues related to the usability of the education program. The PrCA education program was then moved to empirical testing through 10 in-depth interviews. The empirical testing was a means to validate the usability of the prototype through system use observation and follow-up interviews with the community. The interviews with the community focused on similar system design constructs relevant to our expert heuristic evaluation (e.g., how similarly does this system function compared to other technologies that you have used previous to using this system?). These interviews exemplified involving the community in all phases of the research process. Details regarding the prototyping process and results from the second phase of focus groups and in-depth interviews can be found elsewhere [44].

2.5 Iterative Design

CBPR, much like UEL, supports the development of interventions/systems through a cyclical and iterative process where any stage of the design process is revisited in order to produce the most usable system. In the development of the PrCA education program, the design from conception to prototype was iteratively orchestrated through multiple focus groups, in-depth interviews, and a heuristic evaluation with the community involved in each of these phases of research. In addition, prior to the research team's future field testing of the system, the PrCA education program will be further revised based on changes recommended during the heuristic evaluation and in-depth interviews described above. Furthermore, following this future field testing (next step), the research team will revisit the design again to make salient changes that could improve the intervention.

2.6 Collect Feedback from Field Use (Next Steps)

Based on findings from the prior heuristic evaluations and empirical testing, the research and development team will make changes necessary to increase the usability and professional value of the PrCA education program. The research team will then pilot the PrCA education program among AA men who did not participate in the development of the system. For the pilot, the PrCA education program will be administered on both tablets and all-in-one, touch screen computers. Men from the design phase will, however, be invited **to participate in this phase of research** by helping recruit other participants for involvement in the pilot. By implementing pre-and post-surveys, the research team can gather information about the system's effect on the research team's posited knowledge and behavioral outcomes (e.g., PrCA knowledge, informed decision making self-efficacy) and the usability of the system based on both general heuristics and overall satisfaction regarding user experience. At the conclusion of our study, we will **disseminate findings and knowledge gained to all partners** through local forums with study participants/stakeholders who will be invited to engage in further discussion regarding where the system would be most accessible to AA men within and beyond the AA faith-based community (Table 1).

Table 1. How CBPR fits into UEL: A summary table

UEL steps	CBPR principles specific to UEL step
(1) Know the User	• Recognize the community as a unit of identity
(2) Competitive Analysis	• Facilitate collaborative partnerships in all phases of the research
(3) Setting Usability Goals	• Build on the strengths and resources within the community
(4) Participatory Design	• Facilitate collaborative partnerships in all phases of the research
(5) Coordinated Design	• Integrate knowledge and action for mutual benefit of all partners
	• Promote a co-learning and empowering process that attends to social inequalities
	• Disseminate findings and knowledge gained to all partners
(6) Prototyping	• Facilitate collaborative partnerships in all phases of the research
(7) Heuristic Analysis	• Promote a co-learning and empowering process that attends to social inequalities
(8) Iterative Design	• Implement a cyclical and iterative process
	• Facilitate collaborative partnerships in all phases of the research
(9) Collect Feedback from the field	• Disseminate findings and knowledge gained to all partners
	• Facilitate collaborative partnerships in all phases of the research

3 Summary/Conclusions

There are multiple strengths and similarities in UEL and CBPR principles. However, using UEL and CBPR principles in concert could lead to stronger computer-based intervention designs for minority populations who may be far less likely to participate in a non-targeted effort to solicit feedback on a product or system design. CBPR emphasizes an equitable partnership between the developer and the community, which is not central to UEL. Conversely, CBPR has not been used extensively in studies focused on the development of computer-based education interventions and cannot be used unaccompanied by a set of usability guidelines. Further research is warranted to assess the impact of the conjunctive use of UEL and CBPR principles to develop technologies for diverse populations to address the prevention of varying diseases.

References

1. Siegel, R., et al.: Cancer Statistics, 2014. Cancer **64**(1), 9–29 (2014)
2. American Cancer Society, Cancer Facts and Figures 2015. 2015: Atlanta, GA
3. American Cancer Society, Prostate Cancer: Early Detection. 2013: Atlanta, GA
4. Briss, P., et al.: Promoting informed decisions about cancer screening in communities and healthcare systems. Am. J. Prev. Med. **26**(1), 67–80 (2004)
5. Schroder, F.H., et al.: Screening and prostate-cancer mortality in a randomized European study. N. Engl. J. Med. **360**(13), 1320–1328 (2009)
6. Andriole, G.L., et al.: Mortality results from a randomized prostate-cancer screening trial. N. Engl. J. Med. **360**(13), 1310–1319 (2009)
7. Welch, H.G., Albertsen, P.C.: Prostate cancer diagnosis and treatment after the introduction of prostate-specific antigen screening: 1986-2005. J. Natl Cancer Inst. **101**(19), 1325–1329 (2009)
8. O' Connor, A.M.: User Manual-Decision Self Efficacy Scale (1995)
9. Bass, S.B., et al.: Relationship of internet health information use with patient behavior and self-efficacy: experiences of newly diagnosed cancer patients who contact the national cancer institute's cancer information service. J. Health Commun. **11**(2), 219–236 (2006)
10. Wakefield, C.E., et al.: Development and pilot testing of an online screening decision aid for men with a family history of prostate cancer. Patient Educ. Couns. **83**(1), 64–72 (2011)
11. Allen, J.D., et al.: A computer-tailored intervention to promote informed decision making for prostate cancer screening among African American men. Am. J. Mens Health **3**(4), 340–351 (2009)
12. Evans, R., et al.: Supporting informed decision making for prostate specific antigen (PSA) testing on the web: an online randomized controlled trial. J. Med. Internet Res. **12**(3), e27 (2010)
13. Patton, M.Q.: Qualitative Research Evaluation Methods. Sage Publications, Thousand Oaks (2002)
14. Israel, B.A., et al.: Review of community-based research: assessing partnership approaches to improve public health. Annu. Rev. Public Health **19**, 173–202 (1998)
15. Schulz, A.J., et al.: A community-based participatory planning process and multilevel intervention design toward eliminating cardiovascular health inequities. Health Promot. Pract. **12**(6), 900–911 (2011)

16. Nielsen, J.: The usability engineering life cycle. Computer **25**(3), 12–22 (1992)
17. Braun, K.L., et al.: Operationalization of community-based participatory research principles across NCI's community networks programs. Am. J. Public Health **102**(6), 1195–1203 (2012)
18. Wallerstein, N., Duran, B.: Community-based participatory research contributions to intervention research: the intersection of science and practice to improve health equity. Am. J. Public Health **1**(100), 10 (2010)
19. Hebert, J., et al.: Interdisciplinary, translational, and community-based participatory research: finding a common language to improve cancer research. Cancer Epidemiol. Biomark. Prev. **18**(4), 1213–1217 (2009)
20. Letcher, A.S., Perlow, K.M.: Community-based participatory research shows how a community initiative creates networks to improve well-being. Am. J. Prev. Med. **37**(6, suppl 1), S292–S299 (2009)
21. Kerner, J.F.: Integrating research, practice, and policy: what we see depends on where we stand. J. Public Health Manage. Pract. **14**(2), 193–198 (2008)
22. Kerner, J.F., et al.: Translating research into improved outcomes in comprehensive cancer control. Cancer Causes Control **1**, 27–40 (2005)
23. Israel, B.A., et al.: Community-based participatory research: policy recommendations for promoting a partnership approach in health research. Educ. Health **14**(2), 182–197 (2001)
24. Israel, B.A., et al.: Critical issues in developing and following community based participatory research principles. In: Wallerstein, N., Minkler, M. (eds.) Community-Based Participatory Research for Health, pp. 53–79. Jossey-Bass, San Francisco (2003)
25. Strong, L.L., et al.: Piloting interventions within a community-based participatory research framework: Lessons learned from the Healthy Environments Partnership. Prog. Community Health Partnerships Res. Educ. Action **3**(4), 327 (2009)
26. Friedman, D.B., et al.: Developing partnerships and recruiting dyads for a prostate cancer informed decision making program: lessons learned from a community-academic-clinical team. J. Cancer Educ. **27**(2), 243–249 (2012)
27. Hackenberg, G., McCall, R., Broll, W.: Lightweight palm and finger tracking for real-time 3D gesture control. In: Virtual Reality Conference (VR). IEEE (2011)
28. Hebert, J.R., et al.: Mapping cancer mortality-to-incidence ratios to illustrate racial and gender disparities in a high-risk population. Cancer **115**(11), 2539–2552 (2009)
29. Holt, C.L., et al.: A comparison of a spiritually based and non-spiritually based educational intervention for informed decision making for prostate cancer screening among church-attending African-American men. Urol. Nurs. **29**(4), 249–258 (2009)
30. Holt, C.L., Wynn, T.A., Darrington, J.: Religious involvement and prostate cancer screening behaviors among southeastern African American men. Am. J. Mens Health **3**(3), 214–223 (2009)
31. Corbie-Smith, G., et al.: Partnerships in health disparities research and the roles of pastors of black churches: potential conflict, synergy, and expectations. J. Natl Med. Assoc. **102**(9), 823–831 (2010)
32. Allicock, M., et al.: Promoting fruit and vegetable consumption among members of black churches, Michigan and North Carolina, 2008–2010. Prev. Chronic Dis. **10**, E33 (2013)
33. Wilcox, S., et al.: The Faith, Activity, and Nutrition (FAN) Program: design of a participatory research intervention to increase physical activity and improve dietary habits in African American churches. Contemp. Clin. Trials **31**(4), 323–335 (2010)
34. Kaplan, S.A., et al.: Stirring up the mud: using a community-based participatory approach to address health disparities through a faith-based initiative. J. Health Care Poor Underserved **20**(4), 1111–1123 (2009)

35. Drake, B.F., et al.: A church-based intervention to promote informed decision-making for prostate cancer screening among African-American men. J. Natl Med. Assoc. **102**(3), 164–171 (2010)
36. Holt, C.L., et al.: Development of a spiritually based educational intervention to increase informed decision making for prostate cancer screening among church-attending African American men. J. Health Commun. **14**(6), 590–604 (2009)
37. Holt, C.L., et al.: A comparison of a spiritually based and non-spiritually based educational intervention for informed decision making for prostate cancer screening among church-attending African-American men. Urol. Nurs. **29**(4), 249–258 (2009)
38. Ford, J.G., et al.: Barriers to recruiting underrepresented populations to cancer clinical trials: a systematic review. Cancer **112**(2), 228–242 (2008)
39. Owens, O.L., et al.: African American men's and women's perceptions of clinical trials research: focusing on prostate cancer among a high-risk population in the South. J. Health Care Poor Underserved **24**(4), 1784–1800 (2013)
40. Venkatesh, V., et al.: User acceptance of information technology: toward a unified view. MIS Q. **27**(3), 425–478 (2003)
41. Owens, O.L., et al.: Digital solutions for informed decision making: an academic-community partnership for the development of a prostate cancer decision aid for African-American men. Am. J. Men's Health (2014). (in Press)
42. Keeker, K.: Improving Website Usability and Appeal. Microsoft Corporation, Redmond (2007)
43. Nielsen, J., Mack, R.L.: Usability Inspection Methods. Wiley, Hoboken (1994)
44. Owens, O.l., et al.: An iterative process for developing and evaluating a computer-based prostate cancer decision aid for African-American men. Health Promot. Pract. 2014. (in Press)

Evaluation of Complex Distributed Multimodal Applications: Evaluating a TeleRehabilitation System When It Really Matters

Carlos Pereira[1,2](✉), Nuno Almeida[1,2], Ana Isabel Martins[1,2], Samuel Silva[1], Ana Filipa Rosa[1], Miguel Oliveira e Silva[1,2], and António Teixeira[1,2]

[1] Institute of Electronics and Telematics Engineering, University of Aveiro, Aveiro, Portugal
cepereira@ua.pt

[2] Department of Electronics, Telecommunications and Informatics Engineering, University of Aveiro, Aveiro, Portugal

Abstract. The evaluation of applications or systems within dynamic environments is complex. The existence of multiple hardware and software items which share the same space can provoke concurrency issues and result in erratic interactions. A sudden change within the environment can result is dramatic changes both to the user and application itself which can pass unnoticed in traditional evaluation methodologies. To verify if a component is compatible with a given environment is of paramount importance for areas like pervasive computing, ambient intelligence or ambient assisted living (AAL). In this paper, a semi-automatic platform for evaluation is presented and integrated with a TeleRehabilitation system in an AAL scenario to enhance evaluation. Preliminary results show the advantages of the platform in comparison with typical observation solutions mainly in terms of achieved data and overall ease of use.

Keywords: Evaluation · Multimodality · TeleRehabilitation

1 Introduction

The design and development of complex multimodal systems, working in multiple devices and deployed in dynamic environments, poses several challenges. Beyond the technical aspects, designing user experience in this context is far from being simple. At this level, tasks and interaction modalities cannot be looked at as isolated phenomena [6]. For example, the use of several modalities simultaneously, as a result of a more complex use of the system, might result in sensory overload [9]; or particular modalities, which in abstract seem suitable options, are disregarded by the user in some (e.g., stressful) situations. Furthermore, these concerns are particularly relevant when the target users might present some level of disability, physical or cognitive, which directly influences how they use the system: an audio warning might not be heard by the user, due to a hearing disability, or multiple tasks crossing might leave the user disoriented [3]. Therefore, integration of proper evaluation, in the development cycles,

J. Zhou and G. Salvendy (Eds.): ITAP 2015, Part II, LNCS 9194, pp. 146–157, 2015.
DOI: 10.1007/978-3-319-20913-5_14

covering different contexts of use and complex tasks, running in its intended (real or simulated) environment, is of paramount importance and should be increasingly introduced, from early on, as a tool to support the development of such systems.

In this article, we present a semi-automatic evaluation platform and its usage applied to the assessment of a TeleRehabilitation system. This platform allows the creation of dynamic evaluation plans and, by continuously assessing context and user performance, provides evaluators with a more complete report of the experience. The collected data also allows inferring the precise timings to trigger questions to assess user performance and/or satisfaction, for example right after failing to complete a task or when the user is idle. The platform distinguishes itself from alternative tools [4,8] by using an ontology at its core and by providing a decoupled manner in which evaluators can integrate other software with it. Additionally, a dedicated user interface (UI) simplifies the creation and deployment of evaluation tests without requiring specific programming knowledge.

2 Supporting the Evaluation of Multimodal Distributed Systems - the DynEaaS Platform

Usual evaluation methods do not fully serve the task of assessing user feedback and performance in regard to applications in highly dynamical environments. Ubiquitous or pervasive systems require adaptable evaluation solutions that do not limit the amount of gathered data. By gathering additional data, evaluators are able to assess a wide range of aspects regarding their applications and take into account the surrounding environment when establishing conclusions.

Dynamic Evaluation as a Service (DynEaaS) (Fig. 1) is an evaluation platform capable of evaluating user performances in dynamical environments by allowing evaluation teams to create and conduct context-aware evaluations. The platform allows evaluators to specify evaluation plans which contain actions that are triggered at precise timings or only when certain conditions are met, thus gathering better contextualized data.

DynEaaS follows a distributed paradigm allowing the evaluator to run multiple evaluations at different locations simultaneously. At each location, the plan is instantiated and applied taking into account user preferences, current context and the environment itself. When applying the plan, DynEaaS constantly evaluates the current context and chooses the best suited conditions to interact with the user.

Within DynEaaS, each user is seen as a user node named EaaS Node which is a part of an evaluation network. An evaluation can be remotely started for a defined set of users. Each evaluation network is defined by a set of criteria which every user node must comply with and is controlled by a central node called EaaS Core. Some examples of criteria can encompass user preferences or interests as well as more structural aspects such as hardware or environment conditions.

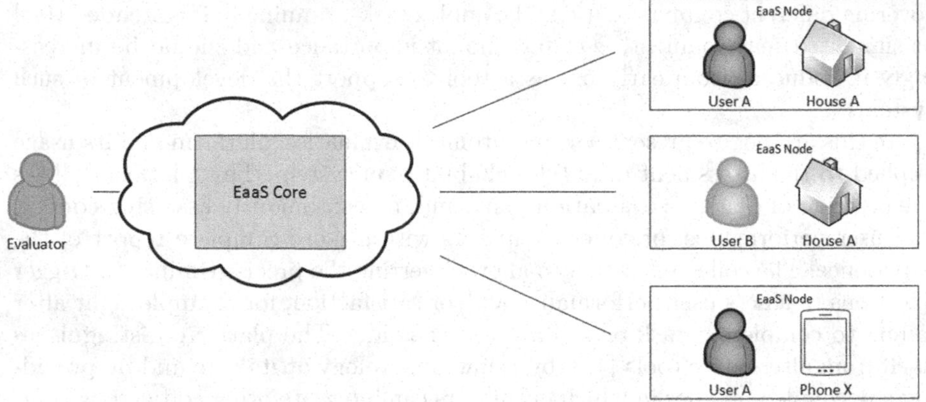

Fig. 1. DynEaaS ecosystem

Results are synchronized in real time. By having access to them, the evaluator is able to analyze current data and have a better grasp over the evaluation current status making small changes to it, if so required.

DynEaaS embraces a International Classification of Functioning, Disability and Health (ICF) [12] based methodology that includes different usability evaluation methods such as questionnaires and performance evaluation. The environmental factors are a central aspect of the ICF based methodology. Using the DynEaaS platform it is possible to assess every situation foreseen by the evaluator concerning a system, a user or the entire environment by defining events triggering actions (e.g., questions). Events can encompass temporal aspects (specific times), environmental aspects (noise, brightness), contextual aspects (persons in the room, interruptions), interaction options (repeated actions), among others, which can be aggregated to create specific evaluation contexts. All data is recorded and can be further analyzed later.

By using ontologies, the platform is highly flexible and can be used in different domains without core changes. Post-evaluation reasoning operations are also possible if required.

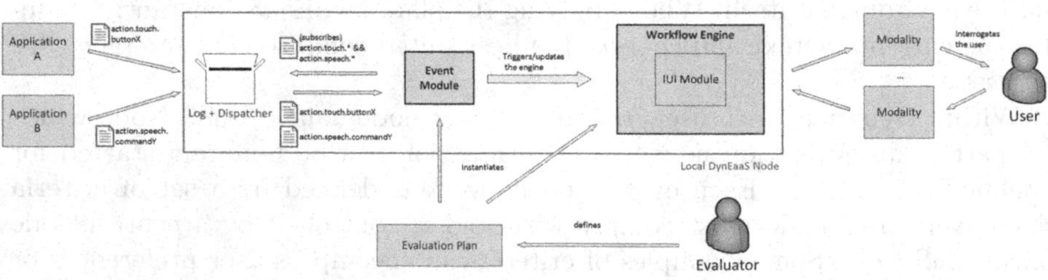

Fig. 2. DynEaaS local architecture exemplification

Locally, each EaaS Node (illustrated in Fig. 2) is composed of a set of services which cooperate to execute evaluation plans. These evaluation plans are created by the evaluator at EaaS Cores and deployed on-demand to selected user nodes.

Each evaluation plan encompasses an unbounded number of workflows with the objective of gathering specific information from the user. Each workflow can be seen as a tree which is started at its root and executed until it reaches all of its leafs. These workflows are executed by the Workflow Engine within the EaaS Node and delivered to the user via associated modalities/user interfaces. The selection of which modality to use falls on the IUI Module based on current context and the evaluation specifications.

Each workflow can contain two types of elements: event rules and inquiries. An inquiry comprises a number of questions to be asked in succession. DynEaaS supports both open-answer questions and multi-answer questions which are created by the evaluator. Event rules on the other hand enable the creation of complex event compositions.

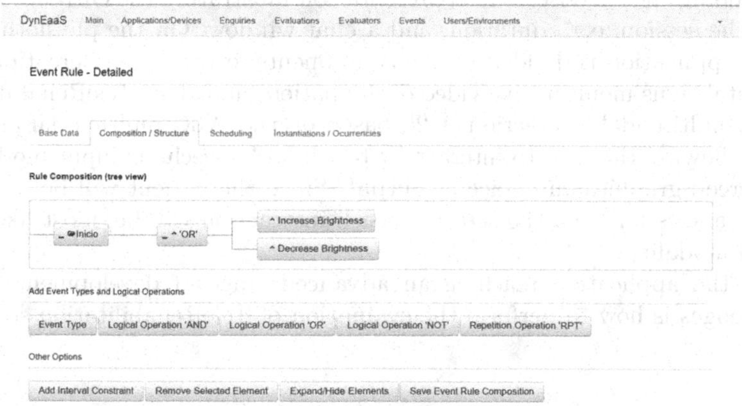

Fig. 3. DynEaaS UI for creating event rules dynamically

In DynEaaS, each event is described by an EventType which defines a routing key for it. These routing keys are used by applications to deliver notifications to DynEaaS using a decoupled message queue (Log+Dispatcher). This message queue is associated with an Event Module which receives selected events (according to active workflows which trigger the engine). EventTypes can also be used to form EventRules using a number of operators such as:

- 'And' and 'Or' Operator - creates a logical operation between two elements (either types or other operators)
- 'Not' Operator - negates an element
- Delay Operator - waits a period of time after or before evaluating an element
- Functor Operator (such as BiggerThan or SmallerThan) - enables the creation of predicate functions that compare arguments inside the events.

Each of these operators (except functor) can be applied to other operators which makes the creation of event rules limitless. The platform is accessible via a graphical UI which enables evaluators to create, design and deploy an evaluation plan to any linked user. Figure 3 demonstrates the UI for the creation of a simple event rule that triggers when either an increase or a decrease on brightness occurs.

3 Evaluation of TeleRehabilitation Using DynEaaS

3.1 TeleRehabilitation Application

TeleRehabilitation [11] is a new service which allows a patient to have a remote session of rehabilitation with a physiotherapist. The system provides different features for the patient and for the physiotherapist (Fig. 4).

Figure 5 illustrates the telerehabilitation system with both user interfaces. On the patient side, the application is divided in four major components: live video of the user doing the exercises, video presentation illustrating the current exercise, state of the session, e.g., duration, and a chat window. On the physiotherapist side, the application is divided in five components: exercise plan creation, plan status, vital signs monitor, live video of the patient and chat. TeleRehabilitation supports multimodal interaction [1,2], based on the W3C multimodal architecture [5], allowing the user to interact by touch and speech, as input modalities, and onscreen graphics and voice as output. Since the patient will be doing the exercises, and is far from the screen, speech interaction will be, most likely, the preferred modality.

With the application reaching an advanced stage of development, one of the challenges is how to perform the evaluation of TeleRehabilitation so that it

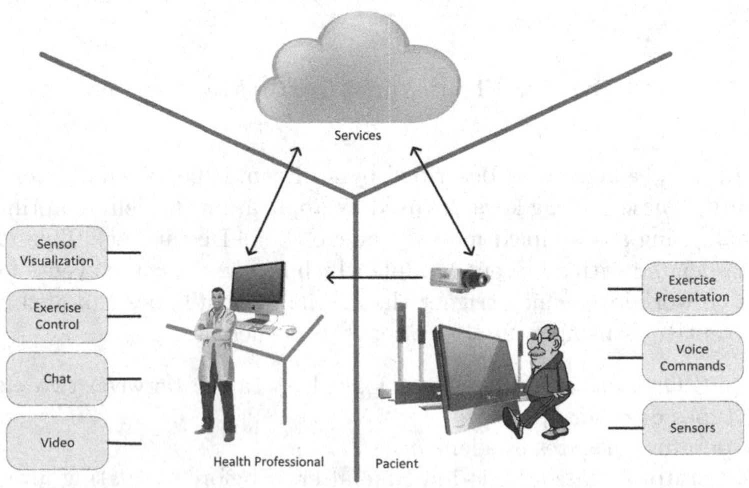

Fig. 4. TeleRehabilitation system architecture

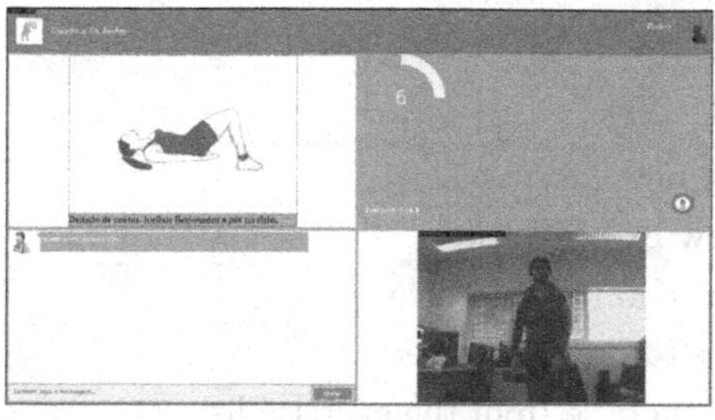

(a) Patient Interface

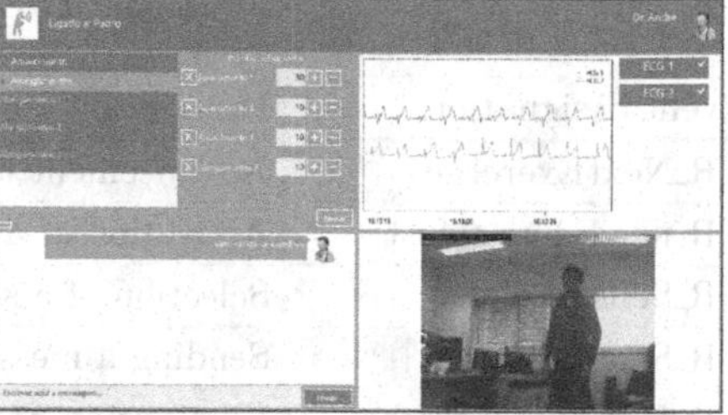

(b) Physiotherapist Interface

Fig. 5. The TeleRehabiliation application user interfaces

can encompass the full complexity of the system, its tasks and true multimodal interaction.

3.2 Specifying the Evaluation Protocol

The TeleRehabilitation system consists of two different modules addressing the two user profiles involved: therapists and patients. This fact makes it more difficult to evaluate the system as a whole, given that it is necessary to perform two evaluations at the same time, one for the patient and one for the physiotherapist.

The system itself requires validation from both users regarding its overall functioning and usability. To do so, we have used the DynEaaS platform with two user nodes, one for the patient and one for the physiotherapist.

In order not to obstruct the user, but at the same time obtain information in precise timings, we have embedded evaluation specific interfaces within both application modules. This way, the user is not required to shift his/her attention from the application and is able to insert information in real time. For this evaluation, users were able to interact using touch, keyboard and mouse or voice commands. The test was set within our Living Lab [10](in the case of the user) and a private room (in the case of the physiotherapist).

The evaluation session itself was composed of several exercises, activated by the therapist and displayed at the user's side. The user was asked to perform the exercises while the therapist observed and sent feedback. The performed sessions had an average duration of 15 min. Each test was accompanied by an evaluator to provide the necessary initial explanation to the user. The evaluator was also asked to compose a critical incidents registration.

Previously to the start of the evaluation, involved event types were specified in DynEaaS (see Table 1). In this case, only events produced by the TeleRehabilitation system have been inserted.

The list of possible events includes simple events like login or session start as well as more specific events such as sending a chat message, receiving current exercise status information or selecting a new exercise.

Based on these event types and also event rules and inquiries, we have created two plans, one for each intervenient. Both plans were set to start at the

Table 1. Event Listing

Event designation	Description
TR_NextExercise	Advancement to a new exercise.
TR_newExerciseList	Activation of a new exercise list.
TR_SensorSelect	Selection of a sensor in the interface.
TR_SendExercise	Sending a message to the other user.
TR_RemoveExercise	Elimination of an exercise from the exercise list.
TR_Login	Successfull authentication.
TR_PreviousExercise	Selection of a previous exercise.
TR_TimeChangeExercise	Changing the time period of an exercise.
TR_SensorZoomReset	Reseting the sensor viewing component.
TR_ExerciseStatus	Indication of the status of the currently active exercise.
TR_SensorZoom	Performing zoom on the sensor component.
TR_ReceiveMsgChat	Receiving a message on the chat component.
TR_SendMsgChat	Sending a message via chat component.
TR_SelectExercise	Selecting an exercise.
TR_endExerciseList	Finishing an exercise list.
TR_SessionStart	Initiating an exercise session.

same time. In order to obtain information from the user with questions, the plan integrates a set of evaluation flows. An evaluation flow depicts a set of linked event rules and inquiries with a specific order. When the evaluation is initialized, evaluation flows are instantiated into workflows and executed in the EaaS Nodes. Following are some examples which illustrate the diversity of the inserted evaluation flows:

- a flow intended to assert the overall opinion of the application after a certain usage. The flow is composed of two elements, the first being an event rule which triggers ten minutes after login, and the second, a question composed of a number of possible answers.
- a flow to assert a possible malfunctioning with the chat component. In case the user presses the 'Send chat message' five times in a row under ten seconds, a question is triggered asking the user the cause of that event. Note that while the first flow will occur due to being associated with time, the probability of this second flow happening is very slim. This helps demonstrate the flexibility of DynEaaS in the sense that it can support both time specific flows like the first while flows like the second one can help depict faults within the application itself.
- a flow to trigger a question when the user surpasses thirty percent of the exercise list. The question itself interrogates the user regarding the exercise demonstrations and its utility.

- a flow to trigger if the user has not used the chat functionality at all after ten minutes. In this case, the user is asked why did he not use that functionality, either by not noticing, not needing it or feeling it is not important.
- another flow operates similarly in regard to voice commands after five minutes.

On the physiotherapist side, we have created another set of evaluation flows, some similar to the ones for the patient (like overall impression of the system), and others to assert specific components on the physiotherapist side (such as inquiring why the physiotherapist did not use certain features).

Overall, both plans aim at gathering information from a single therapy session, covering both sides of application use simultaneously (therapist and patient).

4 Results

Before performing a high number of evaluation sessions, a preliminary test was performed that, besides collecting evaluation data, should serve to validate the methodology, integration of DynEaaS with the application and assess the relevance of the defined evaluation plans. On this test, we have prepared a room for the therapist, and another for the patient and ran it for 15 min. An observer was present to take notes on the session from the patient side, and DynEaaS was placed running on both users.

Figure 6 shows both users during the initial test of the system. At the end of this test we reached two main conclusions. First, both DynEaaS plans were not extracting as much information as we desired. The truth was that the created plans were small. Initially, we feared that a high number of evaluation flows could constantly disrupt/distract the user from using the system and, therefore, created evaluation plans with a very limited scope. However, given the gathered results, we found that half of the actual workflows within both plans were dependent of the user himself and did not activate because the user had not fulfilled the necessary conditions.

The second conclusion was that the embedded interfaces within the system did not suit the system itself. Asking the user to answer the question with a keyboard and mouse lowered the user's usability dramatically.

(a) User View

(b) Physiotherapist View

Fig. 6. A TeleRehabiliation session

Taking this in mind, we prepared a second trial which complemented these aspects. To tackle the issue with keyboard and mouse, we inserted a new interface into TeleRehabilition which enabled the user to answer all DynEaaS solicitations using speech.

4.1 Analyzing Obtained Results

In both sessions, the number of triggered workflows was very similar. Both users performed the login step, the requested exercises and used the available interaction modalities successfully. In session one, the number of detected events however was much smaller than in session two, especially concerning the chat component which indicated that patient two interacted with the therapist more often.

Either in session one and two, the therapist created a 12 step exercise list for the patient to complete which allowed us to compare timings between both. Results from DynEaaS showed that when reaching the 30 % percent of exercises performed, both patients found the exercise component to be clear and helpful in regard to its demonstration.

The results captured by the DynEaaS show good acceptance by both users. They were engaged within the rehabilitation session and indicated that they were satisfied with the interaction. These results are in compliance with previous usability evaluation test used to assess the preceding versions of the Telerehabilitation [7]. The previous test was made according with the traditional approach. The users followed a session script while the evaluator observed and collected data about the interaction. At the end of the session, the users completed a usability questionnaire regarding the system.

Evaluators claimed that when comparing the results of the evaluation made with DynEaaS and the previous one made with a traditional approach, it is possible to understand the practical value of DynEaaS as with a minor effort the evaluator has access to a greater amount of data regarding user experience.

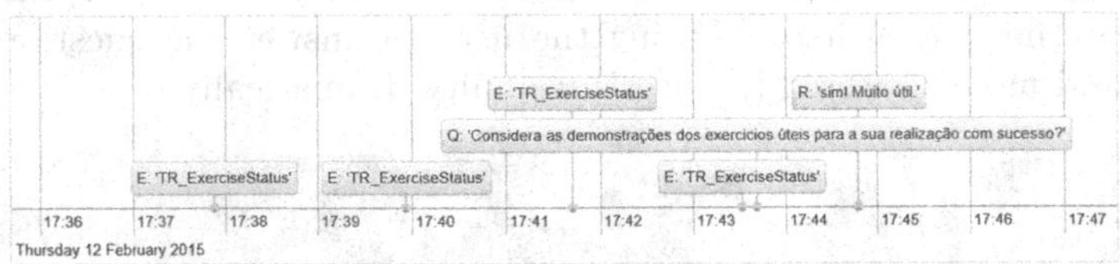

Fig. 7. DynEaaS UI showing results for a workflow in a timeline

An example of the added value to the evaluation process is the timeline generated from DynEaaS (Fig. 7). The figure illustrates a timeline generated from DynEaaS which allowed us to check the times that both patients took when performing the '30 % percent' workflow. Another interesting result that DynEaaS provided, concerns the overall opinion of the user after 10 min using the system. Figure 8 presents two graphics, the first regarding the first session and the second concerning the second. The major difference from the first session to the second was the inclusion of speech. Results show that the amount of time that the patient took to provide the necessary user credentials (marked by 'Login' in Fig. 8) decreased by half from the first to the second session. This is also true when analyzing the timings for answering a question in the same workflow. Based on these results, we were able to confirm the importance and usefulness of speech.

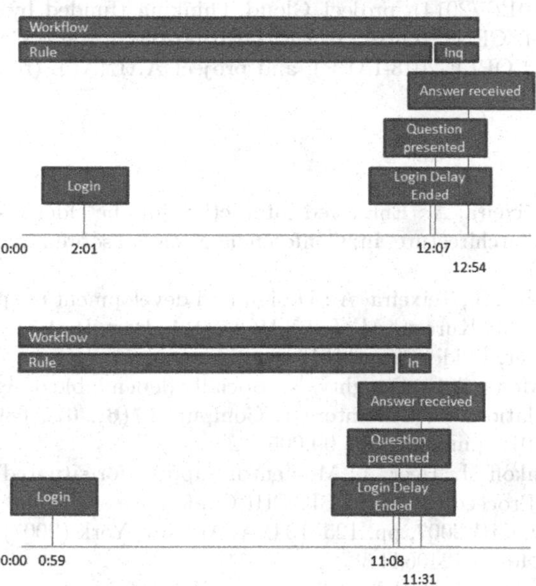

Fig. 8. Comparison between the two users concerning a specific workflow

In both sessions, observation reports indicated that the test itself went accordingly to what was expected, which also indicated that the user was engaged by the application.

5 Conclusions

The usage and flexibility of DynEaaS for evaluating the TeleRehabilitation system was proved to be very helpful. The creation of automatic workflows which trigger according to specific events allowed the extraction of valuable information from the user in real situations. For instance, DynEaaS allowed us to verify that the patient, when confronted with the ability to use speech interfaces, does so, even when speech recognition is not perfect.

In the future we intend to create more test cases with a higher number of users. While the presented case study was performed singularly and without concurrent applications, the compatibility of other software and hardware elements should be also asserted, preferably in non-controlled environments.

Additionally, the application of DynEaaS in other scenarios is also an objective as well as its enhancement, majorly by exploring the automatic generation of inquiries based on domain specific ontologies.

Acknowledgments. Research partially funded by IEETA Research Unit funding (PEst-OE/EEI/ UI0127/2014), project Cloud Thinking (funded by the QREN Mais Centro program, ref. CENTRO-07-ST24-FEDER-002031), Marie Curie Actions IRIS (ref. 610986, FP7-PEOPLE-2013-IAPP), and project AAL4ALL (ref. QREN 13852).

References

1. Almeida, N., Teixeira, A.: Enhanced interaction for the elderly supported by the w3c multimodal architecture. In: Conferência Nacional sobre Interacção. Vila Real, Portugal (2013)
2. Almeida, N., Silva, S., Teixeira, A.: Design and development of speech interaction: a methodology. In: Kurosu, M. (ed.) HCI 2014, Part II. LNCS, vol. 8511, pp. 370–381. Springer, Heidelberg (2014)
3. Blythe, M.A., Monk, A.F., Doughty, K.: Socially dependable design: The challenge of ageing populations for hci. Interact. Comput. **17(6)**, 672–689 (2005). http://dx.doi.org/10.1016/j.intcom.2005.09.005
4. Carter, S., Mankoff, J., Heer, J.: Momento: Support for situated ubicomp experimentation. In: Proceedings of the SIGCHI Conference on Human Factors in Computing Systems, CHI 2007, pp. 125–134. ACM, New York (2007). http://doi.acm.org/10.1145/1240624.1240644
5. Dahl, D.: The w3c multimodal architecture and interfaces standard. J. Multimodal User Interfaces **7**(3), 171–182 (2013)
6. Hollender, N., Hofmann, C., Deneke, M., Schmitz, B.: Review: Integrating cognitive load theory and concepts of human-computer interaction. Comput. Hum. Behav. **26(6)**, 1278–1288 (2010). http://dx.doi.org/10.1016/j.chb.2010.05.031
7. Martins, A.I., Queirós, A., Cerqueira, M., Alvarelhão, J., Teixeira, A., Rocha, N.: Assessment of Ambient Assisted Living Services in a Living Lab Approach: a Methodology based on ICF (2012)
8. Meschtscherjakov, A., Reitberger, W., Tscheligi, M.: Maestro: Orchestrating user behavior driven and context triggered experience sampling. In: Proceedings of the 7th International Conference on Methods and Techniques in Behavioral Research, MB 2010, pp. 29:1–29:4. ACM, New York (2010). http://doi.acm.org/10.1145/1931344.1931373
9. Oviatt, S., Coulston, R., Lunsford, R.: When do we interact multimodally?: Cognitive load and multimodal communication patterns. In: Proceedings of the 6th International Conference on Multimodal Interfaces, ICMI 2004, pp. 129–136. ACM, New York (2004). http://doi.acm.org/10.1145/1027933.1027957
10. Teixeira, A., Rocha, N., Pereira, C., et al.: The living usability lab architecture: Support for the development and evaluation of new aal services for the elderly. In: Ambient Assisted Living Book. CRC Press (2011)

11. Teixeira, A., Pereira, C., e Silva, M.O., Alvarelhao, J., Silva, A., Cerqueira, M., Martins, A.I., Pacheco, O., Almeida, N., Oliveira, C., Costa, R., Neves, A.J.R., Queiros, A., Rocha, N.: New telerehabilitation services for the elderly. In: Isabel Maria Miranda, M.M.C.C. (ed.) Handbook of Research on ICTs for Healthcare and Social Services: Developments and Applications. IGI Global (2013)
12. World Health Organization: International Classification of Functioning, Disability and Health (2001)

Innovative Technology-Based Healthcare and Support Services for Older Adults: How and Why Industrial Initiatives Convert to the Living Lab Approach

Maribel Pino[1(✉)], Caroline Moget[2], Samuel Benveniste[3,5], Robert Picard[4], and Anne-Sophie Rigaud[1]

[1] Hôpital Broca, Assistance Publique Hôpitaux de Paris, Université Paris Descartes, EA 4468, LUSAGE Living Lab, Paris, France
{maribel.pino, anne-sophie.rigaud}@brc.aphp.fr
[2] SESIN, Marseille, France
cmoguet@sesinsud.com
[3] CEN STIMCO, Paris, France
samuel.benveniste@censtimco.org
[4] Conseil Général de l'Economie, Ministère de l'Economie, de l'Industrie et du Numérique, Paris, France
Robert.PICARD@finances.gouv.fr
[5] CRI, MINES ParisTech, Paris, France
samuel.benveniste@mines-paristech.fr

Abstract. To support older adults with age-related or chronic diseases living in the community, suppliers are increasingly turning to Personal Health Systems (PHS) for remote care delivery. Despite the advantages of PHS, implementing these systems brings on several challenges on the technical level, but also related to the diversity of end-users, the characteristics of the ecosystem, the innovation process itself, regulatory and social aspects. To discuss these issues, we study two different PHS currently under implementation and deployment by two French companies: a telehealth service for frail older adults living at home and a GPS-based monitoring service to deal with wandering and disorientation of persons with dementia. We describe and compare problematic situations faced by these companies on three levels - demand, supply, and context- and explain why they decided to evolve towards a Living Lab approach to improve technology acceptance and social and economic return on investment.

Keywords: Living-lab · Innovation · Healthcare · PHS · User involvement · Older adults

1 Introduction

Healthcare systems in Europe currently face many challenges due, in part, to the general background of the economic crisis resulting in limited public expenditure, budget cuts, and fiscal austerity [1]. Population ageing is another key factor putting a strain on healthcare systems, particularly in a context of healthcare providers shortage.

J. Zhou and G. Salvendy (Eds.): ITAP 2015, Part II, LNCS 9194, pp. 158–169, 2015.
DOI: 10.1007/978-3-319-20913-5_15

Therefore, dealing with questions such as how to achieve and maintain a good health status throughout the life cycle, and how to deal with common chronic diseases and disabilities in old age, seems fundamental [2].

An individual's health status results from the interaction between genetic and environmental factors [3]. Understanding these interactions, and the extent to which they contribute to the risk of illness, is important for the development of preventive and therapeutic measures supporting a healthy, active and independent life throughout an individual's existence. Innovative approaches for reaching better health outcomes at the population level may seek to improve the identification of risk factors, prevention strategies, diagnostic procedures, and enhance care quality and efficiency. Health policies are critical for the implementation of these innovative approaches because they guide initiatives and contribute to shape services and resources. In this context, the use of Information and communications technologies (ICTs) for health promotion and disease prevention has been growing rapidly in recent years, mainly in high-income countries [4].

The use of ICT in the healthcare context is expected to improve cost-effectiveness, safety, quality, availability and continuity of care delivery. Therefore, to better support elderly populations, commonly affected by age-related or chronic diseases, service suppliers are increasingly turning to remote care delivery systems, of which Personal Health Systems (PHS) are a major component. PHS refer to a number of ICT-based tools, such as wearable, implantable, and portable systems, that automatically acquire, monitor and analyze health-related data in a continuous and unobtrusive way. Health data is then coupled with expert biomedical or psychosocial knowledge for the prevention or treatment of a condition. PHS also take into account individual and environmental information to offer the most appropriate response to the user. Responses can range from the delivery of information (e.g., personalized nutrition advice) to remote or personal assistance (e.g., call centers, point-of-care systems) [5].

Within the eHealth area, PHS focus on providing individualized and quality-controlled services that empower individuals to have an active role in their own healthcare regardless of their location [6]. Consequently, PHS are expected to improve quality of care, process efficiency and care delivery costs, either in public or private settings. Finally, it is worth noting that from an industrial point of view, PHS provide new business opportunities in Europe and globally, with a potential to bring a significant return on investment (ROI) and generate savings in resources [7].

PHS are diverse (e.g., telehealth, health information exchange, communication, mobile and assistive technologies, etc.) and cover different situations (e.g., emergency, prevention, regular therapy, home monitoring, nutrition support, etc.). Due to their wide range of applications, PHS appear particularly interesting for delivering home care and related services to older adults who want to continue living at home for as long as possible. However, their design and implementation brings on several challenges, of course on the technical level, but also related to the diversity of needs, capabilities, preferences and goals of end-users, to the characteristics of the social and physical environment in which they live, or to the features of the local ecosystem (e.g., organizational complexities, political aspects, regulatory restrictions or insufficiencies).

In this paper we provide a general analysis on the industrial processes for the development and implementation of PHS that specifically target older adults with particular health and social care needs. First we provide some background information and summarize a number of challenges that healthcare technology companies may encounter when developing PHS. Then we introduce two PHS developed by French companies that are either under current development or already deployed. The first one is a telehealth service for frail older adults living at home. The second is a Global Positioning System (GPS) to deal with wandering and disorientation of persons with dementia. For each example we describe challenging situations encountered by these companies at different stages of the product development life cycle. We also explain how these challenges could be more successfully addressed by the implementation of Living Lab principles of open innovation, real-life experimentation, user involvement, and stakeholder partnerships. Finally, we build on these case studies to provide an analysis on how stakeholders in this industry sector may take advantage of Living Lab methods at different points of the product cycle.

1.1 Challenges Faced in the Development of PHS

Challenges faced by healthcare technology companies when developing PHS for elderly individuals can be grouped into three categories described in this section.

From the Demand Side: Tailoring Systems to Users. PHS users are very diverse including older adults, family members, informal or formal caregivers, among others. Because a wide range of persons may interact with PHS, these systems should be adaptable to various needs, capacities, limitations, preferences, and goals.

Several factors that may directly or indirectly hinder acceptance and adoption of PHS among older adults have been documented in the literature: (a) having a limited technology experience [8, 9]; (b) age-related changes in visual, auditory, motor and cognitive function, that render difficult the use of technological products [10–12]; (c) slowness in technology adoption compared to younger adults [13]; (d) being very selective in the choice of technologies they use (e.g., more frequent use of health care devices than entertainment technologies) [9]; (e) psychological aspects such as low self-confidence when using technological products, or having a negative perception of these products (e.g., being unnecessary) [13–15]; (f) assistive technology products conveying a negative connotation or appearing stigmatizing (e.g., highlighting disability) [16]; (g) ethical concerns regarding the use of PHS (e.g., mistrust, respect of privacy, dignity, autonomy) especially when the primary user has cognitive impairment; and (h) the high heterogeneity observed among elderly individuals (e.g., geographic, demographic, psychographic, and behavioral characteristics) which makes it difficult to draw a good picture of consumer segments [17].

All these factors represent a serious challenge for the development and implementation of PHS for older adults. Therefore, these systems must be designed with a strong concern of customization regarding elderly individuals and stakeholders around them. Consequently, participative and user-centered methodologies appear to be the most promising design approaches to address these issues.

From the Supply Side: Promoting a Collaborative Market Orientation. In order to keep up to date with globalization, technological change, and the rapid shift in industry boundaries, a new model for market orientation has emerged over the past years: the "open innovation" model. Contrary to classic hierarchical models of "closed innovation" in which one organization controls entirely the R&D process, owning the intellectual property of the production, the "open innovation" model refers to cooperation among multiple stakeholders who share their perspectives to foster innovation (e.g., cross-product, cross-firm and cross-industry business models) [18, 19]. The rationale behind this approach is that, when developing new products, the choice of involving multiple stakeholders, and combining their knowledge, methods, and technology, can bring an added value to the product.

Cooperation for the development of PHS within an open-innovation model implies including several firms in the sector, healthcare providers, suppliers, researchers, and end-users, among others. These partnerships may involve public, private and civic sectors of society. However, different risks associated to open innovation activities have been identified, for instance: loss of knowledge, high coordination costs, loss of control, high complexity, and conflicting interests. Some barriers to open innovation activities have been highlighted as well, such as the difficulty establishing effective partnerships, the unbalance between open innovation activities and daily business, insufficient time and financial resources, and intellectual property issues [20].

The higher created value for all stakeholders that can be achieved by properly conducted open innovation, when compared to traditional approaches, justifies the creation of specialized, independent organizations to deal with these issues. By employing solid and structured methodologies, it is indeed possible to collect and organize knowledge to prevent its loss, balance interests objectively to resolve conflicts, coordinate efforts to reduce costs, and mitigate negative interferences of the innovation process with the core activities of partners.

The Context: Legal, Social and Policy Issues in Innovation. Legal, social and policy issues may arise at different stages of the innovation process, from the design of PHS to their implementation in home or institutional settings. These questions do not only concern decision-makers, legislators, and policy-makers (e.g., adapting existing laws to new healthcare practices) but also users (e.g., patients, families, caregivers, health professionals) and manufacturers [21]. From a broad perspective, stipulations at this level may support or hinder industrial processes, research, and the diffusion of proven technologies.

A widely acknowledged legal challenge to the implementation of PHS systems is the respect of patient's rights regarding privacy and data protection. In the European context, it is worth reminding that there is a move towards greater integration. Therefore, cross-border collaborations for technology development and implementation, patient mobility, and the sharing of health records that results from it, require all the reflection on legal aspects for the development of PHS at the region level. However, up to now there is a lack of a unified body of legislation for eHealth in Europe [21].

With respect to social aspects, one key issue regarding the adoption of PHS is the degree of ICT readiness of potential users. A recent European [22] study pointed out that new health inequalities are emerging due to the impact of "traditional determinants of health" on ICT readiness. Therefore, e-Inclusion policies related to "ICT for Health" are needed to ensure that individuals with low socio-economic status, low technology experience, and more prone to health problems, are able to benefit from these types of technologies, in particular regarding elderly persons.

Here too, independent organizations able to federate all stakeholders, balance their interests through objective measures and synthesize these data to inform policy makers are needed. These organizations could particularly help to speed-up the necessary evolution of the legal and regulatory context, which today is slowed down by conflicting interests at the highest levels and the lack of a proper space for their resolution.

2 Two French Case Studies of PHS

In this section we give more concrete examples of the aforementioned challenges based on two case studies about the development and implementation of PHS. These studies cover different stages of the design and development cycle, and were chosen because they illustrate well the problematic situations faced by companies in the PHS sector.

2.1 SESIN and the Hadagio Telehealth System

SESIN is a French content management software publisher created in 1976. It has recently expanded its activities to e-health. The company is based in Marseille but is present in other French regions, in some African countries and in Brazil. Within the framework of a French Ministry of Health call for promoting health and independent living through ICT, the company conceived the project "Hadagio" in 2012.

Hadagio is a PHS intended to provide medical and social services such as tele-consultation, remote monitoring, social digital space, to frail elderly living in the community. The detection of unusual biological or behavioral patterns can automatically trigger an alarm notifying an informal caregiver or other care provider. The main goal of Hadagio is to improve health outcomes in older adults by supporting self-care and coordinated care. Overall, support services provided by the system are expected to prevent worsening of frailty and some of its adverse outcomes. The solution may be installed on tablets or smartphones and is expected to be used by patients, family members, and care providers. With the aim of ensuring acceptance and usability of the system, the company decided to give a particular attention to ergonomics throughout the design process of the system. A classical user-centered approach, structured into five phases, was used for the conception of the system (Fig. 1).

Although user-centered design methods were used to facilitate the appropriation of the system by users, and a satisfactory usability of interfaces was achieved, several barriers to acceptance still emerged. For instance, in Phase II-b (Fig. 1), an informative booklet was designed to ease the recruitment of participants for the pilot assessment (Phase V). The booklet introduced the system and presented a number of fictional scenarios illustrating how Hadagio could be used to support health and social care in elderly individuals. Results from the Phase I, and supporting literature on this topic, were used for this purpose. However, when gathering the opinions of older adults on

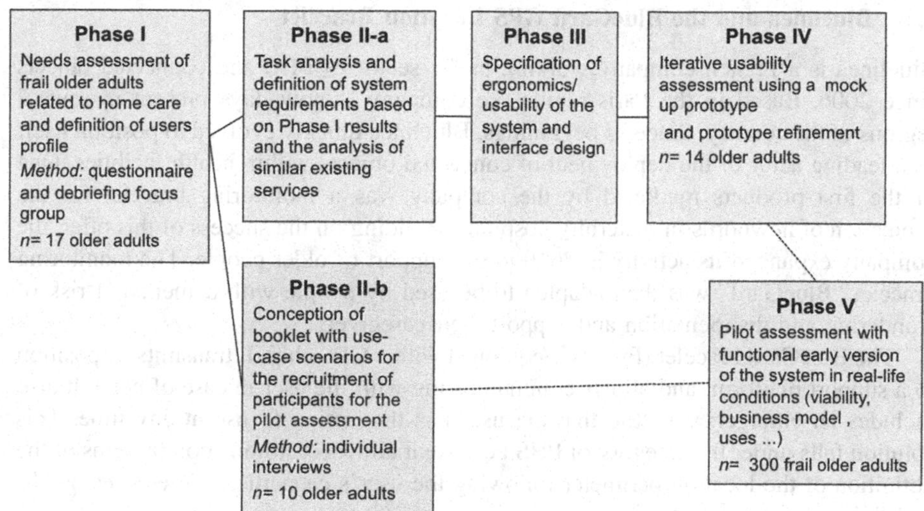

Fig. 1. Phases of design and evaluation of the Hadagio system

the information presented in the booklet, the project team noticed a low acceptance of the system. Participants' concerns pertained to different aspects:

- Technical feasibility: *"Remote health monitoring using sensors is fine, but how does one process data from sensors for all the patients? It's a huge job!"*
- Reliability: *"How do we prevent accidental triggering of alarms? We don't want emergency workers to come for nothing."*
- Intrusiveness: *"What type of sensor does the system use? Cameras? I do not want cameras at my home!"*
- Practical aspects: *"For tele-consultation, how does it work for payment, orders...? We must be there for that!"*
- Mobility: *"How does it work when we go on vacation? We must take our sensors with us?"*

Participants' feedback showed that the situations presented in the booklet appeared to be, first, far from their reality, and second, created a conflicting perspective with the way they wish to live at home and take care of their health. Older adults failed to perceive the usefulness of the system, which prevented them to imagine themselves as future users. The company acknowledged that because of its innovative character, implementing a system such as Hadagio would require a change of current self-care practices that could not be predicted neither promoted without the involvement of potential users. It was then decided to work more closely with older adults for the conception of more realistic use-case scenarios that would influence in a positive way the intention of use. This means giving them a more active and expert role and recognizing their right to decide over things affecting them.

2.2 Bluelinea and the BlueGard GPS Location Bracelet

Bluelinea is a French company working in the sector of PHS and connected objects since 2006. Based in the Paris region the company is nowadays present in several regions of the country. Since its beginnings, Bluelinea quickly evolved to position itself as a leading actor of the deployment of connected objects within health facilities. One of the first products marketed by the company was a monitoring bracelet for the protection of newborns in maternity hospitals. Building on the success of this offer, the company expanded its activity in 2010 to the support of older people. The monitoring bracelet "BlueGard" was then adapted to be used by people with dementia at risk of wandering and disorientation and support their caregivers.

The BlueGard bracelet (Fig. 2) is equipped with a GPS chip. It transmits its position to a support platform, and allows communicating with the user in case of need. It also includes an emergency button that the user has the option to use at any time. This solution falls under the category of PHS because it allows customization in terms of the definition of the location perimeter following the user's capacities, preferences, goals, and living situation.

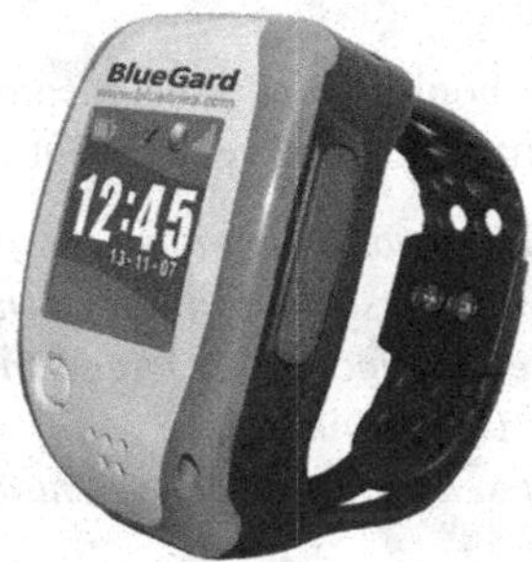

Fig. 2. The "BlueGard" bracelet for monitoring the location of persons with dementia

The main purpose of BlueGard was to support older adults with dementia living in the community and help them continue living at home, with safety and independence, for as long as possible. The service was also intended to give respite and alleviate the stress of family members and informal caregivers of persons with dementia. A secondary use anticipated for this system was to provide healthcare institutions for older adults (e.g., retirement homes, geriatric hospitals) with a support service to prevent elopement and improve resident's safety.

However, the offer did not reach the deployment level originally anticipated by the company. Nowadays approximately 1000 units are distributed each year, with a mean number of 300 active users at a given time and around 50 to 60 alarms triggered each day. Contrary to expectations, 70 % of users are in healthcare institutions, with only 30 % living at home. Several reasons can explain this situation:

- *Social environment characteristics*: absolute need of a caregiver at home to recharge the bracelet, informal caregiver being too old, or not having the possibility to pick up the person with dementia after he or she was located following an elopement episode (e.g., not having a car).

- *Technology-related*: size of the bracelet, negative design (e.g., stigmatizing), reduced autonomy (e.g., need to be charged at least 3 h everyday).
- *Service introduced too late*: the offer does not appear to be effective at later stages of dementia. The company has observed that families frequently look for a support solution after experiencing one or several elopement episodes, when usually other responses would be needed (e.g., institutionalization).
- *Ethical and regulatory aspects*: Some particular and institutional clients worried about the idea of infringing the autonomy and privacy of the person with dementia.
- *Costs*: No clear model of financial support for families taking care of a person with dementia, requiring changes at the policy level.

Yet, by being very attentive to users' and market feedback "after-the-fact" even though no proper co-creation approach was used in the beginning, the service could also be refined throughout the years. For example, improving the definition of the monitoring and location area according to each individual's needs. Also, a partnership with local cab companies was established, to help caregivers who did not have the possibility to pick up the person with dementia in case of elopement. The company has also gradually developed and applied an ethics charter defining high-level principles for the provision of remote monitoring in dementia. Nevertheless, the organization acknowledged that the lack of a structured approach to use data collection and analysis hindered the identification and implementation of critical modifications that would have helped to reach higher market penetration.

3 The Living Lab Approach as a Solution

The Living Lab approach is a recent but potentially influential stream in the field of innovation research that is structured around five basic principles [23]:

- *Openness:* The conception and evaluation process of a product or service should be public and anyone who considers him/herself potentially impacted can get involved in the operation.
- *Influence:* All parties involved must have a balanced influence on the final result, meaning that no stakeholder should be able to stir the project according only to his/her own goals.
- *Reality:* The conception and evaluation of the solutions should be based on quantitative and qualitative evidence collected as ecologically as possible. This means involving actual users, focusing on actual issues and testing solutions in real-life using the organizational and logistic setup projected for the final solution.
- *Value creation:* The conception and evaluation process should create value for everyone involved. Thus, the focus should not be only on economic value, but also on the social impact of the solution.
- *Sustainability:* Conception and evaluation should be an integral part of the project throughout its entire lifespan, meaning that the proposed solution should evolve and be re-evaluated thanks to feedback from the field. This makes it necessary to have

sustainable conception and evaluation processes, able to be self-funded through a re-investment of part of the value created.

With respect to the PHS examples here presented, while neither firm has truly applied a complete Living Lab approach, both have taken steps to operate according to some of its core principles. In this section we explain how a full implementation of Living Lab methodologies, at different moments of the product cycle (e.g., development and deployment), may positively impact the innovation process in both companies.

3.1 SESIN and the Hadagio Telehealth System

To allow potential users better imagine the conditions for a future use of Hadagio, SESIN intends to engage users in a process of *creative mediation* [24]. This method proclaims that making potential users participate in the writing of usage scenarios for innovative technologies helps them having a more clear representation of their usefulness and start shaping an intention to use them [24]. In this method, first, some services of the system are selected. Then, draft scenarios are presented to potential users, with "problematic" and "adjustment" situations without including the system. Participants are asked to complete these draft scenarios by imagining they play the main role in them. This practice may help participants identify and define unmet needs that could be potentially met by a product or service. In a second time, the system is included in the storyboard. Participants are then invited to imagine potential problems when using the system and possible solutions. Based on these elements, more realistic scenarios can be co-designed having constraints and solutions articulated in a coherent story.

This technique should provide a concrete framework to help prospective users to build a personalized scenario that fits well with their needs, goals, and preferences. For SESIN such a method is expected to be more effective for identifying determinants of technology acceptance than a questionnaire survey. For its implementation, a Living Lab approach appears as a particularly appropriate response because it offers a set of tools, methods and infrastructures [25] that effectively support participatory research for the construction of product usage scenarios. For this reason SESIN has decided at this point of the design cycle to move to Living Lab methodologies.

3.2 Bluelinea and the BlueGard GPS Location Bracelet

As part of Bluelinea further development of the BlueGard bracelet, the Living Lab approach, to which the company has recently turned, is expected to prove very useful. First, at the user level, the participatory approach recommended by the Living Lab can help improve product acceptability in terms of improved product appearance (e.g., more positive design), specifications of the system (e.g., improving their autonomy to reduce the need to recharge frequently), and training needs, as part of a co-design work. Openness and user involvement may also help the company to anticipate other potential partners, instead of discovering them afterwards, as it was the case with partnership with the cab company.

The Living Lab can also contribute to the improvement of the BlueGard service by putting in place a systematic approach to quality-controlled usage data collection and analysis. This is expected to help the company better demonstrate the profits of supply and better position itself in the market by better informing and assuring decision-makers (e.g., managers of healthcare organizations, caregivers) with respect to legal risks, and their tradeoffs with respect to safety/risks, benefits and costs.

It is worth noting that GPS systems for monitoring the location of persons with dementia seem to be better positioned in other countries than France by local dementia associations. For Bluelinea, the Living Lab approach can also help at the regulatory level to improve awareness of existing technology-based solutions regarding wandering and disorientation problems of persons with dementia. In order to demonstrate cost-effectiveness of the offer, necessary to be supported by local health authorities, Living Lab methodologies are also expected to contribute to the ROI study, the analysis of data related to users' enrollment, technology and operating costs, personnel or staffing costs. This strategic choice was made by the company to overcome an "opportunistic" approach and be in line with healthcare policies regarding the implementation of evidence-based practices.

4 Conclusion

In this paper, we have explained how two French firms developed very different PHS using approaches that were partly in accordance with Living Lab principles but did not fully implement this kind of approach. While original strategies used by both companies did address some challenges in interesting ways, and truly moved to personalization, which is rarely the case, technology acceptance and market take-up has remained low for both.

We have explained why we think that a more rigorous Living Lab approach would have produced better results, and how future versions of these two PHS will benefit from such a move. With these two examples, we have illustrated how innovative companies can benefit from this approach throughout the entire innovation process: concepts should be tested with both users and experts to generate feedback; mock-ups should be reviewed by users in realistic contexts to help generate useful, adequate scenarios; early prototypes should be tested in model environments and then in the real-world to iterate over the design, specifications and accompanying service; more mature solutions should be deployed in the real world as soon as possible with systematic logging and analysis of generated data and user feedback for gradual improvement; and finally companies and Living Labs should join forces to push authorities to improve regulatory and policy context by providing real-world, scientific evidence for the economic and social benefits that their solutions bring. That is why some of the authors of this paper have created the independent, neutral and participative French Forum of Living Labs for Healthy and Independent Living (www.forumllsa.org), in order to support this effort towards closer collaboration between stakeholders.

Thanks to this open, ethical yet efficient process, we think that effective and acceptable PHS for older adults will finally emerge and be deployed, generating the public health and economic benefits that they have long been expected to produce.

Acknowledgments. We thank Laurent Levasseur, Alexis Westermann, and Nathalie Mouret (Bluelinea) and Henri Noat (SESIN) for the support provided for this work.

References

1. Mladovsky, P., Srivastava, D., Cylus, J., Karanikolos, M., Evetovits, T., Thomson, S., McKee, M.: Health policy responses to the financial crisis in Europe. In: Policy Summary, vol. 5. World Health Organization (2012)
2. Rechel, B., Grundy, E., Robine, J.-M., Cylus, J., Mackenbach, J.P., Knai, C., McKee, M.: Ageing in the European union. Lancet **381**, 1312–1322 (2013)
3. Coll, C.G., Bearer, E.L., Lerner, R.M.: Nature and Nurture: The Complex Interplay of Genetic and Environmental Influences on Human Behavior and Development. Psychology Press, Taylor & Francis Group, New York (2014)
4. Howitt, P., Darzi, A., Yang, G.Z., Ashrafian, H., Atun, R., Barlow, J., Wilson, E.: Technologies for global health. Lancet **380**, 507–535 (2012)
5. Maglaveras, N., Bonato, P., Tamura, T.: Guest editorial. Special section on personal health systems. IEEE trans. inf. technol. biomed. publ. IEEE Eng. Med. Biol. Soc. **14**, 360–363 (2010)
6. Schartinger D., Giesecke, S., Heller-Schuh, B., Amanatidou, E., Schreir G., Miles, I., Pombo-Juárez, L., Saritas, O., Kastner, P., Könnölä, T.: Personal Health Systems. State of the art. Deliverable 1.1. Report on state-of-the-art and policy recommendations. Personal Health Systems Foresight Project (2013)
7. Baum, P., Abadie, F.: Market Developments–Remote Patient Monitoring and Treatment, Telecare, Fitness/Wellness and mHealth. Strategic Intelligence Monitor on Personal Health Systems, Phase 2. JRC Scientific and Policy Reports, European Commission, Joint Research Center (2013)
8. Eisma, R., Dickinson, A., Goodman, J., Mival, O., Syme, A., Tiwari, L.: Mutual inspiration in the development of new technology for older people. In: Proceedings of Include, pp. 252–259. London (2003)
9. Olson, K.E., O'Brien, M.A., Rogers, W.A., Charness, N.: Diffusion of technology: frequency of use for younger and older adults. Ageing Int. **36**(1), 123–145 (2011)
10. Marquié, J.C.: Perception visuelle et vieillissement [Visual perception and ageing]. L'année psychologique. **86**, 573–608 (1986)
11. Kelley, C.L., Charness, N.: Issues in training older adults to use computers. Behav. Informn Technol. **14**, 107–120 (1995)
12. Lauverjat, F., Pennequin, V., Fontaine, R.: Vieillissement et raisonnement: une approche multifactorielle (Ageing and thinking: a multifactorial approach). Année psychol **105**, 225–247 (2005)
13. Czaja, S.J., Charness, N., Fisk, A.D., Hertzog, C., Nair, S.N., Rogers, W.A., Sharit, J.: Factors predicting the use of technology: findings from the center for research and education on aging and technology enhancement. Psychol. Aging **21**, 33–352 (2006)

14. Melenhorst, A.S., Rogers, W.A., Caylor, E.C.: The use of communication technologies by older adults: exploring the benefits from the user's perspective. In: Proceedings of the Human Factors and Ergonomics Society 45th Annual Meeting, pp. 221–225. SAGE Publications, Minneapolis (2001)
15. Specht, M., Sperandio, J.C., de la Garza, C.: L'utilisation réelle des objets techniques du quotidien par les personnes âgées (The real use of daily technologies by older adults). Réseaux **17**, 97–120 (1999)
16. Doyle, J., Bailey, C., Scanaill, C.N., van den Berg, F.: Lessons learned in deploying independent living technologies to older adults' homes. UAIS. **13**, 191–204 (2014)
17. van der Zanden, L.D., van Kleef, E., de Wijk, R.A., van Trijp, H.: Understanding heterogeneity among elderly consumers: an evaluation of segmentation approaches in the functional food market. Nutrition res rev. **27**, 159–171 (2014)
18. Chesbrough, H.W.: Open Innovation: The new Imperative for Creating and Profiting from Technology. Harvard Business School Press, Boston (2003)
19. Velu, C., Barrett, M., Kohli R., Oliver Salge T.: Thriving in Open Innovation Ecosystems: Towards a Collaborative Market Orientation (2013) Working paper. Cambridge Service Alliance, University of Cambridge, UK (2013)
20. Van de Vrande, V., De Jong, J.P., Vanhaverbeke, W., De Rochemont, M.: Open innovation in SMEs: Trends, motives and management challenges. Technovation **29**(6), 423–437 (2009)
21. George, C., Whitehouse, D., Duquenoy, P.: Assessing legal, ethical and governance challenges in eHealth. In: eHealth: Legal, Ethical and Governance Challenges, pp. 3–22. Springer, Berlin Heidelberg (2013)
22. Lupiañez, F., Maghiros, I., Abadie, F.: Citizens and ICT for Health in 14 European Countries: Results from an Online Panel, in Strategic Intelligence Monitor on Personal Health Systems, Phase 2. JRC Scientific and Policy Reports, European Commission, Joint Research Center (2013)
23. Bergvall-Kareborn, B., Hoist, M., Stahlbrost, A.: Concept design with a Living Lab approach. In: 42nd HICSS Hawaii International Conference on System Sciences, pp. 1–10 (2009)
24. Gentès, A.: Médiation créative: scénarios et scénarisations dans les projets d'ingénierie des TIC [Creative mediation: scenarios and storyboarding in ICT engineering projects]. Hermès. **50**, 83–89 (2008)
25. Feurstein, K., Hesmer, A., Hribernik, K.A., Thoben, K.D., Schumacher, J.: A new development strategy. In: Feurstein, K. (ed.) European Living Labs – A new approach for human centric regional innovation, pp. 1–14. Wissenschaftlicher Verlag Berlin, Berlin (2008)

Developing Radical-Digital Interventions to Tackle Loneliness Amongst the Elderly

Dhruv Sharma[1(✉)], Lynne Blair[2], and Stephen Clune[3]

[1] HighWire Centre for Doctoral Training, Lancaster University, Lancaster, UK
d.sharma2@lancaster.ac.uk
[2] School of Computing and Communications, Lancaster University, Lancaster, UK
l.blair@lancaster.ac.uk
[3] Imagination Lancaster, Lancaster University, Lancaster, UK
s.clune@lancaster.ac.uk

Abstract. Loneliness is a growing issue amongst older people and one popular approach to tackling it is by developing non-medical interventions such as befriending services, mentoring provisions, social clubs, etc. Our analysis reveals that these interventions are predominantly *incremental-physical* in nature and that there is a lack of *radical-digital* ones. In this paper we discuss the properties of digital technologies that can be potentially helpful for the elderly and we suggest that social innovation provides a robust theoretical framework to conceive radical-digital loneliness interventions. We also draw parallels between loneliness interventions based on social innovation and the emerging 'sharing economy' in the digital world and discuss the role of third paradigm of HCI research in this area.

Keywords: Elderly · Loneliness · Interventions · The third paradigm · Radical-digital

1 Introduction

Because humans are social animals, our social relationships are very important for our emotional fulfilment, behavioural adjustment and mental wellbeing [1]. Disruption to these relationships can cause exceedingly unpleasant experiences associated with insufficient discharge of the need for human intimacy, called 'loneliness' [2]. Loneliness can be equated to 'perceived isolation' [3] or can be more precisely defined as the distressing feeling that results from, and comes with, discrepancies between one's desired and actual social relationships [4, 5]. Loneliness can be severely detrimental to health and quality of life of an individual [6–8]. Frans De Waal, a leading anthropologist, has highlighted the importance of human company in our lives. He opines that, "Next to death, solitary confinement is our most extreme punishment. Our bodies and minds are not designed for lonely lives. We become hopelessly depressed in the absence of human company and our health deteriorates" [9]. Weiss refers to loneliness as a "a gnawing chronic disease without redeeming features" that can instigate depression [8]. Loneliness should not be confused with living alone as many who live alone life fully integrated as well as socially active lives [10]. However it has been observed that loneliness is more common amongst people who live alone [11–13].

J. Zhou and G. Salvendy (Eds.): ITAP 2015, Part II, LNCS 9194, pp. 170–180, 2015.
DOI: 10.1007/978-3-319-20913-5_16

Results from an English longitudinal study of ageing by the Office for National Statistics, UK (ONS) suggest that 25 per cent of those aged 52 and over felt lonely sometimes. An additional 9 per cent of these respondents reported that they 'often' felt lonely [14]. Therefore age-related loneliness is a major social issue as it is increasing alongside an upward global population trend which predicts that nearly 22 % of the world population will be aged 60 years or over by 2050 [15]. This 'silver tsunami' [16] represents an unprecedented growth of the elderly population and is likely to exert socio-economic pressure globally in the form of healthcare needs [17, 18]. Researchers have long discussed loneliness' close association with ageing [19–22]. They have also suggested that those over 80 years of age are more vulnerable to experiencing it [23, 24]. Recent surveys conducted in the USA, the UK and Japan, etc. reveal this plight of the elderly as many older people report experiencing loneliness 'often' [25–27].

As a society we have been trying to tackle this seemingly impenetrable problem of loneliness amongst older adults for some time. For example, some of the strategies examined by Cattan et al. in their systematic review of interventions aimed at reducing loneliness amongst older people were developed nearly 30 years ago [7]. The fact that we are still trying to address similar (if not the same) issues at present, highlights a clear need to reflect upon our existing approach to mitigating loneliness so that we can develop more effective loneliness interventions. However, age-related loneliness is a 'complex concept' [28] and it is important to conduct rigorous research in this area to enhance our understanding of preventing, moderating or reducing loneliness amongst the elderly.

Previously we have suggested that there is an under-representation of digital technologies in loneliness interventions for the elderly [29]. This is in spite of digital technologies affording [30] several qualities that can ease age-related factors contributing to loneliness such as mobility challenges, audio-visual problems, etc. In this paper we highlight that the current thinking around developing 'digital interventions' predominantly adopts an *incremental* approach. We then discuss a gap in knowledge exemplified by the lack of *radical-digital* [29] interventions. In order to highlight the untapped potential of radical-digital technologies, we draw parallels from the rise of a 'sharing economy' [31] in the digital world and suggest that the elderly could benefit from being involved in it. We also propose that experimentation in this area can provide a provocative test-bed for HCI research in the third-paradigm [32].

2 Mapping Loneliness Interventions

According to cognitive theory of loneliness, loneliness can be manipulated; hence interventions have been developed to implement mitigation strategies [7]. These interventions mostly operate as services offering befriending, mentoring, information dissemination, etc. In their review, Windle et al. point out, "Just as the range of wellbeing services is extensive, so too is the available literature examining how well they work" [33]. Thus there are no standardised *formulae* that guarantee the success of loneliness interventions. The vast variety of interventions can broadly be classified as either being medical or non medical in their approach. Of the non-medical variety, many interventions operate as services that either provide companionship, information or support to the elderly and, in this paper, we focus on such non-medical interventions.

In order to highlight gaps in our existing understanding of how to prevent, reduce or alleviate age-related loneliness, we examined existing interventions in this area. The reviewed loneliness interventions were identified using an online ethnographic method. They were logged using a specially designed pattern recognition template and coding questions were developed to pigeonhole them into the following categories:

a. Incremental or Radical
b. Digital or Physical
c. Preventative, Supportive or Remedial
d. One to one, Group based or Community based

Using this method, all the interventions were logged onto the template, coded using the questions and mapped onto individual grids to arrive at a characteristic visualisation for each intervention.[1] All such individual visualisations were then transferred onto a single grid as shown in Fig. 1 for analysis.

This early analysis of loneliness interventions has revealed a gap in research in the form of a lack of interventions that are 'radical' as well as digital in nature. The majority of the interventions we reviewed fall in the *incremental-physical* category. Before we begin to consider this gap further, it is important to unpack the meaning of 'radical' interventions. Manzini suggests that incremental innovations represent our existing ways of 'thinking and doing'. On the contrary, innovations that fall outside our current ways of 'thinking and doing' represent radical innovation [34]. Also, Norman and Verganti define *incremental* innovation as "improvements within a given frame of solutions" or "doing better what we already do" and *radical* innovation as "a change of frame" or "doing what we did not do before" [35]. This is akin to Dryzek's [36] 'reformist' versus 'radical' departures in environmental discourses. Reformist departures are similar to incremental approaches as they seek solutions within familiar modes of rational management, while radical departures argue for a comparatively significant movement away from industrial modes of living and being.

3 Exploring Radical-Digital Interventions

While radical-digital interventions may not, in the end, prove to be a 'silver-bullet' solution to the problem, the idea that they are underrepresented, as can be seen in the preliminary analysis, suggests that we do not know much about their potential strengths as well as possible weaknesses. An initial approach to exploring this opportunity could be to critically examine existing loneliness interventions in order to identify what separates the radical from the incremental and then finding ways of enabling their *digitisation*.[2] However a mere lack of the use of digital technologies in developing

[1] Coding questions were developed in order to aid categorisation. The coding method has been discussed in detail in our previous work *Radicalising the designer: Combating age-related loneliness through radical-digital interventions (in press)* [29].

[2] The Oxford Dictionary defines digitisation as "The conversion of text, pictures, or sound into a digital form that can be processed by a computer". Here we mean meeting the aims and objectives of radical interventions that are *physical* in nature by using digital technologies involving the elderly.

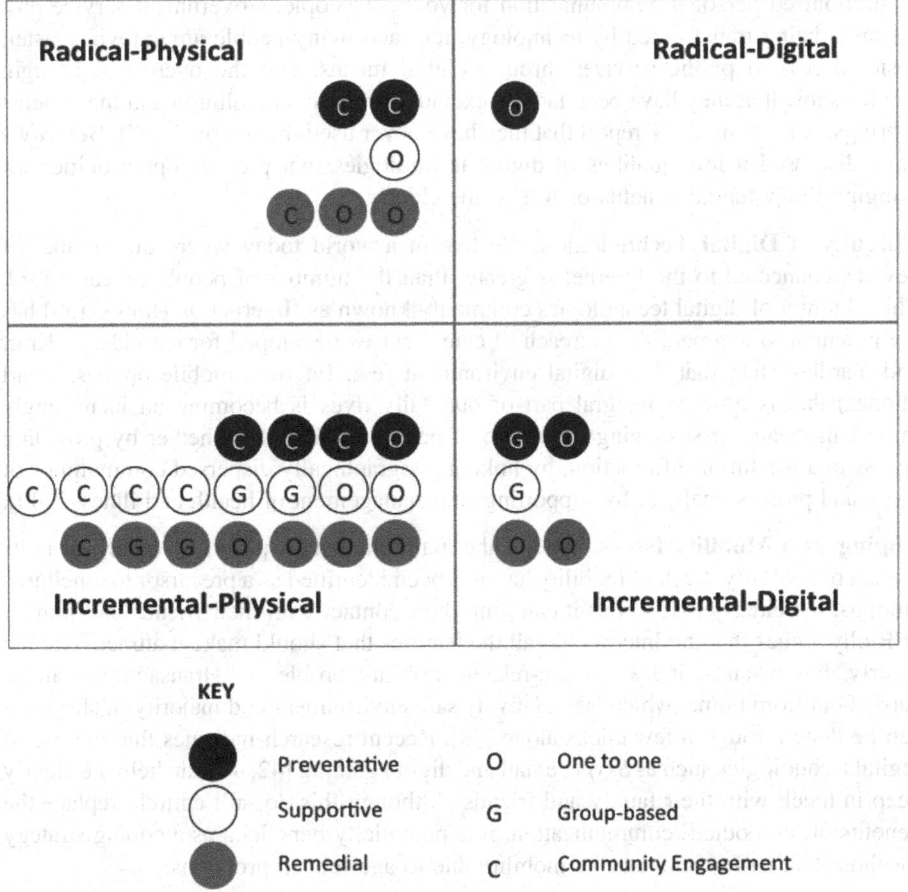

Fig. 1. Mapping all the interventions onto a single grid.

loneliness interventions cannot be the sole justification for 'investing' in this area. Therefore this paper highlights the qualities that digital technologies possess, which can help in coping with challenges posed by old age. We begin by looking at key properties of ICT that could be of significant value in easing age-related challenges. We then look at digital loneliness interventions and suggest that they are predominantly incremental in nature. We point out that the growth of the online sharing economy [31] can provide a good framework to develop radical-digital interventions.

3.1 Harnessing the Digital

Technological developments in the last decade or so have completely transformed the way we interact and communicate with each other. However a large proportion of older people seem to be neglected from this digital revolution. "Internet communication systems such as email and social networking sites like Facebook and Twitter have revolutionised personal communication for younger people. Government service provision is being transformed by technology, too, and many people are enjoying faster, easier access to public services through digital means. Not the over-65 s, though: studies show that they have been largely excluded from this revolution and the benefits it brings. A startling 70 % report that they have never used the internet" [37]. Below we have discussed a few qualities of digital technologies that provide opportunities for bringing the potential benefits of ICT to the elderly.

Ubiquity of Digital Technologies. We live in a world today where the number of devices connected to the Internet is greater than the number of people on earth [38]. This ubiquity of digital technologies commonly known as 'Internet of Things' [39] has the potential to augment the outreach of care services developed for the elderly. Kraft and Yardley state that "the digital environment (e.g. Internet, mobile phones, smart phones) that is now an integral part of our daily lives is becoming an increasingly important means of sustaining the health of people worldwide, whether by providing access to a wealth of information, by linking geographically dispersed communities of peers and professionals, or by supporting self-management of health and illness" [40].

Coping with Mobility Issues. One of the main challenges posed by older age is its impact on mobility. Lack of mobility has also been identified as a precursor to loneliness amongst the elderly [41, 42] as it can limit their contact with their friends and family. O'Reilly argues that the Internet has all the features that should make it attractive to the elderly. For instance it lessens age-related mobility problems – transactions can be carried out from home, which is a relatively safe environment and majority of shopping can be done through a few clicks alone [43]. Recent research indicates that the use of digital technologies such as *Skype*, email and digital gaming [42, 44] can help the elderly keep in touch with their family and friends. Although this doesn't entirely replace the benefits of 'embodied' communication, it is potentially beneficial as a coping strategy for those that suffer from lack of mobility due to age-related problems.

Providing Alternate Infrastructure. Recent socio-economic developments in the UK have severely impacted rural areas due to the closure of shops, post offices, bus routes, etc. [45]. By removing these 'social opportunities', this has impacted the quality of life of older people as they have become further isolated. It can be argued that the lack of a hard infrastructure can be negated by the use of a soft infrastructure. For example, farmers in rural India overcome the challenge of a lack of roads and transport facilities by using their mobile phones to settle their deals [46]. Although a different context, it still highlights the potential of using digital technologies in overcoming infrastructural challenges. Moreover digital technologies can be easily (and cheaply) modified, altered or customised in comparison to physical structures.

4 Reframing Perception of the 'Elderly'

Gaver et al. have pointed out that, "There is a kind of disciplinary hubris in the assumption that HCI (Human Computer Interaction) can define systems that reflect comprehensive understandings of users, whether in terms of tasks, problems or communities of use" [47]. The third paradigm challenges such predisposition as it elucidates the importance of use and usage of a system within context. Here we argue that loneliness interventions for the elderly based on social innovation fit within the sharing economy and that this creates a shared context that can provide an interesting opportunity to test ideas from the third paradigm in HCI.

4.1 Social Innovation in a Digital World

As introduced earlier, the majority of existing interventions are incremental and direct in their approach [29]. Someone is identified as lonely, therefore befriended or recommended to an expert service provider. These approaches focus on the underlying symptom of loneliness, i.e. the deficiency of human company, rather than a more holistic context such as envisioning a cultural milieu that nurtures meaningful human interactions.

A more radical approach can be found in the literature on social innovation, where the elderly are viewed as a desirable resource that has a unique offering that would be of benefit to society. Upon a closer examination of the interventions reviewed, we found that most of the radical interventions provide the elderly users something more than *someone to speak to* or the *information* they may require. With the exception of PARO, a robotic seal that brings the known benefits of animal therapy to elderly care, all the other radical interventions that were reviewed appear to treat the elderly as *providers* rather than as *recipients* alone. For example, the elderly have a crucial role to play in *GoodGym*. They *provide* the necessary motivation for keen runners to stay committed to running. Similarly, in *Speaking Exchange*, their role is not of a service *user* alone but it is one that entails offering support to help non-native English speakers brush up their English speaking skills. *Homeshare* is another great example where by giving someone a house to live-in, older people contribute to other peoples' wellbeing while being cared for simultaneously.

What these interventions actually provide the elderly is an opportunity to have a new role to play in the society, one where they can act as solutions to someone else's problems. Manzini encourages the idea of looking at problems as solutions to inspire Social Innovation [48]. Therefore by building loneliness interventions where the elderly person's role is not restricted to being a *user* of that service, but one where they can offer support or help to someone else, we can begin to create loneliness interventions that are radical. Such radical interventions can then move into the digital realm through the use of ICT.

4.2 Social Innovation in a Sharing Economy

As Tonkinwise points out, sharing is something that we have always been doing in families, between friends, through government and with infrastructures [31] but more recently, the growth of the sharing economy has been propelled by the rise of Internet. "The ease with which individuals, even strangers, can now connect, exchange, share information, and cooperate is truly transformative. That's the promise of the sharing platforms about which virtually everyone agrees. But technologies are only as good as the political and social context in which they are employed. Software, crowdsourcing, and the information commons give us powerful tools for building social solidarity, democracy, and sustainability. Now our task is to build a movement to harness that power" [49].

Loneliness interventions based on social innovation are also closely associated with the sharing economy. Whether it is living in the same house in *Homeshare*, relying on a matching system to satiate seemingly unrelated personal objectives in *GoodGym* or sharing experiences online via *Speaking Exchange*, all these interventions rely on some form of a 'shared experience' to solve social problems. This suggests that social innovation can become a vehicle for encouraging older adults' involvement in the sharing economy. However, while we argue that the sharing economy combined with social innovation presents great potential to inspire the building of a framework for developing radical-digital loneliness interventions, if 70 % of the target population have not used the Internet – access to the market requires an alternative strategy. The emergence of the third paradigm of HCI research provides a promising trajectory that this line of work could potentially benefit from.

4.3 The Third Paradigm of HCI Research

Harrison et al. begin their discussion of the third paradigm by recognising that embodied interaction is a 'key underlying' theme [32]. They opine that embodiment also plays an important role in other approaches to interaction. For instance, human factors practitioners pay attention to such aspects as the ergonomics of a mouse or the suitability of fonts and their sizes for specific purposes. They also suggest that cognitively based work in HCI focuses on physical constraints that guide interface design such as the speed at which humans react to a particular interface. They argue that embodiment in the third paradigm is based on a different stance. Seeking inspiration from phenomenology, "it takes as central that the way in which we come to understand the world, ourselves, and interaction derives crucially from our location in a physical and social world as embodied actors" [32]. In their review of embodiment in HCI research thus far, they bring to fore our fixation with visual, auditory and physical abilities of users. They argue that, "design can also support other senses and physical abilities such as action-centered skills and motor memory. Embodiment refocuses attention from the single-user/singe-computer paradigm that has recently dominated HCI towards collaboration and communication through physically shared objects" [32]. In his work on intergenerational digital games between grandparents and their grandchildren, Loos has also pointed out some of these issues in designing for shared experiences. He suggests that taking age-related factors such as declining vision, useful field of view, vision-motor ability and hearing is not sufficient for designing such games [44] and recommends a more 'human-centred research procedure' in the form of workshops involving both younger and older adults to capture mutual expectations from such games.

As HCI researchers, if we are to design for such joint experiences, then the third paradigm becomes extremely relevant as it emphasises the importance of users 'situated' [50] within their contexts. In case of loneliness interventions based on social innovation, users' contexts are shared ones. Therefore skills with a social science lineage which inherently study people in their contexts, such as ethnography, ethnomethodology and sociology, etc. might gain a more prominent place in relation to other approaches such as human factors and usability research which presently occupy more space in a HCI practitioner's toolbox.

Dillahunt points out that "technological platforms and applications that promote the sharing economy (e.g. AirBnB, TaskRabbit), and job creation (e.g. oDesk, MTurk), and trading (e.g. Craigslist) are relatively understudied within HCI" [51]. Therefore we imply that HCI community would benefit from an engagement with the elderly population prone to loneliness, as it would allow for experimentation within the rapidly evolving sharing economy space in the backdrop of the third paradigm.

5 Conclusion

This paper discusses the social problem of loneliness, which is increasing amongst older people as an unprecedented number of people are beginning to reach retirement age globally. We have examined our existing approach to mitigating loneliness through non-medical interventions. Our review reveals that the predominant tactic we deploy in alleviating loneliness is *incremental-physical* in nature. We identify a gap in this area in the form of lack of *radical-digital* interventions and advocate experimentation in this area to uncover their strengths and/or possible limitations.

We present key properties of digital technologies that can help in coping with age-related challenges. For instance, ubiquity of digital technologies, their ability to negate the challenge of mobility presented by old age and their disposition as a potential substitute for hard infrastructure. We suggest that social innovation provides a compelling theoretical framework to develop radical interventions and that the use of ICT can potentially enhance their impact. By highlighting the similarities between loneliness interventions based on social innovation and the rapidly evolving 'sharing economy', we recommend that developing such interventions provides a great foundation for HCI research into shared experiences. We conclude by positing that the HCI community would benefit from looking into the third paradigm for inspiration on how to plan and execute research for such shared experiences.

References

1. Hughes, M.E., et al.: A short scale for measuring loneliness in large surveys results from two population-based studies. Res. Aging **26**(6), 655–672 (2004)
2. Weiss, R.S.: Loneliness: The experience of emotional and social isolation. MIT Press, Cambridge (1973)
3. Cacioppo, J.T., Hawkley, L.C., Thisted, R.A.: Perceived social isolation makes me sad: 5-year cross-lagged analyses of loneliness and depressive symptomatology in the chicago health, aging, and social relations study. Psychol. Aging **25**(2), 453 (2010)

4. Perlman, D., Peplau, L.A.: Loneliness. In: Friedman, H.S. (ed.) Encyclopedia of Mental Health, Vol 2, pp. 571–581. Academic Press, San Diego (1998)
5. Pinquart, M.: Loneliness in married, widowed, divorced, and never-married older adults. J. Soc. pers. relat. **20**(1), 31–53 (2003)
6. Lynch, J.J.: The Broken Heart: The Medical Consequences of Loneliness. Basic Books, New York (1977)
7. Cattan, M., et al.: Preventing social isolation and loneliness among older people: a systematic review of health promotion interventions. Ageing soc. **25**(01), 41–67 (2005)
8. Stuart-Hamilton, I.: The Psychology of Ageing: An Introduction. Jessica Kingsley Publishers, Philadelphia (2012)
9. Waal, F.B.M.: Our Inner Ape: The Best and Worst of Human Nature. Granta, London (2006)
10. Leikas, J., et al.: Life-based design to combat loneliness among older people. J. Community Inform. **8**(1), 7–14 (2012)
11. Havinghurst, R.: Ageing in western society. In: The Social Challenge of Ageing. pp. 15–44. Croom Helm, London (1978)
12. Hunt, A.: The Elderly at Home-a Study of People Aged 65 and Over Living in the Community in England 1976. HM Stationery Office, London (1978)
13. Wenger, G.C.: Loneliness: a problem of measurement. In: Ageing in modern society, pp. 145–167. Croom Helm, Beckenham (1983)
14. Beaumont, J.: Measuring National Well-being - Older People and Loneliness. Office for National Statistics, UK (2013)
15. Rutherford, T.: Population ageing: statistics, in House of Commons library (2012). www.parliament.uk/topics/PopulationArchive. Accessed 2 Jan 2013, Social and General Statistics
16. Cacioppo, J.T., Patrick, W.: Loneliness: Human Nature and the Need for Social Connection. WW Norton & Company, New York (2008)
17. Dychtwald, K., Flower, J.: Age Wave: The Challenges and Opportunities of an Aging America. Bantam Books, New York (1989)
18. O'Connor, J.: Age-related loneliness is a ticking time bomb waiting to explode. Inside Time: The National Newspaper for Prisoners and Detainees 2014. http://insidetime.co.uk/articleview.asp?a=1773&c=agerelated_loneliness_is_a_ticking_time_bomb_waiting_to_explode. Accessed 25 Sep 2014
19. Sheldon, J.H.: The Social Medicine of Old Age: Report of an Enquiry in Wolverhampton. Oxford University Press, Oxford (1948)
20. Halmos, P.: Solitude and privacy: a study of social isolation its causes and therapy, vol. 15. Psychology Press, Hove (1998)
21. Dykstra, P.A., Van Tilburg, T.G., de Jong Gierveld, J.: Changes in older adult loneliness results from a seven-year longitudinal study. Res. Aging **27**(6), 725–747 (2005)
22. Dykstra, P.A.: Older adult loneliness: myths and realities. Eur. J. Ageing **6**(2), 91–100 (2009)
23. Kaasa, K.: Loneliness in old age: psychosocial and health predictors. Norsk epidemiologi **8** (2), 195–201 (1998)
24. Demakakos, P., Nunn, S., Nazroo, J.: 10. Loneliness, relative deprivation and life satisfaction. Retirement, health and relationships of the older population in England, p. 297 (2006)
25. Hawkley, L.C., Cacioppo, J.T.: Aging and loneliness downhill quickly? Curr. Dir. Psychol. Sci. **16**(4), 187–191 (2007)
26. Kim, O., et al.: Loneliness, depression and health status of the institutionalized elderly in Korea and Japan. Asian Nurs. Res. **3**(2), 63–70 (2009)

27. Marsh, S.: Fourteen ways councils can help combat loneliness. Public Leaders Network: Insight, news, comment and jobs in policy and leadership 2014. http://www.theguardian.com/local-government-network/2014/apr/14/fourteen-ways-councils-can-help-combat-loneliness. Accessed 14 Sep 2014
28. Murphy, F.: Loneliness: a challenge for nurses caring for older people. Nurs. older people **18** (5), 22–25 (2006)
29. Sharma, D., Blair, L., Clune, S.: Radicalising the designer: combating age-related loneliness through radical-digital interventions. In: Proceedings of Cumulus: Virtuous Circle, Milan, Italy (2015)
30. Gaver, W.W.: Technology affordances. In: Proceedings of the SIGCHI Conference on Human Factors in Computing Systems, ACM (1991)
31. Tonkinwise, C.: Unpredictable Conveniently Awkward Sharing 2015. http://www.academia.edu/10605747/What_Futurists_should_learn_from_the_Inconvenience_of_Sharing. Accessed 15 Feb 2015
32. Harrison, S., Sengers, P., Tatar, D.: Making epistemological trouble: third-paradigm HCI as successor science. Interact. Comput. **23**(5), 385–392 (2011)
33. Windle, K., Francis, J., Coomber, C.: Preventing loneliness and social isolation: interventions and outcomes, pp. 1–16. Social Care Institute for Excellence, London (2011)
34. Manzini, E.: DESIS Network, making things happen. Design Issues, **30**(1) pp. 57–66 (2014)
35. Norman, D.A., Verganti, R.: Incremental and radical innovation: design research vs technology and meaning change. Des. Issues **30**(1), 78–96 (2014)
36. Dryzek, J.S.: The politics of the earth: environmental discourses. Oxford University Press, Oxford (2005)
37. Independent Age. Older People, Technology and Community: The Potential of Technology to Help Older People Renew or Develop Social Contacts and to Actively Engage in their Communities 2010. http://www.cisco.com/web/about/ac79/docs/wp/ps/Report.pdf. Accessed 16 Feb 2015
38. Frey, T.: Replacing Our Physical Infrastructure with Digital Infrastructure. FuturistSpeaker.com: Challenging your thinking, pushing your imagination, creating the future 2012. http://www.futuristspeaker.com/2012/11/replacing-our-physical-infrastructure-with-digital-infrastructure/. Accessed 16 Feb 2015
39. Das, R., Harrop, P.: The Internet of Things: massive new markets for automated location, tracking, authentication and barcode replacement. Total Asset Visibility, IDTechEx Ltd. (1999)
40. Kraft, P., Yardley, L.: Current issues and new directions in Psychology and Health: What is the future of digital interventions for health behaviour change? (2009)
41. Milligan, C., Passey, D.: Ageing and the use of the internet: current engagement and future trends 2011. http://www.nominettrust.org.uk/sites/default/files/NT%20SoA%20-%20Ageing%20and%20the%20use%20of%20the%20internet_0.pdf. Accessed 16 Feb 2015
42. Age UK. Digital inclusion evidence review 2013. http://www.ageuk.org.uk/Documents/EN-GB/For-professionals/Research/Age%20UK%20Digital%20Inclusion%20Evidence%20Review%202013.pdf?dtrk=true. Accessed 16 Feb 2015
43. O'Reilly, P.: Use of Internet Banking by the Elderly - time to rise to the challenge 2008. http://www.researchgate.net/researcher/2014977975_Paidi_OReilly. Accessed 16 Feb 2015
44. Loos, E.: Designing meaningful intergenerational digital games. In: International Conference on Communication, Media, Technology and Design (2014)
45. Commission for Rural Communities. Social isoltion experienced by older people in rural communities 2012. http://www.agenda-efa.org.uk/site/wp-content/uploads/2012/09/Executive-Summary-Social-isolation-experienced-by-older-people-in-rural-communities.pdf. Accessed 16 Feb 2015

46. The Centre for Knowledge Societies, Mobile Development Report, India (2006)
47. Gaver, W., et al.: The prayer companion: openness and specificity, materiality and spirituality. In: Proceedings of the SIGCHI conference on Human factors in computing systems. ACM (2010)
48. Association, I.D. Ezio Manzini-Keynote: Design for Social Innovation and Sustainability 2010. http://vimeo.com/9660466. Accessed 01 Sep 2014
49. Schor, J.: Debating the Sharing Economy. Great Transition Initiative: Toward a transformative vision and praxis 2014. http://greattransition.org/publication/debating-the-sharing-economy. Accessed 17 Feb 2015
50. Suchman, L.A.: Plans and situated actions: the problem of human-machine communication. Cambridge University Press, New York (1987)
51. Dillahunt, T.: Toward a deeper understanding of sustainability within HCI, CHI 2014 (2014)

Effects of Using Care Professionals in the Development of Social Technology for Elderly

Marie Sjölinder[1(✉)] and Isabella Scandurra[2]

[1] SICS Swedish ICT, Box 1263, 164 29 Kista, Sweden
marie@sics.se

[2] School of Business, Örebro University, 701 82 Örebro, Sweden
Isabella.Scandurra@oru.se

Abstract. In some situations when developing technology for elderly, the intended users are too fragile and cannot participate themselves in the design process. The aim with this study was to investigate the use of care personnel as mediators for the elderly in the design process. The system that was developed was an information and communication technology system for sharing information and for keeping in touch with friends and family. Initially the care personnel misunderstood the need of technology among the elderly. During the project the care personnel changed their view and suggested new ways of using the technology. When the devices where placed in the rooms of the elderly the usage was low, but when the system was used in the dining areas as something to gather around, e.g. to show each other pictures of friends and family, the system became a success.

Keywords: Social technology · Welfare technology · Elderly · Community-based participatory research · Co-participatory design · Community networks · Professional-patient relations

1 Introduction

There is an increasing social isolation among elderly today. Loneliness and social isolation can, however, be addressed in several ways using different interactive electronic services. One of the most important issues in reducing social isolation is the existence of social networks [1]. The possibilities to communicate with friends and relatives through computers and Internet can increase the social network, and social isolation can be reduced [1, 2]. Several studies have shown the importance for older adults to be able to communicate with family members and friends enabled through new communication technology [2, 3]. Although it may seem different, in Sweden the Internet usage pattern does not differ between older and younger daily users; Internet is mostly used for e-mailing, searching news and gathering practical information [3]. Technology also provides opportunities for older adults to gain new knowledge from other generations. The Internet usage among older adults is increasing [3] and the possibility to communicate with children and grandchildren through Internet and e-mail is important for older adults. Among many elderly, Internet has also become an

J. Zhou and G. Salvendy (Eds.): ITAP 2015, Part II, LNCS 9194, pp. 181–192, 2015.
DOI: 10.1007/978-3-319-20913-5_17

important source for getting health information. For elderly using digital health information this is an opportunity to increase the feeling of control over the own health [4]. It empowers people in terms of both being more educated in the area, and of having the possibility to share experiences with others [5].

Also, the quick development in the area of mobile communication in the last decade has provided many new possibilities for communication and for sharing our everyday life with each other. Many new services and applications are targeted towards elderly and have interfaces that are considered easy to use. However, daily usage decreases from generation to generation as a function age. The older a citizen is, the less he/she uses Internet services [3]. The low rate of usage at high ages could become a society problem, where more and more public services are accessed via different communication technology tools.

The digital divide could be addressed in several ways [4] by different and alternative (non-traditional web browsers) information and communication technology (ICT) solutions. Unfortunately, literature reports on numerous failures when trying to deploy novel technology to elderly user groups. Some explanations to this could be that the services are not perceived to be meaningful enough or that they, despite efforts from the developer team, are perceived too cumbersome or difficult to use. A further challenge when developing services for the oldest group is to involve the users in the design process.

In this action research project, elderly care professionals were invited to co-design novel services as they are experienced in age-related impairments. The services were provided through an innovative mobile communication device connected to the TV, which worked as an interactive large screen remotely controlled.

The objective of this work was two-fold. The aim of the project was to investigate how the device and the social interactive applications could be further developed and appropriated among elderly at a nursing home, while at the same time the researchers developed and applied an iterative co-design technique with engagement of older adults and the care personnel that supported in conveying the needs of the elderly.

2 Research Approach

Present action research study adheres to Cooperative design [6, 7] as one of the Human-Computer Interaction (HCI) research theories that regards system development with user participation and that considers designing a social process. From research literature we know that usability aspects should be brought in early in the development process [6, 8]. Previous research also presents several methods to engage users with the aim to create future environments, e.g. future workshops [9]. Other methods to bring future needs analysis into system development are iterative prototyping and scenario-based design, preferably applied together with potential users in a collaborative approach [7, 10].

The degree of user participation may vary. Regardless of activation degree, in cooperative design developers and practitioners/users are seen as actively cooperating partners. Together they aim to reduce uncertainty and risk in the development of novel systems, where a detailed conception of exactly which future needs should be supported, often lacks [6, 9].

In this study the approach was to involve the end users as much as possible, but when this inclusion was not possible also involve the care personnel. However, this is only an option when the information not can be gathered from the elderly themselves. Using older adults' extensive experience when trying to meet their needs can be more successful for promoting a new product or service, rather than relying on interaction patterns based on the computer paradigm [11].

This work aimed to increase the competence of the municipality care personnel while at the same time increase the knowledge of the industry partner of the end-users of their system. By collaboration with the research team, the company also got a chance to improve their methodological skills. In this environment, problem-owners, researchers, elderly users and developers of novel ICT services worked together in a user-centered and participatory design approach [12].

3 Method and Materials

The project (called IPPI, as the device involved), in which this study was conducted, was carried out during 2010 and 2011 and was financed by the Swedish agency for innovation systems, Vinnova. The work was a part of gathering knowledge regarding social technology tools and interacting eHealth services among different older user groups and in different contexts [13]. As a part of the development of a co-design technique, present study investigated the usage of elderly care personnel as mediators of the elderly users' needs. This work was conducted during the implementation and testing phase of the IPPI project together with old adults and care personnel at a nursing home.

3.1 Study Site and Participants

The nursing home (Väsbygården) was situated outside Stockholm, Sweden, in Vallentuna municipality. It consisted of four departments of which all participated in the study, although to various extent. Each division contained approximately 20 apartments and a dining room for meals in common. For each division, an employee responsible for the IPPI project was appointed by the operations manager. The project team at site further consisted of the registered nurse, the janitor, the reception and the nutrition managers as well as the operations manager. In all, there were nine care personnel responsible for different parts of the project execution. Project members from academia (the authors of this paper) were working closely with the development company who contributed with a project leader, a test leader and a developer. Five end-users were involved as test participants in the project. Other elderly tried the services but not as frequent users. The project team met approximately every two weeks during the latter part of the project, from January to June 2011 and there were both internal and external funding to reimburse the nursing home for time loss and to hire substitutes for the care personnel when necessary.

According to our knowledge, it is not common that a municipality project in elderly care is so well equipped with care personnel and resources as this project was. The care personnel took on different roles; recruiting elderly, information to the relatives, display of food or menus, information about activities for the residents, teaching activities to the rest of the care personnel as well as medication and technology experts. These responsibilities contributed to the creation of new content and new services of the device. The entire setting was prominent and cheerful and all involved care personnel was appointed as "IPPI ambassadors" in relation to the residents or their relatives.

3.2 Study Design

In general, there is a need to develop technology towards the demands of older adults in the future. There is, consequently, a need to develop technology towards elderly already today; however for some people in this target group it could be difficult to imagine possibilities with the new technology. Many of the elderly also suffer from age-related decline, both with respect to physical and cognitive abilities that make it difficult to be involved in the design of new services and new technology.

Inspired by Boyd-Graber et al. [14] and their work regarding using people close to the intended user in the design process, our aim was to investigate to which extent people familiar with elderly persons' presuppositions could contribute regarding needs and usage of technology. In the work conducted by Boyd-Graber et al. [14] staff that worked close to users with aphasia was involved in the design process. This study showed that overall it worked well since supporting staff was very familiar with the user groups' needs and demands. However, some difficulties were found regarding the testing of prototypes since it was impossible to imagine another person's usage context all the way and in all details [14].

One of the goals of the IPPI project was to develop an interactive ICT system for elderly users with possibilities to share information and to keep in touch with friends and family. In this case, the majority of the elderly at the nursing home was too fragile and they could not participate themselves in the project. Hence, in the study we investigated the use of care personnel as mediators for the needs of the elderly. Contradictory to the Boyd Graber et al. [14] study, focus was not on the design process, but particularly on the needs and actual use of social technology. The study was explorative in a sense that the authors wanted to get a first understanding of to which extent care personnel could represent different categories of elderly in terms of attitudes towards and usage of technology.

Workshop Activities. On an every two weeks basis during 6 months, the project team was gathered in 2-4 h workshops with different content. Once a common agreement on vision and goals was reached, other workshops iteratively handled:

- the needs and demands of the elderly,
- the needs and demands of the care personnel,
- the needs and demands of the relatives,
- eHealth and communication services,
- potential improvements of the device and services.

The researchers and the industry partner's project leader planned and lead the workshops together, using different techniques. Personas [15], brainstorming techniques [16] and semi-structured interviews were used to gather information from the different groups about themselves, but also to gather what they thought about the needs and attitudes of the other groups.

Every meeting had a formal agenda, always containing: (1) What was decided last time? (2) Where are we now? (3) Where to go next? (4) How to get there? In that way, a truly cooperative work was established and the process was transparent to all participants.

Personas were created by the care personnel. This method was previously successfully used by one of the authors in another project [17], by then in a clinical setting by home care personnel. At that time, the home care personnel agreed to mix medical conditions and characteristics of deceased persons they had been involved with and in that way they created completely new personas, but with the possibility to remember those persons and their characteristics and behaviors. In the study presented here, the care personnel worked with a template of characteristics such as age, gender, social situation, preferred hobbies, previous life in terms of work and family situation as well as medical history, current conditions, medication etc. The only restriction was that the care personnel should create three personas describing different categories of elderly living at a Swedish nursing home.

Brainstorming sessions were held with the care personnel. The aim with these sessions was to suggest new relevant services for the device.

Information from the elderly was gathered by the researchers through individual semi-structured interviews, which often were held during a conversation over coffee. Although the company staff had made a good impression on the elderly, we choose not to involve them in the interviews in order to let the users speak freely about the device and its services.

The collected material was analyzed with regard to differences and similarities; what the elderly had described and what the care personnel had thought about the elderly. Although the care personnel knew the residents well, the comparison needed to be performed on a more general level and the researchers turned to the respondents once more to verify that the interpretations and abstraction passages were correct.

3.3 The Device

Research suggests that use of a TV as platform would reduce new users' uncertainty [2, 12]. Based on this previous research, the TV-platform was believed to have a relative advantage over computers and mobile phones in terms of users' self-reported motivations for starting and continuing to use the system. Hence, this project was built around an innovative mobile communication device called "ippi" (Fig. 1) that was connected to the TV, which worked as an interactive large screen remotely controlled.

When the device was connected to an ordinary TV, the TV could receive and send photos, videos, sounds and text messages to and from mobile phones and computers. The technology behind was based on the mobile phone network for communication. There was a SIM-card in the device, requiring the device to be placed within GSM coverage. It was also possible to send e-mails through the device.

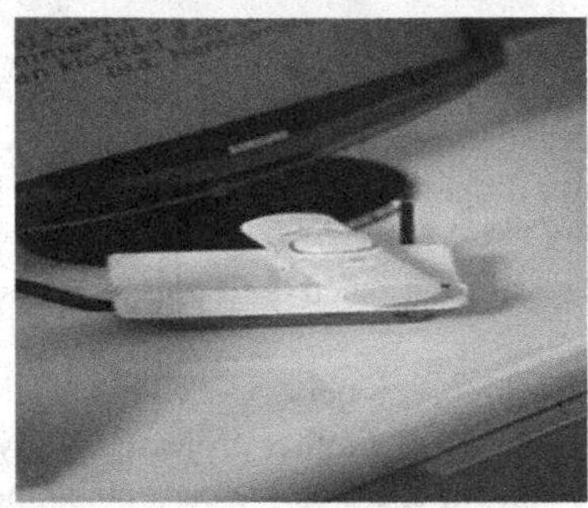

Fig. 1. The novel communication device, called "ippi", connected to the TV-set

The device was considered easy to install; it was plugged into the TV and to the power connector. When a message had been received, the device flashed like an answering machine. The message could be opened with one press on the main button of the remote control. The user of the device could answer the message by writing a text or by sending a voice message. The device could be used for communication between friends and relatives, but also for care-giving purposes, e.g. to inform the older adults which nurse was scheduled to come, which social care services or other activities, which medication etc. were scheduled for that day.

The device had been iteratively developed over three years. The studied (and latest) version consisted of three different user modes addressing different user groups, as designed by the development company. User mode 1 consisted of a limited amount of functionality and was aimed to address the basic needs of elderly without technology experience living at nursing homes. User mode 2 was targeted to a more active user group that still lived on their own, but with nursing or home help support. Some of the most advanced functionalities had been closed to make the device easy to use for people without technology experience. The aim with user mode 3 was to provide full possibilities for mobile communication (text messages, e-mail, sending pictures etc.) for a cognitively active senior living on their own, with or without support from the municipality. These target groups were handled in different studies in the project. In the case study described in this paper user mode 1 was initially used.

Five devices were placed in the residents' apartments and five in dining areas, one in each department and one in the reception, to provide the possibility to refine broadcasting services at the nursing home as well as electronic communication between friends, relatives and the residents.

4 Results

Meetings were held with elderly and workshops with care personnel at the nursing home. The different perspectives of the elderly and the care personnel are presented below.

4.1 Services Suggested and Developed for the Device

The intended main usage of the device was social interaction with friends and relatives, but many other suggestions for services that could be useful for elderly and care personnel came up during the project. For example information services as news, sports and TV-guides were suggested. An important condition of these services was that they should be context-dependent so that they would provide information that was not possible to get elsewhere, i.e. in many cases a local anchor was desired. Local information about activities at the nursing home was a service that was suggested and quickly developed and deployed. An administrative web site of the device was used for broadcasting personal invitations to activities and to administer sign ups for these activities. This service turned out to increase participation at the nursing home activities. A slideshow (shown in the reception) with photos from these activities also turned out to be much appreciated by the elderly.

Based on ideas from the elderly and the care personnel quizzes, riddles and a memory game were developed and introduced at the nursing home. These services were mainly used when the elderly were gathered at common meetings and support was given by the care personnel. There were several other suggestions for services to develop, such as making appointments or order food. However, in an evaluation the most desired services turned out to be the ones that supported social activities, therefore the development company decided to firstly focus on these services.

4.2 Developing Personas with the Care Personnel

To get descriptions of different subgroups of users, a task was given to create a number of personas that represented elderly living at a Swedish nursing home. The care personnel were responsible of the development of the personas. The participants started their work with the personas based on the initial characteristics and thought of some of the elderly living at the nursing home and created the persona descriptions from them. The task seemed to be very fun and engaging. The descriptions were developed with very little input from the researchers, whose task was to write down the descriptions of the personas for further use.

Important in the work was to create a balance between describing real characteristics and behavior and at the same time avoiding descriptions that potentially could point out someone particular. Compared to persona creations in the other project previously mentioned [17] using living role models for the personas was a delicate task. When reflecting upon the two choices; if possible, creating personas using memories of deceased residents was considered preferable by the care professionals, with regard to both ethics and time consumption. The development of the persona descriptions however forced the care personnel to reflect on their residents. To think of a person as he or she used to be was a learning experience, as well as to reflect on the entire person in a salutogenic manner, beyond all medical conditions. It also contributed to gaining a new perspective of the residents since the care personnel was forced to think about them as possible users of new technology.

4.3 Attitudes Towards Technology Among the Care Personnel

In the workshops with the care personnel we asked the participants about their own attitudes towards technology, and how they perceived the attitudes towards technology among the elderly. They all answered positively with respect to the care personnel's own attitudes towards technology. They all had own computers and smart phones, and they were positive towards using ICT in the daily work with the residents.

Regarding how the care personnel perceived attitudes and needs for technology among the elderly the results were less encouraging. Compared to the answers given by the elderly themselves, the care personnel underestimated the technology experience and overlooked that many of the elderly once had worked with technology in different environments. Since the care personnel placed large focus on what they thought about previous experience of computers and its importance for using the device, they initially selected test participants for the project based on technology interest and computer experience. This turned out to be unfortunate, since the selected persons already were included in the digital world and did not see any need for further devices providing the same services.

It was clear that the care personnel did not quite understand for which resident the device could be useful. It was not, as the care personnel had expected, the computer savvy elderly that needed the services the most. On the contrary, when the devices were given to elderly that had no previous experience of new technology but were curious to get a communication channel with people outside the nursing home the new technology became a useful tool. This result is in line with previous studies [2] and may show that sometimes care personnel act as gatekeepers preventing without any clear reason that the elderly are exposed to new technology.

Finally, in the discussions with the care personnel it was also clear that many thoughts about the potential need for technology among the elderly were discussed from the care personnel's point of view. The technology was discussed in terms of how it could be useful in their work with the elderly, rather than how it could be useful for the elderly themselves.

4.4 The Perspective of the Elderly Living at the Nursing Home

The number of elderly participants varied during the project due to illness, changed living conditions and misleading expectations. One expectation was that the device was a tool to increase social interaction. New communication tools often merely provide a new channel for social interaction. The sender and the receiver need to be there. In one case, the resident wanted to communicate more with his family, and was consequently disappointed when the device did not increase this communication. However, for many of the elderly participants the technology strengthened the contact with family and friends, especially for those who had relatives living far away.

In meetings with the elderly it was shown that they appreciated to get messages from their grandchildren, especially when sent to a TV in a public area so they could show other people the messages and the pictures. The possibility to share information about children and grandchildren turned out to be one of the most important needs for the device to fulfill among the elderly. By using the device together with others or with care personnel, there was also the possibility to get support when answering the messages. This way of using the device in public was not at all considered by the developers. From the beginning, the device was supposed to be used by only one person, or by a couple. This novel usage scenario was taken further with different folders created for each user and by informing relatives that their messages were shown in public. This also forced the developers to rethink their idea of user modes, as easy access to individual settings became important.

Another appreciated category of services was "games and quizzes". These services were also used together with others in dining areas or at meetings. Many of the residents desired content that was related to previous times or to history. Personal historical information or information that the person felt he/she had a relationship to was especially appreciated. Other historical content were, at least by some participants, described as not relevant and uninteresting. This reveals another preconception suggesting that most elderly people are interested in history or in things that have happened in the past.

With respect to the device and its interaction ways, some elderly thought it was difficult to use the remote control, especially if one had difficulties with the fine motor skills of the hand. Further, the use of the remote for messaging instead of a keyboard was, by some elderly, perceived as inhibitory since it introduced an unequal situation where the elderly person could not communicate at the same level as the person on the other side (friend, relative etc.). This experience places a focus on the negative aspects of trying to develop easy-to-use devices for elderly. Ways of producing text that are common today was preferable compared to this device designed for "easy clicking".

Further, the user modes had a good intention, but it was questioned and caused irritation. When selecting a user mode for someone, this is done based on stereotypes and without understanding the situation of this person or his motivation to use the device. This can be wrong in both ways, either a too complicated interface is provided or an interface that will be perceived as childish and without possibilities to access all the functionalities that this person regards as needed. The entire concept of user modes needs to be reconsidered. The elderly demand easy access to settings in order to individually build up shortcuts to meaningful functionality instead of pre-designed user modes.

4.5 Evolution During the Project

In the beginning of the project large efforts by the care personnel were placed in getting the devices out to different users. After a while it turned out that the devices were not used as much as expected. The users had got stuck in handling the devices or they lacked the motivation to use them. There were also examples of elderly not having anyone to communicate with through the device.

This initial phase led to the insight among the care personnel that they should aim for participants with rich social network rather than participants with computer experience. The engagement of relatives and grandchildren became a key component, and work with involving the relatives started at the nursing home. Lists of relatives and contact information were gathered and the elderly got help with creating contact lists on their devices.

However, the key to a successful usage lies within the social interaction; that the user actually receives interesting messages and photos, and with a certain frequency. In an evaluation regarding contact with relatives and friends, it turned out that the contact had increased a bit, but not that much as expected. The participants had too small social networks for using the device for communication only with people outside the nursing home compared to their expectations.

Based on an idea from the care personnel more devices were placed in the dining areas of the nursing home. This turned out to be a success and the general usage increased. The main benefit of the device turned out to be social interaction between the residents, and not as expected, interaction with people outside the nursing home. This resulted in positive effects by both elderly and care personnel, when realizing how technology can be used and appropriated when elderly users were given the opportunity to start using novel technology in their own ways, as stated previously by e.g. Wyatt [18] and Östlund [2].

5 Discussion and Conclusions

The aim with this study was to investigate the use of care personnel as mediators for the elderly in the design process. The complexity of the design process is acknowledged, especially when developing towards end-users with whom it is difficult to relate and whose world of experience is different from that of the researcher/designer [19]. The agile co-design method and the care personnel's growing insights about the user groups' need for social technology finally led to succeeding in involving user groups with different impairments and to keep their interest throughout the design process.

However, several initial misunderstandings with respect to the users' preconditions and needs led to a loss of interest from the users. The first selection of participants done by the care personnel were performed based on computer experience, which turned out to be completely wrong since the persons using computers did not need an additional device. The role of the care personnel in the work with selecting elderly participants could be viewed from several perspectives. It could be argued that they protect the elderly from "being used" in different projects and by companies developing products. On the other hand, when the participation of the elderly is arranged by care personnel, it might be harder to convey the elderly users' needs in order to influence the development of new products and services. There is no legal barrier for approaching the elderly users directly, however to be able to conduct a fruitful project within a nursing home, the "externals" have to work with the "internal" care personnel, and as shown in this study the cooperation with the care personnel was irreplaceable from many other perspectives. Similar to Boyd-Graber's results [14] the mediators, in this case the care personnel had difficulties in understanding usage context. Although the study initially showed that the care professionals had difficulties in understanding which elderly could benefit from using the device and which services could be meaningful for the elderly, during the project the care personnel broadened their view of the elderly person as a user of technology. When the care personnel could see other social needs, the technology became used in a meaningful way.

The involvement of the care personnel led to new ideas not thought of initially. The device was originally intended as a device for single usage. But a success factor was achieved when the care personnel placed the devices in the dining areas and used it for social activities and for sharing information together. The possibility to show pictures of friends and family supported the need for a contact with the life outside the nursing home, showing that the residents were more than old patients. From this perspective, the device was not viewed as proprietary in the same way as a mobile phone is an individual property. Similar to the conclusions by Barkhuus and Brown [20], the device became something to socialize around and the TV metaphor shines through with its possibilities to gather around something in common.

This work resulted in many lessons learnt. One could argue that several aspects of this could have been done differently, but it was the hands on experiences that led to the actual insights and the successful results at the end regarding where and how to use the device. As a result of the increased usage in the dining areas of the nursing home, the authors conclude that it may be more fruitful to dare to provide the novel technology in different settings to see what happens, rather than trying to figure out impaired elderly citizens' needs through someone else. A current trend is that much work regarding service development is conducted from a broad perspective in test beds with a large number of ongoing projects only in Sweden. In these environments it will be particularly important to take into account results like the ones from this study, showing that it is not enough to ask care personnel about elderly users needs for technology. The users themselves have to be involved regardless of difficulties related to physical and cognitive limitations.

Acknowledgements. We would like to thank all participants at the nursing home for their hard work and engagement. We also would like to thank the entire project team and the people working with developing the device. Finally we thank the Swedish agency for innovation systems, Vinnova and RnD Seniorium for supporting the project with funding and resources.

References

1. McConatha, D.: Aging Online: Toward a Theory of e-Quality. In: Morrell, R.W. (ed.) Older Adults Health Information and the World Wide Web, (pp. 21–41). Lawrence Erlbaum Associates, New Jersey (2002)
2. Östlund, B., Lindén, K.: Turning older people's experiences into innovations: Ippi as the convergence of mobile services and TV viewing. Gerontechnology **10**(2), 103–109 (2011)
3. Findahl, O.: The Swedes and the Internet. Stockholm: SE-foundation for Internet infrastructure, pp. 14, 30, 31 (2011)
4. Hall, A.K., Bernhardt, J.M., Dodd, V., Vollrath, M.W.: The Digital Health Divide: Evaluating Online Health Information Access and use Among Older Adults. Health Educ Behav. ePub ahead of print, August. PMID: 25156311 (2014)
5. O'rourke K., Heckman J., Elwood D.: Development and Exploration of a Multifaceted Social Platform to Improve Patient Education, Communication, and Activity. Medicine 2.0 (2012)

6. Greenbaum, J., Kyng, M.: Design at work Cooperative design of computer systems, pp. 3–24. Lawrence Erlbaum Associates, New Jersey (1991)
7. Schuler, D., Namioka, A.: Participatory Design Principles and Practicies, pp. 41–77 Lawrence Erlbaum Associates Inc, London (1993)
8. Constantine, L., Lockwood, L.: Software for Use: A practical guide to the Essential Models and Methods of Usage-Centered Design. Addison-Wesley (1999)
9. Jungk, R., Müllert, N.: Future Workshops: How to Create Desirable Futures. Institute for Social Interventions, London (1987)
10. Scandurra, I., Hägglund, M., Koch, S.: From user needs to system specifications: Multi-disciplinary thematic seminars as a collaborative design method for development of health information systems. J. Biomed. Inform. **41**(4), 557–569 (2008)
11. Dickinson, A., Dewsbury, G.: Designing computer technologies with older people. Gerontechnology **5**(1), 1–3 (2006)
12. Scandurra I., Sjölinder M.: Participatory Design With Seniors: Design of Future Services and Iterative Refinements of Interactive eHealth Services for Old Citizens. Med 2.0 2013 2 (2), e12 (2013). doi:10.2196/med20.2729
13. Scandurra I.: Sustainable and Quality-based Communication Services in Elderly Care. R&D Seniorium Report 2011:03. Stockholm (2011) (in Swedish)
14. Boyd-Graber, J., Nikolova, S.S., Moffatt, K.A., Kin, K.C., Lee, J.Y., Mackey, L.W., Tremaine, M.M., Klawe, M.M.: Participatory design with proxies: Developing a desktop-PDA system to support people with aphasia. Computer-Human Interaction (2006)
15. Cooper, A.: The Inmates Are Running the Asylum. Macmillan Publishing Co., Inc, Indianapolis (1999). ISBN 0672316498
16. Shneiderman, B., Plaisant, C.: Designing the User Interface: Strategies for Effective Human-Computer Interaction, 5th edn. Pearson Addison-Wesley, Boston (2009)
17. Scandurra, I., Hägglund, M., Koch, S.: Specific demands for developing IT systems for shared home care - a user centred approach. J. Qual. Life Res. **3**(2), 171–175 (2005)
18. Wyatt S.: Non-users also matter: the construction of users and non-users of the Internet, in: Oudshoorn N., Pinch T. (eds.) How Users Matter: The Co-construction of Users and Technology, Cambridge, MA, USA, pp. 67–79 (2003)
19. Crilly, N., Maier, A., Clarkson, P.J.: Representing artefacts as media: modelling the relationship between designer intent and consumer experience. Int. J. Des. **2**(3), 15–27 (2008)
20. Barkhuus, L., Brown, B.: Unpacking the television: user practices around a changing technology. ACM Trans. Comput-Hum. Interact. **16**(3), 1–22 (2009)

More Light! Improving Well-Being for Persons Suffering from Dementia

Charlotte A. Sust[1(✉)], Peter Dehoff[2], Christina Hallwirth-Spörk[3], Dieter Lang[4], and Dieter Lorenz[5]

[1] ABoVe GmbH, Freiburg, Germany
cas@abovegmbh.de
[2] Zumtobel GmbH, Dornbirn, Austria
peter.dehoff@zumtobel.com
[3] Caritas Socialis, Vienna, Austria
christina.hallwirth-spoerk@cs.or.at
[4] Osram GmbH, Munich, Germany
dieter.lang@osram.com
[5] Technische Hochschule Mittelhessen, Campus Giessen, Giessen, Germany
dieter.lorenz@suk.thm.de

Abstract. Daylight regulates the wake-sleep cycle by acting on specific receptors of the retina that are sensitive to the blue component of the spectrum. Especially in the winter months, the amount of daylight exposure is insufficient for adequate control of the circadian rhythm in many people because they increasingly stay indoors. This is particularly true for elderly or mobility-impaired persons, as well as for residents of care homes, where prevailing levels of illuminance and colour temperature are frequently too low. This not only has negative consequences for the residents' cognition, but also impairs their sleep-wake rhythms. Starting from the hypothesis that suitably designed, biologically effective artificial lighting can compensate for the lack of daylight and lead to regulation of the wake-sleep rhythm, a study comprising approximately 60 participants investigated whether an improvement in the mental and emotional condition of the residents can be achieved. Appropriate lighting was installed in four wards of two Caritas Socialis care homes in Vienna and from October 2012 until April 2013: basic illumination (static, 300 lux, 3000 K) and intervention illumination (dynamic, 800-1200 lux, 3000-6500 K) were alternated (roughly every four weeks). The results indicated that agitated behavior (as measured by the Cohen-Mansfield Agitation Inventory) increased with basic illumination and decreased in the intervention situation. Communicative behavior (observation inventory) was likewise positively influenced, particularly the non-verbal component.

Keywords: Biologically effective lighting · Dementia · Well-being · Field study

1 Dementia and Light/Illumination

1.1 Dementia, Care and Well-Being

Demographic trends have given rise to the increase in the number of dementia patients: age is to some extent the greatest risk factor for dementia [1]. Although many dementia

J. Zhou and G. Salvendy (Eds.): ITAP 2015, Part II, LNCS 9194, pp. 193–200, 2015.
DOI: 10.1007/978-3-319-20913-5_18

patients may initially remain in their own familiar environment, the need for care increases with the progression of the disease. In the late stages of dementia, transfer to a care institution is usually inevitable given the care and assistance requirements [5]. Both informal, caregiving relatives as well as care personnel in the institutions face great challenges in this process. If, in the care and support of those with age-related physical limitations, the compensation of relatives and/or caregivers may become exhausted, such a transfer can easily contribute in a comparatively simple way to the well-being of the patient. These patients can report their well-being relatively simply and immediately to their caregivers and in turn contribute to the job satisfaction of caregivers. This is clearly more complex in the care of dementia patients. On the one hand, the patient may not be able to interpret the caregiving activity, which can cause confusion and anxiety, consequently leading to frustration and aggressive behavior. On the other hand, it is difficult for the caregivers to assess the behavior and mental state of the persons in their care and to arrange their living conditions in such a way that they can feel comfortable. The cycle of reciprocal positive reinforcement is thus frequently difficult with dementia patients.

There is, therefore, a range of approaches to arranging the living and ambient conditions so that dementia sufferers can feel comfortable, although they cannot, or only to a limited extent, communicate this verbally, but tend to react non-verbally or emotionally. These approaches include, for example, various care concepts (e.g. resource activation, basal stimulation, non-pharmacological therapies (occupational therapy, physiotherapy, music therapy) as well as organisational procedures (recurring structures) and last but not least, ambient spatial design [5, 10].

1.2 Dementia and Light/Illumination

The lighting situation is an important aspect of environmental design, and indeed, in several respects is crucial for the elderly, particularly for dementia sufferers. First of all, it means a considerable relief for the elderly when higher illuminance levels can be put into effect. In many existing nursing homes, illuminance levels are too low or so unfavourable that visual orientation is limited and many fine motor activities (crafts, handicrafts) cannot be carried out, or only with great effort.

But yet a further aspect of lighting or illumination can be used to contribute to the well-being of people with dementia. About a decade ago, a receptor in the retina of the eye was detected that responds particularly sensitively to the blue component of daylight and triggers the sleep-wake rhythm through the output of corresponding enzymes [3, 6, 8, 9]. Particularly in the winter months, for many people the amount of daylight exposure is insufficient for adequate control of the wake-sleep rhythm because they increasingly remain indoors. This is also especially true for elderly or mobility-impaired persons, as well as for (dementia-suffering) residents of care homes, where, in addition to levels of illuminance frequently being too low, colour temperatures with a relatively low blue component of the spectrum prevail. That is, the sleep-wake rhythm, which is already frequently disrupted in people with dementia, is more strongly affected by environmental conditions. As a result, the residents sleep less restoratively, which contributes to impairments in mental and physical well-being.

If, then, artificial lighting can compensate for the biologically active effects of insufficient daylight exposure and thereby stabilise the sleep-wake rhythm, this should lead to more restorative sleep and thus ultimately improve the mental and emotional condition, i.e. well-being of the residents. Since the first results from pilot studies were promising [9], a larger study was launched with about 60 participants in order to achieve more robust results.

2 Design and Implementation of the Field Study

Inherently, the question posed in this study is of the operationalisation of well-being, since the subject group of dementia sufferers investigated was not, or not sufficiently able to provide verbal self-reporting. Therefore, a number of aspects were considered which allowed for conclusions to be made on well-being, whereby mainly two aspect are addressed here:

- Communication: earlier studies [9] had already demonstrated that residents in the lighting situation communicated more with fellow residents, relatives and caregivers. In the present investigation, these aspects are augmented by non-verbal communication such as smiling and physical contact as well as communication with "virtual" partners (imagined counterparts, soft toys, dolls and similar). An increase in communication was interpreted as a gain in social participation with positive effects on well-being.
- Agitation: if agitated behaviour is understood to be a reaction to confusion, frustration and/or anxiety, it may be assumed that a reduction in such behaviour suggests a higher degree of relaxation and well-being.

2.1 Investigation Procedure

As shown, a number of different procedures were used in order to obtain an overall impression of the lighting effects. Care personnel - because of their more intensive knowledge of the subjects - as well as external observers and measuring instruments were employed.

The verbal and non-verbal communication behavior of the residents was recorded by observers, who noted the frequency according to predetermined criteria - such as general communication with fellow residents, relatives, volunteers or caregivers, smiling, eye contact, and the like. The observers were first familiarised with the instrument in a workshop, followed by a supervised observation week in the use of the instrument.

The assessment of agitated behaviour was carried out by care personnel, as they are more intensively in contact with the residents over a longer time period. One team of caregivers per ward was appointed to assess the residents at regular intervals (six times in all) using the Cohen-Mansfield Agitation Inventory (CMAI), after having been prepared for this procedure at a workshop [4].

Moreover, using the observation inventory, further behavioural aspects were determined, such as length of stay and mobility in the illuminated area, participation in social activities (crafts, singing etc.), independence in eating and drinking and expressions of emotional state.

In each case, in addition to the CMAI, the Cornell Depression Scale was applied at the same time. Moreover, on the days prior to the observations, the caregivers on night duty also kept a record during their monitoring rounds (as a rule, three) of whether the residents were found to be asleep or awake or were woken up by this.

As an instrumental measurement method, twelve beds were equipped with sensors for non-contact measurement of sleep and movement, and 40 of the residents investigated were willing to wear Actiwatches (generally 24 h over the entire study period) for recording their movement (actigraphy).

2.2 Illumination Conditions

On all wards, a lighting situation was created for the communal areas, in which the residents could stay under daylight-like conditions during the morning and early afternoon hours. These ceilings were equipped with corresponding flat illumination which enabled the implementation of different lighting situations (Fig. 1).

Fig. 1. Illuminated ceiling in the communal area (Caritas Socialis Old People's and Care Home, Rennweg).

In each case, two different lighting situations were implemented: a basic version with an illuminance of 500 lux and a warm white colour temperature (3000 K), and an intervention situation with a higher illuminance (1200 lux) and a daylight-like spectrum (approx. 6500 K) during the time from 09.00 to 15.00 h, and then from the afternoon (15.00 h) with a reduced light intensity (800 lux) and warm white color temperature (3000 K). The lighting conditions were programmed via a corresponding automated control unit.

2.3 Procedure

The investigation was carried out on four wards in two Caritas Socialis care homes in Vienna, two of the wards in Kalksburg, a south-westerly suburb (23rd District) and one ward distributed over two floors in Rennweg in the 3rd District (which was treated as two wards for observation and evaluation, see below).

Both light situations were implemented alternately, starting in October 2012 with the basic version (BL1), November 2012 to early January 2013: intervention situation (LS1), from January 2013 to February 2013: basic variant (BL2) February to March 2013: intervention situation (LS2), March to mid-April: basic version (BLvZ, BLnZ, respectively, before/after time change).

The observations were carried out on Tuesdays to Thursdays, between 10.30 and 13.00 h as well as between 14.00 and 17.00 h. In the period from 15 December 2012 to 6 January 2013 no observations took place. During the nights before the observations the night duty staff recorded, according to specified criteria, whether they found the residents asleep or awake during their rounds.

2.4 Subjects

The investigation started with 58 subjects (approx. 25 % men), of whom approximately two thirds (N = 38) participated in the entire investigation. The average age was 83 years and the subjects were predominantly single.

3 Report and Discussion of Selected Results

From the wide range of data, two aspects are discussed below, which, as detailed at the outset, can be interpreted as indicators of an improvement in well-being.

3.1 Agitation

The CMAI to survey agitated behavior was filled in a total of six times by the specially dedicated teams of each ward. Here, the CMAI subscales "physically aggressive behavior," "physically non-aggressive behavior," "verbal aggression" and "hoarding/hiding," are also combined in one overall value. The data were analysed by means of parameter-free rank analysis of variance (Fig. 2 includes the representation of rank sums) [2].

Except for the subscale hoarding/hiding, all scales show significant reductions (0.05) in agitated behavior in the intervention situations calculated with the CMAI. That is, when the lighting situation is returned to the basic variant, agitated behavior increased again. This is particularly dramatic in the midwinter situation: the lighting situation (LS1) in the second week of January was returned to the basic variant (BL2)

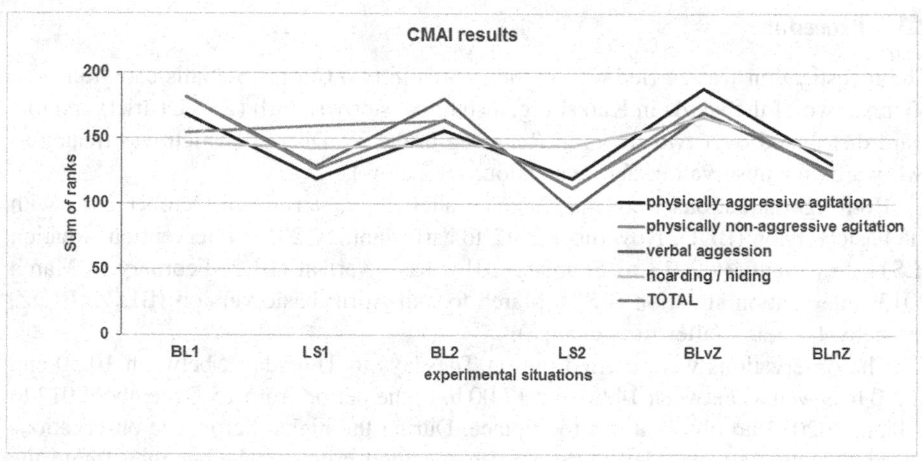

Fig. 2. Results of the subscales and the total value of the CMAI for residents participating over the entire period (BL: Basic lighting situation, LS: Intervention situation; vZ/nZ: before/after time change).

and thus the values in the CMAI rose immediately, while with the onset of next intervention situation the values fell again.

3.2 Communication

Similar results can also be observed when considering the values for communicative behavior, in particular the non-verbal behavior. Especially when the dementia is far advanced, the non-verbal level becomes increasingly significant. For example, it is easier for a dementia sufferer to respond with a smile instead of a verbal response. Even the conversation with an imagined counterpart or with a doll viewed as a child is no less real and satisfying for people with dementia than with a real person, in particular because they largely control the scope of verbal interaction themselves here.

Overall, non-verbal communication behavior demonstrated more clearly that in the lighting intervention situations communication is more frequent. Here, too, the significant drop could be seen in the midwinter period when returning from the intervention situation to the basic variant (Fig. 3). The second lighting situation did not have the anticipated positive effect, at least on verbal communication, but could only stabilise the situation here; a slight increase in non-verbal communication was, however, brought about. Here, seasonal effects may have played a role but also the fact that during the second intervention situation, significant changes occurred through several incidences of new occupancy on three wards within a four-week period. On the ward least affected, a significant increase in communication could be recorded (Fig. 4).

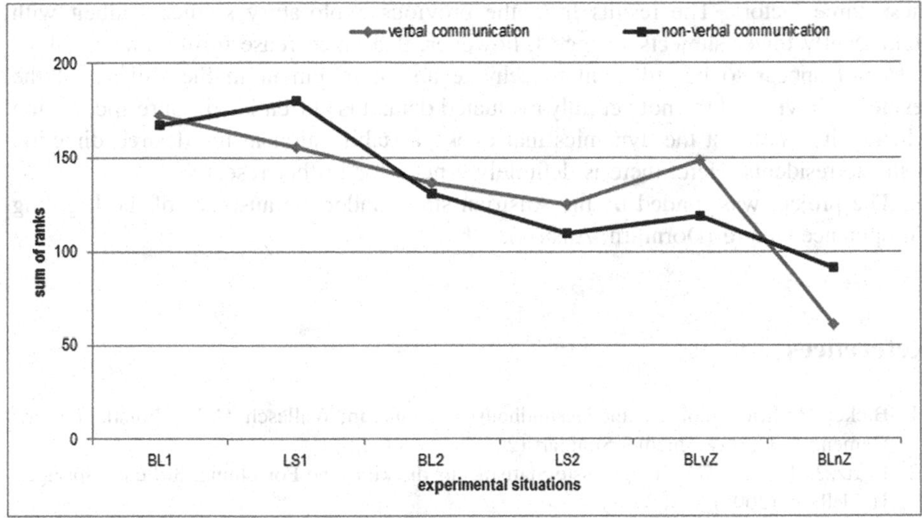

Fig. 3. Results of the frequency of verbal and non-verbal communication for residents participating over the entire period (B: Basic lighting situation, LS: Intervention situation; vZ/nZ: before/after time change).

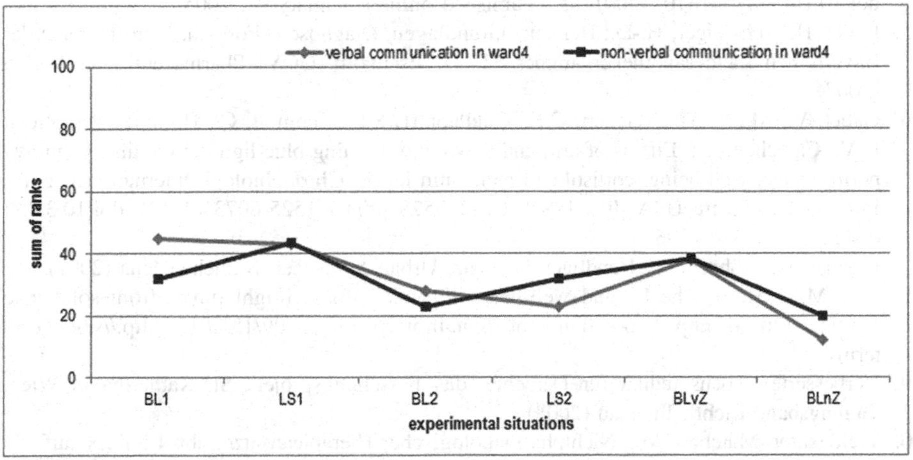

Fig. 4. Results of the frequency of verbal and non-verbal communication for residents participating over the entire period in ward 4 (B: Basic lighting situation, LS: Intervention situation; vZ/nZ: before/after time change).

4 Conclusion and Outlook

Based on the data analysed so far, it is not yet possible to unambiguously determine whether the improvement that occurred was due to the increased illumination or the dynamics of the lighting situation or the higher color temperature or the combination of these three factors. The results from the previous exploratory studies - albeit with significantly fewer subjects - suggest, however, that an increase in illuminance alone does not appear to be sufficient to achieve an improvement in the welfare of the residents. In view of the not yet fully evaluated data, it is currently still pure speculation whether it is not just the dynamics that evoke a stabilisation in the desired direction with the residents. Here, there is definitely a need for further research.

The project was funded by the Austrian state, under the auspices of the Lighting Competence Centre (Dornbirn, Austria).

References

1. Bickel, H.: Epidemiologie und Gesundheitsökonomie. In: Wallesch, C.-W., Förstl, H. (eds.) Demenzen. Gustav Thieme, Stuttgart (2005)
2. Bortz, J., Lienert, G.: Kurzgefasste Statistik für die klinische Forschung, 3rd edn. Springer, Heidelberg (2008)
3. Brainard, G.C., Hanifin, J.P., Greeson, J.M., Byrne, B., Glickman, G., Gerner, E., Rollag, M.D.: Action spectrum for melatonin regulation in humans: evidence for a novel circadian photoreceptor. J. Neurosci. **21**(16), 6405–6412 (2001)
4. Cohen-Mansfield, J., Marx, M.S., Werner, P.: Agitation in elderly persons: an integrative report of findings in a nursing home. International Psychogeriatrics, **4**(4), 221–240 (1992). doi:10.1017/S1041610292001285; (Published online): January 07, 2005
5. Förstl, H., Schweiger, H.-D.: Demenz. Grundlagen, Diagnostik. Formen. Schriftenreihe der Bayerischen Landesapothekerkammer, H. 74. Eschborn: GOVI Pharmazeutischer Verlag (2007)
6. Gabel, V., Maire, M., Reichert, C.F., Chellappal, S.L., Schmidt, C., Hommes, V., Viola, U.V., Cajochen, C.:. Effects of artificial dawn and morning blue light on daytime cognitive performance, well-being, cortisol and melatonin levels. Chronobiology International, 1–10, Informa Healthcare USA, Inc. ISSN: 0742–0528 print / 1525-6073 (2013). doi:10.3109/07420528.2013.793196
7. Kastner, U., Löbach, R.: Handbuch Demenz. Urban & Fischer, München Jena (2007)
8. Rea, M.S.: Human health and well-being: Promises for a bright future from solid-state lighting. (2013). http://proceedings.spiedigitallibrary.org/ on 09/13/2013. http://spiedl.org/terms
9. Verbesserte Lebensqualität für Demente: das Forschungsprojekt St. Katharina in Wien, Tagungsband Licht , Ilmenau (2008)
10. Weidekamp-Maicher, M.: Nichtpharmakologische Therapieansätze: ihr Einfluss auf die Lebensqualität Demenzkranker und die Rolle der Messinstrumente. Z Gerontol Geriat, 2013. **46**, 134–143 (2009). doi:10.1007/s00391-012-0341-3

The Design of Pain Management and Creative Service for Older Adults with Chronic Disease

Wang-Chin Tsai[1(✉)], Chia-Ling Chang[2], and Hsuan Lin[1,3]

[1] Department of Product and Media Design, Fo Guang University, Yilan, Taiwan
forwangwang@gmail.com

[2] Department of Creative Product Design and Management, Far East University, Tainan, Taiwan
idit007@gmail.com

[3] Department of Cultural Creative Design, Tainan University of Technology, Tainan, Taiwan
te0038@mail.tut.edu.tw

Abstract. Chronic Disease is expected to affect approximately 3 million older adults by the year 2030 in Taiwan. It is one of the top causes of disability, mobility problems, and chronic pain among older adults. With so many individuals affected, it is important to identify how to effectively manage the pain associated with chronic pain disease. The purpose of the present research was to understand the factors and needs critical to the successful management of chronic pain and to create the management and service tools currently available to the older adults. We conducted structured interviews with subject matter experts, target user, and brainstorming for the pain management development. All of the process reviewed were found to be current chronic problem pain lacking in several key areas, such as failing to include critical variables and difficulty integrating the data collected into a meaningful representation of one's pain experience. Resolving these issues will improve the quality of life for individuals suffering from chronic pain. The researches provides 3 pain care system concepts through the convenience of household devices combined with cloud computing technology, touch interface and information design (The Pain Tracker, The Pain Helper, The Pain Exerciser). According to older patients with chronic pain, considering the both of physiological and psychological part of the demand to conduct innovative service design, the health care self-management concept will enhance the better quality of life of older chronic patients.

Keywords: Chronic pain · Older adults · Pain management

1 Introduction

According to the statistical data from the Ministry of the Interior (2012), Taiwan, published at the end of May 2012 (the 101st year of the Republic of China), 10.14 % of Taiwan's population was older than 65 years. The proportion of elderly persons in the population was estimated to reach 19.7 % (Ministry of the Interior, 2010) by 2031 (the 120th year of the Republic). With the rapid increase in the elderly population, the

J. Zhou and G. Salvendy (Eds.): ITAP 2015, Part II, LNCS 9194, pp. 201–210, 2015.
DOI: 10.1007/978-3-319-20913-5_19

health of the elderly has become a concern. Statistical analysis showed that chronic illnesses account for nine of the top 10 causes of death among the elderly in Taiwan (Department of Health, 2009). Moreover, according to data from the Statistics Office of the Ministry of the Interior (2000), 76.06 % of the elderly citizens have chronic illnesses. Based on this disease pattern, chronic illnesses can be considered as the leading cause of death and a major threat to the health of the elderly. Although age itself is not an illness, the physiological changes and reduced functionality that come with it increase the risks of health problems and disabilities. In addition, health problems in the elderly are often complicated by comorbidity, concomitancy, concurrency, and cumulative or additive conditions. They are also mostly chronic in nature. In view of this, the Department of Health (2011) has been actively promoting chronic illness prevention and health maintenance plans in recent years. It has also promoted awareness of the measures to prevent chronic illness and maintain health in order to popularize and elevate the quality of care of the elderly with chronic illnesses.

Of the chronic illnesses in the elderly, pain is the most common symptom and has the greatest effect on their quality of life. Pain can exacerbate the symptoms of an illness and cause unexpected bodily changes. For example, pain in a patient with a heart condition may trigger myocardial infarction. A clinical documentation indicated "soaring blood pressure due to pain, causing the patient to suffer intracranial hemorrhage," which is a life-threatening condition. Pain can also reduce patient quality of life. An investigation by Partners Against Pain (PAP) in the United States found that once pain occurs, the basic functions of life deteriorate. The most common effect of pain is insomnia, which occurs in 56 % of cases, followed by emotional effects in 51 % of cases. Furthermore, pain causes the inability to operate a vehicle in in 30 % of cases, lack of sex drive in 28 %, and loss of appetite in 7 %. In addition, pain can cause economic losses. The US Center for Disease Control and Prevention conducted a statistical census on health among US citizens and discovered that approximately 76 million Americans have chronic pain distress (Davis and White 2008*), far exceeding the number of patients with diabetes, heart disease, and cancer. In terms of medical expenses and loss of productivity, chronic pain costs Americans an average of $100 billion per year.*

Chronic pain can limit a sufferer's activities, is associated with social isolation and depression, presents challenges to sense of self, and can dramatically affect quality of life (Berman et al. 2009*). Older people with chronic pain are likely to experience more physical impairments and interference with activities than younger people, and patterns of pain location tend to broaden with age. Widespread pain may especially affect the progression of disability and impaired mobility (Blondal and Halldorsdottir* 2009*). The subjective experience of chronic pain, in particular negative thinking and stress, can play an important role in the management of pain, communication of pain to others, and treatment outcomes and can exacerbate pain or the disease process leading to pain. Self-care strategies for managing stress, facilitating positive coping behaviors, or reducing anxiety may be especially effective for mediating psychological and social components of pain management (Foster* 2007*). For instance, behavioral-cognitive therapies often focus on maladaptive coping responses, perceived helplessness, and low self-efficacy for pain management (Hirsh* et al. 2009*). These therapies, including mind-body approaches, have demonstrated benefits for a wide variety of pain* *conditions, particularly interventions with multiple components or approaches. They have been associated with reductions in pain frequency, pain intensity, pain duration, depression, anxiety, and medication use, as well as improvements in self-efficacy, ability to control pain, coping, activity levels, and health-related quality of life (Medynskiy and Mynatt* 2010*).*

There is growing evidence that older adults will use and benefit from technological complementary and alternative medicine and mind-body therapies (Borders et al. 2005*). Future cohorts of baby boomers may be more inclined to use such therapies because there are more older adults are likely to turn to the cloud technology for health information. Delivering self-care pain management service* via *the cloud technology may be of particular benefit for people in chronic pain who are isolated or have difficulty leaving the home (Peat* et al. 2001*). Technological access to self-care pain management service overcomes previously identified barriers to participation among older people such as lack of transportation, inability to travel, time conflicts, and reluctance to participate in a group or associate with other frail individuals. The benefits of technological self-care pain management service for a variety of health conditions appear to be comparable to in-person interventions. For instance, a cloud technology -based chronic disease self-management program demonstrated improvements in self-efficacy and health status, and a web-based stress management intervention showed reduced stress and improvements in ability to manage stress. Technological self-care pain management service addressing pain due to a variety of conditions have also been associated with decreased pain and increased control over pain; reduced catastrophizing of pain and maladaptive coping; reduced disability and improved role function; reduced depression and perceived stress; decreased physician visits and time spent in hospitals; and increased work hours.*

With the imminent aging of societies and the increasing tendency of illnesses to become chronic, more elderly people will develop chronic illnesses in the future (Van Baar et al. 1998*). Perfecting self-care of pain will not only satisfy the health needs of the elderly but also help them achieve their maximum potential within their limitations due to their diseases, maintain their health and independence, increase their control over their lives, and help them achieve their optimal physiological, psychological, and social conditions. Therefore, self-management of pain in chronic illnesses is a most basic level of health care for the elderly and the most important self-care strategy.*

2 Technological Self-Care Pain Management Service Design Process

2.1 Prospective Science and Technology

This prospective plan anticipates the use of mobile medical technology and applications, combined with various mobile and wearable devices equipped with relevant hardware and software for information security and functional authentication. Mobile medical care overturns the traditional health-care relationships. Its application is no longer confined to face-to-face treatments at fixed locations or to computer terminals. The development of mobile medicine is aimed toward overcoming the limitations of time and space, and combining mobile equipment with the hospital information system (HIS) in order to implement mobile medical care. It will instantaneously provide elderly patients with chronic diseases with all types of pain information, record-keeping systems, and querying via the cloud infrastructure.

With the full development of key technologies, including WiMAX, RFID, Sensor, and RF, the aim is to use these technologies to integrate all pain self-monitoring and management systems. With the cooperation of remote care centers, the elderly population can be offered comprehensive, instantaneous pain management care. Family members can use remote medical care application software on their cell phones to check on any facet of their elder's chronic illness pain management status at any time and place, even overseas. Families can then work together to promote the health of their elders and improve family interaction.

2.2 Design Process

The design process included the following steps: design concept and scope, existing product analysis, brainstorming and creative thinking, concept sketches, design concept revision, and concept solidification procedures. Then, the design concepts were finalized and presented.

A. Design concept and scope
This stage of the design work was based on the basic goal and direction of the design. Creative concepts were proposed according to the concept schemata derived from lifestyle analyses and approved in order to fix the scope and direction of the design (Fig. 1).

Fig. 1. Image *board for the design concept and scope*

B. Brainstorming and creative thinking
After converging on chronic pain and lifestyles of the elderly, we conducted the first-stage brainstorming and creative thinking session to identify forward-looking design concepts and key words (Fig. 2).

C. Concept sketch
We sorted through the concepts generated in the previous step, narrowing down the options and selecting the most innovative concept directions. We ended up with three major conceptual directions for product development.

D. Design concept revision
After repeated proposals to amend the concepts, we invited a professional designer to suggest improvements of the three conceptual products and to supplement or correct any conceptual deficiencies (Fig. 3).

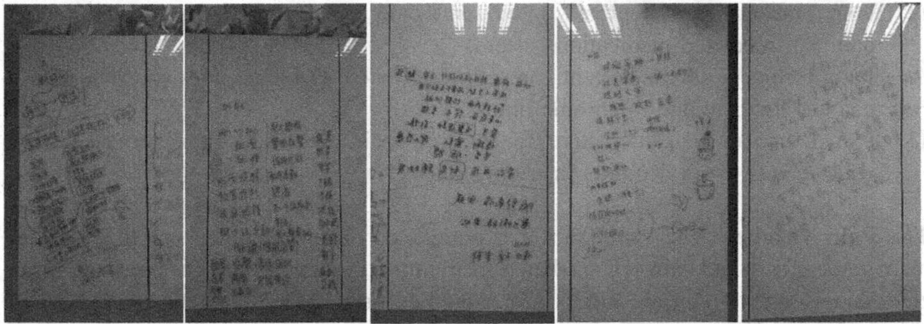

Fig. 2. The *outcome of brainstorming*

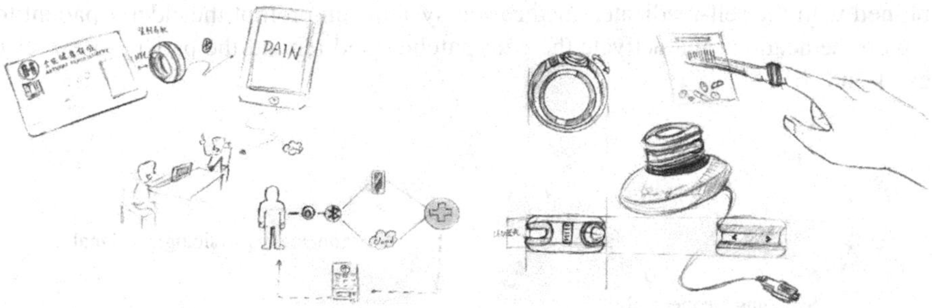

Fig. 3. Design *concept sketches*

E. Solidification of the concepts
   We further revised the three concepts from the previous steps and solidified their details in this step. We used three-dimensional (3-D) software rendering to present the integration of specific modes of operation, technology applications, visual design, and aesthetic appearance.

3 Design Results

3.1 3 Concepts for the Technological Self-Care Pain Management Service

By using the convenience of intelligent, wearable devices; physiological detection technology; wireless communications; and cloud-based medical care technology, we devised products and information interface designs. Based on the physiological and psychological needs of elderly patients with pain due to chronic illness, we innovated the service design and constructed a series of pain management and service products, which we called "The Pain Project." The Pain Project includes the following:

(1) Pain Tracker – an integrated, intelligent, pain management ring and automated pain self-mediated medication system.
(2) Pain Helper – an intelligent, prescription patch machine with touch-sensitive patches for pain due to chronic illness.
(3) Pain Exerciser – an interactive, far-infrared, pain and health management device with somatosensory motion instrumentation.

The Pain Tracker. The Pain Tracker is composed of an integrated, intelligent, pain management ring and pain self-mediated medication system. At the onset of pain in an elderly person with chronic illness, the ring measures the sympathetic physiological signals created by the autonomic nervous system. It records the time of the onset of pain, the frequency of pain, and the R-R high- and low-frequency changes. The elderly person can also twist the ring to view a subjective pain index and record a vocal description of the chronic pain symptoms. The information can be transmitted over the cloud to an assisting physician for an accurate evaluation of the pain condition. This combined with the self-medicated medication system can prompt the elderly patient to take pain medications and activate the pain patches, and remind the patient to exercise (Figs. 4 and 5).

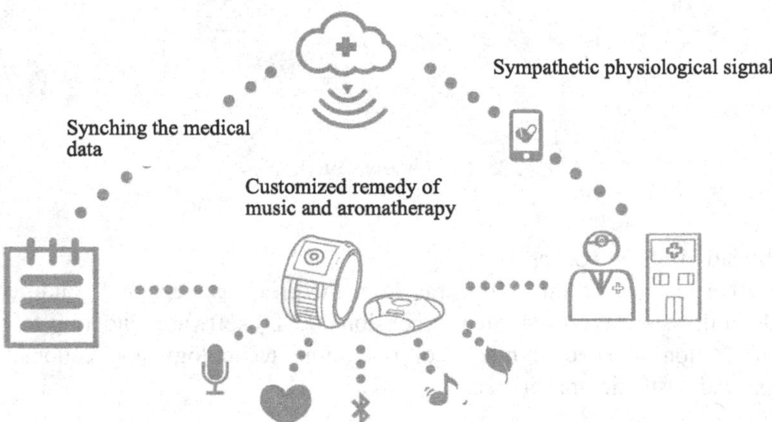

Fig. 4. The *framework of pain tracker service*

The Pain Helper. The Pain Helper is an intelligent, prescription patch machine for pain in chronic illness that is available in pharmacies. It offers intelligent pain-relieving patches to elderly patients with different levels of chronic illness-related pain. When the Pain Helper receives the pain signal from the Pain Tracker, the patient's prescription data is sent over the cloud, and the machine can immediately make an intelligent pain patch tailored to the patient's need. On the screen, it can display relevant health education information. The machine has different built-in pain medications that can be refilled or replaced. When the elderly patient pushes the sensing pad on the intelligent patch, the chronic pain medication is evenly distributed onto the patch and the

Fig. 5. Prototype *of pain tracker*

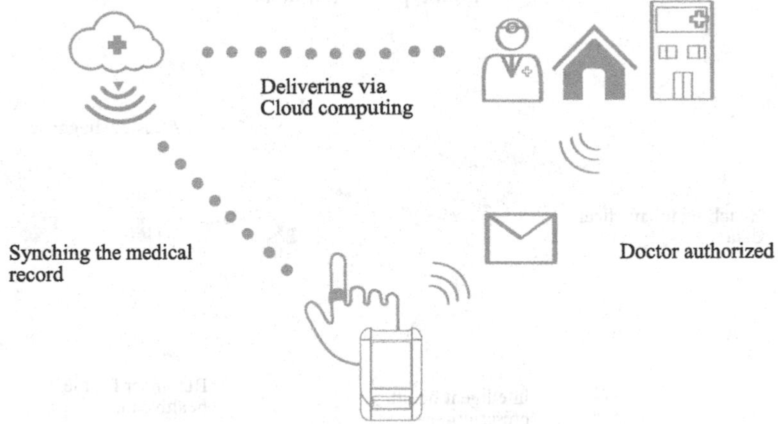

Fig. 6. The *framework of pain helper service*

time-recording function is activated. This helps the patient use the patch correctly (Figs. 6 and 7).

The Pain Exerciser. *The Pain Exerciser is an intelligent device that offers hand and foot exercises and far-infrared treatment to elderly people with chronic illness-related pain. Through a 3-D floating laser projection technology, it creates images of different sports themes. Paired somatosensory devices on the hands and feet detect posture and control the projected image. It promotes peripheral blood circulation. Combined with far-infrared treatment, it improves the oxygen supply efficiency of the body and the*

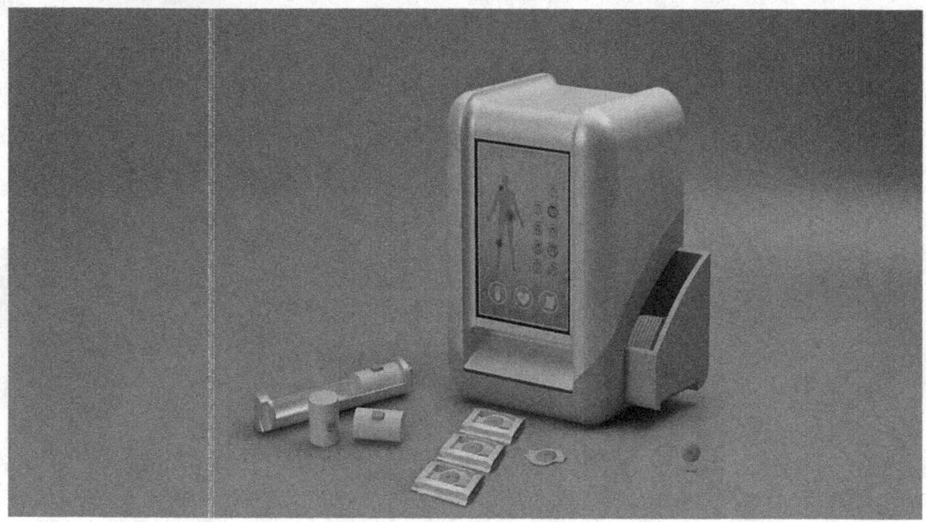

Fig. 7. Prototype *of pain helper*

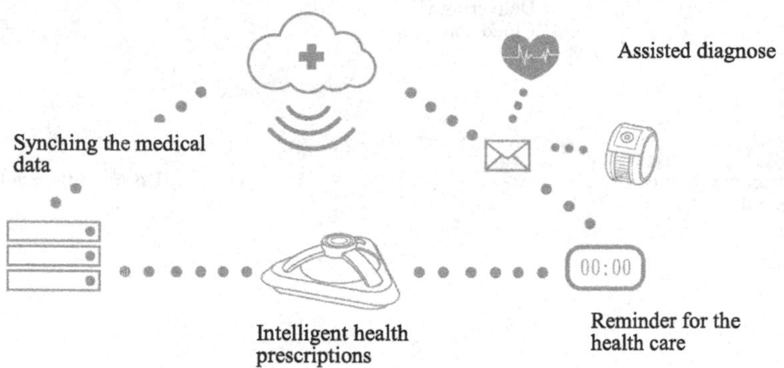

Fig. 8. The *framework of pain exerciser service*

effectiveness of exercise for the treatment of chronic illness-related pain. Relevant exercise data are also simultaneously recorded by the Pain Tracker to provide the physician with auxiliary clinical pain data for diagnosis (Figs. 8 and 9).

This research specifically aimed to emphasize the importance of understanding and managing chronic pain among the elderly. It combined academic research with design practice. Moreover, it supports interdisciplinary design creativity and exemplifies the synergy between the humanities and sciences.

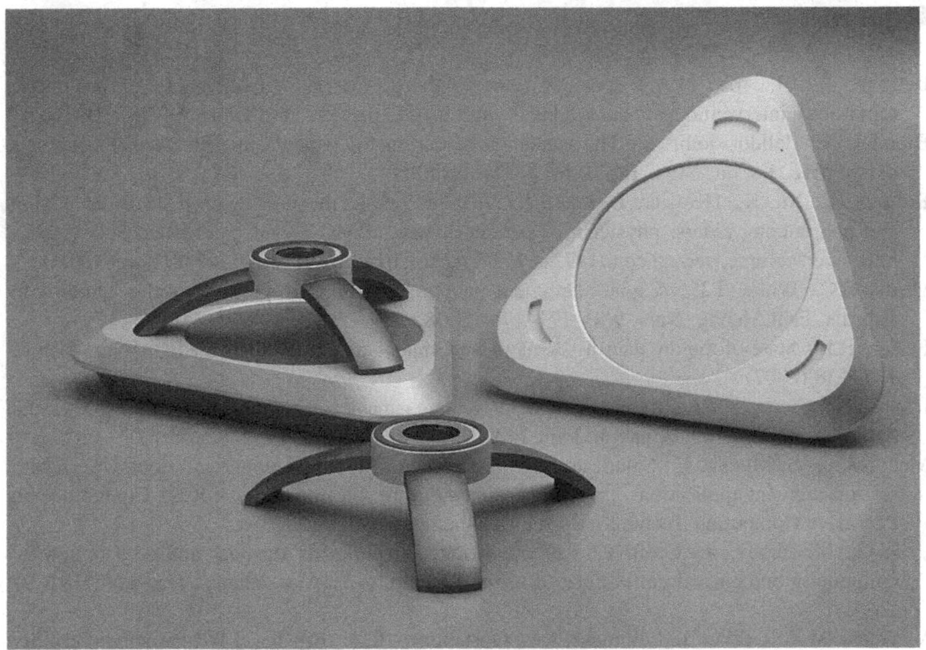

Fig. 9. Prototype *of pain exerciser*

4 Conclusion

This study has demonstrated that older adults will use and can benefit from a relatively technological self-care pain management service that provides easy to use mind-body self-care techniques. Such an intervention may empower older adults in chronic pain to engage in self-care, focus on managing pain in a positive way, and integrate what they learn into their daily routines. Thus, a technological self-care pain management service intervention can be suitable for older adults who have various and multiple health problems. Although this study targeted older adults, such interventions are also amenable for use by adults of younger ages, as the techniques and exercises are not specific to older people. Reaching those in chronic pain can be a challenge, as pain often limits mobility and leads to social isolation and depression, thereby undermining motivation to engage in self-care or attend educational sessions. Those who are unwilling or unable to set to hospital or who are reluctant to learn techniques in a group setting may especially appreciate the convenience and privacy of technological self-care pain management service. Offering mind-body self-care techniques via the technology is a promising strategy for complementing medical care and insight medication for older adults and others in chronic pain.

Acknowledgments. This research was received partly financial support from the National Science Council of the Republic of China Government, under Grant No. NSC 102-2218-E-431 - 001 - The authors would like to acknowledge the contributions of Dr. Dai-We Ro in providing guidelines and advices for medical consultation of this paper.

References

Berman, R.L.H., Iris, M.A., Bode, R., Drengenberg, C.: The effectiveness of an online mind-body intervention for older adults with chronic pain. J. Pain **10**(1), 68–79 (2009)

Blondal, K., Halldorsdottir, S.: The challenge of caring for patients in pain: from the nurse's perspective. J. Clin. Nurs. **18**(20), 2897–2906 (2009)

Borders, T., Xu, K., Heavner, J., Kruse, G.: Patient involvement in medical decision-making and pain among elders: physician or patient-driven?. BMC Health Serv. Res. **5**(4) (2005). http://www.biomedcentral.com/1472–6963/5/4. doi:10.1186/1472-6963-5-4 (Retrieved)

Davis, G.C., White, T.L.: A goal attainment pain management program for older adults with arthritis. Pain Manag. Nurs. **9**(4), 171–179 (2008)

Foster, R.L.: State-of-the-art pain assessment and management. J. Spec. Pediatr. Nurs. **12**(3), 137–138 (2007)

Hirsh, A.T., George, S.Z., Robinson, M.E.: Pain assessment and treatment disparities: a virtual human technology investigation. Pain **143**(1–2), 106–113 (2009)

Medynskiy, Y., Mynatt, E.: Salud! an open infrastructure for developing and deploying health self-managment applications. In: Paper presented at the 4th International ICST Conference on Pervasive Computing Technologies for Healthcare, Munich (2010)

Peat, G., McCarney, R., Croft, P.: Knee pain and osteoarthritis in older adults: a review of community burden and current use of primary health care. Ann. Rheum. Dis. **60**(2), 91–97 (2001)

Van Baar, M.E., Dekker, J., Lemmens, J.A., Oostendorp, R.A., Bijlsma, J.W.: Pain and disability in patients with osteoarthritis of hip or knee: the relationship with articular, kinesiological, and psychological characteristics. J. Rheumatol. **25**, 125–133 (1998)

The Design of Mobile Technology to Support Diabetes Self-Management in Older Adults

Laura A. Whitlock, Anne Collins McLaughlin(✉), Maurita Harris, and Jessica Bradshaw

North Carolina State University, Raleigh, NC, USA
{lawhitlo,anne_mclaughlin,mtharri6,jlbrads3}@ncsu.edu

Abstract. Type 2 diabetes is a concern for older adults and an increasing concern for society as the percentage of older persons rises across the globe. Though potentially deadly, it is a disease that responds well to self-management through behavior: adherence to dietary guidelines, medication regimens, and exercise. However, older persons with type 2 diabetes tend to self-manage poorly, despite educational initiatives. Based on a review of the challenges faced by persons with type 2 diabetes and the state of existing highly rated diabetes self-management applications, we propose a list of design practices and core features most needed in mobile technologies designed to support the self-management of diabetes in older adults.

Keywords: Older adults · Aging · Chronic health condition · Type 2 diabetes · Mobile technology · App · Support

1 Introduction

In the United States and across the world, the number of older persons compared to younger has reached a level never before seen in human history. The United Nations has described the current trend in global population aging as unprecedented, pervasive, and enduring, and has stated it will have profound implications for many facets of human life (UN, 2001). In the United States alone the population of adults aged 65 and older is expected to nearly double from 37 million in 2005 to 72 million in 2030 (He, Sengupta, Velkoff, & DeBarros, 2005). With the benefit of extended lifespan comes a longer amount of time when people may experience age-related health conditions. Ideally, the extended years the current and future generations are expected to experience will be vibrant and marked by extended independence. However, to achieve this goal society and technology will need to be adapted to the higher percentage of older adults in the population, particularly technology that focuses on the management and amelioration of age-related diseases and their effects on physical and psychological health.

Chief among age-related diseases is type 2 diabetes, estimated to affect ~ 27% of older adults in the United States in diagnosed or undiagnosed form (Cowie et al. 2009). Furthermore, it is also estimated that an additional 40 % of older adults have prediabetes (Cowie et al. 2009), a state of elevated blood glucose that does not yet qualify as diabetes but indicates an increased risk of developing diabetes as well as an increased

J. Zhou and G. Salvendy (Eds.): ITAP 2015, Part II, LNCS 9194, pp. 211–221, 2015.
DOI: 10.1007/978-3-319-20913-5_20

risk of heart disease and stroke. Due in part to diet and in part to the larger percentage of older adults, type 2 diabetes is increasing worldwide, noted by the World Health Organization as the "slow-motion catastrophe" of a rising trend in chronic, noncommunicable disease (Chan 2011). It is currently the seventh leading cause of death in the United States (CDC 2011). With two-thirds of the older adult population of the United States estimated to either be at risk of diabetes or to already have the disease, it is one of the greatest health concerns facing older adults today and in the foreseeable future.

Type 2 diabetes has serious health consequences if not managed and treated, as the pancreas fails to regulate insulin in response to dietary sugars. Over time, elevated blood glucose raises the risk of heart and kidney diseases, stroke, blindness, limb dysfunction, amputation, and chronic pain as the result of nerve damage. A four-community epidemiological study found that older adults with diabetes experienced substantial comorbidity with report visual problems, major physical disability, and hospitalizations during the past year (Moritz et al. 1994). Low blood sugar levels bring their own dangers as well, including high rates of Alzheimer's disease and dementia (Yaffe et al. 2013). Despite these dangers and side effects from the disease, there is hope for those suffering from type 2 diabetes. Studies of self-management find diabetes symptoms can be controlled and the onset of the disease delayed in high-diabetes risk persons who keep tight control of their blood sugar levels through diet and exercise (DPPRG, 2002; Lindström et al. 2003).

1.1 Challenges of Self-Management

However, persons with type 2 diabetes do not tend to control their blood sugar levels well, including even the most health-literate older adults (Boren 2009; Klein & Meininger 2004; Shigaki et al. 2010). A meta-analysis of ~ 10,000 patients found that even after a self-management training program, improvements in blood sugar levels were small - indicating that type 2 patients need more than education (Klein et al. 2013).

Problems with effective self-management appear to be both cognitive and motivational in nature. Type 2 diabetes is notable because of the necessity for patients to manage their own condition by actively engaging in self-management behaviors (Skinner et al. 2006). These behaviors include self-monitoring of blood glucose via at-home glucometers, medication adherence (including for some, administering insulin shots as needed), adherence to a diet appropriate for the individual's level of insulin resistance and medication use, physical activity, and visiting healthcare practitioners for diabetes-related health checks. Some of these self-management behaviors are cognitively complex and involve processes like problem detection and identification, sensemaking, decision making, and planning/replanning (Klein & Lippa 2008). Because of these cognitive requirements, successful self-management is not an easy rule-based procedure. It necessitates "the fitting of complex and sometimes contradictory information into a coherent picture that generates a reasonable action strategy" (Klein & Lippa 2012), a dynamic control task that patients are often unable to understand and perform (Klein & Lippa 2008).

Persons with diabetes who experience trouble with this dynamic control task will likely experience even greater trouble in the future due to the apparent causal link between poor diabetes control and cognitive decline. Poor diabetes control is associated with both diagnosed and undiagnosed cognitive dysfunction (Munshi et al. 2006), and current findings suggest that poor diabetes control precedes cognitive decline in older adults. A four-year prospective study of cognitive change in older adults found that women with impaired glucose tolerance at baseline had four times the risk of major cognitive decline on a verbal fluency test after the four year period when compared to women with normal glucose tolerance at baseline (Kanaya, Barrett-Connor, Gildengorin, & Yaffe, 2004). A meta-analysis of prospective studies of cognitive decline in persons with diabetes found a 1.6-fold increase in the odds of future dementia (Cukierman, Gerstein, & Williamson, 2005). These findings suggest that poorly managed diabetes can rob patients of the abilities most needed to manage their disease well.

Furthermore, because the patient must choose to engage in these behaviors on his or her own, the emotional and motivational factors affecting self-management behavior are especially important when considering how to improve diabetes management. Major depression in persons with diabetes is associated with worse self-management, including less physical activity, poorer diet, and lower rates of medication adherence (Lin et al. 2004). This is particularly concerning since diabetes is in itself associated with a higher risk of depression than that of the nondiabetic population (Anderson, Freedland, Clouse, & Lustman, 2001; Peyrot & Rubin 1997). The stress of managing diabetes may directly contribute to depression; more frequent blood glucose self-monitoring can be associated with negative psychological well-being outcomes including higher levels of distress, worries, and depressive symptoms (Franciosi 2001). There is also some evidence that improving individuals' capacity to cope with stress can improve diabetes management. A randomized controlled trial found that teaching acceptance coping strategies to adults with diabetes improved both self-reported self-management behaviors and HbA1c values, an indicator of glycemic control over time (Gregg, Callaghan, Hayes, & Glenn-Lawson, 2007).

2 Supporting Self-Management via Technology

The development and use of smartphone applications ("apps") to assist with diabetes self-management is a rapidly growing area, driven in part by increases in smartphone adoption. Smartphone ownership has consistently increased since their introduction and as of 2011, over 85 % of Americans owned one (Tran, Tran & White, 2012). As adoption increases, smartphones have become more affordable and utilized across the socio-economic spectrum (Liang, et al., 2010; Nundy, Dick, Solomon & Peeka, 2013). Related directly to diabetes self-management, smartphones allow users to track and manage their diabetes in a variety of environments. Indeed, users noted they would rather use a mobile phone than be "tied down" to a home computer (Harris, et al., 2010). Such immediacy of tracking encourages consistent and frequent measurements for self-management (Baron, McBain, & Newman, 2012; Lyles, et al., 2011; Nundy, et al., 2013). An additional benefit comes from the displays on these phones, as they allow graphical and tabular displays of information, which can aid understanding of the complex and dynamic system that is diabetes management (Årsand & Tatara, 2010; Harris, et al., 2010). When compared to paper logbooks, a traditional method of self-management, smartphone users made fewer errors, were more likely to log information, reported ease of noticing trends (Harris, et al., 2010), and found smartphones more motivational (Rao, Hou, Golnik, Flaherty & Vu, 2010). Smartphone benefits are not exclusive to diabetes management with the FDA predicting that by 2015, 500 million people will be using mobile health applications (El-Gayar, Timsina, Nawar & Eid, 2013).

Studies have shown smartphone apps improve diet and exercise (Tran, Tran & White, 2012), increase the frequency of blood glucose logging (Lyles, et al., 2011), and provide much needed feedback on a more frequent basis from healthcare providers (Harris, et al., 2010). When feedback was provided automatically via smartphones, users reported elevated motivation to self-manage (Nundy, Dick, Solomon & Peeka, 2013). The connection with health care providers works both ways, as there are fewer needed appointments when communication of levels and management comes through an app (Lyles, et al., 2011). However, despite the promise of smartphone apps to improve diabetes self-management, a number of challenges remain regarding their use. This is particularly true when considering older adult users, and the design of existing apps often fails to take older users' capabilities and limitations into account (Whitlock & McLaughlin, 2012).

2.1 General Design Recommendations

It is possible to describe the desirable features of a technology to support the tracking and management of blood glucose levels from a review of the literature. First, the technology should be mobile and usable in a variety of environments, particularly environments linked to eating and exercise. Designs should consider age-related changes in perception, cognition, and movement control and be tested with a representative sample of the target population. Second, the technology should provide accurate and up-to-date information regarding available carbohydrates and their potential effects, medications, and blood sugar historical trends. Third, the technology should encourage good self-management behaviors beyond simply providing information to the user, reducing stress related to the disease when possible. Fourth, the technology should provide or be a conduit of emotional support during self-management decision-making. Last, the technology should scaffold the user during decision-making in a complex and dynamic system. These features can be broken down into specific recommendations for blood glucose tracking applications on smartphones ("apps").

In terms of content, the app must track blood glucose levels, nutrition, medication use, and physical activity (Baron, McBain, & Newman, 2012; El-Gayar, Timsina, Nawar & Eid, 2013; Liang, et al., 2010). Optimally, blood glucose levels would be tracked in immediate form and historical data/trends would also be available. Nutritional information should include tracking of foods eaten with amounts and a count of the carbohydrates (Årsand & Tatara, 2010). Tracking of physical activity should be detailed enough to assist with weight management but also provides inputs useful to informing patterns of blood glucose levels. Tracked data must be displayed in uncluttered, high-contrast graphical visualizations that allow the user to discern relationships and patterns between tracked variables and resulting blood glucose levels.

In terms of education, adaptive training should be offered through the app. This could be as simple as automated messages from health care providers (Harris, et al., 2010) to connections with other users best able to answer specific questions in a timely manner. This mimics the benefits that have been found for the use of online forums by persons with chronic health conditions (Eysenbach et al. 2004).

It is also desirable that apps provide a support structure, both for emotional support and decision support. One study found that among older adults with diabetes, those who reported greater social support were likely to have fewer impairments on the ADLs and IADLs, to have better self-rated health, shorter duration of diabetes, were less likely to feel depressed and to have trouble with stress, and less likely to have had a heart attack (Zhang, Norris, Gregg, & Beckles, 2007). The support structure should include a reminder system that prompts the user for readings and tracking information (Baron, McBain, & Newman, 2012; El-Gayar, Timsina, Nawar & Eid, 2013) but with the understanding that reminders alone do not guarantee adherence (Brath, et al., 2012). Support should extend beyond the app and social networks of the user and also allow communication with health-care providers that are part of the team helping the user to manage type 2 diabetes (Baron, McBain, & Newman, 2012; El-Gayar, Timsina, Nawar & Eid, 2013; Liang, et al., 2010).

The app should motivate the user in the face of an ambiguous, complex, dynamic task that offers few if any instances of immediate feedback. Elevated blood sugar levels tend to be severe before symptoms are noticed by patients, meaning that an older adult can be off optimal levels for long periods of time before acute symptoms act as feedback. Time spent off optimal levels permanently damages the body. Thus, apps can step in to provide the feedback and rewards not offered by the condition itself.

The last recommendations for app design center on usability. The app should be adaptable to the changing health, knowledge, and performance of the user (Årsand et al. 2012). To improve the mobility of the app, it should sync across devices as to be readily available and accessible even when a smartphone is not. Usability should be tested with older adults with type 2 diabetes throughout app development. Adherence to older adult design guidelines assists in the initial designs and directions (Pak & McLaughlin, 2010; Rogers, Fisk, Charness, Czaja, & Sharit, 2009) but there is no substitution for testing representative and long-term tasks with the target population. Pak and McLaughlin offer guidelines for usability testing with older adults (Pak & McLaughlin 2010).

2.2 Analysis of Existing Apps

We examined three apps selected on the basis of published usability ratings identifying them as among the most usable of diabetes self-management apps available on the Android market (Demidowich et al. 2012). The three apps were *Glucool Diabetes*, *OnTrack Diabetes*, and *Dbees.com*. *Glucool Diabetes* is available as both a free and a premium ($4.99) version, with 126 reviews and an average user rating of 3.6 stars. *OnTrack Diabetes* is available for free, with 5,455 ratings and an average user rating of 4.4 stars. *Dbees.com* is available for free, with 415 ratings and an average user rating of 4.0 stars.

A commonality shared by all of these apps was that each tended to offer major features that users expect in current diabetes tracking apps, for example tracking multiple variables (blood glucose, food, physical activity, etc.) and exporting data to a spreadsheet. However, features were not always implemented in accordance with usability principles. Graphs were sometimes cluttered (Fig. 1, right) and often did not contain appropriate labels (Fig. 1, right; Fig. 3, right). For one app the website implementation did not load correctly when viewed on the mobile device used for testing (Fig. 2, right).

No app was designed using guidelines for the needs of older users, and older users who experience physical or cognitive side-effects of diabetes are likely to find their use especially problematic, e.g. reading tiny labels on graphs. Some apps provided both tracking and up-to-date information on dietary choices, but none included information analysis support to help users interpret causes behind trends in the data. No apps provided the social support or communication with healthcare providers beyond data transfer that is recommended in the literature. No apps provided emotional or decision support to the user and showed no adaptation. No apps provided education during their use.

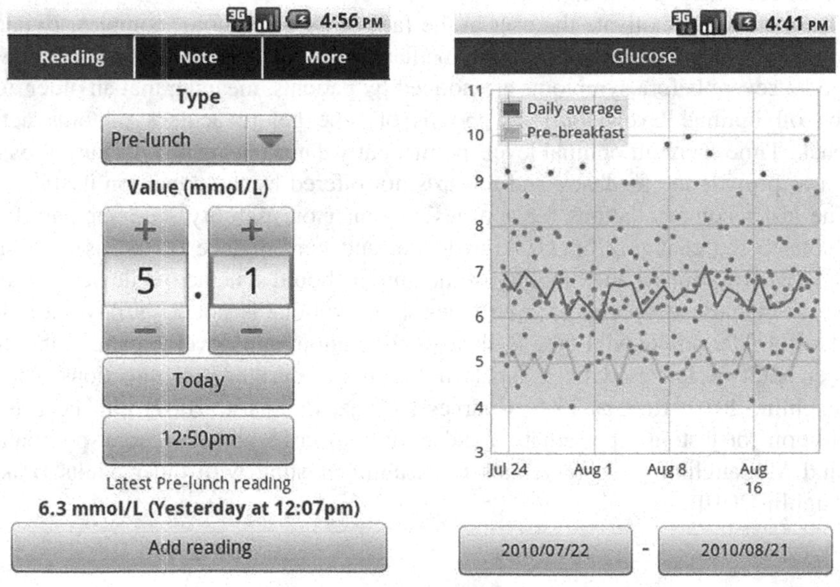

Fig. 1. Glucool *Diabetes* app, with tracking input screen (left) and historical graphical summary of blood glucose (right).

It is important to note that despite their occasional usability challenges, these apps are highly useful to many users, as evidenced by their ratings and number of downloads. Many of them are the efforts of programmers highly invested in the management of diabetes, who have dedicated a great deal of time to the features of these apps. We are grateful for these efforts, as they are a first step toward diabetes management applications created using a human factors and participatory design process.

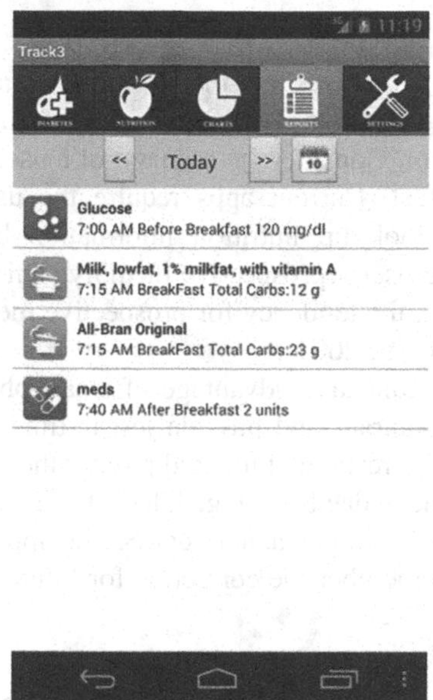

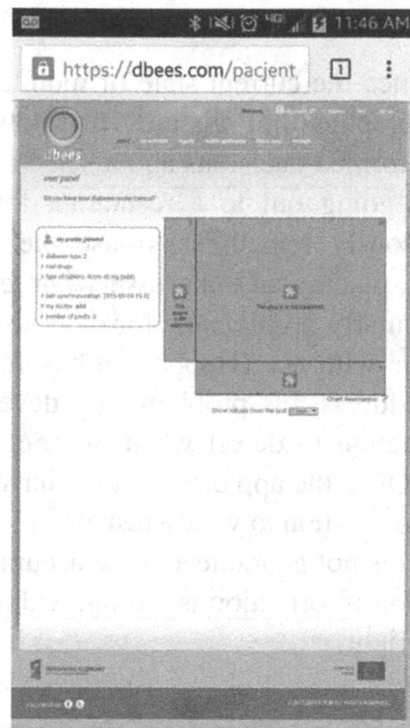

Fig. 2. *Dbees.com app*, with daily summary screen (left) and failed attempt to view graphical data on the integrated website on a Samsung Galaxy S4 mobile device (right).

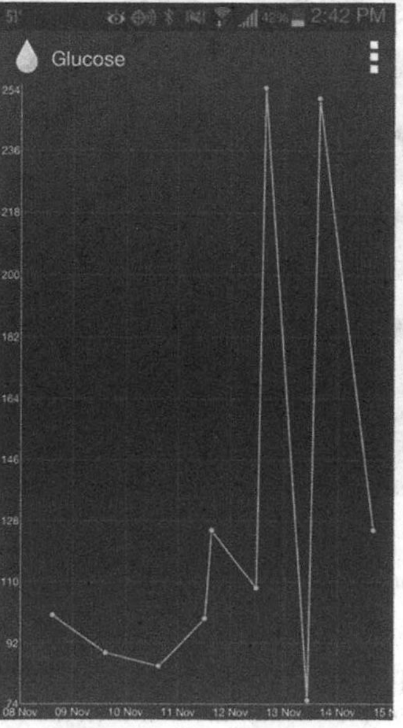

Fig. 3. *OnTrack Diabetes* app, with daily summary screen (left) and historical graphical summary of blood glucose (right).

2.3 Future Directions

To advance the current state of mobile apps for diabetes self-management we advise the development of features that lower the cognitive and time costs of making better-informed decisions about self-management. Consider the scenario of a user with diabetes going out to a restaurant for breakfast. Current apps require the user to spontaneously remember to use the app to look up nutrition information before ordering, placing an unnecessary burden on the user's prospective memory. This may be particularly problematic for older users given the tendency for prospective memory to decline with age (Huppert, Johnson, & Nickson, 2001).

To address this problem, app developers could take advantage of smart phones' GPS function to detect when users enter a restaurant and provide just-in-time intervention Once the app detects users have entered a restaurant it could prompt them with a push notification to view a restaurant-specific menu database (Fig. 4, left). Because GPS detection is not guaranteed to be accurate, users should be able to correct the app when its location information is wrong, and have it remember the correction for future visits (Fig. 4, right).

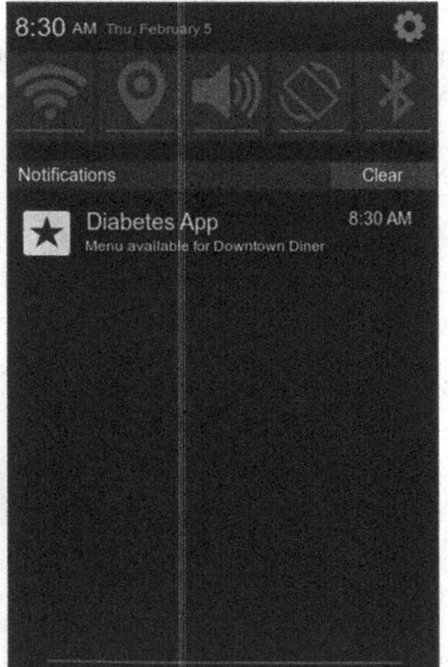

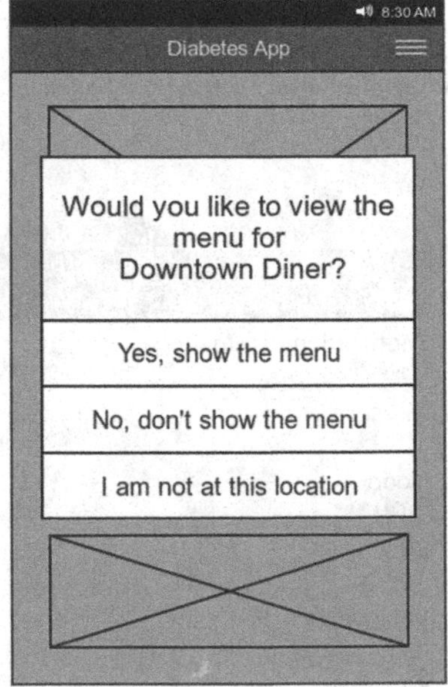

Fig. 4. Prototypes of push notification feature (left) and screen allowing user to choose to view the menu or correct the GPS location (right).

App developers could also utilize crowd-sourced diabetes knowledge by allowing users to rate restaurant menu items in terms of appropriateness for a healthy diabetes diet (Fig. 5, left). Users can consult the ratings to quickly determine the best choices on the menu. After selecting a menu item, users are given the nutrition information with

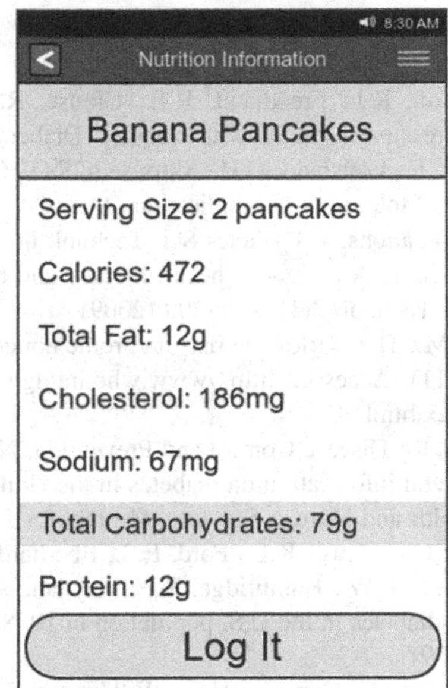

Fig. 5. Prototypes of crowd-sourced menu nutrition ratings (left) and menu item nutrition information with carbohydrates highlighted (right).

carbohydrate content highlighted, and can add it to their food log with a single touch (Fig. 5, right).

Although accuracy of crowd-sourced information is a potential concern, a previous study of a diabetes internet forum found that recommendations given by users on the forum were in agreement with best practice clinical guidelines 91 % of the time (Hoffman-Goetz et al. 2009). This suggests that user-sourced information in the context of diabetes may reach high accuracy. Crowd-sourced menu ratings could also be independently assessed for accuracy by professionals, e.g. nutritionists, or by "super users" singled out for their high level of diabetes knowledge.

Features like these that reduce the cognitive burden of making informed self-management decisions are likely to be particularly helpful for users experiencing age- and diabetes-related cognitive decline. We furthermore recommend that developers utilize the lessons learned from building apps that track and display food, exercise, and blood glucose levels to make apps that also:

- Are created using design guidelines for older adult usability
- Are tested with older users
- Allow two-way communication between users and healthcare providers
- Contain motivational features such as gamified rewards and social support
- Contain educational features, such as tutorials and online social networks of other patients and healthcare professionals
- Provide just-in-time decision support when diet, exercise, or medication decisions must occur

References

Anderson, R.J., Freedland, K.E., Clouse, R.E., Lustman, P.J.: The prevalence of comorbid depression in adults with diabetes. Diabetes Care **24**(6), 1069–1078 (2001)

Årsand, E., Frøisland, D.H., Skrøvseth, S.O., Chomutare, T., Tatara, N., Hartvigsen, G., Tufano, J.T.: Mobile health applications to assist patients with diabetes: lessons learned and design implications. J. Diabetes Sci. Technol. **6**(5), 1197–1206 (2012)

Boren, S.A.: A review of health literacy and diabetes: opportunities for technology. J. Diabetes Sci. Technol. **3**(1), 202–209 (2009)

Chan, M.: The worldwide rise of chronic noncommunicable diseases: A slow-motion catastrophe (2011). Accessed http://www.who.int/dg/speeches/2011/ministerial_conf_ncd_20110428/en/index.html

Centers for Disease Control and Prevention. National diabetes fact sheet: National estimates and general information on diabetes in the United States, 2011. Atlanta, GA: U.S. Department of Health and Human Services, Centers for Disease Control and Prevention (2011)

Cowie, C.C., Rust, K.F., Ford, E.S., Eberhardt, M.S., Byrd-Holt, D.D., Li, C., Williams, D.E., Gregg, E.W., Bainbridge, K.E., Saydah, S.H., Geiss, L.S.: Full accounting of diabetes and pre-diabetes in the U.S. population in 1988-1994 and 2005-2006. Diabetes Care **32**, 287–294 (2009)

Cukierman, T., Gerstein, H.C., Williamson, J.D.: Cognitive decline and dementia in diabetes – systematic overview of prospective observational studies. Diabetologia **48**, 2460–2469 (2005)

Demidowich, A.P., Lu, K., Tamler, R., Bloomgarden, Z.: An evaluation of diabetes self-management applications for Android smartphones. J. Telemedicine Telecare **18**(4), 235–238 (2012)

Diabetes Prevention Program (DPP) Research Group: The Diabetes prevention program (dpp) description of lifestyle intervention. Diabetes Care **25**(12), 2165–2171 (2002)

Eysenbach, G., Powell, J., Englesakis, M., Rizo, C., Stern, A.: Health related virtual communities and electronic support groups: systematic review of the effects of online peer to peer interactions. Br. Med. J. **328**, 1–6 (2004)

Franciosi, M., Pellegrini, F., De Berardis, G., Belfiglio, M., Cavaliere, D., Di Nardo, B., Nicolucci, A.: The impact of blood glucose self-monitoring on metabolic control and quality of life in type 2 diabetic patients: an urgent need for better educational strategies. Diabetes Care **24**(11), 1870–1877 (2001)

Gregg, J.A., Callaghan, G.M., Hayes, S.C., Glenn-Lawson, J.L.: Improving diabetes self-management through acceptance, mindfulness, and values: a randomized controlled trial. J. Consult. Clin. Psychol. **75**(2), 336–343 (2007)

He, W., Sengupta, M., Velkoff, V.A., DeBarros, K.A.: 65 + in the United States, 2005. US Department of Commerce, Economics and Statistics Administration, US Census Bureau (2005)

Hoffman-Goetz, L., Donelle, L., Thomson, M.D.: Clinical guidelines about diabetes and the accuracy of peer information in an unmoderated online health forum for retired persons. Inf. Health Soc. Care **34**(2), 91–99 (2009)

Klein, H.A., Jackson, S.M., Street, K., Whitacre, J.C., Klein, G.: Diabetes self-management education: miles to go. Nurs. Res. pract. **2013**, 1–15 (2013)

Klein, H.A., Lippa, K.D.: Type 2 diabetes self-management: Controlling a dynamic system. J. Cogn. Eng. Decis. Making **2**(1), 48–62 (2008)

Klein, H.A., Lippa, K.D.: Assuming control after system failure: Type II diabetes self-management. Cogn. Technol. Work **14**, 243–251 (2012)

Klein, H.A., Meininger, A.R.: Self management of medication and diabetes: cognitive control man and cybernetics systems. IEEE Trans. Sys. Hum. **34**(6), 718–725 (2004)

Lin, E.H.B., Katon, W., Von Korff, M., Rutter, C., Simon, G.E., Oliver, M., Ciechanowski, P., Ludman, E.J., Bush, T., Young, B.: Relationship of depression and diabetes self-care, medication adherence, and preventive care. Diabetes Care **27**(9), 2154–2160 (2004)

Lindström, J., Louheranta, A., Mannelin, M., Rastas, M., Salminen, V., Eriksson, J., Tuomilehto, J.: The finnish Diabetes prevention study (DPS) lifestyle intervention and 3-year results on diet and physical activity. Diabetes Care **26**(12), 3230–3236 (2003)

Logroscino, G., Kang, J.H., Grodstein, F.: Prospective study of type 2 diabetes and cognitive decline in women aged 70-81 years. BMJ **328**(7439), 548–553 (2004)

Moritz, D.J., Ostfeld, A.M., Blazer, D., Curb, D., Taylor, J.O., Wallace, R.B.: The health burden of diabetes for the elderly in four communities. Public Health Rep. **109**, 782–790 (1994)

Munshi, M., Grande, L., Hayes, M., Ayres, D., Suhl, E., Capelson, R., Lin, S., Milberg, W., Weinger, K.: Cognitive dysfunction is associated with poor diabetes control in older adults. Diabetes Care **29**(8), 1794–1799 (2006)

Pak, R., McLaughlin, A.: Designing displays for older adults. CRC Press, Boca Raton (2010)

Peyrot, M., Rubin, R.R.: Levels and risks of depression and anxiety symptomatology among diabetic adults. Diabetes Care **20**(4), 585–590 (1997)

Shigaki, C., Kruse, R.L., Mehr, D., Sheldon, K.M., Ge, B., Moore, C., Lemaster, J.: Motivation and diabetes self-management. Chronic illness **6**(3), 202–214 (2010)

Skinner, T.C., Carey, M.E., Cradock, S., Daly, H., Davies, M.J., Doherty, Y., Heller, S., Khunti, K., Oliver, L.: Diabetes education and self-management for ongoing and newly diagnosed (DESMOND): process modelling of pilot study. Patient Educ. Couns. **64**, 369–377 (2006)

United Nations. World Population Ageing: 1950–2050 (2001)

Whitlock, L.A., McLaughlin, A.C.: Identifying usability problems of blood glucose tracking apps for older adult users. In: Proceedings of the Human Factors and Ergonomics Society Annual Meeting, 56(1), pp. 115–119

Yaffe, K., Falvey, C.M., Hamilton, N., Harris, T.B., Simonsick, E.M., Strotmeyer, E.S., Schwartz, A.V.: Association between hypoglycemia and dementia in a biracial cohort of older adults with diabetes mellitus. JAMA Intern. Med. **173**(14), 1300–1306 (2013)

Design and Fabricate Neckwear to Improve the Elderly Patients' Medical Compliance

Xiaolong Wu(✉), Young Mi Choi, and Maysam Ghovanloo

School of Industrial Design, School of Electrical Computing Engineering, Georgia Institute of Technology, Atlanta, GA 30332—0250, USA
{xwu86, Christina.choi, mgh}@gatech.edu

Abstract. According to the estimation of the US National Council for Patient Information and Education, there is millions of prescription written each year, but only half of them are correctly followed by patients. Non-compliance with medicine prescription will result in higher medical cost, more hospitalizations, more complicated pill dosage, and even a threat to life. In order to improve elderly people's medical compliance, a new approach that utilizes microelectronics technology in wearable neckwear has been proposed. The sensors in the neckwear are able to detect whether the user has actually taken the pill and which pills the user has taken. During the design iteration, elderly participants' medication related behavioral data and their opinions towards the neckwear reminder concept were first gathered by interviews. The result has demonstrated that wearable neckwear seemed to be a potential solution to improve elderly people's medication compliance. Then a set of physical (non-functional) prototypes was created based on the initial survey input. Usability testing was conducted in order to measure elderly people's preferences in relation to shape, comfort, desirability, ease of use and other factors. This paper documented the development of this prototype and focused on the design challenges that have been encountered, and how the problems have been solved.

Keywords: Medical compliance · Wearable

1 Introduction

Medical compliance, which is commonly defined as the degree to which a patient follow the medical prescription [1]. Non-compliance with the medicine prescription is becoming a major cost of the medical care in each therapeutic area. According to the estimation of the US National Council for Patient Information and Education, even though there is millions of prescription written each year, only half of them are followed by the patients [3]. Among the patients who have difficulty in the compliance with the prescription, the elderly people with kidney transplantation gains a special concern. Because of aging, the elderly patients are commonly suffering the loss of their physical dexterity, cognitive skills, and memory. In the meantime, they must take a great amount of pills in different dosage, at different time everyday to keep their body function properly [2]. The non-compliance with medicine will result in higher medical cost, more hospitalizations, more complicated pill dosage, and even a threat to life.

J. Zhou and G. Salvendy (Eds.): ITAP 2015, Part II, LNCS 9194, pp. 222–234, 2015.
DOI: 10.1007/978-3-319-20913-5_21

Theofilou [2] stated that the mental factors that caused the non-compliance are depression, less structured daily life, and social isolation. And for the physical side, the small label reading and understanding, child resistant container, and short-term memory also prevent the elderly people from complying with the prescription.

In order to improve elderly patients' compliance with prescription, different interventions have been provided. A simple dosage regime along with reducing the daily pill-taking frequency, and makes it easier for the patients to remember when to take pills, have been proven to be effective. Special cues have been selected to help the elderly patients memorize the time when they need to take pills. Increasing the communication between the doctor and the patients also helps in educating the elderly patients and reduce their depression. This paper mainly focuses on utilizing microelectronics technology to create a new way to reminder and monitor the pill-taking frequency of the elderly patients, and conducting usability test about it.

2 Previous Work

With the development of the electronics, they have been using to improve the medical adherence with a focus on reminding and monitoring. According to Cramer's [4] article, the development of the microelectronics has significantly affected the field of medicine compliance, especially in the area of monitoring, and the electronic monitoring has been proven to be the most sensitive method available for measuring medication non-adherence.

2.1 Category

Most of the reminding and monitoring technology above has been categorized as automated detection and reminder system. It means that the patient in the system is a passive receiver, he doesn't need to interact with the system, instead, the system automatically monitors and generates data. According to Granger's [5] article, he pointed out that there is no significant improvement by the automated detection/reminder itself. A research project has been conducted by Christensen, which utilized a Pharmaceutical database technology-a system working on filling and refilling pills, and transferring data between the doctor and the patient. The research result has shown that the patients did not react consistently to the technology, and only the automated system itself was ineffective for improving the compliance with the medicine. Besides the automated detection and reminder system, another main category is the in-person system in which the patient uses a device as an assistant [5]. Some research results have shown that it also did not improve patients' adherence to medical prescription. For instance, an in-home telemonitoring system has been used to allow the patients themselves to generate and respond to their own medical data. The biggest challenge for in-person system is the user error, which means users may report wrong data by mistake. Moreover, Christensen [13] concluded that there was no big significance between the control group and the group with the in person system in terms of medical adherence.

Even though neither the automated system nor the in-person system has proven to be effective in terms of improving elderly patient's medical adherence, the combination of both the systems has shown its advantage in improving the patients' medical adherence, generating better clinical outcome, improving patients and the caregivers' satisfaction, and increasing patients' awareness of their diseases. Floerkemeier [6] has conducted a project that combined smart pill packages with mobile phones. There are sensors and microcontroller on the blister pack, when a user remove a pill from the pack, the sensors will detect the removal event, and it will send a message to the phone and the caregiver, indicating whether the user has taken the pill. Besides reminding and monitoring, he also stated that the smart package should have the function of warning the user about a dangerous dose combination, or the pill is out of date.

2.2 Devices

According to Naditz's [12] article, there are mainly three types of monitoring and remaindering devices: the large, in-home units; a smaller, battery-powered pillbox that can be put in the pocket; and the newly wearable devices. They each have their own advantages and disadvantages.

Home-based microelectronic monitoring systems have been developed to organize, distribute pills, monitor and remind the patients remotely. A mechanical device called Compu-Med [4], is able to automatically distribute pills. It provides both audio and visual reminder, and it is able to print out the data log on paper. Another device called Dosing Partner has also been developed. It tried to improve the compliance by sending the pill-taking data to the caregiver everyday. In this way, if a caregiver finds out that the patient missed one dose or being significantly late for one time, he will communicate with the patient immediately. The features of home-based microelectronic monitoring system, such as, recording the pill-taking behavior, and sending the pill-taking data to the caregivers and family members has ensured the compliance with medicine of the elderly people, and in the meantime, it significantly saved the cost of nursing-home care. However, since the sizes of those facilities are relatively bulky, the usage has been greatly limited.

In order to increase the usage of the microelectronics and to make the reminder portable, nowadays, pill containers have shifted from regular plastic boxes to containers with process chips embedded in. The smart pillbox is able to record the time and to count the open frequency by detecting the movement of the bottle cap or the inhaler. Besides the regular beeping and flashing functions, now the smart pillbox also utilized recorded voice, such as, the voice of the patient's daughter, to reminder the patients to take pills on time. In order to prevent overdosing and ensure the pill taking frequency, a pillbox named uBox [9] was developed by Massachusetts Institute of Technology. It records every opening time, when it's not reach a certain time, the opener remains close and it can't be open by others. However, even though the smart pillbox becomes smaller and portable, in terms of pill storage, it is impractical to store all the pills in a container since some kinds of pills are required to be stored in a sealed blister.

Bleser [7] also conducted a usability test about a device called the Helping Hand. It is a handheld device with a process chip, and it stores blisters inside. When the user needs to take pills, he moves the blister out of the device, take the pills and re insert the blister into the device. The Helping Hand device provides both acoustic and visual feedback to the users. It provides acoustic reminder to the user at the pill-taking time and if the device detects that the user doesn't follow the prescription, the light on the device will change color. The pill-taking frequency data can also be printed out to let both the caregivers and the patients see the pattern. Bleser's usability testing mainly focused on three aspects, user performance, user satisfaction, and acceptability. The result showed that even though generally the participants tend to like the device, there were three main obstacles. The first one was that some participants found that the acoustic reminder was too light to hear. Second one was that it requires certain level motor skill to manipulate the device, such as re inserting the blister back into the device. The third obstacle was that the device can only store one kind of pills. It's useless for the users who have to take several kinds of pills per day.

Moreover, people tend to have social stigma with the hand held or in pocket reminder devices. They don't want other people to know they are taking pills; therefore, they fear to be away from home and refuse to use the pillbox in public, which caused the noncompliance with the medicine.

In order to address the social stigma and shift from the outside the patients to the inside of the patients, along with the development of wearable computing technology, the existing sensors with the capabilities of physiological sensing, biochemical sensing, and motion sensing were utilized in health care devices. They have been widely used in the fields of medical monitoring and feedback system, monitoring social networking to reinforce healthy behavior, and to early detect the symptoms of depression and dementia [8].

Wristwatches have been programmed to remind the elderly people in a more discreet way. Different approaches have been utilized based on the watch. One is providing audio to the elderly people to remind them to take pills. However, it turns out that some elderly people are also suffering from the loss of hearing, and they may not be able to hear the reminding audio. Moreover, because of the short memory issue, under some circumstances, even people have heard the reminder, they will easily forget about it after a few seconds. In order to ensure that the elderly patients read the reminder, another approach has been developed. Instead of only producing audio reminder, it displays a short message on the watch screen, indicating the required medicine the users need to take. Also, it provides a more discreet reminder-vibration on the user's wrist, so the user can use it in public and others won't be aware of it. However, the performance of the reminder is unpredictable, since it does not implement monitoring system, so it cannot detect whether the users have followed the reminding contents or whether the elderly patients have taken the right dosage.

One project about a memory glass has also been conducted by Pentland [8] in MIT Thrill lab. The glass works as a personal memory assistant. It can store users' data and utilize sound and visual cues to remind the users under certain circumstance. He stated that the difference between the glass and the other reminders is that the glass is a context-awareness device. It means that the glass will react to different environment, and also it is personalized. He also stated that since the main obstacle of the traditional reminder is that people naturally tend to resist being reminded to perform tasks, the advantage of the glass is that it is able to provide subliminal cues directly to the users' threshold of perception-eyes. Therefore, the users may react based on the cues while they are not even aware of it. However, even though the glass has to some extent addressed the context-awareness issue, and it works effectively in terms of reminding people, there is still a social stigma about the head up device. Besides, it currently doesn't have the monitoring function, so it may be useless for the patients who require special care and attention.

2.3 Previous Study

In conclusion, with the development of technology, the medical reminder is shifting from an in-home bulky device to a smaller, portable device. The role of the patients shifts from a passive receiver to an active manipulator. Many complicated issues, such as, multiple dosage distribution, discreet reminding, require to be portable, and context awareness, have been addressed by the current healthcare products. However, there are still some issues remaining unsolved. For example, the biggest drawback of the current reminder/monitor device is that it is able to remind the patient to take pills and to detect whether the pills have been taken out of the pillbox; it is impossible to tell whether the patient has actually swallowed them. Furthermore, the current products are not able to tell whether the patients have taken the correct dosage.

- Patients tend to have social stigma with wearable products that show their diseases to the public. Therefore, the new design of the wearable product should address this problem by designing a user- friendly shape and material. In the meantime, it should look appealing to both the user and others.
- The micro electronic device should be able to detect whether the user has taken the pill, instead of the action of taking the pill out of the pillbox.
- There should be a smooth interaction between the user and the device, either passively receiving information or actively finding information has been proven to be less effective.
- The device should be portable, in order not to limit the activity of the user.
- The device should be able to identify different kinds of pills.
- There should be no special motor skill requirement for the user to manipulate the device since most of the end users are elderly people, and they are losing their motor skill as aging.
- The reminding approaches should be obvious enough for the users.
- The device should be context-awareness.

Therefore, based on the requirements, the author proposed a new combination of a smart necklace and a smartphone application concept. Since the micro controller is shifted from outside (bottles) to be on the users' body, it does not require motor skill to perform tasks any more. Moreover, compared with the head up device, the neckwear is smaller and can be hided inside the collar.

3 Data Collection

3.1 Interview

Based on the concept, interviews have been conducted among twenty elderly people. The subjects aged from 66 to 96 years old. To gain their perspective views of the new WEAMS (Wireless and Wearable Event Detection and Adherence Monitoring System) concept [10], their medication regimen, the current reminder system they are using, the usability issues they have, and their opinions towards the neckwear reminder, have been gathered during the phone interview session. And all the phone interviews have been recorded and transcribed for analyzing. The analyzed interview data demonstrated the following facts.

- People tend to have fewer adherences with their medicine as time flies.
- Very few subjects have realized the importance of taking pills on time.
- A connection between the reminder system and their daily routine is essential for elderly people to take their regimen on time. However, once the connection is broken by travels or short days visits, it's difficult for them to remember to take pills.
- Even though most of the current reminders in the market utilize both visual and audio feedback, half of the subjects reported that they only relied on their own memory, and they thought they were able to feel the difference if they missed a dosage.
- One big issue of the reminder system is that it should be integrated into the elderly people's daily life without making them look/behave different. Also the reminder system should be able to distinguish different pill sources.
- As for the neckwear concept, the subjects seemed to appreciate the benefits from wearing it, however, they did not regard their conditions as serious enough to wear it. Besides, they also worried about their privacy, which meant that they were being monitoring by their doctors all the time. Most of them also have social stigma, and some of them even worried about the waterproof issue.

3.2 Initial Prototypes Testing

Since the interview results have indicated that elderly people tend to accept the WEAMS concept, several appearance conceptual models have been made to further gain users' perspectives. The appearance models of the neckwear are based on the analysis of the phone interview data. Generally there is a locking mechanism on the neckwear, which enables the user to put it on and take it off easily. It is intentionally made tiny, which is used to reduce the social stigma the users may have. Also it is designed lightweight to make the users feel comfortable.

Six devices have been tested in a controlled environment, half of the devices are appearance models and the rest of them exist monitoring devices. The first appearance prototype is called Adjustable. It utilized a clasp mechanism to fit for different sizes of the neck. The shape of it is also designed to avoid resting on users' collarbone, so it can reduce the discomfort when the user is wearing it. The Snap one utilized a slipcover that there is a locking mechanism inside. The third one is called Magnetic, which used small magnets for locking. The three exist devices are Jawbone Up wristband, MIO alpha watch, and BodyMeida FIT armband.

Twelve subjects whose average age is 77.7 were involved in the test. The test procedure consisted of two parts. The first part included the users' current medication evaluation, medication adherence, medication management, using wearable systems, consumer preferences, and their physical strength. The second part included the device evaluation and ranking. The three prototypes were evaluated first, and then the three exist devices. All the devices have been evaluated in terms of ease of use, comfort, and physical characteristics. Subjects were asked to wear it to perform several tasks, and then evaluate each device via Likert Scale. In the ranking session, the subjects were asked to rank the three prototypes and three exist devices based on their appearance, comfort, and overall preferences.

The test result showed that Magnetic was significantly better than the other two in terms of ease of usability field. There was no significant difference among the three prototypes in terms of comfort and desirability. However, Magnetic was a slightly better. As for the ranking, in terms of appearance, there was significant difference among the three prototypes. Both Magnetic and Adjustable were preferred. In terms of comfort, Magnetic was preferred over Snap. As for the overall preference, there was no significant difference between Adjustable and Magnetic, but they both are preferred over Snap. Magnetic clasping mechanism tends to be more intuitive to the user, and it's easy to use since it require less motor skill and strength. Even though in the comfort and desirability fields, there was no significant difference among the three prototypes, Magnetic concept is always ranking high. As for the appearance, the result has demonstrated that the users preferred simply design features.

3.3 Limitations

Since the prototypes in the test were only appearance model, there were several limitations of the data. First of all, the prototypes did not simulate the actual weight of the final product. Since the final concept requires the neckwear to work for at least one week continuously, the battery of the neckwear is relatively large and heavy. Besides, the appearance model did not include the size and shape of the sensors. Therefore, based on the initial testing data, a functional prototype was created.

4 Design

The design and fabrication of the working prototype was undertaken by a graduate industrial design student. According to Jayaraman's book [11], there were eight principles for wearable product design; comfortable, no skin irritation, lightweight, breathable, moisture absorption, easy to wear and take off, easy to access body, and maintain range of motion. The design challenge for the necklace was how to arrange those electronics in the necklace to make it work effectively and efficiently, in the meantime, appealing and comfortable.

4.1 Material

In order to make the necklace user friendly, several kinds of materials were considered in the very beginning of project. Besides lightweight, since the necklace should fit different users' neck diameters, the material must not be too rigid. Also, since there are sensors and batteries fixed in it, the necklace should not be too soft in case the electronics would vibrate inside or the users would break it by accident. Moreover, it should not hurt the skin since the users will wear it all day long. Finally silicone material was chosen in this project since it is relatively light, rigid and skin-friendly. Then different types of silicone have been tested. The number of silicone represents its rigidness. Silicone with the rigidness of 30 was the first one to test and it turned out to be too soft, it was difficult to maintain its shape after it became solid. Then silicone with the rigidness of 60 was tested and the rigidness of it perfectly fulfilled the requirement (shown in Fig. 1). Therefore, the silicone with the rigidness of 60 was used for the necklace body.

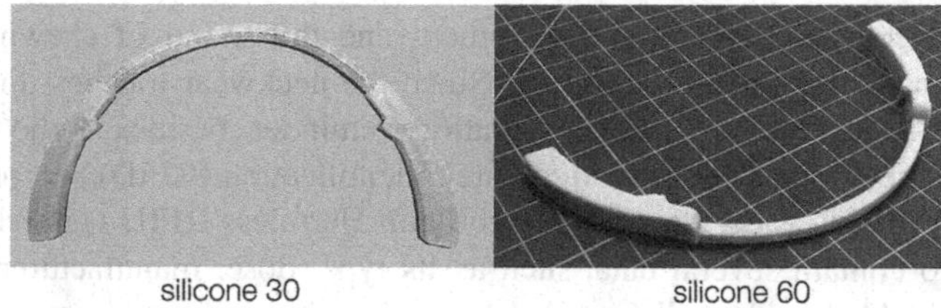

Fig. 1. It shows the difference between the silicone 30 and silicone 60. Silicone 30 is too soft to stay on users' neck.

In order to create a necklace that fits different users, the diameter of the neckwear should be flexible. Therefore, a pair of connector that allowed the users to adjust the size of the necklace has been made. Since the RFID sensor should go around the neck with a closed loop, and all the other sensors in the front necklace body should connect back to the power source and the main process chip, there are eight wires in total for each side. Therefore, a pair of connector that works both as a clasping mechanism, and connecting the wires inside, was created. To ensure the connector attach the silicone body tightly, several "T" shape hooks were created on the connector. Therefore, all these hooks were embedded in the silicone body before the silicone became dry.

4.2 Connecting Mechanism

To allow wires to connect each other, small conductors were used inside the connectors. (Shown in Fig. 2) To make a stable connection, besides the conductor, extra magnets have been used on the connectors, and a tilt connecting surface was used instead of flat one. When the user attaches the male part to the female part, the magnet on each part automatically attach to each other. And the tilt surface increased the connecting interface. However, even though the attaching and detaching was easy, it still required some motor skills to perform that action. Therefore, reducing the time that users need to take it on/off is very important, which required a power source that was able to last for one week. After testing, two AAA batteries were selected for the neckwear.

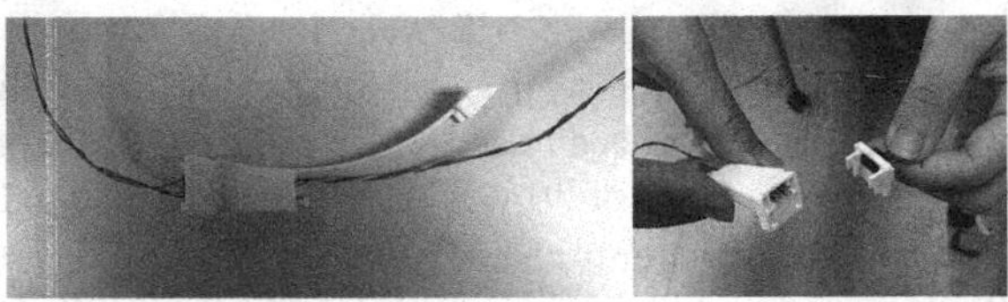

Fig. 2. It shows the connector with wires coming through and conductors inside

4.3 Sensors

In order to collect the user's throat movement and the sound of chewing, two bio microphones and a flex sensor were used. Since the neckwear touches directly to the user's skin, it was able to provide vibration reminder besides audio and visual reminders. The neckwear with radio frequency identification (RFID) and other sensors aims at solving the dose personalization problem. Harmless RFID tags which are pre programmed to contain several data, such as its type, dose, manufacturer and expire date, were embedded in the pill capsule. An inert polymer based coating material is used to protect the tag from decomposing in the process of falling in the user's body [10]. The RFID reader in the neckwear is used to detect the RFID tag to see whether the pills go through the throat. Moreover, combining with a flex senor and a biotical microphone that are used to detect the chewing sound and the movement of the throat, the RFID reader is able to accurately detect whether the user has taken pills. The neckwear also addressed the portable issue since users can wear it to wherever they go, it read the pills directly and it didn't need an extra carrier. A smart phone connected to the neckwear can receive data. Therefore, both the patients and the caregivers will be able to know whether the patients have taken pills on time.

4.4 Social Stigma

In order to address the social stigma issue, the necklace was designed light-weighed and small. Both the batteries and the process chips were located in the back part of the body, which was hidden behind the neck. (Shown in Fig. 3) To make the user feel comfortable, the back part of the neckwear follows the contour of the user's neck, and the batteries are located in both side of the neckwear separately.

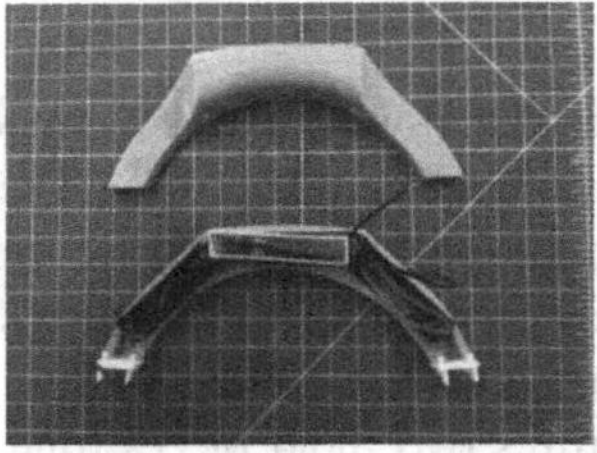
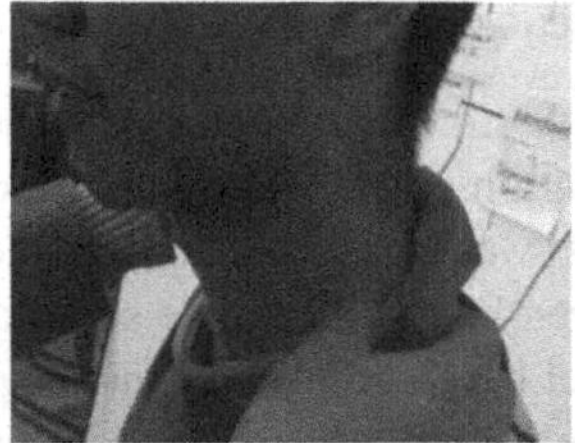

Fig. 3. It shows the connector with wires coming through and conductors inside

4.5 Final Design

The final design of the neckwear is shown in Fig. 4. The front part of the neckwear was used to hold the shape; the flex sensor and microphones were located directly to users' necks. The connectors on either side ware used as both connecting mechanism and conductor points. Two AAA batteries and a board sit in the back part of the neckwear, which can be hidden by users' necks.

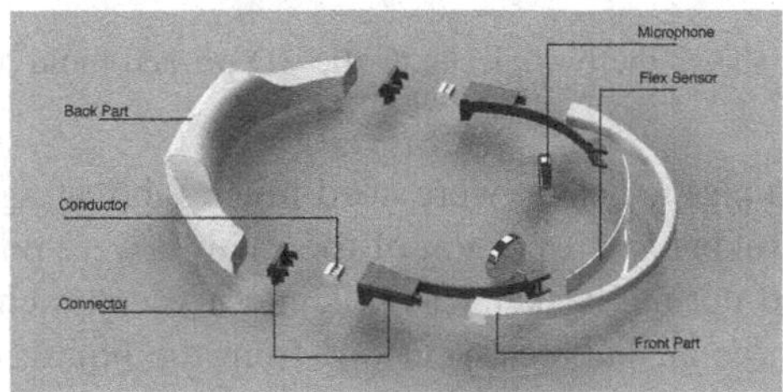

Fig. 4. It shows how the neckwear is assembled, and the location of each item

5 Fabrication

5.1 Connector

Since the connector is still in the prototype phase, and it only required low volume production, 3D printing technique was used. Therefore, the connector model was all made of ABS plastic (shown in Fig. 5).

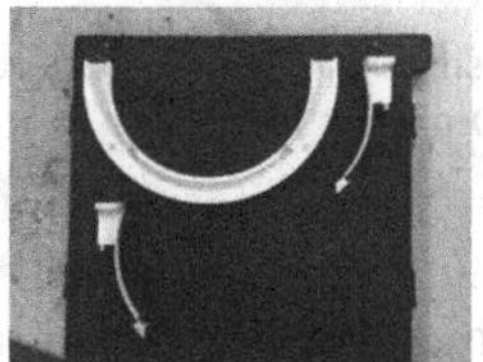
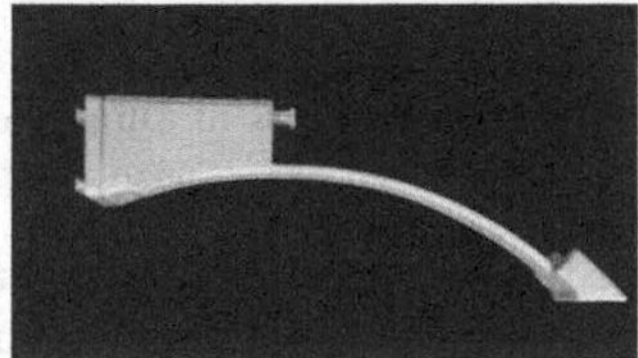

Fig. 5. It shows a 3D printed, plastic connector. The gears on the connector will be embedded in the silicone model.

5.2 Neckwear Body

In order to save time and the cost, instead of traditional way of silicone model making, in design iteration phase, 3D printing method was used in this project. The 3D printed plastic molds were used to replace the urethane molds, because a urethane mold requires sixteen hours to become solid, and the material itself is too costly. The whole silicone model has been divided into several parts to build. And since the inside of the silicone model is hollow, each model part requires two mold pieces (one female and one male) to create. And there were two holes of each mold pieces to let the air go in and out (Fig. 6).

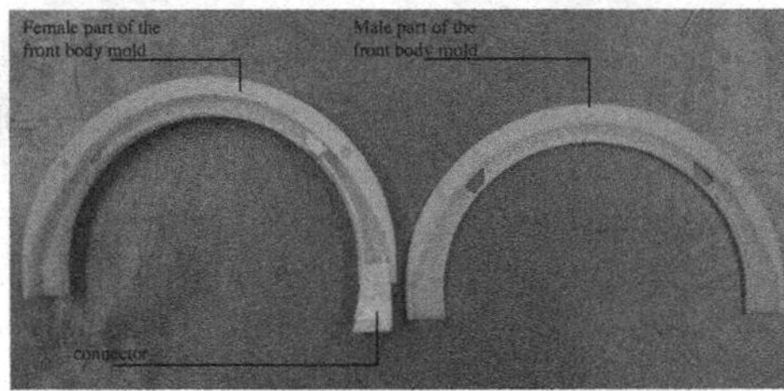

Fig. 6. The picture shows the two pieces of the 3D printed mold and one connector

A small scale and a plastic beaker were used in the fabricating process. At first, 10 portion of the silicone rubber and 1 portion of the catalyst were poured into the beaker, after they totally mixed up; the beaker was put into a vacuum chamber for degasing. During the time when the air bubbles went out from the liquid, the universal release was spray painted on the molds to avoid silicone rubber and plastic mold sticking to each other. As soon as most of the air bubbles vanished, the silicone liquid was poured into the mold slowly (Shown in Fig. 7).

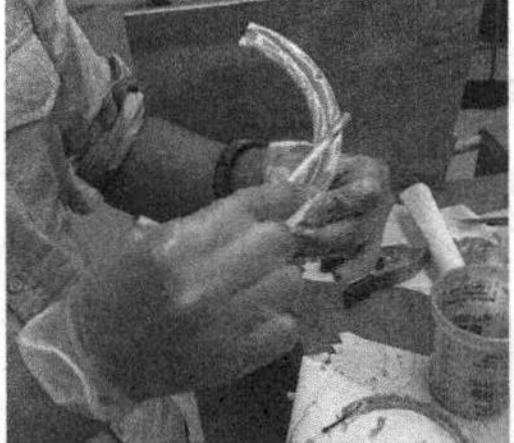

Fig. 7. The picture on the left demonstrates how the silicone was measured on the scale. The picture on the right shows the process of filling the 3D printed mold.

After a piece of the female part mold was full of silicone liquid, the mold was covered by its male part. Two clamps were used to tighten the two parts. Then after 16 h' drying time, the silicone liquid became solid, and a piece of the model has been created. This process was repeated again to create the other part of the necklace model.

In order to keep the wires in position inside the model and make the connecting part strong, the wires and the hook of the connector were seated in the mold before silicone liquid was poured into.

After each body has been created, a silicone proxy was used to attach the two pieces of the back part together. The finished silicone model is shown in Fig. 8.

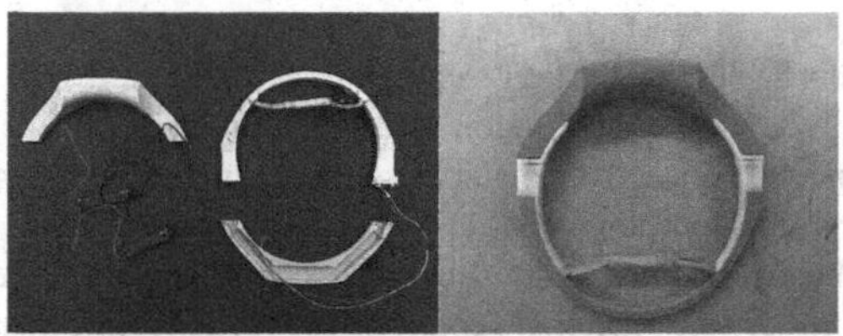

Fig. 8. The picture on the left shows a dissembled view of the fabricated model. The picture on the right shows an assembled one.

5.3 Microphone Shell

Since the neckwear is in charge of telling whether the patient has swallowed the pills, a bio-microphone and a piece of flex sensor are used. In order to better hold the electronic devices, a piece of silicone shell is specifically designed (Shown in Fig. 9).

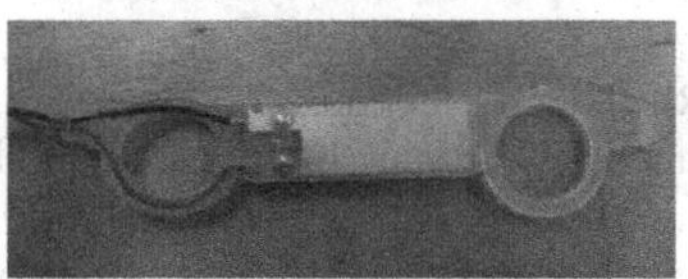

Fig. 9. The picture shows a finished silicone part with flex sensor in it. The two holes on both sides are for microphones.

In order to make the flex sensor embedded in the shell, the flex sensor with all the wires connected was pre positioned in the mold before the silicone gets dry. When the silicone shell gets dry, two microphones are placed inside the two circles. To make the silicone shell strongly attach to the front part, a "T" shape is made on both end of the shell. Before the front part is made, the shell has been seated inside the mold, with the "T" shapes stuck inside the mold. Besides, all the wires (microphone, RFID wires, and the flex sensors) have been connected to the conductors.

6 Future Work

Limited by the electronic technology, the battery currently used in the prototype is relatively big and heavy; this issue can be solved by the advancement of technology. The connector in the neckwear is an existing product; it did not fit the neckwear well.

A customized connector may need to be developed. Moreover, the neckwear was only fabricated, and was tested within real environment. Users' perspectives about the functional prototype need to be collected for further design iteration.

References

1. Kriens, L.M.: Improving medication adherence in the elderly using a medication management system (Doctoral dissertation, Tilburg University) (2012)
2. Theofilou, P.: Noncompliance with medical regimen in haemodialysis treatment: A case study. Case Reports in Nephrology (2011)
3. Rogers, P.G., Bullman, R.: Prescription medicine compliance: a review of the baseline of knowledge-a report of the national council on patient information and education. J. Pharmacoepidemiol. Binghamton **3**, 3–36 (1995)
4. Cramer, J.A.: Enhancing patient compliance in the elderly. Drugs Aging **12**(1), 7–15 (1998)
5. Mann, W.C., Ottenbacher, K.J., Fraas, L., Tomita, M., Granger, C.V.: Effectiveness of assistive technology and environmental interventions in maintaining independence and reducing home care costs for the frail elderly: a randomized controlled trial. Arch. Fam. Med. **8**(3), 210 (1999)
6. Floerkemeier, C., Siegemund, F.: Improving the effectiveness of medical treatment with pervasive computing technologies. In: Workshop on Ubiquitous Computing for Pervasive Healthcare Applications at Ubicomp. October 2003
7. De Bleser, L., Matteson, M., Dobbels, F., Russell, C., De Geest, S.: Interventions to improve medication-adherence after transplantation: a systematic review. Transpl. Int. **22**(8), 780–797 (2009)
8. Starner, T., Mann, S., Rhodes, B., Levine, J., Healey, J., Kirsch, D., Pentland, A.: Augmented reality through wearable computing. Presence: Teleoperators Virtual Environ. **6** (4), 386–398 (1997)
9. Naditz, A.: Medication compliance—helping patients through technology: modern "smart" pillboxes keep memory-short patients on their medical regimen. Telemedicine e-Health **14** (9), 875–880 (2008)
10. Choi, Y.M., Olubanjo, T., Farajidavar, A., Ghovanloo, M. Potential barriers in adoption of a medication compliance neckwear by elderly population. In: 2013 35th Annual International Conference of the IEEE on Engineering in Medicine and Biology Society (EMBC), pp. 4678-4681. IEEE, July 2013
11. Jayaraman, S., Kiekens, P., Grancaric, A.M. (eds.): Intelligent Textiles for Personal Protection and Safety. IOS press, Amsterdam (2006)
12. Naditz, A.: Medication compliance—helping patients through technology: modern "smart" pillboxes keep memory-short patients on their medical regimen. Telemedicine e-Health **14** (9), 875–880 (2008)
13. MacLaughlin, E.J., Raehl, C.L., Treadway, A.K., Sterling, T.L., Zoller, D.P., Bond, C.A.: Assessing medication adherence in the elderly. Drugs Aging **22**(3), 231–255 (2005)

Home and Work Support

Psychosocial Approach of Skills Obsolescence in Older Workers: Contribution of Methodological Triangulation

Florence Cros(✉), Marc-Eric Bobillier Chaumon, and Bruno Cuvillier

Laboratoire GRePS, Université Lumière Lyon 2, 5 Avenue Pierre Mendès France, 69500 Bron, France
{Florence.Cros,Marc-Eric.Bobillier-Chaumon, Bruno.Cuvillier}@univ-lyon2.fr

Abstract. Information and Communication Technologies have spread rapidly these last decades. The employment sphere has not been unaffected by these technological developments. One of the greatest risks of computerization is the rise of inequalities between two kinds of workers: those who have knowledge, an easy practice of ICT and those who do not. Older workers constitute a major part of this second kind of workers. They represent a group that is disadvantaged by technological developments. How may the widespread use of ICT in the workplace impact on older workers' activity? In attempting to answer this question, we will focus on the notion of skills obsolescence. The aim of this article is to focus on methodological triangulation to understand the dynamic construction of skills.

Keywords: ICT · Older workers · Skills obsolescence · Methodological triangulation

1 Introduction

Current society is characterized by two major facts. First, since the 2000s, in France, demographic development heads towards a massive aging of population. Indeed, a better access to health care and quality of life leads to an increase in life expectancy [1]. The main consequence on the professional sphere is the necessity of extending people's working lives. Second, Information and Communication Technologies (ICT), implemented in most of companies' services [2], aim to augment productiveness: they are expected to make companies more efficient and competitive. ICT require new professional demands [3], practices and skills [4]. However, this demographic observation leads researchers to question relationships between work, aging and ICT. Studies reveal that older workers are disadvantaged when using ICT in the workplace [5–7]. In spite of the available resources, older workers would not be efficient with ICT [8]. Another well-known result refers to older workers' ability to learn. These different facts and stereotypes bring about questioning on the notion of skills obsolescence. It would be a major risk for workers, including older people whose skills have been weakened.

J. Zhou and G. Salvendy (Eds.): ITAP 2015, Part II, LNCS 9194, pp. 237–246, 2015.
DOI: 10.1007/978-3-319-20913-5_22

To sum up, the aim of this paper is to bring a psychosocial view on skills obsolescence. Indeed, it would be relevant to consider older workers real activity to bring a new light to this notion, with mainly studies in the field of economics. For this research, we set up various qualitative methods that will allow us to access working situations, in their social, cultural and historical dimensions. Thanks to this methodological triangulation approach, we will try to see if it is really possible to talk about skills obsolescence in the case of older workers activity. If necessary, does a transfer of skills exist between younger and older workers?

2 Aging, ICT and Skills Obsolescence

2.1 Main Characteristics of Aging

Usually, aging is associated with weakening, loss and an ineluctable involution of cognitive and physical performances. This pessimistic perspective presents a deterioration of the individual's different functional abilities (sensory, cognitive, breathing…). In its biological aspect, aging is defined as the degradation of cells functioning. This diffuse and uninterrupted phenomenon [9] manifests itself as a set of stable, abrupt and ineluctable conditions. This slow degradation causes a restriction of human functioning and more precisely of cognitive performances [10]. This decline of cognitive performances influences information processing and especially the ability to inhibit information [11]. Therefore, the capacity to realize produce relevant and coherent complex tasks is limited [12]. This phenomenon reduces a person's resistance and adaptability facing context pressures. However human organism components are not subject to the similar laws. Temporal evolution differs and the body development by cell multiplication provokes an important inter-individual variability, which explains why at the beginning decline is imperceptible. Such changes become detectable at the age of 40/45 and are obvious at 60. Concurrently to these biological phenomena, the individual will develop skills, automatic reflexes and experience [12]. Whenever the situation makes it possible adjustments enable individual to offset, even slow down, the effects of aging. American developmental psychologists supported this perspective and developed the *lifespan developmental psychology* [13]. Conceptual changing occurs with the notion of development: according to these authors, development goes on even during adulthood. In conclusion, aging is defined as a nonlinear developmental process. It results from an immutable interaction between cultural and biological dimensions [14].

2.2 ICT Effects on Older Workers Activity

ICT are considered as a factor of performance, modernity, progress and growth. They have submerged the various professionals' spheres [2, 15]. Beyond its economical functions, ICT show a potential to improve working conditions and well- being at work by extending human capacities [16]. This optimistic vision, related to new work modalities, is balanced by a pessimistic vision, related to a loss of autonomy and flexibility [17]. Indeed, ICT implementation has disrupted work organizations and constantly requires developing new flexible and innovative professional practices

[4, 18, 19]. Consequently, workers have to adapt their skills [20]. If new ICT do not require specific skills, workers become machine-operators who only have to press a button. He is subjected to a devaluation of qualifications [17]. This is how ICT may also have deleterious effects on workers especially already weakened ones. Indeed, many studies notice the diminution of adaptation abilities of older workers [21]. Beyond the use of ICT, it may appear that organizational changes, inducted by recurrent developments, constitute a threat for the oldest workers [22]. In spite of available resources, implementation of ICT leads older workers to a major negative shock [6–8]. Therefore, qualifications suffer from an "encapsulation phenomenon" [23] and would not protect older workers anymore [8]. This phenomenon causes information to be segregated in particular areas. Skillfulness requirement also reconsiders older worker's experience [24], which gives them expertise, an advantage compared to flexibility.

All of these analyses show that the risk of skills obsolescence appears to be major among older workers. Continual modification resulted in rapid ICT evolutions, which increased this risk. Workers have to constantly update their skills and knowledge to remain employable [25]. Skills obsolescence is generally associated to deficiency and decrease of human capital. This notion is defined in 1975 [26] « *as negative changes in capital values that are solely a function of chronological time. Obsolescence occurs because stocks of knowledge available to society change from time to time* » (p. 199). Therefore, obsolescence is not only due to aging, innovations also contribute to this process. Two main types of obsolescence have already been distinguished [27, 28]: technical and economic. Technical skills obsolescence refers to the deterioration of physical and cognitive skills associated to disease, weakening or aging. Economic skills obsolescence manifests itself as irrelevance of previously required skills, which lost their market value. Mainly studied in the field of economics, skills obsolescence is evaluated by various methods. Four main methods have been observed [27]. Among these, authors tell the difference between direct and indirect methods. On one hand, direct methods refer to tests and questionnaires [29]. On the other hand, indirect methods aim for productivity measure [28] and probability to be taken out of the workforce. Even if these measures are robust, they do not allow us understanding the dynamic interaction between older workers and ICT. Moreover, the probability to remain employed in spite of skills obsolescence cannot be appreciated.

3 Research Question

As we have seen above, aging is a complex phenomenon that involves interactions between biological and cultural dimensions. These characteristics' main effect is to increase inter-individual variability. ICT developments and its various repercussions accentuate older workers' difficulties. As soon as problems occurred, employment retention was threatened. However, it is made possible by skills development. However, the risk of skills obsolescence is considerable, in particular for weakened people such as older workers. Similarly, many studies have shown that aging increases the risk of obsolescence. Developmental approach of aging leads us to question which methods and models should be used to evaluate skills obsolescence. As a result of its biological and cultural dimensions, aging is a dynamic process. This means that older workers' behavior does not only depend on intrinsic capacities. These workers also take into consideration environment's features, which influence the way they act. This psychosocial approach of older workers defines each individual based on his capacities, cultural affiliations, norms and the role he has in society. So, in this psychosocial perspective, we can formulate our research question as follows: how can we understand the construction of skills obsolescence during older workers' actual activity? This study will focus on the case of train dispatchers to determine whether they are affected by skills obsolescence. Moreover, we will interest in the conditions that enable older workers to continue to work with ICT.

Concerning the model used to give us some elements of answer: activity models developed by Russian psychologists in 1920s appear to be relevant. One of the principal contributions of activity theories is related to the role and place of the individual who is considered as an actor, situated in the social, cultural and historical context of fulfillment of his activity. In line with Vygotski, Leontiev and Luria's research, Engeström [30] developed the "activity system model" or "Engeström's triangle" (see Fig. 1.). Based on Leontiev's notion of activity, Engeström adds a social and collective dimension to the subject-object-instrument relation. According to this model, a permanent and dynamic process of development characterizes activity, which is not limited to a space-time frame. Aiming to understand the developmental perspective of activity, Engeström emphasizes on dialectical contradictions, which he considers as the potential developmental origins of both activity and individual.

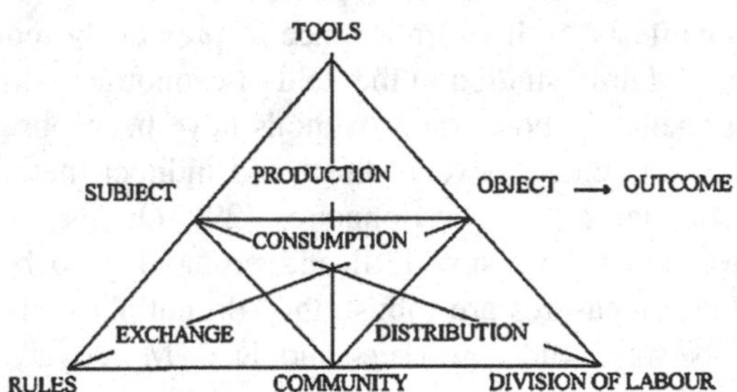

Fig. 1. The basic structure of human activity (Engeström, 1987, p. 78)

4 Methodology

4.1 Context of the Study

The current demographic context leads French companies to wonder about older workers. Our study focuses on the case of the French railway company, which deals with this situation in an intergenerational cooperation perspective. Moreover, massive and continual deployment of ICT defines this company as an innovative one.

More precisely, this research (*currently under development*) concentrates on train dispatchers and ticket inspectors. In this paper, we will focus on train dispatchers.

These agents' profession is about making sure that the train traffic is safe in the area. The underlying objective to this activity is to avoid incident. For this purpose, their work is based on knowing a set of very precise security rules. Agents do not have any room for maneuver, which reduces with successive technical evolutions. We observe that three ways to fulfill the required tasks are identified. The first consists in train shunting. An agent is on the rails and turns the point to run the train. His or her job designation is pointsman. The second way is automated shunting. In this case, agent is situated in the signal box and has to press buttons to open railroad crossing and allow train traffic. A certain number of railroad stations are still fitted with these two systems in France. Finally, computerized shunting has been implemented in the earliest 2000s. Train dispatchers have to enter codes, called "dialogs", to realize inherent tasks of train traffic. Using this system makes the work more complex but the physical load of the profession has significantly reduced.

Therefore, we can see that technical developments lead to many changes in the profession. Both naming and contents have evolved.

During our observations, we noticed that agents use four different tools. All of them belong to computerized shunting. The perimeter extends on three other railroad stations, which are operated by remote control. Each tool has a particular function and completes the others to insure the safety of the traffic. Agents must have to successively juggle with these tools. The first one is an assistance computer. It allows agents to see the time departure of trains in railroad stations on the two ends of the line. Another computer enables agents to deal with a remote control station. To manage two remote control stations and the one they are located in, agents use three other computers that are equipped with system more recent than the other one. Finally, a computer enables agents to enter stops, departures and arrivals of trains. Using these tools, agents have an overall view of the traffic coming from and to their area. Once the train goes inside the area, it can be accurately located. This way, agents may anticipate the opening of signals to make the traffic easier.

Concerning our study's population, it is constituted with six train dispatchers, a unit director and a manager. The six agents work in two different railroad stations that are similar in term of functioning. All of them are men and aged from 25 to 55. The choice to question a unit director and a manager is related to complement agents' profession view.

4.2 Description of the Methodological Triangulation

Many authors have already proved the contribution of methodological triangulation in social sciences [31]. Described as "methods crossing" [32] rather than merely juxtaposition, triangulation enables researchers to understand the complexity of work situations. The various methods used lead to a certain level of quality and subtlety for data. Triangulation confers qualitative methods scientific validity and, *in fine*, precision, spread and depth [33]. Consequently, the originality of our study can be found in the choice of methods that we will make triangulate. The objective is to combine prescribed work and real work.

Research process has been thought in three phases. During each of them, we use different methods.

The first consists in the meeting with train dispatchers. *Semi-structured interview* seems to be the most relevant to get to know well agents. This type of interview has been chosen thanks to the possibility it opens about what thematic to broach. The second decisive element in this choice is the freedom offered to the interviewee. Topics proposed deal with agent's career path, profession, difficulties and ICT connections. Finally, this interview enables researcher to access to prescribed work.

Direct observation of activity and *verbalizations* [34] are at the heart of the second phase. The interests of these methods combination can be found in the access offered to the two parts of activity. On one hand, what is observable in activity and, on the other hand, a part of mental activity leading to tasks realization. Researcher gave agents instructions: he had to do his job as usual and if he wanted, he could clarify what he was doing-. Beforehand, we checked the possibility to interrupt his activity to ask about some actions or points that seemed relevant. These verbalizations are respectively called simultaneous and interrupting. Therefore, real activity of agents, that means what they really do in their work, is understood thanks to these three methods.

Finally, the last phase corresponds to *clarifying interview technique* [35]. It aims to lead the individual to conceptualize his actions. However, conceptualization is not an immediate process; this type of interview assists the individual in awareness. At this moment, he is in an "invocation situation". This enables him to access to implicit dimensions relative to a pre-reflective level. Clarifying techniques allow researcher to understand reasons and meanings of actions and make them comprehensible. More precisely, a few days after observations, we met agents again. We suggested discussing about some situations previously chosen. The selection was made regarding some relevant standards and interests compared to the research question. In this case, we focused on some tasks that involved distinct ways of doing according to agents. These situations could reflect technical, practical or theoretical expertise. They also referred to different types of incident. For example, it could be lateness, an opening of railroad crossing that failed or even point's dysfunction because of the frost.

5 Expected Results

5.1 Main Expectations

In a general way, the objective of this study is to understand the development of older workers' activity, using ICT. This study's expectations are positioned at different levels. Firstly, analysis of data should allow us to identify skills involved in activity. Thanks to the crossing of methods, we will determinate three types of skills: prescribed skills, skills we think we have and real skills applied. The first goal is related to an individual perspective. Secondly, we aim to observe in what way the use of the computerized system does not only depend on the agent, but also on interactions he may have with other individuals in the company. This is a more collective perspective. Finally, the third level is related to the impact using a computerized system on the agent's experience. It refers to a developmental dimension. These expectations should be fulfilled by the methods we use in triangulation.

5.2 First Analyzes

We can add some reflections based on the first analyzes made on the collected data. Firstly, the objective of this research is to understand how skills obsolescence builds up. This developmental approach leads us to consider the older worker as an actor of his working situation. Aging is not intrinsically endured; it is the product of a continual interaction between biological and cultural components.

Older workers may have at their disposal resources that enable them to work in ICT-reliant environments. Considering older worker real activity, can we talk about skills obsolescence? If not, what are the conditions that enable them to be skillful in their profession, including through the use of ICT?

In spite of technical changes and aging, preliminary analyzes suggest a lack of skills obsolescence. Two main dimensions appear to be relevant conditions to prevent this process. Firstly, intergenerational cooperation is shown in a collective activity form. It will lead us to explore more fully the role of the collective dimension in skills development. The second factor refers to an abstract notion: "due course". This subjective characteristic defines the good time to enter dialogs to enable train traffic. Differences observed between train dispatchers show in what way experience and sense of activity is important in skills development.

As a consequence, these two dimensions seem to enable older workers to remain employed in these ICT-reliant working situations. It must be noted that these results emerged from preliminary analyzes. Confirmation of these results will depend on finalization of data collection and an extensive analysis.

Intergenerational Cooperation. The first element that seems favorable towards skills development is *intergenerational cooperation*. Few indicators have been noticed during observations in railroad stations. The oldest workers know practical skills thoroughly while the youngest ones have theoretical skills, which are related to absolutely necessary and rigorous safety rules. Experiential knowledge, mainly possessed by older workers, refers to technical and complex cases. Moreover, we observed that the oldest also possess theoretical skills. However, their ways of doing are more often based on their experience than on safety rules. Indeed, during a complex situation, Mr. H., aged 55, had to regulate train traffic because of a delay. Therefore, he must enter the correct dialogs to enable trains to cross each other. MR. H.'s verbalizations indicated that the situation was problematic. There is a negligible risk of incident. He adds he already had to face this case a long time ago. We assumed that he possesses the solution to the problem. Mr. D., aged 39, interrupted his older colleague's action by saying "*are you sure of this?*" and checked security rules before approving his colleague's decision. Therefore, the skills necessary to traffic system's use seem to depend on an interaction between practical and theoretical dimensions. We can observe that the knowledge of context variables is not sufficient for actions. The skills acquisition related to the use of traffic system depends on interaction between these two dimensions. We could say that a collective organization allows workers - young and older – to become more skillful. On one hand, older worker's skills are accentuated and approved by current safety rules; on the other hand, younger worker's skills are expanded and illustrated by a real situation. Skills are constructed during the use of this technological traffic system. More precisely, collective skills [36] seem to take a major role in the efficient use of the system. It would be relevant to look into collective skills in depth in our further analyzes.

Do the Things in "Due Course". The second piece of information that tends towards a lack of skills obsolescence is the notion "due course". Indeed, various ways of doing have been observed during computerized traffic system's uses. The expedient moment to enter a dialog in the system is the origin of these differences. That is why we observed three main ways to proceed. First, certain agents entered dialogs gradually. Second, others got the dialogs ready and confirmed in "due course". Finally, some of them pre-empted by entering dialogs in a period of time considerably superior to trains arrivals. This notion of "due course" emerged during interruptive verbalizations. We aim to extend our understanding of this notion thanks to clarifying interview techniques. The definition of this notion is different for each train dispatcher. It comes under a subjective reading of security rules. Indeed, agents explained that these rules only prescribe to enable train traffic. Being skillful in this profession means to be able to line up a train without incident. This involves opening signals at the good moment, allowing trains to cross each other, inserting delays in traffic … Since situations are complex and variable, the expedient moment will be different, depending on the agent's interpretation of the situation.

For the most part of older workers, dialogs are entered gradually. According to Mr. D, aged 52: "this way of doing allow us to avoid providing a safety procedure in case of incident". On the contrary, younger workers' practices depend on two modalities. The first one refers to an anticipated input of dialogs. In this case, the validation is done only few seconds before train passage. The second corresponds to the complete input during a specific timeframe. This method is used more often when there is not much traffic. As Mr. C., aged 29 explains: "It is 3 PM o'clock, I enter until 5 PM o'clock like that I can work on other things".

Rooms for maneuver given by the safety rules allow worker to develop appropriate skills to achieve their activity. Their ways of doing will depend on the knowledge that one specific agent has of the system and variables of the situation. These ones are not stuck in time; they progress thanks to their room of maneuver. From these observations, we highlighted the interest of the "due course" notion. Some authors studied the role of these entities that allow professional activities to be effectively organized. They are called "pragmatical concept" [37]. It would be interesting to question more precisely the role of this concept in older workers' skills development in further analyzes.

References

1. United Nations, Department of Economic and Social Affairs. http://esa.un.org/wpp/
2. Bobillier Chaumon, M.E.: Evolutions Techniques et Mutations du Travail: Emergence de Nouveaux Modèles d'Activité. Le. Travail Humain **66**, 163–194 (2003)
3. Vacherand-Revel, J.: Preface. In: Vacherand-Revel, J., Dubois, M., Bobillier Chaumon, M.E., Kouabenan, D.R., Sarnin, P. (eds.) Nouvelles Pratiques de Travail: Innovations Technologiques, Changements Organisationnels, pp. 7–10. L'Harmattan, Paris (2014)

4. Aubert, P., Caroli, E., Roger, M.: New technologies, organization and age: firm-level evidence. Econ. J. **116**, 73–93 (2006)
5. Caroli, E.: Internal versus external labor flexibility: the role of knowledge codification. Nat. Inst. Econ. Rev. **201**, 107–118 (2007)
6. Daveri, F., Maliranta, M.: Age, Technology and Labour costs. Discussion Paper, 1010, The Research Institute of the Finnish Economy (2006)
7. Friedberg, L.: The impact of technological change on older workers: evidence from data on computer use. Ind. Lab. Relat. Rev. **56**, 89–120 (2003)
8. Czaja, S., Sharit, J.: Age differences in the performance of computer based knowledge, personality and motives. In: Cooper, C.L., Robertson, I.T. (eds.) International Review of Industrial and Organizational Psychology, vol. 16, pp. 1–36. Wiley, Chichester (1993)
9. Millanvoye, M.: Le Vieillissement de l'Organisme avant 60 ans. In: Marquié, J.C., Paumès, D., Volkoff, S. (eds.) Le Travail au Fil de l'Âge, pp. 175–209. Octarès, Toulouse (1995)
10. Salthouse, T.A.: What and when of cognitive aging. Cur. Dir. Psychol. Sci. **13**, 140–144 (2003)
11. Hasher, L., Zacks, R.T.: Working memory, comprehension and aging: a review and a new view. In: Bower, G.H. (ed.) The Psychology of Learning and Motivation, pp. 193–226. Academic, New York (1988)
12. Welford, A.T.: Changes of performance with age : an overview. In: Charness, N. (ed.) Aging and Human Performance, pp. 333–369. Wiley, New York (1995)
13. Goulet, L.R., Baltes, P.B.: Life-span Developmental Psychology: Research and Theory. Academic Press, New York (1970)
14. Lecerf, T., de Ribaupierre, A., Fagot, D., Dirk, J.: Psychologie Développementale du Lifespan : Théories, Méthodes et Résultats dans le Domaine Cognitif. Gerontologie et Société. **123**, 85–107 (2007)
15. CAS: L'Impact des TIC sur les Conditions de Travail. La Documentation Française, Paris (2012)
16. Oosterlaken, I.: Design for development: a capability approach. Design Issues 25, 91102 (2009)
17. Vendramin, P., Valenduc, G.: Technologies et Flexibilité. Les Défis du Travail à l'Ere du Numérique. Liaisons, Paris (2002)
18. Caroli, E.: New Technologies, Organizational Change and the Skill Bias: What Do We Know? Economics Paper from University Paris Dauphiné (2001)
19. Greenan, N.: Organisational change, technology, employment and skills: an empirical study of french manufacturing. Camb. J. Econ. **27**, 287–316 (2003)
20. Marquié, J.C., Thon, B., Baracat, B.: Age influence on attitudes of office workers faced with new computerized technologies. App. Ergon. **25**, 130–142 (1994)
21. Teiger, C.: Penser les Relations Âge / Travail au Cours du Temps. In: Marquié, J.C., Paumès, D., Volkoff, S. (eds.) Le Travail au Fil de l'Âge, pp. 15–72. Octarès, Toulouse (1995)
22. Molinié, A.F., Gaudart, C., Pueyo, V.: La Vie Professionnelle: Âge Experience et Santé à l'Epreuve des Conditions de Travail. Octarès, Toulouse (2012)
23. Rybash, J.M., Hoyer, W.J., Roodin, P.A.: Adult Cognition and Aging. Pergamon, New York (1986)
24. Volkoff, S., Molinié, A.F., Jolivet, A.: Efficaces à Tout Âge? Vieillissement Démographique et Activités de Travail. Centre d'Etudes de l'Emploi, Paris (2000)
25. Pazy, A.: Updating in Response to the Experience of Lacking Knowledge. App. Psychol. **53**, 436–452 (2004)
26. Rosen, S.: Measuring the obsolescence of knowledge. In: Thomas Juster, F. (eds.) Education, Income and Human Behavior. pp. 199–232. McGraw Hill, New York (1975)

27. De Grip, A., Van Loo, J.: The economics of skills obsolescence: a review. In: De Grip, A., van Loo, J., Mayhew, K. (eds.) The Economics of Skills Obsolescence. Research in Labor Economics, vol. 21, pp. 1–26. JAI Press (2002)
28. Neuman, S., Weiss, A.: On the effects of schooling vintage on experience-earnings profiles: theory and evidence. Eur. Econ. Rev. **39**, 943–955 (1995)
29. Van Loo, J., De Grip, A., De Steur, M.: Skills obsolescence, causes and cures. Int. J. Manpower **22**, 121–137 (2001)
30. Engeström, Y.: Learning by expanding: an activity theoretical approach to developmental research. Orienta-Konsultit, Helsinki (1987)
31. Leplat, J.: De l'Etude de Cas à l'Analyse de l'Activité. Pistes **4**, 2 (2002)
32. Yin, R.K.: Case Study Research. Design and Methods, 2nd edn. Sage Publications, London (1994)
33. Denzin, N.K., Lincoln, Y.S.: Collecting and Interpreting Qualitative Material. Sage, Thousand Oaks (1998)
34. Newell, A., Simon, H.: Human Problem Solving. Prentice-Hall, Englewood Clifs (1972)
35. Vermersch, P.: L'entretien d'Explictation. ESF, Paris (1994)
36. Montmollin, de M.: Sur le Travail. Choix de Textes (1967-1997). Editions Octarès, Toulouse (1997)
37. Samurcay, R., Pastré, P.: La Conceptualisation des Situations de Travail dans la Formation des Compétences. Éducation Permanente. **123**, 13–31 (1995)

HAVAS: The Haptic Audio Visual Sleep Alarm System

Ali Danesh(✉), Fedwa Laamarti, and Abdulmotaleb El Saddik

MCRLab, University of Ottawa, Ottawa, ON K1N 6N5, Canada
{aahma078,flaamart,elsaddik}@uottawa.ca
http://www.mcrlab.uottawa.ca

Abstract. Sleep inertia is a transitional state of decreased performance or disorientation that occurs immediately after awakening [1]. We introduce HAVAS as a potential prevention measure to sleep inertia. It is a haptic audio visual alarm system that determines an optimal awakening time by considering the sleep stages. It consists of two major parts: Smart Bed Sheet and Smart Phone App. The design principles, methodology, and implementation are explained in detail in the following pages. Additionally, a comparison is drawn between the proposed system and those from similar studies. Moreover, the results of preliminary feasibility tests are presented at the end.

Keywords: Sleep inertia · Sleep stages · Sleep monitoring

1 Introduction

Scientists have been studying sleep for several centuries but modern sleep research started almost a hundred years ago when Berger recorded a human's electroencephalogram (EEG) during sleep for the first time. Loomis introduced Non-Rapid Eye Movement (NREM) by documenting its EEG patterns in 1937. Next, Kleitman and Aserinsky described the Rapid Eye Movement (REM) in 1953. Furthermore, they proposed the existence of a correlation between dreaming and the REM stage of sleep. Then, Kleitman defined a basic sleep cycle and the all night sleep stage architecture. Since then, scientists have been studying sleep disorders based on the properties of the stages of sleep [3,4].

The architecture of a normal sleep includes 5 or 6 cycles. Each cycle takes approximately 90 minutes and follows a sequence of sleep stages. Figure 1 shows the progress of sleep stages across a night in a normal young adult [5, Figure 2-7] with 5 cycles that each of them has two phases: REM and NREM. While human's brain is active in REM phase, it relaxes during the NREM. NERM can be divided into four stages. Stage 1 and 2 are considered to be "light sleep" and the other two stages are called "deep sleep".

However, people suffer from sleep disorders like "sleep inertia" which is a transitional state of lowered arousal occurring immediately after awakening from sleep and producing a temporary decrement in subsequent performance." [1].

J. Zhou and G. Salvendy (Eds.): ITAP 2015, Part II, LNCS 9194, pp. 247–256, 2015.
DOI: 10.1007/978-3-319-20913-5_23

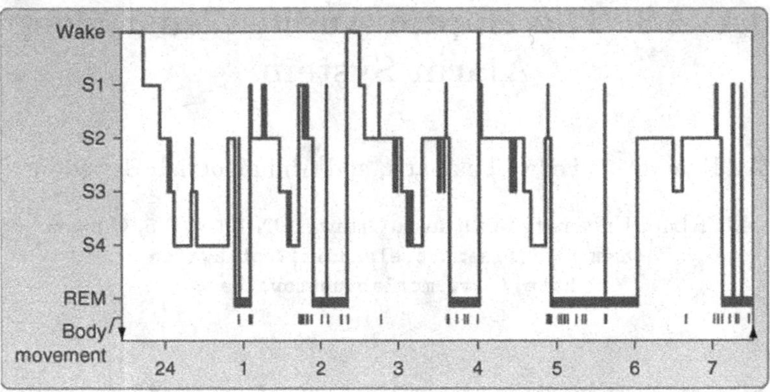

Fig. 1. The progression of sleep stages across a single night in a normal young adult [5, Figure 2-7].

Recently, Santhi et al. studied the effect of morning sleep inertia in alertness and performance [2]. Their results shows that although all cognitive processes are impaired upon awakening, alertness and sustained attention are more affected than working memory and cognitive throughput. Factors like abrupt awakening can cause sleep inertia. Studies have proven that the stage of sleep in which a person was engaged prior to awakening affects sleep inertia. Of the possible scenarios, awakening during light sleep produces the least severe case of sleep inertia while doing so during deep sleep produces the most severe one. Awaking during REM leaves people in a middle ground. Sleep inertia can last anywhere from a few minutes to 4 hours [1].

The present study introduces HAVAS, which is a tangible, portable and embedded alarm system. The system is made of only two parts both of them are light - which makes it portable. The first part is smart bed sheets that can monitor sleep stages using a grid of pressure sensors. In addition, it has a grid of miniature vibrotactile actuators in order to tickle the user at the designated awakening time. The second part is a smartphone app, which controls the bed sheet and provides audio and visual feedbacks. The following sections present the details of the proposed system and results of feasibility test.

2 Related Work

There are many research studies and commercial products that monitor sleep cycles in order to overcome sleep disorders. They can be categorized into four groups: smartphone apps, accessories, cloths and mattresses/pads. A brief review on them is presented here. Smartphone apps use the sensors inside the phone to monitor the sleep stages [6]. Thus, the smartphone has to be kept on the mattress all night. This may not be convenient for some users and it does not work if two or more people share their bed. However, they are portable and easy to use. There is also the possibility of embedding sensors into either accessories such as bracelets [7], watches [8], etc. in the second group or into clothing (e.g. jacket [9]) for the third group. The second and third group are more accurate than the first group since they attach the sensor directly to the user and they are not affected by a third person in cases two or more people sleep on the same mattress. However, most people do not like to wear accessories or extra pieces of cloth when they sleep. The last group is mattresses/pads [10,11]. Since people had already incorporated these items in their sleeping rituals, it requires no adaptation to begin using one with sensors. Also, since they cover the entire bed, they can distinguish between two or more people on the bed and monitor their sleep separately except when they hug each other. However, mattresses and pads are not generally portable.

3 System Design

To begin with, we designed a questionnaire to study some of people's sleep habits. 34 people of an average age of 28.4 years (sd. = 2.87) participated in our study with the following gender distribution: 59 % male and 41 % female. They were university students and employees with different backgrounds in engineering, science, economics, accounting, etc. Table 1 shows their answers to three of the questions posed. Accordingly, 59 % of participants do not take their cellphones to bed. Also, 94 % of people wear neither accessories (including bracelets and watches) nor extra piece of clothing (e.g. jackets, etc.) while sleeping. As regards the provided definition of sleep inertia and its symptoms, it was revealed that 94 % of participants experience sleep inertia at least once a month while 30 % of them suffer from it on a weekly basis. These answers show two significant points. First, this study suggests that a high percentage of participants suffer from sleep inertia. Second, most of the aforementioned solutions reviewed in the literature review would not help them without requiring a change in their sleeping habits since the majority of participants do not take cellphones or wear extra pieces of cloth and accessories when they go to bed. As a result, we decided to work on a solution that uses a component from the bed; one that stems from the last group of solutions in our literature review: mattresses and sleeping pads.

The most beneficial property of the final group of sleep-monitoring products (mattresses and sleeping pads) is that almost everyone uses at least one of them when they want to sleep so they do not need to adapt to an extra device or gadget. However, the main drawback is that they are not portable. As such, people cannot use them when they are away from their homes. To solve this problem, we decided to use bed sheets since they are light and portable but also offer the same convenience that comes with being commonly used when sleeping, much like mattresses and sleeping pads.

HAVAS implements the proposed architecture of Collaborative Haptic Audio Visual Environment (C-HAVE) with emphasis on haptic modality [12]. As Fig. 2 presents the architecture of the proposed system, it involves two parts that are tied together via a Bluetooth connection. The smart bed sheet is responsible of monitoring the sleep stages during the night and provides tangible feedback to

Table 1. The answers to three questions of the user survey.

Question	Answers
Do you take your cellphone in the bed?	Yes: 41 %
	No: 59 %
Do you wear any of these items when you go to bed?	Accessories (e.g. bracelet, watch): 6 %
	Extra Cloths (e.g. jacket, etc.): 0 %
	None: 94 %
How often do you suffer from sleep inertia suffer from sleep inertia when you get up?	Never: 6 %
	Once a month: 35 %
	Once in two weeks: 29 %
	Once a week: 24 %
	More: 6 %

the user at the designated alarm time. The smartphone application, on its end, has two responsibilities. First, it stores the alarm time and controls the smart bed sheets by sending it the commands. Second, it provides audio and visual feedback to the user.

3.1 Bed Sheet Design

Bed sheets have two physical attributes: they are light and thin. In order to keep both of these properties, the proposed solution embedded a grid of resistive pressure sensors and miniature vibration motors in the smart bed sheet. These sensors and actuators are spread out across the bed sheet to cover its entire area. Said sensors are also connected to a processing and communication interface, which receives the data they captured and controls the actuators.

Sleep stages are usually defined using EEG signals however several studies indicate that there is a correlation between the amount of body movements and sleep stages [13,14]. Equation 1 shows the all of the sleep stages sorted by the amount of body movements taking place. Using the pressure sensors, the smart bed sheet captures the body movements and monitors the sleep progress.

$$DeepSleep(S_3, S_4) < S_2 < REM < S_1 \tag{1}$$

Algorithm 1 presents the steps of sleep monitoring. The processing unit of the bed sheet captures the pressure sensor values and performs a pre-processing to eliminate the noise in the data. Then, it counts the number of body movements in 10 minute time periods. 10 minute time windows were chosen since each sleep stage takes 10 to 20 minutes in a normal 90 minutes sleep cycle. After counting the movements, their average is calculated. On average, the number of body movements changes between 0.1 (deep sleep) and 0.4 (S_1) movements per minute [14]. Then, the current stage of sleep is updated. This value is used at the alarm time. The other responsibility of the bed sheet is to provide haptic

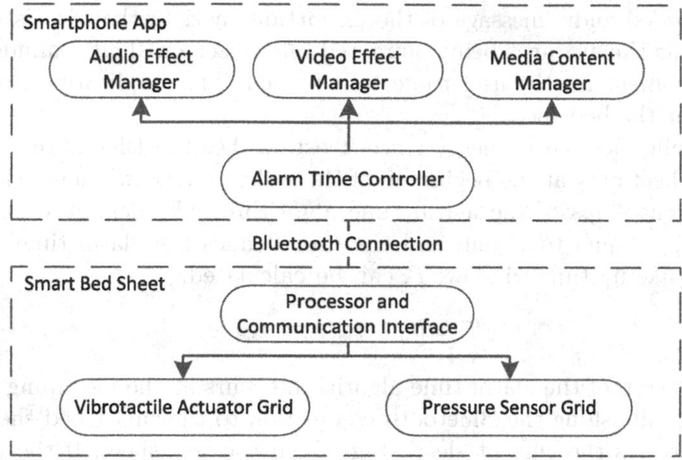

Fig. 2. The abstract architecture of the proposed system.

feedback at the alarm time. This is executed using the vibrotactile actuators. Algorithm 2 describes the abstract alarm time algorithm, which is explained in the following subsection.

Algorithm 1. The abstract algorithm of monitoring sleep stages.

```
while It is not alarm time do
    Read the value of pressure sensors
    Process the captured data and remove the noise
    Compare the new values to the old ones to detect the movements
    if There is a movement then
        Update the number of movements
    end if
    Calculate the average number of movements in the last 10 minutes
    Update the current sleep stage
end while
```

3.2 Smartphone Application

The second part to this sleep-monitoring system is a smartphone application whose main responsibility is to manage the alarm system. Users set the alarm time using this app and it controls the bed sheet at the designated alarm time. The app also offers several other interesting features. It provides two types of alarm sounds: the traditional and usually unpleasant sound of a buzzer and a personalized audio message. The latter option allows users to select an audio file and an avatar for the alarm from either their local or cloud storage (e.g. Dropbox). As such, users can choose to be awoken with a recorded message from a loved one instead of the annoying sound of an alarm. When the audio file ends, a recorded audio message of the important tasks of that day is played to the user while the avatar is being animated on the screen. This reminder can be an encouragement for the user to get out of bed. This application can also be used without the bed sheet.

This application saves energy since it establishes the Bluetooth connection to the bed sheet only at the beginning of the wake up time window. Algorithm 2 shows different steps of the alarm time algorithm. The default value of time window, t_w, is equal to 15 min and the user defines the alarm time value, t_a. Then, the wake up time window, T, can be calculated.

$$T = [t_a - t_w, t_a + t_w] \tag{2}$$

The first step of the alarm time algorithm occurs at the beginning of T and consists of establishing the Bluetooth connection to the smart bed sheet. Next, the app retrieves the current sleep stage from the bed sheet. If the user is in a light sleep, it starts the alarm and sends the bed sheet the command that makes it begin tickling the sleeper. If the user is not in a light sleep, it sends the bed sheet the poke command. Poking the user is essentially a very gentle and short tickle that stimulates the brain in order to change the sleep stage to light sleep, so that the user can then be awaken in light sleep which will help avoid sleep inertia. Then, it waits until t_a. At that time, it checks the sleep stage again. If the user is not in the light sleep, it pokes the user for the second time to change the sleep stage, and waits until the end of T. At the end of T, which means the end of the time allowed by the user, whether the user is in light sleep or not, it starts the alarm and haptic feedback on the bed sheet. It turns them off only when the user leaves the bed. There exist some commercial products similar to HAVAS that force users to leave their bed at the designated alarm time. However, HAVAS has advantages over them. First, it does not need extra space for chasing process (unlike products like Clocky Alarm [15]). Second, people who have auditory diseases can feel the tangible feedback alarm and use this system as well.

4 Implementation

We have built a functional prototype to evaluate the feasibility of the proposed system. An Arduino Mega 2560 is used to process the captured data. Also, only 5 pressure sensors are embedded into this prototype. Each sensor was connected to the supply voltage V_{cc} at one side, and it was connected to an Analogue-to-Digital Converter (ADC) port of a microcontroller and ground via an offset resistor (10kΩ) on the other side. Interlink Elec. FSR 406, which is a force sensitive resistor, was selected as the pressure sensor. The vibrotactile feedback is embedded into the prototype by using Precision Haptic C10-100 motors. BlueSMiRF Gold was used to connect the Arduino board to the smartphone (Fig. 3). Moreover, we developed the smartphone application on the Android platform and ran it on an Android phone to test the system. Figure 4 presents the personalized message recording and the simple avatar pages.

Algorithm 2. The abstract algorithm of awakening for the beginning of T.

```
Initialize the Bluetooth connection
while The user is in bed do
    if (The user is in light sleep) or (It is the end of T) then
        Start the alarm and vibration
        while The user is in the bed do
            Increase the intensity of vibration and the volume of sound
        end while
    else
        Poke the user
        Wait for t_w minutes
    end if
end while
Stop the vibration and alarm
```

5 Results

The prototype device was used to conduct a few preliminary tests in order to evaluate the feasibility of the proposed system. Portability of the system was one of the main principles in our design. Thus, HAVAS was tested on three different types of mattress in order to see whether the mattress can affect the functionality of the system or not. We asked each person to lie on the selected mattresses with the same posture. Table 2a shows the results of this test. The average values of

Fig. 3. The setup of the prototype system.

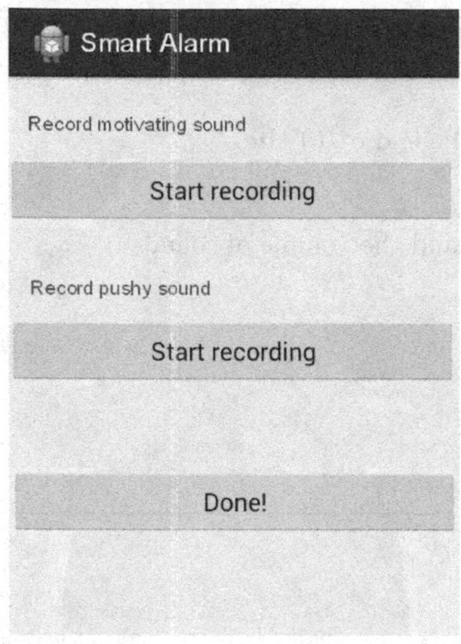

(a) Select audio file page

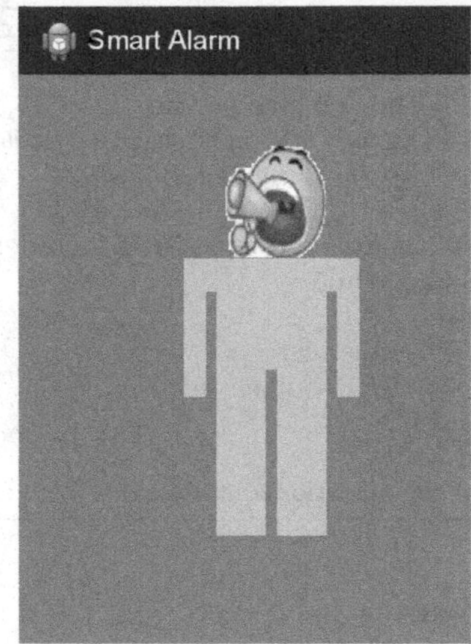

(b) Basic avatar at alarm time

Fig. 4. Two screen shots from the developed app.

captured data are on the same range. Hence, the proposed system is portable and can be used on various mattresses.

Table 2. The results of the feasibility tests.

(a) The mattress type test

Mattress Type	Avg. of ADC Value
Spring	598.95
Sofa Bed	545.05
Foam	642.36

(b) The bed state experiment

Bed State	Avg. of ADC Value
Empty	0
Sitting	397.99
Lying	598.95

Table 2b shows the average of ADC values for three scenarios: empty bed, sitting on the bed, and lying on the bed. Each participant performed these scenarios on the same mattress (i.e. spring mattress). It is clear that the average for the empty bed is much less than the other two while sitting values and lying values are in different ranges.

Figure 5 shows the ADC values during body movement at 0.01 second time intervals. In this experiment, the user turned from supine position to right log. Using the changes on values, HAVAS counts the number of movements and monitors the progress of the sleep cycle. The haptic feedback test was the last conducted experiment. As Fig. 6 shows, the user experienced the vibrotactile feedback in this order: two gentle short vibration pulses (0.5 second) at the beginning and middle of t_w and one vibration of a continuously rising intensity at the end of the alarm t_w.

We discussed the sharing bed problem earlier, but there is another concern regarding the proposed system. Bed sheets are usually washed frequently. However, it is not easy to wash objects that have electronic parts. This smart bed sheet can be used as a mattress cover and placed under a normal bed sheet in order to reduce the need to wash.

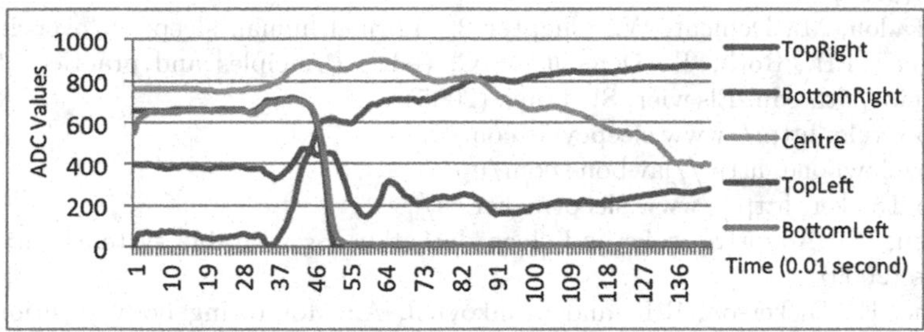

Fig. 5. The ADC values while a user is changing his posture from supine to right log.

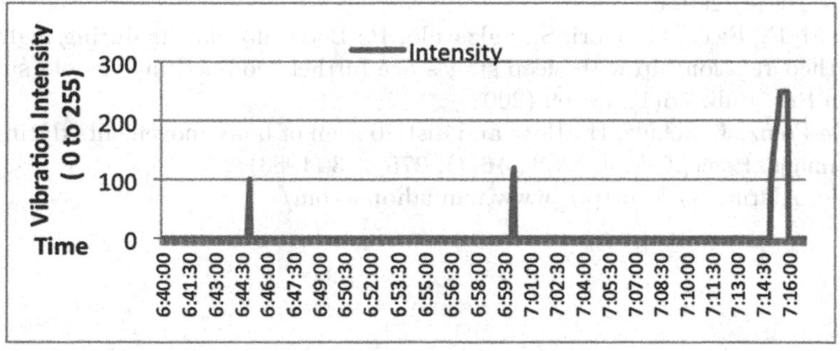

Fig. 6. The vibrotactile feedback test result.

6 Conclusion and Future Work

We have presented a smart portable alarm system that can help eliminate sleep inertia by addressing sleep stages. This system uses embedded sensors to monitor the progress of the sleep cycles and finds an optimal awakening time during the predefined time window. Then, it provides tangible, audio, and visual feedbacks to the users in order to wake them up. Moreover, we conducted some preliminary tests to validate the feasibility of the proposed system and were met with conclusive results. However, an extensive trial is needed to evaluate the accuracy of sleep stage detection and study the effect of provided haptic feedback in long term uses.

References

1. Tassi, P., Muzet, A.: Sleep inertia. Sleep Med. Rev. **4**(4), 341–353 (2000)
2. Santhi, N., Groeger, J.A., Archer, N.S., Gimenez, M., Schlangen, L.J.M., Dijk, D.J.: Morning sleep inertia in alertness and performance: effect of cognitive domain and white light conditions. PLoS One **8**(11), e79688 (2013)
3. A brief history of sleep research. http://www.stanford.edu/~dement/history.html/
4. Dement, W.C.: The study of human sleep: a historical perspective. Thorax **53**, S2–7 (1998)
5. Carskadon, M., Dement, W.: Chapter 2 - normal human sleep: an overview. In: Kryger, M.H., Roth, T., Dement, W.C. (eds.) Principles and practice of sleep medicine, 5th edn. Elsevier, St. Louis (2005)
6. Sleep Cycle. http://www.sleepcycle.com/
7. Up by Jawbone. http://jawbone.com/up
8. Sleep Tracker. http://www.sleeptracker.ca/
9. Karlen, W.: Adaptive wake and sleep detection for wearable systems. In: Ph.D. thesis (2009)
10. Hoque, E., Dickerson, R.F. and StankovicJ, A.: Monitoring body positions and movements during sleep using wisps. In: Wireless Health (2010)
11. Mack, D., Alwan, M., Turner, B., Suratt, P. and Felder, R.: A passive and portable system for monitoring heart rate and detecting sleep apnea and arousals - preliminary validation. In: Distributed Diagnosis and Home Healthcare (2006)
12. El Saddik, A.: The potential of haptics technologies. IEEE Instrum. Meas. Mag. **10**(1), 10–17 (2007)
13. Giganti, F., Ficca, G., Gori, S., Salzarulo, P.: Body movements during night sleep and their relationship with sleep stages are further modified in very old subjects. Brain Res. Bull. **75**(1), 66–69 (2008)
14. Wilde-Frenz, J., Schulz, H.: Rate and distribution of body movements during sleep in humans. Percept. Mot. Skills **56**(1), 275–283 (1983)
15. Clocky Alarm Clock. http://www.nandahome.com/

CogniWin – A Virtual Assistance System for Older Adults at Work

Sten Hanke[1,6(✉)], Hugo Meinedo[2], David Portugal[3], Marios Belk[3,4], João Quintas[5], Eleni Christodoulou[3,6], Miroslav Sili[1], Miguel Sales Dias[2], and George Samaras[4]

[1] Health and Environment Department, Biomedical Systems, AIT Austrian Institute of Technology GmbH, Vienna, Austria
sten.hanke@ait.ac.at

[2] Microsoft Language Development Center, Lisboa, Portugal

[3] Citard Services Ltd., Nicosia, Cyprus

[4] Department of Computer Science, University of Cyprus, Nicosia, Cyprus

[5] Instituto Pedro Nunes, Coimbra, Portugal

[6] University of Geneva, Computer Science Centre (CUI)/Institute of Information Service Science, Geneva, Switzerland

Abstract. This paper presents an innovative virtual assistant system, which aims to address older adults' needs in a professional environment by proposing promising and innovative virtual assistance mechanisms. The system, named CogniWin, is expected to alleviate eventual age related memory degradation and gradual decrease of other cognitive capabilities (*i.e.* speed of processing new information, concentration level) and at the same time assist older adults to increase their learning abilities through personalized learning assistance and well-being guidance. In this paper we describe the overall system concept, the technological approach, the methodology used in the elicitation of user needs, and describe the first pre-trials' evaluation.

1 Introduction

Virtual assistance systems can play an important role for increasing the productivity in professional work environments where employees are engaged in complex computerized tasks, which require an intensive cognitive effort and high levels of concentration. Virtual assistance providing easy to understand and self-adaptive guidance is paramount to increase the user's efficiency when interacting with computers. For older adults, aged 55 and above with expectations for an active professional future, virtual assistance can provide even greater benefits [1].

Typically, when working in highly computerized environments, members of this age group are required to attain new knowledge and adapt their capabilities to cope with fast software changes in their organizations. This often results in hesitating behavior and anxiety, which can cause long-term discomfort and frustration at the workplace [2].

CogniWin proposes to continuously track different biometric measurements, aiming to implicitly extract information about the user physiological status, such

J. Zhou and G. Salvendy (Eds.): ITAP 2015, Part II, LNCS 9194, pp. 257–268, 2015.
DOI: 10.1007/978-3-319-20913-5_24

as arousal states in stressfull conditions, while interacting with the computer. Advanced monitoring is achieved combining data input from three devices: An instrumented intelligent mouse, an eye tracker, and the Microsoft Kinect One for Windows.

Besides acquiring real-time data from different sources, the system captures information about the actions that are being performed by the user, and provides a repository to store important user-related contextual information obtained a priori, such as health profile and user capabilities. Thus, the system is able to transmit knowledge for both existing and new employees and automatically adapt and improve by capturing, saving and learning daily activities, as well as contextualizing them.

Multi-sensor data fusion will drive advanced behavior analysis to aid in real-time user interaction analysis and recognition of abnormal behaviors. This will in turn trigger adequate personalized well-being advice actions, assisting the user to quickly achieve predetermined goals and improve performance.

In order to address CogniWin's objectives, the project tackles technological innovation beyond the state-of-the-art in the following areas: (*i*) Development of an affordable intelligent mouse integrating multiple sensors to measure physiological parameters and corresponding software to analyze the collected data, in order to provide personalized support to the user; (*ii*) Design and development of a user profile based on specific metrics of cognitive processing parameters, which greatly influence the execution of computerized tasks; (*iii*) Design and development of adaptive and natural user interfaces based on user context and on their related cognitive model; (*iv*) Development of innovative context-aware ICT services for active and adaptive on-demand support and access to integrated information, guidance and well-being advice, promoting increased performance and problem-solving abilities to older adults with a minimum of support from other people.

2 The CogniWin Architecture

The architecture can be broken down in four separate layers: **hardware**, which is closely connected to the **lower level components**, including device drivers and the database. The **higher level components**, used to analyze and store data and finally **user interface components**, for user interaction.

The hardware and lower level components layer includes: (*i*) Knowledge repository and database; (*ii*) Eye tracker; (*iii*) Intelligent mouse; (*iv*) Microsoft Kinect One for Windows. The higher level components include: (*i*) Behavioral analysis; (*ii*) Contextual recorder; (*iii*) Data fusion; (*iv*) Cognitive model; (*v*) Application model. Finally, the user interface components include: (*i*) Well-being advisor; (*ii*) Personal learning assistant. Figure 1 shows the overall logical architecture of the CogniWin system.

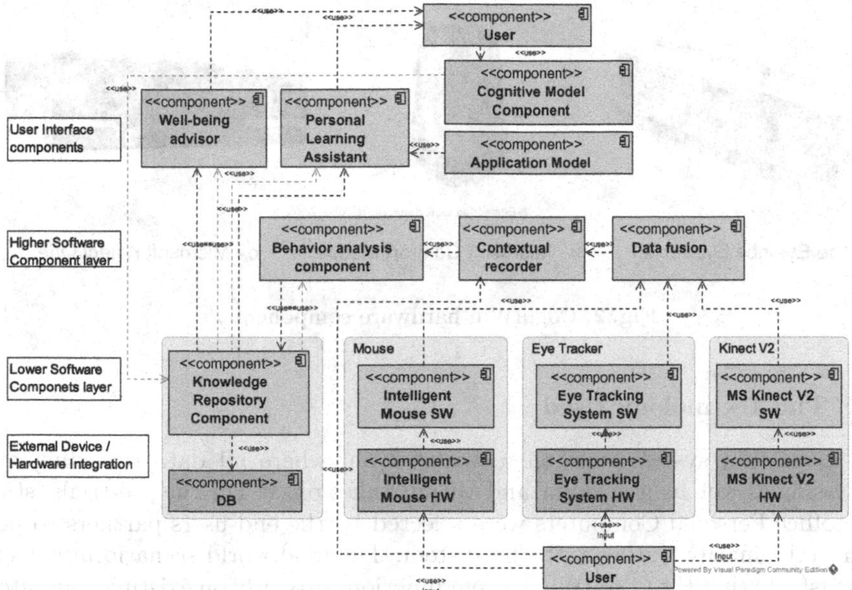

Fig. 1. The overall CogniWin architecture.

2.1 The CogniWin Components

The hardware integration and lower level software components comprise the basic layer of the architecture. Lower level software components are usually drivers (*i.e.* intelligent mouse, eye tracker, Kinect One) of the hardware components which are connected to the PC. The **database** is the central place of data storage in the CogniWin system. A special part of the database is the **knowledge base** which contains and manages all the information about the individual users performance. This component receives inputs from the contextual recorder and the data fusion components. This last one combines data from the eye tracker, the intelligent mouse and the Microsoft Kinect One. These two components are in the higher software layer.

Microsoft Outlook [3] and Citard Active [4] (running in Google Chrome) are the client applications currently supported by the **application module**. As the CogniWin system should be usable with many more applications, each one will need a custom application model. This model contains information about all possible tasks as well as interaction points (buttons) and metadata, such as the application name and version. The contextual recorder is able to detect the active window and store the corresponding application name and version. By searching through this metadata, the personal learning assistant is then able to find a suitable application model.

Fig. 2. CogniWin hardware components.

2.2 The Technology Used

The CogniWin system runs on a workstation, where all data recording and processing as well as user input and output takes place. For the pre-trials, standard office Personal Computers were selected by the end-users partners to perform preliminarily testing with the system. This real world scenario intends to demonstrate that the CogniWin system functions properly on existing computers without the need to buy new expensive hardware. The **Workstation** requires at least two free USB 3.0 ports to connect the eye tracker and the Kinect One for Windows and one USB 2.0 port for the intelligent mouse. It should be a 64-bit machine with a minimum of 4GB of RAM. Since the algorithms used by the eye tracker and the Kinect One are computationally intensive, the workstation should at least have a mid-range processor.

The **Eye Tracker** (Fig. 2a) is a product of "THEEYETRIBE" [5]. It has a small form factor ($20 \times 1.9 \times 1.9$ cm) and can be used together with desktops, laptops and tablets. It does not need a dedicated power supply, and it can even be used on the go. The tracking works by illuminating the face of the user with infrared LEDs and capturing video footage of it. The video is analyzed with eye tracking algorithms which extract gaze related data. This technology is suitable for most environments, but is best used indoors without direct sunlight on the device. It supports screen sizes of up to 24″ and has two sampling rates: 30 Hz and 60 Hz.

The **Intelligent Mouse** (Fig. 2b) is developed in the scope of the CogniWin project. It embeds sensors to measure the galvanic skin response (GSR), grip force, heart rate, temperature, and trembling. It can be used to detect user stress, anxiety, fatigue, lack of confidence and more, [6–8].

The **Microsoft Kinect One** (Fig. 2c) is a depth sensor device developed by Microsoft, which has been intensively used in research lately, due to its use in innovative natural human computing solutions across a variety of industries. It encompasses depth sensing technology based in time-of-flight (TOF) of infrared light, a built-in color camera, an infrared (IR) emitter, and a microphone array, enabling it to sense the location and movements of people as well as their voices.

The CogniWin system supports the Microsoft Windows Operating System. A relational database management system is used in connection with the knowledge repository as data storage. The knowledge repository works as an abstraction layer, decoupling the database from all other components. This enables the use of other languages than SQL to store data, since only the knowledge repository deals with the database itself. CogniWin also makes use of RabbitMQ 3.42, which is a message broker enabling communication between the different components. For example the eye tracker component will send its data asynchronously via RabbitMQ to the data fusion component, which will process it and send it to the knowledge repository for permanent storage which can be then requested by the well-being advisor.

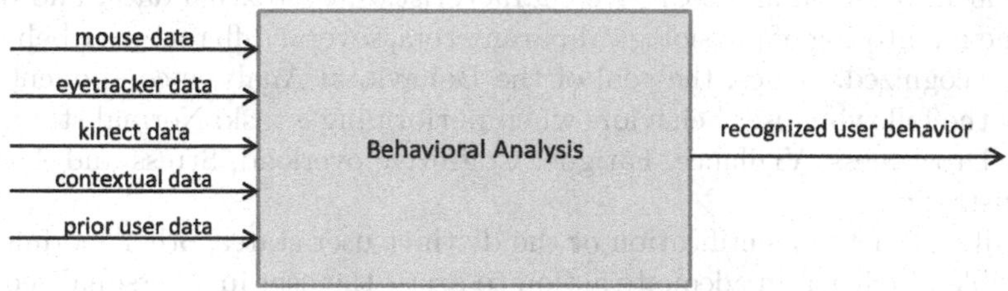

Fig. 3. Behavior analysis component overview.

3 User Behavior Analysis

In order to provide personalized support to the user, the CogniWin system must be able to perceive and contextualize the user behavior. Having this in mind, several cues are extracted from the sensors and devices at the lower level of the architecture, which are combined with user's task performance data and prior knowledge to assess the user's state and trigger assistance (*cf.* Fig. 3).

When using the intelligent mouse endowed with an advanced embedded sensor suite, the system will continuously monitor and measure physiological parameters [9], such as the galvanic skin response and sweat of the hand of the user, gripping force, heart rate, temperature, and measurements of shaking or hand trembling. Figure 2b illustrates the first prototype of the intelligent mouse based on a common model from Microsoft. Additional measurements are provided via the contactless eye-tracker, namely, eye gaze point, pupil size, blinking rate, fixation rate and duration, saccades rate and duration, and maximum velocity. Moreover, the Microsoft Kinect One [10] can eventually be leveraged to extract other information, *e.g.* user's posture, facial expressions, gesture interpretation, and voice tone.

As seen above, user-related information can be extracted using the lower level devices. However, it is also crucial to extract task-related information, therefore enabling CogniWin to contextualize the user's task, assess its performance and infer on the user behavior. To this end, the Contextual Recorder component will be responsible to log the user's keyboard and mouse events, and identify which task, process or services the user is running so as to determine the context according to the actions performed. This is based on log trails, screenshots, mouse motion and key-loggers.

The Knowledge Repository will collect the data extracted by the Contextual Recorder, and also retain the older adults' know-how, as well as their health profile. This will allow the system to learn and adapt to the user specificities, as well as providing personalized assistance.

The user interaction with the system results in the combination of the outcomes of the aforementioned modules via the Sensor Fusion component. By means of advanced behavioral analysis and reasoning algorithms, considering prior health, personal and cognitive characteristics, contextual data, and online real-time monitoring of physiological parameters, several different user behaviors will be recognized. Hence, the goal of the Behavioral Analysis component is to identify the following user behaviors when performing a task: Normal state, Hesitation, Drowsiness, Vigilance, Fatigue, Cognitive overload, Stress and Anxiety, and Frustration.

Finally, after the identification of the distinct user states, other modules are responsible to trigger an adequate action to assist the user in a personalized way, as seen in the next section.

4 User Support

The features of personalized assistance and guidance in the CogniWin system are provided essentially by two components, respectively the Personal Learning Assistant (PLA) and the Well-Being Advisor (WBA).

4.1 Personal Learning Assistant (PLA)

The PLA module provides personalized tips and advice (textual, video, audio) on contextualized tasks based on the users cognitive characteristics, on the identification of the ongoing working activity and based on integrated indicators (*e.g.* time per task, tasks organization, level of concentration, etc.) thus aiding the user to achieve goals and improve performance. The PLA will intervene in case of detecting abnormal user performance so as to provide adaptive support and guidance services to reduce the anxiety and stress level of the user.

The PLA system addresses mistakes and hesitations of employees while performing tasks by providing them a contextual help or a step-by-step procedure for their tasks achievement. A common case is when the end users already know how to use a system but find difficulty in certain tasks. It also provides suggestions for recovering from mistakes or suggestions for performing options when hesitations are detected.

The PLA is a top layer service working in close connection with the Knowledge Repository, the Contextual Recorder and the end users' cognitive model. It compares at runtime, users activities with their specific record of tasks and historical activities. The PLA will display a help invitation, once it detects:

- First time Task
- Decreased performance
- On user request

These are taken into account in order to refine users preferences and their corresponding cognitive model for upcoming tasks.

First Time Task (FTT). Based on the past recorded events (x,y mouse position, active software, action) the system is able to detect if the user is doing the associated task for the first time or not. In the first case, the system will display a help invitation describing the action undertaken by the user and the list of associated documents, videos or pictures stored in the Knowledge Repository. The user can either choose the most suitable form of help or decline the invitation. Based on cognitive models the PLA will feature the most suitable form of help. If the user chooses another form, the preferences will be taken into account for the next PLA invitation. Since this is a FTT, no user personalized metrics are yet associated with it. The basic comparison point will be the median stored metrics (if any) resulting from different users while dealing with this task. Otherwise, the user performance will be stored as reference and associated to the task.

Example: The user places the mouse on x,y (screen spec) corresponding to the "create an automatic reply" (Task) on outlook (active window) and clicks on it (trigger). The help display window appears and invites the user to choose between a tutorial, a video or some pictures showing different scenarios. Based on the user's cognitive model, the video will be the first link followed by the pictures and finally the tutorial.

Decreased Performance (DP). The algorithm to detect DP assumes that the user has completed the task previously and that there is a record in the database associating it to the user. In this case (DP) the time between each click will be longer than the median time stored in the database. Depending on the median value, a minimal time should be specified for each task before considering that the user needs help. For example, if it takes around 10 seconds to click on the next link after having chosen "create an automatic reply", the help invitation will not be displayed immediately after the median time is exceeded. In order to keep it friendly, we will display it only after the median time has been exceeded by 15 seconds.

On User Request. During the user's activity, the system is continuously monitoring the active window and the mouse position. Once the user clicks on the PLA icon, in the active task bar, the PLA will display help according to the user's current activity. As it can be difficult to determine exactly for which tasks the help is being requested, the invitation will display all existing information associated to the active window screen.

4.2 Well-Being Advisor

The Well-Being Advisor (WBA) is a top layer component, along with the Personal Learning Assistant. It interacts with the computer users and provides personalized advice to prevent unwanted age related health situations and to alleviate eventual decrease of cognitive capabilities, thus effectively preserving and improving the users well-being.

The WBA addresses unwanted situations that are known to substantially reduce the users productivity such as tiredness, incorrect sitting position, anxiety and stress, also preventing health related work absences. The WBA makes use of the advanced monitoring sensors from the CogniWin system (*e.g.* the intelligent mouse and the eye tracker). These devices measure several physiological and visual parameters which in turn enables the WBA to analyze the output and provide personalized support. The WBA also takes into consideration the users health related characteristics by checking a profile previously stored in the system database.

When the user is too tired the productivity will decrease. The Well-Being Advisor will address user tiredness following two distinct approaches: promoting regular work breaks, and actively detecting when the user exhibits tiredness symptoms.

Promoting Regular Work Breaks. Tiredness symptoms can be partially mitigated by promoting work breaks at regular intervals. This is based on the idea that frequent breaks can improve mental agility [11] and prevent the user from draining all its energies. One of the most well know time management methods following this idea is the "Pomodoro Technique" [12] which uses a timer to break down work into intervals, traditionally 25 min in length, separated by short breaks. CogniWin implements this method allowing the user to configure the work and pause intervals. Furthermore, we intent to combine this static method with information from the active sensors to allow more flexible decision making. For instance, we can anticipate a short pause if the sensors detect tiredness or delay the pause if the system knows the user is concentrated and being productive.

Active Detection of Tiredness Symptoms. Using information from the eye tracker sensor it is possible to determine when the user is too tired for work or even if the user has fallen asleep. The WBA continuously monitors the eye tracker measurements, filtered by the Data fusion and Behavior Analysis components and decides when to advise the user to take a break.

Anxiety and Stress. Anxiety and stress are two well-known factors responsible for causing health and productivity degradations on workers [13]. Older users can feel more anxious or stressed when dealing with frequent software changes or when facing new computer tasks. The CogniWin system issues a warning message proposing a short break or stress reducing exercises when it detects that the user is experiencing high levels of anxiety or stress. To perform this task, CogniWin takes advantage of the physiological sensors continuously measuring the users Galvanic Skin Response (GSR) which is a direct indication for the anxiety and stress levels being experienced by the person, again filtered by the Data fusion and Behavior Analysis modules [9].

5 Evaluation

The initial system evaluation will take place in the pre-trail phase of the project, during February 2015. The Pre-trials evaluation will: *(i)* Provide feedback to the CogniWin developers, on topics such as the validation of the architecture and the specification of all individual modules. This will ensure that as early as possible in the project, we obtain invaluable insight about most of the concepts and usability issues, which undoubtedly can make for much more robust final prototype implementations, *(ii)* Provide input to the CogniWin developers regarding the user interface from the high-level modules (Personal Learning Assistant and Well-being Advisor). We will analyze the users real interactions to determine if the proposed assistance is well accepted and what adjustments will be needed, *(iii)* Validate and provide feedback for the evaluation metrics themselves (both automatic and user feedback). Adjustments to the evaluation metrics, methodology and tools will be made following the pre-trial results.

5.1 Pre-trials Installation

The pre-trial pilot hardware and software will be installed and evaluated at the premises of Orbis Medisch en Zorgconcern, Netherlands [14] and ArgYou AG, Switzerland [15], the two end-users organizations of the project consortium. In the case of Orbis Medisch en Zorgconcern, the pre-trial systems will be tested on two separate facilities, both situated in the city of Sittard-Geleen in the Nederlands. One of the facilities is the Orbis Medical Centre (OMC), a general regional hospital, built in 2009 and presently one of the most advanced hospitals in Europe. The other facility is the Orbis Hoogstaete, a modern elderly care center. For both, the pre-trials will be performed in conference-rooms and will run on all-in-one PCs with mouse, keyboard and the eye-tracking device. The target application is the Citard Active software, normally used by the administrative staff. Orbis participates with seven volunteer users that will have the opportunity to test the system and also fill-in the questionnaire at the end of the trial period.

The user group is composed by adults aged 55 or older, with or without light physical or cognitive age related limitations, who are engaged in computerized tasks that require an intensive cognitive effort and a high level of concentration. For the Orbis Hoogstaete facility, this specifically includes care coordinators, occupational therapists, and animation employees. For the Orbis Medical Centre the users are office administrative employees.

In the case of ArgYou AG, the pre-trial systems will be tested in the CogniWin office at ArgYou AG in Berne, Switzerland. For the pre-trial, all-in-one PCs with intelligent mouse, keyboard and eye-tracking device are available. Microsoft Outlook software will be available on each PC. All the participants of the trials are included in the following criteria: over 50 years-old and working with branch specific knowledge (tourism, banking, hotel business, food and beverage industry, insurance companies, etc.). All participants will sign an informed consent which is specified by the project's privacy protection plan.

Table 1. Overview of the evaluation objectives.

Goals	Module	Type	Indicators
a. User improved the work efficiency (decreased performance)	PLA	objective	The number of executed computerized standard tasks increases, i.e., more tasks will be accomplished within the same time period
b. User improved the work efficiency (first time task)	PLA	objective	The average duration of a computerized task decreases, indicating that over certain period of time the person obtained help from the system and managed to be more efficient for subsequent similar tasks
c. The system provided useful help	PLA, WBA	objective	The average number of times the CogniWin modules were triggered and that the person accepted the assistance increases
d. The user perceived the help as useful	PLA, WBA	subjective	The timing of the assistance is evaluated as correct by over 60 % of the end users
e. The user perceived the help as useful	PLA, WBA	subjective	The appearance of the assistant is well accepted (score > 6 at range 1 – 10)
f. The system improved the user's work wellness	WBA	objective	The average measured anxiety and stress level reduces
g. The user perceived that its work wellness improved	WBA	subjective	The questionnaire responses indicate that the user's anxiety and stress level has reduced

5.2 Evaluation Goals and Methods

After a initial preparatory phase, the CogniWin functionalities available for the Pre-trial will be activated. During this phase the CogniWin system will collect data and interact with the user to provide assistance. After the Pre-trial ends, all automatically collected data will be analyzed to calculate the objective evaluation indicators. The user will be requested to fill an online questionnaire at the end of the Pre-trial for assessing subjective evaluation aspects such as measuring the user acceptance and satisfaction with the new input devices and the CogniWin system.

Table 1 represents the evaluation goals and the corresponding indicators that will be calculated for assessing the project objectives. We divided the evaluation into subjective indicators, obtained from the user's responses to the online questionnaire and objective indicators, calculated from the stored data. At the time of writing this article, the results of the pre-trials evaluation are not available yet, and will be the subject of deep analysis in the short-term future.

6 Conclusion and Future Work

The paper presents the first prototype implementation of the CogniWin system, an innovative virtual assistant to support and motivate older adults that work on computerized activities, to remain active and productive by providing personalized learning assistance and well-being guidance. The consortium recognizes the importance of supporting this target user group in their work environment, and the CogniWin system is an answer to such challenge, aiming to effectively enabling older adults to cope better with software changes in their workplace and organizations. The paper describes in detail the different modules of the CogniWin system, as well as the methodology developed to evaluate the first pre-trial tests performed with real end-users. It is also noteworthy that our implementation is not restricted to a generic help functionality. The help provided is adjusted to address the user's preferences and to take into consideration previous interactive sessions, where the user successfully completed the planed tasks. Additionally, the measurement of physiological and performance parameters, when using the CogniWin system, will help the user to obtain optimized support as well as perform automated detection when unwanted situations occur. During the second project year, we will focus on enhancing the system with more functionality which has been planned in the scope of the project. This implementation especially involves the implementation of more enhanced data fusion and behavioral analysis components, as well as a cognitive model. These components will enable the system to address the person's needs in a more optimized way. The aim is that the Cogniwin system gets self-learning functionalities to provide the user (or user groups) the best and unobtrusive support possible. In the cognitive model component we plan to group behaviors and preferences of individual users but also user groups. Depending on these specifications also new users will be supported in an optimized way. The cognitive model will take the information into account gathered from the behavior analysis as well as the contextual recorder. The first results have shown that a system like CogniWin is appreciated by the user and can be helpful to support them in their daily work with the computer. Especially when there is a difficult software systems involved. Anyway we think that it will be very important to provide the user an optimized support. Otherwise the system can easily be considered as annoying and will not be used. To be able to provide this optimized support on individual level, we first gather unobtrusive data (intelligent mouse, eye tracker, contextual recorder) and on the other side provide high self-learning capabilities of the system as well as a complex behavior and data analysis. Both facts are considered as being helpful to provide a highly accepted system which will be used and is efficiently supporting the older people at work.

Acknowledgment. This work was partially carried out in the frame of the CogniWin project, funded by the EU Active and Assisted Living Joint Program (AAL 2013-6-114).

References

1. Camarinha-Matos, L.M., Afsarmanesh, H.: Virtual communities and elderly support. In: Advances in Automation, Multimedia and Video Systems, and Modern Computer Science, pp. 279–284 (2001)
2. Kanfer, R., Ackerman, P.L.: Aging, adult development, and work motivation. Acad. Manag. Rev. **29**(3), 440–458 (2004)
3. Microsoft Outlook (2015). http://www.microsoft.com/en-us/outlook-com
4. Citard Active (2015). http://citard-serv.com/products-cascn.php
5. The Eye Tribe (2015). https://theeyetribe.com
6. Sun, D., Paredes, P., Canny, J.: MouStress: detecting stress from mouse motion. In: ACM SIGCHI Conference on Human Factors in Computing Systems (CHI 2014), ACM Press, Toronto, 26 April – 1 May 2014
7. Pedro, S., Quintas, J., Menezes, P.: Sensor-based detection of alzheimers disease-related behaviors. In: The International Conference on Health Informatics (ICHI), Springer. Vilamoura, November 2013
8. Kaklauskas, A., et al.: Web-based biometric computer mouse advisory system to analyze a user's emotions and work productivity. Eng. Appl. Artif. Intell. **24**(6), 928–945 (2011)
9. Belk, M., Portugal, D., Christodoulou, E., Samaras, G.: CogniMouse: on detecting users task completion difficulty through computer mouse interaction. In: Extended Abstracts of the ACM SIGCHI Conference on Human Factors in Computing Systems (CHI 2015), ACM Press, Seoul, 18–23 April 2015 (in Press)
10. Microsoft Kinect One for Windows. http://www.microsoft.com/en-us/kinectforwindows
11. Tambini, A., Ketz, N., Davachi, L.: Enhanced brain correlations during rest are related to memory for recent experiences. Neuron J. Neurosci. **65**(2), 280–290 (2010)
12. Cirillo, F.: The Pomodoro Technique, Creative Commons (2009)
13. Theorell, T.: Workplace Stress causes and consequences. The American Institute of Stress. http://www.stress.org/workplace-stress-causes-and-consequences
14. Orbis Medisch en Zorgconcern. https://www.orbisconcern.nl/home/
15. ArgYou AG. http://www.argyou.com

Developing Mobile Application Design of Virtual Pets for Caring for the Elderly

Hsiu Ching Laura Hsieh(✉)

Department of Creative Design,
National Yunlin University of Science and Technology, Douliu, Taiwan
laurarun@gmail.com

Abstract. In the population ageing society, the companionship and care of the elderly, the medical system, and the consumer trend cannot be neglected. The contact with the external and the ones caring about oneself is essential for the elderly. This study aims to develop application with the functions of healthcare and accompanying, and the accessibility design is included in the interface, where virtual pets are the major communication media to assist the elderly in using mobile application. The required functions and contents in mobile application as well as the preference for the interface and models of interaction for the elderly are investigated in this study. It aims to ease and convince the elderly of the easy use. In the process of cultivating and training the virtual pet mobile application, the elderly could be accompanied and reduced the sense of loneliness; in the further use and interaction with virtual pet mobile application, the physical and metal conditions of the elderly could be real-time monitored and recorded to assist monitoring stations in managing the physical conditions of the elderly and nursing personnel in periodical checks. This research is preceded as following. First, literatures are reviewed. Second, Focus Group Interview is utilized for concluding the application contents and functions and the requirements and preference of the elderly for virtual pets. Third, an application experimental prototype is designed according to such requirements and preference. Fourth, the questionnaire, aiming to test the usability of the elderly, is filled. Fifth, the principles and suggestions for mobile application design suitable for the elderly are concluded based on the test results and analyses. The research outcome would assist in and contribute to the accessibility design of mobile application and the application to medical care by providing possible solutions for insufficient caring manpower in ageing societies and uneven distribution of medical resources.

Keywords: Mobile application · Virtual pet · Virtual elder care · Accessibility

1 Introduction

According to the research of World Health Organization, population ageing is a global problem in the 21st century. Taiwan has stepped in the ageing society since 1993 and the aged population above the age of 60 was 17.4 % of total population in 2013. The Executive Yuan estimated that the ratio would reach 37.5 % by 2056 [4]. In the population ageing society, the companionship and care of the elderly, the medical

J. Zhou and G. Salvendy (Eds.): ITAP 2015, Part II, LNCS 9194, pp. 269–277, 2015.
DOI: 10.1007/978-3-319-20913-5_25

system, and the consumer trend cannot be neglected. The contact with the external and the ones caring about oneself is essential for the elderly. Jive Software, a famous software company in the USA, indicated in 2011 that the probability of the elderly suffering from dementia in poor social networking environment was 60 % higher than the others in active environments [7]. To solve the problems of senses of accompanying and security, a lot of people choose pets to be the companions. Plenty of research on animal-assisted therapy has been studied in the world. In addition to real pets, the application and development of virtual pets could also be transferred into an option of senior care. To solve insufficient medical human capital and resources, the software which allows the elderly applying the mobile application to the medical network real-time interaction software is developed to observe the physical and mental conditions of the elderly. It could be a kind of highly feasible nursing in the future. Integrating virtual pets to replace inflexible machines or nursing personnel allows developing handy mobile application contents for nursing and accompanying the elderly.

The elderly healthcare in Taiwan has become critical as the aging society is forming. Nevertheless, the uneven distribution of physicians between rural and urban has resulted in the lack of medical resources in remote areas [2]. According to the physical conditions of the elderly, it is not easy for them leaving houses for health checks. Besides, the elderly loneliness is caused by the children not being able to take care of their parents because of work or residence in different places. The elderly with self-care functions could effectively reduce the health problems and enhance the health and welfare [6]. For this reason, a virtual pet-based mobile application for caring for the elderly with the functions of self-care and company is developed in this study. It allows the elderly knowing the health conditions, real-time sharing the results with friends and relatives through smartphones, and reducing the loneliness by raising virtual pets. The mobile application prototype is designed, according to the elderly characteristics, for the experimental test to discuss whether the user interface and functions conform to the elderly demands. In this study, the interface characteristics of satisfaction, memorability, error rate, and efficiency are discussed.

2 Literature Review

2.1 Mind and Body Functions of the Elderly

Lee [8] concluded the degenerating functions of the elderly with the age as below.

- **Motive function:** Easy to fall due to reducing strength, low balance, longer operation time for the elderly than for the youth, but less errors because the elderly request higher operation accuracy than operation speed; however, the antagonistic relationship between operation speed and accuracy could not be used for explaining the reason of the elderly being sluggish.
- **Perception function:** (1)Vision. By increasing the time, the errors increase in the green-blue area, especially with low illuminance, while the error rate is lower in the red-yellow area. The elderly perceive narrower chroma that the color discrimination is worse when the color value is close. (2) Hearing. The elderly do not comprehend

the computer voice, cannot distinguish the location of high frequency and temporary sound, but could distinguish low frequency and temporary sound. 3) Haptic perception. Convex marks are more easily recognized than concave marks with haptic perception.

- **Cognitive function:** The elderly could reduce the dependence on work memory through practice. The use of event-oriented prospective memory interface could enhance the compatibility between interface elements.

2.2 The Principles of Mobile Application Interface Design

Shneiderman [9] proposed this collection of principles that are derived heuristically from experience and applicable in most interactive systems after being properly refined, extended, and interpreted. (1) Strive for consistency. (2) Enable frequent users to use shortcuts. (3) Offer informative feedback. (4) Design dialog to yield closure. (5) Offer simple error handling. (6) Permit easy reversal of actions. (7) Support internal locus of control. (8) Reduce short-term memory load.

2.3 The Usability of Interaction Design

Based on Nielsen [2], the usability is defined as the following. (1) Learnability: has to do with how quickly and easily users can begin to do productive work with a system, which is new for them. Learnability is how quickly and easily users can reach a level of proficiency in using the system. (2) Efficiency: Efficiency is the number of tasks per unit of time that the user can perform using the system. (3) Satisfaction: is the subjective opinion that users form about the system (or about some parts of it). It is the most elusive usability attribute, as it is completely dependent on subjective opinion of users. (4) Error rate: This refers to the errors made during the use of the system and how easy it is to recover from them [2]. (5) Memorability: This refers to the ease of remembering the way a system must be operated. Nielsen [2] describes this as the characteristic of a system that allows the user to return to the system after some period of not having used it, without having to learn everything all over again. According to above statements, the mobile application prototype of virtual pets for caring and accompanying the elderly is constructed. The application interface is further tested to conform to the demands of the elderly in Taiwan. The user interface characteristics of satisfaction, errors, learnability, and efficiency are tested in this experiment.

3 Methods

The methods are introduced as following. First, literatures are reviewed. Second, Focus Group Interview is utilized for concluding the mobile application contents and functions and the requirements and preference of the elderly for virtual pets. Third, an mobile application experimental prototype is designed according to such requirements and preference. Fourth, the questionnaire, aiming to test the usability of the elderly, is filled. Fifth, the principles and suggestions for application design suitable for the elderly are concluded based on the test results and analyses.

3.1 Focus Group Interview

Focus Group Interview is utilized for concluding the elderly demands and preference for the mobile application functions and virtual pets. Six elderly participants (aged above 65) are living in Taiwan. From the Focus Group Interview results, the elderly need to tell the mobile application from other programs that pop-up windows are better for the reminder. In regard to the preference for virtual pets, most elderly prefer dogs and cats, especially small dogs with big eyes and big ears. In terms of functions, the reminders of medication and exercise records are favored, and menu records are convenient for the elderly rapidly finding the demands. Most elderly are satisfied with the function to contact the friends and relatives and expect virtual pets to present the functions of looking after the house, security guard, and emergency treatment.

3.2 Constructing Mobile Application Prototype and Questionnaire Design

The prototype of mobile application is constructed and the questionnaire is designed according to the elderly demands and preference in the previous step. Figure 1 shows the application test structure. The test in this study combines care records with pets.

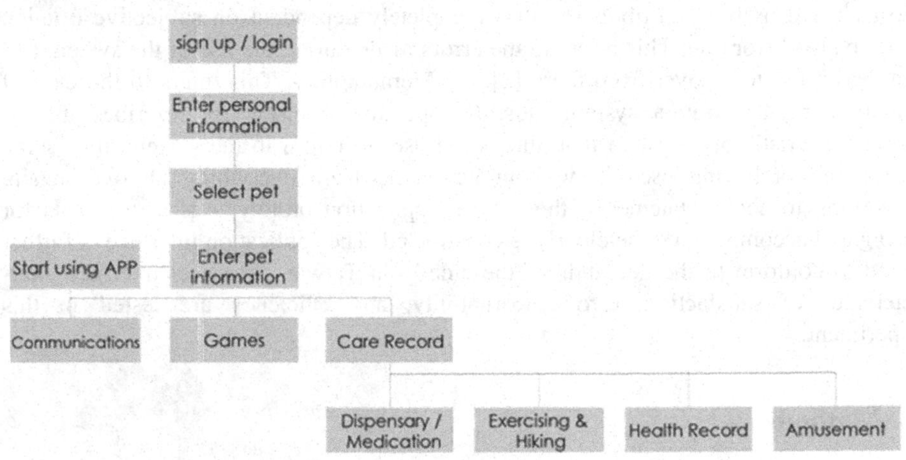

Fig. 1. Mobile application structure

When starting using the application, the major function is divided into communication, games, and care record, where the pet is the helper of such functions.

- Communication: After accumulating for a period of time, it would remind the user to contact with the friends and relatives.
- Games: The brain training games are utilized for slowing down functional degeneration.
- Care record: It is classified into four categories.
  (1) Pharmaceutical Dispensary/Medication: It is used for selecting the variety of medication and recording time. Pet feedback would be acquired after completing the task (Fig. 2).
  (2) Exercise and Hiking: It is used for selecting exercise or pet walking and recording time. Pet feedback would be acquired after completing the task (Fig. 2).

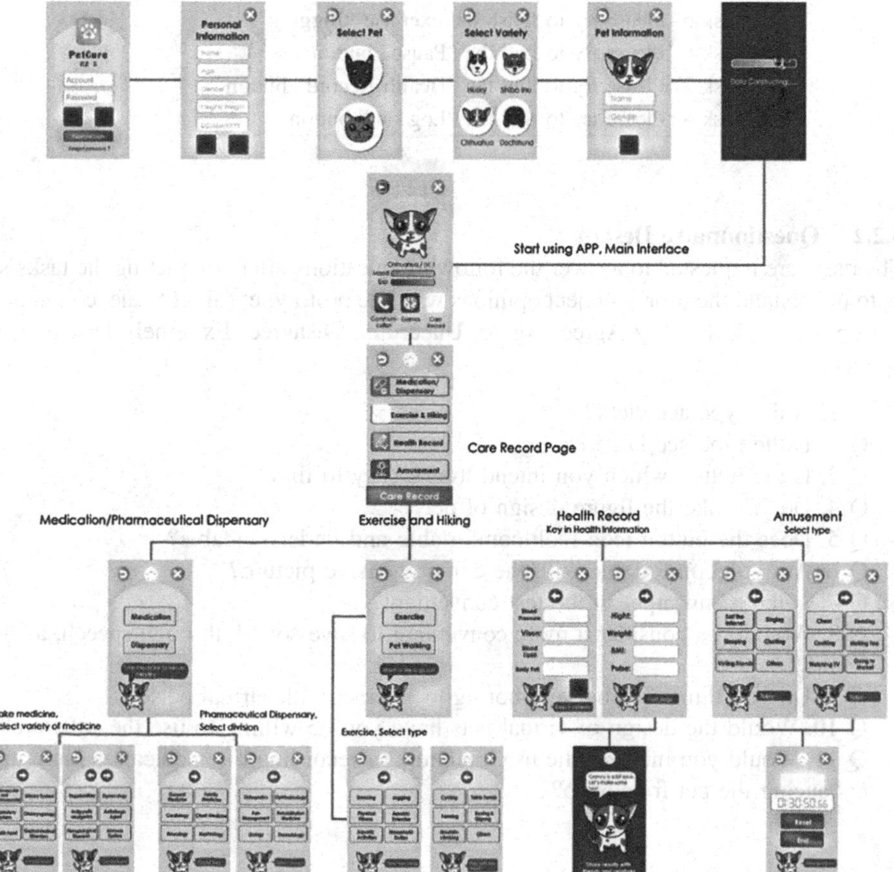

Fig. 2. Mobile application prototype

(3) Health Record: It is used for inputting personal health record, and pet feedback would be acquired (Fig. 2).
(4) Amusement: It is used for selecting amusement and recording time, and pet feedback would be acquired (Fig. 2).

3.2.1 Task Assigned

Total eight tasks are executed by the participants. A testing staff would inform the participants about the tasks, while the other testing staff would record the process. All the tasks are preceded by time and count (Table 1).

Table 1. Task assigned

Task 1	Please try to find the "Care Record" page
Task 2	Please try to find the "Medication/Dispensary" button
Task 3	Please try to find the medication "Antiallergic"
Task 4	Please try to find the "Exercise" button
Task 5	Please try to finish the exercise "Jogging"
Task 6	Please try to find the "Pause" button
Task 7	Please try to find the "Health Record" button
Task 8	Please try to find the "Log out" button

3.2.2 Questionnaire Design

The users are requested to answer the following questions after completing the tasks so as to understand the user's subject opinions with the prototype. Likert Scale, containing the options of Extremely Agree, Agree, Uncertain, Disagree, Extremely Disagree, is applied.

- Q 1. Is the typeface clear?
- Q 2. Is the typeface large enough?
- Q 3. Is the button which you intend to use easy to find?
- Q 4. Do you like the figure design of pets?
- Q 5. Does the button icon look comfortable and understandable?
- Q 6. Are you comfortable with the comprehensive picture?
- Q 7. Is the menu input in the test convenient?
- Q 8. Would you consider it more convenient to save sound, through speech, as the record?
- Q 9. Do you think it being less boring to interact with virtual pets?
- Q 10. Would the design of virtual pets have you be willing to use the software?
- Q 11. Would you increase the use intention by recording the medication habit and enhancing the pet friendship?

- Q12. Would you be happy when the pet learns new skills (sitting down, shaking hands, and so on)?
- Q13. Hence, would you be more motivated to use the application program?
- Q14. Could the pet reminder help you remember to take medicine?
- Q15. Do you think the reminder function being convenient?
- Q16. Do you need the pet reminder function?

3.3 Participants in User Test

Among the total 12 participants, 2 of them are below 60-year-old and 10 are above 65-year-old. The average age is 66.5. All of the elderly live in Taiwan, and 6 of them have the experiences in using smart phones, while the rest 6 do not.

3.4 Results of User Test

Table 2 shows the test results of efficiency and learnability. For Task 1, the carebutton is searched with text explanation. The tested interface efficiency reveals the average speed 3.1 s, with certain efficiency. Tasks 2–7 contain the horizontal menu with the same information structure that the operation procedures are similar. From Table 2, the time for the participants executing from Tasks 2–3 to Tasks 4–6 and then Task 7 decreases obviously. It presents the easy learnability of the interface system for the participants learning the standard procedure in the similar operations. Task 8 relates to the testing efficiency, from which the average speed appears 15.6 s, and most participants could not immediately find the log-out button, because the icon does not show additional text explanation. Additional texts or icon improvement therefore are required for the low readability.

Table 2. Analysis of user task by time

	Subject 01	Subject 02	Subject 03	Subject 04	Subject 05	Subject 06	Subject 07	Subject 08	Subject 09	Subject 10	Subject 11	Subject 12	Average
Task 1	1	1	1	5	6	1	1	6	9	3	2	1	3.1
Task 2	9	12	4	5	4	4	9	17	6	5	6	11	7.7
Task 3	1	2	1	2	2	2	6	1	2	2	2	2	2.1
Task 4	10	12	2	7	5	5	6	4	5	3	9	5	6.1
Task 5	2	1	2	1	1	2	4	2	1	1	1	1	1.6
Task 6	2	1	1	1	1	1	1	1	1	1	1	1	1.1
Task 7	1	2	6	5	1	1	2	2	2	1	1	1	2.1
Task 8	6	9	8	12	3	30	56	10	12	5	16	20	15.6

Table 3 displays the test results of error rate and learnability. No error appears on Task 1, revealing that a button with icon and text is the optimal design. Horizontal menus with the same information structure are used for Tasks 2–7 that the operation procedures are similar. Errors merely appear on Tasks 2–3, but not on Tasks 4–7 that the learnability is also proven. Merely icons, without text explanation, are shown for the buttons in Task 8 that the error rate is high. Comparing Task 1 and Task 8, text explanations might be as important as icons for the elderly.

Table 3. Analysis of user task by count

	Subject 01	Subject 02	Subject 03	Subject 04	Subject 05	Subject 06	Subject 07	Subject 08	Subject 09	Subject 10	Subject 11	Subject 12
Task 1	1	1	1	1	1	1	1	1	1	1	1	1
Task 2	2	3	2	2	2	2	2	2	2	2	3	2
Task 3	1	1	1	1	1	1	1	1	1	1	1	1
Task 4	2	2	2	2	2	2	2	2	2	2	2	2
Task 5	1	1	1	1	1	1	1	1	1	1	1	1
Task 6	1	1	1	1	1	1	1	1	1	1	1	1
Task 7	1	1	1	1	1	1	1	1	1	1	1	1
Task 8	1	1	2	1	1	2	2	2	2	1	1	1

Table 4 shows the questionnaire result, which is divided into usability and interactive emotion. Questions 1–7 in the first part are related to usability (typeface, button, pet figure, icon, comprehensive picture, and menu input), while questions 8–16 in the last part are related to interactive emotion (demands for sound record, pet interactivity, and pet reminder). With Likert 5-point Scale, the questions are scored 1–5 for the options of Extremely Disagree to Extremely Agree for the satisfaction. Overall speaking, the average score is above 4, presenting that the mobile application conforms to the elderly demands and satisfaction.

Table 4. Analysis of overall questionnaire result

Question No	Subject 01	Subject 02	Subject 03	Subject 04	Subject 05	Subject 06	Subject 07	Subject 08	Subject 09	Subject 10	Subject 11	Subject 12	Mean
1	4	4	4	4	4	4	4	4	4	4	4	5	4.1
2	4	4	4	4	5	4	4	4	4	4	4	4	4.1
3	4	4	4	4	4	4	4	4	4	4	4	5	4.1
4	5	4	4	4	5	3	4	4	5	4	4	4	4.2
5	5	4	4	4	4	4	4	4	4	4	4	4	4.1
6	5	4	4	4	4	4	4	4	5	4	4	5	4.3
7	5	3	4	4	4	4	4	4	5	4	4	5	4.2
8	5	4	4	5	5	5	4	4	4	4	4	4	4.3
9	4	4	4	4	4	4	4	4	3	4	4	5	4.0
10	5	4	4	4	4	4	4	4	4	4	4	5	4.2
11	5	4	4	4	5	5	3	4	4	4	4	5	4.3
12	5	4	4	4	4	4	4	4	4	4	4	5	4.2
13	5	3	4	4	4	4	4	4	5	4	4	5	4.2
14	5	4	4	4	4	4	4	4	4	4	4	4	4.1
15	5	4	4	4	4	5	4	4	5	4	4	5	4.3
16	5	4	4	4	4	4	4	4	4	4	4	4	4.1

4 Discussion and Conclusion

After the test, the experimental result and the predicted effect are generally satisfactory. It is found that images marked with texts are more easily recognized by the user to enhance the efficiency of interface use. As a result, texts might be more important than images for the elderly. When preceding tasks with the same model, the time spent would be reduced and the error rate is also decreased, showing that the mobile application prototype interface conforms to the elderly demands and preference. The overall learnability is high. Having the participants look for images without texts, it is found that the elderly can hardly recognize the function of such images that the error rate is high. It is suggested that image should be added texts in the successive interface design to decrease the error rate. The overall questionnaire survey reveals high satisfaction of the participants with the interface. Besides, the designed image of the visual pet is friendly that it indeed could enhance the participants' pleasure using the interface.

According to the experimental result, the participants commonly consider voice records or direct use of button being more convenient than text input. Pet interactivity could enhance the participants' use motivation. The questionnaire data show the demands for the prompt function of medical treatment, exercise, and contact which therefore could be completed. In regard to the final suggestion, the elderly in Taiwan reveal distinct opinions about pet functions, with which looking after the house, security guard, and emergency rescue could be combined. The experimental results reveal that the design of virtual pets actually could enhance the elderly willingness to use the mobile application, and the elderly indeed have the demands for caring and contact functions. The elderly preference for pet image and interactivity could be further developed and designed. Besides, the elderly in Taiwan can correctly identify the buttons with texts on mobile phones. The research results could help designers and design developers develop interactive interface for the elderly.

References

1. Akinagac, S., Tsuneo K.: Healing effect of virtual pet. Psychol. Res. **8**, 39–44
2. Chen, C.Y., Yang, Y.C.: Taiwan Geriatr. Gerontol. **2**(3), 209–224 (2007)
3. Díaz-Bossini, J.M., Moreno, L.: Accessibility to mobile interfaces for older people. Procedia Comput. Sci. **27**, 57–66 (2014)
4. Fan, G.J., Hsu, Y.H.: Socio-economic impacts of population aging in taiwan. Taiwan Geriatr. Gerontol. **5**(3), 149–168 (2010)
5. Hiroko, K.: What kind of influence does online virtual pets have on people. Jpn. Soc. Educ. Inf. **25**(2), 3–14 (2009)
6. Hoy, B., Wagner, L., Hall, E.: Self-care as a health resource of elders: an integrative review of the concept. Scand. J. Caring Sci. **21**(4), 456–466 (2007)
7. Kivimäki, T., Kölndorfer, P, Vainio, A.-M., Pensas, H., Vuorela, T., Garschall, M., Vanhala, J.: User interface for social networking application for the elderly. In: Proceedings of the 6th International Conference on Pervasive Technologies Related to Assistive Environments, Rhodes Island, Greece, 29–31 (2013)
8. Lee, C.F.: Product design for the elderly users. J. Des. **11**(3), 65–79 (2006)
9. Nielson, J.: Why you only need to test with 5 users (2000). http://www.useit.com/alertbox/2000319.html
10. Shneiderman, B., Plaisant C.: Designing the User Interface: Strategies for Effective Human-Computer Interaction. Addison-Wesley, MA
11. Wang, M.T.: Possible design directions of healing toys for caring the aging group. J. Des. **17**(2), 1–24 (2012)
12. Wu, K.C., Tsao, H.Y., Tsai, C.Y.: Introduction to tablet PC APP for the elderly. In: Conference of Gerontechnology and Service Management, 13–14 (2013)

Implementing the SimpleC Companion: Lessons Learned from In-Home Intervention Studies

Chantal Kerssens[1(✉)], Renu Kumar[2], Anne Edith Adams[2,3], Camilla C. Knott[4], and Wendy A. Rogers[3]

[1] eyiApp, LLC, Atlanta, GA, USA
chantal@eyiApp.com
[2] SimpleC, LLC, Atlanta, GA, USA
{rkumar,aadams}@simpleC.com
[3] Georgia Institute of Technology, Atlanta, GA, USA
wendy@gatech.edu
[4] Aptima, Inc., Washington, DC, USA
ccknott@aptima.com

Abstract. This paper provides insights from our experiences that would guide the implementation of home- and community-based intervention studies, in particular field tests of technology in older adults with varying degrees of cognitive impairment and their informal (family) caregivers. Critical issues include recruitment in a vulnerable and frail population, intervention and protocol design, environmental and technology-specific barriers to implementation, and facilitators of success. Our experiences and recommendations should be relevant to a broad range of longitudinal field tests, particularly those with older adult populations.

Keywords: Assistive technology · Caregivers · Dementia · Seniors · Disease management · Caregiver burden · Recruitment · Retention · Applied research · Field test · mHealth · Healthcare technology

1 Introduction

The SimpleC Companion ('Companion') is a behavior and symptom management technology designed specifically for older adults, yet also suitable for younger individuals who have an assistive need. Assistive needs may be defined as behaviors, symptoms or routines that are suboptimal and can benefit from an intervention such as reminding, redirecting, calming or stimulation. Common Companion interventions, for example, include scheduled reminders to take medications, drink water, eat something (healthy), complete an exercise routine, or get ready for important events such as paying bills, doctors visits or activities of daily living (ADL, e.g., getting up, getting dressed, oral hygiene, toileting, bathing). These reminders are embedded in a salient sequence of audiovisual stimuli that typically include a combination of images, music and voice recordings of trusted individuals. The different media reinforce what the person should do or accomplish, for instance showing people exercising together in a

J. Zhou and G. Salvendy (Eds.): ITAP 2015, Part II, LNCS 9194, pp. 278–289, 2015.
DOI: 10.1007/978-3-319-20913-5_26

gym or class to prompt someone to exercise. Pleasing music and an introductory, personal message help the person gently orient, be reminded and motivated to take action. Similarly, many common behavior and mood symptoms, such as depression, apathy, agitation, and sleep difficulties can be mitigated by music and pictures that are positive and personally relevant and that calm, redirect or engage (e.g., a beautiful beach scene paired with the sound of rolling ocean waves to help induce sleep). The 'shows' play for a period of time (e.g., 30 min).

Companion interventions are based on individual needs, preferences, and routines, and are used by healthy older adults as well as persons with mild cognitive impairment or dementia. The interface is simple and intuitive in its design to accommodate users with limited computer literacy and/or impairments common in late life, such as altered vision, hearing, motor and cognitive function.

2 Intervention Goals and Overview

We set out to test the Companion technology and concept in a home- and community-based environment to prepare for serving the unique market of older adults or others with assistive needs living at home. Although the Companion has been a commercial product since 2009 and is used by more than 650 residents of retirement facilities across eight U.S. states, it was never tested in-home with individual families and persons in need of support. We were particularly interested in determining whether the physical environment of the home (multiple rooms, floors, and occupants) would be conducive to a wellness technology like the Companion; whether similar or different user needs existed in this market; and whether a mobile, tablet-based platform is preferable in this market. Specifically, we aimed to assess the usability of the Companion across different levels of cognitive impairment (none, mild, moderate), and its usefulness to care recipients and caregivers. Given this focus, several small samples of caregiving dyads were selected.

Table 1. Study characteristics

	A	B	C
Duration	3 weeks	12 weeks	3 weeks
Touch screen	stationary, 21″	stationary, 21″	tablet, 10″
N (dyads)	7	5	7

Within dyads, the care recipient (CR) was defined as the person for whom the Companion was personalized; the caregiver (CG) was defined as the spouse, partner or adult child taking prime responsibility for or interest in the wellness and/or care of the CR. In all three studies (A, B, C), dyads completed a telephone screen, a baseline assessment (in-home) and a life story and needs interview (in-home) prior to receiving their personal Companion. Once installed in the home, dyads used the Companion 3 or 12 weeks on a large, stationary touch screen or tablet (Table 1). During the intervention period, participants were contacted regularly (weekly) to answer questions, address problems and accommodate user requests for changes, if any. Post-intervention, the CGs and CRs completed technology adoption questionnaires and a goal attainment scale, and were interviewed.

Protocols were reviewed and approved by an independent institutional review board (Sterling IRB, Atlanta, GA). All participants gave written informed consent or assent if unable to sign consent.

3 Recruitment

3.1 The D-word: Dementia

Although there is a great need for studies that evaluate the usability, feasibility, and efficacy of technology-based interventions for persons with dementia (PWD) and mild cognitive impairment (PMCI), these individuals are often excluded from participation given their impairment and the ethical and methodological questions it raises: To what extent can they provide consent, answer questions and properly follow directions? By explicitly recruiting them into our studies and making accommodations to ensure our methods were ethical and would yield valid and valuable results, we were excited as a scientific team to approach PWD and PMCI and offer them a role and voice in our work. Implicitly, we expected dyads to be excited too and eager to participate, especially because we offered a solution and help free of charge. Instead, we met many a cold shoulder. As we quickly learned, dementia is surrounded by stigma, misconceptions, and uncertainty and may have legal ramifications, all of which are barriers to recruitment. Dementia is the D-word.

To many people, dementia implies ‘losing your mind’, your identity, your dignity and indeed that is often how the disease is portrayed even by professionals who know the syndrome well: It is scary and robs you of everything. What many fail to see or do not know, is that it may take years or decades before advanced impairment sets in and even then, there are vast individual differences in how the disease manifests itself and abilities are lost. Meantime, technology and other resources can help maintain or train functions so as to mitigate disease progress and relieve care recipients and caregivers alike. Early on however, that is not what people know or want to hear when they have received a diagnosis or are coming to terms with one. In essence, you as a researcher are a messenger and reminder of bad news, which nobody likes no matter how good your story or solution is. This makes it particularly difficult to recruit healthy and pre-symptomatic older adults, who fear the prospect of dementia and do not want to hear or think about it. Ironically, it is this demographic that may benefit most from early intervention. The implication is to carefully craft your message and materials. Focus on common problems and concerns, such as sleep, nutrition and exercise, in higher functioning individuals who still feel strong, capable and unimpaired. Once you caught their interest and eye, they may volunteer information that conveys the real need, and chances increase you discover other needs in a non-threatening manner. In lower functioning individuals, the same probes may be given with different details: in this group, the concern is not so much whether grocery shopping and cooking is completed independently and regularly, but rather that prepared meals are consumed 3 times a day and the person is motivated to come to the table and participate in meals. Either way, both groups are struggling with nutrition, maintaining weight and healthy routines. This can be addressed respectfully and appropriately when you know your audience and the difficulties they or their families commonly face.

In the absence of a diagnosis, it may also not be clear that a problem is a problem. Consequently, people may not identify with your recruitment message and efforts even when it applies to them and they are good study candidates. We all forget to turn off the light sometimes and may have trouble remembering a face or name. When do we call it or recognize it as a problem? In the face of slow but gradual decline, it may be particularly difficult for older adults to decide that something is wrong and they or a loved-one need help. Not uncommonly, a crisis or adverse event is the wake-up call to seek guidance, advice or help. In our experience, many seniors are reluctant to discuss their needs or difficulties or will dismiss or ignore tell tale signs. Our own studies included several individuals who tested positive for MCI or dementia using a quick screening tool, without having an official diagnosis. This reality and grey area raises a host of ethical questions and should caution researchers to tread carefully: do not assume people know they have a problem or want to know. Researchers should also be creative and flexible in their approach: Develop several narratives (use cases) that allow different target users to self-identify, to recognize the potential merit of your technology or intervention, and to develop an interest in participating. We found that a focus on activities and concerns rather than on a diagnosis or disorder was more palatable to participants. Describe common struggles or omissions, such as paying bills on time and getting up a decent time every morning. Many older adults, especially when they are retired and/or have lost their life companion and live alone, struggle with these routines that have the potential to become a real threat to health and wellness. PWD face these struggles too, but by focusing on the activity and routines (or lack thereof) rather than the disease, everybody can self-identify in one way, shape or form, and join the conversation without risking stigmatization.

In the continuing care retirement communities (CCRCs) where we initially recruited amongst independently living residents who tend to be relatively healthy, we felt a reluctance to discuss assistive needs with us because admitting to such needs may alter the level of care a couple receives from the CCRC, increase their monthly costs, and possibly force both or one of the partners to move to a higher level of care, outside the home. Even when we explained that all data were and would be treated confidentially, and study participation was unlikely to have negative consequences, there was a palpable reluctance to discuss assistive needs. Researchers should attempt to understand the dynamics that are at play in the communities where they recruit, be it financial, social, legal, or otherwise, before they start recruiting. This will help avoid painful errors and save time in the end. Having community advocates or informants, preferably inside the target population, will help to get started and to develop narratives and support. Organize regular 'wine & cheese' events to build rapport, observe the dynamic and group, and identify individuals who may help your cause and those who will not. Engaging both groups of stakeholders (the Pros and the Cons) is vitally important as they each inform what makes or breaks a successful field trial. In one of our communities, for instance, the residents were unhappy about the rollout and cost of

Internet services. When we came in and prided ourselves on being ‘wireless’ and mobile, many residents scoffed and had a bad taste in their mouth fully beyond our control. Identifying the gems that will help your effort or the ways around local barriers is essential to a good, successful trial. Subsequently, focus groups can help identify themes and narratives further.

3.2 Two More D-S: Deficits and Decline

Although a focus on dementia can make it extra difficult to recruit study participants, as discussed above, the notion of assistive technology (AT) itself implies something is ‘off’ and needs ‘correcting’. Whereas this may not be a problem for individuals with an obvious and/or relatively harmless impairment or disability, it can be an unpleasant surprise or raise concerns or suspicions in someone who is not aware of a problem or who does not perceive their behavior or functioning to be problematic. In many ways, our work as AT researchers and developers implicitly sends a message that the user is in need of support, which may be at odds with the user’s perception, belief system, and functional status. Throughout our studies with older adults living independently at home, we sensed a desire in users to focus on health, wellness and independence, as opposed to deficits and decline. This implies that our message and solutions should be positively phrased and framed. In a high-functioning but older user, for instance, a reminder may be referred to as a ‘Note to Self’, which sounds less dysfunctional and stereotypical of this age group. Instead of talking about problems, disease, and symptoms, one can inquire about ‘wellness concerns and needs’, which many of us have regardless of age and health status. In addition, our technology solutions and interventions should offer a range of self-improvement options so users can envision improvement and set personal goals, if need be in consultation with others including AT and clinical teams. Even in households where dementia or other disorders such as Parkinson’s disease were evident, caregivers and care recipients in our studies invariably wanted to improve functional status, not merely maintain it. In many instances this is feasible too and thus should be encouraged and supported using AT interventions. Our message and support should be realistic yet optimistic.

3.3 Gender Differences in Coping May Affect Sample Composition

The older demographic we targeted in this research behaved very much along stereotypical gender lines where men tend to avoid discussing personal problems or experiences, whereas women will. The net result of this dynamic is that women tend to reach out for help more than men, which skews samples and data: Our caregivers tended to be female (71 % overall) and our care recipients male (53 %), which is at odds with the statistic that women are more likely to develop dementia, and that the majority of our participants were traditionally married couples. As such, we expected more female CR and more male CG. Although women may traditionally be more inclined to assume the caregiver role, for instance for parents, our observations do raise the issue that female CRs and male CGs are underrepresented in our studies and data, and hence our product development and design. One way to avoid this is to recruit in a non-random fashion, which has its own set of limitations but may be worthwhile depending on the size of the sample and research aim(s).

3.4 Frailty and Distress

Older adults inherently are more likely to have (chronic) physical ailments and impairments such as limited eyesight, hearing, mobility and altered motor function. These add up to lesser or larger degrees of frailty, which should be factored into our research designs and approaches. In our studies, we screened (per self-report) for chronic conditions, vision, hearing, mobility and fine motor impairments, and capped their occurrence and extent in both caregivers and care recipients. However, that did not prevent samples from being frail or having major functional obstacles that stand in the way of successfully completing studies with participants once enrolled. At an average age of 72 for caregivers (range, 49–89 yrs) and 82 for care recipients (range, 60–90 yrs), visual impairments were common (CG: 82 %–CR: 94 %), walking difficulties were common (24 %–71 %), hearing difficulties were common (18 %–35 %) and fine motor problems were not uncommon (6 %–24 %). These rates are typical of the general population, which means that a good number of your older participants will wear or use assistive devices to compensate for functional loss, such as glasses, hearing aids and canes, all of which may affect the adoption and usability of your AT product or solution. In our case, for example, people must be able to hear and see our intervention shows, which are useless otherwise.

Frailty also affects the cadence of recruitment and completion of implementation studies, especially in research that involves repeat assessments and home visits. Each visit may take longer depending on frailty and the time between visits may be longer than expected or desired. We had to reschedule many appointments due to illness, adverse events (e.g., falls), and unexpected surgeries. This can create serious practical challenges and delays when assessments depend on more than one member of the research team who each have busy calendars. Additionally, frailty is a risk factor for attrition and loss to follow-up, which was significant in our sample despite screening precautions: In our first two studies (A, B), attrition approached or exceeded 50 % (1 in every 2 dyads that had been screened, evaluated and included), which is a huge loss of effort, resources and data. In response, we became much more vigilant and open about potential problems and red flags, such as distress and frailty, and more straightforward and strict in our decisions not to include particular dyads. In many instances, the study was simply not a good fit given the circumstances of interested dyads and the demands of the study. Even though we did not require participants to come our office and made home visits instead, participating in a study takes time and effort. Some dyads, we sensed or it was clear, would not be able to comply with those demands and expectations, and the study would be a burden on all rather than source of support and relief. In those circumstances, researchers should be open and honest with themselves and study candidates that participation is not a safe or the study a good fit, even when all formal recruitment criteria have been met.

In addition to frailty, families or households dealing with dementia quickly face considerable distress. Young caregivers, such as adult children, tend to work (fulltime) jobs and/or have children of their own, which creates a lot of pressure across the board. Caregiving in and of itself is also very distressing given the limitations it places on time and movement, and is a big source of distress in young and old family caregivers alike. Older caregivers, however, may have been taking care of their loved-one for years and experience physical and other limitations themselves, which adds to their frailty and exhaustion. In our studies we curtailed the level of distress experienced by caregivers, per self-report and formal measures, yet this did not prevent samples from being distressed, worn-out and desperate. Our caregivers on average scored in the bottom 25 to 50 % of the distress scales, and formally were deemed "mildly distressed", yet many struggled with making themselves available to us, and frequently were in an unpredictable or low mood. Researchers in-field need to be aware of this and be able to show and experience compassion by being kind, cordial and patient time and time again. This is difficult and therefore, not a job for just anyone. Team leads should pay close attention to their 'field officers' and the (life) experience and personality they bring to the table.

4 Intervention and Protocol Design

4.1 Efficacy vs. Efficiency

In helping families manage chronic disease and challenging symptoms and behaviors in daily life, in particular dementia, individualized interventions are more effective than one-size fits all approaches [1]. Music, for instance, can mitigate agitation or apathy in PWD extremely well, but more so if it is tailored to the individual and pleases or moves him or her. Likewise, reminders for key routines or events depend on personal schedules. The SimpleC Companion, therefore, was expressly developed with personalization in mind. Not only are interventions tailored to match individual preferences and schedules, the scope and focus of interventions entirely depends on the specific area(s) of need or interest: Is it sleep, behavior, mood, an ADL, exercise or a combination that is in need of support? Accordingly, a 'therapy menu' is created and tailored to meet individual preferences, schedules, and needs. This individualized approach is associated with great adoption and efficacy in longitudinal studies of the Companion at home, proving the concept that AT can successfully deliver non-pharmacological interventions and help manage complex diseases, but the approach also depends on the input from key stakeholders.

For the Companion, we need information about the symptoms and needs, about preferences and routines. Although not difficult to provide in essence, the time it takes families or facilities to gather and relay this information can create a bottle-neck and barrier to implementation. Research protocols in general should weigh the need for personalization or information against the demands it places on the informant(s). This holds especially for longitudinal research in older, frail adults.

After several participating dyads recanted in rapid succession one month, we streamlined our protocol in several ways:

- We became bolder in our screening and recruitment decisions, as discussed;
- We limited the number of phone calls or emails about a particular piece of information we needed to two, thereby giving participants room and time to respond while putting the onus on them rather than us. Although unnerving at first, loosening the reigns and putting responsibility in participants' hands, the strategy by and large worked really well and no dyad recanted since;
- We limited the number of home visits prior to installing the Companion to two, and limited the overall number of hours per visit to two. This put a clear boundary on our imposition and intrusion of peoples' homes and time, which is a good practice in general and forces research teams to make choices about what is essential vs. desirable.
- We developed ways, in part as a business, to work with limited information on individual needs, preferences and routines to deliver a 'minimum viable intervention'. This comes down to focusing on top priorities and using the information you do have wisely. For instance, whereas personal photos and videos are always more effective than generic in engaging people, it is still better to put together an album or video on a topic of interest using generic material than to have no album or video at all. Rarely if ever were participants disappointed in the initial result or therapy menu we offered them, and no adverse reactions ever occurred.
- Rather than trying to address all user requests and needs early on, we allowed ourselves to make changes after the initial install, thereby tweaking the intervention to tailor it further without necessarily changing its essence or goal. This removed a lot of stress to deliver upfront on both our end and the participants'.

5 Barriers to Implementation

5.1 Environmental Barriers

For AT solutions like ours that depend on the Internet to send and receive information to devices in the field, such as therapy updates and therapy usage information, the limited availability of Internet or spotty network reception in remote and rural areas can be a problem. In our sample of private homes, 1 in 4 households did not have a wireless internet connection, which we subsequently provided using a router or by establishing a cellular Internet connection through a provider with good local coverage. Research teams need to plan for the added cost of setting up and maintaining these connections as well as the optimal data plan.

Introducing a piece of technology to the home also raises the question where it will be placed, and whether existing furniture can accommodate it. If not, the research team may have to provide new furniture. In two of our studies that used a 21″ touch screen as opposed to tablet to deliver interventions, we provided different types of side and coffee tables because existing ones were inadequate (e.g., flimsy, too low). Equipment placement and requirements depends on where and how the technology will be used, which may depend on user needs. If sleep is a concern, for instance, the device/intervention should be available in the bedroom. Needs sometimes compete (e.g., in addition to sleep, a person should hydrate and eat better which calls for the intervention to be available in the living room), but mobile applications and technologies render such situations less and less problematic fortunately.

Not unique to our or AT studies, but a common barrier to study progress and completion are the holidays, especially towards the end of the year. Teams should plan on scheduling difficulties and changes, and associated delays. In one particularly memorable holiday experience, a caregiver asked us to remove the Companion from her living room, which ended the trial and the couple's access to the intervention despite the husband's enjoyment and benefit, because the wife needed the spot for the Christmas tree. One cannot argue with that…

Environmental barriers also include people's daily habits and routines and how they spend their time and where inside the house. We asked the question where and when people tend to relax while at home to gauge where something like the Companion would best be used for personal enjoyment and engagement. Other technologies, such as computers and television, compete for time and interest and are a common distractor and thus barrier to adoption and use of a new technology-based intervention. After mapping a typical day and week, couples may have to be advised on 'wellness scenarios' that include recommendations on how and when to use the (AT) intervention ideally.

Finally, we consider household dynamics an important barrier to implementation that must be considered and addressed. In some cases we decided not to include couples or dyads because their expectations were unrealistic, their problems and needs were excessive, or problems and needs could not be addressed by an intervention like ours. One wife was tired of picking up after her husband and wanted us to help with that (which we could), but also that he speak to her more openly and often after many years of marriage. We could not help with that. In a few other instances, couples disagreed on what the problem was and how to move forward. They had to be excluded from further participation for lack of common ground and focus. When dealing with human subjects, especially more than one, for extended periods of time and addressing personal needs and issues, researchers must be prepared to recognize and draw a line. Being open, honest, and realistic as a team early on about the risk:benefit ratio of study participation, helps.

5.2 Technology-Specific Barriers

Many older adults perceive new technology such as tablets as gadgets that serve entertainment, not daily function or wellness. This premise creates an instant disconnect between the AT developer and user that must be overcome through education (e.g., recruitment materials) using relevant yet simple everyday use case scenarios that resonate with many older users and that 'disarm' and spark curiosity.

Older adults may also give up more easily on trying a new technology or learning how to use it, thinking they are natural misfits when their actions are not immediately successful. This lack of confidence or 'self-efficacy' in using new technologies is reinforced by watching others, often younger generations, use new technologies effortlessly and constantly. Repeat training and positive reinforcement is essential in making older adults feel at ease with new technologies such as the Companion, even when the design interface is relatively simple and intuitive.

This generation is used to physical buttons and not necessarily familiar with the notion of touch screens. Consequently, many are intimidated by touch screen technologies. Not only are they afraid to break the surface, they are very reluctant to simply touch the screen, which may go back to the days when glass surfaces (television, cameras, windows) were not to be touched. When first introducing a touch screen-based technology to a user or audience, therefore, it helps to bring demo devices along so people can touch and play with it to get familiar and comfortable with the basic notion. Additionally, researchers should plan on explaining and practicing basic touch screen operations, such as touching (using one finger as opposed all five of one hand at the same time) swiping (in a straight as opposed to diagonal line), tapping (lifting one finger up and down relatively quickly but not too quickly, as opposed to holding a finger down on the screen or waiting too long between repeat touches), and enlarging or zooming if applicable. In many instances training and reinforcement of 'good touch screen behavior' is required, even in high-functioning, unimpaired older adults.

The good news is that in our experience many impaired older adults, including those with advanced dementia, quickly develop motor memory for these simple operations and can learn to navigate a touch screen technology and menu like the SimpleC Companion. We have several very impaired users who keep themselves busy and positively engaged for hours per day using the Companion. This, in turn, relieves caregivers, and gives them joy and peace of mind that something meaningful is going on while they are not there or cannot attend to their loved-one. The value of this cannot be overstated.

Conditions such as Parkinson's disease may further keep older adults from using touch screen technologies effectively, and screening for such conditions and other, more common, physical impairments is advised, as already discussed.

One immediate implication of these barriers is that trials should allow sufficient time for older or unfamiliar users to warm up to the technology, its application, and its regular, daily use. Most of our "3-week" trials were extended to give people more time to use the technology as intended and to experience its usefulness properly. Fortunately, once people experience the benefit and/or joy, they are staunch adopters and advocates.

5.3 Facilitators of Success

One overarching theme that was a challenge for all studies was attrition. In addition to some of the strategies already discussed, we recommend the following for successful recruitment and retention of a diverse, representative sample of community-dwelling older adults for (AT) field studies:

- Focus on symptoms and needs rather than specific diagnoses. People may not have a diagnosis and a diagnosis does not necessarily matter. What matters is the symptom and the everyday need or challenge it creates.
- Be aware that counting symptoms or disease burden using standardized measures may underestimate the level of impairment and caregiver burden. Frailty and

distress are much more than a simple addition of physical ailments and should be sampled through direct interaction with dyads.

- Consider the overall challenges faced by the specific dyad. Additional considerations include comorbidities, other family members to help out, jobs, social and financial support, and interpersonal dynamics.
- Minimize the added burden of study participation. No more than two visits prior to implementation.
- Have contingency plans for unexpected circumstances, such as a care recipient who does not want to participate or couples disagreeing at various points in time, to augment dyad participation and retention. Have options and narratives available to assessors in the field.
- Incorporate flexibility in the protocol design. Enable assessors to stop an assessment prematurely or exceed time restrictions if suitable and appropriate without jeopardizing the essence and goal of the intervention.
- Allow time for pilot testing the intervention in a representative environment with representative participants, to develop the right messages and identify advocates.
- Work with your local and state government representatives (e.g., local county senior services centers) to spread the word about your work, and to get invited to community events. The goal is to get in front of as many people as possible.
- Identify community outreach coordinators at local governments and universities to help recruit amongst minority populations.
- Capitalize on existing community networks for recruitment.
- Hire an ethnically-diverse research staff to maximize your connection with different constituents on all levels (language, customs, routines, ethics, etc.).
- Have a dedicated person for home-visits and office phone calls.
- Keep interactions with the team as consistent as possible so rapport can build and a relationship between the research team and the participants can develop.
- Develop a method to assess the characteristics of the home and peoples routines, especially for technology interventions.
- Select and train assessors/assessment team on how to put people at ease and reduce stress (e.g., entering the home, sensitivity training).
- Plan for a best case scenario timeline and add in a factor 1.5 to account for unforeseen circumstances that are likely to occur.
- Develop meaningful and intervention-specific outcome measures. Standardized outcome measures will underestimate the benefits and gains following an individualized intervention. Goal attainment scaling is an individualized outcome measure that assesses individual gain meaningfully. For various applications, see [2, 3].

6 Conclusions

Field studies are desperately needed and can have tremendous positive impact, but are also challenging. Our goal in this paper was to provide lessons learned from our experience but in a general enough way that others can implement the strategies that we found helpful. Over 50 % of participants are using the SimpleC Companion long after their trial ended, demonstrating the criticality of the technology and concept for quality of life and well-being.

Although the experiences and recommendations provided herein were derived from experiences with our particular system, they have broader relevance to field studies with assistive technologies in general, as well as older adults and those with physical and/or cognitive limitations.

Acknowledgements. The work reported in this publication was supported by the National Institute On Aging of the National Institutes of Health under Award Number R44AG042206 awarded to SimpleC, LLC (Principal Investigator: Kerssens). The content is solely the responsibility of the authors and does not necessarily represent the official views of the National Institutes of Health.

We thank all our community partners for their support of this project and their key role in recruitment. No partner is named specifically to protect the identity of study participants.

References

1. Cohen-Mansfield, J.: Nonpharmacologic interventions for inappropriate behaviors in dementia: a review, summary, and critique. Am. J. Geriatr. Psychiatry. **9**(4), 361–381 (2001)
2. Gordon, J.E., Powell, C., Rockwood, K.: Goal attainment scaling as a measure of clinically important change in nursing-home patients. Age Ageing **28**(3), 275–281 (1999)
3. Ruble, L., McGrew, J.H., Toland, M.D.: Goal attainment scaling as an outcome measure in randomized controlled trials of psychosocial interventions in autism. J. Autism Dev. Disord. **42**(9), 1974–1983 (2012)

Investigation of Sensitivity of Foot Soles to Vibrational Stimuli: First Results for Developers of Information Interfaces

Stefan Lutherdt(✉), Eva Kaiser, Tim Kirchhofer, Philipp Wegerich, and Hartmut Witte

Technische Universität Ilmenau, Ehrenbergstr 29, 98693 Ilmenau, Germany
stefan.lutherdt@tu-ilmenau.de

Abstract. This paper gives the first results of basic researches to identify parameters and requirements for the development of a vibrational interface in shoe soles. This interface is an integral part of a system to support orientation and navigation of elderly in new and/or unfamiliar environments. To meet the requirements of the later users it is necessary to know the restrictions, basics and needs of this new technology. For these analyses a test bench was developed to examine the sensitivity of the user's foot sole to vibrational stimuli, and to determine the amount of information which could be transmitted. Another result of first test runs is the possibility to decrease the number of vibrational actuators beneath the foot sole.

Keywords: Foot sole · Vibro-tactile stimuli · Mechanoreceptors · Vibrational interface for orientation · Elderly

1 Motivation

The change in the demographical pyramid is one reason for the increasing number of age caused diseases. Therefore it is reasonable to develop new devices to help the elderly to obtain quality of life and independence.

In the last years researches more and more focused on vibro-tactile stimulation, especially in the field of interface design. Throughout the years more improvements were achieved due to different studies on the devices used, the target group and the application area on the human body. Initially, the actuators were embedded in a belt [1, 2]. This stimulation zone provides a large contact area with the actuator, and consecutively the capability to realize a high information load. Due to the density of receptors this solution delivers a usable device for many target groups, but not for elderly people.

Another area for the application of vibro-tactile stimuli has been considered to be helpful, the foot sole. In the study of [3] a vibro-tactile prototype shoe was designed for examination of navigational skills, only with the aid of those stimuli. The addressed group described in [3] mainly were blind people. The LECHAL shoe (shown in Fig. 1 [4]), a commercial solution for navigation by vibrational stimulation, was also first dedicated to blind people, now it can be used for sports and wellness, for tracking activities and vital parameters.

J. Zhou and G. Salvendy (Eds.): ITAP 2015, Part II, LNCS 9194, pp. 290–299, 2015.
DOI: 10.1007/978-3-319-20913-5_27

 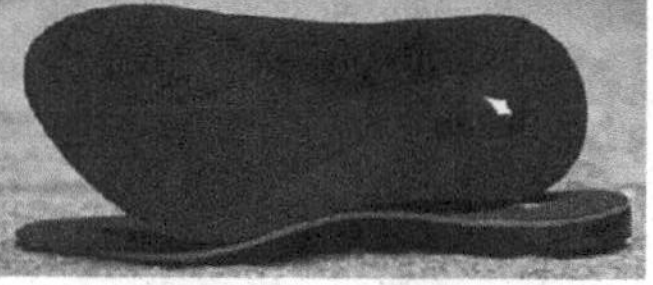

Fig. 1. LECHAL (Hindi for "bring me home"), left: version as a whole shoe with integrated vibration sole; right: sole-only version to integrate vibration stimuli into any kind of shoe [4].

The present study concentrates on the interface in the foot sole. The main reason is the familiarity with the device. For the target group of elderly people, who may have a starting memory disorder, it is important to use a device which they are already familiar to, and which is used on a daily basis. To realize the given requirements the implementation of the interface in a shoe sole was the best option to ensure the usage for elderly people. To realize a user fitted device it is necessary to research the basics.

The aim of the study was the fundamental research concerning the vibro-tactile sensibility of the foot sole in loaded condition and the possible transmittable information for an user fitted device.

2 Propaedeutics

The human skin is not only the largest organ but also the largest sensory system of the human body. It integrates four different senses with the responsible receptors: thermal perception (heat and cold) are sensed by thermoreceptors; perception of pain (nociceptors), and mechanoreceptors, sensitive for mechanical stimuli (necessary for haptic and tactile perception). Tactile perception mainly is aroused by vibration and/or pressure and shear forces. Haptic perception beyond that always has an active component and additionally uses kinesthetic receptors (proprioceptors) in muscle fibers and tendons (e. g. Golgi tendon organ).

As vibrational stimulation is a mechanical stimulation we focus on the mechanoreceptors embedded in the skin, valuable for tactile perception. There are four types of mechanoreceptors, each has its own anatomical structure and physiological function. They are classified in two categories. The first is their adaptivity to the stimulus, the second is the size of the receptive field [3, 6–8].

The receptors are fast or slow adapting. The fast adapting receptors are sensitive for texture and vibration, and the slow ones for dynamic pressure. The size of the receptive field is defined as that skin area which is allocated to one receptor. There are two types of mechanoreceptors with different receptive fields called type I and II. Receptors of type I are small and have defined boundaries, while type-II receptors have large receptive areas with diffuse boundaries. In summary four types of mechanoreceptors can be found: fast adapting I (FA I), fast adapting II (FA II), slow adapting I (SA I), slow adapting II (SA II). The FA I and FA II receptors are sensitive for vibration within different frequency ranges. FA I are mainly aroused between 10 Hz and 100 Hz, while the FA II mechanoreceptors are most sensitive in the range of 100 Hz–300 Hz [7, 8].

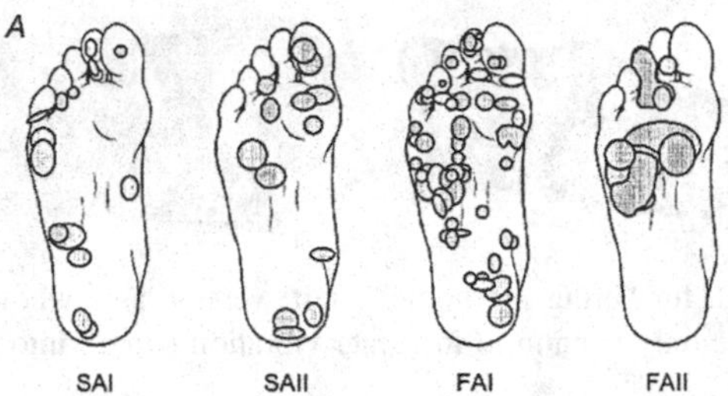

Fig. 2. Position of the receptive fields of the four different receptors on human foot sole [6]

Figure 2 shows, that there is no exact border between the main zones of different types of mechanoreceptors at the foot sole, which makes it difficult to define a receptive field for an exclusive stimulus. In conclusion there always more than one type of receptor is aroused by a given stimulus, and it is difficult to directly arouse a specific receptive field.

To develop an interface which gives adequate stimuli to the foot sole it is necessary to know the range of frequencies as well as the allocation of receptors in the foot sole skin. The following tests focus to provide corresponding data.

3 Design of Experiment

In dependence on anatomical and physiological conditions we used a flexible design of vibro-tactile actuators shown in Fig. 3. The four vibro-tactile actuators used in the study can be arranged in order to anatomical varieties of the volunteers (foot length and width). Additionally they are aligned in those areas which are in ground contact during rolling motion of the foot. The actuators can stimulate the mechanoreceptors in the range between 100 Hz and 225 Hz, because the addressed receptors are of FA II type.

3.1 Design of the Test Bench

The test bench (shown in Fig. 4) is a base body made from alloy with 14 holes for the embedding of the actuators, so the foot is placed plantar on the base body of test bench. It is possible to adapt the test bench for each foot size from 36 to 45 (European Sizes) by switching of alloy distance plates. A back stopper ensures that each subject takes the same and adequate position above the actuators.

The control of the actuators has been realized via USB-6008 from National Instruments®, and by LabView®. The current work bench is controlled by an Arduino Mega™ and an electronic conductor board with drivers for each actuator. The controller gets its program from a PC-based software with internal database via I^2C bus.

The vibration actuators used are eccentric rotating mass (ERM) motors in coin format (pancake motors Pico Vibe 10 mm) from Precision Microdrives™ [9]. The working range is given by the performance characteristics according to Fig. 5.

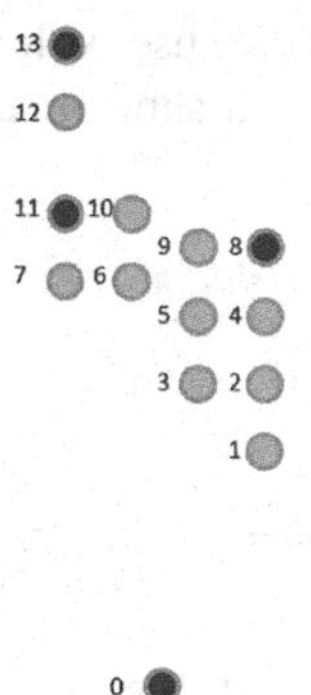

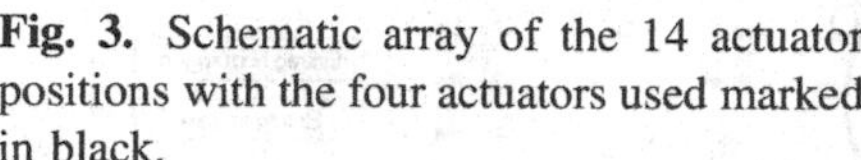

Fig. 3. Schematic array of the 14 actuator positions with the four actuators used marked in black.

Fig. 4. Test bench with four actuators on right foot, two NI USB-6008 for each side; left side has no foot size adaptation (that means size 36), right sight is adapted for size 40.5

To validate these characteristics we also determined the real vibration frequencies by a measurement of the resulting noise, and a following frequency analysis. The main spectral part in FFT was the vibration frequency of the motors evoked by the rotating mass.

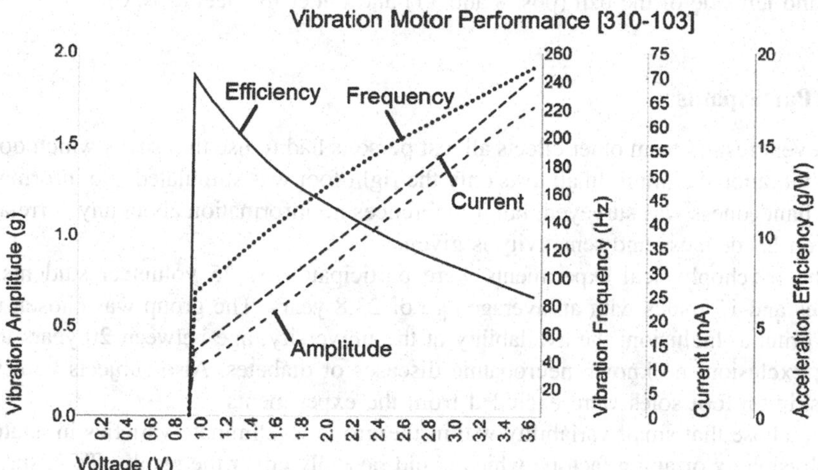

Fig. 5. Performance characteristics of the used ERM coin motors (own image after [9])

For a better control of the test bench and also a better administration of the later experiments a software program with a graphical user interface (GUI) shown in Fig. 6 was developed and tested. With this program it is possible to change all the parameters of each actuator, to combine them to sequences and save this combination for later experiments. If a special set-up of parameters already exists the user will give a hint. By that it is possible to execute a broad variety of tests within a short time.

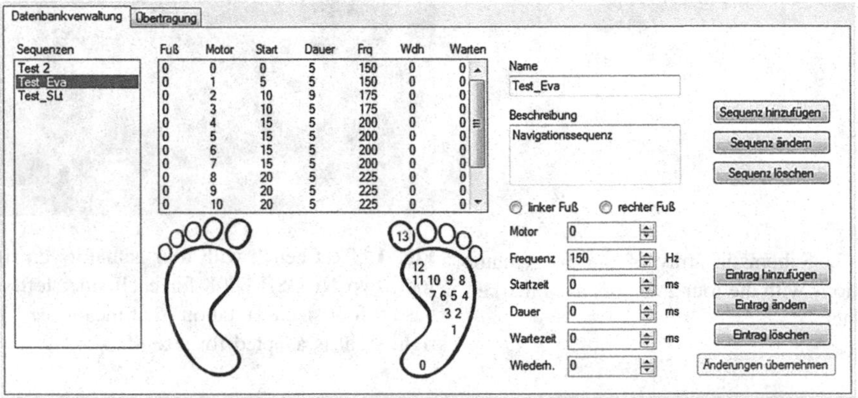

Fig. 6. Screenshot of GUI of software to control the test bench

Pretests had shown that actuators placed directly next to another had a poor spatial resolution, so we reduced the number of actuators in the final tests to only four. These four actuators used were placed, as shown in Figs. 3 and 4, beneath the *Hallux* (pos. 13), right and left side of the ball (pos. 8 and 11) and under the heel (pos. 0).

3.2 Participants

To prevent results from other effects all test persons had to use thin socks which do not damp vibrational stimuli. In all tests only the right foot was stimulated. No information about handedness was surveyed, but in references no information about any correlation between handedness and sensitivity is given.

The psychophysical experiments were participated by 25 volunteer students, 10 females and 15 males with an average age of 23.8 years. The group was chosen with some criteria. Inclusion: the availability at the university, age between 20 years to 30 years; exclusion: no known neuropathic diseases or diabetes. Also subjects with very hard skin on foot soles were excluded from the experiments.

We chose that small variability within the group to eliminate varieties in anatomy and physiology or aging factors, which could possibly cover the results. To ensure the requested criteria each participant had to complete a form which retrieved the necessary information.

3.3 Sensitivity Tests

With regard to the development of the information interface it was primarily important to get a better knowledge of the spatial resolution of the sensitivity of vibro-tactile stimulation of the foot sole. Therefor three experimental tests were designed and performed. All data underlay tests of normal distribution (Kolmogorov-Smirnoff-test) and tests of significance (Student's t-test) performed.

Experiment 1. The purpose of this first test was to examine the spatial resolution of the foot sole. One actuator stimulated the corresponding receptive field at a frequency of 150 Hz. The participant had to recognize at which position the mechanoreceptors were arousen.

To apply the stimulation the test person had to place both feet on the test bench, so its weight was equally applied at both feet. After its verbal answer another motor was started, while the first shut down. The experiment was repeated three times for each actuator. The main questions to be answered through this experiment were, if there are differences between males and females, and how do the volunteers feel the arousal at their foot soles. The focus of interest here is, if they are able to differentiate the diverse stimuli (spatial and time discrimination).

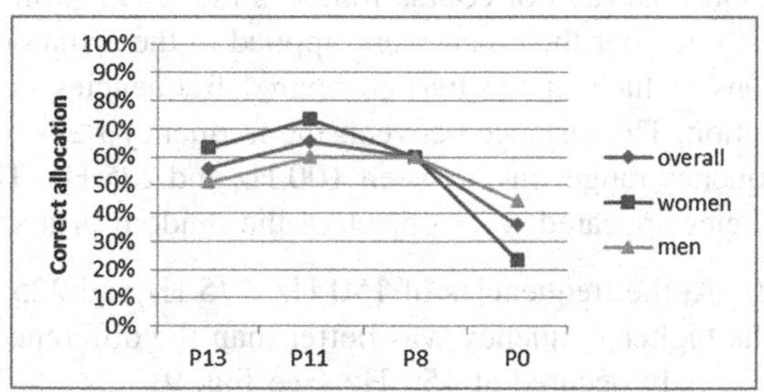

Fig. 7. Comparison of correct identification of given stimuli beneath the foot sole (male – female, different points of stimulation, cf. Fig. 6).

Results. There was no significant difference between men and women. But the results show, that the rate of identification at the heel was significantly worse than the rate of the other three points (see Fig. 7, P0 and Fig. 8). A probable explanation might be the thickness of the callus at the heel, which has influence on the stiffness of the skin and changes the modulus of elasticity. This influences the perception of the pressure to lower degrees and consequently the stimulation of the mechanoreceptors. In addition the stimulated FA II receptors have barely any receptive field on the heel (see Fig. 2), so the sensitivity for frequencies in the chosen range may be lower compared to those on the forefoot.

The results of differences between left and right side of foot are not comparable to other studies. This might be eliminated by further tests with a larger amount of probands, the current results not explainable at this time.

Experiment 2. As a second test only one actuator was focused on in each trial. Whether the one at Position 1, Position 2 or Position 4. Position 3 was negligible because of the rather similarity with Position 2. The aim in this experimental set was to

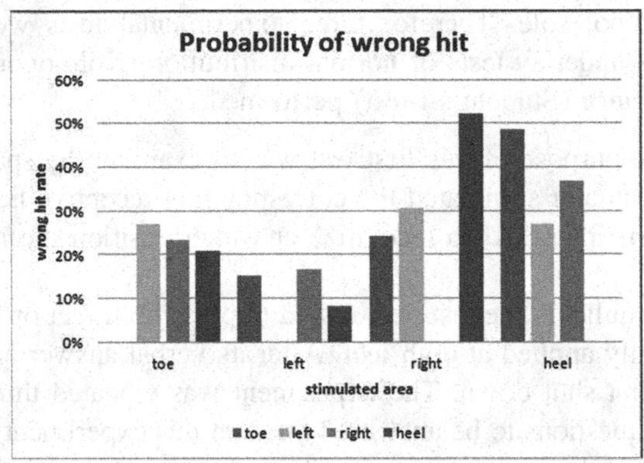

Fig. 8. Observed frequency of wrong recognition at different areas of foot sole

analyze if the subjective perception of different frequencies matches the law of Weber/Fechner and Stevens (and of course matches the readings in literature).

Two frequencies, one after the other, were applied to the actuators. The participant gave a verbal response which of the two compared frequencies is, subjectively, the more intensive vibration. The distance between the frequency steps were 25 Hz, 50 Hz and 75 Hz. The frequency range was between 100 Hz and 225 Hz. The order in which the different frequencies appeared was subject of the random principle.

Results. Step 25 Hz: At the frequencies of 150 Hz, 175 Hz and 225 Hz the sensitivity from the lower to the higher frequency was better than the difference up to down, but significant differences only occured at 150 Hz (see Fig. 9).

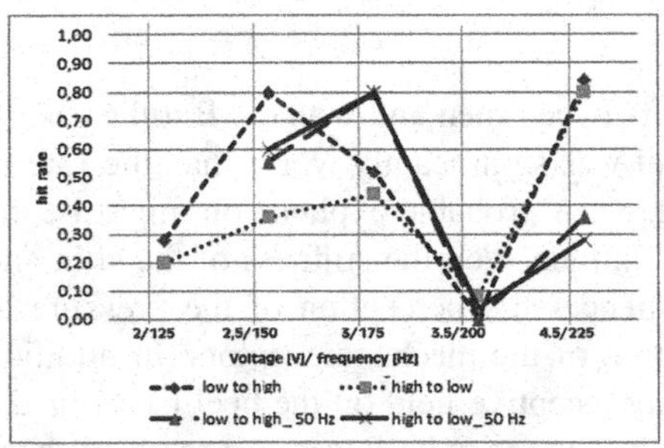

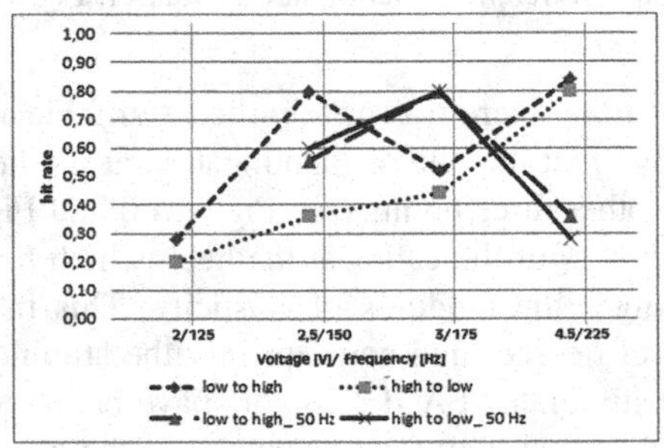

Fig. 9. Test results of experiment 2 (alteration of frequencies upwards and downwards)

Step 50 Hz: Within the test set the results were similar, but the hit rate at a frequency of 225 Hz was not as good as it was by the step size of 25 Hz. The first test set compared the sensitivity at 200 Hz with the sensitivity at 225 Hz. Because of the poor recognition of the lower frequency it was easier to feel the difference in the second test set. Within the second set the compared frequencies were 175 Hz and 225 Hz.

Both showed in the first set a similar recognition rate, so it is more difficult to distinguish between these two frequencies.

The results for a frequency of 200 Hz (3.5 V) were significantly "worse" than the other results (level of significance: $\alpha = 0.05$). This single effect does not match with the expected result, and also with results in other references, in which the maximum of sensitivity reported is at 200 Hz. Thus the right diagram in was drawn without data at 3.5 V ($\triangleq$200 Hz).

Probably this is a summation of several physiological effects. One of these might be the pressure on the foot the participant felt in this study (provoked by own weight), which surely changes the sensitivity, due to the pre-stress of the arches of the foot and the exciting effect on other receptors.

The participants also claimed that the surface of the device used was very (to) cold. With a change of the temperature, a change of the sensitivity threshold goes along. The sensitivity of mechanoreceptors is closely coupled with the ambient temperature. If the temperature decreases, also the sensitivity decreases but the threshold of sensitivity grows [5].

Step 75 Hz: In the last test set the effects were similar to those described in the first two step sizes. Most evident is again the loss of sensitivity at a frequency of 200 Hz.

Experiment 3. The last test was supposed to examine the relation between spatial resolution capacity and the changing of frequencies on the foot sole. Therefore the three most outstanding frequencies in the pretests were used (100 Hz, 150 Hz and 200 Hz). Two actuators were applied at the same time with the same frequency and had to be differed. Similarly to the other experiments the participants' feedback was verbal.

Results. As shown in Fig. 2 the actuator at Position 13 (P13) in combination with the one at Position 11 (P11) had the best spatial resolution capacity, as well as the combination of P13 and P8 where the results were only a little worse. The combination of P11 or P8 with P0 resulted in poor values. A possible explanation can be the lack of FA II receptors at the heel or a combination of multiple effects which provoked a crosstalk of mechanoreceptors and as a result of this the sensitivity decreased. The combination of P13 and P0 showed comparatively bad results. As in test run 1, in the individual tests a transmission occurred from the heel to the toe, this also might explain the outcome. The thicker epidermis causes a stronger attenuation. This results in a superposition of various effects, which may be an explanation for the decline of the hit rate. As mentioned before, also the temperature and the irritation of the other receptors could be the reason for these effects. Another point mentioned by the participants was the unpleasant and uncomfortable kind of standing on the device for the duration of the experiments.

4 Conclusion and Outlook

The results provided give an overview of the basic research on the sensitivity of foot soles to a vibrational stimulation. A second experimental pass is currently processed with varied parameter sets. The load on the foot sole is minimized to that the foot sole only comes in contact with the test bench surface (and actuators), so the resolution capability might increase because of the reduced or totally missing pre-stress of the foot sole.

Furthermore, the duration of one test set is shortened to the minimum length possible, and the cold metal plate is covered by a thermal isolating felt mat to avoid an influence of the temperature on the receptors in the foot sole.

To gain the necessary information for elderly people a third test set starts with the participation of people in the age between 70 years and 80 years with none or slight memory disorder. With this group of respondents we will also perform tests to determine the amount of information which can be transferred by the vibrational interface.

Pretests had shown that actuators placed directly next to each other had a poor spatial resolution capacity, so consequently the placement of two actuators will be used to increase the intensity of the stimulus. The number of motors can be reduced to at least ten (five at each side) vibrational actuators. The frequency range chosen showed results and effects which need to be evaluated. The difference between hit rate of men and women was also investigated, but a significant disparity could not be proven and won't be considered in further experiments (level of significance: $\alpha = 0.05$).

Another result of these first tests is that it is not possible to give vibrational stimuli during stand phase (not exceeding then unspecific vibrations for warning), so an intermediate change of vibrational stimuli from left to right side and back has to be realized. The foot contact can be detected with pressure sensors in the shoe soles, and the available time for information delivery can be calculated as a function to gait velocity (time of rolling motion of one foot is given by different references via gait diagrams).

The foot sole provides a good alternative for a stimulation area for the transmission of information on the human body. Because of various limitations e.g. the small useable space on the foot sole (and inside of shoes), or the decrease of sensibility during aging process, the design of a useful device for elderly people is still a great challenge.

Acknowledgement. This study was supported by the German Government with grant of Federal Ministry of Education and Research. The grant was given from funding program IKT 2020 ("Technologies adapting to people – innovative interfaces between human beings and technological systems").

References

1. Ho, C., Tan, H.Z., Spence, C.: Using spatial vibrotactile cues to direct visual attention in driving scenes (2008). http://www.soft.uni-linz.ac.at/Teaching/_2008SS/SeminarPervasiveComputing Vibrotactile/Begleitmaterial/Related%20Work/2005_Using%20spatial%20vibrotactile%20cues%20to%20direct%20visual%20attention%20in%20driving%20scenes_HoTan.pdf. Accessed June 2014
2. van Erp, Jan B.F., van Veen, Hendrik A.H.C., Jansen, C., Dobbins, T.: Waypoint navigation with a vibrotactile waist belt. ACM Trans. Appl. Percept. **2**(2), 106–117 (2005)

3. Velazquez, R., Bazan, O., Magana, M.: A shoe-integrated tactile display for directional navigation, S. 1235–1240
4. LECHAL, Ducere Technologies, Telangana, India. http://lechal.com/shoe-design.html. Accessed January 2015
5. Schlee, G.: Der Einfluss der Temperatur der Fußsohle, des Blutflusses im Fußbereich und des Schuhwerks auf die plantare Fußsensibilität (2010)
6. Kennedy, P.M., Inglis, J.T.: Distribution and behaviour of glabrous cutaneous receptors in the human foot sole. J. Physiol. (Lond.) **538**(Pt 3), 995–1002 (2002)
7. Johannson, R.S., Valbo, A.B.: Tactile sensory coding in the glaborous skin of the human hand. In: Elsevier Biomedical Press, January 1983
8. Gekle, M.: Taschenlehrbuch Physiologie. 70 Tabellen. Stuttgart: Thieme (2010)
9. Preciscion Microdrives Limited (London, UK). http://catalog.precisionmicrodrives.com/order-parts/product/310-103-10mm-vibration-motor-3mm-type. Accessed January 2015

Robotic Interfaces Design

Avatar and GUI Competing for Older User's Attention

Angie L. Marin Mejia(✉)

Tokyo, Japan
angielorena@gmail.com

Abstract. In the Human Robot Interaction field, developers choose among different solutions to portray a face, ranging for mechanical solutions, or avatars displayed on screens attached to the robot's body. Those designs are commonly displayed separately, being a mechanical head and a tablet size screen, or a screen with the avatar's face and a different one for the Graphical User Interface. The user interactions with the avatar and the GUI are noticeably divided by screen, and interaction designers can make use of design guidelines for computer systems during their design process. However, when the Avatar and Graphical User Interface are displayed together in the same screen, visual and interactive features compete for user's attention, increasing the complexity and affecting users' impression of the robotics system.

It is known that prior knowledge affects older user's interactions, and navigation structures for can be applied trying to elicit that prior knowledge. However, when it comes to robots and elderly people, interaction designers should consider a robot's embodiment as a variable in the interaction equation, whether they are making decisions for the avatar or the GUI.

Designers have little empirical research to guide them in creating such combined models for robotics interfaces and older adults. The fashion in which the visual interfaces of a robot are designed could make the difference in how often and ease individuals use that technology. The true challenge in designing a robotic interface for a system that displays an avatar and a Graphical User Interface in the same screen is representing a GUI Interaction structure without affecting the state of the embodied agent or avatar.

The present research approaches this issue. Different Robotic Interfaces designs for Avatar + GUI with older adults as users are analyzed. The study reported in this paper, implements a robotic female Avatar and Graphical User Interface of our own design. Both designs share the same screen on Homemate, a consumer robot developed to assist the elderly with errand services, communication, entertainment capabilities, and that employs a screen instead of head, allowing us to explore whether these design considerations of Avatar + GUI produce any effect in older adults impressions of an assistant robot.

Keywords: Robotics · Interface · Design · Avatar · Elderly · User experience · Interaction · GUI · UX · Older adults

J. Zhou and G. Salvendy (Eds.): ITAP 2015, Part II, LNCS 9194, pp. 300–310, 2015.
DOI: 10.1007/978-3-319-20913-5_28

1 Introduction

There have been numerous studies about how the interfaces should be designed for older adults. A good portion of those studies are oriented to web based applications or operative systems.

The ageing population is a global concern that affects all the aspects of the technological development [1, 2], and in the robotics field, increase the demand for new and improved robotics systems and applications designed to support older adult's needs.

Robots that are developed to be used for regular consumers, Consumer-robots, alternate from mechanical heads to animated visual elements displayed on screens to portray a face. Those visual elements that animated represent facial expressions and information, are commonly known as conversational agents and avatars [3].

Since those agents or avatars, could play a very important role in how people interact with technology, require to be designed in a proper way.

In the design field, while avatars and customized images are a common terminology as on-screen representations of social presence in mobile technology or Internet. The problematic related to the older adults' technological use of graphical user interfaces is a core theme to be investigated [4, 5].

Nowadays, the vast majority of the available Interaction design guidelines for Graphical User interfaces are for web based and mobile applications, which results in interfaces that bring interaction challenges to designers developing for robotic systems.

This discovery motivate us to research into the conception of Interaction design considerations for robotics interfaces in which two different design solutions, avatar design and GUI design conciliate in the same display portrayal. In the interface design for a robotic system, design decisions represent the state of embodied agents or avatars and the Graphical User interface that allows the user to command and interact with the robot itself.

2 Literature Review

Several researchers have conducted studies regarding the use of new technological interfaces by the older adults [6–8]. In our research, we focus on the design of a structure that integrates the display of an avatar and a GUI in the same screen for a robotic interface, the possible design structures, and the resultant perceptions of the elderly towards the robotics system.

Prior to the study, researchers demonstrated that embodied agents and avatars are interpreted to have social presence for users [9]. Furthermore they also have investigated about the effects of graphic representation level.

Avatars can be designed in a wide range of possibilities; however, in the case of a humanlike avatar to mediate the human-computer interaction, the social aspects of interaction become more explicit. The entire visual design of the avatars (form features, clothing, facial expression, and gestures), express information and reflect contents in the same way as human–human social interaction [10, 11].

HCI studies have examined how new technology can be integrated in older user lives. From Internet searching [12], game play in tablets [13], smart TVs [14] to Social networking, a set of guidelines were provided to build applications aimed to help older adults interaction experience [15–17]. However, in Human Robot Interaction, designers lack sufficient guidelines to ensure that avatars and GUI design decisions will play an efficient role in the user experience and the general impression of the robot. And the designs of those interfaces bring even more complicated interaction challenges to users aged 65 and above.

Very interesting things were found while reviewing previous research, but many questions are still there. For instance, although different design considerations for the elderly have been explored in HCI, none of these studies have explored the applicability of those considerations for robotics interfaces and, more specifically, the possible resultant interactions of a Graphical User Interface integrated with an avatar as the robots face.

The advents of interaction with robotics systems express the need to specify effective, reliable and consistent design guidelines for robotics interfaces. There is little research to guide the creation of avatars and robotics graphical user interfaces for interaction designers. In our case, the findings of the following research contribute into the interaction design guidelines for "Homemate", an assistant robot developed for the Korus Tech project in the Intelligent Systems Research Institute.

2.1 Research Question and Hypothesis

The primary purpose of this study is to demonstrate that interaction decisions, in terms of how an avatar and a graphical user interface are displayed in the same screen, affect user's positive or negative impressions towards the robotics system. In our case, being the users, older adults.

Hence our main research question can me summarized as follows: For older adults, controlled by the type of interface design, what is the relationship between the avatar + GUI design and the level of engagement, learnability of the interface and avatar recognition as a robotic agent.

Therefore, we hypothesize:

- H1: Interface Design with visual dominance of the avatar will allow the users to perceive the robot as an agent and not merely as a user interface.
- H2: Interface Design with visual dominance of the GUI, displaying the totality of the system of icons, will allow older users to identify an icon task with more efficiency.
- H3: Since icons offer strong visual and spatial cues and it is much easier to learn them and to remember their location in the interface structure, and older users have age–related vision complications, the no inclusion of textual elements will allow us to create a less complex visual interface helping from visual attention to icons recognition.

- H4: Interface Design with categorization of robot' tasks, will allow a visual dominance of the avatar and a simultaneous display of GUI with animated menus.

3 Method

A number of methodologies can be used when involving the elderly in the Interaction design process. For instance, focus groups, surveys, interviews, observational studies, and controlled experiments have all been used to study older users experience with new technologies. Many of those methodologies are applied into the participatory Design (PD) approach, which facilitates interaction evaluation to collect and to analyze feedback from intended users, and makes possible their integration through all the interaction design and development process, rather than finishing an interface design and conducing a posterior user testing on it.

Four interface structures were applied to the design of Homemate robot interface during the time of approximately eighteen months. Focus groups of older adults from the Jogno Senior Welfare Service Center interacted with the first stages of the robotic interface design in a controlled scenario.

Asking older adults what they prefer as part of a usability test may offer important information about their subjective response to a given design. However assigning simple interaction tasks, allow us to do a much better job of collecting missing information and helping to achieve consensus on design decisions.

In our prior experience, older adults were in some way reluctant to participate in paper and pencil questionnaires, and to recruit participants for more elaborated experimental designs could be a time-consuming task without a meaningful difference in the outcome given the characteristics of the study. Therefore we decided to implement a reaction card method [18] during the testing of the last two versions of the robotic interface, followed by a series of interviews to the participants and video recordings for a posterior observation and analysis.

Since the participants have no English fluency, the cards were previously translated to Korean language by a Korean native speaker.

3.1 Reaction Card Method

Developed by Microsoft, the Reaction Card method was originally designed to collect the information related to the emotional response and desirability of a design or product. This method is commonly used in the field of software design.

The older adults are asked to describe the robotic interface using any number of 118 words, targeted in a 60 % positive and 40 % negative/neutral balance. Below is an example of these cards "Fig. 1".

Each word is placed on a separate card. After viewing a design or product the participant is asked to pick out the words they feel are relevant. The moderator would then ask the participant to describe their rationale for their selection in a short interview.

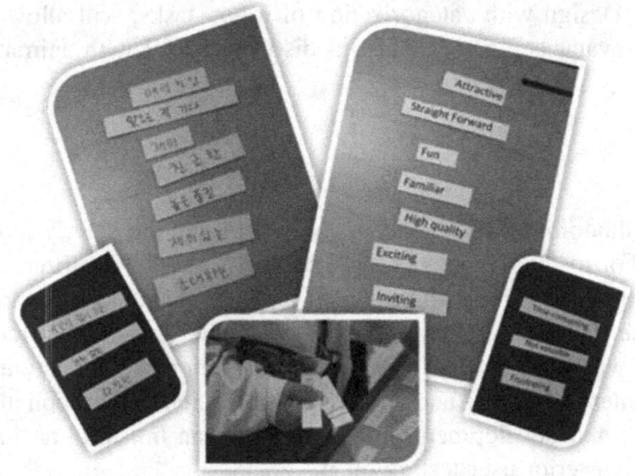

Fig. 1. Example of reaction cards

3.2 Participants and Stimulus Materials

Twenty four participants from the Jongno Senior Welfare Service Center in Seoul, South Korea were recruited to participate in the Reaction Card Desirability test. N = 24 (8 Males, 16 Females).

Since the robot for this study has a small screen size, the two elements of the avatar + GUI were designed to fit screen dimensions and a good legibility on distance. We should keep in consideration that most of the Korean older adults tend to get very close to the screen regardless the use of eye glasses (Fig. 2).

Fig. 2. Homemate robot from inteligent systems research institute (Left) and Robotic interface evaluated (Right).

For a better understanding, we can describe the Robotic Interface designs layout for visual dominances "Fig. 3".

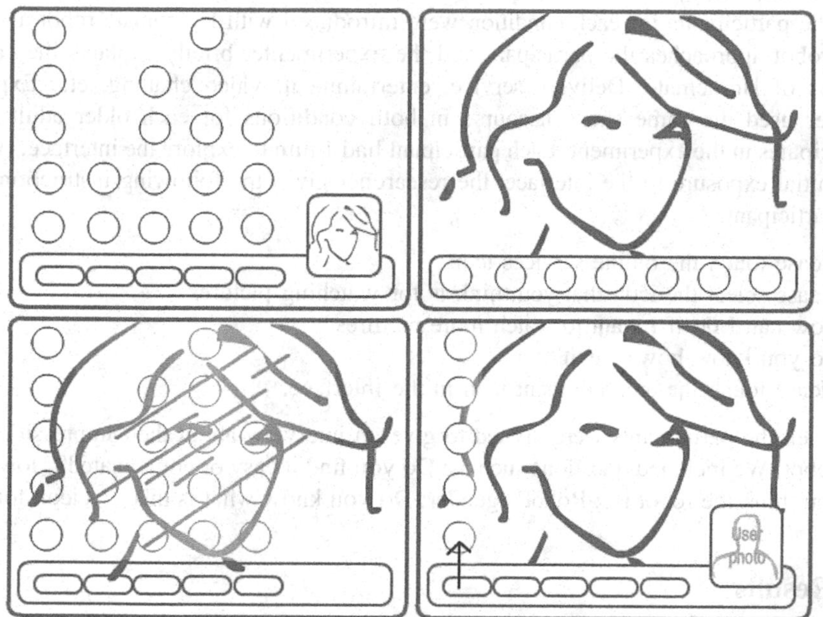

Fig. 3. Robotic interface design structure types

3.3 Manipulation/Independent Variables

Type of Interaction Design:

- GUI dominance on avatar. (full system of icons at once)
- Avatar dominance on GUI
- Intercalating Avatar/GUI
- Avatar dominance and GUI displayed in categories

3.4 Measurements/Dependent Variables

- Perceived Efficiency of the interface
- Perceived Complexity of the Interface
- How intuitive is the interface (Icons recognition, Interface ease of use and learning)
- Recognition of the embodied agent (avatar)
- Desirability

3.5 Procedures

A controlled scenario was prepared in one of the coffee areas in the elderly center. Context was designed to reduce distractions and allow free interaction with the robot and the interface.

The participants for each condition were introduced with Homemate robot avatar. The robot approaches the participant and the experimenter briefly explains the capabilities of Homemate: Delivery service, entertainment, video chatting, etc. Experimenter used the same short discourse in both conditions for each older adult that participates in the experiment. Each participant had 1 min to explore the interface. After the initial exposure to the interface, the researcher gives the following instructions to the participant:

- Please touch the online services icon
- Please select the icon that you think is for watching pictures
- How can I do if I want to watch more pictures?
- Do you know how to exit?
- Please touch the entertainment icon in the interface.

Then the participants were invited to give an interview about their impressions of the robot. We included questions such as: Do you find it easy or complicated? How old do you think the robot is?; Robot's gender; Do you know what is this ___ icon for?…

4 Results

4.1 Based on Interviews and Observational Analysis of the Interaction

Information of great value was collected during the interviews and the observation of the interaction videos. How the participants referred to the robot, whether as a machine, computer or robot. Depending on the applied interface they change their behavior towards the robot having a friendlier attitude with the avatar dominance or stressed attitude with the GUI dominance.

Participants were willing to interact with the robot for longer periods of time when the robot was displaying the Avatar and the categorized GUI structure. Older adults were enthusiastic about trying it again but found complicated to learn and remember what each icon was for. It could be solved by adding task-descriptive text, but then it will bring more elements to the screen that can make complicated the visualization of the avatar.

Auditory feedback was also included for each interaction, but we found it not relevant for the recognition of the icons.

However we found that the inclusion of fading textual information during the touching gesture could help in the recognition and recalling of the icons tasks. This was a very important finding for our design process, allowing us to take advantage of textual aids without keeping them present during all the time of the interaction.

4.2 Based on the Reaction Cards Method

Positive Card Selections:

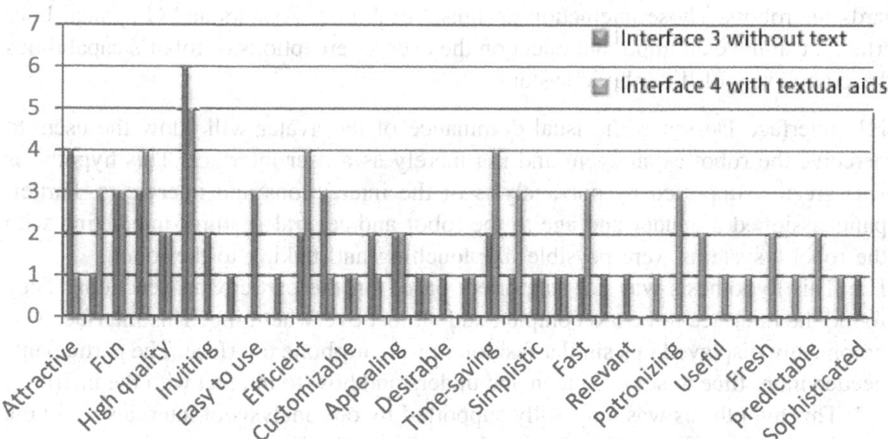

Fig. 4. Avatar dominance on GUI with categories and No textual aids compared with Avatar dominance on GUI with categories and with textual aids.

In general, participants expressed very positive opinions about the two last versions of the robotic interface designs. Selections such as Attractive, Exciting, Usable, Fun, were very popular Avatar dominance on GUI with categories "Fig. 4". However, while the inclusion of textual fading elements help into making more valuable, fast, time saving and efficient the interface, negative impressions for complexity and confusing interface also increase "Fig. 5".

Negative Card selections:

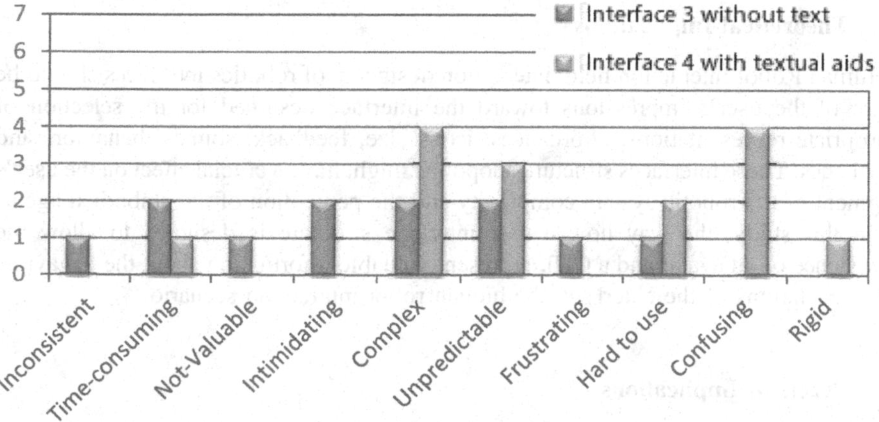

Fig. 5. Avatar dominance on GUI with categories and No textual aids compared with Avatar dominance on GUI with categories and with textual aids.

4.3 Hypotheses Testing

The results from our observations indicated that interaction structures for robotics interfaces are judged to inherently affect the positive impressions of older adults towards the robots. Those interaction designs, combining Avatars and Graphical User Interfaces, can have an important effect on the user's perceptions of robot's capabilities or the complexity of the robotic system.

- H1: Interface Design with visual dominance of the avatar will allow the users to perceive the robot as an agent and not merely as a user interface. This hypothesis was greatly supported by our analysis of the interactions and interviews. Participants assigned a gender and age to the robot and several gestures interacting with the robotic systems were possible like touching and talking to the robot.
- H2: This hypothesis was not supported, based on the participants reactions. They found the interface to be too complex and almost overwhelming. This interface was graphically displayed in a similar fashion of a smartphone interface. The participants needed more time to see each icon and understand how to interact with the interface.
- H3: This hypothesis was not totally supported by our analysis of interviews and the reaction cards information. Although a more simple and clean interface was designed by no including textual information. The participants faced complications to identify and remember some of the icons that represented complicated robot capabilities or services. This could be due to that level of affordance required for those icons representations is difficult to achieve.
- H4: This hypothesis was supported by our analysis of interviews and Reaction Cards information. By keeping the avatar full screen but presenting a GUI in categories, we found a more intuitive way for the elderlies to interact with the interface without losing the robotic agent sense.

5 Discussion

5.1 Theoretical Implications

In Human Robot Interaction field, interaction designers of robotics interfaces should be aware of the user's impressions toward the interface designed for the selection of appropriate representations, affordances, icons size, feedback, sounds, behaviors and visual cues. These interfaces structure adoptions might have a crucial effect on the user's judgment of the robotic system complexity and the perception of the embodied agent.

In this study, the way how a user interface structure is designed to allow the coexistence of an avatar and a GUI, represent valuable information about the behaviors and expectations of the elderly in the human robot interaction scenario.

5.2 Practical Implications

Interaction Design studies for Robotics Interfaces, offer tremendous valuable information for designers of interfaces for the elderly. How a scenario in which an avatar and a GUI share the same screen can be structured for the better performance of the system and an intuitive interaction experience. Considerations such as the use of fading elements to reduce the visual load on the learner in reading text can guide interaction designers in the process. These quick exposures of fading text can help ensure that needed material that may otherwise get excluded from an overtaxed visual modality is processed. Similar considerations are equally important as occurs with less complex interfaces in terms of amount of icons shown in the interface.

The present study contributed in the development and interaction design for a cognitive consumer robot "Homemate" from the Korus Tech Project in the Intelligent Systems Research Institute In Sungkyunkwan University. Homemate tobot displays an Avatar + Interface in a screen instead of head. This robot has a female voice and gives assistance to the elderly for different scenarios such as Errand service for water, beverages, etc. facilitates communication through video chatting, entertainment such as games and karaoke, health assistance and online services such as Facebook photo albums.

Additionally, while in HCI Interaction Guidelines concerning interface design for the elderly, there is not a deep understanding whether the same principles can be applied for HRI and interfaces involving Avatars and Graphical User Interfaces.

Furthermore, with the aging of our society, older adults have been becoming in one of the one of main targets for the robotic industry, therefore investigate which is the more reliable way to achieve user expectations about robots, from the interaction design to the technical and engineering implications that it conceives is strongly needed.

5.3 Limitations and Future Research

The findings in this current study could provide a set of design considerations to help guide interaction designers in creating effective robotic interfaces for older adults, but still are there some concepts to be tested regarding affordances and user learning avatar or GUI assistance.

In robotics systems, task analysis plays a very important role for early input into the design process designing for older adults. Such analysis can help into identify information needs and expectations, visual and auditory requirements, focused attention elements and aids for retaining information. This information provides a starting point for identifying problems that older users could face during the interaction with the robotic interface.

In addition, we can consider a comparative study with American older adults, customization of the system of icons and perhaps conduct a future experiment considering senior adults with cognitive disabilities and applying a similar reaction card methodology.

Few limitations of the study should be acknowledged in order to interpret its findings effectively. First, while there are several assistant robots for older adults, our focus in this study was on Homemate Consumer Robot that has only one screen which plays the role of robot's head. Second, the subjects were Korean older adults without including individuals with serious physical or psychological disabilities.

References

1. Lutz, W., Sanderson, W., Scherbov, S.: The coming acceleration of global population ageing. Nature **451**(7179), 716–719 (2008)
2. Goldstein, J.R.: How population age. In: Uhlenberg, P. (ed.) International Handbook of Population Aging, pp. 7–18. Springer, New York (2009)
3. Breazeal, C.: Designing Sociable Machines. The MIT press, Cambridge (2001)
4. Gregor, P., Newell, A.F., Zajicek, M.: Designing for dynamic diversity: interfaces for older people. In: Proceedings of the Fifth International ACM Conference on Assistive Technologies. ACM (2002)
5. Shyam Sundar, S., Behr, R.A., Oeldorf-Hirsch, A., Nussbaum, J.F.: Retirees on facebook: can online social networking enhance their health and wellness? In: Proceedings of the 29th Annual CHI Conference on Human Factors in Computing Systems (CHI 2011), pp. 2287–2292. ACM, May 2011
6. Ellis, R.D., Allaire, J.: Modeling computer interest in older adults: the role of age, education, computer knowledge, and computer anxiety. Hum. Factors: J. Hum. Ergon. Soc. **41**(3), 345–355 (1999)
7. Redish, J., Chisnell, D.: Designing web sites for older adults: A review of recent literature. Prepared for AARP December (2004)
8. Hawthorn, D.: Cognitive aging and human computer interface design. In: 1998 Australasian Computer Human Interaction Conference, Proceedings. IEEE (1998)
9. King, W.J., Ohya, J.: The representation of agents: anthropomorphism, agency, and in-telligence. In: Proceedings of CHI, pp. 289–290 (1996)
10. Oren, T.: Guides: characterizing the interface. In: Laurel, B. (ed.) The Art of Human-Computer Interface Design. Addison-Wesley Publishing Company, Reading (1990)
11. Don, A.: Anthropomorphism: from eliza to terminator 2. In: Proceedings of CHI, pp. 67–70 (1992)
12. Jayroe, T.J., Wolfram, D.: Internet searching, tablet technology and older adults. Proc. Am. Soc. Inf. Sci. Technol. **49**(1), 1–3 (2012)
13. Pedell, S., Beh, J., Mozuna, K., Duong, S.: Engaging older adults in activity group settings playing games on touch tablets. In: Proceedings of the 25th Australian Computer-Human Interaction Conference: Augmentation, Application, Innovation, Collaboration, pp. 477–480. ACM (2013)
14. Coelho, J., Guerreiro, T., Duarte, C.: Designing tv interaction for the elderly-a case study of the design for all approach. In: Biswas, P., Duarte, C., Langdon, P., Almeida, L., Jung, C. (eds.) A Multimodal End-2-End Approach to Accessible Computing, pp. 49–69. Springer, New York (2013)
15. Gomes, G., Duarte, C., Coelho, J., Matos, E.: Designing a facebook interface for senior users. Sci. World J. **2014**, 8 (2014)
16. Hawthorn, D.: Designing Effective Interfaces for Older Users. The University of Waikato (2006)
17. Reddy, G.R., et al.: Intuitive use of complex interface structure, anxiety and older users. Lecture Notes in Computer Science (LNCS), IFIP and Springer (2013)
18. Mertens, A., Koch-Körfges, D., Schlick, C.M.: Designing a user study to evaluate the feasibility of icons for the elderly In: Mensch & Computer 2011, Oldenbourg Wissenschaftsverlag GmbH, pp. 79–90 (2011)
19. Benedek, J., Miner, T.: Measuring desirability: new methods for evaluating desirability in a usability lab setting. In: Proceedings of Usability Professionals Association (2003)

An Adaptable AR User Interface to Face the Challenge of Ageing Workers in Manufacturing

Maura Mengoni(✉), Matteo Iualè, Margherita Peruzzini, and Michele Germani

Polytechnic University of Marche, Ancona, Italy
{m.mengoni,m.iuale,m.peruzzini,m.germani}@univpm.it

Abstract. In the last years introducing measures to face age discrimination and increasing work safety in production environments have become crucial goals. The present research proposes an innovative user interface exploiting Augmented Reality techniques to support frail people, mainly elderly, in everyday work on complex automated machines. It adapts its functionalities according to the user skill, tasks, age, and cognitive and physical abilities thanks to a set of knowledge-based configuration rules. A case study is described to illustrate the methodology to manage the complexity of configuration rules and the resulting developed platform.

Keywords: Human-computer interaction · Accessibility · User-centred design · Adaptation · Augmented reality

1 Introduction

Numerous studies claim that in 2050 more then one-third of the European population will be over the age of 65 and around half of workers will be aged over 50. The participation rates of older workers in production and operative roles will have an impact on economic growth and manufacturing efficiency because the mild deficiencies they are usually affected (e.g. reduction in sight, mobility, force, concentration, memory) can significantly decrease their performance and increase the risk of injury [1]. As a consequence improving the job quality, introducing measures to face age discrimination, increasing ergonomics and work safety have become crucial goals. Moreover, today processes in manufacturing become more and more automated and machines more and more complex to achieve short cycles and customized goods. Most of them embed computer-based and web interfaces. Despite the advantages, user interfaces (UIs) could represent a barrier for computer laymen and elderly people, acting as inhibitors to usage rather than facilitators as they are generally not appropriate, unfamiliar and acceptable for elderly [2].

In this context, the present research aims at developing an assisted production environment to support frail people working on complex machines by using an innovative human-computer interface that adapts its functionalities according to the user skill, tasks, age, cognitive and physical abilities. The implementation of set of

J. Zhou and G. Salvendy (Eds.): ITAP 2015, Part II, LNCS 9194, pp. 311–323, 2015.
DOI: 10.1007/978-3-319-20913-5_29

knowledge-based configuration rules guarantees adaptation and easy information access. The interface is context-sensitive thanks to the implementation of Augmented Reality (AR) techniques to display the right digital information according to the workspace and the machine the user is in front of and to the tasks he/she has to perform.

The design of the Adaptable User Interface (AUI) follows a user-centred design approach, that starts from the identification of target users and the classification of their frailties, then analyses the context of use and the external events affecting human-computer interaction, correlates the identified user frailties with the UI elements to properly configure their features. Multiple interlinked 3D matrices are used to manage the complexity of the configuration variables. The overall system architecture is then defined and implemented. A preliminary system prototype is developed. Preliminary tests to demonstrate the AUI usability are carried out on a particular case study represented by tasks to control a wood working machine and perform ordinary maintenance on it.

2 Related Work

Nowadays usability and ergonomics issues have become crucial for manufacturing due to the increasing age of technical operators as a consequence of the aging trend of the global population [3, 4]. Contemporarily machines are becoming more digitalised and technologically advanced requiring high mental abilities that inevitably decrease with age [5]. In technological-oriented sectors the deterioration of health and functional status can strongly affect the job performance [6]. For instance, reduction in sight and memory can highly affect the user performance when high reactivity is required and the hard working conditions obstacle the use of glasses or the closing up to the target items. On the basis of literature review, four classes of frailties can be identified for elderly: visual, auditory, motor and cognitive. For each class, some accessibility problems can be defined and some solutions offered by traditional systems can be found in literature [6]. However, when machines are complex and require a very high-skilled interaction, the proposed solutions seem not be easily integrated in such machines and not appropriate for the elderly. In this context, the introduction of assistive technologies based on adaptable and adaptive user interfaces can positively benefit Human-Machine Interaction (HMI).

Adaptive User Interfaces (AUI) are defined as "systems that adapt what they displays and available actions to the user's current goals and abilities by monitoring the user status, the system state and the current situation" [7]. They allow improving HMI mainly by offering a set of functions supporting the user in its own tasks in respect of usability design principles [8]. Practically, AUIs generally facilitate the user performance, minimize the need to request of assistance, help users in dealing with complex machines and avoid cognitive overload problems by conveying the right information to the user, both in case of able-bodied and impaired people. In the context of HMI, being adaptive means that the system is able to automatically adapt its features to the user in a transparent way [9]. In all cases the basic and distinctive characteristic of an AUI is its capability to dynamically tailor itself to the abilities, skills, requirements and preferences of the users, to the different contexts of use, as well as to the changing characteristics of users, as they interact with the system [10]. In order to be adaptive, the interface has to support the various "special" input and output data and dynamically reconfigure its main elements: (1) layout (colors, fonts, graphical compositions in general); (2) contents (information and data provided and managed at different levels of detail); and (3) feedback (interaction way to provide alerts and notifications). A good classification of AUI patterns and a deep analysis of adaptation mechanisms is provided by Nilsson [11].

A tool to make AUI context-sensitive is represented by Augmented Reality (AR), whose advantage is to overlays computer-generated information (e.g. textual data, 3D models, simulations, etc.) on the real world environment, enhancing the person's performance in and his/her perception of the world [12]. The displayed information and overlaid image are context-sensitive, which means that they depend on the objects recorded and recognized by a camera embedded into a portable and wearable device (e.g. web camera, Smartphone, Head-Mounted Display). Chi et al. [13] classified the AR enabling technologies in cloud computing environment for data management, localization technologies to identify the postures of subjects, portable devices and ubiquitous applications and finally natural user interface for the manipulation of digital contents avoiding communication via indirect input devices. One of the strongest and most promising application domains is actually manufacturing. AR can actually assist and enhance both manufacturing and product development, leading to shorter lead-time, reduced cost and improved quality. AR-aided manufacturing can be classified according to the activities connected with the production of an artefact (i.e. factory layout planning, robot control and programming, machine tools, measuring, testing and diagnose of parts, product assembly/disassembly, manipulation, transport and store devices, machine maintenance) [14]. Nee et al. [15] proposed an extensive overview of AR applications in manufacturing. The main critical aspects in AR-aided manufacturing concern both the technology and the application. Despite recent advances in technology, most of AR systems are laboratory-based implementations. Crucial technological challenges regard real-time tracking and computation, synchronization and related latency between real and virtual worlds, realisms of displayed objects, the performance of mobile devices and the usability of current HMD [15].

3 The Adaptable User Interface: From Design to Prototyping

3.1 The Interaction Design Approach

The proposed approach derives from the findings of Lee et al. [16] that successfully used a Quality Functional Deployment (QFD) correlation method to map the UI design components with the user needs of able-bodied persons. However, in the present research the correlation has an additional degree of complexity due to the elderly frailties to be taken into account and to the operational context that is represented by production machines. To solve this problem correlation is set into a 3D space made of the three main elements characterizing Human-Machine Interaction. These elements are the User, the Interface and the Environment. They lie respectively on x-y-z axes (Fig. 1). Each dimension is then the result of further correlations among elements defining them. For instance, the User dimension is achieved by relating the user frailties with the individual profile determined by his/her skill, education and age. The Environment dimension is defined by the context of work and the tasks to be performed.

The combination of the three dimensions results into a set of configuration rules able to adapt the interface features in a dynamic and interactively way. Rules derive from the correlation among user characteristics (e.g. age, frailties, skills, education), context of use (e.g. machine control, maintenance, assembly, training) and machine environment (e.g. tasks, position, external events). They are logical relations able to dynamically set the interface item characteristics and their degree of freedom considering the interaction style, graphics, dynamics and semantics (e.g. colour, icon and text size, shape, relative position, audio feedback). In this way when the operator posture and its position are recognized by the AR localization technologies, the system is able to link the tasks to be executed and as a consequence the contents to be displayed and then to infer which items of the interface will be used and reconfigured to be appropriate for use.

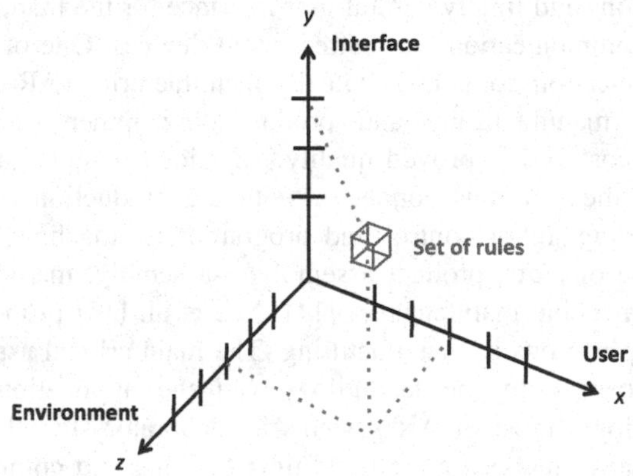

Fig. 1. User-interface-environment space for AUI

As mentioned before, a set of matrices are used to decompose the problem into different steps, each of which manages a set of data that are related each other by means of a specific correlation matrix as summarized in Fig. 2.

The first step regards the definition of the User characteristics dimension (i.e. x-axis). For that purpose it is necessary the fulfillment of Matrix 2, correlating the user profile, set in Matrix 1, and his/her frailties. A user profile is determined by his/her skill, education and age. Each kind of information is categorized into a 5-point scale, where 1 is the lowest level and 5 is the highest level, according to the Likert scale method [17]. The categories proposed in this study are described in Table 1.

The next step is the correlation between the user profile and his/her frailties (i.e. Matrix 2). Frailty classification is based on the model proposed by Clegg et al. [6] that consists of four classes: visual, auditory, motor and cognitive. The frailty classes and categories considered for this study are shown in Table 2.

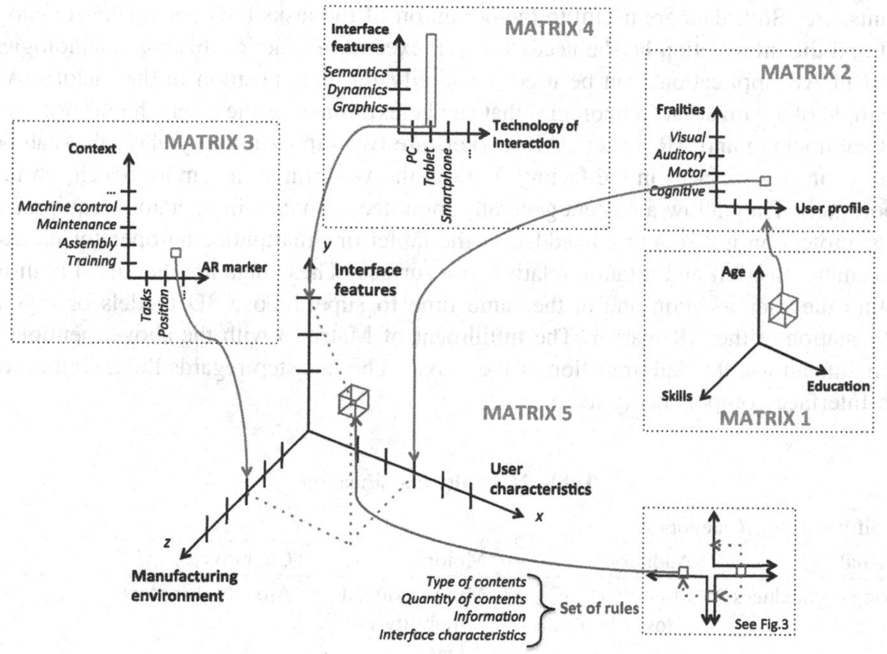

Fig. 2. Research approach for AUI in manufacturing

Table 1. User characteristics categorization

User characteristic	Categories				
	1	2	3	4	5
Skill	Difficulties in using digital / web interfaces ad interacting with technology	Basic use of digital / web interfaces (only)	Medium use of digital / web interfaces (with low knowledge)	Good knowledge and use of digital /web interfaces	High familiarity with technological devices and digital /web interfaces
Education	Elementary school	High school /college	Master / degree	Technical master / degree	Master /PhD in technical disciplines
Age	Over 70	65–70	55–65	40–55	18–40

The second step regards the definition of the Environment elements (i.e. z-axis). The environment is determined by the context of application (e.g. layout planning, maintenance operations, machine control, assembly) and the specific location of the operator in the factory, in front of the machine and its parts, within specific areas of the plants, etc. Both data are useful to the definition of the tasks the operator has to carry out and the information he/she needs for task execution. The localization technologies used in AR applications can be used to identify the user position in the factory. An example of localization technologies that can be exploited for the research purpose uses optical tracking and AR makers. AR markers are two-dimensional symbols that can be placed on key surfaces in the factory (e.g. on the wall, on an assembly bench, on the floor, etc.). They allow a camera generally mounted on a certain operator's equipment (e.g. protection glasses) or embedded in the tablet or Smartphone an operator has, to determine position and rotation relative to a surface. These data are then used both to define the user location and at the same time to superimpose 3D models or digital information at the AR marker. The fulfillment of Matrix 3 with the above-mentioned elements allows the determination of the z-axis. The last step regards the definition of the Interface components (y-axis).

Table 2. Frailty classification

Frailty Classes /Categories			
Visual	Auditory	Motor	Cognitive
Long-sightedness	Minor hearing loss (26-40 dB)	Minor reduced mobility of legs	Anxiety disorders
Short-sightedness	Medium hearing loss (41–55 dB)	Medium-High reduced mobility of legs	Memory problems
Far-sightedness & Astigmatism	Medium-High hearing loss (56–70 dB)	Minor reduced weight lift (<25 kg)	Difficulties in concentrating and processing large amounts of information
Contrast Sensitivity	High hearing loss (71–90 dB)	Medium reduced weight lift (<15 kg)	
Color-blindness	Sever hearing loss (>90 dB)	Highly reduced weight lift (<6 kg)	

A human-computer interface and in general a UI refers to the modalities through which people interact with computational technologies. These include different data input and output devices [18]. Input is how a person communicates his/her needs to the computer (e.g. keyboard, trackball, finger for touch sensitive screens, gestures, voice for spoken instructions). Output is how the computer conveys the result of its computations and requirements to the users (e.g. display screen, sound and haptic displays). Due to the variety and complexity of means for communication, the analysis of the main interface components is limited to Graphic User Interfaces (GUI) for web applications [16, 19], as follows:

- Interaction style, which is the method by which the user and the computer communicate each other. Among them, three have been selected: (i) command line - it requires the user to press a function key into a designed entry area on a screen; (ii) menu selection - it is a set of options or choices from which the user must choose by using a pointing device or keystroke. Labels must be meaningful and understandable to be effective; and (iii) form fill-in - it is useful for easily entering and collecting information.
- Graphics, which refers to styling fonts, size and distribution of elements, colours and shape of icons and their relative position in the graphic interface area. In particular among graphics the research focus is on the following elements: Menu, Frame, Navigation bar, Icons and buttons, and Text. They can differ in terms of colours, size and arrangement.
- Semantics, which comprehends the used language, metaphors and meaning of the words in texts.
- Dynamics, which concerns the sequence of displaying a series of icons, texts as well as the modality to navigate across the information hierarchical structure.

According to the adopted I/O devices, the interaction style, graphics and dynamics can vary. For instance the frame of graphics will be different in case of touchpad or mobile phones. This variation is expressed according a 0–1-3–9 scale according to the following meaning:

0 – functionality not available;
1 – functionality implementation at low level;
2 – functionality implementation at average level;
3 – functionality implementation level at high level.

Such correlation is presented in Matrix 4 (Fig. 2). When the technology is defined, such features can be established and mapped on the y-axis in Matrix 5. Once identified the patterns of Matrix 5, the definition of the knowledge-based rules can start. Rules consider that the interface can be described by means of its logical sections or pages and, for each of them, a set of items are defined. The rules will indicate how such items will be adapted when certain conditions will occur according to the usual syntax of the *if-then-else* logics, which are common across many programming languages. For instance, the interface can be described by its main pages and page sections, and items can be changed according to specific conditions. The mechanism to define the set of adaptive rules is described in Fig. 3.

For a specific user with a particular role located into certain environmental, each interface item will be configured by a set of rules describing:

- *type of contents* to be presented by the interface (i.e. text, video, pictures, acoustic messages, etc.), that mainly depends on the specific task to be executed, the operator skills and role, the specific content of application and scopes, user frailties and finally the interface semantics;
- *quantity of contents* shown by the interface (i.e. full details, partial or minimum level of detail), that depends on the task to be executed, the user profile, the specific content of application and scopes;

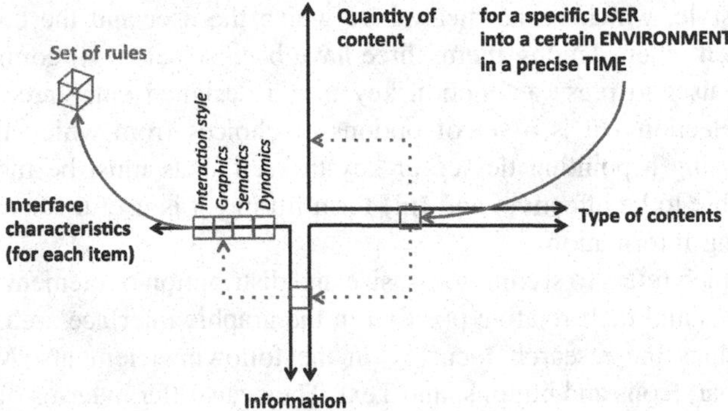

Fig. 3. Rules for the definition of the interface feature

- *information* to be displayed, that consists of data to be shown to the user depending on his/her role and education profile, the specific context and the tasks;
- *interface characteristics* for each specific item of the interface, that refer to how the interface features are configured in term of font, text, icons, color, navigation way (i.e. bigger font, higher contrast, red color, round shapes). They are mainly influenced by the specific user physical and cognitive frailties.

3.2 The AUI Architecture and the Preliminary Prototype

The overall system architecture is reported in Fig. 4. It implements the proposed methodology for UI configuration. It allows the reader to focus on the research objectives and to identify the main system modules.

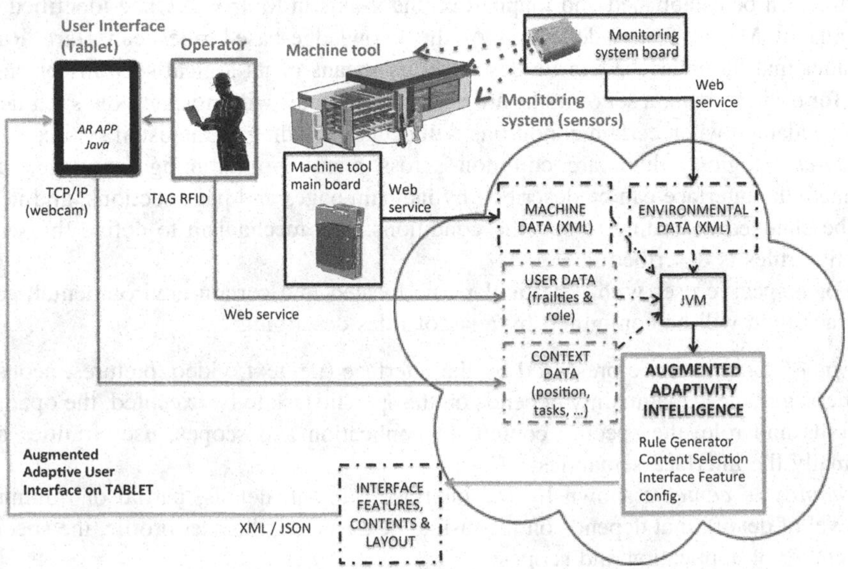

Fig. 4. Overall system architecture

The main modules are:

- a machine main board, that collects and sends data about the specific machine to a server by web services;
- a monitoring system board, that collects data about the manufacturing environment thanks to a dedicated sensor network and sends those data to a server by web services;
- a RFID tag placed on the operator, that monitors the user behaviours and sends data to the central system engine on the server;
- a web-based UI visualized on tablet, that represents the HW-SE user interface where adaptivity is enabled;
- an AR application based on Java to manage the tablet webcam and the Augmented Reality contents on the tablet interface;
- an Augmented Adaptivity Intelligence on the server side, that allows the data collected from the other modules to be managed, the knowledge-based rules to be created according to the proposed method and the interface features to be then configured. It exploits a Java Virtual Machine and web
- a Java Virtual Machine (JVM) to merge data and create/configure the web-based interface visualized by the tablet.

According to such architecture, a preliminary AUI prototype is developed. It is a web-based interface running on tablets that includes a commercial AR application, used by operators in manufacturing context. The system uses RFID tags to identify the specific operator and recover information about its characteristics (i.e. skills, age, education and frailties). In the case study, the machine tool is a machine dedicated to wood processing; it is composed by a loading-unloading area where the operator can load/unload the piece of wood to be processed, and a closed area within which the piece of wood is processed. All data coming from the machine are stored in the machine tool main board. A set of sensors are embedded in the machine to measure vibration and noise, smoke, and dust. All these sensors send data via wireless connection to the machine main board and the monitoring system board located close to the machine; from the boards data are sent via web-services to the central server. The Java Virtual Machine (JVM) on the server side accepts those data and interprets them through XML files that are parsed and stored into database. As soon as the interface webcam is activated and recognizes the AR marker, specific information about the position on the machine and/or the task to be performed are sent to the JVM. These data, combined with the user profile, are used by the augmented adaptivity intelligence to generate specific rules, select proper contents and configure UI features. These new data are sent back to the Augmented AUI trough XML and/or JSON files.

4 A Use Case to Assess the AUI Performance

An industrial case study offered by a large-sized company producing machines for working wood, metal and glass is presented in the paper to demonstrate the approach applicability, validity and potentiality. The industrial partner aimed to realize an AUI integrated in a pilot machine that assists operators with frailties in everyday task execution. In particular, the pilot machine is represented by a woodworking machine, which is living a rapid technological evolution but where the age of the operators is increasing due to the lack of new generations involved. According to the proposed method, the case study is described in terms of:

- *context*: machine control and basic operations for windows furniture production;
- *tasks*: tasks mainly consists of machine loading and unloading, labelling of the machined piece of wood and monitoring of the working conditions;
- *target users*: we consider an operator with a basic role (i.e. Op1), who takes care about the load and unload of the machine, machine status monitoring and alert identification. In our case he is a man of 60 years old (3) with a medium level of education (3) and high skills (5). About its frailties, he is long-sighted and cannot lift more than 25 kg;
- *interface features*: the features to be designed and adapted are described in Table 3. A set of sections are defined and, for each of them, a list of items to be configured in their graphics, dynamics and semantics when possible.

Table 3. Interface features to be adapted

Interface sections	Interface features
Header	F1. Multicolour status bar for environmental parameters
	F2. Multicolour status bar for machine parameters
Load /Unload main page	F3. Loading minutes
	F4. Information about the part processed
	F5. Part volume
	F6. Part weight
	F7. Load button
	F8. Unload button
	F9. Information about parts that have been already loaded
	F10. Label to be put on the part processed
Detailed information page	F11. Information about parts to be loaded next
	F12. Information about running process
Video control panel page	F13. Video about manual lading information
	F14. Video about automatic lading information
	F15. Video about machine internal movements
	F16. Video about machine external locking clamps
Detailed diagram pages	F17. Diagram of dusts
	F18. Diagram of steams /fumes
	F19. Diagram of sound pressure
	F20. Diagram of vibrations
	F21. Diagram of internal noises
	F22. Combined graphs
Multi-level pages	F23. Multi-level information
Alert	F24. Alert and warning messages

In order to preliminary demonstrate the AUI usability and acceptability, preliminary usability tests are carried out. 5 sample users aged from 60 to 65 are involved. At the beginning the machine is properly programmed; the users are asked to execute their tasks about Op1 functions. It means that they are asked to perform tasks such as (T1) Read the status of the environment, (T2) Read the status of the machine, (T3) Load/unload the parts, (T4) Read the next part label to be loaded, (T5) Supply staples and labels, (T6) Recognize an alert and its typology. During task execution a set of metrics are measured and ad hoc questionnaires submitted to the sample users. Quantitative metrics are as follows: execution time, number of errors or percentage, task completion. Qualitative metrics regard perceived simplicity in use and provided information comprehensibility. Judges are expressed according to 1–5 scale. Figure 5 shows a user involved in the experimental testing using the AUI on the tablet and collecting information about the tasks and environment by pointing the AR marker. As soon as the webcam of the tablet recognizes the AR marker (highlighted in the red circle), the system is able to automatically recognize if and when the operator has to load/unload a new piece of wood and help him/her during the operation by providing additional information (i.e. how to load or unload the piece in the right way, check to verify).

Fig. 5. Experimentation: AR application reading the marker positioned on the machine tool

From the results of the experimental phases, it can be stated that introducing assistive technology can really bring advantages to both operators and companies. Operators can work more safely and with better performances, and the company can benefit of the improved productivity. Table 4 shows the average results on all tasks for Op1.

Table 4. Usability test and results

Metrics	Unit. of meas.	Traditional system without AUI (average)	New system with AUI (average)	Improvement
Execution time	Sec.	45	33	−26 %
Number of errors	No.	5	1	−80 %
Task completion	%	60 %	85 %	+41 %
Simplicity in use	1–5 judge	3,0	4,2	+40 %
Comprehensibility	1–5 judge	2,8	4,5	+60,0 %
Order perceived	1–5 judge	2,5	3,9	+56 %
Intuitiveness	1–5 judge	2,1	3,5	+66 %
Pleasure in use	1–5 judge	3,0	4,6	+53 %

5 Conclusion and Future Work

The paper presents an approach for designing AUI to support elderly in using machines in manufacturing. The key element of this approach is the use of a set of 3D correlation matrices able to link the User, the Interface and the Environment and define then some knowledge-based rules to configure the AUI components. The proposed approach enables the interface to change itself on the basis of the user demands, his/her cognitive and physical abilities and the tasks he/she has to perform. The approach has been applied in case of wood working machines. A software platform has been developed and preliminary tested. Future work will be focused on the demonstration of the approach reliability by collecting further case histories and on the analysis of the platform usability and acceptability.

References

1. Skirbekk, V., Loichinger, E., Baraket, B.: The aging of the workforce in European countries: demographic trends, retiment projections and retirement policies. In: Borman, W.C., Hedge, J.W. (eds.) The Oxford Handbook of Work and Aging. Oxford University Press, New York (2012)
2. Doyle, J., Skrba, Z., McDonnell, R., Arent, B.: Designing a touch screen communication device to support social interaction amongst older adults. In: 24th BCS International Conference on Human-Computer Interaction. BCS International Conference on Human-Computer Interaction (HCI-2010), United Kingdom (2010)

3. Ageing in the Twenty-First Century: A Celebration and A Challenge, Published by the United Nations Population Fund (UNFPA), New York, and HelpAge International, London. http://unfpa.org/ageingreport. Accessed 1 February 2015
4. The Organization for Economic Co-Operation and Development: Live longer, work longer (2006). http://www.oecd.org/employment/livelongerworklonger.htm
5. National Telecommunications and Information Administration: Americans in the Information Age (2000). http://www.ntia.doc.gov/ntiahome/fttn00/Falling.htm#67
6. Clegg, A., Young, J., Iliffe, S., Rikkert, M.O., Rockwood, K.: Frailty in elderly people. The Lancet **381**(9868), 752–762 (2013)
7. Rothrock, L., Koubek, R., Fuchs, R., Haas, M., Salvendy, G.: Review and reappraisal of adaptive interfaces: toward biologically inspired paradigms. Theor. Issues Ergon. Sci. **6**(2), 157–172 (2002)
8. Norman, D.A.: The Design of Everyday Things. Basic Books, New York (1998)
9. Schneider-Hufschmidt, M., Malinowski, U., Kuhme, T.: Adaptive User Interfaces: Principles and Practice. Elsevier Science Inc., New York (1993)
10. Stephanidis, C., Paramythis, A., Sfyrakis, M., Stergiou, A., Maou, N., Leventis, A., Paparoulis, G., Karagiannidis, C.: Adaptable and Adaptive User Interfaces for Disabled Users in the AVANTI Project. Intelligence in Services and Networks: Technology for Ubiquitous Telecom Services (1998)
11. Nilsson, E.G.: Design patterns for user interface for mobile applications. Adv. Eng. Softw. **40**, 1318–1328 (2009)
12. Milgram, P., Takemura, H., Utsumi, A., Kishino, F.: Augmented reality: a class of displays on the reality-virtuality continuum. In: International Conference on Telemanipulator and Telepresence Technologies, vol. 2351, pp. 282–292 (1994)
13. Chi, H.L., Kang, S.C., Wang, X.: Research trends and opportunities of augmented reality applications in architecture, engineering and construction. Autom. Constr. **33**, 116–122 (2013)
14. Marcincin, J.N.: Selected applications of virtual reality in manufacturing. J. Technol. Plast. **36**(1), 25–34 (2011)
15. Nee, A.Y.C., Ong, S.K., Chryssolouris, G., Mourtzis, D.: Augmented reality applications in design and manufacturing. CIRP Ann. Manufact. Technol. **61**(2), 657–679 (2012)
16. Lee, Y.C., Chao, Y.H., Lin, S.B.: Structural approach to design user interface. Comput. Ind. **61**(7), 613–623 (2010)
17. Likert, R., Hayes, S.: Some Applications of Behavioural Research. Unesco, Paris (1957)
18. Galiz, W.O.: The Essential Guide to User Interface Design: An introduction to GUI Design Principles and Techniques, 2nd edn. Wiley Publishing, Indianapolis (2002)
19. Huang, S.M., Shieh, K.K., Chi, C.F.: Factors affecting the design of computer icons. Int. J. Ind. Ergon. **29**, 211–218 (2002)

Development of Caricature Robots for Interaction with Older Adults

Jeffrey Sebastian[1,2(✉)], Chih-Yin Tai[1,2], Kim Lindholm[1], and Yeh-Liang Hsu[1,2]

[1] Gerontechnology Research Center, Yuan Ze University, Zhongli, Taiwan
[2] Mechanical Engineering Department, Yuan Ze University, Zhongli, Taiwan
jkingsl6@yahoo.com

Abstract. This paper proposes a concept of combining the techniques of classic animation and robotic design to create a simple robot capable of interacting with older adults, denominated *"caricature robots"*. A caricature robot can be described as "a non-humanoid robot that can show simplified humanoid motions in exaggerated ways". To achieve that illusion, three key elements should be met in a caricature robot: *functionality, simplicity in motion and personality*. While interaction for every older adult can be different, users are allowed to personalize their caricature robot by creating their own set of motions and personas that suits their personal taste. This is made possible through the "Body Cerebellar and Brain" control structure and the MotionClips software developed in this research. MusicMouth is used to exemplify caricature robots. Through the advantage of customization and personalization, caricature robots present a range of scenarios.

Keywords: Interaction · Caricature robots · Robotic motion design

1 Caricature Robots

From the appearance design, robots can be divided into humanoid robots and nonhumanoid robots. Humanoid robots are designed to imitate human-like appearance and movement. For example, Honda's Asimo in Fig. 1(a) contains basic setup of trunk, hips, upper and lower limbs and head. Its movement implementation intends to emulate human motions, including basic walking, grabbing things, arm movement and even dancing. Many non-humanoid companion robots are designed to resemble pets. For example, Paro, described by Guinness world records as the "world's most therapeutic robot of its kind" www.parorobots.com has a pet-like appearance. As shown in Fig. 1(b), it is designed as a seal covered in soft fur like a stuffed animal.

These robots are designed to have a personality, which is expressed by their robotic motion. Paro for example, shows soothing movements and eye blinking which denote a "cute" personality. Asimo, in contrast to Paro, presents more aggressive movements that show a jovial personality, a younger, almost childlike spirit. For robots like Paro, their "personality" or set of motions have been embedded in it, a set of reactions that are triggered by the users to simulate interaction. The limitation with this embedded

J. Zhou and G. Salvendy (Eds.): ITAP 2015, Part II, LNCS 9194, pp. 324–332, 2015.
DOI: 10.1007/978-3-319-20913-5_30

Fig. 1. (a). Asimo http://asimo.honda.com (b). Paro

personality is obvious when trying to distinguish one Paro from another, due they will all be the same and could not be adapted to the different needs or requirements to each individual person who would interact with it. Over the past few decades, robotics has been moving forward in aiding older adults in their daily tasks. Modern medicine as well has been using robotic assistance for several tasks in homecare and medical applications.

There are some important needs for older adults and dementia care that robotics can cover, as numbered below:

- Reminiscence therapy: Therapy based on recollecting past experiences or events through an audio-visual experiences [2, 3].
- Memory aid: Through audio-visual reminders and assets to keep the oriented while doing their daily tasks [2].
- Communication: Research has shown that demented patients have express they feel lonely [4, 5], although this problem is not exclusive for demented patients but also between the elderly population of the world.

The work presented in this paper describes a new approach using caricature robots for interaction with elderly people. A caricature robot as "a non-humanoid robot that can show simplified humanoid motions and emotions in exaggerated ways." A lab-based evaluation, in which 16 older adults aged 52 to 80 interacted with the facilitator through a caricature robot, showed positive results on acceptance of the caricature robot. The levels of anxiety of the older adults were low while interacting with a caricature robot based on their heart rate; also the level of concentration while interacting with caricature robot is high based on the record from an eye tracker. This evaluation was carried internally at the Gerontechnology Research Center during the process and development of the caricature robot concept, these results will be published in an upcoming paper. This paper presents the development of "caricature robots" and how they can become part in the daily lives of older adults.

2 Method, Materials and Concepts

This research intends in a simplistic way to present personalities in caricature robots that can be adapted to the different older adults who come across interacting with them. While interaction for every older adult can be different, users are allowed to personalize their caricature robot by creating their own set of motions and personas that suits their personal taste. This is made possible through the "Body Cerebellar and Brain" control structure and the MotionClips software developed in this research. A set of "rules" or elements were defined for the creation of caricature robots, these elements we defined as the "key elements" that every caricature robot must contain to be denominated as caricature robots. These key elements are Functionality, Simplicity in motion and personality. To be able to explain these key elements we will use the Music Mouth project in this paper to aid us not only in the definition of our concept of caricature robots and their key elements, but the scenarios in which it can be used and how it can be included in the daily lives of older adults for interaction.

2.1 Three Key Elements for Defining a Caricature Robot

Caricature robots, while being non complicated robots; they achieve interaction and can become part of households due to their unique characteristics, that do not rely on the esthetics only but on their core function and motion design to be able to express emotions through simple mechanisms. These key elements combined in a caricature robot are:

Functionality. The first element of a caricature robot is its functionality, which is the crucial factor of determination on how to include a caricature robot into a household. This is what will determine where the robot will be placed, how it will be used and how it can aid in one way or another. The inherent functionality, for example, photo frame holders, trashcans, lamps and more, brings a full range of possibilities on how to include caricature robots to our daily lives at home.

Simplicity in Motion. In a caricature robot, the mechanisms added to the original functionality to facilitate robotic movements are expected to be simple but allow movements for expressive motions. In contrast with most humanoid robots that contain sophisticated mechanisms to achieve humanoid movements, a caricature robot intends to use a small amount of degrees of freedom to achieve expressive motions.

Personality. The personality of a caricature robot relies mainly on the design of motion. In particular, the movement exaggeration is a crucial part to show the personality of a caricature robot. The design of motion can be fully based on principles of cartoon character design used by animators and artists around the world. *"Disney Animation: The Illusion of Life"* [6], considered in the industry as the "Bible" of animation, describes the motion and animation principles for cartoon characters, that could be combined in a robotic body to achieve almost life-like expression in the non-humanoid robot. These principles are:

- Squash and stretch
- Anticipation
- Staging
- Straight ahead and pose to pose animation
- Follow through and overlapping action
- Slow-out and slow-in

- Arcs
- Secondary Action
- Timing
- Exaggeration
- Solid drawing
- Appeal

Through the design of motion, caricatures are able to give life to unanimated objects like lamps, carpets [7] and even a toaster [8]. Of all 12 principles above, the "solid drawing" principle is the only one that cannot be fully applied to a mechanical body yet can be used in the facial expression design.

2.2 Music Mouth for Illustrating the Characteristics of a Caricature Robot

"MusicMouth" shown in Fig. 2 is used as an example to illustrate the three characteristics of a caricature robot. MusicMouth's core functionality is to be a speaker, which is a common appliance in many homes. Simple elements of motion were added to this speaker, including an up-and-down motion that simulates the "mouth" and the side-to-side motion that turns the "body" around. These two degrees of freedom keep this robot simple but are enough to express personality. Personality was added through the motions and visual elements added to the robot. MusicMouth opens and closes its mouth when an audio input is detected. By taking an ordinary object as the speaker and converting it into a caricature robot, more scenarios are possible. This speaker now can use its personality and motions to be a more life-like speaker, an in-call avatar, or just and "interactive partner" which converts digital source into physical motion. This first step on developing this caricature robot was to find a basic common element in a home that wouldn't be invasive, that would be functional and that could be inserted in homes easily. The conversion of the ordinary speaker into a caricature robot was based on a simple design process of the addition of servo motors and controllers that would react to the input received and, along with the speaker generate an output that could give this "illusion of life" through the key element number 3 described before in this paper, Personality. We recently finished the real prototype Fig. 3 of MusicMouth in which we could test the different features that can help us create user scenarios in which such caricature robot can be used to interact with older adults.

Fig. 2. Musicmouth with different visual aids to define personality

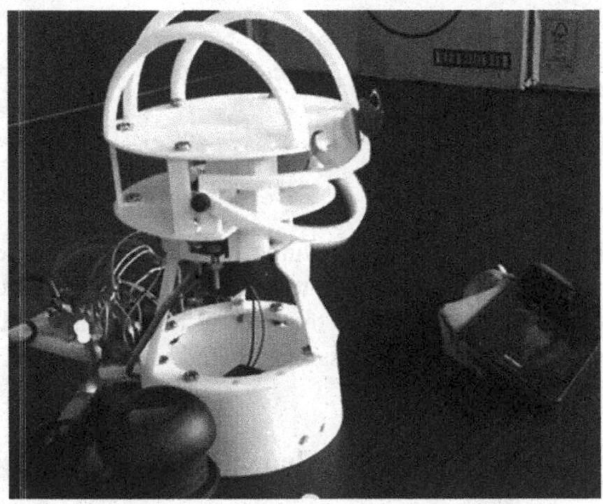

Fig. 3. Musicmouth first prototype

3 Software Development and Discussion

While interaction for every older adult can be different, users are allowed to personalize their caricature robot by creating their own set of motions and personas that suits their personal taste. This is made possible through the "Body Cerebellar and Brain" control structure and the MotionClips software developed in this research.

3.1 Developed Software – The "Body, Cerebella and Brain" Control Structure

MusicMouth is based on the "Body, cerebella and brain" control structure that keeps the whole set of commands and instructions on the software of the system yet not on the hardware. MusicMouth's input can be from music, a Motionclip file or any other audio input available into the application and a micro processing unit controls it, which is ready to receive and execute the different commands from the input application. This allows customization to happen inside the application for persona creation and intensity of interaction. This can also allow easy update on the system without the need of changing anything on the hardware. To facilitate this customization to the users, an application to go along with these caricature robots has been created called Motionclips, which allows the user to create audio and video files with a set of motion commands assigned by the end-user to fit his needs and ways of interaction (Fig. 4).

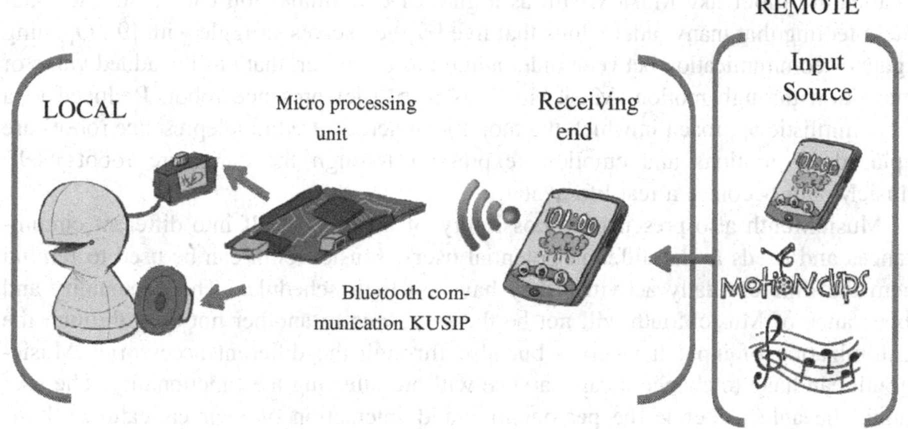

Fig. 4. Control structure of MusicMouth

MotionClips is an application that allows the end-user to create and send custom video and audio content with e-motions (electronic motions) through a caricature robot. This content is saved in a "video + motion" and "audio + motion" format that caricature robots recognizes. This format setting is simply a video or an audio file that carries along with it a command file that will trigger motions of the robotic body of the caricature robot to play along with the video and audio content. MotionClips can also be employed to share audio content with motions through MusicMouth. This simple case-scenario takes two users living afar. MotionClips allows the creation of custom animated motions to accompany an audio clip. When this audio + motion is shared to a caricature robot, the robot will reproduce those motions predetermined by the remote user during while the audio clip is being reproduced.

3.2 Music Mouth and Usage Scenarios for Older Adults

MusicMouth as a caricature robot can be used in many different scenarios based on the features that were added to this home speaker, now transformed into a robot. MusicMouth was created and designed to give life to the sounds emitted by the speaker, bringing a new way to not only hear the intensity of the sound interaction but also add a visual value of such intensity. We will now discuss a couple of scenarios where MusicMouth is used for interactivity. Not only presenting himself as an interactive music speaker which as shown in the image converts the audio input received from a smart device through Bluetooth and converts it to motion and expression while also amplifying the sound signal. MusicMouth does the opposite of what current technology trends are doing; MusicMouth converts a digital input into an analog output. In the second scenario we hold two ends in this "visual equation" in which the caregiver can communicate with the older adult through MusicMouth. This scenario is being applied to older adults who by many different circumstances live in solitude and are not able to keep constant communication with their caregiver, family members, friends etc. Using a caricature robot like MusicMouth as a gate of communication can aid to the loneliness feeling that many older adults that live by themselves struggle with [9]. Opening a gate of communication between older adult and caregiver, that has the added value of interaction through motion, MusicMouth is also a telepresence robot. Reduced to a very simplistic approach in which the monitor or screen used in telepresence robots are replaced by motions and emotions expressed through the caricature robot itself; MusicMouth becomes a real life avatar.

MusicMouth also presents the possibility of adapting itself into different circumstances and needs to the different potential users. MusicMouth can be used to remind them the different daily activities they have on their schedules. The personality and appearance of MusicMouth will not be the same one to another not only through the customization of input it receives but also through the different accessories MusicMouth can have to change its appearance without affecting the functionality. The user should be able to define the personalities and interaction of their caricature robots. MusicMouth can be an aid to elders living alone, not only being a gate of communication with their caregivers or family members but also being a personal reminder for their daily chores and important tasks as taking medication and more. These reminders and tasks can be programmed by the caregiver or family into their own smart device which is connected to MusicMouth, keeping a simple yet interactive way of communicating with their loved ones.

4 Conclusions

Caricature robots open up the possibility to engage older adults in an interactive way of communicating with their loved ones. Caricature robots are defined by three elements, functionality, simplicity in motion and personality, all of the above based on the main objective that the creators of caricature robots desired for this project, to have a useful robot that can be put in homes without being complicated to build or operate. Caricature robots are not intended to be complicated robots or robots with a humanoid behavior, they are simple robots that are capable of expression. The video + motion and audio + motion format created for caricature robots allow users to interact remotely with their loved ones. Customization and persona creation allows caricature robots to differentiate themselves from other available robots allowing the user to define how and where these caricature robots interact with them. The interaction with older adults through caricature robots goes beyond the local scenario. These robots intend to be an open gate of communication between families or caregivers with simple robots that are not invasive and can be included at homes. For our future works we are to implement MusicMouth and other Caricature Robots in home environments designed for elders suffering with dementia in Taiwan, opening a gate of communication between them and their families that usually are separated in great distances due work locations and more. Caricature robots are now in development but they represent a new option in robotic design for households where older adults live, by being daily use objects by themselves through their functionality element of design, we wouldn't present objects that are unfamiliar to them. We can take a picture frame, a speaker, a phone holder and more common objects and add these key elements of caricature robots as shown with

MusicMouth and turn them into robots with personalities. The "cute" factor of their design is a non-threatening one, which allows older adults to feel more relaxed around them as shown before in the lab-based experiment. Caricature robots not only intend to be a feasible and sensible option to include robots at home, but also intend to be the gate of communication and interactivity that is absent in many households where older adults reside alone. MusicMouth and other Caricature robots have been 3d printed, being this, a gate of possibilities for many to be able to obtain customize and print their own, cutting down the costs of production to a minimal, making it affordable and reachable even in places where technology is not an option due to lack of financial resources. Knowing that not every older adult gets acquainted easily with new technology, caricature robots allow a wide range of possibilities in customization, allowing the users and caregivers to adapt them to their own needs and taste. We believe that caricature robots are a good open door to finally allow robots into our daily lives without being intrusive or obsolete "toys" without functionality. Caricature robots do not intend to denigrate our older adult community by designing technology "specially for them", we believe that older adults are an active community that like to play with technology as well, and caricature robots is technology for everyone to use, that is simple yet we kept the "Fun" factor on them for everyone to enjoy. Caricature robots as mentioned before, are to be useful in homes, are to be non-threatening and reachable to anyone who would like to own one to have a home care system through a simple "robotic friend", caricature robots.

References

1. Asimo, The World's Most Advanced Humanoid Robot. (n.d.). ASIMO by Honda. Retrieved March 3, 2014, from http://asimo.honda.com. Figure 2(b). Paro therapeutic robot
2. World Health Organization, Dementia a Public Health Priority. WHO publications, United Kingdom (2012). ISBN: 978 92 4 156445 8
3. Technology and Health Care, A review of the role of assistive technology for people with dementia in the hours of darkness, IOS press, vol. 17, number 4 (2007)
4. Proceedings of the 2011, HRI 2011, Workshop Social Robotic Telepresence, ISTC-CNR Consiglio Nazionale delle Ricerche Istituto di Scienze e Tecnologie della Cognizione Via S. Martino della Battaglia, 44–00185 Rome, Italy (2011)
5. Kane, M., Cook, L.: Dementia 2013: The Hidden Voice of Loneliness. Alzheimers Society, London (2013)
6. Thomas, F., Johnston, O., Thomas, F.: The Illusion of Life: Disney Animation, pp. 306–312. Hyperion, New York (1995)
7. Disney, W. (Director). Aladdin (2 DVD Special Edition): Disney (1992)
8. Disch, T.M. (Director). Walt Disney presents The brave little toaster : Walt Disney Home Video (1988)
9. Alzheimer's society, Dementia 2013: The hidden voice of Lonelines, Alzheimer Society, United Kingdom (2013)
10. Yamane, K., Ariki, Y., Hodgins, J.: Animating non-humanoid characters with human motion data. In: Proceedings of the 2010 ACM SIGGRAPH/Eurographics Symposium on Computer Animation, pp. 169–178. Eurographics Association, July 2010

11. Kwon, E.S.: A study on the color emotion with visual tactility. In: International Conference on Colour Emotion Research and Application Proceedings, pp. 30–36. Chulalongkorn University Press (Bangkok, 2002)
12. Jenkins, C., Smythe, A.: Reflections on a visit to a dementia care village: Catharine Jenkins and Analisa Smythe discuss what the UK can learn from a Dutch model of care, where residents live in an environment carefully crafted to emulate their previous lifestyles. Nursing older people (2013)
13. Tsai, T.C., Hsu, Y.L., Ma, A.I., King, T., Wu, C.H.: Developing a telepresence robot for interpersonal communication with the elderly in a home environment. Telemedicine and e-Health **13**(4), 407–424 (2006)
14. NHI Public Access, Author Manuscript, Intelligent assistive Technology applications to dementia care: Current capabilities Limitations and future challenges. Ashok, J., Bharucha, M.D., Vivek Anand, B.S., Jodi Forlizzi, Ph.D., Mary Amanda Dew, Ph.D., Charles F. Reynolds III, M.D., Scott Stevens, Ph.D., and Howard Wactlar, M.S. Department of Psychiatry, University of Pittsburgh School of Medicine, Western Psychiatric Institute and Clinic (AJB, MAD, CFR); and Carnegie Mellon University (VA, JF, SS, HW), Pittsburgh, PA. (2009)

Computer Input Devices and the Elderly: A Musculoskeletal Disorder Focus

Alvaro D. Taveira(✉) and Sang D. Choi

Department of Occupational and Environmental Safety and Health, University of Wisconsin–Whitewater, Whitewater, USA
taveiraa@uww.edu

Abstract. The aging process carries important implications for the design of human-computer interfaces. Decreases in vision, motor control and muscle force combined with a higher vulnerability to musculoskeletal disorders and to degenerative diseases should be taken in consideration when designing and selecting computer input devices for the elderly. This study reviews the recent research literature on computer input devices and their adequacy to the elderly user. Significant findings from evaluative studies are summarized, and recommendations are provided.

Keywords: Computer input devices · Aging · Older · Elderly · MSDs

1 Introduction and Significance

The fast aging of many western and eastern societies and their increasing reliance on information technology create a compelling need to reconsider older users' interactions with computers. Computers are critical for productive and independent living (Charness 2001). Older adults are increasingly using computers (Ball and Hourcade 2011), but they often face challenges and lag behind younger users (Ji et al. 2010; Czaja and Lee 2003). Barriers include lack of familiarity, feelings of inadequacy, declining visual and motor skills (Carpenter and Buday 2007; Mann et al. 2005). Computers allow the elderly to stay employed, informed, intellectually active, and socially integrated (Taveira and Choi 2009).

Older adults often use computer input devices in different ways when compared to younger ones. These differences in usage style can be attributed to aging effects as well as to limited familiarity with computers. Hsiao and Cho (2012) studied healthy young and older adults performing a series of mouse tasks. A three dimensional motion capture system and electromyographic analysis were used to obtain kinematic and kinetic data. Compared with young adults, the older users had greater amplitude of muscle activity in forearm, and greater cranial-cervical angle and neck flexion (forward head posture). Consequently, the older adults might be at greater risk of developing musculoskeletal disorders (Hsiao and Cho 2012).

Many older adults suffer from vision reducing eye disease (Leonard et al. 2005), and less efficient visual processing. Age-related changes affecting computer usage include reduced muscle strength and range of motion (ROM), difficulty executing fine

J. Zhou and G. Salvendy (Eds.): ITAP 2015, Part II, LNCS 9194, pp. 333–340, 2015.
DOI: 10.1007/978-3-319-20913-5_31

movements, as well as increased incidence of arthritis and neurological disorders (Jochems et al. 2013). Size constraints in handheld devices further aggravate these issues (Díaz-Bossini and Moreno 2014; Zhou, Rau and Salvendy 2012).

The purpose of this review is to synthesize the available research on computer input devices from a perspective of older users, with an emphasis on mitigation and accommodation to musculoskeletal disorders (MSDs).

2 Methods

Using a systematic approach to literature searching, the authors first defined an initial set of keywords to guide the identification of relevant studies. Two librarians were engaged in the process of identifying and searching appropriate databases. The search was conducted primarily using electronic sources, supplemented by books and other printed materials retrieved from a network of libraries. Studies published in English were drawn from peer-reviewed journals, conference proceedings, edited books, and a variety of web-based sources.

3 Discussion of Results

Input devices sense physical properties of the user (e.g., motions, touch, voice, etc.) and convert them into predefined signals to the computer. Input devices must comply with the users' anatomic, biomechanical, perceptual, and cognitive needs and capabilities. Epidemiological studies have associated long hours of computer use with elevated rates of MSDs in the arms and neck (Gerr, Marcus, and Monteilh 2004). Furthermore, since the prevalence of several MSDs increases with age (Woolf and Pfegler 2003), additional caution in the design and selection of input devices for this population is justified. Older adults are in general slower in movement and make more submovements (Hertzum and Hornbaek 2010; Nichols, Rogers, and Fisk 2006) when operating input devices.

3.1 Keyboards

Although the association between typing and MSDs is somewhat mixed (Gerr et al. 2004), the conventional QWERTY keyboard design affects upper limbs postures (Rempel et al. 2007; Swanson et al. 1997). Typing postures are also influenced by the nature of tasks performed and the workstation configuration.

Older adults are slower typists, particularly novices, but not necessarily less accurate (Bosman and Charness 1996). Users with rheumatoid arthritis, a common illness among older adults, tend to apply high force keystrokes. They move their hands to strike keys and tend to maintain their wrists and fingers in a fixed position. These keyboarding styles appear to reduce typing productivity and have the potential to put stress on joints already affected by the disorder (Baker, Gustafson and Rogers 2010).

Mann et al. (2005) found that "larger keys" was the most common improvement request among older users. Scarce evidence exists on the benefits of alternative keyboard designs on MSD prevention, although there is some evidence that users suffering from hand-wrist pain may experience improvement in soreness and function with a split keyboard geometry (Tittiranonda et al. 1999). For handheld computers older adults prefer a physical keyboard to on-screen ones (Zhou, Rau and Salvendy 2012).

3.2 Pointing Devices

Pointing devices allow the user to control cursor positioning and to select, activate, and drag items on display. Web interaction, for example, involves frequent pointing and selecting tasks, commonly surpassing keyboard use. The pointing device design and its operational characteristics, along with the workstation configuration, and the nature, duration and pace of the tasks, affect body postures. General concerns relating to the usage of pointing devices by the elderly include prolonged static postures of the back and shoulders, frequent wrist motions and excessive forearm pronation and wrist deviation.

Mouse. The mouse is the most commonly used non-keyboard input device with desktop computers (Atkinson, Woods, Haslam, and Buckle 2004). Intensive mouse use has been associated with increased risk of upper extremity MSDs, including carpal tunnel syndrome (Keir, Bach, and Rempel 1999). Various aspects of mouse control such as moving, clicking, fine-positioning, and dragging may be difficult for older people due to declining motor control and coordination. Increased susceptibility toward disabling conditions, such as arthritis, compounds the problem. Sandfeld and Jensen (2005) indicated that the combination of small target sizes and high mouse gain reduced performance severely, as measured by working speed and hit rate, and this was especially pronounced in the elderly group. In addition, muscle activation levels were found to be generally higher among older users. Mouse usage speed was found to be negatively affected by age, as well as by age-related impairments (Baker and Rogers 2010)

Touchpad. A touch pad is a flat panel that senses the position of a finger or stylus, and is commonly found as an integrated pointing device on portable computers such as laptops, notebooks, and PDAs. For older adults using portable computers, the small pad dimension poses some challenges due to the size mismatch with the screen. Elderly users may also experience difficulty with the complex motor skills involved in tapping the touch pad (Wood, Willoughby, Rushing, Bechtel, and Gilbert 2005). Armbrüster et al. (2007) showed that older users were significantly slower than younger ones when executing touchpad tasks. Hertzum and Hornbaek (2010) comparing young (12–14 years), adult (25–33 years), and elderly (61–69 years) participants' performance in pointing tasks with mouse and touchpad concluded that all three age groups were slower and made more errors with the touchpad than the mouse, but the touchpad slowed down elderly participants more than young participants, who in turn were slowed down more than adult participants.

Trackball. Users with low strength, poor coordination, wrist pain, or limited ROM, may prefer a trackball to a mouse (Wobbrock and Myers 2006). Trackballs need little space in which to operate, unlike mice, which have large desktop footprints. Trackballs can be embedded in consoles or keyboards, making them suitable for public terminals since they cannot be easily removed (Wobbrock and Myers 2006). Chaparro et al. (1999a) concluded that the trackball might be better for the elderly when performing prolonged and repetitive actions. Chaparro et al. (1999b) suggested that the mouse may be a better device than the thumb-controlled trackball, but that a finger-ball design may offer benefits to the elderly.

Touchscreens. Touch screens allow direct user input on a display. Input signals are generated as the user moves a finger or stylus over a transparent touch-sensitive surface placed over the display. Older adults generally have positive opinions about touchscreens (Mitzner et al. 2010, Chung et al. 2010), but are less likely to use them (Fisk et al. 2012). A performance study by Findlater et al. (2013) found that older adults were significantly slower than younger adults in general with the touchscreen reduced performance gap relative to the desktop and mouse. Indeed, the touchscreen resulted in a significant movement time reduction of 35% over the mouse for older adults, compared to only 16% for younger adults. Error rates also decreased for the touchscreen. Finally, Chang, Tsai, Chang, and Chang (2014) found that performance on touch panel operations was much worse among elderly users as compared to that of young users. The authors also indicated that touchscreen size had a significant effect on operating performance, with elderly users having difficulty performing drag and scale tasks on smaller screens.

Trackpoint. A trackpoint, a small isometric joystick placed between the letter keys G, H and B on the computer's keyboard, is a common input device in laptop and notebook computers. It senses force from the fingertip, which results in a cursor movement specified by a non-linear transfer function. Research has shown that for older adults the trackpoint seems to be quite challenging to master and rather difficult to operate (Armbruster, Sutter, and Ziefle 2007).

3.3 Hands-Free Input

Voice. Voice input may be helpful to older users in a number of situations, either as the sole input mode or jointly with other control means. Speech based input may be appropriate, when the user's hands or eyes are busy, when interacting with handheld computers with limited keyboards or (touch) screens, and for users with perceptual or motor impairments (Cohen and Oviatt 1995). Jastrzembski et al. (2005) reported that speech recognition was preferred over light pens although with longer response times. No age effects within device type were found (i.e., voice versus light pens). In conjunction with other input modes voice can reduce errors, facilitate corrections, and increase flexibility of handheld devices (Cohen and Oviatt 1995). Speech recognition may enable older adults to interact effectively with a number of computerized appliances, and eliminate, reduce, or supplement the use of keyboards or other physical input devices. Voice input seems to be appropriate when quick user input is required for descriptive information, and when minimal training is possible. However, vocal fatigue may be a concern (Welham and Maclagan 2003).

Eye Tracking. Eye-tracking devices employ a camera or an imaging system to visually track some feature of the eye and determine the location of the user's gaze. Eye-tracking devices allow the user to look and point simultaneously, with item selection achieved typically by eye blinking. These devices free the hands to perform other tasks, nearly eliminate device acquisition time, and minimize target selection time. This technology might benefit older users with limited manual dexterity. Significant constraints to its wide application include cost, need to maintain steady head postures, frequency of calibrations, portability, and difficulty to operate. Other relevant problems include unintended item selection and poor accuracy, which limits applications involving small targets (Oyekoya and Stentiford 2004). Morris, Saponas and Tan (2010) indicate that eye tracking technology, which can be incorporated in handheld devices, holds significant potential not only for motor-impaired users, but also for collecting information about a user's attention. Significant challenges remain to distinguish between gazes signifying attention to a target from the ones intended as deliberate inputs.

Gestural Input. Gesture controlled user interface (GCUI) affords realistic opportunities for specific application areas, and especially for users who are uncomfortable with more commonly used input devices (Bhuiyan and Picking 2009). Using Natural User Interfaces, more specifically using gestures or movements on a multi-touch device, can be a good alternative to overcome these difficulties (Loureiro and Rodrigues 2011). Gestural input can address difficulties found in the keyboard and mouse and improve accessibility (Loureiro and Rodrigues 2011; Bhuiyan and Picking 2009). Stößel, Wandke, and Blessing (2010) investigated whether finger gesture input is a suitable input method, especially for older users (60+) with respect to age-related changes in sensory, cognitive and motor abilities. They found that older users are a little slower, but not necessarily less accurate than younger users, even on smaller screen sizes, and across different levels of gesture complexity. This indicates that gesture-based interaction could be a suitable input method for older adults.

4 Conclusions

Increasing numbers of older adults are engaged with computers, but these users still trail the rate of participation of younger individuals and they often meet with difficulties in their interactions with this technology. The smaller and less efficient usage of computers by the elderly can be potentially attributed to the inadequate design and/or selection of input devices. Aging is commonly associated with a number of decrements in perceptual, biomechanical and physiological capacities, which can affect human-computer interaction. Reductions in vision, fine motor control and strength coupled with an increased susceptibility to musculoskeletal disorders and overall incidence of degenerative disorders must be considered when designing and selecting input devices for the older user. Evidence suggests that conventional keyboards with larger keys are preferred. Older users may find computer mice challenging to operate, and lower mouse sensitivity (speed) and larger icons (targets) are recommended. Trackballs may offer an alternative for the elderly performing continued and repetitive pointing tasks. In laptops touchpads may reduce performance among the elderly, but are still preferable to the trackpoint, which is not recommended. Voice input has the potential to improve computer interaction among older users, either as a sole or a supplemental mode. Other forms of input such as gaze and gestures hold great promise but limited evidence exists as to their adequacy to the elderly user.

References

Armbrüster, C., Sutter, C., Ziefle, M.: Notebook input devices put to the age test: the usability of trackpoint and touchpad for middle-aged adults. Ergonomics **50**, 426–445 (2007)

Baker, N.A., Gustafson, N.P., Rogers, J.: The association between rheumatoid arthritis related structural changes in hands and computer keyboard operation. J. Occup. Rehabil. **20**(1), 59–68 (2010). doi:10.1007/s10926-009-9216-x

Baker, N.A., Rogers, J.C.: Association between computer use speed and age, impairments in function, and touch typing training in people with rheumatoid arthritis. Arthritis Care Res. **62** (2), 242–250 (2010). doi:10.1002/acr.20074

Ball, R., Hourcade, J.P.: Rethinking reading for age from paper and computers. Int. J. Hum. Comput. Interact. **27**(11), 1066–1082 (2011). doi:10.1080/10447318.2011.555319

Bhuiyan, M., Picking, R.: Gesture-controlled user interfaces, what have we done and what's next (2009). Retrieved on October 3 2014 from. http://www.glyndwr.ac.uk/computing/research/pubs/sein_bp.pdf

Bosman, E.A., Charness, N.: Age related differences in skilled performance and skill acquisition. In: Blamchard-Fields, F., Hess, T.M. (eds.) Perspectives on Cognitive Change in Adulthood and Aging, pp. 428–453. McGraw-Hill, New York (1996)

Carpenter, B.D., Buday, S.: Computer use among older adults in a naturally occurring retirement community. Comput. Hum. Behav. **23**(6), 3012–3024 (2007). doi:10.1016/j.chb.2006.08.015

Chang, H.-T., Tsai, T.-H., Chang, Y.-C., Chang, Y.-M.: Touch panel usability of elderly and children. Comput. Hum. Behav. **37**, 258–269 (2014). doi:10.1016/j.chb.2014.04.050

Chaparro, A., Bohan, M., Fernandez, J., Choi, S.D., Kattel, B.: The impact of age on computer input device use: psychophysical and physiological measures. Int. J. Ind. Ergon. **24**, 503–513 (1999a)

Chaparro, A., Bohan, M., Fernandez, J., Kattel, B., Choi, S.D.: Is the trackball a better input device for the older computer user? J. Occup. Rehabil. **9**(1), 33–43 (1999b)

Charness, N.: Aging and communication: human factors issues. In: Charness, N., Parks, D.C., Sabel, B.A. (eds.) Communication, Technology and Aging: Opportunities and Challenges for the Future. Springer, New York (2001)

Chung, M.K., Kim, D., Na, S., Lee, D.: Usability evaluation of numeric entry tasks on keypad type and age. Int. J. Ind. Ergon. **40**(1), 97–105 (2010). doi:10.1016/j.ergon.2009.08.001

Cohen, P.R., Oviatt, S.L.: The role of voice input for human-machine communication. Proc. Natl. Acad. Sci. U.S.A. **92**, 9921–9927 (1995)

Czaja, S.J., Lee, C.C.: Designing computer systems for older adults. In: Jacko, J.A., Sears, A. (eds.) The Human-Computer Interaction Handbook: Fundamentals, Evolving Technologies and Emerging Applications. Lawrence Erlbaum Associates, Mahwah (2003)

Díaz-Bossini, J.-M., Moreno, L.: Accessibility to mobile interfaces for older people. Procedia Comput. Sci. **27**, 57–66 (2014). doi:10.1016/j.procs.2014.02.008

Findlater, L., Froehlich, J.E., Fattal, K., Wobbrock, J.O., Dastyar, T.: Age-related differences in performance with touchscreens compared to traditional mouse input. In: Proceedings of the SIGCHI Conference on Human Factors in Computing Systems, pp. 343–346 (2013)

Fisk, A.D., Rogers, W.A., Charness, N., Czaja, S.J., Sharit, J.: Designing for older adults: principles and creative human factors approaches. CRC Press, Boca Raton (2012)

Gerr, F., Marcus, M., Monteilh, C.: Epidemiology of musculoskeletal disorders among computer users: lesson learned from the role of posture and keyboard use. J. Electromyogr. Kinesiol. **14**, 25–31 (2004)

Hertzum, M., Hornbaek, K.: How age affects pointing with mouse and touchpad: a comparison of young, adult, and elderly users. Int. J. Hum. Comput. Interact. **26**(7), 703–734 (2010). doi:10.1080/10447318.2010.487198

Hsiao, L., Cho, C.Y.: The effect of aging on muscle activation and postural control pattern for young and older computer users. Appl. Ergon. **43**(5), 926–932 (2012)

Jastrzembski, T., Charness, N., Holley, P., Feddon, J.: Aging and input devices: voice recognition performance is slower yet more acceptable than a lightpen. In: Proceedings of the Human Factors and Ergonomics Society 49th Annual Meeting; Orlando, FL, pp. 167–171 (2005)

Ji, Y.G., Choi, J., Lee, J.Y., Han, K.H., Kim, J., Lee, I.K.: Older adults in an aging society and social computing: a research agenda. Int. J. Hum. Comput. Interact. **26**(11–12), 1122–1146 (2010). doi:10.1080/10447318.2010.516728

Jochems, N., Vetter, S., Schlick, C.: A comparative study of information input devices for aging computer users. Behav. Inf. Technol. **32**(9), 902–919 (2013). doi:10.1080/0144929x.2012.692100

Keir, P.J., Bach, J.M., Rempel, D.: Effects of computer mouse design and task on carpal tunnel pressure. Ergonomics **42**, 1350–1360 (1999)

Leonard, V.K., Jacko, J.A., Pizzimenti, J.J.: An exploratory investigation of handheld computer interaction for older adults with visual impairments. In: ASSETS 2005, October 9–12, Baltimore, MD, USA (2005)

Loureiro, B., Rodrigues, R.: Multi-touch as a natural user interface for elders: a survey. In: 6th Iberian Conference Information Systems and Technologies (CISTI), pp. 1–6 (2011)

Mann, W.C., Belchior, P., Tomita, M.R., Kemp, B.J.: Computer use by middle-aged and older adults with disabilities. Technol. Disabil. **17**, 1–9 (2005)

Mitzner, T.L., Boron, J.B., Fausset, C.B., Adams, A.E., Charness, N., Czaja, S.J., Dijkstra, K., Fisk, A.D., Rogers, W.A., Sharit, J.: Older adults talk technology: technology usage and attitudes. Comput. Hum. Behav. **26**(6), 1710–1721 (2010)

Morris, D., Saponas, T.S., Tan, D.: Emerging input technologies for always-available mobile interaction. Found. Trends Hum. Comput. Interact. **4**(4), 245–316 (2010). doi:10.1561/1100000023

Oyekoya, O.K., Stentiford, F.W.M.: Eye tracking as a new interface for image retrieval. BT Technol. J. **22**(3), 161–169 (2004)

Rempel, D., Barr, A., Brafman, D., Young, E.: The effect of six keyboard designs on wrist and forearm postures. Appl. Ergon. **38**, 293–298 (2007)

Sandfeld, J., Jensen, B.R.: Effect of computer mouse gain and visual demand on mouse clicking performance and muscle activation in a young and elderly group of experienced computer users. Appl. Ergon. **36**, 547–555 (2005)

Stößel, C., Wandke, H., Blessing, L.: Gestural interfaces for elderly users: help or hindrance? Gesture Embodied Commun. Hum. Comput. Interact. **5934**, 269–280 (2010)

Swanson, N.G., Galinsky, T.L., Cole, L.L., Pan, C.S., Sauter, S.L.: The impact of keyboard design on comfort and productivity in a text-entry task. Appl. Ergon. **28**(1), 9–16 (1997)

Welham, N., Maclagan, M.: Vocal fatigue: current knowledge and future directions. J. Voice **17** (1), 21–30 (2003)

Wobbrock, J.O., Myers, B.A.: Trackball text entry for people with motor impairments. In: Proceedings of the CHI 2006, ACM Press, pp. 479–488 (2006)

Wood, E., Willoughby, T., Rushing, A., Bechtel, L., Gilbert, J.: Use of computer input devices by older adults. J. Appl. Gerontol. **24**(5), 419–438 (2005)

Woolf, A.D., Pfleger, B.: Burden of major musculoskeletal conditions. Bull. World Health Organ. **81**(9), 646–656 (2003)

Zhou, J., Rau, P.L.P., Salvendy, G.: Use and design of handheld computers for older adults: a review and appraisal. Int. J. Hum. Comput. Interact. **28**(12), 799–826 (2012). doi:10.1080/10447318.2012.668129

Development of Automatic Speech Recognition Techniques for Elderly Home Support: Applications and Challenges

Michel Vacher[1(✉)], Frédéric Aman[1], Solange Rossato[2], and François Portet[2]

[1] Laboratoire D'Informatique de Grenoble, GETALP, CNRS, F-38000 Grenoble, France
{Michel.Vacher,Frederic.Aman}@imag.fr
[2] Laboratoire D'Informatique de Grenoble, GETALP, University Grenoble Alpes, F-38000, Grenoble, France
{Solange.Rossato,Francois.Portet}@imag.fr
http://www.liglab.fr/util/annuaire

Abstract. Vocal command may have considerable advantages in terms of usability in the AAL domain. However, efficient audio analysis in smart home environment is a challenging task in large part because of bad speech recognition results in the case of elderly people. Dedicated speech corpora were recorded and employed to adapted generic speech recognizers to this type of population. Evaluation results of a first experiment allowed to draw conclusions about the distress call detection. A second experiments involved participants who played fall scenarios in a realistic smart home, 67 % of the distress calls were detected online. These results show the difficulty of the task and serve as basis to discuss the stakes and the challenges of this promising technology for AAL.

Keywords: Automatic speech recognition · Aged voices · Home automation · Vocal command · Distress call · Ambient assisted living

1 Introduction

Life expectancy has increased in all countries of the European Union in the last decade. In the beginning of 2013, 9 % of the people in France were at least 75 years old. The number of dependent elderly people will increase by 50 % by 2040 according to INSEE institute [12]. The notion of dependency is based on the alteration of physical, sensory and cognitive functions having as a consequence the restriction of the activities of daily living, and the need for help or assistance of someone for regular elementary activities [7]. While the transfer of dependant people to nursing homes has been the *de facto* solution, a survey shows that 80 % of people above 65 years old would prefer to stay living at home if they lose autonomy [10].

J. Zhou and G. Salvendy (Eds.): ITAP 2015, Part II, LNCS 9194, pp. 341–353, 2015.
DOI: 10.1007/978-3-319-20913-5_32

The aim of Ambient Assisted Living (AAL) is to compensate the alteration of physical, sensory and cognitive functions, that are cause of activity restrictions, by technical assistance or environmental management through the use of Information and Communication Technology (ICT)[1] as well as to anticipate and respond to the need of persons with loss of autonomy while AAL solutions are being developed in robotics, home automation, cognitive science, computer network, etc.

We will focus on the domain of smart homes [6,11,25] which are a promising way to help elderly people to live independently. In the context of AAL, the primary tasks of the smart homes are the followings:

- *to support disabled users* via specialized devices (rehabilitation robotics, companion robot, wheelchair, audio interface, tactile screen, etc.);
- *to monitor the users* in their own environment at home thanks to home automation sensors or wearable devices (accelerometer or physiological sensors recording heart rate, temperature, blood pressure, glucose, etc.);
- *to deliver therapy* thanks to therapeutic devices;
- *to ensure comfort and reassurance* thanks to intelligent household devices, smart objects and home automation.

It is worth noting that, within this particular framework, intelligent house equipment (e.g., motion sensors) and smart leisure equipment (interactive communication systems and intelligent environmental control equipments) are particularly useful in case of emergency to help the user to call his relatives, as well as transmitting automatically an alert when the user is not able to act himself. At this time, an other research domain related to energy efficiency is emerging.

Techniques based on very simple and low cost sensors (PIR)[13] or on video analysis [19] are very popular, however they can not be used for interaction purpose unless they are completed by a tactile device (smart phone), while Vocal-User Interface (VUI) may be well adapted because a natural language interaction is relatively simple to use and well adapted to people with reduced mobility or visual impairment [27]. However, there are still important challenges to overcome before implementing VUIs in a smart home [36] and this new technology must be validated in real conditions with potential users [25].

A rising number of recent projects in the smart home domain include the use of Automatic Speech Recognition (ASR) in their design [4,5,9,15,16,22,26] and some of them take into account the challenge of Distant Speech Recognition [23,34]. These conditions are more challenging because of ambient noise, reverberation, distortion and acoustical environment influence. However, one of the main challenges to overcome for successful integration of VUIs is the adaptation of the system to elderly. From an anatomical point of view, some studies have shown age-related degeneration with atrophy of vocal cords, calcification of laryngeal cartilages, and changes in muscles of larynx [24,32]. Thus, ageing voice is characterized by some specific features such as imprecise production of consonants, tremors and slower articulation [29]. Some authors [1,37] have reported

[1] http://www.aal-europe.eu/.

that classical ASR systems exhibit poor performances with elderly voice. These few studies were relevant for their comparison between ageing voice vs. non-ageing voice on ASR performance, but their fields were quite far from our topic of automation commands recognition, and no study was done in French language, except for pathologic voices [14].

In this paper, we present the results of our study related to a system able to detect the call of elderly for emergency when they are in a distress case.

2 State of the Art

A large number of research projects were related to assistive technologies, among them House_n [18], Casas [8], ISpace [17], Aging in Place [31], DesdHIS [13], Ger'Home [41] or Soprano [39]. A great variety of sensors were used like wearable video cameras, embedded sensors, medical sensors, switches and infrared detectors. The main trends of these projects were related to activity recognition, health status monitoring and cognitive stimulation. Thanks to recent advances in microelectronics and ICT, smart home equipments could operate efficiently with low energy consumption and could be available at low prices.

Regarding speech technologies, the corresponding studies and projects are in most cases related to smart homes and assistive technologies. Table 1 summaries their principal characteristics[2]. Among these projects, COMPANIONABLE, COMPANIONS and DIRHA, while aiming at assisting elderly people, mostly performeded studies including typical non-aged adults; the greatest of the SWEET-HOME studies were related to adult voices but some aged and visually impaired people took part in one experiment. Automatic recognition of elderly speech was mainly studied for English by Vipperla et al. [38] and for Portuguese by Pellegrini et al. [26]. These two studies confirmed that the performances of standard recognizers decrease in the case of aged speakers. Vipperla et al. used the SCOTUS speech corpus which is the collection of the audio recordings of the proceedings of the Supreme court of the United States of America. This corpus allowed them to analyze the voice of a same speaker over more than one decade. By contrast, ALADIN, HOMESERVICE, and PIPIN considered the case of Alzheimer's voices, which is a more difficult task than for typical voice because of the cognitive and perceptual decline affecting this part of the population since it may impact the grammatical pronunciation and flow of speech which current speech recognizers can not handle.

Figure 1 describes the general organisation of an Automatic Speech Recognition systems (ASR), the decoder is in charge of phone retrieval in a sequence of feature vectors extracted from the sound, the simplest and more commonly used are Mel-Frequency Cepstral Coefficients (MFCCs) [40]. Phones are the basic sound units and are mostly represented by a continuous density Hidden Markov Model (HMM). The decoder tries to find the sequence of words $\widehat{W}$ that match the input signal $\mathbf{Y}$:

$$\widehat{W} = \arg\max_{W} [p(\mathbf{Y}|W)\, p(W)] \tag{1}$$

[2] The correspondence between project number and reference is given in Table 2.

Table 1. Speech recognition technologies in smart homes for assistive technologies

Project or study	Users	Characteristics of the voice	Conditions of record	Studio or smart home	Vocabulary
S1 [21]	Adults	Neutral: vocal command (wheelchair)	Close	Boston Home	Large
S2 [26]	Elderly	Neutral: ageing well	Close	MLDC corpus	Large
S3 [38]	Elderly	Professional: defense speech	Close	Supreme Court (US)	Large
P1 [15]	Dysarthric	Realistic: vocal command	Close	Studio	Short and adaptative
P2 [23]	Adults	Neutral: vocal command	Distant	SmH	Large
P3 [5]	-	Neutral: Dialog companion	Close	-	Large
P4 [22]	Adults	Neutral: control of appliances/devices	Distant home	DIRHA	Large
P5 [9]	Dysarthric	Neutral: vocal command (assistive technologies)	Microphone array	-	Short
P6 [16]	Adults	Neutral: alarm confirmation	Micro. phone	-	"yes" / "no"
P7 [4]	Dysarthric	Realistic: environmental control	Close	UA-speech corpus	Short
P8 [34]	Adults/ elderly	Neutral: home automation	Distant	DOMUS	Medium
P9 (This study)	Elderly	Neutral/expressive call for help	Short	Medical institutions	Short

The likelihood $p(\mathbf{Y}|W)$ is determined by an Acoustic Model (AM) and the prior $p(W)$ by a Language Model (LM). ALADIN is based on principles radically different from those of classical ASRs and uses a direct decoding thanks to Non-negative Matrix Factorization (NMF) and does not use any AM or LM.

ASRs have reached good performances with close talking microphones (e.g. head-set), but the performances decrease significantly as soon as the microphone

Table 2. Studies and projects related to speech recognition of aged people

Proj.	Principal author or acronym	Ref.	Proj.	Acronym	Ref.
S1	Li, W.	[21]	P4	DIRHA	[22]
S2	Pellegrini, T.	[26]	P5	HOMESERVICE	[9]
S3	Vipperla, R.	[38]	P6	PERS	[16]
P1	ALADIN	[15]	P7	PIPIN	[4]
P2	COMPANIONABLE	[23]	P8	SWEET-HOME	[34]
P3	COMPANIONS	[5]	**P9**	**CIRDO**	**(This study)**

is moved away from the mouth of the speaker (e.g., when the microphone is set in the ceiling). This deterioration is due to a broad variety of effects including reverberation and presence of undetermined background noise. Distant speech recognition is the major aim of DIRHA, COMPANIONABLE and SWEET-HOME. The SWEET-HOME project aimed at controlling an intelligent home automation system by vocal command, and a study done in this framework showed that good performances can be obtained thanks to Acoustic Models trained on the same conditions as the target model and using multiple channels [35].

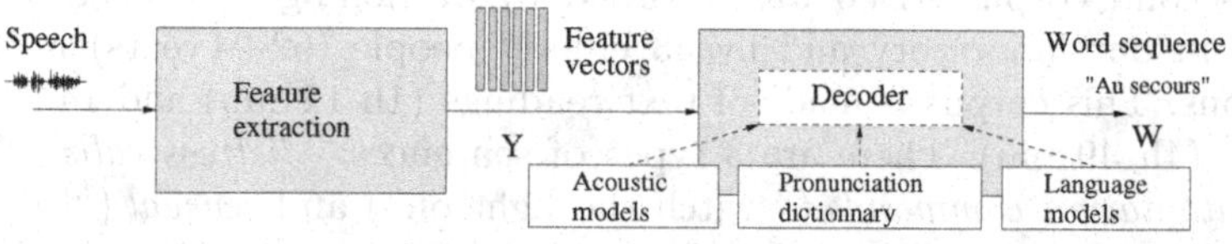

Fig. 1. Architecture of a classical ASR

Studies in the Natural Language Processing (NLP) domain require the use of corpora which are essential at all steps of the investigations and particularly during the model training and the evaluation. To the best of our knowledge, very few corpora are related to ageing voices in French [14]. The different available corpora are stems of projects related to the study of French language like the "Corpus de Français Parlé Parisien des années 2000[3]". This corpus is made of recordings of inhabitants of different districts of Paris in order to study the influence of French spoken language over France and the French speaking world. The "Projet Phonologie du Franais Contemporain[4]" is a database of records according to the region or the country. The records of 38 elderly people (above 70 years old) are included, each record is made of a word list, a small text and two interviews. Other available sources come from videos of testimonies of Shoah survivals and recorded in the framework of "Mmorial de la Shoah[5]" which

[3] http://ed268.univ-paris3.fr/syled/ressources/Corpus-Parole-Paris-PIII.

[4] http://www.projet-pfc.net/.

[5] http://www.memorialdelashoah.org/.

collect testimonies and organize conferences. These videos are not annotated. This corpus is then a collection of interviews and spontaneous speech.

As no study was done with the purpose of facilitating the communication and the detection of distress calls and given that no corresponding corpus exists in French, the first challenge was to record speech corpora uttered by aged people in order to study the characteristics of their voices and explore ways to adapt ASR systems in order to improve their performances for this population category. The second challenge was related to the evaluation of the usability and the acceptance of systems based on speech recognition by their potential users in a smart home.

3 Corpus Acquisition and Analysis System

Therefore, in a first step, we recorded two corpora AD80 and ERES38 adapted to our application domain. ERES38 was used to adapt the acoustic models of a standard ASR and we evaluated the recognition performances on the AD80 corpus. Moreover, we drawed some conclusions about the performance differences of ASR between non-aged and elderly speakers.

The first corpus ERES38 was recorded by 24 elderly people (age: 68-98 years) in French nursing homes. It is made of text reading (48 min) and interviews (4h 53 min). This corpus was used for acoustic model adaptation.

The second corpus AD80 was recorded by 52 non-aged speakers (age: 18-64 years) in our laboratory and by 43 elderly people (62-94 years) in medical institutions. This corpus is made of text readings (1h 12 min) and 14,267 short sentences (4h 49 min). There are 3 types of sentences: -*distress calls* ("I fell"), -*home automation commands* ("switch the light on") and -*casual* ("I drink my coffee"). The distress calls are the sentences that a person could utter during a distress situation to request for assistance, for example after he fell. The determination of a list of these calls is a challenging task. Our list was defined in collaboration with the GRePS laboratory after a bibliographical study [2] and in the prolongation of previous studies [36].

This corpus was used firstly for ASR performance comparison between the two groups (aged/non-aged) and in a second step to determine if acoustic model adaptation could allow the detection of distress or call for help sentences. It was necessary to assess the level of loss of functional autonomy of the 43 elderly speakers. Therefore, a GIR [30] score was obtained after clinicians filled the AGGIR grid (French national test) to classify the person in one of the six groups: GIR 1 (total dependence) to GIR 6 (total autonomy).

The last corpus is the Cirdo-set corpus [3]. This corpus was recorded in the Living Lab of the LIG laboratory by 13 young adults (32 min 01 s) and 4 elderly people (age: 61-83 years, 28 min 54 s) which played 4 scenarios relative to *fall*, one to *blocked hip* and two True Negative (TN) scenarios. These scenarios included calls for help which are identical to some of the corresponding sentences of AD80. The audio records of the Cirdo-set corpus were then used for evaluation purpose of call for help detection in realistic conditions. These are full records, therefore the speech events have to be extracted thanks to an online analysis system. This process will be presented in Sect. 4. Moreover, the recording microphone was set in the ceiling and not as usual at a short distance in front of the speaker but in Distant Speech conditions.

The corpora were processed by the ASR of the CMU toolkit Sphinx3 [20]. The acoustic vectors are composed of 13 MFCC coefficients, their first and second derivatives. The Acoustic Model (AM) is context-dependent with 3-state left-to-right HMM. We used a generic AM trained with BREF120, a corpus made of 100 hours of French speech. The language model was a 3-gram-type LM resulting from the combination of a generic language model (with a 10 % weight) and the domain one (with 90 % weight). The generic LM resulting from French news collected in the Gigaword corpus was 1-gram with 11,018 words. The domain LM trained from the AD80 corpus was composed of 88 1-gram, 193 2-gram and 223 3-gram.

The target is that only the sentences of interest could be recognized by the system (i.e., not when they are receiving a phone call from their relatives) [27]. Therefore, only two categories of the sentences are relevant to the system and must be taken into consideration: home automation commands and calls related to a distress situation. The other sentences must be discarded and it is therefore necessary to determine whether the resulting output from the ASR is part of one of the two categories of interest thanks to a measure distance. This measure is based on a Levenshtein distance between each output and typical sentences of interest. In this way, casual sentences are excluded.

4 Adaptation of the System to Elderly Voices and Detection of Distress Calls

To assess ASR performances, the most common measure is the Word Error Rate (WER) which is defined as follows:

$$WER = \frac{S + D + I}{N} \tag{2}$$

S is the number of substitutions, D the number of deletions, I the number of insertions and N the number of words in the reference. As shown in Table 3, when performing ASR using the generic acoustic model on the distress/home automation sentences of the AD80 corpus, we obtained an average WER of 45.7 % for the elderly group in comparison with an average WER of 11 % for the non-elderly group. These results indicate a significant decrease in performance for elderly speech and we can notice an important scattering of the results for this kind of voice as well as a higher recognition rate for women as supported by the state of the art. It is thus clear that the generic AM is not adapted to the elderly population and then specific models must be used.

Thanks to a Maximum Likelihood Linear Regression (MLLR), the text readings of the ERES38 corpus were used to obtain 3 specific aged AMs from the generic AM: AM_G (men and women), AM_W (women) and AM_M (men). Table 4 gives the obtained results and indicates a significant improvement of

Table 3. WER using the generic acoustic model AM

Subject	Non-elderly	Elderly	Difference
Women	10.4 % (27 speakers)	40.3 % (32 speakers)	+29.9 %
Men	11.7 % (25 speakers)	61.3 % (11 speakers)	+49.6 %
Average	11.0 %	45.7 %	34.7 %
Standard deviation	6.4 %	16.8 %	10.4 %

the performances. An ANOVA analysis allowed us to conclude that: (1) there is no significant difference between generic and specific models for non-aged speakers; (2) the difference between generic and specific models is significant; (3) there is no significant difference between the specific models (AM_G, AM_W, AM_M) and thus the use of a unique global model is possible. In the case of aged speaker, the dispersion of the performances is very important whatever acoustic model is chosen (e.g., $WER_{AM\_G} = 17.4\,\%$ and $\sigma_{AM\_G} = 10.3\,\%$). This dispersion is due to bad performances encountered with some speakers, they are those who suffer of an important loss of functional autonomy (GIR 2 or 3) and then are less likely to live alone at their own home.

Table 4. WER using the specific acoustic models (*** : $p < 0.001$)

Subject	AM (generic)	AM_G (global)	AM_W (women)	AM_M (men)
Non-aged women	10.4 %	7.6 %	7.3 %	-
Non-aged men	11.7 %	11.1 %	-	11.8 %
Elderly women	40.3 %	14.6 %***	15.4 %***	-
Elderly men	61.3 %	25.7 % ***	-	22.3 %***

As reported in Sect. 3, only sentences related to a call for help or home automation management have to be analysed, the other one (i.e., casual) being rejected. Every sentence whose distance to the distress category was above a threshold th was rejected.

For our study, we considered the sentences of AD80 uttered by elderly speakers, namely 2,663 distress sentences, 434 calls for caregivers and 3,006 casual sentences. The ASR used AM_G as model. The threshold th of the filter was chosen in such way that the sensibility Se and the specificity Sp were equal ($th = 0.75$, $Se = Sp = 85.7\,\%$). It should be noted that, due to the WER, 4 % of the selected sentences were put in the correct category but did not correspond to the sentence as it was pronounced. Regarding the distress sentences and calls to caregivers, 18 % were selected with confusion. Consequently, the main uncertainty concerns above all the way in which the call must be treated.

5 Evaluation of the Detection in Real Conditions with the Audio Components of the Cirdo-Set Corpus

For the evaluation of the detection of distress calls *in situ*, we used the Cirdo-set corpus which was recorded in a Living Lab. In order to extract the sentences pronounced by the speakers during the scenarios, we used CirdoX, an online audio analyser in charge of detecting the audio events and discriminating between noise and speech. The diagram of CirdoX is presented Fig. 2. CirdoX is able to capture signal from microphones or to analyse previous audio records on 8 channels, we used it in a mono-channel configuration. The detection of each audio event is operated online thanks to an adaptive threshold on the high level components of the wavelet transform of the input signal. Each audio event is then classified into speech or noise. The GMM classifier was trained with the Sweet-Home corpus [33] recorded in a smart home. The ASR was Sphinx3 as mentioned above.

CirdoX detected 1950 audio events including 322 speech events, 277 of them were calls for help. 204 were analysed as speech and 73 as noise mainly due to a strong presence of environmental noise at the moment of the record. Because of the distant speech conditions, the acoustic model was adapted with sentences of the Sweet-Home corpus recorded in similar conditions [33]. Regarding the calls for help sent to the ASR, the WER was 49.5 % and 67 % of the calls were detected. These results are far from perfect but they were obtained under harsh conditions. Indeed, the participants played scenarios which included falls on the floor and the participants generated a lot of noise sounds which were often mixed with speech. Therefore, the performances would have been better if the call were uttered after the fall.

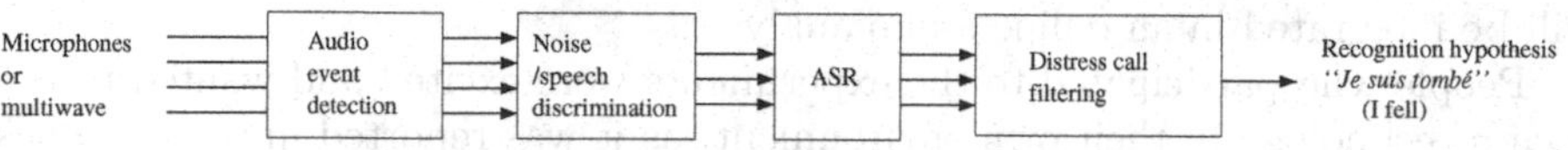

Fig. 2. Architecture of the CirdoX online analyser

Moreover, these results were obtained using a classical ASR as Sphinx but significant improvements were made recently in speech recognition and incorporated in the KALDI toolkit [28]. Off line experiments were done in this framework on the "Interaction Subset" of the Sweet-Home corpus [35]. This corpus is made of records in a smart home equipped with a home automation system including more than 150 sensors and actuators. The home automation network is driven by an Intelligent Controller able to take a context aware decision when a vocal command is recognised. Among other things, the controller must choose what room and what lamp are concerned. The corresponding sentences are home automation vocal commands pronounced by participants who played scenarios of the everyday life. They asked for example to switch on the light or to close the curtains while they are eating breakfast or doing the dishes.

The speech events, for instance 550 sentences (2559 words) including 250 orders, questions and distress calls (937 words), were extracted using PATSH, an online audio analyser which is similar to CirdoX. The original ASR performance with a decoding on only one channel was WER=43.2 %, DER=41 % [34], DER being defined as the Detection Error Rate of the home automation commands. Thanks to 2 more sophisticated adaptation techniques, namely Subspace GMM Acoustic Modelling SGMM) and feature space MLLR (fMLLR) significant improvement were brought which led to WER=49 %, DER=13.6 %. The most important contribution to the DER was due to missed speech utterances at the detection or speech/sound discrimination level. This significant improvement from the experimental condition was obtained in off line conditions and the most important effort must be related to adapt and integrate these new techniques in an online audio analyser, i.e. CirdoX.

6 Conclusion

Regarding the technical aspect, our study showed first of all that thanks to the record of a short corpus by elderly speakers (ERES38, 48 min), it is possible to adapt the acoustic models (AM) of a generic ASR and to obtain recognition performances in the case of elderly voices close to those of non-aged speakers (WER about 10 % or 15 %), except for elderly affected by an important level of loss of functional autonomy. Therefore the detection of distress sentences is efficient and the sensibility is 85 %. Our experiment involving the Cirdo-set corpus recorded in *in-situ* conditions gave lower results due to the harsh conditions, the participants falling as they called for help and only 67 % of the calls were detected. However new adaptation techniques may improve significantly the results as soon as they will be integrated in an online audio analyser.

People who participated to the experiments were excited and wanted to use such a technology in their own environment, as it was reported in some studies [27]. However, the use of a short vocabulary is necessary in order to obtain good performances, so an important difficulty is related to the difficulty of defining which sentences would be pronounced during a fall or a distress situation. Thanks to the collaboration with the GRePS laboratory some of those were incorporated in the AD80 corpus but it is not sufficient for a real application. There is no adequate corpus and the potential users exhibit great difficulties in remembering the sentences they pronounced in such situations. Therefore an important effort will consist in the necessary adaptation of the language models (ML) to the user in the long life term.

Acknowledgments. This work is part of two projects supported by the French National Research Agency (Agence Nationale de la Recherche), SWEET-HOME (ANR-09-VERS-011) and CIRDO (ANR-10-TECS-012). The authors would like to thank elderly and caregivers who agreed to participate in the recordings.

References

1. Baba, A., Lee, A., Saruwatari, H., Shikano, K.: Speech recognition by reverberation adapted acoustic model. In: ASJ General Meeting. pp. 27–28 (2002)
2. Chaumon, M.B., Bekkadja, S., Cros, F., Cuvillier, B.: The user-centered design of an ambient technology for preventing falls at home. Gerontechnol. **13**(2), 169 (2014)
3. Bouakaz, S., Vacher, M., Bobillier-Chaumon, M.E., Aman, F., Bekkadja, S., Portet, F., Guillou, E., Rossato, S., Desserée, E., Traineau, P., Vimon, J.P., Chevalier, T.: CIRDO: smart companion for helping elderly to live at home for longer. Innovation Res. BioMed. Eng. (IRBM) **35**(2), 101–108 (2014)
4. Casanueva, I., Christensen, H., Hain, T., Green, P.: Adaptive speech recognition and dialogue management for users with speech disorders. In: Interspeech 2014, pp. 1033–1037 (2014)
5. Cavazza, M., de la Camara, R.S., Turunen, M.: How was your day? A companion ECA prototype. In: AAMAS. pp. 1629–1630 (2010)
6. Chan, M., Esètve, D., Escriba, C., Campo, E.: A review of smart homes- present state and future challenges. Comput. Meth. Programs Biomed. **91**(1), 55–81 (2008)
7. Charpin, J.M., Tlili, C.: Perspectives démographique et financières de la dépendance, Rapport du groupe de travail sur la prise en charge de la dépendance. Technical report, Ministre des solidarits et de la cohsion sociale, 60 p., Paris (2011)
8. Chen, C., Cook, D.J.: Behavior-based home energy prediction. In: IEEE Intelligent Environments, pp. 57–63 (2012)
9. Christensen, H., Casanueva, I., Cunningham, S., Green, P., Hain, T.: HomeService: voice-enabled assistive technology in the home using cloud-based automatic speech recognition. In: 4th Workshop on Speech and Language Processing for Assistive Technologies, pp. 29–34 (2013)
10. CSA: Les français et la dépendance. http://www.csa.eu/fr/s26/nos-sondages-publies.aspx (2003). Accessed 12 March 2013
11. De Silva, L., Morikawa, C., Petra, I.: State of the art of smart homes. Eng. Appl. Artif. Intell. **25**(7), 1313–1321 (2012)
12. Duée, M., Rebillard, C.: La dépendance des personnes âgées : une projection en 2040. Données sociales - La société française, pp. 613–619 (2006)
13. Fleury, A., Vacher, M., Noury, N.: SVM-based multi-modal classification of activities of daily living in health smart homes: sensors, algorithms and first experimental results. IEEE TITB **14**(2), 274–283 (2010)
14. Gayraud, F., Lee, H., Barkat-Defradas, M.: Syntactic and lexical context of pauses and hesitations in the discourse of Alzheimer patients and healthy elderly subjects. Clin. Linguist. Phonetics **25**(3), 198–209 (2011)
15. Gemmeke, J.F., Ons, B., Tessema, N., Van Hamme, H., Van De Loo, J., De Pauw, G., Daelemans, W., Huyghe, J., Derboven, J., Vuegen, L., Van Den Broeck, B., Karsmakers, P., Vanrumste, B.: Self-taught assistive vocal interfaces: an overview of the ALADIN project. In: Interspeech 2013, pp. 2039–2043 (2013)
16. Hamill, M., Young, V., Boger, J., Mihailidis, A.: Development of an automated speech recognition interface for personal emergency response systems. J. Neuro-Engineering Rehabil. **6**(1), 1–26 (2009)
17. Holmes, A., Duman, H., Pounds-Cornish, A.: The iDorm: gateway to heterogeneous networking environments. In: International ITEA workshop on Virtual Home Environments, pp. 20–37 (2002)

18. Intille, S.S.: Designing a home of the future. IEEE Pervasive Comput. **1**(2), 76–82 (2002)
19. König, A., Crispim, C., Derreumaux, A., Bensadoun, G., Petit, P.D., Bremond, F., David, R., Verhey, F., Aalten, P., Robert, P.: Validation of an automatic video monitoring system for the detection of instrumental activities of daily living in dementia patients. J. Alzheimer's Dis. **44**(2), 675–685 (2015)
20. Lee, K.F., Hon, H.W., Reddy, R.: An overview of the SPHINX speech recognition system. IEEE TASSP **38**(1), 35–45 (1990)
21. Li, W., Glass, J., Roy, N., Teller, S.: Probabilistic dialogue modeling for speech-enabled assistive technology. In: SLPAT 2013, pp. 67–72 (2013)
22. Matassoni, M., Astudillo, R.F., Katsamanis, A., Ravanelli, M.: The DIRHA-GRID corpus: baseline and tools for multi-room distant speech recognition using distributed microphones. In: Interspeech 2014, pp. 1613–1617 (2014)
23. Milhorat, P., Istrate, D., Boudy, J., Chollet, G.: Hands-free speech-sound interactions at home. In: EUSIPCO 2012, pp. 1678–1682, August 2012
24. Mueller, P., Sweeney, R., Baribeau, L.: Acoustic and morphologic study of the senescent voice. Ear Nose Throat J. **63**, 71–75 (1984)
25. Peetoom, K.K.B., Lexis, M.A.S., Joore, M., Dirksen, C.D., De Witte, L.P.: Literature review on monitoring technologies and their outcomes in independently living elderly people. Disabil. Rehabil. Assistive Technol. **10**(4), 1–24 (2014)
26. Pellegrini, T., Trancoso, I., Hämäläinen, A., Calado, A., Dias, M.S., Braga, D.: Impact of age in ASR for the elderly: preliminary experiments in european portuguese. In: Torre Toledano, D., Ortega Giménez, A., Teixeira, A., González Rodríguez, J., Hernández Gómez, L., San Segundo Hernández, R., Ramos Castro, D. (eds.) IberSPEECH 2012. CCIS, vol. 328, pp. 139–147. Springer, Heidelberg (2012)
27. Portet, F., Vacher, M., Golanski, C., Roux, C., Meillon, B.: Design and evaluation of a smart home voice interface for the elderly - acceptability and objection aspects. Pers. Ubiquit. Comput. **17**(1), 127–144 (2013)
28. Povey, D., Ghoshal, A., Boulianne, G., Burget, L., Glembek, O., Goel, N., Hannemann, M., Motlicek, P., Qian, Y., Schwarz, P., Silovsky, J., Stemmer, G., Vesely, K.: The Kaldi Speech Recognition Toolkit. In: ASRU 2011 (2011)
29. Ryan, W., Burk, K.: Perceptual and acoustic correlates in the speech of males. J. Commun. Disord. **7**, 181–192 (1974)
30. Site officiel de l'administration française: Allocation personnalise d'autonomie (Apa): grille Aggir. http://vosdroits.service-public.fr/F1229.xhtml
31. Skubic, M., Alexander, G., Popescu, M., Rantz, M., Keller, J.: A smart home application to eldercare: current status and lessons learned. Technol. Health Care **17**(3), 183–201 (2009)
32. Takeda, N., Thomas, G., Ludlow, C.: Aging effects on motor units in the human thyroarytenoid muscle. Laryngoscope **110**, 1018–1025 (2000)
33. Vacher, M., Lecouteux, B., Chahuara, P., Portet, F., Meillon, B., Bonnefond, N.: The Sweet-Home speech and multimodal corpus for home automation interaction. In: The 9th edition of the Language Resources and Evaluation Conference (LREC), pp. 4499–4506. Reykjavik, Iceland (2014)
34. Vacher, M., Lecouteux, B., Istrate, D., Joubert, T., Portet, F., Sehili, M., Chahuara, P.: Experimental evaluation of speech recognition technologies for voice-based home automation control in a smart home. In: SLPAT, pp. 99–105 (2013)
35. Vacher, M., Lecouteux, B., Portet, F.: Multichannel automatic recognition of voice command in a multi-room smart home : an experiment involving seniors and users with visual impairment. In: Interspeech 2014, pp. 1008–1012 (2014)

36. Vacher, M., Portet, F., Fleury, A., Noury, N.: Development of audio sensing technology for ambient assisted living: applications and challenges. Int. J. e-Health Med. Commun. **2**(1), 35–54 (2011)
37. Vipperla, R.C., Wolters, M., Georgila, K., Renals, S.: Speech input from older users in smart environments: challenges and perspectives. In: Stephanidis, C. (ed.) UAHCI 2009. LNCS, vol. 5615, pp. 117–126. Springer, Heidelberg (2009)
38. Vipperla, R., Renals, S., Frankel, J.: Longitudinal study of ASR performance on ageing voices. In: Interspeech 2008, pp. 2550–2553 (2008)
39. Wolf, P., Schmidt, A., Klein, M.: SOPRANO - an extensible, open AAL platform for elderly people based on semantical contracts. In: 3rd Workshop on Artificial Intelligence Techniques for Ambient Intelligence, ECAI 2008 (2008)
40. Young, S.: HMMs and Related speech Recognition Technologies. In: Benesty, J., Sondhi, M.M., Huang, Y. (eds.) Handbook of Speech Processing, pp. 539–557. Springer, Heidelberg (2008)
41. Zouba, N., Bremond, F., Thonnat, M., Anfosso, A., Pascual, E., Mallea, P., Mailland, V., Guerin, O.: A computer system to monitor older adults at home: preliminary results. Gerontechnol. J. **8**(3), 129–139 (2009)

Aging Working Population: Hearing Impairment a Growing Challenge for the Working Environment

Verena Wagner(✉) and K. Wolfgang Kallus

Institute of Psychology, University of Graz, Graz, Austria
{verena.wagner,wolfgang.kallus}@uni-graz.at

Abstract. Population developments raise expectations of an aging working population. These create new challenges for the working world. One is to deal with age-related impairments such as hearing impairment which impacts performance due to impairment of speech comprehension, memory performance and can lead to safety risks. In order to compensate this proactively a basic question has to be answered: Are problems in auditory processing and memory performance due to deficits in peripheral hearing or due to age-related or secondary deficits in central processing components? Two studies were conducted to check the role of peripheral factors. Young normal hearing participants have to perform a verbal memory task under different hearing conditions that simulate hearing impairment. The results show significant effects of induced hearing impairment and provide further evidence that verbal memory performance deficits of hearing impaired are based on a peripheral hearing loss/early processing stages and maybe less on central processing components.

Keywords: Aging working population · Hearing impairment · Verbal memory performance

1 Introduction

The population developments in Western industrialized nations raise expectations of an aging of the working population. These create new challenges for the working world. One of the challenges is to deal with age-related impairments such as loss in hearing capacity. The results of a Finnish survey study [1] with participants aged from 54 to 66 years show that 37 % of the participants reported hearing difficulties and 43 % reported difficulties in following a conversation under noisy conditions. Furthermore, it was shown that self-reported hearing loss can be strongly associated with the audiometric measurement in the range of audibility of 4 to 8 kHz. Data of the WHO suggest that 53 % of the people which are 45 years old and older are hearing impaired [2]. This underlines the importance of research in this area for the working world that will be increasingly shaped by older employees.

Various studies have shown that hearing impairment impacts not only the quality of life of the concerned person itself [3–6] as well as all persons with whom the concerned person communicates [7], but also the (job) performance of those affected [8] due to

J. Zhou and G. Salvendy (Eds.): ITAP 2015, Part II, LNCS 9194, pp. 354–364, 2015.
DOI: 10.1007/978-3-319-20913-5_33

impairment of speech comprehension and memory performance. Furthermore, uncorrected reduced hearing can lead to safety risks in everyday situations as well as in the workplace e.g. because warning and/or information signals or environmental noises cannot be heard well enough [9] or instructions are misunderstood. The National Academy on an Aging Society [5] reports that in America only 67 % of the working-age population with impaired hearing is employed whereas, 75 % of the working-age population without hearing impairment is employed. Also, hearing impaired people are often employed in jobs like farming, craft and repair, machine operators or transportation and fewer of them are employed in occupations like administrative, professional, service and/or sales. Furthermore, 18 % of Americans with hearing impairment aged between 51 and 61 are retired whereas only 12 % of the normal hearing Americans go into retirement the same early. In addition hearing impairment can be the result of occupational noise exposure (e.g. in airfield personnel, military personnel) [10].

Impairment of speech comprehension [11] is accompanied by impaired short-term memory, and by more recent theories the transfer from short-term memory to long-term memory, a partial function of the working memory due to losses in the acoustic perception [12–15]. Boxtel et al. [12] suggest "(…) that verbal memory function may be underestimated in individuals with mild to moderate degree of hearing loss." (p. 152). Also, selective attention seems to be impaired by hearing difficulties [16]. Performance comparisons of normal hearing people and people with hearing impairments show performance penalty of selective attention already in mild hearing impairment from 17.5 dB [17].

A number of studies suggest that information processing of people with hearing impairment can often be executed without error, but the information processing is associated with significantly increased effort. McCoy et al. [18] use the so-called "effortfulness hypothesis" [19] to explain deficits in memory performance of hearing impaired people: A hearing impaired must expend a higher performance effort respectively more cognitive resources to achieve the same perceptual performance as a normal hearing person, which leads to lower available process resources to encode the content. The argumentation of McCoy et al. [18] bases on the results of Rabbitt's experiments [20] with noise masked spoken digits. Normal hearing participants showed a poorer recall frequency for digits that were noise masked than for digits without noise. Also, the recall of the first half of a digit list, no matter if they are presented with or without noise masking, was significantly better if the second half of the list was presented without noise masking than with noise masking. Rabbitt [20] explained the results by an increase of effort that is necessary to discriminate between the spoken digits and the noise which leads to less available information processing resources to rehearse and memorize the digits. Also, differences in memory performance between normal hearing and mild hearing impaired participants were shown, even if hearing impaired participants were able to initially recall the used words. McCoy et al. [18] were able to experimentally proof the hypothesis of additional efforts which are needed by hearing impaired. They investigated the recall performance of sets of three words of two different hearing groups: a "better hearing group" (pure tone averages less or equal to 25 dB in the better ear; max. mild hearing impairment) and a "hearing loss group" (pure tone averages greater than 25 dB in the better ear). The results of the serial reproduction task show no memory deficits for words at the final position but for words at the antepenultimate position, and only if the words had low semantic similarity. Thus, the result provides an argument not only for the "effortfulness hypothesis", but also for the "top-down" compensation of such deficits through long-term memory processes. Wingfield, Tun and McCoy [21] emphasize that the effect of the effort must be very powerful because of influencing the memory performance of a really short set of three words.

Frisina and Frisina [22] tested the speech recognition performance of younger (18 – 19 years old) and older adults without hearing impairment and older adults with hearing impairment (three groups: graded degrees of mild high-frequency hearing loss, presbycusis; older adults: 60–81 years old) in quiet and in noisy conditions. Under quiet conditions, younger and older normal hearing adults do not differ in their speech recognition performance. Concerning the four groups of elderly participants the results show that the performance of normal hearing older participants was significant better than the performance of all three elderly hearing impaired groups. Also, the group with the least hearing impairment did perform better than the two other groups with more degree of hearing impairment. But the results look different if noise was added to the presented words: For noise conditions a significant age-affect can be shown for speech recognition performance. In the noise condition younger normal hearing participants perform significant better than older participants without hearing impairment. In addition the performance advantage under quiet conditions of normal hearing older adults compared to older adults with hearing impairment (three groups) disappeared for spondee words and for target words in sentences with supportive context. Only for target words in sentences without supportive context, a better performance of the normal hearing older adults than of all three hearing impaired groups can be shown. Frisina and Frisina [22] point out that the performance differences under noise between normal hearing younger and older participants cannot be explained on differences in peripheral hearing loss. Due to the absence of performance differences between the two normal hearing groups under the quiet conditions they suggest a brainstem auditory dysfunction. The performance deficits of the hearing impaired groups under noise condition can be interpreted as result due to a peripheral hearing loss, a central auditory processing dysfunction due to age and a peripheral hearing-loss induced plasticity occurring at brainstem and cortical levels.

Wong et al. [23] found a neurophysiological proof of the "effortfulness hypothesis": In a word identification task younger and older adults had to identify words in a quiet and two noise conditions (multi-talker babble noise). In comparison to the younger group, older adults show a decreased activation in the auditory cortex but an increased activation in areas that are associated with attention and the working memory, especially under conditions with minor signal-to-noise ratio. Unfortunately, the degree of hearing impairment was not explicitly included resp. not reported in the work of Wong et al. [23].

Often, studies with participants suffering of hearing impairment do investigate samples which consist of elderly people but the results of different research groups indicate that the association between hearing acuity and the performance in a verbal memory task was not dependent on the age of the participants [e.g. 12].

Complementary to the investigation of performance differences of hearing impaired people, some research groups study the impact of hearing aids. Their results give a first indication that the correction of peripheral hearing loss with a hearing aid leads to an increase of working memory capacity [e.g. 24].

Eckert et al. [25] tested 15 normal hearing participants aged from 21 to 75 years in a voice recognition task. To simulate hearing conditions of people with high frequency hearing loss and to vary word intelligibilities, four different low-pass filter conditions were investigated. The results show that the correct word recognition was equivalent across age but did very between the four hearing conditions (% of correct word recognition for low pass filter frequency cutoff 3150 Hz > 1600 Hz > 1000 Hz > 400 Hz).

The findings presented above indicate that different processes contribute to the performance deficits associated with hearing loss. It is necessary to develop a clear and detailed picture of the processes involved to cope with problems that might be associated with reduced hearing proactively. Preventive interventions, training and rehabilitation that improve technical aids have to be developed. For the willingness to use them, and the provision of technical assistive devices, a basic question has to be answered: Are problems in auditory processing and memory performance primarily due to the peripheral hearing loss/early processing stages or are they basically caused by age-related or secondary deficits in central processing components/higher cognitive functions (physiological and/or anatomical changes) of hearing impaired people. Despite many studies, the question has not been definitively answered. Therefore, two studies were carried out: A laboratory experiment and a group study. In both studies young normal hearing participants have to perform a verbal memory task under different hearing conditions that simulate hearing impairment (induced hearing impairment). Young adults were chosen in the first instance to exclude a possible age-effect on information processing (see also [12]).

Both studies tested two research questions: (1) Can differences in the verbal memory performance of normal hearing young adults be shown, depending on different simulated impaired hearing conditions (quiet, interrupted, distorted, background noise) and normal volume (loud = control condition)? (2) If differences in the verbal memory performance exist, which of the four different simulated hearing conditions do lead to which performance difference?

If significant differences in the verbal memory performance of normal hearing young adults can be shown due to induced hearing impairment, this would be a strong indication for a central role of peripheral hearing impairments/impairments of early processing stages. In this case, the use of (well adapted) hearing aids could really improve the situation of hearing impaired.

2 Method

2.1 Study 1: Laboratory Experiment

A laboratory experiment with repeated measures was chosen for Study 1. The study was conducted in an experimental laboratory of the department of psychology of the University of Graz, Austria.

Participants. In total, 31 young adults participated in Study 1. The sample consists of 18 women and 13 men aged between 20 and 31 years with an average age of 24.00 years (*SD* = 2.22). All study participants have a higher level of education (24 with a general qualification for university entrance, 7 with a university degree). The participation in the study was voluntary and all participants provided an informed consent.

Materials. To measure the verbal memory performance five different word lists of the German version [26] of the Auditory Verbal Learning Test (AVLT) [27, 28] were presented via headphones (AKG K240 studio headphones). The Auditory Verbal Learning Test has been successfully used in a study of Boxtel et al. [12]. Every used word list consists of 15 different nouns with low phonetic and semantic similarity. The used playback interval was two seconds per word. The verbal memory performance was operationalized with two performance measures: number of correctly reproduced words and number of errors (frequency of called words that were not part of the particular word list).

Overall, five different hearing conditions (within factors) were investigated in Study 1: four conditions of hearing impairment induced by e.g. reduced volume or additional noise with the levels: quiet, interrupted, distorted, background noise and one control condition (not reduced, loud). To induce these different conditions of hearing impairment the audio files of four of the five word lists have been modified with the help of the software Audacity®. The word list used for the "quiet condition" (induced conductive hearing loss, simulation of the auditory impression of a person with mild to moderate hearing loss) has been reduced in volume on 7 % of the base volume which was used for the word lists of all other conditions. This leads to a sound pressure level of 39 dB for the "quiet condition" and of 65 dB for all other conditions (measured at the headphones, sound pressure level meter SL-100, Voltcraft®). A sound pressure level of 65 dB can be described as normal conversational level. To create an effect of masking of parts and interruptions within of the presented words ("interrupted condition"), 20 % of the total word duration was masked by a silence sequence for each word of the word list of the "interrupted condition". Care was taken not to remove important parts for proper word recognition to avoid malapropisms. For the "distorted condition" (simulation of an age-related change in the periodic encoding) one of the five word lists was divided into two separate audio tracks. With the help of the software Audacity®, the frequencies of the two audio tracks were modified. All frequencies of the first audio track were enhanced by 12 % and all frequencies of the second audio track were reduced by 12 %. After that, both tracks were reassembled into a single track, which leads to a distorted hearing effect. To simulate hearing conditions that can be found in everyday situation, background noise typical for a situation when two persons meet in a café were added as a second audio track to the word list used in the "background noise condition". The two different audio tracks of the "background noise condition" were presented dichotic which means that each audio track was presented at one of the participant's ears.

Procedure. The participants were asked to reproduce all 15 words of the heard word list immediately after the presentation of the whole list. For this, they had a maximum reproduction time of two minutes. Each participant has to hear and reproduce all five tested word lists (five trials/hearing conditions) during the laboratory experiment (repeated measure). The order of the five word lists was permuted over all participants. In order not to make the experiment too strenuous a short break (three minutes) in which the participants could recover, was inserted between the trials.

Statistical Analysis. Analyses of variance with repeated measures were performed for calculating the results. A significance level of 5 % was adopted for the results.

2.2 Study 2: Group Study

Study 2 was planned as replication of Study 1 and was conducted as group study as part of two different courses for undergraduate students at the Hochschule Ruhr West - University of Applied Sciences in Bottrop, Germany.

Participants. The sample of Study 2 consists of 30 participants with normal hearing abilities. Overall, 6 women and 24 men aged between 19 and 29 years (M = 21.73, SD = 2.33) take part in this study. The participation in the study was voluntary and all participants provided an informed consent.

Materials. In order to ensure that Study 2 replicates Study 1, the materials used in Study 2 were, with the exception of the presentation of the word lists, not different from the materials described under the material section of Study 1 (see 2.1 for more details). Due to the execution of Study 2 as group study, the audio tracks of the five different word lists were presented via loudspeakers and not via headphones. Also, the presentation via loudspeakers leads to a change in the presentation mode of the "background noise condition" from a dichotic presentation (Study 1) to a binaural presentation.

Procedure. Study 2 replicated the procedure of Study 1 (see Study 1 for more details). Due to the execution of Study 2 as group study the verbal reproduction of the words after hearing each word list used in Study 1 was changed into a written one.

Statistical Analysis. Analyses of variance with repeated measures were performed for calculating the results. A significance level of 5 % was adopted for the results.

3 Results

3.1 Study 1: Laboratory Experiment

Correct Word Reproduction. An analysis of variance with repeated measures shows that the number of correctly reproduced words was significantly better in the "control condition (loud)" than in the "distorted condition", $F(4, 27) = 3.67$, $p = .041$ (post-hoc test: Sidak, $p < .05$). No significant differences can be shown for all other hearing conditions. The mean values of all five conditions are shown in Table 1.

Number of Errors. To show differences of the five hearing conditions in the second verbal memory performance measure, the numbers of errors which is defined as frequency of called words that were not part of the particular word list, an analysis of variance with repeated measures was calculated. The result show no significant number of error differences for the five different hearing conditions, $F(2.78, 83.31) = 1.89$, *ns* (see Table 1).

Table 1. Study 1: Mean correct word reproduction and mean number of errors per each hearing condition.

		Hearing condition				
		Quiet	Interrupted	Distorted	Background noise	Control (loud)
Correct word reproduction	M	8.19	8.90	**8.35**	9.16	**9.45**
	(SD)	*(3.05)*	*(2.75)*	*(2.68)*	*(2.19)*	*(2.92)*
Number of errors	M	0.97	0.45	0.61	0.55	0.58
	(SD)	*(1.11)*	*(0.57)*	*(0.88)*	*(0.81)*	*(0.99)*

3.2 Study 2: Group Study

Correct Word Reproduction. The result of an analysis of variance with repeated measures shows that there are some significant differences in the verbal memory performance measured by the number of correctly reproduced words for the five different hearing conditions, $F(4, 26) = 36.55$, $p < .0001$. Post-hoc analyses (Sidak, $p < .05$) show that the number of correctly reproduced words was significantly better in the "control condition (loud)" than in the three conditions "interrupted", "background noise" and "quiet". Also, the number of correctly reproduced words was significant higher in the "distorted condition" than in the two conditions "background noise" and "quiet" and significant higher for the "interrupted condition" than for the two hearing conditions "background noise" and "quiet" (see Fig. 1).

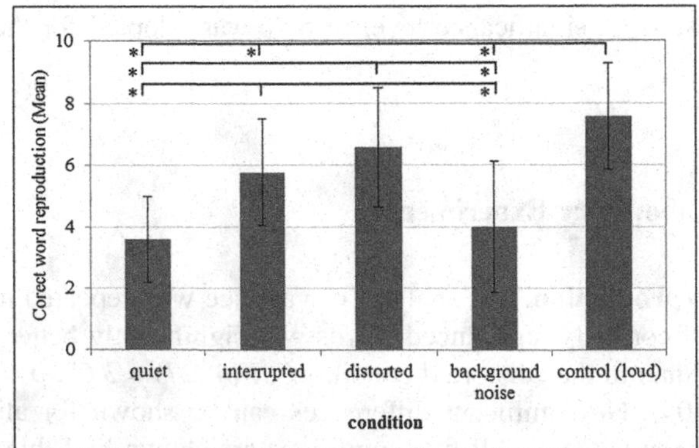

Note. * … $p < .05$, Sidak

Fig. 1. Study 2 – Mean correct word reproduction of the five hearing conditions

Number of Errors. An analysis of variance with repeated measures shows that the number of errors (frequency of called words that were not part of the particular word list) was significantly higher in the two conditions "quiet" and "background noise" than in the "control condition (loud)", $F(4, 26) = 4.37$, $p = .008$ (post-hoc test: Sidak, $p = .041$, see Fig. 2).

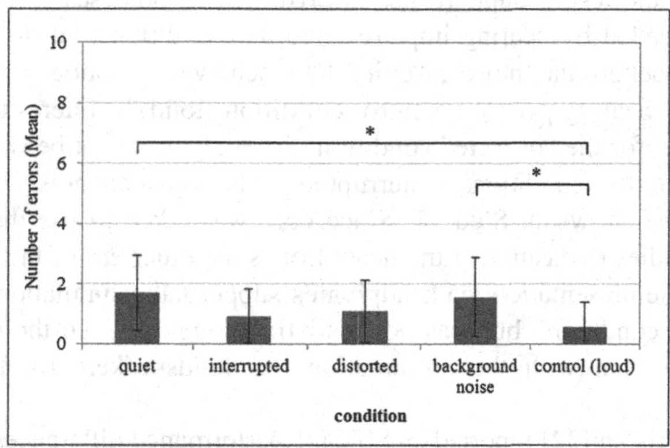

Note. * … $p < .05$, Sidak

Fig. 2. Study 2 – Mean number of errors of the five hearing conditions

4 Discussion

In both studies an effect of induced hearing impairment on the verbal memory performance of normal hearing young adults can be shown. Whereas in Study 1 only a significant better number of reproduced words in the "control condition (loud)" compared to the "distorted condition" (simulation of an age-related change in periodic encoding) and no differences in the number of errors made by the participants can be shown, Study 2 resulted in more differences between the varied hearing conditions. The three conditions of induced hearing impairment "interrupted" (masking effect), "background noise" (everyday situation) and "quiet" (simulation of the auditory impression of a person with mild to moderate hearing loss) results in a poorer verbal memory performance (correct word reproduction) of the participants than the "control condition (loud)". Also, the number of errors was significant higher for the two induced hearing impairment conditions "background noise" and "quiet" than for the "control condition (loud)". Overall, the results show that quantitative effects ("loud", "quiet") as well as qualitative effects ("distorted", "interrupted", "background noise") of hearing impairment on the verbal memory performance can be simulated for normal hearing young adults.

The results show that the association between hearing acuity and performance found by Boxtel et al. [12] using the same verbal memory task can be shown for normal hearing young adults under simulated hearing loss, too. For this reason, the results of the two studies provide further evidence that differences in the verbal memory performance can be attributed to a peripheral hearing loss/early processing stages and not primarily on central processing components/higher cognitive functions. Also, they are consistent with the results of Eckert et al. [25] which were able to show an impact of simulated hearing conditions (by low-pass filtering) on the percentage of correct word recognitions in normal hearing participants.

Furthermore, the results support the "effortfulness hypotheses" [18, 19] that additional effort is needed by hearing impaired people (conditions: "distorted condition", "interrupted", "background noise", "quiet") to achieve the same perceptual performance as normal hearing people ("control condition (loud)"). Interestingly, the effect that can be shown for the "distorted condition" in Study 1 cannot be shown in Study 2 and the effect for the conditions "interrupted", "background noise" and "quiet" in Study 2 cannot be shown in Study 1. Since care was taken to use the same volume levels in both studies (measured at the headphones/the outer ear of the participants), it is possible that the presentation via headphones supports the simulation of impairment in the "distorted condition" but was not realistic enough to give the participants the same impression than with the presentation via loudspeakers for the other three conditions.

Frisina and Frisina [22] reported significant performance differences between three groups of hearing impaired elderly participants in a speech recognition task. The least impaired group did perform better than the two groups with more degree of hearing impairment. The performance differences that can be shown for the "distorted condition" and the two conditions "background noise" and "quiet" as well as between the "interrupted condition" and the two conditions "background noise" and "quiet" in Study 2 may reflect this too. An interpretation of these effects can be that the "background noise condition" and the "quiet condition" both simulate hearing conditions of greater hearing loss than the two conditions "distorted" and "interrupted". These results indicate that the concomitants of hearing loss in speech perception are due to complex distortion of perception and not only to volume factors.

To sum it up, the results of the two studies provide further evidence that differences in the verbal memory performance are due to a peripheral hearing loss/early processing stages and not primarily on the impairment of central processing components/higher cognitive functions. The exclusion of possible age-related effects by investigating only young adult participants supports this. The results provide an opportunity to simulate hearing impairment and learn more how to develop new ways of interventions, trainings and rehabilitation as well as for the development of future human-machine-interfaces and technical assistive devices. Also, the research of Lehrl et al. [24] supports the importance of future research in the field of hearing aid design and the fitting of hearing aids. However, the results support the well-known fact on the subject of hearing impairment: A hearing aid that just increases volume/the sound pressure level will not be efficient and may potentially result in discomfort rather than in better performance. As the results of qualitative changes indicate, sound perception is an important secondary component, which also might be primarily due to early process stages of speech perception. Therefore, more research is needed to understand how memory performance demands of hearing impaired people can be improved with the help of new and modern hearing aids. To increase the possibilities of employment of hearing impaired, future studies have to think about occupationally specific hearing conditions to characterize them and to improve the fitting of hearing aids in these special situations. This may have a big impact on employees in working environments like open-plan offices, jobs with customer contact, consulting, teaching and so on as well as for employees in working environments with sound emission (e.g. construction areas, machine operator, airfield personnel,…) or acoustically difficult rooms (e.g. classroom, auditorium, conference room,…). A better fitting of hearing aids may also help to increase the willingness to wear them and improve the present situation that many hearing impaired people do not use a hearing aid or do not use it regularly (see also [5]).

Acknowledgments. We thank Prof. Dr. Stefan Geisler for the permission to ask undergraduate students of the Hochschule Ruhr West - University of Applied Sciences to participate in Study 2, the undergraduate students Till Schües [29], Lisa Nußhold [30] and Johannes Riener [31] for their support in conducting Study 1, and all participants who participated in the two studies.

References

1. Hannula, S., Bloigu, R., Majamaa, K., Sorri, M., Mäki-Torkko, E.: Self-reported hearing problems among older adults: prevalence and comparison to measured hearing impairment. J. Am. Acad. Audiol. **22**(8), 550–559 (2003)
2. Behnke, B.: Betriebliche Gesundheitsförderung älterer Arbeitnehmer. GRIN, Norderstedt (2009)
3. Dalton, D.S., Cruickshanks, K.J., Klein, B.E., Klein, R., Wiley, T.L., Nondahl, D.M.: The impact of hearing loss on quality of life in older adults. Gerontologist **43**(5), 661–668 (2003)
4. Mathers, C., Smith, A., Concha, M.: Global burden of hearing loss in the year 2000. Global Burdon of Disease. World Health Organization, Geneva (2000)
5. National Academy on an Aging Society: Hearing loss: A growing problem that affects quality of life. Challenges of the 21st Century: Chronic and Disabling Conditions 2, 1–6, December 1999
6. Slawinski, E.B., Hartel, D.M., Kline, D.W.: Self-reported hearing problems in daily life throughout adulthood. Psychol. Aging **8**(4), 552–561 (1993)
7. Jennings, M.B., Shaw, L.: Impact of hearing loss in the workplace: raising questions about partnerships with professionals. Work **30**(3), 289–295 (2008)
8. Nachtegaal, J., Festen, J.M., Kramer, S.E.: Hearing ability in working life and its relationship with sick leave and self-reported work productivity. Ear Hear. **33**(1), 94–103 (2012)
9. Morata, T.C., Themann, C.L., Randolph, R.F., Verbsky, B.L., Byrne, D.C., Reeves, E.R.: Working in noise with a hearing loss: perceptions from workers, supervisors, and hearing conservation program managers. Ear Hear. **26**(6), 529–545 (2005)
10. Yankaskas, K.: Prelude: noise-induced tinnitus and hearing loss in the military. Hear. Res. **295**, 3–8 (2013)
11. Baskent, D., Eiler, C.L., Edwards, B.: Phonemic restoration by hearing-impaired listeners with mild to moderate sensorineural hearing loss. Hear. Res. **260**, 54–62 (2010)
12. Boxtel, M.P.J., van Beijsterveldt, C.E.M., Houx, P.J.L., Anteunis, J.C., Metsemakers, J.F.M., Jolles, J.: Mild hearing impairment can reduce verbal memory performance in a healthy adult population. J. Clin. Exp. Neuropsychol. **22**(1), 147–154 (2000)

13. Pearman, A., Friedman, L., Brooks, J.O., Yesavage, J.A.: Hearing impairment and serial word recall in older adults. Exp. Aging Res. **26**(4), 383–391 (2000)
14. Rönnberg, J., Danielsson, H., Rudner, M., Arlinger, S., Sternäng, O., Wahlin, A., Nilsson, L.G.: Hearing loss is negatively related to episodic and semantic long-term memory but not to short-term memory. J. Speech Lang. Hear. Res. **54**(2), 705–726 (2011)
15. Rudner, M., Rönnberg, J., Lunner, T.: Working memory supports listening in noise for persons with hearing impairment. J. Am. Acad. Audiol. **22**(3), 156–167 (2011)
16. Lin, F.R., Ferrucci, L., Metter, E.J., Yang, A., Zonderman, A.B., Resnick, S.M.: Hearing loss and cognition in the baltimore longitudinal study of aging. Neuropsychol **25**(6), 763–770 (2011)
17. Neijenhuis, K., Tschur, H., Snik, A.: The effect of mild hearing impairment on auditory processing tests. J. Am. Acad. Audiol. **15**(1), 6–16 (2004)
18. McCoy, S.L., Tun, P.A., Cox, L.C., Colangelo, M., Stewart, R.A., Wingfield, A.: Hearing loss and perceptual effort: downstream effects on older adults' memory for speech. Q. J. Exp. Psychol. Sect. A: Hum. Exp. Psychol. **58**(1), 22–33 (2005)
19. Kahneman, D.: Attention and Effort. Prentice-Hall Inc., New Jersey (1973)
20. Rabbitt, P.M.A.: Channel-capacity, intelligibility and immediate memory. Q. J. Exp. Psychol. **20**(3), 241–248 (1968)
21. Wingfield, A., Tun, P.A., McCoy, S.L.: Hearing loss in older adulthood: what it is and how it interacts with cognitive performance. Curr. Dir. Psychol. Sci. **14**(3), 144–148 (2005)
22. Frisina, D.R., Frisina, R.D.: Speech recognition in noise and presbycusis: relations to possible neural mechanisms. Hear. Res. **106**, 95–104 (1997)
23. Wong, P.C.M., Jin, J.X., Gunasekera, G.M., Abel, R., Lee, E.R., Dhar, S.: Aging and cortical mechanisms of speech perception in noise. Neuropsychol **47**, 693–703 (2009)
24. Lehrl, S., Funk, R., Seifert, K.: Erste Hörhilfe erhöht die geistige Leistungsfähigkeit. Offene kontrollierte Anwendungsbeobachtungsstudie als Pilotstudie. HNO **53**, 852–862 (2005)
25. Eckert, M.A., Walczak, A., Ahlstrom, J., Denslow, S., Horwitz, A., Dubno, J.R.: Age-related effects on word recognition: reliance on cognitive control systems with structural declines in speech-responsive cortex. J. Assoc. Res. Otolaryngol. **9**, 252–259 (2008)
26. Helmstaedter, C., Lendt, M., Lux, S.: VLMT Verbaler Lern- und Merkfähigkeitstest. Beltz Test GmbH, Göttingen (2001)
27. Lezak, M.D.: Neuropsychological Assessment. Oxford University Press, New York (1983)
28. Rey, A.: Ikxamen Clinique en Psychologie. Presses Universitaires de France, Paris (1964)
29. Schües, T.: Auswirkungen von Hörbeeinträchtigung auf die verbale Gedächtnisleistung. Experimentelle Untersuchung zu Möglichkeiten der Induzierung von leichter Schalleitungsschwerhörigkeit und Schallempfindungsschwerhörigkeit und damit verbundene negative Auswirkungen auf die verbale Gedächtnisleistung (bachelor's thesis). University of Graz, Institute of Psychology, Graz (2013)
30. Nußhold, L.: Einflüsse von induzierter Hörbeeinträchtigung auf das verbale Gedächtnis (bachelor's thesis). University of Graz, Institute of Psychology, Graz (2013)
31. Riener, J.: Induzierte Hörbeeinträchtigung und verbales Gedächtnis. Die verbale Gedächtnisleistung normalhörender Personen bei leisen und unterbrochenen Wörtern (bachelor's thesis). University of Graz, Institute of Psychology, Graz (2013)

Smart Environments and AAL

Spatial Modeling Factors in Sensor-Based Ambient Assisted Living Technologies Designed for Ageing Populations

Dua'a Al-Hajjar, Reem Al Ehaidib, Sarah Al Muhanna, May Al Sohibani, and Areej Al-Wabil(✉)

College of Computer and Information Sciences, Prince Sultan University, Riyadh, Saudi Arabia
{dhajjar,awabil}@pscw.psu.edu.sa

Abstract. In this paper, we synthesize research on the different emerging Ambient Assisted Living (AAL) sensor-based technologies and examine the spatial parameters that are used in these systems. Different lenses in examining the AAL literature are considered, such as the chronological development in sensor-based AAL and the human factors in the design of sensor-based AAL in various contexts. Relevant metrics and standards in AAL design are highlighted. A comparative prospective of these metrics and how they are applied in recent studies and systems are also discussed. The paper presents a categorization of those technologies based on their selection of the spatial information to obtain a clearer understanding of the relationship between spatial modeling and the accuracy of these technologies. Implications for the design of AAL and situated interaction in AAL contexts are discussed.

Keywords: AAL sensors · AAL human factors · Spatial metrics

1 Introduction

Technologies in every aspect of daily living have been evolving to adapt to smarter environments [1]. One of the main goals of smart environments is to provide adequate support and improve the abilities of its occupants and give the users the ability to live an independent life. Ageing involves progressive decline of cognitive, sensory and physical abilities. This consequently has led to a proliferation of Ambient Assisted Living (AAL) research as it became more viable and important for a growing population. Recent studies have shown the impact of AAL technologies on the quality of life for people with visual impairments [2], and with mobility impairments [3]. According to the aging statistics that are provided by the Administration for Community Living (ACL) in the US [4], the older population (persons 65 years or older) represented 12.9 % of the U.S. population; i.e. around 40 million. However, the ACL is expecting that in 2030, there will be about 72.1 million older persons, more than twice their number in 2000. An increase in aging rates is also accompanied by an increase of dependency levels and of life expectancy levels that increase complexity of ageing issues [3].

J. Zhou and G. Salvendy (Eds.): ITAP 2015, Part II, LNCS 9194, pp. 367–376, 2015.
DOI: 10.1007/978-3-319-20913-5_34

AAL technologies have the potential to provide ageing populations with autonomy, mobility, and independence and consequently improve their quality of life. Smart environments could be the most useful solutions for elderly people who need assistance in their Activities of Daily Living (ADL) by alleviating the caregivers from the burden of some responsibilities and simplifying the tasks executed by the elderly [5]. In this context, evidence suggests potential contribution via technology solutions and the need to develop cost-effective solutions for improving care for the elderly in a non-intrusive way, which can, in turn, improve their independent living in their own environments at home [3].

Ambient Assisted Living (AAL) is a term that includes concepts, products, and services, which improve the interaction between technical and social systems to increase quality of life in all areas. AAL solutions mainly aim at supporting people with special needs through technology. AAL technology intends to accomplish that via intelligent interaction with surrounding environments mediated by devices [3]. These systems are important for physically impaired and elderly people to maintain an independent living in their own homes. They help in improving their living in several domains: sensing, reasoning, acting, communication, and interaction. Therefore, AAL is an important application of the emerging Smart Homes field. Information and Communication Technology (ICT) provides several solutions for improving daily life and health condition [6]. Some of these solutions are technologies that monitor the elderly and aim to enhance their sight and hearing senses [7], reduce the risk of falls and detect falls while navigating [8, 9], provide a social network platform for the elderly [10], assist in sleeping [11, 12], and track their daily routine [13].

In the context of AAL for the elderly, this paper examines the different emerging AAL sensor-based technologies studies and proposed systems, concentrating on the selection of spatial parameters that are used in those studies. A synthesis of human factors in the design of sensor-based AAL in previous work is also reported. Relevant metrics and standards to this field are presented; for example, the sensor type, patient dependence level, sensor detection range, and number of sensors. A comparative prospective of these metrics and how they are being followed in recent studies and systems are also discussed [14]. Further, the paper presents a categorization of those technologies based on their selection of the spatial information to get a clearer understanding on the importance of carefully deciding spatial information and their impact on the accuracy of the study's results [15, 16]. Implications for the design of AAL and situated interaction in AAL contexts are discussed.

2 Sensor-Based AAL Technologies

In recent years, varied approaches have been reported for categorizing sensor-based technologies designed for the elderly. The authors in [17] summarized the state-of-the-art AAL technologies, techniques, and tools. In their paper, they categorized the main AAL technologies into: ambient sensors used in smart environments, assistive smart home projects, mobile and wearable sensors and assistive robotics. They organized nine ambient sensors in a table based on measurement (e.g. motion, identification, and pressure) while taking data format (e.g. numeric, image, and sound) into account, whereas assistive smart home projects were arranged according to the educational institution where they were first employed; for instance, CASAS project at Washington State University, DOMUS project at the University de Sherbrooke, and House_n project at the MIT. Wearable and mobile sensors that are equipped in AAL technologies were categorized in the paper according to the measured properties. The required data rate used to detect activities is also shown in the wearable and mobile sensors categorization tables. For example, accelerometer and gyroscope capture acceleration and orientation; therefore, a high sampling rate is needed to detect activities such as running while other physiological measurements such as body temperature will not change abruptly so occasional data sampling will suffice. In addition, assistive robots were categorized into three categories in the paper; robots assisting with ADL activities, robots assisting with instrumental activities of daily living (IADL), and robots assisting with enhanced activities of daily living (EADL). The authors also reviewed the different computational techniques that support AAL tools such as the activity recognition and context modelling techniques.

Innovative AAL designs included monitoring sensors and spatial wireless monitoring solutions. Most of the wireless sensors operate using communication standards such as WiFi, Bluetooth, and ZigBee. In addition, there are a few proprietary solutions that were spatially adopted for biomedical monitoring applications (e.g. [18]). Information and communication technologies (ICT) are being developed continuously to meet the challenges that emerge in medical, healthcare or social contexts. The authors in [19] described the methodological considerations for wireless sensor networks (WSNs) in AAL environments by detailing the following sections: specification of open distributed systems, specification of requirements, and development and evaluation process. The authors also concluded that applying distributed and open paradigm to a distributed biomedical sensor network paradigm will result in improving the power autonomy without affecting the system operations. Research has shown that AAL systems can provide some independence and autonomy for individuals with impairments to make their lives much easier. Different approaches could be adopted to develop AAL systems that involve the use of multi-sensor data fusion techniques. Other research projects (e.g. [20]) were examined ambient sensors solutions that are used in AAL environments by considering spatial-temporal aspects. In [20], the authors discussed the challenges of estimating the accuracy of user's position in environment. They provided a novel approach to solve this issue using an advanced system. This paper focused on RESIMA system, which assists people with sensory disability and those who suffer from visual impairment in indoor environment in particular. RESIMA system, which is an intelligent assisted system based on several sensors those were used to monitor user's status and position. In addition, this system exploited technologies and tools such as Wireless Sensor Network, user-environment interaction (UEI), user-environment contextualization (UEC), decision support system (DSS), and graphical user interface (GUI). They were adopted in order to establish RESIMA system. They aim to manage the interaction of user by sending notification to the user about obstacles or services existed, along with high spatial resolution.

In examining recent additions to the extant knowledge base in AAL sensor technologies, we first considered categorizing the AAL technologies according to the services provided by each technology. Two questions guided the enquiry: 'What are the main issues reported in the literature with regards to AAL sensor technologies in general and to the elderly in specific?' and 'What insights have emerged in AAL sensor technologies for the elderly?'

A number of services emerged as distinct categories in this domain (listed in Table 1):

- Cognitive reinforcement services that enhance the cognitive functions of the user.
- Patient-specific home care services include social reinforcement services, services capable to detect abnormalities, and services capable of monitoring several disease risk factors.
- General home care services include medication reminder services, information services, notification systems for emergency response and intrusion, as well as alarm services in cases of abnormal health conditions

Table 1. Categorization of AAL sensor-based services

Project/System	Services/Application Domains			Reference
	Cognitive Reinforcement	Patient-Specific Home Care	General Home Care	
HERA	✓	✓	✓	Spanoudakis [21]
AALISABETH		✓		Culmone [22]
Fall Preventive iTV Solution		✓		Aal [8]
UMBS		✓		Walsh [11]
eWatch		✓		Maurer [23]
EMERGE		✓	✓	Stelios [24]
GERHOME		✓		Zouba [25]
Autominder	✓		✓	Pollack [26]
Maya MedMinder	✓			Alzheimer's Association [27]
Distributed Vision-Based Analysis System		✓		Aghajan [9]
RGB-D Camera			✓	Jungong [1]
Smart House		✓		Barger [28]
SOPRANO			✓	Klein [29]
Health Informatics System		✓	✓	Suryadevara [16]

One lens in examining the literature is to look at the chronological developments in the field over the past two decades. In this field, it is interesting to note that AAL research has appeared in journals and conferences related to other fields as sub-research topics in consumer electronics [1, 28], mechatronics [22], medicine and biology [11] [21], artificial intelligence [26, 29], multimedia [24], pervasive computing [9], and sensor technologies [16, 18, 23]. Other AAL research for the elderly was included in conferences related to technologies assisting people with special needs such as the International Conference on Computers Helping People with Special Needs. AAL research matured as a standalone discipline and started appearing in conferences and journals in 1994. The first conference that was conducted to explore the use of computing and information technologies to help persons with disabilities and older adults was the ASSET'94, the International ACM/SIGCAPH Conference on Assistive Technologies and it was in 1994. Around a decade later in 2003, other conferences were started such as the AAATE 2003 by the Association for the Advancement of Assistive Technology in Europe. Another conference is the International Conference on Ubiquitous Computing and Ambient Intelligence UCAml, which was first launched in 2005 in Spain. Also, the first Smart Objects and Ambient Intelligence conference was held in 2005, and it explored AAL tools and techniques for augmenting environments with smart, networked, interacting objects [30]. The PErvasive Technologies Related to Assistive Environments (PETRA) conference focuses on computational and engineering approaches to improve the quality of life by providing solutions for the in-home care of the elderly as well as for the care of people with Alzheimer's, Parkinson's and other disabilities or traumas. PETRA was first conducted in 2008. Further, the first volume of the Journal of Ambient Intelligence and Smart Environments was published in January 2009. The journal covers broad areas such as sensors, human cantered interfaces, and societal applications within the field of smart environments and ambient intelligence. Recently, several research groups have been established to tackle AAL issues such as Ambient Intelligence Group CITEC in Bielefeld University [31], AMBIT research group in Artesis University College of Antwerp [32], AmIVital [33], iAMEA International Ambient Media Association [34], and NTT [35].

Of particular interest to the AAL community for the elderly are new insights related to human factors and ergonomics. Early AAL technologies for the elderly focused on providing cognitive, physical, and assistive home services to the elderly. Many of the early-developed technologies overlooked the human factors and issues involved. For example, lack of privacy and security of the elderly or their caretakers, usability of these technologies, user-friendliness, personalization and obtrusiveness were among the issues that emerged from using the AAL technologies. The sensitivity of these technologies and responsiveness needed have called for further research into the field to resolve the issues. A development in maturity of awareness within different stakeholder groups and a development of interest in research in the AAL sensor-based technologies field can be observed. Finally, for the professionals interested in issues of spatial modelling factors, limited effort has been reported. The review of existing literature about AAL sensor-based technologies revealed that spatial modelling factors are still vastly unexplored. The following section examines these factors in more depth.

3 Relevant Metrics and Standards in AAL

The research is designed to propose a categorization of the AAL sensor-based technologies based on their spatial information to obtain a clearer understanding on the importance of considering spatial information in AAL design, and their impact on the accuracy on the systems. The research is exploratory in nature. The following process is followed: first, the collection of archived papers to collate the spatial design considerations in AAL. A synthesis of human factors in the design of sensor-based AAL in previous work is reported and the implications for the design of AAL and situated interaction in AAL contexts elaborates described.

When deciding to localize AAL system, we should consider some metrics addressing accuracy, efficiency, and result optimization. In this section, we discuss the metrics observed from the surveyed research papers and the properties related to each metric (summarized in Table 2). The distance is a one of the metrics that must be taken into consideration. The distance value varies based on the purpose of designing the AAL system. For example, an AAL system that allows the elderly to avoid collisions requires different distance measurements than a system designed for localization sensors nodes aim. In this matter, there have been experiments reported in [20] which were conducted to test the system performance in collision avoidance and to test the services exploitation. The authors observed that successful result of collision avoidance is proportional to the distance between the user's position and obstacles. They concluded that in this case the optimized result is 86 % in 0.75 m. On the other hand, they noted that the successful result of services exploitation is optimized for a specific distances between the service and user's position. These specific values are appropriate to the user and service positions that assure that the positioning is within an appropriate range. The overall result of both tests illuminated that the reliable UEI functionality when the value of compatible distance between user's position and obstacle/service is (~ 1 m) and the optimized resolution of the localization system is (~ 4 cm). In addition, the authors considered other metrics to conduct their experiment such as the distance between two nodes, area size, height of nodes, and the number of nodes used based upon the area size.

With regards to the distance between a user and a node, research has shown that the accuracy of distance between the user and nodes could have an influence on the system accuracy for estimating the user's position [36]. The sensor's range and coverage ability are important factors to be considered when setting the sensors' position [36]. This also affects the number of sensors placed in a specific area. The range of coverage for sensors is also an important factor in design. Sometimes, the radio frequency wave cannot pass through barriers so designers/architects increase the number of sensors in that area [36, 37].

The distance, area size, and height metrics play a role that is emphasized in AAL research papers. The authors in [24] specified the exact position measurements for the sensors in order to evaluate the suggested localization platform for ambient assisted living in an indoor environment, this platform was part of the EMERGE system. There were four Ubisense sensors (Ubisensors) positioned on the ceiling of ordinary office with an area dimension of 6.5 m × 13.45 m × 2.70 m. The coordinates for the first, second, third, fourth sensor were (5.25 m × 0.70 m × 2.75 m), (5.24 m × 12.53 m × 2.52 m), (0.55 m × 11.86 m × 2.52 m), and (5.25 m × 0.70 m × 2.54 m) consecutively with battery powered tags (Ubitag) attached at a height of 1 m. Thus, in this paper the authors considered the area size and high metrics.

Table 2. Metrics of sensor-based Ambient Assisted Living technologies

Metric	Purpose	Properties	Optimized value
Distance	Collisions avoidance/Services exploitation	- Distance between user's position and obstacle/service	~1 m
		- UEI algorithm	
	Distribution of sensor nodes	Distance between two nodes	~4 m
	Accuracy of localizing user position	Distance between the user and node	
	Data transition (Inter-ban)	- Distance between sensors located on user's body and the device	> = 10 m
		- Inter-Ban communication using Bluetooth or WiMedia protocol	
		- Distance between sensors located on user's body and the device	> = 20 m
		- Inter-Ban communication using ZigBee protocol	
Number of nodes	Accuracy of determining the user position and ensuring to cover the operating range of the user	Relying on area's size, and sensor' range ability	7 nodes
Area's size	Accuracy, and homogenous performance of the localization system	Considering the width and length of area	8.60 m × 7.10 m
			6.5 m × 13.45 m
Height	Localization of nodes/energy	Nodes	~3.0 m
		Energy (Ubitag)	1.0 m
Sensor' Range	Coverage range of the sensors	Depending on sensor type	~5 m

There are several IEEE 802.15 standards that can be used to transmit data from sensors located on the user's body to a handheld device. The communication between sensors located on user's body and the device is known as inter-BAN communication. According to [17], some of these standards and the suitable range for the inter-BAN communication are: IEEE 802.15.1 protocol (Bluetooth) and IEEE 802.15.3 protocol (WiMedia) with a range less than 10 m, and IEEE 802.15.4 protocol (ZigBee) with a range less than 20 m.

4 Conclusions

This paper presented insights from the different lenses in examining the AAL literature and categorizing the technologies based on their selected spatial metrics. Challenges and trends in AAL technologies have become apparent and need to be considered by developers prior to designing spatial configurations for AAL environments and interaction design of such spaces (e.g. social interaction [38]). And one of the important challenges that the designers of an AAL environment must address is privacy. The reason is that in order to achieve context-awareness, adaptability and anticipatory behavior in an AAL environment, it needs to contain historical and current data about individual's daily activities and preferences [39]. The perception of privacy violation varies according to factors such as age, cultural background, and level of support an individual requires in order to live independently [40, 41]. Along with privacy comes security; an issue of how to secure the AAL environment from malicious attacks and hacks [42]. This paper aids developers in understanding the spatial design considerations for creating AAL environments for ageing populations, and contributes towards future research in spatial modeling and simulations for AAL.

References

1. Han, J., Pauwels, E.J., De Zeeuw, P.M., De With, P.H.: Employing a RGB-D sensor for real-time tracking of humans across multiple re-entries in a smart environment. IEEE Trans. Consum. Electron. **58**(2), 255–263 (2012)
2. Ando, B.: Measurement technologies to sense "users in the environment" for ambient assisted living. IEEE Inst. Meas. Mag. **15**(6), 45–49 (2012)
3. Cunha, D., Trevisan, G., Samagaio, F., Ferreira, L., Sousa, F., Ferreira-Alves, J., Simoes, R.: Ambient assisted living technology: comparative perspectives of users and caregivers. In: IEEE 15th International Conference on e-Health Networking, Applications & Services (Healthcom), Lisbon (2013)
4. Administration for Community Living, "Administration on Aging Aging Statistics," ACL (2012). http://www.aoa.gov/Aging_Statistics/. Accessed 14 October 2014
5. Wan, J., O'Grady, M.J., G. O'Hare, M.: Towards a scalable infrastructure for ambient assisted living. In: IEEE Third International Conference on Consumer Electronics, Berlin (2013)
6. Amaro, F., Gil, H.: ICT for Elderly People: « Yes, 'They' Can! » . In: *e*-CASE & e-Tech International Conference, Tokyo, Japan (2011)
7. AAL Joint Programme, "AAL Newsletter September," Ambient Assisted Living Joint Programme - Newsletter, pp. 1–2 (2013)
8. Aal, K., Ogonowski, C., Rekowski, T.V., Wieching, R., Wulf, V.: A Fall Preventive iTV Solution for Older Adults. Siegen, Germany (2014)
9. Aghajan, H., Augusto, J.C., Wu, C., McCullagh, P., Walkden, J.-A.: Distributed vision-based accident management for assisted living. In: Okadome, T., Yamazaki, T., Makhtari, M. (eds.) ICOST. LNCS, vol. 4541, pp. 196–205. Springer, Heidelberg (2007)
10. Alzheimer's Association, "Technology Improving Lives of People with Dementia." Memory Matters 14(1), 3 (2014)

11. Walsh, L., McLoone, S., Behan, J., Dishongh, T.: The Deployment of a Non-Intrusive Alternative to Sleep/Wake Wrist Actigraphy in a Home-Based Study of the Elderly. In: 30th Annual International Conference of the IEEE Engineering in Medicine and Biology Society (EMBS), Vancouver (2008)
12. Adami, A.M., Pavel, M., Hayes, T.L., Singer, C.M.: Detection of movement in bed using unobtrusive load cell sensors. IEEE Trans. Inf Technol. Biomed. **14**(2), 481–490 (2010)
13. Kaluža, B., Gams, M.: Analysis of daily-living dynamics. J. Ambient Intel. Smart Env. **4**(5), 403–414 (2012)
14. Andrushevich, A., Kistler, R., Bieri, M., Klapproth, A.: ZigBee/IEEE 802.15.4 Technologies in Ambient Assisted Living Applications. In: 3rd European ZigBee Developers' Conference (EuZDC), Munich, Germany (2009)
15. Alemdar, H., Durmus, Y., Ersoy, C.: Wireless healthcare monitoring with rfid-enhanced video sensor networks. Int. J. Distrib. Sens. Netw. **2010**, 10 (2010)
16. Suryadevara, N.K., Chen, C.-P., Mukhopadhyay, S.C., Rayudu, R.K.: Ambient Assisted Living Framework for Elderly Wellness Determination through Wireless Sensor Scalar Data. In: Seventh International Conference on Sensing Technology (ICST), Wellington (2013)
17. Rashidi, P., Mihailidis, A.: A survey on ambient-assisted living tools for older adults. IEEE J. Biomed. Health Inf. **17**(3), 579–590 (2013)
18. Figueiredo, C.P., Gama, Ó.S., Pereira, C.M., Mendes, P.M., Silva, S., Domingues, L., Hoffmann, K.P.: Autonomy suitability of wireless modules for ambient assisted living applications. In 2010 Fourth International Confere on Sensor Technologies and Applications (SENSORCOMM), Venice (2010)
19. Estudillo-Valderrama, M.A., Roa, L.M., Reina-Tosina, J., Román-Martínez, I.: Ambient Assisted Living: A Methodological Approach. In: 32nd Annual International Conference of the IEEE Engineering in Medicine and Biology Society (EMBS), Buenos Aires (2010)
20. Andò, B., Baglio, S., Lombardo, C.O.: RESIMA: an assistive paradigm to support weak people in indoor environments. IEEE Trans. Inst. Meas. **63(11)**, 2522–2528 (2014)
21. Spanoudakis, N., Grabner, B., Kotsiopoulou, C., Lymperopoulou, O., Moser-Siegmeth, V., Pantelopoulos, S., Sakka, P., Moraitis, P.: A novel architecture and process for Ambient Assisted Living - the HERA approach. In: 2010 10th IEEE International Conference on Information Technology and Applications in Biomedicine (ITAB), Corfu, (2010)
22. Culmone, R., Falcioni, M., Giuliodori, P., Merelli, E., Orru, A., Quadrini, M., Ciampolini, P., Grossi, F, Matrella, G.: AAL domain ontology for event-based human activity recognition. In: IEEE/ASME 10th International Conference on Mechatronic and Embedded Systems and Applications (MESA), Senigallia (2014)
23. Maurer, U., Smailagic, A., Siewiorek, D.P., Deisher, M.: Activity recognition and monitoring using multiple sensors on different body positions. In: International Workshop on Wearable and Implantable Body Sensor Networks (BSN 2006), Cambridge (2006)
24. Stelios, M.A., Nick, A.D., Effie, M.T.: An indoor localization platform for ambient assisted living using UWB. In: The 6th International Conference in Advances in Mobile Computing and Multimedia (MoMM 2008), Linz, Austria (2008)
25. Zouba, N., Bremond, F., Thonnat, M., Anfosso, A., Pascual, É., Mallea, P., Mailland, V., Guerin, O.: Assessing computer systems for monitoring elderly people living at home. In: The 19th IAGG World Congress of Gerontology and Geri-atrics, Paris (2009)
26. Pollack, M.E., Brown, L., Colbry, D., McCarthy, C.E., Orosz, C., Peintner, B., Ramakrishnan, S., Tsamardinos, I.: Autominder: an intelligent cognitive orthotic system for people with memory impairment. Robot. Aut. Syst. **44**(3), 273–282 (2003)
27. Association, Alzheimer's: Memory Matters. Technol. Imp. Lives People Dementia **14**(1), 1–8 (2014)

28. Barger, T.S., Brown, D.E., Alwan, M.: Health-status monitoring through analysis of behavioral patterns. IEEE Trans. Syst., Man, Cyb. **35**(1), 22–27 (2005)
29. Klein, M., Schmidt, A., Lauer, R.: Ontology-centred design of an ambient middleware for assisted living: the case of SOPRANO. In: Towards Ambient Intelligence: Methods for Cooperating Ensembles in Ubiquitous Environments (AIM-CU), 30th Annual German Conference on Artificial Intelligence (KI 2007), Osnabrück (2007)
30. AMI Conferneces, Smart Objects & Ambient Intelligence, 12–14 October 2005. http://www.ami-conferences.org/2005/. Accessed 5 December 2014
31. CITEC, Ambient Intelligence Group (2011). http://www.cit-ec.de/ami. Accessed 5 December 2014
32. Artesis University, AMBIT in Artesis University College of Antwerp (2013). http://www.artesis.be. Accessed 5 December 2014
33. Valero, Z., Ibáñez, G., Naranjo, J.C., García, P.: Am IVital: digital personal environment for health and well-being. Wireless Mob. Comm. Healthcare **55**, 160–167 (2011)
34. Ambient Media Association, "iAMEA - International Ambient Media Association" (2013). http://www.ambientmediaassociation.org. Accessed 5 December 2014
35. NTT Communication Science Laboratories, "Ambient Intelligence" (2008). http://www.brl.ntt.co.jp/cs/ai/index.html. Accessed 5 December 2014
36. Bruno, A., Salvatore, B., La Malfa, S., Marletta, V.: A sensing architecture for mutual user-environment awareness case of study: a mobility aid for the visually impaired. IEEE Sens. J. **11**(3), 634–640 (2011)
37. Alcantara, J.A., Lu, L.P., Magno, J.K., Soriano, Z., Ong, E., Resurreccion, R.: Emotional narration of children's stories. In: Nishizaki, S.-Y., Numao, M., Caro, J., Suarez, M.T. (eds.) Theory and Practice of Computation. PICT, vol. 5, pp. 1–14. Springer, Heidelberg (2012)
38. Alaoui, M., Ting, K.L.H., Lewkowicz, M.: The urge for empirically-informed design of social-oriented aal applications – the example of 2 aal projects. In: 5th International Conference on Software Development and Technologies for Enhancing Accessibility and Fighting Information exclusion DSAI, Troyes, France (2014)
39. Friedewald, M., Da Costa, O., Punie, Y., Alahuhta, P., Heinonen, S.: Perspectives of ambient intelligence in the home environment. Telematics Inform. **22**(3), 221–238 (2005)
40. Cooka, D.J., Augustob, J.C., Jakkulaa, V.R.: Ambient intelligence: Technologies, applications, and opportunities. Pervasive Mob. Comput. **5**(4), 277–298 (2009)
41. O'Connell, P.L.: "Korea's High-Tech Utopia, Where Everything Is Observed," New York Times, 5 October 2005. http://www.nytimes.com/2005/10/05/technology/techspecial/05oconnell.html?ex=1286164800&en=4a368c49e8f30bd2&ei=5088. Accessed 28 December 2014
42. Friedewald, M., Vildjiounaite, E., Punie, Y., Wright, D.: Privacy, identity and security in ambient intelligence: A scenario analysis. Telematics Inform. **24**(1), 15–29 (2007)

Modeling the Interaction and Control of Smart Universal Interface for Persons with Disabilities

Shady Aly[1(✉)], Ghassan Kbar[2], Mohammed Abdullah[3], and Ibraheem Al-Sharawy[1]

[1] Industrial Engineering Department, College of Engineering, King Saud University Riyadh, Riyadh, Kingdom of Saudi Arabia
saly@ksu.edu.sa, eng.isharawy@gmail.com

[2] Riyadh Techno-Valley, King Saud University Riyadh, Riyadh, Kingdom of Saudi Arabia
gkbar@ksu.edu.sa

[3] Riyadh, Kingdom of Saudi Arabia
eng.muhamed.abdullah@gmail.com

Abstract. A little if not rare work has been considered empowering the PWD with smart universal assistive technologies at the workplace. Most researches focus on specific or single impairment condition such as smart solutions for blind or low vision persons, physically disabled persons (PDP), deaf or mute persons, and mostly with home or building places. This paper present the models of interaction and control of a universal interface solution for PWD, called SMARTUNIVERS. The SMARTUNIVERS is currently being developed within the of SMARTDISABLE's research project activities implemented at the Riyadh Techno Valley, King Saud University, Riyadh, KSA. IT includes two smart interface modules: Smart Help (SMARTHELP) and Smart editor (SMARTED-IT). The SMARTHELP module provides personalized smart help and communication services for the PWD at workplace. The SMARTEDIT module is a multimodal editor interface that provides the capability for wide spectra of PWD groups (11 groups with various combination of disabilities) to edit documents using multi-model ways of interactions and commanding through use of speech recognition engine, text-to-speech, Mic, virtual mouse/keyboard and Braille keyboard. We shall present in this paper the high level design of the SMART-UNIVERS and the two smart component modules, together with the interaction models and scenarios for some typically covered PWD groups. The SMART-UNIVERS provides a flexible dynamic interface that adjusts itself according to the impairment conditions associated with the eleven supported groups of PWD.

Keywords: Ambient Assisted Living (AAL) · Smart workplace · Persons With Disability (PWD) · Human Computer Interaction (HCI)

J. Zhou and G. Salvendy (Eds.): ITAP 2015, Part II, LNCS 9194, pp. 377–388, 2015.
DOI: 10.1007/978-3-319-20913-5_35

1 Introduction

The recent advances in Ambient Assistive living technologies [1] bear great potentiality for realizing effective and efficient social inclusion of peoples with disabilities (PWD). Instead of being a heavy burden on the nations' economy and society, they can become productive through designing adequately smart workplace environment full of intelligent devices and interfaces in order for these PWDs to smartly access, control and interact with these objects and carry out normal person's office tasks. This can be achieved through smartly integrating advanced human computer interaction (HCI) technologies within all objects of the workplace environment.

In fact, one important justification of this article and its related previously linked research efforts from the authors, is that, in spite of its significance on the nation's economy and its social dimensions, the issue of inclusion of PWDs with workplaces environment have not been tackled in previous researches concerned with developing smart environment for disable persons. Most work have focus on home or outdoor assistive technologies. But still obvious neglection of significance of social inclusion of PWDs at workplace. Over and above, most developed smart solutions and assistive technologies were not comprehensive, as they address specific or combination cases of disability, such as smart solutions for blind or low vision persons, physically disabled persons (PDP), deaf or mute persons, and mostly with home or building places.

This paper is organized as follows. In next section, we cover the literature review of relevant technological solution for PWD. Section 3, presents and describes the SMARTUNIVERS interaction and control liked to its interface module windows. Then in Sect. 4, we describe the major guidelines and standards of interface design process upon which the design of SMARTUNIVERS is based and their realizations, and finally a conclusion is given in Sect. 5.

2 Literatures Review

In this section, we review the literatures relevant to smart solutions for PWD, with particular focus on the data and information models developed for smart applications. Workplace environment Related to the utilization of assistive technology to aid persons with neuromuscular disabilities, Chang et al. [2] used a location-based task prompting system to assess the possibility of training two individuals with cognitive impairments in a supported employment program. They concluded that data showed that the two participants significantly increased their target response, thus improving vocational job performance during the intervention phases. Hakobyan et al. [3] conducted a research on making mobile phones and other handheld devices accessible via touch and audio sensory channels for the visually impaired persons. Kbar & Aly [4] proposed smart assistive technologies at the workplace consisting of an integrated and connected set of smart software and hardware technologies to empower the Physically disabled persons with the capability to access and effectively utilize the ICTs in order to execute knowledge rich working tasks with minimum of effort and with sufficient comfort level. Their proposed technology solution for PWD includes smart help and smart editors through using voice recognition that enables them to edit and document their work smartly through animating of the mouse cursor movement to track the editing without the need to use their hands. It also enables PWD to get help from the network using smart help engine that is based on voice recognition.

Relevant to the utilization of smart software to empower the PWD in the workplace, Chang et al. [5] assessed the possibility of training three people with cognitive impairments using a computer-based interactive game. They designed a game to provide task prompts in recycling scenarios, identify incorrect task steps on the fly, and help users learn to make corrections. The results showed that the three participants considerably increased their target response, which improved their vocational job skills during the intervention phases and enabled them to maintain the acquired job skills after intervention. Angkananon et al. [6] focused on designing accessible mobile learning interactions involving disabled people using a newly developed Technology Enhanced Interaction Framework. Their framework was developed to help design technological support for communication and interactions between people, technology, and objects particularly when disabled people are involved.

Lancioni et al. [7] built a computer aided telephone to help person with motor and visual disability to make phone calls to his work college or his family. The system communicates with user through voice commands to select the person he want to call, the user activate a micro-switch by his hand to perform a call or to hang up the call. The system help visual impaired individuals to perform calls with no need to press numeric keypad which could cause miss typing of phone number. However, the system was not portable and requires the use of hands to control the micro-switch. Halawani Zaitun [8] built a software system that help deaf. The system captures the speech through speech recognition system, and digitizes the speech then converts it to Arabic sign language. The Arabic sign language output is a pre-saved images of equivalent avatar for each alphabet and words in the recognized language. Addressing the needs of motor disability, Peixto et al. [9] designed and implemented a voice control system to a wheelchair movement, the author used voice commands such as go to start chair movement and measure the frequency of humming to change the chair speed, also for controlling chair rotation user could say turn left command and then use humming to control the rotation angle. Yang et al. [10] designed a system to help people with motor disability to use blinking to control virtual keyboard. The scanning keyboard was designed to be controlled by blinking left eye and right eye simultaneously. The pseudo electromyography (EMG) signal generated from a user's blink was acquired by a Bluetooth headset and transmitted to a PC through wireless transmission. Hawley et al. [11] built a prototype of voice-input voice-output system that helps individuals with speech disability to improve the conversation with other individuals. The system receives the keywords such as 'want', 'water', 'drink' from the user then user press a button that allow system to generate a speech output which will generate "can I have a drink of water please." The final phrase is then spoken by speech synthesizer. Considering visual impaired individuals the research is targeting indoor navigation systems such in Jain [12] built a wearable device that consists of wall modules deployed in building and, user end comprising of a waist-worn device coupled with a mobile phone. The network of infrared-based wall units retrofitted at specific locations in the building. The sensors transmit the unique IR tags corresponding to their location perpendicular to the direction of motion of the user. All the information is conveyed to the user via the

Text-to-Speech (TTS) engine of the mobile application, and also displayed in a large font size to provide for someone with partial vision. Vibration alerts are used to provide continuous feedback for being on the right track. Addressing the needs of individuals with speech impairment, Padmanabhan & Sornalatha [13] presented an artificial speaking system, the system depend on wearable flex sensor and accelerometer that measure the finger angles and tilting angle of hand while making the gestures (i.e., English alphabets gestures). The system recognizes the gestures and translates it to speech through a speaker output. In 2014, Jamil et al. [14], developed eye tracking system to control powered wheel chair to support impaired people who cannot drive wheel chair manually or unable to move joy-sticks because of lack of physical ability. User's eye moments were translated to screen position through a camera. Once user moves his eyeball, the wheel chair will follow the direction according to eye movement. Also, relevant to this research is the work done in [15] concerning adaptive interactive solutions, and proposed adoptive interaction support to adjust level of interaction based on quality of context, in ambient aware environment. Another related work is the development of RFID-based multi-media system [16], which involves design and experimentation of RFID-based magic stick for children use in interacting with environment for learning and game playing.

The above literature reveals that indeed, a very few if not rare work has been considered empowering the PWD with smart universal assistive technologies at the workplace. Most researches focus on specific or single impairment condition such as smart solutions for blind or low vision persons, physically disabled persons (PDP), deaf or mute persons, and mostly with home or building places.

In this paper, we will explain briefly the high level design of the universal interface called SMARTUNIVERSE that covers several kinds and combinations of disabilities. The user interface, interaction and control of the developed SMARTUNIVERS is described in the following sections.

3 Interactions and Control of SMARTUNIVERS

In this section, we introduce the interaction and control of the SMARTUNIVERS. The SMARTUNIVERS is currently being developed within the of SMARTDISABLE's research project activities implemented at the Riyadh Techno Valley, King Saud University, Riyadh, KSA. IT includes two smart interface modules: Smart Help (SMARTHELP) and Smart editor (SMARTEDIT). The SMARTHELP module provides personalized smart help and communication services for the PWD at work services. The smart help services mainly enable the PWD to get help information about the locations, directions, building information, etc. The smart communications enable the PWD to make a call using Voice over IP (VOIP) with colleagues and other persons in building to ask for help or intervention. In addition the SMARTHELP also support Auto Emergency Response to assist PWD in getting immediate help through Auto Emergency server as well as getting personal assistant from caregiver.

The SMARTEDIT module is a multimodal editor interface that is provides the capability for wide spectra of PWD groups. The SMARTUNIVERS and its two component modules will make use of voice and speech recognition engines, text to speech, virtual mouse/keyboard and Braille keyboard to cover the requirements of wide spectra of PWD defined groups with various combination of impairments, including physically disabled persons (PDP), partially blind or low vision, deaf, mute and combinations of these kinds of capabilities or disability together, in a customized adaptive way. PWD user profile setup is a common part for the SMARTHELP and SMARTEDIT that supports user initial and customized profile setup and adopt the interface display parameters (color, fonts, etc.) and environments (speaker volume, Mic volume, virtual mouse, and virtual keyboard) according to the requirements of the PWD based on the predefined and stored profile.

Developing a unified interface that is relevant for many users especially for People with Disability is a challenging task as it requires knowing the needs for different group and adjust the interface accordingly. We have identified 11 groups that are relevant for PWDs to support a combination of different impairment conditions including visual, hearing, speaking, and motor impairments. Different interface parameters will be modified to satisfy these conditions including Mic and Speaker volume level, font type, color and size, window background and foreground color, and Window size for command and displaying result. Table 1 presents the 11 groups according to different impairment conditions, where some of the combination has been eliminated as user must see or partially see as we don't target the blind group in this project. For each group, following the PWDs group standards guidelines, a set of defined interface design parameters including text type, size and color, volume level, and window color will adjust dynamically according to different group.

Table 1. The identified 11 groups of various impairments

Requirement	Category	group 1	group 2	group3	group4	group5	group6	group7	group 8	Group 9	Group 10	Group 11
must	**See**	√	√	√	√	√	√	×	×	√	√	√
Must is can't fully see	**Partially see**	×	×	×	×	×	×	√	√	×	×	×
Optional if see & must if partially see	**hearing**	×	×	√	√	×	√	√	√	×	×	×
must if not moving hand & Could be if move hand	**Speak**	√	×	√	×	√	√	√	×	√	×	√
must if not speaking & Could be if speaking	**Move hand**	×	√	×	√	√	√	×	√	×	√	√
Optional if see & must if partially see	**Partially hear**	×	×	×	×	×	×	×	×	√	√	√

3.1 SMARTUNIVERS' User Interaction and Flow of Control

Figure 1 illustrates the Use Case diagram of the SMARTUNIVERS. As indicated, There are five use cases that constitute the SMARTUNIVERS modules: Enter user

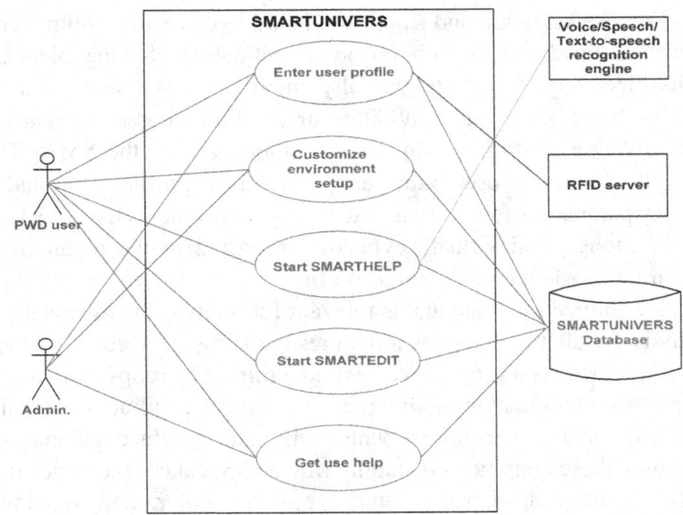

Fig. 1. Use Case of PWD user's interaction with SMARTUNIVERS functions

profile, Customize environmental set, Start SMARTHELP, Start SMARTEDIT, Get use help. The user triggers the five use cases (red lines) and the application Admin interacts with the three use cases out of them to provide help and support to the user, and in some cases assist in user profiling and pre-established environmental setup. The SMARTUNIVERS interface communicates with an integrated speech recognition engine. It also interacts with the RFID which add automatic identification of user profile. The SMARTUNIVERS's database contains all use cases related entities.

3.2 The Flow of Control of the Unified Interface

The following flow chart at Fig. 2 describes the interface of users to setup his/her profile and the environment. Where users supposed to have an account in order to use the system, and for the first time the system requested him/her to enter their details which will be used for the user profile as shown in Figs. 3, 4, 5 and 6. Once the user enters his/her details she/he can login in the system and use it according to default environment setup that will be done according to group he/she belongs to. In addition to the dynamic interface setup, security has been considered in the interface to allow authenticated user to use the program and connect to the network as shown in Figs. 7 and 8, where user can be authenticated through 3 different methods. User will be authenticated using RFID and optional security keyword, normal login with password, and Voice recognition (Figs. 4 and 5).

3.3 Main Unified Interface

The main user interface is shown in Fig. 7, where user can customize his/her user profile as well as environment setup as shown in Figs. 8 and 9. In window 8, (Fig. 8),

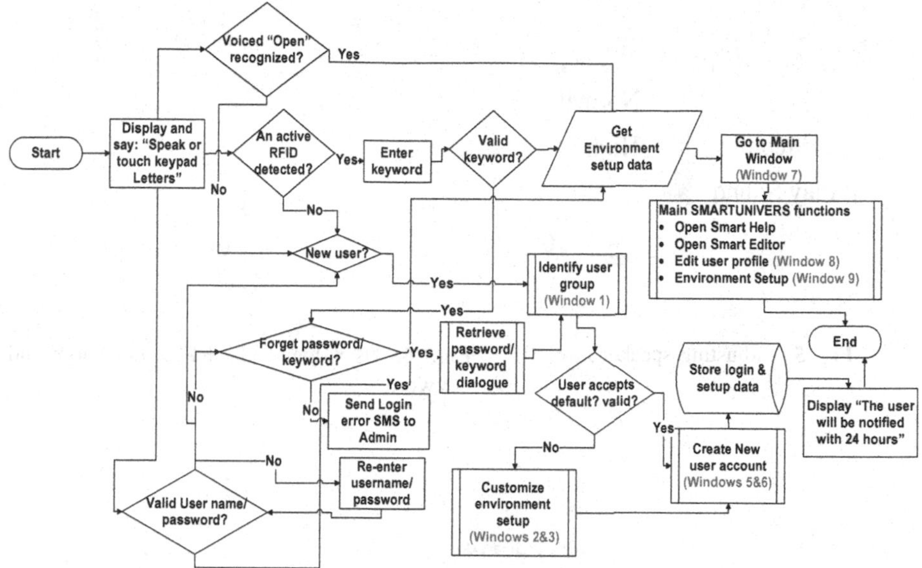

Fig. 2. The control flow chart of user interaction

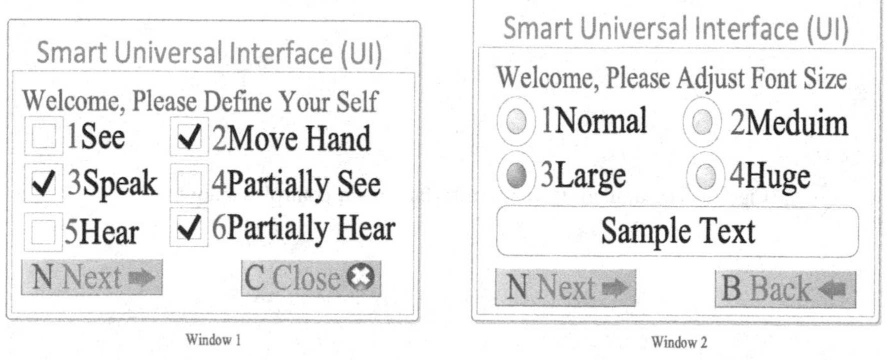

Fig. 3. Defining user basic user group window

Fig. 4. Adjusting font size options

the common interface is to service on the two applications (Smart Help and Smart Editor) which identifies the user and the group of that user and the setting needed by that group to be able to use the applications.

Common Interface Components:

User Profiler. Contains user information like (name, phone, age …) and the PWD group that user belong to and if the user will use the default setting to its group or not. Through this module window 8 (Fig. 8) we can do these options:

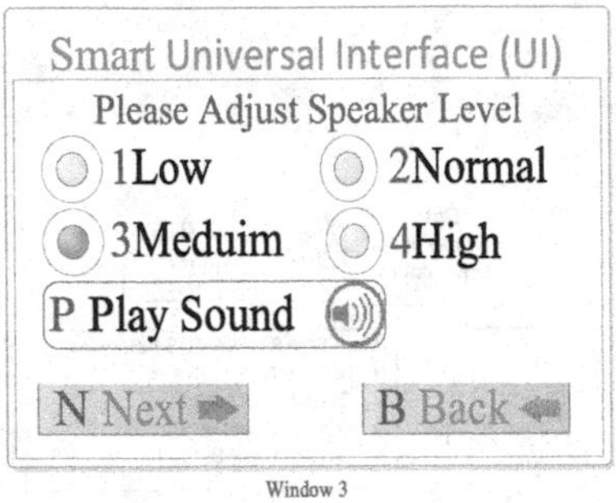

Smart Universal Interface (UI)
Please Adjust Speaker Level
1Low
2Normal
3Meduim
4High
P Play Sound
N Next
B Back
Window 3

Fig. 5. Adjusting speaker level

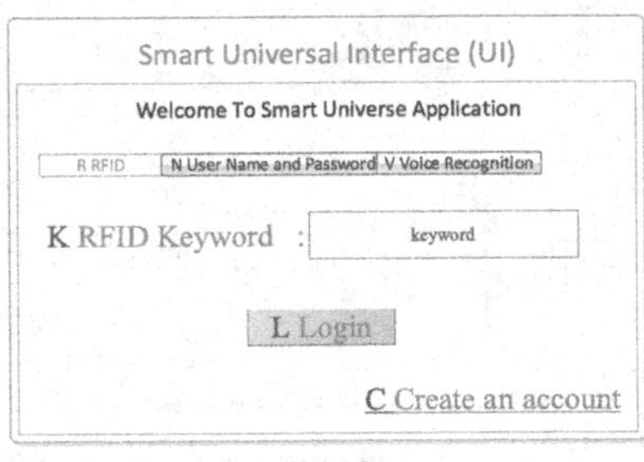

Fig. 6. User login via RFID detection and keyword

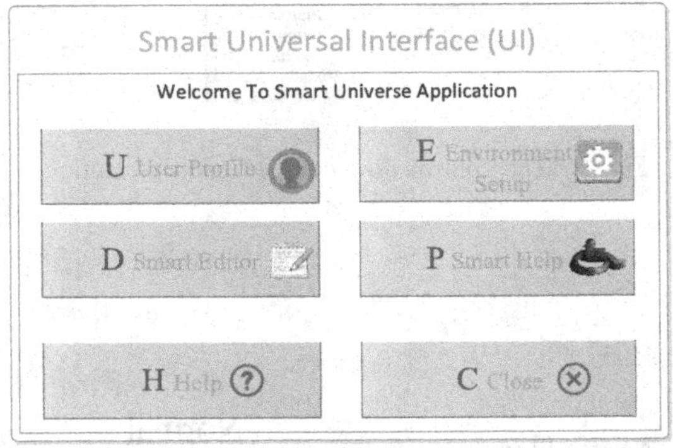

Fig. 7. The unified universal interface main control window

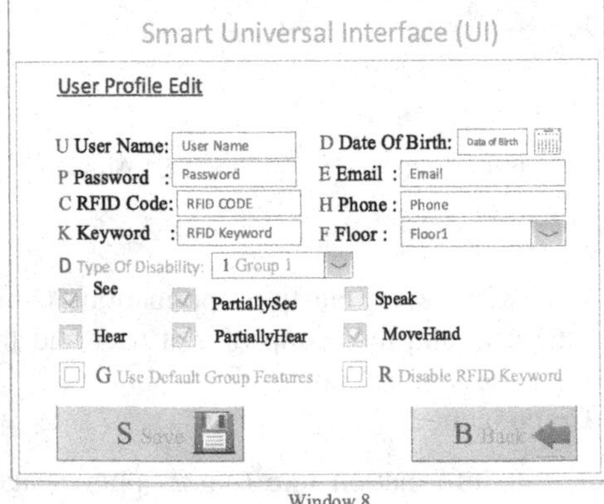

Fig. 8. User profiler module window

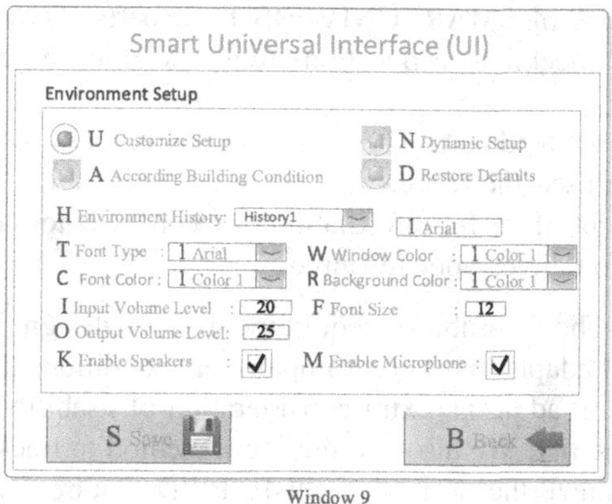

Fig. 9. Environmental setup module window

- Add a new user profile
- Edit current user profile

Environment Setup. Contains the setting that help the PWD group to use the application like (Input volume level, output volume level, enable input through mike, enable output through speakers, font size, and font color) as shown in Window 9 Fig. 9. For each group there will be a default setting and user can customize one for him, but at any time if the user needs to return to default setting can do this throw the button Restore Defaults in the Environment setup Window.

Smart Editor. Used to open Smart Editor application in another window and still running and send the user id to smart editor application to get all information and setting about that user from database throw it.

Smart Help. Used to open Smart Help application in another window and still running and send the user id to smart editor application to get all information and setting about that user from database throw it which has been covered by Kbar & Aly in [15]

Help. Used to open a document describe how to use the common window and its function. The user can read this document or listen to it according to its need.

Close. Used to close the common window itself.

4 Considerations for the Designed SMARTUNIVERS

In order to optimize our universal interface design, several considerations and standards for the design of user interface has been taken into account [16]. Among these significant considerations are the usability:

- Usability testing with real PWD users. Giving typical users some tasks to perform and recording what they do and what they think of the resource.

- Usability evaluations of SMARTUNIVERS by experts. They might make use of formal guidelines, checklists or questions (e.g. 'usability inspections' or 'heuristic evaluation')
- Gathering PWD user feedback. These approaches involve seeking feedback from users after they've used the resource.
- Usage logging. A lot of useful information is recorded automatically by the server or software used to deliver your resource.

Pertaining to the above usability requirements, our design is based on flexible dynamic interface that adapts to different impairment conditions that would satisfy the needs of PWD users. In addition, extra consideration of usability has been addressed through expert in disability. We also use the login method to track the performance of the interface and optimize the design to satisfy PWD requirement conditions, where different logging statements will be recorded to track the performance of the system as well as collecting automatic feedback from users to further analyze them and improve the interface.

On the other hand, we considered also, ISO 13407 which focuses on the processes involved in developing a high-quality and usable interface. It advocates four main steps:

- Specify the context of use. Understand who will be using the resource and how they will be using it.
- Specify user, organizational requirements, and the tasks that must be supported.
- Produce design solutions to meet the requirements identified in Step 2.
- Evaluate designs against user requirements. Check that the development does in fact meet the requirements and targets you have identified in earlier steps.

Responding to the above requirements, we have considered the four guidelines for high quality user interface as specified by the ISO 13407. Where the whole design interface has been done according to the need of PWDs to satisfy their requirement conditions at the workplace as has been described in the next previous section. We are planning to involve PWD users to evaluate the interface and give us their feedback, in addition to involve them in testing the interface once a prototype has been built. This will allow us to improve the design to satisfy PWD needs. Note that our design support 11 groups with different impairment conditions with adaptable unified interface that adjust the interface environment setup according to user group conditions as well as the working environment conditions associated with floor location, weather and day conditions.

A most significant issue that we considered also, is ensuring accessibility of the developed SMARTUNIVERS. The Disability Discrimination Act gave certain rights to people with disabilities in the areas of employment, housing, and access to goods or services, but it excluded education.

Taking accessibility requirement, actually, our design is considering accessibility for PWD at the work environment through considering both desktop and smart phones. The interface will be dynamically setup according to user and group profile. In addition, PWD users can customize the environment setup according to his/her preference. Two main programs will be supported to maximize the accessibility of users at the work environment which are Smart help that allows users to search for relevant information at the workplace such as location, building information, and employee's information. In addition PWD users will be able to communicate with other users and care giver as well as setting up personal note and reminder to remind him/her about future activities. The Smart help and Smart editor can be driven by users through voice control, mouse, and keyboard.

5 Conclusion

The proposed universal interface paves a great road toward inclusion of various groups of disables persons with different combinations of impairments. We have presented the SMARTUNIVERS, which is a smart universal interface that suits eleven groups of persons of various kinds of disabilities. It provides two main smart solutions. The smart help (SMARTHELP) and smart editor (SMARTEDIT). We have focused only on the interaction and control of the SMARTUNIVERS. The SMARTUNIVERS will make use of voice and speech recognition engines, text to speech, virtual mouse/keyboard and Braille keyboard to cover the requirements of wide spectra of PWD defined groups. The proposed solution will smartly identify the PWD user profile and adopt the interface display parameters (color, fonts, etc.) and environments (speaker volume, Mic volume, virtual mouse, and virtual keyboard) according to the requirements of the PWD based on the predefined and stored profile. Finally, the SMARTUNIVERS satisfy the usability, accessibility requirements of the defined PWDs groups.

Acknowledgment. This work was supported by NSTIP strategic technologies program number (12-ELE3220-02) in the kingdom of Saudi Arabia.

References

1. Rashidi, P., Mihailidis, A.: A survey on ambient-assisted living tools for older adults. IEEE J. Biomed. Health Inf. **17**(3), 579–590 (2013)
2. Chang, Y.J., Wang, T.Y., Chen, Y.R.: A location-based prompting system to transition autonomously through vocational tasks for individuals with cognitive impairments. Res. Dev. Disabil. **32**, 2669–2673 (2011)
3. Hakobyan, L., Lumsden, J., O'Sullivan, D., Bartlett, H.: Mobile assistive technologies for the visually impaired. Surv. Ophthalmol. **58**, 513–528 (2013)
4. Kbar, G., Aly, S.: SMART Workplace for Persons with Disabilities (SMARTDISABLE). In: 4th International Conference on Multimedia Computing and Systems (ICMCS 2014), pp. 996–100. IEEE Explore, April 2014
5. Chang, Y.J., Kang, Y.S., Liu, F.L.: A computer-based interactive game to train persons with cognitive impairments to perform recycling tasks independently. Res. Dev. Disabil. **35**, 3672–3677 (2014)
6. Angkananon, K., Wald, M., Gilbert, L.: Applying technology enhanced interaction framework to accessible mobile learning. Procedia Comput. Sci. **27**, 261–270 (2014)
7. Lancioni, G.E., O'Reilly, M.F., Singh, N.N., Sigafoos, J., Oliva, D., Alberti, G., Lang, R.: Two adults with multiple disabilities use a computer-aided telephone system to make phone calls independently. Res. Dev. Disabil. **32**, 2330–2335 (2011)

8. Halawani, S.M., Zaitun, A.B.: An avatar based translation system from arabic speech to arabic sign language for deaf people. Int. J. Inf. Sci. Edu. **2**(1), 13–20 (2012)
9. Peixoto, N., Nik, H.G., Charkhkar, H.: Voice controlled wheelchairs: fine control by humming. Comput. Methods Programs Biomed. **112**, 156–165 (2013)
10. Yang, S., Lin, C., Lin, S., Lee, C.: Design of virtual keyboard using blink control method for the severely disabled. Comput. Methods Programs Biomed. **111**(2), 410–418 (2013)
11. Hawley, M.S., Cunningham, S.P., Green, P.D., Enderby, P., Palmer, R., Sehgal, S., O'Neill, P.: A Voice-Input Voice-Output Communication Aid for people with severe speech impairment. IEEE Trans. Neural Syst. Rehabil. Eng. **21(1)** (2013)
12. Jain D.: Path-guided indoor navigation for the visually impaired using minimal building retrofitting. In: Proceedings of the 16th International ACM SIGACCESS Conference on Computers & Accessibility, pp. 225–232 (2014)
13. Padmanabhan V., Sornalatha, M.: Hand Gesture recognition and voice conversion system for dumb people. Int. J. Sci. Eng. Res. **5(5)**, May 2014
14. Mohamad Jamil, M.H., Al-Haddad, S.A.R., Kyun Ng, C.: A flexible speech recognition system for cerebral palsy disabled. In: Abd Manaf, A., Zeki, A., Zamani, M., Chuprat, S., El-Qawasmeh, E. (eds.) ICIEIS 2011, Part I. CCIS, vol. 251, pp. 42–55. Springer, Heidelberg (2011)
15. Hossain, M.A., Shirehjini, A.A.N., Alghamdi, A.S., El Saddik, A.: Adaptive interaction support in ambient-aware environments based on quality of context information. Multimedia Tools Appl. **67**(2), 409–432 (2013)
16. Karime, A., Hossain, M.A., Rahman, A.M., Gueaieb, W., Alja'am, J.M., El Saddik, A.: RFID-based interactive multimedia system for the children. Multimedia Tools Appl. **59**(3), 749–774 (2012)
17. Kbar, G., Aly, S., Alsharawy, I., Bhatia, A., Alhasan, N., Enriquez, R.: Smart help at the workplace for persons with disabilities (SHW-PWD). Int. J. Comput. Inf. Syst. Control Eng. **9**, 1586–1592 (2015)
18. JISC Guide, "Graphical User Interface Design: Developing Usable and Accessible Collections". http://www.jiscdigitalmedia.ac.uk/guide/graphical-user-interface-design-developing-usable-and-accessible-collection. Accessed 25 Jan 2015

Signing Off: Predicting Discontinued ICT Usage Among Older Adults in Assisted and Independent Living

A Survival Analysis

Ronald W. Berkowsky[1], R.V. Rikard[2], and Shelia R. Cotten[2(✉)]

[1] University of Miami Miller School of Medicine, Miami, FL, USA
rxb285@med.miami.edu
[2] Michigan State University, East Lansing, MI, USA
{rvrikard, cotten}@msu.edu

Abstract. While previous research examining digital inequality among older adults has exposed factors that prevent older adults from using information and communication technologies (ICTs), less has been done focusing on factors that may contribute to ICT discontinuation. This investigation uses data from a randomized controlled intervention study to examine possible predictors of discontinued ICT usage among older adults in assisted and independent living communities. Survival analysis shows that participating in a non-technology activities intervention can increase the odds of stopping the use of ICTs over time. In addition, an increase in the number of instrumental activities of daily living (IADLs) an individual needs assistance with was associated with increased odds of discontinuing ICT use. Results suggest that those promoting continued usage of ICTs among older adults in assisted and independent living need to address the social activities that may prevent use and account for the increasing frailty of residents over time.

Keywords: ICTs · Aging · Assisted living · Independent living · Digital divide

1 Introduction

With the increase in prevalence of information and communication technologies (ICTs), such as Internet-connected computers and smartphones, in everyday life as well as the increase in research that suggests ICTs may benefit individual users with regards to health [1–4], researchers have turned their attention to addressing the so-called "digital divide" – the inequalities in access and use of ICTs. By addressing multiple levels of the digital divide, applied researchers can ensure that all populations will be able to reap the potential benefits of using ICTs. One particular population that is at risk of experiencing the negative consequences of the divide is that of older adults aged 65+ [5]. Although the number of older adults who are using ICTs is increasing [6], their usage levels pale in comparison to younger groups. While research examining the digital divide has focused on the factors that prevent older adults from using ICTs or the attitudes that may dissuade initial use [7–15], less has focused on the factors that

J. Zhou and G. Salvendy (Eds.): ITAP 2015, Part II, LNCS 9194, pp. 389–398, 2015.
DOI: 10.1007/978-3-319-20913-5_36

influence a previously using older adult to discontinue ICT use, particularly older adults who reside in continuing care retirement communities (CCRCs) such as assisted and independent living communities. Using data from a longitudinal study that centered on examining ICT use in older adults in CCRCs, the purpose of this investigation is to identify predictors of discontinued ICT use for this special population. Results may provide insight on measures applied researchers and CCRC staff may take in promoting continued ICT use so that older adults in these communities can continue to reap the benefits of their use.

1.1 Background

ICTs have the potential to enhance the health of users. Applications provide users with tools to help manage, cope with, or even treat a variety of physical and mental health issues such as diabetes, asthma, weight control, smoking cessation, and depression [1, 2, 16]. In addition to providing tools to assist in managing health, ICTs have also been found to have a more direct impact on health and quality of life. For older adults, ICT use has been found to have a significant association with decreased depression [3] and decreased loneliness [17]. Yet while older adults may potentially benefit from ICT use with regards to health and quality of life, the percentage of older adults who report using ICTs is much lower compared to other cohorts. The Pew Research Center reports that while the percentage of older adults who go online has increased between 2001 and 2013 from 15 % to 59 %, it trails in comparison to the general population where 86 % report using the Internet [6, 18].

Researchers of digital inequality have identified various facets of the "digital divide" that help to explain why older adults are less likely to use ICTs despite the potential benefits of use. These go beyond simple explanations of access and also focus on attitudes towards technology and aging. A sample of the reasons older adults do not use ICTs include perceived lack of relevance, perceptions of being too old to learn, embarrassment of abilities, cognitive declines, and issues with vision/hand dexterity [7–15]. As such, some applied researchers looking to explore and potentially decrease the digital divide and enhance the well-being of older populations have attempted to address these through the use of intervention-based investigations [19, 20].

While a considerable amount of literature is devoted to the training of older adults to use ICTs and examining trends in usage, less has focused on examining discontinued ICT use. What motivates an older adult ICT user to stop using a computer and/or the Internet? Previous work suggests that attitudes towards computers such as interest, utility, and control have a significant relationship with discontinuation of ICT use [21] as well as demographic characteristics, as those with low incomes and racial/ethnic minorities are more likely to stop using ICTs [20]. However, to our knowledge no study has examined trends in ICT discontinuation and possible predictors of discontinuation in the context of CCRCs. Residents of CCRCs, specifically assisted and independent living, are a unique subset of the older adult population in that they are typically more physically and cognitively impaired than the general older adult population [22] and they are at risk of lower levels of social support and higher levels of loneliness and social isolation [23, 24].

The focus of this investigation is to determine what factors may predict discontinued ICT use among older adults in assisted and independent living. We focus our attention on factors that are especially salient to residents of these communities: social support and relationships (as residents are at a risk for decreased social contact) and health and functional limitations (as residents tend to have increased physical and cognitive impairments) [22–24]. We hypothesize that individuals in assisted and independent living with decreased levels of support and worse health will be more likely to stop using ICTs over time. We also hypothesize that individuals who take part in a technology-based intervention designed to teach assisted and independent living residents the basics of using a computer and the Internet will be less likely to stop using computers over time.

2 Method

Data for this investigation come from the ICTs and Quality of Life Study, a multi-site randomized controlled intervention study designed to assess the effect of ICT use on the quality of life of older adults residing in assisted and independent living. Nineteen CCRCs located in a medium-sized metropolitan city within the Deep South of the US were randomized into one of three study arms: an ICT arm wherein study participants were given an 8-week training course in the basics of using desktop/laptop computers and the Internet; an Activities Control (AC) arm wherein participants engaged in recreational activities with study personnel such as musical sing-alongs and trivia games; and a True Control (TC) arm wherein no intervention was conducted at the CCRC. Potential participants were screened for cognitive impairment using the Mini-Mental State Examination [25]. Initial recruitment yielded a sample of 313 participants: 101 in the ICT arm, 112 in the AC arm, and 93 in the TC arm.

Participants in the ICT arm engaged in an 8-week introductory course of using computers and the Internet. Two 90-minute classes were held in the CCRC each week using a portable computer lab, along with an additional optional 90-minute "office hours" session where participants could receive more one-on-one instruction with the instructors. The ICT classes started with the basics of using a computer – how to turn one on and off, how to use the keyboard, how to use the mouse, how to open a program – and increased in difficulty over time to cover topics like using email, searching for information online, using social networking sites (e.g. Facebook, Twitter), and using video/recreational websites (e.g., Hulu, Youtube). Each class was led by a graduate student instructor who was assisted by at least one additional graduate student, oftentimes two or three depending on the size of the class. Instruction was supplemented with a custom-made training manual that contained all the lessons covered in the classes that participants could keep. Desktop computers were provided at each CCRC and installed in common areas for participants to use once the classes were complete should they not own or have access to a personal computer (one desktop computer per every five participants).

Both qualitative and quantitative data were collected over the course of the study, although for the purposes of this investigation the analysis is limited to the quantitative data. Quantitative data were derived from a series of surveys conducted with each participant in-person with a member of the study team. Five surveys were administered over the course of approximately 14 months. After baseline, a survey was administered after the intervention (in the case of the ICT and AC arms) or approximately eight weeks after the initial (in the case of the TC arm) and then at 3-, 6-, and 12-month post-intervention follow-ups. Survey questions covered a number of topics, including participant health and well-being, social support and social life in and outside of the CCRC, ICT use, and basic demographics, among others.

2.1 Analytic Technique

The purpose of this investigation is to determine what factors may contribute to an older adult's decision to stop using ICTs. We employ survival analysis as an analytic technique to track ICT usage and identify these factors among the participants of the study. Survival analysis was designed for longitudinal data on the occurrence of an event or a discrete change from one state to another [26, 27]. In general, longitudinal data cannot be analyzed using conventional multivariate methods such as linear regression. The endpoint of the time period of interest or duration is usually right-censored for the occurrence of an event; in other words, the event of interest has not occurred during the period of observation and all that is known about the duration is that it exceeds the observation period [28]. Given the design of the ICTs and Quality of Life Study, the survival analysis examines when the participant stopped using ICTs and what predicts the event of interest.

Cox proportional hazards regression is commonly employed to model survival data. However, the introduction of time-dependent covariates into a Cox regression model will result in non-proportional hazards. Moreover, there are further concerns about the complexity involved in the practical interpretation of the resulting coefficients and in the robustness of the models. Therefore, we employ the flexible parametric model estimation procedure in Stata developed by Lambert & Royston [29]. The advantages of the flexible parametric model estimation over the Cox model are the ease with which smooth predictions can be made, the modeling of complex time-dependent effects, investigation of absolute as well as relative effects, and the incorporation of the expected event for relative survival models [29, 30].

2.2 Measures

Event of Interest. Responses to two questions were used to create the event indicator that a participant stopped using an ICT device. First, participants were asked if they ever use a computer at least occasionally (response options were "yes" or "no"). The value of the response options were recoded to a dichotomous indicator (0 = yes, 1 = no). Second, participants were asked how many times in the past week they used a computer/Internet to search for information. A response value of zero (0) was recoded to a value of one (1) and all response values greater than zero were collapsed and recoded as zero (0). The dichotomous response values for both items were cross tabulated to correctly assign whether the participant continued to use an ICT device (i.e., 0) or if the participant stopped using ICT devices (i.e., 1) for the five time periods.

Independent Variables. The study arm (i.e., ICT, AC, and TC) variable was recoded into three separate variables with dichotomous indicators (i.e., 1/0). In the analyses, the TC group is the excluded or comparison category. The social support measure uses a modified version of the MOS Social Support Survey [31] but without the items assessing help with meals and support with chores as these are addressed elsewhere. Response values were averaged across 18 items and higher average values indicate a higher level of social support. The participant's age was recorded at her/his last birthday. Participants were asked marital status and the response options include: currently married, widowed, divorced, separated, and never married. Marital status was recoded into a dichotomous indicator for either currently married or not (i.e., 1 = currently married, 0 = widowed, divorced, separated, and never married). Participants

Table 1. Descriptive statistics

	Mean	S.D.	Minimum	Maximum
ICT Group	0.33	0.47	0.00	1.00
AC Group	0.37	0.48	0.00	1.00
TC Group	0.30	0.46	0.00	1.00
Age	81.96	8.38	51.00	102.00
Social Support Scale				
Time 1	3.72	0.80	0.94	4.72
Time 2	3.75	0.77	1.17	4.72
Time 3	3.74	0.80	0.94	4.72
Time 4	3.78	0.78	0.94	4.72
Time 5	3.80	0.83	0.22	4.72
Currently Married				
Time 1	0.14	0.35	0.00	1.00
Time 2	0.13	0.33	0.00	1.00
Time 3	0.13	0.33	0.00	1.00
Time 4	0.12	0.33	0.00	1.00
Time 5	0.11	0.31	0.00	1.00
Self-Reported Health Status				
Time 1	3.11	1.04	1.00	5.00
Time 2	3.08	1.02	1.00	5.00
Time 3	2.98	1.00	1.00	5.00
Time 4	2.94	0.99	1.00	5.00
Time 5	2.99	0.98	1.00	5.00
IADLs Scale				
Time 1	3.33	1.34	0.00	8.00
Time 2	3.33	1.37	0.00	6.00
Time 3	3.38	1.22	0.00	8.00
Time 4	3.06	1.32	0.00	7.00
Time 5	3.22	1.29	0.00	7.00

Source: ICTs and Quality of Life Study. N = 313

were asked to rate their health with the response options: excellent, very good, good, fair, and poor. The corresponding response values were recoded so that the highest value indicates an excellent level of self-reported health. To assess the participants Instrumental Activities of Daily Living (IADLs), participants were asked if they received eight types of assistance at their living facility. The eight types of assistance include: medicine management, transportation, meal preparation, household chores, sitting services, financial assistance, shopping, or other not listed. Responses were recoded into a dichotomous indicator (i.e., 1/0) for each type of assistance. Affirmative responses to the eight types were summed so that higher values indicate a higher level of assistance needed.

3 Results

3.1 Descriptive Statistics

Table 1 displays the descriptive statistics for all predictors in the analysis. At baseline there were a total of 313 participants who began the study. Approximately 33, 37, and 30 percent of participants were assigned to the ICT, AC, and TC arms, respectively. On average, participants were 82 years of age. The average value of the social support scale increased from 3.72 at Time 1 to 3.80 at Time 5. The percent of respondents currently married decreased from 14 percent to 11 percent over the course of the study. The average value of participants self-reported health status decreased during the course of the study, although the score was relatively high as the range of 2.94-3.11

Table 2. Flexible parametric survival analysis. Hazard ratios for stopped using ICT devices

	Model 1		Model 2		Model 3	
ICT Group	0.731		0.857		0.792	
	(0.153)		(.180)		(0.169)	
AC Group	1.351		1.644	**	1.471	*
	(0.253)		(0.312)		(0.284)	
Social Support			0.835		0.908	
			(0.083)		(0.095)	
Age					1.012	
					(0.009)	
Currently Married					0.853	
					(0.209)	
Self-Reported Health Status					0.944	
					(0.077)	
IADLs					1.269	***
					(0.078)	
LR chi-square	10.44	*	14.72	**	34.49	***

Source: ICTs and Quality of Life Study. * $p < 0.05$, ** $p < 0.001$, *** $p < 0.0001$. Standard errors reported in parentheses.

corresponds with good/very good health. While self-reported health declined, the average number of IADLs residents reported needing assistance with was relatively stable over the five points in time.

A series of flexible parametric regression models are presented in Table 2. The coefficient for each predictor is the hazard ratio or rate that a participant stopped using an ICT device during the 14 months. Therefore, a significant positive coefficient increases the hazard rate that a participant stopped using ICT devices, while a negative coefficient decreases the hazard rate and increases expected duration that the participant will continue to use an ICT device. In Model 1, the ICT and AC study arm groups are not significant. The social support measure enters Model 2 and the hazard rate for the AC group is significant. Participants in the AC group have a 64 % higher rate that they will stop using ICT devices compared to the TC group. Model 3 adds the participants' age, current marital status, self-reported health status, and IADLs scale measures. Participants in the AC group have a 47 % higher rate that they will stop using ICT devices compared to the TC group. Moreover, as IADL level increases participants have a 27 % higher rate that they will stop using ICT devices.

4 Conclusion

While research examining the digital divide has explored the factors that may contribute to preventing an older adult from using ICTs [7–15], far less has focused on the factors associated with discontinuing the use of ICTs over time, particularly in the context of CCRCs. This investigation sought to identify factors that could potentially predict whether or not an individual living in assisted or independent living would cease using ICTs. We hypothesized that social support and relationships as well as health considerations may contribute to a resident's decision to stop using a computer or the Internet. Our results suggest that while health in the form of functional limitations may motivate residents to discontinue ICT usage, social support may have less of an impact than we thought. Moreover, we had an unexpected finding in that residents in the AC group of the study had increased odds of discontinuing ICT use.

Regarding the unexpected finding, it is possible that the significantly higher rate that a participant in the AC group will stop using ICT devices is a result of engaging in activities with other participants. AC group participants engaged in recreational activities with study personnel such as musical sing-alongs and trivia games. Therefore, AC group members may have lost interest in using ICT devices given the level of other activities they engage in. A previous investigation using data from this study found that participating in any activity, regardless of whether it was an ICT activity or a recreational activity, was associated with increased quality of life [32]; as such, participants in the AC group may have been taking advantage of the benefits of participation (whether these benefits were social or psychological in nature) to the point that they did not perceive a need or simply did not want to engage with ICTs.

Self-rated health was not found to be a significant predictor of discontinuing the use of ICTs. However, as a respondent's number of IADLs that required assistance increased, so too did the likelihood that the respondent would stop using ICTs. This shows that while a subjective measure of health (self-reported health) did not serve as a significant predictor, a more objective measure of functional limitations did. This indicates that while an individual residing in assisted or independent living may feel healthy, limitations that prevent them from being able to carry out IADLs without assistance may also be contributing to their inability to use ICTs. It could be that these increased limitations translate into a direct physical or cognitive complication of using ICTs (e.g., an individual who requires assistance with household chores may also find it difficult to use a keyboard or a mouse), or it could be that the limitations suggest that the respondent refocuses their energies on activities they find more important to their daily life.

Research has shown that there is potential for older adults to use ICTs to better their health and well-being [1–3], [16, 17], and thus it is important for applied researchers to not only identify what factors are preventing older adults from getting online initially but also what factors may motivate them to sign off. The investigation using data from a longitudinal intervention-based study suggests that participating in recreational/non-technology-related activities and increased functional limitations may contribute to discontinued ICT use among older adults in assisted and independent living. As such, applied researchers and CCRC staff looking to bridge the digital divide and keep these residents online will need to account for these factors.

Acknowledgements. The project described was supported by Award Number R01AG030425 (PI, Shelia Cotten) from the National Institute on Aging. The content is solely the responsibility of the authors and does not necessarily represent the official views of the National Institute on Aging or the National Institutes of Health.

References

1. Cole-Lewis, H., Kershaw, T.: Text messaging as a tool for behavior change in disease prevention and management. Epidemiol. Rev. **32**, 56–69 (2010)
2. Kaltenthaler, E., Parry, G., Beverly, C., Ferriter, M.: Computerised cognitive-behavioural therapy for depression: systematic review. Br. J. Psychiatry **193**, 181–184 (2008)
3. Cotten, S.R., Ford, G., Ford, S., Hale, T.M.: Internet use and depression among retired older adults in the us: a longitudinal analysis. J. Gerontol. Ser. B Psychol. Sci. Soc. Sci. **69**, 763–771 (2014)
4. Slegers, K., Van Boxtel, M.P.J., Jolles, J.: Effects of computer training and internet usage on the well-being and quality of life of older adults: a randomized, controlled study. J. Gerontol. Ser. B Psychol. Sci. Soc. Sci. **63**, 176–184 (2008)
5. Millward, P.: The 'Grey Digital Divide': Perception, Exclusion and Barriers of Access to the Internet for Older People. First Monday 8 (2003). http://firstmonday.org/ojs/index.php/fm/article/view/1066/986
6. Smith, A.: Older Adults and Technology Use. Pew Research Center (2014). http://www.pewinternet.org/files/2014/04/PIP_Seniors-and-Tech-Use_040314.pdf
7. Boulton-Lewis, G.M., Buys, L., Lovie-Kitchin, J.: Learning and active aging. Educ. Gerontol. **32**, 271–282 (2006)
8. Boulton-Lewis, G.M., Buys, L., Lovie-Kitchin, J., Barnett, K., David, L.N.: Ageing, learning, and computer technology in australia. Educ. Gerontol. **33**, 253–270 (2007)

9. Broady, T., Chan, A., Caputi, P.: Comparison of older and younger adults' attitudes towards and abilities with computers: implications for training and learning. Br. J. Educ. Technol. **41**, 473–485 (2010)
10. Gatto, S.L., Tak, S.H.: Computer, internet, and e-mail use among older adults: benefits and barriers. Educ. Gerontol. **34**, 800–811 (2008)
11. Hanson, V.L.: Influencing technology adoption by older adults. Interact. Comput. **22**, 502–509 (2010)
12. Purdie, N., Boulton-Lewis, G.: The learning needs of older adults. Educ. Gerontol. **29**, 129–149 (2003)
13. Renaud, K., Ramsay, J.: Now what was that password again? a more flexible way of identifying and authenticating our seniors. Behav. Inf. Technol. **26**, 309–322 (2007)
14. Selwyn, N., Gorard, S., Furlong, J., Madden, L.: Older adults' use of information and communications technology in everyday life. Ageing Soc. **23**, 561–582 (2003)
15. Timmerman, S.: The role of information technology in older adult learning. New Dir. Adult Continuing Educ. **1998**, 61–71 (1998)
16. Tran, J., Tran, R., White, J.R.: Smartphone-based glucose monitors and applications in the management of diabetes: an overview of 10 salient 'apps' and a novel smartphone-connected blood glucose monitor. Clin. Diabetes **30**, 173–178 (2012)
17. Cotten, S.R., Anderson, W.A., McCullough, B.M.: Impact of internet use on loneliness and contact with others among older adults: cross-sectional analysis. J. Med. Internet Res. **15**, e39 (2013)
18. Fox, S., Rainie, L., Larsen, E., Horrigan, J., Lenhart, A., Spooner, T., Carter, C.: Wired Seniors: A Fervent Few, Inspired by Family Ties. Pew Research Center (2001). http://www.pewinternet.org/~/media//Files/Reports/2001/PIP_Wired_Seniors_Report.pdf.pdf
19. Berkowsky, R.W., Cotten, S.R., Yost, E.A., Winstead, V.P.: Attitudes towards and limitations to ict use in assisted and independent living communities: findings from a specially-designed technological intervention. Educ. Gerontol. **39**, 797–811 (2013)
20. Choi, N.G., DiNitto, D.M.: The digital divide among low-income homebound older adults: internet use patterns, ehealth literacy, and attitudes toward computer/internet use. J. Med. Internet Res. **15**, e93 (2013)
21. Zhang, J., Umemuro, H.: When Older Adults Start and Stop to Use Technologies: Long Term Study on Technology Usage, Computer Attitudes and Cognitive Abilities of Japanese Older Adults. Gerontechnology 11 (2012). http://www.iaarc.org/publications/fulltext/When_older_adults_start_and_stop_to_use_technologies_Long_term_study_on_technology_usage,_computer_attitudes_and_cognitive_abilities_of_Japanese_older_adults.pdf
22. Golant, S.M.: Do impaired older persons with health care needs occupy us assisted living facilities? an analysis of six national studies. J. Gerontol. Ser. B: Psychol. Sci. Soc. Sci. **59**, S68–S79 (2004)
23. Adams, K.B., Sanders, S., Auth, E.A.: Loneliness and depression in independent living retirement communities: risk and resilience factors. Aging Mental Health **8**, 475–485 (2004)
24. Winstead, V., Anderson, W.A., Yost, E.A., Cotten, S.R., Warr, A., Berkowsky, R.W.: You can teach an old dog new tricks: a qualitative analysis of how residents of senior living communities may use the web to overcome spatial and social barriers. J. Appl. Gerontol. **32**, 540–560 (2013)
25. Folstein, M.F., Folstein, S.E., McHugh, P.R.: Mini-mental state: a practical method for grading the cognitive state of patients for the clinician. J. Psychiatr. Res. **12**, 189–198 (1975)
26. Allison, P.D.: Survival Analysis Using SAS A Practical Guide. SAS Institute. SAS Press, Cary (2010)
27. Singer, J.D., Willett, J.B.: Applied Longitudinal Data Analysis: Modeling Change and Event Occurrence. Oxford University Press, Oxford (2003)

28. Rabe-Hesketh, S., Everitt, B.: Handbook of Statistical Analyses Using Stata. Chapman and Hall/CRC, Boca Raton (2003)
29. Lambert, P.C., Royston, P.: Further development of flexible parametric models for survival analysis. Stata J. **9**, 265–290 (2009)
30. Royston, P.: Flexible parametric alternatives to the cox model, and more. Stata J. **1**, 1–28 (2001)
31. Sherbourne, C.D., Stewart, A.L.: The MOS social support survey. Soc. Sci. Med. **32**, 705–714 (1991)
32. Winstead, V., Yost, E.A., Cotten, S.R., Berkowsky, R.W., Anderson, W.A.: The impact of activity interventions on the well-being of older adults in continuing care communities. J. Appl. Gerontol. **33**, 888–911 (2014)

Understanding the Socio-Domestic Activity: A Challenge for the Ambient Technologies Acceptance in the Case of Homecare Assistance

Salima Body-Bekkadja(✉), Marc-Eric Bobillier-Chaumon, Bruno Cuvillier, and Florence Cros

Laboratoire GRePS (EA4163), Université de Lyon 2, 69676 Bron Cedex, France
{salima.bekkadja,marc-eric.bobillier-chaumon, bruno.cuvillier,florence.cros}@univ-lyon2.fr

Abstract. Due to the global aging of population, fatal domestic accidents increase. In this paper we describe a user-centered design process of a new pervasive technology (CIRDO). The aim of this technology is to empower the elderly people by the detection of their physical falls and to alert family or caregivers. Two different studies were performed. First, we analyzed the actual risk situations. Second, social acceptance was investigated for the different stakeholders involved. Altogether 63 older adults and 38 other stakeholders were subjected to interviews, focus groups, and were observed in user tests. Falls are mostly due to environments, internal factors, external resources, and social factors. Falling scenarios were identified to configure the future device. All stakeholders proved to have different views as to the acceptability of CIRDO, depending on previous experience, trajectory, needs and objective (support, assistance, care, prevention…) Therefore they have specific expectations and fears with regard to the system.

Keywords: Pervasive technology · Social acceptance · Domestic activity · Elderly people · Risk situations

1 Introduction

Our society is experiencing an aging of its population, explained among others by the increase in life expectancy. In parallel, lifestyles change, involving new living conditions for the elderly People (EP) and their families. New needs in terms of dependency care and support are to be elaborated [1]. Indeed, because of the psychological, social or financial costs incurred by the institutional placement of EP, many of them prefer to stay at home, despite physical, psychological or cognitive difficulties. According to a study by ALTIVIS [2], fear of falling ranks second after that of dependence. The consequences of falling are serious, including motor and psychosocial levels [3, 4]. The possibilities offered by gerontechnologies suggest innovative solutions in support of EP. Besides home-care and home-hospitalization as well as the development of autonomy, gerontechnologies aim at rehabilitating or mitigating some deficiencies [5, 6] and improving elderly people's quality of life [7–9].

J. Zhou and G. Salvendy (Eds.): ITAP 2015, Part II, LNCS 9194, pp. 399–411, 2015.
DOI: 10.1007/978-3-319-20913-5_37

Ambient technologies are less intrusive than conventional remote support or monitoring systems, and tend to blend into the living environment [1]. Indeed, they are able to anticipate users' needs by using environment data and then propose appropriate solutions [10]. Moreover, these technologies have been proved less stigmatizing since they do not need to be worn, unlike telemonitoring bracelets, which equate subjects with their handicaps and weakness; Caradec [11] called them *"old age markers"*.

The CIRDO research project (funded by ANR and CNSA[1]) is part of this socio-technical context. It gathers several scientific and industrial partners and aims to develop an ambient technology that fosters keeping dependent EP at home, by means of the automated analysis of their activities.

CIRDO means in French "Compagnon Intelligent obéissant au Doigt et à l'Oeil", that is to say, a device that obeys your every word.

1.1 Presentation of the Technological Device CIRDO

The objective of CIRDO is to provide a relatively discreet technological prosthesis to solve the problem posed by the home-care of very elderly persons faced with the risk of falling.

Technically, the device is composed of a camera(s) and microphone(s) dispersed in the domestic space, and is based on the detection of human activities via video and audio sensors. For practical purposes, the sensors are exclusively located in the living room. The system evaluates in real time and independently (without external human intervention) abnormal, dangerous or risky (falls, immobility, calls for help, accidents) domestic situations and is able to automatically alert family or caregivers if necessary.

1.2 The Theoretical Framework

Defined as "the fact of unintentionally coming to rest on the ground or other lower level" [2], a fall entails a phenomenon that is difficult to comprehend. The studies by [3] show that the elderly underestimate the risks they face. The bias in this self-assessment may be due to a sense of superiority, optimism or the illusion of invulnerability. This denial can influence how the elderly perceive the usefulness and relevance of protection devices such as CIRDO. Findings from the study [12] carried out by INPES[2] show that fall risks are significant. Almost a quarter of people aged between 65 and 75 years old had fallen in the last twelve months prior to the study. These falls represent almost 80 % of everyday life accidents. They are involved in over 60 % of domestic accidents and are responsible for approximately 9300 deaths each year among persons aged 65 years and above. However, these data are generally underestimated as the elderly often forget that their falls [13]. Moreover, age, gender and health status can affect the type and severity of the fall [4]. Falling leads to limited

---

[1] ANR : (French) National Research Agency
CNSA : (French) National Solidarity Fund for Autonomy.

[2] National Institut of prevention and health education.

outings and increased isolation, and drives elderly people into a state of relative dependence. They are drawn into a dangerous spiral that makes it difficult for them to remain at home and increases the deleterious effects of aging [14].

However, these impairments are neither ineluctable nor irreversible if the elderly are in an environment that is safe and suitable for them and their relatives. This implies that a different perspective must be contemplated in the process of senescence among the elderly. The onset of disability does not reside in the individual alone. It also depends on the interaction between individuals and their environment and specifically, on the incompatibility between the living conditions of the environment and the needs of the vulnerable people. If the environment is not modified to adapt individuals with a "impairment", then they will be faced with an impediment. Such a situation would be non-existent if the environment was adapted to them [15, 16].

Two models can be distinguished in this perspective [17]. The first is the "integrative" model in which reducing disability involves working on the individual through rehabilitation or equipment. The second is a "participative" model where the environment compensates for an individual's shortcomings and therefore transforms the situation into a source of development and autonomy. Naturally, the CIRDO project falls within the second approach as it seeks to adapt the life environment to the risk situation of the dependent elderly. This pervasive technology seeks to transform a situation with obstacles into a suitable situation. We will now turn to this by analyzing the contributions of technology.

New ways in which aging can be supported and falls prevented are necessary to enable the elderly to maintain their autonomy and delay institutionalization. Possibilities opened up by gerontechnology suggest that innovative solutions to assist elderly persons exist. Besides maintenance, hospitalization at home and autonomy development, gerontechnology also aims at rehabilitating, attenuating some deficiencies [5, 6] and improving the quality of life of the elderly [7–9].

Pervasive assistive technologies are less intrusive than conventional systems of remote assistance or surveillance as they tend to blend into the living environment [1]. They are thus able to anticipate the users' needs using data from the environment and propose an appropriate solution [11]. Moreover, these technologies are less stigmatizing because they do not have to be worn, unlike remote surveillance bracelets known as "markers of old age" [12] which equate subjects to their shortcomings and to some form of weakness.

In the second part of this research, we assume from the theory of the Engeström system of activities [18], that the integration of CIRDO in elderly people system of life would not be trivial and would lead to a major reconfiguration of the system of activity (SoA) in presence, each registering as develops Engeström: (i) a community (composed of the elderly and their peer but also family carers, professional speakers), each (ii) rules universe (what to do or not do at home, tasks to do or delegate, safety instructions to follow …) and may be related to (iii) some division of work (who does what,, who intervenes when and with whom to help the elderly, to assist the cure).

Engeström has also identified three tension levels within these SoA and on which we can rely to better identify potential reconfigurations caused by the implementation of CIRDO : (i) tensions within each element of SoA; (ii) tensions between some elements of the SoA. (iii) tensions between different interacting SA (the EP, the family caregiver who crosses the professional caregivers system at home ….) (Fig. 1).

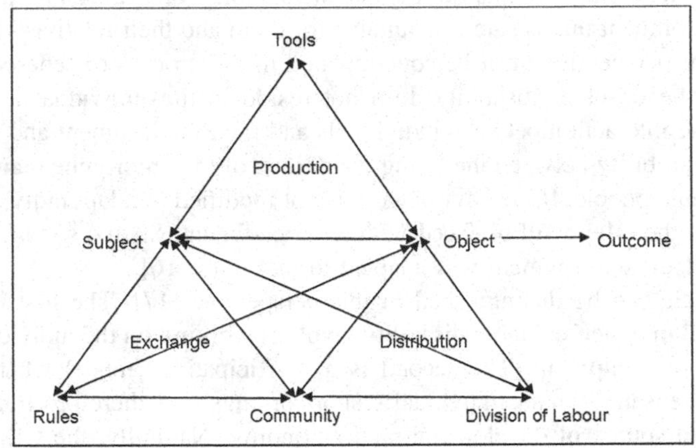

Fig. 1. Model of the activity systems (According to Engeström, 1987)

If these three tension levels have effects on the activities and the final acceptance of CIRDO, they nevertheless constitute the real source of the development of the SoA, based on its dynamic innovation and evolution.

Referring to the SoA for our prospective analyzes seems essential and allows us to direct the research problem on two levels of analysis:

- Firstly, in the domestic environment: we assume that the analysis of the activities of daily living (ADLs) -in elderly people and the associated risks (inventory situations falls) provides information essential for the design of the device, its methods of introduction in the domestic sphere and the adjustments to be made.
- Secondly, in terms of socio-domestic environment of the elderly: we seek to evaluate how the activity, as well as the forms and quality commitment of family carers and professionals can be disrupted by the introduction of the device. Indeed, on the basis of the AS model, it is expected that this may not necessarily be the same purposes of the system or the same practices that are perceived /expected by each player at home.

Ultimately, the tensions, the risk of non-convergence between activity systems should therefore be designed, worked so CIRDO can really fit in and be accepted by the various stakeholders.

To carry out this study, we developed a method, through a methodological triangulation approach: the first study aims to understand and model the processes of domestic falls, from a description of EP's daily activities. Finally, a second study explores the conditions of the system acceptance by the elderly, the family and the caregivers.

2 The Methodology Implemented

2.1 Approach to Understand Falls and Risk Factors for the Elderly, at Home

We have first interviewed 65 elderly people (average of 85 years old, 90 % women) to know their backgrounds and living conditions, in terms of autonomy, needs, isolation and social links with the environment. We also asked them to accurately describe a typical day. The critical incident method [19] was also used to identify the specific circumstances of incidents (causes, modalities) and their consequences.

Then, we focused on actual observations of risk situations. From these 65 elderly, we have selected six seniors with most representative falls descriptions. These people were able to physically and mentally replay their falls, filmed by "tripod" and "embedded" (subcam) cameras. After re-reading him or her the circumstances of the fall, we asked the person to re-act the scene and verbalize simultaneously what they did, said and felt when they fell. We also intervened (via interruptive verbalization) to ask them to specify actions, words or circumstances of the fall (What did you say at the time? What did you do once on the ground).

Finally, we asked them to comment the different scenes previously filmed, by consecutive verbalization.

2.2 Approach to Explore the Device Social Acceptance

In order to identify how each home-care stakeholder perceived CIRDO's contributions and potential risks from the perspective of its own activity system, we developed a methodology that enable us to have the richest and most varied data possible about these experiences.

We added to the first observations and interviews (with the elderly people), semi-structured interviews and focus groups that were conducted with home-care stakeholders (19 professional caregivers, nurses and 19 family members, from 19 years to 62 years, 80 % of women) to better understand their activity (*what they had to do, what they did, what they could not do /no longer do*), the difficulties to perform their activity, as well as the way they understood how their own activity is connected with the other stakeholders'. Finally, after presenting them the aims of CIRDO, we sought, through focus groups, to see how the device could become a resource or a constraint to their activities, including the issues that had been raised before. All these interviews lasted one hour on average and were conducted, whenever possible, either in the elderly people's homes (in a discrete secluded room), or in caregivers' professional organization. They were recorded and fully transcripted to facilitate subsequent analysis.

Based on these interviews, activity assays were performed on the more specific craft of professional home-caregivers. We have conducted an initial series of three field analyzes to better understand this activity and grasp the nature and diversity of tasks performed (operational /relational tasks, contacts with family, with others stakeholders…).

We also "monitored" the activity of two EP equipped with telecare devices (medallion and bracelet). They had to complete a self-reported grid of activities – for 7 days, from sunrise to sunset indicating nature, duration, difficulty, location and time of their domestic, relational and recreational activities. They also indicated the conditions of use of the remote alarm device. Ultimately, we asked them to comment each of these episodes. Finally, we resorted to another technique, the Wizard of Oz method, in order to evaluate the conditions of use of a CIRDO demonstrator. We presented it to 6 elderly persons in their homes. These were asked to simulate an incident (i.e. stuck on the couch with a blocked hip) and interact with a demonstrator that detected a hazardous situation (e.g. *"I detect an abnormal situation. Do you need help?"*). We developped this prototype in the form of a webcam and a microphone connected to a computer. Prerecorded alert sentences were triggered by the researcher, based on the EP's behaviors and calls. This approach has enabled us to evaluate users' reactions in almost real situations

3 Results

3.1 Understand and Specify the Process of Falls

This study aimed at understanding the falling process (by analyzing daily activities within elderly people's homes), in order to:

- identify the different nature of Activity of Daily Living,
- define the different falling profiles
- identify the factors involved
- develop falling scenarios to set parameters and test CIRDO (for further analyses in the second study)

All these objectives aim to gather data for adjusting all the parameters of the device, both videos and audios.

In fact, we were able, using behavioral (key postures) and verbal (key words) descriptors to define much more parameters of automatic detection of falls by the CIRDO system.

The factors involved in understanding ADL and the risks faced by the elderly.

The first part of the study consisted in identifying the different activities of daily living to determine how these situations could turn into a fall. We analyzed the factors that could transform an activity that a priori was normal, into an abnormal and dangerous situation. The analysis enabled us to identify 8 major ADL groups that individuals perform over the course of their day: household activities, food, recreation, rest, mobility, care and hygiene, communication and health. Carrying out these domestic activities requires the mobilization of two types of resources: intrinsic (dispositional) and extrinsic (situational). While intrinsic resources involve the specific characteristics of the elderly, extrinsic resources refer to what the environment provides to enable an individual to achieve a given objective. The interaction between these two conditions defines the context in which the action takes place.

ADL can become "risky" if at least one of these two conditions is absent. This is notably the case when internal functions (motor, perceptual…) of the elderly fail due to a natural (generalized fatigue, hip problems) and/or provoked (taking sleeping pills) weakness. This is what happened, for instance, to one person we studied, a 83 years old woman who fell in her kitchen. Conscious but unable to alert her relatives or trigger the remote alarm device that was in her bedroom, she remained immobilized for close to 36 h. It is her cleaning lady who finally found her. "*At home, I had taken my sleeping pills and I was taking my juice bottle to the fridge. I was wearing my nightgown then as I approached the kitchen door, I felt myself slip; I said 'oh, you're falling'. I felt my head explode as it touched the ground. I didn't quite feel my leg at the time. I felt, but later when I wanted to move it, I suffered too much. I couldn't turn, I couldn't go anywhere, the phone was close by, it was in the entrance hall and so was I…*".

The physical resources of the situation can also be limited (insufficient lighting) or inappropriate (dented carpets, high stairs) and can thus be dangerous. These resources thus become obstacles to the normal carrying out of activities and create a second example of risk situations as the case of our 89-year-old woman who fell in her kitchen shows. After her slipper caught on a screw protruding from the parquet floor, she remained on the floor for a long time, stunned, before managing to get up after several attempts: "*I caught on something. There was something protruding, a screw. Incidentally, it's still slightly protruding because it was fixed askew. So I was eating there, I had my tray and as I was passing, I had soles with laces, so the tip of the sole caught, and I found myself lying down, I glided against the doorpost*".

Moreover, the social circumstances that include individuals' trajectories and the experiences of the elderly persons and their entourage can also have an impact on falling. They can condition risk taking or on the contrary, restrict it. Consequently, if a fall is experienced or shared with a third party, some elderly persons can implement strategies to avoid or prevent falling. This was the case of an 88 years old woman who got rid of all visible cables in her home following a friend's accident.

Accidents can also occur due to non-compliance with the allocation of chores at home. The elderly person takes the task of the absent professional helper, exposing him or herself to risk. This was the case with a 78-year-old woman who decided to move the plants in her living room because her helper was late; she got knocked out against the edge of her fireplace.

Finally, elements in one's personal and social history can also increase the risk of accidents as the following example shows. An 80-year-old woman who wanted to clear the table got her foot caught in the stairs leading to her bay window and fell, cracking a rib. As she mentioned in the description of her story, she could have let go of the plates she was carrying in order to recover her balance. However, she preferred to protect the plates as "*they were part of the family history, passed down from generation to generation*". This fall thus stemmed from situational circumstances (stairs too high, pile of plates reducing mobility), dispositional conditions (reduced motor skills, lack of attention linked to fatigue) and social circumstances (do everything to preserve family assets). Here, social data took precedence over the woman's own safety and protection.

The comparative analysis of 28 falling situations (selected based on spatial and social criteria: see method) revealed three broad categories of falls: Falling (flopping onto the ground from a static posture, whether standing or lying on a couch), slipping (loss of balance as one is moving) and stumbling (loss of verticality induced by stumbling on an obstacle – a cane, carpet or stairs).

Falls primarily occurred in the living room (13 falls), as this is where various activities were centralized (meals, rest, recreation, relaxation, telephone). Frequent actions and displacements also took place in this room. Other falls (7) occurred in transitional spaces (corridors, stairs or the door between the living room and kitchen or balcony) that had to be crossed and required mobility. This confirms the fact to evaluate CIRDO only in living rooms. The "falling" situations account for more than half of risky situations (57 %). Slipping (17) and stumbling (19) are quit equal. These results provide some interesting insight into the kind of falls that we have to analyze and formalize to allow CIRDO to detect them.

Situational conditions were the most common factors responsible for falls (19 implications). Only 8 cases were related to personal weaknesses. These results suggest that accidents are more the result of the inadequacy of the environment than individual weaknesses. Respondents spoke of their behavior and their level of consciousness after the accident. In 13 of the cases reported, the elderly people were quite conscious and active. They crawled, attempted to get up, cling onto furniture or call for help. In such a context, CIRDO would be able to identify this behavior and engage in dialogue with the person in need (via a microphone). In 5 cases, the elderly persons were rather inert and unconscious. This would entail visual detection and a CIRDO diagnosis with an automated alert. Finally, in 11 situations, the people were able to immediately get up without any specific repercussions or traumatism. In this case, CIRDO would be able to detect that the fall had no harmful effects on the person and/or make the person orally validate that he or she is ok.

Based on the falling simulations by the 6 subjects, we were able to develop 12 scenarios of falls according to the Personas method. On one hand, we described the conditions of the fall, (the person's characteristics, the activity performed, the location, the circumstances of the fall…) on the other hand, the modalities of the fall. We paid particular attention to the different limbs mobilized in the fall (upper/lower limbs), the direction and the magnitude of each movement (arm lifted upwards/downwards, body to the right/left…), the speed (speed and direction of the body), the elderly person's reaction while on the ground (trying to get up, crawling…) and the approximate time of (in)action (duration immobilized on the ground). Phrases of alarm were also identified at different moments of the fall "*Damn, what's happening to me, Oh no…*). For example, this is the scenario of falls using the Personas method (brief):

> *"She gets up in the middle of the night to drink a glass of water in the kitchen. She is walking in the dark when suddenly her foot slips on the floor. She loses her balance and her whole body swings backward. She exclaims "ouaahhhhhhh!!!" Her body bends to the right side. First her right knee hits the ground forcefully, then her whole body. She finds herself on her back, arms extended behind her head."*

These scenarios were used for two types of application. Using falling scripts, the first scenario sought to provide specific details on the different actions and postures that lead to falls. We defined this as "key postures". We also identified the "key words" spoken. The designers used these indicators to calibrate CIRDO's video and audio sensors. All these descriptors are clues which enable the camera and microphone to identify and distinguish fall situations from normal behavior.

The second application was used to replay the scenarios with 22 voluntary actors including the elderly and younger voluntary adults equipped with an old age simulator. This device hampers mobility and reduces vision and hearing when worn.

The simulations were conducted on an experimental platform similar to a living-lab (the Domus platform at the *Université de Grenoble*). Equipped with audio and video sensors and a two-way mirror, this room was configured to resemble an independent living community. We were thus able to reconstruct the scenes of incidents by adapting the living environment to the different scenarios that we sought to simulate (dented carpet, falling from a sofa…). The purpose of these experiments was also to test the first version of the CIRDO demonstrator in order to improve the parameters of detection and validate the detection algorithms.

3.2 Acceptance of the Device by the Elderly and Their Social Environment

The reading grid offered by Engeström's system of activity has shown an ambivalent positioning by these different actors: based on their experiences, their career and needs, each of them (elderly, professional counselors, family) has a different view of the object of their activity (support, help, care, prevention, control), and therefore has specific expectations and fears (Fig. 2).

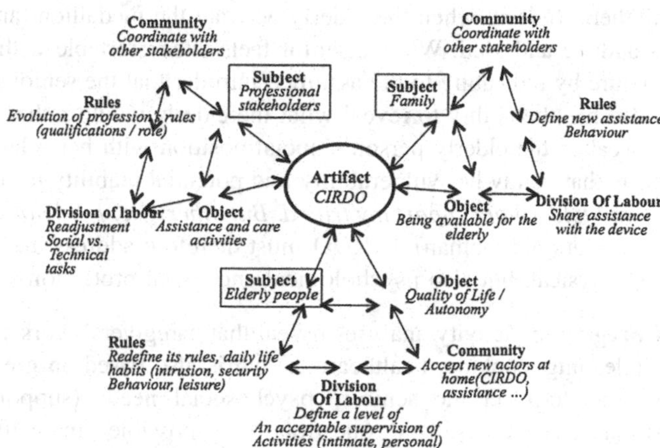

Fig. 2. Model of the activity systems integrating these different actors (According to the Engeström's Model, 1987).

The Seniors: Self-activity statements made on the use of remote alarm systems by EP indicate contrasted positions for the seniors.

First, the remote alarm system can be used according to a subjective estimation of risk: in that, it becomes dangerous because the elderly could put themself in danger more often for there is a device ready to ask for help. In this context, CIRDO would provide a continuous and discrete supervision, able to overcome the erroneous judgments associated with risk taking.

On the contrary, the elderly could feel less freedom at home, and would do nothing in order not to trigger the alarm. This assessment itself is not risk-free, as falling is unpredictable. Even though the senior does everything to not fall, once more, the device doesn't prevent from falling.

In a second case, the elderly is extremely dependent on the medallion and cannot do anything without wearing the system. Here, the discretion and non-intrusiveness of an ambient environment like CIRDO may paradoxically cause rejection, because people would feel insufficiently protected. How can the senior know that the device is still on and be sure that his family will be aware of what would happen?

Simulated uses of CIRDO with the Wizard of Oz method also indicate seniors' fear to make their homes more accessible and losing control in case of accident; particularly: who to warn after a fall? Who should be involved and how? Indeed, these Seniors are alone and not only dread an internal domestic risk (falls and accidents), but also fear outside intrusion (thieves, salesmen) *"Firefighters, well, er, they will break down the door, won't they? What will they do? I don't want to have my door broken!"* or *"If they (firefighters) break down the door and they take me away, I cannot just leave my house opened to intruders* "The new device may forces the elderly person to redefine compromises about security, domestic and protection priorities.

But, on the other hand, from experiences with their devices and experiences, such as medallion, seniors have described new potential uses of the devices. For example, the devices can be a new way to prevent themselves from intruders or discourage the latter to "harm" them. Indeed, when the elderly activate the medallion, an agent calls the elderly: it's audible and loud. When a senior feels uncomfortable with a situation, this call can reassure by indicating to the assumed intruder that the senior is not alone.

Because it also has the ability to reveal what the elderly would rather keep secret, the system can weaken the elderly person's social position with her relatives. It may provide them facts that betray her vulnerability and potential inability to live alone. *"I fell in the street and told no-one, apart my friend. But otherwise, I did not say anything to my family."* (86years old woman). CIRDO must therefore address the challenge of securing seniors' physical, but also psychological and social protections.

Professional Caregivers: Activity analyses reveal that caregivers' work is to perform technical tasks (cleaning, cooking, healthcare…) but is also based on great emotional and relational work to meet the seniors' psychosocial needs (support, listening, attention, assistance…). Caregivers question the possible intensification and re-engineering risks of their activity, with the new system. They imagine their work being supervised by it, forcing them to make a choice between technical tasks (the prescribed tasks of the job, the Cure), and the empathic accompaniment of people (the actual service activity, the Care). They also fear a reduced scope of action (a system substitution for regular visits or diagnoses).

Coordination appears to be essential to face the multiplicity of professionals and the scattering of their interventions over time. In this context, CIRDO could have an important role to play in providing a digital liaison diary role by facilitating and enhancing cooperation, ensuring the best possible articulation and continuity of the care process.

Our interviews and focus group also show that CIRDO creates an ambivalent feeling among caregivers: stakeholders assume CIRDO will allow better recognition of their activity by making its reality, complexity and difficulty more visible to the eyes of the family or their own managers. It could also protect them from their "client's" abusive behavior as much as by their own corporation.

In contrast, the CIRDO project could help raise the status of the home help profession. These stakeholders may well contribute to setting the system more finely during its implementation, thanks to their intimate knowledge of EP's habits, risks and practices (e.g. which types of video and /or audio-sensors to install, in which room and at which angle). Likewise, they could be more involved in the definition of the digital liaison notebook: its nature, function and recipient(s). In addition to using their expertise, these professionals can also develop upstream an essential mediating function to get EP and families to accept the device.

Thus, these inputs would contribute significantly to repositioning this exchange, through enriching and expanding their activities (system setup, support to change, usage tips, besides mere operational tasks). But that would require a parallel rise in qualifications and training.

Analysis of the Conditions of the Acceptance of CIRDO by the Family. Notwithstanding its so-called "natural" feature, aid is time-consuming for many, or even, for some, a serious burden because some of the providers could themselves be resorting to such support (some "children" are 65 years old, indeed).

Families deem CIRDO as a potential "competitor": automatic alarm triggering deprives caregivers of their ability to assess the severity of the incident and the adequate alert level that should ensue. They also feel guilty of not being constantly present to assist, support or reassure their loved ones. These concerns can also be interpreted as the fear of being replaced by these devices, even though the caregiver system would not be changed and /or altered by the introduction of CIRDO.

CIRDO would be useful to caregivers by constantly watching over EP and release caregivers of their perpetual burden. Seen as prosthesis, it would reassure everyone, family and relatives. In this sense, CIRDO might well meet one of family caregivers' needs: to be protected from their own failure to be present and intervene.

4 Conclusion

The purpose of the article was double. We have shown how psychology can help and lead the design of a new pervasive technology, by scrutinizing the causes and consequences of falls and by exploring the social acceptance of the elderly system of life.

The approach we used presented first, daily life activities and falls at home, and secondly how each home stakeholder considers the impact of this new device on their respective trade systems and between them.

We have shown that, depending on their experience, backgrounds and needs, each stakeholder in the home (EP, professional help and family) has a different vision of the purpose of their activities (support, help, care, prevention, control…) and therefore has specific expectations and fears vis-à-vis the system. The function and purpose of the latter are (implicitly) heterogeneous since various stakeholders interpret them differently. Their perceptions may be partial, conflicting, or partially contradictory [20]. The whole difficulty in CIRDO design and implementation is a matter of adjusting to a socio-domestic system that is different every time, given (i) the diversity of EP's at risk activities [21], and (ii) the differing interests of the various stakeholders. The latter also turn out to be powerful mediators in the eventual use and adoption of the system.

References

1. Bobillier-Chaumon, M.-E., Ciobanu, R.: Les nouvelles technologies au service des personnes âgées: entre promesses et interrogations. Psychologie Française **54**(3), 271–285 (2009)
2. Gaucher, J., Ribes, G.: Étude Altivis : analyse de données. Paris : Institut Silver Life. Retrieved from www.silverlife-institute.com/upload/etude_altivis_1182436620.pdf (2006)
3. Ballinger, C., Payne, S.: The construction of the risk of falling, among and by older people. Ageing Soc. **22**(3), 305–321 (2002)
4. Todd, C.J., Ballinger, C., Whitehead, S.: A Global Report on Falls Prevention: Reviews of Socio-Demographic Factors Related to Falls and Environmental Interventions to Prevent Falls Amongst Older People Living in the Community. World Health Organization, Geneva (2007)
5. Buiza, C., Soldatos, J., Petsatodis, T., Geven, A., Etxaniz, A., Tscheligi, M., et al.: *Pervasive computing and cognitive training for ageing well*. Hermes. **5518**, 756–763 (2009). doi:10.1007/978-3-642-02481-8
6. Hage, B.: Bridging the digital divide: the impact of computer training, internet and e-mail use on levels of cognition, depression, and social functioning in older adults. Gerontechnology **7**(2), 118 (2008). doi:10.4017/gt.2008.07.02.054.00
7. Bronswijk, J.E.M.H., van Bouma, H., Fozard, J.L.: Technology for quality of life: an enriched taxonomy. Gerontechnology **2**(2), 169–172 (2002). doi:10.4017/gt.2002.02.02.000.00
8. Blaschke, C.M., Freddolino, P.P., Mullen, E.: Ageing and technology: a review of the research literature. British J. Soc. Work **39**(4), 641–656 (2009)
9. Bobillier-Chaumon, M.-E., Michel, C., Tarpin-Bernard, F., Croisille, B.: Can ICT improve the quality of life of very mature adults living in residential home care units? from actual impacts to hidden artifacts. Behav. Inf. Technol. 33(6), 574-590. (2013). http://www.tandfonline.com/doi/abs/10.1080/0144929X.2013.832382#.UpIOneJEmsM
10. Gaver, B., Strong, R.: Feather, scent and shaker: supporting simple intimacy. *In: Proceedings. of the Extended Abstract of the Conference. on CSCW*. ACM, Cambridge, USA (1996)
11. Caradec, V.: Vieillissement et usage des technologies. Une Perspective Identitaire et Relationnelle. Réseaux **96**, 45–95 (1999)
12. Institut National de Prévention et d'Education pour la Santé. Mieux Prévenir les chutes chez les personnes âgées. La Santé de L'homme.; 381: 22-29. (2006)
13. Cummings, S.R.N.M., Nevitt, M.C., Kidd, S.: Forgetting falls. the limited accuracy of recall of falls in the elderly. J. Am. Geriatr. Soc. **36**(7), 613–616 (1988)
14. Fontaine, R., Pennequin, V.: De la vieillesse optimale à la vieillesse réussie. Psychologie Française. **42**(4), 345–353 (1997)

15. Vanderheiden, G.C.: Design for people with functional limitations resulting from disability, aging, and circumstance. In: Salvendy, G. (ed.) Handbook of Human Factors and Ergonomics, pp. 2010–2052. John Wiley & Sons, New York (1997)
16. Newel, A.F, Gregor, P.: User sensitive inclusive design. In: Actes du colloque Interaction Homme Machine & Assistance, Metz, France. (2001)
17. Ebsersold, S.: Le champ du handicap, ses enjeux et ses mutations : du désavantage à la participation sociale. Handicap. **94–95**, 149–164 (2002)
18. Engeström, Y. *Learning by expanding : an activity-theoretical approach to developmental research*. Helsinky, Orienta-Konsultit (1987)
19. Flanagan, J.: The critical incident. Psychol. Bull. **51**, 327–358 (1954)
20. Otjacques, B., Krier, M., Feltz, F., Ferring, D., Hoffmann, M.: Designing for older people: a case study in a retirement home. In: Leitner, G., Hitz, M., Holzinger, A. (eds.) USAB 2010. LNCS, vol. 6389, pp. 177–194. Springer, Heidelberg (2010)
21. Rowe, J.: Fall prevention: core characteristics and practical interventions. Home Health Care Manage. Pract. **23**(1), 20–26 (2010)

The Wearable Multimodal Monitoring System: A Platform to Study Falls and Near-Falls in the Real-World

Tracy Jill Doty[1(✉)], Bret Kellihan[2], Tzyy-Ping Jung[3], John K. Zao[4], and Irene Litvan[5]

[1] Center for Military Psychiatry and Neuroscience Research, Walter Reed Army Institute of Research, Silver Spring, MD 20902, USA
tracy.j.doty2.ctr@mail.mil

[2] Research Engineering and Support Branch, DCS Corporation, Alexandria, VA 22310, USA
bkellihan@dcscorp.com

[3] Swartz Center for Computational Neuroscience, Institute for Neural Computation, University of California at San Diego, La Jolla, CA 92093, USA
jung@sccn.ucsd.edu

[4] Department of Computer Science, National Chiao Tung University, Hsinchu, Taiwan
jkzao@pet.cs.nctu.edu.tw

[5] Movement Disorders Center, University of California at San Diego, La Jolla, CA 92093, USA
ilitvan@ucsd.edu

Abstract. Falls are particularly detrimental and prevalent in the aging population. To diagnose the cause of a fall current medical practice relies on expensive hospital admissions with many bulky devices that only provide limited diagnostic information. By utilizing the latest wearable technology, the Wearable Multimodal Monitoring System (WMMS) presented here offers a better solution to the problem of fall diagnostics and has the potential to predict these falls in real-time in order to prevent falls or, at least, mitigate their severity. This highly integrated system has been designed for real-life long-term monitoring of movement disorder patients. It contains multiple wearable and wireless biosensors that simultaneously and continuously monitor cardiovascular, autonomic, motor, and electroencephalographic (EEG) activity, in addition to receiving critical patient feedback about symptoms. Initial pilot data show that the system is comfortable and easy to use, and provides high quality data streams capable of detecting near-falls and other motor disturbances.

Keywords: Wireless electroencephalography · Skin conductance response · Electrodermal activation · Heart-rate variability · Blood pressure · Wearability · Fall prediction

1 Introduction

One in three adults aged 65 and older fall each year [1]. Older adults are hospitalized for fall-related injuries five times more often than they are for injuries from other causes [2]. With the population aging, the number of falls and the related costs will increase.

J. Zhou and G. Salvendy (Eds.): ITAP 2015, Part II, LNCS 9194, pp. 412–422, 2015.
DOI: 10.1007/978-3-319-20913-5_38

Falls are more frequent in patients with advanced Parkinson's disease (PD) and they occur at even earlier stages and more frequently in patients with atypical parkinsonian disorders [3–5]. About half of PD patients who fall will require medical care for fall-related injuries, and many never recover to their pre-fall motor and independence baseline [4, 6].

Current medical practice for diagnosing falls relies on expensive hospital admissions to determine if cardiologic, blood pressure, balance, gait, or seizure disturbances caused a fall. Patients are connected for short periods to bulky, single-function devices that can provide only limited diagnostic information as this information is confined to the hospital setting after a fall has occurred. Currently, advanced technologies may allow using inexpensive and wearable multisensor devices on outpatients to determine the causes of their near-falls and falls as well as collect other critical diagnostic information in a daily life setting.

Only recently has technology evolved to allow scientists to continuously record multiple data streams from the body in everyday life in a comfortable and unobtrusive way. This technology has been used for real-world applications such as stress monitoring [7], as well as gait and vital sign assessment and fall detection (see review [8]). The Wearable Multimodal Monitoring System (WMMS) improves upon previous technology by integrating and synchronizing multiple data streams in real-time while also recording valuable patient feedback via a smartphone. The system is an extension of on-going work to build a Multi-Aspect Real-world Integrated Neuroimaging (MARIN) system to study stress [9, 10]. The WMMS takes advantage of the original MARIN system architecture by utilizing some of the same devices, and also includes new devices and mobile applications specifically engineered for the study of falls in movement disorder patients. Our multimodal monitoring system is aimed to diagnose the causes of falls and near-falls so appropriate treatments can be undertaken to prevent subsequent occurrences.

2 The Wearable Multimodal Monitoring System (WMMS)

The Wearable Multimodal Monitoring System (WMMS) is a highly integrated system designed for real-life long-term monitoring of patients susceptible to falls. It uses several state-of-the-art microelectronics and communication technologies in a mobile, wireless data collection and computing platform with multiple, wearable biosensors that simultaneously and continuously monitor cardiovascular, autonomic, motor, and neurological activity in the daily life environment. We chose these modalities as they can capture the most common causes of intrinsic falls unrelated to accidents. In addition, the system requests and receives critical patient feedback about symptoms and other outcome measures. It is envisioned that the data collected by this system will be suitable for the creation of algorithms that can go beyond diagnosis, to the prediction of falls. These algorithms could then be implemented in next-generation systems to alert the patient when conditions and behaviors exist that increase their risk of falling.

2.1 Components

Peripheral Monitoring Devices. The WMMS contains five commercially available devices (Fig. 1). (1) The Zephyr Bioharness 3 is a chest band that is capable of monitoring heart rate, EKG/R-R intervals, respiration rate, posture, and 3-axis accelerations. The data will allow us to determine whether abnormal heart rhythms or heart ischemia cause patient symptoms (lightheadedness or syncope) and/or falls. (2) The Empatica E3 is a small wrist-worn device containing a 3-axis accelerometer and optical temperature sensor, as well as an electrodermal activity sensor and a photoplethysmography sensor, which measure physiological arousal that will be used to determine autonomic disturbances. (3) The MINDO 4-channel wireless EEG Headset is a 4-channel wireless EEG monitoring system equipped with dry electrodes to monitor syncope-related decrease or seizure-related increase in brain activity. The headset can provide up to 256 samples per second from each EEG channel. (4) The BodyDyn 10-DOF Wireless Body Motion and Posture Monitor is the prototype of a wearable body motion and posture monitoring system that will be used to determine if gait disturbances are the possible cause of a fall or near-fall. It will be also used to determine whether motor disturbances such as tremors, dyskinesias, dystonia and freezing are possible causes of falls and near-falls. Each device can provide up to 100 samples per second of 3D linear accelerations data points, 3D angular acceleration data points, 3D magnetic flux, and barometric pressure. These small, unobtrusive sensors will be affixed to clothing or other devices at locations including the wrists, chest, waist, back, and ankles. While the four devices outlined above stream data wirelessly to the smartphone in real-time, (5) the HealthStats BPro ABPM Watch records data locally and those data are then added to the other datastreams post hoc. The BPro is an ambulatory blood pressure monitoring (ABPM) system in the form of a wristwatch used to measure blood pressure (BP) and heart rate (HR) and to determine whether drops in BP or HR can cause falls and near-falls (orthostatic hypotension). It uses modified applanation tonometry to measure the pressure pulses detected at the radial artery in the wrist every 5 to 15 min.

Handheld Electronic Device. An Android smartphone serves both as the data hub for the sensors and the graphic user interface for the patient. The WMMS uses several Android-based applications. The main widget provides an event monitoring panel which allows the patient to log notes for salient events and answer related questions. Additionally, the WMMS includes three interactive applications designed to assess symptom severity and a suite of inventories that gauges non-motor functions (i.e., mood).

Event Monitoring Panel. The event monitoring panel is a widget that is available to the patient when the phone is turned on. It includes six different buttons that the patient can select to log salient events (right center of Fig. 1): falls and near-falls, medication, loss of consciousness, meals, dizziness, and tremors or dyskinesias. When selecting a button, the patient is directed to answer questions about the event. Each button follows a pathway of questions designed by clinicians to capture important associated information in a uniform way. This information will be helpful in the development of fall prediction algorithms, because it provides subjective information that adds context to the continuous physiological data streams.

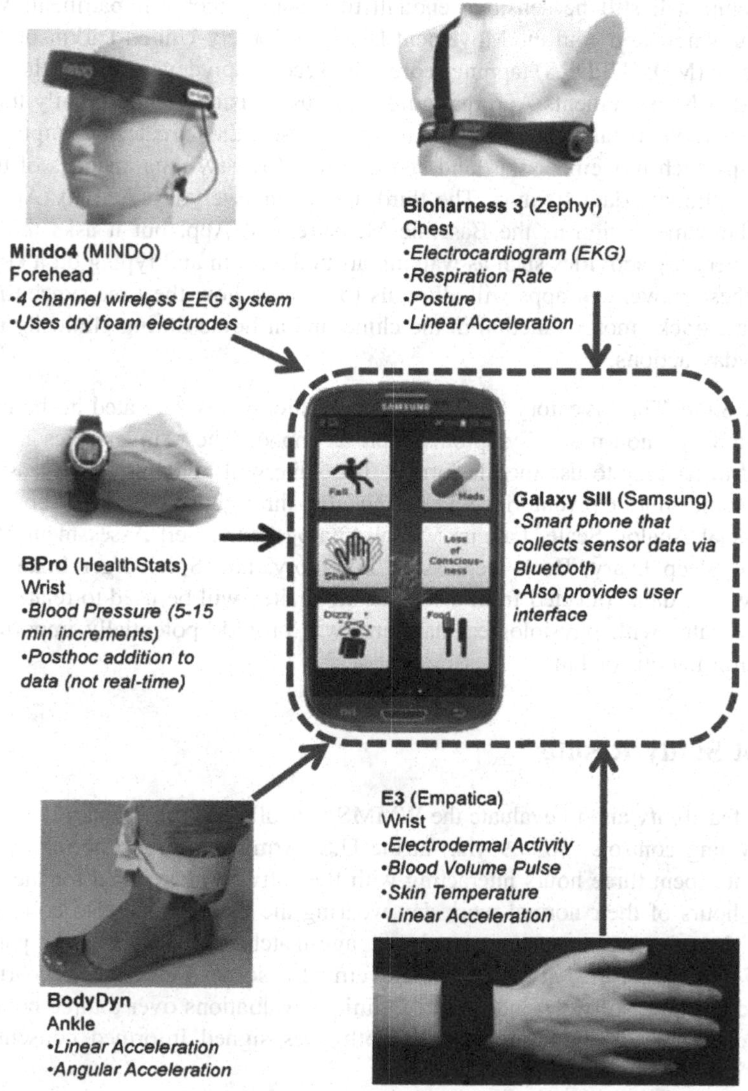

Fig. 1. The Wearable Multimodal Monitoring System (WMMS)

Applications. In order to collect data about symptoms throughout the day, we have developed three interactive apps that can be easily accessed by the patient. The first app is our mobile version of a force transducer based tapping task. The parameters replicate those of a study of Huntington's Disease patients where outcome measures (variability of tapping intervals and tap frequency) were found to be sensitive enough to distinguish between carriers (pre-manifest) and age-matched healthy controls [11]. This task has also been performed with PD patients with success [12]. The task is performed via a touch screen and does not utilize a force transducer; however, we expect that this mobile setup will still be sensitive enough to quantify motor impairment. We will compare this new app with the Movement Disorder Society-United Parkinson Disease Rating Scale (MDS-UPDRS) tapping score. The second app developed for the WMMS is a Baseline Measurements App that guides the user visually and verbally through a series of movements taken from clinical motor scales. It then creates an output file that time stamps each movement start and end to allow for easy data analysis of the time synced multimodal data streams. The third app is an Everyday Activity App which follows the same design as the Baseline Measurement App, but it asks the user to perform everyday activities such as walking around a room and typing on a keyboard. Both of these movement apps will allow us to explore how the time-synced multimodality data tracks motor function in the clinic and at home during clinically relevant and everyday actions.

Inventory Suite. The Inventory Suite contains questionnaires validated in the literature for the study of non-motor symptoms such as mood. These inventories have been translated to an easy to use mobile format. The suite will be deployed at least once a day, but some shorter inventories will be repeated throughout the day. It contains the Stress Visual Analog Scale, Fatigue Visual Analog Scale, Self-Assessment Manikin, Pittsburgh Sleep Diary, Beck Depression Inventory, and Spielberger State Anxiety Inventory. The data collected from these questionnaires will be used to relate different perceived states with physiological data and will provide potentially important predictive information for falls.

3 Pilot Study Results

To show feasibility and to evaluate the WMMS we collected preliminary data from six healthy young controls (36 ± 9 yrs.) at the U.S. Army Research Laboratory (ARL). Participants spent three hours interacting with the software developed for the WMMS and four hours of their normal work day wearing the system. We also collected preliminary data from three patients and one age-matched healthy control participant (65.2 ± 7.6 yrs.) recruited at the UCSD Movement Disorder Center. These participants interacted with the software and received clinical evaluations over a three hour period under close supervision. Participants at both sites signed informed consent before entering into the study.

3.1 Comfort Ratings/Ease of Use

To determine ease of use we employed the well-established Visual Analog Scale (VAS) [13, 14] to assess comfort of the whole system and of individual sensors separately. The Android handheld device calculated a number from 0-100 corresponding to the location of the cursor as placed on the line by the participant. The three patients and one age-matched control at UCSD rated the WMMS at 90 ± 7 % of the perceived comfort visual analog scale (PC-VAS), and this rating did not after three hours of wear (Fig. 2). Healthy young adults at ARL rated the system initially as less comfortable (75 ± 12 % of the PC-VAS; compared to patients), but these ratings also did not change over seven hours of wear. These preliminary results indicate that the system's high comfort level was maintained even while being worn over extended durations. All pilot users were asked if the system was comfortable upon first placement, and all users replied that the system was comfortable. Therefore, we believe that healthy adults and patients have different thresholds for comfort that is in turn reflected in different initial PC-VAS ratings. All participants also reported that the WMMS was esthetically acceptable, unobtrusive, and easy to use.

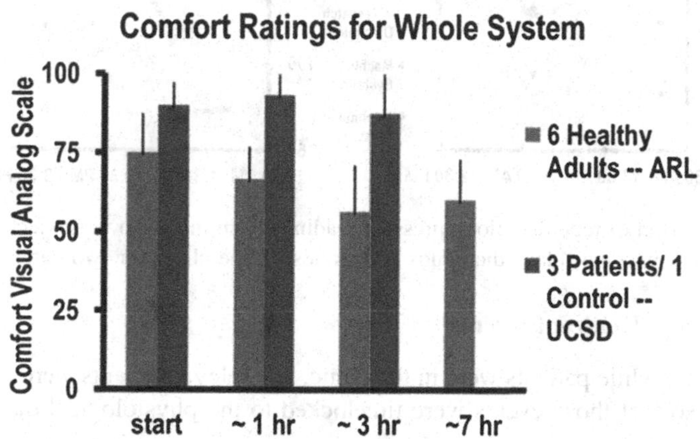

Fig. 2. Comfort Ratings (from the PC-VAS) at intervals during the pilot study

3.2 Quality of WMMS Data Compared to Medical Instruments

One of the goals of the pilot study held in the clinic was to compare the quality of data collected from the WMMS to data collected from gold-standard medical instruments.

Heart Rate and Rhythm. There were no substantial differences between the EKG readings (heart rate, rhythm, and waves) from the Bioharness and the EKG machine (Illustrated in Fig. 3 for two patients).

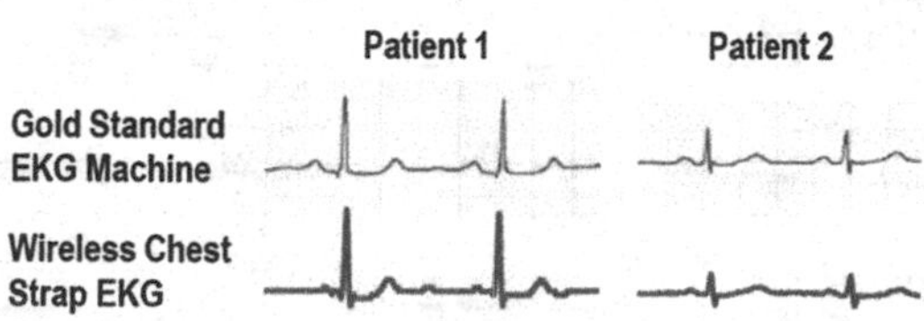

Fig. 3. Comparison of simultaneously recorded EKG traces from the standard wired EKG machine and the wireless chest strap (i.e. the Bioharness) of the WMMS.

Blood Pressure. Figure 4 shows an example of the BPs obtained from the WMMS and a standard cuff BP machine for two patients. While the BP fluctuated throughout the day, the blood pressure taken by the machine at intermittent intervals (three times for

Patient 1 and twice for Patient 2) was very close to the reading given by the wristwatch device (i.e. the BPro). It is important to note that the starting value for both devices is the same because the wristwatch requires an initial calibration value from the blood pressure machine.

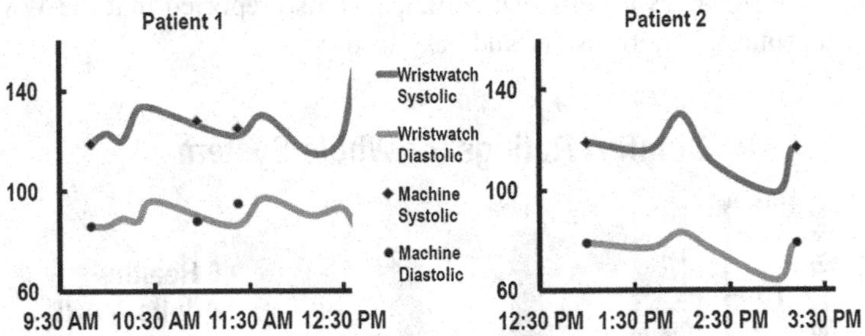

Fig. 4. Comparison of recorded blood pressure readings from the BPro wristwatch (solid lines) and the standard machine (black diamonds and circles) in the clinic for two patients.

3.3 Capturing Relevant Events

During the time while patients were in the clinic, any relevant events were noted on the smartphone, so that those events were timelocked to the physiological data streams.

Tremor. During the pilot study in the clinic one patient displayed behavior that was identified clinically as tremor at rest typically observed in parkinsonism. The accelerometer outputs (from three devices) that corresponded to this time period can be found in Fig. 5 (right panel). Compared to normal movement without tremor (left panel), the tremor is shown by the regular oscillation in the leg and hand in contrast to normal movement patterns where acceleration increases and decreases without an oscillation pattern.

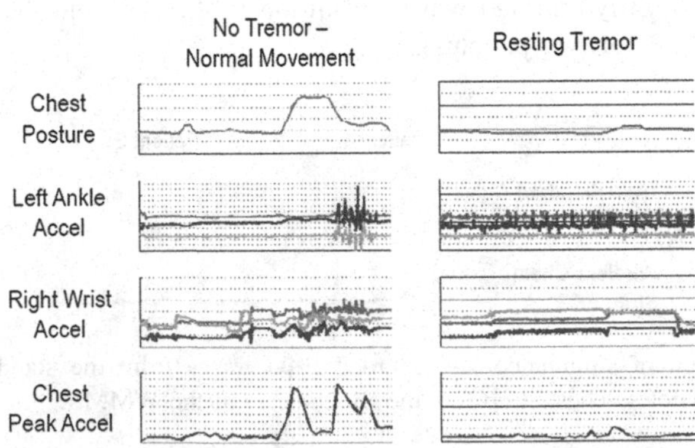

Fig. 5. Accelerometer data streams for one patient during normal movement with no tremor (left panel) and a resting tremor (right panel).

Near-fall. One patient experienced two near-falls due to balance impairment, and these events were captured in the multimodal data stream. Figure 6 compares the accelerometer streams for one of the near-falls (left panel) with the same ten second time period where the patient sat down and stood back up again according to instructions in the Baseline Measurements App (right panel). The near-fall created a large but brief increase in peak acceleration values from the chest sensor (where the patient sat down abruptly to catch the fall). This brief but sharp increase is not seen when the patient sits down and stands up normally. These data demonstrate that the WMMS can distinguish between different types of actions, including distinguishing falls and near-falls from normal actions. Moreover, the lack of simultaneous or preceding EKG and blood pressure abnormalities (not shown) excluded the cardiovascular and autonomic systems as potential causes for the near-fall and pointed to postural instability as a cause of this near-fall.

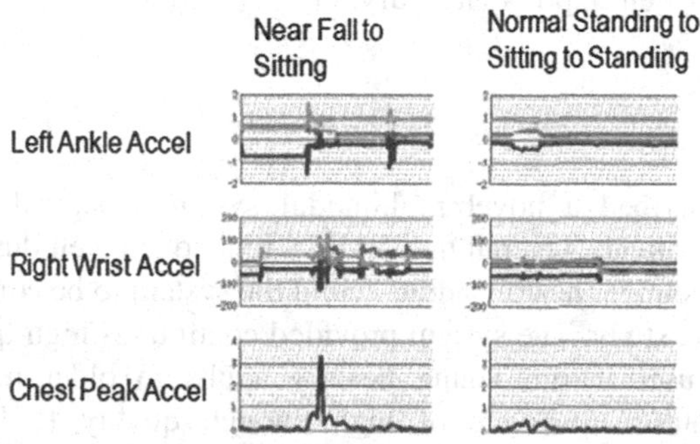

Fig. 6. Accelerometer data streams for one patient during a near-fall to sitting (left panel) and during normal standing to sitting (right panel).

4 Fall Prediction Algorithm Development

Successful fall detection algorithms have been developed using acceleration data collected from various parts of the body utilizing techniques such as less sensitive simple threshold based algorithms [15] or more complex and precise machine learning algorithms [16] including the use of Bayesian models [17]. While a wide literature has established that basic fall detection is a relatively simple process requiring only acceleration data from a few sites on the body, fall prediction algorithms have not yet been attempted on real-world data. Moreover, to our knowledge diagnosing the multiple causes for a fall has not been attempted. The WMMS offers an integrated view as it will utilize real-world continuous multimodal data streams collected on healthy controls and fall-prone subjects to begin to build prediction profiles for the various causes of falls. These profiles could be used for the prediction and intervention of falls in this population and the ageing population at large. We will use the recently validated definition of near-falls by Maidan et al. [18]: A stumble event or loss of balance that would result in a fall if sufficient recovery mechanisms were not activated. At least two of the following mechanisms should be activated to be determined as a near-fall:

(1) unplanned movement of arms or/and legs; (2) unplanned change in stride length, (3) lowering of the center of mass, (4) unplanned change in stride velocity and (5) trunk tilt.

Once fall and near-fall events are identified via user input and/or basic fall detection algorithms, we will then utilize the rich multimodal dataset (including those data obtained through the pathways, questionnaires, and motor apps) to probe for which preceding features are predictive of falls. We will do this by applying recent ground-breaking machine learning techniques [19–23] to these multimodal data streams. Techniques include but are not limited to fuzzy logic [24] and Bayesian probability models [17]. The techniques will not only mine physiological and physical activities from multimodal sensors, but also handle context awareness, and subject specific models and personalization. Once an optimal fall prediction algorithm has been created, it will then be deployed in real-time on the smartphone and will trigger questions for the user or an emergency call to the study coordinators or 911 if questions are left unanswered or the patient reports an injury.

5 Conclusion

This paper has described a novel multimodal system designed to study falls in movement disorder patients. Overall the WMMS functioned well during the short pilot study. Patients and younger healthy adults found the system to be comfortable and easy to use throughout the study. The system provided continuous high-quality datastreams from a variety of users (from young healthy adults to older movement disorder patients). These datastreams were of high enough quality to be comparable to gold-standard medical equipment and to discriminate between events of interest and normal movement patterns. Moving forward, we aim to continue to collect data for the pilot study and to incorporate any advances in technology in order to update the system. For example, we chose the HealthStats BPro to measure blood pressure because it is the best non-cuff semi-continuous blood pressure device available on the market. However, during the pilot study we noted that the device lacked sufficient data collection frequency to accurately measure sudden blood pressure drops. New emerging technology utilizing Pulse Transit Time (PTT) [25, 26] may provide an alternative option. The WMMS employs a very flexible architecture and can be modified to incorporate new sensor technology as it becomes available. With continued improvement and data collection, we can deploy fall detection algorithms and initialize fall prediction algorithm development. We believe the WMMS holds the promise of safer and more independent living, not only for movement disorder patients but also for the ageing population at large.

Acknowledgements. This research was sponsored by the Army Research Laboratory (ARL) under Cooperative Agreement W911NF-10-2-0022 and the ARL Postdoctoral Fellowship Program administered by Oak Ridge Associated Universities. This material has been reviewed by the Walter Reed Army Institute of Research, and there is no objection to its presentation and/or publication. The views and conclusions contained in this document are those of the authors and should not be interpreted as representing the official policies, either expressed or implied, of the

Department of the Army of the Department of Defense or the U.S. Government. The U.S. Government is authorized to reproduce and distribute reprints for Government purposes notwithstanding any copyright notation herein.

References

1. Tromp, A.M., Pluijm, S.M., Smit, J.H., Deeg, D.J., Bouter, L.M., Lips, P.: Fall-risk screening test: a prospective study on predictors for falls in community-dwelling elderly. J. Clin. Epidemiol. **54**(8), 837–844 (2001)
2. Alexander, B.H., Rivara, F.P., Wolf, M.E.: The cost and frequency of hospitalization for fall-related injuries in older adults. Am. J. Public Health **82**(7), 1020–1023 (1992)
3. Wenning, G.K., Ebersbach, G., Verny, M., Chaudhuri, K.R., Jellinger, K., McKee, A., Poewe, W., Litvan, I.: Progression of falls in postmortem-confirmed parkinsonian disorders. Mov. Disord. **14**(6), 947–950 (1999)
4. Wielinski, C.L., Erickson-Davis, C., Wichmann, R., Walde-Douglas, M., Parashos, S.A.: Falls and injuries resulting from falls among patients with Parkinson's disease and other parkinsonian syndromes. Mov. Disord. **20**(4), 410–415 (2005)
5. Williams, D.R., Watt, H.C., Lees, A.J.: Predictors of falls and fractures in bradykinetic rigid syndromes: a retrospective study. J. Neurol. Neurosurg. Psychiatr. **77**(4), 468–473 (2006)
6. Gazibara, T., Pekmezovic, T., Tepavcevic, D.K., Tomic, A., Stankovic, I., Kostic, V.S., Svetel, M.: Circumstances of falls and fall-related injuries among patients with Parkinson's disease in an outpatient setting. Geriatr Nurs **35**(5), 364–369 (2014)
7. Kusserow, M., Amft, O., Troster, G.: Monitoring Stress Arousal in the Wild. IEEE Pervasive Comput. **12**(2), 28–37 (2013)
8. Khusainov, R., Azzi, D., Achumba, I.E., Bersch, S.D.: Real-time human ambulation, activity, and physiological monitoring: taxonomy of issues, techniques, applications, challenges and limitations. Sensors **13**(10), 12852–12902 (2013)
9. Kellihan, B., Doty, T.J., Hairston, W.D., Canady, J., Whitaker, K.W., Lin, C.-T., Jung, T.-P., McDowell, K.: A real-world neuroimaging system to evaluate stress. In: Schmorrow, D.D., Fidopiastis, C.M. (eds.) AC 2013. LNCS, vol. 8027, pp. 316–325. Springer, Heidelberg (2013)
10. Doty, T.J., Hairston, W.D., Kellihan, B., Canady, J., Oie, K.S., McDowell, K.: Developing a wearable real-world neuroimaging system to study stress. In: *2013 6th International IEEE/EMBS Conference on Neural Engineering (NER)*, pp. 786–789 (2013)
11. Bechtel, N., Scahill, R.I., Rosas, H.D., Acharya, T., van den Bogaard, S.J.A., Jauffret, C., Say, M.J., Sturrock, A., Johnson, H., Onorato, C.E., Salat, D.H., Durr, A., Leavitt, B.R., Roos, RCa, Landwehrmeyer, G.B., Langbehn, D.R., Stout, J.C., Tabrizi, S.J., Reilmann, R.: Tapping linked to function and structure in premanifest and symptomatic Huntington disease. Neurology **75**(24), 2150–2160 (2010)
12. Reilmann, R., Ellerbrock, M., Sass, C., Heger, T., Berg, D., Maetzler, W.: Quantitative motor (Q-Motor) deficits in tapping (digitomotography) distinguish Parkinson's disease from control subjects and correlate to the UPDRS III-A step towards objective outcomes for motor deficits in clinical trials? Mov. Disord. **28**, S174–S175 (2013)
13. McCormack, H.M., de L. Horne, D.J., Sheather, S.: Clinical applications of visual analogue scales: a critical review. Psychol. Med. **18**(4), 1007–1019 (1988)
14. Wewers, M.E., Lowe, N.K.: A critical review of visual analogue scales in the measurement of clinical phenomena. Res. Nurs. Health **13**(4), 227–236 (1990)

15. Bourke, A.K., O'Brien, J.V., Lyons, G.M.: Evaluation of a threshold-based tri-axial accelerometer fall detection algorithm. Gait Posture **26**(2), 194–199 (2007)
16. Özdemir, A.T., Barshan, B.: Detecting falls with wearable sensors using machine learning techniques. Sensors **14**(6), 10691–10708 (2014)
17. Zhang, M., Sawchuk, A.A.: Context-aware fall detection using a Bayesian network. In: Proceedings of the 5th ACM International Workshop on Context-Awareness for Self-Managing Systems, pp. 10–16, New York, NY, USA (2011)
18. Maidan, I., Freedman, T., Tzemah, R., Giladi, N., Mirelman, A., Hausdorff, J.M.: Introducing a new definition of a near fall: intra-rater and inter-rater reliability. Gait Posture **39**(1), 645–647 (2014)
19. Broccard, F.D., Mullen, T., Chi, Y.M., Peterson, D., Iversen, J.R., Arnold, M., Kreutz-Delgado, K., Jung, T.-P., Makeig, S., Poizner, H., Sejnowski, T., Cauwenberghs, G.: Closed-loop brain–machine–body interfaces for noninvasive rehabilitation of movement disorders. Ann. Biomed. Eng. **42**(8), 1573–1593 (2014)
20. Bellazzi, R., Ferrazzi, F., Sacchi, L.: Predictive data mining in clinical medicine: a focus on selected methods and applications. WIREs Data Mining Knowl. Discov. **1**(5), 416–430 (2011)
21. Müller, K.-R., Krauledat, M., Dornhege, G., Curio, G., Blankertz, B.: Machine learning and applications for brain-computer interfacing. In: Smith, Michael J., Salvendy, Gavriel (eds.) HCII 2007. LNCS, vol. 4557, pp. 705–714. Springer, Heidelberg (2007)
22. Sow, D., Turaga, D.S., Schmidt, M.: Mining of sensor data in healthcare: a survey. In: Aggarwal, C.C. (ed.) Managing and Mining Sensor Data, pp. 459–504. Springer, US (2013)
23. Sullivan, T.J., Deiss, S.R., Jung, T.-P., Cauwenberghs, G.: A brain-machine interface using dry-contact, low-noise EEG sensors. In: IEEE International Symposium on Circuits and Systems, ISCAS 2008, pp. 1986–1989 (2008)
24. Boissy, P., Choquette, S., Hamel, M., Noury, N.: User-based motion sensing and fuzzy logic for automated fall detection in older adults. Telemedicine e-Health **13**(6), 683–694 (2007)
25. Chung, E., Chen, G., Alexander, B., Cannesson, M.: Non-invasive continuous blood pressure monitoring: a review of current applications. Front. Med. **7**(1), 91–101 (2013)
26. Thomas, S.S., Nathan, V., Zong, C., Akinbola, E., Aroul, A.L.P, Philipose, L., Soundarapandian, K., Shi, X., Jafari, R.: BioWatch #x2014; a wrist watch based signal acquisition system for physiological signals including blood pressure. In: 2014 36th Annual International Conference of the IEEE Engineering in Medicine and Biology Society (EMBC), pp. 2286–2289 (2014)

Smart Textiles as Intuitive and Ubiquitous User Interfaces for Smart Homes

Julian Hildebrandt, Philipp Brauner(✉), and Martina Ziefle

Human-Computer Interaction Center, RWTH Aachen University,
Campus Boulevard 57, 52074, Aachen, Germany
{hildebrandt, brauner, ziefle}@comm.rwth-aachen.de

Abstract. Textile user interfaces for smart homes offer novel intuitive input gestures and may lower acceptance barrier for technophobic or elderly people. To understand the users' requirements of smart textile input devices, an Adaptive Conjoint Analysis with the attributes wearability, functionality, haptic, location, and components was carried out with 100 participants. The attributes were rated with different importances. Users request non-wearable textile input devices with no noticeable electronics for the living room. Gender, but no age effects were identified, as women prefer health applications, whereas men prefer media control. In summary, the device needs to be individually tailored to the user's requirements to achieve high acceptance.

Keywords: Smart textiles · Technology acceptance · Design space · User centered design · Conjoint · Smart home

1 Introduction

Marc Weiser's vision of Ubiquitous Computing [1] is slowly becoming a reality. As early as in 1991, Weiser envisioned the appearance of different smart input devices in form of walls (table-size displays), pads (tablets), and tabs (smart phones) and smart appliances that can be controlled via a network. The envisioned input devices already penetrated the market and smart appliances currently spread in domestic, commercial, and industrial environments. Television and other media, lights, or smart heating control, washing machines and refrigerators are just some of many devices that are increasingly connected to the "Internet of Things" and that are accessible via tablets or smart phones, or by other smart appliances nearby.

While the road to the future may seem straight ahead, one should not forget about our past. In human history textiles have been used for over 30.000 years [2, 3] and accompany us every day since then [4]. Textiles are typically perceived as warm, fashionable, and pleasurable and come in uncountable forms, materials, functionalities, sizes, and colors. Still, textiles have rarely been used as input or output devices for computing machinery, leaving the field to inflexible and cold devices of plastic, metal, or glass.

Using textiles as input devices is an innovative research field [5, 6], at least out of two reasons. One reason is methodological by nature: Creating a novel input device or even a set of input devices that combine smart sensors and actuators can be seemingly

J. Zhou and G. Salvendy (Eds.): ITAP 2015, Part II, LNCS 9194, pp. 423–434, 2015.
DOI: 10.1007/978-3-319-20913-5_39

integrated in textiles surfaces, such as in pillows, blankets, or in couches. Contrary to currently available computing technology, these devices ought to be soft and smooth, and may be cuddled – technology characteristics that could open out into a completely positive connoted devices. The second reason refers to novel application contexts, which go much beyond he traditional field of applications of input devices. Also, new user groups currently not interested in computing technology could be addressed [7]. In particular, smart textile user interfaces may be a way for reaching social inclusion of elderly and technophobic people and allow them to handle technology with a well-known material (fabrics) in their personal home environment [8, 9].

1.1 Smart Textiles as Input Devices

Textiles are defined as smart, if they have intrinsic properties that are not normally associated with traditional textiles and can respond to environmentally stimuli. In contrast to that, the term functional textile refers to textiles that have specific functions added by specific materials or coatings. Distinguish characteristic is the integration of electronics in the textile architecture. There are three distinct hierarchical categories of smart textiles depending on the closure between fabrics and electronics: Textiles made of fibers and yarns to reach wearable computing, textiles with woven or embroidered fabrics and yarns to: The first category contains textiles that are made of fibers and yarns that build a single functionality in combination with conventional components (e.g., wearable computing). With textiles of the second category functions are achieved by the use of the textile itself resulting from a closer connection (embroidery and weaving) between fabric and electronic components. Third categories textiles are developed to offer functions on the fiber level by implementing the electronic device deep into textiles fabrics. Current challenges are mechanical flexibility, washability, power supplies and product development and commercialization [10]. Due to flexibility, closeness to human body and the possibility of very discreetness, smart textiles can apply to a very wide range of tasks like health, security and smart homes [11].

Karrer et al. [12] created PinStripe, a poloshirt with electric sensors in a sleeve for measuring a continuous value based on grasping and deforming. Possible applications were seen in controlling mobile devices or music, but also in safety-critical contexts. From a technical and or electronic point of view, the development of smart textiles is at an advanced stage [13, 14]. Current research discussions are directed to the integration of novel sensors into smart clothing [15] and wearables [16]. Also, [12, 17] are focusing on novel interaction technologies.

Because of their closeness to human body, smart textiles can also react to implicit input like temperature and breathing frequency. Najafi [18] created SmartSox, a pair of socks that can measure temperature, pressure and hallux range of motion to avoid diabetic feet. All patients perceived the socks as comfortable and had no problems while walking with them.

Smart textiles are increasingly used for different application scenarios, as e.g. motion sensing [19] or sports [20] or even within the education context [21], in which efforts were made to tailor teaching anatomy and physiology to children with smart wearables. Stark [22] developed SnapToTrace, a textile component kit that can be used to learn computational systematics and coherences for youths by rearranging textile input- and output components on a base mat. Also, smart textiles find their way into caring and health monitoring contexts ([5, 23, 24]).

1.2 The Missing Keystone: Usability, User Diversity and Acceptance

While the potential of textiles in different application domains is widely acknowledged still the research and technology development is mostly technology driven. Yet, the impact of user requirements and the general acceptance of devices in close distance to persons did not adequately receive attention. Sparse knowledge is known about the impact of user diversity on acceptance of textiles [5, 25, 26]. However, the integration of users in the technology development is indispensable for the success of textile input devices and therefore a mandatory requirement for sustainable solutions.

Recent research directed to personal medical devices revealed that user diversity – in terms of gender, technology generation and technical self-confidence – is impacting not only the ease of using devices but also the degree to which users are willing to use technology in their home environment. Especially the perceived barriers when confronted with novel technologies and the prevailing aloofness towards consequences when using technology in the close environment is much higher in women compared to men [27, 28]. Age and technology generation is especially sensible to the perception of the usefulness of the novel technology and the susceptibility to stigmatizing by device design, as elderly feel being marked as old and ill [29]. Another meaningful outcome in this context is that devices implemented at home are very differently accepted depending on the respective location and the room [30].

Another critical issue is the way of how technology acceptance is assessed [7, 31]. To gain knowledge about users preferences and the acceptance of the technology, conventional methods like conceptualization of dimensions like "importance of placement on the human body" or compositional traditional technology acceptance models [32, 33], reach their limits due to functional dependencies within a possible design space of textile input devices. What is needed for the question regarding the acceptance of smart textiles in the home environment is a holistic evaluation of ecologically more valid decision scenarios, in which different single factors are weighed against each other, and the possibility of direct simulations. That's why we took usage of an adaptive conjoint analysis, a methodology where incompletely described concepts are compared with each other to calculate part-worth utilities of every possible attribute. As far as we know, this is the first approach to evaluate technology acceptance using ACA using technology decomposing attributes and levels (in comparison see [34]).

2 Method

2.1 Measuring Technology Acceptance via Conjoint-Analysis

Conjoint analysis in general is a multivariate analysis method for measuring customer's preferences in a decompositional way: well-defined concepts of products are compared against each other to decompose their part-worth utilities for every *level* and relative importances for every *attribute* of a product or service. In this context, *attribute* is a property of a product or service and *level* is a concrete manifestation of an attribute, i.e. green would be a level of the attribute color. Because of the similarity to a real buying situation Conjoint Analysis is very widespread in marketing disciplines to perform trade-off analysis and market simulations.

The Adaptive Conjoint Analysis (ACA) method used in this study consists of several steps. In contrast to other conjoint methods, ACA is a hybrid method consisting of a compositional part also. The ACA is made up of four steps, the first two being compositional, the third being decompositional and the forth being for calibration. In the first step, called ACA Rating, every level of an attribute is rated from desirable to undesirable. In the second step, called ACA Importance, the importance of these ratings is measured by rating the importance of the difference between the most desired level and the least desired level from ACA Rating. During these steps, relative importance are created and updated with every given answer. In the third step, called ACA Pairs a comparison between two products takes place on a 9-Point rating-scale, while the amount of levels starts at two and increases to an upper limit. During this step, part-worth utilities and are created and updated with every given answer. The concepts presented to the participant are assumed to have nearly equal desirability. In the last step, called ACA Calibration, fully described concepts are rated from 0 to 100 to calculate the predictive value of the method [35].

Besides marketing analysis, Conjoint Analysis can be used to provide decision criteria or concrete practical guidelines for designers of technical systems [36]. ACA was chosen for this study to avoid cognitive or creative overload that could occur in a comparison of fully defined concepts. In addition to that underestimation of pricing and bad mimicry of buying situations does not matter in this context, indeed we assume that a gradually decision between two concepts fits better in this context of technology acceptance [34].

2.2 Characteristics of the Sample

Overall 100 people aged 18 to 73 years (M = 31.8; SD = 11.5) participated in the study (41 % of female, 59 % male).

Self-efficacy in Interacting with Technology (SET): Participants reported an average SET of M = 3.8/6 points max (SD = 1.2). A two-way analysis of variance with *age* and *gender* as independent variables and *SET* as dependent variable yielded in a significant effect of gender on SET ($F_{1,99} = 16.7$, $p < .001$) with men reporting considerable higher technical self-efficacy (M = 5.3, SD = .9) than women (M = 4.4, SD = 1.2). No age effects on technical self-efficacy were found.

Liking of Textiles: The index for assessing the linking of textiles achieved a moderate internal reliability of α *(100, 4 items) = .635*. On average, participants reported an affinity of M = 3.27 (SD = 0.94). Again, a two-way ANOVA with *age* and *gender* as independent variables and the *textile index* as dependent variables revealed a significant effect of gender ($F_{1,99} = 8.3$ $p < .05$, $\eta^2 = .079$), but no effect of age ($F_{1,99} = .417$, $p = .520 > .05$, ns.) on liking of textiles. Specifically, women reported a higher affinity towards textiles (M = 4.5, SD = .8) than men (M = 3.9, SD = 1.0).

Experience with textiles: 73 % of participants had heard or read about smart textiles and 15 % had actual experiences in any form with smart textiles. Interestingly, there is a significant relationship between persons with smart textiles experience and technical self-efficacy ($F_{1,98} = 7.4$, $p < .05$,), with experienced persons having higher self-efficacy scores also having more experience with smart textiles.

2.3 Study Design

The study was realized in an online survey with an average completion time of 15 min. The survey started with a brief motivation of the research. Next, demographic information was recorded (age, gender, educational level, (last) occupation). In addition, participants were surveyed regarding individual factors that are known to impact the interaction with and evaluation of technology.

Self-efficacy in interacting with technology (SET) on a Beier's scale [37]. SET has been identified as an pivotal psychological construct that explains the users' effectiveness, efficiency [38], learnability [39], user satisfaction, and acceptance in interacting with electronically devices. Also, participants' inclination towards textile surfaces was surveyed, in order to control for individual differences in the liking of textiles. These aspects were captured using 6-point Likert scales (0 to 5, 5 max.).

Table 1. Attributes and Levels

Attribute	**Level**
Wearability	Wearable
	Non-wearable
Functionality	Health function
	Media controlling
	Smart home controlling
Components	Box
	Smartphone
	Textile
Haptic	Soft
	Medium
	Hard
Room	Bedroom
	Kitchen
	Living room

Attributes and dimension of the Conjoint Analysis were taken from prior research [26], in which a design space of possible factors (spatial context, users, tasks, application scenarios) were explored (see Table 1). The five factors with the highest impact on further prototyping decisions were chosen: *Wearability* (wearable/non-wearable), *Functionality* (remote controlling of media /smart home technology /health technology), *Components* (textile only /communication with smartphone needed /box of hardware needed). The other two attributes are *Haptic* of the textile (hard /medium / soft) and *Room* of usage (bedroom /kitchen /living room).

In ACA Rating and ACA Importance the evaluations were measured on a scale from 0 to 5. The upper limit for the number of attributes in ACA pairs was set to three, there were six questions with two and three attributes each. ACA Calibration consisted of five concepts. Addressing the fact that there are no functional dependencies none of the 162 possible products were excluded from the study. An exemplary question set is shown in Fig. 1.

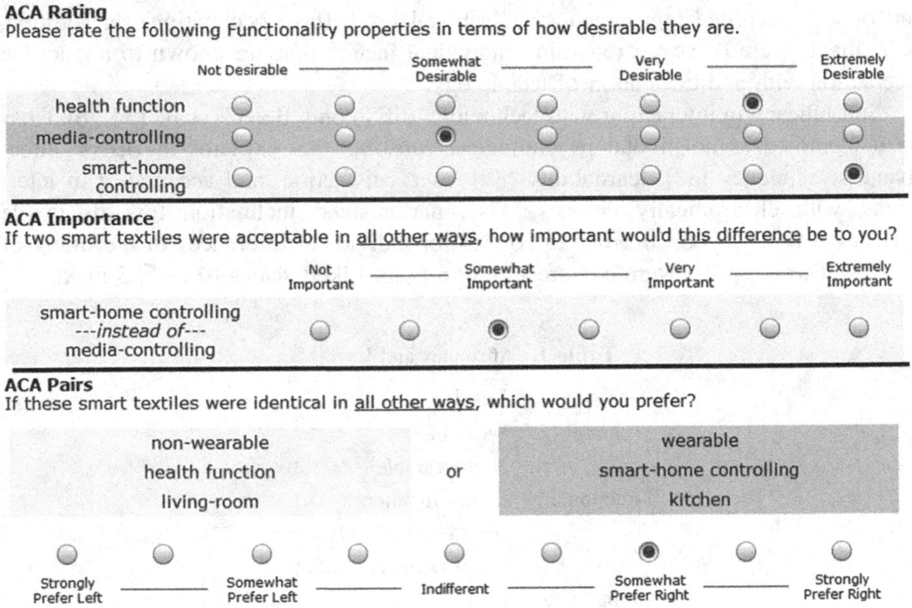

ACA Rating
Please rate the following Functionality properties in terms of how desirable they are.
Not Desirable — Somewhat Desirable — Very Desirable — Extremely Desirable
health function
media-controlling
smart-home controlling

ACA Importance
If two smart textiles were acceptable in all other ways, how important would this difference be to you?
Not Important — Somewhat Important — Very Important — Extremely Important
smart-home controlling
---*instead of*---
media-controlling

ACA Pairs
If these smart textiles were identical in all other ways, which would you prefer?
non-wearable
health function
living-room
or
wearable
smart-home controlling
kitchen
Strongly Prefer Left — Somewhat Prefer Left — Indifferent — Somewhat Prefer Right — Strongly Prefer Right

Fig. 1. Illustration of exemplary ACA questions

3 Results

First, the relative importance of the five dimensions is shown. Finally, for each of the five dimensions the rating of the individual levels is presented and gender differences will be discussed.

3.1 Relative Importance and Part-Worth Utilities

The participants of attach different importance to the five considered dimensions of a textile input device. Specifically, *Components* is rated as the most important attribute (24.6 %), followed by *Room* (22.5 %) and *Functionality* (22.0 %). *Haptic* (18.7 %) and

Wearability (12.2 %) were found to be least important to the subjects. What is noteworthy in this context is that the order of importance across criteria is not affected by user diversity (neither age nor gender). Figure 2 shows the relative importance of the five attributes.

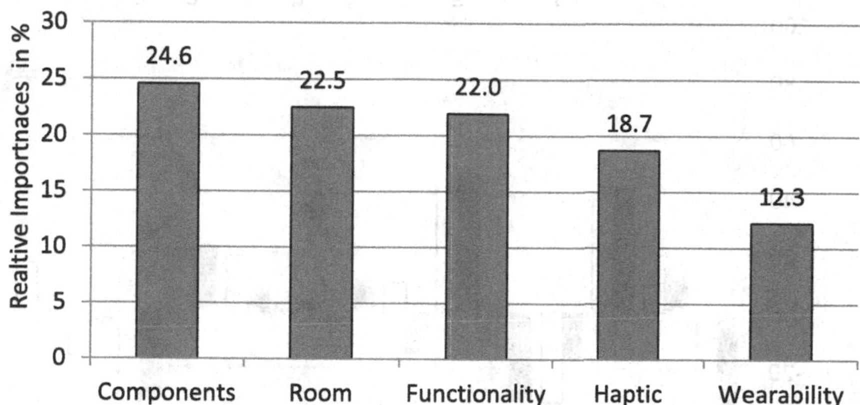

Fig. 2. Relative importance of smart textile attributes

3.2 The Impact of User Characteristics on the Evaluation of Textiles.

In the following sections the preferences for the individual levels for each attribute are discussed in order of relative importance. Figure 3 illustrates the part-worth utilities separated by gender.

In the *Component* attribute the level *textile* was strictly preferred by men (43.10) and women (40.69) over the other levels *smartphone* (men 15.08; women 9.41) and *box*, which was strictly disliked by men and women (men −58.18; women −50.10).

Regarding *Room*, a strong preference for using the technology in the *living room* was reported by both genders (47.14 men; 42.79 women). A contrasting gender effect in the evaluation of *bedroom* and *kitchen* was found: women disliked a device the *kitchen* (−11.31) less than the *bedroom* (−31.48) as a location for use of smart textiles; men in contrast disliked the *bedroom* (−16.34) less than the *kitchen* (−30.81).

Evaluation of the attribute *Functionality* revealed gender preferences: men favored smart textiles to control *media* (11.8), while women favored *health functionalities* (10.0). In contrast to that, men disliked *health functions* (−14.6) and women disliked *media functionalities* (-12.7). *Smart home* controlling was tendentially rated positively by both men (3.8) and women (2.7).

As regards *Haptic* of the device, *medium hard* was favored most by men (23.1) and women (20.8), but women liked *soft* textiles (19.4) just marginally less. The *hard* option was disliked by both genders, with women's rating (−40.2) being more negative than men's (−31.0).

Regarding *Wearability* women reported a stronger preference for *non-wearables* (15.9) than men (5.2).

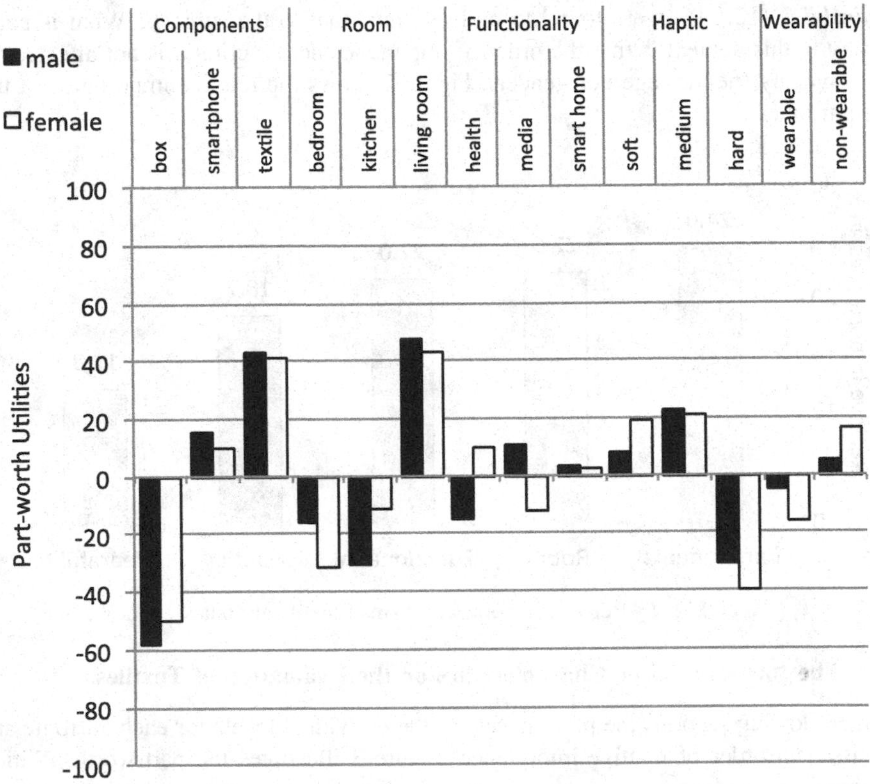

Fig. 3. Part-worth utilities for every level, separated by gender

4 Discussion

The study investigated the users' requirements of the different aspects of a textile input device. The research motivation was to contribute to the undeveloped knowledge about the usefulness of a textile input device that can be implemented in the home context. Different from other social science approaches, in which acceptance for or against a specific technology is assessed by using single factors approach, we simulated the decision process in real world scenarios by using conjoint analysis. Methodologically, the main objective is to simulate decision processes and to decompose the preference of a product or scenario as a combined set of attributes into separate utilities of the attributes and respective attribute levels. From a theoretical point of view this approach mimics the real procedure: Characteristically, acceptance is a "product" out of perceived benefits and at the same time barriers and they weigh those factors depending on their individual situation and perspective.

On the base of previous research, we predefined five aspects of a textile input device that have been identified as important on a single factors level [26].

The conjoint findings corroborate that users assign different levels of importance to the five investigated aspects of the design of a textile input device. Participants evaluate the technical realization as the most important aspect of the device. Here, users clearly oppose a product with a noticeable electronics or a battery pack and they prefer a device with seamlessly integrated electronics or – as a temporary solution – that the computing logic is outsourced into a smartphone wirelessly connected to the device. The second most important criteria for users are the operational area of the device. Users predominantly prefer a device specifically designed for the living room and the two other alternatives, kitchen and bedroom, were disdained by the users. The latter mimics findings according to which rooms at home have different sensibilities and tolerance towards the integration of technology. The third most important criterion is the actual functionality of the device. However, users did not clearly prefer one possible function to the other, meaning that some users want a textile for controlling the smart home, whereas others want to control music or other media. This shows that there is not the tendency for "one function for all" but a tendency for the wish to individually tailor the functionality to own needs and to control the functionality, which is implemented in the device.

What is quite astounding in data outcomes is the fact that user diversity – at least in those facets that were under study here – did not have major impact on acceptance. Beyond the fact, that women dislike smart textiles in the bedroom more than in the kitchen, and vice versa for men, neither age, nor gender nor the level of technical self-competence did modulate the order of importance regarding the evaluation criteria. In addition, age is not related to self-efficacy in interacting with technology, nor does age influence the preferred appearance of a prospective textile input device. This contradicts on a first sight a huge body of research outcomes according to which women are more reluctant to use and like novel technology in their private space [27] or a decreasing openness to novel technology with increasing age [40].

This missing effect of user diversity might be based on three reasons:

The first reason is directed to the textile as input device as a well-known and deeply anchored material. If this assumption is right then the disadvantage of a technical device as a foreign artifact and disliked in the private sphere may be compensated by a highly appreciated technology. More so, this result would then open up a huge success to cope with the challenge developing technical assistance for an aging society: appreciated technology that is not stigmatizing persons with a lower technical competency.

The second reason could lie in the evaluation dimensions, which were under study. To evaluate the functional design space and more or less design aspects of a novel technology might not be sensitive to diversity as such. If so then we have strong arguments to assume that those functions might follow a "design for all" approach, at least in the respective functionalities implemented in the device. Third, a quite simple reason could regard the speculation that this is an effect of the comparably young sample, which might not be representative for the whole group of older and possibly handicapped users. On the base of the present finding we cannot decide which of the reasons might be correct. Future studies could continue in this line of research, addressing many more facets.

In this context, first, we will have to find out whether these devices are accepted at all and if they are preferred over conventional input devices. The concurrently realized focus groups and the previous survey discussed the benefits and barriers of such a device and premises for a successful adoption process.

Second, most participants were recruited via social networks, mostly Facebook or personal emails. This led to a sample askew to younger and more technophile people. A subsequent study must therefore investigate if the presented tradeoffs are comparable with an older and less tech-savvy sample. Furthermore, we have of course to elaborate the range of the design space. So far, only few selected elements were investigated in this study. Subsequent studies must address additional characteristics – such as weight, for a holistic understanding how users balance the pros and cons across these dimensions.

What we can say is that textile input devices offer excellent opportunities for younger and older persons to control the increasingly widespread smart devices in domestic environments. The presented trade-off analysis is one of several important columns of this line of research. In parallel focus groups multiple realizations of possible textile input devices as low fidelity prototypes are investigated. Following the results from this study and earlier work, these prototypes are targeted as a smart remote for home automation and media control for the living room in a smart home. From the technical perspective, the users' requirement that the necessary sensor and actuator technology must be seemingly integrated in the device (i.e., without a noticeable electronic brick and battery pack) is one of the toughest challenges.

Acknowledgement. This project is funded by the German Ministry of Education and Research under the project No. 16SV6270.

References

1. Weiser, M.: The computer for the 21st century. Sci. Am. **265**, 94–104 (1991)
2. Kvavadze, E., Bar-Yosef, O., Belfer-Cohen, A., Boaretto, E., Jakeli, N., Matskevich, Z., Meshveliani, T.: 30,000-year-old wild flax fibers. Science **325**, 1359 (2009)
3. Robinson, S.: History of Dyed Textiles. MIT Press, Cambridge (1970)
4. Riello, G., Parthasarathi, P.: The Spinning World - A Global History of Cotton Textiles, 1200-1850. Oxford University Press, Oxford, Boston (2011)
5. Van Heek, J., Schaar, A.K., Trevisan, B., Bosowski, P., Ziefle, M.: User requirements for wearable smart textiles. Does the usage context matter (medical vs. sports)? In: Proceedings of the 8th International Conference on Pervasive Computing Technologies for Healthcare. (2014)
6. Ziefle, M., Brauner, P., Heidrich, F., Möllering, C., Lee, K., Armbrüster, C.: Understanding requirements for textile input devices individually tailored interfaces within home environments, pp. 587–598
7. Lenert, L., Kaplan, R.M.: Validity and interpretation of preference-based measures of health-related quality of life. Med. Care. **38**, II138–I150 (2000)
8. Holzinger, A., Röcker, C., Ziefle, M.: From smart health to smart hospitals. In: Holzinger, A., Röcker, C., Ziefle, M. (eds.) Smart Health. LNCS, vol. 8700, pp. 1–20. Springer, Heidelberg (2015)
9. Mennicken, S., Huang, E.M.: Hacking the natural habitat: an in-the-wild study of smart homes, their development, and the people who live in them. In: Kay, J., Lukowicz, P., Tokuda, H., Olivier, P., Krüger, A. (eds.) Pervasive 2012. LNCS, vol. 7319, pp. 143–160. Springer, Heidelberg (2012)

10. Cherenack, K., van Pieterson, L.: Smart textiles: challenges and opportunities. J. Appl. Phys. **112**, 091301 (2012)
11. Axisa, F., Schmitt, P.M., Gehin, C., Delhomme, G., McAdams, E., Dittmar, A.: Flexible technologies and smart clothing for citizen medicine, home healthcare, and disease prevention. IEEE Trans. Inf Technol. Biomed. **9**, 325–336 (2005)
12. Karrer, T., Wittenhagen, M., Lichtschlag, L., Heller, F., Borchers, J.: Pinstripe: eyes-free continuous input on interactive clothing. In: Proceedings of the 2011 annual conference on Human factors in computing systems - CHI 2011, pp. 1313–1322 (2011)
13. Park, S., Jayaraman, S.: Smart textile-based wearable biomedical systems: a transition plan for research to reality. IEEE Trans. Inf. Technol. Biomed. **14**(1), 86–92 (2010)
14. Schwarz, A., Van Langenhove, L., Guermonprez, P., Deguillemont, D.: A roadmap on smart textiles. Text. Prog. **42**, 99–180 (2010)
15. Dunne, L.: Smart clothing in practice: key design barriers to commercialization. Fashion Practice J. Des. Creative Process Fashion Ind. **2**, 41–66 (2010)
16. Chan, M., Estève, D., Fourniols, J.-Y., Escriba, C., Campo, E.: Smart wearable systems: current status and future challenges. Artif. Intell. Med. **56**(3), 137–156 (2012)
17. Baurley, S.: Interactive and experiential design in smart textile products and applications. Pers. Ubiquit. Comput. **8**(3-4), 274–281 (2004)
18. Najafi, B.: SmartSox: a smart textile to prevent diabetic foot amputation. In: Qatar Foundation Annual Research Forum Proceedings, BIOP 2013 (2013)
19. Mattmann, C., Amft, O., Harms, H., Tröster, G., Clemens, F.: Recognizing upper body postures using textile strain sensors. In: Proceedings - International Symposium on Wearable Computers, ISWC, pp. 29–36 (2007)
20. Helmer, R.J.N., Mestrovic, M.A., Farrow, D., Lucas, S., Spratford, W.: Smart textiles position and motion sensing for sport, entertainment and rehabilitation. Adv. Sci. Technol. **60**, 144–153 (2008)
21. Norooz, L., Froehlich, J.: Exploring early designs for teaching anatomy and physiology to children using wearable e-textiles. In: Proceedings of the 12th International Conference on Interaction Design and Children - IDC 2013, pp. 577–580. ACM Press, New York, USA (2013)
22. Stark, L.: SnapToTrace : a new e-textile interface and component kit for learning computation. In: Proceedings of the 6th International Conference on Tangible and Embedded Interaction, 2012, pp. 399–400. ACM (2012)
23. Zięba, J., Frydrysiak, M.: Textronics system for breathing. Measurement **15**, 105–108 (2007)
24. Lymberis, A., De Rossi, D.: Wearable eHealth Systems for Personalised Health Management - State of the Art and Future Challenges. IOS Press, Amsterdam (2004)
25. Schaar, A.K., Ziefle, M.: Smart clothing: perceived benefits vs. perceived fears. In: 2011 5th International Conference on Pervasive Computing Technologies for Healthcare (PervasiveHealth) and Workshops, pp. 601–608 (2011)
26. Ziefle, M., Brauner, P., Heidrich, F., Möllering, C., Lee, H.-Y., Armbrüster, C.: Understanding requirements for textile input devices: individually-tailored interfaces within home environments. In: Proceedings of Universal Access in Human-Computer Interaction, HCII 2014, pp. 589–600 (2014)
27. Ziefle, M., Schaar, A.K.: Gender differences in acceptance and attitudes towards an invasive medical stent. Electron. J. Health Inf. **6**, 1–18 (2011)
28. Wilkowska, W., Ziefle, M.: Privacy and data security in e-Health: requirements from the user's perspective. Health Inf. J. **18**, 191–201 (2012)

29. Schaar, A.K., Ziefle, M.: Technology acceptance by patients: empowerment and stigma. In: van Hoof, J., Demiris, G., Demiris, E.J.M. (eds.) Handbook of Smart Homes, Health Care and Well-Being, pp. 1–10. Springer, Heidelberg (2014)
30. Wilkowska, W., Himmel, S., Ziefle, M.: Perceptions in smart home technologies: do user assessments vary depending on the chosen research method? In: Proceedings of the Human-Computer Interaction International, 2015 (2015)
31. Spagnolli, A., Guardigl, E., Orso, V., Varotto, A., Gamberini, L.: Measuring user acceptance of wearable symbiotic devices: validation study across application scenarios. In: Jacucci, G., Gamberini, L., Freeman, J., Spagnolli, A. (eds.) Symbiotic 2014. LNCS, vol. 8820, pp. 85–96. Springer, Heidelberg (2014)
32. Davis, F.D.: A technology acceptance model for empirically testing new end-user information systems: Theory and results. Management. Ph.D., 291 (1985)
33. Venkatesh, V., Morris, M.G., Davis, G.B., Davis, F.D.: User acceptance of information technology: toward a unified view. MIS Q. **27**, 425–478 (2003)
34. Pagani, M.: Determinants of adoption of third generation mobile multimedia services. J. Interact. Mark. **18**(3), 46–59 (2004)
35. Software, S.: Technical paper: ACA. Design. 98382, 0–26 (2008)
36. Kowalewski, S., Arning, K., Minwegen, A., Ziefle, M., Ascheid, G.: Extending the engineering trade-off analysis by integrating user preferences in conjoint analysis. Expert Syst. Appl. **40**, 2947–2955 (2013)
37. Beier, G.: Kontrollüberzeugungen im Umgang mit Technik [Locus of control when interacting with technology]. Report Psychologie. **24**, 684–693 (1999)
38. Arning, K., Ziefle, M.: Understanding age differences in PDA acceptance and performance. Comput. Hum. Behav. **23**, 2904–2927 (2007)
39. Brauner, P., Leonhardt, T., Ziefle, M., Schroeder, U.: The effect of tangible artifacts, gender and subjective technical competence on teaching programming to seventh graders. In: Hromkovič, J., Královič, R., Vahrenhold, J. (eds.) ISSEP 2010. LNCS, vol. 5941, pp 61–71. Springer, Heidelberg (2010)
40. Wilkowska, W., Ziefle, M.: Which factors form older adults' acceptance of mobile information and communication technologies? In: Holzinger, A., Miesenberger, K. (eds.) USAB 2009. LNCS, vol. 5889, pp. 81–101. Springer, Heidelberg (2009)

Designing an Indoor Navigation System for Elderly People's Capabilities

Mathias Källström(✉), Sondre Berdal, and Suhas Govind Joshi

Department of Informatics, University of Oslo, Oslo, Norway
{mathiapk, sondrejb}@student.matnat.uio.no,
joshi@ifi.uio.no

Abstract. The elderly population is increasing and the need of smart home technology and customized health-care solutions is growing rapidly. A common symptom of old age is cognitive impairment, which can in some cases lead to the inability of self-navigation. Numerous indoor navigation systems have proposed to solve such problems. However, previous developers have only to a minor extent included elderly in the design process, despite the user group's complex needs. The solution presented in this paper is based on using recognizable aids and abstractions to ensure that the new proposed system is something elderly users can relate to and feel comfortable with. Other solutions often require wearable modules, or constant interaction, whereas this system does not require any of the two. In addition to our solution we present five implications when designing an indoor navigation system for elderly people.

Keywords: Indoor navigation · Cognitive impairment · Elderly people · Assisted living · Positioning

1 Introduction

The elderly population is increasing throughout the world and the average life expectancy is higher than ever before in human history. In Norway the population aged 65 years or older constitutes approximately 15 % of the total population. The growing number of older citizens are placing new stresses on communities and increases the need for health-care, in-home care giving and appropriate housing [1]. The majority of older adults prefer to live independently for as long as they possibly can. Supporting older adults to remain in their own homes and communities is also favored by policy makers and health providers to avoid the costly option of institutional care [1]. A common symptom of old age is cognitive impairment. However, the impact of cognitive impairment is relative to each individual; therefore, it is hard to categorize the needs of elders, and their ability to take care of themselves, by age. One symptom of cognitive impairment is disorientation and the inability of self-navigation in familiar and unfamiliar indoor environments. Nowadays there are many commercial and non-commercial systems with the aim of providing reliable indoor positioning e.g. InfSoft, Nextome and MazeMap. However, most of them are not considering the complex needs of elderly users. In this paper we propose a system which aims to improve the well-being of elders and help them become more independent by

J. Zhou and G. Salvendy (Eds.): ITAP 2015, Part II, LNCS 9194, pp. 435–445, 2015.
DOI: 10.1007/978-3-319-20913-5_40

introducing an indoor navigation system using Bluetooth technology that is specially designed for their capabilities. By using this system elderly people will be able to move around in known and unknown buildings unsupervised as well as feeling safe and independent. Our design can work as a tool to let elders live independently for a longer period of time.

The structure of this paper is as follows; we start this paper by introducing related work about technology and prior research on elderly and cognitively impaired people. This is followed by our research context and our choice of method. Then we present our results and discuss them in light of prior research and related work. Thereafter we present our design as well as five implications when designing an indoor navigation system for elderly people. After this we present a discussion on designing new technology for elderly people, as well as a discussion regarding our results and findings.

2 Related Work

2.1 Positioning

The demand for a reliable indoor-positioning system for commercial and practical use is high, therefore many technologies has been approached to reach a satisfactory level of accuracy. Over the last few years many different frequency-based technologies has been used for indoor positioning, such as Bluetooth, Radio Frequency Identification (RFID), Ultra Wideband (UWB) and Wireless Fidelity (Wi-Fi) [3]. The most favored solution uses Wi-Fi access-points, mostly because it already exists in most infrastructures and it is therefore easy and affordable to implement [4]. Studies by Tsirmpas et al. [2] and Ozdenizci et al. [5] suggest that implementing the indoor-navigation system into the environment with RFID and near field communication (NFC) tags is a solid solution; however, this has not shown to satisfy all the requirements from the consumers. Technologies like Wi-Fi, Bluetooth, and UWB have been the favorable for on-the-go navigation indoors. Studies indicate that Bluetooth is the technology that gives the best precision with an increased number of sensors [3], however a recent study by Aoki et al. [6] has informed us that Personal Handy-phone System (PHS) technology can be utilized for indoor-navigation in hospitals. Because PHS operates at a different frequency band it does not interfere with equipment in hospitals and care facilities.

2.2 Elderly and Cognitively Impaired People

Most commercial navigation systems today depends on the user being able to read visible output, therefore developing indoor and outdoor navigation systems for blind people are still being researched. In 2004, Ran et al. [7] developed an indoor/outdoor navigation system "Drishti" for blind people that presented intriguing results. This system has an inconvenience by requiring the user to wear several components like a small computer, headsets and ultrasound tags in order to use it. Research concerning navigation aids for elderly people is also something that is in development [2, 6, 8]. However, recurring problems from these studies are a lack of representative sampling, or user involvement when developing the solution and is something that has influenced our methods when developing our proposed system. However, to design such a complicated system for unexperienced users has proved to be difficult. Culén et al. [9] researched on cognitive and bodily mastering while observing a smart-gym in use by elders. They found that elderly people are often not familiar with the most common icons and symbols used in everyday technology for younger people. This lack of familiarity may lead to insecurity, less self-efficacy and in some cases a denial to the use of technology at all. Mary Zajicek [10] presented research concerning aspects of HCI research for older people that in addition to lack of familiarity, they also experience a wide range of age related impairments, including loss of vision, hearing, memory and mobility, the combined effects of which contribute to loss of confidence and difficulties in orientation and absorption of information. According to Williams et al. [11] simplicity is key when designing visual displays for elderly people - while visual displays for teenagers might need flash and bounce to attract their attention, too much color and action in a display will confuse and frustrate an elderly user. This is something we have kept in mind when designing our proposed system.

3 Method

3.1 Research Context

To conduct our fieldwork we cooperated with a residential care facility in Oslo. The age of the residents varied from 64 to 101 years, with an average of 84 years. This facility target seniors with an increased need of greater security, activity and opportunities for social interaction. The facility consists of 91 smart-home apartments which are controlled by a central computer system and smart-home systems to stabilize heat/ventilation as well as monitoring stove activity, water, smoke sensors, outdoor camera calling system and lock system. In addition to the central computer system each apartment is equipped with a tablet which can be used for regular web surfing, as well as checking the dinner schedule for the in-house restaurant or schedules for local activities. The facility has big common areas for different activities, and it has a specially equipped gym, hairdresser, library, physiotherapist office and so forth (Fig. 1).

Fig. 1. Common areas in the facility

3.2 Direct Observations, Interviews and Surveys

Initially we observed the residents in their natural environment. This gave us insight in their daily routines and activities. We used questionnaires to get qualitative data from both staff and residents on what requirements they felt was important for our proposed system. We also interviewed both residents and staff with the purpose of providing in-depth knowledge of their different perspectives. This was to retrieve information about the resident's habits with technology and their relationship with it.

3.3 User Testing

We wanted to involve our primary and secondary users early in the design-process. This was accomplished by presenting paper sketches of our design and inviting residents and staff to discuss and contribute with constructive criticism.

We designed an experiment with the intention to see if our system would act as a distraction or disturbing factor. Participants were represented by both sexes and were asked to walk a given distance with a walker which had an iPad attached to it. The participants walked the same distance with, and without the screen turned on. When the screen was on it showed unique pictures every five seconds and the participants were asked to say out loud what was displayed. This was to simulate the use of our system, where the users will have to watch the screen while walking. We hypothesized that there would be a difference in time spent walking a given distance when watching the screen compared to just walking the distance (Fig. 2).

When we had a functional prototype we wanted to investigate different user scenarios to see how potential users would interact with the system. Due to the low level of mobility from the participant group we used screenshots from the system. The participants were given tasks in a controlled environment. This way we could find ambiguities and what parts of the interface that needed adjustments for better understanding of it as a whole. The tasks were aimed to test if the system had a satisfactory level of affordance; could elderly people use the basic functions in the system with no

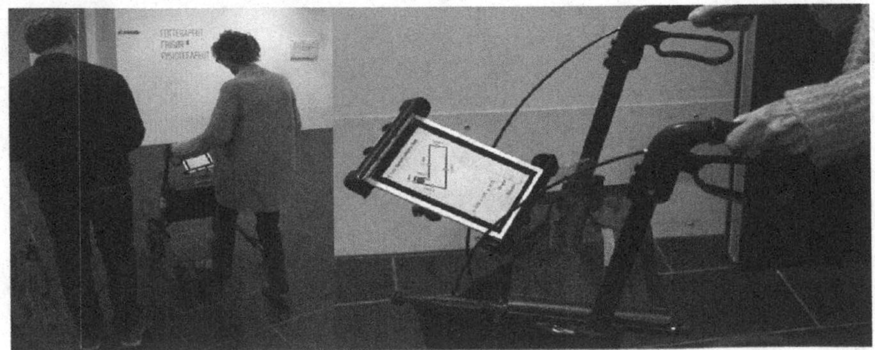

Fig. 2. A participant walking with the prototype

Fig. 3. User involvement during the summative test

training. During this test we measured time spent on each task, and the participants were encouraged to "think out loud" (Fig. 3).

Lastly we conducted a test in a natural environment. The goal was to test the application in a real time situation, with the main target uncovering errors in both software and design. Participants was tasked to walk a given route in the room, by doing this we could see how often the positioning was updated and if there were any interference or inaccuracies in the signal received. We recruited three participants, although we recognize that the pool of participants was small, it served its purpose.

4 Results

4.1 Observations, Interviews and Surveys

Many of the residents expressed reluctance towards new technology, and during a conversation with one of the volunteers at the facility the word technophobia came up when talking about the relationship between the residents and technology. Observations indicated that around 90 % of the residents used special aids for support when walking. This gave us the idea to attach our proposed system to the residents most used pre-existing aid, which was the walker.

Results from the questionnaires showed that the opinions differed slightly among the involved parties on what functions to be considered when developing the system (Fig. 4). However the question about whether a user should have the freedom of adding a new destination produced an interesting result. 85 % of the residents asked felt that this function was necessary, while only 20 % of the staff and none of the volunteers had the same opinion. There was also a disagreement within the groups on whether the system should have a surveillance function. Because of the disagreements, we could not move forward with all the functions we initially proposed to the user-groups. Anyhow it was clear that our system has to be easily operable due to low technical understanding,

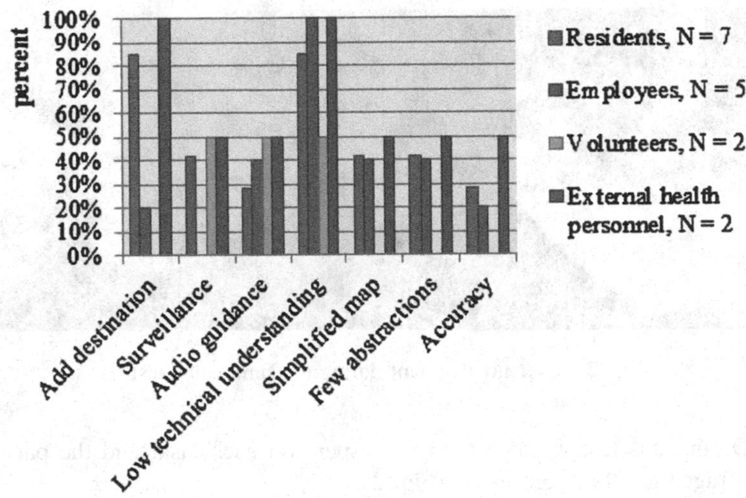

Fig. 4. Opinions on functions to be included when developing the system

4.2 Experiment

In Table 1 we have the results from the experiment. The table shows how much time each participant (P1-10) spent on each task with each condition of the independent variable (with/without screen). The time was measured in seconds. The total number of participants was 10, five from the care facility, as well as five participants from the control group recruited at another similar residential care facility in Oslo.

From the results in Table 1 we can see that the participants walked slightly slower when they had to watch the screen as they walked, compared to when they only had to walk the distance. To analyze the results we conducted a test of normality to confirm that the data was normally distributed which is a necessary assumption to be able to perform a paired sample t-test. The results from the paired samples t-test is shown in the figure below.

The results shown in Fig. 5 are from the care facility and the control group twinned together. The t-test reveals that it's a strong correlation between the two variables with a Pearson's r value of 0.956. The t-test also revealed a Sig. (2-Tailed) value, this value can tell us if there is a statistical significant difference between the two conditions when

Table 1. Results from the experiment

	Experimental group	N = 5		Control group	N = 5
Participant	*With screen*	*Without screen*	Participant	*With screen*	*Without screen*
P1	25s	20s	P6	43s	37s
P2	28s	28s	P7	45s	41s
P3	35s	32s	P8	52s	44s
P4	43s	38s	P9	31s	28s
P5	44s	36s	P10	30s	31s

Paired Samples Correlations

N	Correlation	Sig.
10	.956	.000

Paired Samples Test

t	df	Sig. (2-tailed)
-4.324	9	.002

Paired Samples Test

Paired Differences				
			95% Confidence Interval of the Difference	
Mean	Std. Deviation	Std. Error Mean	Lower	Upper
-4.10000	2.99815	.94810	-6.24475	-1.95525

Fig. 5. Results from paired samples t test

the value is less than or equal to .05. With a Sig. (2-Tailed) value of .002 we can therefore conclude that there is a statistically significant correlation between time spent walking when watching the screen compared to just walking the distance. By looking at the results from Table 1 we can see that watching the screen has a negative effect on time spent walking a given distance for the users.

4.3 Test of Interface

We have summarized the most interesting data points from one of the summative tests in the table below (Table 2). It shows average task completion time, range and whether the task was completed or not. We did not include standard deviation or variance because our goal was to test the prototypes functions and intuitiveness, and normal distribution was therefore irrelevant. The data was collected from five potential users at the care facility, as well as five participants from the control group recruited at another similar residential care facility in Oslo. The total number of participants was 10.

Table 2. Results from the summative test of interface.

	Experimental group		N = 5	Control Group		N = 5
Task	*Average*	*Range*	*Not completed*	*Average*	*Range*	*Not completed*
Start application	12,8s	21s	0	6,4s	9s	0
Choose destination	15,4s	17s	0	3,2s	6s	0
Find yourself on the map	28,6s	36s	0	28,6s	18s	2
Find destination	24s	15s	1	9,2s	13s	0
Understanding distance	36,5s	39s	1	28s	79s	0
Find the amount of exits	10s	16s	1	16,6s	21s	0
Go back, and delete destination	26,8s	37s	0	48,8s	54s	0

The summative test of interface showed that the participants could complete most of the tasks asked, with a success rate of 92.85 %. The table show high variation between participants in time spent on most tasks, and with an average task completion time higher than what we could expect. It also shows that some participants did not complete all tasks. This implicates that some tasks were either not properly described or they were too hard to execute. From this we drew the conclusion that our interface needed to be simpler and cleaner. We also have to look at what symbols and text is the most descriptive and find something they can relate to.

5 Implications for Design

As a result of these tests we found that some of the abstractions and assumptions were too unfamiliar, and caused some comprehension trouble. The questionnaire-results (Fig. 4) indicated that it was close to a mutual agreement that the system should consider the low technical understanding of the user group. This was reflected in the user-tests as we observed that most participants had problems with either the technology or the interaction due to lack of experience with similar equipment and interfaces.

By reviewing our Table 2 we have found a high completion rate and a satisfying time completion rate in four out of seven tasks, while three tasks showed a time completion rate below our desired level. The functions that the participants had few too none problems in completing, was the tasks of starting the application, choosing destination, finding destination and arguably finding the amount of exits. The latter had a satisfying time completion ratio, but one participant didn't complete the task. The functions in the system that need be further tested are a representative icon for the user, how we present the distance from user to destination and going back in the application. We discovered one flaw in the system which was that the back button was written in English, and not in our native language Norwegian. This is possibly one of the reasons this task had such high range and average completion time. The symbol for deletion was often easily interpreted,however, this is a function we need to think about implementing, as elders with cognitive disabilities or dementia might delete destinations by accident.

We discovered through our experiment that the screen had a negative effect on time spent walking a given distance. However, the goal of our proposed system is to serve as an aid for indoor navigation. This implicates getting the user to his or hers desired destination independently and safely, the time spent doing so is not equally important.

As a final result we present five implications for designing our system.

The system should:

A. **Avoid advanced settings and features**
B. **Use familiar abstractions and terminology**
C. **Integrate with pre-existing aids**
D. **Contain few distractions, colors and contrasts (keep it simple)**
E. **Contain few customization options (constraints)**

Figure 6 shows the transformation from sketch to the final prototype. The change of design is built on implication C. We also found that they used the platform we wanted to place the iPad for placing objects or as a mobile resting place.

Figure 7 shows the transformation of our tablet's navigation interface. The changes from first to final prototype is affected by removing unnecessary, distracting information (implication A and D) while gaining functions e.g. making exits clearer and gaining destination point (implication 2).

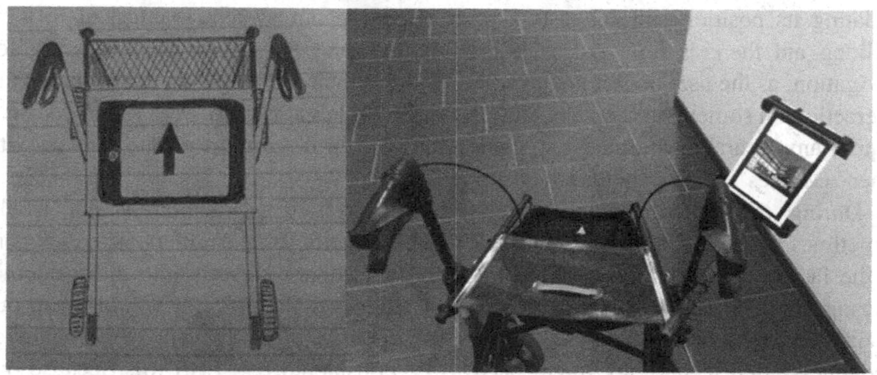

Fig. 6. The prototype - first sketch to last prototype

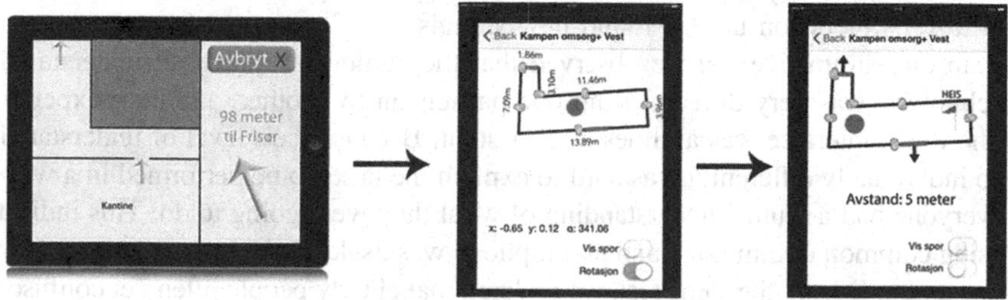

Fig. 7. The tablet navigation interface - first sketch to last prototype

6 Discussion

In the related work section we mentioned systems that used NFC and RFID technology for indoor navigation [2, 5]. They integrated the navigation system into the environment by having several reference points in the building. This way the users had to use an identification module in order to use the system. The system using NFC required the user to interact with the reference points in the building using their personal digital assistant (PDA) or mobile devices to get instructions on where to go. This implies that every user must remember to bring certain equipment in order to use the system. It also requires physical interaction during the navigation to update the users' current location. The system using RFID is a very intricate system which, in addition to a tracking module, requires the user to wear earplugs for auditory feedback. For elderly people with hearing impairments this might block other environmental sounds which could cause the user to miss important information concerning their surroundings. It might also conflict with other hearing aids. Another problem concerning these solutions is that they present a brand new activity which an elderly user might not relate to. Culén et al. [9] found in their research on cognitive and bodily mastering that this lack of familiarity may lead to insecurity, less self-efficacy and in some cases a denial to the use of technology at all. In our proposed system, the only interaction needed is to choose destination. After that the user can simply watch the screen as it is constantly updating its position and suggests a route. Because our system is attached to their walking aid there is little risk of forgetting to bring the equipment necessary for navigation, as the user do not go anywhere without their walking aids. It also bases the interaction on something they already feel comfortable with. Also, our system does not require any wearable equipment so there is no risk for discomfort or interference with other activities the user might attend to.

During our experiment we found that our system's Bluetooth signal would sometimes suffer interference from other nearby Bluetooth transmitters. The elevators in the facility are programmed to send auditory feedback directly into the resident's hearing aids, via Bluetooth. This means that whenever the elevator would open, our navigation system would be thrown of course. To prevent this, another frequency-based technology might need to be considered e.g. PHS [6]. Because our system uses signal strength to determine the user's position, and Bluetooth signals are easily weakened or blocked by physical phenomenon, the accuracy of the positioning data will therefore vary. We also found that when walking around corners the system would lose its precision until it found new signals.

From our summative test we observed that the participant's level of understanding the technology was very different from one participant to another, and their experience with the touch-interface was at times non-existent. Because their level of understanding was so individually different it was hard to explain the tasks to be performed in a way so that everyone had a mutual understanding of what they were going to do. This indicated that using common terminology and assumptions was useless when communicating with the user group. During the same test, we realized that elderly people often get confused if the interface has too many objects and abstractions presented at the same time. We found that the more accurate the abstractions were, and the fewer choices that were presented at a time, the users would have a higher level of understanding of how to interact with the interface. This corresponds with a previous study by Williams et al. [11] concerning the considerations when designing human computer interfaces for elderly people. Their study indicates that elderly people often have less sensitivity to contrasts in color, and having multiple pictures or wallpaper patterns increases the risk of confusing a user. They concluded that in general, simplicity is key when designing visual displays for elderly people, as too much action in a display will confuse and frustrate an elderly user.

In the result section, we presented five implications for designing an indoor navigation system for elderly people. These implications are based on the results from the questionnaires, observations, interviews and tests, as well as related work regarding developing an interface for elderly people. We regard these implications as key points when designing an indoor navigation system for elderly users. These implications may be of use in similar circumstances, considering most of them concern physical and cognitive conditions of elderly people.

7 Conclusion

In our paper we propose a system with the aim to make indoor navigation easier for elderly and cognitively impaired people. We have used three different data gathering methods, and we have conducted three user tests as well as an experiment, to gain a deeper understanding of elderly users and their perspective on technology. All tests were conducted in natural environments with real users to assure realistic data. Using our results we present five implications for design when designing for elderly users. Our results indicate that elderly people can use our proposed system with a task completion ratio of 92.5 %. This system aims to improve the well-being of elders and help them become more independent by introducing a familiar design and integrating it with a pre-existing aid.

References

1. Crews, D.E., Zavotka, S.: Aging, disability, and frailty: implications for universal design. J. Physiol. Anthropol. **25**(1), 113–118 (2006)
2. Tsirmpas, C., Rompas, A., Fokou, O., Koutsouris, D.: An indoor navigation system for visually impaired and elderly people based on Radio Frequency Identification (RFID). Information Sciences (2014)
3. Renaudin, V., Yalak, O., Tomé, P., Merminod, B.: Indoor navigation of emergency agents. Eur. J. Navig. **5**(3), 36–45 (2007)
4. Cheng, J., Yang, L., Li, Y., Zhang, W.: Seamless outdoor/indoor navigation with WIFI/GPS aided low cost inertial navigation system. Phys. Commun. **13**, 31–43 (2014)
5. Ozdenizci, B., Ok, K., Coskun, V., Aydin, M.N.: Development of an indoor navigation system using NFC technology. In: 2011 Fourth International Conference on Information and Computing (ICIC), pp. 11–14. IEEE, April 2011
6. Aoki, R., Yamamoto, H., Yamazaki, K.: Android-based navigation system for elderly people in hospital. In: 2014 16th International Conference on Advanced Communication Technology (ICACT), pp. 371–377. IEEE, February 2014
7. Ran, L., Helal, S., Moore, S.: Drishti: an integrated indoor/outdoor blind navigation system and service. In: Proceedings of the Second IEEE Annual Conference on Pervasive Computing and Communications, 2004. PerCom 2004, pp. 23–30. IEEE, March 2004
8. Tervonen, J., Asghar, Z., Parviainen, E., Nissinen, H., Ylipelto, M., Shikur, H., Yamamoto, G.: Design for all case study: a navigation aid for elderly persons. In: 2014 International ICE Conference on Engineering, Technology and Innovation (ICE), pp. 1–5. IEEE, June 2014
9. Culén, A.L., Finken, S., Bratteteig, T.: Design and interaction in a smart gym: cognitive and bodily mastering. In: Holzinger, A., Ziefle, M., Hitz, M., Debevc, M. (eds.) SouthCHI 2013. LNCS, vol. 7946, pp. 609–616. Springer, Heidelberg (2013)
10. Zajicek, M.: Aspects of HCI research for older people. Univ. Access Inf. Soc. **5**(3), 279–286 (2006)
11. Williams, D., Alam, U., Ahamed, S.I., Chu, W.: Considerations in designing human-computer interfaces for elderly people. In: 2013 13th International Conference on Quality Software (QSIC), pp. 372–377. IEEE July 2013

Exploring Use Cases of Smart Presence for Retirement Communities

Karina R. Liles(✉), Rachel E. Stuck, Allison A. Kacmar, and Jenay M. Beer

University of South Carolina, Columbia, SC, USA
{lileskr, stuckr, akacmar}@email.sc.edu, jbeer@cse.sc.edu

Abstract. The goal of this study was to understand what employees of continuing care retirement communities (CCRC) think about the smart presence technology. To better understand their perceptions of the benefits, concerns, and adoption criteria for smart presence systems we have conducted a needs assessment with CCRC employees (N = 23) who were given first-hand experience operating the smart presence system, BEAM, as a local and a pilot user. From the interview data, the most commonly mentioned use case was interaction with others such as doctors, staff, and patients, family, friends, and guests and conduct/attend meetings. From the questionnaire data, the highest uses cases were entertainment (e.g. playing games), interaction for CCRC group activities, and receive remote visits and tours. Findings from this study can guide designers in identifying ways in which smart presence can be integrated into a CCRC environment and used by the employees. Future directions are also considered.

Keywords: Performance · Design · Human factors

1 Introduction

Smart presence technology allows individuals to communicate and interact with each other without being physically in the same space. The use of this technology has historically been in the workplace; however, there is potential for smart presence technology to be used in retirement communities. As we explore the uses of this technology in retirement communities, we must consider the acceptance of smart presence technology by the employees (e.g., nurses, staff, administration). Retirement community employees' perspectives of smart presence technology will influence their own as well as the older adults' adoption rate, as well as the nature the system may be used. Furthermore, by understanding the user's needs, designers can develop user-centered and user friendly systems. Retirement communities, broadly defined, include nursing homes, assisted living facilities, independent living and continuing care retirement communities (CCRCs). For this research, the retirement communities of interest were CCRCs. CCRCs were chosen because smart presence can impact a range of residents and employees that require/offer a range of medical care.

J. Zhou and G. Salvendy (Eds.): ITAP 2015, Part II, LNCS 9194, pp. 446–455, 2015.
DOI: 10.1007/978-3-319-20913-5_41

1.1 Defining Older Adults and Continuing Care Retirement Communities (CCRCs)

Individuals over the age of 65 are typically categorized as older adults. However, it is important to note that individual differences exist and the group of people over 65 years of age is very diverse. Thus, we can think about older adults as two major categories: (1) the younger-old group that is comprised of older adults between the ages of 65 and 75, and (2) the older-old group that is comprised of older adults over the age of 75 years old. This categorization is necessary as there are huge differences in capabilities and limitations between the groups (i.e. a 65 year old versus an 85 year old). Between 2000 and 2010, the population over age 65 grew at 15.5 %, a faster rate than the population under age 45. Overall, the population in the older ages grew at a faster rate than the population in the younger ages [1].

Older adults live in various housing arrangements. Most live in their home with a spouse while approximately 30 % live alone. Women aged 85 and older are most likely to live alone. Almost 50 % of women over age 75 live alone [2]. About 32 % of older adults live with other relatives [3]. There is a small percentage of older adults who live in institutional care (i.e., nursing homes, assisted living) and a majority of those residents are 85 years of age or older [2, 4]. People are living longer, remaining more active into older age, and staying in their homes longer before finding the need for institutional care.

One approach to providing care for the duration of older adulthood is continuing care retirement communities (CCRCs). CCRCs are communities for older adults that meet a wide range of needs. Healthy and independent older adult residents are able to live in apartments, condominiums, or homes depending on the individual community. With this approach, the CCRC offers a community where neighbors are at the same life stage and residents can feel at ease and secure. As a person ages and needs change, the CCRC is designed to meet those new needs. For example, CCRCs offer assisted living for persons needing some assistance with activities of daily living (ADLs), and they have skilled care for those who may need more intensive care. There are many benefits to living in this type of setting. The senior never needs to leave what they come to identify as their community allowing them to age-in-place. Aging-in place is a goal for many older adults; meaning they have the ability to age in their own home and/or community safely [5–7]. Living in one setting for the duration of one's remaining life, such as in a CCRC, means having the assurance that guidance and assistance will be provided in each step of the aging process. Lastly, family and friends can feel comfortable knowing their loved one has care and housing regardless of future changes in ability.

1.2 Smart Presence for Older Adults and Health Care

Promoting health and independence in later years requires more than access to adequate housing. Assistive technology has much promise in increasing older adults quality of life. One such technology is smart presence. Smart presence systems are used to foster communication among individuals using audio and video via a teleoperated device [8].

It offers the sensation of being present at a given location without physically being there. Video conferencing simultaneously transfers audio and video in two or more locations. With this setup, users interact with each other using a stationary apparatus. Unlike traditional video conferencing technologies, smart presence technologies such as the BEAM offer much more including mobility through teleoperation control. Currently the BEAM (and similar devices) are primarily used in the work place allowing companies to interact with others (i.e. clients, employees and teammates) as a means to conduct business in different locations. Although smart presence technology was originally designed and marketed for office settings, there is potential for use cases outside of the work place.

Older adults typically prefer to age-in-place and smart presence technologies have the potential to assist them in completing tasks they cannot perform of choose not to perform. Thus possibly helping older adults maintain their independence by reducing healthcare needs, providing everyday assistance and promoting social interaction [8]. Smart presence has potential for increase social interaction and social connectedness. Social connectedness is the concept in which an individual is actively involved with others or activities in which the involvement promotes comfort and wellbeing and reduces anxiety [9, 10]. Social connectedness is vital for successful aging as it can directly affect a person's probability of disease and disease-related disability, cognitive and physical function and active engagement with life.

In addition to being beneficial to older adults, there is potential for smart presence to positively impact health care workers that work in CCRCs. The general nature of smart presence makes it simple to transfer its application from office environments to other domains. The smart presence devices has been proven useful for meetings as well as conducting conversations while doing something as simple as walking down a hallway [11]. However, little research has investigated the use of smart presence in CCRC settings. It is important to understand how smart presence might fit into the CCRC health care setting, because without the support and buy-in from CCRC employees, the system may never be used to its fullest potential. Thus, we aim to identify specific use cases for smart presence as an initial step in assessing how to best implement this technology.

2 Goals of Research

It is critical that a human computer interaction (HCI) needs assessment is conducted on CCRC employees to better understand how smart presence can be deployed into this market. For this HCI needs assessment, we employed a multi-method approach and collected both quantitative and qualitative data. The quantitative data from the questionnaires provided an indication of how participants' felt the BEAM could be used. The qualitative data from the structured interviews helped us understand the user's perceptions to use smart presence technology. This is the first study dedicated for use specifically in CCRCS. This paper focuses on understanding CCRC employees' views on how a smart presence system may be used.

3 Methods

3.1 Participants

There were 23 participants in this study, 74 % identified themselves as White/Caucasian, 17 % as Black/African American, and 9 % as other. Of the total number of participants, 6 were male and 17 female. The average age of participants was 51.31 years with the ages ranging from 24-70 years of age (SD = 12.66). All participants were employees of CCRCs. The average number of years working in geriatrics was between 1-41 years (M = 13.24, SD = 10.93). Their positions within the company span across four categories: Administration, Activities, Nursing and Other (see Table 1).

Table 1. Work area/position

Area	Count
Administration *(includes 11 Directors)*	11
Activities *(includes 1 activities coordinator, excludes 3 directors of activity services)*	1
Nursing *(includes 1 RN, 1 LPN & 3 CNAs)*	5
Other *(includes 2 Chaplains, 1 Marketing employee, 1 Human Resources employee, 1 IT Support Engineer & 1 Office Manager)*	6

3.2 Platform

In this study, we used two Suitable Technologies BEAM Pro smart presence systems. Going beyond traditional video conferencing products, BEAM removes the constraints of a screen by coupling high-end video and audio with the freedom of mobility. This combination provides a rich experience that connects people. Using two BEAM smart presence systems, participants were able to see the BEAM driven on site (as a local user), and were able to drive a BEAM residing off site (as a pilot user). This gave participants the opportunity to experience the clarity, usability, and capabilities of the system.

3.3 Demonstrations

Two demonstrations were used in this study to allow participants to experience the BEAM both as a local and pilot user. In the local demonstration, a secondary researcher controlled the BEAM and held a conversation with the participant, located in the CCRC (see Fig. 1). The conversation included topics about the participant's day, their job, etc. During this demo, participants had a chance to see the BEAM design, screen size, video/audio quality, and mobility.

Next, during the second demonstration, the participants logged into a BEAM located remotely in a USC office (see Fig. 2). The participants interacted with a researcher, who gave instructions to drive the BEAM through an obstacle course.

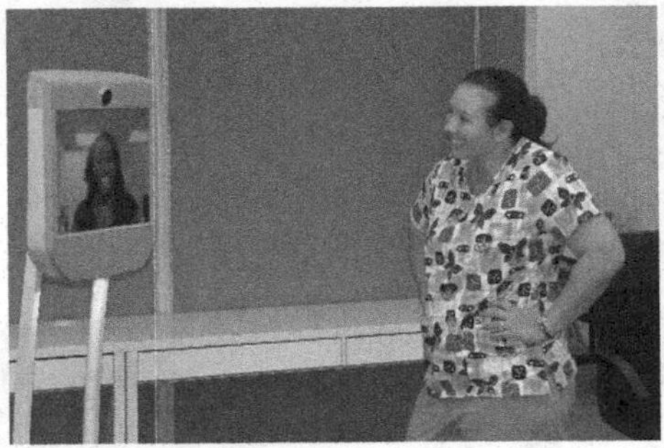

Fig. 1. Participant as local user

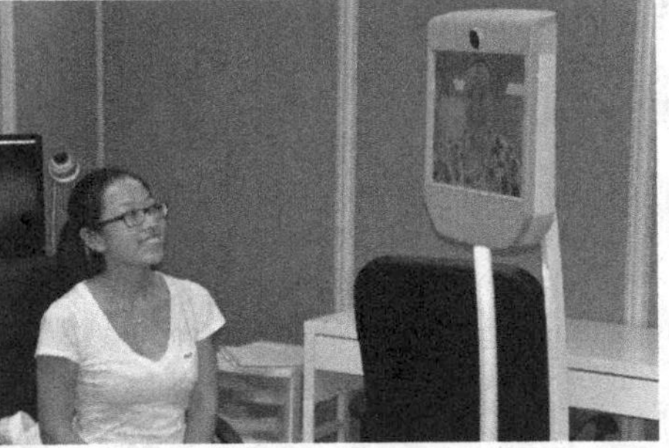

Fig. 2. Participant as pilot user

The obstacle course consisted of items and furniture commonly found in work and CCRC settings (such as tables, chairs, trashcans) as well as traffic cones and tape on the floor to indicate the direction the participants moved the BEAM. This set up was used to ensure consistency and control across all participants. A similar experience with BEAM is critical for comparing data across participants.

3.4 Materials

Interview Script. We developed a five-part interview script to collect qualitative and quantitative data regarding CCRC employees' preferences for using the BEAM system in their facility. The design of the interview script followed the methodology provided by Fisk and colleagues [12] and included a systematic development of the interview questions, materials, selection of the interview environment, recruitment of participants, and training of interview moderators. The interviews were conducted one-on-one, in a closed office or conference room. The script was semi-structured, meaning that there were a set order of questions, however, we did not restrict the participant if he/she diverted topic and discussed new ideas during the interview.

Questionnaires. The participants completed the usage checklist questionnaire. This Likert questionnaire captured participants' opinions about the feasibility of using the BEAM in CCRCs for a variety of administration, activities, nursing, and resident use tasks. For each given task, participants indicated their level of agreement for usage of the BEAM. For example, the checklist stated "I would use BEAM to…Conduct/attend meetings" and participants selected one of the answer choices: 1 = strongly disagree, 2 = disagree, 3 = neither agree or disagree, 4 = agree, or 5 = strongly agree.

3.5 Procedure

On arrival to the interview, participants provided written informed consent. They were informed that the discussion would be digitally recorded and later transcribed for analysis. The moderator then discussed the goals and topic of the interview, and allowed the participant to complete the pre-demonstration questionnaire regarding their opinion of the BEAM. The interview then followed a semi-structured order so that all participants would have the same flow of discussion:

- Formal introduction of researcher and co-researchers
- Demonstration of the BEAM; participant as a local user, followed by participant as a pilot user
- Discussion regarding the participants reactions to BEAM (e.g. How would you find the BEAM beneficial to you? Do you feel the BEAM can make an impact on the residents? How often do you think you would use the BEAM?)
- Post-demonstration questionnaire

At the conclusion of the semi-structured interview, the participants were thanked and compensated monetarily for their time. Only interview data about use cases are included in this report.

4 Results

4.1 Data Analysis

The interview transcripts were analyzed according to a coding scheme to identify patterns and themes from the discussions. To do this, first the audio recordings were transcribed verbatim with the participant's personal information omitted. Next, transcripts were segmented into units of analysis. A segment was defined as a statement or description that included the following dimensions: any utterance in which a thought, feeling, or opinion was related to attitudes and acceptance toward smart presence. Additionally, segments were created for any utterance that represented a potential use case.

Next, a coding scheme was developed to categorize each segment. A coding scheme is an organized categorization of the information in the interviews. The coding scheme was largely organized as benefits and concerns for use of the smart presence in CCRCs. The coding scheme was based on both the literature and the nature of the participant comments. In other words, it included themes already known to be related to attitudes about or use of smart presence [8]. Also an iterative category generation strategy was used. In this approach, the first segment was coded either on a category already included in the coding scheme, or assigned a new category label determined by the researcher that described the general idea of that segment (i.e., a bottom-up approach).

Coders were calibrated by conducting three rounds of independent coding on the same four randomly selected transcripts. Each round was followed by discussion of discrepancies and revision to the coding definitions. The final round of reliability resulted in an average of 87 % agreement between the two coders. Percent agreement was calculated as the percentage at which different coders agreed and remained consistent with their assignment of particular codes to particular data. There is no standard or base percentage of agreement among qualitative researchers, but 85 % seems to be a minimal acceptable benchmark [13]. After inter-coder agreement was met, the remaining transcripts were divided among the two coders to code independently.

The questionnaire data was entered into the statistical software SPSS and analyzed using both descriptive and nonparametric statistics. The criterion of $p < .05$ was used to determine statistical significance.

4.2 Understand CCRC Employees' Views on How a Smart Presence System May Be Used

Use Cases Mentioned in Interview. After operating the BEAM as a pilot and local user, participants were asked to consider uses for the BEAM in their role at the CCRC. Figure 3 depicts the mentioned use cases for BEAM in CCRCs by CCRC employees and the percentage of participants who mentioned each particular use case.

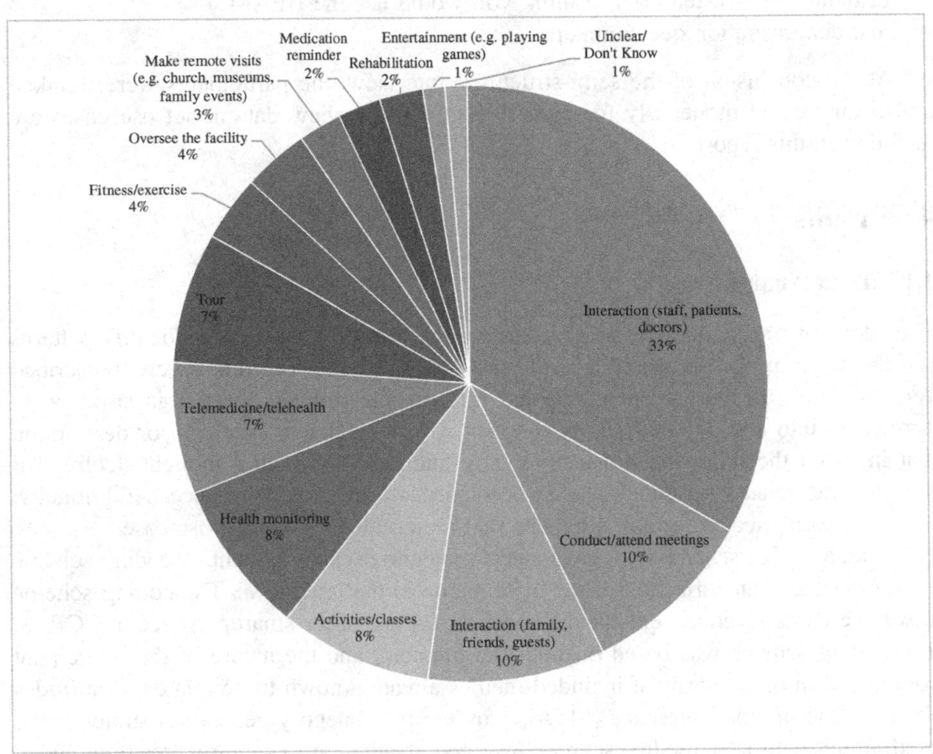

Fig. 3. Use cases (percentages represent number of times mentioned)

The most commonly mentioned use case was heath care-based interaction with doctors, staff, and patients. The two second highest use case categories (tied) were social interaction with others such as family, friends, and guests, as well as to use the BEAM to conduct/attend meetings. Overall, participants indicated that the BEAM would be most used for interaction with others. Although the aforementioned use cases were the most commonly mentioned, nearly half of the remaining responses ranged in nature. Participants expressed interest in using the BEAM for a variety of uses, such health monitoring, holding classes, and telemedicine.

BEAM Usage Checklist Questionnaire. In this questionnaire, we pre-identified 22 use cases, split them into categories: administration, activities, nursing, and resident use. We asked participants to indicate their level of agreement for using the BEAM to complete each task. The mean responses are depicted in Fig. 4. As the figure conveys, participants thought that the BEAM can be used for a variety of tasks. Each task mean was rated above a 3.0 (3 = neither agree nor disagree), indicating an openness to use the BEAM for all 22 tasks.

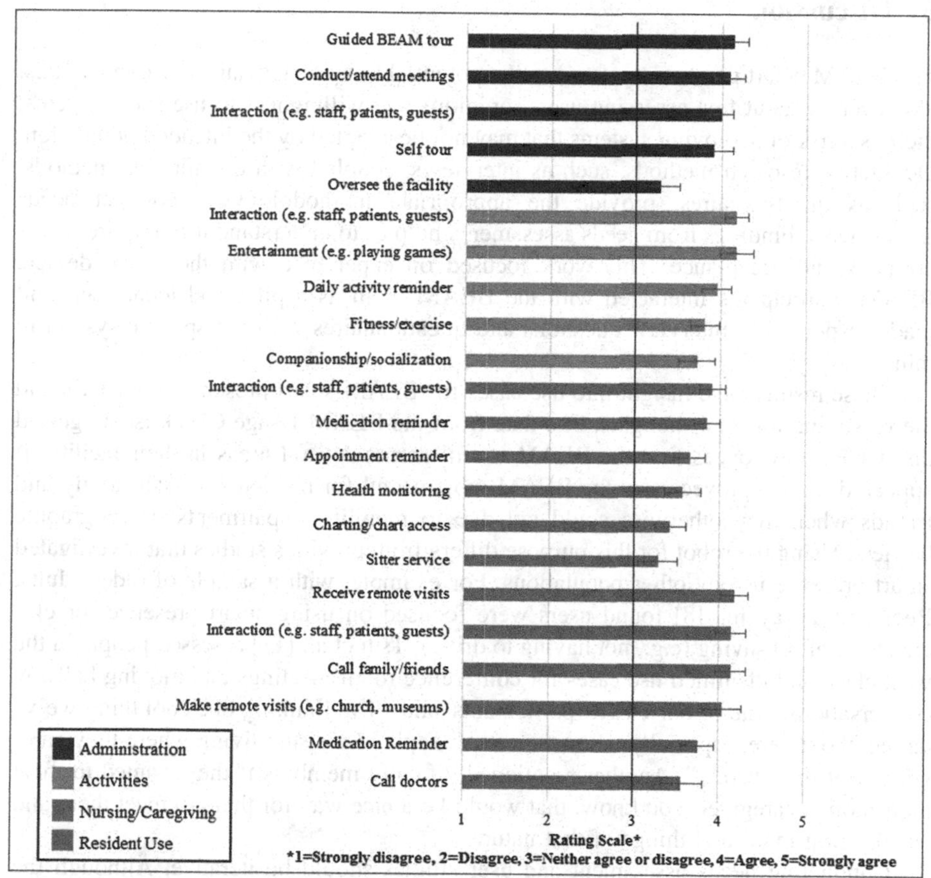

Fig. 4. BEAM usage checklist

Below we list the top 5 use cases chosen from this checklist. Some tasks were tied for the number one and two slot.

1. Entertainment (e.g. playing games) (M = 4.18, SE = 0.19),

   Interaction (e.g. staff, patients, guests) for activities (M = 4.18, SE = 0.14), Receive remote visits (M = 4.18, SE = 0.16);

2. Guided BEAM tour (M = 4.14, SE = 0.17),

   Call family/friends (M = 4.14, SE = 0.18),
   Interaction (e.g. staff, patients, guests) for resident use (M = 4.14, SE = 0.18);

3. Conduct/attend meetings (M = 4.09, SE = 0.17);
4. Make remote visits (e.g. church, museums) (M = 4.05, SE = 0.22); and
5. Interaction (e.g. staff, patients, guests) for administration (M = 4.00, SE = 0.14).

5 Discussion

The BEAM smart presence system has the potential to be beneficial for use in CCRCs. However, without first assessing users' opinions and willingness to use such systems, there is a risk of deploying systems that may not be adopted by the intended population. Qualitative research methods, such as interviews, coupled with quantitative methods, such as questionnaires, provide the appropriate methodology to conduct needs assessments. Findings from needs assessments help us to understand user requirements, attitudes and acceptance. This work focused on experience with the actual device, BEAM. Participants interacted with the BEAM, both as a pilot and local user, and made responses to interview questions and questionnaires with the specific system in mind.

These results gave insight into use cases for BEAM smart presence in CCRCs and the reasoning for their thoughts. The data from the BEAM Usage Checklist suggested that CCRC employees find the BEAM useful across several areas in their facility. It appeared that employees saw the BEAM most useful for residents to visit family and friends when they otherwise could not due to mobility impairments or geographic barriers. Using the robot for this purpose differs from previous studies that investigated smart presence use by other populations. For example, with a sample of older adults, Beer and Takayama [8] found users were focused on using smart presence for efficiency or effort saving (e.g., not having to drive); Tsui et al. [11] assessed people in the workplace and identified use cases for conference room meetings and moving hallway conversations. One of our CCRC participants said, "I'm thinking one cool thing we've talked about here, especially when there are people in assisted living where they can't get out of their bed…". Another mentioned, "family members if they wanted to meet their mom's caregiver, you know, that would be a nice way for them to meet them and check in on mom and things of that nature."

Conducting needs assessment and user studies should be iterative. Although the current study provides insight to this user population's suggested uses for this system, it is critical for future work to be conducted to ensure that future designs are effective. In this study, we learned the use of smart presence from the employee's perspective; however, it will be useful to review the attitudes of the residents and family members who will most likely benefit from smart presence. In fact, the goals of retirement communities are centered on the residents' needs and wellbeing. The participants made it clear that the facility's primary purpose is to accommodate the residents. In terms of methodology, it would be ideal if future work could also provide long-term experience with a smart presence system applied to the top use cases mentioned in this study. In addition to having the interviews, this would enable longitudinal and ethnographic studies that can use observations to learn about how smart presence can be used in retirement communities. It is important to ensure that the technology fits well into the environmental workspace, so longer-term studies would be critical in assessing sustained adoption.

Finally, future studies could incorporate usability aspects such as situation awareness, mental maps, immersion, and social connectedness as measures to assess whether BEAM is "just like being there." The present study provides ample evidence that the technology would be welcomed into retirement communities (attitudinal and intentional acceptance); next steps to assess adoption and actual long-term system use will prove to be just as exciting.

Acknowledgements. This research was supported by Suitable Technologies Educational Foundation, via the University of South Carolina, Department of Computer Science and Engineering Assistive Robotics and Technology Lab. ART Lab is affiliated with the SmartHOME^{TM}, a research initiative of the South Carolina SeniorSMART^{TM} Center of Economic Excellence. Special thank you to Benjamin Aaron and Blakeley Hoffman for their help with this project, as well as Bob Bauer from Suitable Technologies.

References

1. Howden, L., Meyer, J.: Age and Sex Composition: 2010–2010 Census Briefs (2011). Retrieved August 1, 2014. http://www.census.gov/prod/cen2010/briefs/c2010br-03.pdf
2. Administration on Aging, U.S. Department on Health and Human Services [AoA] (2009). A profile of older Americans (2009). http://www.aoa.gov/aoaroot/aging_statistics/profile/2009/docs/2009profile_508.pdf
3. Fields, J.: America's families and living arrangements: 2003 (Current Population Reports P20–553). Retrieved from U. S. Census Bureau website (2003). http://www.census.gov/prod/2004pubs/p20-553.pdf
4. Administration on Aging, U.S. Department on Health and Human Services [AoA] (2011). A profile of older Americans: 2011. http://www.aoa.gov/aoaroot/aging_statistics/Profile/2011/docs/2011profile.pdf
5. AARP. Beyond 50.05 survey (2005). Retrieved February 13, 2009. http://assets.aarp.org/rgcenter/il/beyond_50_05_survey.pdf
6. Gitlin, L.: Conducting research on home environments: Lessons learned and new directions. Gerontologist **43**(5), 628–637 (2003)
7. Lawton, M.P.: Aging and performance of home tasks. Hum. Factors **32**(5), 527–536 (1990)
8. Beer, J.M., Takayama, L.: Mobile remote presence systems for older adults: acceptance, benefits, and concerns. In: Proceedings of the 6th ACM/IEEE International Conference on Human-Robot Interaction HRI 2011, pp. 19–26 (2011)
9. Hagerty, B.M., Lynch-Sauer, J., Patusky, K.L., Bouwsema, M.: An emerging theory of human relatedness. J. Nurs. Scholarsh. **25**(4), 291–296 (1993). doi:10.1111/j.1547-5069.1993.tb00262.x
10. Rowe, J., Kahn, R.: Successful aging. Nurs. Adm. Q. **37**(4), 433 (1997)
11. Tsui, K.M., Desai, M., Yanco, H.A.: Exploring Use Cases for Telepresence Robots. Lowell, MA (2010)
12. Fisk, A.D., Rogers, W.A., Charness, N., Czaja, S.J., Sharit, J.: Designing for Older Adults: Principles and creative Human Factors Approaches, 2nd edn. CRC Press, Boca Raton (2009)
13. Saldana, J.: The Coding Manual for Qualitative Researchers, 2nd edn. Sage Publications, London (2013)

A Meta User Interface for Understandable and Predictable Interaction in AAL

Aida Mostafazadeh, Ali Asghar Nazari Shirehjini(✉), and Sara Daraei

Sharif University of Technology, Tehran, Iran
amostafazadeh@ce.sharif.edu, shirehjini@sharif.edu,
s_daraei@dena.sharif.edu

Abstract. The aim of this paper is the design and development of a novel user interface to interact with a meta system. Our focus is rather on interacting with Ambient Intelligence as a whole, which would for example enable users to influence the overall behavior and attributes of dynamic device compositions. We call such interfaces Meta User Interfaces. The design details of a proposed user interface as well as a cognitive walkthrough evaluation are presented in this paper.

Keywords: Ambient Intelligence · System image · Transparency · Predictability · Overriding default behavior · Human-environment interaction

1 Introduction

Ambient Intelligence (AmI) refers to a new paradigm of interaction where humans and other "smart players" interact with, and are supported by, their smart surroundings [1]. Smart players refer to entities acting in smart surroundings. Examples include humans, animals, smart factory machines, autonomous robots, and other intelligent autonomous systems. Examples of intelligent autonomous systems are home robot vacuums, security and surveillance systems, smart home energy management systems, or enhanced digital media equipment. They are designed to work on their own to support a domain specific task, in most cases without depending on infrastructure support coming from their operation environment. Smart surroundings are everyday living or operation environments of these autonomous systems. Smart surrounding are physical spaces that have been instrumented to provide natural interaction capabilities and useful behaviors such as rule based automation, statistically learned adaptations, etc.

The concept of Ambient Intelligence has been widely adopted. It is proved to be effective in terms of making life easier [2] supporting healthier living [3], or reducing the in-house energy consumption [4, 5]. Much valuable research reported successful deployments of AmI within various application domains such as independent living, energy-aware production, or smart health.

To make AmI happen, first everyday objects must transform into networked information appliances [6]. This is done by augmenting everyday objects and devices with sensing, communication, and networking technology to support a specific task. Next, available information appliances and smart players form together "ad hoc

J. Zhou and G. Salvendy (Eds.): ITAP 2015, Part II, LNCS 9194, pp. 456–464, 2015.
DOI: 10.1007/978-3-319-20913-5_42

ensembles". A generic architecture supporting ensemble creation is presented in [8]. This last step orchestrates entities available in a smart surrounding to offer a coherent behavior [8] and collective intelligence [9] (cf. Fig. 2). In doing so, a composition of systems is created. The coherently acting devices that implement a higher level collective intelligent behavior are compositional parts of Ambient Intelligence. We use the concept of meta systems [10] to refer to such compositions. In other words, Ambient Intelligence can be considered as a meta-system with intelligence that *governs* multiple information systems (information appliances) to support various autonomous systems (the smart players) residing and acting within the same physical space. Figure 1 shows the relationships among different components of ambient intelligence environment.

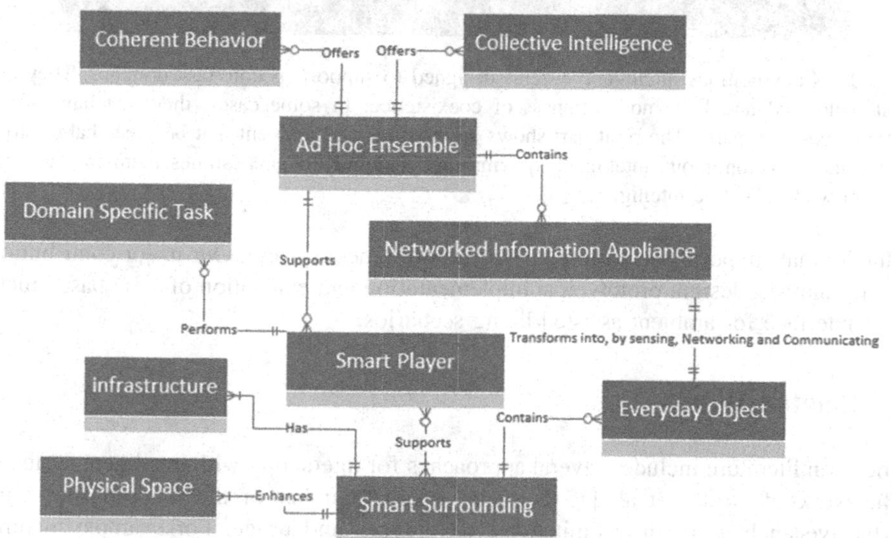

Fig. 1. AmI is a meta system composed by the physical space, networked information appliances, sensors, and infrastructure that are seamlessly integrated into the physical space with the autonomous intelligent systems – the smart players – residing and interacting with it [8].

The important question that arises here is: how would users interact with such a meta-system that implements a higher level collective intelligent behavior [11]? Please note the conceptual difference to the situation where people would interact with *N* stand-alone systems, each exposing a limited intelligent assistance for a very specific task domain. For this later case, many useful user interfaces have been presented [12, 13]. But can we use traditional UIs to interact with above explained meta systems?

We use the term Meta User Interface (MetaUI) to refer to user interfaces that support performing tasks at the meta system level. While a significant amount of important research covers interaction issues on the *device level,* to the best of our knowledge no research has studied the interaction between a human (smart player) and a meta system. In this paper, we present the user centric analysis and design of a

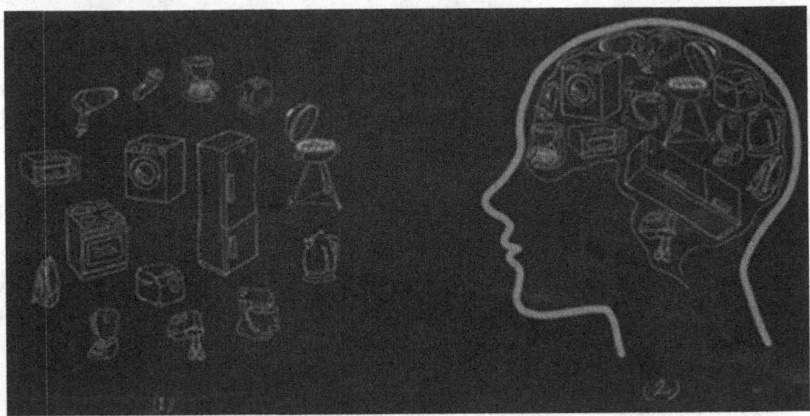

Fig. 2. N autonomous intelligent systems designed to support specific task domains. They are just collocated and have no awareness of coexistence. In some cases, they just have some interactions (left part). The right part shows an instrumented ambient that becomes habitat to a multitude of autonomous intelligent systems that dynamically orchestrates them into a meta system with collective intelligence [8].

MetaUI that supports performing operations on a meta system. Our major contribution is the analysis, design, prototypical implementation and evaluation of a 3D based meta user interface for ambient assisted living scenarios.

2 Related Work

The open literature includes several approaches for interacting with intelligent systems. The work of Ardoti et al. [15] surveys a large number of these approaches with extensive analysis of their limitations, advantages and usage. For example, natural speech and gesture based interfaces are commonly used to interact with smart objects such as the work in [14]. Much research has been done in the area of context recognition which is a key element for implementing context aware interaction. The work in [7] discusses group activity recognition. An approach for measuring location is presented in [20]. Anwar Hossain et al. [19] present an adaptive interaction framework based on quality of context information to address wrong automations and to deal with uncertainty. However, the focus of related work is on directly interfacing single parts of an environment such as a smart TV or intelligent kitchen devices. In contrast, we aim at interfacing the meta system as a whole, rather than focusing on controlling its compositional parts. By doing so, we address the common problems of interaction with smart environments such as over-automation, missing ability to override default behavior, lack of predictability and observability etc., which are rather attributes of/subject to meta system interaction.

Many researchers have studied the topic of interaction with intelligent systems and discussed interaction issues. In this work, we analyze these studies to elaborate requirements, which then will be used to design an appropriate MetaUI. The lack of control and over automation have been reported as a major weakness of fully automated interaction [16] because people do not accept a fully automated environment, and in fact want to always be in control. As Sheridan states in his study [16], over automation negatively affects the acceptance of automated systems. According to [16], there are 10 degrees "to express the level of automation in an adaptive system". Since Ambient Intelligence is a concept related to automation, in order to ensure user acceptance, a Meta User Interface must have the ability to change the level of automation (cf. Table 1, Requirement #1). Another basic requirement for any kind of user interface is to provide perceivable affordances. Users must be able to figure out possibilities of interaction, as soon they face anything they want to work with [6]. This is regardless of the interaction is automated or explicit interfaces have disappeared. Therefore, user interfaces for AmI need to be *explorable* in a way they can understand how they can work their smart surrounding (cf. Table 1, Requirement #2). Another issue is the relatively low reliability of automatic system behaviors that lead into distrust [17].

Whether a specific automatic system behavior is reasonable or not, users need to be aware of their existence. They want to be informed when important things go on in their spaces [18] (cf. Table 1, Requirement #3). This is because, if actions initiated by the system are not visible to users, or when users fail to explain what exactly triggered certain automatic behaviors, they might be confused [6]. Further, a lack of *visibility* and *understandability* can cause negative mental responses such as anger [6]. In addition, it can lead into incomplete or incorrect mental models, which would negatively affect interaction performance and cause misunderstandings. Therefore, when interacting with Ambient Intelligence users need some means of support for visibility and understandability, in a way they perceive and reason about automatic behaviors of their surroundings (cf. Table 1, Requirement #4). Users also want to predict how the Ambient Intelligence will react upon certain user activities or in case certain events would happen. Empirical studies provide scientific evidence that the lack of predictability leads into distrust [17]. Thus, another requirement for the proposed MetaUI is to support users with predicting automatic behaviors of Ambient Intelligence (cf. Table 1, Requirement #5). In a recent research [19] we discussed that a mixed-initiative approach is the key to increase user acceptance and trust in AmI environments (cf. Table 1, Requirement #6).

Table 1. Requirements elaborated to design Meta User Interfaces

Number	Requirement
1	Level of automation
2	Explorability
3	Understandability
4	Visibility
5	Predictability
6	Mixed-Initiative

Considering these evidences, we propose an interaction approach to overcome the mentioned weaknesses. Next we explain the architecture of our system.

3 Design of a Meta User Interface

To design the MetaUI, we conducted an empirical user study to understand tasks a MetaUI needs to support. The study and the results have been presented by Khojasteh and Shirehjini (2014) in [21]. In this section, we describe the architectural components of the proposed system for interfacing meta systems that expose a collective intelligent behavior.

Notice that we explicitly distinguish between those tasks performed on the level of single devices, which we refer to as *device level* tasks, and tasks that are internal to a meta system. An example for device level tasks is when an elderly person turns on his smart TV to play a social game with his grandson. Therefore, operations such as turning on and off devices, or changing the behavior of a smart entity (e.g. assistive home robot) are not subject matter of meta interaction, because the scope of the interaction does not go behind affecting a single autonomous intelligent system. In contrast, other tasks such as adjusting the level of automation for an entire house are influencing the attributes of the meta system, thus can be considered as operations performed on the meta system level. The Meta UI is composed of the environment 3D representation, a behavior manager, to create, alter and delete behaviors, and an action manager to supervise the active, previously active or soon to be activated behaviors (cf. Fig. 3).

3.1 Behavior Manager

The behavior manager provides necessary functionalities to create new behaviors. In addition, it allows for the meta system to *download* or learn additional behaviors. A behavior in our system is a set of actions that the meta system executes to satisfy a set of post conditions. In order to describe a new behavior user needs to declare a set of preconditions and post conditions from the list of all the rules in the environment. A rule refers to an environmental or temporal event or events related to user actions. For example "if a person enters the room" is a rule and can be the precondition to some specific behaviors that user requires the system to accomplish if someone enters the room. Using the pre and post conditions, representation of environment state, before and after the completion of the behavior can be automatically visualized (cf. Fig. 3) User can make use of this component by tapping on the automation button as shown in Fig. 3.

Through the behavior manager users can edit downloaded behaviors, or create new rules from the scratch. Furthermore, it assists users with overriding and changing existing behaviors. The behavior manager maintains three *behavior lists.* These lists represent all the automatic responses that the meta system can currently offer. This section along with the next part satisfies Requirement #2, since it allows users to explore the system behaviors.

3.2 Action Manager

In order to make the meta system level actions visible and predictable (Requirements #4, #5), the MetaUI implements an *action manager* component, containing the three behavior lists. For each behavior represented in the lists, a declaration part can be represented, which shows the preconditions and post conditions for that behavior along with the rule that activates the behavior. As you can see in Fig. 3, the "Medicine Reminder" behavior is activated when the "time event" happens and alters the environment from the state that is depicted in *before* section to the state that is represented in the *after* section.

The first list that is shown in the lower left part of Fig. 3 represents the behaviors that took place in the past, which are either done successfully or has been terminated by the user or the system due to confliction, dissatisfaction or directly by the user. The second list contains the behaviors that are currently taking place and altering the environment. User is supposed to be able to conclude the reason of each alteration in the environment and match them to the currently performing behaviors using the declaration part of behaviors. The 3D visualization of before and after states helps towards this goal. The third list represent the behaviors that will *probably* take place in

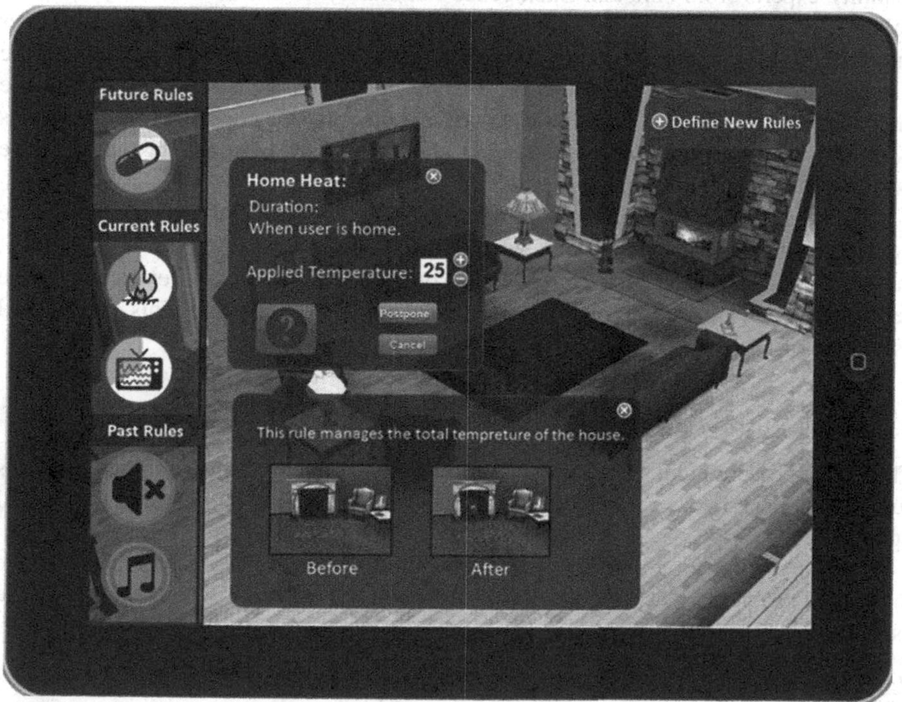

Fig. 3. The proposed meta user interface provides an image of Ambient Intelligence meta systems. It is designed to support visibility, predictability, overriding default behavior, conflict handling, and perceived control in presence of system initiated automated behaviors (implicit interaction).

the future, we use the term *probably* because the possibility for a behavior to take place depends on the conditions of the environment, and each behavior has a probability at any specific time, which is a number in the range of 0 to 100. This probability is used to augment the corresponding icons of each behavior, as shown in the upper left part of the Fig. 3.

Furthermore there are options represented for each behavior, users can cancel or postpone an ongoing behavior, prevent the system from activating a behavior and perceive the reasons for terminated past actions in case of a confliction.

Each list would appear on the screen if the user taps on the buttons which are labeled as *past*, *now* and *future*, user can also make the lists disappear by tapping again on the same buttons.

4 Evaluation

As a means to usability evaluation a cognitive walkthrough was selected to evaluate our design. Using cognitive walkthrough early prototypes can be evaluated, the ease of learning can be estimated and the reasons to possible errors can be discovered. The evaluation was performed by a group consisting of the writers of this paper and two usability experts from Ambient Intelligence Laboratory of Sharif University of Technology. As the first step of the process, we distinguished the users of our Meta User Interface, and the identified main tasks to evaluate, and for each task we defined the correct action sequence. Afterwards the experts stepped through each task to evaluate the possibility to achieve them. For each task experts provide success or failure stories as to why the expected users would either choose or fail to choose the action as we assumed in the action sequence.

The process and the results are depicted in Table 2. After analyzing the results we figured out that the first step, which was to find the list icon and tap on it, had failed; meaning that the users either cannot figure out the availability and existence of the behavior lists, or cannot interpret the icons corresponding to each list. This can be fixed using one of the two options:

1. Redesign the icons.
2. Make the lists visible at the startup.

The first approach might seem more facile, but to prevent any future usability problems such as the ones that we captured, we changed the prototype and applied the second option (Table 2).

Thus a second prototype (cf. Fig. 3) was built in order to overcome the above mentioned problems. The differences that distinguished this prototype from the last are as follows.

- The Action Manager is visible by default, it can disappear later on as user wants.
- The Action Manager contains a one-columned list.
- The one-columned Action Manager is decomposed horizontally into 3 sections corresponding to past, present and future actions.

Table 2. The cognitive walkthrough shows that the first steps were problematic

Task	Failed Step
Define new behavior	1st
Postpone an action that's going to trigger	1st
Find out what conflicts has happened in the system	1st
Find out the result of a behavior	1st
Cancel an ongoing action	1st
Define new behavior	1st

As you might notice, the Action Manager is one-columned in the latter prototype; since the Action Manager is visible by default, having only one column leads to covering less space. Moreover, the list decomposition is horizontal thus the list can represent the actions whilst having one column and less width as a result, which allows the Action Manager to cover a smaller space.

We conducted a second walkthrough, with the same user assumptions and the same task. The new prototype leads to changes in action sequences for each tasks, therefore we altered the sequences accordingly.

5 Conclusion

In this paper, we have presented a Meta User Interface that is designed to satisfy 6 main requirements that are considered essential according to our literature study. The design of the User Interface and the evaluation of the prototype were explained. There are aspects of this system that are planned for future work. First, a task migration feature will be included in the system. Another future work is a wizard of Oz evaluation of the system with the features against a system without them. Also, automatically generating visualizations for behaviors will be considered in the future work. Also we tend to include some features to enable the behaviors to be downloaded and installed on the system; therefore the user can install new behaviors on her system as she can install apps on her smart phone.

References

1. Aarts, E., Encarnaçao, J.: The Emergence of Ambient Intelligence. Springer, Berlin (2006)
2. Friedewald, M., et al.: Perspectives of ambient intelligence in the home environment. Telematics Inform. **22**(3), 221–238 (2005)
3. Kleinberger, T., Becker, M., Ras, E., Holzinger, A., Müller, P.: Ambient intelligence in assisted living: enable elderly people to handle future interfaces. In: Stephanidis, C. (ed.) UAHCI 2007 (Part II). LNCS, vol. 4555, pp. 103–112. Springer, Heidelberg (2007)
4. Heo, N., Varshney, P.K.: Energy-efficient deployment of intelligent mobile sensor networks. IEEE Trans. Syst. Man Cybern. Part A Syst. Hum. **35**(1), 78–92 (2005)

5. Zamora-Izquierdo, M.A., Santa, J., Gómez-Skarmeta, A.F.: An integral and networked home automation solution for indoor ambient intelligence. IEEE Pervasive Comput. **9**(4), 66–77 (2010)
6. Norman, D.A.: Yet another technology cusp: confusion, vendor wars, and opportunities. Commun. ACM **55**(2), 30–32 (2012)
7. Gordon, D., Hanne, J.H., Berchtold, M., Nazari Shirehjini, A.A., Beigl, M.: Towards collaborative group activity recognition using mobile devices. Mob. Netw. Appl. **18**(3), 326–340 (2013)
8. Kirste, T.: Smart environments. In: Aarts, E., Encarnação, J. (eds.) True Visions, pp. 321–337. Springer, Heidelberg (2006)
9. Kennedy, J., Kennedy, J.F., Eberhart, R.C.: Swarm Intelligence. Morgan Kaufmann, San Francisco (2001)
10. Palmer, K.D., Meta-systems Theory (2006) http://holonomic.net
11. Maes, P.: How to do the right thing. Connection Sci. **1**(3), 291–323 (1989)
12. Park, Y.T., Sthapit, P., Pyun, J.-Y.: Smart digital door lock for the home automation. In: TENCON 2009–2009 IEEE Region 10 Conference. IEEE (2009)
13. Warner, A.F., Suchecki, M.T.: Smart bed system and apparatus. Google Patents (2006)
14. Coutaz, J.: Meta-user interfaces for ambient spaces. In: Coninx, K., Luyten, K., Schneider, K.A. (eds.) Task Models and Diagrams for Users Interface Design. LNCS, vol. 4385, pp. 1–15. Springer, Heidelberg (2007)
15. Ardito, C., et al.: Interaction with large displays: a survey. ACM Comput. Surv. (CSUR) **47** (3), 46 (2015)
16. Sheridan, T.B.: Adaptive automation, level of automation, allocation authority, supervisory control, and adaptive control: distinctions and modes of adaptation. IEEE Trans. Syst. Man Cybern. Part A Syst. Hum. **41**(4), 662–667 (2011)
17. Jian, J.-Y., Bisantz, A.M., Drury, C.G.: Foundations for an empirically determined scale of trust in automated systems. Int. J. Cogn. Ergon. **4**(1), 53–71 (2000)
18. Van Welie, M., Trætteberg, H.: Interaction patterns in user interfaces. In: Proceedings of. Seventh Pattern Languages of Programs Conference: PLoP (2000)
19. Hossain, M.A., Shirehjini, A.A.N., Alghamdi, A.S., El Saddik, A.: Adaptive interaction support in ambient-aware environments based on quality of context information. Multimedia Tools Appl. **67**(2), 409–432 (2013)
20. Nazari Shirehjini, A., Shirmohammadi, S.: A high precision sensor system for indoor object positioning and monitoring. In: IEEE International Workshop on Robotic and Sensors Environments, 2009. ROSE 2009, IEEE (2009)
21. Khojasteh, N., Nazari Shirehjini, A.A.: Experimental analysis and design of a meta user interface for smart homes. B.Sc Thesis, Sharif University of Technology, Computer Engineering Department, Tehran, Iran (2014)

Giving Elderly Access to Smart Environments

Providing Adaptive User Interfaces Based on Web Components, the Universal Remote Console and the Global Public Inclusive Infrastructure

Lukas Smirek, Alexander Henka(✉), and Gottfried Zimmermann

Stuttgart Media University, Nobelstraße 10, 70569 Stuttgart, Germany
{smirek, henka}@hdm-stuttgart.de, gzimmermann@acm.org

Abstract. An increasing number of devices and applications from the Smart Home and Ambient Assisted Living domain are leaving the experimental state and are reaching commercial viability. These developments come with great opportunities, but also with challenges for elderly and disabled people. In this paper, we propose a holistic approach, using concepts of the Global Public Infrastructure (GPII), the Universal Remote Console (URC) and the upcoming technology of Web Components, to build personalized and adaptive user interfaces for people with special needs. The goal is to provide for everyone the interface fitting best his or her needs. In this paper we present the preliminary result of our approach and discuss its impact on the design of adaptive user interfaces.

Keywords: Human computer interaction · Accessibility · Elderly users · GPII · URC · AAL · Smart home · Web components · Adaptive user interfaces

1 Introduction

We face a world with an increasing presence of information and communication technologies (ICT) in everyday life situations. ICT products are available in public spaces, at work and in our homes. Also the technical interconnections and interdependencies of ICT products are continuously increasing. Consequently, we are approaching a world of so-called smart environments. This trend yields a high potential to support us in our daily life and to make it more comfortable.

This is true for "regular" users but also for people with special needs like people with disabilities or elderly people. Several studies [1–3] have illustrated the potential of providing smart environments for elderly people and that elderly are willing to use them as a support for retaining an independent life. What also needs to be considered in this scenario, is that ICT products are not only getting richer in functionality, but also in complexity [4] involved with new challenges for the design of user interfaces [5]. Different users have different needs, preferences and requirements, regarding the usage of an ICT product. This is of special importance when considering elderly people, where accessibility issues can change over time and the skill level of interacting with ICT products varies broadly [6]. One approach of providing user interfaces to a

J. Zhou and G. Salvendy (Eds.): ITAP 2015, Part II, LNCS 9194, pp. 465–475, 2015.
DOI: 10.1007/978-3-319-20913-5_43

heterogeneous user group, with changing requirements, are so called *adaptive user interfaces* [7], which accommodate the needs and preferences of a distinct user.

However, it must be taken into account that the smart home market is still an emerging and consequently a very volatile market with a lot of different technologies. As pointed out in [8], it is very important that the choice of a certain adaptation engine does not restrict the users' opportunities to connect to multiple smart home technologies rather than to a single one. Instead, an appropriate adaptive user interface platform for smart homes and Ambient Assisted Living (AAL) applications must be able to provide adaptive user interfaces upfront so that a heterogeneous user group can access the system, while at the same time it must be able to integrate different smart home technologies in the backend so that users can benefit from all available technologies.

In this paper, we describe an approach using concepts of the *Global Public Infrastructure* (GPII) [9], the *Universal Remote Console* (URC) [10, 11] and the upcoming technology of *Web Components* [12], to build personalized and adaptive user interfaces for people with special needs. We propose an approach to build adaptive user interfaces, using self-adapting user interface widgets on the basis of Web Components. Beside the adaptation logic, the user interface widgets will comprise mechanisms to connect to GPII and to the URC framework. The connection to GPII enables the component to get access to the users personal preference set [13] with which the component adapts its appearance to the user's preferences and personal needs. We use URC for the adaptation at design time and for connecting to different devices and services in a smart-home environment (e.g., a television, HVAC device). URC introduces an abstract user interface layer for any device or service, called a *user interface socket*. Concrete user and device specific interfaces can be build upon this socket layer taking the user's needs and contextual parameters, such as the device being used, into account.

The remainder of this paper is structured as follows. Section 2 provides an overview of related work. Section 3 describes the adaptation mechanisms of GPII and URC. Section 4 illustrates the concept of our approach. Section 5 provides a discussion on our work, displays envisioned benefits, and offers an outlook on the current status and next steps.

2 Related Work

Today, it is widely agreed that smart homes and the concept of AAL can bring great benefits for a wide spectrum of users. Mavrommati and Darzentas present an overview on HCI issues related to Ambient Intelligence [14]. Nevertheless, Saizmar and Kim claim that HCI research in smart homes is limited and biased to specific situations [15]. Abascal et al. criticize that, although many scenarios have been described in the field of ambient intelligence, the interface between the user and the system still remains unclear [16]. In order to improve acceptance of Ambient Intelligence and to make it capable to provide better life quality in a non-obtrusive way, Casas et al. point out the necessity to combine ongoing Ambient Intelligence technological developments with user-centered design techniques [17].

In the same vein, Mavrommati and Darzentas point to the necessity of focusing on a more user centered HCI perspective [14]. Studies have shown that elderly people are willing to use Smart Home technologies for the purpose of a longer independent life [1, 18]. It is acknowledged that Ambient Assisted Living technologies have the potential of providing safe environments for elderly people [2].

Nevertheless, at the moment, many technologies do not yet meet the needs of elderly people and current solutions overemphasize the importance of smart devices while either neglecting or lacking real implementations on the side of human interaction and human power [17]. Therefore, several authors have argued for a more user-centered view in the Ambient Assisted Living domain [17, 19, 20].

Kleinberger et al. [21] and Abascal et al. [17] are concerned with the design of appropriate user interfaces in the field of Ambient Assisted Living. Their conclusion is that natural and adaptive interfaces can bring great benefits to this field.

The PIAPNE Environment [16] is an adaptive Ambient Assisted Living system for elderly people based on three models: A user model (capabilities, permissions), a task model (user activity) and a context (environment) model. The system consists of multiple layers, including a middleware layer to bridge different network technologies and an intelligent service layer to which intelligent applications (interfaces) can be connected.

The MyUI project [22] provides a framework for self-adaptive user interfaces. The project follows the approach that user interface developers create an abstract application interaction model that is rendered at runtime according to a user profile and environmental conditions. It uses an interactive TV set as a communication point. MyUI allows only controlling one device at the time, with a dedicated user interface. Responding to multiple devices in a single user interface in order to execute scenarios in a smart home environment is not within the project's scope. A scenario that falls under this condition would be dimming the lights, switching on TV and blue-ray player with one command; hence, enabling "cinema mode".

3 Providing a Suitable User Interface for Everyone

In 2010, Sloan et al. illustrated in their work the potential and benefits of adaptive web user interfaces for the elderly [24]. However, they pointed out the necessity for frameworks and environmental settings to accommodate this adaptation process and that an appropriate system was still missing at that time. By now, The GPII and the URC framework provide appropriate solutions to close this gap of missing foundation technologies.

3.1 The Global Public Inclusive Infrastructure

The GPII serves as a foundation to support adaptation of user interfaces across devices by transferring settings from one device or service to another. The vision of the GPII is to provide personalized, self-adaptive user interfaces to all people, including those facing accessibility barriers when using the Internet or other electronic services.

Independent of age, disability or literacy, people shall be enabled to use the full advantage of the Internet and with that having the chance to access typical features and applications of our modern world.

In order to benefit from this infrastructure users have to customize their private devices like PCs, smart phones, etc., according to their own needs. The GPII uses the settings from the user's personal device and stores them as a so-called *personal preference set*. The user's preferences contain information like the need for increased font size, a scanning keyboard, or volume settings. The preference set is stored in the cloud. From now on the user can use every device connected to the GPII. Typical examples are ticket machines, computers in public libraries or applications running on any platform. The adaptation process is conducted by transferring the user's needs and preferences from one system or application to another. The adaptation process comprises preparation at runtime as well as design time. If a user expresses the need for a larger font size, a specific color theme or magnification, this can easily be done at runtime.

However, more complex adaptations like content adaptations (e.g. the provision of sign-language videos to describe content for deaf people) need to be prepared when designing the application; since sign language videos cannot be automatically generated for the corresponding content at runtime [30].

In several studies it was illustrated that the elderly can benefit from assistive technologies and the conformance of user interfaces to accessibility guidelines [25, 26]. However, elderly users face also issues due to different perception models or strategies in the meaning making process [27–29].

As it was stated in [23], the elderly rely on familiar interaction patterns and tend to use them more frequently rather then to search for alternative interaction flows to accomplish their goals. When confronted with semantic barriers where they cannot apply their familiar interaction concepts they rather blame themselves than the application's design. Therefore, the elderly have preferences and needs in which an adaptation must be conducted on the content's semantic level [23] and as described, semantic content adaptation is hard to undertake without design time preparations. Zimmermann et al. [31] illustrated that user interfaces can be modeled as layered systems, consisting of three layers: presentation and input events, structure and grammar, and content and semantics; hence, in an attempt to provide a strongly user-centered adaption one has to consider runtime and design-time adaption [30].

3.2 The Universal Remote Console

The Universal Remote Console (URC) focuses mainly on electronic devices that can be found in smart home environments and in the AAL domain. URC provides pluggable, portable and personalized user interfaces; hence, people can control any target device or service with a controller-device and with a user interface, which best fits their needs.

In order to enable pluggable user interfaces, every target has to provide an abstract description of its user interface functionality - the *user interface socket description*, or just "*socket description*". A socket description is basically an API description of a devices' operating interface and contains information about properties that can be accessed by a user, in the form of variables (e.g., the temperature of a thermostat), commands that can be sent to the device (e.g., changing the channel on a TV) and notifications that are dispatched by the target (e.g., reminder function of a calendar). Based on these socket descriptions, one can either develop personalized user interfaces for different user groups or additional resources for existing user interfaces.

User interface resources are associated with dedicated socket elements and can be any user interface component, e.g. supplemental labels for multi-language support, additional help texts or instructions to sign language videos. User interfaces and user interface resources are stored on a resource server and are downloaded on demand at runtime. In a usage scenario, a user connects their controller device, e.g., a smartphone running a URC client, via the URC system to a target. Based on their specific controller device, a list of appropriate user interfaces is then presented for the user to choose from. The chosen user interface is automatically downloaded from the resource server and virtually plugged into the socket exposed by the target.

Targets of the same class (like TVs) could all expose a basic common socket, containing common functionality. A person can therefore exchange their device while retaining its familiar user interface. This usage of personalized user interfaces can also be seen as an asset for the elderly, since they can continue to use their well-known user interfaces, without being afraid of using new technologies; therefore, pluggable user interfaces can accommodate different perception models or meaning making strategies.

4 Concept of the Envisioned Approach

We propose an approach to provide self-adapting user interface components, so-called widgets. Each widget is intended to execute a certain task, like one for the log-in to a device, or another one representing a simple switch. All widgets together form a set of building blocks that can be used to create more complex user interfaces. We decided to use the upcoming technology of *Web Components* [32] for implementing the different building blocks, in order to be as platform independent as possible and to be able to define independent components with clear interfaces.

Web Components provide the potential to define and use and arbitrary HTML elements that extend the element space of HTML. For example, one can define a "login element" consisting of two form elements for user name and password, and a button that performs the login action. Grouping these elements by using a nested element structure, a web author can better characterize the semantics of this component, using only one sophisticated HTML element. This new element internally consists of the same three elements (two form elements and a button), but those are hidden inside the widget. Web Components are an umbrella term for three concepts: *Custom Elements* [34], *Shadow DOM* [33] and *HTML Import* [35].

Custom Elements is an API that allows defining and registering arbitrary HTML elements in the web browser. Hereby, web authors can define their own library of HTML elements.

Shadow DOM characterizes the internal DOM tree of HTML elements. Complex elements make use of internal elements, e.g., to form the control components like a "play", "fast-forward" or "mute" button in the HTML5 video element. So far, only the web browser was permitted to manipulate the internal structure of HTML elements. By the Shadow DOM specification a developer gains access to this internal DOM tree. The API of the Shadow DOM can be used to hide and manipulate the implementation details of arbitrary HTML elements, i.e., the Shadow DOM represents the structure and appearance of a Custom Element and is exposed to a user.

HTML Imports is a mechanism that allows importing HTML documents or individual elements from different documents during runtime. HTML Imports provide the foundation to build libraries of arbitrary HTML elements, which can hereby be reused in multiple HTML documents. The import of the HTML elements can also be carried out from remote sources. We can utilize this to store HTML templates adjusted for dedicated user groups and devices on a server like the URC's resource server and download the appropriate templates during runtime.

One of the Web Component's benefits is their web-based foundation; thus, their platform independence and runtime adaptability. Assistive technologies such as screen readers interact with web pages as the browser renders them; therefore, Web Components and elements in the Shadow DOM are accessed just as any other element and their accessibility depends equally on accessible design and its conformance to accessibility guidelines.

As stated in our previous work, URC and the GPII can be an asset for providing adaptable user interfaces in smart home environments [30, 36]. Web Components can be a connector that accommodates the need for runtime adaptation, platform independence and the connection to URC sockets via common web communication methods. Also, they allow for reloading of resources to conduct deeper adaptations if the options for simple adaptations (e.g., increasing font-size) are exhausted. Figure 1 illustrates the interplay of the involved technologies.

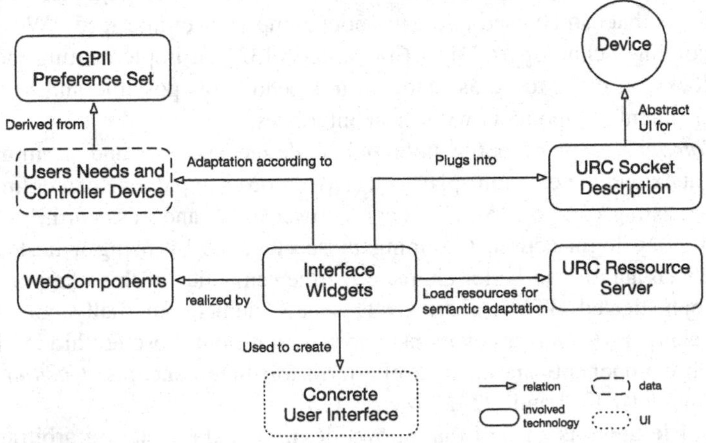

Fig. 1. Overview of the concept and the interplay of the involved technologies

The widgets should be defined using Custom Elements and structured to map the URC socket elements. Therefore, widgets should not contain any specific description of their appearances on a user interface in their names. Instead they should be described by functionality. So, instead of having a "list" element, we would have a "select-one-of-many" element. The concrete appearance depends on the used controller device and the specific user needs and preferences derived from the GPII. In order to accommodate these requirements, each widget must provide the following requirements:

- Some internal adaptation logic to shape its representation. The principle is to adapt the widgets by the means of the user's personal preferences. Simpler adjustments, like changing font-size or color theme, can be directly conducted by the widgets by using common web techniques such as JavaScript and CSS. Also, some more complex adaptations like substituting list-menus for radio buttons can be done by the widget itself, using JavaScript.
- Some appropriate logic to connect to one or several socket elements, so that a target can be controlled. To connect a URC socket to a specific widget, we can set an attribute on the widget that point to the specific element in the socket.
- Procedures enabling the connection to the GPII infrastructure to get access to a user's preference set to perform required adaptations, or – if the widget cannot perform the required adjustments – to download a new and suitable widget appearance from the URC resource server, based on the users preferences and needs, as proposed in [30].

To compensate for insufficient content adaptations, as described in Sect. 3, we propose to use the URC resource server to store alternative widget appearances. If the accommodation of the user needs requires semantic adaptions, e.g., in case of simple interfaces or the usage of sign-language videos, alternative widget appearance versions can be downloaded during runtime and substituted in the widget's Shadow DOM. A user now sees the exchanged and therefore adapted version of the widget. In order to function as a valid substitution, the alternative widget appearances have to satisfy the same interaction paradigm as the original one. If a certain socket element is augmented with a widget using checkboxes to express the functionality of switching on and off a light, an alternative widget appearance has to augment the same functionality.

The example in Listing 1 illustrates our proposed widgets, using an example of augmenting a socket element for light control. The identifier in the attribute "socket-element" specifies the augmented socket element. Switching the light on or off is a boolean operation, since the light can either be on or off. Therefore, the socket can only be augmented by user interface components and interaction pattern that express this behavior (e.g., checkboxes, radio buttons and rocker-switch shaped pictograms that are showing the state of the light in a graphical way, as shown in Fig. 2).

Listing 1: Illustration of the widget usage in an application.

```
<html>
  <head>[...]</head>
  <body>
    <h1>Light Control</h1>
    <boolean-switch socket-element=http://lightController/OnOFF/>
  </body>
</html>
```

Fig. 2. Examples for the appearance of a widget, which is augmenting the on/off functionality of a socket to switch lights.

The left interface in Fig. 2 shows a checkbox as a very basic user interface. The interface on the right illustrates a more descriptive user interface by using a graphic imitation of a rocker-switch. However, they both rely on the very same widget (cf. Listing 1) with only the appearance in the Shadow DOM exchanged.

5 Discussion and Conclusion

The integration of URC and GPII in predefined widgets provides several benefits for users and developers. Users can profit from user interfaces that adapt to their individual needs and also include semantic adaptions by substituting the appearance of a widget to provide the individually preferred interaction pattern; furthermore, the concept of sockets makes it possible to exchange targets while still providing a familiar user interface.

Due to the set of predefined widgets developers have a base for developing appropriate interfaces for different user groups. Because of the widgets' internal adaptation mechanisms, they do not need to address a different user interface for every user group.

The combination of URC and GPII results in a stronger adaptation mechanisms. URC provides only the possibility to build personalized user interfaces or exchange some parts of it, but does not provide any adaptation mechanisms or user preference sets, like GPII does.

On the other hand, GPII can benefit from the inclusion of the URC to allow changes at runtime. So far, in the GPII, all required sources for the adaptation must be available before runtime, which leads to a rather closed system. Here, the URC resource server can bring additional value to the system by making additional resources available at runtime. While many resources can be prepared at design time, there are some cases in which the need for additional resources occurs at runtime.

A further advantage of this system is the provision of additional resources by third parties, e.g., assistive technology experts can provide sign-language videos for specific user groups and sockets. When uploaded to a resource server, they become available for user interfaces. But third-party contributions bears also security risks such as injecting malware into the system. In order to cope with security problems, one could think about a review process for resources, like in an app store for mobile applications. So far, such techniques are not yet available and also GPII security framework is under development.

Another issue is the acceptance of adaptive user interfaces by developers. By using self-adaptive user interfaces that adapts on the clients' side, the influence on the final appearance of the user interface is shifted from the developer to the renderer; which can break the design and function of user interfaces.

By using widgets, developers still have at least some freedom of choice how certain elements are rendered, located and behave on the final user interface and with that the acceptance for our approach increases.

The main tasks to be accomplished in the future are to provide an appropriate security framework and to widen the set of available widgets; furthermore one could think about a totally automated user interface generation process by parsing a URC socket description and, based on the result, choosing appropriate widgets.

Acknowledgments. The research leading to these results has received funding from the European Union Seventh Framework Program (FP7/2007-2011) under grant agreement no. 610510, Prosperity4All ("Ecosystem infrastructure for smart and personalized inclusion and PROSPERITY for ALL stakeholders"). This publication reflects only the authors' views and the European Union is not liable for any use that may be made of the information contained herein.

References

1. Demiris, G., et al.: Older adults' attitudes towards and perceptions of smart home technologies: a pilot study. Informatics for Health and Social Care **29**, 87–94 (2004). [Hrsg.] Informa UK Ltd. UK
2. Sun, H., et al.: Promises and challenges of ambient assisted living systems. In: Sixth International Conference on Information Technology: New Generations, 2009, ITNG 2009, pp. 1201–1207. IEEE (2009)
3. Den Ouden, E.: Development of a design analysis model for consumer complaints: Revealing a new class of quality failures. Eindhoven University of Technology, Eindhoven (2006)
4. Richter, K., Hellenschmidt, M.: Interacting with the ambience: Multimodal interaction and ambient intelligence. Interaction **19**, 20 (2004)
5. Rich, C.: Building Task-Based User Interfaces With ANSI/CEA-2018. Computer **42**(8), 20–27 (2009)
6. Abou-Zahra, S., Brewer, J., Arch, A.: Towards bridging the accessibility needs of people with disabilities and the ageing. In: Proceedings of the 2008 International Cross-disciplinary Conference on Web Accessibility (W4A), pp. 83–86 (2008)
7. Peissner, M., Schuller, A., Ziegler, D., Knecht, C., Zimmermann, G.: Requirements for the successful market adoption of adaptive user interfaces for accessibility. In: Stephanidis, C., Antona, M. (eds.) UAHCI 2014, Part IV. LNCS, vol. 8516, pp. 431–442. Springer, Heidelberg (2014)
8. Maestre, J.M., Camacho, E.F.: Smart home interoperability: the DomoEsi project approach. Int. J. Smart Home **3**(3), 31–44 (2009)

9. Global Public Inclusive Infrastructure, Jan 2015. http://gpii.net/
10. OpenURC Aliance. OpenURC, Feb 2015. http://www.openurc.org
11. ISO/IEC 24752 Information Technology user interfaces Universal Remote Console 5 parts (2008)
12. W3C, Introduction to Web Components, 07 Nov 2014. http://www.w3.org/TR/2013/WD-components-intro-20130606/
13. Iglesias-Pérez, A., Loitsch, C., Kaklanis, N., Votis, K., Stiegler, A., Kalogirou, K., Serra-Autonell, G., Tzovaras, D., Weber, G.: Accessibility through preferences: context-aware recommender of settings. In: Stephanidis, C., Antona, M. (eds.) UAHCI 2014, Part I. LNCS, vol. 8513, pp. 224–235. Springer, Heidelberg (2014)
14. Mavrommati, I., Darzentas, J.: An overview of AmI from a User Centered Design perspective. In: 2nd IET International Conference on IET, vol. 2, pp. 81–88 (2006)
15. Saizmaa, T., Kim, H.-C.: A holistic understanding of HCI perspectives on smart home. In: Networked Computing and Advanced Information Management, vol. 2, pp. 59–65 (2008)
16. Abascal, J., Fernández de Castro, I., Lafuente, A.L., Cia, J.M.: Adaptive interfaces for supportive ambient intelligence environments. In: Miesenberger, K., Klaus, J., Zagler, W.L., Karshmer, A.I. (eds.) ICCHP 2008. LNCS, vol. 5105, pp. 30–37. Springer, Heidelberg (2008)
17. Casas, R., Blasco Marín, R., Robinet, A., Delgado, A.R., Yarza, A.R., McGinn, J., Picking, R., Grout, V.: User modelling in ambient intelligence for elderly and disabled people. In: Miesenberger, K., Klaus, J., Zagler, W.L., Karshmer, A.I. (eds.) ICCHP 2008. LNCS, vol. 5105, pp. 114–122. Springer, Heidelberg (2008)
18. Demiris, G., Oliver, D., Dickey, G., Skubic, M., Rantz, M.: Findings from a participatory evaluation of a smart home application for older adults. Technol. Health Care **8**(2), 111–118 (2008)
19. Henkemans, O.B., Caine, K., Rogers, W., Fist, A.: Monitoring for independent living: user-centered design of smart home technologies for older adults. In: Proceedings of the Med-e-Tel Conference for eHealth, Telemedicine and Health Information and Communication Technologies, pp. 368–373 (2007)
20. Röcker, C.: User-centered design of intelligent environments: requirements for designing successful ambient assisted living systems. In: Proceedings of the Central European Conference of Information and Intelligent Systems (CECIIS 2013), pp. 4–11 (2013)
21. Kleinberger, T., Becker, M., Ras, E., Holzinger, A., Müller, P.: Ambient intelligence in assisted living: enable elderly people to handle future interfaces. In: Stephanidis, C. (ed.) UAHCI 2007 (Part II). LNCS, vol. 4555, pp. 103–112. Springer, Heidelberg (2007)
22. MyUI Consortium. MyUI project Official Web Page, Jan 2015. http://www.myui.eu/
23. Pernice, K., Estes, J., Nielsen, J.: Senior Citizens on the Web, 2nd Edition | Research Report by Nielsen Norman Group. Nielsen Norman Group (2013)
24. Sloan D., Atkinson, M.T., Machin, C., Li, Y.: The potential of adaptive interfaces as an accessibility aid for older web users. In: Proceedings of the 2010 International Cross Disciplinary Conference on Web Accessibility (W4A), New York, NY, USA, pp. 35:1–35:10 (2010)
25. Affonso de Lara, S.M., Watanabe, W.M., dos Santos, E.P.B., Fortes, R.P.M.: Impro-ving WCAG for elderly web accessibility. In: Proceedings of the 28th ACM International Conference on Design of Communication, New York, NY, USA, pp. 175–182 (2010)
26. Dickinson, A., Arnott, J., Prior, S.: Methods for human – computer interaction research with older people. Behav. Inf. Technol. **26**(4), 343–352 (2007)

27. Abou-Zahra, S., Brewer, J., Arch, A.: Towards bridging the accessibility needs of people with disabilities and the ageing community. In: Proceedings of the 2008 International Cross-Disciplinary Conference on Web Accessibility (W4A), New York, NY, USA, pp. 83–86 (2008)
28. Arch, A.: Web accessibility for older users: successes and opportunities (Keynote). In: Proceedings of the 2009 International Cross-Disciplinary Conference on Web Accessibililty (W4A), New York, NY, USA, pp. 1–6 (2009)
29. Leitner, M., Subasi, Ö., Höller, N., Geven, A., Tscheligi, M.: User requirement analysis for a railway ticketing portal with Emphasis on Semantic Accessibility for older users. In: Proceedings of the 2009 International Cross-Disciplinary Conference on Web Accessibililty (W4A), New York, NY, USA, pp. 114–122 (2009)
30. Zimmermann, G., Henka, A., Strobbe, C., Mack, S., Landmesser, A.: Towards context-driven user interfaces in smart homes - the Cloud4all project's smart house demo. Presented at the CENTRIC 2013, Venice, Italy, pp. 98–103 (2013)
31. Zimmermann, G., Vanderheiden, G.C., Strobbe, C.: Towards deep adaptivity – a framework for the development of fully context-sensitive user interfaces. In: Stephanidis, C., Antona, M. (eds.) UAHCI 2014, Part I. LNCS, vol. 8513, pp. 299–310. Springer, Heidelberg (2014)
32. World Wide Web Consortium (W3C). WebComponents, Jan 2015. http://www.w3.org/wiki/WebComponents/
33. World Wide Web Consortium (W3C, 2015a). Shadow DOM, W3C Editor's Draft, 23 January 2015. http://w3c.github.io/webcomponents/spec/shadow/
34. World Wide Web Consortium (W3C, 2015b). Custom Elements, W3C Editor's Draft, 25 January 2015. http://w3c.github.io/webcomponents/spec/custom/
35. World Wide Web Consortium (W3C, 2015c). HTML Imports, W3C Editor's Draft, 23 January 2015. http://w3c.github.io/webcomponents/spec/imports/
36. Smirek, L., Zimmermann, G., Ziegler, D.: Towards universally usable smart homes - how can MyUI, URC and openHAB contribute to an adaptive user interface platform? Presented at the IARIA Conference, Nice, France, pp. 29–38 (2014)

Communication, Games and Entertainment

Baby Boomers and Gaze Enabled Gaming

Soussan Djamasbi(✉), Siavash Mortazavi, and Mina Shojaeizadeh

User Experience and Decision Making Research Laboratory,
Worcester Polytechnic Institute, 100 Institute Road, Worcester, MA, USA
{01609djamasbi,01609smortazavi,
01609minashojaei}@wpi.edu

Abstract. Despite common belief, Baby Boomers form a sizable population of gamers. Paying attention to how this generation experiences a game can help companies that target this group of users increase their market share. To address this need, this study examines Baby Boomers' reaction to a new way of manipulating objects in a game, namely with their eyes. In particular, the study focuses on testing the impact of two different gaze activation strategies on Baby Boomers' interaction experience of a game. We tested two gaze enabled games that provided different levels of flexibility in their respective gaze activation strategies. Our results showed that Baby Boomers had a significantly better interaction experience with the game that had a more flexible gaze activation strategy.

Keywords: Activation strategy · Gaze interaction · User experience · Game play · Baby boomers · Human technology interaction · HCI

1 Introduction

Older users form nearly half of the adult gamers in the US, and the number of this group of gamers is growing [5, 6, 9]. According to a recent report by the Entertainment Software Association [4], the number of gamers that were 50 or older increased by 32 % in this past year alone. Thus, understanding preferences of the older generation users can provide valuable insight for developers who are planning to design for this growing target market.

Motivated by this need, in a recent study we examined the reaction of Baby Boomers to several gaze interaction methods for a single player memory game [1]. As high quality eye tracking devices are becoming more readily available and affordable [2], using gaze as a new way to interact with games is becoming more and more viable and interesting. Because we use our eyes to attend to objects in our visual field, using gaze to manipulate objects may provide an engaging game experience for many users.

The preliminary results of our recent study showed that older users did not enjoy using their gaze to manipulate objects in the memory game as much as their younger counterparts did [1]. The full analysis of our data suggested that a more flexible way to activate game objects may help to improve the experience of gaze interaction for Baby Boomers.

J. Zhou and G. Salvendy (Eds.): ITAP 2015, Part II, LNCS 9194, pp. 479–487, 2015.
DOI: 10.1007/978-3-319-20913-5_44

To test this possibility, in this study we examined the reactions of Baby Boomers to two different gaze activation strategies, which afford different levels of flexibility to users to manipulate game objects. This examination required the development of a new gaze enabled game that had a more flexible activation strategy than the memory game that we used in our previous study. In the following sections, we provide a brief background for the two gaze enabled games that were used in this current study.

2 Background

The preliminary analysis of our most recent gaze interaction study showed that older users did not enjoy gaze as a way to interact with game objects in a single player PC memory game [1]. Compared to their younger counterparts, Baby Boomers rated the likability of gaze as selection/activation method much less favorably. Additionally, Baby Boomers gave low scores when asked to rate the naturalness of gaze as a method to interact with the game [1].

The full analysis of the data suggested that Baby Boomers may have had a poor gaze interaction experience because of the activation strategy that we used in the game. For example, Baby Boomers' average ratings for ability to activate game objects with gaze was quite low, 1.5 on a 7-point scale with 1 denoting low and 7 denoting high ratings. Similarly, their average rating for their ability to adjust to the activation strategy was 1.5 on a 7-point scale, again a very low score. The analysis of user comments as well as the review of the experimenter's observation logs supported the above ratings. These analyses suggested that the activation strategy used in the previous study made it challenging for users to view game objects without activating them. This in turn suggested that affording users a more flexible gaze strategy to activate target objects in the game is likely to improve the game experience for older users, who seemed to have a harder time with gaze interaction than their younger counterparts did.

To test this possibility, we designed and developed a new game, Space Shooter, which was a suitable choice for the development of a more flexible gaze activation strategy. We conducted a laboratory experiment to compare the impact of each of the two gaze activation strategies on their respective game experience. In the following sections, we provide a brief explanation for the two games and their activation strategies.

2.1 Simon

Simon is a single player memory/puzzle game. There are four game objects (squares) in this game that can be activated by a user if the user looks at them for a brief period (e.g., 500 ms). The objective of this game is to activate a set of game objects that are selected by the computer in a specific order. Every time a user activates a sequence of objects correctly, the computer increases the length of the sequence by one and thus challenges the user to play a more difficult round. If the player fails to activate the squares in the correct sequence, the player loses the game. Figure 1 displays a screenshot of the Simon game.

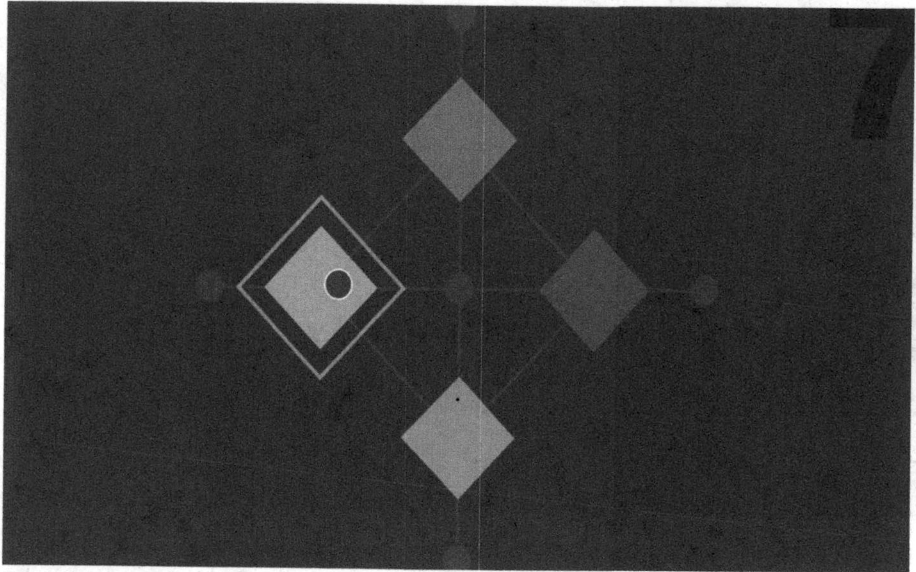

Fig. 1. A screenshot of the gaze enabled Simon game. The colorful squares are the objects of the game. The red circular dot represents a user's gaze point during the gameplay. To activate an object (e.g., the yellow square in the above scenario) the player has to directly look at the target object (Color figure online).

2.2 Space Shooter

Space Shooter is an action shooter game. There are three types of game objects in this game: spaceships, care packages, and cannons. The objective of the game is to destroy spaceships while saving the care packages that appear on the screen by activating (or deactivating) the three cannons that are available in the game (Fig. 2). In other words, while all game objects play an important role in the game, the user can activate only cannons. Unlike the Simon game, activating cannon does not require the player to look at the cannon directly. Instead, the player can activate a cannon by looking at the game scene. The activation strategy is set up in a way to fire the cannon on the game scene that is closest to player's gaze. The player receives points when he/she destroys a spaceship and loses points if he/she destroys a care package.

2.3 Activation Strategy

The strategy for selecting the game objects in the Simon game requires users to look directly at the target (e.g., a specific square). Our analysis of the data from a previous study [1] showed that Baby Boomers had a hard time controlling game objects with this activation strategy. Activating objects by directly looking at them makes it hard for users to view objects without activating them. This strategy also limits the player's viewing area when the player attempts to activate an object because the player can only

Fig. 2. A screenshot of the Space Shooter game. The cannons (bottom of the screen), spaceships (robot in upper right hand corner of the screen), and the care packages (Red Cross package in the middle left part of the screen) are the objects of the game. However, only cannons can be activated with gaze. The gray circular dot with the "+" sign represents a user's gaze point during the gameplay. To activate a cannon (in this case the middle cannon) the player does not need to look at the cannon directly. For example, in the above scenario, the player can activate the middle cannon by looking anywhere in the middle of the screen (anywhere in the scene between the two blue dashed lines) (Color figure online).

attend to the object that he/she intends to activate. By expanding the activation area for an object, users can manipulate their desired objects while following other objects in the game. For this reason, the activation strategy in Space Shooter affords players more flexibility in controlling game objects. Players can activate cannons by looking at any area where the desired cannon is located. This allows users to activate the target cannon without restricting their ability to follow the movement of other game objects, i.e., the spaceships and care packages. We expect this flexibility in activation strategy to provide a better sense of control. Because Baby Boomers had a difficult time to control their gaze interaction in our previous study, we expect this strategy to provide older users with a better gaze interaction experience.

3 Methodology

Data from two different games, Simon and Space Shooter, was collected from five participants (2 male, 3 female), resulting in a sample of 10 sets of data. The participants ranged in age from 54 to 71. Each participant played both games in a counterbalanced order.

3.1 Measurements

In order to compare the differences in gaze activation strategies between the two games, we adopted interview questions from the ImmersiveNess of Games (ING) instrument by Norman [11]. Because we were interested in examining the impact of activation strategy on interaction experience, we used only the items that captured reactions to the activation method. We modified the items to match the gaze interaction method in our games. The following interview questions measured users' subjective experiences of the activation strategy on a 7-point scale:

- *Perceived control* measured the degree to which users were able to control their interaction with the game. Higher scores indicated better control.
- *Perceived naturalness* measured the degree to which interactions felt natural to users. Higher scores indicated experiences that were more natural.
- *Perceived ability to activate* measured the degree to which it was easy for the users to activate an object with their eyes. Higher scores indicated higher levels of perceived ability.
- *Adjustment to the activation method* measured the degree to which users felt they were able to adjust to using their eyes as an activation method. Higher scores indicated higher perceived adjustment.

3.2 Procedure

The experiment was conducted in a laboratory setting. Each participant was engaged in a 15-second calibration procedure. Tobii × 30 eye tracking system and Tobii SDK was used to develop both games used in our study. The experimenter provided the participants with a brief explanation of the game. Each participant played both games in a counterbalanced order. The experiment was not timed. Participants played the games as long as they wished to play and at their own pace. After each game, participants completed a survey using the measures discussed in the previous section. After playing both games, users were asked to rank the two games from most favorite to least favorite and explain their experience with the game.

4 Results

We used paired t-tests to compare the experiences of the two activation strategies used in this study. The results of the t-tests showed that of the two activation strategies, the more flexible strategy used in the Space Shooter game was rated significantly more favorable. As shown in Table 1, the mean ratings for the perceptions of control (2.00 vs. 5.20), naturalness (2.30 vs. 5.00), ability to activate an object (2.40 vs. 5.60), and ability to adjust to the activation method (2.00 vs. 6.40) were all significantly higher for the more flexible activation strategy. The p-values for the aforementioned variables were all significant at the 0.01 level. The average ratings for the less flexible activation strategy were in the low range of the scale because they were all smaller than 3 on a 7-point scale with 1 denoting the lowest and 7 denoting the highest or best experience [1]. The mean values for the more flexible activation strategy, on the other hand, were all in the high range (larger than 5) [1]. These results show that the impact of the two activation strategies on interaction experience were significantly different.

Table 1. Paired t-test comparing the experience of the less flexible activation strategy used in the Simon game with the experience of the more flexible activation strategy used in the Space Shooter game.

	Less flexible activation strategy (Simon)	More flexible activation strategy (Space shooter)	Significance
Control	2.00 (0.70)	5.20 (0.84)	t = 5.49 p = 0.005
Naturalness	2.30 (1.04)	5.00 (0.94)	t = 3.38 p = 0.028
Ability to activate	2.40 (0.55)	5.60 (1.52)	t = 4.35 p = 0.012
Adjustment to the activation method	2.00 (1.00)	6.40 (0.89)	t = 6.49 p = 0.003

After playing both games, the users ranked the games. The results showed that all users (100 %) ranked Space Shooter as their more favorite game. When participants were asked to explain their preferences, while 40 % indicated they liked both games almost equally well, they all indicated that it was much easier for them to control objects in the Space Shooter game. For example, they stated: “I liked Space Shooter, it was easier to play, I felt in control” or “Simon was hard to control” or “I was confused when playing Simon, hard to focus my eyes where I wanted to.”

5 Discussion and Conclusion

The results of this study show that activation strategy can have a significant impact on the gaze interaction experience. As indicated by the results, the self-reported ability to activate game objects and to adjust to the activation method was significantly higher for the more flexible activation strategy. Participants’ perceived ability to activate objects was in the high range when they played the game that had a more flexible gaze activation strategy. Their ratings for the same variable were in the low range when they played the game with the less flexible activation strategy. Participants also indicted that it was significantly easier for them to adjust to the gaze activation strategy that provided more flexibility.

Activation strategy also had a significant impact on participants’ perception of control. Participants’ self- reported ability to control the game was in the high range for the more flexible activation strategy and in the low range for the less flexible activation strategy. Additionally, the results showed that activation strategy influenced participants’ perception of the naturalness of gaze as a new way to manipulate objects in the game.

The above results revealed that participants rated the interaction experience of the less flexible activation strategy rather poorly (the mean values were all on the low range of the scale), while they rated the interaction experience of the more flexible activation strategy quite favorably (the mean values were all on the high range of the scale).

These results were supported by the analysis of interviews and observations. All participants favored the interaction experience of the more flexible game. Their comments indicated that perception of control was an important issue in their interaction experience.

The results taken together, show that the flexibility of the gaze activation strategy significantly and positively affected the interaction experience of the game. The results suggest that developing a flexible strategy for gaze controlled games is likely to make these types of games more fun and playable for older users.

Given the upward trend in the development of low-cost high quality eye tracking devices [2], and hence the increased viability of gaze interaction in gaming [1], along with the growing number of Baby Boomer gamers, the results of our study have important theoretical and practical implications. From a theoretical point of view, the results extend gaze control studies, particularly those that focus on investigating older users' preferences [1, 7, 13, 14]. The results also extend research that focuses on experience design for older adults in general [3, 8–10] and gaming in particular [1, 12].

From a practical point of view, the results of this study provide insight for designing appealing gaze activation strategies for older users. The results suggest that expanding the screen areas for activating an object is likely to increase older users' ability to adjust to gaze interaction and thus improve their perception of control and naturalness of gaze interaction. The results suggests that designing flexibility in the activation strategy is likely to provide a more positive user experience for gaze enabled games for older users.

6 Limitations and Future Research

As with any controlled laboratory study, the results are limited to the setting. We compared the interaction experience of the two games without focusing on performance. Had we required users to achieve a desired level of performance, we may have observed different results. In our study, participants could play as long as they wished. Requiring a time limit could affect our results. Participants in our study were new to gaze enabled games. Experience or long-term exposure to gaze interactive games or interfaces may influence how older users experience a gaze enabled game. Through exposure to gaze enabled devices and practice, users can master controlling objects with their gaze more effectively. This in turn, can improve their experience of gaze enabled games.

Sample size was another limitation of our study. Nevertheless, our results showed significant differences in experience of the two games. We also focused on Baby Boomers. Future studies with larger sample sizes are needed to see whether flexibility in selection is as favorable among younger users as it is among older users.

7 Contribution

The results of this study have important theoretical and practical implications. The results provide evidence that older users, at least initially, find gaze interaction more controllable and natural when the strategy for activating an object is more flexible. These results provide a first step in scientific examination of gaze activation methods in gaming. Our results showed that older users had significantly higher levels of perceived control, naturalness, ability to activate, and ability to adjust to the activation method for the more flexible activation strategy. From a practical point of view, the results provide valuable insight for developing a more successful gaze interaction experience for older adults.

References

1. Djamasbi, S., Mortazavi, S.: Generation Y, baby boomers, and gaze interaction experience in gaming In: Proceedings of the 48th Hawaii International Conference on System Sciences (HICSS), Computer Society Press (2015)
2. Djamasbi, S.: Eye Tracking and Web Experience. AIS Trans. Hum. Comput. Interact. **6**(2), 37–54 (2014)
3. Djamasbi, S., Siegel, M., Skorinko, J., Tullis, T.: Online viewing and aesthetic preferences of generation Y and baby boomers: testing user website experience through eye tracking. Int. J. Electr. Commer. (IJEC) **15**(4), 121–158 (2011)
4. Entertainment Software Association: Essential facts and the computer & video game industry (2014) http://www.theesa.com/wp-content/uploads/2014/10/ESA_EF_2014.pdf. Accessed 13 October 2014
5. Entertainment Software Association: Essential facts and the computer & video game industry. Washington, DC (2013) http://www.theesa.com/facts/pdfs/esa_ef_2013.pdf. Accessed 13 June 2014
6. Entertainment Software Rating Board (ESRB): How much do you know about video games? (2014) http://www.esrb.org/about/video-game-industry-statistics.jsp. Accessed 13 June 2014
7. Isokoski, P., Joos, M., Spakov, O., Martin, B.: Gaze controlled games. Univ. Access Inf. Soc. **8**(4), 323–337 (2009)
8. Loos, E.F., Romano Bergstrom, J.: Older adults. In: Schall, A.J., Romano Bergstrom, J. (eds.) Eye Tracking in User Experience Design, pp. 313–329. Elsevier, Amsterdam (2014)
9. Loos, E.F.: Generational use of new media and the (ir)relevance of age. In: Colombo, F., Fortunati, L. (eds.) Broadband Society and Generational Changes, pp. 259–273. Peter Lang, Berlin (2011)
10. Loos, E.: In search of information on websites: a question of age? In: Stephanidis, C. (ed.) Universal Access in HCI, Part II, HCII 2011. LNCS, vol. 6766, pp. 196–204. Springer, Heidelberg (2011)
11. Norman, K.L.: Development of instruments to measure immerseability of individuals and immersiveness of video games. Technical Report LAPDP-2010-03, HCIL Technical Report 12-5-10, University of Maryland, College Park, MD 20742 (2010)
12. Pearce, C.: The truth about baby boomer gamers a study of over-forty computer game players. Games Cult. **3**(2), 142–174 (2008)

13. Prensky, M.: Digital natives, digital immigrants. On the Horizon MCB University Press, vol. 9, no 5 (2001) http://www.marcprensky.com/writing/Prensky%20-%20Digital%20Natives%20Digital%20Immigrants%20-%20Part1.pdf. Accessed 13 June 2014
14. Schneider, N., Wilkes, J., Grandt, M., Schlick, C.M.: Investigation of input devices for the age-differentiated design of human-computer interaction. In: Proceedings of the Human Factors and Ergonomics Society Annual Meeting, vol. 52, no. 2, pp. 144–148. Sage, London (2008)

Assessing Older Adults' Usability Challenges Using Kinect-Based Exergames

Christina N. Harrington(✉), Jordan Q. Hartley, Tracy L. Mitzner, and Wendy A. Rogers

Human Factors and Aging Laboratory, Georgia Institute of Technology, Atlanta, GA, USA
{cnh, jhartley3, tracy, wendy}@gatech.edu

Abstract. Exergames have been growing in popularity as a means to get physical exercise. Although these systems have many potential benefits both physically and cognitively, there may be barriers to their use by older adults due to a lack of design consideration for age-related changes in motor and perceptual capabilities. In this paper we evaluate the usability challenges of Kinect-based exergames for older adults. Older adults rated their interaction with the exergames system based on their perceived usefulness and ease-of-use of these systems. Although many of the participants felt that these systems could be potentially beneficial, particularly for exercise, there were several challenges experienced. We discuss the implications for design guidelines based on the usability challenges assessed.

Keywords: Older adults · Exergames · Usability · Interface evaluation

1 Introduction

The use of commercially designed exergames for physical activity has become widely accepted among a large audience of "wellness gamers" as a means of cognitive and physical stimulation [1]. Exergames are defined as interactive, exercise-based video games where players engage in physical activity via an onscreen interface [2]. These games can be played at home via a player interacting with a computer-simulated competitor, or in a multiplayer mode to encourage social connectivity. Exergames use body movement and gestures as input to responsive motion-detection consoles such as the Nintendo Wii and Balance Board, or Microsoft Xbox 360 with Kinect. As motion is detected via a WiiMote or Kinect sensor, users can manipulate on-screen items of the game while following structured instructions of exercises or challenges to obtain virtual scores or advance through simulated levels. These games are often used to simulate sports or exercise-based activities, driving, or puzzles. Although typically marketed to younger adults, exergames have potential for older adults because of the many benefits of engaging in physical and cognitive exercise across the lifespan and the fact that they can be used indoors and at-home. However, it is unclear whether these systems are useful for and useable by older adults.

J. Zhou and G. Salvendy (Eds.): ITAP 2015, Part II, LNCS 9194, pp. 488–499, 2015.
DOI: 10.1007/978-3-319-20913-5_45

1.1 Potential Benefits of Exergames

Exergames have potential benefits for various target users within the population. Beyond a source of fun and leisure entertainment, exergames present opportunities to increase physical and cognitive functioning in both younger and older adults. In a 2010 survey conducted on adults aged 22 and older, 68 % of participants who played exergames reported that they began a new fitness activity after playing the games [3].

Research studies have examined the effects of exergame use in the rehabilitation of lower-extremity and upper-limb functioning of stroke patients [6, 8], as well as spinal cord injury rehabilitation [7]. Recent studies have also identified the potential benefits of exergames for the older adult population. Exergames may be a viable means to promote physical activity among older adults with the potential to improve function, balance, and muscle training [1]. Improving gait and balance through the use of exergames can reduce the risk of falls for older adults [12]. In a home-based intervention utilizing the Dance-Dance Revolution games, participants experienced improved stepping ability as well as other neuropsychological factors associated with falls [2]. Exergames may be an effective approach to encouraging positive lifestyle changes in this population by introducing vigorous physical activity to those who might otherwise be sedentary [3, 9].

In addition to potential physical benefits, exergames present a new opportunity for older adults to socialize [4]. Exergames often offer players the experience to engage in game simulation with one other player or against a computer-simulated opponent. By increasing social interaction these games have the potential to decrease prevalence of depression [5], and increase intergenerational interaction [4]. Exergames provide an opportunity for physical activity in the familiar environment of one's home, facilitating meaningful social interaction while eliminating some barriers to exercise and socialization, such as transportation access [15].

Lastly, exergames have the potential to increase cognitive functioning among the older adult population [10]. Active games that simulate sports, exercise, driving, or puzzles require various cognitive capacities. Malliot, Perrot and Hartley found that there are significant benefits on executive control and process of speed tasks in the cognitive domain of older adults that are active with exergames [3]. Spence and Feng [11] identified some of the more prevalent sensory, perceptual, and cognitive functions that are exercised during exergames and normal video game play such as analytical, memory, attention, and visuomotor functions. Consequently, exergames may benefit these functions as well. The potential to affect cognitive functioning may come at a cost if cognitive demands exceed capabilities.

1.2 Cognitive Demand and Usability Challenges

Although exergames aim to make physical activity more appealing and engaging, there appears to be a lack of consideration of age-related limitations. Most of the systems currently on the market are not designed to accommodate for older adults' physical and cognitive abilities or limitations (e.g., impairments in visual and auditory perception, or loss of sensorimotor skills) [13]. Exergames can be complicated due to players engaging in multiple activities simultaneously. These systems place demands on working memory [15], and require a great deal of learning and information processing [16] which may prove difficult for older adults. Previous studies assessing the cognitive demands of video games and exergames demonstrated that players must activate multiple mental models simultaneously utilizing perceptual and motor skills, such as holding a cursor steady while reading information or observing a demonstration [12, 15].

Older adult users of exergames report some of the more common usability challenges to be the fast-pace of the programs themselves, and confusion in navigating the interface [14]. McLaughlin et al. highlighted that some of the more prevalent challenges faced by older adults when using exergames include difficulty in reading text, discernment of objects from the background interface, and difficulty in activating icons and display elements [15]. In addition, there is a lack of training support provided for older adults utilizing exergames [17]. Understanding the cognitive demand that exergames systems place on older adults can guide the development of better-designed systems as well as training approaches. The present study focused on usability challenges associated with these systems for older adults.

1.3 Study Overview

Much of the previous literature published on exergames has primarily focused on the perceived health benefits of these games for healthy older adults as well as those with physical and sensory impairments. In particular, there has been an emphasis on studying the effectiveness of exergames in rehabilitation and balance training. Few studies have examined the usability challenges faced by older adults actually utilizing exergames. Thus it is beneficial to identify these challenges and how they translate into design recommendations to provide older-user-friendly exergames systems.

The objective of this study was to identify usability challenges of Kinect-based exergames for older adults. We present an error analysis from a study of 20 healthy older adults participating in two separate exergames programs. Our goal was to identify the challenges and misinterpretations of operating the system through the common errors experienced by participants. In particular, we identified which aspects of these programs older adults found challenging. Results are discussed in terms of perceived usability and perceived ease-of-use of the Kinect-based exergames systems, as well as participants' opinions regarding the system. These errors, along with the older adults' opinions concerning the use of exergames, were used to derive implications and guidelines for the design of instructions for exergames systems.

2 Method

2.1 Participants

Participants included 10 older adults (five male/five female) aged 60–69 (M = 66.2; SD = 1.40) and 10 older adults (five male/five female) aged 70–79 (M = 74.6; SD = 2.72). Participants were recruited from the Human Factors and Aging Laboratory

Participant Registry at the Georgia Institute of Technology. Pre-screening calls were conducted to ensure participants would be able to perform the necessary actions and had no previous experience with the Microsoft Xbox 360 with Kinect system.

2.2 Materials

Questionnaires. Prior to participation, each participant completed four questionnaires: (1) a Health Questionnaire [18]; (2) a Demographics Questionnaire [18]; (3) a Technology Experience Questionnaire [19]; and (4) a Video Game Experience Questionnaire [28]. The Health and Demographics Questionnaires assessed participant's overall health and collected background information including age, gender, race, and education as well as any vision, hearing, or mobility limitations. The Technology Experience Questionnaire assessed use and familiarity with various technologies. The Video Game Experience questionnaire was adapted from Boot et al. [28] to assess level of familiarity with video games and their gaming habits.

Additional questionnaires were given after the completion of each individual program session to assess participant satisfaction and performance. A 5-item questionnaire assessed satisfaction with motion/gesture controls for navigation. A 7-item questionnaire assessed satisfaction with the in-program activity. Both questionnaires used a scale ranging from 1 "strongly disagree" to 7 "strongly agree".

After completing both exergame programs, each participant completed three questionnaires pertaining to the overall system. Two questionnaires used the Technology Acceptance Model (TAM) scales of perceived usefulness and perceived ease-of-use adapted from Davis [21] and Davis et al. [22] respectively. The first questionnaire assessed perceived usefulness and included the following items assessed on a Likert scale ranging from 1-*strongly disagree* to 7-*strongly agree*: (1) My interaction with the system was clear and understandable, (2) I would find the system useful in my daily life, (3) Using the system in my daily life would make me more physically active, (4) Using the system would make it easier for me to be physically active, and (5) Using the system would improve my daily life. The second questionnaire, assessing perceived ease-of-use, included the following items assessed on the same Likert scale: (1) I found the system easy to use, (2) I found the system flexible for me to interact with, (3) It was easy for me to become skillful at using the system, (4) I found it easy to get the system to do what I wanted it to do, and (5) Learning to operate the system was easy for me. The third questionnaire, the System Usability Scale, was adapted from Brooke [20].

This paper will focus on the data obtained from the two questionnaires relating to perceived usefulness and perceived ease-of-use.

Interviews. After each program participants were interviewed to assess their attitudes and opinions about the programs. Participants were also interviewed after completing both programs to assess their experience with the overall system. During interviews participants were asked to describe what they liked and did not like about each program and their reasoning behind their responses. Additionally, participants were asked if they would have benefited from additional help or instruction throughout the program.

The goal of these interviews was to determine where participants felt the most frustrated and what type of help would be most beneficial.

2.3 Procedure

After completing consent forms, participants were introduced to the Microsoft Xbox 360 with Kinect system, which included the basics of the Kinect sensor and the optimal location for the participant to stand. Sessions began with researchers giving details of what would be required of the participant. Participants were notified that they could discontinue at any time if they felt they could not complete an activity. Each participant was assessed individually during sessions that lasted from 1.5 to 3 h. During this time, two video cameras recorded the participant. One was positioned in front of the participant to record the actions. The other was placed several feet behind the participant to record the television screen.

Participants then began one of two programs, *Body and Brain Connection* [23] or *Your Shape Fitness Evolved* [24]. Participants were pre-assigned to a program order so that 50 % of the males and females received *Body and Brain Connection* as their first program. Researchers provided hints correlating to the task being completed when initial errors were made. For example, the task of turning on the Xbox was accompanied by the hint: "*Press the round silver 'Power' button on the Xbox console to turn the Xbox on. The 'Power' button looks like a circle with a line through the top.*" A script was used to ensure that hints and instructions were consistent across all participants. The hints were pre-determined by assessing what possible errors participants could make while performing a task. Upon finishing the first program, participants completed the relevant questionnaires and were interviewed about the program they just completed.

Completion of the second program consisted of the same format: engaging in the program activities, the post-program questionnaires, and a post-program interview. Both programs required participants to perform the following overall tasks: turn on the Xbox system, load the disc, start the program, play the program, review the results of the program, eject the disc, and turn off the Xbox system.

Following interaction with the exergame systems each participant was given questionnaires concerning overall system measures and asked questions concerning attitudes and opinions of their overall experience with the system. All interview responses were audio recorded for later transcription.

2.4 Data Analysis

The coding scheme was developed by reviewing a sample of participant videos, in addition to observations made by researchers, to determine all possible participant errors that could occur for each task. The errors were then grouped into a comprehensive set of categories to minimize redundancy.

The coding scheme assessed three aspects for every task: initial errors, whether or not hints were given after initial errors were made, and whether participants corrected these initial errors or not. Three rounds of independent coding were conducted to calibrate the two coders. The final round yielded a high level of agreement and reliability (r = .91). The video assessments were then divided evenly, with regard to sex and age of the participant, between two coders for independent coding.

For purposes of this study interview data was analyzed for important quotes addressing usefulness and ease-of-use of the system.

3 Results

3.1 Potential of Exergames

Older adults were generally positive about the potential benefits of exergames as evident by the results of the TAM Perceived Usefulness questionnaire. There was not much difference in the perceived usefulness of the Kinect-based exergames systems between the '60–69' age group and the '70–79' age group. Most participants (n = 15) reported that they perceived these systems to be useful. Figure 1 details the frequency of agreement on the perceived usefulness of exergames for each age group.

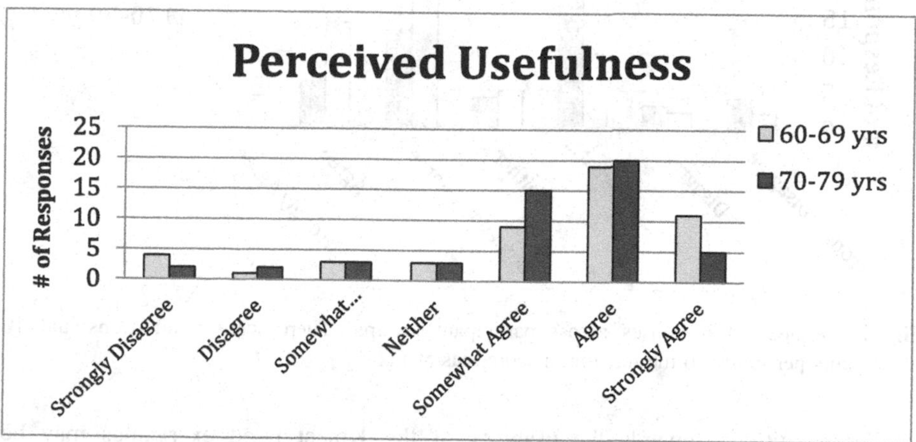

Fig. 1. Number of responses across participant groups (There were 5 questions and 10 participants per group resulting in a maximum of 50)

Many participants felt that the health aspect of exergame activities was potentially beneficial even though this was their initial interaction with the system. Of the participants sampled, 75 % were above the neutral mark in their agreement with statements about the perceived usefulness of exergames systems. In the interviews participants responded that the exergames were a useful means to engage in exercise, commenting that exergames would be "*good for physical activity*" and can help to "*keep you active*". As mentioned before, exergames allow for users to engage in physical activity in the familiar environment of their home. Participants found this to be a perceived benefit of these games commenting: "*it would help with my physical regimen as rainy days, crummy days, [I] can't go out to walk*".

3.2 Ease-of-Use

Although many participants reported positive perceptions about the potential benefits of exergames, there were mixed responses to the perceived ease-of-use of the systems. A majority of participants in the 60–69 age group somewhat agreed that these programs were user friendly, whereas most of the 70–79 age group somewhat disagreed with the ease-of-use of these games. Figure 2 details the frequency of agreement with perceived ease-of-use of the Kinect-based exergames across groups.

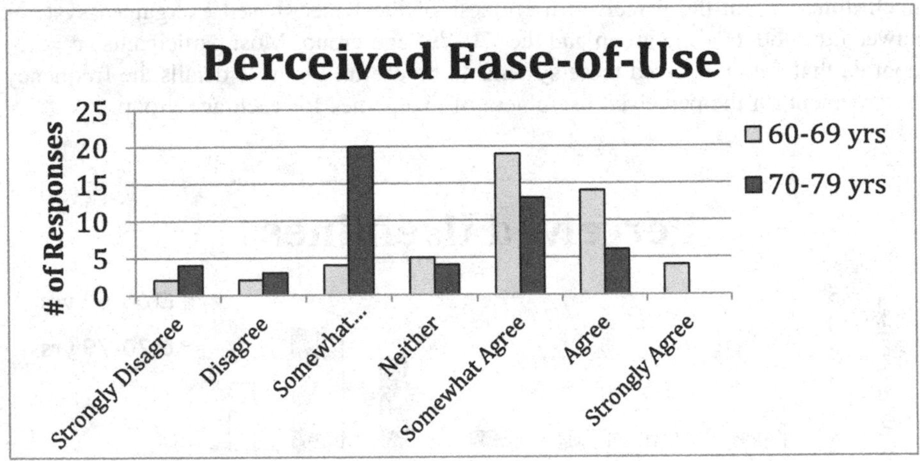

Fig. 2. Number of responses across participant groups (There were 5 questions and 10 participants per group so the maximum score was 50)

These attitudes towards the usability of the Kinect-based exergames may be attributed to the complexity of the system interface, and the difficulty in navigating controls during the game. Participants commented on aspects of the system interface concerning feedback, level of intuitiveness, and clarity of instructions when assessing how easy the programs were to use. Users made descriptive comments of their interactions such as: "*sometimes the instructions were a little cryptic*" or that "*often it was unclear what they wanted me to do, I was confused*".

3.3 Common Task Errors

Throughout usability testing of the exergame programs, many older adults had difficulties performing the tasks essential to initiating and navigating the in-program activities. Our error analysis assessed which task errors occurred most frequently.

For each program, tasks included opening the Xbox tray, inserting the program disc, closing the Xbox tray, starting the Kinect system, initializing the game, choosing the one-player mode, selecting a particular activity, navigating through instructions, completing the actual activity, reviewing results, navigating back to the main menu, ending the program and ejecting the disc. Tasks were listed sequentially and coded based on a participant's actions during the program. Table 1 lists the possible task errors made during each program. The top panel shows the initial errors that were made and the bottom panel shows the errors that were made after a hint was provided.

Table 1. Mean percentage of errors (Standard deviation)

Error	*60–69 yrs*	*70–79 yrs*
Initial errors		
Wrong button	9 % (.08)	18 % (.14)
Could not locate button	2 % (.04)	4 % (.04)
Button not completely triggered	11 % (.05)	13 % (.04)
No action	10 % (.06)	9 % (.05)
Out of range of sensor	3 % (.04)	2 % (.02)
Participant had issues	56 % (.26)	50 % (.22)
After-hint errors		
Wrong button	2 % (.04)	3 % (.04)
Could not locate button	1 % (.02)	1 % (.02)
Button not completely triggered	3 % (.03)	5 % (.04)
No action	0 (.01)	1 % (.01)
Out of range of sensor	2 % (.02)	0
Participant had issues	26 % (.23)	24 % (.23)

There were almost no errors in turning the Xbox system on and off or closing the disc tray. Many participants however did make an error when initially opening the tray, often due to the inability to discern the button on the Xbox console. There were also several errors in starting up the Body and Brain Connection and Your Shape Fitness Evolved programs, and starting up the individual activities within the program. Many participants also made errors in reviewing their results at the conclusion of the activity (most participants did nothing (*no action*) due to misinterpretation of instructions).

We also found game-specific error trends. The majority of errors in Body Brain Connection were participants discerning which button to press and disambiguation of on-screen instruction, whereas the majority of the errors associated with the Your Shape Fitness Evolved program were issues with completely triggering the button. Participants were often not clear on the force required to activate the button to move to the next screen, oftentimes having to repeat this action several time. These errors were more associated with the perceptual and motor abilities of participants.

While certain task errors were more common than others, it is important to note that every participant made at least one error related to the initiation of the program or carrying out the actual exergame activity.

4 Discussion

Exergames have the potential to become an effective way to engage both healthy and rehabilitating individuals in physical activity. Recently, these systems have been used to supplement regular physical activity regimens, or introduce older adults to a feasible way to engage in exercise. Evidence suggests that benefits of exergames range from improved balance or gait [12], to increased working memory and reaction to processing speed tasks [3]. Due to the perceived benefits of these systems, it is beneficial to understand the potential usability challenges associated with exergames for older adults. This study assessed the usability challenges experienced by older adults using the Microsoft Xbox 360 with Kinect program, with the goal of developing design guidelines to reduce common errors and issues with ease-of-use.

4.1 Key Observations

Observations during usability testing of the Kinect-based exergames system yielded insights into the causes of task errors. The majority of older adults had difficulty learning to use gesture controls and navigating the menus in the actual program. This was a learning hurdle that was typically overcome after initial interaction with the system, but many participants struggled to identify the on-screen hand icon to activate the game. In addition, participants often had to repeat gestures several times to fully trigger a button or navigational control, often commenting that the system was not correctly sensing them. This lead to the repeated need for instructional hints that somewhat mitigated task difficulties.

Participants found the on-screen instructions difficult to understand and insufficient for detailing how to perform a particular activity. The complexity of elements on-screen made it hard for users to discern which buttons were supposed to be pressed or which were shown as a part of an instructional demonstration. Participants commented that they were often unable to tell when the instructions concluded or when they were able to begin the actual activity. Consequently many participants attempted to initiate the activity while the instructions screen was still present. This was a source of frustration for many users.

Few differences were observed for the task errors made by the '60–69' age group and the '70–79' age group other than the higher mean average of wrong buttons attempted. Overall most participants benefited from having verbal hints during the programs to correct errors as they were made. Although task errors such as opening the disc tray or starting the Body Brain Connection or Your Shape Fitness Evolved programs were seen often across participants, they were typically corrected after a participant's initial interaction with one of the programs. Thus familiarity may be a key factor in usability of Kinect-based exergames for older adults. The natures of errors were also observed to be different between the games (e.g., ability to punch out calories vs. ability to stamp results at the end of an activity).

Results of this study supported previous findings from other studies assessing the usability of exergames for older adults. Similar to findings of previous studies [14, 15, 17] users experienced trouble with discernment among interface elements and activating buttons.

4.2 Implications for Design Guidelines

Although most of the older adults in this study perceived potential benefits of exergames systems, the frequency of task errors indicate a need for training and/or redesign to make these systems more user-friendly. The older adults we observed found the overall system inflexible and difficult to operate. Thus, there is need to further develop guidelines for older adults to successfully utilize exergames.

Understanding the perceptual, motor, and cognitive challenges faced by older adult users of exergames can prove beneficial to designing systems that are user friendly for users of all ability levels. Exergames, much like traditional video games, place a considerable amount of cognitive demand on the users [15, 16, 27]. However, unlike video games, exergames require users to divide their efforts between motor and cognitive domains, which may prove particularly difficult for older adults due to age-related changes. Although previous research has addressed the usability and design of exergames systems [1, 3, 8, 13, 15, 25, 26], there is a need to better account for age-related changes that may affect system usability. Based on the areas of usability challenges faced by older adults, designers should develop interfaces that are less complex and dense for the end-user.

Exergames have benefit in being a motivational and rewarding avenue to engage in physical activity, but oftentimes they lead to frustration due to the inability to adequately navigate gesture controls or interpret instructions. One recommendation to address these challenges might be to minimize information presented on the screen to account for varying levels of psychomotor abilities. Exergames should be developed with attractive and user-friendly interfaces that are not complex but are easy to interpret. Minimizing the amount of information that is presented on a single screen will allow for older adults to better perceive information [16], thus making instructions and commands easier to follow. Additionally, providing helpful information and feedback at the appropriate times throughout the program will also prove beneficial to older adults. As seen by our results, many participants were unsure of what action was supposed to take place at a particular time. This would be best addressed by having smaller on-screen instructional gestures present during each activity to serve as guidance and reinforcement. These implications are relevant not only to Xbox but to all exergame consoles utilizing gesture control.

In conclusion, there are numerous perceived cognitive and physical benefits to the use of exergames by older adults. Reducing the barriers to use of these systems while still allowing for them to be challenging is a necessary research endeavor to ensure the continued use of these systems. The next steps in this research program are to develop helpful instructions for exergames in the form of a quick start guide, and ultimately evaluate the usability of this guide with older adult exergamers.

Acknowledgments. This research was supported in part by a grant from the National Institutes of Health (National Institute on Aging) Grant P01 AG17211 under the auspices of the Center for Research and Education on Aging and Technology Enhancement (CREATE; www.create-center.org). We also would like to acknowledge the National Institute on Disability and Rehabilitation Research (Department of Education) Grant H133E130037 under the auspices of the Rehabilitation and Engineering Research Center on Technologies to Support Successful Aging with Disability (TechSAge; www.techsage.gatech.edu). We thank Brian Jones, the director of the Aware Home Research Initiative for the use of their facilities during testing, and Laura Barg-Walkow for her help in reviewing this paper.

References

1. Nawaz, A., Waerstad, M., Omholt, K., Helbostad, J.L., Vereijken, B., Skjaeret, N., Kristiansen, L.: Designing simplified exergame for muscle and balance training in seniors: a concept of ′out in nature′. In: 8th International Conference on Pervasive Computing Technologies for Healthcare, Oldenburg, Germany, 20–23 May 2014
2. Schoene, D., Lord, S.R., Delbaere, K., Severino, C., Davies, T.A., Smith, S.: A randomized controlled pilot study of home-based step training in older people using videogame technology. PLoS ONE **8**(3), e57734 (2013). doi:10.1371/journal.pone.0057734
3. Maillot, P., Perrot, A., Hartley, A.: Effects of interactive physical-activity video-game training on physical and cognitive function in older adults. Psychol. Aging **27**(3), 589–600 (2012). doi:10.1037/a0026268
4. Velazquez, A., Martinez-Garcia, A., Favela, J., Hernandez, A., Ochoa, S.: Design of exergames with the collaborative participation of older adults. In: Proceedings of the 2013 IEEE 17th International Conference on Computer Supported Cooperative Work in Design, pp. 521–526 (2013). doi:10.1109/CSCWD.2013.6581016
5. Rosenberg, D., Depp, C.A., Vahia, I.V., Reichstadt, J., Palmer, B.W., Kerr, J., Jeste, D.V.: Exergames for subsyndromal depression in older adults: a pilot study of a novel intervention. Am. J. Geriatr. Psychiatry **18**(3), 221–226 (2010)
6. Saposnik, G., Teasell, R., Mamdani, M., et al.: Effectiveness of virtual reality using Wii gaming technology in stroke rehabilitation: a pilot randomized clinical trial and proof of principle. Stroke **41**(7), 1477–1484 (2010)
7. Chien-Yen, C., Lange, B., Mi, Z., Koenig, S., Requejo, P., Noom, S., Sawchuk, A., Rizzo, A.: Towards pervasive physical rehabilitation using microsoft kinect. In: 6th International Conference on Pervasive Computing Technologies for Healthcare, pp. 159–162 (2012). doi:10.4108/icst.pervasivehealth.2012.248714
8. Borghese, N.A., Pirovano, M., Lanzi, P.L., Wüest, S., de Bruin, E.D.: Computational intelligence and game design for effective at-home stroke rehabilitation. Games Health J. **2** (2), 81–88 (2013)
9. Leiberman, D.A., Chamberlin, B., Medina, E.: The power of play: innovations in getting active summit 2011: a science panel proceedings report from the american heart association. Circulation **123**, 1–10 (2011)
10. Green, C.S., Li, R., Bavelier, D.: Perceptual learning during action video game playing. Top. Cogn. Sci. **2**, 202–216 (2010). doi:10.1111/j.1756-8765.2009.01054.x
11. Spence, I., Feng, J.: Video games and spatial cognition. Rev. Gen. Psychol. **14**, 92–104 (2010). doi:10.1037/a0019491
12. Pigford, T.: Feasibility and benefit of using the nintendo wii fit for balance rehabilitation in an elderly patient experiencing recurrent falls. J. Stud. Phys. Ther. Res. **2**(1), 12–20 (2010)

13. Quiroga, M.A., Herranz, M., Gomez-Abad, M., Kebir, M., Ruiz, J., Colom, R.: Video games: do they require general intelligence? Comput. Educ. **53**, 414–418 (2009). doi:10.1016/j.compedu.2009.02.017
14. Marinelli, E.C., Rogers, W.A.: Identifying potential usability challenges for xbox 360 kinect exergames for older adults. Proc. Hum. Factors Ergon. Soc. Annu. Meet. **58**(1), 1247–1251 (2014). SAGE Publications
15. McLaughlin, A., Gandy, M., Allaire, J., Whitlock, L.: Putting fun into video games for older adults. Ergon. Des. Q. Hum. Factors Appl. **20**(2), 13–22 (2012)
16. Brox, E., Luque, L.F., Evertsen, G.J., Hernández, J.E.G.: Exergames for elderly: social exergames to persuade seniors to increase physical activity. In: 2011 5th International Conference on Pervasive Computing Technologies for Healthcare (PervasiveHealth), pp. 546–549, IEEE, May 2011
17. Whitlock, L.A., McLaughlin, A.C., Allaire, J.C.: Training requirements of a video game-based cognitive intervention for older adults: lessons learned. In: Proceedings of the Human Factors and Ergonomics Society 54th Annual Meeting, Human Factors and Ergonomics Society, Santa Monica, pp. 2343–2346 (2010)
18. Czaja, S.J, Charness, N., Dijkstra, K., Fisk, A.D., Rogers, W.A., Sharit, J.: Background questionnaire. Technical report, No. CRE-ATE-2006-02 (2006)
19. Barg-Walkow, L.H., Mitzner, T.L., Rogers, W.A.: The technology experience profile (TEP): assessment and scoring guide (HFA-TR-1402). School of Psychology, Human Factors and Aging Laboratory, Georgia Institute of Technology, Atlanta, GA (2014)
20. Brooke, J.: SUS: a quick and dirty usability scale. In: Jordan, P.W., Thomas, B., Weerdmeester, B.A., McClelland, A.L. (eds.) Usability Evaluation in Industry. Taylor and Francis, London (1996)
21. Davis, F.D.: Perceived usefulness, perceived ease of use, and user acceptance of information technology. MIS Q. **13**(3), 319–340 (1989)
22. Davis, F.D., Bagozzi, R.P., Warshaw, P.R.: User acceptance of computer technology: a comparison of two theoretical models. Manag. Sci. **35**(8), 982–1003 (1989)
23. Body and brain connection [Video game]. Namco Bandai Games America Inc., Santa Clara, CA (2010)
24. Your shape fitness evolved 2012 [Video game]. Ubisoft Entertainment, San Francisco, CA (2011)
25. Silva, P.A., Nunes, F., Vasconcelos, A., Kerwin, M., Moutinho, R., Teixeira, P.: Using the smartphone accelerometer to monitor fall risk while playing a game: the design and usability evaluation of dance! don't fall. In: Schmorrow, D.D., Fidopiastis, C.M. (eds.) AC 2013. LNCS, vol. 8027, pp. 754–763. Springer, Heidelberg (2013)
26. Wüest, S., Borghese, N.A., Pirovano, M., Mainetti, R., van de Langenberg, R., de Bruin, E.D.: Usability and effects of an exergame-based balance training program. GAMES HEALTH Res. Dev. Clin. Appl. **3**(2), 106–114 (2014)
27. Mendes, F.S., Pompeu, J.E., Lobo, A.M., da Silva, K.G., Oliveira, T.P., Zomignani, A.P., Piemonte, M.P.: Motor learning, retention and transfer after virtual-reality-based training in Parkinson's disease – effect of motor and cognitive demands of games: a longitudinal, controlled clinical study. Physiotherapy **98**(Special Issue on Advancing Technology including papers from WCPT), 217–223 (2012)
28. Boot, W.R., Kramer, A.F., Simons, D.J., Fabiani, M., Gratton, G.: The effects of video game playing on attention, memory, and executive control. Acta Psychol. **129**(3), 387–398 (2008)

Play for the Elderly - Effect Studies of Playful Technology

Henrik Hautop Lund(✉)

Technical University of Denmark, Building 326, 2800 Kgs., Lyngby, Denmark
hhl@playware.dtu.dk

Abstract. This paper addresses play for the elderly, and how playware can act as a play force that pushes people into a play dynamics. Play is a free and voluntary activity that we do for no other purpose than the play and enjoyment. Nevertheless, we may observe collateral effects of play amongst the elderly, e.g. in terms of health effects. The paper presents both qualitative and quantitative studies of the effect of play amongst elderly. For instance, it is shown how playful training on modular interactive tiles show statistical significant effects on all the test measures of elderly functional abilities (e.g. balancing, strength, mobility, agility, endurance) after merely 13 group training sessions during which each elderly play (exercise) for just 12–13 min. Hence, the statistical significant effects are obtained after just 2–3 h of total playing time with such playful technology. In play, the elderly seem to forget about time and place (e.g. forget about their possible fear of falling and physical limitations), and thereby achieve the remarkable collateral effect on their health.

Keywords: Play · Playware · Elderly · Effect · Modular technology

1 Introduction

Play is a free and voluntary activity that we do for no other purpose than play itself. We do not play to achieve a certain outcome or product, but we play for the pleasure and enjoyment that we feel while playing. Nevertheless, under various circumstances, we may observe certain effects of play. For the one who plays, these effects are not the primary reason to engage in play. Therefore, we term such effects the collateral effects of play. The collateral effects of play can be educational achievements, motor skill enhancement, cognitive and physical rehabilitation, etc. These collateral effects of play can be significant and important, but it is essential to understand that play is a self-sustaining phenomenon which carries its purpose in itself. Compared to other human activities, in its pure form, play does not lead to anything; it neither creates nor produces anything, except for play:

– Play is a free, voluntary activity indulged for its own sake, and although creative, play is unproductive and non-utilitarian. Play has boundaries of space and time, and takes place temporarily outside ‘regular life,’ with its own course and meaning [1].

Likewise the French play theoretician Roger Caillois emphasizes the unproductive and voluntary nature of play:

J. Zhou and G. Salvendy (Eds.): ITAP 2015, Part II, LNCS 9194, pp. 500–511, 2015.
DOI: 10.1007/978-3-319-20913-5_46

- Play is characterized as free (not obligatory); separate (isolated in space and time); uncertain (indeterminable); unproductive (without material production); governed by rules (contingent conventions); and make-believe (suspension of disbelief) [2].

Huizinga describes play as a separate life sphere, which existence cannot and shall not be legitimized with outer purposes. The notion of play as a separate life sphere is summarized by Gadamer: When human beings engage themselves in playing, an "ontological shift" occurs where we, so to speak, move to another stage of being. This particular stage of being is characterized by the fact that the player as subject is incorporated in the act of playing as the object of the act. Therefore, in the end play is not dependent on the subject who plays but of the subject submitting itself to something which involves the subject as if it was an object. Rephrased, it is "play that plays the player", and we are thus attracted to play by a basic force. Gadamer describes this force as the fundamental "motion" of the universe as such ([3]:103–04). By submitting oneself to play, the player goes through a separation from ones status as a rational being and instead becomes a part of what Gadamer calls the "natural" uncertain and purposeless motion which influences the universe. This philosophical description in reality shows, in spite of the level of abstraction, a phenomenon which we are able to recognize as a common experience with play activities in which we experience that the play takes over when we actively engage in it – and however possesses the necessary skills. We forget about time and place when in play.

Though society has often viewed play as a childish and frivolous activity, we all engage in play over our entire lifespan, and engage in such play activities in which we forget about time and place just for the enjoyment and pleasure of play itself. Sport, sex, games, art, and scientific research activities can in many cases be described as playful activities in which the subject performs an ontological shift forgetting about time and place, and in which the activity has its own course and meaning. The play activity provides life fulfilling enjoyment and meaning to the player. The player can be of all ages. It appears limiting and exclusive to define such life fulfilling enjoyment as an activity for children and youth alone. Play is, for everybody, a fundamental activity submitted to free will. In the act of playing, we manage our lives at our own choice, as we create the special form of lived life outside the "regular" life where (lust for) life and happiness as the essence of play rules. When we play we become, in the words of the philosopher Friedrich Schiller, "a whole and complete human being":

- For, to speak out once for all, man only plays when in the full meaning of the word he is a man, and he is only completely a man when he plays. […] I promise you that the whole edifice of aesthetic art and the still more difficult art of life will be supported by this principle [4].

In the following, we will examine play amongst older adults. Especially, we will examine how the design and development of playful technology in the form of playware mediates playful interaction, and results in significant collateral effects of play in the health of the older adults.

2 Designing Play and Playware for Older Adults

We use countless methods to achieve the moods of play, and knowledge of those methods and competencies in using them are indispensable if one wants to play. As the American psychologist Michael J. Apter expresses it: One of the most interesting things about play is the tremendous variety of devices, stratagems and techniques which people can use to obtain the pleasures of play ([5], p. 18). And it could be added that it is similarly interesting which great economic investments people are willing to make to obtain playful experiences.

Some of the methods to achieve play we know, for example, as games, which we either learn, for instance from parents, peers etc., or buy as with computer games. Other methods are embedded in play equipment like the swing or the roller coaster. Both play equipment and games can be described as instruments or "tools" that are specialized in creating play, and when someone is using these tools, they assist in creating and regulating those physical and mental states of tension that we define as play.

If one wishes to design and develop play facilities or if one wishes to create play products, it is important to have an understanding of which games and play products will function and why some function and others do not. This understanding can be gained by studying what we call the play-dynamics which are activated through games and play-facilities. We define play-dynamics as follows, as we take our point of departure in concepts from the description of dynamic forces in the world of physics:

- A play-dynamic is the dynamic effect of the play-force which affects the player by placing this person in a state of playing.

The play-force can for example be a motion, a competition, a danger or a joke which initiates a dynamic in which the player raise from the rational reality to a state of playing. The play-force is the influence and the effect becomes a dynamic play condition. Games and other tools function exactly by manifesting a force of play which can initiate a play-dynamic.

We can design play technology, called playware, which act as a play force bringing the user into a play-dynamic. *Playware* has been defined as intelligent hardware and software that creates play and playful experiences for users of all ages [6, 7]. Playware-tools are tools with a "behaviour" that initiates play force (e.g. a motion, in the case of sensorimotor play) via interaction. This is the basis for the play dynamic to emerge through which the users are brought into a state of playing. R&D in playware has led to numerous applications in various areas such as rehabilitation [8], playgrounds [7], education [9], art [10], and sport [11]. In all such cases, users interact with the playware as a free and voluntary activity that they engage in for the pleasure of play, even if the activity may be shown to have collateral effects e.g. in terms of health and skills. Modular playware has been proposed as of particular interest to develop solutions for such varied areas of application, since modularity may facilitate easy assembly and adaptation of the playware to different interaction modalities [12].

We can outline several guidelines for the design and development of modular playware [12], which should help in the designing playware that acts as a play force to bring the user into play dynamics. Important features of this design approach are modularity, flexibility, and construction, tangible interaction and immediate feedback to stimulate engagement, activity design by end-users, and creative exploration of play activities. These features permit the use of such modular playware by many users, including older adults who often could be prevented from using and taking benefits from modern technologies. The objective is to get anybody moving, exchanging, experimenting and having fun, regardless of their cognitive/physical ability levels.

3 Designing Modular Playware for Dementia Treatment

As an example of design of modular playware following these guidelines, together with P. Marti's group at University of Siena, we designed and developed novel tools for dementia treatment based on activity analyses together with therapists and elderly in an Italian home care [13, 14]. We developed modular playware tools to become part of a "multi-sensory room", i.e. a space augmented by innovative technologies, that can be configured for different therapeutic activities and needs and that provide sensory stimulation. The modular playware design features allow for space re-configurability and adaptivity, which should support customized therapeutic interventions, and involve dementia affected users in the interaction with the solutions. The objective of such environment is to obtain an optimal level of stimulation of dementia affected patients through their playful engagement, active participation and intrinsic motivation in the therapeutic activity, and favouring the emergence of personal meanings (memories, interpretations, narratives) eased by the dynamic configurations of the environment.

The modular playware we designed each has a physical expression (Light and Sound Cylinders and RollingPins). Each module can process and communicate with its surrounding environment (to neighbouring modules and/or through sensing or actuation). The overall behaviour emerges from the user's coordination of a number of modules. The Light and Sound Cylinders and RollingPins developed for the non-pharmacological therapeutic treatment were designed as modular playware in order to allow very easy and understandable physical operation by dementia affected patients and therapists.

In particular, the RollingPins are semi-transparent plastic tubes capable of measuring their orientation and the speed of their rotation. They provide feedback in the form of RGB light, sound and vibration. The RollingPins are able to communicate with each other or with other devices equipped with the same radio communication technology. The RollingPins are usually used in pairs, as the local feedback of a RollingPin can be set depending not only on its own speed and orientation, but also on the speed and the orientation of the peer RollingPin. The system is used as a facilitator and mediator of social dynamics during the normal therapy to counteract social isolation that can result in dementia through the loss of social skills.

The RollingPins embody by design a dialogic component supporting non-verbal communication between therapist and patient. They can be manipulated (e.g. grasped, rolled and shaken), and each of these actions can produce feedback (visual, audio, tactile, smell as a local or environmental output in the multi-sensory room). The RollingPins communicate with each other, and by doing this they influence each other.

Each time a RollingPin is manipulated, it produces an output (visual, auditory or tactile) both locally and remotely on the peer device, influencing its behaviour.

The therapeutic interventions in the multi-sensory room include the presence of a therapist. The therapist coordinates the session by defining the protocol, the setting, the most appropriate level of stimuli according to patients' needs, and also supports the patient in remaining involved in the activity. In order to assess if non-verbal and gesture-based exchange can engage the dementia patient and sustain effective communication and coordination between therapist and patient, an experiment was designed to compare the use of the RollingPins in two conditions:

Individual Modality: with the RollingPins used as independent devices, interactive but not communicating with each other.

Dialogic Modality: with the RollingPins communicating with each other.

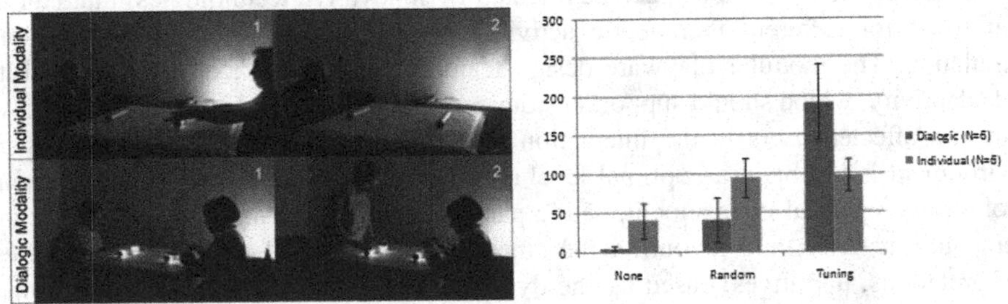

Fig. 1. The RollingPins used in individual modality and dialogic modality. The diagram shows mean values in seconds of behavioral indicators (None, Random, Tuning) of the dementia patients actions with the RollingPins in dialogical and individual modality tests.

It was found in interventions with elderly dementia patients [13, 14] that using the RollingPins, the patients participated in the activity, coordinating their behaviour with the therapist and imitating the same interaction patterns generated by the therapist. Figure 1 shows physical engagement with the RollingPins in individual modality and dialogic modality, with statistical significant differences between the two modalities. Marti et al. [14] concluded that the use of simple units, easy to manipulate without explicit instruction, puts the subjects at ease and provides them with minimal but clear stimuli to both have a pleasurable experience and perform the tasks that better suit their problem. Furthermore, a dynamic, flexible and configurable system has proved to be a key factor for obtaining an optimal stimulation tailored to the specific needs of each patient.

Further, regarding the intervention with dementia patients, it was concluded that "The results of the experiment demonstrate the positive effects of the use of the RollingPins on engagement, coordination and motivation in regards to therapy in the dialogic condition. In particular, we observed that, differently from the patients working in the individual modality, the patients working in the dialogic modality established with the therapist a non-verbal dialogue based on sensory-motor imitation of the pattern generated by the therapist" [14].

To test for the modular playware mediating play thereby triggering intrinsic motivation in the patients, at the end of the session, the patients were asked to answer a standard version of the Intrinsic Motivation Inventory (IMI). The means of the Interest/Enjoyment and Perceived Competence scores were found to be higher in the dialogic condition than in the individual one. The Interest/Enjoyment means difference was significant ($t = 1.95$, $p = 0.041$), which is a critical scale in assessing the emergence of the intrinsic motivation. This indicates that the modular playware designed as the RollingPins indeed mediates playful interaction, which the patients engage in for their own enjoyment.

4 Designing Modular Playware for Functional Ability Enhancement of Older Adults

As another example of the design of modular playware following the design guidelines, we designed and developed modular interactive tiles for enhancing functional abilities – in particular balancing skills – of older adults. There are many functional abilities which are of high importance for elderly to retain and possibly improve in order to perform activities of daily living and in order lower health risks, e.g. related to illness and falls. These functional abilities include mobility, agility, balancing, strength and endurance. Due to the importance of such functional abilities for the health and daily activities of people, a number of training methods are used to address the prevention of loss of these abilities and to address the rehabilitation of these abilities. We hypothesize that if the training methods and training equipment is designed in the form of modular playware for retention and rehabilitation of functional abilities of elderly, it may motivate elderly to perform training which after just few training sessions can provide significant effects on the broad range of functional abilities necessary for elderly health and for elderly to perform their daily activities.

In order to verify this hypothesis, effect studies of such collateral effects of play among elderly is needed. Therefore, we will outline the design of a modular playware technology aimed at improving functional abilities among elderly and related studies of effect of playful modular interactive tiles training amongst community-dwelling elderly.

4.1 Material - Modular Interactive Tiles

The modular interactive tiles [8] are a distributed system of electronic tiles which like building blocks can be attached to one another to form the overall system (Fig. 2). Each tile is self-sufficient of processing power (an ATmega1280) and each one has a battery that lasts approximately 30 h in use. This makes the usage of the tiles very flexible because the tiles do not need a computer, a computer monitor or external power source. When connected to one another to form a playfield, the modular tiles communicate to their neighbors through four infra-red (IR) transceivers located on the sides. One tile has an XBee radio communication chip, with which it can communicate to other devices that have an XBee chip, for example a game selector box (or a PC that has an USB XBee dongle connected).

Fig. 2. The modular interactive tiles can be assembled in different configurations for different playful exercises and levels.

When playing on the tiles, the subject provides the tiles with an input in the form of pressure measured by a force sensitive resistor which is located in the center of each tile. The tile can then react by turning on 8 RGB LEDs which are mounted with equal spacing between each other in a circle inside the tile. In the present intervention, the tiles were placed on the floor (though there is also an option to place them on a wall with magnets on the back of the tiles).

Therapists may use the interactive modular tiles to provide playful treatment for a large number of patients who receive hospital, municipality or home care, although the tiles can as well be used for prevention with elderly or for fitness with normal people. Nielsen and Lund [15] described the use of the modular tiles with cardiac patients, smoker's lung (COLD) patients and stroke patients in hospitals and in the private homes of patients and elderly. Through a qualitative research methodology of the new practice with the tiles, it was found that therapists are using the modular aspect of the tiles for personalized training of a vast variety of elderly patients modulating exercises and difficulty levels, that in physical games there are individual differences in patient interaction capabilities and styles, and that modularity allows the therapist to adapt exercises to the individual patient's capabilities [15]. The aspect of adaptivity was further explored by Lund and Thorsteinsson [16].

4.2 Interventions and Results

We have performed several tests for the effect on functional abilities of elderly from playful training with the modular interactive tiles over a short period of time, e.g. [17]. In one study, 16 community-dwelling elderly aged 63–95 years (mean 83.2 years of age) participated in 13 group training sessions on the modular interactive tiles over a period of 16 weeks in two senior activity centers in Gentofte (Copenhagen), Denmark. The training with the modular interactive tiles were set up to be an activity which like any other activities in the senior activity centers, the elderly could sign up to. Each individual elderly performed training on the modular interactive tiles 12–13 min during each session. The elderly participants were tested with the Senior Fitness Test [18, 19] (Chair-to-stand (CS), 8 ft Timed Up and Go (TUG), 6 Minute Walking Test (6MWT)) and an extra balancing test (Line Walk (LW)) before and after the intervention (pre-tests and post-tests after 13 sessions). The pre- and posttests were performed by Sundhedsdoktor, an independent third-party not involved with the training, and post-test was performed blinded from the pre-test results.

A research assistant would guide the training of the group on the modular interactive tiles, using 10–12 tiles for each session. In the group sessions, the elderly rotated between playing on the modular interactive tiles for a few minutes, and resting until it was their turn on the modular interactive tiles again.

During some of the sessions, the tiles would be split into two smaller platforms (with 6 tiles each) to allow parallel interaction of two elderly on two different platforms. Other part of the session would be on a larger platform of tiles, on which elderly would interact individually. The individual platforms where formed as squares of 9 tiles or as a horseshoe with the elderly player standing in the middle.

The games used for the training were Colour Race, Final Countdown, Reach, Island Game, Concentration Game Colour, and Simon Says. The last two games are memory games that may potentially challenge both physical and mental skills, whereas the first four games are also challenging mobility, balancing, endurance, and reaction. Indeed, most games are designed to challenge several physical and cognitive abilities simultaneously while playing the games.

The protocol for the sessions were that the elderly participants started out with playing Colour Race of 2 × 4 round with each round lasting for 30 s, given a two minute workout at a time followed by a break while the rest of the eldery were training. Afterwards, the game Final Countdown was applied in a slow version in order for the elderly participants to feel success with their playing. Again the training was 2 × 2 min, in a pace that the elders could set themselves. In the informal sessions, Reach, Island and Simon Says were used depending on the wishes and mood of the eldery while maintaining a two minute play, though Island has a fixed length of 1.5 min. The Concentration Game Color game was put on as a finale game, not least because this game seemed to entertain the eldery a lot, and thus motivated them to play for longer. In general each eldery got at least 12 min of training, but due to the nature of playing, some elders forgot time and in the informal sessions were allowed to continue to play games as Concentration Game Colour for longer time without breaks.

The sessions were preformed in small rooms with the tiles in the middle, surrounded by small mattress and the eldery placed on chairs along the edge. The setup had the advantage that the elders could engage with each other while playing, thus also motivate and making sure all participated.

The games required variations in the both movements of the players, such as the length of steps, moving forward and backwards, turning around, and in the speed, because of the elements of competition that is central for the games. These were important elements, due to the motivation of the elderly participants, as they lost track of time, and gave into playing the games.

Table 1 shows the results of the pre- and posttests of the elderly participants. All tests showed a statistical significant improvement of performance between pre-test and post-test at level $P < 0.001$ (Wilcoxon Signed Rank Test). The average improvement was 24 % on CS, 21 % on 8-ft TUG, 29 % on 6MWT, and 66 % on LW. Further, several subjects improved so that they transferred from one health risk level to another health risk level (according to the Rikli and Jones' criterion reference points [19]) increasing at least one level. In total, 63 % of the subjects improved their health risk level according to at least one of the three tests of the Senior Fitness Test.

As confirmed by the quantitative data, also qualitative observations found the subjects to be much more mobile at post-test, and it was found that three subjects who performed the pre-tests with orthopedic aids (rollator, walker and cane), would perform the post-test without these aids or using these much less.

Table 1. Results of pre-test and post-test of the 13 sessions training with modular interactive tiles for "2. Cross-generational playful training" (16 elderly subjects).

Test	Pre-test	Post-test	Average improvement	Significance level	Level improvements
CS	9.9	12.3	24 %	P < 0.001	7
TUG	11.7 s	9.3 s	21 %	P < 0.001	6
6MWT	269.8 m	347.9 m	29 %	P < 0.001	5
LW	3.8	6.3	66 %	P < 0.001	NA

In another study, 12 community-dwelling elderly (average age: 79 (66–88)) with smaller balancing problems participated in a small randomized controlled study to test for dynamic balancing using the Dynamic Gait Index (DGI) test. The intervention was performed at the Lyngby-Taarbaek municipality (Copenhagen, Denmark) physiotherapy training unit. A therapist blinded to the intervention perform random lottery to assign the elderly to either the control group (6 persons) or the intervention group (6 persons). The control group continued to perform their daily activities during the experimental period of 2 months, whereas the intervention group performed playful training on the modular interactive tiles of average 12.5 group sessions during the 2 months. DGI tests were performed as pre-tests and post-tests for both control group and intervention group.

The test score for control group and intervention group is presented in Table 2. The score in the control group and the tiles training group did not differ at baseline (DGI mean score: 18.3 vs. 19.0), but there was significant difference in change of DGI score after the 2-months period with the control group decreasing DGI score by 9.3 % and tiles training group increasing DGI score by 12.3 %. A two way repeated measures ANOVA (Student Newman-Keuls method) resulted in no statistical significant differences at baseline and in control group performance over time, whereas there is statistical significant increase in performance of tiles training group over time ($p < 0.05$) and statistical significant difference between control group and tiles training group after intervention ($p < 0.05$). DGI mean score after intervention was 16.6 for the control group compared with 21.33 for the tiles training group, i.e. −9.3 % vs. +12.3 %.

Table 2. Results of the DGI pre-test and post-test after two months of the 12.5 sessions training with modular interactive tiles for "3. Formal playful training".

	Pre-test	Post-test	Average improvement	Significance level
Control group	18.3	16.6	−9.3 %	NS
Tiles training group	19.0	21.3	12.3 %	P < 0.05

The community dwelling elderly with balancing problems seemed to be at high risk of falling if not subject to any training, whereas those who performed training increased their dynamic balancing abilities. A DGI score of < 19 is associated with impairment of gait and fall risk [20, 21], so the statistical significant difference between DGI score of 16.6 of the control group and DGI score of 21.33 of the tiles training group is important.

5 Discussion and Conclusion

The effect studies show important collateral effects of play. Qualitative observations indicate that the elderly participants are having fun and that they meet to play for their own enjoyment and pleasure. They enter into play as a free and voluntary activity with no other purpose that the play itself, and for the life fulfilling enjoyment and meaning that it provides to the elderly participants. The observations indicate that the ontological shift happens for the participants. They enter into a new status when they are playing, forgetting about time and place, and thereby most importantly for obtaining the documented collateral health effects of play, they forget about the fear of falling, fear of getting out of balance, their normal physical limitations, etc. We observe that often, when the elderly citizens are on the modular interactive tiles, they jump around much more freely and fast than when they move around normally.

Hence, the tiles' light pattern and performance seem to act as a play force which pushes the elderly user into a play dynamics. The tiles light up in the pattern needed to be performed by the user, and the tiles are providing immediate feedback to the user. As found by Nielsen and Lund in a study of playful training on tiles with elderly stroke patients: "the features of the modular interactive tiles allow for a combination of physical and cognitive training of elderly" [15]. The features based upon the modular playware design seem to be among those which results in the tiles acting as a play force. They distinguish the modular interactive tiles from other exergaming systems and other training methods, and may be among the reasons that may explain the success of the modular interactive tiles for improving the functional abilities of the community-dwelling elderly.

Compared with other training methods, it is extraordinary that the playful training on modular interactive tiles show statistical significant effects on all the test measures of elderly functional abilities after merely 13 group training sessions during which each elderly exercise for just 12–13 min. Hence, the statistical significant effects are obtained after just 2–3 h of total training time on the modular interactive tiles. This can be compared to other training methods and interventions typically reporting 13–25 h of training for showing statistical significant effects [22].

Further, even when such other training methods show statistical significant effects after the longer period of, for instance, 25 training sessions, the effects are often on only one or two of the functional abilities that are included in the tests in the present work. Contrary, the tests with modular interactive tiles training show comprehensive statistical significant effect on all test measures which test for dynamic balancing, strength, mobility, agility, and endurance.

The design, development and testing of modular playware (e.g. as RollingPins and modular interactive tiles) has shown that such tools may act as play forces to push the users into play dynamics. The users engage in play with such playware as a free and voluntary activity with no other purpose than play itself, but simply for the pleasure and enjoyment. For instance, in the case of the modular interactive tiles, it seems to be the case that the elderly participants forget about their possible fear of falling and physical limitations when playing, and thereby achieve the remarkable collateral effect on their health in terms of balancing skills, endurance, strength, etc. Hence, as has been shown in this paper, playing may lead to important collateral effects. These collateral effects of play are shown to be significant and important, especially in the area of health. At the same time, it is important to remember that play is a self-sustaining phenomenon which carries its purpose in itself.

Acknowledgement. The author would like to thank Prof.ssa Patrizia Marti, University of Siena and her group, staff and elderly at Casa Protetta Albesani, staff and elderly at the senior activity centers Tvaerbommen and Vennerslund, children from the kindergarten, Sundhedsdoktor, Gentofte municipality, Lyngby-Taarbaek municipality, physiotherapists of Lyngby-Taarbaek municipality, Kirsten Skyhøj, volunteers from Ældre Sagen in Lyngby, and especially J. Jessen who assisted several interventions.

References

1. Huizinga, J.: Homo Ludens (1938). Beacon Press, Boston (1971)
2. Caillois, R.: Man, Play and Games (1958). University of Illinois Press, Champaign (2001)
3. Gadamer, H.-G.: Truth and Method. Crossroad, New York (1989)
4. Schiller, F.: Letters Upon The Aesthetic Education of Man. Courier Corporation, Chelmsford (1795)
5. Apter, M.J.: A structural phenomenology of play. In: Kerr, J.K., Apter, M.J. (eds.) Adult Play. Routledge, New York (1991)
6. Lund, H.H., Jessen, C.: Playware - Intelligent technology for children's play. Technical report TR-2005-1, June, Maersk Institute, University of Southern Denmark (2005)
7. Lund, H.H., Klitbo, T., Jessen, C.: Playware technology for physically activating play. Artif. Life Robot. J. **9**(4), 165–174 (2005)
8. Lund, H.H.: Modular robotics for playful physiotherapy. In: Proceedings of IEEE International Conference on Rehabilitation Robotics, pp. 571–575. IEEE Press (2009)
9. Lund, H.H., Marti, P.: Physical and conceptual constructions in advanced learning environments. Interact. Stud. **5**(2), 269–299 (2004)
10. Lund, H.H., Ottesen, M.: RoboMusic – a behavior-based approach. Artif. Life Robot. J. **12** (1–2), 18–23 (2008)
11. Lund, H.H., Thorsteinsson, T.: Social playware for mediating teleplay interaction over distance. Int. J. Artif. Life Robot. **16**(4), 435–440 (2012)
12. Lund, H.H., Marti, P.: Designing modular robotic playware. In: Proceedings of 18th IEEE International Symposium on Robot and Human Interactive Communication (Ro-Man 2009), pp.115–121. IEEE Press (2009)

13. Marti, P., Lund, H.H., Bacigalupo, M., Giusti, L., Mennecozzi, C.: A multi-sensory environment for the treatment of dementia affected subjects. J. Gerontechnol. **6**(1), 33–41 (2007)
14. Marti, P., Giusti, L., Lund, H.H.: The role of modular robotics in mediating nonverbal social exchanges. IEEE Trans. Rob. **25**(3), 602–613 (2009)
15. Nielsen, C.B., Lund, H.H.: Adapting playware to rehabilitation practices. Int. J. Comput. Sci. Sport **11**, 1 (2012)
16. Lund, H.H., Thorsteinsson, T.: Adaptive playware in physical games. In: Proceedings of the 6th International Conference on Foundations of Digital Games 2011. ACM (2011)
17. Lund, H.H., Jessen, J.D.: Effects of short-term training of community-dwelling elderly with modular interactive tiles. Games For Health: Res. Dev. Clin. Appl. **3**(5), 277–283 (2014)
18. Rikli, R.E., Jones, C.J.: Development and validation of a functional fitness test for community-residing older adults. J. Aging Phys. Act. **7**(2), 129–161 (1999)
19. Rikli, R.E., Jones, C.J.: Senior Fitness Test Manual. Human Kinetics, Champaign (2001)
20. Shumway-Cook, A., Woollacott, M.: Motor Control: Theory and Applications. Wilkins & Wilkins, Baltimore (1995)
21. Shumway-Cook, A., Baldwin, M., Polissar, N.L., Gruber, W.: Predicting the probability for falls in community-dwelling older adults. Phys. Ther. **77**, 812–819 (1997)
22. Sherrington, C., Whitney, J.C., Lord, S.R., Herbert, R.D., Cumming, R.G., Close, J.C.T.: Effective exercise for the prevention of falls: a systematic review and meta-analysis. J. Am. Geriatr. Soc. **56**(12), 2234–2243 (2008)

TwitterIDo: What if My Shopping Bag Could Tell My Friends I'm Out Shopping

Elena Nazzi(✉) and Tomas Sokoler

IT University of Copenhagen, Rued Langaards Vej 7,
2300 Copenhagen, Denmark
{elna,sokoler}@itu.dk

Abstract. In this paper, we explore the use of augmented everyday artefacts to make seniors' everyday activities more visible in local communities to strengthen existing face-to-face social interactions or open new ones. We ground the twitterIDo idea in a three-year research project. We involved seniors as co-designers and we explored twitterIDo in a living lab with a community of senior citizens. Through a set of interactive prototypes of augmented everyday artefacts and dedicated displays, we engaged senior co-designers in in-situ enactments and workshops. Experiencing the possibilities of our idea, the seniors envisioned the use of the interactive prototypes to support their collaboration in shopping activities. We reflect on how promoting social interaction by making everyday activities more visible became instrumental to support collaboration, offering the seniors a clear purpose to make their shopping activities more visible.

1 Introduction

Society is increasingly looking at digital technology to guarantee quality of life for a growing older population. Because quality of life is a complex mix of physical, emotional and social aspects [9], research and industry are exploring novel technologies to support communication between seniors, their caregivers, family members and friends. Our research investigates through design explorations a future where artefacts used by the seniors in their everyday activities are augmented with digital technology to be able to communicate the on-going activity to other seniors. Through this communication, the everyday activities are made more visible, thereby strengthening existing possibilities for social interaction in local communities of seniors, or open new ones. We name this approach twitterIDo. What if a senior lady could let her friends know she is out shopping simply by picking up her shopping bag and going shopping? What if her shopping bag could communicate clues on her owner's shopping activity?

People often needs a good excuse to initiate a conversation with acquaintances or strangers in occasional encounters [15]. Moreover, the changes that often characterize senior life affect the quality and quantity of their social interactions. For some seniors, initiating social interactions may become intimidating, thus finding good occasions and good excuses becomes important [10]. Examples

J. Zhou and G. Salvendy (Eds.): ITAP 2015, Part II, LNCS 9194, pp. 512–523, 2015.
DOI: 10.1007/978-3-319-20913-5_47

of such good excuses can come from everyday activities. Let's think about shopping: noticing someone with bags full of grocery can offer a point for a conversation on the deals in the local supermarket, if not an occasion to help a neighbour to carry home his/her bags. TwitterIDo explores the potential for the design of systems that expand the role of everyday activities as openers of social interaction by making these activities more visible. In particular twitterIDo relies on augmented everyday artefacts to communicate on-going activities and dedicated displays to notice these activities.

This paper presents twitterIDo and our exploration of making the shopping activities of a local community of seniors more visible with twitterIDo technologies. In a living lab [6] comprising over a year of co-design activities, we used a series of interactive prototypes in in-situ enactments, portraying the seniors' own activities, situations and environment. Most interventions looking at seniors' social interaction and well-being focus on strict relations and supporting an emotional idea of caring and keeping an eye on each other [10]. Our findings show that our seniors envisioned twitterIDo as useful to collaborate around shopping activities. Making their shopping activities more visible can have a valuable practical purpose. In this paper, we focus on seniors' everyday activities, artefacts and social networks, and we explore what if social interaction becomes the means that supports a more practical purpose for seniors doing an activity together. We propose a design approach that shifts the attention from caring to supporting everyday activities, and that takes advantage of everyday artefacts to communicate such activities.

2 Related Works

Research in HCI and gerontechnology is increasingly looking at supporting social interaction among seniors, their caregivers and their families [4,8,10,14]. Sociological studies highlight the importance of tickets to talk, or resources, for initiating social interaction in occasional encounters [15]. Svensson and Sokoler [16] design digital technology for social interaction among seniors around TV watching, building on how everyday activities can offer a "resource of information about the state of affairs within a community that may help turn a casual encounter between people into an opening for social interaction [16]. Building on [16] we assume that if activities are more visible, more seniors can notice them, and potentially have additional openings for social interaction.

Mobile devices, smartphones and tables and Internet of Things technologies are increasingly available, making easier and easier to embed technology into our everyday life. It is a question of how to design these technologies to fit the everyday situations of seniors and offer them a concrete benefit in their everyday life. Our work is in line with Brereton's call [3] for designing technology that builds on the habituated artefacts that already are part of a senior's life. The everyday artefacts that seniors use in their everyday activities are the starting point of our designs. Recent research projects are exploring more tangible and situated ways to bring the potential of social networking in the seniors everyday environments [5]. TwitterIDo stands on the same grounds. Moving away from text interfaces, we explore tangible ways to notice and make everyday activities visible, trying to translate what happens in on-line social networking and make its benefits meaningful for seniors [12].

3 TwitterIDo

The first formulation of twitterIDo emerged during the concept-development phase of the SeniorInteraktion project. This 3-year research project was dedicated to design novel welfare technologies based on reciprocal exchange and social interaction among seniors in local communities. The project was driven by a research-through-design approach and co-design methods, and by a research interest towards tangible and social computing technologies for seniors' everyday life. Investigating the seniors' attitudes towards social interaction technologies through co-design workshops [1,7], we gathered insights that offered the ground for refining twitterIDo and start its exploration. Here a simple scenario:

> Marie is an active 75-years-old woman. She enjoys having walks around the neighbourhood and she shops almost everyday. She often shares shopping favours with other 4 senior neighbours. This morning she takes her shopping-rollator and walks to her local shop. Her augmented shopping-rollator[1] communicates a new shopping update to her shopping group.
>
> Peter is at home having breakfast, when he puts the last portion of milk in his coffee. He will need some milk for his half-morning coffee but he doesn't have time to go to the shop. He is a member of Marie's shopping group. He glances at his tablet display and sees that someone is out shopping. He picks it up and notices that Marie is out shopping. Peter decides to ask Marie to buy him some milk. Peter takes his mobile device, swipes it over the shopping magnet on the fridge and activates his shopping app. He finds Marie's contact, calls her and asks for milk inviting her over for coffee when back from the shop.
>
> Lise is a neighbour of Marie and Peter. She moved in since two months and she does not know many other residents. Lise goes out for a walk. Passing through the entrance hall she takes a look at the Community Display. There are a couple of new offers on display and she stops to take a look at them. While she is in the entrance hall, Marie enters with her shopping-rollator full of bags of groceries. Lise takes the chance to ask Marie about one of the offers on display and they start a nice conversation.

In this scenario, the augmented shopping-rollator communicates when it is in use, and a family of dedicated displays–the shopping tablet at home, the mobile device and the Community Display in the entrance hall–help the seniors to notice shopping activities. These displays offer a dedicated way to keep in

[1] a 4-wheeled walking aid.

contact with each other in different situations. Simple additional clues on ongoing shopping activities are available for the seniors to interpret and act upon or simply to ignore. The augmented rollator and the screens are additional resources to strengthen existing ways of noticing everyday activities and interacting in face-to-face encounters. The augmented everyday artefacts offer familiar tangible interfaces to interact with digital technology, while the family of displays aim to facilitate the access and relevance of activity clues depending on situations, locations and content.

Differentiating between personal and semi-public displays, detailed information is communicated to a trusted and interested audience, while anonymous information are available in common areas of the local community. TwitterIDo supports both the community to get an overview of ongoing activities and small groups of seniors to be connected on the basis of a specific activity. In the scenario, the activity of shopping is useful for Marie and Peter that are part of the same shopping group, but also for Lise even if she is not part of this small group.

TwitterIDo builds on the following assumptions:

1. everyday activities have the potential of creating openers of social interaction in occasional encounters and digital technology can contribute to augment their potential;
2. making these everyday activities more visible, we can expand the potential of everyday activities to offer openings for social interaction;
3. augmenting everyday artefact to communicate on-going activities, we can offer seniors a way to make their activities more visible that is familiar and situated in what they do.The seniors can communicate about what they do by simply doing it and the communication is enhanced by the meaning that the artefacts carry with them [3].
4. we support communication in the local community and in particular we look at smaller activity-based groups of seniors that, within this local community, share an interest and practice on specific activities. Brandt et al. [1] call these gropus"communities of everyday practice", groups of seniors doing a particular everyday activity together.

4 Interactive Prototypes

Throughout the living lab, we designed a set of interactive prototypes of augmented shopping rollators, dedicated displays and their communication infrastructure. The following paragraph introduces the interactive prototypes and their functionalities. We decided to not replicate all the functionalities through the different displays because we aim to tailor the interface and interaction design to the situation of use: the common areas, the home or while on the go and shopping. Finally we designed two types of personal displays, mobile phone and tablet. They are dedicated to a particular activity and meant to strengthen the connection between seniors with their activity group rather than with the larger local community.

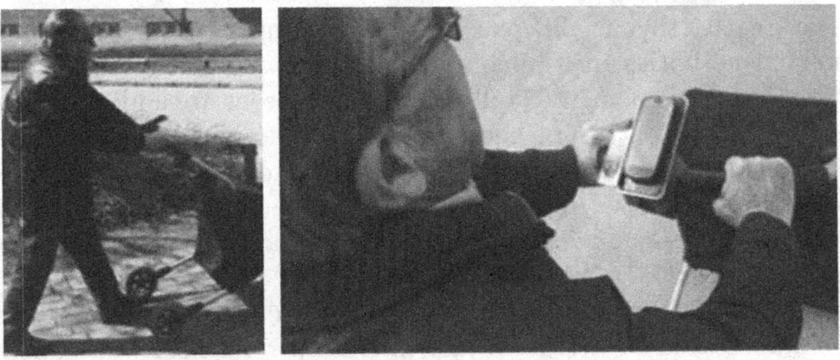

Fig. 1. MyShoppyBagRollator in use during an activity of the living lab

MyShoppyBagRollator. MyShoppyBagRollator is a 4-wheeles rollator augmented with sensors and equipped with an nfc-enabled interactive dock (Fig. 1). The augmented rollator is able to communicate when it is in use. Here its functionalities:

1. MyShoppyBagRollator is ON when a senior places his mobile device on the interactive dock. The sensors on the rollator detect when the rollator is in use, and, using the mobile device as gateway, the rollator communicates on-going shopping activity. Each activity cue is notified to the system and available for shopping friends over personal displays (mobile and tablet) and on the Community Display.
2. The augmented rollator is OFF when it is not paired with the mobile device. When OFF, MyShoppyBagRollator is a normal non-augmented rollator, it does not communicate and doesn't offer access to shopping activities of other seniors while on the go. Thus the seniors remain in control of what they disclose and when.

Community Display. The Community Display is a big screen (32 or 40 in.) positioned in the entrance hall of the community building (Fig. 2). Built with a

Fig. 2. The Community Display: main page, during co-design activities and details of the shopping page.

web interface, the Community Display shows on-going and planned activities in the community. Here its functionalities:

1. The main page offers an overview of the on-going activities. It offers a list of the most frequent activities showing the number of seniors/artefacts currently involved in a particular activity. From the main page are available also planned activities and seniors can leave digital comments.
2. Selecting one of the activities, a dedicated page offers more details on the activity. For example, the shopping activity page offers 4 views: how many people are currently out shopping and how many offers have been posted recently; a gallery of offers posted by residents in the last week; a summary of the week activities, and finally a list of supermarkets where people is currently shopping.
3. All the activity information on the Community Displays is anonymous, except the explicit comments created by the seniors. Anonymity supports the seniors' concerns for privacy but still offers insights and cues over on-going activities and events' attendance.

Fig. 3. Details of MyShoppyMobile and while in use

MyShoppyMobile. MyShoppyMobile is a mobile device implemented with an application running on Android phones (Fig. 3). Here its functionalities:

1. When paired with MyShoppyBagRollator, the mobile device turns into MyShoppyMobile, a shopping dedicated mobile device. This shopping device has 5 functionalities: make noticeable shopping activities when paired with the rollator; notice shopping activities and new offers with real-time notifications; make noticeable interesting offers allowing the seniors to take pictures and post offers when at home or on the go; browse pictures of interesting offers posted by their shopping friends; directly contact their shopping friends through voip calls (we used Skype).
2. The shopping application is ON when the device is on the dock of MyShoppyBagRollator, or when swiped over an NFC shopping-tag available as fridge magnet or embedded in the weekly deal magazine.
3. MyShoppyMobile becomes a dedicated device to connect seniors with their activity group. ideally, when coupled with different artefacts, MyShoppyMobile offer access to the specific activity such artefact is related to.

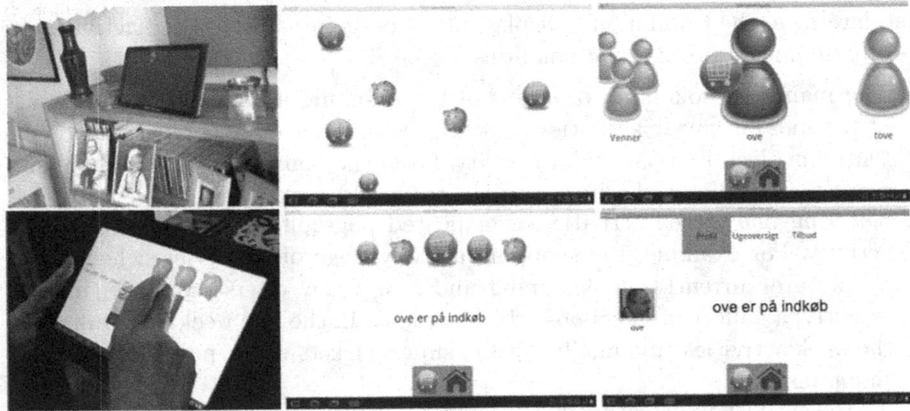

Fig. 4. MyShoppyTab with details from its ideal positioning within the house and screenshots of its interface.

MyShoppyTab. MyShoppyTab is a tablet device implemented with an application running on Android tablets. MyShoppyTab is meant for the home and has two modalities: ambient display and browsing device (Fig. 4). Here its functionalities:

1. When left on the shelf, MyShoppyTab is an ambient display. It shows a glanceable animation collecting real-time notifications of on-going activities within one's own shopping group.
2. When the senior picks up MyShoppyTab or touches the screen, the view reveals details these on-going activities: the latest offers posted and which seniors are currently out shopping.
3. Pressing the dedicated icon, the seniors can enter the browsing mode. In browsing mode, MyShoppyTab offers two functionalities: noticing active members of the shopping group; browsing through the history of activities and offers of the shopping group members and ones' own activities and offers.

5 Method

Our research is based on research-through-design, complemented with a co-design approach. To best investigate the possibilities of twitterIDo, we established a living lab with a community of seniors living in an apartment building in Valby, in the suburbs of Copenhagen. The format of the living lab gave us a vantage point to explore twitterIDo in real life settings and thus best explore its possibilities. The living lab activities lasted over a year from Spring 2011 to Spring 2012. The senior community was composed of 51 seniors living alone or with their spouse, independently in their own apartments. The building, composed of three connected blocks, included common spaces, such as a common dining room and kitchen for common events, a petanque court, a laundry room with a small library, and a leisure room with gym and leisure equipment. The senior residents were quite diverse, ranging from 65 to 98 years old. In general, the computer literacy of the residents was quite low, and only a few residents had a personal computer and an Internet connection. Although all the seniors had age related issues, we avoided targeting any specific issue, but we considered the needs of the participants as they emerged.

5.1 Procedure

The living lab offered a favourable setting to engage the seniors as co-designers in our exploration. It provided the familiar and known setting necessary for the seniors to relate our ideas to concrete situations in their everyday life. Throughout the living lab, we sketched and used the interactive prototypes to make the concept of twitterIDo concrete for the seniors. These prototypes were iteratively refined and used in in-situ enactments of everyday familiar scenarios and situations. These interactive prototypes and first person enactments were our main tools to start a dialogue with the seniors.

The living lab included over 20 design activities between open workshops and design meetings. The attendance to the open workshops varied from 20 to 7 senior participants, while design meetings involved from 2 to 5 seniors in more focused activities. Overall we aimed to engage the larger possible number of residents, but soon emerged a small group of engaged seniors with whom we decided to conduct focused design meetings in addition to the open workshops.

We can group the twitterIDo explorations in three groups of design activities. First, we introduced the shopping scenario to the larger community to generate discussions in relation to opportunities and to generate the common interest. In this phase, our demonstrations and discussions revolved around a very simple sketch of an augmented rollator able to communicate to the Community Displays when it was in use.

Second, we unfolded the shopping scenario presented earlier in three workshops, one for each of the locations of the seniors (home, shared areas, shop). We conducted the first workshop in a private apartment with 2 seniors; the second workshop in one of the three entrance halls with a group of 11 seniors; and for the third workshop we went to a local supermarket with 3 seniors [11]. In these workshops we discussed concretely the possibilities for noticing and making shopping activities noticeable, engaging the seniors to position tablet devices in their private apartments and imagining their use, discussing the role of the Community Displays for their everyday routines, or trying to post pictures of offers from the shop.

Third, from the insights gathered with the seniors we provided them a set of technologies to try out in first person. Thus we organized a scenario enactment inspired from [2]. We engaged 5 seniors to enact a series of scripted scenes taking place in different locations and following the interactions between the seniors, the technology and their neighbours. In these scenes we let the seniors interact with the technology and with each other with the assistance of researchers and the feedback of other seniors. We asked the seniors to imagine what if they had the technology we designed together and what if they could connect with their shopping group while doing their shopping activities. The researchers motivated the seniors to reflect on their experience and their practices. The scenes were open to be discussed and re-enacted to fix what was odd and not working for the seniors and thus find better possibilities.

6 Findings

We collected pictures, videos and researchers' notes from informal discussions, activities and observations through the co-design activities. We analysed the data to identify key themes and get insights into how the seniors related their experience of the interactive prototypes with their own ways of shopping and socially interact with their neighbours. Could twitterIDo technologies be a meaningful resource for the seniors and fit with their everyday situations? The data analysis revealed that the seniors envisioned different ways to collaborate over shopping thanks to the additional possibilities to make their shopping activities visible and the additional ways to notice these activities. Our senior participants were very interested in new, everyday and affordable solutions for moving around in the city because the municipality was removing their service-bus. Collaborating and helping each other were their ways to deal with the new situation and they were interested to explore if digital technology could contribute. We report the comments from some of our senior co-designers: Ove (male), Birgit (female), Tove (female), Torben (male) and Åse (female), all in their '70s.

Doing Favours to Each Other. Our senior co-designers offered different examples of their practices of sharing shopping favours with each other. We built our workshops and in-situ enactments on these examples and the seniors took the occasion to relate their engagement with the interactive prototypes of twitterIDo with more examples of their everyday practices. During the early workshops the seniors were concerned about privacy issues and the possible distance that screens and digital communication can introduce between people. But they opened to new possibilities when the seniors started to engage with the interactive prototypes. They started to relate their experiences in our scenarios to their own practices.

Ove and Birgit reported a simple example. Not long before one of our meetings, Ove bought some medicines for Birgit at the pharmacy. The pharmacy is quite far from the residence of our seniors and Birgit has problems with her knees. They interact face-to-face to share their shopping plans sometimes, and when there is a need and an opportunity, they help each other. For both Ove and Birgit knowing when one of their shopping-friends is at the pharmacy is very convenient and can give a chance to ask him/her favours. Ove and Birgit used the pharmacy example as a possible scenario where making the activity more visible can help them find opportunities to do favours to each other, without aiming to replace their face-to-face interactions but being one of the many available resources.

Coordinating Shopping Arrangements. In the scenario enactment, Torben came up with the garden shop example. Torben and his wife own a car that they use to move around and go shopping. When they go to the garden shop they ask their neighbours if they need anything. The garden shop is far, and some gardening items can be difficult to find in the local shops and carry home. Torben and his wife receive requests before, but also phone-calls while they are at the garden shop. Similarly to the pharmacy example, this example generated reflections among the seniors. Tove convened that twitterIDo-technologies could help Torben and his neighbours with garden shopping: "It might be easier this way" Tove commented. She referred to noticing when Torben is at the garden shop, but also to posting and noticing offers and keep in contact when out and about. As Torben said: "Knowing who is at the shop makes you interact more easily, if you know you need something you can call". In addition to Torben telling his neighbour about his trips to the garden shop, new interactions can happen if his group of garden-lovers could notice when he is at the shop. The seniors imagined a sort of mutual agreement for which if a member of the shopping group is shopping, he/she is also available and open to interact with his/her shopping friends.

Finding Opportunities to Save Money and Spending Time Together. While the examples of the pharmacy and the garden shop are improvised arrangements, the seniors reported also examples of regular shopping arrangements. Åse used to go shopping with one of her neighbours, sharing offers too big for only one person, and exchanging shopping tips. Although not all the other senior participants had similar shopping arrangements, they could easily relate to Åse's example and to the convenience of sharing shopping offers and tips. Ove and Åse offered another example of sharing shopping tips: "Let's take the example of the other day when you [Åse] came with that chocolate, which was on sale for 29 kr., right. Well, I bought four of those. So that piece of information was a good one for sharing". in the scenario enactment, Torben posted a picture of the offer on sausages. It was recognized to be a great offer on sausages"the best you can find, especially for those money" as Åse said. Ove and Torben were particularly interested to see their own pictures and offers on the Community Displays and personal displays. Noticing interesting offers has the practical purpose to help seniors to save money. At the same time, building on personal expertise and interests, posting offers can be engaging for the seniors because they can offer and recognize their own contributions.

As we can expect, what is an interesting offer can be very subjective. During the scenario enactment, Tove and Åse mentioned that they would be more interested in noticing offers on clothes rather than groceries from the Community Displays. Tove explained that: "If somebody is standing there we would also go and check, and start a little conversation maybe" ... "If it is something interesting we can also sit here and talk". Tove added that she could imagine that if two seniors meet in the entrance hall and like the offers on display, they might even decide to go shopping and spend some time together. These reflection point out that cues become valuable occasions for social interaction depending on the people who notices them.

7 Discussions and Conclusions

Our explorations provide insights on the seniors' attitudes towards twitterIDo technology in real-life settings. These insights help us reflect on how communication technology can fit in seniors' everyday life and be meaningful for their everyday practices, as Ostlund [13] advocates. Through our activities it became clear that seniors needed a practical purpose to make their shopping activities more visible through technology. Thus we aimed our activities and interactive prototypes at exploring these practical purposes. The seniors progressively shifted our understanding of twitterIDo technologies. The interactive prototypes became resources for collaborating on shopping activities, and social interaction became the instrument to achieve a better collaboration. The primary motivations for making everyday shopping activities more visible were practical solutions useful for everyday situations.

Previous work has explored communication technology to make everyday activities more visible with family, friends and caregivers [4,10,14]. The attention has often focused on keeping an eye on each other and explicitly creating occasions for social interaction [8,10], [eg.] TwitterIDo provides seniors with technology to collaborate in everyday activities. In line with Svensson and Sokoler's ticket to talk TV [16], in twitterIDo the quest for social interaction is not explicit because the attention is shifted to the activity, to shopping and helping each other shopping. In twitterIDo the focus lies on the activity communicated, on the everyday artefacts that communicate this activity, and last but not least on groups of seniors interested in such activity. Brandt et al. [1] report on how seniors' social interaction often develop around "communities of everyday practice" groups of seniors and neighbours that share an interest or practice in an everyday activity. TwitterIDo supports such everyday networks of seniors rather than focusing on care, friendship or family relations.

Our findings show that twitterIDo offers a valid design approach for supporting social interactions among senior peers in local communities. This design approach proposes to turn the attention to specific activities, moving away from social interaction per-se and further explore how digital technology can support seniors doing activities together, supporting more practical purposes of why seniors would choose to make their activities more visible.Rather than aiming for generalizing our research, we invite other researchers interested in designing for senior social interaction to translate the idea of twitterIDo into their own situations, thus generating new designs that focus on making everyday activities more visible, exploit the everyday artefacts and look at social interaction as an instrument for supporting more practical purposes.

Acknowledgments. Thanks to all the senior participants, the researchers and partners of the Senior Interaction project that made these explorations possible.

References

1. Brandt, E., Binder, T., Malmborg, L., Sokoler, T.: Communities of everyday practice and situated elderliness as an approach to co-design for senior interaction. In: OZCHI 2010, pp. 400–403. ACM (2010)
2. Brandt, E., Grunnet, C.: Evoking the future: drama and props in user centered design. In: Proceedings of Participatory Design Conference (PDC 2000), pp. 11–20 (2000)
3. Brereton, M.: Habituated objects: everyday tangibles that foster the independent living of an elderly woman. Interact. Mag. **20**, 20–24 (2013)
4. Consolvo, S., Roessler, P., Shelton, B.E.: The carenet display: lessons learned from an in home evaluation of an ambient display. In: Mynatt, E.D., Siio, I. (eds.) UbiComp 2004. LNCS, vol. 3205, pp. 1–17. Springer, Heidelberg (2004)
5. Cornejo, R., Favela, J., Tentori, M.: Ambient displays for integrating older adults into social networking sites. In: Kolfschoten, G., Herrmann, T., Lukosch, S. (eds.) CRIWG 2010. LNCS, vol. 6257, pp. 321–336. Springer, Heidelberg (2010)
6. Følstad, A.: Living labs for innovation and development of information and communication technology: a literature review. eJOV: Electron. J. Virtual Organ. Netw. **10**, 99–131 (2008)
7. Foverskov, M., Binder, T.: Super Dots: making social media tangible for senior citizens. In: Proceedings of the 2011 Conference on Designing Pleasurable Products and Interfaces, DPPI 2011. No. c (2011)
8. Garattini, C., Wherton, J., Prendergast, D.: Linking the lonely: an exploration of a communication technology designed to support social interaction among older adults. Univ. Access Inf. Soci. **11**(2), 211–222 (2011)
9. Hirsch, T., Forlizzi, J., Hyder, E., Goetz, J., Stroback, J.: The ELDer project: social, emotional, and environmental factors in the design of eldercare. In: CUU 2000 Proceedings of the Conference for Universal Usability, pp. 72–80. Washington DC (2000)
10. Morris, M.E., Lundell, J., Dishongh, T., Needham, B.: Fostering social engagement and self-efficacy in later life: studies with ubiquitous computing. In: Markopoulos, P., De Ruyter, B., Mackay, W. (eds.) Awareness Systems Advances in Theory, Methodology and Design, chap. 14, pp. 335–349. Human-Computer Interaction Series, Springer, London (2009)
11. Nazzi, E., Bagalkot, N.L., Nagargoje, A., Sokoler, T.: Concept-driven interaction design research in the domain of attractive aging: the example of walky. In: Articulating Design Thinking, pp. 227–245. Paul rodge edn. (2012)
12. Nef, T., Ganea, R.L., Müri, R.M., Mosimann, U.P.: Social networking sites and older users - a systematic review. Int. Psychogeriatr./IPA **25**(7), 1041–1053 (2013)
13. Ostlund, B.: Design Paradigms and Misunderstood Technology: The case of older. Young Technologies in Old Hands-An International View on Senior Citizen's, pp. 1–28. DJOF Publishing, Copenhagen (2005)
14. Riche, Y., Mackay, W.: PeerCare: supporting awareness of rhythms and routines for better aging in place. Comput. Support. Coop. Work (CSCW) **19**(1), 73–104 (2010)
15. Sacks, H.: Lectures on Conversation: Volumes I and II. Blackwell, Oxford (1992)
16. Svensson, M., Sokoler, T.: Ticket-to-talk-television: designing for the circumstantial nature of everyday social interaction. In: NordiCHI 2008: Proceedings of the 5th Nordic Conference on Human-Computer Interaction: Building Bridges (2008)

Designing Cross-Age Interaction Toys for Older Adults and Children

Wang-Chin Tsai[1(✉)], Chi-Hsien Hsu[2], and Kung-Chih Lo[1]

[1] Department of Product and Media Design, Fo Guang University, Yilan, Taiwan
forwangwang@gmail.com, kclo@mail.fgu.edu.tw

[2] Department of Culture-Based Creative Design, National Taitung Junior College, Taitung, Taiwan
assahl6@gmail.com

Abstract. This paper describes the process of using a co-participatory design method to produce a toy prototype for children and adults. Based on suggestions from both groups, co-participatory design activities were organized around a single guiding principle: to construct an interesting and creative toy to help both generations interact with each other. Our findings support the usefulness and necessity of this design method and illustrate how designers could implement them in future work. Two industrial designers, six older adults (three male and three female, aged 65–75), and six children (3 male and 3 female, aged 6–10) were involved in the co-participatory design process, which was conducted via daily dialogue, scenario creation, and semi-structured interviews. This research described a co-participatory design process that included designers, children, and older adults. Data gathered from the process revealed that children had creative design ideas that considerably improved the interactive toy. This enabled the designer team to achieve a better empathic understanding of older and younger users, and to work on a project that was grounded in the interests of both target groups.

Keywords: Co-participatory design · Older adults · Children · Toy

1 Introduction

The global trend of an aging population, the market of older consumer market is increasingly large. According to Ministry of Interior predicts that the next 40 years, Taiwan will accelerate the aging of the forecast, Table 1 is the stream of the aging in Taiwan. Related to age and type of product consumption in the rapid increases in older industries is a growing potential market. Characteristics of research and development for the elderly, and the function of reasonable, good quality products have become competitive in the market for development opportunities. From the ergonomic point of view, give full consideration to older people's physical characteristics, psychological characteristics, designed for the elderly to use the comfortable, convenient, safe, healthy products is the social development needs.

J. Zhou and G. Salvendy (Eds.): ITAP 2015, Part II, LNCS 9194, pp. 524–532, 2015.
DOI: 10.1007/978-3-319-20913-5_48

Table 1. The stream of the aging in Taiwan

Year	Total population (million persons)	Age structure (%)			Dependency ratio		
		0–14 years	15–64 years	65 years and over	(%)	Young age population ratio (%)	Old age population ratio (%)
2006	22.9	18.17	71.88	9.95	39.13	25.28	13.85
2018	23.3	12.50	73.14	14.36	36.73	17.10	19.63
2030	22.8	10.59	65.56	23.85	52.54	16.16	36.38
2050	18.9	7.85	55.43	36.72	80.42	14.17	66.25

With the economy and society going through transformation and the trend of aging population, the family structure has changed rapidly (Fig. 1). Besides, people nowadays are busy with their work and mostly form dual-earner families. The phenomenon of "grandparent family" is becoming increasingly common, and grandparents and grandchildren (elderly and children) are spending more and more time together, which makes it mostly the elderly and children keeping each other's company at home. However, while children and older people are gaining influence they can still be considered in a broad sense as groups of vulnerable people. In many cases, they have less control of their lives and are more dependent on others to help out with various kinds of things than the average population. In addition to this, they may also have various kinds of cognitive and physical restrictions. For these reasons the term "vulnerable generations" will be used to denote the group of children and elderly as a whole. In line with their increased influence, there is a growing awareness of the needs of vulnerable generations. Innovative use of design specifically targeted towards these groups' special needs can contribute greatly to the improvement of their wellbeing, preventing them from facing difficult or stressful situations. Moreover, less work has been spent on developing teaching modules for design methods and practices aiming at

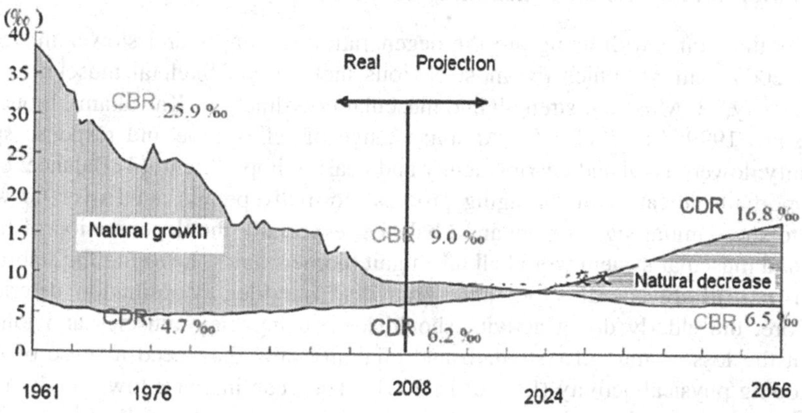

Fig. 1. Population changes and projection in taiwan: 1961-2056 (Source: population projection 2008-2056 in Taiwan, R.O.C., Council of economic planning and development, 2008.)

covering the needs of elderly and children. Accordingly, more work is needed on design for these groups. To improve the design practice in the area of design for elderly and children it is necessary to not only study and improve methodology, but also how to transfer the gained knowledge to new generations of designers to ensure its use in design. A combination of current research practices and design explorations and methods can be used to suggest new approaches to design for children and older people and to modernize the design curriculum with a specific focus on both older people and children.

2 Literature Reviews

2.1 Toy Design for the Aged and Trans-Generational Society

Seniors toy that is developed specifically for older toys, and some activities can help the elderly wrist, waist, and some have educational functions, for old hands-on brain, slow thinking, degradation, prevention of Alzheimer's disease. Psychologists believe that staying at home for elderly people have a tendency to a return to innocence. The curiosity of the elderly with special emphasis on toys to satisfy their spiritual needs; some of the elderly living alone, if they can cultivate interest in favorite toys, flavoring agents will increase the number of life for people with mild dementia of the elderly, not only can improve the quality of life, but also promote health and longevity. In Western countries developed for adults and older toys, toy market has become hot. In the United States, 40 percent of the toys are specifically designed for adults. Japan is also a lot of toys in the development of new features for the elderly, such as electric toys, playground common "combat crocodile," attach a blood pressure measurement function, as both entertainment and sports features, not only for stroke patients future nursing home can also be used. In this respect, Taiwan is still in the blank.

2.2 Physical and Mental Functioning of the Elderly

Changes that come with aging are the degeneration of senses and slower movement (Wang 2009), among which the most obvious include: (1) Skeletal muscle: reduced bone density, (2) Muscular strength and muscular coordination (Kawakami, Inoue, and Kumashiro 1999; Lin 2008); (3) Action: change of reflex time and response speed; (3) acuity: lower visual and hearing acuity and hearing impairment; (4) Balance: one of the important indicators of the aging process, normally people aged over 60 would begin to show initial signs of impaired balance, especially the degeneration of bones, joints and muscular system would all affect gait biomechanics, lowering the stability of gait (14); (5)Body coordination: hand-brain and hand-leg coordination deteriorate. Therefore, the elderly doing activity should keep using their muscles and joints to prevent the loss of muscular strength and pliability, and they need a sense of safety when doing physical activity (Lu and Li 2001). They can increase lower body muscle and strengthen muscular endurance by simply walking or knee bend. Besides, exercises can improve the balance of the elderly, especially those with instant vertical or horizontal movement can help with the sense of balance.

Mentally, the elderly also go through some apparent changes with age, including poorer memory and judgment, and failure to achieve what they are originally familiar with (Hsieh 2007). The mental characteristics of the elderly are as follows: (1) logic: logical reasoning is an important indicator of understanding cognitive development and intelligence (Bjorklund 2000; Siegler, 1998); (2) memory: poorer memory, failure to achieve what they are originally familiar with; (3) creativity: when people get older, the ability to repress gets weaker, which unleashes their creativity and makes them stronger artistically.

2.3 Physical and Mental Condition of the Children

The study looks into the physical and mental condition of 3-12-year-old children raised by cross-generational parenting. This stage lays the foundation for children's growth physically, mentally or in character development. So if their physical and mental growth can be enhanced through the interactive toys for grandparents and grandchildren, it will be very beneficial to their future development (Marcus, Selby & Rossi, 1992). The movement skills developed by children aged 3-7 are basic locomotor and non-locomotor skills, such as running, sliding, bending, turning, hopping on one foot and hopping on both feet, jumping over, dodging, swaying, swinging, and stretching. When they turn 8-9 years old, they perform these fundamental skills more easily and efficiently, and start to develop complicated locomotor, non-locomotor, and manual skills. In the meantime, due to an increase in body strength during this period, accompanied by growth in perception and cognition, children are able to complete coordinated movement more quickly and accurately. 10- to 12-year-olds emphasize more special movement skills needed in competition, dancing or gymnastics (Lin, 2004).

In terms of psychological development theory, with regard to creativity: children aged over 3 years have endless inspiration, and 3- to 5-year-olds can find association between different concepts, expressing their imagination or ideas through analogy and comparison; 4- to 6-year-olds try to turn analogical concepts into actual concepts that apply to the outside world. In respect of spatial perception: 3- to 7-year-olds can use themselves as the center to feel the things in the surrounding, and gradually develop spatial concepts. A 3-year-old child can already distinguish the direction of up and down; a 4-year-old can distinguish front and back; a 5-year-old can start using himself/herself as the center to distinguish left and right; and a 6-year-old can correctly distinguish up and down, front and back. 6- to 10-year-olds have the abstract spatial and temporal concepts

3 Co-Participatory Toy Design and Development

3.1 Co-Participatory Toy Design and Development

We recruited older adults by sending flyers to community associations. People who were interested then called us and we conducted a phone interview with each one to understand their family structure. We collected a small amount of demographic data during these interviews and subsequently invited them to join us for a pilot session.

In total, ten grandparent families came to the first session. Two weeks later, six grandparent families agreed to join the whole participatory design. The sample participants consisted of married older adults and spread over urban and rural locations in Taiwan with different socio-economic backgrounds. Participants missed a few design meetings due to scheduling conflicts. This step involved identifying key groups of end-users and forming a participatory design team of intended users. The goal of this step was to open chances of cooperation between intended users and the designers.

Two industrial designers, Six grandparent families: including six older adults (three male and three female, aged 65–75), and six children (3 male and 3 female, aged 6–10) were involved in the participatory design .The methods employed here were dialogue, scenario creation, and asking semi-structured interviews. As none of the participants have experienced a participatory design session in their lives, almost all were very shy at the beginning. The designers had to make them imagine themselves in some related scenarios to be able to start the session. Narratives and metaphors were considered positive language use for this activity to elicit tacit knowledge and to allow the designers to gain insight into the mindset of the users. The participants provided ideas and defined their exact needs and preferences towards the current interaction toy design based on their past using experiences and scenario creation with their own words.

How do we access co-participatory design?

There are many ways we can learn from older adults and children about their ideas, memories, their current experiences and their ideal experiences:

- We can listen to what older adults and children say.
- We can interpret what older adults and children express, and make inferences about what they think.
- We can watch what older adults and children do.
- We can observe what older adults and children use.
- We can uncover what older adults and children know.
- We can reach toward understanding what older adults and children feel.
- We can appreciate what older adults and children dream.

Through analysis from the conducted dialogue, scenario creation, and asking semi-structured interviews, this research proposes the design concepts for toys targeted at older adults and children, and then conducts toy design accordingly. The concepts are as follows:

(1) Safety first (10 clues from the Coding Scheme)
To varying degrees, the judgment, cognitive ability and ability to respond of the old people weaken and children, thus in the process of using the product, they inevitably make mistakes. In case a threat to physical and mental health occurs, they usually are unable to escape the danger. Therefore, toys for the seniors and children should be fault-tolerant. So that, the old people and children even make a mistake, there will be no danger. Here the reduction of operation process and the set of message for safe operation is an effective way to ensure the safety of the seniors with toys for these two generations.

(2) Moderate difficult (12 clues from the Coding Scheme)
The design of toys for the old and children should be of moderate difficulty, and the purpose is to arouse their interest in playing. If too simple, it would not enhance the interest of the seniors and children and thus would not achieve the aim of exercising the brain; if too difficult, it would be strenuous for them to learn, and consequently cause a sense of failure which is not conducive to their mental health.

(3) Easy to identify (8 clues from the Coding Scheme)
The interaction toy should have a familiar form and an understandable functional theory for the old and children. It should also be equipped with an interface in keeping with the experience and habits of the seniors and children. Besides, the toys that need interface design, should take into account the graphic symbols, size, color, clarity of sound, light intensity.

(4) Facilitate communication (13 clues from the Coding Scheme)
People's feelings need to vent and exchange, especially for the seniors and children. For them, emotional communication is indispensable to maintain their vitality, and improve the quality of life. Playing with toys, there are many ways for the old and young to choose, such as: taking turns to participate, working together and racing in the game. The development of multiple-persons playing toys is to create a harmonious environment in which they can talk when play. So the core of toy-development is to involve the participants as much as possible. For the participating ways, common collaborative participatory approach is the best, which is more conducive to conversation, and get to know some new friends. In this way the seniors and children can expand their social circle with emotional exchange.

(5) The effect for keeping fitness and developing intelligence (15 clues from the Coding Scheme)
Increasing with age, people's organ recession becomes an objective physiological phenomenon. In order to maintain good physical function and mental state, and improve the quality of life, fitness puzzle is a very important content in the lives of older persons and children. Body-building that can achieve with playing toys is the most basic needs of older persons. Old people and children by playing intellectual toys can effectively prevent Alzheimer's disease and enhance eye-hand coordination, so to maintain the flexibility of the seniors and children mind is the main direction of the toy development.

(6) Cultural connotations (9 clues from the Coding Scheme)
Life experiences bring the old people with more comprehensive concept of life, and good inheritance for the children, thus toys with a certain ideological and cultural depth usually put them in recollecting and thinking of issues. While the old emphasize the toy's inherent fun, and show great interest in the toys with cultural connotations. Of course, this culture must be familiar with the elderly and children has gone deep into the ideological deep.

According to the above results and considering the revival of motor function and divergent creativity, the cross-age interaction toy design (Fig. 2) in the study is set up as a pieces assembled toy for three reasons: (1) the process of different game type

Fig. 2. Cross-age interaction toys: game house

involves movement of the whole body; (2) the process of different game type can develop the users' creative thinking; (3) the different game type of the game can be determined by the users' physical strength, which makes it suitable for both the elderly and children. The toy feature are as follows:

1. The game starts with spinning the spinner.
2. Four different types of games are available.
3. Different turntables are designed for a variety of game combinations.
4. The direction of the spinner shall define the structure of the game.
5. The wood texture gives forth a warm and safe impression.
6. The cake-shaped toy attracts curiosity of little children, evoking their interest to play (Figs. 3 and 4, Table 2).

Fig. 3. Playing and interaction scenario

Fig. 4. Game type: from left to right: arithmetic games, mapping games of color and shape, reward games of action activity, copy games of charades

Table 2. Use process

Illustration	description
	Process1: selecting the game type and set aside the tuning panel
	Process2: then play rock-paper scissor game to make the order
	Process3: turning the panel to choose different test question
	Process4: Starting the game

4 Conclusion

In the Taiwan aging society, elderly population grows, and many elders take the responsibility of taking care of children in the family. Thus, childhood of many are filled with wonderful memories shares with their grandparents. With such background, this design seeks to find fun and creative elements that benefit both elders and children: interactive educational toys simulate brain exercise of the elders, prevent degeneration of their brain function, and at the same time, inspire the imagination of children, and strengthen hand-eye coordination. This toy is designed to enhance the relationship between the elders and their grandchildren and build good memories.

References

Birren, J.E., Schroots, J.F.: Handbook of the Psychology of Aging, 6th edn. Academic Press, Waltham (2005)

Bjorklund, D.F.: Children's Thinking: Developmental Function and Individual Difference, 3rd edn. Wadsworth / Thomson Learning, Belmont (2000)

Chen, C.N.: Leisure activities and life satisfaction among taiwanese elderly. J. Popul. Stud. **26**, 96–136 (2001)

Dickinson, A., Arnott, J., Prior, S.: Methods for human-computer interaction research with older people. Behav. Inf. Technol. **26**(4), 343–352 (2007)

Fisk, A.D., Rogers, W.A., Neil, C., Czaja, S.J., Joseph, S.: Designing for Older Adults-Principles and Creative Human Factors Approaches. CRC Press, USA (2004)

Freudenthal, A.: The Design of Home Appliance for Young and Old Consumer. Delft University, Netherlands (1999)

Hannon, P.O.: An Investigation of the Impact of Short-Term Quality Intergenerational Contact On Children's Attitudes toward Older Adults. Unpublished doctoral dissertation. The university of Pennsylvania State (2004)

Kawakami, M., Inoue, F., Kumashiro, M.: Design of a work system considering the needs of aged workers. Exp. Aging Res. **25**(4), 477–483 (1999)

Kazemek, F., Logas, B.: Spiders, kid curlers, and white shoes: telling and writing stories across generations. Read. Teach. **53**(6), 446–451 (2000)

Kline, D.W., Scialfa, C.T.: Sensory and perceptual function: basic research and human factors implication. In: Fisk, A.D., Rogers, W.A. (eds.) Handbook of Human Factors and the Older Adult, vol. 3, pp. 27–54. Academic Press, San Diego (1997)

Kosnik, W., Winslow, L., Kline, D., Rasinski, K., Sekuler, R.: Visual changes in daily life throughout adulthood. J. Gerontol. Psychol. Sci. **43**, 63–70 (1988)

Lu, L., Chen, H.H.: An exploratory study on role adjustment and intergenerational relationships among the elderly in the changing taiwan. Res. Appl. Psychol. **12**, 221–249 (2002)

Wang, H.S.: Exercise and physical activity for older adults. Am. Coll. Sports Med. MSSE **41**(7), 1510–1530 (2009)

Wu, M.T., Chan, Y.S.: The effects of aging and exercise intervention on balance control in the elderly. Taiwanese Gerontol. Forum. **2**, 1–12 (2009)

A Slow Game Design for Elderly with Their Family and Friends

Yi-Sin Wu and Teng-Wen Chang(✉)

National Yunlin University of Science and Technology, Douliu, Taiwan
{m10234017, tengwen}@yuntech.edu.tw

Abstract. After preliminary studies, based on horticultural activities, to propose amendments. Through interviews with elderly people, exploring the life and discuss the literature review, and found that the most affect elderly living alone is the quality of interaction with the community, rather than quantity. The concept of community nurseries, proposed to the original game, the family cannot help activities, through interaction with neighborhood friends, let elderly care by being converted into active share.

Keywords: Elderly platform · Community nursery · Neighborhood and friends

1 Introduction

In recent decades, an old man alone, the number and proportion of the population are rising. The challenges arising out of these changes fell on the shoulders of each family. An old man alone needs to learn and lifestyle changes. Those young simple things, such as: to see a doctor, to pass the time, to maintain physical strength, all with the decline of physical function, and it becomes difficult to manage. Klinenberg pointed out that age, a person, isolated, not only make people vulnerable in case of illness or crisis, it could dramatically reduce our quality of life [1].

In the beginning, researcher is the use of horticultural activities to promote interaction with elderly and family. Especially horticultural activities can provide hearing, touch, smell, sight and taste of the five senses stimulation, has anti-aging, maintain normal physiological function, chronic disease treatment and rehabilitation, and certainly worth the existence of self-expanding social contact surface and prevent or against the loss wisdom psychosis effect [2].

Last year, the researchers conducted interviews with elderly living alone. After exploring the elderly living alone in a variety of situations in life, and to analyze the context of their lives, was found that, to live alone and lonely are different things. The impact of social interaction is the loneliest of quality, rather than quantity [1]. So researchers tried a new way of human interaction patterns, Increase the range of elderly living alone and social interaction, the original single (family) in the direction of extension of the two directions, family and neighborhood friends.

J. Zhou and G. Salvendy (Eds.): ITAP 2015, Part II, LNCS 9194, pp. 533–540, 2015.
DOI: 10.1007/978-3-319-20913-5_49

2 Reference

The internet of social things is a vision, for the next decade, the social networking will bring the wisdom of the things connected. And might rewrite the market economy, subvert industrial operation, then our life is about to face a huge change [3]. Through the social networking, people and objects, human and human, the relationships will be more closely, we are able to share our information, entertainment, tools and programs. Explore the social networking literature review and projects, to get the internet of social things' meaning and guidelines.

2.1 An Internet of Social Things

The researchers believe, research and design of the Internet of things, are a benefit from community to broaden understanding of things [4]. Through two project modification of the design: the installation of communication layers in the original project, after the attempt to understand and discovery, the communication layer does have a role in social relations.

Researchers explore the literature and case analysis, proposed a significance and guidelines. The key is that the user should be further considered, and follow the society understanding of things and attention. The first, in the design practice, need to be considered for potentially non-human users of new IoT devices. The second is that to observe the user's social life, and proposed a new human-computer interaction research methods. By ethnography to explore the significance of those items to help humanity, maintain relationships, and work together. At the same time, we are concerned with the expansion of the relationship between humans and objects.

2.2 Habituated Objects: Everyday Tangibles that Foster the Independent Living of an Elderly Woman

The study showing the elderly habituated objects [5]. Researchers through interviews, an 82-year-old woman, Maria. Though Maria is amblyopia, but in execution by hip surgery, she remained independent lives. The researchers observed focus on how she put objects at home. With the change of time and social relations, when the woman is already accustomed to using these items in life, what these objects are related to each other. By understanding the user's habits, and how to improve these habits of elderly person's independence, will allow us to better understand how to design in the internet of social things.

Maria has many items and equipment, and how these objects to perform their functions at home (Fig. 1 Maria goods record). Researchers asked her, the most important and most beloved items, and the emergence of a diverse and interesting list: magnifying glasses, shoes, tea-bag squeezer, big-screen TV, computer, key-on-a-string, free bus pass, sturdy shoes, and so on. With insight, these important items, will likely be converted to a tangible interaction design.

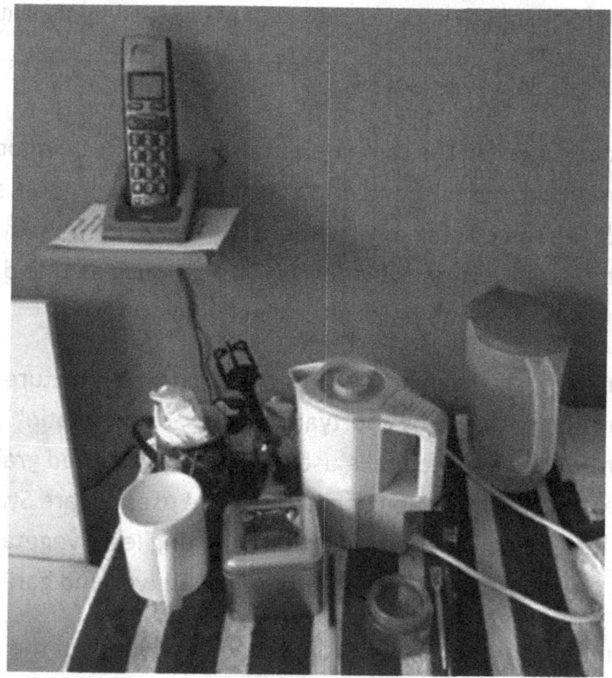

Fig. 1. The kettle, tea and tea-bag squeezer. Used for habitual morning tea in get up.

3 Personal Interview: Increased Social Activity Through Horticultural Activities

Through interviews with elderly, to get the planted habits in daily life. The researchers found that, elderly mostly planting vegetables and fruits in the outdoor, such as: leafy vegetables and sweet potatoes. And there is a phenomenon of supply exceeds. But fruits and vegetables cannot be stored for too long, so the elderly will be through give family, friends and neighborhood residents to consume, Thus, to increase opportunities for social activities of elderly and neighbor (Fig. 2).

Box 1. Interview excerpt during user research. Translated by the authors.

Interview with Ms. Wu. (74-year-old)

Ms. Wu has been living in the same neighborhood, from childhood to youth. Even married, her husband is in the same neighborhood, so Ms. Wu had never left the same living environment. Although in the same environment, she will leisure activities as interest, such as Line dance, Chinese shadow boxing, and horticultural activities.

Since the marriage, she lived in Taiwan's traditional architecture-courtyard houses. An atrium enclosed by courtyard houses, called "patio". In the past, the farm will be used to make use of this plaza to dried grain. Ms. Wu use this space to grow fruits and vegetables. She uses square Styrofoam boxes made into a small vegetable garden, planting leafy vegetables and shallow root class, such as: sweet potato leaves, chives and garlic.

This community has a good interaction. Ms. Wu said that, if the number of the leek plant too more, she will distribute them to other residents. Besides, her place of residence with their children closer, so often have intercourse, she will also give children the harvest. When Ms. Wu was not at home a long time, but also play the advantages of neighborhood to help each other.

Fig. 2. The image record the planting of chives and other plants.

4 To Enhance the Elderly Social Interaction by Slow Game

In the first edition of the game design, the researchers planted strawberries, set up the lights in the planting, make a pot like lamp, and placed in the living room. Elderly and families to interact with the physical potted and phone. Different gardening activities will correspond to different interaction mechanisms, when the families' complete indication of the action, the message will be passed to the real potted and display different light to indicate elderly gardening activities.

But the results were not as expected. So the researchers were revised, the slow game design is divided into families and neighborhood friends. Using a cross-ways to enhance "quality" and "quantity" in social interaction. And in the following, to description the a conception of elderly interaction with neighborhood friends:

4.1 Slow Game with Neighborhood Friends

In the semi-rural area in Taiwan, there is a lot of unused space. The researchers observed that, the general situation is dumping of soil on the idle space, become community nurseries. And in the community nurseries surrounding, will be placed benches, chairs, is a field for elderly to gathering and chatting.

And horticultural activities rely on the exchange experience and sharing of plant species, because of the different plants have different life cycle length, the environment, and so many different natural factors, lead to different kinds of plant cultivation techniques. Because of horticultural activities (horticulture therapy) has also been applied to the education institution, the elderly and children's centers, psychiatric hospitals, rehab centers, medical institutions or communities. Is an ancillary therapy, by actual contact, to enhance physical, psychological, cognitive knowledge and economic of benefits.

So, the researchers combined horticultural activities and slow the game to become the community nurseries planting tasks. Selection of outdoor planting, like as vegetables, fruits, etc. The plants require a lot of natural light in order to bloom and bear fruit, such as onions, leeks, and tomatoes. Elderly by tilling the soil, planting, watering and other activities to promote coordination of muscle. And more importantly, is through the support each other to achieve the mission objectives. In this idle space, not only harvest vegetables, but also harvest friendship between neighborhoods and elderly.

5 Prototyping

Using the elderly's TV, and installed the set-top boxes. Elderly can click the button to enter the game of the main screen on the platform. Elderly using the TV remote control keys and the enter key to operate. Into the game's main interface, you can see three options: "Family", "Neighborhood Friends" and "The tasks field guide." "Family" and "Neighborhood Friends" is different, you can enter after the selection (Fig. 3 The gaming platform main screen). Besides, setting "The tasks field guide", will record the plants growth conditions, to facilitate elderly to sharing the experiences.

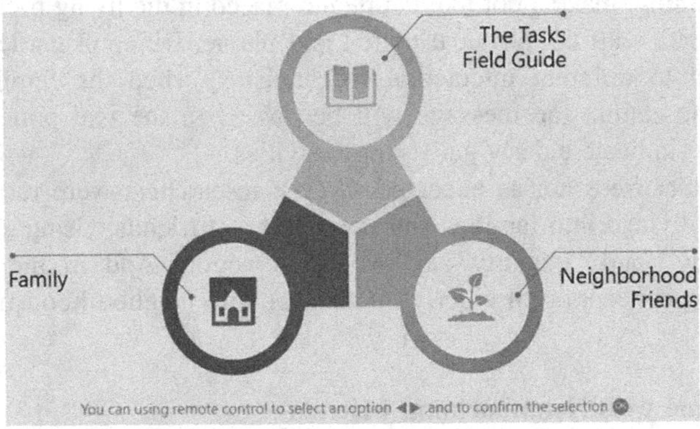

Fig. 3. The gaming platform main screen.

5.1 How to Play the Game with Neighborhood Friends

Community nursery allow elderly gathered and let elderly challenge the tasks in the system, the tasks including fruits and vegetables except peak season and. Elderly can choose a task to challenge, such as tomatoes, leeks, and cucumbers. Once the task is to confirm and begin, the TV interface with neighborhood friend's page, there will be a map of the plant growth processes.

5.2 Scenario

Use prototyping simulation elderly using processes. When the elderly to open a new challenge. After click the neighborhood friend's option, select the challenge of entering the picture. The game will show three combinations, elderly can pick through their wishes.

Then there are these fruits and vegetables planting process, Depending on fruits and vegetables, the system will be show different. These activities include: (1) Seeding, (2) Watering (3) Weeding (4) Fertilizing (5) Draining (6) Remove out weak plants (7) Platform (8) Harvesting. To follow the planting instructions process to complete the task. Process will record temperature and humidity and other environmental related information. The following simulation elderly challenging the task:

- Elderly choose sweet potatoes, cabbage and carrots in this task, and then press the OK button on the remote control (Fig. 4 Elderly selection task).
- Elderly into the planting process, showing sweet potatoes activity indicator. (Fig. 5 Sweet Potatoes activities indicate). In this page, can display temperature and rain in the past.

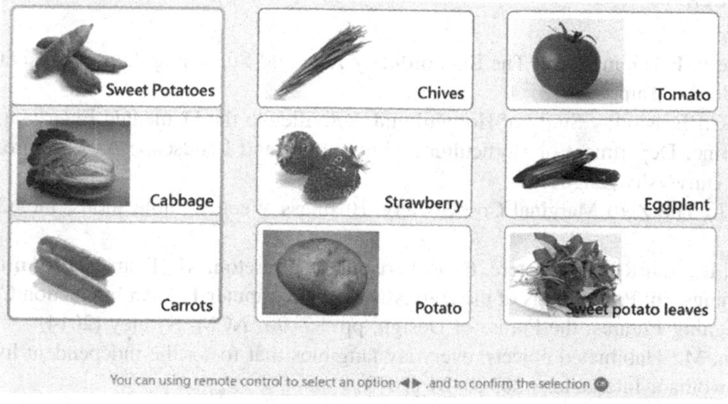

Fig. 4. Elderly selection task.

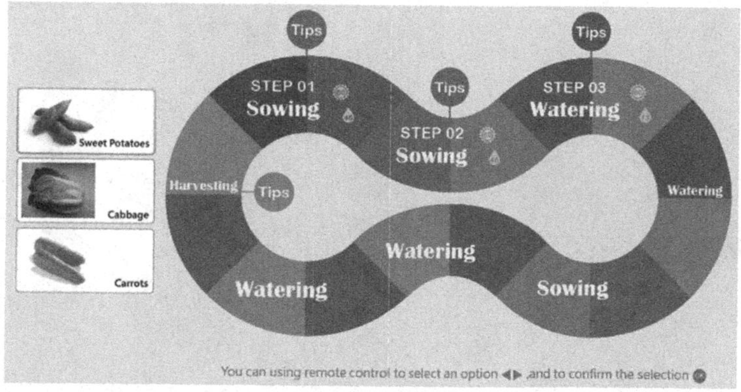

Fig. 5. Sweet Potatoes activities indicate.

6 Conclusion

This study will attempt to improve the elderly's gut reaction to the platform. Elderly's gardening tool in life, through the design making the tool becoming an icon. Then through the instructions and interactive television platforms, especially TV built-in speaker, the sound can be included as part of the interaction should be more in line with elderly.

And through social networking, elderly to work together through community nurseries, to relieve physical and mental discomfort, is a new concept. But in addition to TV platform, for elderly watch tasks and the plant records. Social networking should focus on the objects surrounding the elderly, get elderly's habits and further tripping of the original framework. In interactive design, to find suitable elderly the internet of social things.

References

1. Klinenberg, E.: Going Solo: The Extraordinary Rise and Surprising Appeal of Living Alone. Azoth Books, Taipei (2013)
2. Liu, Y.-C.: Feasibility Study of Horticultural Activities to the Demented Elderly at A Senior Care Home. Department of Horticultural Horticulture and Landscape Architecture. National Taiwan University (2010)
3. Rifkin, J.: The Zero Marginal Cost Society. Business Weekly Publications, Inc, Cambridge (2014)
4. Nansen, B., van Ryn, L., Vetere, F., Robertson, T., Brereton, M., Douish, P.: An internet of social things. In: Proceedings of the 26th Australian Computer-Human Interaction Conference on Designing Futures: the Future of Design, pp. 87–96. ACM, Sydney (2014)
5. Brereton, M.: Habituated objects: everyday tangibles that foster the independent living of an elderly woman. Interactions **20**, 20–24 (2013)

Author Index

Printed in the United States
By Bookmasters

Lecture Notes in Computer Science **8962**

Commenced Publication in 1973
Founding and Former Series Editors:
Gerhard Goos, Juris Hartmanis, and Jan van Leeuwen

More information about this series at http://www.springer.com/series/7407

Ivan Dimov · Stefka Fidanova
Ivan Lirkov (Eds.)

Numerical Methods and Applications

8th International Conference, NMA 2014
Borovets, Bulgaria, August 20–24, 2014
Revised Selected Papers

Springer

Editors
Ivan Dimov
Institute of Information
and Communication Technologies
Bulgarian Academy of Sciences
Sofia
Bulgaria

Ivan Lirkov
Institute of Information
and Communication Technologies
Bulgarian Academy of Sciences
Sofia
Bulgaria

Stefka Fidanova
Institute of Information
and Communication Technologies
Bulgarian Academy of Sciences
Sofia
Bulgaria

ISSN 0302-9743 ISSN 1611-3349 (electronic)
Lecture Notes in Computer Science
ISBN 978-3-319-15584-5 ISBN 978-3-319-15585-2 (eBook)
DOI 10.1007/978-3-319-15585-2

Library of Congress Control Number: 2015931374

LNCS Sublibrary: SL1 – Theoretical Computer Science and General Issues

Springer Cham Heidelberg New York Dordrecht London

Printed on acid-free paper

Springer International Publishing AG Switzerland is part of Springer Science+Business Media (www.springer.com)

Preface

The International Conference on Numerical Methods and Applications is a traditional forum for scientists from all over the world providing an opportunity to share ideas and establish fruitful scientific cooperation. The aim of the conference is to bring together leading international scientists of the numerical and applied mathematics community and to attract original research papers of very high quality. The papers in this volume were presented at the eighth edition of the International Conference on Numerical Methods and Applications (NMA 2014) held in Borovets, Bulgaria, during August 20–24, 2014. The conference was organized by the Institute of Information and Communication Technologies at Bulgarian Academy of Sciences. The Institute of Mathematics and Informatics at Bulgarian Academy of Sciences and Faculty of Mathematics and Informatics at St. Kliment Ohridski University of Sofia were co-organizers of this traditional scientific meeting. Over 100 participants from 22 countries attended the conference. Seventy-six talks, including five invited and keynote talks, were presented. This volume contains 34 selected papers. During NMA 2014, a wide range of problems concerning recent theoretical achievements in numerical methods and their applications in mathematical modeling were discussed. Specific topics of interest were the following: Numerical methods for differential and integral equations; approximation techniques in numerical analysis; numerical linear algebra; hierarchical and domain decomposition methods; parallel algorithms; Monte Carlo methods; computational mechanics; computational physics, chemistry, and biology; engineering applications. Six special sessions where organized namely: Monte Carlo and Quasi-Monte Carlo Methods; Metaheuristics for Optimization Problems; Advanced Numerical Methods for Scientific Computing; Advanced Numerical Techniques for PDEs and Applications; Solving Large Engineering and Scientific Problems with Advanced Mathematical Models; Numerical Simulations and Back Analysis in Civil and Mechanical Engineering.

The success of the conference and the present volume are due to the joint efforts of many colleagues from various institutions and organizations. We express our deep gratitude to all the members of the Scientific Committee for their valuable contribution to forming the scientific spirit of the conference, as well as for their help in reviewing the submitted papers. We are also grateful to the staff involved in the local organization.

December 2014

Ivan Dimov
Stefka Fidanova
Ivan Lirkov

Organization

NMA 2014 was organized by the Institute of Information and Communication Technologies at Bulgarian Academy of Sciences.

Scientific Committee

Andrey Andreev	Bulgaria
Emanouil Atanassov	Bulgaria
Radim Blaheta	Czech Republic
Jan Buša	Slovak Republic
Raimondas Čiegis	Lithuania
Pasqua D'Ambra	Italy
Ivan Dimov	Bulgaria
Stefka Dimova	Bulgaria
István Faragó	Hungary
Miloslav Feistauer	Czech Republic
Stefka Fidanova	Bulgaria
Krassimir Georgiev	Bulgaria
Alexei Goolin	Russia
Snezhana Gocheva-Ilieva	Bulgaria
Jean-Luc Guermond	USA
Stefan Heinrich	Germany
Raphaèle Herbin	France
Oleg Iliev	Germany
Boško Jovanović	Serbia
Sergey Korotov	Spain
Johannes Kraus	Austria
Nataša Krejic	Serbia
Raytcho Lazarov	USA
Ivan Lirkov	Bulgaria
Svetozar Margenov	Bulgaria
Pencho Marinov	Bulgaria
Svetoslav Markov	Bulgaria
Piotr Matus	Belarus
Peter Minev	Canada
Thomas Müller-Gronbach	Germany
Mihail Nedjalkov	Bulgaria
Kalin Penev	UK
Bojan Popov	USA
Milena Racheva	Bulgaria
Stefan Radev	Bulgaria

Pedro Ribejro	Portugal
Karl Sabelfeld	Russia
Joachim Schöberl	Germany
Siegfried Selberherr	Austria
Blagovest Sendov	Bulgaria
Khristo Semerdzhiev	Bulgaria
Slavcho Slavchev	Bulgaria
Michail Todorov	Bulgaria
Vidar Thomee	Sweden
Petr Vabishchevich	Russia
Ivan Yotov	USA
Ludmil Zikatanov	USA

Local Organizers

Chairperson: Ivan Dimov
Stefka Fidanova
Tzvetan Ostromski
Rayna Georgieva
Jean Michel Sellier

Contents

Invited Papers

Monte Carlo and Quasi-Monte Carlo Methods

Metaheuristics for Optimization Problems

Numerical Simulations and Back Analysis in Civil and Mechanical Engineering

Contributed Papers

Invited Papers

A Note on Local Refinement for Direction Splitting Methods

T. Gornak[1,2], O. Iliev[1,2], and P. Minev[3(✉)]

[1] Department of Flows and Materials Simulation, Fraunhofer Institute for Industrial Mathematics, Fraunhofer-Platz 1, 67663 Kaiserslautern, Germany
[2] Germany and Technical University of Kaiserslautern, Kaiserslautern, Germany
[3] Department of Mathematical and Statistical Sciences, University of Alberta, Edmonton, AB T6G 2G1, Canada
minev@ualberta.ca

Abstract. In this note we propose a grid refinement procedure for direction splitting schemes for parabolic problems that can be easily extended to the incompressible Navier-Stokes equations. The procedure is developed to be used in conjunction with a direction splitting time discretization. Therefore, the structure of the resulting linear systems is tridiagonal for all internal unknowns, and only the Schur complement matrix for the unknowns at the interface of refinement has a four diagonal structure. Then the linear system in each direction can be solved either by a kind of domain decomposition iteration or by a direct solver, after an explicit computation of the Schur complement. The numerical results on a manufactured solution demonstrate that this grid refinement procedure does not alter the spatial accuracy of the finite difference approximation and seems to be unconditionally stable.

1 Introduction

Adaptive grid refinement is a very desirable feature of any algorithm for approximation of PDEs since the adaptivity can greatly reduce the overall costs while preserving the optimal convergence rate of the method. Most algorithms for h refinement are based on unstructured grids since they provide a very natural framework for local refinement without the need of introduction of hanging nodes. There is a large amount of literature devoted to this subject and, without claiming comprehensiveness, we would refer the reader to [1–3], just to name a few of the most important articles in this area. Structured grid local refinement has in fact been introduced earlier than the one on unstructured grids. It necessarily involves hanging nodes on the interface of refinement and therefore it involves some extra conditions following from the need to balance the fluxes across the interface of refinement. To our knowledge, the earliest refinement algorithm in the context of Cartesian cell-centred finite volume discretizations was introduced in [6]. It allows for a conservative approximation provided that at the interface of refinement each coarse-grid cell has exactly three refined neighbours. The recent advances in Discontinuous Galerkin methods allowed for easy

I. Dimov et al. (Eds.): NMA 2014, LNCS 8962, pp. 3–12, 2015.
DOI: 10.1007/978-3-319-15585-2_1

development of h-refinement strategies involving hanging nodes without such geometric restrictions (see [8] and the references therein).

The purpose of the present note is to propose an algorithm for local refinement on Cartesian grids involving hanging nodes, if the time discretization is performed with a direction splitting scheme. This combination has the potential to yield a very simple and fast solution method for parabolic equations and unsteady incompressible flow. The most important feature of the combination of local Cartesian refinement and direction splitting is that the Schur complement for the unknowns corresponding to the interfaces of refinement can be computed explicitly and has a diagonal structure that allows for an easy solution. The actual algorithm for local refinement on Cartesian finite difference (or finite volume) grids that we employed bears some similarities to the Cartesian grid refinement proposed in [5], however, it is applied on grid blocks rather than on individual lines. In addition, here we combine it with a direction splitting algorithm which allows to construct a direct method for the solution of the overall system, thus avoiding costly iterations usually involved in methods based on Schur complements in the presence of hanging nodes.

2 Grid Refinement with Direction Splitting

2.1 Direction Splitting Procedure

To explain the basic ideas we first consider the two-dimensional heat equation in a domain $\Omega = [0, X] \times [0, Y]$:

$$\frac{\partial u}{\partial t} = \frac{\partial^2 u}{\partial x^2} + \frac{\partial^2 u}{\partial y^2} + f(x, y, t) \text{ in } \Omega \times (0, T], \tag{1}$$

and its Peaceman-Rachford discretization

$$\begin{aligned} (I - \frac{\tau}{2}\delta_x^2)u_h^{n+1/2} &= (I + \frac{\tau}{2}\delta_y^2)u_h^n + \frac{\tau}{2}f_h^{n+1/2} \\ (I - \frac{\tau}{2}\delta_y^2)u_h^{n+1} &= (I + \frac{\tau}{2}\delta_x^2)u_h^{n+1/2} + \frac{\tau}{2}f_h^{n+1/2}, \end{aligned} \tag{2}$$

where I is the identity operator, τ is the time step, u_h is the vector of the discrete solution, and $\delta_i^2 u_h, i = x, y,$ is a suitable discretization of the second derivative of u in the corresponding direction. All considerations below can be applied to any of the other direction splitting schemes available in the literature (see [10] for a comprehensive presentation of such schemes).

2.2 Difference Operators with Local Refinement

Since this local refinement procedure is intended for the use in the context of direction splitting procedures that require the discretization of one dimensional spatial operators only, we demonstrate it here in one direction, on a refined strip. It can likely be extended to a refinement containing an internal two-dimensional refined patch of a rectangular shape. The considerations in [6] clearly indicate that with a proper approximation of the fluxes across the interface of refinement the positivity of the discrete operator, and therefore the stability of the scheme, can be maintained. However, this case needs a further investigation and is not considered in the present note. Such a refinement would be particularly needed if the procedure is to be extended to three dimensions.

The 1D local refinement is illustrated in Fig. 1. The procedure starts with a initial uniform grid of size h. Suppose that we identify a subdomain where the gird has to be refined. It can be identified either before the start of the computations, due to some *a priori* knowledge of the solution behaviour, or during the solution process by means of an *a posteriori* error estimator. In the subdomain where refinement is needed the grid size is lowered to $h/2$ which naturally produces some hanging nodes at the interface which, in terms of notations in Fig. 1, have indices $k + 1/2$ on line $j + 1$. All nodes of the fine grid on such lines and of the coarse grid on the neighbouring lines, e.g. line j, will be referred to as interface nodes. In all internal (non-interface nodes) (k, l) we employ the standard central difference for approximation of the second derivatives:

$$\delta_x^2 u_{k,l} = u_{k+1,l} - 2u_{k,l} + u_{k-1,l}, \quad \delta_y^2 u_{k,l} = u_{k,l+1} - 2u_{k,l} + u_{k,l-1}. \tag{3}$$

In [5] the authors propose to modify the central difference approximation only in the hanging nodes of type $(i + 1/2, j + 1)$ using a linear interpolation in the "ghost" node $((i + 1/2, j)$. In the context of Fig. 1 this would mean to use the following vertical difference in $(i + 1/2, j + 1)$:

$$\delta_y^2 u_{i+1/2,j+1} = u_{i+1/2,j+2} - 2u_{i+1/2,j+1} + 0.5(u_{i+1,j} + u_{i,j}). \tag{4}$$

Note that the resulting approximation of the second derivative looses symmetry and the resulting 1D discrete operator is likely non-positive (at least we were not able to prove positiveness). It somehow seem to still provide approximation and stability in the multidimensional case as verified in [5]. However, since the positiveness of the 1D discrete operators is key for the stability of most direction splitting schemes, the Peaceman-Rachford scheme is only conditionally stable with such an approximation. Our numerical experience seems to suggest that the stability condition is of the type $\tau \sim h^2$ which is typical for fully explicit schemes. On the other hand, the so-called locally one dimensional schemes proposed by Yanenko, [11], Sect. 2.3, seem to retain unconditional stability with such 1D discrete operators. However, these schemes have some issues with their accuracy in this case and therefore we will not discuss them further in this paper. Nevertheless, since the hanging node difference (4) yields a very simple splitting scheme in which the solution in any given direction can be performed independently on any grid line, this option deserves some further attention.

Key in proving positiveness for second order difference operators is the ability to sum by parts the product of its action with an arbitrary element of the corresponding Hilbert space (see [9], Sect. 2.3.1). This usually requires the continuity across the interface of refinement not only of the solution (imposed by 4) but, more importantly, the continuity of the fluxes. To this end, we employ an approximation which approximately guarantees this, however, it links the interface nodes in a non-tridiagonal fashion. Therefore, the resulting system can no longer be split so easily direction-wise. More precisely, in terms of the notations in Fig. 1, the second vertical difference in interface nodes of type (i, j) is given by:

$$\delta_y^2 u_{i,j} = \left(\frac{1}{4}u_{i-1/2,j+1} + \frac{1}{2}u_{i,j+1} + \frac{1}{4}u_{i+1/2,j+1}\right) - 2u_{i,j} + u_{i,j-1}. \tag{5}$$

In all interface nodes of type $u_{i,j+1}$ we use the approximation

$$\delta_y^2 u_{i,j+1} = u_{i,j+2} - 2u_{i,j+1} + \left(\frac{1}{2}u_{i-1,j} + \frac{1}{2}u_{i+1,j}\right), \tag{6}$$

and in all nodes of type $u_{i-1/2,j+1}$ we use:

$$\delta_y^2 u_{i-1/2,j+1} = u_{i-1/2,j+2} - 2u_{i-1/2,j+1} + \left(\frac{1}{2}u_{i-1,j} + \frac{1}{2}u_{i,j}\right). \tag{7}$$

Our numerical experience indicates that the Peaceman-Rachford scheme with the interface differences (5)–(7) provides an unconditionally stable discretization for parabolic problems. Since this scheme is not extendable to 3D problems, one can use alternatively the scheme proposed by Douglas, [4], employed in the discretization of the Navier-Stokes equations described in Sect. 2.4. Note that in the 3D case the finite difference operators (5)–(7) must be properly adjusted. This 3D procedure has not been tested yet and its stability and accuracy properties need to be further investigated.

2.3 Solution of the Resulting Linear System

As it can be easily observed, the approximations (5)–(7) couple the interface unknowns not only along vertical lines and therefore spoil the tridiagonal structure of the resulting linear system. Nevertheless, the system for all internal unknowns is still tridiagonal and we can still exploit this advantageous feature in a solution procedure of a domain decomposition type.

One possible option is the following iterative procedure which is easy to implement on both, serial and parallel computers. To explain it, let us decompose the system into 2×2 blocks corresponding to internal (U_i) and interface (U_s) unknowns.

$$\begin{bmatrix} A_{11} & A_{12} \\ A_{21} & A_{22} \end{bmatrix} \begin{bmatrix} U_i \\ U_s \end{bmatrix} = \begin{bmatrix} F_i \\ F_s \end{bmatrix}$$

The matrix A_{11} that corresponds to the internal unknowns is still tridiagonal in case of both, the horizontal and vertical sweeps comprised in the direction splitting (2). The matrix A_{22} is five-diagonal but with an appropriate renumbering the diagonals off the main diagonal can be brought very close to it. Then the iterative solution procedure proceeds as follows. Starting with an initial guess for U_s^0 (superscripts denote the iteration level), repeat for $k = 0, \ldots,$ until the convergence criterion is met:

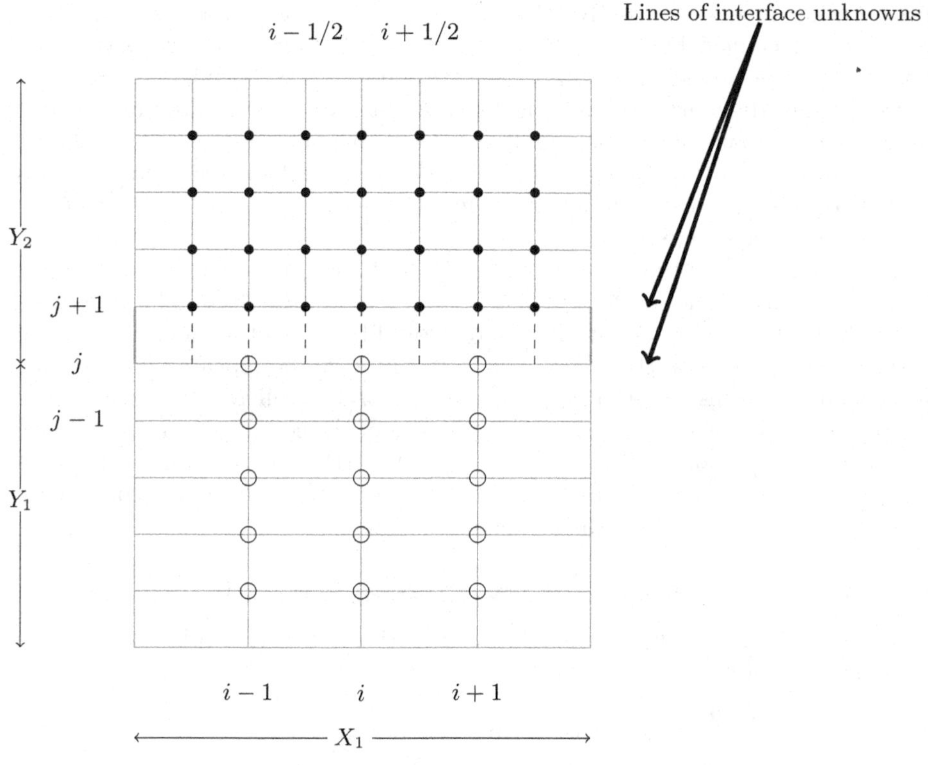

Fig. 1. Interface of refinement with hanging nodes.

1. Solve the equations for internal unknowns:

$$A_{11}U_i^{k+1} = F_i - A_{12}U_s^k$$

2. Solve equation for interface unknowns:

$$A_{22}U_s^{k+1} = F_s - A_{21}U_i^{k+1}.$$

This iterative procedure convergences fast because of the nice structure of the matrix. However, if the matrix structure is time-independent we can take a further advantage of the relatively simple structure of the matrix and completely eliminate the iteration. Note that each interface unknown is connected to exactly one internal unknown. This allows us to compute explicitly the Schur complement matrix $A_{22} - A_{21}A_{11}^{-1}A_{21}$ with relatively little effort at the beginning of the computations. Indeed, consider one particular line of internal nodes in the direction in which we currently solve. The edge nodes of such a line can either have a interface neighbour or be a boundary node. In any case, the part of the matrix A_{12} corresponding to this type of unknowns has at most two nonzero entries, in two different columns, corresponding to the eventual link of the edge nodes with interface nodes. Solving twice the tridiagonal system corresponding to these internal unknowns with a right hand side given by these columns yields the part of $A_{11}^{-1}A_{12}$ corresponding to the link of the two edges with the (eventual) two interface neighbours.

Multiplying it by the corresponding part of A_{21} yields easily the part of $A_{21}A_{11}^{-1}A_{21}$ corresponding to the interface nodes bordering the two internal edge nodes. Note that each such interface node would have exactly one link with one of the internal nodes on the edges. This procedure can be repeated on each line of internal unknowns and as a result we can construct explicitly the entire Schur complement $A_{22} - A_{21}A_{11}^{-1}A_{21}$ at the beginning of the computation. It will have a very sparse but non-tridiagonal structure. Nevertheless, its solution is not a particular problem since in case of a d-dimensional problem, it will correspond to a linear system of a $d-1$-dimensional problem.

2.4 Direction Splitting for the Navier-Stokes Equations

The proposed refinement procedure with direction splitting can be extended to solve the unsteady Navier-Stokes equations:

$$\begin{cases} \dfrac{\partial \mathbf{u}}{\partial t} + (\mathbf{u}\cdot\nabla)\,\mathbf{u} - \nu\Delta\mathbf{u} + \nabla p = \mathbf{f} \text{ in } \Omega \times (0,T) \\ \nabla\cdot\mathbf{u} = 0 \text{ in } \Omega \times (0,T), \end{cases} \tag{8}$$

One such possible scheme is proposed by [7]. It can be summarized as follows.

Pressure predictor. Compute a pressure predictor by setting $p^{\frac{1}{2}} = 0$ and for $n \geq 0$:

$$p^{*,n+\frac{1}{2}} = p^{n-\frac{1}{2}} \tag{9}$$

Velocity update. Updating the velocity field using direction splitting technique due to Douglas [4]. Initializing the algorithm with $\mathbf{u}^0 = \mathbf{u}_0$, for $n > 0$, the velocity is updated as follows:

$$\begin{aligned} &\frac{\xi^{n+1} - \mathbf{u}^{n+1}}{\Delta t} + (\mathbf{u}^n\cdot\nabla)\mathbf{u}^n - \nu\Delta\mathbf{u}^n + \nabla p^{*,n+\frac{1}{2}} = f(t^{n+\frac{1}{2}}) \\ &\frac{\nu^{n+1} - \xi^{n+1}}{\Delta t} + \frac{\nu}{2}\partial_{xx}(\nu^{n+1} - \mathbf{u}^n) = 0 \\ &\frac{\mathbf{u}^{n+1} - \nu^{n+1}}{\Delta t} + \frac{\nu}{2}\partial_{yy}(\mathbf{u}^{n+1} - \mathbf{u}^n) = 0 \end{aligned} \tag{10}$$

Pressure update. The pressure is updated by solving $Ap^{n+\frac{1}{2}} = \dfrac{1}{\Delta t}\nabla\cdot u^{n+1}$, where A is a direction splitting operator of the following form $A = (1-\partial_{xx})(1-\partial_{yy})$.

$$\begin{aligned} \psi - \partial_{xx}\psi &= -\frac{1}{\Delta t}\nabla \cdot u^{n+1} \\ p^{n+\frac{1}{2}} - \partial_{yy}p^{n+\frac{1}{2}} &= \psi \end{aligned} \tag{11}$$

All implicit steps in this scheme require the solution of one dimensional problems only. Therefore, the proposed refinement procedure is easy to adapt to each of the equations of the scheme. The spatial discretization was performed using a collocated grid for all variables. It is not *inf-sup* stable but for the parameters involved in this problem it did not exhibit spurious modes in the pressure due to the stabilization provided by the operator A in the pressure equation. Nevertheless, the generally appropriate setting would be to use staggered grids. Although the two velocities and pressure variables are located in staggered positions the refinement procedure can be applied on the grid corresponding to each of these variables.

2.5 Numerical Results

Test Case with a Manufactured Solution. We use the following manufactured solution of the heat equation to test the stability and accuracy of the proposed refinement procedure:

$$u(x, y, t) = exp(-t)\sin(\pi x)\sin(\pi y) \tag{12}$$

The tests were performed using two different grids on two different domains: the one illustrated in Fig. 1 with dimensions $X_1 = 1, Y_1 = 1, Y_2 = 1$, and another one which is similar but has another course region of size 1 added on top. In both cases, the analytic solution was used as a Dirichlet boundary condition and the source term was adjusted so that the above function satisfies the equation.

Table 1 shows the maximum and the L^2 norm of the error between the analytic and numerical solutions. The scheme on both grids clearly exhibits a second order spatial convergence rate in the L^2 norm.

Table 1. L^∞ and L^2 errors in the domain depicted in Fig. 1 (left panel) and in the domain domain with an additional coarse region on top (right panel).

h	$\|u_h - u\|_{L_\infty}$	$\|u_h - u\|_{L_2}$
0.1	0.069	0.001
0.05	0.032	0.0002
0.025	0.013	4.2e-5

h	$\|u_h - u\|_{L_\infty}$	$\|u_h - u\|_{L_2}$
0.1	0.08	0.002
0.05	0.035	0.00018
0.025	0.018	5.1e-5

Numerical Results for the Lid Driven Cavity Problem. The procedure for the Navier-Stokes equations is tested on the 2D lid driven cavity problem. The computational domain is $\Omega = (0, 2)^2$. The boundary conditions for the horizontal component of the velocity are given by: $u|_{x=0,1,y=0} = 0$, $u|_{y=1} = 1$, and for its vertical component by: $v|_{\partial\Omega} = 0$. The Reynolds number is $Re \approx 1$ and the time step is $\tau = 0.001$. The grid in the lower half of the domain has a coarse grid size $1/20$ and the upper of the domain is gridded with a grid size $1/40$.

We show in Fig. 2 the horizontal and vertical profiles of the velocity alongside the vertical (CD) and horizontal (A_1B_1) lines through the centre of the cavity. Since the grid is constructed so that the horizontal centre line is part of the coarse grid and the line above it, which we denote by A_2B_2, is the first line of refinement, we also provide the v-profile along the refined line. It clearly does not contain fluctuations that would indicate instabilities and is almost identical to the profile on the coarse grid line below it.

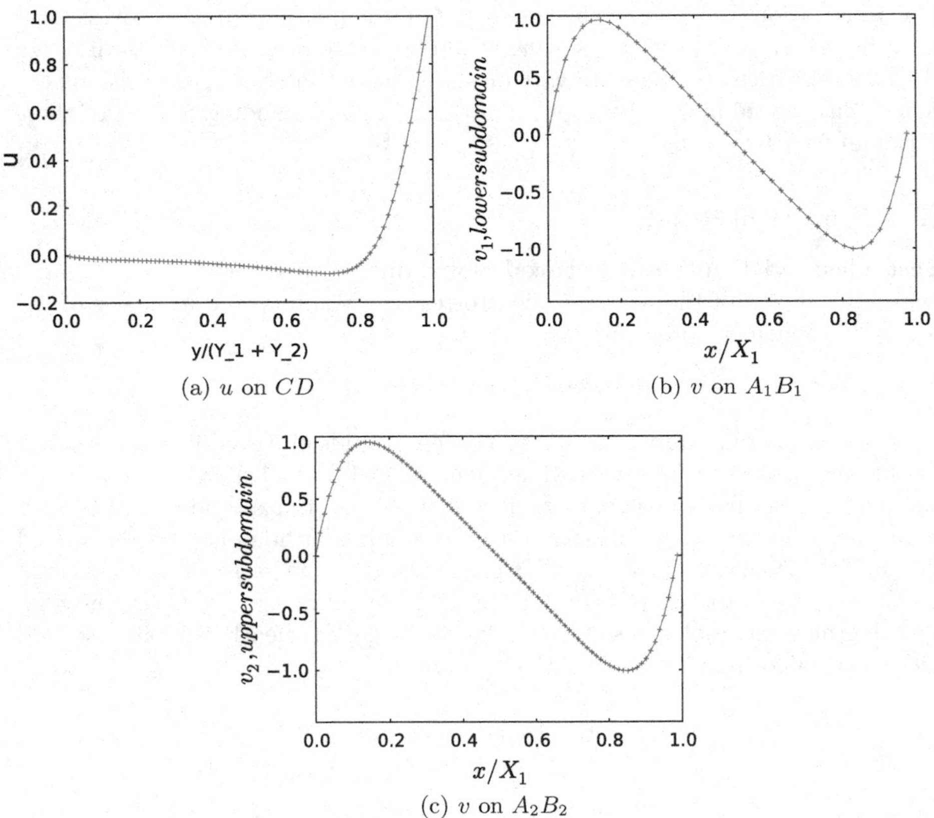

(a) u on CD

(b) v on A_1B_1

(c) v on A_2B_2

Fig. 2. Velocity profiles in a lid driven cavity problem.

3 Conclusions

One of the major objections against the use of direction splitting schemes is that they cannot be used on grids other than regular Cartesian grids. This prevents the use of locally refined grids and therefore in some cases eliminates the advantage of speed that these schemes have. This is particularly true if the problems under consideration require small grid sizes only in a fraction of the computational domain, like boundary layer problems for example. In this note we propose a new grid refinement procedure which can successfully be applied in conjunction with the Peaceman-Rachford and Douglas direction splitting schemes. It introduces hanging nodes but the resulting linear systems have very small deviations from the classical tridiagonal structure, only in the nodes at the interfaces of refinement. The possibilities for such a refinement are demonstrated on a strip that contains a refined and a coarse domains. Further 2D or 3D patch refinement would require an additional adjustment of the fluxes in the corner nodes that is to be studied further.

The resulting linear system can be solved in two possible ways. First, we can use an iteration to solve the Schur complement system corresponding to the interface unknowns, which at each iteration step requires the solution of a tridiagonal system corresponding to all internal nodes. Because of the simple structure of the matrices resulting from the direction splitting procedure it is also possible to compute explicitly the Schur complement matrix once, at the beginning of the computations, and then solve the corresponding linear system with a direct method. This can be done even in case of three-dimensional problems since the Schur complement matrix corresponds roughly to a two-dimensional subproblem and is quite sparse. Therefore its solution by a direct method is not a particular problem.

The grid refinement technique discussed in this paper can be easily extended to the case of the incompressible Navier-Stokes equations, in combination with the direction splitting procedure introduced in [7]. Indeed, this procedure requires only the solution of one dimensional linear systems in each direction for both, the pressure and the velocity. Although it employs staggered grids for these unknowns, the refinement procedure described in this paper naturally introduces a staggered refined grid and therefore its implementation is straightforward.

References

1. Binev, P., Dahmen, W., DeVore, R.: Adaptive finite element methods with convergence rates. Numer. Math. **97**, 219268 (2004)
2. Carstensen, C., Rabus, H.: An optimal adaptive mixed finite element method. Math. Comp. **80**, 649667 (2011)
3. Dörfler, W.: A convergent adaptive algorithm for Poisson equation. SIAM J. Numer. Anal. **33**, 11061124 (1996)
4. Douglas, J.J.: Alternating direction methods for three space variables. Numer. Math. **4**(1), 41–63 (1962). http://dx.doi.org/10.1007/BF01386295
5. Durbin, P., Iaccarino, G.: An approach to local refinement of structured grids. J. Comp. Phys. **181**, 639–653 (2002)
6. Ewing, R., Lazarov, R., Vassilevski, P.: Local refinement techniques for elliptic problems on cell-centered grids: I. Error analysis. Math. Comp. **56**, 437–461 (1991)
7. Guermond, J.L., Minev, P.: A new class of splitting methods for the incompressible Navier-Stokes equations using direction splitting. Comput. Methods Appl. Mech. Engrg. **200**, 2083–2093 (2011)
8. Riviére, B.: Discontinuous Galerkin methods for solving elliptic and parabolic equations. SIAM (2008)

9. Samarskii, A.: The Theory of Difference Schemes. Marcel Dekker Inc., New York (2001)
10. Samarskii, A., Vabishchevich, A.: Additive Schemes for Problems of Mathematical Physics (in Russian). Nauka, Moskva (1999)
11. Yanenko, N.N.: The Method of Fractional Steps: The Solution of Problems of Mathematical Physics in Several Variables. Springer, Heidelberg (1971)

On Positivity Preservation in Some Finite Element Methods for the Heat Equation

V. Thomée(✉)

Mathematical Sciences, Chalmers University of Technology
and the University of Gothenburg, 412 96 Gothenburg, Sweden
thomee@chalmers.se

Abstract. We consider the initial boundary value problem for the homogeneous heat equation, with homogeneous Dirichlet boundary conditions. By the maximum principle the solution is nonnegative for positive time if the initial data are nonnegative. We study to what extent this property carries over to some piecewise linear finite element discretizations, namely the Standard Galerkin method, the Lumped Mass method, and the Finite Volume Element method. We address both spatially semidiscrete and fully discrete methods.

Keywords: Heat equation · Finite element method · Positivity preservation

1 Introduction

We consider the following model problem for the homogeneous heat equation, to find $u = u(x,t)$ for $x \in \Omega$, $t \geq 0$, satisfying

$$u_t = \Delta u \quad \text{in } \Omega, \quad u = 0 \quad \text{on } \partial\Omega, \quad \text{for } t \geq 0, \quad \text{with } u(\cdot, 0) = v \quad \text{in } \Omega, \tag{1}$$

where Ω is a polygonal domain in $\mathbb{R}^2$. The initial values v are thus the only data of the problem, and the solution of (1) may be written $u(t) = E(t)v$ for $t \geq 0$, where $E(t) = e^{\Delta t}$ is the solution operator. By the maximum principle, $E(t)$ is a nonnegative operator, so that

$$v \geq 0 \quad \text{in } \Omega \quad \text{implies} \quad E(t)v \geq 0 \quad \text{in } \Omega, \text{ for } t \geq 0. \tag{2}$$

Our purpose here is to discuss analogues of this property for some finite element methods, based on piecewise linear finite elements, including, in particular, the Standard Galerkin (SG), the Lumped Mass (LM), and the Finite Volume Element (FVE) method. For general information about these methods, and especially error estimates, see Thomée [7], Chou and Li [3], and Chatzipantelidis, Lazarov and Thomée [1,2]. We consider both spatially semidiscrete and fully discrete approximations.

I. Dimov et al. (Eds.): NMA 2014, LNCS 8962, pp. 13–24, 2015.
DOI: 10.1007/978-3-319-15585-2_2

The basis for the methods studied is the variational formulation of the model problem, to find $u = u(\cdot, t) \in H_0^1 = H_0^1(\Omega)$ for $t \geq 0$, such that

$$(u_t, \varphi) + A(u, \varphi) = 0, \quad \forall \varphi \in H_0^1, \ \text{ for } t \geq 0, \quad \text{with } u(0) = v, \tag{3}$$

where $(v, w) = (v, w)_{L_2(\Omega)}$ and $A(v, w) = (\nabla v, \nabla w)$. The finite element methods are based on regular triangulations $\mathcal{T}_h = \{K\}$ of Ω, with $h = \max_{\mathcal{T}_h} \operatorname{diam}(K)$, using the finite element spaces

$$S_h = \{\chi \in \mathcal{C}(\overline{\Omega}) : \chi \text{ linear on each } K \in \mathcal{T}_h;\ \chi = 0 \quad \text{on } \partial\Omega\}.$$

The spatially semidiscrete SG method consists in using (3) restricted to S_h, and the corresponding LM and FVE methods on variational formulations in which the first term (u_t, φ) has been modified, or to find $u_h(t) \in S_h$ for $t \geq 0$, such that

$$[u_{h,t}, \chi] + A(u_h, \chi) = 0, \quad \forall \chi \in S_h, \ \text{ for } t \geq 0, \quad \text{with } u(0) = v_h, \tag{4}$$

where $[\cdot, \cdot]$ is an inner product in S_h, approximating $(\cdot, \cdot)$. The specific choices of $[\cdot, \cdot]$ in the LM and FVE cases will be given in Sect. 2 below.

We now formulate (4) in matrix form. Let $Z_h = \{P_j\}_{j=1}^N$ be the interior nodes of $\mathcal{T}_h$, and $\{\Phi_j\}_{j=1}^N \subset S_h$ the corresponding nodal basis, with $\Phi_j(P_i) = \delta_{ij}$. Writing

$$u_h(t) = \sum_{j=1}^N \alpha_j(t) \Phi_j, \quad \text{with } v_h = \sum_{j=1}^N \widetilde{v}_j \Phi_j,$$

the semidiscrete problem (4) may then be formulated, with $\alpha = (\alpha_1, \ldots, \alpha_N)^T$,

$$\mathcal{M}\alpha' + \mathcal{S}\alpha = 0, \ \text{for } t \geq 0, \quad \text{with } \alpha(0) = \widetilde{v}, \tag{5}$$

where $\mathcal{M} = (m_{ij})$, $m_{ij} = [\Phi_i, \Phi_j]$, $\mathcal{S} = (s_{ij})$, $s_{ij} = A(\Phi_i, \Phi_j)$, and $\widetilde{v} = (\widetilde{v}_1, \ldots, \widetilde{v}_N)^T$. The mass matrix $\mathcal{M}$ and the stiffness matrix $\mathcal{S}$ are both symmetric, positive definite. The solution of (5) can be written, with $\mathcal{E}(t)$ the solution matrix,

$$\alpha(t) = \mathcal{E}(t)\, \widetilde{v}, \quad \text{where } \ \mathcal{E}(t) = e^{-\mathcal{H}t}, \quad \mathcal{H} = \mathcal{M}^{-1}\mathcal{S}. \tag{6}$$

We note that the semidiscrete solution $u_h(t) \in S_h$ is ≥ 0 (> 0) if and only if, elementwise, $\alpha(t) \geq 0$ (> 0).

It was shown in Thomée and Wahlbin [8] that, for the semidiscrete SG method, the discrete analogue of (2) does not hold for small $t > 0$. However, in the case of the LM method, it is valid if and only if the triangulation is of Delaunay type; it had been shown already in Fujii [5] that nonnegativity holds for triangulations with all angles $\leq \frac{1}{2}\pi$. For the FVE method we will show here that the situation is the same as for the SG method, i.e., that $\mathcal{E}(t) \geq 0$ does not hold for small $t > 0$.

In cases where the solution operator is not nonnegative for all positive times, we shall also discuss if it becomes nonnegative for larger time, or if $\mathcal{E}(t) \geq 0$ for $t \geq t_0 > 0$; the smallest such t_0, if it exists, will be referred to as the *threshold of positivity*. Clearly, this is particularly interesting if t_0 is relatively small.

We also study fully discrete schemes based on time stepping in the spatially semidiscrete methods. With k a time step, we consider approximations of the solution matrix $\mathcal{E}(t) = e^{-t\mathcal{H}}$ in (6) at $t_n = nk$ of the form $\mathcal{E}_k^n$, where $\mathcal{E}_k = r(k\mathcal{H})$, with $r(\xi)$ a rational function satisfying certain conditions. We will be particularly concerned here with the Backward Euler and (0, 2) Padé time stepping methods, corresponding to $r(\xi) = 1/(1+\xi)$ and $r(\xi) = 1/(1+\xi+\frac{1}{2}\xi^2)$, respectively.

In Schatz, Thomée and Wahlbin [6] some positivity results were obtained for fully discrete schemes related to those for the spatially semidiscrete SG and LM methods, and some of these are extended here to include also the FVE method.

After the introductory Sects. 1 and 2, the positivity properties of the spatially semidiscrete methods are analyzed in Sect. 3, and then, in Sect. 4, of the fully discrete methods. In Sect. 5 we give a concrete example, with Ω the unit square, using the most basic uniform triangulation $\mathcal{T}_h$, with the stiffness matrix corresponding to the 5-point finite difference Laplacian. Computations in MATLAB are used to elucidate our theoretical results, and to determine actual positivity thresholds.

The author gratefully acknowledges the help of Panagiotis Chatzipantelidis with the computer experiments and the figures.

2 The Spatially Semidiscrete Methods

We begin our discussion of the semidiscrete problem (4), or (5), by observing that for the stiffness matrix $\mathcal{S} = (s_{ij})$, which is common to all cases of (4), simple calculations show, see, e.g., [4],

$$s_{ij} = (\nabla\Phi_i, \nabla\Phi_j) = \begin{cases} \sum_{K\subset\text{supp}(\Phi_i)} h_i^{-2}|K|, & \text{if } i = j, \\ -\frac{1}{2}\sin(\alpha+\beta)/(\sin\alpha\sin\beta), & \text{if } P_i, P_j \text{ neighbors}, \\ 0, & \text{otherwise}. \end{cases} \tag{7}$$

Here h_i is the height of K with respect to the edge opposite the vertex P_i, and α and β are the angles opposite the edge P_iP_j, see Fig. 1. We assume throughout that the triangulations $\mathcal{T}_h$ are such that the corresponding $\mathcal{S}$ are irreducible matrices.

We now turn to the three different semidiscrete versions of (4) mentioned above, and specify the corresponding discrete inner products $[\cdot,\cdot]$ on S_h.

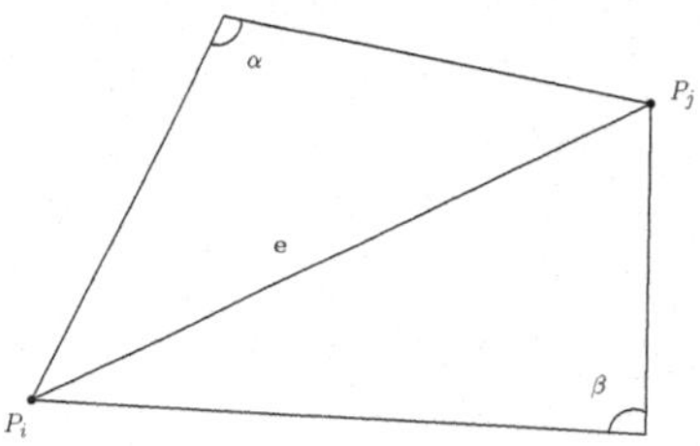

Fig. 1. An interior edge $\mathbf{e} = P_iP_j$.

The *Standard Galerkin* (SG) method is defined by (4) with $[\cdot,\cdot] = (\cdot,\cdot) = (\cdot,\cdot)_{L_2(\Omega)}$, and we find for the mass matrix, with $|V| = \text{area}(V)$,

$$m_{ij} = m_{ij}^{SG} = (\Phi_i, \Phi_j) = \begin{cases} \frac{1}{6}|\text{supp}(\Phi_i)|, & \text{if } i = j, \\ \frac{1}{12}|\text{supp}(\Phi_i\Phi_j)|, & \text{if } P_i, P_j \text{ neighbors}, \\ 0, & \text{otherwise}. \end{cases} \tag{8}$$

The *Lumped Mass* (LM) method uses (4) with $[\cdot,\cdot] = (\cdot,\cdot)_h$, where the latter is defined by quadrature: with $\{P_{K,j}\}_{j=1}^3$ the vertices of the triangle K, we set

$$(\psi, \chi)_h = \sum_{K\in\mathcal{T}_h} Q_{K,h}(\psi\,\chi), \quad \text{with } Q_{K,h}(f) = \tfrac{1}{3}\,|K| \sum_{j=1}^{3} f(P_{K,j}) \approx \int_K f\,dx.$$

In the matrix formulation (5), this means that $\mathcal{M} = \mathcal{D} = (d_{ij})$, with $d_{ij} = (\Phi_i, \Phi_j)_h = 0$ for $j \neq i$, so that $\mathcal{D}$ is a diagonal matrix.

To define the spatially semidiscrete *Finite Volume Element* (FVE) method, following [2], we note that a solution of the differential equation $u_t = \Delta u$ in (1) satisfies the local conservation law

$$\int_V u_t\,dx - \int_{\partial V} \frac{\partial u}{\partial n}\,ds = 0, \quad \text{for } t \geq 0, \tag{9}$$

for any $V \subset \Omega$, with n the unit exterior normal to ∂V. The semidiscrete FVE method is then to find $u_h(t) \in S_h$, for $t \geq 0$, satisfying

$$\int_{V_j} u_{h,t}\,dx - \int_{\partial V_j} \frac{\partial u_h}{\partial n}\,ds = 0, \ \text{ for } j = 1, \ldots, N, \ t \geq 0, \quad \text{with } u_h(0) = v_h, \tag{10}$$

where the V_j are the so called control volumes, defined as follows, see Fig. 2. For $K \in \mathcal{T}_h$, let b_K be its barycenter, and connect b_K with the midpoints of the edges of K, thus partitioning K into three quadrilaterals K_l, $l = j, m, n$, where P_j, P_m, P_n are the vertices of K. The control volume V_j is then the union of the quadrilaterals K_j, sharing the vertex P_j. The equations (10) thus preserves (9) for any union of control volumes.

To write (10) in weak form, we introduce the finite dimensional space

$$Y_h = \{\eta \in L_2 : \ \eta|_{V_j} = \text{constant}, \ j = 1, \ldots, N; \ \eta = 0 \text{ outside } \cup_{j=1}^N V_j\}.$$

For $\eta \in Y_h$, we multiply (10) by $\eta(P_j)$, and sum over j, to obtain the Petrov–Galerkin formulation

$$(u_{h,t}, \eta) + a_h(u_h, \eta) = 0, \quad \forall \eta \in Y_h, \ t \geq 0, \quad \text{with } u_h(0) = v_h, \tag{11}$$

where

$$a_h(\chi, \eta) = -\sum_{j=1}^{N} \eta(P_j) \int_{\partial V_j} \frac{\partial \chi}{\partial n}\,ds, \quad \forall \chi \in S_h, \ \eta \in Y_h. \tag{12}$$

In order to rephrase this as a pure Galerkin method, we shall introduce a new inner product on S_h. Let $J_h : \mathcal{C}(\Omega) \to Y_h$ be the interpolant defined by $(J_h v)(P_j) = v(P_j)$, $j = 1, \ldots, N$. The following lemma then holds, see [3].

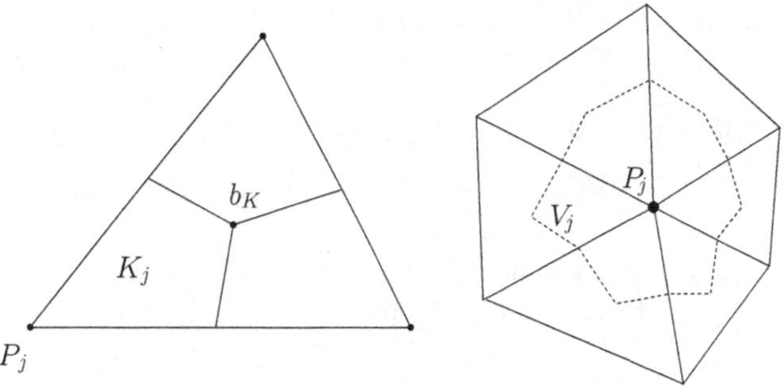

Fig. 2. A triangle $K \in \mathcal{T}_h$ and a patch Π_j around a vertex P_j

Lemma 1. *The bilinear form* $(\chi, J_h\psi)$ *is symmetric, positive definite on* S_h, *and*

$$a_h(\chi, J_h\psi) = (\nabla\chi, \nabla\psi) = A(\chi, \psi), \quad \forall \chi, \psi \in S_h. \tag{13}$$

We now define the inner product $\langle \chi, \psi \rangle = (\chi, J_h\psi)$, for $\chi, \psi \in S_h$. By (13), the Petrov-Galerkin equation (11), (12) may then be written in the Galerkin formulation (4), with $[\cdot,\cdot] = \langle \cdot,\cdot \rangle$, and the mass matrix $\mathcal{M} = (m_{ij})$ in (5) is

$$m_{ij} = m_{ij}^{FVE} = \langle \Phi_i, \Phi_j \rangle = \begin{cases} \frac{11}{54}|\mathrm{supp}(\Phi_i)|, & \text{if } i = j, \\ \frac{7}{108}|\mathrm{supp}(\Phi_i\Phi_j)|, & \text{if } P_i, P_j \text{ neighbors}, \\ 0, & \text{otherwise.} \end{cases} \tag{14}$$

We note that the FVE mass matrix is more concentrated on the diagonal than that of SG. In fact, with $\mathcal{D}$ the diagonal mass matrix of LM, we have

$$\mathcal{M}^{FVE} = \tfrac{2}{9}\mathcal{D} + \tfrac{7}{9}\mathcal{M}^{SG}. \tag{15}$$

3 Positivity Preservation in the Spatially Semidiscrete Methods

In this section we shall consider the general spatially semidiscrete problem (4), in matrix form (5), where $\mathcal{S}$ is the stiffness matrix, and $\mathcal{M} = (m_{ij})$, $m_{ij} = [\Phi_i, \Phi_j]$, is the mass matrix. We assume that $[\cdot,\cdot]$ is such that either $m_{ij} > 0$ for all neighbors P_i, P_j, or such that $m_{ij} = 0$ for all neighbors P_i, P_j. In the former case $\mathcal{M}$ is a nondiagonal matrix, and in the latter diagonal. We shall make the technical assumption that $\mathcal{T}_h$ has a strictly interior node, P_j say, such that any neighbor of P_j has a neighbor which is not a neighbor of P_j; we shall refer to such a triangulation as *normal*. Note that $\mathcal{T}_h$ is normal if it has a strictly interior node P_j, with all its neighbors strictly interior, such that the associated patch Π_j is convex. In the case of a nondiagonal mass matrix we have the following negative result, which was shown in [8] for the SG method.

Theorem 1. *Assume that $\mathcal{T}_h$ is normal and that $\mathcal{M}$ is nondiagonal. Then the solution matrix $\mathcal{E}(t) = e^{-\mathcal{H}t}$ for (5) cannot be nonnegative for small $t > 0$.*

Proof. Assume that $\mathcal{E}(t) \geq 0$ for small $t > 0$. Then $h_{ij} \leq 0$ for $i \neq j$ since

$$\mathcal{E}(t) = e^{-\mathcal{H}t} = \mathcal{I} - \mathcal{H}t + O(t^2) \geq 0, \quad \text{as } t \to 0.$$

Let P_j be the strictly interior node in the definition of a normal $\mathcal{T}_h$. We shall show that $h_{ij} = 0$ for $i \neq j$. If this has been proven, then

$$s_{ij} = \sum_{l=1}^{N} m_{il} h_{lj} = h_{jj} m_{ij}, \quad i = 1, \ldots, N, \tag{16}$$

with $h_{jj} \neq 0$, and hence the jth columns of $\mathcal{S}$ and $\mathcal{M}$ are proportional. Since P_j is strictly interior, we have $\sum_{i=1}^{N} \Phi_i = 1$ on $\operatorname{supp}(\Phi_j)$ and hence $\sum_{i=1}^{N} s_{ij} = \sum_{i=1}^{N} (\nabla\Phi_i, \nabla\Phi_j) = (\nabla 1, \nabla\Phi_j) = 0$. Together with $\sum_{i=1}^{N} m_{ij} > 0$, this contradicts (16) and thus shows our claim.

It remains to show that $h_{ij} = 0$ for $i \neq j$. Consider first the case that P_i is not a neighbor of P_j, so that $m_{ij} = s_{ij} = 0$. Since $\mathcal{S} = \mathcal{M}\mathcal{H}$, we find $s_{ij} = \sum_{l \neq j} m_{il} h_{lj} = 0$, and since $h_{lj} \leq 0$ for $l \neq j$, we have $m_{il} h_{lj} \leq 0$ and hence $m_{il} h_{lj} = 0$ for $l \neq j$. In particular, $h_{ij} = 0$. When P_i is a neighbor of P_j, it has a neighbor P_q which is not a neighbor of P_j and hence $s_{qj} = \sum_{l \neq j} m_{ql} h_{lj} = 0$, now implying $h_{ij} = 0$ since $m_{qi} > 0$ (where we have used that $\mathcal{M}$ is nondiagonal). This completes the proof.

This result thus covers the SG and FVE methods, but not the LM method, which has a diagonal mass matrix. We recall that an edge $\mathbf{e}$ of $\mathcal{T}_h$ is a Delaunay edge if the sum of the angles α and β opposite $\mathbf{e}$ is $\leq \pi$ (see Fig. 1), and that $\mathcal{T}_h$ is a Delaunay triangulation if all *interior* edges are Delaunay. Using (7) this shows that $\mathcal{T}_h$ is Delaunay if and only if $s_{ij} \leq 0$ for all $i \neq j$. But this is equivalent to $\mathcal{S}$ being a Stieltjes matrix, i.e., a symmetric, positive definite matrix with nonpositive off-diagonal entries. The following result was shown in [8].

Theorem 2. *The LM solution matrix $\mathcal{E}(t) = e^{\mathcal{H}t}$, $\mathcal{H} = \mathcal{D}^{-1}\mathcal{S}$, is nonnegative for all $t \geq 0$ if and only if $\mathcal{T}_h$ is Delaunay.*

Proof. As in the proof of Theorem 1 we find that $\mathcal{E}(t) \geq 0$ for $t \geq 0$ implies $h_{ij} \leq 0$ for $i \neq j$, and hence, since $\mathcal{S} = \mathcal{D}\mathcal{H}$, that $s_{ij} \leq 0$ for $i \neq j$, so that $\mathcal{T}_h$ Delaunay.

On the other hand, if $\mathcal{T}_h$ is Delaunay, then $\mathcal{S}$, and hence also $\mathcal{D}+k\mathcal{S}$, is Stieltjes, which implies $(\mathcal{I} + k\mathcal{H})^{-1} = (\mathcal{D} + k\mathcal{S})^{-1}\mathcal{D} \geq 0$ for all $k \geq 0$, where we have used the fact that if $\mathcal{A}$ is a Stieltjes matrix, then $\mathcal{A}^{-1} \geq 0$. Hence

$$\mathcal{E}(t) = \lim_{n\to\infty} (\mathcal{I} + \frac{t}{n}\mathcal{H})^{-n} \geq 0, \text{ for all } t > 0.$$

We recall that if $\mathcal{A}$ is a Stieltjes matrix which is also irreducible, then $\mathcal{A}^{-1} > 0$. In particular, if $\mathcal{T}_h$ is Delaunay, we have $\mathcal{S}^{-1} > 0$. Returning to the general case, we then also have $\mathcal{H}^{-1} = \mathcal{S}^{-1}\mathcal{M} > 0$. Since $\mathcal{G} = \mathcal{H}^{-1} = \mathcal{S}^{-1}\mathcal{M}$ is symmetric and positive definite with respect to the inner product $\mathcal{M}v\cdot w = \sum_{i=1}^{N}(\mathcal{M}v)_i w_i$, it has eigenvalues $\{\kappa_j\}_{j=1}^{N}$, with $0 < \kappa_{j+1} \le \kappa_j$, and orthonormal eigenvectors $\{\varphi_j\}_{j=1}^{N}$, with respect to this inner product. Recall that by the Perron-Frobenius theorem, if $\mathcal{G} > 0$, then $\varphi_1 > 0$ and $\kappa_j < \kappa_1$ for $j \ge 2$. Note that $\{\varphi_j\}_{j=1}^{N}$ are then also the eigenvectors of $\mathcal{H}$, with corresponding eigenvalues $\lambda_j = 1/\kappa_j$, $j = 1,\ldots,N$, and thus $\lambda_j > \lambda_1$ for $j \ge 2$. We may write

$$\mathcal{E}(t)\widetilde{v} = \sum_{l=1}^{N} e^{-\lambda_l t}(\mathcal{M}\widetilde{v}\cdot\varphi_l)\,\varphi_l. \tag{17}$$

We now return to the general semidiscrete problem (4), or (5), and show that, if $\mathcal{G} = \mathcal{H}^{-1} > 0$, then there exists $t_0 \ge 0$ such that $\mathcal{E}(t) > 0$ for $t > t_0$. This result was incorrectly stated in [6], without the positivity assumption.

Theorem 3. *If $\mathcal{G} = \mathcal{H}^{-1} > 0$, then there is a $t_0 \ge 0$ such that the solution matrix $\mathcal{E}(t) = e^{-\mathcal{H}t}$ for (5) is positive for $t > t_0$.*

Proof. It suffices to show that $\mathcal{E}(t)e_j > 0$ for large t, for the finitely many unit vectors $\{e_j\}_{j=1}^{N}$. But, since $\varphi_1 > 0$ and $\mathcal{M}e_j\cdot\varphi_1 > 0$, we find by (17), for t large,

$$\mathcal{E}(t)e_j = \sum_{l=1}^{N} e^{-\lambda_l t}(\mathcal{M}e_j\cdot\varphi_l)\,\varphi_l = e^{-\lambda_1 t}\big((\mathcal{M}e_j\cdot\varphi_1)\,\varphi_1 + O(e^{-(\lambda_2-\lambda_1)t})\big) > 0.$$

4 Fully Discrete Methods

In this section we study time discretizations of the semidiscrete problem (4), or (5). We thus consider approximations of the solution matrix $\mathcal{E}(t) = e^{-t\mathcal{H}}$ in (6) at $t_n = nk$, with k a time step, of the form $\mathcal{E}_k^n$, where $\mathcal{E}_k = r(k\mathcal{H})$, with $r(\xi)$ a rational function satisfying certain conditions.

We begin with the *Backward Euler* (BE) method, to find $U^n \in S_h$, $U^n \approx u_h(t_n)$, for $n \ge 0$, such that

$$[\frac{U^n - U^{n-1}}{k}, \chi] + A(U^n,\chi) = 0, \quad \forall\chi\in S_h, \text{ for } n \ge 1, \quad \text{with } U^0 = v_h. \tag{18}$$

In matrix formulation, with $U^n = \sum_{j=1}^{N}\alpha_j^n\Phi_j$, this takes the form

$$(\mathcal{M}+k\mathcal{S})\alpha^n = \mathcal{M}\alpha^{n-1} \quad\text{or}\quad \alpha^n = \mathcal{E}_k\alpha^{n-1}, \quad \text{for } n\ge 1, \quad \text{with } \alpha^0 = \widetilde{v},$$

where $\mathcal{E}_k$ the time stepping matrix

$$\mathcal{E}_k = (\mathcal{M}+k\mathcal{S})^{-1}\mathcal{M} = (\mathcal{I}+k\mathcal{H})^{-1} = r_{01}(k\mathcal{H}), \quad \mathcal{H} = \mathcal{M}^{-1}\mathcal{S}, \tag{19}$$

using $r(\xi) = r_{01}(\xi) = 1/(1+\xi)$. The fully discrete solution is thus $\alpha^n = \mathcal{E}_k^n\widetilde{v}$.

We first have the following time discrete analogue of Theorem 1, see [6].

Theorem 4. *Assume that $\mathcal{T}_h$ is normal and $\mathcal{M}$ nondiagonal. Then the BE time stepping matrix $\mathcal{E}_k = (\mathcal{I} + k\mathcal{H})^{-1}$ cannot be nonnegative for small $k > 0$.*

Proof. If we assume $\mathcal{E}_k \geq 0$ for $k > 0$ small, we would have, for any $t > 0$,

$$\mathcal{E}(t) = e^{-\mathcal{H}t} = \lim_{n\to\infty} (\mathcal{I} + \frac{t}{n}\mathcal{H})^{-n} = \lim_{n\to\infty} \mathcal{E}^n_{t/n} \geq 0, \tag{20}$$

in contradiction to Theorem 1.

For the Backward Euler Lumped Mass method the mass matrix is diagonal, and the following analogue of Theorem 2 was shown in [6].

Theorem 5. *For the BE LM method, $\mathcal{E}_k \geq 0$ for all $k > 0$ if and only if $\mathcal{T}_h$ Delaunay.*

For the nonnegativity of $\mathcal{E}_k$ for larger k, the following holds, where, as in the semidiscrete case, positivity properties of $\mathcal{H}^{-1}$ enter.

Theorem 6. *For $\mathcal{E}_k = (\mathcal{I} + k\mathcal{H})^{-1}$ to be nonnegative for k large, it is necessary that $\mathcal{H}^{-1} \geq 0$. If $\mathcal{H}^{-1} > 0$, then there exists $k_0 \geq 0$ such that $\mathcal{E}_k > 0$ for $k > k_0$.*

If $\mathcal{E}_{k_0} \geq 0$, then $\mathcal{E}_k \geq 0$ for $k \geq k_0$. Thus $\{k : \mathcal{E}_k \geq 0\}$ is an interval $[k_0, \infty)$.

Proof. We write $\mathcal{E}_k = \varepsilon(\varepsilon\mathcal{I} + \mathcal{H})^{-1}$, with $\varepsilon = 1/k$, and note that thus $\mathcal{E}_k \geq 0$ for k large implies $(\varepsilon\mathcal{I} + \mathcal{H})^{-1} \geq 0$ for $\varepsilon > 0$ small. But $(\varepsilon\mathcal{I} + \mathcal{H})^{-1} \to \mathcal{H}^{-1}$ as $\varepsilon \to 0$, and hence $\mathcal{H}^{-1} \geq 0$. On the other hand, if $\mathcal{H}^{-1} > 0$, then $(\varepsilon\mathcal{I} + \mathcal{H})^{-1} > 0$ for ε small, and hence $\mathcal{E}_k > 0$ for k large.

For the last statement in the theorem we show that if $(\varepsilon_0\mathcal{I} + \mathcal{H})^{-1} \geq 0$, with $\varepsilon_0 > 0$, then $(\varepsilon\mathcal{I} + \mathcal{H})^{-1} \geq 0$ for $\varepsilon \in [0, \varepsilon_0]$. With $\delta = \varepsilon_0 - \varepsilon > 0$, we may write

$$(\varepsilon\mathcal{I} + \mathcal{H})^{-1} = (\varepsilon_0\mathcal{I} + \mathcal{H} - \delta\mathcal{I})^{-1} = (\varepsilon_0\mathcal{I} + \mathcal{H})^{-1}(\mathcal{I} - \mathcal{K})^{-1}, \quad \text{where } \mathcal{K} = \delta(\varepsilon_0\mathcal{I} + \mathcal{H})^{-1}.$$

Here $\mathcal{K} \geq 0$, by assumption, and, if δ is so small that, for some matrix norm $|\cdot|, |\mathcal{K}| = \delta|(\varepsilon_0\mathcal{I} + \mathcal{H})^{-1}| < 1$, then $(\mathcal{I} - \mathcal{K})^{-1} = \sum_{j=0}^{\infty} \mathcal{K}^j \geq 0$, and therefore $(\varepsilon\mathcal{I} + \mathcal{H})^{-1} \geq 0$. But if $(\varepsilon\mathcal{I} + \mathcal{H})^{-1} \geq 0$ for $\varepsilon \in (\varepsilon_1, \varepsilon_0]$, with $\varepsilon_1 \geq 0$, then $(\varepsilon_1\mathcal{I} + \mathcal{H})^{-1} \geq 0$. Hence, by the above, $(\varepsilon\mathcal{I} + \mathcal{H})^{-1} \geq 0$ for some $\varepsilon < \varepsilon_1$, and thus the smallest such ε_1 has to be $\varepsilon_1 = 0$.

When $\mathcal{E}_k \geq 0$ for large k, we refer to the smallest k_0 such that $\mathcal{E}_k \geq 0$ for $k \geq k_0$ as the *threshold of positivity* for $\mathcal{E}_k$. Thus, by the last statement of Theorem 6, in the BE case the positivity threshold is the smallest k for which $\mathcal{E}_k \geq 0$.

The following result from [6] gives precise values of k for $\mathcal{E}_k$ to be guaranteed to be nonnegative, under a sharper conditions than $\mathcal{H}^{-1} > 0$, namely if $s_{ij} < 0$ for P_i, P_j neighbors, or $\alpha + \beta < \pi$ for each edge $\mathbf{e} = P_iP_j$ of $\mathcal{T}_h$ (see Fig. 1).

Theorem 7. *If $s_{ij} < 0$ for all neighbors P_iP_j, then $\mathcal{E}_k \geq 0$ if*

$$k|s_{ij}| \geq m_{ij}, \quad \forall j \neq i. \tag{21}$$

Proof. (21) implies that $m_{ij} + ks_{ij} \leq 0$ for all $j \neq i$, so that $\mathcal{M} + k\mathcal{S}$ is a Stieltjes matrix. Hence $(\mathcal{M} + k\mathcal{S})^{-1} \geq 0$, and thus $\mathcal{E}_k \geq 0$ by (19).

Thus $\mathcal{E}_k \geq 0$ if $k \geq \max(m_{ij}/|s_{ij}|)$, with max taken over all neighbors P_i, P_j. If $\{\mathcal{T}_h\}$ is a quasiuniform family, and $\alpha + \beta \leq \gamma < \pi$ for all P_iP_j, then $\mathcal{E}_k \geq 0$ if $k \geq ch^2$ with $c = c(\{\mathcal{T}_h\})$. Note that since $m_{ij}^{SG} = \frac{7}{9} m_{ij}^{FVE}$ for P_i, P_j neighbors, by (15), the above lower bound is smaller for FVE than for SG, by a factor 7/9.

Now consider, more generally, a fully discrete solution $\alpha^n = \mathcal{E}_k^n \widetilde{v}_h$, $n \geq 0$, of (5) defined by a time stepping matrix $\mathcal{E}_k = r(k\mathcal{H})$, where $r(\xi)$ is a bounded rational function for $\xi \geq 0$ approximating $e^{-\xi}$ for small ξ, so that

$$r(\xi) = 1 - \xi + O(\xi^2), \quad \text{as } \xi \to 0. \tag{22}$$

We may write

$$\mathcal{E}_k \widetilde{v} = r(k\mathcal{H})\widetilde{v} = \sum_{l=1}^{N} r(k\lambda_l)(\mathcal{M}\widetilde{v} \cdot \varphi_l)\, \varphi_l.$$

As in Theorem 4, $\mathcal{E}_k$ cannot be nonnegative for small k and $\mathcal{M}$ nondiagonal [6].

Theorem 8. *Assume that $\mathcal{T}_h$ is normal and $\mathcal{M}$ nondiagonal. Let $\mathcal{E}_k = r(k\mathcal{H})$, with $r(\xi)$ satisfying (22). Then $\mathcal{E}_k$ cannot be nonnegative for small k.*

Proof. Using (22), the result follow as in Theorem 4 from

$$\lim_{n\to\infty} \mathcal{E}_{t/n}^n = \lim_{n\to\infty} \Big(\mathcal{I} - \frac{t}{n}\mathcal{H} + O(\frac{t^2}{n^2})\Big)^n = e^{-t\mathcal{H}} = \mathcal{E}(t), \quad \text{for any } t > 0.$$

For nonnegativity of $\mathcal{E}_k = r(k\mathcal{H})$ for larger k we first show that if $\mathcal{H}^{-1} > 0$, this requires that $r(\xi) \geq 0$ for large ξ.

Theorem 9. *Let $\mathcal{H}^{-1} > 0$ and let $\mathcal{E}_k = r(k\mathcal{H})$. Then a necessary condition for $\mathcal{E}_k$ to be nonnegative for large k is that $r(\xi) \geq 0$ for large ξ.*

Proof. With λ_1, φ_1 the first eigenvalue and the corresponding eigenvector of $\mathcal{H}$, we have $\mathcal{E}_k\varphi_1 = r(k\lambda_1)\varphi_1$, and thus, since $\lambda_1 > 0$, $\varphi_1 > 0$, for $\mathcal{E}_k\varphi_1$ to be nonnegative for large k it is necessary that $r(k\lambda_1)$ be nonnegative for large k, showing our claim.

A typical and interesting example is the (0, 2) Padé approximation $r_{02}(\xi) = 1/(1 + \xi + \frac{1}{2}\xi^2)$. However, the Padé approximations $r_{11}(\xi) = (1 - \frac{1}{2}\xi)/(1 + \frac{1}{2}\xi)$ and $r_{12}(\xi) = (1 - \frac{1}{3}\xi)/(1 + \frac{2}{3}\xi + \frac{1}{6}\xi^2)$ are negative for large ξ, and hence the corresponding $\mathcal{E}_k$ cannot be nonnegative for large k when $\mathcal{H}^{-1} > 0$.

We now assume that $r(\infty) = 0$. If $r(\xi) \geq 0$ for large ξ, we may then write

$$r(\xi) = c\xi^{-q} + O(\xi^{-q-1}), \quad \text{as } \xi \to \infty, \quad \text{with } q \geq 1,\ c > 0. \tag{23}$$

We show the following result, generalizing the first part of Theorem 6.

Theorem 10. *Assume that (23) holds. Then $\mathcal{H}^{-q} \geq 0$ is a necessary condition for $\mathcal{E}_k = r(k\mathcal{H}) \geq 0$ for large k. If $\mathcal{H}^{-q} > 0$, then $\mathcal{E}_k = r(k\mathcal{H}) > 0$ for large k.*

Proof. Both statements of the theorem follow since, by (23),

$$\mathcal{E}_k = ck^{-q}(\mathcal{H}^{-q} + O(k^{-1})), \quad \text{as } k \to \infty. \tag{24}$$

The result shows, in particular, that $\mathcal{E}_k = r_{02}(k\mathcal{H}) > 0$ for large k if $\mathcal{H}^{-2} > 0$. We complete this section by showing that for this method, the negative conclusion of Theorem 8 holds also for the LM method, even though $\mathcal{M}$ is then diagonal, under the not very restrictive assumption that $\mathcal{T}_h$ is *4-connected* in the following sense: There exists a path $\mathcal{P}$ in Z_h consisting of four connected edges P_mP_n, with $s_{mn} \neq 0$, and such that the endpoints P_i, P_j of the path cannot be connected by a path with fewer than four edges.

Theorem 11. *Assume that $\mathcal{T}_h$ is Delaunay and 4-connected. Then, for the LM method, $\mathcal{E}_k = r_{02}(k\mathcal{H})$ cannot be nonnegative for small k.*

Proof. We have, by Taylor expansion of $r_{02}(\xi)$,

$$\mathcal{E}_k = r_{02}(k\mathcal{H}) = \mathcal{I} - k\mathcal{H} + \tfrac{1}{2}k^2\mathcal{H}^2 - \tfrac{1}{4}k^4\mathcal{H}^4 + O(k^5), \quad \text{as } k \to 0.$$

We shall show that if $P_iP_pP_qP_rP_j$ is a path $\mathcal{P}$ as above, then $(\mathcal{E}_k)_{ij} < 0$ for small k. For this we write $\mathcal{H} = \mathcal{D}^{-1}\mathcal{S} = \mathcal{V} - \mathcal{W}$, where $\mathcal{V}$ is a positive diagonal matrix and $\mathcal{W}$ has elements $w_{mn} = -s_{mn}/d_{mm} > 0$ when P_m, P_n are neighbors with $s_{mn} \neq 0$, with the remaining elements 0. (Recall that since $\mathcal{S}$ is Stieltjes, $\mathcal{W} \geq 0$.) It follows that $(\mathcal{H}^4)_{ij} = \sum_{l_1,l_2,l_3} h_{il_1}h_{l_1l_2}h_{l_2l_3}h_{l_3j}$ and, by our assumption on the path $\mathcal{P}$ connecting P_i and P_j, none of the nonzero terms have factors from $\mathcal{V}$. Hence $(\mathcal{H}^4)_{ij} \geq w_{ip}w_{pq}w_{qr}w_{rj} > 0$. In the same way, since P_j cannot be reached from P_i in less than four steps, $(\mathcal{H}^l)_{ij} = 0$ for $l = 0, 1, 2, 3$. Hence $(\mathcal{E}_k)_{ij} = -\frac{1}{4}k^4(\mathcal{H}^4)_{ij} + O(k^5) < 0$ for k small.

5 A Numerical Example

In this final section we present a numerical example to illustrate our theoretical results. For a family of uniform triangulations of the unit square $\Omega = (0,1) \times (0,1)$, we study the positivity properties of the spatially semidiscrete, the Backward Euler, and the $(0,2)$ Padé methods, using the SG, FVE and LM spatial discretizations. The triangulations $\mathcal{T}_h$ of Ω are defined as follows: Let M be a positive integer, $h = 1/(M+1)$, and set $x_j = y_j = jh$, for $j = 0, \ldots, M+1$. This partitions Ω into squares $(x_j, x_{j+1}) \times (y_m, y_{m+1})$, and we may define a triangulation $\mathcal{T}_h$, by connecting the nodes (x_j, y_m), (x_{j+1}, y_{m-1}). The number of interior vertices is $N = M^2$, and $\max_{\mathcal{T}_h} \operatorname{diam}(K) = \sqrt{2}h$. We note that $\mathcal{T}_h$ is normal, Delaunay, and 4-connected (if $M \geq 3$).

To determine the stiffness and mass matrices, let $\zeta_0 = (x_j, y_m)$ be an interior vertex of $\mathcal{T}_h$ and let $\{\zeta_j\}_{j=1}^6$ be the surrounding (including possibly boundary) vertices, numbered counterclockwise, with $\zeta_1 = (x_{j+1}, y_m)$, and $\{\Psi_j\}_{j=0}^6$ the corresponding basis functions, see Fig. 3. The contributions corresponding to ζ_0 to $\mathcal{S}$ are then given by (cf. (7))

$$(\nabla\Psi_0, \nabla\Psi_j) = \begin{cases} 4, & j = 0, \\ -1, & j = 1, 2, 4, 5, \\ 0, & j = 3, 6, \end{cases}$$

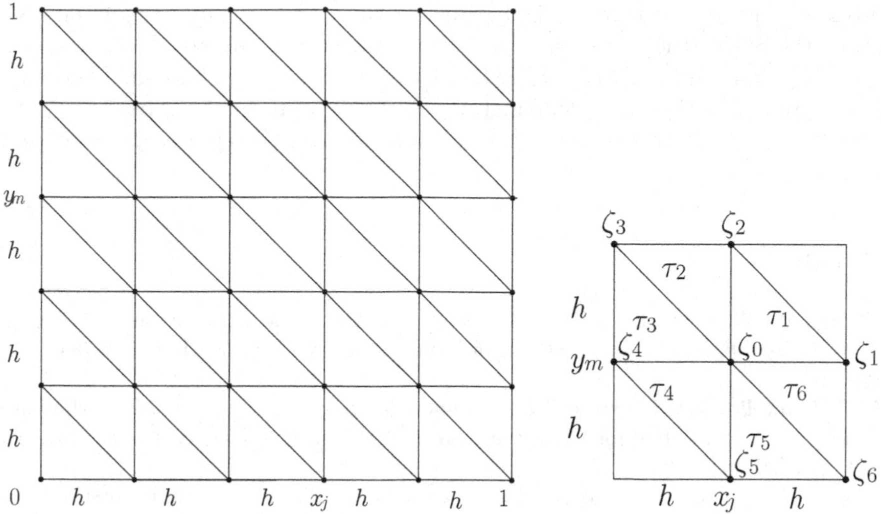

Fig. 3. *Left*: The unit square Ω with the symmetric triangulation $\mathcal{T}_h$.*Right*: The patch at ζ_0.

and to the mass matrices $\mathcal{M}$ for the SG and FVE methods by

$$(\Psi_0, \Psi_j) = \tfrac{1}{2}h^2 \begin{cases} 1, & j=0, \\ \frac{1}{6}, & j=1,\dots,6, \end{cases} \quad \text{and} \quad \langle \Psi_0, \Psi_j \rangle = \tfrac{1}{2}h^2 \begin{cases} \frac{11}{9}, & j=0, \\ \frac{7}{54}, & j=1,\dots,6. \end{cases}$$

Note that since the sum of the angles opposite a diagonal edge is π, the corresponding elements s_{ij} of the stiffness matrix vanish. We observe that $\mathcal{S}$ is an irreducible Stieltjes matrix, so that $\mathcal{S}^{-1} > 0$, and hence the matrices $\mathcal{H}^{-1} = \mathcal{S}^{-1}\mathcal{M}$ for the SG, FVE and LM methods are all positive. Thus the results of Theorems 3, 6, 9, and 10 concerning positivity for large t and k all apply. However, since some $s_{ij} = 0$ for P_i, P_j neighbors, this does not hold for Theorem 7.

Table 1. Positivity thresholds for the numerical example in Sect. 5.

	Semidiscrete		Backward Euler		(0,2) Padé		
h	SG	FVE	SG	FVE	SG	FVE	LM
0.10	0.046	0.043	0.0053	0.0045	0.025	0.024	0.020
0.05	0.035	0.031	0.0013	0.0011	0.023	0.023	0.021
0.025	0.021	0.019	0.0003	0.0003	0.022	0.022	0.022

In Table 1 we show some computed positivity thresholds t_0 for $\mathcal{E}(t)$, and k_0 for $\mathcal{E}_k = r_{01}(k\mathcal{H})$ and $\mathcal{E}_k = r_{02}(k\mathcal{H})$, for the SG, FVE, and in the case of $r_{02}(k\mathcal{H})$ also the LM method. The numbers indicate that for the spatially semidiscrete problem, the positivity thresholds diminish with h, and are smaller for the FVE than for the SG method. For the BE method the thresholds are small, with the ratio k_0/h^2 approximately 0.54 for SG and 0.45 for FVE, even though Theorem 7 does not apply. For the $(0, 2)$ Padé method the thresholds do not appear to diminish with h, and also to be independent of the choice of the spatial discretization method.

References

1. Chatzipantelidis, P., Lazarov, R.D., Thomée, V.: Some error estimates for the lumped mass finite element method for a parabolic problem. Math. Comp. **81**, 1–20 (2012)
2. Chatzipantelidis, P., Lazarov, R.D., Thomée, V.: Some error estimates for the finite volume element method for a parabolic problem. Comput. Methods Appl. Math. **13**, 251–279 (2013)
3. Chou, S.H., Li, Q.: Error estimates in L^2, H^1 and L^∞ in covolume methods for elliptic and parabolic problems: a unified approach. Math. Comp. **69**, 103–120 (2000)
4. Drăgănescu, A., Dupont, T.F., Scott, L.R.: Failure of the discrete maximum principle for an elliptic finite element problem. Math. Comp. **74**, 1–23 (2004)
5. Fujii, H.: Some remarks on finite element analysis of time-dependent field problems. In: Theory and Practice in Finite Element Structural Analysis, pp. 91–106. University of Tokyo Press, Tokyo (1973)
6. Schatz, A.H., Thomée, V., Wahlbin, L.B.: On positivity and maximum-norm contractivity in time stepping methods for parabolic equations. Comput. Methods Appl. Math. **10**, 421–443 (2010)
7. Thomée, V.: Galerkin Finite Element Methods for Parabolic Problems, 2nd edn. Springer, Heidelberg (2006)
8. Thomée, V., Wahlbin, L.B.: On the existence of maximum principles in parabolic finite element equations. Math. Comp. **77**, 11–19 (2008)

Monte Carlo and Quasi-Monte Carlo Methods

Optimized Particle Regeneration Scheme for the Wigner Monte Carlo Method

Paul Ellinghaus(✉), Mihail Nedjalkov, and Siegfried Selberherr

Institute for Microelectronics, TU Wien, Vienna, Austria
ellinghaus@iue.tuwien.ac.at

Abstract. The signed-particle Monte Carlo method for solving the Wigner equation has made multi-dimensional solutions numerically feasible. The latter is attributable to the concept of annihilation of independent indistinguishable particles, which counteracts the exponential growth in the number of particles due to generation. After the annihilation step, the particles regenerated within each cell of the phase-space should replicate the same information as before the annihilation, albeit with a lesser number of particles. Since the semi-discrete Wigner equation allows only discrete momentum values, this information can be retained with regeneration, however, the position of the regenerated particles in the cell must be chosen wisely. A simple uniform distribution over the spatial domain represented by the cell introduces a 'numerical diffusion' which artificially propagates particles simply through the process of regeneration. An optimized regeneration scheme is proposed, which counteracts this effect of 'numerical diffusion' in an efficient manner.

1 Introduction

The Wigner formalism expresses quantum mechanics, which normally is formulated with the help of wave functions and operators, in terms of functions and variables defined in the phase-space. This reformulation in the phase-space facilitates the reuse of many classical concepts and notions.

The Wigner transform of the density matrix operator yields the Wigner function, $f_w(x,p)$, which is often called a quasi-probability function as it retains certain properties of classical statistics, but suffers of negative values. The associated evolution equation for the Wigner function follows from the von Neumann equation for the density matrix, which for the illustrative, one-dimensional case is written as

$$\frac{\partial f_w}{\partial t} + \frac{p}{m^*}\frac{\partial f_w}{\partial x} = \int dp' V_w(x, p-p') f_w(x, p', t) \,. \tag{1}$$

If a finite coherence length is considered – the implications and interpretation of which is discussed in [2,5] – the semi-discrete Wigner equation results and the momentum values are quantized by $\Delta k = \pi/L$ and the integral is replaced by a summation. Henceforth, the index q refers to the quantized momentum, i.e. $p = \hbar(q\Delta k)$.

I. Dimov et al. (Eds.): NMA 2014, LNCS 8962, pp. 27–33, 2015.
DOI: 10.1007/978-3-319-15585-2_3

Equation (1) is reformulated as an adjoint integral equation (Fredholm equation of the second kind) and is solved stochastically using the particle-sign method [4]. The latter associates a + or – sign to each particle, which carries the quantum information of the particle. Furthermore, the term on the right-hand side of (2) gives rise to a particle generation term in the integral equation; the statistics governing the particle generation are given by the Wigner potential (i.e. the kernel of the Fredholm equation), which is defined here as

$$V_w\left(x,q\right) \equiv \frac{1}{i\hbar L}\int_{-\mathbf{L}/2}^{\mathbf{L}/2} ds\, e^{-i2q\Delta k\cdot s}\left\{V\left(x+s\right)-V\left(x-s\right)\right\}. \tag{2}$$

A generation event entails the creation of two additional particles with complementary signs and momentum offsets q' and q'', with respect to the momentum q of the generating particle. The two momentum offsets, q' and q'', are determined by sampling the probability distributions $V_w^+(x,q)$ and $V_w^-(x,q)$, dictated by the positive and negative values of the Wigner potential in (2), respectively:

$$V_w^+\left(x,q\right) \equiv \max\left(0,\, V_w\right); \tag{3}$$

$$V_w^-\left(x,q\right) \equiv \min\left(0,\, V_w\right). \tag{4}$$

The generation events occur at a rate given by

$$\gamma\left(x\right) = \sum_q V_w^+\left(x,q\right), \tag{5}$$

which typically lies in the order of $10^{15}s^{-1}$. This rapid increase in the number of particles makes the associated numerical burden become computationally debilitating, even for simulation times in the order of femtoseconds.

The notion of particle annihilation is used to counteract the exponential increase in the number of particles, due to particle generation. This concept entails a division of the phase space into many cells – each representing a volume $(\Delta x\Delta k)$ of the phase space – within which particles of opposite sign annihilate each other: Consider a cell (i,q) within the phase-space, which encompasses all particles with a momentum of $\hbar\,(q\Delta k)$ and a position within the spatial domain $\Omega_i = \left[x_i,\, x_i+\Delta x\right]$. The particles within the cell are considered identical and indistinguishable, i.e. any positive particle may annihilate any negative particle in the cell and vice versa. Within the cell (i,q), let there be P_i particles with a positive sign and Q_i particles with a negative sign which are summed up to yield a remainder of particles, $R_i = P_i - Q_i$; $|R_i|$ particles, each carrying the sign of R_i, are regenerated within the cell.

The $|R_i|$ particles that survive the annihilation procedure should, ideally, replicate the same distribution in cell (i,q) as represented by the $(P_i + Q_i)$ particles before the annihilation step. Since the momenta are quantized and a single value is shared amongst all particles within a cell, the distribution in the k-space can be recovered after annihilation. The positions of the particles, however, are real-valued, which prompts a closer inspection of the regeneration process to retain this information.

2 Particle Regeneration Schemes

The straight-forward approach to regeneration – leaning on the assumption of identical, indistinguishable particles used for the annihilation – would be to spread the $|R_i|$ particles uniformly in space, over the domain Ω_i. This approach, however, leads to a 'numerical diffusion' of particles, which causes the global particle ensemble to propagate at a different rate than dictated by its k-distribution. The evolution of a minimum uncertainty wave packet, defined as

$$f_w(x,k) = \mathcal{N}^{-\frac{(x-x_0)^2}{\sigma^2}} e^{-(k-k_0)^2\sigma^2}, \tag{6}$$

with $x_o = -50\,\text{nm}$, $k_0 = 6\left(\frac{\pi}{50}\right)\text{nm}^{-1}$ and $\sigma = 10\,\text{nm}$, is compared in Fig. 1 using three different approaches: (i) an analytical solution, (ii) a Monte Carlo approach without any re-generation and (iii) a Monte Carlo approach with a (forced) regeneration procedure at each time step. A typical time step, for simulations in which annihilation is required due to particle generation, of 0.1 fs is chosen. It is evident that approaches (i) and (ii) correspond exactly, however, the wave packet which is subjected to the regeneration procedure spreads out faster. This discrepancy is solely due to the regeneration procedure and is analyzed in the following.

Consider an ensemble of N particles, with positions $\{p_j\}$ $j = 1\dots N$, $p_j \in \Omega_i$, within the cell (i,q) at time t_0. The mean position of the ensemble at time t_0 is

$$\begin{aligned} \bar{p}_0 &= \frac{1}{N}\sum_{j=1}^{N} p_j \\ &= x_i + \frac{1}{N}\sum_{j=1}^{N} \delta x_j, \end{aligned} \tag{7}$$

where the position is expressed as $p_j = x_i + \delta x_j,\ \delta x_j \in [0, \Delta x]$. The particles of the ensemble evolve (drift) for a time period Δt, whereafter the mean position of the ensemble at time t_1 is

$$\begin{aligned} \bar{p}_1 &= \frac{1}{N}\sum_{j=1}^{N} p_j + v_j \Delta t \\ &= x_i + \frac{1}{N}\sum_{j=1}^{N} \delta x_j + v_j \Delta t, \end{aligned} \tag{8}$$

where v_j denotes the velocity of particle j, which is assumed to be small enough such that the particle remains within the bounds of the cell for one time step. Since we only have a single discrete momentum value associated with the cell, the velocity of all particles within the cell is the same (v_m). Therefore,

$$\bar{p}_1 = \bar{p}_0 + v_m \Delta t. \tag{9}$$

Now, suppose that before the particle evolution commences an annihilation step is performed, whereafter N' particles are regenerated within the cell with positions

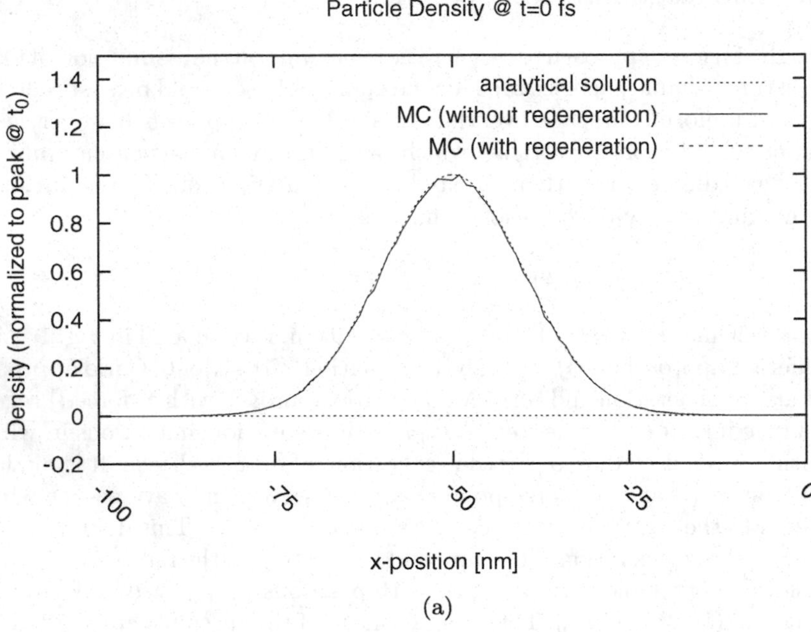

(a)

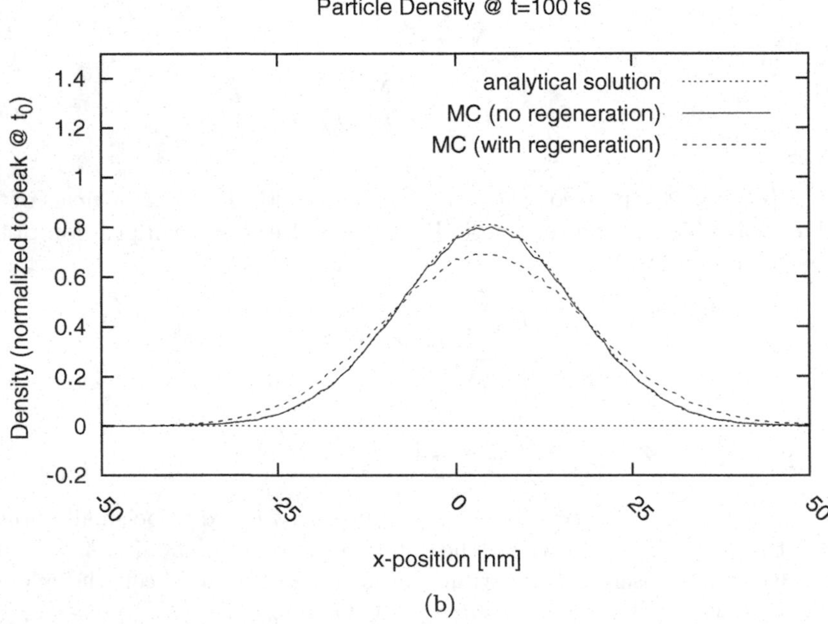

(b)

Fig. 1. Comparison of a wave packet evolved from (a) 0 fs to (b) 100 fs, using an analytical solution and a Monte Carlo (MC) approach without and with the regeneration process (repeated every 0.1fs).

$\{p'_j\}$ $j = 1 \ldots N' \leq N$. If the particles are uniformly distributed over the cell, one imposes

$$\bar{p}'_0 = \frac{x_i + x_{i+1}}{2} = x_i + \frac{\Delta x}{2}. \tag{10}$$

Consequently, the mean position of the ensemble at time t_1 will be

$$\bar{p}'_1 = x_i + \frac{\Delta x}{2} + v_m \Delta t, \tag{11}$$

which, when compared to (9), introduces an artificial propagation/retardation depending on the spatial distribution of particles before the annihilation procedure.

The original spatial distribution of the particles within a cell can be perfectly recovered, if all (infinitely many) of the moments of the distribution before the annihilation are known (and the Carleman's condition [1] for uniqueness is satisfied). The mean position represents the first moment of the local distribution and already retains the most important information. By uniformly distributing the particles over a distance Δx around the pre-annihilation mean, the 'numerical diffusion' is effectively remedied, albeit with some added 'noise', as shown in Fig. 2. This 'noise' is attributed to the fact that the uniform distributions of neighbouring cells overlap.

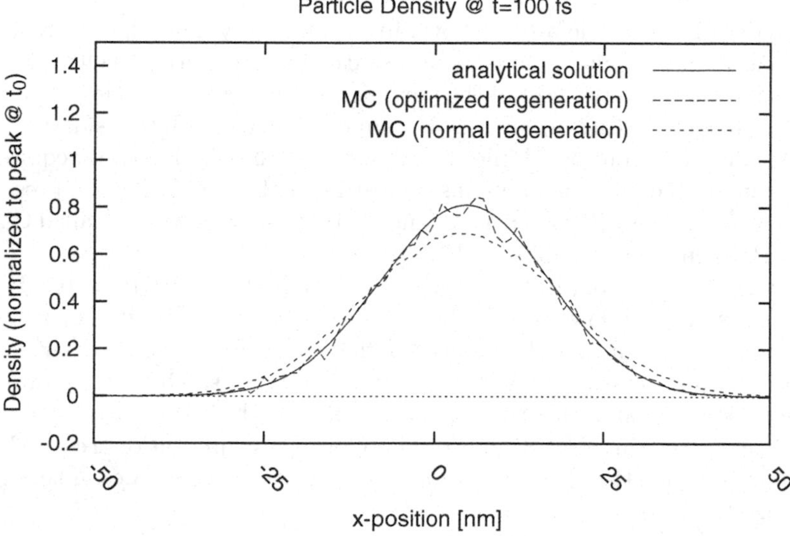

Fig. 2. Comparison of wave packets evolved for 100 fs using an optimized regeneration scheme and the conventional regeneration process; analytical solution shown by the solid line.

If, in addition to the mean, the second moment of the distribution – the standard deviation – is also calculated the particles can be regenerated using e.g. a

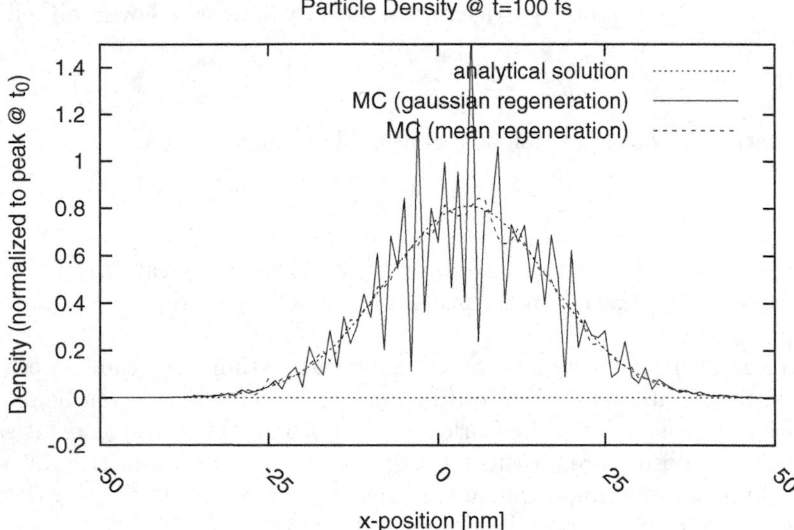

Fig. 3. Comparison of wave packets evolved for 100 fs using regeneration schemes based on a Gaussian distribution and a mean with uniform distribution (as in Fig. 2); the analytical solution is shown for comparison.

Gaussian distribution. The result, shown in Fig. 3, is very noisy, however, since a Gaussian distribution poorly models the actual distribution in each cell in this specific case and concentrates most of the particles in cell in a small region. The quality of the regenerated distribution may be refined indefinitely, by considering more moments of the distribution. While the increase in computation time required to calculate additional moments remains almost negligible (<1 % for the presented cases), to recover a distribution from (some of) its moments – the so-called Classic Moment Problem [1,6] – is quite challenging.

A flexible distribution, like the generalized Lambda distribution (GLD) [3], which can assume a wide variety of shapes is well-suited to describe an arbitrary distribution quite accurately. The GLD is defined using four parameters which are based on the first four moments of the distribution and solving up to four non-linear equations, making the computational effort high, if this process must be repeated for each cell in the phase space. Therefore, the computational costs should be weighed against the gained advantages and other techniques, like simply decreasing Δx.

3 Conclusion

It has been shown that an artificial propagation/retardation of particles arises when solving the semi-discrete Wigner equation, using the signed-particle method. This 'numerical diffusion' arises, if the particle regeneration process does not consider the spatial distribution of particles, within a phase-space cell, prior to annihilation. Calculating the mean value of the particles within a cell – the first moment of the distribution – before regenerating them has emerged as an efficient approach to counteract the 'numerical diffusion'. Fitting the distribution using more moments is not trivial and incurs considerable computational costs.

Acknowledgement. This research has been supported by the Austrian Science Fund through the project *WigBoltz* (FWF-P21685-N22).

References

1. Akhiezer, N.: The Classical Moment Problem: And Some Related Questions in Analysis. University Mathematical Monographs, Oliver & Boyd, London (1965)
2. Ellinghaus, P., Nedjalkov, M., Selberherr, S.: Implications of the coherence length on the discrete wigner potential. In: Abstracts of the 16th International Workshop on Computational Electronics (IWCE), pp. 155–156 (2014)
3. Karian, Z., Dudewicz, E.: Fitting Statistical Distributions: The Generalized Lambda Distribution and Generalized Bootstrap Methods. Taylor & Francis, New York (2010)
4. Nedjalkov, M., Schwaha, P., Selberherr, S., Sellier, J.M., Vasileska, D.: Wigner quasi-particle attributes - an asymptotic perspective. Appl. Phys. Lett. **102**(16), 163113 (2013)
5. Nedjalkov, M., Vasileska, D.: Semi-discrete 2D wigner-particle approach. J. Comput. Electron. **7**(3), 222–225 (2008)
6. Shohat, J.A., Tamarkin, J.D., Society, A.M.: The Problem of Moments. Mathematical Surveys and Monographs. American Mathematical Society, Providence (1943)

Sensitivity Analysis of Design Parameters for Silicon Diodes

J.M. Sellier(✉), Rayna Georgieva, and Ivan Dimov

Institute of Information and Communication Technologies,
Bulgarian Academy of Sciences, Acad. G. Bonchev 25A, 1113 Sofia, Bulgaria
{jeanmichel.sellier,rayna}@parallel.bas.bg, ivdimov@bas.bg

Abstract. In this work, a sensitivity study of the Boltzmann equation describing electron transport in one-dimensional Silicon diodes is performed. We focus on the variability of the model outputs according to the variability of input parameters connected to the geometry, temperature and doping concentration of the device. A number of numerical experiments exploiting the Boltzmann Monte Carlo method have been carried out to compute global sensitivity measures. The most popular variance-based sensitivity analysis approaches, such as the Sobol method and Fourier Amplitude Sensitivity Test (FAST), have been applied. First-order and total sensitivity indices in the context of FAST and Sobol methods have been computed. Furthermore, in order to estimate the interaction effects, the calculation of higher-order sensitivity indices have been performed. Based on the numerical results, we are able to classify the inputs according to their influence over the output variability. This allows a systematic approach to give physical interpretations and insights on the design parameters of a diode, which is hardly accessible otherwise.

1 Introduction

As a standard procedure, before the actual manufacturing, engineers design semiconductor devices basing themselves on mathematical models implemented in TCAD (Technology Computer Aided Design) tools. This eventually allows the calculation of the electrical characteristics. In this work, we focus on the Boltzmann Monte Carlo (MC) method and apply it to the simulation of a $n_S^+ - n - n_D^+$ diode to calculate the corresponding current-voltage curves (also known as IV curves). Our aim is to understand how the IV curve is eventually affected by the choice of several physical parameters involved in the design of a selected device. In particular, we focus on the following parameters: lengths and doping concentrations for source, channel and drain, and lattice temperature. While the effects of some of these parameters are somehow predictable, based on the designer experience, no systematic study has been carried out explaining in a rigorous way what is the *degree* of influence and *how* they affect the functionality of the device.

In this work, we perform a sensitivity analysis study focusing on Silicon diode devices. This is a simplified, but realistic, case study which can be used as

I. Dimov et al. (Eds.): NMA 2014, LNCS 8962, pp. 34–43, 2015.
DOI: 10.1007/978-3-319-15585-2_4

a mathematical laboratory. Sensitivity analysis is a powerful tool to study how uncertainty in the output of a model (numerical or otherwise) can be apportioned to different sources of uncertainty in the model input [6]. The general procedure for sensitivity analysis can be described in the following few steps:

- definition of probability distributions for the parameters under study,
- generation of samples according to the defined probability distributions using a sampling strategy,
- sensitivity analysis of the output variance in relation to the variation of the inputs.

This paves the way towards more sophisticated studies involving devices such as MOSFETs (Metal On Silicon Field Effect Transistor), double-gates transistors, nanowires, etc.

2 Approaches and Tools

Our investigation consists of simulating several instances of a one-dimensional (1D) diode, using the Boltzmann MC method [3]. Then we apply the Sobol [9] and the FAST (Fourier Amplitude Sensitivity Test) approaches, two reliable variance-based tools which provide global sensitivity analysis. In this section, a brief description of the utilized mathematical models, the applied sensitivity analysis approaches, and the involved software tools is given.

The Boltzmann MC method is based on the particle nature of electrons, i.e. classical billiard balls, which is completely described by two vectors, the position r and the pseudo-wave vector k [3]. At each time step, the two vectors are evolved according to the main phenomena affecting the dynamics of a classical particle. The evolution consists of two steps, the interaction with the electrostatic potential (drift) and the interactions with lattice phonons (scattering) as implemented in [10]. A outer self-consistent loop couples the Boltzmann model to the Poisson equation to include the effects of an electrostatic potential during the simulation.

Variance-based sensitivity methods are a useful tool for an advanced study of relations between the input parameters of a model, output results and internal mechanisms regulating the system under consideration. They deliver global, quantitative and model-independent sensitivity measures and are efficient computationally speaking. Its computational cost for estimating all first-order and total sensitivity measures is proportional to the sample size and the number of input parameters. In Sobol approach the variance of the square integrable model function is decomposed into terms of increasing dimension. The sensitivity of model outputs over each parameter, or parameter interaction, is measured by its contribution to the total variance. An important advantage of this approach is that it also allows the computation of higher-order interaction effects in a way similar to the computation of the main effects. The total effect of a fixed parameter can be calculated by means of only one MC integral per factor.

Consider a scalar model output $u = f(x)$ corresponding to a number of non-correlated model parameters $x = (x_1, x_2, \ldots, x_d)$ with a joint probability density function (p.d.f.) $p(x) = p(x_1, \ldots, x_d)$. In Sobol approach [9], the parameter importance is studied via numerical integration in the terms of analysis of variance (ANOVA) model representation [6,9]:

$$f(x) = f_0 + \sum_{\nu=1}^{d} \sum_{l_1<\ldots<l_\nu} f_{l_1 \ldots l_\nu}(x_{l_1}, x_{l_2}, \ldots, x_{l_\nu}), \quad \text{where } f_0 = \int_\Omega f(x)dx = const,$$

$f(x)$ is a square integrable model function, and $\int_0^1 f_{l_1 \ldots l_\nu}(x_{l_1}, \ldots, x_{l_\nu})dx_{l_k} = 0$, $1 \le k \le \nu$, $\nu = 1, \ldots, d$. The quantities $\mathbf{D} = \int_{U^d} f^2(x)dx - f_0^2$, $\mathbf{D}_{l_1 \ldots l_\nu} = \int f^2_{l_1 \ldots l_\nu} dx_{l_1} \ldots dx_{l_\nu}$ are called variances (total and partial variances, respectively). Based on the above assumptions about the model function and the output variance, the following quantities $S_{l_1 \ldots l_\nu} = \frac{\mathbf{D}_{l_1 \ldots l_\nu}}{\mathbf{D}}$, $\nu \in \{1, \ldots, d\}$ are called Sobol global sensitivity indices [8,9]. Nevertheless, the calculating of the integrals defined by the formulas described above requires integration of different integrands which is not computationally efficient. A procedure for computing global sensitivity indices of the input parameters overcoming this disadvantage has been proposed by Sobol [9]. Let $x = (y, z)$, where y is the subset which the measure of influence we are interested in, and z is the complementary subset of inputs. The computation of global sensitivity indices is based on the following representation of the variance $\mathbf{D}_y$: $\mathbf{D}_y = \int f(x)\, f(y, z')dxdz' - f_0^2$ (see [9]). This approach is more efficient since it utilizes only one integrand (i.e. the model function). The total variance corresponding to the subset y is $\mathbf{D}_y^{tot} = \mathbf{D} - \mathbf{D}_z$. Then, the total sensitivity index of a particular input parameter x_i, $i = 1, \ldots, d$, is defined as $S_i^{tot} = 1 - \mathbf{D}_i^{tot}/\mathbf{D}$. The mathematical treatment of the problem of providing global sensitivity analysis consists in evaluating total sensitivity indices and in particular Sobol global sensitivity indices of corresponding order. It leads to computing multidimensional integrals (from the mathematical representation of variances) of the following type $I = \int_\Omega g(x)p(x)\, dx$, $\Omega \subset \mathbf{R}^d$, where $g(x)$ is a square integrable function in Ω and $p(x) \ge 0$ is a p.d.f., such that $\int_\Omega p(x)\, dx = 1$. A more detailed description of the Sobol approach can be found in [2].

The Fourier Amplitude Sensitivity Test is a procedure that has been developed for uncertainty and sensitivity analysis [1,5]. This procedure provides a way to estimate the expected value and variance of the output variable and the contribution of individual input factors to this variance. An advantage of FAST is that the evaluation of sensitivity estimates can be carried out independently for each factor using just a single set of runs because all the terms in a Fourier expansion are mutually orthogonal. The main idea behind the FAST method is to convert the d-dimensional integral in x into a one-dimensional integral in s by using the transformation functions G_i for $i = 1, \ldots, d$, namely

$$x_i = G_i(\sin \omega_i s),$$

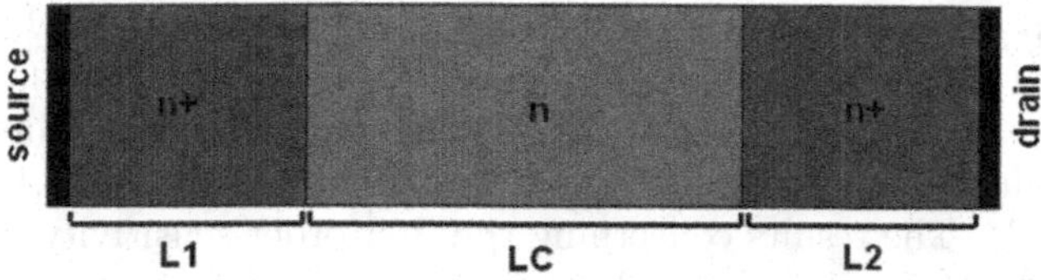

Fig. 1. Description of the device input parameters.

where $s \in (-\pi, \pi)$ is a scalar variable and $\{\omega_i\}$ is a set of integer angular frequences. For properly chosen ω_i and G_i, the expectation of Y can be approximated by

$$\mathbf{E}(Y) = \frac{1}{2\pi} \int_{-\pi}^{\pi} f(s) \mathrm{d}s,$$

where $f(s) = f(G_1(\sin \omega_1 s), \ldots, G_k(\sin \omega_d s))$. Application of the FAST method involves: (1) defining the ω_i and G_i, and (2) evaluating the original model at a sufficient number of points. This allows numerical evaluations of the integrals for the Fourier coefficients in the expression of the variance of Y. The computation of the total indices using Extended FAST (EFAST) was proposed in [7]. The basic idea behind the computation of the total indices is to consider the frequences that do not belong to the set $\{p_1\omega_1, p_2\omega_2, \ldots, p_d\omega_d\}$, for $p_i = 1, 2, \ldots, \infty$ and $\forall i = 1, 2, \ldots, d$. As in the Sobol indices, the total indices are computed by using the formula $S_i^{tot} = 1 - \mathbf{D}_{\sim i}^{FAST} / \mathbf{D}^{FAST}$, where the symbol "$\sim i$" is used to represent "all but i".

3 Analysis of Numerical Results and Discussion

In this section, we present the results of a sensitivity analysis study of the Boltzmann MC method applied to a one-dimensional diode. For our case study we use the following set of model inputs $\mathrm{x} = (x_1, x_2, \ldots, x_7)$ (Fig. 1): $[(x_1, x_2, x_3)\text{:}]$ length of the source/channel/drain $L_1, L_c, L_2 \in [50\,\text{nm}; 500\,\text{nm}]$; $[(x_4, x_5, x_6)\text{:}]$ doping of the source/channel/drain $n_1^+, n, n_2^+ \in (0; 10^{24}/m^3]$; $[x_7\text{:}]$ temperature $T_L \in (0; 300\,\text{K}]$. The output provided for each simulation is the current-voltage curve, which is affected by the choice of the above parameters.

Firstly, random samples of various sizes have been generated in the corresponding range by using the software SimLab. A uniform distribution has been used for all the variables. An important assumption here is that the input parameters are independent. That is why two main variance-based sensitivity analysis approaches, EFAST and Sobol, have been applied. In particular, quasirandom sequences have been used for the Sobol method. The model output has been produced by simulating the diode by means of the Boltzmann MC method. One model run takes an averaged 4 h (see below) for a complete current-voltage curve. For 0 **V** applied voltage we do not perform any calculation for the reasons that it would require a very large number of particles due to high MC noise. It is also known that a diode does not provide any current if there is no voltage.

Using the produced model values first-order and total sensitivity indices have been computed through the both approaches (EFAST and Sobol), and all the higher-order indices - by the second one. The computations have been done for 10 different values of the applied voltage in the interval [0.005 **V**; 0.05 **V**] with a step = 0.005 **V**. The results concerning the first-order sensitivity indices of all input parameters, for various applied voltages, as well as the sum of all first-order sensitivity indices obtained by both approaches are presented in Table 1. The results concerning the total sensitivity indices of the input parameters, for various applied voltages, obtained by both approaches are presented in Table 2. Furthermore, a graphical representation of some of the results is given on Figs. 2 and 3.

One observes that some negative values of sensitivity indices appear which is not acceptable from the theoretical point of view. These negative values are due to numerical errors in the estimates. Such negative values can be encountered when the analytical sensitivity indices are close to zero (i.e. for unimportant inputs). Since both approaches are performed numerically by a MC method, the choice of the sample size is important since it affects the quality of the estimates. The increase of the sample size reduces the probability of having negative estimates. This is confirmed by our results concerning both first-order and total sensitivity indices - indeed negative values disappear or become smaller. The results corresponding to higher sample size show higher stability and a more reliable interpretation from physical point of view.

As one can see from the results, the difference between first-order and total sensitivity index for a particular input parameter is significant. Moreover, the sum of all first-order sensitivity indices (see Table 1) is smaller than 1 generally. It demonstrates non-additivity of the mathematical model. Nevertheless, one can conclude that when the applied voltage increases then the noise decreases as well as the additive feature of the model appears stronger (see Table 1). On the other side, the non-additivity defines an important contribution of higher-order sensitivity indices. In this case, it is reasonable and crucial to apply Sobol approach to estimate higher-order interaction effects. The results of some higher-order sensitivity indices are presented in Table 3. When the applied voltage is 0.025 **V** just indices with values larger than 0.1 are given, and for the applied voltage equal to 0.05 **V** just indices with values larger than 0.2 are given. The results confirm that some of the higher-order sensitivity indices are significant. In general, there is a reasonable assumption that quite often in high dimensional models small subsets of input variables have the main impact upon the output [4]. In such cases, a low dimensional approximation of the model function can be rather efficient - constants, terms of first and second order. Obviously, in our particular case this assumption does not hold and a higher dimensional approximation should be done to reach satisfied accuracy of estimates.

The classification of input parameters according to their importance on variability of model output is different for various values of the applied voltage. For example, the most important parameter when the applied voltage is 0.01 **V** is the temperature (x_7), for 0.025 **V** and 0.05 **V** - doping concentration of the source (x_4). Theoretical expectations about insignificant influence of two parameters

(x_3, length of drain, and x_6, doping concentration of drain) have been fully confirmed by the numerical experiments performed by both approaches, in case of well-designed diodes. One observes a complete consistency of results obtained through both approaches for higher values of the applied voltage. This demonstrates the stability of the process. On the other hand, the values of the sensitivity indices are totally different (or most of them) corresponding to both approaches (EFAST and Sobol). Nevertheless, it is possible to capture some main trends about the model sensitivity with respect to the inputs under consideration. Indeed, for some particular values of the applied voltage the order of the inputs according to their importance is the same following both approaches.

Table 1. First-order sensitivity indices of input parameters for various applied biases.

Input parameter	Sensitivity analysis algorithm	Applied voltage				
		0.01 **V**	0.02 **V**	0.03 **V**	0.04 **V**	0.05 **V**
$L^1_{n^+}$	EFAST (N = 2023)	0.0052	0.0094	0.0116	0.0102	0.0119
	EFAST (N = 8463)	0.0072	0.0120	0.0124	0.0115	0.0109
	Sobol (N = 8192)	**−0.0019**	0.0123	0.0032	0.0169	0.0095
L_c	EFAST (N = 2023)	0.0144	0.0202	0.0203	0.0248	0.0192
	EFAST (N = 8463)	0.0065	0.0124	0.0156	0.0160	0.0161
	Sobol (N = 8192)	0.0159	0.0159	0.0113	0.0261	0.0270
$L^2_{n^+}$	EFAST (N = 2023)	0.0050	0.0090	0.0116	0.0115	0.0118
	EFAST (N = 8463)	0.0012	0.0202	0.0182	0.0191	0.0251
	Sobol (N = 8192)	0.0358	0.0394	0.0299	0.0327	0.0480
n^+_1	EFAST (N = 2023)	0.0804	0.1697	0.2314	0.2758	0.3153
	EFAST (N = 8463)	0.1356	0.2062	0.2485	0.2464	0.2744
	Sobol (N = 8192)	0.2908	0.3494	0.3525	0.3322	0.3287
n	EFAST (N = 2023)	0.1292	0.1714	0.1925	0.1942	0.1903
	EFAST (N = 8463)	0.0685	0.1307	0.1536	0.1672	0.1702
	Sobol (N = 8192)	0.0251	0.0719	0.1130	0.1182	0.1456
n^+_2	EFAST (N = 2023)	0.0231	0.0538	0.0897	0.1044	0.1142
	EFAST (N = 8463)	0.0250	0.0671	0.1044	0.1198	0.1205
	Sobol (N = 8192)	**−0.074**	**−0.080**	**−0.023**	0.011	**−0.186**
T_L	EFAST (N = 2023)	0.2363	0.1528	0.1077	0.0809	0.0735
	EFAST (N = 8463)	0.2321	0.1501	0.1015	0.0848	0.0717
	Sobol (N = 8192)	0.4517	0.2940	0.1997	0.1454	0.1339
$\sum_{i=1}^{7} S_i$	EFAST (N = 2023)	0.4936	0.5863	0.6648	0.7018	0.7362
	EFAST (N = 8463)	0.4761	0.5987	0.6542	0.6648	0.6889
	Sobol (N = 8192)	0.8193	0.7829	0.7096	0.6825	0.6927

Table 2. Total sensitivity indices of input parameters for various applied biases.

Input parameter	Sensitivity analysis algorithm	Applied voltage				
		0.01 **V**	0.02 **V**	0.03 **V**	0.04 **V**	0.05 **V**
$L^1_{n^+}$	EFAST (N = 8463)	0.24098	0.15490	0.10906	0.0790	0.06518
	Sobol (N = 8192)	0.11423	0.07849	0.05948	0.01684	0.03752
L_c	EFAST (N = 8463)	0.23312	0.14259	0.10686	0.09010	0.08175
	Sobol (N = 8192)	0.05125	0.06564	0.05008	0.02898	0.04780
$L^2_{n^+}$	EFAST (N = 8463)	0.22747	0.15018	0.12360	0.12642	0.13380
	Sobol (N = 8192)	0.01452	0.04936	0.06305	0.05954	0.09558
n_1^+	EFAST (N = 8463)	0.40971	0.43636	0.46368	0.47965	0.49756
	Sobol (N = 8192)	0.57327	0.54756	0.51006	0.51141	0.54596
n	EFAST (N = 8463)	0.38861	0.37535	0.36536	0.35421	0.34555
	Sobol (N = 8192)	0.16944	0.29911	0.33115	0.35345	0.35190
n_2^+	EFAST (N = 8463)	0.37590	0.33134	0.31337	0.29585	0.27607
	Sobol (N = 8192)	0.04515	0.21131	0.29304	0.29162	0.30383
T_L	EFAST (N = 8463)	0.61409	0.37597	0.26454	0.22038	0.18282
	Sobol (N = 8192)	0.73363	0.41965	0.30164	0.22137	0.19096

Table 3. Higher-order sensitivity indices of input parameters obtained by Sobol approach for various applied biases (N = 8192).

Sensitivity measure	Applied voltage is 0.025 **V**	Sensitivity measure	Applied voltage is 0.05 **V**
S_{67}	0.1854	S_{16}	0.2383
S_{3467}	0.1024	S_{26}	0.2257
S_{12356}	0.1083	S_{36}	0.2004
S_{23567}	0.1239	S_{56}	0.3003
		S_{67}	0.2035
		S_{1367}	0.2175

For example, when the applied voltage is 0 **V**, then the parameters x_7 and x_6 are the most important and x_3 is the less important.

In comparing the results, corresponding to computations by EFAST for different sample sizes, a better consistency has been observed. The estimates for both techniques (EFAST and Sobol) have been computed for similar sample sizes and in the both cases they are based on MC approach. However, the dimension of the integrals of the quantities of interest is strongly different. In the first case the integral is one-dimensional, while in the second case it is 8-dimensional for first-order sensitivity indices, and 13-dimensional for total sensitivity indices.

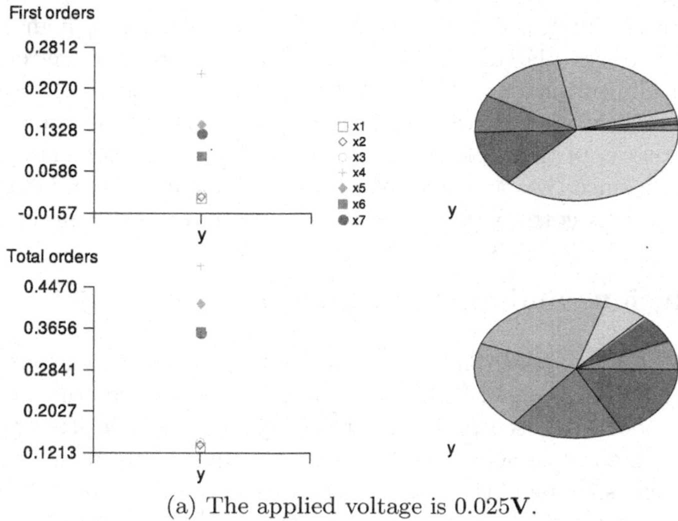

(a) The applied voltage is 0.025**V**.

Fig. 2. Graphical representation of first-order and total sensitivity indices obtained by EFAST for various applied biases (N = 8463).

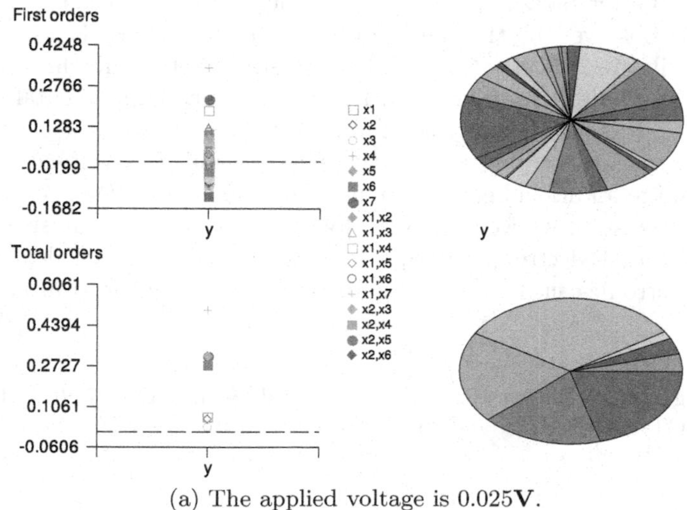

(a) The applied voltage is 0.025**V**.

Fig. 3. Graphical representation of first-order and total sensitivity indices obtained by Sobol approach for various applied biases (N = 8192).

This, obviously, leads to different amount of variances and thus to different accuracy of numerical approximation. For smaller applied voltages, bigger fluctuations in the results for different sample sizes appear due to high MC noise. This forces us to use a larger sample size in order to reach a more reliable estimate of multidimensional integrals. On the other side, the results show that, for EFAST, additive model feature appears for smaller values of the applied voltage. Therefore, in this case higher-order effects should be computed by the Sobol approach since they are represented by higher dimensional integrals (8 to 13-dimension). This corresponds, again, to the need of a larger sample size.

4 Conclusions and Future Plans

In this work, the results from sensitivity analysis provided for semi-classical transport in a diode are described. A number of numerical experiments with the Boltzmann model have been performed to compute global sensitivity measures. The following main comments and conclusions can be drawn: (1) The mathematical model is non-additive; (2) It is reasonable to compute higher-order sensitivity indices via Sobol approach since some of them seem to be significant; (3) It is known that, for well designed diodes, x_3 (drain length) and x_6 (drain doping concentration) should not affect the simulation results. In our study, we put ourselves in a very general situation where the source and drain dopings are not necessarily equal. Thus we are able to draw broader conclusions; (4) We observe that less MC noise appear for higher applied voltages ($0.035\,\mathbf{V} - 0.05\,\mathbf{V}$) and results are more consistent. This can be explained by the fact that, in this case, we have better Boltzmann MC convergence [3]; (5) Two concurrent physical effects are observed: on the one hand temperature, which relaxes the system towards equilibrium, on the other hand electrostatic potential, which drives the system out of equilibrium. This is in accordance with experimental measurements. Indeed, it is well-known that if no potential is applied, the electrons will simply relax towards equilibrium (lattice energy) and, if a voltage is applied, they will acquire additional energy provided by the electric field.

As a further step, we would like to focus on sensitivity analysis studies of more sophisticated electron transport models applied to actual devices issued from nanoelectronics such as double-gates and single-electron transistors, nanowires, etc.

Acknowledgment. This work has been supported by the EC FP7 Project AComIn (FP7-REGPOT-2012-2013-1), and the Bulgarian NSF Grants DMU 03/61/2011 and DCVP 02/1/2010.

References

1. Cukier, R., Fortuin, C., Shuler, K., Petschek, A., Schaibly, J.: Study of the sensitivity of coupled reaction systems to uncertainties in rate coefficients. I. Theory. J. Chem. Phys. **59**, 3873–3878 (1973)

2. Dimov, I.T., Georgieva, R., Ivanovska, I., Ostromsky, T., Zlatev, Z.: Studying the sensitivity of pollutants' concentrations caused by variations of chemical rates. J. Comput. Appl. Math. **235**, 391–402 (2010)
3. Jacoboni, C., Reggiani, L.: The Monte Carlo method for the solution of charge transport in semiconductors with applications to covalent materials. Rev. Mod. Phys. **55**(3), 645–705 (1983)
4. Rabitz, H., Alis, O.F., Shorter, J., Shim, K.: Efficient input-output model representation. Comput. Phys. Commun. **117**(1–2), 11–20 (1999)
5. Saltelli, A., Chan, K., Scott, M.: Sensitivity Analysis. Probability and Statistics. Wiley, New York (2000). ISBN: 978-0-470-74382-9
6. Saltelli, A., Ratto, M., Andres, T., Campolongo, F., Cariboni, J., Gatelli, D., Saisana, M., Tarantola, S.: Global Sensitivity Analysis: The Primer. Wiley, Hoboken (2008)
7. Saltelli, A., Tarantola, S., Chan, K.: A quantitative model-independent method for global sensitivity analysis of model output source. Technometrics Arch. **41**(1), 39–56 (1999)
8. Sobol, I.M.: Sensitivity estimates for nonlinear mathematical models. Math. Model. Comput. Exp. **1**(1993), 407–414 (1993)
9. Sobol, I.M.: Global sensitivity indices for nonlinear mathematical models and their Monte Carlo estimates. Math. Comput. Simul. **55**(1–3), 271–280 (2001)
10. Sellier, J.M.: GNU Archimedes. www.gnu.org/software/archimedes. Accessed 11 February 2014

Balancing of Systematic and Stochastic Errors in Monte Carlo Algorithms for Integral Equations

Ivan Dimov, Rayna Georgieva, and Venelin Todorov(✉)

IICT, Bulgarian Academy of Sciences, Acad. G. Bonchev 25 A, 1113 Sofia, Bulgaria
{idimov,rayna}@parallel.bas.bg, dvespas@mail.bg

Abstract. The problem of balancing of both systematic and stochastic error is very important when Monte Carlo algorithms are used. A Monte Carlo method for integral equations based on balancing of systematic and stochastic errors is presented. An approach to the problem of controlling the error in non- deterministics methods is presented. The problem of obtaining an optimal ratio between the number of realizations N of the random variable and the mean value k of the number of steps in each random trajectory is discussed. Lower bounds for N and k are provided once a preliminary given error is given. Meaningful numerical examples and experiments are presented and discussed. Experimental and theoretical relative errors are presented. Monte Carlo algorithms with various initial and transition probabilities are compared. An almost optimal Monte Carlo algorithm is discussed and it is proven that it gives more reliable results.

1 Introduction

The Monte Carlo method is a powerful tool in many fields of mathematics, physics and engineering. It is known that the algorithms based on this method give statistical estimates for the functional of the solution by performing random sampling of a certain random variable whose mathematical expectation is the desired functional.

In general, Monte Carlo numerical algorithms may be divided into two classes: direct and iterative algorithms. The direct algorithms contain only a stochastic error. For example, evaluating integrals can be performed by direct Monte Carlo algorithms. Iterative Monte Carlo algorithms deal with an approximate solution obtaining an improved solution with each iteration of the algorithm. In principle, they require an infinite number of iterations to obtain the exact solution, but usually an approximation with k significant figures is satisfactory. Iterative algorithms are preferred for solving integral equations and large sparse systems of algebraic equations (such as those arising from approximations of partial differential equations). In the latter case there are two errors - stochastic and systematic. The systematic error depends both on the number of iterations performed and the characteristic values of the iteration operator, while the stochastic errors depend on the probabilistic nature of the algorithm. In order to

I. Dimov et al. (Eds.): NMA 2014, LNCS 8962, pp. 44–51, 2015.
DOI: 10.1007/978-3-319-15585-2_5

obtain good results the stochastic error r_N must be approximately equal to the systematic error r_k that is

$$r_N = O(r_k).$$

The problem of balancing of the errors is closely connected with the problem of obtaining an optimal ratio between the number of realizations N of the random variable and the mean value k of the number of steps in each random trajectory [3]. The problem of balancing of both systematic and stochastic error is very important when Monte Carlo algorithms are used. The balancing of errors (both, systematic and stochastic) allows to get an approximation of the quantity of interest in the most efficient way by fixing the number of samples N and the number of iterations k if the error is fixed.

2 Monte Carlo Algorithms

2.1 Monte Carlo Method for Integral Equations

We study the Fredholm integral equation of the second kind:

$$u(x) = \int_{\Omega} k(x, x') u(x')\, dx' + f(x) \text{ or } u = \mathcal{K}u + f, \tag{1}$$

where

$$x, x' \in \Omega \subset \mathbb{R}^d,\ u(x), f(x) \in L_2(\Omega),\ k(x, x') \in L_2(\Omega \times \Omega)$$

and $\mathcal{K}$ is the integral operator. We want to construct a Monte Carlo algorithm to evaluate the linear functional from the solution, denoted by the following expression:

$$J(u) = \int \varphi(x) u(x) dx = (\varphi, u). \tag{2}$$

We assume that $\varphi(x) \in L_2(\Omega)$. We construct a Monte Carlo method for integral equations based on discrete Markov chains. Define a set of permissible densities:

$$\pi(x),\ p(x, x') :\ \pi(x) \geq 0,\ p(x, x') \geq 0,$$

$$\int_{\Omega} \pi(x)\, dx = 1,\ \int_{\Omega} p(x, x')\, dx' = 1,\ x \in \Omega \subset \mathbb{R}^d.$$

In correspondance with the initial and transition probabilities we define a discrete Markov chain $T_k : x_0 \to x_1 \to \cdots \to x_k$ [4] with length k started from the initial state x_0. Let $u^{(0)} \equiv f$ is the approximate initial solution. It is well known that a Monte Carlo algorithm for integral equations is given by the following expressions [7]:

$$E\theta_k[\varphi] = \left(\varphi, u^{(k)}\right),\ \theta_k[\varphi] = \frac{\varphi(x_0)}{\pi(x_0)} \sum_{j=0}^{k} W_j f(x_j),$$

$$W_0 = 1,\ W_j = W_{j-1} \frac{k(x_{j-1}, x_j)}{p(x_{j-1}, x_j)},\ j = 1, \ldots, k,$$

$$\left(\varphi, u^{(k)}\right) \approx \frac{1}{N}\sum_{n=1}^{N} \theta_k[\varphi]_n.$$

2.2 A Probabilistic Error Estimate

The probabilistic error is $r_N \le 0.6745\sigma(\theta)\dfrac{1}{\sqrt{N}}$ [4], where N is the number of the realizations of the random variable θ and $\sigma(\theta) = (D\theta)^{1/2}$ is the standard deviation of the random variable θ for which $E\theta_k[\varphi] = \left(\varphi, u^{(k)}\right) = \sum_{j=0}^{k}(\varphi, \mathcal{K}^{(j)} f)$, where for point $x = (x_0, \ldots, x_j) \in G \equiv \Omega^{j+1} \subset \mathbb{R}^{d(j+1)}$, $j = 1, \ldots, k$:

$$(\varphi, \mathcal{K}^{(j)} f) = \int_\Omega \varphi(x_0)\mathcal{K}^{(j)} f(x_0) dx_0$$

$$= \int_G \varphi(x_0)k(x_0, x_1)\ldots k(x_{k-1}, x_j) f(x_j) dx_0 dx_1 \ldots dx_j = \int_G F(x)dx,$$

where

$$F(x) = \varphi(x_0)k(x_0, x_1)\ldots k(x_{k-1}, x_j) f(x_j),\ \ x \in G \subset \mathbb{R}^{d(j+1)}.$$

Taking into account that $D\sum_{j=0}^{k}\theta_k^{(j)} \le \left(\sum_{j=0}^{k}\sqrt{D\theta_k^{(j)}}\right)^2$, and using the variance properties we have the following inequalities [5]:

$$r_N \le \frac{0.6745}{\sqrt{N}}\sum_{j=0}^{k}\left(\int_G \left(\mathcal{K}^{(j)}\varphi f\right)^2 p dx - \left(\int_G \mathcal{K}^{(j)}\varphi f p dx\right)^2\right)^{1/2}$$

$$\le \frac{0.6745}{\sqrt{N}}\sum_{j=0}^{k}\left(\int_G \left(\mathcal{K}^{(j)}\varphi f\right)^2 p dx\right)^{1/2} = \frac{0.6745}{\sqrt{N}}\|\varphi\|_{L_2}\|f\|_{L_2}\sum_{j=0}^{k}\left\|\mathcal{K}^{(j)}\right\|_{L_2}.$$

In this case the estimate simply involves the L_2 norm of the integrand. Finally, we obtain the following estimate for the probable error:

$$r_N \le \frac{0.6745\|f\|_{L_2}\|\varphi\|_{L_2}}{\sqrt{N}\left(1 - \|\mathcal{K}\|_{L_2}\right)}.$$

2.3 A Systematic Error Estimate

Consider the sequence $u^{(1)}$, $u^{(2)}, \ldots,$ defined by the recursion formula $u^{(k)} = \mathcal{K}u^{(k-1)} + f, k = 1, 2, \ldots$. The formal solution of the Eq. (1) is the truncated Neumann series $u^{(k)} = f + \mathcal{K}f + \cdots + \mathcal{K}^{(k-1)} f + \mathcal{K}^{(k)} u^{(0)}, k > 0$, where $\mathcal{K}^{(k)}$ means the kth iteration of $\mathcal{K}$, $u^{(k)} = \sum_{i=0}^{k-1}\mathcal{K}^{(i)} f + \mathcal{K}^{(k)} u^{(0)}$.

We define the k - residual vector of the systematic error $r^{(k)}$: $r^{(k)} = f - (I - \mathcal{K})\, u^{(k)} = (I - \mathcal{K})\left(u - u^{(k)}\right)$.

By the definition of $r^{(k)}$: $r^{(k)} = f - u^{(k)} + \mathcal{K}u^{(k)} = u^{(k+1)} - u^{(k)}$ and $r^{(k+1)} = u^{(k+2)} - u^{(k+1)} = \mathcal{K}u^{(k+1)} + f - \mathcal{K}u^{(k)} - f = \mathcal{K}\left(u^{(k+1)} - u^{(k)}\right) = \mathcal{K}r^{(k)}$.

We have $r^{(0)} = u^{(1)} - u^{(0)} = \mathcal{K}u^{(0)} + f - u^{(0)} = \mathcal{K}f$, $r^{(k+1)} = \mathcal{K}r^{(k)} = \mathcal{K}^{(2)}r^{(k-1)} = \cdots = \mathcal{K}^{(k+1)}r^{(0)}$.

So we obtain $u^{(k+1)} = u^{(k)} + r^{(k)} = u^{(k-1)} + r^{(k-1)} + r^{(k)} = \cdots = u^{(0)} + r^{(0)} + \cdots + r^{(k)} = u^{(0)} + r^{(0)} + \mathcal{K}r^{(0)} + \mathcal{K}^{(2)}r^{(0)} + \cdots + \mathcal{K}^{(k)}r^{(0)} = u^{(0)} + \left(I + \mathcal{K} + \cdots + \mathcal{K}^{(k)}\right) r^{(0)}$ [1].

If $\|\mathcal{K}\|_{L_2} < 1$ then the Neumann series $u = \sum_{i=0}^{\infty} \mathcal{K}^{(i)} f$ is convergent and $u^{(k+1)} \xrightarrow{k\to\infty} u$. Therefore, from $u^{(k+1)} = u^{(0)} + \left(I + \mathcal{K} + \cdots + \mathcal{K}^{(k)}\right) r^{(0)}$ and $k \to \infty$ we have $u = u^{(0)} + (I - \mathcal{K})^{-1} r^{(0)}$. After simple transformations $u = \mathcal{K}u + f = \mathcal{K}u^{(0)} + \mathcal{K}(I - \mathcal{K})^{-1} r^{(0)} + f = u^{(1)} + \mathcal{K}(I - \mathcal{K})^{-1} r^{(0)}$.

After k iterations one obtains: $u = u^{(k)} + \mathcal{K}^{(k)}(I - \mathcal{K})^{-1} r^{(0)}$. Using the Cauchy-Schwarz inequality:

$$r^{(k)} = \left\| u - u^{(k)} \right\|_{L_2} \leq \frac{\|\mathcal{K}\|_{L_2}^{k} \left\|r^{(0)}\right\|_{L_2}}{1 - \|\mathcal{K}\|_{L_2}} \leq \frac{\|\mathcal{K}\|_{L_2}^{k} \|f\|_{L_2} \|\mathcal{K}\|_{L_2}}{1 - \|\mathcal{K}\|_{L_2}} = \frac{\|\mathcal{K}\|_{L_2}^{k+1} \|f\|_{L_2}}{1 - \|\mathcal{K}\|_{L_2}}.$$

Finally, we obtain the following estimate for the systematic error:

$$\left|(\varphi, u) - \left(\varphi, u^{(k)}\right)\right| \leq \|\varphi\|_{L_2} \left\| u - u^{(k)} \right\|_{L_2} \leq \frac{\|\varphi\|_{L_2} \|f\|_{L_2} \|\mathcal{K}\|_{L_2}^{k+1}}{1 - \|\mathcal{K}\|_{L_2}}.$$

3 Balancing of the Errors

3.1 Error Balancing Conditions

Let δ be the preliminary given error to solve the problem under consideration (2). We suppose that

$$r_N \leq \frac{0.6745 \|\varphi\|_{L_2} \|f\|_{L_2}}{\sqrt{N}\left(1 - \|\mathcal{K}\|_{L_2}\right)} \leq \frac{\delta}{2}, \quad r_k \leq \frac{\|\varphi\|_{L_2} \|f\|_{L_2} \|\mathcal{K}\|_{L_2}^{k+1}}{1 - \|\mathcal{K}\|_{L_2}} \leq \frac{\delta}{2}.$$

Theorem 1. *For a Fredholm integral equation (1) the lower bounds for N and k for the Monte Carlo algorithm with a balancing of the errors are:*

$$N \geq \left(\frac{1.349 \|\varphi\|_{L_2} \|f\|_{L_2}}{\delta\left(1 - \|\mathcal{K}\|_{L_2}\right)} \right)^2, \quad k \geq \frac{\ln \frac{\delta\left(1 - \|\mathcal{K}\|_{L_2}\right)}{2\|\varphi\|_{L_2} \|f\|_{L_2} \|\mathcal{K}\|_{L_2}}}{\ln \|\mathcal{K}\|_{L_2}}.$$

The proof of the two inequalities leads directly from the above assumption where the probable and systematic errors are bounded by the half of the preliminary given error. In addition to that, we can obtain an optimal ratio between k and N by using the theorem:

Corollary 1. *For a Fredholm integral equation (1) the lower bounds for N and k for the Monte Carlo algorithm with a balancing of the errors are:*

$$N \geq \left(\frac{1.349 \|\varphi\|_{L_2} \|f\|_{L_2}}{\delta \left(1 - \|\mathcal{K}\|_{L_2}\right)} \right)^2, \quad k \geq \frac{\ln \dfrac{0.6745}{\|\mathcal{K}\|_{L_2} \sqrt{N}}}{\ln \|\mathcal{K}\|_{L_2}}.$$

In fact, the two obtained lower bounds for k are equivalent if N is equal to the smallest natural number for which the first inequality in the theorem holds because in this case one can easily see that the estimate for the systematic error is smaller than the estimate for the probable error and the corollary follows directly.

4 Numerical Examples and Results

To illustrate the balancing of errors we give two examples representing Fredholm integral equation of the second kind.

4.1 Example 1

The first example is:

$$u(x) = \int_{\Omega} k(x, x') u(x') \, dx' + f(x),$$

$\Omega \equiv [0,1]$, $k(x, x') = \frac{1}{6} e^{x+x'}$, $f(x) = 6x - e^x$, $\varphi(x) = \delta(x)$. The exact solution is $u(x) = 6x$. We would like to find the solution in just one point - the middle of the interval. In order to apply the theorem we evaluate the L_2 norms: $\|\varphi\|_{L_2} = 1$, $\|\mathcal{K}\|_{L_2} = 0.5324$, $\|f\|_{L_2} = 1.7873$. Our Monte Carlo algorithm starts from $x_0 = 0.5$ so the exact solution is 3 and $\pi(x) = \delta(x)$. We make 20 algorithm runs on Intel Core i5-2410M @ 2.3 GHz.

In Table 1 we present different values for δ and estimates of N and k by the theorem are presented. The values of N and k are set to the smallest possible natural numbers for which the inequalities in the theorem hold.

We compare Monte Carlo methods with various transition probabilities. The initial probability is the δ - function. First, we choose the transition probabilities to be constant functions and after that we choose them to be proportional to the kernel. The latter choice of the transition probabilities leads to an Almost Optimal Monte Carlo (MAO) algorithm [2].

The first two columns with the expected relative error and the computational time measured in seconds are for the case when the transition probabilities are constant functions and the last two columns are for the case when MAO is used. One can easily see that the latter method gives better results.

We can see the comparison between the expected relative error and the experimental relative error for the two Monte Carlo algorithms on Fig. 1. It directly leads that experimental relative error confirms the expected relative error.

Table 1. Relative error and computational time for the first example with the balancing of errors (different transition probabilities).

δ	N	k	Expected rel. error	Experimental rel. error	Time (sec.)	Experimental rel. error	Time (sec.)
0.1	2659	6	0.0333	0.0137	11	0.0132	5
0.03	29542	8	0.01	0.0039	62	0.0036	42
0.02	66468	9	0.0067	0.0022	140	0.0020	70
0.0075	472659	10	0.0025	0.001	1167	9.3671e-04	529
0.007	542593	11	0.00233	6.9639e-04	1562	6.3582e-04	614
0.005	1063482	11	0.00167	6.4221e-04	4412	6.2479e-04	2202

4.2 Example 2

We study the following example taken from neuron networking:

$$u(x) = \int_{\Omega} k(x, x')u(x')\, dx' + f(x),$$

$\Omega \equiv [-2, 2]$, $k(x, x') = \dfrac{0.055}{1 + e^{-3x}} + 0.07$, $f(x) = 0.02\left(3x^2 + e^{-0.35x}\right)$, $\varphi(x) = 0.7((x + 1)^2 \cos(5x) + 20)$.

We want to find (φ, u), where $\varphi(x) = 0.7((x + 1)^2 \cos(5x) + 20)$. The exact solution is 8.98635750518 [6]. This integral equation describes the procedure of teaching of neuron networks. In order to apply the theorem we evaluate the L_2 norms:

$\|\varphi\|_{L_2} = 27.7782$, $\|\mathcal{K}\|_{L_2} = 0.2001$, $\|f\|_{L_2} = 0.2510$. The L_2 norm of the kernel is smaller than this in the previous example, so we can expect that smaller values of k will be needed to obtain the balancing of the errors. We make 20 algorithm runs on Intel Core i5-2410M @ 2.3 GHz.

In Tables 2 and 3 we give δ different values and estimates N and k by the theorem. The values of N and k are set in the same way as in the first example.

We compare Monte Carlo method with various initial and transition probabilities. The first two columns with the expected relative error and computational time in seconds, are for the case when the initial and transition probabilities are constant functions and the last two columns are for MAO algorithm.

One can easily see that the MAO gives much better results than the Monte Carlo algorithm with constant probabilities for larger values of N and k. For smaller values the Monte Carlo algorithm with constant probabilities gives better results, but the results obtained with MAO are closer to the expected theoretical error. Using MAO we see that experimental relative error confirms the expected relative error. We also see that in the MAO algorithm the computational time is bigger because we use the acceptance-rejection method for modelling the initial probability. In our example this is not necessary for the transition probabilities because the kernel is a function of only one variable and

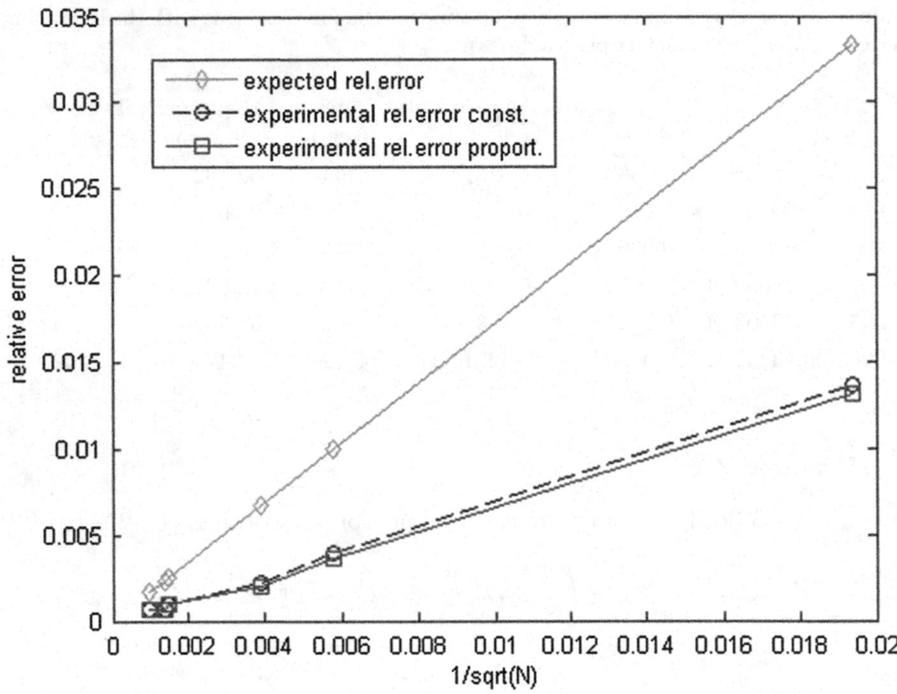

Fig. 1. Experimental and expected relative error.

Table 2. Relative error and computational time for the third example with the balancing of errors (constant probabilities).

δ	N	k	Expected relative error	Experimental relative error	Time (sec.)
0.4	865	2	0.0445	0.0397	3
0.2	3457	2	0.0223	0.0396	12
0.1	13827	3	0.0111	0.0025	23
0.05	55306	3	0.00556	0.0021	100
0.028	176357	3	0.00312	0.0022	260

when we set the transition probability to be proportional to the kernel we obtain that it is equal to a constant function.

To summarize, we can see that in the case when the initial probability is different from δ - function MAO gives much better results than the Monte Carlo with constant probabilities, and in the case when the initial probability is δ - function the above two methods give closer results but again MAO has the edge as expected.

Table 3. Relative error and computational time for the third example with the balancing of errors (different initial and transition probabilities).

δ	N	k	Expected rel. error	Experimental rel. error	Time (sec.)	Experimental rel. error	Time (sec.)
0.4	865	3	0.0445	0.0052	3	0.0239	5
0.2	3457	4	0.0223	0.0094	9	0.0121	23
0.1	13827	4	0.0111	0.0113	28	0.0086	46
0.05	55306	5	0.00556	0.0177	132	0.0032	222
0.028	176357	5	0.00312	0.0176	448	0.0031	540
0.02	345659	6	0.00233	0.0202	901	0.0013	1090

5 Conclusion

Monte Carlo method based on balancing of the systematic error and probability error is presented. Lower bounds for N and k are obtained. Numerical examples and results are discussed. Monte Carlo algorithms with various initial and transition probabilities are compared. Experimental relative errors confirm expected theoretical errors. Monte Carlo algorithms with probabilities chosen to be proportional to the function from the linear functional under consideration and the kernel, respectively, give more reliable results.

Acknowledgments. This work was supported by the Bulgarian National Science Fund under the grant FNI I 02/20 Efficient Parallel Algorithms for Large-Scale Computational Problems.

References

1. Curtiss, J.H.: Monte Carlo methods for the iteration of linear operators. J. Math. Phys. **32**, 209–232 (1954)
2. Dimov, I.: Minimization of the probable error for some Monte Carlo methods. In: Proceedings of International Conference on Mathematical Modeling and Scientific Computation, Albena, Bulgaria, Sofia, Publishing House of the Bulgarian Academy of Sciences, pp. 159–170 (1991)
3. Dimov, I.: Monte Carlo Methods for Applied Scientists, 291 p. World Scientific, London (2008)
4. Dimov, I., Atanassov, E.: What Monte Carlo models can do and cannot do efficiently? Appl. Math. Model. **32**, 1477–1500 (2007)
5. Dimov, I., Karaivanova, A.: Error analysis of an adaptive Monte Carlo method for numerical integration. Math. Comput. Simul. **47**, 201–213 (1998)
6. Georgieva, R.: Computational complexity of Monte Carlo algorithms for multidimensional integrals and integral equations. Ph.D thesis, Sofia (2003)
7. Sobol, I.: Numerical Methods Monte Carlo. Nauka, Moscow (1973)

Metaheuristics for Optimization Problems

Slot Machines RTP Optimization with Genetic Algorithms

Todor Balabanov(✉), Iliyan Zankinski, and Bozhidar Shumanov

Institute of Information and Communication Technologies,
Bulgarian Academy of Sciences, acad. G. Bonchev Str, Block 2, 1113 Sofia, Bulgaria
todorb@iinf.bas.bg
http://www.iict.bas.bg/

Abstract. Slot machine RTP optimization problem is usually solved by hand adjustment of the symbols placed on the game reels. By controlling the symbols distribution, it is possible to achieve the desired return to player percent (RTP). Some other parameters can also be adjusted (for example, the free spins frequency or the bonus game frequency). In this paper RTP optimization automation, based on genetic algorithms, is proposed.

Keywords: Slot machines · RTP · Genetic algorithms · Optimization

1 Introduction

Slot machines are electronic gambling devices that offer wide variety of games. They are mainly found at casinos and some bars. Slot machines are relatively inexpensive to be run compared to the roulette, blackjack or poker, that is why they have become a very popular and a very profitable form of gambling. The game consists of three or five reels which spin when the button is pushed. The game pays off according to the patterns of symbols visualized on the screen after the spin stop. The main scope of this paper is related with the symbols distribution on the machine reels. On each reel there are ordered symbols (usually represented by numbers in mathematical models). The order, in which the symbols are presented on the reel, is of discrete probability distribution. According to the symbols distribution, different winning combinations can appear on the game screen. The mathematicians, who develop slot machine reels, have the task to select such discrete probability distribution, which will produce a certain RTP. The value of RTP (return to player) is calculated by division of the money won by the money lost, multiplied by one hundred. The RTP value is very important for slot machine vendors, because this is the main gambling game parameter which is under government regulation. The RTP value has the mathematical meaning of an expected value. Another interesting parameter of the slot machine games is volatility, but this parameter is not discussed in this study, because it is rarely taken into account in government regulations. The approach proposed for symbols discrete distribution optimization can be very appropriate for mathematicians who are working on the design of new slot gambling games.

I. Dimov et al. (Eds.): NMA 2014, LNCS 8962, pp. 55–61, 2015.
DOI: 10.1007/978-3-319-15585-2_6

2 Slot Machine Reels

In this section a brief review of the basic concepts of the slot machines and of the game reels in particular will be given.

The slot machines are based on the concept of spin reels. At the beginning the slot reels were mechanical and the spin of the reels was done by a manual pull of the game handle. Nowadays most of the slot machines are computerized and the game reels are only virtual, so that the stops are selected by Random Number Generator, RNG (for more information refer to [1]). In most of the games five independent reels are presented, but there are also variants with three or more than five reels. After the push button is hit, the reels start a spin and one by one each reel stops. The winning of the player is calculated according to the combinations of symbols presented on the screen. Each game has its own pay table, which is visible for the player usually on a separate screen. Some symbols are presented on the reels more often than others. Less frequent symbols form less often winning combinations and hence, the winning for the player is bigger.

The main characteristic of each slot machine is the RTP percentage. This parameter is calculated by the ratio between the won and the lost money, multiplied by one hundred. The RTP can be from 80 % in Las Vegas up to 98 % in some EU state members. For example, the fruit machines in the United Kingdom are obliged by a law to pay out a minimum percentage within a short period of time [2]. Usually the RTP is above 90 %. In order to achieve the desired RTP, the mathematicians and the game designers are working in collaboration to populate game reels with proper symbols in a proper discrete distribution (for more information refer to [3]).

3 Genetic Alghorithms

Genetic algorithms (GAs) are search heuristic algorithms inspired by the process of natural selection [4,5]. GAs are routinely used to select points (candidate solutions) from the solutions space. By application of the techniques for inheritance (crossover), mutation and selection, the generated solutions get closer to the optimum. GAs are classified also as population based algorithms because each point in the solution space represents an individual inside the GA population. Each individual has a set of properties which are subject to mutation and modification (usually a crossover). The traditional representation of the properties is binary, as a sequence of zeros and ones, but other encodings are also possible (a binary tree for example).

The optimization usually starts with a randomly generated population of individuals, but this may vary across implementations. The optimization process is iterative and the population in each iteration is called generation. A fitness value is calculated for each individual of the generation. The fitness value usually represents the objective function which is subject to optimization. The fittest individuals in the population are selected (according to a selection rule) and recombined (crossover and/or mutation) to form a new generation. This new generation is used at the next iteration of the algorithm. The algorithm termination is usually achieved either by reaching the maximum number of generations or by reaching the desired level of the fitness value.

In order to run GAs, the researcher should provide: 1. Genetic representation of the solution space (the solution domain); 2. An appropriate fitness function to evaluate the solution domain. Once these two conditions are met, GAs can proceed with the population initialization and the iterative population improvement by repetitive application of the selection, crossover, mutation and individuals evaluation.

4 The Model Proposed

In the model proposed every individual consists of slot machine symbols (given as numbers), distributed on the reels. Each symbol on the reels is represented by a single integer number in such a way, that the symbol and its position on the reel are significant. The solution domain is finite and discrete. Each position in each reel must be a single integer number from the list of possible game symbols.

The population initialization is usually done by random generation, but the model proposed in this paper uses initial reels configuration in order to initialize the population. The initialization is done by the addition of random noise to the initial reels configuration (see [6] for more details). The population size is a subject of experimental estimation and may vary from several individuals to hundreds or thousands of individuals.

During the selection process the individuals are selected according to their fitness value. Some selection methods prefer the best individuals, but other methods just take a random subset of the population. The fitness function is problem dependent and it is defined over the genetic representation as a measure of the quality of the solution represented. In the model proposed, the absolute difference between the desired RTP and the obtained RTP is used as a fitness function. Monte-Carlo simulation is used for the RTP obtained in order to estimate the slot machine performance in 100 000 or 1 000 000 separate runs. The rule of elitism is also applied so that the best individual would survive among the generations.

For the crossover operation a pair of parent individuals are selected (individuals that are part of the selected population subset). A single point cut is used in order to recombine the attributes of the first and the second parent, in order to create the child individual. Additional research is needed to determine whether it is better to use more than two individuals as parents. After the crossover, a mutation is applied over the child. The mutation is realized by random selection of the symbol, changed by another randomly selected symbol.

As a termination criterion the maximum number of the generations is used and also manual observation/termination of the process is implemented. The final solution, found by GA, is an integer vector. This vector is directly used as slot machine symbols distribution. For example, if there is a slot game with 5 reels (visible on the screen as 5 columns and 3 rows), and on each reel 63 symbols are available, the final GA solution would be an integer vector of 5×63 values (refer to [6] for more details).

Table 1. Slot machine pay table. Each column represents the winning of one particular symbol (9 possible symbols in this game). The sixth row shows the winning of the symbols when the combination is of 5 symbols, the fifth row shows the winning for a combination of 4 symbols, and so on.

0	0	0	0	0	0	0	0	0
0	0	0	0	0	0	0	0	0
0	0	0	0	0	0	0	0	2
15	10	10	8	8	5	5	4	3
70	40	25	20	18	15	12	10	10
750	400	300	200	180	150	120	100	75

5 Experiments and Results

The experiments have been done with non-commercial slot machine (5 reels with 3 symbols visible on the screen for each of the reels) with a particular pay table and combination lines. The game has a pay table shown in (Table 1) which is valid for five winning lines shown in (Table 2). All winning combinations are paid from left to right. The lowest winning is 2 for a combination of 2 symbols (the last column, row 3 of Table 1). The highest winning is 750 - for a combination of 5 symbols (the first column, the last row of Table 1). The model of the slot machine considered has 9 symbols which can form winning combinations on the screen. The slot game pay table is presented in this way in order to use the row indices as a number of the symbols on a particular winning line. For example, if there is a winning line consisting of 4 symbols of symbol type 3 on the screen, this means that the winning for this combination is 25 (third column, fifth row). All experiments were done with elitism rule, a population size of 17, a maximum number of generations 213, and one million separate simulation game runs accomplished in ten separate sessions for the fitness value estimation. The crossover probability is about 90 %. The mutation probability is 100 % and only one value in the chromosome is changed. More information about GA parameters can be found in [6]. As initial reels distribution, handmade reels with 90.88 % RTP have been used.

It is visible that GA convergence is pretty fast and in about 51 generations, the optimal goal is achieved (Fig. 1 - Target RTP 90 %). Because of the discrete nature of the process, the optimization is done in separate steps, visible in generations 6, 8, 15, 19, 31 and 51. In the second experiment, the target RTP of 91 % is very close to the initial RTP and the convergence is with small steps around the 15-th generation and the 67-th generation (Fig. 1 - Target RTP 91 %). The third experiment has a target RTP of 92 % and it is obvious how the optimization process follows (Fig. 1 - Target RTP 92 %). A few steps have been done in generations 7, 15, 41, 55, 63 and 71. In some of the cases (Fig. 1 - Target RTP 93–99%) it is interesting to point the initial difference from the target percent with respect to the 97 % target RTP optimization (an initial difference of more than 5) and the 99 % target RTP

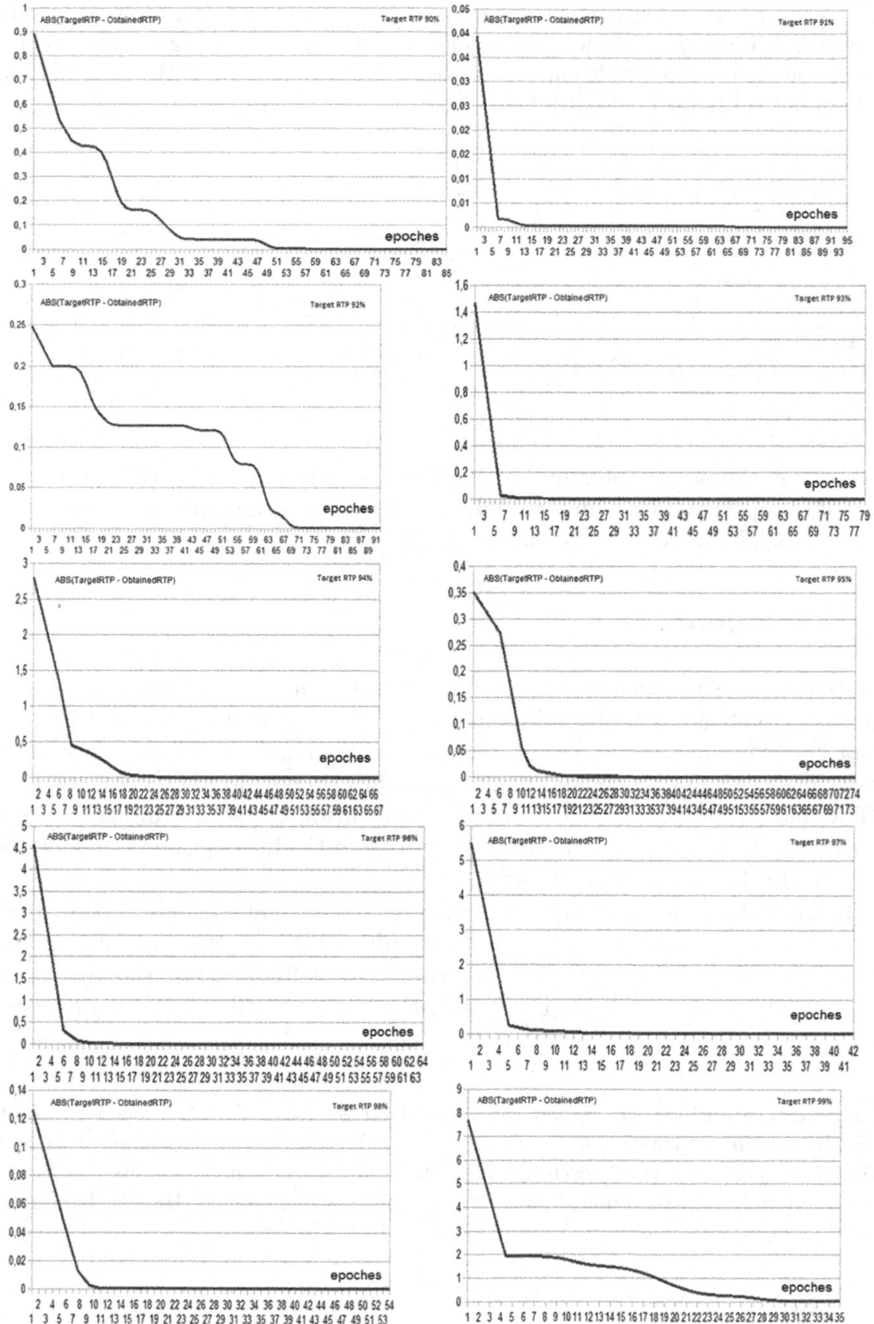

Fig. 1. GA convergence for different target RTPs. On the axes: x is the number of generations, y ABS (TargetRTP-ObtainedRTP).

Table 2. Slot machine winning combinations. The first row shows that symbols must be presented on the middle row of the game screen (the top row has index 0, the middle row has index 1 and the bottom row has index 2). The second winning line is presented in the second row (all symbols must be positioned in the top row of the game screen) and so on for third, forth and fifth line.

1	1	1	1	1
0	0	0	0	0
2	2	2	2	2
0	1	2	1	0
2	1	0	1	2

optimization (an initial difference of almost 8). The initial difference for the 98 % target RTP optimization is much smaller, because in each experiment the initial difference is calculated after the first generation.

6 Conclusions

All experiments show that using GA may be very efficient and improve the slot games development by better adjustment of RTP. As already shown (Fig. 1) in half of the experiments the convergence was very fast, while in the other half - slower. These results are related to the probabilistic nature of GA.

The main disadvantage of GA based optimization is the time of fitness value calculation. In the slot reels optimization problem the fitness value is calculated by relatively slow game simulations.

The biggest advantage of GA based optimization is the possibility to optimize more than one parameter. In this study only RTP has been optimized, but considering multicriteria optimization, the symbol frequencies, the free spins frequency, the bonus game frequency and the game volatility can be optimized as well.

Acknowledgements. This research is supported by AComIn "Advanced Computing for Innovation", Grant 316087, sponsored by FP7 Capacity Programme, Research Potential of Convergence Regions (2012–2016), the European Social Fund and the Republic of Bulgaria, the Operational Programme Development of Human Resources 20072013, Grant BG051PO001-3.3.06-0048 from 04.10.2012.

References

1. Brysbaert, M.: Algorithms for randomness in the behavioral sciences: a tutorial. Behav. Res. Methods Instrum. Comput. **22**(1), 45–60 (1991)

2. Parke, J., Griffiths, M.: The psychology of the fruit machine: the role of structural characteristics (revisited). In: Paper Presented at the Annual Conference of the British Psychological Society, Surrey, England (2001)
3. Osesa, N.: Bitz and Pizzas optimal stopping strategy for a slot machine bonus game. OR Insight **22**, 31–44 (2009)
4. Eiben, A.E: Genetic algorithms with multi-parent recombination. In: PPSN III: Proceedings of the International Conference on Evolutionary Computation. The Third Conference on Parallel Problem Solving from Nature, pp. 78–87 (1994). ISBN 3-540-58484-6
5. Ting, C.-K.: On the mean convergence time of multi-parent genetic algorithms without selection. In: Capcarrère, M.S., Freitas, A.A., Bentley, P.J., Johnson, C.G., Timmis, J. (eds.) ECAL 2005. LNCS (LNAI), vol. 3630, pp. 403–412. Springer, Heidelberg (2005)
6. Balabanov, T: Slot Genetic Algorithm. http://drive.google.com/file/d/0Bz5a6NKy7qNiYi1jS01ZVnFOV1U

Hierarchical Topology in Parallel Differential Evolution

Petr Bujok(✉)

Department of Informatics and Computers, Faculty of Computer Science, University of Ostrava, 30. dubna 22, 70103 Ostrava, Czech Republic
petr.bujok@osu.cz

Abstract. A new differential evolution (DE) algorithm with a parallel hierarchical topology (HDE) is proposed. The main goal of the paper is to study how the performance of the algorithm is influenced by the use of parallel migration model. The hierarchical model has several control parameters and the influence of these parameters setting is also studied. The performance of HDE algorithm is compared with non-parallel DE algorithm on CEC2013 benchmark suite. Experimental results show that the HDE outperforms the non-parallel DE algorithm significantly in 27 out of 28 test problems.

Keywords: Differential evolution · Parallel model · Hierarchical topology · CEC2013 benchmark suite

1 Introduction

In a lot of fields of research and industry there are problems that need to be optimized. Such optimization can be performed by several methods. In the case of problems where analytical solutions are not possible, biologically inspired optimization algorithms are often able to find an acceptable solution. A major group of biologically inspired algorithms are evolutionary algorithms (EA), which are typified by using randomization and thus can be successful in problems where a deterministic solution is not possible.

Optimization is generalized to search the global minimum of the problem, which is simply defined (1). The global minimization problem is formed as follows:

$$\text{minimize } f(\boldsymbol{x}), \ \ \boldsymbol{x} \in \Omega, \ f(\boldsymbol{x}) : \Omega \rightarrow \mathbb{R}, \ \Omega \subseteq \mathbb{R}^D, \tag{1}$$

where $f(\boldsymbol{x})$, $\boldsymbol{x} = (x_1, x_2, \ldots, x_D)$ is the real-value objective function and D is the dimension of the problem.

The search space is boundary-constrained (2) for many continuous problems, i.e. the domain Ω is defined by:

$$\Omega = \prod_{i=1}^{D} [a_i, b_i], \ \ a_i < b_i \ . \tag{2}$$

I. Dimov et al. (Eds.): NMA 2014, LNCS 8962, pp. 62–69, 2015.
DOI: 10.1007/978-3-319-15585-2_7

The aim of this paper is to study the influence of migration in hierarchical parallel model on the performance of DE algorithm. The increase of search performance is crucial in very hard problems that are defined by the CEC2013 test suite [6]. Any possible improvement of the search speed is important for getting an acceptable solution in reasonable time. That is why the influence of migration in EA is worth studying. This paper is not focused on physical parallel implementation but on the influence of migration in a hierarchical model. Thus, comparative experiments are carried out on a single-processor PC in a pseudo-parallel mode.

The paper is organized in the following manner. General ideas of differential evolution algorithm with pseudo-code are described in Sect. 2. The description of the parallel models used in EA is summarized in Sect. 3. The novel DE algorithm is presented in Sect. 4. Settings of experiments are given in Sect. 5. The results of the novel algorithm on CEC 2013 problems are depicted in Sect. 6 and some conclusions are made in Sect. 7.

2 Differential Evolution

Differential evolution (DE) proposed by Storn and Price [11] is a population-based optimization algorithm for single-objective problems with a real-valued objective function [9]. Possible solutions in DE are represented as vectors with real-number components, $\boldsymbol{x} = (x_1, x_2, \ldots, x_D)$, D is the dimension of the problem. The population is placed in the search space $\Omega = \prod_{j=1}^{D}[a_j, b_j]$, $a_j < b_j$, $j = 1, 2, \ldots, D$ and evolves during the search to the state of higher fitness. The solution of the problem is the global minimum point $\boldsymbol{x}^*$ satisfying condition $f(\boldsymbol{x}^*) \leq f(\boldsymbol{x})$, $\forall \boldsymbol{x} \in \Omega$.

The population of the size N is developed step-by-step from generation P to generation Q. The evolutionary operators, i.e. mutation, crossover, and selection, are applied in the development of generation Q. A new trial point is created from a mutant point $\boldsymbol{u}$ generated by using a kind of mutation and from the current point of the population by the application of the crossover. Better point from the couple of $\{\boldsymbol{x}_i, \boldsymbol{y}\}$, based on the value of the objective function, is selected to the new generation Q.

The DE algorithm has been studied intensively in recent period. A comprehensive summary of recent results in DE research is available in [8] and [5]. Several kinds of mutation and crossover were suggested as well as some adaptive or self-adaptive DE variants. The aim of the paper is to apply a hierarchical parallel model with the standard DE algorithm to achieve higher performance.

3 Parallel Differential Evolution

Three standard parallel models are typically used in parallel EAs: *master-slave*, *diffusion* and *migration*. More details of the models can be observed in [4,7]. When the migration model is considered, the interconnection among islands called *topology* [1,10] is an important feature influencing the performance of the algorithm. The migration models with various topologies were also applied in parallel DE [2,3,12,13].

3.1 Hierarchical Approach

Performance of the parallel models depends on several mentioned control parameters, particularly on the topology. The topology defines interconnection of the independent parts of the population, which is typically divided in the parallel models. Commonly used topologies in distributed computing are only with one level (ring, net topologies) or with two levels (star topology). These topologies applied in the DE environment were compared in [1,2]. The aim is to use more than two levels of independent development, which can increase the performance of DE algorithm. A hierarchical topology has more than two levels and it is similar to a tree topology. Some applications of a hierarchical topology in EA are in [14,15].

4 Proposed Hierarchical Algorithm

A hierarchical topology with more than two levels is applied to standard DE algorithm. Two different settings of hierarchical approach in a parallel DE algorithm are depicted in Fig. 1. Both variants of hierarchical DE (HDE) algorithm have three levels: low, middle and high level. The DE algorithm starts at the low level, where many small sub-populations are situated. After several generations individuals are selected from the low level, they fill several sub-populations at the middle level. After some DE generations at the middle level are selected individuals that are placed into one high level sub-population. The difference between the two proposed HDE algorithms is the algorithm illustrated on the left performs one 'low-to-high' round whereas the algorithm on the right performs many rounds. The first variant ('*One-Way*' abbreviated) uses only one way communication, from the lower level to the higher level. In the second variant ('*Both-Way*' abbreviated) the communication is performed in both ways, i.e. from the lower to higher level and from the highest to the lowest level. A pseudo-code of the 'One-Way' HDE algorithm is depicted in Algorithm 1. At first, k sub-populations are uniformly initialized at the low-level of the model.

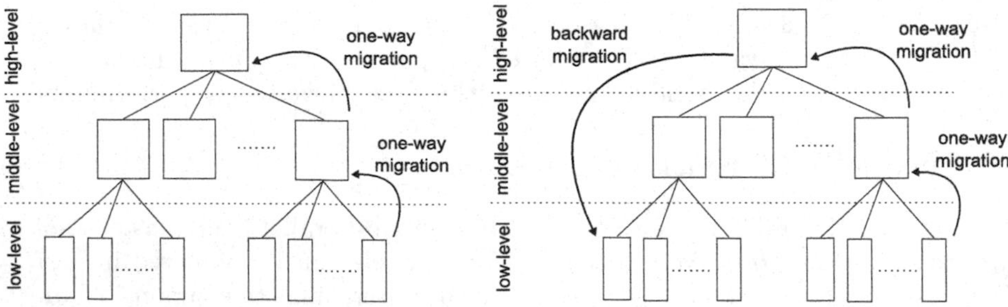

Fig. 1. Topology with three levels of independent development and with 'one-way' (left) or 'both-way' (right) migration.

Algorithm 1. Hierarchical One-Way Differential Evolution Algorithm

```
initialize sub-populations P_L, L = 1, 2, ... k
for each low-level sub-population do
  perform llg generations of each low-island by DE
end for
migrate selected individuals from low to middle level
for each middle-level sub-population do
  perform mlg generations of each middle-island by DE
end for
migrate selected individuals from middle to high level
while stopping condition not reached do
  develop high-level sub-population by DE
end while
```

All sub-populations are independently evolved by a standard DE algorithm during several generations. The development of the low-level sub-populations stops if the difference between the best and the worst function value is less than ε_{ll} or the number of generations is llg at the most. The best individuals from the low-level sub-populations are inserted to the sub-populations at the middle level. The middle level sub-populations are developed until the difference between the best and the worst function value is less than ε_{ml} or for mlg generations at most. The best individuals are selected in the middle-level and inserted to the high-level sub-population. The development of the high-level sub-population stops when the total number of the function values reaches the predetermined limit. The 'Both-Way' HDE in a pseudo-code is presented in Algorithm 2. At the beginning k sub-populations are uniformly initialized at the low-level. The sub-populations are evolved by standard DE until the difference between the best and the worst function value is less than ε_{ll} or for llg generations at the most. Then the best individuals of the low-level sub-populations are selected and inserted to the middle-level sub-populations. The development of the middle-level sub-populations runs until the difference between the best and the worst

Algorithm 2. Hierarchical Both-Way Differential Evolution Algorithm

```
initialize sub-populations P_L, L = 1, 2, ... k
while stopping condition not reached do
  for each low-level sub-population do
    perform llg generations of each low-island by DE
  end for
  migrate selected individuals from low to middle level
  for each middle-level sub-population do
    perform mlg generations of each low-island by DE
  end for
  migrate selected individuals from middle to high level
  perform hlg generations of each high-island by DE
end while
```

function value is less than ε_{ml} or for mlg generations at the most. Then the best points are selected from the middle-level and placed into the high-level sub-population. The high-level sub-population is developed for hlg generations or until the difference between the best and the worst function value is less than ε. Then the second part of the migration is performed. The best individuals are selected from the high-level sub-population and they are moved back into all of the low-level sub-populations. The remaining parts of the low-level sub-populations are initialized and then the development continues.

5 Experiments

Experimental setting follows the requirements given in the report [6], where 28 minimization problems with search range $[-100, 100]^D$ are defined. We can expect that this test suite will become one of the most relevant benchmark required for publishing new single-objective optimization algorithms. The algorithms are implemented in Matlab 2010a and all computations were carried out on a standard PC with Windows 7, Intel(R) Core(TM)2 CPU 6320, 1.86 GH 1.87 GH, 2 GB RAM.

The tests were carried out at the level of dimension, $D = 30$, 51 repeated runs per the test function. The run of the algorithms stops if the number of the function values reaches the prescribed value $D \times 10^4 = 3 \times 10^5$. The values of the function error less than 1×10^{-8} are treated as zero in further processing because such a value of the error is considered sufficient for an acceptable approximation of the current solution.

The number of low-level sub-populations was set to $k = 100$ (for both HDE) and the size of the sub-populations for all levels was set to $N_p = 10$. It results in the total population size $N = 1000$, that is initialized. The population size for non-parallel DE was the same, i.e. $N = 1000$. The non-parallel DE algorithm uses '*DE/randrl/1/bin*' strategy and the control parameters $F = 0.8$ and $CR = 0.8$. HDE algorithms use the same strategy with *randrl* mutation and *binomial* crossover. The control parameters F and CR for HDE are combined from the values $F = [0.4, 0.5, 0.6, 0.7, 0.8]$ and $CR = [0, 0.1, 0.2, 0.3, 0.4, 0.5, 0.6, 0.7, 0.8, 0.9]$ in such a way that they form 50 couples of $\{F, CR\}$. Each low-level sub-population has one pair of the values $\{F, CR\}$. The middle-level sub-populations take only every fifth couple out of the 50 couples used at the low-level. The high-level sub-population takes the values from $\{F, CR\}$ randomly. The number of the best individuals copied from the high-level to the low-level is 5. The maximal number of generations for 'One-Way' HDE is set $llg = 50$ and $mlg = 2000$. For the 'Both-Way' HDE these parameters are set $llg = 20$, $mlg = 200$ and $hlg = 2000$. The remaining HDE parameters are set $\varepsilon_{ll} = 0.1$, $\varepsilon_{ml} = 0.01$ and $\varepsilon = 1 \times 10^{-8}$.

6 Results

The complete results of non-parallel DE and two HDE algorithms are depicted in Table 2, where the best and the worst values, the mean and the median

Table 1. Comparison of Algorithm Performance by Kruskal-Wallis Test.

F	Best	2nd best	Worst	p-value
1	Both-Way, One-Way		DE	0.000000
2	Both-Way	One-Way	DE	0.000000
3	One-Way, Both-Way		DE	0.000000
4	Both-Way	One-Way	DE	0.000000
5	Both-Way	One-Way	DE	0.000000
6	One-Way, Both-Way		DE	0.000000
7	One-Way	Both-Way	DE	0.000000
8	DE	One-Way	Both-Way	0.000000
9	One-Way, Both-Way		DE	0.000000
10	Both-Way	One-Way	DE	0.000000
11	One-Way, Both-Way		DE	0.000000
12	One-Way, Both-Way		DE	0.000000
13	One-Way, Both-Way		DE	0.000000
14	One-Way	Both-Way	DE	0.000000
15	Both-Way	One-Way	DE	0.000000
16	Both-Way	One-Way	DE	0.000068
17	One-Way	Both-Way	DE	0.000000
18	Both-Way	One-Way	DE	0.000000
19	One-Way, Both-Way		DE	0.000000
20	Both-Way	One-Way	DE	0.000002
21	Both-Way, One-Way		DE	0.000000
22	One-Way	Both-Way	DE	0.000000
23	Both-Way	One-Way	DE	0.000000
24	One-Way	Both-Way	DE	0.000000
25	One-Way	Both-Way	DE	0.000000
26	One-Way	Both-Way	DE	0.000000
27	One-Way, Both-Way		DE	0.000000
28	One-Way	Both-Way	DE	0.000000
DE	1	0	27	
One-Way	8	10	0	
Both-Way	9	8	1	

values and the standard deviations are computed from 51 runs for each of 28 problems. A robust comparison is given in Table 1, where results of the Kruskal-Wallis statistical test are to be found. Bellow this table are the counts of the separate wins (and second and third place) for each of the algorithms. We can observe in the 'Best' column that the HDE algorithms perform significantly better than the non-parallel DE in the most of the CEC 2013 test problems. Only in the case of problem $F8$, the HDE variants are outperformed by non-parallel DE. The performance of the HDE algorithms is very similar in most problems. The time consumption caused by parallelism was measured on three functions (unimodal $F1$, multimodal $F11$ and composition $F22$). It was found that the increase of time consumption due to migration in parallel algorithms is negligible compared to the time burden of the function evaluations.

Table 2. Results for $D = 30$.

	DE					One-Way HDE					Both-Way HDE				
F	Best	Worst	Median	Mean	Std	Best	Worst	Median	Mean	Std	Best	Worst	Median	Mean	Std
1	3601.62	5551.63	4800.51	4700.71	419.338	1.02E-07	3.32E-03	1.38E-05	2.46E-04	6.63E-04	8.99E-07	7.3E-04	6.38E-05	1.08E-04	1.51E-04
2	8.29E+07	2.22E+08	1.77E+08	1.71E+08	3.02E+07	200942	1.89E+06	658471	744611	366087	224940	3.24E+06	1.18E+06	1.28E+06	620904
3	1.47E+10	2.7E+10	2.28E+10	2.22E+10	2.68E+09	354555	1.03E+08	1.89E+07	2.48E+07	2.41E+07	147065	1.1E+08	1.21E+07	2.04E+07	2.27E+07
4	46422.1	88578.7	71604.8	70659.2	8681.84	361.308	5158.64	1121.29	1431.67	976.604	711.35	7257.43	2216.92	2509.07	1340.27
5	268.3	380.134	339.051	331.542	30.9724	6.35E-07	2.46E-03	1.52E-04	3.92E-04	5.74E-04	3.15E-05	4.93E-03	7.73E-04	1.2E-03	1.19E-03
6	304.324	475.335	396.691	390.953	38.291	15.5684	80.0683	16.5797	25.3721	19.8145	14.8079	29.1838	16.7327	17.8782	3.21394
7	107.903	150.798	131.887	132.593	9.50139	15.9236	70.5053	29.2281	31.7466	11.5651	4.85197	47.5617	19.5351	21.8303	10.7848
8	20.7853	21.0222	20.9554	20.9469	5.48E-02	20.7338	21.1105	21.0051	20.9974	6.2E-02	20.8511	21.0447	20.956	20.9642	4.21E-02
9	37.4208	41.6637	39.3993	39.3079	1.00508	13.5672	33.3474	27.1861	25.7345	5.14426	15.4553	31.7739	24.443	23.9064	4.48867
10	769.443	1368.78	1177.62	1179.48	120.598	3.53E-02	6.57E-01	2.18E-01	2.69E-01	1.7E-01	5.02E-02	1.39051	4.34E-01	5.15E-01	3.15E-01
11	212.719	290.172	269.912	266.829	14.1586	6.32E-07	3.97984	9.95E-01	1.08988	1.0707	5.37E-05	2.98577	9.95E-01	6.95E-01	7.34E-01
12	275.866	331.922	314.57	310.302	14.9351	30.8441	131.337	67.6571	69.7118	25.0143	33.8936	90.4471	64.0185	63.4454	11.0568
13	266.278	345.239	313.231	310.232	16.2713	48.2148	177.087	108.602	111.811	32.3431	55.9903	147.501	107.648	108.622	18.7605
14	6087.09	7110.64	6729.99	6694.33	268.008	5.38357	155.8	31.4029	39.9993	34.4463	1.39594	147.324	14.6633	20.279	22.0824
15	6604.38	7813.7	7393.24	7343.73	281.869	2950.23	6152.43	4172.04	4217.233	762.332	3754.99	6698.03	5438.03	5366.98	602.277
16	1.70271	2.9483	2.40509	2.43265	2.6E-01	1.16544	3.17991	2.03882	2.10693	4.54E-01	1.49287	2.80433	2.27746	2.26963	3.03E-01
17	508.741	709.994	629.68	630.1124	36.1681	30.8907	34.3771	32.0057	32.1467	8.38E-01	30.466	33.0938	30.9895	31.0638	4.63E-01
18	536.328	693.962	633.712	630.728	40.1224	61.8073	158.597	104.153	105.415	22.0827	142.601	204.124	172.789	171.049	14.5508
19	177.754	857.209	485.643	460.978	149.684	1.38247	2.85813	2.1021	2.07646	3.66E-01	1.35404	2.44827	2.05881	2.00137	2.58E.01
20	12.6303	13.7237	13.4328	13.3724	2.32E-01	11.3614	15	14.5373	14.1492	1.0744	11.4713	15	15	14.8031	7.2E-01
21	1431	1948.6	1738.14	1735.52	86.9899	200	443.544	300.002	294.822	86.5614	200	443.551	300.006	314.6298	101.128
22	6043.33	7471.3	7041.04	7028.39	248.216	31.6648	268.706	145.843	145.825	39.503	23.9542	297.195	134.19	131.198	42.287
23	6645.47	8151.93	7596.73	7581.09	278.157	3094.21	5639.53	4064	4183.01	610.674	2892.21	6328.15	5236.47	5120.89	622.935
24	292.757	310.552	304.83	304.47	3.28261	214.167	280.726	251.249	249.853	17.7791	208.28	273.698	234.067	235.41	14.0852
25	311.919	327.943	322.425	321.856	3.27453	251.297	306.495	282.78	281.118	10.1783	250.487	288.326	269.987	270.829	11.3379
26	208.231	222.253	215.758	215.966	3.02812	200.032	352.398	200.087	203.086	21.326	200.021	200.255	200.068	200.077	4.44E-02
27	1264.33	1368.83	1330.61	1326.2	26.8724	612.186	1112.48	944.453	927.558	134.494	592.646	1129.38	881.147	899.160	95.5671
28	1773.7	2204.93	2092.37	2085.2	75.9944	300	300.43	300.019	300.055	8.05E-02	100.219	300.016	300.002	296.086	27.9754

7 Conclusion

In this paper two novel algorithms are proposed and compared with a reasonable non-parallel DE algorithm. Based on the comparison given by the CEC 2013 benchmark problems the HDE algorithms performs better in most of the test problems. The comparison shows that the results of the HDE algorithms with standard non-adaptive DE variants are not able to outperform all adaptive DE in the case of the CEC 2013 test problems. Promising results of the HDE variants indicate that a hierarchical approach have a considerable potential.

Acknowledgments. This work was supported by the University of Ostrava from the project SGS15/PřF/2014.

References

1. Bujok, P.: Parallel models of adaptive differential evolution based on migration process. In: Aplimat, 10th International Conference on Applied Mathematics, pp. 357–364, Bratislava (2011)
2. Bujok, P.: Synchronous and asynchronous migration in adaptive differential evolution algorithms. Neural Netw. World **23**(1), 17–30 (2013)
3. Bujok, P., Tvrdík, J.: Parallel migration model employing various adaptive variants of differential evolution. In: Rutkowski, L., Korytkowski, M., Scherer, R., Tadeusiewicz, R., Zadeh, L.A., Zurada, J.M. (eds.) EC 2012 and SIDE 2012. LNCS, vol. 7269, pp. 39–47. Springer, Heidelberg (2012)
4. Cantu-Paz, E.: A survey of parallel genetic algorithms. http://neo.lcc.uma.es/cEA-web/documents/cant98.pdf (1997)
5. Das, S., Suganthan, P.N.: Differential evolution: a survey of the state-of-the-art. IEEE Trans. Evol. Comput. **15**, 27–54 (2011)
6. Liang, J.J., Qu, B., Suganthan, P.N., Hernandez-Diaz, A.G.: Problem definitions and evaluation criteria for the CEC 2013 special session on real-parameter optimization (2013). http://www.ntu.edu.sg/home/epnsugan/
7. Nedjah, N., Alba, E., de Macedo Mourelle, L.: Parallel Evolutionary Computations. Studies in Computational Intelligence. Springer, New York (2006)
8. Neri, F., Tirronen, V.: Recent advances in differential evolution: a survey and experimental analysis. Artif. Intell. Rev. **33**, 61–106 (2010)
9. Price, K.V., Storn, R., Lampinen, J.: Differential Evolution: A Practical Approach to Global Optimization. Springer, Heidelberg (2005)
10. Ruciński, M., Izzo, D., Biscani, F.: On the impact of the migration topology on the island model. Parallel Comput. **36**, 555–571 (2010)
11. Storn, R., Price, K.V.: Differential evolution - a simple and efficient heuristic for global optimization over continuous spaces. J. Glob. Optim. **11**, 341–359 (1997)
12. Tasoulis, D.K., Pavlidis, N., Plagianakos, V.P., Vrahatis, M.N.: Parallel differential evolution. In: IEEE Congress on Evolutionary Computation (CEC), pp. 2023–2029 (2004)
13. Weber, M., Tirronen, V., Neri, F.: Scale factor inheritance mechanism in distributed differential evolution. Soft Comput. Fusion Found. Methodol. Appl. **14**(11), 1187–1207 (2010)
14. Wu, S.X., Banzhaf, W.: A hierarchical cooperative evolutionary algorithm. In: Proceedings of the 12th Annual Conference on Genetic and Evolutionary Computation, GECCO 2010, pp. 233–240. ACM, New York (2010)
15. Zaharie, D., Petcu, D., Panica, S.: A hierarchical approach in distributed evolutionary algorithms for multiobjective optimization. In: Lirkov, I., Margenov, S., Waśniewski, J. (eds.) LSSC 2007. LNCS, vol. 4818, pp. 516–523. Springer, Heidelberg (2008)

On Meme Self-Adaptation in Spatially-Structured Multimemetic Algorithms

Rafael Nogueras and Carlos Cotta(✉)

Dept. Lenguajes y Ciencias de la Computación, ETSI Informática, Universidad de Málaga, Campus de Teatinos, 29071 Malaga, Spain
ccottap@lcc.uma.es

Abstract. Multimemetic algorithms (MMAs) are memetic algorithms that explicitly exploit the evolution of memes, i.e., non-genetic expressions of problem-solving strategies. We consider a class of MMAs in which these memes are rewriting rules whose length can be fixed during the run of the algorithm or self-adapt during the search process. We analyze this self-adaptation in the context of spatially-structured MMAs, namely MMAs in which the population is endowed with a certain topology to which interactions (from the point of view of selection and variation operators) are constrained. For the problems considered, it is shown that panmictic (i.e., non-structured) MMAs are more sensitive to this self-adaptation, and that using variable-length memes seems to be a robust strategy throughout different population structures.

1 Introduction

Memetic algorithms [8] are a pragmatic integration of population-based global search techniques and trajectory-based local search techniques [6]. They rest on the notion of *meme* [2], which within this optimization context translates to computational problem-solving procedures. While different possibilities have been defined in the literature, such procedures are usually local-search techniques. Furthermore, they are often fixed or pre-defined and therefore the MA can be regarded as operating with static implicit memes. This fact notwithstanding, the explicit management of memes has been around for some time now – cf. [7] –, and can be found in, e.g., multimemetic algorithms (MMAs) [5]. Therein, each solution carries memes determining the way self-improvement is conducted. Such memes are themselves subject to evolution and hence conform a self-adaptive search approach.

While early population-based algorithms often used a panmictic approach, whereby any two solutions within the population could interact for reproductive purposes, more general population structures have been in use in the last decades – see e.g. [1,4]. However, the deployment of such structures on MMAs has been less explored. Some steps to fill this gap were firstly taken in [9], in which an idealized model of spatially-structured MMAs was defined, hinting at

I. Dimov et al. (Eds.): NMA 2014, LNCS 8962, pp. 70–77, 2015.
DOI: 10.1007/978-3-319-15585-2_8

the usefulness of spatial structures in this context (the slower convergence of the population buying time for good memes to express themselves). These findings have been also validated elsewhere on actual MMAs using fixed-length memes. Here we turn our attention to the use of memes of self-adaptive complexity in combination with spatially structured populations, analyzing comparatively their effectiveness in this context. To do so, let us firstly define the particular multimemetic scenario we have considered. This is done next.

2 Multimemetic Approach

As mentioned above, the core idea of MMAs is the explicit treatment of memes within the evolutionary process. Hence, we shall firstly describe the representation of memes, before getting into the deployment of spatial structure on MMAs.

2.1 Meme Representation and Self-Adaptation

Memes are taken to be non-genetic expressions of problem-solving strategies and as such can be represented in many ways depending on the level of abstraction and problem dependance considered. Following some ideas posed by Smith [10] in the context of pseudoboolean function optimization, we consider in this work memes expressed as pattern-based rewriting rules [*condition*→*action*] as follows: let $[C \rightarrow A]$ be a meme, where $C, A \in \Sigma^r$ with $\Sigma = \{0, 1, \#\}$ and $r \in \mathbb{N}$. In this ternary alphabet '#' represents a wildcard symbol; now, let $g_1 \cdots g_n$ be a genotype; a meme $[C \rightarrow A]$ could be applied on any genotypic substring into which the condition $C = c_1 \cdots c_r$ fits, i.e., for which $g_i \cdots g_{i+r-1} = c_1 \cdots c_r$ (for the purpose of this comparison, wildcard symbols in the condition match any symbol in the genotype). If the meme were to be applied on position i, its action would be to implant the action $A = a_1 \cdots a_r$ in that portion of the genotype, i.e., letting $g_i \cdots g_{i+r-1} \leftarrow a_1 \cdots a_r$ (in this case, the interpretation of wildcard symbols is as don't-change symbols, that is, keeping unchanged the corresponding symbol in the genotype). In order to avoid positional bias, the order in which the genotype is scanned to check for potential meme application sites is randomized. If a match is found the meme is applied and the resulting neighboring genotype is evaluated. A parameter w determining the maximal number of meme applications per individual is used to keep the total cost of the process under control. The best neighbor generated throughout the precess is kept if it is better than the current genotype.

The main advantage of having memes linked to individuals is giving the algorithm the ability to discover appropriate neighborhoods definitions for the corresponding solution, so as to effectively exploring neighboring points. Such neighborhoods can evolve alongside solutions, providing a self-adaptive means to boost the search by means of this dynamic definition of the local improvement mechanism. This self-adaptation is not limited to the actual definition of the neighborhood for a certain fixed *radius* (i.e., Hamming distance) but can also involve this radius itself. To do so, the length r of the meme is defined within a certain interval $\{l_{\min}, \cdots, l_{\max}\}$. Initially, each meme has a random length in that range. Subsequently, in each evolutionary step before a certain meme is going to be mutated and then applied, its length can be incremented or decremented by one much like in [10]. This is done with a certain probably p_r (in the case of increasing the meme length, a new random symbol is appended in the rightmost position; if the length is decreased the rightmost symbol in the meme is removed). By doing so, the length of the rewriting rule can be dynamically adjusted by evolutionary means, thus providing a self-adaptive control of its complexity: long memes are powerful tools for performing large jumps in the search space but, on the other hand, they are more specific and hence can have lower applicability. It is up to the algorithm to discover the appropriate meme complexity in each moment.

2.2 Spatial Structure

The spatial structure of the population can be regarded as a topological structure upon which individuals in the population are projected. More precisely, let T be this topological structure, comprising μ sites (μ being the population size), each of them identified by an index $i \in \{1, \cdots, \mu\}$. We can characterize this structure using a Boolean $\mu \times \mu$ matrix S. Each entry S_{ij} represents the interaction potential between two sites in the structure. More precisely, let S_{ij}= `true` if, and only if, the individual at the i-th site can interact with the individual at the j-th site.

In this work we consider interaction matrices induced by a particular spatial arrangement of individual sites in a grid: let $\mu = a \times b$; each site i can then be represented by a pair of coordinates $(i_x, i_y) \in \{1, \cdots, a\} \times \{1, \cdots, b\}$. Now, let $d : (\{1, \cdots, a\} \times \{1, \cdots, b\})^2 \to \mathbb{N}$ be a distance measure between sites. Given a certain neighborhood radius ρ, we take $S_{ij} \Leftrightarrow (d(i,j) \leqslant \rho)$, i.e., two sites can interact if they are within a certain distance threshold. Different spatial structures arise from the use of alternative distance measures. We have considered the following possibilities:

1. Panmixia: $d(\cdot, \cdot) = 0$.
2. Moore neighborhood: $d((i_x, i_y), (j_x, j_y)) = \max(|i_x - j_x|, |i_y - j_y|)$.
3. von Neumann neighborhood: $d((i_x, i_y), (j_x, j_y)) = |i_x - j_x| + |i_y - j_y|$.

The above operations are modulo coordinate ranges so as to make them toroidal. Figure 1 illustrates these spatial structures.

3 Experimental Analysis

In order to analyze the impact of meme self-adaptation on the MMAs described in previous section we have considered two pseudoboolean optimization problems. These are described in Sect. 3.1; subsequently we shall analyze the results in Sect. 3.2.

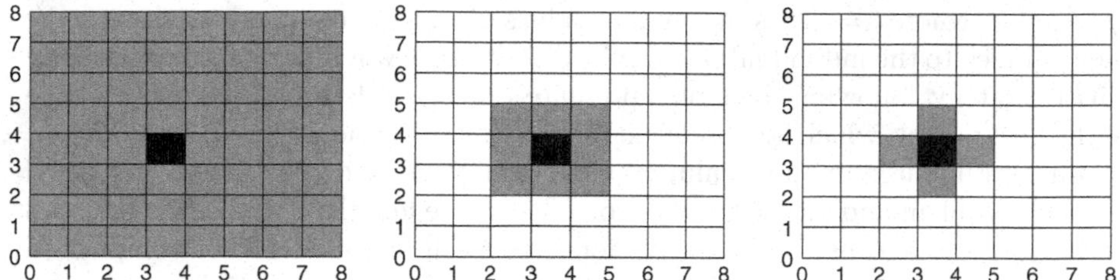

Fig. 1. Illustration of the different neighborhoods considered. The black cell indicates an arbitrary individual and the grey cells denotes its neighbors. From left to right: panmictic, Moore and von Neumann. In the last two cases, $\rho = 1$.

3.1 Benchmark and Settings

The functions considered in the test suite are Deb's trap function [3] (TRAP) and Watson et al.'s hierarchical if-and-only-if function [12] (HIFF). These are defined as follows. Consider firstly the TRAP function. A basic 4-bit trap is defined as

$$f_{trap}(b_1 \cdots b_4) = \begin{cases} 0.6 - 0.2 \cdot u(b_1 \cdots b_4) & \text{if } u(b_1 \cdots b_4) < 4 \\ 1 & \text{if } u(b_1 \cdots b_4) = 4 \end{cases} \quad (1)$$

where $u(s_1 \cdots s_i) = \sum_j s_j$ is the unitation (number of 1 s in a binary string) function. A higher-order problem can be built by concatenating k such traps, and defining the fitness of a $4k$-bit string as the sum of the fitness contribution of each block. In our experiments we use $k = 32$ subproblems (i.e., 128-bit strings, $opt = 32$).

As to the HIFF function, it is a recursive epistatic function based of the interaction of increasingly large building blocks. It is defined for binary strings of 2^k bits by using two auxiliary functions $f : \{0, 1, \times\} \to \{0, 1\}$ (to score the contribution of building blocks), and $t : \{0, 1, \times\} \to \{0, 1, \times\}$ (to capture their interaction), where '$\bullet$' denotes a *null* value. These are defined as:

$$f(a, b) = \begin{cases} 1 & a = b \neq \bullet \\ 0 & \text{otherwise} \end{cases} \qquad t(a, b) = \begin{cases} a & a = b \\ \bullet & \text{otherwise} \end{cases}$$

These two functions are combined as follows:

$$\text{HIFF}_k(b_1 \cdots b_n) = \sum_{i=1}^{n/2} f(b_{2i-1}, b_{2i}) + 2 \cdot \text{HIFF}_{k-1}(b'_1, \cdots, b'_{n/2}) \quad (2)$$

where $b'_i = t(b_{2i-1}, b_{2i})$ and $\text{HIFF}_0(\cdot) = 1$. We have considered $k = 7$ (i.e., 128-bit strings, $opt = 576$).

We consider MMAs as described in Sect. 2, with a population size of $\mu = 100$ individuals. These MMAs follow a generational reproductive plan with binary tournament for parent selection, one-point crossover ($p_X = 1.0$), bit-flip mutation

($p_M = 1/\ell$, where $\ell = 128$ is the number of bits), local-search (conducted using the meme linked to the individual) and replacement of the worst parent (an inherently elitist strategy, following the model presented in [9]). Offspring inherit the meme of the best parent, which is subsequently subject to mutation with probability p_M. A run is terminated upon reaching 25,000 evaluations, and 20 runs are performed for each problem and algorithm. We consider meme lengths bounded by $l_{\min} = 3$ and $l_{\max} = 9$, and use $p_r = 1/l_{\max}$ for length self-adaptation. For comparison purposes we also consider fixed-length memes ($r \in \{3, 6, 9\}$). Spatially structured MMAs consider a 10×10 grid and a neighborhood radius $\rho = 1$.

3.2 Experimental Results

The numerical results of the different MMAs are shown in Table 1. Qualitatively, panmictic MMAs (regardless of meme lengths) seem to perform comparatively worse than the corresponding Moore/von Neumann versions, thus supporting the positive impact that the slower convergence induced by the latter spatial structures has on the final results. This is further supported by the slight superiority of the MMA with von Neumann topology over the MMA with Moore topology, which has a faster convergence rate, both at the genotypic and the memetic level – see Fig. 2.

Let us now focus on the effect of meme lengths. If we firstly observe the results of using fixed-length memes, it seems that the intermediate value $r = 6$ offers the best tradeoff between memetic richness and meme specificity among the values considered. This offers a first gauge to the way meme lengths self-evolve. Indeed,

Table 1. Results (20 runs) of the different MMAs on the two problems considered. The number of time the optimum is found (n_{opt}), the median ($\tilde{x}$), the mean ($\bar{x}$) and the standard error of the mean (σ_x) are indicated.

Topology	r	TRAP			HIFF		
		n_{opt}	$\tilde{x}$	$\bar{x} \pm \sigma_x$	n_{opt}	$\tilde{x}$	$\bar{x} \pm \sigma_x$
Panmictic	3	5	30.4	29.5 ± 0.5	1	390.0	404.1 ± 14.9
	6	9	30.4	29.6 ± 0.5	4	382.0	420.3 ± 20.4
	9	3	28.4	28.7 ± 0.5	2	362.0	382.0 ± 16.6
	3–9	8	29.0	29.2 ± 0.6	8	456.0	475.3 ± 20.8
Moore	3	8	31.2	30.4 ± 0.4	5	444.0	460.0 ± 17.0
	6	10	31.2	30.0 ± 0.5	8	456.0	476.4 ± 19.7
	9	7	29.8	29.8 ± 0.4	6	456.0	449.0 ± 21.4
	3–9	11	32.0	30.8 ± 0.4	7	460.0	471.8 ± 19.5
von Neumann	3	6	30.8	30.1 ± 0.5	9	464.0	501.0 ± 16.9
	6	13	32.0	30.9 ± 0.4	12	576.0	518.4 ± 17.0
	9	10	31.8	30.4 ± 0.4	9	464.0	491.7 ± 18.6
	3–9	15	32.0	31.2 ± 0.3	12	576.0	515.6 ± 18.1

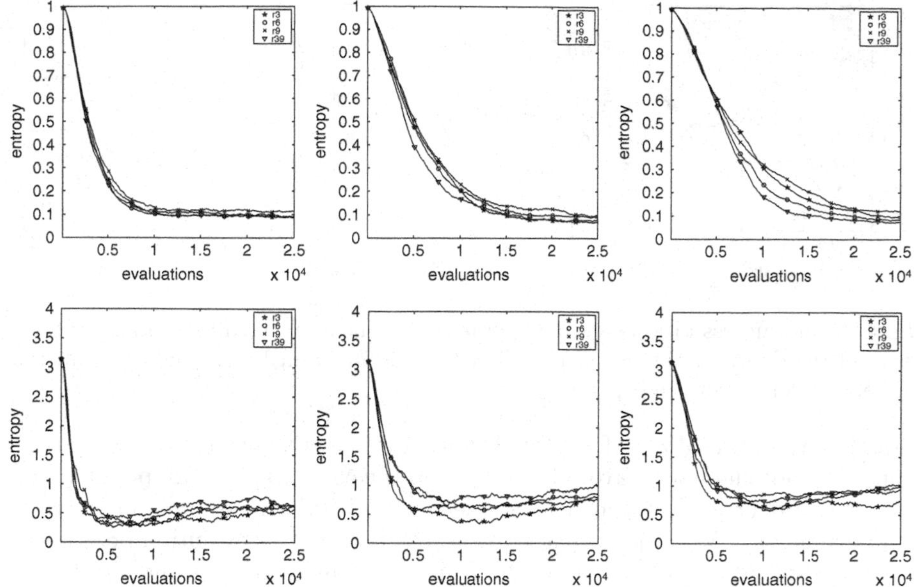

Fig. 2. Evolution of diversity of the different MMAs on the TRAP function. The top row corresponds to genetic diversity and the bottom row to memetic diversity. From left to right: panmictic, Moore, and von Neumann topology.

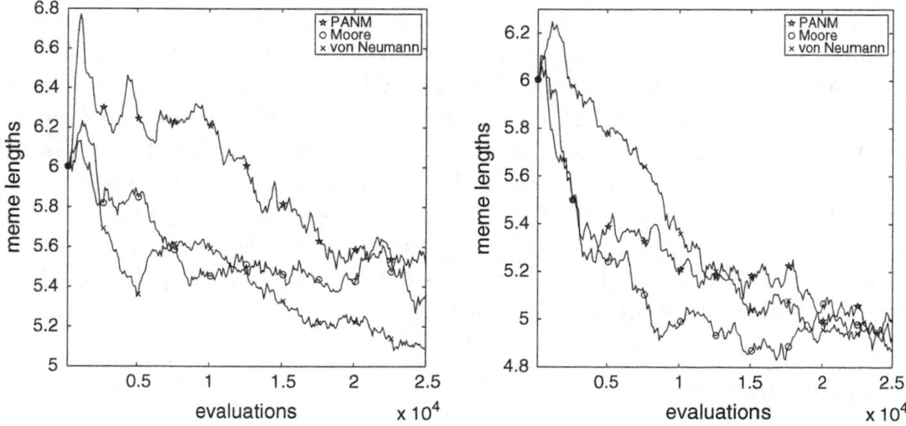

Fig. 3. Evolution of meme lengths in self-adaptive MMAs with different topology. (Left) TRAP. (Right) HIFF.

if we take a look at Fig. 3 we can see that average meme lengths oscillate around values close to 6, indicating the fully self-adaptive MMA seems to be locating this area of memetic interest. This is further vindicated by the fitness results and the number of times the optimum is found (Quade test indicates that in both cases at least one algorithm performs significantly different, $\alpha = 0.05$) by each

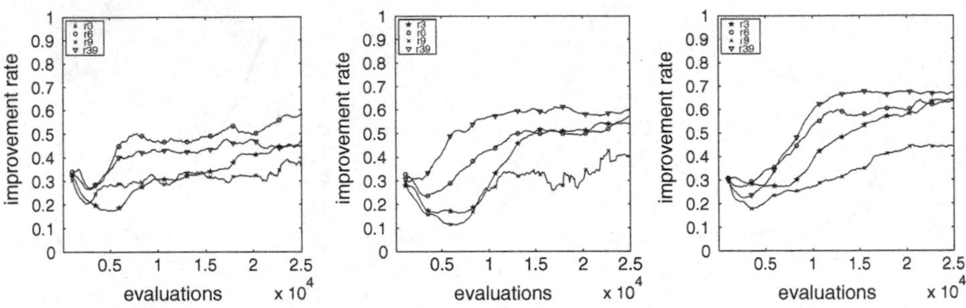

Fig. 4. Meme success ratio (percentage of meme applications resulting in an improvement) of the different MMAs on the TRAP function. From left to right: panmictic, Moore, and von Neumann topology.

algorithm: the MMA_{3-9} performs analogously or better than the MMA_6 (the difference is more marked in favor of MMA_{3-9} in the case of panmictic population). The general decreasing trend of meme lengths in this MMA_{3-9} is an interesting phenomenon. We conjecture it is due to the fact that as evolution progresses, the algorithm starts to locate optimal or near-optimal solutions and the role of memes might be changing from being a search artifact (trying to find search directions to the optimal) to function as an error-correcting mechanism (correcting perturbations introduced by mutation on already (near-)optimal solutions), i.e., their role turns from exploratory to exploitative. This interpretation is consistent with the meme success rates (percentage of meme applications that result in an improvement) shown in Fig. 4. Notice that these follow an upwards trend (and that the values for MMA_{3-9} are normally superior to the remaining MMAs, in particular for non-panmictic populations), which may be indicating this active role as the result of error correction (fitness values are rather stable in those later evolution stages, and hence a high success rate would rather be interpreted as lower-quality solutions being repaired back to known optima than to the discovery of new better solutions). The evolution of diversity also fits nicely in this picture since – as seen in Fig. 2 – the genetic diversity seems to decrease faster for the fully self-adaptive MMA (more clearly in the case of von Neumann topology), while memetic diversity stays comparatively higher.

4 Conclusions

It is well known that parameterization is a major issue in memetic algorithms [11], even more so if we consider MMAs which need additional parameters controlling meme representation. For this reason, the study of self-adaptation mechanisms alleviating this parameterization problem is of paramount interest. We have studied a class of spatially-structured MMAs featuring self-adaptation of meme lengths. The results obtained on two problems and three topologies (panmictic, Moore and von Neumann) indicate that the self-adaptation of meme lengths is not detrimental and sometimes even beneficial, although mainly in the case of panmictic population. We attribute this latter effect to the non-panmictic

MMAs being more robust to suboptimal parameterization. At any rate, self-adaptation of meme lengths globally seems an adequate strategy for the problems considered, since it does not penalize performance and saves configuration time. Needless to say, further experimentation on other problems would be useful to confirm these findings. Work is underway in this direction. Another line for future development implies the use of other population structures, as well as analyzing the scalability of the approach.

Acknowledgements. This work is partially supported by MICINN project ANYSELF (TIN2011-28627-C04-01), by Junta de Andalucía project DNEMESIS (P10-TIC-6083) and by Universidad de Málaga, Campus de Excelencia Internacional Andalucía Tech.

References

1. Collins, R.J., Jefferson, D.R.: Selection in massively parallel genetic algorithms. In: Belew, R.K., Booker, L.B. (eds.) Fourth International Conference on Genetic Algorithms, pp. 249–256. Morgan Kaufmann, San Diego (1991)
2. Dawkins, R.: The Selfish Gene. Clarendon Press, Oxford (1976)
3. Deb, K., Goldberg, D.E.: Analyzing deception in trap functions. In: Whitley, L.D. (ed.) Second Workshop on Foundations of Genetic Algorithms, pp. 93–108. Morgan Kaufmann, Vail (1993)
4. Gorges-Schleuter, M.: ASPARAGOS: an asynchronous parallel genetic optimization strategy. In: Schaffer, J.D. (ed.) Third International Conference on Genetic Algorithms, pp. 422–427. Morgan Kaufmann, San Francisco (1989)
5. Krasnogor, N., Blackburne, B.P., Burke, E.K., Hirst, J.D.: Multimeme algorithms for protein structure prediction. In: Merelo Guervós, J.J., Adamidis, P.A., Beyer, H.-G., Fernández-Villacañas, J.-L., Schwefel, H.-P. (eds.) PPSN 2002. LNCS, vol. 2439, pp. 769–778. Springer, Heidelberg (2002)
6. Moscato, P.: On evolution, search, optimization, genetic algorithms and martial arts: towards memetic algorithms. Technical Report Caltech Concurrent Computation Program, Report 826, California Institute of Technology, Pasadena, CA, USA (1989)
7. Moscato, P.: Memetic algorithms: a short introduction. In: Corne, D., Dorigo, M., Glover, F. (eds.) New Ideas in Optimization. McGraw-Hill's Advanced Topics in Computer Science Series, pp. 219–234. McGraw-Hill, London (1999)
8. Neri, F., Cotta, C., Moscato, P.: Handbook of Memetic Algorithms. Studies in Computational Intelligence, vol. 379. Springer, Heidelberg (2012)
9. Nogueras, R., Cotta, C.: Analyzing meme propagation in multimemetic algorithms: initial investigations. In: 2013 Federated Conference on Computer Science and Information Systems, pp. 1013–1019. IEEE Press, Cracow (2013)
10. Smith, J.E.: Self-adaptative and coevolving memetic algorithms. In: Neri, F., Cotta, C., Moscato, P. (eds.) Handbook of Memetic Algorithms. SCI, vol. 379, pp. 167–188. Springer, Heidelberg (2012)
11. Sudholt, D.: Parametrization and balancing local and global search. In: Neri, F., Cotta, C., Moscato, P. (eds.) Handbook of Memetic Algorithms. SCI, vol. 379, pp. 55–72. Springer, Heidelberg (2012)
12. Watson, R.A., Pollack, J.B.: Hierarchically consistent test problems for genetic algorithms: summary and additional results. In: 1999 IEEE Congress on Evolutionary Computation, pp. 292–297. IEEE Press, Washington, DC (1999)

An Ant Algorithm for the Partition Graph Coloring Problem

Stefka Fidanova[1(✉)] and Petrică C. Pop[2]

[1] Bulgarian Academy of Sciences, Sofia, Bulgaria
stefka@parallel.bas.bg

[2] Department of Mathematics and Computer Science, North University Center at Baia Mare, Technical University of Cluj-Napoca, Cluj-Napoca, Romania

Abstract. In this paper we propose an Ant Colony Optimization (ACO) algorithm for the partition graph coloring problem (PGCP). Given an undirected graph $G = (V, E)$, whose nodes are partition into a given number of the node sets. The goal of the PGCP is to find a subset $V^* \subset V$ that contains exactly one node for each cluster and a coloring for V^* so that in the graph induced by V^*, two adjacent nodes have different colors and the total number of used colors is minimal. The performance of our algorithm is evaluated on a common benchmark instances set and the computational results show that compared to a state-of-the-art algorithms, our ACO algorithm achieves solid results in very short run-times.

1 Introduction

In this paper we consider the partition graph coloring problem, denoted by PGCP. Given an undirected graph $G = (V, E)$ and a partition of its nodes into p node sets $V_1, \ldots, V_p$, the *partition graph coloring problem* consists in finding a subset $V^* \subseteq V$ containing exactly one node from each node set V_i, $i \in \{1, ...p\}$ and such that the chromatic number of the graph induced in G by V^* is minimum.

The considered problem belongs to a class of combinatorial optimization problems commonly referred to as generalized network design problems (GNDPs) or generalized combinatorial optimization problem (GCOPs). This class of problems is obtained in a natural way, generalizing many combinatorial optimization problems by considering a related problem on a clustered graph (i.e. a graph whose nodes are partitioned into node sets), where the original problem's feasibility constraints are expressed in terms of the clusters, i.e., node sets instead of individual nodes. For more information concerning to this class of optimization problems we refer to [4,11].

In the last period several generalized combinatorial optimization problems have been studied such as the generalized minimum spanning tree problem, the generalized traveling salesman problem, the generalized vehicle routing problem, the partition graph coloring problem, the generalized fixed-charge network

I. Dimov et al. (Eds.): NMA 2014, LNCS 8962, pp. 78–84, 2015.
DOI: 10.1007/978-3-319-15585-2_9

design problem, etc. All such problems belong to the class of $\mathcal{NP}$-complete problems, they are harder to solve in practice than their original counterparts and recently a lot of research is emphasized on them especially due to their interesting properties and important real-world applications in telecommunication, network design, scheduling problems, resource allocation, transportation problems, software engineering, etc.

The PGCP was introduced by Li and Simha and it was motivated by considering the joint problem of routing and assignment in wavelength division multiplexing optical networks [9]. The same authors proved that the problem is $\mathcal{NP}$-complete. Demange *et al.* [1,2] considered this type of graph coloring problem in the framework of generalized network design problems and named it selective graph coloring problem. They investigated as well some special classes of graphs including split graphs, bipartite graphs and q-partite graphs and settled the complexity status of the PGCP in these particular classes.

Due to its practical applications and its complexity, the PCGP has generated an important interest, being proposed exact and heuristic algorithms: Li and Simha [9] designed two groups of heuristic algorithms: one-step algorithms including *onestep Largest-First*, *onestep Smallest-Last* and *onestep Color-Degree* and two-steps algorithms including *twosteps Largest-First*, *twosteps Smallest-Last* and *twosteps Color-Degree*, Frota *et al.* [5] described a branch-an-cut algorithm for PGCP, Hoshino *et al.* [8] proposed an integer programming model and a branch-and-price algorithm to solve it, Noronha and Ribeiro [10] described a Tabu Search algorithm. Recently, Pop *et al.* [12] proposed a memetic algorithm (MA) which uses two different solution representations for the genetic operators and for the local search procedure.

The aim of this paper is to present an efficient ant colony algorithm for solving the PGCP.

The remainder of the paper is organized as follows. Section 2 provides some definitions and notations used throughout the paper and formally state the partition graph coloring problem. Section 3 describes the ACO framework. Section 4 presents and analyses the results of the preliminary computational experiments and finally, the last section concludes the paper.

2 Definition of the Partition Graph Coloring Problem

We start this section with some basic definitions concerning graph coloring. For more details we refer for example to [7].

Let $G = (V, E)$ an undirected graph and $V' \subseteq V$ then the *graph induced by* V' is obtained from the graph G by deleting the nodes of $V \setminus V'$ and the all the edges incident to at least one node from the set $V \setminus V'$.

A *vertex k-coloring* of the graph G is a mapping $c : V \to \{1, ..., k\}$ with the property that $c(u) \neq c(v)$ for all the edges $(u, v) \in E$. The number $c(u)$ or $c(v)$ is called the *color* of u or v. A graph that can be assigned a k-coloring is *k-colorable.*

The *vertex-coloring problem* consists in finding a vertex-coloring of G with minimum k. The smallest number of colors needed to color a graph G is called *chromatic number.*

Formally, the partition graph coloring problem is defined on an undirected graph $G = (V, E)$ with the set of nodes V and the set of edges E. The set of nodes is partitioned into p mutually exclusive nonempty subsets, called clusters, $V_1, \ldots, V_p$ with $V_1 \cup \cdots \cup V_p = V$ and $V_i \cap V_j = \emptyset$ for all $i, j \in \{1, \ldots, p\}$ and $i \neq j$. The PGCP consists of finding a set $V^* \subset V$ such that:

1. $|V^* \cap V_i| = 1$, i.e., V^* contains exactly one node from each cluster V_i for all $i \in \{1, \ldots, p\}$,
2. the graph induced by V^* is k-colorable where k is minimal.

The PGCP reduces to the classical graph coloring problem when all the clusters are singletons.

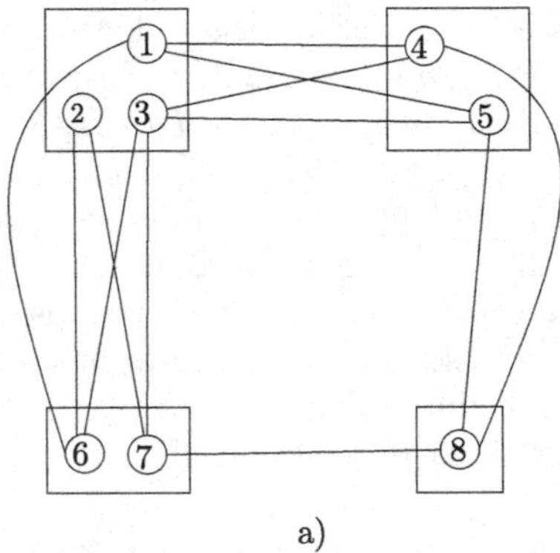

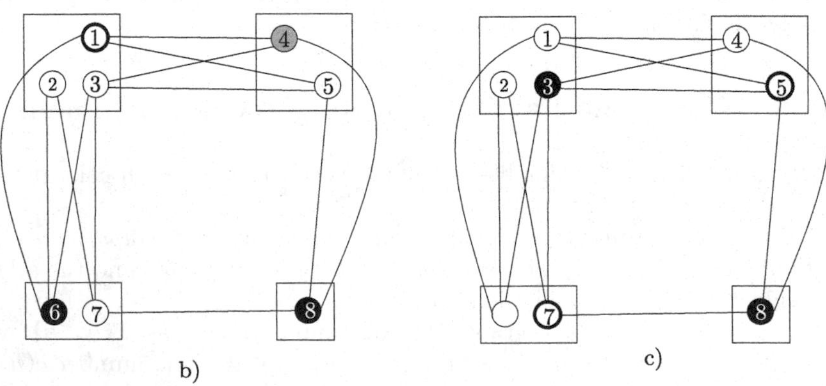

Fig. 1. (a) An instance of the PGCP, (b) A feasible solution with three colors, (c) An optimal solution with two colors

An illustration of the PGCP, a feasible solution with three colors and an optimal solution with two colors is shown in Fig. 1.

In this example the graph $G = (V, E)$ has 8 nodes partitioned into 4 clusters. A feasible solution for the PGCP making use of three colors is represented. The optimal solution makes use of two colors: the first is used to color the nodes 3 and 8 and the second for the nodes 5 and 7.

3 The ACO Algorithm

Ant Colony Optimization is one of the most successive metaheuristic methods. The main idea comes from collective intelligence of real ant when they look for a food. The problem is solved collectively by the whole colony. This ability is explained by the fact that ants communicate in an indirect way by laying trails of pheromone. If the pheromone trail within a particular direction is higher, the probability of choosing this direction is higher.

The ACO algorithm was proposed by Marco Dorigo [3]. It uses a colony of artificial ants that behave as cooperative agents in a mathematical space where they are allowed to search and reinforce pathways (solutions) in order to find the optimal ones. The problem is represented by graph and the ants walk on the graph to construct solutions. The solutions are represented by paths in the graph. After the initialization of the pheromone trails, the ants construct feasible solutions, starting from random nodes, and then the pheromone trails are updated. At each step the ants compute a set of feasible moves and select the best one (according to some probabilistic rules) to continue the rest of the tour. The transition probability $p_{i,j}$, to choose the node j when the current node is i, is based on the heuristic information $\eta_{i,j}$ and the pheromone trail level $\tau_{i,j}$ of the move, where $i, j = 1, \ldots, n$.

$$p_{i,j} = \frac{\tau_{i,j}^a \eta_{i,j}^b}{\sum\limits_{k \in Unused} \tau_{i,k}^a \eta_{i,k}^b},$$

where $Unused$ is the set of unused nodes of the graph. The higher the value of the pheromone and the heuristic information, the more profitable it is to select this move and resume the search. In the beginning, the initial pheromone level is set to a small positive constant value τ_0; later, the ants update this value after completing the construction stage. ACO algorithms adopt different criteria to update the pheromone level.

The pheromone trail update rule is given by:

$$\tau_{i,j} \leftarrow \rho \tau_{i,j} + \Delta \tau_{i,j},$$

where ρ models evaporation in the nature and $\Delta \tau_{i,j}$ is the new added pheromone which is proportional to the quality of the solution.

In our implementation every ant begins to create their solution starting from random cluster V_j and it chooses a random node v_{ij} from the cluster as a first node of the solution. This first node is colored with color number 1. The ants will deposit their pheromone on the nodes of the graph. It means that the node is suitable to represent the cluster. Our heuristic information is $\eta_{ij} = \frac{1}{w_{ij}}$, where w_{ij} is the weight of the node (number of the edges which entry in the node). Thus the ants will prefer nodes with less weight. The ant chooses to include the node with a highest value of the transition probability according all clusters and nodes in the clusters with which the current node is related by edge. Let the maximal number of colors till the current step is C. We chose the minimal number from the interval $[1, C]$, as a color for the new node, thus this color to be different from the colors of neighbor nodes. If it is impossible, the number of the color of the next node becomes $C + 1$. After the ant chooses some node we decrease the number of uncolored clusters with one. We repeat procedure for including new nodes in the solution till the number of uncolored clusters becomes 0.

We update the pheromone, at the end of every iteration, using the rule:

$$\tau_{ij} = \begin{cases} \rho\tau_{ij} + \frac{1-\rho}{C} & \text{if the node is colored} \\ \tau_{ij} & \text{if the node is not colored} \end{cases}$$

If some of the clusters is isolated, no one of its nodes is neighbor with nodes from other clusters, than we chose a random node from it and we color it with a color number 1.

4 Experimental Results

The developed algorithm has been coded in C++ language and experiments were run on a Intel Core i4 PC with 3.4 GHz. The parameters are fixed as follows: $\rho = 0.5$, $a = 1$, $b = 1$, number of used ants is 3 and the number of iterations is 10. We used the Rand-set of instances [6] that was also used in [5]. It contains randomized instances with 20 to 120 nodes partitioned into 10 to 60 clusters, respectively. We performed 30 independent runs for each instance and determined the average and standard deviations of the final objective values.

Table 1. Experimental results on instances with different size

Instance set		B&C		MA1			MA2			ACO		
Nodes	Density	LB	UB	Aver	SD	Time	Aver	SD	Time	Aver	SD	Time
20	0.5	3	3	3.00	0.00	0.02 s	3.00	0.00	0.14 s	2.55	0.325	0.003 s
40	0.5	4	4	4.50	0.51	0.10 s	4.00	0.00	0.60 s	3.47	0.258	0.004 s
60	0.5	5	5	5.96	0.20	0.31 s	5.63	0.49	2.00 s	4.25	0.267	0.008 s
70	0.5	6	6	6.86	0.40	0.53 s	6.06	0.24	3.33 s	4.47	0.499	0.012 s
80	0.5	6	6	7.66	0.48	0.80 s	6.94	0.29	4.90 s	4.89	0.404	0.014 s
90	0.5	6	7	8.22	0.42	1.21 s	7.55	0.50	7.49 s	5.42	0.307	0.015 s
100	0.5	6	7	8.90	0.30	1.74 s	7.93	0.30	11.04 s	5.24	0.469	0.017 s
120	0.5	7	8	10.26	0.44	3.41 s	9.22	0.43	21.05 s	6.08	0.49	0.023 s

Table 2. Experimental results on instances with different density

Instance set		B&C		MA1			MA2			ACO		
Nodes	Density	LB	UB	Aver	SD	Time	Aver	SD	Time	Aver	SD	Time
90	0.1	2	3	3.13	0.33	0.22 s	3.09	0.29	1.37 s	3.00	0.013	0.015 s
90	0.2	3	4	4.71	0.45	0.52 s	4.41	0.49	3.24 s	3.98	0.044	0.015 s
90	0.3	4	5	6.06	0.24	0.78 s	5.52	0.56	4.90 s	4.55	0.283	0.015 s
90	0.4	5	6	7.59	0.49	1.07 s	6.79	0.83	6.54 s	4.88	0.313	0.015 s
90	0.5	6	7	8.22	0.42	1.21 s	7.55	0.50	7.49 s	5.42	0.307	0.015 s
90	0.6	8	8	10.98	0.34	1.88 s	10.50	0.87	11.95 s	4.80	0.542	0.015 s
90	0.7	10	10	12.93	0.38	2.37 s	12.39	1.12	14.83 s	5.22	0.32	0.015 s
90	0.8	12	12	15.55	0.51	3.38 s	15.18	0.80	20.98 s	5.00	0.483	0.015 s
90	0.9	16	16	17.69	0.86	7.38 s	17.27	0.98	45.75 s	4.11	0.538	0.015 s

We compare our ACO algorithm with two variants of memetic (MA1 and MA2) algorithms [12] and Branch and Cut (B&C) approach [5]. Table 1 contains experimental results on instances with 20 – 120 nodes and an edge density of 0.5, while Table 2 contains results on instances with 90 nodes and an edge density of 0.1 – 0.9. Each line corresponds to a set of 5 different instances. Both tables show the instance characteristics, the lower and upper bounds obtained by the branch and cut (B&C) approach within two hours run-time, followed by the average objective values of the final best solutions, their standard deviations, and the run-time in seconds for the MA1, MA2 and ACO algorithms.

We observe that ACO algorithm achieves better results than two memetic algorithms. The difference is larger for larger instances as well as for instances with larger density. The ACO running time is much less than the other mentioned algorithms. We will note that ACO is a constructive method and avoids conflicts creating only feasible solutions. ACO achieves better solutions than B&C too. Thus our ACO algorithm performs better than memetic algorithms because achieves better solutions with less running time. It is very important when it comes to time-critical applications and large instances due to its excellent scalability.

5 Conclusions and Future Work

This paper has presented a novel method for solving the partition graph coloring problem, namely Ant Colony Optimization (ACO) algorithm. Computational experiments on common benchmark instances sets show that although the ACO is not always able to find the optimal solutions, it produces solid results with very low run-times and therefore has excellent scalability when it comes to large instances.

We compare our ACO algorithm with two memetic algorithms, and can conclude that it performs superiorly, achieving better solutions with less run time.

For future work, we want to augment our ACO approach with effective local search algorithms in order to improve the quality of the solutions.

Acknowledgments. This work was supported by a grant of the Romanian National Authority for Scientific Research, CNCS - UEFISCDI, project number PN-II-RU-TE-2011-3-0113 and by the Bulgarian National Science Fund under the grants Efficient Parallel Algorithms for Large Scale Computational Problems and InterCriteria Analysis A New Approach to Decision Making.

References

1. Demange, M., Monnot, J., Pop, P., Ries, B.: Selective graph coloring in some special classes of graphs. In: Mahjoub, A.R., Markakis, V., Milis, I., Paschos, V.T. (eds.) ISCO 2012. LNCS, vol. 7422, pp. 320–331. Springer, Heidelberg (2012)
2. Demange, M., Monnot, J., Pop, P.C., Ries, B.: On the complexity of the selective graph coloring problem in some special classes of graphs. Theoret. Comput. Sci. **540–541**, 89–102 (2014)
3. Dorigo, M., Gambardella, L.M.: Ant colony system: a cooperative learning approach to the traveling salesman problem. IEEE Trans. Evol. Comput. **1**(1), 53–66 (1997)
4. Feremans, C., Labbé, M., Laporte, G.: Generalized network design problems. Eur. J. Oper. Res. **148**, 1–13 (2003)
5. Frota, Y., Maculan, N., Noronha, T.F., Ribeiro, C.C.: A branch-and-cut algorithm for the partition coloring problem. Networks **55**(3), 194–204 (2010)
6. Frota, Y., Maculan, N., Noronha, T.F., Ribeiro, C.C.: Instances for the partition graph coloring problem. http://www.ic.uff.br/celso/grupo/pcp.htm.
7. Kubale, M.: Graph Colorings. American Mathematical Society, Ann Arbor (2004)
8. Hoshino, E.A., Frota, Y.A., de Souza, C.C.: A branch-and-price approach for the partition coloring problem. Oper. Res. Lett. **39**(2), 132–137 (2011)
9. Li, G., Simha, R.: The partition coloring problem and its application to wavelength routing and assignment. In: 1st Workshop on Optical Networks (2000)
10. Noronha, T.F., Ribeiro, C.C.: Routing and wavelength assignment by partition colouring. Eur. J. Oper. Res. **171**(3), 797–810 (2006)
11. Pop, P.C.: Generalized Network Design Problems. Modeling and Optimization, De Gruyter Series in Discrete Mathematics and Applications, Germany (2012)
12. Pop, P.C., Hu, B., Raidl, G.R.: A memetic algorithm with two distinct solution representations for the partition graph coloring problem. In: Moreno-Díaz, R., Pichler, F., Quesada-Arencibia, A. (eds.) EUROCAST. LNCS, vol. 8111, pp. 219–226. Springer, Heidelberg (2013)

Multi-exchange Neighborhoods for the Capacitated Ring Tree Problem

Alessandro Hill(✉)

ANT/OR - Operations Research Group, Department of Engineering Management, University of Antwerp, Prinsstraat 13, 2000 Antwerp, Belgium
alessandro.hill@uantwerpen.be

Abstract. A *ring tree* is a tree graph with an optional additional edge that closes a unique cycle. Such a cycle is called a *ring* and the nodes on it are called *ring nodes*. The *capacitated ring tree problem* (CRTP) asks for a network of minimal overall edge cost that connects given customers to a depot by ring trees. Ring trees are required to intersect in the depot which has to be either a ring node of degree two in a ring tree or a node of degree one if the ring tree does not contain a ring. Customers are predefined as of *type 1* or *type 2*. The type 2 customers have to be ring nodes, whereas type 1 customers can be either ring nodes or nodes in tree sub-structures. Additionally, optional Steiner nodes are given which can be used as intermediate network nodes if advantageous. Capacity constraints bound both the number of the ring trees as well as the number of customers allowed in each ring tree. In this paper we present first advanced neighborhood structures for the CRTP. Some of them generalize existing concepts for the TSP and the Steiner tree problem, others are CRTP-specific. We also describe models to explore these multi-node and multi-edge exchange neighborhoods in one or more ring trees efficiently. Moreover, we embed these techniques in a heuristic multi-start framework and show that it produces high quality results for small and medium size literature instances.

Keywords: Capacitated ring tree problem · Network design · Local search

1 Introduction

The design of cost efficient networks under capacity constraints is of undoubted importance for applications in various industries. Especially in the field of transportation and telecommunication significant cost savings were achieved through the application of appropriate optimization models in the last decades. Topologically, many networks are based on fundamental structures such as trees or rings. The extensively studied *minimum weight spanning trees* (MSTs) assure connectivity such that a unique path between any two nodes in the network exists,

This research was partially supported by the Interuniversity Attraction Poles (IAP) Programme initiated by the Belgian Science Policy Office (COMEX project).

I. Dimov et al. (Eds.): NMA 2014, LNCS 8962, pp. 85–94, 2015.
DOI: 10.1007/978-3-319-15585-2_10

whereas the *capacitated minimum spanning tree problem* (CMSTP) [2] asks for such a tree of minimal total edge costs while limiting the number of nodes of sub-trees connected to a depot by a single edge. In practice, the integration of optional intermediate *Steiner nodes* is highly relevant and is facilitated by the well-known *Steiner tree problem* (STP) [7]. On the contrary, a prominent ring based optimization problem is the *travelling salesman problem* (TSP), asking for a travel cost minimizing sequence in which each customer of a given set should be visited before returning to a depot. Such a *tour* is required for each vehicle starting from the depot in the *vehicle routing problem* (VRP) [3]. The need for multiple vehicles arises from the commonly limited transport capacity to deliver or pick up goods from or to the customers. Beyond these concepts, the recent *capacitated ring tree problem* (CRTP) [5] integrates the ring structure and the tree structure into an optimization model under consideration of capacities and the useful Steiner nodes. The implemented *ring tree* structure is defined to be either a tree, a ring or a ring with additional disjoint trees attached to some of its nodes. Moreover, certain customers are prespecified to be of type 2 and thus required to be contained in sub-rings in ring trees. The remaining type 1 customers can be such *ring nodes* or nodes in sub-trees. Additional capacity constraints bound the total number of customers on each ring tree as well as the number of ring trees originating from the depot. Figure 1 shows a feasible network that satisfies these requirements and minimizes the overall edge costs, i.e. the objective function. The CRTP is NP-hard as are its special cases, the STP and the TSP, but computationally even more challenging [5]. For most real world applications heuristic solution approaches are indispensable due to the size limits for efficient exact algorithms. Therefore, in this paper we generalize known neighborhood structures for the purely tree [1] and purely ring based [6] special cases by treating the ring tree case. Furthermore, the CRTP gives rise to interesting structured neighborhoods on its own that we introduce and show how to efficiently explore. We embed these techniques in a multi-start heuristic framework and show its efficiency on a set of literature instances.

After a formal definition of the CRTP in Sect. 2 we introduce the novel neighborhoods and corresponding exploration techniques in Sect. 3. The embedding of these ideas in a multi-start heuristic is described in Sect. 4 before we close with our conclusion in Sect. 5.

2 The Capacitated Ring Tree Problem

In the following we give a formal definition of the CRTP using basic graph theoretic notation. We consider a network $\mathcal{N}$ synonymous with an undirected simple graph with node set $V[\mathcal{N}]$ and edge set $E[\mathcal{N}]$. The graph obtained after the removal of a node $v \in V[\mathcal{N}]$ is denoted by $\mathcal{N} \backslash v$.

Definition. *We are given a set of nodes* $V = U_2 \dot\cup U_1 \dot\cup W \dot\cup \{d\}$ *where the nodes in* U_t *correspond to type* t *customers, nodes in* W *are Steiner nodes and* d *represents a central depot. The cost of connecting two nodes* $u \neq v$ *in* V *by an edge* $e = \{u, v\}$ *is* $c_e > 0$. *A solution for the CRTP is a network* $\mathcal{N}$ *obtained from*

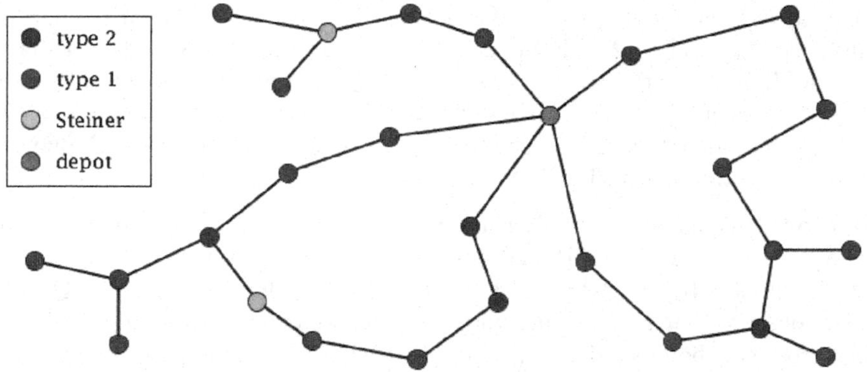

Fig. 1. A CRTP solution with 24 customers in 3 ring trees.

the union of a set of rings $\mathcal{R} = \{R_1, ..., R_k\}$ *and a set of trees* $\mathcal{T} = \{T_1, ..., T_l\}$ *on* V *such that*

- *each type 2 customer is contained in exactly one ring,*
- *each type 1 customer is contained in exactly one ring or tree,*
- *each Steiner node is contained in at most one ring or tree,*
- *each ring contains the depot* d*,*
- *each tree contains either the depot* d *or a node of a ring,*

and $\mathcal{N}$ *is capacity feasible, i.e.*

- *the number of connected components in* $\mathcal{N}\backslash d$ *is at most* m *and*
- *the number of type 1 and type 2 customers in each connected component of* $\mathcal{N}\backslash d$ *does not exceed* q*.*

The CRTP asks for such a network of minimal total edge cost $c(\mathcal{N}) = \sum_{e \in E[\mathcal{N}]} c_e$*.*

From each connected component of $\mathcal{N}\backslash d$ we obtain a *ring tree* Q by adding the depot d and the edges connecting d and Q in $\mathcal{N}$. Such a ring tree forms either a tree or a ring with disjoint trees attached to it. Figure 1 illustrates a solution network based on 2 rings and 4 trees according to our definition of the CRTP.

3 Neighborhood Structures

In the following we elaborate several structured neighborhoods for the CRTP and explain how to efficiently explore them. They partially generalize existing concepts for the TSP, VRP, STP and CMSTP but we also introduce CRTP-specific neighborhoods that do not have non-trivial counterparts in these specializations. For the sake of simplified descriptions we introduce some notation which refers to a CRTP solution network $\mathcal{N}$ unless explicitly stated differently. Let $U = U_1 \cup U_2$ be the set of all customers. For a ring tree $\mathcal{Q} \subseteq \mathcal{N}$ we denote the set of neighbors of a node $v \in V[\mathcal{Q}]$ in Q as $N_{\mathcal{Q}}[v]$. Let $P_{\mathcal{Q}}[u, v]$ be the set of paths that connect two distinct nodes $u, v \in V[\mathcal{Q}]$. We recall that if $\mathcal{Q}$ contains a ring then $|P_{\mathcal{Q}}[u,v]| \leq 2$, otherwise $\mathcal{Q}$ is a tree and thus $|P_{\mathcal{Q}}[u,v]| = 1$. Then we define $T_{\mathcal{Q}}[u,v]$ as the set of *path trees* of $\mathcal{Q}$ obtained from extending each path $\mathcal{P} \in P_{\mathcal{Q}}[u,v]$ by the non-ring structures in $\mathcal{Q}$ attached to the nodes of $\mathcal{P}$. Finally, for a node set $X \subset V$ we define $\Delta_{\mathcal{Q}}[X]$ as the set of edges with one end in X and the other end in $V[\mathcal{Q}] \backslash X$.

1-edge-opt. In contrast to purely ring-based models, a 1-edge-opt neighborhood can be defined for the CRTP by considering the feasible removal of an edge $e \in E[\mathcal{Q}]$ followed by the insertion of an edge $e' \notin E[\mathcal{Q}]$ for each ring tree $\mathcal{Q} \subseteq \mathcal{N}$. We first observe that given a ring without type 2 customers, the edge with the highest cost can be deleted and $\mathcal{N}$ is still feasible. Therefore, we assume that each ring in $\mathcal{N}$ contains a type 2 customer. In the case that e is a ring edge e' is required to *repair* the destroyed ring if possible. The ring-tree-opt neighborhood below will cover this case. Thus let $e = \{u, v\}$ be a non-ring edge of $\mathcal{Q}$ and let u be the node on each path from v to d. Then the deletion of e creates two connected components of $\mathcal{Q}$, one containing d and another one that contains v, more precisely a tree $\mathcal{T}_v$. To establish a valid solution we consider the insertion of each re-connecting edge $e' \in \Delta_{\mathcal{Q}}[V[\mathcal{T}_v]]$ subject to adherence to the capacity constraints. In particular, we may create a new (ring)tree by allowing e' to be incident to d.

2-edge-opt. The prominent TSP-tailored edge swaps can be applied to each ring in $\mathcal{N}$. In a similar manner ties can be broken by facilitating capacity-feasible re-combinations of two distinct ring trees $\mathcal{Q}_1$ and $\mathcal{Q}_2$ as known for the VRP. More specifically, for two ring edges $e = \{u, v\} \in E[\mathcal{Q}_1]$ and $e' = \{w, x\} \in E[\mathcal{Q}_2]$ we consider their replacement by $\{u, w\}$ and $\{v, x\}$ or $\{u, x\}$ and $\{v, w\}$. Figure 2 illustrates such an improvement move. If both edges are incident to d the neighborhood is empty. By allowing $\mathcal{Q}_1 = \mathcal{Q}_2$ and avoiding sub-tours we obtain the mentioned 2-opt for the TSP.

Moreover, we consider the deletion of two non-ring edges followed by the reconnection of the cut-off sub-trees $\mathcal{T}_1 \subseteq \mathcal{Q}_1$ and $\mathcal{T}_2 \subseteq \mathcal{Q}_2$ to other ring trees as depicted in Fig. 3. We hereby partially generalize the 1-edge-opt neighborhood. Since we regard the capacity constraints such a move can have an ejecting effect with respect to attached sub-trees when for instance reconnecting $\mathcal{T}_1$ to $\mathcal{Q}_2$. Finally, taking into account the removal of an edge e in a ring $\mathcal{R} \subseteq \mathcal{Q}_1$ and a non-ring edge $e' \in E[\mathcal{Q}_2]$ yields the remainder of this neighborhood. Let $\mathcal{T}_2$

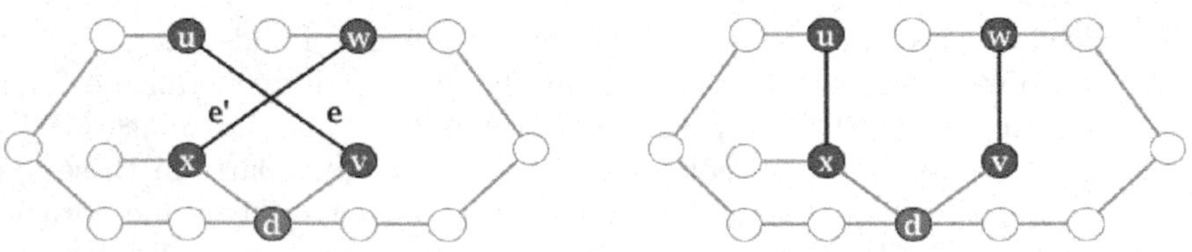

Fig. 2. A 2-edge-opt improvement based on the ring edges $\{u, v\}$ and $\{w, x\}$.

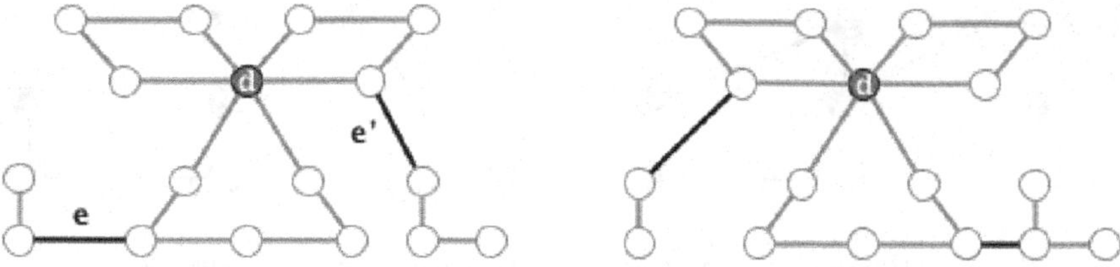

Fig. 3. A 2-edge-opt improvement based on the non-ring edges e and e'.

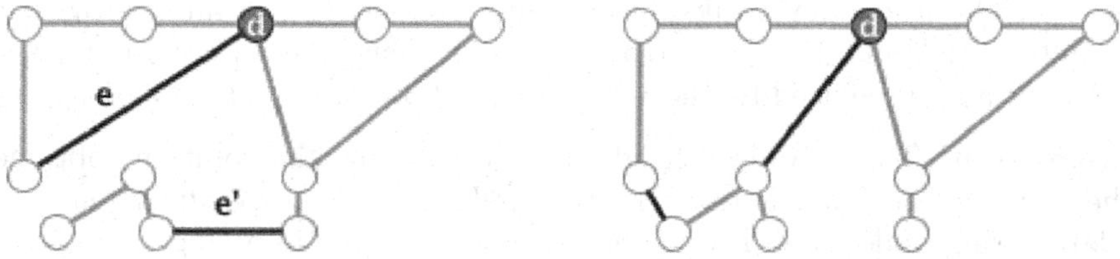

Fig. 4. A 2-edge-opt improvement based on a ring edge e and a non-ring edge e'.

be the sub-tree of $\mathcal{Q}_2$ induced by e' as in the 1-edge-opt neighborhood. The corresponding modification of $\mathcal{Q}_1$ in $\mathcal{N}$ corresponds to the replacement of a e by a path tree obtained from $\mathcal{T}_2$, whereas $\mathcal{Q}_2$ is reduced by $\mathcal{T}_2$. Figure 4 shows such a transformation.

1-node-opt. We consider moving a single customer node u from its current ring tree $\mathcal{Q}_1$ to a ring tree $\mathcal{Q}_2$. Obviously, the capacity of $\mathcal{Q}_2$ needs to be sufficient when performing such an operation. We ensure the preservation of the ring tree structure after the extraction of u from $\mathcal{Q}_1$ by the incorporation of a MST on the neighbors $N_{\mathcal{Q}_1}[u]$. Note that the degree of the depot has to be limited by m minus the number of current ring trees beside $\mathcal{Q}_1$ to satisfy the ring tree capacity m. Although the *degree constrained minimum spanning tree problem* (DCMSTP) is known to be NP-hard in general this special case can be solved polynomially using a Prim's algorithm in a slightly modified version starting from d. If u is of type 1 it may be inserted into $\mathcal{Q}_2$ either as a leaf or as an intermediate node that splits an edge $\{v, w\}$ into edges $\{v, u\}$ and $\{u, w\}$. Type 2 customers may only be inserted in this edge replacing manner into a ring instead.

2-node-opt. We consider swapping two customers that are not necessarily in distinct ring trees. This neighborhood can be constructed by intersecting two 1-node-opt spaces.

Steiner-node-opt. This neighborhood is inspired by known STP improvement moves and consists of all the feasible solutions obtained after deleting or inserting a single Steiner node. Certainly, a Steiner leaf node can simply be removed, whereas a node with degree 2 can be replaced by an edge connecting both neighbors if this results in an overall cost reduction. For an arbitrary Steiner node $x \in V[\mathcal{Q}]$, the re-connection can be accomplished by a MST on $N_{\mathcal{Q}}[x]$ as for the

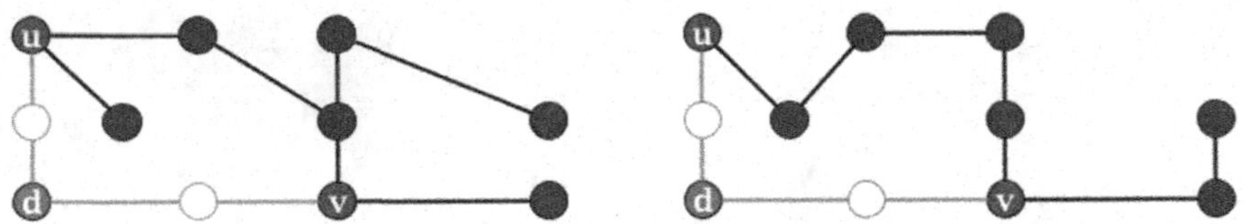

Fig. 5. A minimum spanning tree based improvement in a ring-tree-opt.

1-node-opt neighborhood. Conversely, we also consider the insertion of a Steiner node $x \notin V[\mathcal{N}]$ into $\mathcal{N}$. We take into account the *splitting* of an existing edge $\{u, v\}$ into $\{u, x\}$ and $\{x, v\}$. Moreover, two incident edges $\{u, v\}$ and $\{u, w\}$ with $u \neq d$ can be replaced by the *star configuration* $\{x, u\}$, $\{x, v\}$ and $\{x, w\}$.

Ring-tree-opt. This advanced neighborhood contains the solutions obtained by the rearrangement of the tree structure induced by two specifically situated mandatory ring nodes. Let $\mathcal{T} \in T_{\mathcal{Q}}(u, v)$ be a path tree in a ring tree $\mathcal{Q} \in \mathcal{N}$ for $\{u, v\} \subseteq U_2 \cup \{d\}$ such that $V[\mathcal{T}] \backslash \{u, v\}$ does not contain type 2 customers or the distributor. Then we can build a DCMSTP on the nodes of $\mathcal{T}$. As in previous neighborhoods a single degree constraint applies when $d \in \{u, v\}$ to avoid the installation of more additional ring trees than allowed. An improving solution in this neighborhood connects u and v by a path tree of less cost as illustrated in Fig. 5. This neighborhood is also valid for nodes u and v such that $V[T_{\mathcal{Q}}(u, v)] \cap U_2 = \emptyset$ and therefore, in particular applicable when $\mathcal{Q}$ is a tree.

Ring-tree-split-opt. This neighborhood contains solutions that can be obtained by *splitting* a ring tree $\mathcal{Q} \subseteq \mathcal{N}$ into two separate ring trees. This presumes enough capacity in $\mathcal{N}$ to install an additional ring tree. Basically, we try to repair a single ring edge removal by the feasible insertion of two new ring-closing edges. As in the ring-tree-opt search let $\mathcal{T}$ be a path tree for two distinct nodes u and v in $V[\mathcal{Q}] \cap (U_2 \cup \{d\})$ with $V[\mathcal{T}] \backslash \{u, v\} \cap \{d\} \cup U_2 = \emptyset$. Then we consider the removal of each ring edge $e \in E[\mathcal{T}]$ followed by the insertion of two edges $\{d, w\}$ and $\{d, x\}$ for $\{w, x\} \subseteq V[\mathcal{T}]$ as shown in Fig. 6. If $u = d$ then $\mathcal{Q}$ splits into a tree and a ring tree, whereas the splitting of a pure tree $\mathcal{Q}$ is contained in the 1-edge-opt neighborhood.

Ejection-chain-opt. Extracting a customer node u_1 from a ring tree $\mathcal{Q}_1$ and inserting it into a ring tree $\mathcal{Q}_2$ might be cost saving but not feasible because $\mathcal{Q}_2$ is capacity tight, i.e. $\mathcal{Q}_2$ contains q customers. However, the ejection of a customer u_2 in $\mathcal{Q}_2$ and its insertion into a ring tree $\mathcal{Q}_3$ can facilitate the move.

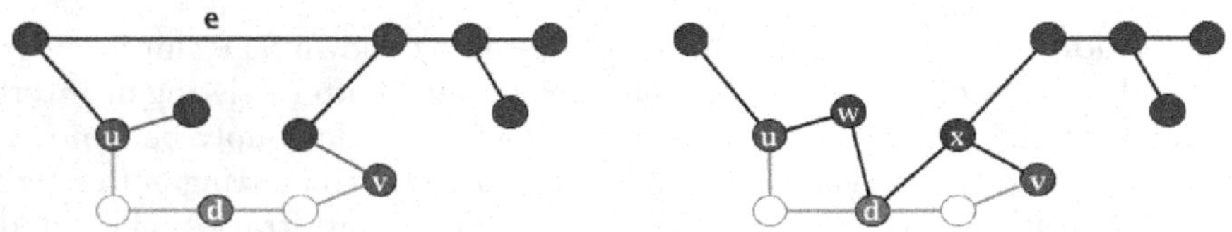

Fig. 6. An improving solution in the ring-tree-split neighborhood.

In this ejection-chain-opt neighborhood we consider all these double node moves for distinct ring trees $\mathcal{Q}_1$, $\mathcal{Q}_2$ and $\mathcal{Q}_3$. Note that if $\mathcal{Q}_3 = \mathcal{Q}_1$ then it corresponds to the 2-nodes-opt neighborhood.

4 A Multi-start Local Search Heuristic

Our heuristic is based on the iterated exploration of the introduced CRTP neighborhoods. We apply the corresponding local searches (LQSs) in a multi-start fashion on a set of start solutions obtained from different initial constructions. For a CRTP instance P, let $\Sigma(P)$ be the procedure that returns a solution pool based on the strategies that we briefly summarize in the following. On the one hand we apply *cluster first, route second* techniques as in [4] to solve the VRP obtained after temporarily declaring all customers type 2. Different cluster distance metrics (e.g. min/max/avg cluster node distance) give rise to multiple solutions that are added to the pool. Then we conversely focus on the design of (partial) rings or (partial) trees based on the computation of MSTs and the construction of *nearest first* TSP routes. We combine these partial networks on the different sets of customers and turn them into a feasible solution by a correction mechanism that repeatedly applies moves similar to the ones described in our local search neighborhoods. Our overall algorithm applies the local searches on each of the solutions in $\Sigma(P)$ in a best-fit fashion until no enhancement can be found. The order in which the different neighborhoods are explored corresponds to the increasing potential structural impact. The resulting *multi-start CRTP heuristic* can be described as follows.

```
Input: CRTP P
;
foreach N' ∈ Σ(P) do
    z ← ∞;
    while c(N') < z do
        z ← c(N');
        LQS(N', Ring-tree-opt);
        LQS(N', 1-edge-opt);
        LQS(N', 2-edge-opt);
        LQS(N', 1-node-opt);
        LQS(N', 2-node-opt);
        LQS(N', Steiner-node-opt);
        LQS(N', Ring-tree-split-opt);
        LQS(N', Ring-tree-join-opt);
        LQS(N', Ejection-chain-opt);
    end
    if c(N') < c(N) then N ← N';
end
return N;
```

We implemented the algorithm in c++ and ran tests on an Intel i7-3667U 2.00 GHz processor unit for the 225 small to medium size instances[1] used in [5]. The type 1 customers in these TSPLIB based instances with $|V| \in \{26, 51, 76, 101\}$ are randomly assigned according to a rate $r_1 \in \{0, 0.25, 0.5, 0.75, 1\}$. Various combinations of m and q with an average customer capacity slack $(mq - |U|)/mq$ of 0.14 make them capacity tight. The computational results are given in Appendix 1. The run time of the heuristic procedure never exceeded 25 s. Table 1 contains the computational results with the first 4 columns indicating the CRTP instance, the type 1 customer rate r_1, the number of nodes $|V|$ and customers $|U|$. The network cost $c(\mathcal{N})$ is then given along with the relative gaps $\Delta_{lb} = [c_{lb}(\mathcal{N}) - c(\mathcal{N})]/c(\mathcal{N})$ and $\Delta_{ub} = [c(\mathcal{N}) - c_{ub}(\mathcal{N})]/c(\mathcal{N})$ to the lower bound $c_{lb}(\mathcal{N})$ and the upper bound $c_{ub}(\mathcal{N})$ obtained by the exact method in [5]. We do not intend to compete with the branch & cut algorithm but rather give an idea of the solution quality obtained by the heuristic. Since we initialized the exact method with the heuristic solution and use the local search techniques along the branch & bound $\Delta_{ub} \geq 0$ holds.

5 Conclusions

We introduced advanced multi-edge and multi-node exchange neighborhood structures for the CRTP. They partially generalize existing concepts for prominent tree and ring based combinatorial optimization problems. We presented suitable models to explore these neighborhoods efficiently and a heuristic framework to turn these techniques into an efficient heuristic. Using this diversifying multi-start algorithm we are able to obtain optimal results in many cases for a set of small and medium sized literature instances. The average gap to known lower bounds is 3.8 %. We suggest this first heuristic approach for the CRTP as a reference for related models and further algorithms.

[1] The instances can be obtained from the author.

Appendix 1

Table 1. Heuristic results for CRTP instances from [5] with type 1 customer rates $r_1 \in \{0, 0.25, 0.5, 0.75, 1\}$ compared to bounds obtained by a branch & cut algorithm.

P	r_1	$\lvert V\rvert$	$\lvert U\rvert$	Δ_{lb}	$c(\mathcal{N})$	Δ_{ub}	P	r_1	$\lvert V\rvert$	$\lvert U\rvert$	Δ_{lb}	$c(\mathcal{N})$	Δ_{ub}	P	r_1	$\lvert V\rvert$	$\lvert U\rvert$	Δ_{lb}	$c(\mathcal{N})$	Δ_{ub}
1	1	26	12	**0**	**157**	**0**	16	1		37	**0**	**304**	**0**	31	1		75	**-1**	478	**1**
	0.75			**-2.3**	215	**2.3**		0.75			-6.6	375	0		0.75			-6.4	551	0
	0.5			**0**	**227**	**0**		0.5			-3.7	378	0.5		0.5			-4.9	564	0
	0.25			**0**	**236**	**0**		0.25			**-0.3**	380	**0.3**		0.25			-3.4	573	1.6
	0			**0**	**242**	**0**		0			**-0.3**	381	**0.3**		0			**-2.1**	584	**2.1**
2	1			**-0.6**	164	**0.6**	17	1			**-0.3**	309	**0.3**	32	1			**-2.4**	494	**2.4**
	0.75			**0**	**207**	**0**		0.75			**-1.6**	369	**1.6**		0.75			-7.4	573	0
	0.5			**0**	**240**	**0**		0.5			-3.8	399	0		0.5			-9.8	612	0
	0.25			**0**	**249**	**0**		0.25			-1.9	404	0		0.25			-5.2	618	0
	0			**0**	**251**	**0**		0			**-1.9**	418	**1.9**		0			-3.7	626	0
3	1			**-1.7**	173	**1.7**	18	1			**0**	**314**	**0**	33	1			**-1.4**	495	**1.4**
	0.75			**-0.8**	244	**0.8**		0.75			-8.2	408	0		0.75			-11.3	623	0
	0.5			**0**	**251**	**0**		0.5			-7	431	0		0.5			-6.1	623	0
	0.25			**0**	**279**	**0**		0.25			-4.5	436	0		0.25			-7.4	656	0
	0			**0**	**279**	**0**		0			**-1.3**	452	**1.3**		0			-4.9	674	0
4	1		18	**0**	**207**	**0**	19	1		50	**-0.3**	377	**0.3**	34	1	101	25	**-1.8**	282	**1.8**
	0.75			**0**	**256**	**0**		0.75			-4.1	436	2.1		0.75			**-4**	327	**4**
	0.5			**0**	**274**	**0**		0.5			-2.7	447	0.4		0.5			-4.6	353	0
	0.25			**0**	**292**	**0**		0.25			**-0.7**	454	**0.7**		0.25			-2	363	0
	0			**-1.3**	305	**1.3**		0			**-2.3**	473	**2.3**		0			**0**	**366**	**0**
5	1			**-1.4**	220	**1.4**	20	1			**-0.5**	386	**0.5**	35	1			**-1.4**	293	**1.4**
	0.75			**0**	**285**	**0**		0.75			-7.7	458	0		0.75			-6.2	367	0
	0.5			**-1.6**	318	**1.6**		0.5			-9.1	493	0		0.5			-9.3	405	0
	0.25			**0**	**334**	**0**		0.25			-6.2	502	0		0.25			-7.5	416	0
	0			**0**	**339**	**0**		0			**-3.9**	513	**3.9**		0			-3.8	425	0
6	1			**-1.7**	231	**1.7**	21	1			**-0.5**	392	**0.5**	36	1			**0**	**299**	**0**
	0.75			**0**	**278**	**0**		0.75			-10.7	501	2		0.75			-8.1	393	0
	0.5			**0**	**336**	**0**		0.5			-9.1	526	0		0.5			-6.2	403	0
	0.25			**0**	**361**	**0**		0.25			-5.3	525	0		0.25			-5.1	429	0
	0			**0**	**375**	**0**		0			-3.5	541	2.8		0			-2.7	452	0
7	1		25	**-1.2**	248	**1.2**	22	1	76	18	**0**	**214**	**0**	37	1		50	**0**	**411**	**0**
	0.75			**0**	**294**	**0**		0.75			**0**	**272**	**0**		0.75			-7.1	492	0
	0.5			**0**	**313**	**0**		0.5			-9.6	318	0		0.5			-5.3	499	0
	0.25			**0**	**327**	**0**		0.25			-4.8	318	0		0.25			-3.9	503	0
	0			**0**	**328**	**0**		0			**0**	**332**	**0**		0			-5.7	523	2.9
8	1			**-5.6**	267	**5.6**	23	1			**-0.9**	235	**0.9**	38	1			**-1.2**	420	**1.2**
	0.75			**-1.3**	315	**1.3**		0.75			-3.1	312	1		0.75			-4.1	480	0
	0.5			**0**	**345**	**0**		0.5			**0**	**336**	**0**		0.5			-6.5	517	0
	0.25			**0**	**357**	**0**		0.25			-2.8	369	0		0.25			-5.7	531	0
	0			**0**	**362**	**0**		0			**-1**	390	**1**		0			-2.3	537	0
9	1			**-3.1**	262	**3.1**	24	1			**0**	**259**	**0**	39	1			**-3.8**	443	**3.8**
	0.75			**-0.9**	322	**0.9**		0.75			**0**	**325**	**0**		0.75			-4.8	505	0
	0.5			**-0.8**	372	**0.8**		0.5			-2.9	379	0		0.5			-6.1	527	0
	0.25			**-0.3**	379	**0.3**		0.25			**0**	**397**	**0**		0.25			-7.3	564	0
	0			**-0.3**	397	**0.3**		0			**-0.7**	451	**0.7**		0			-3.6	574	0
10	1	51	12	**0**	**156**	**0**	25	1		37	**0**	**320**	**0**	40	1		75	**-1**	516	**1**
	0.75			**-2**	196	**2**		0.75			-6.8	390	0		0.75			-6.6	594	0
	0.5			**0**	**215**	**0**		0.5			-7.4	402	0		0.5			-3.8	592	0
	0.25			**0**	**222**	**0**		0.25			-3.3	403	0		0.25			-4	612	0
	0			**0**	**242**	**0**		0			**-1**	413	**1**		0			**-2.6**	622	**2.6**
11	1			**-2.5**	163	**2.5**	26	1			**-3**	336	**3**	41	1			**-0.6**	519	**0.6**
	0.75			**0**	**209**	**0**		0.75			-5	402	0		0.75			-6.2	595	0
	0.5			**0**	**230**	**0**		0.5			-9.8	455	0		0.5			-4.2	607	0
	0.25			**0**	**238**	**0**		0.25			-9.2	460	0		0.25			-2.6	619	0
	0			**0**	**251**	**0**		0			-2.6	458	0		0			-2.8	642	0.5
12	1			**-1.2**	172	**1.2**	27	1			**-0.9**	343	**0.9**	42	1			**-1.3**	529	**1.3**
	0.75			**0**	**203**	**0**		0.75			-8.7	446	0		0.75			-10.6	653	0
	0.5			**0**	**251**	**0**		0.5			-9.9	473	0		0.5			-7.3	645	0
	0.25			**0**	**278**	**0**		0.25			-10.9	497	0		0.25			-7.1	670	0
	0			**0**	**279**	**0**		0			-5.6	506	0		0			-5.8	689	0
13	1		25	**-1.2**	248	**1.2**	28	1		56	**-3**	395	**3**	43	1		100	**0**	**555**	**0**
	0.75			-4	305	1		0.75			-7.6	462	0		0.75			-6.2	652	0
	0.5			**0**	**312**	**0**		0.5			-8.1	477	0		0.5			-5.5	660	0.5
	0.25			**0**	**322**	**0**		0.25			-2.4	472	1.5		0.25			-1.9	656	1.2
	0			**0**	**328**	**0**		0			**-3.8**	495	**3.8**		0			**-2.9**	683	**2.9**
14	1			**-5.6**	267	**5.6**	29	1			**-3.2**	402	**3.2**	44	1			**-0.7**	568	**0.7**
	0.75			**-5.3**	321	**5.3**		0.75			-9.7	488	0		0.75			-5.9	663	0
	0.5			-3.1	352	0		0.5			-10.4	520	0		0.5			-6.7	690	0
	0.25			**0**	**357**	**0**		0.25			-7.4	532	0		0.25			-3.8	691	1.2
	0			**0**	**362**	**0**		0			-5.4	543	1.5		0			-2.3	700	0
15	1			**-3.1**	262	**3.1**	30	1			**-3.6**	414	**3.6**	45	1			**-1**	576	**1**
	0.75			-2.2	339	1.2		0.75			-11.9	533	0		0.75			-9.5	695	0
	0.5			-3.5	372	0.5		0.5			-11	554	0		0.5			-6	717	0
	0.25			-3.9	387	0		0.25			-8.2	558	0		0.25			-5.6	730	0
	0			**-1.8**	397	**1.8**		0			-2.6	561	0.7		0			-4.6	743	0

References

1. Ahuja, R.K., Orlin, J.B., Sharma, D.: Multi-exchange neighborhood structures for the capacitated minimum spanning tree problem. Math. Program. **91**, 71–97 (2000)
2. Amberg, A., Domschke, W., Voß, S.: Capacitated minimum spanning trees: Algorithms using intelligent search. Comb. Optim. Theory Pract. **1**, 9–39 (1996)
3. Golden, B., Raghavan, S., Wasil, E.A.: The Vehicle Routing Problem: Latest Advances and New Challenges. Operations research/Computer Science Interfaces Series. Springer, New York (2008). http://www.worldcat.org/oclc/254177374
4. Hill, A., Voß, S.: An equi-model matheuristic for the multi-depot ring star problem. Research paper, University of Antwerp, Faculty of Applied Economics (2014). http://EconPapers.repec.org/RePEc:ant:wpaper:2014015
5. Hill, A., Voß, S.: Optimal capacitated ring trees. Research paper, University of Antwerp, Faculty of Applied Economics (2014). http://EconPapers.repec.org/RePEc:ant:wpaper:2014012
6. Lin, S., Kernighan, B.W.: An effective heuristic algorithm for the traveling-salesman problem. Oper. Res. **21**(2), 498–516 (1973). http://pubsonline.informs.org/doi/abs/10.1287/opre.21.2.498
7. Voß, S.: Steiner tree problems in telecommunications. In: Resende, M.G.C., Pardalos, P.M. (eds.) Handbook of Optimization in Telecommunications, pp. 459–492. Springer, US (2006). http://dx.doi.org/10.1007/978-0-387-30165-5_18

Hebbian Versus Gradient Training of ESN Actors in Closed-Loop ACD

Petia Koprinkova-Hristova(✉)

Institute of Information and Communication Technologies,
Bulgarian Academy of Sciences,
Acad. G. Bonchev Str. bl.25A, 1113 Sofia, Bulgaria
pkoprinkova@bas.bg

Abstract. The present work continues investigations on combination between Adaptive Critic Design (ACD) approach - a gradient-based optimization technique - and a more biologically plausible associative or Hebbian learning. Echo state network (ESN) was used as adaptive critic element that was trained minimizing temporal difference error. While in the previous work the actor was a time profile of the action variable, here investigations are extended to the closed loop (feedback) control scheme. The actor is another ESN network and its inputs are some of the process state variables while its output is the value of the controlled variable. The only trainable connections of the actor - from its reservoir to the readout - are trained to minimize (maximize) the critic output. Comparison between backpropagation of utility approach that is gradient descent algorithm and a Hebbian learning law is made. These two approaches are tested on a task for optimization of a complex nonlinear process for bio-polymer production. The obtained results are compared with respect to the convergence speed as well as to the obtained solution, i.e. reached local optima.

Keywords: Reinforcement Learning · Hebbian learning · Adaptive Critic Design · Echo State Networks

1 Introduction

Adaptive Critic Designs (ACD) [12] originate from one side as a method approximating Bellman's dynamic programming [2,3] and from the other side as gradient version of associative learning from experience called Reinforcement Learning (RL) [1]. During the last thirty years theoretical developments in this field led to numerous variations of optimal control approaches [10]. The core of the methods is approximation of Bellman's equation via neural network called heuristic adaptive critic. Training of a critic is done minimizing temporal difference (TD) error [18] thereby mimicking the brains ability to learn how to predict future outcomes on the basis of previous experience without awaiting the final results from future actions. The key component of ACD training and solving the optimization task is the backpropagation method that is gradient algorithm based

I. Dimov et al. (Eds.): NMA 2014, LNCS 8962, pp. 95–102, 2015.
DOI: 10.1007/978-3-319-15585-2_11

on the chain rule of derivative calculation [20]. In contrast, the RL from [1] uses Hebbian or associative learning law for both critic and controller (called actor in terms of RL) networks. Usually the critic is trained off-line since it needs a collection of a variety of data from the beginning to the end of several process runs. Combination between off-line and on-line learning is also considered [13]. True on-line applications of ACD approaches, however, needs very fast training algorithms [14]. In highly non-linear environments the necessity for additional feedback connections arises, which further complicates the on-line training. In such cases the application of backpropagation trough time (BPTT) [20] is an alternative. However, it is impossible to be used in an on-line mode. Instead of that the Extended Kalman Filter (EKF) method [4] is usually applied, which is more complicated and resource demanding. Hence it is crucial to work towards finding simply trainable recurrent network structures for ACD schemes.

In search of fast trainable neural network architectures in [7,8] it was proposed to use recently developed class of Recurrent Neural Networks (RNNS) called Echo State Networks (ESNs) [4]. Their structure incorporates a dynamic reservoir of neurons that is generated randomly and a fast trainable readout layer. These allow on-line adaptation via Recursive Least Square (RLS) method [4] as well as calculation of needed derivatives with much less computational effort [8].

From biological point of view however, the gradient learning is considered as non-plausible. It is claimed that associative learning algorithms like Hebbian law are closer to the biological neurons behavior. That is why in [9] it was proposed to incorporate associative learning laws within ACD scheme. That was done via training of actor with associative manner like in [1]. However in [9] the actor was not entire network structure but only time profile of the control variable and hence the control loop was without feedback from the object output. Here the investigation is extended to the closed-loop version of ACD using ESN structure for the actor and two training approaches - gradient and associative - were used for its adaptation. The developed algorithms are tested on a task for optimization of a complex nonlinear process for bio-polymer production. The obtained results are compared with respect to the convergence speed as well as to the obtained solution, i.e. reached local optima.

2 Problem Formulation

2.1 ACD Approach with Closed-Loop Control

The ACD scheme in the case without available model of the process under control that is called heuristic dynamic programming [10] adopted with some changes from [16] is given on Fig. 1 below. The vector $State(k)$ represents the state vector of the process under control, $a(k)$ is the control variable (or vector). The critic ESN has to be trained to predict the discounted sum of future values of utility

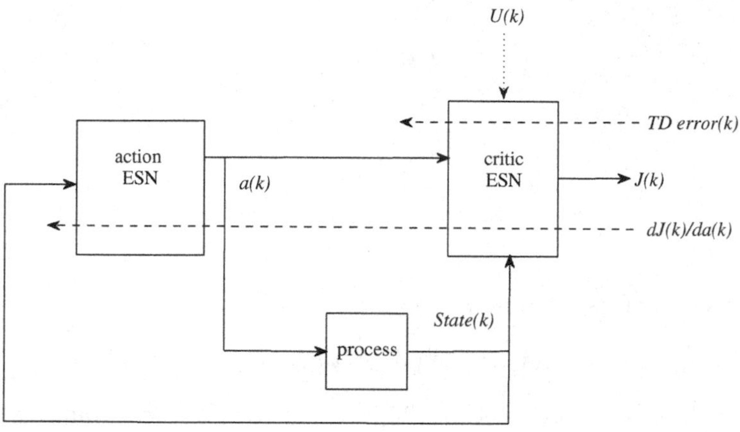

Fig. 1. ACD scheme with closed-loop control and ESN actor.

function $U(k)$ by approximating Bellman's equation as follows:

$$J(State(k), a(k)) = \sum_{t=0}^{k} \gamma^t U(State(t), a(t)) \tag{1}$$

where γ is discount factor taking values between 0 and 1.

The action ESN represents the controller that has to be adjusted so as generated by it control actions maximize (minimize) the utility function. The feedback connection from the process state to the controller can include the full state vector or some of state variables. The dashed lines represent the training cycles of critic and actor respectively.

The critic network is trained using RLS method to minimize the TD error defined in [18]:

$$TDerror(k) = J(k) - U(k) - \gamma J(k+1) \tag{2}$$

Concerning the action ESN, it has to be trained so as to generate proper control actions. In the classical ACD it is done via backpropagation of utility [20] that is gradient descent training. Here it is compared with biologically plausible associative learning algorithm adopted from early RL scheme [1]. Both algorithms are described bellow but first a short introduction to mathematical description of ESN structure is presented.

2.2 ESN Description

ESNs are a kind of recurrent neural networks that arise from so called reservoir computing approaches [11]. The basic ESN structure is shown in Fig. 2 below.

The ESN output vector denoted here by $out(k)$ (it will be $J(k)$ or $a(k)$ for critic and action networks respectively) for the current time instance k is usually

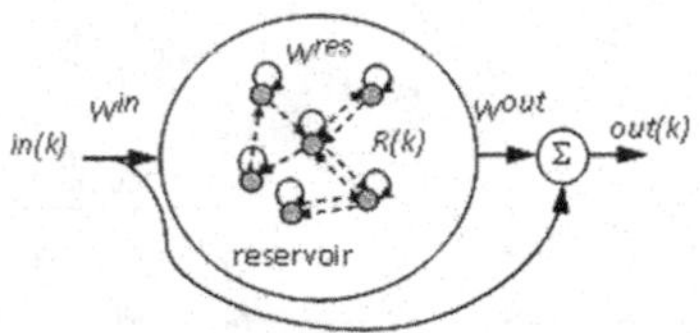

Fig. 2. Echo state network structure.

a linear function of its input and current state:

$$out(k) = f^{out}(W^{out}[in(k), R(k)]) \tag{3}$$

Here, $in(k)$ is a vector of network inputs and $R(k)$ a vector composed of the reservoir neuron states; f^{out} is a linear function (usually the identity), W^{out} is a $n_{out} \times (n_{in} + n_R)$ trainable matrix (here n_{out}, n_{in} and n_R are the sizes of the corresponding vectors out, in and R). The neurons in the reservoir have a simple sigmoid output function f^{res} (usually hyperbolic tangent) that depends on both the ESN input $in(k)$ and the previous reservoir state $R(k-1)$:

$$R(k) = f^{res}(W^{in} in(k) + W^{res} R(k-1)) \tag{4}$$

Here W^{in} and W^{res} are $n_{in} \times n_R$ and $n_R \times n_R$ matrices that are randomly generated and are not trainable. There are different approaches for reservoir parameter production [11]. A recent approach used in the present investigation is proposed in [15]. It is called intrinsic plasticity (IP) and suggests initial adjustment of these matrices, aiming at increasing the entropy of the reservoir neurons outputs. For on-line training, the RLS algorithm [4] was used.

2.3 Gradient Training of ESN Actor

Following derivatives calculation algorithm from [8] and backpropagating derivatives from output of the critic to the output of actor, training rule for actor's output weights W_a^{out} becomes:

$$W_{ai}^{out}(k) = W_{ai-1}^{out}(k) \pm \alpha \frac{\partial J_i(k)}{\partial a_i(k)} R_{ai}(k) \tag{5}$$

Here i denotes the iteration number and $0 < \alpha < 1$ is learning rate. The sign (+ or −) in the above equation depends on whether the optimization task is to maximize or to minimize the utility function.

2.4 Associative Training of ESN Actor

Following [1] learning rule of Associative Search Element (ASE) and formulas from [9] the associative learning rule for actor's output weights W_a^{out} becomes:

$$W_{ai}^{out}(k) = W_{ai-1}^{out}(k) \pm \alpha J_i(k) e_{ai}(k) \tag{6}$$

where $e_{ai}(k)$ denotes the eligibility trace of all neurons in the reservoir of the action ESN. According to [1] and accounting for specificity of the ACD scheme used here, the eligibility traces become:

$$e_{ai}(k) = \delta e_{ai-1}(k) + (1-\delta)a_i(k)R_{ai}(k) \tag{7}$$

where $0 < \delta < 1$ is decay rate of the trace.

3 Simulation Experiment Description

3.1 PHB Production Process

The object under consideration here (PHB production process) is biotechnological process with mixed culture cultivation. During it the sugars (glucose) are converted to lactate by the microorganism *L.delbrueckii* and then the lactate is converted to PHB (poly-β-hydroxybutyrate) by the microorganism *R.euthropha*. The main process product (PHB) is biodegradable polymer used as thermoplastic in food and drug industry. In [19] quite a complete mathematical model of the process has been developed and different control strategies were exploited separately or in combination. The model consists of seven nonlinear ordinary differential equations. More details can be found in [6,19]. This model was used as process simulator in our simulation experiment. The target product outcome is the subject of optimization in present study.

3.2 Optimization Task for PHB Production

The main goal of the process is to maximize the outcome of the final product Q. Hence the utility function at each time step k will be:

$$U(k) = Q(k)V(k) \tag{8}$$

and the aim of optimization procedure will be to maximize the overall outcome by the end of process, i.e.:

$$U_{sum} = \sum_{k=0}^{N} Q(k)V(k) \tag{9}$$

Vector $State(k)$ includes all main process state variables, i.e.:

$$State(k) = (X_1(k), S(k), P(k), X_2(k), N(k), Q(k)) \tag{10}$$

where X_1 and X_2 denote concentrations of two microorganisms; P is the intermediate metabolite (lactate) concentration; N is the nitrogen source concentration; S is sugar source concentration.

The applied control scheme is described in more detail in [6,19]. We suppose that all concentration controllers work properly and that they are able to follow the set points. Hence the optimization task to be solved is to determine the proper values of these set points at each moment. The control vector consists of the three set points of the main control variables as follows:

$$a(k) = (S^*(k), N^*(k), DO^*(k)) \tag{11}$$

Here DO is dissolved oxygen concentration in the cultural broth.

Following the ACD scheme from Fig. 1, for each control variable a corresponding ESN action network was trained using both gradient and associative rules described above. In present work we choose to have only one input of each action ESN - the key intermediate metabolite P since it is on-line measurable and its concentration is of crucial importance for process trend.

4 Results and Discussion

For the ESN critic training and simulation a Matlab toolbox from [17] with our improvements for IP training as in [15] was used. The critic network has 9 inputs (6 for the process state variables plus 3 for the control actions), 10 reservoir neurons and 1 output. The action networks have one input, one output and 5 neurons in the reservoir each. All reservoir neurons have hyperbolic tangent output function. The initial set point profiles were taken from [6]. Detailed optimization algorithm can be found in [5]. It consists of consecutive critic and actor training iterations. Here for comparative purpose simple gradient algorithm without any improvement (such as momentum term or variable speed) was used. After every cycle of a critic plus an action training iteration parameter γ is slightly increased until it become equal to 0.5. During first 1000 iterations γ reaches its maximal

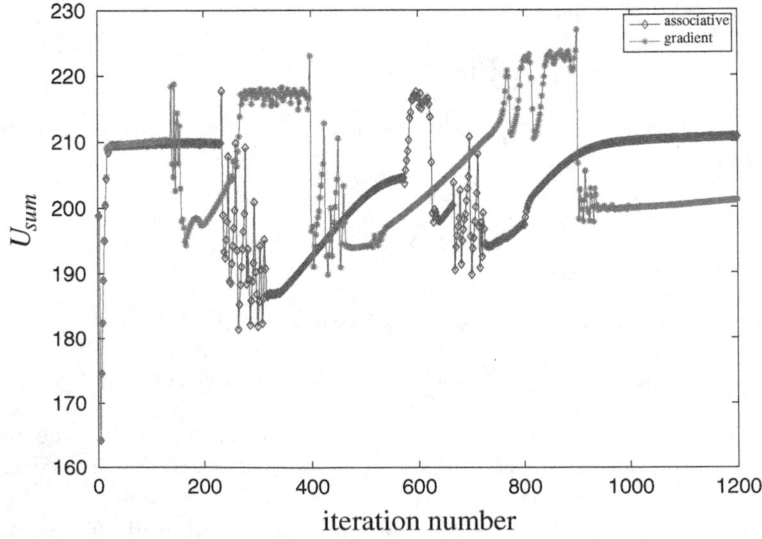

Fig. 3. Change of utility function value during iterative optimization.

value and within the rest of 200 iterations it was constant. Figure 3 represents the change of the value of the utility function during iterative optimization for both gradient and associative learning algorithms. Since in previous work [9] it was observed that the procedure is too sensitive to big changes in discount factor, here a small step of 0.001 was used.

It was observed that although at the beginning the gradient algorithm looks faster and it reaches bigger utility values in comparison with the associative one, by the end of iterations associative algorithm gives bigger outcome in comparison with the gradient one. Looking at convergence speed it seems almost the same for both algorithms especially after discount factor reaches its maximum value. Further improvement of both algorithms could be achieved by using variable learning rate that will allow to prevent observed now big variations of the utility values during iterations. In both cases the trained actors have stable work. There was not observed uncontrolled increase of trained weights - a problem that was observed in the case of RLS training procedure before.

5 Conclusions

The carried out simulation investigations showed that both gradient and associative learning algorithms fit well to training of readout connections of the ESN actor in ACD scheme. Associative learning can be consider as the better algorithm in comparison with the gradient one because: it achieved bigger utility value; it is more biologically plausible; during the iterations it showed slightly smaller variations of the utility function and better convergence characteristics.

Acknowledgments. The research work reported in the paper is partly supported by the project AComIn, grant 316087, funded by the FP7 Capacity Programme (Research Potential of Convergence Regions).

References

1. Barto, A.G., Sutton, R.S., Anderson, C.W.: Neuronlike adaptive elements that can solve difficult learning control problems. IEEE Trans. Syst. Man Cybern. **13**(5), 834–846 (1983)
2. Bellman, R.E.: Dynamic Programming. Princeton University Press, Princeton (1957)
3. Bertsekas, D.P., Tsitsiklis, J.N.: Neuro-Dymanic Programming. Athena Scientific, Belmont (1996)
4. Jaeger, H.: Tutorial on training recurrent neural networks, covering BPPT, RTRL, EKF and the "echo state network" approach. GMD Report 159, German National Research Center for Information Technology (2002)
5. Koprinkova-Hristova, P., Palm, G.: Adaptive Critic Design with ESN critic for bioprocess optimization. In: Diamantaras, K., Duch, W., Iliadis, L.S. (eds.) ICANN 2010, Part II. LNCS, vol. 6353, pp. 438–447. Springer, Heidelberg (2010)
6. Koprinkova-Hristova, P.: Knowledge-based approach to control of mixed culture cultivation for PHB production process. Biotechnol. Biotechnol. Equip. **22**(4), 964–967 (2008)

7. Koprinkova-Hristova, P., Oubbati, M., Palm, G.: Adaptive Critic Design with echo state network. In: Proceedings of 2010 IEEE International Conference on Systems, Man and Cybernetics, Istanbul, Turkey, 10–13 October, pp. 1010–1015 (2010)
8. Koprinkova-Hristova, P., Oubbati, M., Palm, G.: Heuristic dynamic programming using echo state network as online trainable adaptive critic. Int. J. Adapt. Control Sig. Process. **27**(10), 902–914 (2013)
9. Koprinkova-Hristova, P.: Adaptive Critic Design and heuristic search for optimization. In: Lirkov, I., Margenov, S., Waśniewski, J. (eds.) LSSC 2013. LNCS, vol. 8353, pp. 248–255. Springer, Heidelberg (2014)
10. Lenardis, G.G.: A retrospective on adaptive dynamic programming for control. In: Proceedings of International Joint Conference on Neural Networks, Atlanta, GA, USA, 14–19 June, pp. 1750–1757 (2009)
11. Lukosevicius, M., Jaeger, H.: Reservoir computing approaches to recurrent neural network training. Comput. Sci. Rev. **3**, 127–149 (2009)
12. Prokhorov, D.V.: Adaptive Critic Designs and their applications. Ph.D. dissertation. Department of Electrical Engineering, Texas Tech. Univ. (1997)
13. Prokhorov, D.: Toward effective combination of off-line and on-line training in ADP framework. In: Proceedings of the 2007 IEEE Symposium on Approximate Dynamic Programming and Reinforcement Learning (ADPRL 2007), pp. 268–271 (2007)
14. Prokhorov, D.: Training recurrent neurocontrollers for real-time applications. IEEE Trans. Neural Netw. **18**(4), 1003–1015 (2007)
15. Schrauwen, B., Wandermann, M., Verstraeten, D., Steil, J.J.: Improving reservoirs using intrinsic plasticity. Neurocomputing **71**, 1159–1171 (2008)
16. Si, J., Wang, Y.-T.: On-line learning control by association and reinforcement. IEEE Trans. Neural Netw. **12**(2), 264–276 (2001)
17. Jaeger, H., Group members: Simple and very simple Matlab toolbox for Echo State Networks. http://www.reservoir-computing.org/software
18. Sutton, R.S.: Learning to predict by methods of temporal differences. Mach. Learn. **3**, 9–44 (1988)
19. Tohyama, M., Patarinska, T., Qiang, Z., Shimizu, K.: Modeling of the mixed culture and periodic control for PHB production. Biochem. Eng. J. **10**, 157–173 (2002)
20. Werbos, P.J.: Backpropagation through time: what it does and how to do it. Proc. IEEE **78**(10), 1550–1560 (1990)

Free Search in Multidimensional Space II

Kalin Penev(✉)

Technology School, Maritime and Technology Faculty, Southampton Solent University, East Park Terrace, Southampton SO14 0YN, UK
Kalin.Penev@solent.ac.uk

Abstract. Recent publications suggest that resolving multidimensional tasks where optimisation parameters are hundreds and more faces unusual computational limitation. In the same time optimisation algorithms, which perform well on tasks with low number of dimensions, when are applied to high dimensional tasks require infeasible period of time and computational resources. This article presents a novel investigation on Differential Evolution and Particle Swarm Optimisation with enhanced adaptivity and Free Search applied to 200 dimensional versions of three scalable, global, real-value, numerical tests, which optimal values are dependent on dimensions number and virtually unknown for variety of dimensions. The aim is to: (1) identify computational limitations which numerical methods could face on 200 dimensional tests; (2) identify relations between test complexity and period of time required for tests resolving; (3) discover unknown optimal solutions; (4) identify specific methods' peculiarities which could support the performance on high dimensional tasks. Experimental results are presented and analysed.

Keywords: Free Search · Differential Evolution · Particle Swarm Optimization · Multidimensional dimensions optimization

1 Introduction

This article presents a novel investigation on two hundred dimensional (200D) versions of three scalable real-value numerical tests. Explored are real coded optimisation algorithms Free Search (FS) [10], Differential Evolution (DE) [15] and Particle Swarm Optimisation (PSO) [3]. It continues the efforts on multidimensional optimisation published earlier [12]. The number of potential solution for 200 dimensions (200D), similarly to one hundred dimensional tests is large. This makes these tasks difficult for identification of the optimal solutions and their clarification with acceptable level of precision.

Substantial research efforts are involved in evaluation and improvement of existing and design of new methods capable of resolving multidimensional tasks [5, 7–9, 12–14, 16, 17].

Publications suggest that assessment of evolutionary methods, is limited to 10, 30, 50 and 100 dimensions [7] and methods which perform well on numerical tests with up to 10, 30 and 50 dimensions are suffering insuperable stagnation on 100 dimensional tests [7, 12]. When applied to multidimensional tasks with hundreds of parameters well-known methods face difficulties such as: - need for large number of objective

I. Dimov et al. (Eds.): NMA 2014, LNCS 8962, pp. 103–111, 2015.
DOI: 10.1007/978-3-319-15585-2_12

function evaluations (OFE); - need for large computational resources; - need for large period of time for calculations; - inability to identify optimal solution; - inability to clarify optimal solution with appropriate level of precision [12]. In summary identification of optimal solutions with acceptable level of precision and within acceptable period of time for more than 100 dimensions seems a great challenge and need additional research efforts.

The aim of this study is also to continue evaluation of DE and PSO with enhanced abilities for adaptation and FS, to avoid stagnation and trapping in local suboptimal solution, to identify minimal number of iterations required to resolve 200 dimensional optimisation tests with acceptable precision. For this purpose three scalable, global, real-value, numerical tests, which optimal values are dependent on dimensions number and virtually unknown for 200 dimensions are used - Schwefel [1], Michalewicz [6] and Norwegian [2] tests.

2 Test Problems

Tests selection uses the following criteria:

- must be scalable to 200 dimensions;
- must be for global optimisation with many local suboptimal solutions;
- must not provide initial knowledge for optimal solution value and location;
- optimal solution must be dependent on dimensions number.

The test, which meets the above criteria and selected for this investigation are presented below.

2.1 Schwefel Test

This test function referred in the literature [1] is:

$$f(x_i) = 418.9829^* n - \sum_{i=1}^{n} x_i \sin\left(\sqrt{|x_i|}\right) \tag{1}$$

where n is the number of dimensions and $-500 \le x_i \le 500$, $i = 1, \ldots, n$. The maximum is dependent on dimensions number and for n = 200 is unknown.

2.2 Michalewicz Test Function

The Michalewicz test function [6] is global optimisation problem. In this study it is transformed for maximization.

$$f(x_i) = \sum_{i=1}^{n} \sin(x_i)(\sin(ix_i^2/\pi))^{2m} \tag{2}$$

where search space is defined as $0 \leq x_i \leq \pi$, i = 1,...,n, $m = 10$. The maximum is dependent on dimensions number and for n = 200 is unknown.

2.3 Norwegian Test Function

Norwegian test function is global test problem [2].

$$f(x_i) = \prod_{i=1}^{n} \left(\cos(\pi x_i^3) \left(\frac{99 + x_i}{100} \right) \right) \tag{3}$$

where search space borders are defined by $-1.1 < x_i < 1.1$, i = 1,...,n. The maximum is dependent on dimensions number and for n = 200 is unknown.

3 Optimization Methods

In this study three optimization methods are used – FS, DE and PSO. In order to clarify the abilities to explore and resolve multidimensional global tasks this section focuses on the event modification of these algorithms.

3.1 Free Search

Free Search is adaptive heuristic method [10] for real coded optimisation. It is based on a conceptual model, which is different from other methods. In Free Search optimisation process of continuous search space is organised in sequence of short explorations within continuous neighbouring area.

Modification strategy for FS is generated according to the Eqs. (4) and (5):

$$x_{tji} = x_{0ji} - \Delta x_{tji} + 2^* \Delta x_{tji}{}^* random_{tji}(0, 1) \tag{4}$$

x_{0ji} is an initial or previous location marked as good. $random_{tji}(0, 1)$ is a random value between 0 and 1. t is current step $t = 1, \ldots, T$, T is the step limit per exploration. Δx_{tji} is the step. The step size generation is:

$$\Delta x_{tji} = R_{ji}{}^* (Xmax_i - Xmin_i)^* random_{tji}(0, 1) \tag{5}$$

where R_{ji} is a variable value of the neighbour space radius $R_{ji} = [Rmin, Rmax]$. $Xmin_i$ and $Xmax_i$ are the search space borders. $random_{tji}(0, 1)$ is a random value between 0 and 1. The search space borders restrict the probability for access to any location within the search space, only. Variation of R_{ji} higher than one exceeds the search space borders and guarantees non-zero probability for access to any location within the search space. It guarantees a probabilistic transaction rule for exploration of the whole space. FS is implemented with a population of 10 individuals and the explorations are 5 steps, for all experiments. The sense is random in the highest 10 % of the sensibility, and the neighbouring space varies from 0.5 to 1.5 with step 0.1 [10].

3.2 Differential Evolution

Differential Evolution could be classified as a simple and powerful real value optimisation method. Explored solutions in DE are called vectors. DE selects from current population target, donor and differential vectors. From these vectors DE generates a new trial vector, which replaces the target vector, if it is better, in the new population. The authors proposed several strategies for generation of a trail vector [15].

In line with the literature target vector is denoted as X_k, differential vectors are X_i and X_j, and differential factor (weight) is F. Every pair of vectors (X_i, X_j) in the primary array defines a difference $X_i - X_j$. These two vectors are usually chosen randomly, their weighted difference is used to perturb another vector in the primary array, X_k':

$$X_k' = X_k + F(X_i - X_j) \tag{6}$$

F scales the difference achieved from $X_i - X_j$. An effective variation of this scheme involves keeping track of the best vector so far noted as X^*. This can be combined with X_k and then perturbed, producing:

$$X_k' = X_k + F(X^* - X_k) + F(X_i - X_j). \tag{7}$$

Several modification strategies are originally proposed:

$$X_k' = X_k + F(X_i - X_j), \tag{8}$$

$$X_k' = X^* + F(X_i - X_j), \tag{9}$$

$$X_k' = X_k + F(X^* - X_k) + F(X_i - X_j), \tag{10}$$

$$X_k' = X^* + F(X_i - X_j + X_n - X_m), \tag{11}$$

$$X_k' = X_k + F(X^* - X_k + X_n - X_m). \tag{12}$$

DE is implemented with population of 10 individuals and explored with strategy at Eq. (12). All individuals are subject of replacement. The crossover probability is 0.5. Differential factor varies from 0.5 to 1.5 with step 0.1.

3.3 Particle Swarm Optimisation

Particle Swarm Optimisation could be classified as real value optimisation method motivated from simulation of social behaviour of a group of individuals [3]. PSO generates new values for all particles (individuals) in the swarm (population). It memorises the previous individual and social (swarm) experience and it uses them for generation of new particles.

Earlier the modification strategy of PSO has been improved by use of the original concept for the so called inertia parameter that increases the overall performance of

PSO [3]. With the addition of the inertia factor, w, [4] the particles are manipulated according to the following equations:

$$v_{id} = w * v_{id} + n_1 * random(0,1) * (P_{id} - x_{id}) + n_2 * random(0,1) * (g_d - x_{id}) \quad (13)$$

$$x_{id} = x_{id} + v_{id} \quad (14)$$

Where the constants n_1 and n_2 determine the relative influence of the social and cognitive components, and are usually both set the same to give each component equal weight as the cognitive and social learning rate. PSO is implemented and explored with inertia parameter. The inertia parameter varies from 0.5 to 1.5 with step 0.1. It has a population of 10 individuals for all experiments. The individual and the social learning factors are 2 for all experiments.

4 Experimental Methodology

Methodology aims to identify minimal number of OFE required to achieve optimal result with acceptable level of precision. Selected test are evaluated in two series of 320 experiments, with start from different random locations. First series are limited to 2.10^6 and second to 2.10^8 OFE. Achieved experimental results are presented and compared for maximal achieved result.

5 Experimental Results

Achieved from two series of 320 experiments results on Schwefel, Michalewicz and Norwegian test functions are presented in Tables 1, 2, 3, and 4 below.

Table 1. Maximal results from 320 experiments

	Function evaluations	FS	DE	PSO
Schwefel	2.10^6	167582	146154	139643
	2.10^8	167592	146372	140457
Michalewicz	2.10^6	199.473	158.7	153.809
	2.10^8	199.612	162.486	156.381
Norwegian	2.10^6	0.553932	0.19664	0.0209277
	2.10^8	1.00007	0.203317	0.021299

Table 2. Mean results from 320 experiments

	Function evaluations	FS	DE	PSO
Schwefel	2.10^6	167577.8906	128025.4094	107220.6172
	2.10^8	167591.9969	131360.6531	108331.9978
Michalewicz	2.10^6	199.3335375	81.97717438	57.07641063
	2.10^8	199.6084094	100.1925019	60.7117175
Norwegian	2.10^6	0.478959472	0.042988971	9.26984E-05
	2.10^8	0.9795565	0.082466566	9.30029E-05

Table 3. Standard deviation from 320 experiments

	Function evaluations	FS	DE	PSO
Schwefel	2.10^6	1.570401894	11641.83834	16045.21447
	2.10^8	0.967082	9190.399551	16166.05376
Michalewicz	2.10^6	0.063176775	35.83038048	40.39638912
	2.10^8	0.001784807	40.55275988	42.02935262
Norwegian	2.10^6	0.026979583	0.072504813	0.001185493
	2.10^8	0.009963986	0.087516196	0.001205768

Table 4. Standard deviation from 320 experiments in % from maximum

	Function evaluations	FS	DE	PSO
Schwefel	2.10^6	0.0000973 %	6.9465358 %	9.5739739 %
	2.10^8	0.0000577 %	5.4837937 %	9.6460772 %
Michalewicz	2.10^6	0.0031649 %	17.9500132 %	20.2374552 %
	2.10^8	0.0000894 %	20.3157925 %	21.0555240 %
Norwegian	2.10^6	2.6977694 %	7.24997380 %	0.1185410 %
	2.10^8	0.9963288 %	8.75100702 %	0.1205683 %

6 Discussion

Analysis of experimental results suggests that on Schwefel and Michalewicz test functions DE and PSO stagnate in suboptimal solutions for all experiments limited to 2.10^6 and 2.10^8 OFE. Reasons for this could be a subject of further research. On Schwefel and Michalewicz test FS achieves optimal solution for all experiments limited to 2.10^6 and 2.10^8 OFE. For experiments limited to 2.10^8 OFE FS refines the precision of the results for Michalewicz test with 0.3 % and for Schwefel test with 0.02 %.

Solving 200 dimensional Schwefel and Michalewicz tests for each run confirms good exploration abilities of FS. It indirectly suggests that these tasks could be resolved within less number of OFE, which could be a subject of further research. For Norwegian test function used implementations of DE and PSO stagnate in suboptimal solutions for all experiments limited to 2.10^6 and 2.10^8 OFE. DE and PSO had also difficulties on 2 dimensional [11] and 100D versions [12] of this test. Reasons for this could be a subject of further research.

In contrast FS confirms its abilities to avoid stagnation and escape from trapping in suboptimal local areas. For the first series of 320 experiments on Norwegian test limited to 2.10^6 OFE FS does not reach optimal solution. However for tests limited to 2.10^8 OFE from 320 runs with different start locations FS reaches 26 times optimal solutions with acceptable precision (above 1.00004). This corresponds to 8 % probability for success. Whether high probability for success will be reached for higher number of OFE could be a subject of further research. Overall this is a good illustration of the effectiveness of FS modification strategy, which guarantees non-zero probability for access to the whole search space during entire optimization process.

Other essential issue is a period of time required for completion of optimization task. For experiments limited to 2.10^8 OFE average periods of time in minutes, from 320 experiments, required for completion of one experiment on Schwefel, Michalewicz and Norwegian test are presented in Table 5 below.

Table 5. Average period of time in minutes for 2.10^8 objective function evaluations

	Function evaluations	FS	DE	PSO
Schwefel	200 000 000	31 min	82 min	221 min
Michalewicz	200 000 000	84 min	131 min	230 min
Norwegian	200 000 000	15 min	62 min	145 min

Time periods in Table 5 are measured on processor Intel i7 3960x overclocked to 4.5 GHz and memory G. Skill TridentX at 1866 MHz, motherboard ASUS Rampage VI and solid state disk - SanDisk Extreme SSD SATA III. Experiments are completed simultaneously in hyper-treading processor mode. The results presented in Table 5 indicate that FS completes the tests faster than DE and PSO. In the same time Table 1 shows that FS reaches optimal solutions and DE and PSO did not.

Achieved results confirm that FS process is more effective than logically and analytically organised search processes on uncertain and unknown global multidimensional problems due to the expiration, during the search process, of the knowledge, on which logical processes are based.

7 Conclusion

This article presents experimental evaluation of FS, DE and PSO on hard global multidimensional tests. Identified are minimal numbers of iterations for which selected test could be resolved with certain probability. Achieved results suggest that FS completed the same number of objective function evaluation for less time than DE and PSO and riches optimal solutions with 100 % probability for Schwefel and

Michalewicz tests and 8 % for Norwegian test, while DE and PSO success is 0 % for all tests. Further investigation could focus on evaluation and measure of time and computational resources sufficient for completion of other multidimensional tasks or for higher number of dimensions until reaching the limits of modern computational systems. Algorithms analysis and improvement could be also subject of future research.

Acknowledgements. I would like to thank to my students Asim Al Nashwan, Dimitrios Kalfas, Georgius Haritonidis, and Michael Borg for the design, implementation and overclocking of desktop PC used for completion of the experiments presented in this article.

References

1. Bäck, T., Schwefel, H.P.: An overview of evolutionary algorithms for parameter optimization. Evol. Comput. **1**(1), 1–23 (1993)
2. Brekke, E.F.: Complex Behaviour in Dynamical Systems, pp. 37–38. The Norwegian University of Science and Technology (2004). http://www.academia.edu/545835/COMPLEX_BEHAVIOR_IN_DYNAMICAL_SYSTEMS. Accessed 29 May 2014
3. Eberhart, R., Kennedy, J.: Particle swarm optimisation. In: Proceedings of the 1995 IEEE International Conference on Neural Networks, vol. 4, pp. 1942–1948. IEEE Press (1995)
4. Eberhart, R., Shi, Y.: Comparing inertia weights and construction factors in particle swarm optimization. In: Proceedings of the 2000 CEC, pp. 84–89 (2000)
5. Hendtlass, T.: Particle swarm optimization and high dimensional problem spaces, In: IEEE Congress on Evolutionary Computation, CEC 2009, pp. 1988–1994 (2009)
6. Hedar, A.-R.: Test functions for unconstrained global optimization (2014). http://www-optima.amp.i.kyoto-u.ac.jp/member/student/hedar/Hedar_files/TestGO_files/Page2376.htm. Accessed 29 May 2014
7. Liang, J.J., Qu, B.-Y., Suganthan, P.N.: Problem definitions and evaluation criteria for the CEC 2014 special session and competition on single objective real-parameter numerical optimization. Technical report 201311, December 2013 (2014). http://www.ntu.edu.sg/home/EPNSugan/index_files/CEC2014/CEC2014.htm. Accessed 16 September 2014
8. MacNish, C., Yao, X.: Direction matters in high-dimensional optimisation. In: IEEE Congress on Evolutionary Computation, pp. 2372–2379 (2008)
9. Noman, N., Iba, H.: Enhancing differential evolution performance with local search for high dimensional function optimization. In: Proceedings of the 2005 Conference on Genetic and Evolutionary Computation, pp. 967–974 (2005)
10. Penev, K.: Free Search of Real Value or How to Make Computers Think. St. Qu, Southampton (2008). ISBN 978-0-9558948-0-0
11. Penev, K.: Adaptive intelligence - essential aspects. J. Inf. Technol. Control **VII**(4), 8–17 (2009). ISSN 1312-2622
12. Penev, K.: Free search – comparative analysis 100. Int. J. Metaheuristics **3**(1), 22–33 (2013)
13. Liu, P., Lau, F., Lewis, M.J., Wang, C.-l.: A new asynchronous parallel evolutionary algorithm for function optimization. In: Guervós, J.J.M., Adamidis, P.A., Beyer, H.-G., Fernández-Villacañas, J.-L., Schwefel, H.-P. (eds.) PPSN 2002. LNCS, vol. 2439, pp. 401–410. Springer, Heidelberg (2002)
14. Liu, P., Lewis, M.J.: Communication aspects of an asynchronous parallel evolutionary algorithm. In: Proceedings of the Third International Conference on Communications in Computing, Las Vegas, NV, 24–27 June 2002, pp. 190–195 (2002)

15. Storn, R.: Constrained optimisation. Dr. Dobb's J. **20**(5), 119–123 (1995)
16. Yanga, Z., Tanga, K., Yaoa, X.: Large scale evolutionary optimization using cooperative coevolution. Inf. Sci. **178**(15), 2985–2999 (2008)
17. Yang, Z., Tang, K., Yao, X.: Differential evolution for high-dimensional function optimization. In: IEEE Congress on Evolutionary Computation, 25–28 September 2007, pp. 3523–3530 (2007)

A Semi-numerical Approach to Radiation Boundary Conditions

Ivan A. Starkov[1(✉)] and Alexander S. Starkov[2]

[1] SIX Research Centre, Brno University of Technology, Technická 12, 616 00 Brno, Czech Republic
starkov@feec.vutbr.cz

[2] Institute of Refrigeration and Biotechnology, University ITMO, Kronverksky pr. 49, 197101 St. Petersburg, Russia

Abstract. The study proposes a new semi-numerical approach to absorbing boundary problem. The developed method relies on the new formulation of generalized impedance boundary conditions. A distinguishing feature of the approach is the possibility to obtain an analytical solution after performing numerical calculations. The accuracy of the presented model was verified by comparing the simulation results with the exact solution for dipole and loop antennas radiation problem. The examples are based on a finite difference scheme but finite element methods can also be used.

Keywords: Radiation boundary conditions · Artificial boundary · Radiation pattern

1 Introduction

Computational procedures based on discretization schemes require the replacement of the condition at infinity by a boundary condition on a finite artificial surface. Unfortunately, reflections or wraparound from such artificial surfaces present a difficulty when running simulations. In other words, direct imposition of the condition at infinity along the numerical grid results in large errors. There are a number of different ways that this problem might be solved and each of them have their own advantages and limitations. Typically, this procedure involves a compromise between efficiency of solution and accuracy of the reformulation.

In this paper we present an accurate derivation of radiation boundary conditions that provide increasingly accurate approximations to the problem in the infinite domain. The main idea of the approach is to replace the absorbing conditions in the usual sense (ABC) on a new semi-analytical formulation of the generalized impedance boundary conditions (SAGIBC). The applicability to a smaller vicinity of the radiation source makes GIBC [1] a very attractive option [2]. The described method allows a significant reduction in the computational costs without accuracy losses and can be used in a wide class of wave equations. Following the standard strategy, we examine the effectiveness of the proposed conditions on the basis of analytic solutions.

I. Dimov et al. (Eds.): NMA 2014, LNCS 8962, pp. 112–119, 2015.
DOI: 10.1007/978-3-319-15585-2_13

2 The Approach

The initial-boundary value problem for vector, or electromagnetic, waves is to find the vector fields uniquely characterized by the Silver-Müller radiation conditions [3]. Maxwell's equations for an isotropic medium demand that the electric $\mathbf{E}$ and magnetic $\mathbf{H}$ fields have an asymptotic

$$\begin{aligned} \mathbf{E}(r,\theta,\varphi) &= \frac{\mathrm{e}^{ikr}}{r}\mathbf{E}_0(\theta,\varphi) + O\left(\frac{1}{r^2}\right), \\ \mathbf{H}(r,\theta,\varphi) &= \frac{\mathrm{e}^{ikr}}{r}\mathbf{H}_0(\theta,\varphi) + O\left(\frac{1}{r^2}\right), \end{aligned} \tag{1}$$

where $\mathbf{E}_0(\theta,\varphi)$ and $\mathbf{H}_0(\theta,\varphi)$ are radiation patterns in spherical coordinates (r,θ,φ), while k is the wave number. Further, we will consider a single component of the vector $\mathbf{E}$ and by E denote the absolute value of the electric field strength. To formulate it more precisely than asymptotic (1) and to obtain an exact formula, the electric field at any point in space $r > 0$ ($r \neq 0$) can be expressed using spherical harmonics expansion [4] as follows

$$E(r,\theta,\varphi) = \sum_{l=0}^{\infty}\sum_{m=-\infty}^{\infty} a_{l,m}\psi_{l,m}(r,\theta,\varphi). \tag{2}$$

Here $a_{l,m}$ are the unknown Fourier coefficients and the spherical harmonics $\psi_{l,m}(r,\theta,\varphi)$ are given by [5]

$$\psi_{l,m}(r,\theta,\varphi) = \sqrt{\frac{\pi}{2kr}}H^{(1)}_{l+1/2}(kr)P^m_l(\cos\theta)\mathrm{e}^{im\varphi}. \tag{3}$$

In (3) $H^{(1)}_{l+1/2}$ is the Hankel function of the first kind and P^m_l the associated Legendre polynomials. These functions are well known and may always be found in literature (see, e.g. [6]).

2.1 Construction of the Generalized Impedance Boundary Conditions

In order to formulate the boundary conditions problem, we can restrict ourselves to consider only N first terms in the expansion (2). This number N corresponds to the amount of grid points on the artificial boundary surface. Obviously, N must be consistent with the indexes $l = 0, ..., L$ and $m = -M, ..., M$. The choice of the optimal number of harmonics depends on the geometry and position of the radiation source. We have chosen that the indexes l and m are defined in the way that $L \times (2M + 1) = N$. This is the easiest and low cost variant for the purposes described in Sect. 3. However, the last relation is not rigorous. This ratio is chosen as an optimal from accuracy and calculation time point of view.

We can assume $L \times 2(M+1) = N$ and account additional harmonic in the expansion (2) in the case of odd L and even number of boundary points.

That is, for the i-th point on the artificial boundary with coordinates (r_i, θ_i, φ_i) we can write down

$$E_i = \sum_{l=0}^{L} \sum_{m=-M}^{M} a_{l,m} \psi_{l,m}(r_i, \theta_i, \varphi_i), \quad i = 1, ..., N. \tag{4}$$

As a next step, let us calculate the derivative along the normal $\mathbf{n}$ to the boundary surface at the point $(r_i, \theta_i, \varphi_i)$

$$\left[\frac{\partial E}{\partial n}\right]_i = \sum_{l=0}^{L} \sum_{m=-M}^{M} a_{l,m}(\nabla \psi_{l,m}(r_i, \theta_i, \varphi_i) \cdot \mathbf{n}_i), \tag{5}$$

with

$$\nabla \psi = \frac{\partial \psi}{\partial r}\mathbf{e}_r + \frac{1}{r}\frac{\partial \psi}{\partial \theta}\mathbf{e}_\theta + \frac{1}{r \sin\theta}\frac{\partial \psi}{\partial \varphi}\mathbf{e}_\varphi. \tag{6}$$

Here $\{\mathbf{e}_r, \mathbf{e}_\theta, \mathbf{e}_\varphi\}$ are the basis vectors of the coordinate system, $\mathbf{n}_i$ is the unit normal vector to the boundary surface at the i-th point, and the dot is a scalar product. Further, we introduce the column matrices $\mathbb{A}$, $\mathbb{E}$, and $\mathbb{E}'$ of the same dimension $1 \times N$ with elements given by unknown coefficients $\{a_m, E_i, [\partial E/\partial n]_i\}$, respectively. To be more precisely

$$\mathbb{A} = \begin{pmatrix} a_{0,-M} \\ a_{0,-M+1} \\ \vdots \\ a_{1,M} \\ \vdots \\ a_{L,M} \end{pmatrix}, \quad \mathbb{E} = \begin{pmatrix} E_1 \\ E_2 \\ \vdots \\ E_N \end{pmatrix}, \quad \mathbb{E}' = \begin{pmatrix} \left[\frac{\partial E}{\partial n}\right]_1 \\ \left[\frac{\partial E}{\partial n}\right]_2 \\ \vdots \\ \left[\frac{\partial E}{\partial n}\right]_N \end{pmatrix}. \tag{7}$$

Additionally, we define matrices $\mathbb{Z}$ and $\mathbb{Z}'$ of size $N \times N$ with components $\psi_{l,m}(r_i, \varphi_i)$ and $\nabla \psi_{l,m}(r_i, \varphi_i) \cdot \mathbf{n}_i$ by relations (8) and (9).

$$\mathbb{Z} = \begin{pmatrix} \psi_{0,-M}(r_1, \theta_1, \varphi_1) & \cdots & \psi_{L,M}(r_1, \theta_1, \varphi_1) \\ \psi_{0,-M}(r_2, \theta_2, \varphi_2) & \cdots & \psi_{L,M}(r_2, \theta_2, \varphi_2) \\ \vdots & \ddots & \vdots \\ \psi_{0,-M}(r_N, \theta_N, \varphi_N) & \cdots & \psi_{L,M}(r_N, \theta_N, \varphi_N) \end{pmatrix}, \tag{8}$$

$$\mathbb{Z}' = \begin{pmatrix} \nabla \psi_{0,-M}(r_1, \theta_1, \varphi_1) \cdot \mathbf{n}_1 & \cdots & \nabla \psi_{L,M}(r_1, \theta_1, \varphi_1) \cdot \mathbf{n}_1 \\ \nabla \psi_{0,-M}(r_2, \theta_2, \varphi_2) \cdot \mathbf{n}_2 & \cdots & \nabla \psi_{L,M}(r_2, \theta_2, \varphi_2) \cdot \mathbf{n}_2 \\ \vdots & \ddots & \vdots \\ \nabla \psi_{0,-M}(r_N, \theta_N, \varphi_N) \cdot \mathbf{n}_N & \cdots & \nabla \psi_{L,M}(r_N, \theta_N, \varphi_N) \cdot \mathbf{n}_N \end{pmatrix}, \tag{9}$$

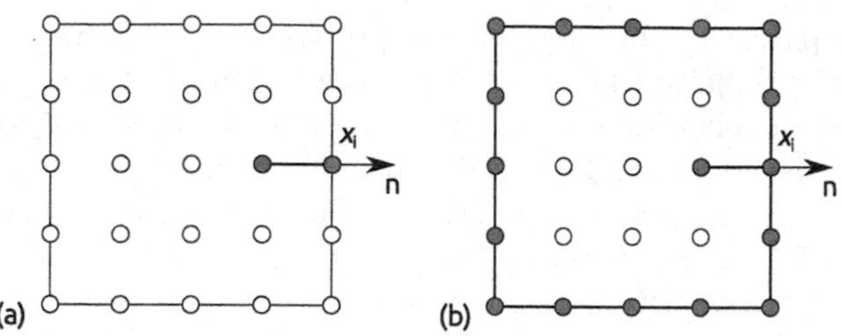

Fig. 1. The geometrical interpretation of the generalized impedance boundary conditions (b). In contrast to ABC (a), there is known exact local relation between the normal components at any point of the boundary with contribution from all other boundary points.

Rewriting Eqs. (4), (5) in the matrix form, we obtain the following system of equations

$$\mathbb{E} = \mathbb{Z}\mathbb{A}, \quad \mathbb{E}' = \mathbb{Z}'\mathbb{A}, \tag{10}$$

from which we can derive the required boundary conditions

$$\mathbb{E}' = \mathbb{Z}'\mathbb{Z}^{-1}\mathbb{E}. \tag{11}$$

Thus, the matrix conditions (11) with $\mathbb{Z}'\mathbb{Z}^{-1}$ as a boundary operator connect the values of the normal derivative of the electric field and the electric field itself in the specified points. The physical sense of these conditions is explained in Fig. 1. The value of the normal derivative is linked to all other boundary points, as opposed to ABC. This kind of relation allows us to achieve high computational efficiency without compromising solution accuracy or numerical stability. Moreover, it is necessary to emphasize that the formula (11) is exact.

2.2 Semi-analytical Generalized Impedance Boundary Conditions

For a far-field calculations it is convenient in (3) to replace the Hankel function by its asymptotic [6]. Then, the electric field at the point (r, θ, φ) is

$$E(r,\theta,\varphi) = \frac{e^{ikr}}{kr} \sum_{l=0}^{M} \sum_{m=-M}^{M} a_{l,m} P_l^m(\cos\theta) e^{i[m\varphi - \pi(l+1)/2]}. \tag{12}$$

The obtained conditions (11) can be easily implemented in numerical schemes, e.g. finite difference or finite element methods. As an output of this numerical procedure we can consider coefficients $a_{l,m}$ calculated from the system $\mathbb{A} = \mathbb{Z}^{-1}\mathbb{E}$. If we are interested in a far field solution, it is possible to perform numerical procedure for a small computational domain (which requires less time and resources). Then, to calculate coefficients $a_{l,m}$ and substitute them in (12) or (2). Here it should be pointed out that boundary operator $\mathbb{Z}'\mathbb{Z}^{-1}$ and coefficients $a_{l,m}$ are calculated once and can be used in further calculations, if necessary.

Let us compare the efficiency of the proposed method with ABC. If the dimensions of the radiation source exceed 3–5 wavelengths then number of operations in the both schemes is practically identical. In this case, the advantage of the SAGIBC is the possibility to obtain more accurate analytical expression for the radiation pattern. It can be demonstrated, using the Kurylev approach [7], that with increasing amount of basic functions (number of grid points) the inaccuracy of the SAGIBC method decreases as ${}^{c_1}/_{l^{3/2}} + {}^{c_2}/_{m^{3/2}}$. In the last expression, c_1 and c_2 are some coefficients dependent on the shape of the emitter. At the same time, the inaccuracy of ABC remains constant and does not tend to zero. Another advantage of SAGIBC can be revealed for sources with size less than the radiation wavelength: a small fraction of computing resources required by other methods to determine the radiation pattern. Simple estimates demonstrate that the number of operations decreases as $1 + {}^{4\pi}/_{V}$, with V as a volume of the source measured in wavelengths. From where we can conclude that the reduction in the computational cost can be significant for an elongated radiation object.

In contrast to the ABC method, the developed conditions are precisely defined. As a consequence, the described model requires less computation demands in order to achieve satisfactory outputs. We have a solution written in the form of a series expansion that gives explicit formulas for the field distribution. This is extremely important, for example, when we need to consider the diffraction of the radiated field on an object. In standard approaches, it is required to switch from the numerical radiation pattern to an analytical one. That is, the computational scheme is incredibly appealing for the analysis of the antenna diffraction problem. For this it is only necessary to introduce additional terms in the right-hand side of the system of Eq. (10). Finally, we have considered three-dimensional model problem but the presented approach can be easily generalized to two space dimensions [8].

3 Model Verification Examples

The governing equations for electromagnetic wave propagation are Maxwell's equations, which can be reduced to the Helmholtz equation. In order to demonstrate the model performance, we restrict ourselves to the scalar case of the latter. As an classical absorption radiation condition that enforces waves to be outgoing, we use [9]

$$\frac{\partial E(r,\theta,\varphi)}{\partial n} - ikE(r,\theta,\varphi) = 0 \tag{13}$$

which mathematically has the form of the Sommerfeld condition but is set at a finite boundary rather than at infinity [10]. The radiation source is represented by an elongated object (the average width-length ratio is 0.1) and a round object (identical length and width). Such a strategy is not new and it has been commonly used in far-field analysis. As the objects, we employ two types of wire antennas.

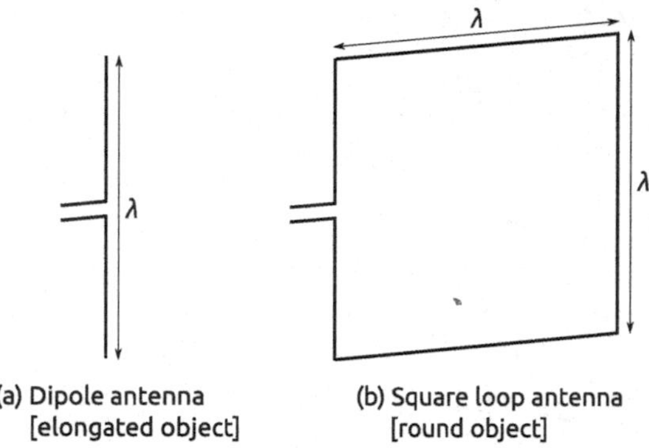

Fig. 2. Schematic representation of (a) dipole and (b) square loop antennas chosen as elongated and round radiation sources, respectively.

Dipole antenna [elongated object]: The first one is the world most popular dipole antenna. It is fed by a two-wire line, where the two currents in the conductors are equal in amplitude but opposite in direction. We consider the case of the total length of the antenna is equal to the wavelength λ of the radiation it is emitting. Since the antenna ends are essentially an open circuit, the current distribution along the length of the dipole is considered sinusoidal [11].

Square loop antenna [round object]: The second example, as a round radiation source, is electrically large loop antenna which has a loop perimeter of four wavelengths. The loop antenna is a conductor bent into the shape of a closed curve with a gap in the conductor to form the terminals. The current distribution is assumed to be sinusoidal and continuous around the loop [12,13]. At low frequencies where physical sizes are large, loops are often square because they are more easily constructed. A simple design of dipole and square loop antennas can be seen in Fig. 2.

In order to solve the Helmholtz equation in a rectangular three-dimensional domain, the standard finite-difference method was used. As the measure of model efficiency, we use a reproduction of the analytic solution [11,12] with precision not less than 5 %. Here we define the absolute error averaged over all points of interest as the modulus of the difference between the analytical and simulated

Table 1. Simulation parameters for different types of conditions.

	ABC		SAGIBC		Improvement [Times]
	Domain size [λ^3]	Grid points	Domain size [λ^3]	Grid points	
Dipole antenna	5.4^3	157264	1.2^3	9261	17.0
Loop antenna	3.2^3	42875	1.1^3	6859	6.3

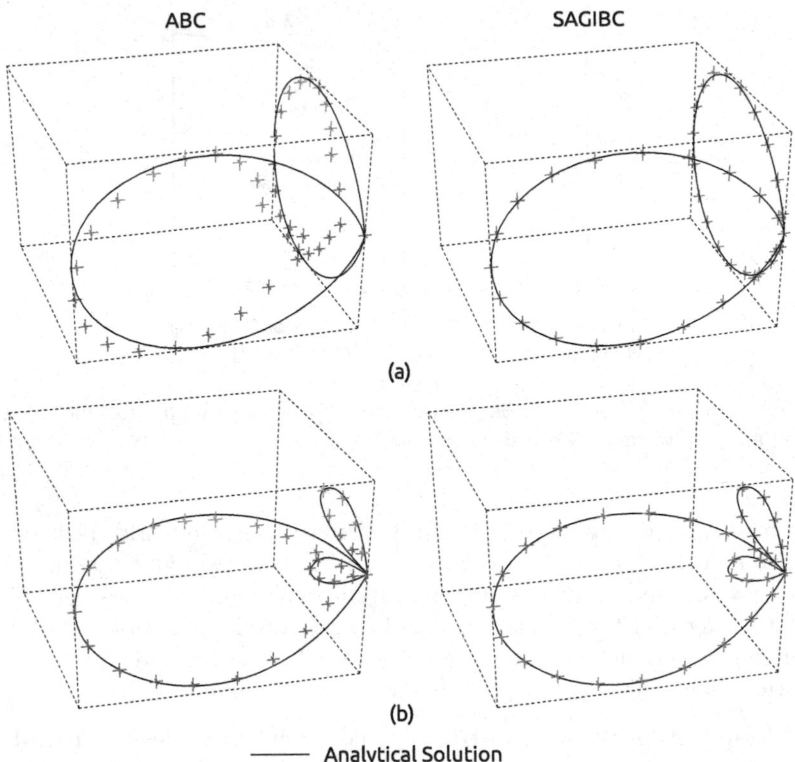

Fig. 3. The normalized 3D radiation patterns for (a) dipole and (b) square loop antennas. The comparison between analytical solution and those obtained from the finite difference method using different boundary conditions (left column – ABC, right column – SAGIBC). The simulations were performed under conditions that are sufficient for the semi-numerical model to fulfill the evaluation criteria (see Table 1). For brevity, in each case the results are presented only for two profiles.

values of the electric field. The parameters used in simulations to achieve such a result are summarized in the Table 1. One can see that calculation procedure with classical ABC (13) requires approximately 17 times more computational resources than SAGIBC for dipole antenna and 6.3 for square loop antenna.

In addition, to compare the accuracy of the approaches we repeat the calculations of the electric field distribution with parameters that are sufficient for the semi-numerical approach to satisfy the evaluation criteria. The normalized radiation patterns calculated by the various schemes are shown in Fig. 3 for more visualization. Note that for graphical reasons only results on two cuts are reported. The curves obtained using SAGIBC at the artificial boundary are significantly better than ABC – the relative error in the radiation pattern can reach 24.4 % in the case of conditions (13).

4 Conclusion

A new approach for constructing radiation boundary conditions has been presented. The main feature of the method is the possibility to obtain an analytical solution after performing numerical calculations. These conditions do not reduce the accuracy of calculations. The magnitude of the error introduced by them is estimated by the accuracy of the electric field on the artificial boundary. The model performance has been demonstrated on the radiation problem of dipole and square loop antennas by the finite difference method. The proposed boundary conditions have lower computational and time demands in comparison with a classical scheme.

Acknowledgments. The paper was funded by the SIX project CZ.1.05/2.1.00/03.0072 and project CZ.1.07/2.3.00/30.0039 of Brno University of Technology. Additionally, this work was supported by Government of Russian Federation, Grant 074-U01.

References

1. Hoppe, D.: Impedance Boundary Conditions in Electromagnetics. Electromagnetics library. Taylor & Francis, London (1995)
2. Haddar, H., Joly, P., Nguyen, H.-M.: Generalized impedance boundary conditions for scattering problems from strongly absorbing obstacles: the case of Maxwell's equations. Math. Models Meth. Appl. Sci. **10**(18), 1787–1827 (2008)
3. Wilcox, C.H.: Spherical means and radiation conditions. Arch. Ration. Mech. Anal. **3**(1), 133–148 (1959)
4. Deakin, A., Rasmussen, H.: Nonreflecting boundary condition for the Helmholtz equation. Comput. Math. Appl. **41**(3), 307–318 (2001)
5. Weber, H., Arfken, G.: Essential Mathematical Methods for Physicists. Academic Press, San Diego (2004)
6. Abramowitz, M., Stegun, I.A.: Handbook of Mathematical Functions: With Formulas, Graphs, and Mathematical Tables. Dover Publications, New York (2012)
7. Kurylev, Y., Starkov, A.: Directional moments in the acoustic inverse problem. In: Chavent, G., Sacks, P., Papanicolaou, G., Symes, W.W. (eds.) Inverse Problems in Wave Propagation, pp. 295–323. Springer, New York (1997)
8. Starkov, I., Raida, Z., Starkov, A.: A new model for radiation boundary conditions. In: Proceedings of the IEEE 24th International Conference Radioelektronika, pp. 1–4 (2014)
9. Cooray, F., Costache, G.: An overview of the absorbing boundary conditions. J. Electromagn. Waves Appl. **5**(10), 1041–1054 (1991)
10. Lui, S.H.: Numerical Analysis of Partial Differential Equations. Pure and Applied Mathematics: A Wiley Series of Texts, Monographs and Tracts. Wiley, New York (2012)
11. Kong, J.: Electromagnetic Wave Theory. Wiley, New York (1986)
12. Prasad, S.: Radiation field of the corner-driven square loop antenna. Technical report, No 283, Cruft Laboratory, Harvard University, February 1959
13. Murakami, Y., Yoshida, A., Ieda, K., Nakamura, T.: Rectangular loop antenna for circular polarization. Electron. Commun. Jpn (Part I: Communications) **79**(3), 42–51 (1996)

Advanced Numerical Methods for Scientific Computing

Spectral Analysis of Geometric Multigrid Methods for Isogeometric Analysis

Clemens Hofreither(✉) and Walter Zulehner

Institute of Computational Mathematics,
Johannes Kepler University Linz,
Altenbergerstr. 69, 4040 Linz, Austria
chofreither@numa.uni-linz.ac.at

Abstract. We investigate geometric multigrid methods for solving the large, sparse linear systems which arise in isogeometric discretizations of elliptic partial differential equations. We observe that the performance of standard V-cycle iteration is highly dependent on the spatial dimension as well as the spline degree of the discretization space. Conjugate gradient iteration preconditioned with one V-cycle mitigates this dependence, but does not eliminate it. We perform both classical local Fourier analysis as well as a numerical spectral analysis of the two-grid method to gain better understanding of the underlying problems and observe that classical smoothers do not perform well in the isogeometric setting.

1 Introduction

Isogeometric analysis (IGA), a numerical technique for the solution of partial differential equations first proposed in [5], has attracted considerable research attention in recent years. The efficient solution of the discretized systems arising in isogeometric analysis has been the topic of several publications [2–4,6,8,9]. In the present paper, our interest lies in geometric multigrid methods for isogeometric analysis. Our aim in this article is mainly to enhance the understanding of multigrid methods for IGA by spectral analysis and more extensive numerical experiments. In particular, we are interested in the effect the spline degree has on the performance of multigrid iteration. The experiments from [4] show that, while convergence rates for standard V-cycle iteration are h-independent as predicted by the theory, they depend strongly on the spline degree p. This effect is more pronounced in higher space dimensions. We investigate this effect in more detail by analyzing the performance of classical smoothers as well as of the coarse-grid correction step for different space dimensions and spline degrees. We also clarify to what extent boundary effects are responsible.

We outline a simple geometric multigrid solver for IGA. After performing some basic iteration number tests both with pure V-cycle iteration and with CG iteration preconditioned by a V-cycle, we perform local Fourier analysis in 1D. We then perform a more detailed numerical spectral analysis of the smoother and the coarse-grid correction step for the eigenfunctions of the discretized problem in order to elucidate the effect that increasing the spline degree has.

I. Dimov et al. (Eds.): NMA 2014, LNCS 8962, pp. 123–129, 2015.
DOI: 10.1007/978-3-319-15585-2_14

2 Geometric Multigrid for Isogeometric Analysis

For space reasons, we cannot present a full IGA framework and instead consider a simple model problem. See, e.g., [5] for more details. Let $\mathcal{V}_h \subset H_0^1(\Omega)$ denote a tensor product B-spline space over $\Omega = [0, 1]^d$. We consider an IGA discretization of the Poisson equation with pure Dirichlet boundary conditions: find $u_h \in \mathcal{V}_h$ such that

$$a(u_h, v_h) = \langle F, v_h \rangle \qquad \forall v_h \in \mathcal{V}_h$$

with the bilinear form and linear functions, respectively,

$$a(u, v) = \int_\Omega \nabla u \cdot \nabla v \, dx, \qquad \langle F, v \rangle = \int_\Omega f v \, dx - a(\tilde{g}, v).$$

Here $\tilde{g} \in H^1(\Omega)$ is a suitable extension of the given Dirichlet data.

In the following, we outline the construction of a simple geometric multigrid scheme for this problem. Let $\mathcal{V}_0$ denote a coarse tensor product spline space over $(0, 1)^d$. Performing uniform and global h-refinement by knot insertion, we obtain a sequence of refined spline spaces $\mathcal{V}_1, \mathcal{V}_2, \ldots$ Let $\mathcal{V}_H$ and $\mathcal{V}_h$ denote two successive spline spaces in this sequence, and let $P : \mathcal{V}_H \to \mathcal{V}_h$ denote the prolongation operator from the coarse to the fine space. One step of the two-grid iteration process is given by a pre-smoothing step, the coarse-grid correction, and a post-smoothing step; i.e., given $u_0 \in \mathcal{V}_h$, the next iterate u_1 is obtained by

$$\begin{aligned} u^{(1)} &:= u_0 + S^{-1}(f_h - A_h u_0), \\ u^{(2)} &:= u^{(1)} + P A_H^{-1} P^\top (f_h - A_h u^{(1)}), \\ u_1 := u^{(3)} &:= u^{(2)} + S^{-\top}(f_h - A_h u^{(2)}). \end{aligned}$$

Here, S is a suitable smoother for the fine-space stiffness matrix A_h.

As usual, a multigrid scheme is obtained by considering a hierarchy of nested spline spaces and replacing the exact inverse A_H^{-1} in the above procedure recursively with the same procedure applied on the next coarser space, until $\mathcal{V}_0$ is reached. We consider only the case of a single coarse-grid correction step, i.e., the V-cycle.

To test the multigrid iteration, we set up the Poisson equation $-\Delta u = f$ with pure Dirichlet boundary conditions on $\Omega = (0, 1)^d$. We choose tensor product B-spline basis functions defined on equidistant knot vectors with spline degrees p in every direction and maximum continuity, i.e., simple interior knots. The right-hand side f and the boundary conditions are chosen according to the exact solution $u(x) = \prod_{i=1}^d \sin(\pi(x_i + 0.5))$.

We then choose a random starting vector and perform V-cycle iteration as described above. In Table 1, left half, we display the iteration numbers required to reduce the initial residual by a factor of 10^{-8} in the Euclidean norm. The h-independence is clearly observed. Furthermore, the scheme is highly efficient for low spline degree p, yielding very low iteration numbers. In higher dimensions, in particular for $d = 3$, we see a dramatic increase in the number of iterations as the spline degree is increased. Very similar results have been observed in [4].

Table 1. V-cycle iteration numbers for the model Poisson problem. Columns from left to right: space dimension d, number of unknowns N, V-cycle iteration numbers for $p = 1$ to 4, iteration numbers for CG preconditioned with V-cycle for $p = 1$ to 4

d	N	V-cycle iteration				PCG iteration			
		p				p			
		1	2	3	4	1	2	3	4
1	~4,1 k	11	8	7	9	7	6	5	6
	~262 k	11	8	7	9	7	5	5	6
2	~66 k	9	11	37	127	6	7	14	27
	~1,05 m	9	11	36	125	6	7	14	27
3	~40 k	9	38	240	1682	6	15	37	100
	~290 k	9	38	236	1564	6	15	37	98

We also test preconditioned conjugate gradient (PCG) iteration with one V-cycle as the preconditioner; see Table 1, right half. The iteration numbers are significantly reduced for the previously unsatisfactory cases with $d = 3$ and high spline degree p. A clear dependence of the iteration numbers on d and p remains.

We remark that the results remain quantitatively very similar for the model problem $-\Delta u + u = f$ with pure Neumann boundary conditions.

3 Local Fourier Analysis

We perform local Fourier analysis (LFA) for the two-grid method in the case $d = 1$ as described in the literature [1, 7]. For this, we set up a space of B-splines of degree p on $\mathbb{R}$ with uniformly spaced knots $\mathbb{Z} \cdot h$ at distances $h = 1$ as well as the corresponding nested coarse space with knots at $\mathbb{Z} \cdot H,\ H = 2h$. We then compute, for p from 1 to 4, the stencils of the variational form of the operator $-\partial_{xx}$ on the fine space,

$$
\begin{gathered}
h^{-1}(-1, 2, -1),\\
h^{-1}(-\tfrac{1}{6}, -\tfrac{1}{3}, 1, -\tfrac{1}{3}, -\tfrac{1}{6}),\\
h^{-1}(-\tfrac{1}{120}, -\tfrac{1}{5}, -\tfrac{1}{8}, \tfrac{2}{3}, -\tfrac{1}{8}, -\tfrac{1}{5}, -\tfrac{1}{120}),\\
h^{-1}(-\tfrac{1}{5040}, -\tfrac{59}{2520}, -\tfrac{17}{90}, -\tfrac{11}{360}, \tfrac{35}{72}, -\tfrac{11}{360}, -\tfrac{17}{90}, -\tfrac{59}{2520}, -\tfrac{1}{5040}),
\end{gathered}
$$

and the stencils of the canonical embedding of the coarse in the fine space,

$$
(\tfrac{1}{2}, 1, \tfrac{1}{2})^\top, (\tfrac{1}{4}, \tfrac{3}{4}, \tfrac{3}{4}, \tfrac{1}{4})^\top, (\tfrac{1}{8}, \tfrac{1}{2}, \tfrac{3}{4}, \tfrac{1}{2}, \tfrac{1}{8})^\top, (\tfrac{1}{16}, \tfrac{5}{16}, \tfrac{5}{8}, \tfrac{5}{8}, \tfrac{5}{16}, \tfrac{1}{16})^\top.
$$

We study the effect of these stencils on the Fourier modes $(\exp(\mathrm{i}\alpha\theta))_{\alpha\in\mathbb{Z}}$ for $\theta \in (-\pi, \pi)$. As usual, the analysis decomposes into two parts, namely the low frequencies $|\theta| < \pi/2$ and the high frequencies $|\theta| \geq \pi/2$. Following the standard procedure, we can compute the symbols of the fine-grid and prolongation operators $\hat{A}_h(\theta) \in \mathbb{C}^{2\times 2}$, $\hat{P}(\theta) \in \mathbb{C}^{2\times 1}$, respectively, based on the stencils above, as well as the derived symbols $\hat{R}(\theta) = \hat{P}(\theta)^* \in \mathbb{C}^{1\times 2}$, $\hat{A}_H(\theta) = \hat{R}(\theta)\hat{A}_h(\theta)\hat{P}(\theta) \in \mathbb{C}^{1\times 1}$ of the restriction and coarse-grid operators, respectively.

4 Numerical Spectral Analysis

In this section, we take an alternative approach to spectral analysis which operates directly on the matrices used in the multigrid method and can therefore capture boundary effects.

We consider the problem $\Delta u = 0, u|_{\partial\Omega} = 0$ with $u = 0$ as its exact solution, and set up a two-grid scheme as above with N unknowns on the fine grid. For a given vector $\mu \in \mathbb{R}^d$, we perform one step of the symmetrized Gauss-Seidel smoother, or one coarse-grid correction step, and measure the Euclidean norm of the result. That is, we compute the error reduction factors

$$r^{\mathrm{S}}(\mu) = \frac{|G_{S^\top} G_S \mu|}{|\mu|}, \quad r^{\mathrm{CGC}}(\mu) = \frac{|(I - P A_H^{-1} P^\top A_h)\mu|}{|\mu|}.$$

As a basis, we choose the generalized eigensystem (μ_j) which satisfies

$$A_h \mu_j = \lambda_j M_h \mu_j, \qquad j = 1, \ldots, N,$$

where M_h is the mass matrix of the fine-grid isogeometric basis. In Figs. 1-3, we analyze the 1D, 2D, and 3D Laplace problem, respectively, using the Gauss-Seidel smoother. Each figure contains one plot each for spline degrees

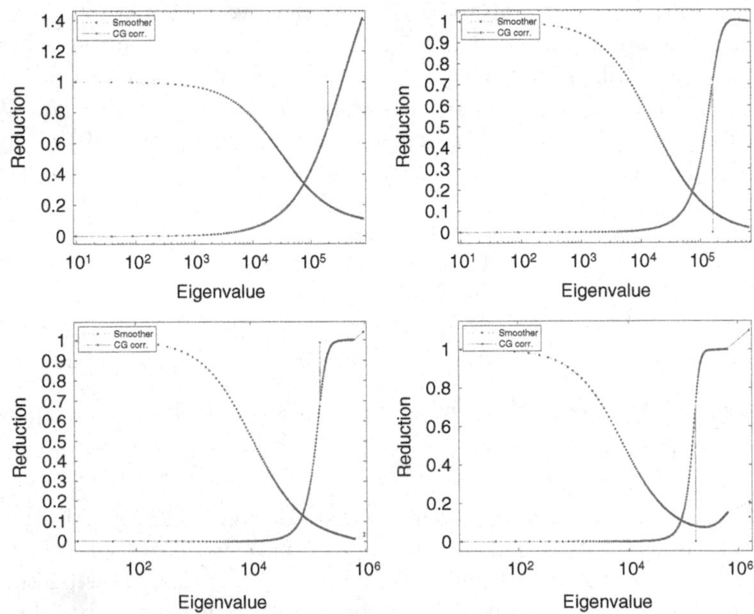

Fig. 1. Error reduction in the basis (μ_j) in 1D with $p = 1, 2$ (top), $p = 3, 4$ (bottom)

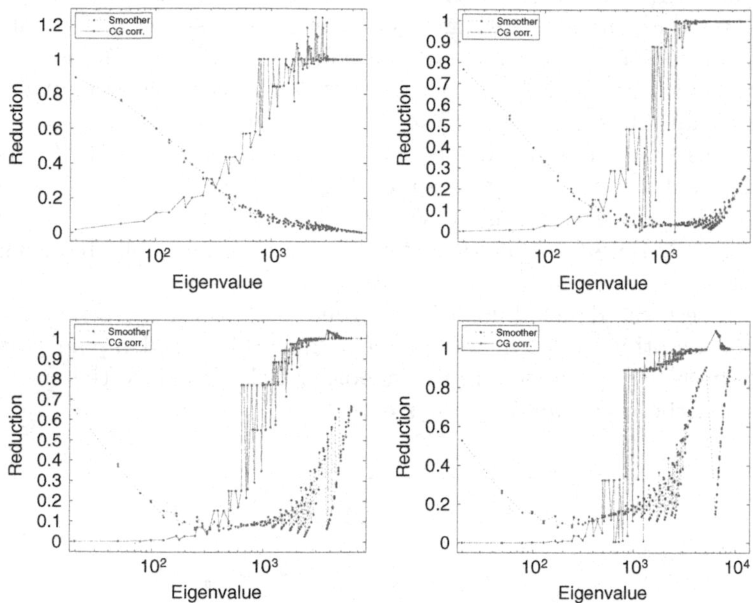

Fig. 2. Error reduction in the basis (μ_j) in 2D with $p = 1, 2$ (top), $p = 3, 4$ (bottom)

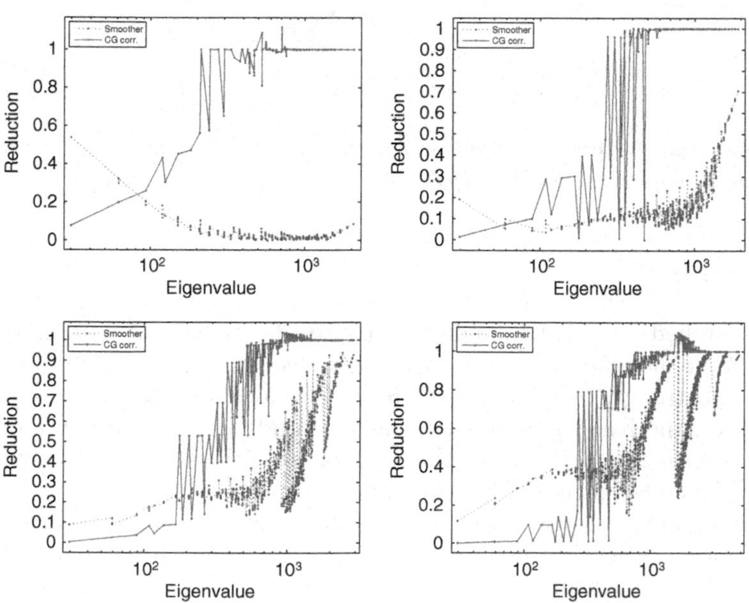

Fig. 3. Error reduction in the basis (μ_j) in 3D with $p = 1, 2$ (top), $p = 3, 4$ (bottom)

$p = 1, 2, 3, 4$. In each plot, we display the error reduction factors $r^{\mathrm{S}}(\mu_j)$ and $r^{\mathrm{CGC}}(\mu_j)$ for the generalized eigenvectors over their respective eigenvalues λ_j. The studied problems were relatively small, up to around $N = 1000$.

Throughout, the coarse-grid correction step reduces the lower part of the spectrum in an efficient manner. The Gauss-Seidel smoother however fails to perform robustly as the spline degree p is increased. Already in 1D, the plot for $p = 4$ suggests difficulties for higher spline degrees. These difficulties start earlier for higher space dimensions, as we see from the plots for $d = 2, p = 4$ as well as $d = 3, p = 3$. Here the smoother starts to become unusable, reducing some high-frequency components by 10 % or less.

We also test the damped Jacobi smoother, $S^{-1} = \tau \operatorname{diag}(A_h)^{-1}$. In Fig. 4, we plot its smoothing rates in the case $d = 2, p = 4$ with damping parameter τ ranging from 0.1 to 1.0. Again, the smoother fails to reduce the error in the upper part of the spectrum, regardless of τ.

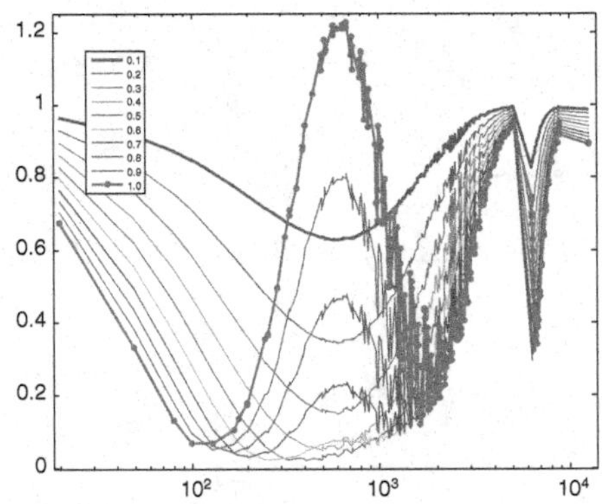

Fig. 4. Smoothing factors for the Jacobi smoother ($d = 2, p = 4$) with different damping parameters τ. x-axis: λ_j, y-axis: $r^{\mathrm{S}}(\mu_j)$

5 Conclusions

We have studied a geometric multigrid method for isogeometric discretizations using a simple model problem. As already observed in [4], V-cycle iteration numbers depend strongly on the spline degree p. The local Fourier analysis indicates that even on the real line without boundary conditions, performance degrades as p is increased. CG iteration preconditioned with one V-cycle predictably improves the convergence in the badly performing cases.

The numerical spectral analysis shows that both the Gauss-Seidel and the damped Jacobi smoother fail to reduce high-frequency error components for higher p. Higher space dimensions compound this problem.

Acknowledgments. This work was supported by the National Research Network "Geometry + Simulation" (NFN S117, 2012–2016), funded by the Austrian Science

Fund (FWF). The first author was also supported by the project AComIn "Advanced Computing for Innovation", grant 316087, funded by the FP7 Capacity Programme "Research Potential of Convergence Regions".

References

1. Brandt, A.: Rigorous quantitative analysis of multigrid, I: Constant coefficients two-level cycle with L_2-norm. SIAM J. Numer. Anal. **31**(6), 1695–1730 (1994)
2. Buffa, A., Harbrecht, H., Kunoth, A., Sangalli, G.: BPX-preconditioning for isogeometric analysis. Comput. Methods. Appl. Mech. Eng. **265**, 63–70 (2013)
3. Collier, N., Pardo, D., Dalcin, L., Paszynski, M., Calo, V.M.: The cost of continuity: a study of the performance of isogeometric finite elements using direct solvers. Comput. Methods Appl. Mech. Eng. **213–216**, 353–361 (2012). http://www.sciencedirect.com/science/article/pii/S0045782511003392
4. Gahalaut, K.P.S., Kraus, J.K., Tomar, S.K.: Multigrid methods for isogeometric discretization. Computer Methods in Applied Mechanics and Engineering **253**, 413–425 (2013). http://www.sciencedirect.com/science/article/pii/S0045782512002678
5. Hughes, T.J.R., Cottrell, J.A., Bazilevs, Y.: Isogeometric analysis: CAD, finite elements, NURBS, exact geometry and mesh refinement. Comput. Methods Appl. Mech. Eng. **194**(39–41), 4135–4195 (2005). http://dx.doi.org/10.1016/j.cma.2004.10.008
6. Kleiss, S.K., Pechstein, C., Jüttler, B., Tomar, S.: IETI - isogeometric tearing and interconnecting. Comput. Methods Appl. Mech. Eng. **247–248**, 201–215 (2012)
7. Trottenberg, U., Oosterlee, C., Schüller, A.: Multigrid. Academic Press, San Diego (2001)
8. Beirão da Veiga, L., Cho, D., Pavarino, L., Scacchi, S.: Overlapping Schwarz methods for isogeometric analysis. SIAM J. Numer. Anal. **50**(3), 1394–1416 (2012). http://epubs.siam.org/doi/abs/10.1137/110833476
9. Beirão da Veiga, L., Cho, D., Pavarino, L., Scacchi, S.: BDDC preconditioners for isogeometric analysis. Math. Models Methods Appl. Sci. **23**(6), 1099–1142 (2013)

Numerical Homogenization of Epoxy-Clay Composite Materials

Ivan Georgiev[1,2](✉), Evgeni Ivanov[3], S. Margenov[1], and Y. Vutov[1]

[1] Institute of Information and Communication Technologies, Bulgarian Academy of Sciences, Acad. G. Bonchev, Bl. 25A, 1113 Sofia, Bulgaria
{ivan.georgiev,margenov,yavor}@parallel.bas.bg

[2] Institute of Mathematics and Informatics, Bulgarian Academy of Sciences, Acad. G. Bonchev, Bl. 8, 1113 Sofia, Bulgaria

[3] Open Laboratory for Experimental Mechanics of Micro and Nanomaterials, Institute of Mechanics, Bulgarian Academy of Sciences, Acad. G. Bonchev, Bl. 4, 1113 Sofia, Bulgaria
ivanov_evgeni@imbm.bas.bg, ivanov_evgeni@yahoo.com

Abstract. The numerical homogenization of anisotropic linear elastic materials with strongly heterogeneous microstructure is studied. The developed algorithm is applied to the case of two-phase composite material: epoxy resin based nanocomposite incorporating nanoclay Cloisite. The upscaling procedure is described in terms of six auxiliary elastic problems for the reference volume element (RVE). A parallel PCG method is implemented for efficient solution of the arising large-scale systems with sparse, symmetric, and positive semidefinite matrices. Then, the bulk modulus tensor is computed from the upscaled stiffness tensor and its eigenvectors are used to define the transformation matrix. The stiffness tensor of the material is transformed with respect to the principle directions of anisotropy (PDA) which gives a canonical (unique) representation of the material properties. Numerical upscaling results are shown. The voxel microstructure of the two-phase composite material is extracted from a high resolution computed tomography image.

1 Introduction

Polymer nanocomposites are generally defined as the combination of polymer matrix and fillers that have at least one dimension in nanometer range. Epoxy based layered silicate nanocomposites are highly versatile polymer systems for the new era of making lighter structural composites for various aerospace and automobile applications. They are known for its outstanding mechanical properties like high elastic modulus, increased strength, barrier effects, flame retardancy, electroconductivity etc. with very small addition of nano particles [11,12]. This is due to the very large surface area of interaction between polymer matrix and nano filler.

Epoxy resins are widely used because of their excellent chemical and heat resistance, high adhesive strength, good impact resistance, high strength and

I. Dimov et al. (Eds.): NMA 2014, LNCS 8962, pp. 130–137, 2015.
DOI: 10.1007/978-3-319-15585-2_15

hardness, and high electrical insulation. Among the thermoset materials, epoxy resins show special chemical characteristics such as absence of byproducts or volatiles during curing reactions, low shrinkage up on curing, curing over a wide temperature range and the control of degree of cross-linking. Layered silicates (nanoclays) are ideal nano reinforcements for epoxy resins, because of their high intercalation chemistry, high aspect ratio, ease of availability and low cost. Epoxy clay nanocomposites have already been used in high performance structural and functional applications such as laminates, adhesives, sealants, tooling, electronics, and construction.

The materials used in this study are epoxy resin Epilox T 19-38/500, hardener Epilox H 10-30, organoclay Cloisite 30B and Tetrachloro aurate (III) trihydrate. The nanofiller is dispersed in the matrix of epoxy resin to create a three-phase nanocomposite by "in situ" polymerization method.

2 Problem Formulation

Let Ω be a parallelepipedal domain representing our reference volume element (RVE) and $\mathbf{u} = (u_1, u_2, u_3)$ be the displacements vector in Ω. Here, components of the small strain tensor are:

$$\varepsilon_{ij}\left(\mathbf{u}\left(\mathbf{x}\right)\right) = \frac{1}{2}\left(\frac{\partial u_i(\mathbf{x})}{\partial x_j} + \frac{\partial u_j(\mathbf{x})}{\partial x_i}\right). \tag{1}$$

We assume that Hooke's law holds. The stress tensor σ is expressed in the form $\sigma_{ij} = s_{ijkl}\varepsilon_{kl}$, where summation over repeating indexes is assumed. The forth-order tensor s is called the stiffness tensor, and has the following symmetry:

$$s_{ijkl} = s_{jikl} = s_{ijlk} = s_{klij}. \tag{2}$$

Often, the Hooke's law is written in matrix form:

$$\begin{bmatrix} \sigma_{11} \\ \sigma_{22} \\ \sigma_{33} \\ \sigma_{23} \\ \sigma_{13} \\ \sigma_{12} \end{bmatrix} = \begin{bmatrix} s_{1111} & s_{1122} & s_{1133} & s_{1123} & s_{1113} & s_{1112} \\ s_{2211} & s_{2222} & s_{2233} & s_{2223} & s_{2213} & s_{2212} \\ s_{3311} & s_{3322} & s_{3333} & s_{3323} & s_{3313} & s_{3312} \\ s_{2311} & s_{2322} & s_{2333} & s_{2323} & s_{2313} & s_{2312} \\ s_{1311} & s_{1322} & s_{1333} & s_{1323} & s_{1313} & s_{1312} \\ s_{1211} & s_{1222} & s_{1233} & s_{1223} & s_{1213} & s_{1212} \end{bmatrix} \begin{bmatrix} \varepsilon_{11} \\ \varepsilon_{22} \\ \varepsilon_{33} \\ 2\varepsilon_{23} \\ 2\varepsilon_{13} \\ 2\varepsilon_{12} \end{bmatrix}. \tag{3}$$

The symmetric 6×6 matrix in (3) is denoted with S and is called also the stiffness matrix. For an isotropic material the matrix S and the tensor s have only two independent degrees of freedom. For orthotropic materials (materials containing three orthogonal planes of symmetry), the matrix S has nine independent degrees of freedom. In the general anisotropic case, S has 21 independent degrees of freedom.

The goal of our study is to obtain homogenized material properties of the epoxy-clay composite. In other words – to find the stiffness tensor of a homogeneous material which would have the same macro-level properties as our RVE.

3 Homogenization Technique

Our homogenization approach follows the numerical upscaling scheme from [1] (see also [2,3,9]). The scheme requires finding Ω-periodic functions $\xi^{kl} = (\xi_1^{kl}, \xi_2^{kl}, \xi_3^{kl})$, k, $l = 1, 2, 3$, satisfying the following equation in a week formulation:

$$\int_{\Omega} \left(s_{ijpq}(x) \frac{\partial \xi_p^{kl}}{\partial x_q} \right) \frac{\partial \phi_i}{\partial x_j} d\Omega = \int_{\Omega} s_{ijkl}(x) \frac{\partial \phi_i}{\partial x_j} d\Omega \tag{4}$$

for an arbitrary Ω-periodic variational function $\phi \in H^1(\Omega)$. After computing the characteristic displacements ξ^{kl}, from (4) we can compute the homogenized elasticity tensor s^H using the following formula:

$$s_{ijkl}^H = \frac{1}{|\Omega|} \int_{\Omega} \left(s_{ijkl}(x) - s_{ijpq}(x) \frac{\partial \xi_p^{kl}}{\partial x_q} \right) d\Omega. \tag{5}$$

From (4) and due to the symmetry of the stiffness tensor (2), we have the relation $\xi^{kl} = \xi^{lk}$. Therefore the solution of only six problems (4) is required to obtain the homogenized stiffness tensor.

The periodicity of the solution implies the use of periodic boundary conditions. Rotated trilinear (Rannacher-Turek) finite elements are used for the numerical solution of (4). This choice is motivated by the additional stability of the nonconforming finite element discretization in the case of strongly heterogeneous materials [4]. Construction of a robust non-conforming finite element method is generally based on application of mixed formulation leading to a saddle-point system. By the choice of non continuous finite elements for the dual (pressure) variable, it can be eliminated at the (macro)element level. As a result we obtain a symmetric positive semi-definite finite element system in primal (displacements) variables. We utilize this approach, which is referred as the *reduced and selective integration* (RSI) [5].

For the solution of the arising linear system, the preconditioned conjugate gradient is used. For the construction of the preconditioner the isotropic variant of the displacement decomposition (DD) [6] was used. We write the DD auxiliary matrix in the form $C_{DD} = \text{diag}(A, A, A)$ where A is the stiffness matrix corresponding to the bilinear form

$$a(u^h, v^h) = \sum_{e \in \Omega^h} \int_e E(e) \left(\sum_{i=1}^{3} \frac{\partial u^h}{\partial x_i} \frac{\partial v^h}{\partial x_i} \right) de. \tag{6}$$

Here $E(e)$ is the elasticity modulus of the material related to the element e.

Such approach is motivated by the second Korn's inequality, which holds for the RSI FEM discretization under consideration. More precisely, in the case of isotropic materials, the estimate $\kappa(C_{DD}^{-1} M) = O((1 - 2\nu)^{-1})$ holds uniformly with respect to the mesh size parameter in the FEM discretization, where ν is the Poisson ratio and M is the stiffness matrix.

As the arising linear systems are large, the problems are solved in parallel. Parallel MIC(0) preconditioner for scalar elliptic systems [7] is used to approximate C_{DD}. Its basic idea is to apply MIC(0) factorization of an approximation B of the stiffness matrix A. Matrix B has a special block structure. Its diagonal blocks are diagonal matrices. This allows the solution of the preconditioning system to be performed in parallel. The condition number estimate $\kappa(B^{-1}A) \leq 3$ holds uniformly with respect to mesh parameter and possible coefficient jumps (see for the related analysis in [7]). Thus we obtain the parallel MIC(0) preconditioner in the form $C_{DDMIC(0)} = \text{diag}(C_{MIC(0)}(B), C_{MIC(0)}(B), C_{MIC(0)}(B))$. More details on applying this preconditioner for the proposed homogenization technique can be found in [1], see also [9].

4 Principal Directions of Anisotropy

We follow the procedure for determining the principal directions of anisotropy (PDA) described in [8]. This is useful for comparison of different materials, because the stiffness matrices (for anisotropic materials) differ in different coordinate systems. A coordinate system is said to coincide with the PDA of the material, when subjected to "all-around uniform pure extension state," forms a "pure tension state." Let us introduce the bulk modulus tensor

$$K = \begin{bmatrix} K_{11} & K_{12} & K_{13} \\ K_{21} & K_{22} & K_{23} \\ K_{31} & K_{32} & K_{33} \end{bmatrix}. \tag{7}$$

The elements of K are defined as $K_{ij} = \sum_{k=1}^{3} s_{ijkk}$ We write the "all-round uniform extension" as $\varepsilon_{ij} = \tilde{\varepsilon}\delta_{ij}$, where $\tilde{\varepsilon}$ is a constant reference strain and δ_{ij} is the Kronecker delta. Then, the stress components are $\sigma_{ij} = K_{ij}\tilde{\varepsilon}$. Hence the principal directions of the tensor K coincide with the stress principal directions. The stress values in these principal directions are $\sigma_{ij} = \lambda_i\tilde{\varepsilon}\delta_{ij}$, where λ_i are the eigenvalues of the tensor K. To ensure uniqueness of the transformation, we order the eigenvalues $\lambda_3 \geq \lambda_2 \geq \lambda_1$, i.e. the biggest eigenvalue is the third and the smallest is the first. With this order, we enforce the material to orient its strongest direction in z axis and its weakest in x. The case of equal eigenvalues, leads to equivalence of the material in two or more directions. The transformation matrix T, which rotates the coordinate system to the one which coincides with the PDA, is given by the corresponding normalized eigenvectors v^i of K:

$$T = \begin{bmatrix} v_1^1 & v_2^1 & v_3^1 \\ v_1^2 & v_2^2 & v_3^2 \\ v_1^3 & v_2^3 & v_3^3 \end{bmatrix}. \tag{8}$$

Now using formula $\bar{s}_{klst} = s_{mnpr}T_{km}T_{ln}T_{sp}T_{tr}$. we are able to rotate the stress tensor. Here summation over repeating indexes is assumed again.

Remark 1. Note that the described homogenization procedure is not limited only for two material composites. It can be applied to any composite, constituted with any number of materials.

5 Numerical Experiments

To solve the above described upscaling problem, a portable parallel FEM code is designed and implemented in C++. The parallelization has been facilitated using the MPI library.

The analyzed test specimens are parts of a high resolution computed tomography image obtained by industrial CT scanning of epoxy-clay composite in IICT. The voxel size is 2.56 μm.

The microstructure of four different RVEs with sizes of $128 \times 128 \times 128$ is shown, see Fig. 1. Material properties were set for the epoxy $E_e = 2.55$ GPa, $\nu_e = 0.35$ and for the clay - $E_c = 3$ MPa, $\nu_c = 0.2$. The iteration stopping criterion is $||\mathbf{r}^j||_{C^{-1}}/||\mathbf{r}^0||_{C^{-1}} < 10^{-6}$, where $\mathbf{r}^j$ is the residual at the j-th iteration step

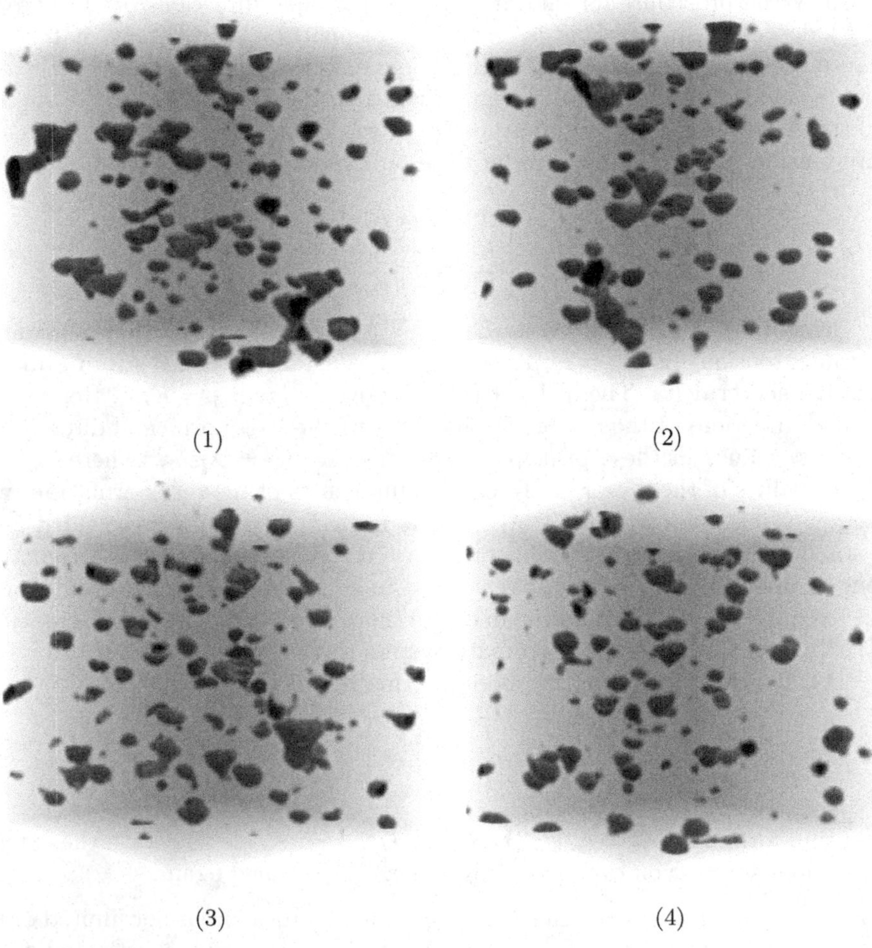

Fig. 1. Speciemens under investigation

of the preconditioned conjugate gradient method and C stands for the used preconditioner.

When the homogenization procedure from Sect. 2 was applied the homogenized tensors for each specimen were obtained. We denote them with S_i^H, where i is the number of the specimen. After applying the transformation procedure, described in Sect. 3, to the stiffness matrices S_i^H, matrices $\bar{S}_i^H$, characterizing the properties of the considered specimens in the coordinate systems aligned with their PDA are obtained. In what follows the matrices $\bar{S}_i^H$ are presented. All values are measured in Pascals.

$$\bar{S}_1^H = \begin{bmatrix} 3.86\times10^9 & 2.03\times10^9 & 2.02\times10^9 & -1.43\times10^5 & 1.59\times10^5 & 1.25\times10^6 \\ 2.03\times10^9 & 3.85\times10^9 & 2.02\times10^9 & 4.08\times10^5 & -1.20\times10^5 & -1.19\times10^6 \\ 2.02\times10^9 & 2.02\times10^9 & 3.82\times10^9 & -2.64\times10^5 & -3.89\times10^4 & -6.19\times10^4 \\ -1.43\times10^5 & 4.08\times10^5 & -2.64\times10^5 & 9.06\times10^8 & -1.36\times10^5 & -1.19\times10^5 \\ 1.59\times10^5 & -1.20\times10^5 & -3.89\times10^4 & -1.36\times10^5 & 9.07\times10^8 & -1.91\times10^5 \\ 1.25\times10^6 & -1.19\times10^6 & -6.19\times10^4 & -1.19\times10^5 & -1.91\times10^5 & 9.11\times10^8 \end{bmatrix}.$$

$$\bar{S}_2^H = \begin{bmatrix} 3.88\times10^9 & 2.05\times10^9 & 2.04\times10^9 & 8.00\times10^4 & -2.50\times10^5 & 2.19\times10^4 \\ 2.05\times10^9 & 3.87\times10^9 & 2.03\times10^9 & -3.73\times10^5 & -2.61\times10^5 & 4.34\times10^4 \\ 2.04\times10^9 & 2.03\times10^9 & 3.84\times10^9 & 2.93\times10^5 & 5.11\times10^5 & -6.54\times10^4 \\ 8.00\times10^4 & -3.73\times10^5 & 2.93\times10^5 & 9.09\times10^8 & -1.80\times10^5 & -2.70\times10^5 \\ -2.50\times10^5 & -2.61\times10^5 & 5.11\times10^5 & -1.80\times10^5 & 9.10\times10^8 & 2.61\times10^4 \\ 2.19\times10^4 & 4.34\times10^4 & -6.54\times10^4 & -2.70\times10^5 & 2.61\times10^4 & 9.14\times10^8 \end{bmatrix}.$$

$$\bar{S}_3^H = \begin{bmatrix} 3.89\times10^9 & 2.05\times10^9 & 2.04\times10^9 & -1.38\times10^5 & 1.05\times10^5 & -3.49\times10^5 \\ 2.05\times10^9 & 3.88\times10^9 & 2.04\times10^9 & -5.77\times10^5 & 3.07\times10^4 & 2.95\times10^5 \\ 2.04\times10^9 & 2.04\times10^9 & 3.85\times10^9 & 7.16\times10^5 & -1.35\times10^5 & 5.36\times10^4 \\ -1.38\times10^5 & -5.77\times10^5 & 7.16\times10^5 & 9.11\times10^8 & -7.24\times10^4 & 8.31\times10^4 \\ 1.05\times10^5 & 3.07\times10^4 & -1.35\times10^5 & -7.24\times10^4 & 9.11\times10^8 & -1.26\times10^5 \\ -3.49\times10^5 & 2.95\times10^5 & 5.36\times10^4 & 8.31\times10^4 & -1.26\times10^5 & 9.16\times10^8 \end{bmatrix}.$$

$$\bar{S}_4^H = \begin{bmatrix} 3.94\times10^9 & 2.09\times10^9 & 2.08\times10^9 & 6.66\times10^3 & -1.52\times10^5 & -5.79\times10^5 \\ 2.09\times10^9 & 3.93\times10^9 & 2.08\times10^9 & 2.12\times10^5 & 3.17\times10^4 & 6.16\times10^5 \\ 2.08\times10^9 & 2.08\times10^9 & 3.91\times10^9 & -2.18\times10^5 & 1.20\times10^5 & -3.67\times10^4 \\ 6.66\times10^3 & 2.12\times10^5 & -2.18\times10^5 & 9.18\times10^8 & -4.12\times10^4 & 5.37\times10^4 \\ -1.52\times10^5 & 3.17\times10^4 & 1.20\times10^5 & -4.12\times10^4 & 9.19\times10^8 & 9.60\times10^3 \\ -5.79\times10^5 & 6.16\times10^5 & -3.67\times10^4 & 5.37\times10^4 & 9.60\times10^3 & 9.22\times10^8 \end{bmatrix}.$$

Interesting fact is that for all four specimens, the transformation matrix was actually a rotation over the z axis. In all 4 specimens the material response is somewhat weeker in the z direction. Currently we don't know if this is an scanning artefact, or real material property.

5.1 Comparison with GeoDict

We used also the specialized software for numerical homogenization GeoDict [10], and more precisely the module ElastoDict, to compare and verify our results.

We run it for the four specimens. The obtained results (matrices) $\bar{S}_i^{H_{GD}}$, $i = 1, \ldots, 4$ are also rotated to the PDA.

$$\bar{S}_1^{H_{GD}} = \begin{bmatrix} 3.86\times10^9 & 2.04\times10^9 & 2.03\times10^9 & -1.35\times10^5 & 3.71\times10^5 & -5.17\times10^5 \\ 2.04\times10^9 & 3.87\times10^9 & 2.03\times10^9 & 1.56\times10^5 & -1.93\times10^5 & 6.15\times10^5 \\ 2.03\times10^9 & 2.03\times10^9 & 3.83\times10^9 & -2.15\times10^4 & -1.53\times10^5 & -5.58\times10^4 \\ -1.35\times10^5 & 1.56\times10^5 & -2.15\times10^4 & 9.08\times10^8 & -1.33\times10^5 & -2.21\times10^5 \\ 3.71\times10^5 & -1.93\times10^5 & -1.53\times10^5 & -1.33\times10^5 & 9.07\times10^8 & -1.10\times10^5 \\ -5.17\times10^5 & 6.15\times10^5 & -5.58\times10^4 & -2.21\times10^5 & -1.10\times10^5 & 9.11\times10^8 \end{bmatrix}.$$

$$\bar{S}_2^{H_{GD}} = \begin{bmatrix} 3.88\times10^9 & 2.06\times10^9 & 2.04\times10^9 & -2.41\times10^4 & 2.03\times10^5 & -2.53\times10^4 \\ 2.06\times10^9 & 3.89\times10^9 & 2.05\times10^9 & 8.95\times10^3 & -7.79\times10^4 & -9.29\times10^4 \\ 2.04\times10^9 & 2.05\times10^9 & 3.85\times10^9 & 2.72\times10^5 & -1.41\times10^5 & 5.85\times10^4 \\ -2.41\times10^4 & 8.95\times10^3 & 2.72\times10^5 & 9.11\times10^8 & 1.71\times10^5 & -3.00\times10^4 \\ 2.03\times10^5 & -7.79\times10^4 & -1.41\times10^5 & 1.71\times10^5 & 9.10\times10^8 & -2.70\times10^4 \\ -2.53\times10^4 & -9.29\times10^4 & 5.85\times10^4 & -3.00\times10^4 & -2.70\times10^4 & 9.15\times10^8 \end{bmatrix}.$$

$$\bar{S}_3^{H_{GD}} = \begin{bmatrix} 3.88\times10^9 & 2.06\times10^9 & 2.05\times10^9 & -5.83\times10^4 & -3.61\times10^5 & -9.47\times10^4 \\ 2.06\times10^9 & 3.89\times10^9 & 2.05\times10^9 & -4.30\times10^4 & 4.63\times10^4 & 1.23\times10^5 \\ 2.05\times10^9 & 2.05\times10^9 & 3.86\times10^9 & 1.27\times10^5 & 3.59\times10^5 & -9.63\times10^4 \\ -5.83\times10^4 & -4.30\times10^4 & 1.27\times10^5 & 9.12\times10^8 & 3.97\times10^4 & 3.93\times10^4 \\ -3.61\times10^5 & 4.63\times10^4 & 3.59\times10^5 & 3.97\times10^4 & 9.12\times10^8 & -1.11\times10^5 \\ -9.47\times10^4 & 1.23\times10^5 & -9.63\times10^4 & 3.93\times10^4 & -1.11\times10^5 & 9.16\times10^8 \end{bmatrix}.$$

$$\bar{S}_4^{H_{GD}} = \begin{bmatrix} 3.94\times10^9 & 2.09\times10^9 & 2.08\times10^9 & -3.71\times10^4 & -1.91\times10^5 & 1.01\times10^5 \\ 2.09\times10^9 & 3.94\times10^9 & 2.08\times10^9 & 3.94\times10^5 & 3.40\times10^4 & -7.29\times10^4 \\ 2.08\times10^9 & 2.08\times10^9 & 3.91\times10^9 & 8.99\times10^3 & 1.63\times10^5 & -2.72\times10^4 \\ -3.71\times10^4 & 3.94\times10^5 & 8.99\times10^3 & 9.20\times10^8 & -3.45\times10^4 & 1.92\times10^4 \\ -1.91\times10^5 & 3.40\times10^4 & 1.63\times10^5 & -3.45\times10^4 & 9.19\times10^8 & -5.32\times10^4 \\ 1.01\times10^5 & -7.29\times10^4 & -2.72\times10^4 & 1.92\times10^4 & -5.32\times10^4 & 9.23\times10^8 \end{bmatrix}.$$

5.2 Discussion

We observe that the results obtained by our code and by the software package GeoDict are very close. Other important observation from the obtained effective elasticity tensors is that on macro-level the material properties are very close to isotropic. Usually this is the desired behavior of composite materials except in the cases when specific structure is assumed. Hence from the isotropic approximation of the elasticity tensors we can calculate the effective elastic module $E_H \approx 2.46$ GPa. Comparing with the elastic module of the epoxy resin $E = 2.55$ GPa we observe that the influence of the "big" nanoclay clusters is relatively small.

In general by CT scanning we can detect only the nanoclay clusters in the micro scale. Since the characteristics of the epoxy resin are influenced also by the nanoclay particles and clusters smaller than 3 μm the nanoidentation elastic module was also used in the numerical homogenization procedure.

In our experiment 48 nanoindentations (4 lines with 12 indentations and spacing of 80 μm) were carried out using Nanomechanical Tester (Bruker, USA).

Each indentation was made with a force of 100 mN. The nanohead of the Nanoindenter performs indentation tests, where the applied load and displacement are continuously monitored, generating load versus displacement data for the test specimen. Young's modulus and hardness are derived from the unload data segments through "in situ" monitoring of the force vs. displacement plot and automatic calculations by utilizing the Oliver-Pharr method. By averaging the obtained results we get the nanodentation module $E_N = 3.37\,\text{GPa}$. Here we observe that the well dispersed nanoclay particles increase the elastic modulus of the modified epoxy resin. Using the value of the nanodentation module E_N in the numerical homogenization procedure we obtain effective elastic module $E_{H_N} \approx 3.25\,\text{GPa}$. This confirm our observation that the influence of the "big" nanoclay clusters to the effective elastic module is rather small.

Acknowledgments. This work is supported in part by Bulgarian NSF Grants DFNI I01/5 and DCVP-02/1, and by the project AComIn "Advanced Computing for Innovation", grant FP7-316087. The second author acknowledged the support from the FP7-280987 NanoXCT project.

References

1. Margenov, S., Vutov, Y.: Parallel MIC(0) preconditioning for numerical upscaling of anisotropic linear elastic materials. In: Lirkov, I., Margenov, S., Waśniewski, J. (eds.) LSSC 2009. LNCS, vol. 5910, pp. 805–812. Springer, Heidelberg (2010)
2. Hoppe, R.H.W., Petrova, S.I.: Optimal shape design in biomimetics based on homogenization and adaptivity. Math. Comput. Simul. **65**(3), 257–272 (2004)
3. Bensoussan, A., Lions, J.L., Papanicolaou, G.: Asymptotic Analysis for Periodic Structures. Elsevier, Amsterdam (1978)
4. Arnold, D.N., Brezzi, F.: Mixed and nonconforming finite element methods: implementation, postprocessing and error estimates, RAIRO. Model. Math. Anal. Numer. **19**, 7–32 (1985)
5. Malkus, D., Hughes, T.: Mixed finite element methods. Reduced and selective integration techniques. Comp. Meth. Appl. Mech. Eng. **15**, 63–81 (1978)
6. Blaheta, R.: Displacement decomposition-incomplete factorization preconditioning techniques for linear elasticity problems. NLAA **1**(2), 107–128 (1994)
7. Arbenz, P., Margenov, S., Vutov, Y.: Parallel MIC(0) preconditioning of 3D elliptic problems discretized by Rannacher-Turek finite elements. Comput. Math. Appl. **55**(10), 2197–2211 (2008)
8. Rand, O., Rovenski, V.: Analytical Methods in Anisotropic Elasticity: With Symbolic Computational Tools. Birkhuser Boston, Boston (2004)
9. Lazarov, B.S.: Topology optimization using multiscale finite element method for high-contrast media. In: Lirkov, I., Margenov, S., Waśniewski, J. (eds.) LSSC 2013. LNCS, vol. 8353, pp. 339–346. Springer, Heidelberg (2014)
10. www.geodict.com
11. Kotsilkova, R.: Thermosetting Nanocomposites for Engineering Application. Rapra Smiths Group, London (2007)
12. Petrova, I., Ivanov, E., Kotsilkova, R., Tsekov, Y., Angelov, V.: Applied study on mechanics of nanocomposites with carbon nanofillers. J. Theor. Appl. Mech. **43**(3), 67–76 (2013)

Isogeometric Analysis for Nonlinear Dynamics of Timoshenko Beams

Stanislav Stoykov(✉), Clemens Hofreither, and Svetozar Margenov

Institute of Information and Communication Technologies,
Bulgarian Academy of Sciences, Acad. G. Bonchev, Bl. 25A,
1113 Sofia, Bulgaria
stoykov@parallel.bas.bg

Abstract. The dynamics of beams that undergo large displacements is analyzed in frequency domain and comparisons between models derived by isogeometric analysis and p-FEM are presented. The equation of motion is derived by the principle of virtual work, assuming Timoshenko's theory for bending and geometrical type of nonlinearity.

As a result, a nonlinear system of second order ordinary differential equations is obtained. Periodic responses are of interest and the harmonic balance method is applied. The nonlinear algebraic system is solved by an arc-length continuation method in frequency domain.

It is shown that IGA gives better approximations of the nonlinear frequency-response functions than the p-FEM when models with the same number of degrees of freedom are used.

Keywords: p-FEM · Bifurcation diagrams · Isogeometric analysis · B-Splines · Continuation method · Nonlinear frequency-response function

1 Introduction

Isogeometric analysis (IGA) is a relatively novel discretization technique which was introduced by Hughes et al. [4]. The key idea of representing both the computational geometry as well as the trial functions using spaces of appropriate spline functions afford the method several interesting advantages. It has been demonstrated that IGA has superior spectral approximation properties compared to standard finite element method (FEM) discretizations [5]. The method has been applied successfully to the structural analysis of various mechanical models [1,3,6]. Recently, nonlinear dynamics of beams in frequency domain has been studied by isogeometric approach [11].

In the current work, a Timoshenko beam model is used for comparison of the nonlinear frequency-response function (NFRF) of models obtained by isogeometric analysis and p-FEM. The equation of motion is derived by the principle of virtual work, Timoshenko's beam theory is assumed and geometrical nonlinearity is taken into account. External harmonic excitation is considered and the response is assumed to be periodic function of time, thus the vector of generalized coordinates is expressed in Fourier series. The frequency-response function

I. Dimov et al. (Eds.): NMA 2014, LNCS 8962, pp. 138–146, 2015.
DOI: 10.1007/978-3-319-15585-2_16

is obtained by the continuation method. It is shown that IGA has better convergence properties than p-FEM in nonlinear dynamic analysis of elastic structures.

2 Isogeometric Analysis

We present very briefly the construction of an isogeometric method in 1D. We begin by setting up a B-spline basis

$$\{B_j : [-1,1] \to \mathbb{R}_0^+\}_j$$

of degree p over an open knot vector which spans the parameter interval $[-1,1]$. *Open* means that the first and last knots are repeated $p+1$ times. The interior knots are repeated at most p times. For the definition of B-splines, see [2,7,9].

To each basis function B_j, we associate a control point (coefficient) $C_j \in \mathbb{R}$ in such a way that we obtain an invertible geometry mapping $F = \sum_j C_j B_j : [-1,1] \to \Omega = [-\ell/2, \ell/2]$, where Ω is an interval representing the beam of length ℓ. The isogeometric basis functions on Ω are given by

$\psi_j(x) := B_j(F^{-1}(x))$ and their span $\mathcal{V}_h := \text{span}\{\psi_j\}$ is the isogeometric trial space on Ω.

Note that in the 1D case it is always possible to choose the control points in such a way that the parametrization F is linear. However, it is also possible to use a nonlinear parametrization, which can be advantageous in certain situations.

For problems in higher space dimensions, NURBS, i.e., rational versions of the B-spline basis functions, are commonly used to represent the geometry. For the one-dimensional geometry of beams, however, we stick to the use of B-splines.

The linear longitudinal equation of motion of beams is used as an example of space discretization using isogeometric analysis:

$$\mu\ddot{u}(x,t) - (EAu'(x,t))' = F_u(x,t) \qquad \forall x \in \Omega, t \in (0,T), \tag{1}$$

where E denotes the elastic modulus, A is the area of the cross section, μ - the mass per unit length, F_u - the longitudinal external load, and $u(x,t)$ the longitudinal displacement, $\ddot{u}(x,t)$ denotes the second derivative with respect to time, and $u'(x,t)$ - the first derivative with respect to x. The variational form of (1) is

$$\int_\Omega \mu\ddot{u}v\,dx + \int_\Omega EAu'v'\,dx = \int_\Omega F_u v\,dx \quad \forall v \in \mathcal{V} \tag{2}$$

with an appropriate test space $\mathcal{V}$. It is assumed that the ends of the beam are fixed, i.e., $u(x) = 0$ at $x = \pm\ell/2$.

The isogeometric discretization of the linear longitudinal equation of motion is obtained by restricting the variational equation (2) to the isogeometric space $\mathcal{V}_{h,0} \subset \mathcal{V}_h$, where the first and last basis function have been removed from $\mathcal{V}_h$ to enforce the essential boundary condition $u(x) = 0$ at $x = \pm\ell/2$. That is, we seek time-dependent coefficients $(q_j^u(t))_j$ such that

$$u_h(x,t) = \sum_j q_j^u(t)\psi_j^u(x) \in \mathcal{V}_{h,0}$$

satisfies (2) for all $v_h \in \mathcal{V}_{h,0}$. Here we write $\psi_j^u := \psi_j$ for the basis functions to make clear that they correspond to the displacement u. Later on, we will use different bases for the transverse displacement and rotation components.

With the stiffness matrix, mass matrix, and load vector, respectively,

$$K_{ij} = \int_{\Omega} EA\psi_j'\psi_i'\,dx, \quad M_{ij} = \int_{\Omega} \mu\psi_j\psi_i\,dx, \quad f_j = \int_{\Omega} F_u\psi_j\,dx,$$

we obtain the system of linear ordinary differential equations

$$\mathbf{M}\ddot{\mathbf{q}}^u + \mathbf{K}\mathbf{q}^u = \mathbf{f}$$

for the vector-valued function $q^u(t)$ of displacement coefficients.

3 An Isogeometric Formulation of Timoshenko Beams

The equation of motion is derived by the principle of virtual work considering Timoshenko's theory for bending. It is assumed that the cross section remains plane after deformation, but the transverse shear strain ε_{xz} is not neglected. We denote the longitudinal and transverse displacements by $u(x,z,t)$ and $w(x,z,t)$, respectively, they depend on space coordinates x and z and on time t. The displacement field on the middle line is expressed as

$$u(x,z,t) = u_0(x,t) + z\phi_y(x,t), \tag{3a}$$

$$w(x,z,t) = w_0(x,t), \tag{3b}$$

where $u_0(x,t)$ and $w_0(x,t)$ denote the longitudinal and transverse displacements on the middle line and $\phi_y(x,t)$ is the rotation of the cross section about y axis. Nonlinearity is taken into account by assuming nonlinear strain-displacement relations. The axial and shear strains are derived from Green's strain tensor and the longitudinal terms of second order are neglected:

$$\varepsilon_x = \frac{\partial u}{\partial x} + \frac{1}{2}\left(\frac{\partial w}{\partial x}\right)^2, \qquad \gamma_{xz} = \frac{\partial w}{\partial x} + \frac{\partial u}{\partial z} + \frac{\partial w}{\partial z}\frac{\partial w}{\partial x}. \tag{4}$$

Elastic isotropic materials are of interest, hence the stresses are related to the strains by Hooke's law,

$$\boldsymbol{\sigma} = \begin{Bmatrix} \sigma_x \\ \tau_{xz} \end{Bmatrix} = \begin{bmatrix} E & 0 \\ 0 & \lambda G \end{bmatrix} \begin{Bmatrix} \varepsilon_x \\ \gamma_{xz} \end{Bmatrix} = \boldsymbol{D}\boldsymbol{\varepsilon},$$

where E is the Young's modulus of the material, G is the shear modulus, $\boldsymbol{\sigma}$ is the vector of stresses, σ_x represents the axial stress, τ_{xz} represents the shear stress and λ is the shear correction factor. In the numerical experiments, $\lambda = \frac{5+5\nu}{6+5\nu}$ is used. The middle line displacements are discretized as

$$u_0(x,t) = \sum_{i=1}^{p_u} \psi_i^u(x) q_i^u(t), \tag{5a}$$

$$w_0(x,t) = \sum_{i=1}^{p_w} \psi_i^w(x) q_i^w(t), \tag{5b}$$

$$\phi_y(x,t) = \sum_{i=1}^{p_{\phi_y}} \psi_i^{\phi_y}(x) q_i^{\phi_y}(t), \tag{5c}$$

where $\mathbf{q}^u(t)$, $\mathbf{q}^w(t)$ and $\mathbf{q}^{\phi_y}(t)$ are coefficient vectors depending on time t. Above, p_u, p_w and p_{ϕ_y} are the numbers of basis functions used for the discretization of each of the displacement components and $\psi_i^u(x)$, $\psi_i^w(x)$ and $\psi_i^{\phi_y}(x)$ are the basis functions for space discretization. For the isogeometric case, these functions are B-spline basis functions, and for the p-FEM, these sets are hierarchical shape functions [8]. The basis functions must satisfy the geometric boundary conditions. The sets of B-splines and hierarchical shape functions used in the current work for the transverse displacement w_0 are shown in Fig. 1.

The equation of motion is derived by the principle of virtual work,

$$\delta W_V + \delta W_{in} + \delta W_E = 0, \tag{6}$$

where δW_V is the virtual work of internal forces, δW_{in} is the virtual work of inertia forces and δW_E is the virtual work of external forces. They are defined as

$$\delta W_V = -\int_V \delta\boldsymbol{\varepsilon}^T \boldsymbol{\sigma}\, dV, \quad \delta W_{in} = -\int_V \rho \delta\mathbf{d}^T \ddot{\mathbf{d}}\, dV, \quad \delta W_E = \int_V \delta\mathbf{d}^T \mathbf{P}\, dV, \tag{7}$$

where $\delta\boldsymbol{\varepsilon}$ is the vector of virtual strains, ρ is the density, $\delta\mathbf{d}$ represents the vector of virtual displacements, $\ddot{\mathbf{d}}$ is the acceleration of a point of the beam and $\mathbf{P}$ is the vector of external forces. Inserting Eqs. (7) into (6), we obtain the equation of motion

$$\mathbf{M}\ddot{\mathbf{q}}(t) + \mathbf{C}\dot{\mathbf{q}}(t) + \mathbf{K}(\mathbf{q}(t))\mathbf{q}(t) = \mathbf{f}(t), \tag{8}$$

where $\mathbf{M}$ is the mass matrix, $\mathbf{C}$ is the damping matrix, $\mathbf{K}$ is the stiffness matrix which depends on the coefficient vector $\mathbf{q}$, and $\mathbf{f}$ is the load vector. A mass proportional and frequency dependent damping is used. The longitudinal inertia is neglected and the degrees of freedom of the equation of motion are reduced, without neglecting the longitudinal displacement.

Since periodic responses are of interest, the coefficient vector is expressed in Fourier series and inserted into the equation of motion (8). The harmonic balance method (HBM) is employed and a nonlinear system of algebraic equations is obtained. The new unknowns are the coefficients of the harmonic functions, from the Fourier series, and the frequency of vibration. The nonlinear algebraic system is solved by an arc-length continuation method in frequency domain.

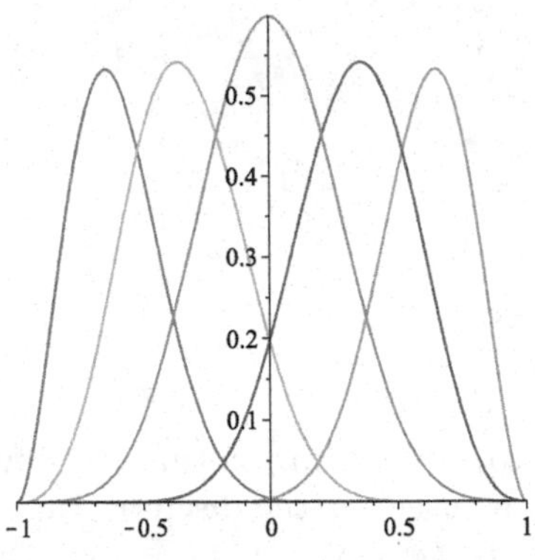

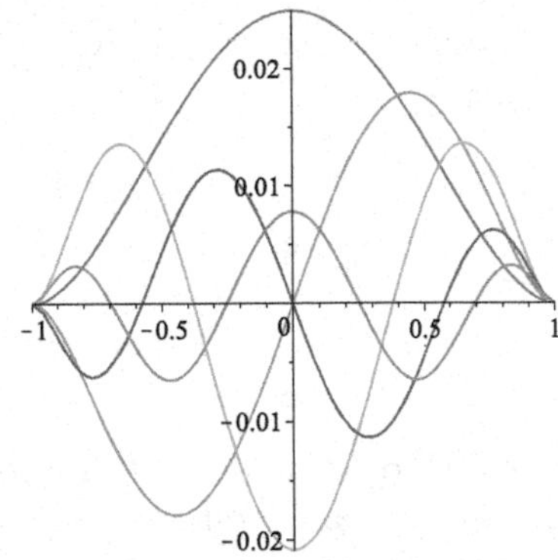

Fig. 1. (a) B-spline basis functions of degree 4, C^3-continuity across element boundaries; (b) hierarchical basis of shape functions, $p = 4$.

4 Results

It has been shown that the isogeometric analysis gives better approximation to the higher natural frequencies than the FEM [5]. Thus, it is expected that space discretization by isogeometric analysis will give better approximations of the nonlinear frequency-response function than discretization by the FEM. In this section, numerical results of Timoshenko beam, obtained by both approaches are compared. B-splines of varying degree are considered in the isogeometric analysis, keeping the highest possible continuity, i.e. C^{p-1}-continuity across element boundaries. The p-FEM is used with hierarchical shape functions [10] and the beam is modeled as one finite element. First, the natural frequencies are presented, and then, the nonlinear frequency-response functions are compared. The beam is assumed to be clamped-clamped with dimensions $l = 0.58\,\text{m}$, $b = 0.02\,\text{m}$, $h = 0.002\,\text{m}$, and isotropic material with properties (aluminum) $E = 70\,\text{GPa}$, $\nu = 0.34$, $\rho = 2778\,\text{kg/m}^3$.

Comparison of Natural Frequencies. The natural frequencies of both approaches are compared, keeping the same number of degrees of freedom. The bending natural frequencies are presented in Table 1, where five functions are used for the transverse displacement w_0 from (5b), and the corresponding derivatives are used for the rotation of the cross section ϕ_y from (5c). In addition, the results are also compared with the converged frequencies from [6].

The last two natural frequencies increase with the order of the B-Splines (Table 1). They are referred as "outlier frequencies" and the reasons for their appearance was discussed in [3]. Nevertheless, the fourth degree B-splines yield better approximations to the natural frequencies than those obtained by the p-FEM (including the higher frequencies). Thus, B-splines of fourth degree will be used in the nonlinear analysis.

The longitudinal natural frequencies are presented in Table 2. Six functions are used for the longitudinal displacement given in (5a). Again, "outlier frequencies" appear in the spectra. In this case, quadratic B-splines are more suitable than higher order B-splines or p-FEM and they will be used in the nonlinear analysis.

Table 1. Comparison of bending natural frequencies (rad/s) obtained by IGA and p-FEM, 10 DOF.

Mode	Converged values	Ref. [6]	IGA p = 3	IGA p = 4	IGA p = 5	p-FEM
1	192.74	192.74	192.79	192.74	192.74	192.74
2	531.24	531.29	532.71	531.47	531.58	531.42
3	1041.27	1041.49	1055.76	1046.73	1041.68	1043.24
4	1720.99	1721.52	1795.28	1865.64	1947.05	1910.51
5	2570.24	2571.47	2668.90	2601.51	2758.14	3041.97

Table 2. Comparison of longitudinal natural frequencies (rad/s) obtained by IGA and p-FEM, 6 DOF.

Mode	Converged values	IGA p = 2	IGA p = 3	IGA p = 4	p-FEM
1	2.7190E+04	2.7191E+04	2.7190E+04	2.7190E+04	2.7190E+04
2	5.4379E+04	5.4436E+04	5.4385E+04	5.4381E+04	5.4379E+04
3	8.1569E+04	8.2106E+04	8.1714E+04	8.1818E+04	8.1728E+04
4	1.0876E+05	1.1156E+05	1.0955E+05	1.0877E+05	1.0947E+05
5	1.3595E+05	1.4415E+05	1.5600E+05	1.6433E+05	1.6214E+05
6	1.6314E+05	1.6421E+05	1.7369E+05	1.8766E+05	2.0673E+05

Comparison of Nonlinear Frequency-Response Functions. Taking into account the results from Tables 1 and 2, and considering that in nonlinear dynamics of elastic structures the higher modes of vibration become important, an isogeometric Timoshenko beam model is generated using five B-splines of degree four for the transverse displacement w_0 and six quadratic B-splines for the longitudinal displacement u_0. The total number of degrees of freedom is 16, and after neglecting the longitudinal inertia the model has 10 DOFs. A nonlinear model with the same number of DOFs is generated by the p-FEM, by using hierarchical set of shape functions. External harmonic force is applied on the middle of the beam in transverse direction, $F_z(t) = 0.035\cos(\omega t)N$. Harmonics up to fifth order are used in the Fourier series, hence the algebraic nonlinear

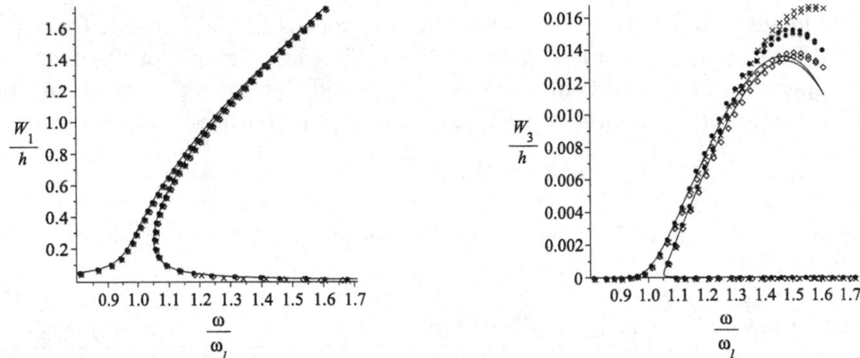

Fig. 2. Comparison of nonlinear frequency-response functions obtained with 10 DOF. (a) amplitude of the first harmonic, (b) amplitude of the third harmonic; — reference results, ××× p-FEM, ••• IGA, $p = 4$ for longitudinal and transverse displacements, ◊◊◊ IGA, $p = 2$ for longitudinal and $p = 4$ for transverse displacements; ω_l - fundamental frequency.

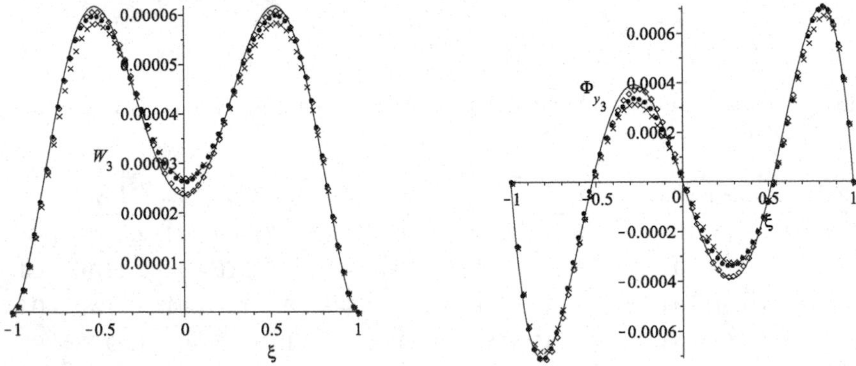

Fig. 3. Comparison of shapes of vibration for point $\omega/\omega_l = 1.45$ from the bifurcation diagram. (a) transverse displacement w_0, (b) rotation of the cross section ϕ_y; — reference results, × × × p-FEM, ••• IGA, $p = 4$ for longitudinal and transverse displacements, ◊◊◊ IGA, $p = 2$ for longitudinal and $p = 4$ for transverse displacements.

equation has 110 DOFs. The bifurcation diagrams of these models are presented and compared in Fig. 2. In addition, a model based on the isogeometric analysis but using B-splines of degree four for the longitudinal and transverse displacement is generated and included in the comparisons. The reference solution is obtained by p-FEM with 15 shape functions for each displacement component. It was verified that the results of this model are converged.

The nonlinear frequency-response function of the first harmonic is approximated very well by both methods, there is no visible difference. The difference appears in the third harmonic (Fig. 2(b)), where it can be seen that the isogeometric analysis yields a better approximation. The better approximation of the nonlinear frequency-response function is consequence of the better approximation of the higher linear frequencies of vibration.

The shapes of vibration of the transverse displacement w_0 and the rotation of the cross section ϕ_y, for point $\omega/\omega_l = 1.45$ from the bifurcation diagram, are shown in Fig. 3.

5 Conclusion

In the current work, the nonlinear frequency-response functions of beams, obtained by two approaches for space discretization, were compared. The equation of motion was derived by the principle of virtual work considering Timoshenko's theory for bending and assuming geometrical type of nonlinearity. For the isogeometric analysis case, the displacement components were expressed by appropriate sets of B-Splines, while for the finite element case, a set of hierarchical shape functions was used and p-version FEM was implemented. It was demonstrated that isogeometric analysis gives better approximation of the NFRF than the p-FEM, when the same numbers of degrees of freedom are used.

Acknowledgments. This work was supported by the project AComIn "Advanced Computing for Innovation", grant 316087, funded by the FP7 Capacity Programme and through the Bulgarian NSF Grant DCVP 02/1.

References

1. Benson, D.J., Bazilevs, Y., Hsu, M.C., Hughes, T.J.R.: Isogeometric shell analysis: The Reissner-Mindlin shell. Comput. Methods Appl. Mech. Eng. **199**(5–8), 276–289 (2010)
2. Cottrell, J.A., Hughes, T.J.R., Bazilevs, Y.: Isogeometric Analysis: Toward Integration of CAD and FEA. Wiley, Chichester (2009)
3. Cottrell, J.A., Reali, A., Bazilevs, Y., Hughes, T.J.R.: Isogeometric analysis of structural vibrations. Comput. Methods Appl. Mech. Eng. **195**(41–43), 5257–5296 (2006)
4. Hughes, T.J.R., Cottrell, J.A., Bazilevs, Y.: Isogeometric analysis: CAD, finite elements, NURBS, exact geometry and mesh refinement. Comput. Methods Appl. Mech. Eng. **194**(39–41), 4135–4195 (2005). http://dx.doi.org/10.1016/j.cma.2004.10.008
5. Hughes, T.J.R., Reali, A., Sangalli, G.: Duality and unified analysis of discrete approximations in structural dynamics and wave propagation: Comparison of p-method finite elements with k-method NURBS. Comput. Methods Appl. Mech. Eng. **197**(49–50), 4104–4124 (2008)
6. Lee, S.J., Park, K.S.: Vibrations of Timoshenko beams with isogeometric approach. Appl. Math. Model. **37**(22), 9174–9190 (2013)
7. Piegl, L., Tiller, W.: The NURBS Book. Monographs in Visual Communications. Springer, Berlin (1997)
8. Ribeiro, P., Petyt, M.: Non-linear vibration of beams with internal resonance by the hierarchical finite-element method. J. Sound Vibr. **224**(4), 591–624 (1999)
9. Schumaker, L.: Spline Functions: Basic Theory. Cambridge Mathematical Library. Cambridge University Press, Cambridge (2007)

10. Stoykov, S., Ribeiro, P.: Nonlinear free vibrations of beams in space due to internal resonance. J. Sound Vibr. **330**, 4574–4595 (2011)
11. Weeger, O., Wever, U., Simeon, B.: Isogeometric analysis of nonlinear Euler-Bernoulli beam vibrations. Nonlinear Dyn. **72**(4), 813–835 (2013)

Advanced Numerical Techniques for PDEs and Applications

Deterministic Solution of the Discrete Wigner Equation

Johann Cervenka(✉), Paul Ellinghaus, and Mihail Nedjalkov

Institute for Microelectronics, TU Wien, Vienna, Austria
cervenka@iue.tuwien.ac.at

Abstract. The Wigner formalism provides a convenient formulation of quantum mechanics in the phase space. Deterministic solutions of the Wigner equation are especially needed for problems where phase space quantities vary over several orders of magnitude and thus can not be resolved by the existing stochastic approaches. However, finite difference schemes have been problematic due to the discretization of the diffusion term in this differential equation. A new approach, which uses an integral formulation of the Wigner equation that avoids the problematic differentiation, is shown here. The results of the deterministic method are compared and validated with solutions of the Schrödinger equation. Furthermore, certain numerical aspects pertaining to the demanded parallel implementation are discussed.

Keywords: Discrete Wigner equation · Integral formulation

1 Introduction

An accurate description of carrier transport in nanoelectronic devices necessitates quantum mechanics to be considered. The Wigner formalism presents a convenient formulation of quantum mechanics in the phase-space, thereby allowing many classical notions and concepts to be reused [3,4].

Basis for the following considerations is the Wigner equation

$$\frac{\partial f(x,k,t)}{\partial t} - \frac{\hbar k}{m^*}\frac{\partial f(x,k,t)}{\partial x} = \sum_m V_w(x,k-k')\, f(x,k',t), \tag{1}$$

which describes the evolution of the Wigner function $f(\mathbf{r},k,t)$, under the influence of the Wigner potential V_w. A detailed explanation to the aspects of the Wigner formalism can be found in [6] for instance. Deterministic solutions of the Wigner equation have huge memory requirements, which has hampered practical implementations in the past. Stochastic methods avoid this problem, albeit usually by trading memory requirements for computation time. A further difficulty with deterministic methods lies in the discretization of the diffusion term in the differential equation, due to the the highly oscillatory nature of Wigner functions in the phase-space. Indeed the commonly used higher-order schemes show very different output characteristics. However, the precision of the deterministic methods make them the only possible approach in cases where physical quantities vary over many orders of magnitude in the phase space.

I. Dimov et al. (Eds.): NMA 2014, LNCS 8962, pp. 149–156, 2015.
DOI: 10.1007/978-3-319-15585-2_17

2 Solution Approach

The developed deterministic approach uses the integral formulation of the evolution Wigner equation. The integral form [5,7] is obtained by considering the characteristics of the Liouville operator on the left-hand-side of (1), which are the Newtonian trajectories $x(\cdot, t)$ initialized with x', k', t':

$$x(x', k', t', t) = x' + \frac{\hbar k'}{m^*}(t - t'). \tag{2}$$

This approach has already been used for development of stochastic solvers, which rely on the corresponding Neumann series of the integral equation [1].

Here, we develop an alternative procedure by first discretizing the variables of the equation by:

$$x = n\Delta x,\ n \in [0, N]; \quad k = m\Delta k,\ m \in [-M, M]; \quad t = l\Delta t,\ l \in [0, L]$$

The numerical task is to calculate the mean value f_Θ – the integral of the solution inside a particular domain indicated by Θ. The indicator function Θ is unity if the phase-space argument belongs to the domain and zero otherwise.

$$f_\Theta(\tau) = \int_0^\tau \mathrm{d}t \sum_n \sum_m f_i(n, m)\, e^{-\int_0^t \gamma(x_i(y))\mathrm{d}y}\, g_\Theta(x_i(t), m, t), \tag{3}$$

where τ is the evaluation time, f_i the initial condition, $x_i(t)$ is the trajectory, initialized by $(n\Delta x, m\Delta k, 0)$, and g_Θ is the so-called forward solution of the adjoint integral equation:

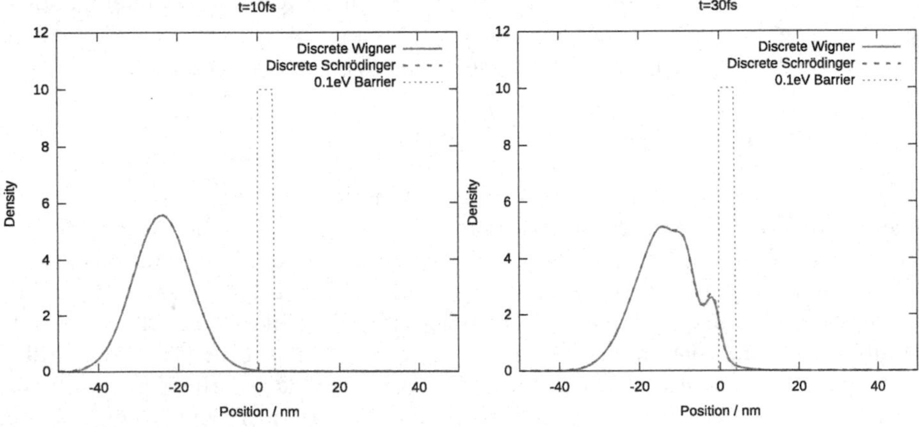

Fig. 1. Density after 10 fs and 30 fs for a wave package propagating through a 4 nm wide and 0.1 eV high potential barrier.

$$g_\Theta(n',m',t') = \Theta(n',m')\,\delta_{t',\tau} + \int_{t'}^{\tau} \mathrm{d}t \sum_m e^{-\int_{t'}^{t}\gamma(x(y))\mathrm{d}y}\,\Gamma(x(t),m,m')\,g_\Theta(x(t),m,t) \tag{4}$$

Within (4) $\gamma(n) = \sum_m V_w^+(n,m)$,

$$\Gamma(n,m,m') = V_w^+(n,m-m') + V_w^+(n,m'-m) + \gamma(n)\delta_{m,m'},$$

and $x(t)$ initialized by $(n'\Delta x, m\Delta k, t)$. All operations involving the time variable are also discretized. In particular, (2) may be expressed as

$$x(n',m,l',l) = \left(n' + int\left(\frac{\hbar m \Delta k \Delta t}{m^*\Delta x}(l-l')\right)\right)\Delta x. \tag{5}$$

For the moment we assume that the integral can be simply substituted by a summation and will return to the problem in the sequel.

3 Numerical Aspects of the Method

The value of f_Θ depends on the particular forward solution g_Θ and the initial condition f_i. The various values forming the initial condition evolve independently from each other in time and then are summated according to (3). Hence, to account for any arbitrary specified initial condition f_i, Eq. (4) must be solved for each domain $\Theta = \delta_{n',u}\delta_{m',v}$ associated to each point (u,v) of the region and evolution time $\tau = l_\tau \Delta t$. The simulation task entails solving

$$f_{u,v}(l_\tau) = \sum_{l=0}^{l_\tau} \Delta t \sum_n \sum_m f_i(n,m)\, e^{-\sum_{j=0}^{l}\gamma(x_i(j))\Delta y}\, g_{u,v,l_\tau}(x_i(l),m,l), \tag{6}$$

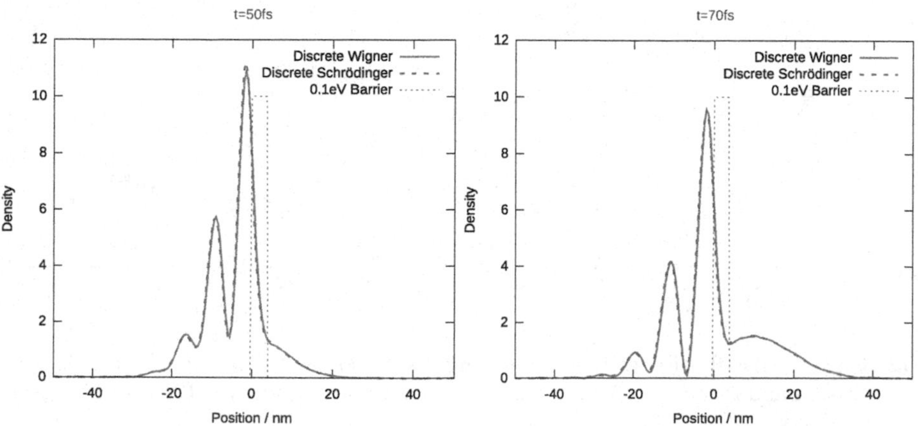

Fig. 2. Density after 50 fs and 70 fs for a wave package propagating through a 4 nm wide and 0.1 eV high potential barrier.

with

$$g_{u,v,l_\tau}(n',m',l') = \delta_{n',u}\delta_{m',v}\delta_{l',l_\tau} + \sum_{l=l'}^{l_\tau} \Delta t \sum_{m} e^{-\sum_{j=l'}^{l} \gamma(x(j))\Delta j}\, \Gamma(x(l),m,m')\, g_{u,v,l_\tau}(x(l),m,l). \quad (7)$$

For simplicity of the formulas we skip the initialization point in the notation of x and keep only the running variable.

Complexity of the Method

A direct implementation of the algorithm is to assemble and solve the equation system (4) of rank $L{\cdot}N{\cdot}2M$ (the number of spatial, momentum and time points) and then to back-insert the solution into (6).

This implies that the following algorithmic steps have to be repeated $L{\cdot}N{\cdot}2M$ times (for each particular indicator):

- assembly of (7) with effort $\mathcal{O}(2M \cdot L \cdot L)$,
- solving a system with rank $L \cdot N \cdot 2M$,
- back-insertion in (6) with effort $\mathcal{O}(L \cdot N \cdot 2M)$,
- the storage of all $g_\Theta(n', m', l')$
- the temporary storage for the equation system (7).

This analysis presents the upper bound for the estimated computational complexity. We suggest some optimizations to reduce the complexity in the following.

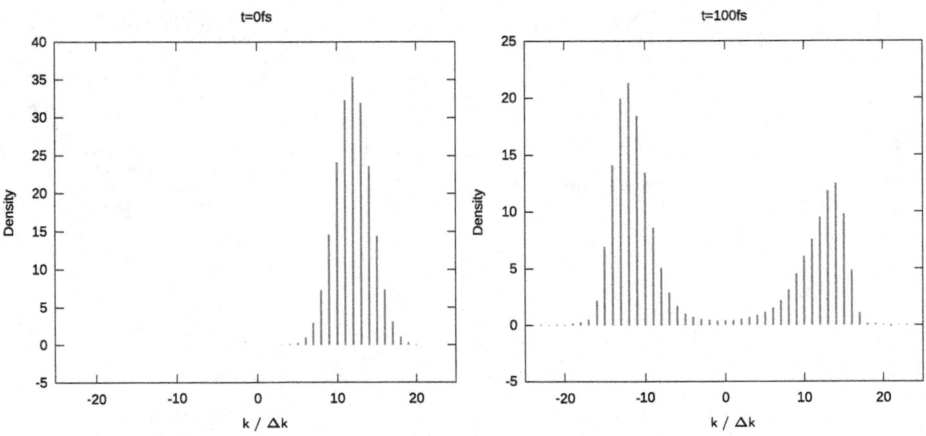

Fig. 3. The k-distribution at initial time and after 100 fs corresponding to Fig. 1. The transmission and reflection of the initially located wave around $k_0 = 12\Delta k$ can be seen.

Aspects of the Time Integration

An important improvement of the computation scheme is made by observing that the time-related quantity δ_{l',l_τ} may be accounted for analytically. Indeed, it may be shown that Eq. (7) becomes

$$g_{u,v,l_\tau}(n',m',l') = e^{-\sum_{j=l'}^{l_\tau}\gamma(x'(j))\Delta t}\delta_{x'(l_\tau),u}\delta_{m',v}$$
$$+\sum_{l=l'}^{l_\tau}\Delta t\sum_m e^{-\sum_{j=l'}^{l}\gamma(x'(j))\,\Delta t\,\omega_j}\,\Gamma(x'(l),m,m')\,g_{u,v,l_\tau}(x'(l),m,l)\,\omega_l, \quad (8)$$

with $x'(l)$ initialized by n', m', l'. With this technique the time dependency in the back-insertion can be omitted and its complexity can be reduced. We note that Eq. (8) corresponds to a newly introduced higher-order integration scheme, since a detailed analysis has shown that higher-order discretization schemes have to be used. The used weights ω_l depend on the discretization of the integration.

Furthermore, examining the equation system (8) enables a recursion scheme where the already obtained forward solution is used to calculate the solution of the next time step. This allows a simplification in the rank of the equation system to $N \cdot 2M$.

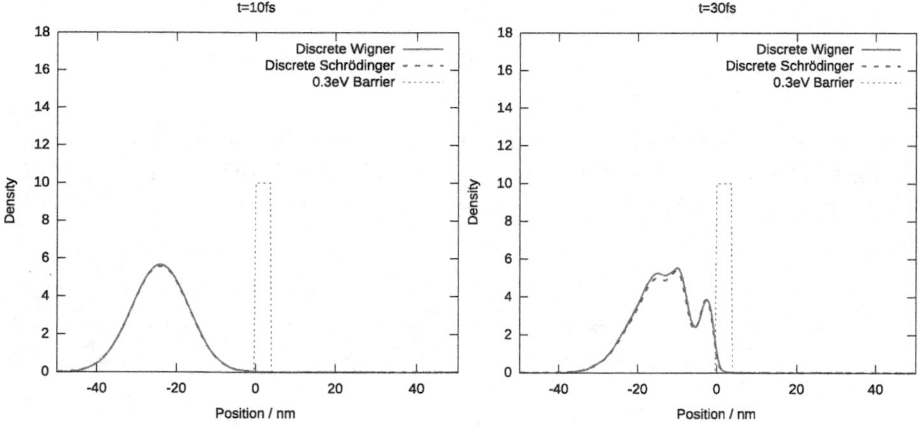

Fig. 4. Density after 10 fs and 30 fs for a wave package propagating through a 4 nm wide and 0.3 eV high potential barrier.

Computational Demands

The process step demanding the most computation time is the assembly of the equation system. The latter weights more heavily as evolution time increases, as the time steps to be summated and the summands in the exponent increase accordingly.

We further utilize the fact that the procedure, applied for each point (u, v, l_τ), depends only on the initial location in phase-space. Therefore, the calculation of a certain point is independent on the processes associated with the rest of the points, making this method well-suited for parallelization as it proceeds without communications between the particular tasks. This enables an easy possibility of combining OpenMP on each node with Message Passing Interface (MPI) over several nodes. The communication overhead is only occasionally incurred when collecting the particular results $f_{u,v}(l_\mathcal{T})$ – this is reflected in the excellent scalability of the parallelization.

The increase of the evolution time brings a corresponding increase of the memory required to retain the history. Thus a serial implementation running on single node quickly reaches its memory limit, thereby limiting both the achievable resolution and simulated time for the simulation. Additionally, a parallel implementation has the advantage of splitting the memory demands between the particular nodes, thereby allowing acceptable time and phase-space resolution to be achieved.

4 Application to a Wave Packet

The time evolution of a wave packet, which captures both particle- and wave-like physical characteristics, is an effective tool to study quantum transport in nanoscale semiconductor devices [2].

As a benchmark problem a minimum uncertainty wave packet [3]

$$\Psi_i(x, t = 0) = e^{-\frac{(x-x_0)^2}{2\sigma^2}} e^{ik_0 x} \tag{9}$$

is chosen, traveling to the right towards a square potential barrier. To apply this setting to the Wigner equation, the distribution of the potential barrier $V(x)$ has to be transformed by

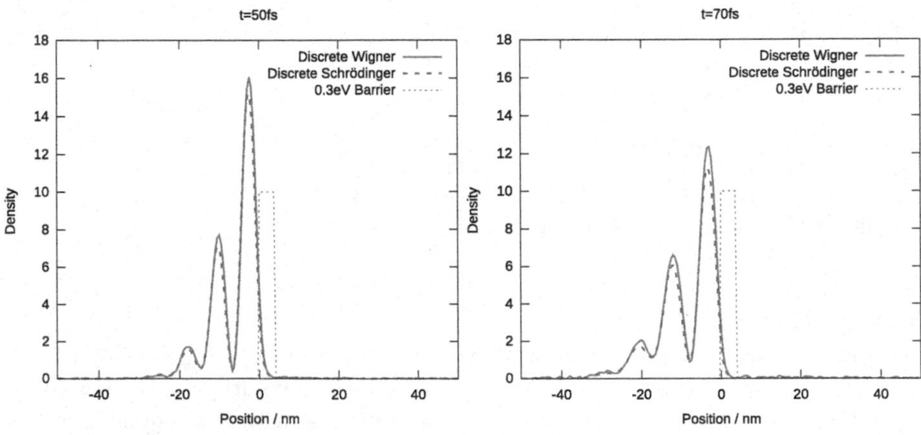

Fig. 5. Density after 50 fs and 70 fs for a wave package propagating through a 4 nm wide and 0.3 eV high potential barrier.

$$V_w(x,m) = \frac{1}{i\hbar}\frac{1}{L_{\text{coh}}} \int\limits_{-L_{\text{coh}}/2}^{L_{\text{coh}}/2} e^{-i2m\Delta ks} \left[V(x+s) - V(x-s)\right] \mathrm{d}s \tag{10}$$

to Wigner space. This formula is very general for the Wigner formalism, e.g. any wave function Ψ or any potential give their Wigner counterparts by such integral transform [6]. Here L_{coh} describes the desired coherence length of the system.

The parameters of the simulation are

- $x_0 = -29.5\,\text{nm}$ the initial position of the peak of the wave packet,
- $\sigma = 10\,\text{nm}$ the standard deviation in space of the initial wave package,
- $k_0 = 12\Delta k$ the speed of the wave packet,
- $\Delta k = \pi/L_{\text{coh}}$ is the chosen spacing in phase-space, with
- $L_{\text{coh}} = 100\,\text{nm}$ the coherence length for the Wigner transformation.

To validate the results of the developed deterministic method, they are compared to the numerical solution of the one-dimensional Schrödinger equation [8]

$$i\hbar\frac{\partial\Psi(x,t)}{\partial t} = \left[-\frac{\hbar^2}{2m}\nabla^2 + V\right]\Psi(x,t). \tag{11}$$

Figures 1 and 2 show the solutions of the Wigner equation, solved by the deterministic method, compared to the solution of the Schrödinger equation for a wave packet traveling through a 4 nm wide, 0.1 eV high barrier at various time steps. A good accordance between the results can be seen. The corresponding distribution in k-space can be seen in Fig. 3. Here, the transmitted and reflected parts of the wave can be clearly observed. The simulations were performed using a 200×50 grid in the phase-space, with a spatial resolution of $\Delta x = 0.5\,\text{nm}$

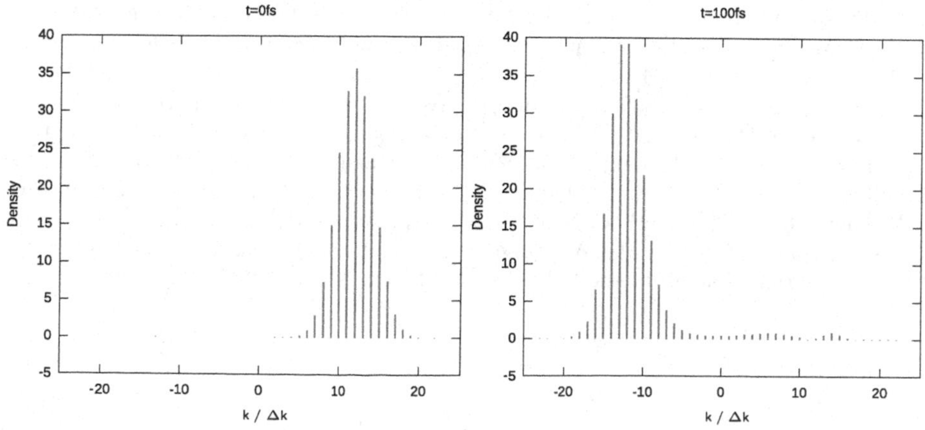

Fig. 6. The k-distribution at initial time and after 100 fs corresponding to Fig. 4. The nearly total reflection of the initially located wave around $k_0 = 12\Delta k$ can be seen.

and $\Delta k = \pi/100\,\text{nm}$. The time discretization used a step-with of $\Delta t = 0.5\,\text{fs}$ to maintain a good accuracy for the transmitted part of the wave packet.

Figures 4 and 5 show the same initial wave approaching a 0.3 eV high barrier. Here, the wave is almost completely reflected. The corresponding k-distribution can be seen in Fig. 6 for 0 fs and 100 fs, which shows nearly the same shape as the former but reversed sign in k-space. Both examples show an excellent accordance between the numerical solution of the Schödinger equation – the mainstay for quantum transport simulations – and the deterministic solution of the Wigner equation.

5 Conclusion and Outlook

A novel method for deterministically solving the Wigner equation has been shown and validated by a comparison with the Schrödinger equation. Several improvements of the history calculation and interpolation schemes seem feasible and offer the most potential for speed-up. In the future the method will be applied to scattering processes and may be useful as pre-conditioner for stochastic Wigner methods.

References

1. Dimov, I.T.: Monte Carlo Methods for Applied Scientists. World Scientific, London (2008)
2. Fu, Y., Willander, M.: Electron wave-packet transport through nanoscale semiconductor device in time domain. J. Appl. Phys. **97**(9), 094311 (2005)
3. Griffiths, D.: Introduction to Quantum Mechanics. Pearson Prentice Hall, Upper Saddle River (2005)
4. Kosik, R.: Numerical challenges on the road to NanoTCAD. Ph.D. thesis, Institut für Mikroelektronik (2004)
5. Nedjalkov, M., Kosina, H., Selberherr, S., Ringhofer, C., Ferry, D.K.: Unified Particle approach to Wigner-Boltzmann transport in small semiconductor devices. Phys. Rev. B **70**, 115319 (2004)
6. Nedjalkov, M., Querlioz, D., Dollfus, P., Kosina, H.: Wigner function approach. In: Vasileska, D., Goodnick, S.M. (eds.) Nano-electronic Devices. Semiclassical and Quantum Transport Modeling, pp. 289–358. Springer, New York (2011)
7. Sellier, J.M.D., Nedjalkov, M., Dimov, I., Selberherr, S.: A benchmark study of the Wigner Monte Carlo method. Monte Carlo Method Appl. **20**(1), 43–51 (2014)
8. Sudiarta, I.W., Geldart, D.J.W.: Solving the Schrödinger equation using the finite difference time domain method. J. Phys. A: Math. Theor. **40**(8), 1885 (2007)

Explicit-Implicit Splitting Schemes for Parabolic Equations and Systems

Petr N. Vabishchevich[1(✉)] and Petr E. Zakharov[2]

[1] Nuclear Safety Institute, 52, B. Tulskaya, 115191 Moscow, Russia
vabishchevich@gmail.com
[2] North-Eastern Federal University, 58, Belinskogo, 677000 Yakutsk, Russia

Abstract. Standard explicit schemes for parabolic equations are not very convenient for computing practice due to the fact that they have strong restrictions on the time step. This stability restriction is avoided in some explicit schemes based on explicit-implicit splitting of the problem operator (Saul'yev asymmetric schemes, explicit alternating direction (ADE) schemes, group explicit method). These schemes are unconditionally stable, however, their approximation properties are worse than the usual implicit schemes. These explicit schemes are based on the so-called alternating triangle method and can be considered as factorized schemes in which the problem operator is split into a sum of two triangular operators that are adjoint to each other.

Here we propose a multilevel modification of the alternating triangle method, which demonstrates better properties in terms of accuracy. We also consider explicit schemes of the alternating triangle method for the numerical solution of boundary value problems for systems of equations. The study is based on the general theory of stability (well-posedness) of operator-difference schemes.

1 Introduction

Explicit schemes have an evident advantage over implicit schemes in terms of computational implementation. This advantage is especially pronounced in the construction of computational algorithms for parallel computing systems. At the same time explicit schemes have the well-known disadvantage that is associated with strong restrictions on the admissible time step. Some promising unconditionally stable explicit schemes, computing the solution as a decomposition in the form of travelling waves, have been known in the literature for a long time. They are based on the decomposition of the problem operator into two operators only one of them being associated with the new time level. That is why such schemes with inhomogeneous approximation in time are called explicit-implicit schemes. Although being unconditionally stable and explicit, however, these schemes are not widely used because they suffer of relatively low accuracy as compared to the standard implicit schemes.

First explicit difference schemes with traveling wave computations for parabolic equations of second order were proposed by Saul'yev in the book [10].

I. Dimov et al. (Eds.): NMA 2014, LNCS 8962, pp. 157–166, 2015.
DOI: 10.1007/978-3-319-15585-2_18

In view of explicit-implicit inhomogeneity of approximation in time, the author called them asymmetric schemes. Further fundamental result was obtained by A.A. Samarskii in the work [7], where these schemes were treated as factorized operator-difference schemes with the additive splitting of the problem operator (matrix) into two terms that are adjoint to each other. Considering a system of first order ordinary differential equations, we split the original matrix into the sum of a lower and upper triangular matrices and this is why the method is called the Alternating Triangle Method (ATM). Further applications of explicit schemes with travelling wave decomposition of the computations for parabolic BVPs can be found in the work of Evans and co-authors [2,3], who named them the Group Explicit (Alternating Group Explicit) method. Recently, the implementation of such schemes on parallel computers has also been actively studied (see, e.g., [17,18]). Explicit schemes of the ATM type have also been applied to time-dependent convection-diffusion problems, see e.g. [4,16].

Another area of significant importance for applications is the case of vectorial systems of PDEs in which the various components of the solution vector are coupled through the operator of the problem. Then it is also possible to decouple the problems for the individual components using explicit-implicit schemes. Schemes of this type for the common parabolic and hyperbolic systems are constructed in [8]. Additive schemes of ATM type for problems of an incompressible fluid with variable viscosity are studied in [14], and for elasticity problems — in [5]. Vector problems of electrodynamics are studied in [11].

2 Spatial Approximation

As a typical example, we study the boundary value problem for a parabolic equation of second order. Let us consider a model two-dimensional parabolic problem in a polygonal region Ω ($\boldsymbol{x} = (x_1, x_2)$). An unknown function $u(\boldsymbol{x}, t)$ satisfies the equation

$$\frac{\partial u}{\partial t} - \sum_{\alpha=1}^{2} \frac{\partial}{\partial x_\alpha}\left(k(\boldsymbol{x})\frac{\partial u}{\partial x_\alpha}\right) = f(\boldsymbol{x}, t), \quad \boldsymbol{x} \in \Omega, \quad 0 < t \leq T, \tag{1}$$

where $k(\boldsymbol{x}) \leq \varkappa$, $\boldsymbol{x} \in \Omega$, $\varkappa > 0$. The equation (1) is supplemented with homogeneous Dirichlet boundary conditions

$$u(\boldsymbol{x}, t) = 0, \quad \boldsymbol{x} \in \partial\Omega, \quad 0 < t \leq T. \tag{2}$$

In addition, we specify the initial condition

$$u(\boldsymbol{x}, 0) = u^0(\boldsymbol{x}), \quad \boldsymbol{x} \in \Omega. \tag{3}$$

The region $\overline{\Omega} = \Omega \bigcup \partial\Omega$ is discretized by a mesh $\overline{\omega}$ consisting of the nodes of a Delaunay triangulation, $\boldsymbol{x}_i$, $i = 1, 2, \ldots, M$. Let ω be the set of all internal nodes and $\partial\omega$ be the set of all boundary nodes, i.e., $\omega = \overline{\omega} \bigcap \Omega$, $\partial\omega = \overline{\omega} \bigcap \partial\omega$. Using the standard finite volume approach, a dual Voronoi grid of control volumes is constructed. The edges of the control volume associated with a given node i, Ω_i, are the line segments produced by intersecting the lines through the midpoints of all line segments connecting i with its immediate neighbours in the Delaunay triangulation, that are perpendicular to these segments.

Control volumes cover the entire computational region, so that

$$\overline{\Omega} = \bigcup_{i=1}^{M} \overline{\Omega}_i, \quad \overline{\Omega}_i = \Omega_i \bigcup \partial\Omega_i, \quad \Omega_i \bigcap \Omega_j = \emptyset,$$

$$i \neq j, \quad i,\ j = 1, 2, \ldots, M.$$

For common edges of control volumes, we use the notation

$$\partial\Omega_i \bigcap \partial\Omega_j = \Gamma_{ij}, \quad i \neq j, \quad i,\ j = 1, 2, \ldots, M.$$

For a node i, we define the set of neighbouring nodes $\mathcal{W}(i)$, whose control volumes have common edges with the control volume for the node i, i.e.,

$$\mathcal{W}(i) = \{j \mid \partial\Omega_i \bigcap \partial\Omega_j \neq \emptyset,\ j = 1, 2, \ldots, M\}, \quad i = 1, 2, \ldots, M.$$

We also introduce the notation

$$V_i = \int_{\Omega_i} d\boldsymbol{x}, \quad l_{ij} = \int_{\Gamma_{ij}} d\boldsymbol{x}, \quad i,\ j = 1, 2, \ldots, M,$$

for the area of the control volume and the length of the edge of a Voronoi polygon, respectively.

For grid functions $y(\boldsymbol{x})$, $w(\boldsymbol{x})$ defined in nodes $\boldsymbol{x} \in \bar{\omega}$ and become zero at the boundary nodes $\boldsymbol{x} \in \partial\omega$, we define the scalar product in $H = L_2(\omega)$ and norm by expressions

$$(y, w) = \sum_{\boldsymbol{x}_i \in \omega} V_i y(\boldsymbol{x}_i) w(\boldsymbol{x}_i), \quad \|y\| = (y, y)^{1/2}.$$

We define the distance between nodes $\boldsymbol{x}_i$, $\boldsymbol{x}_j$:

$$d(\boldsymbol{x}_i, \boldsymbol{x}_j) = \left[\sum_{\alpha=1}^{2} \left(x_i^{(\alpha)} - x_j^{(\alpha)} \right) \right]^{1/2},$$

and the midpoint of the segment joining these nodes:

$$\boldsymbol{x}_{ij} = \left(x_{ij}^{(1)}, x_{ij}^{(2)} \right), \quad x_{ij}^{(\alpha)} = \frac{1}{2} \left(x_i^{(\alpha)} + x_j^{(\alpha)} \right), \quad \alpha = 1, 2.$$

We define an elliptic operator

$$\mathcal{A}u = - \sum_{\alpha=1}^{2} \frac{\partial}{\partial x_\alpha} \left(k(\boldsymbol{x}) \frac{\partial u}{\partial x_\alpha} \right).$$

The corresponding grid elliptic operator, which refers to the internal node of the computational grid $\boldsymbol{x}_i \in \omega$, is defined in accordance with the integro-interpolation method of integration over the control volume Ω_i:

$$\mathcal{A}u = (\mathcal{A}u)_i \approx -\frac{1}{V_i} \int\limits_{\Omega_i} \mathcal{A}u \, d\boldsymbol{x}. \tag{4}$$

For the flow vector, we use the expression $\boldsymbol{q} = -k(\boldsymbol{x})\operatorname{grad} u$ such that $\mathcal{A}u = \operatorname{div} \boldsymbol{q}$. Taking this into account for the right-hand side of (4), we obtain

$$\int\limits_{\Omega_i} \mathcal{A}u \, d\boldsymbol{x} = \int\limits_{\partial\Omega_i} (\boldsymbol{q}, \boldsymbol{n}) d\boldsymbol{x}. \tag{5}$$

Difference approximation of the normal component of the flow on the edge of γ_{ij} we denote $\boldsymbol{q}_{ij}^h$ and, therefore, from (4), (5) for the difference operator we obtain the representation

$$(Ay)_i = \frac{1}{V_i} \sum_{j \in \mathcal{W}(i)} l_{ij} q_{ij}^h, \quad \boldsymbol{x}_i \in \omega. \tag{6}$$

As usual for the finite volume method we use the simplest approximations for the normal flux at point $\boldsymbol{x}_{ij}$:

$$q_{ij}^h = -k(\boldsymbol{x}_{ij}) \frac{y_j - y_i}{d(\boldsymbol{x}_i, \boldsymbol{x}_j)}. \tag{7}$$

From (6), (7), we obtain the required representation for the difference operator of diffusion transport:

$$(Ay)_i = -\frac{1}{V_i} \sum_{j \in \mathcal{W}(i)} l_{ij} k(\boldsymbol{x}_{ij}) \frac{y_j - y_i}{d(\boldsymbol{x}_i, \boldsymbol{x}_j)}, \quad \boldsymbol{x}_i \in \omega. \tag{8}$$

For grid functions $y_i \equiv y(\boldsymbol{x}_i) = 0, \; w_i = 0, \; \boldsymbol{x}_i \in \partial\omega$, we have

$$(Ay, w) = \sum_{\boldsymbol{x}_i \in \omega} \sum_{j \in \mathcal{W}(i)} l_{ij} k(\boldsymbol{x}_{ij}) q_{ij}^h w_i = -\sum_{\boldsymbol{x}_i \in \omega} \sum_{j \in \mathcal{W}(i)} l_{ij} k(\boldsymbol{x}_{ij}) \frac{y_j - y_i}{d(\boldsymbol{x}_i, \boldsymbol{x}_j)} w_i.$$

The summation over all edges of Voronoi polygons for all internal nodes can be given in a more convenient form

$$(Ay, w) = \frac{1}{2} \sum_{\boldsymbol{x}_i \in \omega} \sum_{j \in \mathcal{W}(i)} \frac{l_{ij} k(\boldsymbol{x}_{ij})}{d(\boldsymbol{x}_i, \boldsymbol{x}_j)} ((y_j - y_i) w_j - (y_j - y_i) w_i)$$

$$= \frac{1}{2} \sum_{\boldsymbol{x}_i \in \omega} \sum_{j \in \mathcal{W}(i)} l_{ij} k(\boldsymbol{x}_{ij}) d(\boldsymbol{x}_i, \boldsymbol{x}_j) \frac{y_j - y_i}{d(\boldsymbol{x}_i, \boldsymbol{x}_j)} \frac{z_j - z_i}{d(\boldsymbol{x}_i, \boldsymbol{x}_j)}.$$

Thereby $(Ay, w) = (y, A^* w)$, i.e., the difference operator (8) is self-adjoint in H. By

$$(Ay, y) = \frac{1}{2} \sum_{\boldsymbol{x}_i \in \omega} \sum_{j \in \mathcal{W}(i)} l_{ij} k(\boldsymbol{x}_{ij}) d(\boldsymbol{x}_i, \boldsymbol{x}_j) \left(\frac{y_j - y_i}{d(\boldsymbol{x}_i, \boldsymbol{x}_j)} \right)^2$$

it is also non-negative ($A = A^* \geq 0$).

Using the grid analog of the Friedrichs lemma [13], we can show that

$$A = A^* \geq \delta E, \quad \delta = \frac{\varkappa}{M_0} E, \tag{9}$$

for grid functions from the space $H = L_2(\omega)$. Here E is the unit (identity) operator in H and the constant

$$M_0 = \frac{l_1^2}{16} + \frac{l_2^2}{16},$$

where l_α, $\alpha = 1, 2$ are the lengths of the sides of a rectangle with sides parallel to the axes, which contains the whole polygon Ω.

After spatial approximations, we come from (1)–(3) to the Cauchy problem for the evolutionary equation of first order:

$$\frac{dv}{dt} + Av = f(t), \quad 0 < t \leq T, \tag{10}$$

$$v(0) = u^0, \tag{11}$$

using the notation $v(t) = v(\boldsymbol{x}, t)$, $\boldsymbol{x} \in \omega$.

3 Approximation in Time

To solve numerically the problem (10), (11), we start our consideration with the two-level scheme. Let τ be a step of a uniform grid in time such that $y^n = y(t^n)$, $t^n = n\tau$, $n = 0, 1, ..., N$, $N\tau = T$. Let us approximate equation (10) by the two-level scheme

$$\frac{y^{n+1} - y^n}{\tau} + A(\sigma y^{n+1} + (1 - \sigma) y^n) = \varphi^n, \quad n = 0, 1, ..., N - 1, \tag{12}$$

with weight $0 < \sigma \leq 1$, where, e.g., $\varphi^n = f(\sigma t^{n+1} + (1 - \sigma) t^n)$. In view of (11), the operator-difference equation (12) is supplemented with the intitial condition

$$y^0 = u^0. \tag{13}$$

The truncation error of temporal approximation of the difference scheme (12), (13) is $O(\tau^2 + (\sigma - 0.5)\tau)$.

Theorem 1. [8,9] *The two-level difference scheme (12), (13) is stable for $\sigma \geq 0.5$, and the finite-difference solution satisfies the estimate*

$$\|y^{n+1}\|_A^2 \leq \|u^0\|_A^2 + \frac{\tau}{2} \sum_{k=0}^{n} \|\varphi^k\|^2. \tag{14}$$

Let us decompose the problem operator A into the sum of two operators:

$$A = A_1 + A_2. \qquad (15)$$

Individual operator terms in (15) must make it possible to construct splitting schemes based on explicit calculations. In the alternating triangle method [7,8], the origional matrix is splitted into the upper and lower matrices, which correspond to the operators adjoint to each other:

$$A_1 = A_2^*. \qquad (16)$$

To solve the problem (12), (13), (15), (16), we can use various splitting schemes [15], where the transition to a new time level is associated with solving subproblems that are described by the individual operators A_1 and A_2. For the above two-component splitting (15), it is natural to apply factorized additive schemes. In this case, we have

$$(E + \sigma\tau A_1)(E + \sigma\tau A_2)\frac{y^{n+1} - y^n}{\tau} + Ay^n = \varphi^n, \quad n = 0, 1, ..., N - 1. \qquad (17)$$

The value $\sigma = 0.5$ corresponds to the classical Peaceman-Rachford scheme [6], whereas for $\sigma = 1$, we obtain an operator analog of the Douglas-Rachford scheme [1].

Theorem 2. [7,8] *The factorized scheme of the alternating triangle method (13), (15)–(17) is unconditionally stable under the restriction* $\sigma \geq 0.5$. *The following a priori estimate holds:*

$$\|y^{n+1}\|_A^2 \leq \|u^0\|_A^2 + \frac{\tau}{2}\sum_{k=0}^{n} \|\varphi^k\|^2. \qquad (18)$$

Special attention should be given to the investigation of the accuracy of the alternating triangle method. The accuracy of the approximate solution of (10), (11) is estimated without considering the truncation error due to approximation in space. The convergence of the factorized scheme of the alternating triangle method (13), (15)–(17) for the problem (10), (11) is studied in the standard way. The equation for the error $z^n = y^n - u^n$ has the form

$$(E + \sigma\tau A_1)(E + \sigma\tau A_2)\frac{z^{n+1} - z^n}{\tau} + Az^n = \psi^n, \quad n = 0, 1, ..., N - 1,$$

with the truncation error ψ^n. By Theorem 2, the error satisfies estimate

$$\|z^{n+1}\|_A^2 \leq \frac{\tau}{2}\sum_{k=0}^{n} \|\psi^k\|^2.$$

The truncation error has the form

$$\psi^n = \psi_S^n + \psi_R^n, \qquad (19)$$

where

$$\psi_S^n = \left(\sigma - \frac{1}{2}\right) \tau A \frac{du}{dt}(t^{n+1/2}) + O(\tau^2),$$
$$\psi_R^n = \sigma^2\tau^2 A_1 A_2 \frac{du}{dt}(t^{n+1/2}) + O(\tau^3). \qquad (20)$$

The first part of the truncation error ψ_S^n is standard for the conventional scheme with weights (12), (13), which converges with the second order with respect to τ for $\sigma = 0.5$, and only with the first order if $\sigma \neq 0.5$.

The scheme of alternating triangle method (17) is a two-level scheme. We construct a three-level modification of this scheme which preserves the unconditional stability but demonstrates a more acceptable accuracy. Such schemes are called here Multi-Level Alternating Triangle Method (MLATM).

Rewrite the scheme (17) as

$$(E + \sigma\tau A)\frac{y^{n+1} - y^n}{\tau} + \sigma^2\tau^2 A_1 A_2 \frac{y^{n+1} - y^n}{\tau} + Ay^n = \varphi^n.$$

Here we have separated the term that corresponds to the standard scheme with weights from the term proportional to τ^2, which is associated with splitting. For this, we replace the term associated with splitting by

$$\sigma^2\tau^2 A_1 A_2 \frac{y^{n+1} - y^n}{\tau} - \sigma^2\tau^2 A_1 A_2 \frac{y^n - y^{n-1}}{\tau} = \sigma^2\tau^3 A_1 A_2 \frac{y^{n+1} - 2y^n + y^{n-1}}{\tau^2}.$$

After this modification the MLATM scheme takes the form

$$(E + \sigma\tau A))\frac{y^{n+1} - y^n}{\tau} + \sigma^2\tau^3 A_1 A_2 \frac{y^{n+1} - 2y^n + y^{n-1}}{\tau^2} + Ay^n = \varphi^n. \qquad (21)$$

As in the standard ATM scheme (17), the transition to a new time level in (21) involves the solution of the problem

$$(E + \sigma\tau A_1)(E + \sigma\tau A_2)y^{n+1} = \xi^n.$$

For the truncation error, now we have the representation (19), where

$$\psi_S^n = \left(\sigma - \frac{1}{2}\right) \tau A \frac{du}{dt}(t^{n+1/2}) + O(\tau^2),$$
$$\psi_R^n = \sigma^2\tau^3 A_1 A_2 \frac{d^2u}{dt^2}(t^{n+1/2}) + O(\tau^4).$$

Thus, the error associated with splitting ψ_R^n decreases by an order of τ (see (20)). Our main result [12] is the following.

Theorem 3. *The scheme of the multilevel alternating triangle method (13), (15), (16), (21) is unconditionally stable under the restriction* $\sigma \geq 0.5$. *The following a priori estimate holds:*

$$\mathcal{E}_{n+1} \leq \mathcal{E}_n + \frac{\tau}{2}\|\varphi^n\|^2_{(E+\sigma\tau A)^{-1}},$$

where

$$\mathcal{E}_{n+1} = \left\| \frac{y^{n+1} + y^n}{2} \right\|_A^2 + \left\| \frac{y^{n+1} - y^n}{\tau} \right\|_{\frac{\tau}{2}E + \sigma^2\tau^3 A_1 A_2 + \frac{\tau^2}{4}(2\sigma - 1)A}^2 .$$

4 Comparison of Numerical Results

We compare the accuracy of the ATM and MLATM schemes on the numerical solution of the model problem. The problem (1)–(3) in Ω is solved at values $T = 0.02, \tau = 0.0005$, with

$$k(\boldsymbol{x}) = 1, \quad \boldsymbol{x} \in \Omega,$$

$$f(\boldsymbol{x}, t) = 1, \quad \boldsymbol{x} \in \Omega, \quad 0 < t \leq T,$$

$$u^0(\boldsymbol{x}) = 0, \quad \boldsymbol{x} \in \Omega.$$

The region Ω is a quarter of the circle with a radius 1 discretized by a triangular mesh with the average distance between nodes equals 0.025 (see Fig. 1).

The error is defined as follows:

$$\varepsilon = \|y_p^n - y^n\|,$$

where y_p^n is the benchmark solution obtained on a fine grid with 24017 nodes and 47456 triangles, where the average distance between nodes equals 0.00625 with $\tau = 0.0000625$ and $\sigma = 0.5$. Figure 2 shows the time history for the error of various schemes. The ATM scheme gives a large error relatively as compared to the implicit scheme, and the error of the MLATM scheme is comparable with the error of the implicit scheme. Since the MLATM scheme is three-level, to calculate the first time level, we apply the implicit scheme. A similar relation is obtained for $\sigma = 0.5$ (see Fig. 3), to calculate the first time level of the MLATM scheme, we use the Crank-Nicholson scheme.

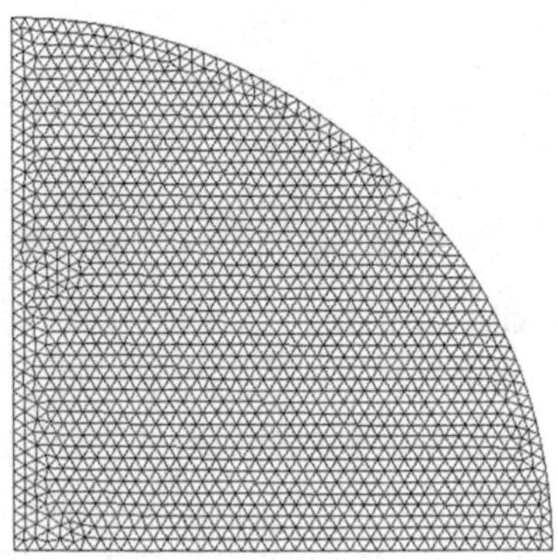

Fig. 1. Computational mesh: 1569 nodes and 2992 triangles

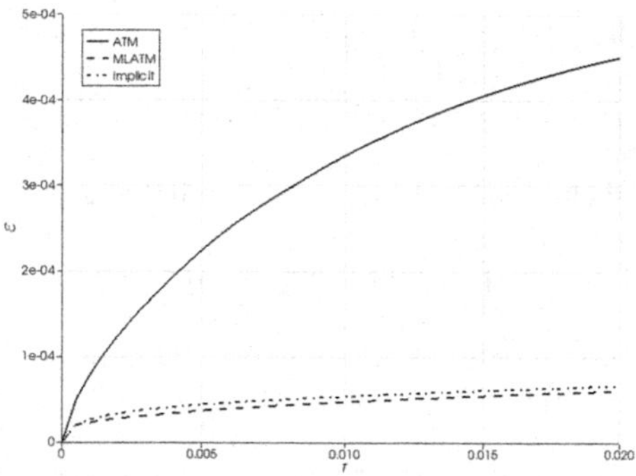

Fig. 2. Time-history of the error at $\sigma = 1$

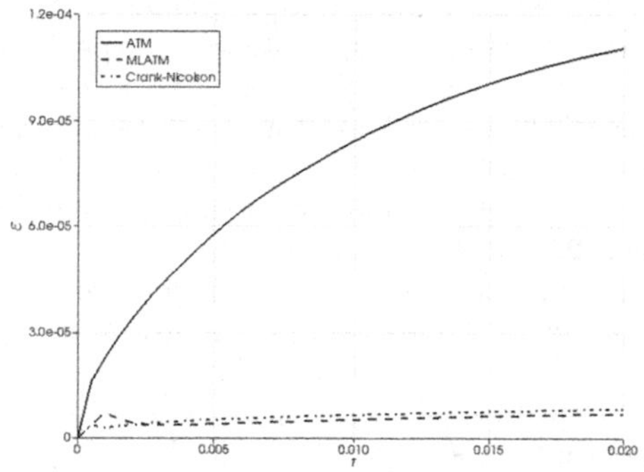

Fig. 3. Time-history of the error at $\sigma = 0.5$

The calculation of the first time level for the MLATM scheme with $\sigma = 1$ is conducted with various schemes. The explicit scheme gives the error jump, but further time levels are not particularly affected and the error is comparable with the error obtained using the exact solution for the first time level. The implicit scheme for the first level also shows the error enough close to the error obtained by using the exact solution. The ATM scheme provides the worst result at using for the first time level.

Acknowledgements. This work was supported by RFBR (project 14-01-00785).

References

1. Douglas, J.J., Rachford, H.H.: On the numerical solution of heat conduction problems in two and three space variables. Trans. Amer. Math. Soc. **82**, 421–439 (1956)
2. Evans, D.J.: Alternating group explicit method for the diffusion equation. Appl. Math. Model. **9**(3), 201–206 (1985)
3. Evans, D.J., Abdullah, A.R.B.: Group explicit methods for parabolic equations. Int. J. Comput. Math. **14**(1), 73–105 (1983)

4. Feng, Q., Zheng, B.: Parallel alternating group explicit iterative method for convection-diffusion equations. In: Proceedings of WSEAS International Conference on Mathematics and Computers in Science and Engineering, pp. 383–387. No. 8. World Scientific and Engineering Academy and Society (2009)
5. Lisbona, F.L., Vabishchevich, P.N.: Operator-splitting schemes for solving elasticity problems. Comput. Meth. Appl. Math. **1**(2), 188–198 (2001)
6. Peaceman, D.W., Rachford, H.H.: The numerical solution of parabolic and elliptic differential equations. J. SIAM **3**, 28–41 (1955)
7. Samarskii, A.A.: An economical algorithm for the numerical solution of differential and algebraic equations. Zh. Vychisl. Mat. Mat. Fiz. **4**(3), 580–585 (1964). in Russian
8. Samarskii, A.A.: The Theory of Difference Schemes. Marcel Dekker, New York (2001)
9. Samarskii, A.A., Matus, P.P., Vabishchevich, P.N.: Difference schemes with operator factors. Kluwer Academic Pub, The Netherlands (2002)
10. Saul'ev, V.K.: Integration of Equations of Parabolic Type. Pergamon Press, Oxford (1964)
11. Vabishchevich, P.N.: Difference schemes for nonstationary vector problems. Diff. Equat. **40**(7), 1000–1008 (2004)
12. Vabishchevich, P.N.: Explicit schemes for parabolic and hyperbolic equations. Appl. Math. Comput. **250**, 424–431 (2015)
13. Vabishchevich, P.N., Samarskii, A.A.: Finite difference schemes for convection-diffusion problems on irregular meshes. Zh. Vychisl. Mat. Mat. Fiz. **40**, 692–704 (2000). in Russian
14. Vabishchevich, P.N., Samarskii, A.A.: Solving the dynamic problems of an incompressible fluid with variable viscosity. Zh. Vychisl. Mat. Mat. Fiz. **40**(12), 1813–1822 (2000). in Russian
15. Vabishchevich, P.N.: Additive Operator-Difference Schemes. Splitting Schemes. Walter de Gruyter GmbH, Berlin (2014)
16. Wang, W.Q.: The alternating segment Crank-Nicolson method for solving convection-diffusion equation with variable coefficient. Appl. Math. Mech. **24**, 32–42 (2003)
17. Zhang, B., Li, W.: Age method with variable coefficients for parallel computing. Parallel Algorithms Appl. **5**(3–4), 219–228 (1995)
18. Zhuang, Y.: An alternating explicit-implicit domain decomposition method for the parallel solution of parabolic equations. J. Comput. Appl. Math. **206**(1), 549–566 (2007)

Solving Large Engineering and Scientific Problems with Advanced Mathematical Models

Solving Two-Point Boundary Value Problems for Integro-Differential Equations Using the Simple Shooting-Projection Method

Stefan M. Filipov[1], Ivan D. Gospodinov[1], and Jordanka Angelova[2(✉)]

[1] Department of Programming and Computer System Application, University of Chemical Technology and Metallurgy, blvd. Kl. Ohridski 8, 1756 Sofia, Bulgaria
[2] Department of Mathematics, University of Chemical Technology and Metallurgy, blvd. Kl. Ohridski 8, 1756 Sofia, Bulgaria
jordanka_aa@yahoo.com

Abstract. In this paper the use of the simple shooting-projection method for solving two-point boundary value problems for second-order ordinary integro-differential equations is proposed. Shooting methods are very suitable for solving such equations numerically, as the integral part of the equation can be evaluated while performing the shooting. The simple shooting-projection method consists of the following steps: First, a guess for the initial condition is made and a forward numerical integration is performed so that an initial value problem solution is obtained, called a shooting trajectory. The shooting trajectory satisfies the left boundary constraint but does not satisfy the right boundary constraint. Next, the shooting trajectory is transformed into a projection trajectory that is an approximate boundary value problem solution. Finally, from the projection trajectory a new initial condition is obtained and the procedure is repeated until convergence, i.e. until the boundary value problem solution is obtained within a prescribed precision.

Keywords: Second order integro-differential equation · Simple shooting-projection method · Iterative guess choice

1 Introduction

This paper studies numerical solutions of two-point boundary value problems (TPBVPs) for integro-differential equations (IDEs) of one independent variable. They arise when the solution of an IDE needs to satisfy boundary conditions (constraints) at two points. The widely applied numerical methods for solving TPBVPs are the shooting methods [2,6,7,10,11] and the references therein. The simple (single) shooting method (SSM) [3,4] is very suitable for solving TPBVPs for IDEs since the integral part can be evaluated while performing the shooting. Typically, in the SSM one starts from the left boundary, makes a guess for the value of the first derivative there, denoted by v_a, and performs numerical integration of the IDE to obtain a shooting trajectory. The shooting trajectory

I. Dimov et al. (Eds.): NMA 2014, LNCS 8962, pp. 169–177, 2015.
DOI: 10.1007/978-3-319-15585-2_19

is a numerical initial value problem (IVP) solution. The end of the shooting trajectory differs from the second constraint by some distance, called *error*, and denoted by $E = E(v_a)$. Next, v_a is corrected and a new shooting trajectory is obtained. The process is repeated until the root of $E(v_a) = 0$ is reached. Thus, any SSM for solving TPBVPs for IDE is, in fact, an iterative root finding method.

The various existing SSMs differ in the way the correction for v_a is performed at each iteration. In most SSMs the new v_a is obtained by subtracting the term E/k from the old v_a, where k is the slope of the line, used by the numerical method, that passes through point $(v_a, E(v_a))_{old}$. The different SSMs employ different values of k. There are two types of such methods - ones that readjust k at each iteration, and others that do not. The methods that readjust k utilize two or more shooting trajectories per iteration. Typical such methods are the simple shooting by Newton's method [5,9] and the simple shooting by secant method [5]. The value of k in the Newton's shooting method is the value of the derivative dE/dv_a evaluated at the current value of v_a. The methods that do not readjust k utilize only one shooting trajectory per iteration. One such method is the constant-slope Newton's method [8], for which the value of k is the value of the derivative dE/dv_a evaluated at the starting (arbitrary) guess value of v_a. Another such method is the simple shooting-projection method [1], for which the value of k is obtained from the boundary constraints only, and thus the method is independent of the starting value of v_a. At each iteration, this method uses the current value of v_a to obtain a shooting trajectory and then finds a projection trajectory that is an approximate TPBVP solution. A new v_a is extracted from this projection trajectory and is used in the next iteration. The simple shooting-projection method was introduced in [1] and was applied for solving TPBVPs for ordinary differential equations. The method was shown to be quite useful since there are cases when it converges whereas most of the prominent shooting methods do not.

This paper demonstrates the applicability of the simple shooting-projection method for solving TPBVPs for ordinary IDEs.

2 Simple Shooting-Projection Method for TPBVPs of Ordinary IDEs

In this section we consider a TPBVP for the second-order ordinary IDE

$$u''(t) = f\big(t, u(t), u'(t), G(t)\big)\,, \quad t \in (a, b) \tag{1a}$$

$$u(a) = u_a \tag{1b}$$

$$u(b) = u_b\,, \tag{1c}$$

where: u is a real valued function of a real independent variable $t \in [a, b]$ (smooth enough); f is a real-valued function of t, u, u' and G in some domain of $\mathbb{R}^4$; $G(t) = \int_a^t g(t, s, u(s), u'(s))\, ds$, where g is integrable in the same domain as f; u_a, $u_b \in \mathbb{R}$ are the values of u at the two boundaries.

The TPBVP may have more than one solution.

The SSMs solve TPBVP (1) by transforming it into the IVP problem (1a), (1b), and an initial condition:

$$u'(a) = v_a \,. \tag{2}$$

Then, the following iterative procedure is used: make a guess for the starting v_a, solve the IVP problem numerically, correct v_a, and repeat until convergence. To solve this IVP numerically, we introduce $v = u'$ and numerically integrate (1a) as a system of two first-order differential equations (in u and v) using the Euler's method and the right-rectangle rule for finding the integral G. Thus, the IVP (1a), (1b), (2) is discretized into the following system of nonlinear algebraic equations:

$$u_i = u_{i-1} + hv_{i-1} \tag{3a}$$

$$v_i = v_{i-1} + hf(t_i, u_i, v_{i-1}, G_i)\,, \qquad i = 2, \ldots, N \tag{3b}$$

$$G_i = h\sum_{j=2}^{i} g(t_i, s_j, u_j, v_{j-1})\,, \tag{3c}$$

where: N is the number of mesh points; $h = (b-a)/(N-1)$ is the step size; $t_i = a + h(i-1)$, $s_j = a + h(j-1)$ are mesh points; $u_i \approx u(t_i)$ and $v_i \approx v(t_i)$; $u_1 = u_a$ and $v_1 = v_a$.

In the case when g does not depend on t Eq. (3c) is replaced by:

$$G_i = G_{i-1} + hg(t_i, u_i, v_{i-1}) \tag{4}$$

The numerical IVP solution, considered as a set of points $\{(t_i, u_i)\}$, $i = 1, 2, \ldots, N$, obtained by Eq. (3), is called a shooting trajectory.

The simple shooting-projection method transforms this shooting trajectory into a projection trajectory $\{(t_i, u_i^*)\}$, $i = 1, 2, \ldots, N$, where:

$$u_i^* = u_i - \big((u_N - u_b)(i-1)\big)/(N-1)\,, \quad i = 1, 2, \ldots, N\,. \tag{5}$$

The projection trajectory, as can be checked, is a solution to

$$u_{i+1}^* - 2u_i^* + u_{i-1}^* = u_{i+1} - 2u_i + u_{i-1}\,, \quad i = 2, 3, \ldots, N-1\,, \text{ and } u_1^* = u_a\,,\ u_N^* = u_b\,.$$

Therefore, it has the same numerical second derivative as the shooting trajectory at all interior points, and satisfies both boundary conditions. This, as shown in [1], insures that the projection trajectory is an approximate solution to the TPBVP (1). Writing Eq. (5) for u_1^* and u_2^*, subtracting u_1^* from u_2^*, and dividing by h, the following expression for finding the new initial condition v_a^* from the old initial condition v_a is found

$$v_a^* = v_a - E(v_a)/k\,, \tag{6}$$

where: $v_a^* = (u_2^* - u_1^*)/h$; $v_a = (u_2 - u_1)/h$; $E(v_a) = u_N(v_a) - u_b$ is the error; $k = b - a$, as explained above, is the value of the slope, used in the simple shooting-projection method.

This is the iterative formula for correcting the initial condition v_a at each iteration of the simple shooting-projection algorithm. The algorithm consists of the following steps:

Step 1: Make a guess for the initial condition v_a.
Step 2: Obtain the shooting trajectory using this v_a.
Step 3: Obtain the projection trajectory.
Step 4: Correct v_a to obtain v_a^* using Eq. (6).
Step 5: Replace v_a in Step 1 with v_a^*.

Note, that Eq. (6) does not contain any projection trajectory points. Therefore, while carrying out the numerical procedure the actual construction of the projection trajectory is not necessary, i.e. Step 3 is virtual. Thus, the simple shooting-projection algorithm repeats steps 1, 2, 4, and 5 until the shooting trajectory satisfies the second boundary constraint within a prescribed tolerance, i.e. $u_N \approx u_b$.

The proposed simple shooting-projection method has the following important features: it uses only one shooting trajectory per iteration; the slope k in the iterative correction formula (6) is constant and its value $b - a$ does not depend on the starting guess v_a; the projection step is a relaxation step.

The first feature leads to computational savings. As will be shown in the Numerical Examples section, the second feature may lead to convergence advantages over methods that adjust the slope at each iteration, such as the secant and the Newton's shooting methods. Also, this feature may lead to convergence advantages over methods that do not adjust the slope at each iteration, such as the constant-slope Newton's shooting method.

Let m be the slope of $E(v_a)$ at its root. As shown in [1], in small enough neighborhood of the root the simple shooting-projection method converges when

$$|1 - m/k| < 1\,. \tag{7}$$

Otherwise the method diverges. The method converges linearly except for the trivial case $m = k$ where the convergence is quadratic.

3 Numerical Examples

The applicability of the simple shooting-projection method for solving TPBVPs for IDEs is demonstrated with four examples.

Example 1. Consider the following TPBVP

$$\begin{aligned} u''(t) &= 3u'(G(t) + 1/3)/u^2\,, && t \in (1,2) \\ G(t) &= \int_1^t u(s)\,ds\,, && u(1) = 1\,, \quad u(2) = 4\,. \end{aligned} \tag{8}$$

This problem has an analytical solution $u(t) = t^2$. Figure 1 shows the evolution of the shooting and the corresponding projection trajectories while solving

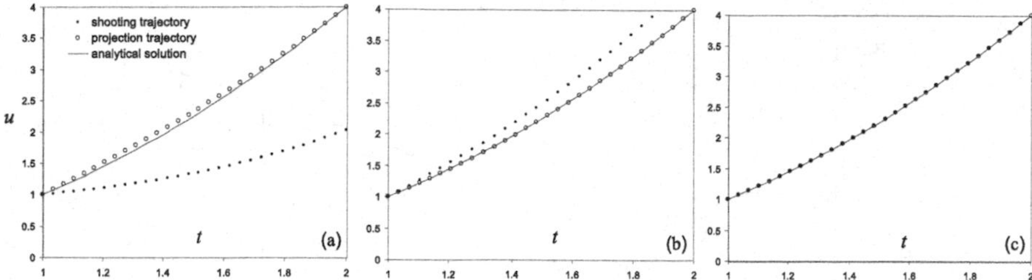

Fig. 1. The solution, the shooting and the projection trajectories obtained for solving TPBVP (8) using the simple shooting-projection method for $v_a = 0.5$ and $N = 30$ at: (a) iteration 1; (b) iteration 2; (c) iteration 4.

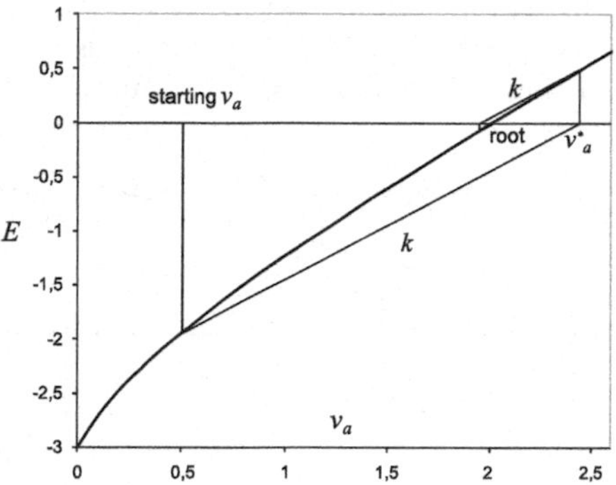

Fig. 2. Converging sequence for solving TPBVP (8) using the simple shooting-projection method for $v_a = 0.5$, $N = 30$. The root of $E = 0$ is $v_a = 2$

problem (8) using the simple shooting-projection method for starting $v_a = 0.5$ and $N = 30$. Equations (3a), (3b) and (4) are used for obtaining each shooting trajectory. The simple shooting-projection method converges in 5 iterations within $|E| < 0.001$. The figure shows that the projection trajectory is a good approximation to the TPBVP solution, shown by solid line.

Figure 2 plots the graph of $E(v_a)$ and the sequence of parallel lines with slope $k = 1$ that lead to the root of E (only two such parallel lines are clearly visible in the figure). The error $E(v_a)$ is found numerically by performing shootings for multiple values of v_a that span the interval $[0, 2.6]$. As can be seen in Fig. 2 the value of the slope k is close to the value of the slope of E at the root.

Example 2. Consider the following TPBVP

$$\begin{aligned} u''(t) &= -u^2 u' G(t)/t^2 \,, \qquad && t \in (1,2) \\ G(t) &= \int_1^t u(s) s e^{-ts}\, ds \,, \quad u(1) = 1 \,, && u(2) = 2 \,. \end{aligned} \tag{9}$$

The problem (9) is solved using the simple shooting-projection method starting from $v_a = 5$. Equation (3) are used for obtaining each shooting trajectory. Figure 3 shows the convergence sequence for finding the root of $E(v_a) = 0$.

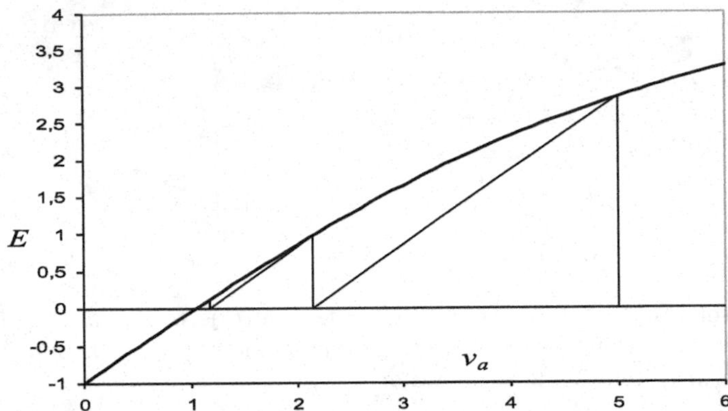

Fig. 3. Converging sequence for solving TPBVP (9) using the simple shooting-projection method for starting $v_a = 5$ and $N = 100$. The root of $E = 0$ is $v_a = 1.0414$

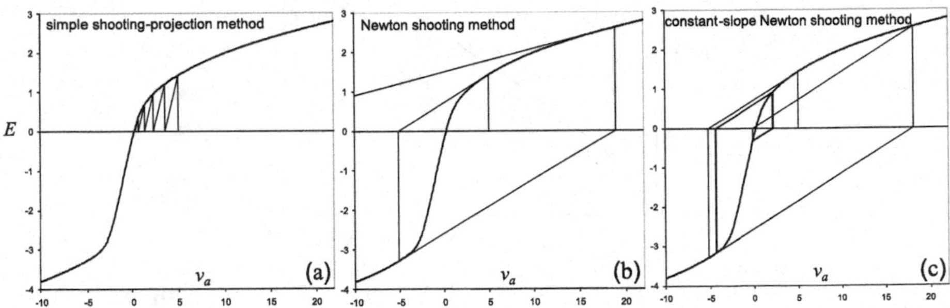

Fig. 4. Solving TPBVP (10) for starting $v_a = 5$ and $N = 100$ using: (a) the simple shooting-projection method converges, (b) the Newton's shooting method diverges, and (c) the constant-slope Newton's method fails to converge. The root of E is $v_a = 0.2258$

The root of E is $v_a = 1.0414$. The method converges in 4 iterations within $|E| < 0.001$.

Example 3. Consider the following TPBVP

$$\begin{aligned} u''(t) &= -3u^2 u' G(t)/t\,, \qquad\qquad t \in (1,2) \\ G(t) &= \int_1^t u^2(s)\,ds\,, \qquad u(1) = 0.7\,, \quad u(2) = 0.9\,. \end{aligned} \tag{10}$$

Three methods are tried for solving TPBVP (10) - the simple shooting-projection method, the Newton's shooting method, and the constant-slope Newton's shooting method. Equation (4) is used for calculating G. Figure 4 compares the convergence of the three methods starting from $v_a = 5$. Figure 4a shows that the simple shooting-projection method converges to the root in 8 iterations within $|E| < 0.001$. Figure 4b shows that the Newton's shooting method diverges.

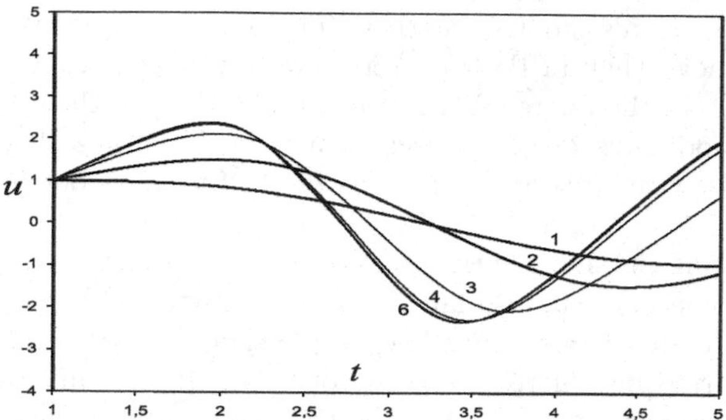

Fig. 5. Evolution of the shooting trajectory while solving TPBVP (11) using the simple shooting-projection method for starting $v_a = 0$ and $N = 1000$

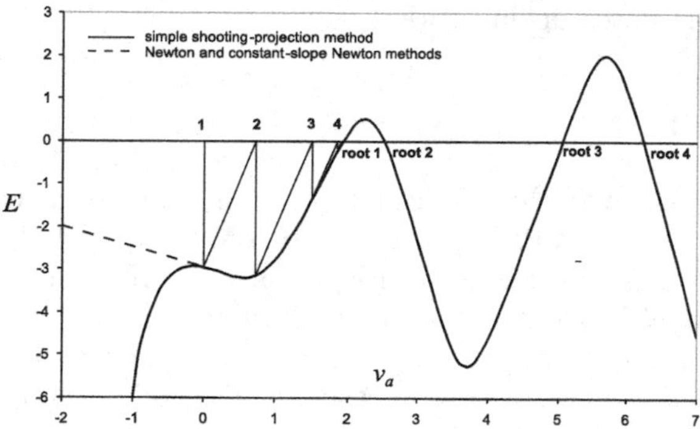

Fig. 6. Solving TPBVP (11) for starting $v_a = 0$ and $N = 1000$. The simple shooting-projection method (solid lines) converges to *root*1 with value $v_a = 1.9287$. Both the Newton's shooting method (dashed line) and the constant-slope Newton's method (the same dashed line) fail to converge to any root

Figure 4c shows that the constant-slope Newton's shooting method oscillates around the root and fails to converge.

Example 4. Consider the following TPBVP

$$\begin{aligned} u''(t) &= -\sinh(uG(t)), \qquad t \in (1,5) \\ G(t) &= \int_1^t (u(s)/s)\, ds, \quad u(1) = 1, \quad u(5) = 2. \end{aligned} \tag{11}$$

Figure 5 shows the evolution of the shooting trajectory while solving TPBVP (11) using the simple shooting-projection method starting from $v_a = 0$. Equation (4) is used for calculating G. The method converges in 6 iterations within $|E| < 0.005$ to the root $v_a = 1.9287$. In the figure, the consecutive shooting trajectories are numbered 1 through 6.

Figure 6 shows the convergence results of solving TPBVP (11) using the simple shooting-projection method, the Newton's shooting method, and the constant-slope Newton's shooting method. The function $E(v_a)$ is found numerically. Figure 6 shows that TPBVP (11) has multiple solutions, corresponding to *root*1, *root*2, etc. in the figure. When started from $v_a = 0$ the simple shooting-projection method finds *root*1, whereas both the Newton's shooting and the constant-slope Newton's shooting methods fail to find any root (see the dashed line in Fig. 6).

After inspecting the shape of the function $E(v_a)$ in Fig. 6 one can see that the secant shooting method will also fail to converge if started from the two initial conditions $v_a = 0$ and $v_a = 0.7358$. The simple shooting-projection method will find *root*1 if started anywhere to the left of *root*2. It will find *root*3 if started anywhere between *root*2 and *root*4. Since the slope, used in the constant-slope Newton's method, depends on the starting v_a the method may or may not find a root depending on the starting value of v_a. Figures 2, 3, 4, and 6 show that the value of $k = b - a$ is close to the value of the slope of E at the root for all four examples, presented in this work.

4 Conclusion

This work demonstrated the applicability of the simple shooting-projection method for solving TPBVPs for IDEs. The results showed that the method is suitable for finding solutions of such equations. There are cases in which the proposed method fails to find a solution, while one or more of the other shooting methods succeed. However, as the third and the fourth examples in the Numerical Examples section show, at certain cases the method outperforms prominent shooting methods, such as the Newton's, the secant, and the constant-slope Newton's methods.

References

1. Filipov, S.M., Gospodinov, I.D.: Simple shooting-projection method for numerical solution of two-point boundary value problems. arXiv:1406.2615 [math.NA]
2. Holsapple, R., Venkataraman, R., Doman, D.: A new, fast numerical method for solving two-point boundary value problems. J. Guidance Control Dyn. **27**, 301–303 (2004)
3. Keller, H.B.: Numerical Methods for Two-Point Boundary-Value Problems. Blaisdell Publishing Co., Waltham (1968)
4. Keller, H.B.: Numerical Methods for Two-Point Boundary-Value Problems. SIAM, Pennsylvania (1976)
5. Press, W.H., Flannery, B.P., Teukolsky, S.A., Vetterling, W.T.: Numerical Recipes in FORTRAN 77: The Art of Scientific Computing, 2nd edn. Cambridge University Press, New York (1992)
6. Ramachandra, L.S., Roy, D.: A new method for nonlinear two-point boundary value problems in solid mechanics. J. Appl. Mech. **68**(5), 778–786 (2001)
7. Roberts, S.M., Shipman, J.S.: Two-Point Boundary Value Problems: Shooting Methods. Elsevier, New York (1972)
8. Steward, G.W.: Afternotes on Numerical Anlysis. SIAM, Philadelphia (1996)

9. Stoer, J., Bulirsch, R.: Introduction to Numerical Analysis, 3rd edn. Springer, New York (2002)
10. Strain, J.: Fast stable deferred correction method for two-point boundary value problems. http://math.berkeley.edu/~strain/228a.F04/bvpdc.pdf
11. Bibliography for Shooting Methods for ODE's. http://mathfaculty.fullerton.edu/mathews/n2003/shootingmethod/ShootingBib/Links/ShootingBib_lnk_3.html

HPC Simulations of the Fine Particulate Matter Climate of Bulgaria

Georgi Gadzhev[1(✉)], Kostadin Ganev[1], Nikolay Miloshev[1], Dimiter Syrakov[2], and Maria Prodanova[2]

[1] National Institute of Geophysics, Geodesy and Geography, Bulgarian Academy of Sciences, Acad. G. Bonchev Str., Bl.3, 1113 Sofia, Bulgaria
{ggadjev,kganev,miloshev}@geophys.bas.bg

[2] National Institute of Meteorology and Hydrology, Bulgarian Academy of Sciences, Sofia, Bulgaria
{dimiter.syrakov,maria.prodanova}@meteo.bg

Abstract. Some extensive numerical simulations of the atmospheric composition fields in Bulgaria have been recently performed. The US EPA Model-3 system was chosen as a modelling tool. The TNO emission inventory was used as emission input. Special pre-processing procedures are created for introducing temporal profiles and speciation of the emissions. The biogenic emissions of VOC are estimated by the model SMOKE. The numerical experiments have been carried out for different emission scenarios, which makes it possible the contribution of emissions from different source categories to be evaluated. The simulations aimed at constructing of ensemble, comprehensive enough as to provide statistically reliable assessment of the atmospheric composition climate of Bulgaria - typical and extreme features of the special/temporal behavior, annual means and seasonal variations, etc. The present one focuses on the results about fine particulate matter. This is a compound with significant impact on human health, so the interest towards it is recently very big.

Keywords: $PM_{2.5}$ · Atmospheric composition climate · Air pollution modeling · US EPA models-3 system · Multi-scale modeling · Emission scenarios · Process analyzes

1 Introduction

Recently extensive studies for long enough simulation periods and good resolution of the atmospheric composition status in Bulgaria have been carried out using up-to-date modeling tools and detailed and reliable input data [7–12].

The simulations aimed at constructing of ensemble, comprehensive enough as to provide statistically reliable assessment of the atmospheric composition climate of Bulgaria - typical and extreme features of the special/temporal behavior, annual means and seasonal variations, etc.

I. Dimov et al. (Eds.): NMA 2014, LNCS 8962, pp. 178–186, 2015.
DOI: 10.1007/978-3-319-15585-2_20

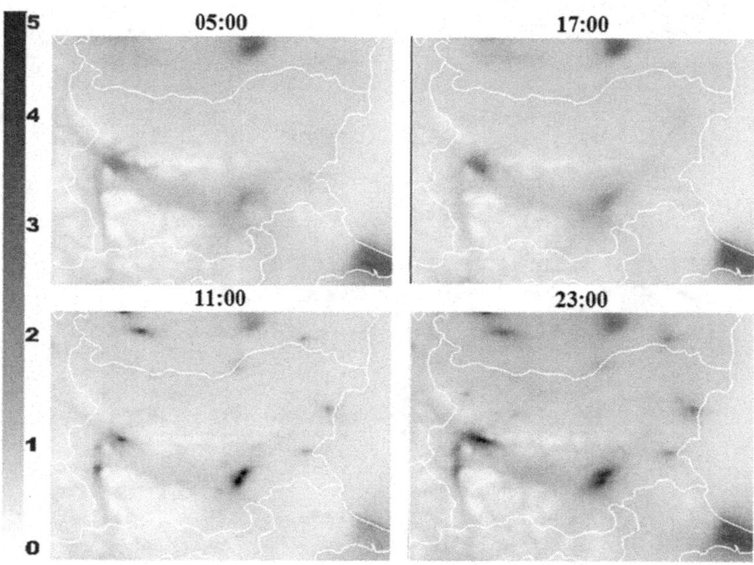

Fig. 1. Maps of mean annual $PM_{2.5}$ concentrations [$\mu g/m^3$] in 05:00, 11:00, 17:00 and 23:00 GMT.

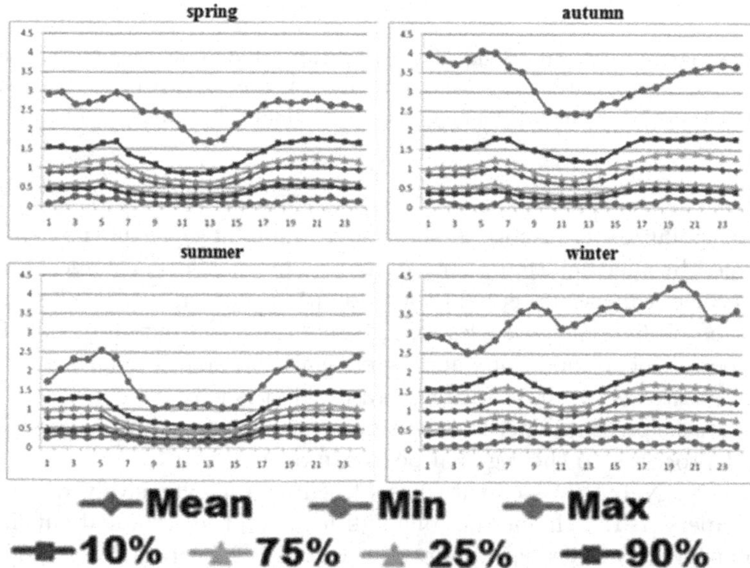

Fig. 2. Seasonal/diurnal variations of $PM_{2.5}$ surface concentrations [$\mu g/m^3$], averaged for the territory of Bulgaria: curves of mean, maximal and minimal values as well as curves show the imaginary concentrations for which the probability of the simulated ones to be smaller is respectively 0.25, 0.75, 0.1 and 0.9.

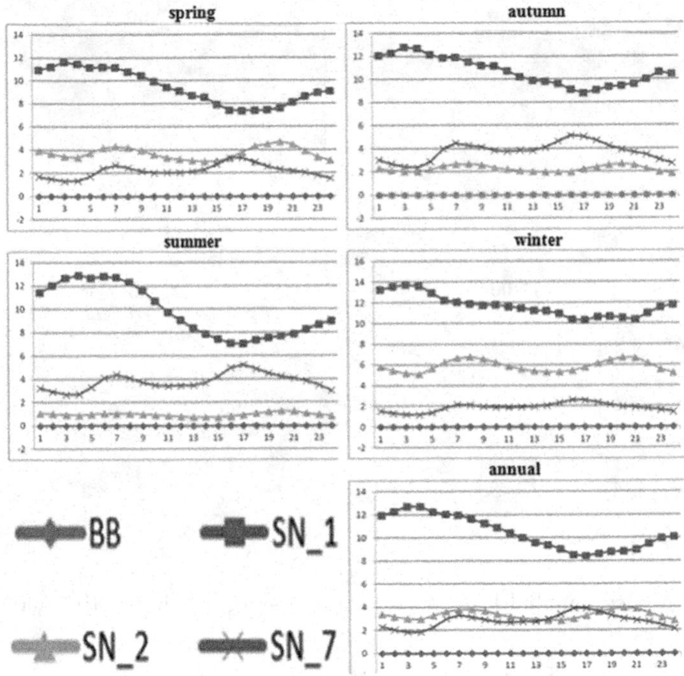

Fig. 3. Seasonal/diurnal variations of contribution of different emission categories to $PM_{2.5}$ surface concentrations [%], averaged for the territory of Bulgaria: BB-biogenic emissions, SN_1-power plants, SN_2-none industrial combustion and SN_7-road transport.

The air pollution transport is subject to different scale phenomena, each characterized by specific atmospheric dynamics mechanisms, chemical transformations, typical time scales etc. The air pollution pattern is formed as a result of interaction of different processes, so knowing the contribution of each for different meteorological conditions and given emission spatial configuration and temporal behavior is by all means important. That is why the one of the important issues in the present paper is to present some evaluations of the contribution of different processes to the regional pollution over Bulgaria.

As the O_3, NOx, SO_2, climate has already been extensively discussed in previous papers [7–12], the present one will focus on the results about fine particulate matter - particles with diameters less then 2.5 μm ($PM_{2.5}$). This is a compound with significant impact on human health, so the interest towards it is recently very big.

2 Methodology

All the simulations are based on the US EPA Model-3 system. The system consists of three components:

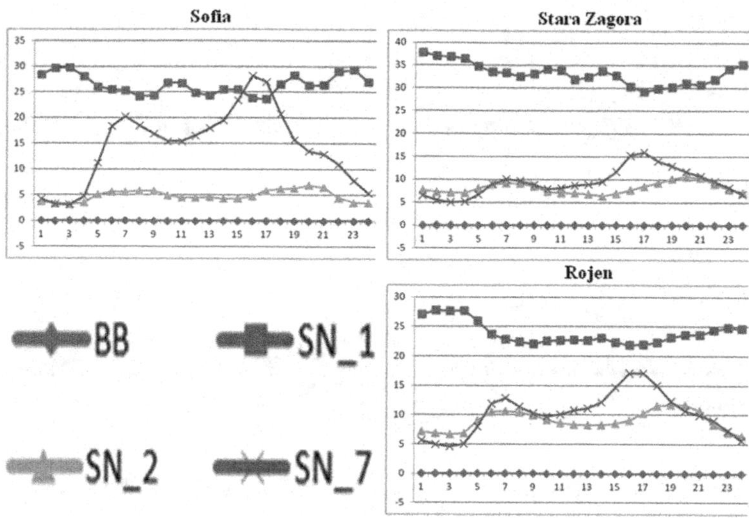

Fig. 4. Annual contribution of different emission categories to $PM_{2.5}$ surface concentrations [%] in different points in Bulgaria: BB-biogenic emissions, SN_1-power plants, SN_2-none industrial combustion and SN_7-road transport.

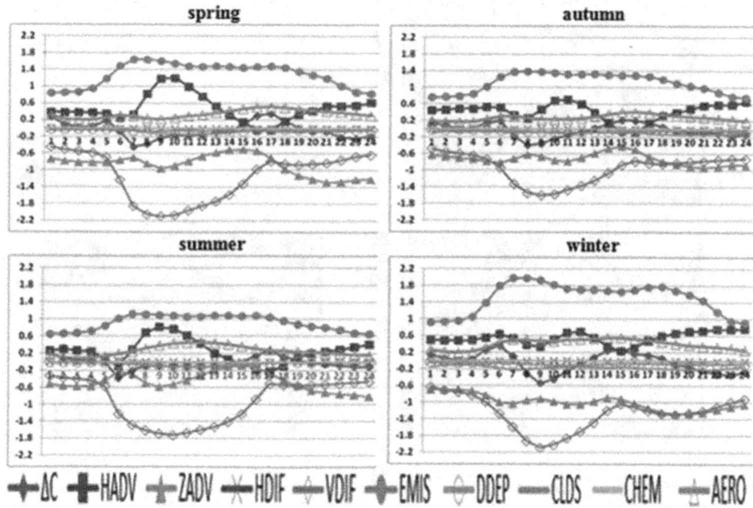

Fig. 5. Seasonal/diurnal variations of contribution of different processes to $PM_{2.5}$ surface concentrations change $\boldsymbol{\Delta}$C [$(\mu g/m^3)/h$], averaged for the territory of Bulgaria.

- MM5 - the 5th generation PSU/NCAR Meso-meteorological Model MM5 [5, 14] used as meteorological pre-processor;
- CMAQ - the Community Multiscale Air Quality System [2,3], being the Chemical Transport Model (CTM) of the system, and

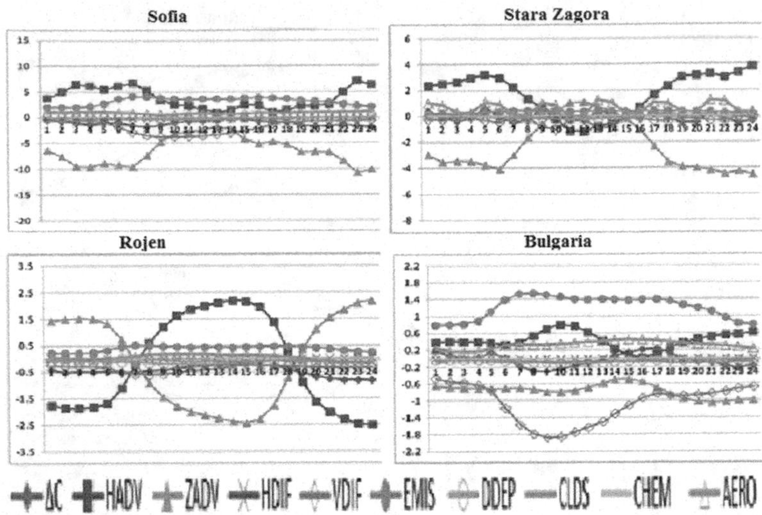

Fig. 6. Annually averaged diurnal variations of contribution of different processes to $PM_{2.5}$ surface concentrations change ΔC [(μg/m^3)/h] in different points in Bulgaria.

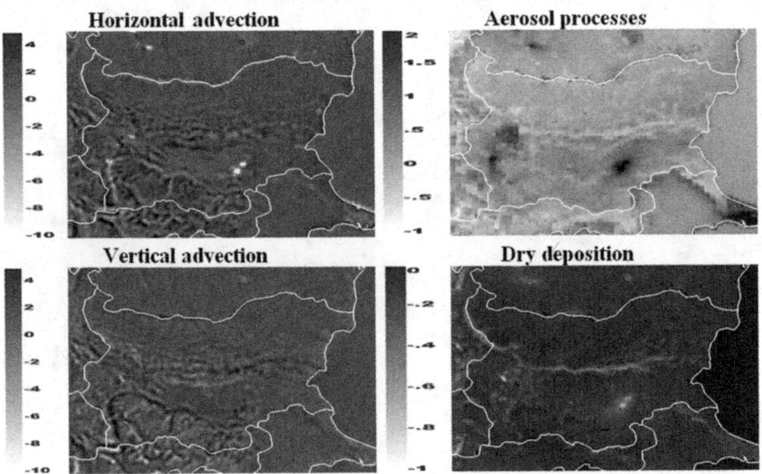

Fig. 7. Mean annual contribution of horizontal and vertical advection, aerosol processes and dry depposition to $PM_{2.5}$ surface concentrations change ΔC [(μg/m^3)/h] in 11:00 GMT.

– SMOKE - the Sparse Matrix Operator Kernel Emissions Modelling System [4] - the emission pre-processor of Models-3 system.

The Models-3 Integrated Process Rate Analysis option was applied to discriminate the role of different dynamic and chemical processes for the air pollution pattern formation. The procedure allows the concentration change for each compound for an hour to be presented as a sum of the contribution of the processes, which determine the concentration. The processes that were considered are: advection, diffusion, mass adjustment, emissions, dry deposition, chemistry, aerosol processes and cloud processes/aqueous chemistry.

The large scale (background) meteorological data used by the study is the NCEP Global Analysis Data with $1^\circ \times 1^\circ$ resolution. By using the nesting abilities of MM5/CMAQ the simulations are downscaled to horizontal resolution of 3 Km for Bulgaria. The TNO high resolution emission inventory [15] is exploited. A detailed description of the emission modeling is given in [9].

Four emission scenarios will be considered in the present paper: Simulations with all the emissions, simulations with biogenic emissions and the emissions of SNAP categories 1 (power plants), 2 (none industrial combustion) and 7 (road transport) for Bulgaria reduced by a factor of 0.8.

As it can be seen from [9] the computer resource requirements are quite big. On the other hand the very nature of the numerical experiments planned make it possible to organise the computations in grid effective manner. The MM5 simulations were carried out in 3-day packages for all the 4 domains, using the two-way nesting mode of the model. This will make total run time of less than 20 h, which means that the successful execution of the jobs on the Grid [1,6] is quite probable.

3 Results, Comments, and Discussion

3.1 $PM_{2.5}$ Concentrations

The most simple atmospheric composition evaluations are, of course, the surface concentrations. By averaging over the 8-year simulated fields ensemble the mean annual and seasonal surface concentrations can be obtained and treated as respective typical daily concentration patterns. Plots of some of these typical annual surface $PM_{2.5}$ concentrations are shown in (Fig. 1) From the plots it can be seen that the typical concentrations for the country are about 0,5 $\mu g/m^3$, and the lowest values are above the mountains during the whole day. The big cities, the big power plants and to some extend the road network are clearly outlined as spots with higher $PM_{2.5}$ surface concentrations. The spatial/diurnal variations in $PM_{2.5}$ fields are well manifested.

The seasonal and diurnal variations of the averaged for the country surface $PM_{2.5}$ concentrations are shown in (Fig. 2), together with the maximal and minimal values and the curves denoted by 0.25, 0.75, 0.1 and 0.9. These curves show the imaginary concentrations for which the probability of the simulated ones to be smaller is respectively 0.25, 0.75, 0.1 and 0.9. Thus the band 0.25-0.75 contains 50 % and the band 0.1-0.9 - 80 % of the possible cases. The plots are self explanatory enough and demonstrate the seasonal and diurnal country mean $PM_{2.5}$ variations. It could be noted that the 80 % band (most of the cases) is way below the maximal possible $PM_{2.5}$ concentrations.

3.2 Contribution of Different Emission Categories to $PM_{2.5}$ Concentrations

The seasonal and diurnal variations of the contribution of different emission categories to the surface $PM_{2.5}$ concentrations, averaged for Bulgaria are given in (Fig. 3). It can be seen that both the seasonal and diurnal variations of the contributions are very well manifested. The emissions from power plants have the major role in surface $PM_{2.5}$ concentrations and the contribution of biogenic emissions is negligible. Annually the contributions of none industrial combustion and road transport are almost equal, while during spring and winter the none industrial combustion (which includes domestic heating) plays greater role than road transport. The contributions of different emission categories have also significant spatial variability (Fig. 4).

3.3 Contribution of Different Processes to $PM_{2.5}$ Hourly Concentration Change

An example of the annually mean special distribution of the processes contribution to the surface $PM_{2.5}$ hourly change ΔC, averaged for Bulgaria is given in Fig. 5.

Very briefly the main characteristics, which can be seen from the plots, are the following: (1) There are well manifested seasonal differences and diurnal variations; (2) The $PM_{2.5}$ concentration change is formed as a rather small sum of processes with larger values and different signs; (3) Averaged for the territory of Bulgaria the impacts of horizontal diffusion and cloud processes/aqueous chemistry are negligible; (4) For all the seasons the vertical diffusion has a large negative impact, especially during the day (more intensive turbulence) - $PM_{2.5}$ transport from ground level to higher atmosphere; (5) The dry deposition has negative impact, but it is almost negligible; (6) For all the seasons the horizontal advection has mostly positive impact - $PM_{2.5}$ inflow trough the country boundary; (7) Horizontal and vertical advection are mostly in counter-phase, tending to compensate each other; (8) The impact of chemical processes is very small, but the impact of aerosol processes is rather significant; (9) The $PM_{2.5}$ emissions play the major role in $PM_{2.5}$ changes.

The contributions of different processes have also significant spatial variability (Fig. 6). It can be seen that their behaviour for Sofia (big city), Stara Zagora (medium size city near Maritza TPPs) and Rojen (mountain site) is qualitatively different and also differs pretty much from the averaged for the country.

A very good idea of how complex and heterogeneous the process contribution fields really are gives (Fig. 7). The slope wind effects can be followed in the horizontal/vertical advection maps, as well as the counter phase behaviour of both advections. The dry deposition contribution is, of course, negative. The absolute values are big, where the $PM_{2.5}$ surface concentrations are big, which is quite natural. It could be significantly big over the mountain ridges, however, where the $PM_{2.5}$ surface concentrations are relatively small. This is an evidence of the complexity of the dry deposition process.

4 Conclusions

The numerical experiments performed produced a huge volume of information, which have to be carefully analyzed and generalized so that some final conclusions could be made. Simulations for emission scenarios concerning the contribution of the other emission categories have to be performed.

The demonstrations, presented in the present paper are concern the $PM_{2.5}$ pollution climate. The major findings so far will be listed below:

- the behavior of the surface $PM_{2.5}$ concentrations, averaged over the ensemble annually, or for the four seasons and over the territory of the country is reasonable and demonstrates effects which can be explained from a point of view of the generally accepted schemes of dynamic influences (in particular the role of turbulent transport and its dependence on atmospheric stability) and/or chemical transformations;
- the emissions from power plants have the biggest contribution to the surface $PM_{2.5}$. Annually the mean for Bulgaria contributions of none industrial combustion and road transport are almost equal, while during spring and winter the none industrial combustion (which includes domestic heating) plays greater role than road transport.
- the results produced by the CMAQ Integrated Process Rate Analysis demonstrate the very complex behavior and interaction of the different processes. The analysis of the behavior of different processes does not give simple answer of the question how the air pollution in a given point or region was formed.
- it seams reasonable the evaluations to be transfered into terms directly measuring the $PM_{2.5}$ influence on human health by introducing Air Quality Indexes [13].

Acknowledgments. The present work is supported by the Bulgarian National Science Fund (grant DCVP-02/1/29.12.2009) and the EC-FP7 grant 261323 (project EGI-InSPIRE).

Deep gratitude is due to US EPA and US NCEP for providing free-of-charge data and software. Special thanks to the Netherlands Organization for Applied Scientific research (TNO) for providing us with the high-resolution European anthropogenic emission inventory.

References

1. Atanassov, E., Gurov, T., Karaivanova, A.: Computational Grid: structure and applications. J. Avtomatica i informatica (in Bulgarian), 3/2006, year XL, 40–43, September 2006
2. Byun, D., Young, J., Gipson, G., Godowitch, J., Binkowski, F.S., Roselle, S., Benjey, B., Pleim, J., Ching, J., Novak, J., Coats, C., Odman, T., Hanna, A., Alapaty, K., Mathur, R., McHenry, J., Shankar, U., Fine, S., Xiu, A., Jang, C.: Description of the Models-3 Community Multiscale Air Quality (CMAQ) Modeling System. In: 10th Joint Conference on the Applications of Air Pollution Meteorology with the A&WMA, Phoenix, Arizona, pp. 264–268 (1998)

3. Byun, D., Ching, J.: Science Algorithms of the EPA Models-3 Community Multiscale Air Quality (CMAQ) Modeling System. EPA Report 600/R-99/030, Washington DC (1999). http://www.epa.gov/asmdnerl/models3/doc/science/science.html
4. CEP: Sparse Matrix Operator Kernel Emission (SMOKE) Modeling System, University of Carolina, Carolina Environmental Programs, Research Triangle Park, North Carolina (2003)
5. Dudhia, J.: A non-hydrostatic version of the Penn State/NCAR Mesoscale Model: validation tests and simulation of an Atlantic cyclone and cold front. Mon. Wea. Rev. **121**, 1493–1513 (1993)
6. Foster, J., Kesselmann, C.: The Grid: Blueprint for a New Computing Infrastructure. Morgan Kaufmann, San Francisco (1998)
7. Gadzhev, G., Syrakov, D., Ganev, K., Brandiyska, A., Miloshev, N., Georgiev, G., Prodanova, M.: Atmospheric Composition of the Balkan Region and Bulgaria. Study of the Contribution of Biogenic Emissions. AIP Conf. Proc. **1404**(200), 200–209 (2011)
8. Gadzhev, G., Ganev, K., Syrakov, D., Miloshev, N., Prodanova, M.: Contribution of Biogenic Emissions to the Atmospheric Composition of the Balkan Region and Bulgaria. IJEP **50**(1–4), 130–139 (2012)
9. Gadzhev, G., Ganev, K., Miloshev, N., Syrakov, D., Prodanova, M.: Numerical Study of the Atmospheric Composition in Bulgaria. CAMWA **65**, 402–422 (2013a)
10. Gadzhev, G., Ganev, K., Miloshev, N., Syrakov, D., Prodanova, M.: Some basic facts about the atmospheric composition in Bulgaria – grid computing simulations. In: Lirkov, I., Margenov, S., Waśniewski, J. (eds.) LSSC 2013. LNCS, vol. 8353, pp. 484–490. Springer, Heidelberg (2014)
11. Gadzhev, G., Ganev, K., Miloshev, N., Syrakov, D., Prodanova, M.: Analysis of the processes which form the air pollution pattern over bulgaria. In: Lirkov, I., Margenov, S., Waśniewski, J. (eds.) LSSC 2013. LNCS, vol. 8353, pp. 390–396. Springer, Heidelberg (2014)
12. Gadzhev, G., Ganev, K., Syrakov, D., Prodanova, M., Miloshev, N.: Some statistical evaluations of numerically obtained atmospheric composition fields in Bulgaria. In: The Proceedings of 15th International Conference on Harmonisation within Atmospheric. Dispersion Modelling for Regulatory Purposes, Madrid, Spain (2013d) (accepted for publishing)
13. Georgieva, I.: Air Quality Index Evaluations for Bulgaria. In: The Proceedings of NMSCAA, Bansko, Bulgaria (2014)
14. Grell, G.A., Dudhia, J., Stauffer, D.R.: A description of the Fifth Generation Penn State/NCAR Mesoscale Model (MM5). NCAR Technical Note, NCAR TN-398-STR, 138 pp. (1994)
15. Visschedijk, A.J.H., Zandveld, P.Y.J., Denier van der Gon, H.A.C.: A High Resolution Gridded European Emission Database for the EU Integrate Project GEMS, TNO-report 2007-A-R0233/B. Apeldoorn, The Netherlands (2007)

Tall RC Buildings Environmentally Degradated and Strengthened by Cables Under Multiple Earthquakes: A Numerical Approach

Angelos Liolios[1], Anaxagoras Elenas[1], Asterios Liolios[1], Stefan Radev[2], Krassimir Georgiev[3], and Ivan Georgiev[3,4](✉)

[1] Department of Civil Engineering Division of Structural Engineering, Democritus University of Thrace, 67100 Xanthi, Greece
aliolios@civil.duth.gr

[2] Institute of Mechanics, Bulgarian Academy of Sciences, Acad. G. Bonchev Str. 8, 1113 Sofia, Bulgaria
stradev@imbm.bas.bg

[3] Institute of Information and Communication Technologies, Bulgarian Academy of Sciences, Acad. G. Bonchev Str. Bl. 25A, 1113 Sofia, Bulgaria
georgiev@parallel.bas.bg

[4] Institute of Mathematics and Informatics, Bulgarian Academy of Sciences, Acad. G. Bonchev Str. Bl. 8, 1113 Sofia, Bulgaria
ivan.georgiev@math.bas.bg

Abstract. A numerical investigation is presented for the seismic analysis of tall reinforced concrete (RC) Civil Engineering structures, which have been degradated due to extreme environmental actions and are strengthened by cable elements. The effects of multiple earthquakes on such RC building frames are computed. Damage indices are estimated in order to compare the seismic response of the structures before and after the retrofit by cable element strengthening, and so to elect the optimum strengthening version.

1 Introduction

Significant strength degradation and damages, caused to Civil Engineering structures by non-usual extreme actions (seismic, environmental etc.), require the use of repairing and strengthening techniques, see e.g. [2,10,21,22]. Among the available such techniques [5,10] the one using cable-like members can be sometimes used as a first strengthening and repairing procedure for RC building frames against earthquake actions [15,24]. These cable-members can undertake tension, but buckle and become slack and structurally ineffective when subjected to a sufficiently large compressive force. Thus the governing conditions take an equality as well as an inequality form and the problem becomes high nonlinear [12].

Regarding the strict mathematical treatment of the problem, the concept of variational and/or hemivariational inequalities can be used and has been successfully applied [18,23]. As concerns the numerical treatment, non-convex optimization algorithms are generally required [12,16].

I. Dimov et al. (Eds.): NMA 2014, LNCS 8962, pp. 187–195, 2015.
DOI: 10.1007/978-3-319-15585-2_21

On the other hand, current seismic codes [7–9] suggest the exclusive adoption of the isolated and rare "design earthquake", while the influence of repeated earthquake phenomena is ignored. This is a significant drawback for the realistic design of building structures. Despite the fact that the problem has been qualitatively acknowledged, few studies have been reported in the literature, especially the last years, regarding the multiple earthquake phenomena, see e.g. [11].

This study presents a numerical approach for the seismic analysis of tall reinforced concrete (RC) building frames, which have been strengthened by cable elements. Emphasis is given to effects of multiple earthquakes. The procedure uses the Ruaumoko structural engineering software [3] and can compare various cable-bracing strengthening versions, in order the optimum one to be chosen.

2 Method of Analysis

2.1 Formulation of the Problem

A double discretization is applied, using the finite element method for space discretization in combination with a time discretization scheme [4]. So, first the structural system is discretized in space by using finite elements. Pin-jointed bar elements are used for the cable-elements. The behaviour of these elements includes loosening, elastoplastic or/and elastoplastic-softening-fracturing and unloading - reloading effects. All these characteristics concerning the cable constitutive law can be expressed mathematically by the relation:

$$s_i(d_i) \in \hat{\partial} S_i(d_i) \tag{1}$$

where s_i and d_i are the (tensile) force (in [kN]) and the deformation (elongation) (in [m]), respectively, of the i-th cable element, $\hat{\partial}$ is the generalized gradient and S_i is the superpotential function, see [18,23]. By definition, relation (1) is equivalent to the following hemivariational inequality, expressing the Virtual Work Principle:

$$S_i^{\uparrow}(d_i, e_i - d_i) \geq s_i(d_i) \cdot (e_i - d_i) \tag{2}$$

Here $S_i^{\uparrow}$ denotes the subderivative of S_i and e_i and d_i are kinematically admissible (virtual) deformations.

Next, dynamic equilibrium for the assembled structural system without cables is expressed by the usual matrix relation:

$$\boldsymbol{M}\ddot{\boldsymbol{u}} + \boldsymbol{C}(\dot{\boldsymbol{u}}) + \boldsymbol{K}(\boldsymbol{u}) = \boldsymbol{p} \tag{3}$$

Here $\boldsymbol{u}$ and $\boldsymbol{p}$ are the time dependent displacement and load vectors, respectively, and $\boldsymbol{M}$ the mass matrix. The damping and stiffness terms, $\boldsymbol{C}(\dot{\boldsymbol{u}})$ and $\boldsymbol{K}(\boldsymbol{u})$, respectively, concern the general non-linear case. When the linear-elastic case holds, these terms have the usual form $\boldsymbol{C}\dot{\boldsymbol{u}}$ and $\boldsymbol{K}\boldsymbol{u}$. Dots over symbols denote derivatives with respect to time.

When cable-elements are taken into account, Eq. (3) becomes

$$\boldsymbol{M}\ddot{\boldsymbol{u}} + \boldsymbol{C}(\dot{\boldsymbol{u}}) + \boldsymbol{K}(\boldsymbol{u}) = \boldsymbol{p} + \boldsymbol{A}\boldsymbol{s}. \tag{4}$$

Here $\boldsymbol{s}$ is the cable stress vector and $\boldsymbol{A}$ is a transformation matrix. For the case of ground seismic excitation $\boldsymbol{x}_g$ only, the loading history term $\boldsymbol{p}$ becomes

$$\boldsymbol{p} = -\boldsymbol{M}\boldsymbol{r}\ddot{\boldsymbol{x}}_g \tag{5}$$

where $\boldsymbol{r}$ is the vector of stereostatic displacements. The above relations (1)-(5), combined with the initial conditions, consist the problem formulation, where, for given $\boldsymbol{p}$ and/or $\ddot{\boldsymbol{x}}_g$, the vectors $\boldsymbol{u}$ and $\boldsymbol{s}$ have to be computed.

Regarding the strict mathematical treatment, by using relations (1) and (2) we can first formulate the problem as a hemivariational inequality one following [18,23] and then investigate it about existence and uniqueness of solution.

2.2 Numerical Treatment for Multiple Earthquakes

Concerning the Civil Engineering praxis, numerical treatments of the problem are required. Such an approach, based on a piecewise linearization of the above constitutive relations as in elastoplasticity [14] is described in [12] for cable-braced RC systems. By using a time-integration scheme, in each time-step a relevant non-convex linear complementarity problem (NC-LCP) of the following matrix form is solved :

$$\boldsymbol{v} \geq \boldsymbol{0}, \quad \boldsymbol{A}\boldsymbol{v} + \boldsymbol{a} \leq \boldsymbol{0}, \quad \boldsymbol{v}^T.(\boldsymbol{A}\boldsymbol{v} + \boldsymbol{a}) = 0. \tag{6}$$

So, the nonlinear Response Time-History (RTH) for a given seismic ground excitation can be computed. For details, see [12]. Similar procedures using optimization methods have been presented in [16].

An alternative approach for treating numerically the problem is the incremental one [13]. On this approach is based the structural analysis software Ruaumoko [3], which uses the finite element method. For the time-discretization, the Newmark scheme is here chosen. Generally, the Ruaumoko software permits an extensive parametric study on the inelastic response of structures. Especially for the case of multiple earthquakes, Ruaumoko has been applied for reinforced concrete planar frames under real seismic sequences [11]. These sequences are recorded by the same station, in the same direction and in a short period of time, up to three days [17]. Comprehensive analysis of the created response databank is employed in order to derive significant conclusions. Ruaumoko provides results which are related to the following critical parameters: local or global structural damage, maximum displacements, interstorey drift ratios, development of plastic hinges and response using the incremental dynamic analysis (IDA) method [25].

2.3 Damage Response Parameters Used for Assessment and Comparison

Among the several response parameters, the focus here is on the overall structural damage index (OSDI). This is due to the fact, that this parameter summarises all the existing damages on columns and beams of reinforced concrete frames in a single valuc, which is useful for comparison reasons [6]. So, after the seismic assessment [10] of the existing RC structure, the OSDI can be used for the choice of the best strengthening cable system.

In the OSDI model after [1,19] the global damage is obtained as a weighted average of the local damage at the section ends of each element or at each cable element. The local damage index is given by the following relation:

$$DI_L = \frac{\mu_m}{\mu_u} + \frac{\beta}{F_y d_u} E_T \tag{7}$$

where, DI_L is the local damage index, μ_m the maximum ductility attained during the load history, μ_u the ultimate ductility capacity of the section or element, β a strength degrading parameter, F_y the yield force of the section or element, E_T the dissipated hysteretic energy. The Park/Ang global damage index is a weighted average of the local damage indices and the dissipated energy is chosen as the weighting function. The global damage index is given by the following relation:

$$DI_G = \frac{\sum_{i=1}^{n} DI_L E_i}{\sum_{i=1}^{n} E_i} \tag{8}$$

where, DI_G is the global damage index, DI_L the local damage index after Park/Ang, E_i the energy dissipated at location i and n the number of locations at which the local damage is computed.

3 Numerical Example

3.1 Description of the Considered RC Structure

The tall, five-storey reinforced concrete frame F0 of Fig. 1 (left) is of concrete class C40/45, has dimensions $L = 5m$ and $h = 3m$ and was designed according to Greek building codes and to current European seismic codes [7–9].

The beams are of rectangular Sect. 30/60 (width/height, in cm) and have a total vertical distributed load 30 KN/m (each beam). The columns have section dimensions, in cm: 40/40.

The frame was initially constructed without cable-bracings. Due to various extreme actions (environmental etc.), corrosion and cracking has been taken place, which has caused a strength and stiffness degradation. The so resulted reduction for the section inertia moments was estimated [20] to be 10 % for the columns and 50 % for the beams. After the seismic assessment [10], it was decided that the frame F0 has to be seismically upgraded. Due to various reasons (serviceability, architectural etc.), the bracing system of ten diagonal cable-elements shown in Fig. 1 (right) was elected. The cable-strengthened frame is denoted as F10. The cable elements have a cross-sectional area $F_c = 18\,cm^2$ and they are of steel class S220 with yield strain $\epsilon_y = 0.2\,\%$, fracture strain $\epsilon_f = 2\,\%$ and elasticity modulus $E_c = 200GPa$. The cable constitutive law, concerning the unilateral (slackness), hysteretic, fracturing, unloading-reloading etc. behaviour, is depicted in Fig. 2.

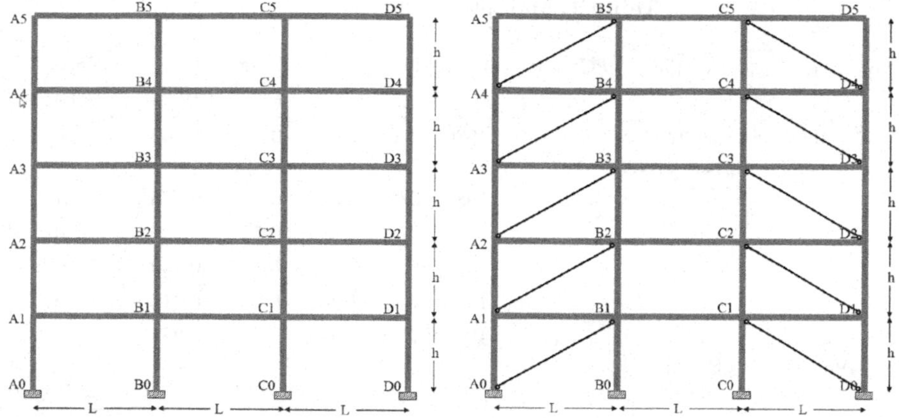

Fig. 1. The initial five-storeys RC frame F0, without cable-strengthening (left) and the RC frame F10, cable-strengthened with 10-braces (right)

3.2 Representative Results

3.3 Multiple Earthquakes Input

The systems F0 and F10 are subjected to a multiple ground seismic excitation, received from PEER database [17] and concerning the Coalinga case of next Table 1. The strong ground motion database consists of five real seismic sequences, which have been recorded during a short period of time (up to three days), by the same station, in the same direction, and almost at the same fault distance. These seismic sequences are namely: Mammoth Lakes (May 1980 - 5 events), Chalfant Valley (July 1986 - 2 events), Coalinga (July 1983 - 2 events), Imperial Valley (October 1979 - 2 events) and Whittier Narrows (October 1987 - 2 events) earthquakes. The complete list of these earthquakes, which were downloaded from the strong motion database of the Pacific Earthquake Engineering

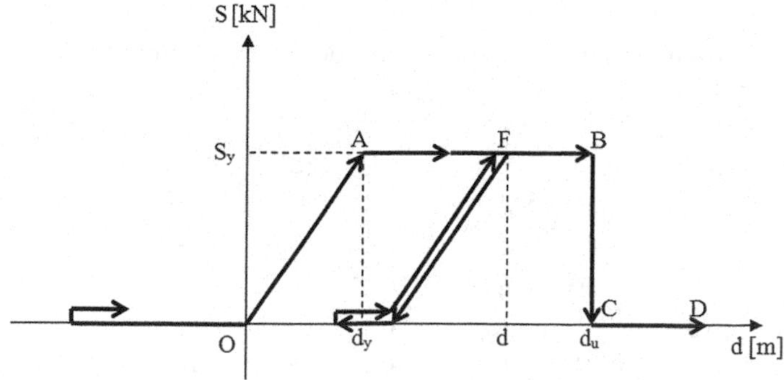

Fig. 2. The diagramme for the constitutive law of cable-elements

Table 1. Multiple earthquakes data

No	Seismic	Station	Comp	Date (Time)	Magn. (M_L)	Rec. $PGA(g)$	Norm. $PGA(g)$
1	Mammoth Lakes	54099 Convict Creek	N-S	1980/05/25 (16:34)	6.1	0.442	0.200
				1980/05/25 (16:49)	6.0	0.178	0.081
				1980/05/25 (19:44)	6.1	0.208	0.094
				1980/05/25 (20:35)	5.7	0.432	0.195
				1980/05/27 (14:51)	6.2	0.316	0.143
2	Chalfant Valley	54428 Zack Broth. Ranch	E-W	1986/07/20 (14:29)	5.9	0.285	0.128
				1986/07/21 (14:42)	6.3	0.447	0.200
3	Coalinga	46T04 CHP	N-S	1983/07/22 (02:39)	6.0	0.605	0.165
				1983/07/25 (22:31)	5.3	0.733	0.200
4	Imperial Valley	5055 Holtville P.O	HPV 315	1979/10/15 (23:16)	6.6	0.221	0.200
				1979/10/15 (23:19)	5.2	0.211	0.191
5	Whittier Narrows	24401 San Marino	N-S	1987/10/01 (14:42)	5.9	0.204	0.192
				1987/10/04 (10:59)	5.3	0.212	0.200

Research (PEER) Center, appears in Table 1. Every sequential ground motion records becomes a single ground motion record (serial array), where between two consecutive seismic events a time gap is applied. This gap is here chosen to be equal to 100 sec, enough to cease the moving of any structure due to damping. Figure 3 shows the time histories of three such simulated seismic sequences. For compatibility reasons with the design process, the seismic sequences are normalized to have PGA=0.2g.

Table 2. Representative response quantities for the frames F0 and F10

FRAMES	EVENTS	DI_G	DI_L	$u_{top}[10^{-2}m]$
(0)	(1)	(2)	(3)	(4)
F0	Event E_1	0.119	0.000	3.811
	Event E_2	0.267	0.182	8.595
	Event $E_1 + E_2$	0.276	0.198	9.571
F10	Event E_1	0.108	0.000	3.345
	Event E_2	0.220	0.175	7.078
	Event $E_1 + E_2$	0.236	0.161	7.255

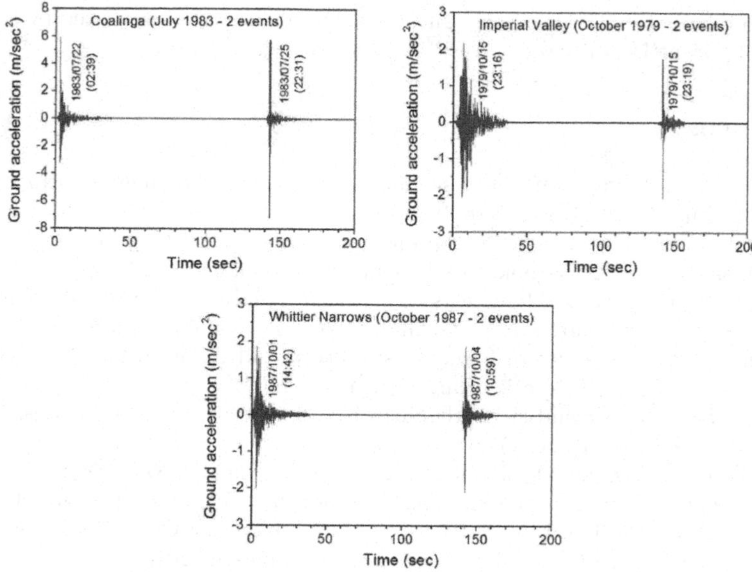

Fig. 3. Ground acceleration records of three simulated seismic sequences

Some representative results of the numerical investigation are presented in next Table 2. The sequence of Coalinga events E_1 (of PGA=0.605 g) and E_2 (of PGA=0.733 g) is denoted as Event $(E_1 + E_2)$. In column (2) the Global Damage Indices DI_G and in column (3) the Local Damage Index DI_L for the bending moment at the left fixed support A0 of the frames F0 and F10 are given. Finally, in the column (4), the maximum horizontal top displacement u_{top} is given. As the above table values show, multiple earthquakes generally increase, in an accumulative way, the response quantities. This holds especially for the damage indices. On the other hand, the strengthening of the frame F0 by 10-bracings, i.e. Frame F10, generally reduces the response values and, in comparison to F0, proves the strengthening effects.

4 Conclusions

The inelastic behaviour of tall planar RC frames, strengthened by cable elements and subjected to sequential strong ground motions, can be numerically investigated by the herein presented approach. As the results of a numerical example have shown, multiple earthquakes generally indicate the need for strengthening. Increased displacement demands are required in comparison with single seismic events. Furthermore, the seismic damage for multiple earthquakes is higher than that for isolated single ground motions. These characteristics, computed by the herein approach, are very important and should be taken into account for the seismic design and strengthening of RC structures.

Acknowledgments. The last three authors acknowledged the supported by the Bulgarian NSF Grant DCVP-02/1 and FP7-316087 project AComIn.

References

1. Ang, A.H.S.: Seismic damage assessment and basis for damage-limiting design. Probab. Eng. Mech. **3**, 146–150 (1998)
2. Bertero, V.V., Whittaker, A.S.: Seismic upgrading of existing buildings. In: 5as Jornadas Chilenas de Sismología e Ingeniería Antisísmica, vol. 1, pp. 27–46 (1989)
3. Carr, A.J.: RUAUMOKO - Inelastic Dynamic Analysis Program. University of Canterbury, Christchurch, New Zealand, Department of Civil Engineering (2008)
4. Chopra, A.K.: Dynamics of Structures: Theory and Applications to earthquake Engineering. Pearson Prentice Hall, New York (2007)
5. Dritsos, S.E.: Repair and strengthening of reinforced concrete structures. University of Patras, Greece (2001)
6. Elenas, A., Liolios, Ast., Vasiliadis, L., Favvata, M., Liolios, Ang.: Seismic intensity parameters as damage potential descriptors for life-cycle analysis of buildings. In: Proceedings of the Third International Symposium on Life-Cycle Civil Engineering (IALCCE 2012). CRC Press, Taylor & Francis, London (2012)
7. EN 1991-1-1, Eurocode 1: Actions on Structures, Part 1–1: General actions-densities, self-weight, imposed loads for buildings, European Committee for Standardization, Brussels, 2002
8. EN 1992-1-1, Eurocode 2: Design of Concrete Structures, Part 1–1: General rules and rules for buildings, European Committee for Standardization, Brussels, 2004
9. EN 1998–1, Eurocode 8: Design of structures for earthquake resistance; Part 1: General rules, seismic actions and rules for buildings 2005; European Committee for Standardization, Brussels, 2005
10. Fardis, M.N.: Seismic design, assessment and retrofitting of concrete buildings: based on EN-Eurocode 8, vol. 8. Springer, Netherlands (2009)
11. Hatzigeorgiou, G., Liolios, A.A.: Nonlinear behaviour of RC frames under repeated strong ground motions. Soil Dynamics and Earthquake Engineering **30**, 1010–1025 (2010)
12. Liolios, Ang, Chalioris, K., Liolios, Ast, Radev, S., Liolios, K.: A computational approach for the earthquake response of cable-braced reinforced concrete structures under environmental actions. In: Lirkov, I., Margenov, S., Waśniewski, J. (eds.) LSSC 2011. LNCS, vol. 7116, pp. 590–597. Springer, Heidelberg (2012)
13. Liolios, Ang, Liolios, Ast, Hatzigeorgiou, G.: A Numerical Approach for Estimating the Effects of Multiple Earthquakes to Seismic Response of Structures Strengthened by Cable-Elements. J. Theor. Appl. Mech. **43**(3), 21–32 (2013)
14. Maier, G.: Incremental Elastoplastic Analysis in the Presence of Large Displacements and Physical Instabilizing Effects. Int. J. Solids Str. **7**, 345–372 (1971)
15. Markogiannaki, O., Tegos, I.: Strengthening of a Multistory R/C Building under Lateral Loading by Utilizing Ties. Appl. Mech. Mater. **82**, 559–564 (2011)
16. Mistakidis, E.S., Stavroulakis, G.E.: Nonconvex optimization in mechanics. Smooth and nonsmooth algorithmes, heuristic and engineering applications. Kluwer, London (1998)
17. Pacific Earthquake Engineering Research Center. PEER Strong Motion Database. http://peer.berkeley.edu/smcat. Last accessed 15 February 2011
18. Panagiotopoulos, P.D.: Hemivariational Inequalities. Applications in Mechanics and Engineering. Springer, Berlin, New York (1993)

19. Park, Y.J., Ang, A.H.S.: Mechanistic seismic damage model for reinforced concrete. J. Struct. Div. ASCE **111**(4), 722–739 (1985)
20. Paulay, T., Priestley, M.J.N.: Seismic Design of Reinforced Concrete and Masonry Buildings. Wiley, New York (1992)
21. Penelis, G.G., Kappos, A.J.: Earthquake resistant concrete structures. CRC Press, London (1997)
22. Penelis, G., Penelis, Gr: Concrete Buildings in Seismic Regions. CRC Press, Penelis (2014)
23. Stavroulakis, G.E.: Computational Nonsmooth Mechanics: Variational and Hemivariational Inequalities, Nonlinear Analysis. Theor. Methods Appl. **47**(8), 5113–5124 (2001)
24. Tegos, I., Liakos, G., Tegou, S., Roupakias, G., Stilianidis, K.: An alternative proposal for the seismic strengthening of existing R/C buildings through tension-ties. In: Proceedings of 16th Pan- Hellenic Concrete Conference, Cyprus (2009)
25. Vamvatsikos, D., Cornell, C.A.: Incremental dynamic analysis. Earthq. Eng. Struct. Dyn. **31**, 491–514 (2002)

Multi-scale Computational Framework for Evaluating of the Performance of Molecular Based Flash Cells

Vihar P. Georgiev[1(✉)] and Asen Asenov[1,2]

[1] Device Modelling Group, University of Glasgow, Glasgow, UK
vihar.georgiev@glasgow.ac.uk
[2] GoldStandartSimulation Ltd., Glasgow, UK

Abstract. In this work we present a multi-scale computational framework for evaluation of statistical variability in a molecular based non-volatile memory cell. As a test case we analyse a BULK flash cell with polyoxometalates (POM) inorganic molecules used as storage centres. We focuse our discussions on the methodology and development of our innovative and unique computational framework. The capability of the discussed multi-scale approach is demonstrated by establishing a link between the threshold voltage variability and current-voltage characteristics with various oxidation states of the POMs. The presented simulation framework and methodology can be applied not only to the POM based flash cell but they are also transferrable to the flash cells based on alternative molecules used as a storage media.

Keywords: Multi-scale modelling · Molecular electronics · Multi-bit non-volatile memory · Polyoxometalates

1 Introduction

In the last few decades the flash cell technology has experienced significant changes, mainly in terms of the physical dimension of devices. This has been achieved primarily by reducing the tunnel oxide thickness in order to improve the programming/erasing performance. However, further scaling of the current NAND flash memory cells faces significant challenges. One of them is the existence of strong coupling between the floating gates in neighbouring cells that can result in cross talk and errors in a write and read operation (Kim 2010; Park 2009). Another challenge is the occurrence of a charge loss in the floating gate that happens due to a trap-assisted tunnelling in the tunnelling oxide, which jeopardises a write/erase cycling process (Amoroso 2013).

In order to overcome these technological issues charge trapping memories have been extensively researched. They are based on storing charge inside a silicon nitride or a high-k dielectric aiming to suppress the floating gate to gate disturbance. The charge trapping memories also provide immunity to localized defects in the tunnelling oxide and corresponding charge leakage (Lu 2012; Ma 2011).

I. Dimov et al. (Eds.): NMA 2014, LNCS 8962, pp. 196–203, 2015.
DOI: 10.1007/978-3-319-15585-2_22

However, the random number and position of the traps creates significant additional variability in the threshold voltage of the programmed flash cells (Amoroso 2010).

An alternative is development of nanocrystal memories where the charge is stored on semiconductor microcrystals embedded in the cell gate dielectric (Compagnoni 2005; Shaw 2005). Although such approach allows storage of multiple charges on a single micro-crystal, these memories also suffer from a significant statistical variability due to the size distribution of the micro-crystals and related different injection conditions (Dimitrakis 2013).

One possible option for an improvement is to replace the nanocrystals with molecules. In principal, a chemical synthesis in combination with a molecular self-assembly of the redox-active molecules can yield a regular distribution (spatially and energetically) of charge-storage centers (Pro 2009; Musumeci 2011). This allows us to scale the memory cell down to a few nanometres, as shown when using the organic redox-active molecules based on ferrocene and porphyrin (Zhu 2013; Paydavosi 2011). However, the organic molecules display low retention time due to the small associated redox potentials. Moreover, incorporation of the organic molecules in the flash memory manufacturing cycle is connected with numerous challenges. Therefore, from the technological point of view, it would be advantageous to find molecules, which are compatible with the standard silicon flash manufacturing. This would simultaneously help to overcome the deficiencies associated with the low retention time of their organic counterparts.

2 Concept and Flash Cell Design

One possible candidate to create the multi-bit molecular based flash cell is the polyoxometalate molecule known also as a POM. These inorganic metal-oxide clusters are formed by early transition metal ions and oxo ligands (Fay 2007). POMs have attractive properties for potential NVM application due to their

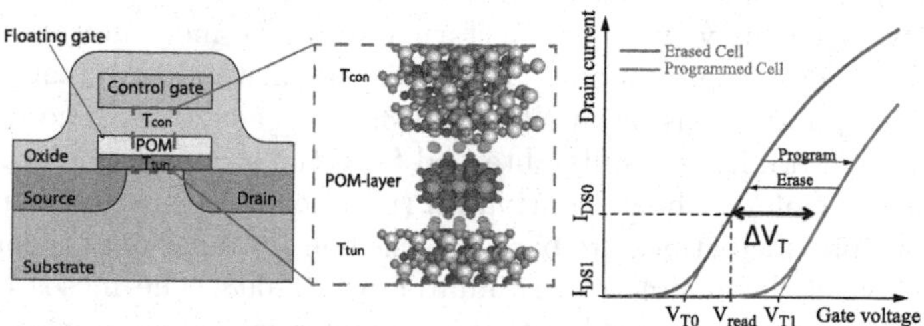

Fig. 1. Left: Schematic representation of a single-transistor BULK memory cell, indicating the aimed substitution of the poly-Si floating gate (FG) with an array of polyoxometalate molecules (POM layer). Right: Transfer characteristics (the source-drain current versus the control gate bias) of the device, illustrating the effect of programming the POM layer, leading to a shift of the voltage threshold (V_T) to higher values of the gate voltage

ability to undergo stable multiple and reversible oxidation/reduction processes. Also, incorporation of regular arrays of numerous POMs into SiO_2 has already been experimentally reported (Shaw 2011). As a result, we decided to concentrate our attention on possible integration of POMs with the floating gate (FG) of the current BULK flash cell architecture Fig. 1.

We consider the BULK flash cell with a gate area of $18 \times 18\,nm^2$ as a template. The density of the POMs could vary significantly depending on the crystal structure, which determines the size of the molecule. In our calculations, that consider the gate area of $18 \times 18\,nm^2$ and the crystal dimensions of the $[W_{18}O_{54}(SO_3)_2]^{4-}$POMs together with the $(CH_3H_7)_4N^+$ cations, we calculate that the optimal density of the molecules is $3 \times 10^{12}\,cm^{-2}$. This density corresponds to nine molecules in the FG, which in our case are arranged in a 3×3 regular planar grid. The molecular layer starts 3 nm above the Si/SiO_2 interface and the entire gate stack is identical to our previously published work (Vilá-Nadal 2013; Georgiev 2014).

The selected POM has three stable and reversible reduction/oxidation states. It is therefore attractive for multi-bit charge storage. We should point out that in the process of chemical synthesis each molecule is surrounded on average by four positive charges (contra cations). Those cations are schematically presented as green points surrounding the molecule in Fig. 1 on the left hand side. The charge of the POM cluster on itself is 4- and each green chain has a single positive charge. On average 4 cations in total surround each POM, which means that the overall charge equals zero. However, with increasing of the oxidation state of the molecule from 4- to 5- the overall charge in the FG increases, which leads to a shift of the voltage threshold (V_T) to higher values of the gate voltage (V_G). The effect of the current-voltage characteristics and V_T is schematically presented in Fig. 1 on the right hand side.

3 Methodology

In this section we will briefly introduce the multi-scale simulation framework which we developed to evaluate the performance of the molecular storage flash memory cells. More details about the simulation methodology can be found in our previous publications (Vilá-Nadal 2013; Georgiev 2014). The multi-scale simulation framework links results obtained from the atomistic molecular simulations (first principle) with the continuum (mesoscopic) transistor simulations. The first principle calculations are based on the density functional theory (DFT) as implemented in the commercial simulator ADF 2008. The mesoscopic transistor simulations are performed with the commercial three-dimensional (3D) numerical device simulator GARAND (GARAND 2014). The simplified simulation flow diagram is presented in Fig. 2. The key component of this flow is the custom-built Simulation Domain Bridge that links the two distinct simulation domains atomistic and continuum.

In our simulation flow the DFT calculations provide the atomic coordinates and charges of a polyoxometalate molecule in a given redox state. It is vital

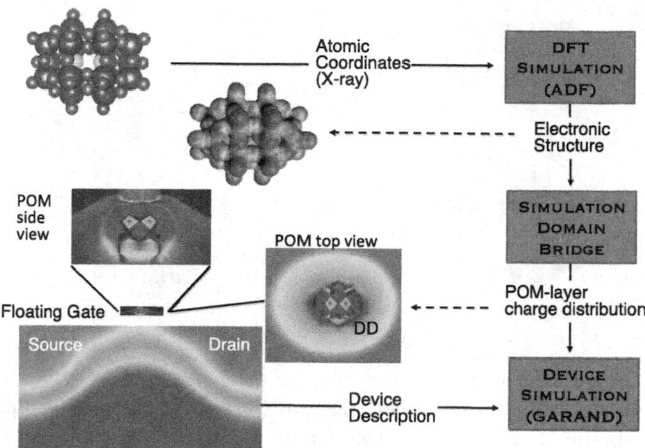

Fig. 2. Simplified block diagram of the simulation methodology, linking the atomistic molecular simulations (first principle) with the continuum (mesoscopic) transistor simulations

		$[W_{18}O_{54}(SO_3)_2]^{4-}$			
		X	Y	Z	MDC-q
1	O	-2.996	1.7533	0	-0.93357
2	O	-0.7393	1.2805	5.1309	-0.952574
3	O	-3.0671	0	6.3752	-0.617707
4	O	-4.6588	2.7977	2.0278	-0.602512
5	O	-2.9898	1.2983	3.7644	-0.910451
6	O	-4.0243	0	1.749	-0.899429
7	O	-1.6958	2.9372	2.0267	-0.944329
8	O	-1.5413	0	1.8242	-0.608756
9	S	0	0	1.2973	1.028495
10	W	-3.2746	1.805	1.9078	2.418012
11	W	-2.1678	0	4.9208	2.470102
12	O	-2.996	-1.7533	0	-0.93357

Fig. 3. Some atomic coordinates and charges of a polyoxometalate molecule in a given redox state obtained from the first principle simulations (DFT)

to consider the presence of cations in the process of fabrication or calculation of the flash cells. For this reason we take into account these positive charges in our work. In the first principle calculations the cations are presented with a continuum solvation model while in the device simulations they are described as 18 point charges around each POM. Some of these atomic charges of the molecule are represented in a table in Fig. 3.

In order to simulate and explore the realistic molecular based memory cells one option is to perform the transistor level simulations based on the continuum approach. In our case we relay on the 3D numerical device simulator GARAND. The data from the DFT calculations is transferred through the in-house built Simulation Domain Bridge as schematically depicted in Fig. 2. The bridge reads

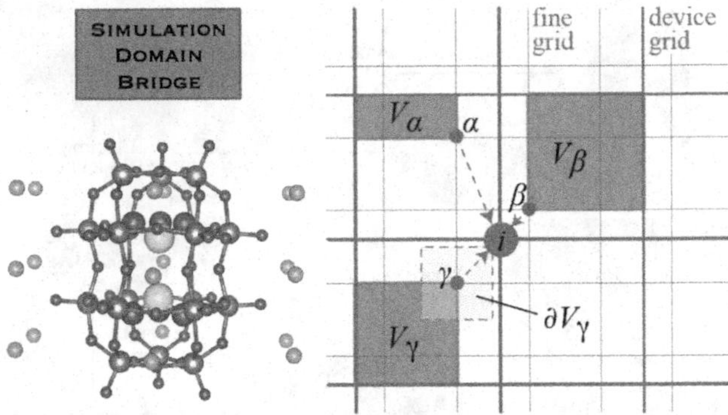

Fig. 4. 2D picture of the cloud-in-cell assignment of charge used from the domain bridge that reads the atomic charges from the DFT simulation and assigns the partial charges to the discretisation grid of GARAND

the atomic charges from the DFT simulation and assigns the partial charges to the discretisation grid of GARAND applying the cloud-in-cell technique. Figure 4 presents a 2D sketch of the cloud-in-cell assignment of charge. The spatial distribution of fractional charges (e.g., alpha, beta and gamma) obtained from the DFT calculations is mapped on the coarser discretisation grid used in the 3D device simulator. A part of each fractional charge is assigned to the node according to an inverse of the volume associated with the opposite node. The obtained electron density of the POM based on the BULK flash cell is presented in Fig. 5. In this way we are able to calculate the current-voltage characteristics (I_D-V_G) and threshold voltage (V_T) of the molecular based flash memory cells for various number, spatial and redox configurations of the POMs in the oxide.

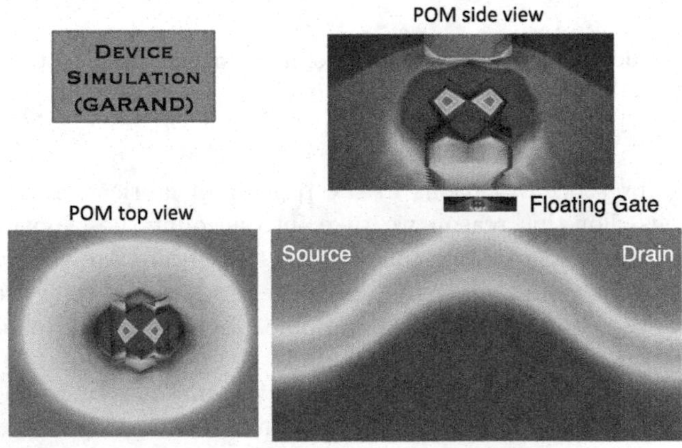

Fig. 5. Visual representation of electron density in the floating gate and in the body of the BULK cell obtained from the 3D numerical device simulator GARAND

Importantly, GARAND allows the introduction of various device architectures, such as BULK, FDSOI, FinFET and Nanowire. It also handles seamlessly intrinsic sources of statistical variability, such as random dopant fluctuation (RDF) and POMs' fluctuation (POMF). This allows us to obtain realistic and reliable evaluation for the POM flash technology. The 3D numerical simulations of the flash cell, performed with GARAND, deploy the drift-diffusion transport formalism and include density-gradient quantum corrections essential for the accurate modeling of the decananometer devices and for the resolution of the discrete localised charges.

4 Flash Cell Performance

In this section we present results of the analysis of the number of the charges in the FG for the BULK POM based flash cell. All transistors have 9 molecules in the FG and they are arranged in a 3×3 grid in the FG as illustrated in Fig. 6. Also, all devices have continuous doping and they are characterised by the absence of any sources of statistical variability. The main focus is on the programming window ΔV_T and the current-voltage (I_D-V_G) characteristics.

In order to investigate the device performance we assume that each POM molecule has three easily accessible redox states. These are the parent (n = 4), 1x reduced (n = 5) and 2x reduced (n = 6) states. Each of these states corresponds to one bit of stored information. The parent flash cell has 0 total charge in the floating gate because the nine POMs charge is neutralised (even though they are negatively charged) by the positively charged cations which are represented by the point charges in our simulations Fig. 4. In the case of the 1x reduced NVM cell the total amount of charges in the FG is -9q (q a unit charge of electron). This corresponds to one extra electron per POM in comparison to the parent configuration. Correspondingly, the 2x reduced transistors have -18q charges in comparison to the parent structure and -9q charges in comparison to the 1x reduced NVM cell. By embedding the charge distributions obtained from

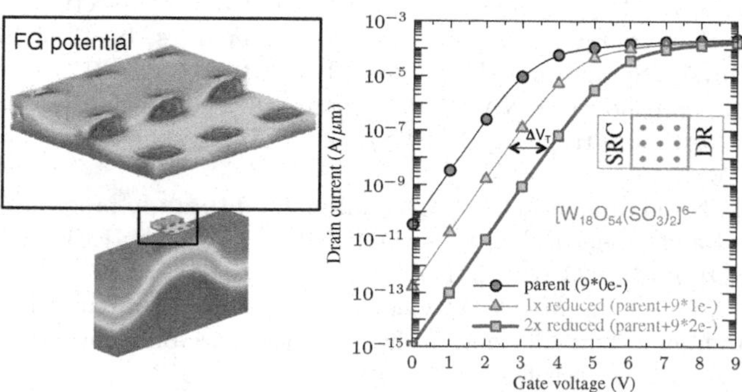

Fig. 6. 3D representation of electron density of the BULK transistor and 3D depiction of the floating gate potential where POMs are arranged in a symmetrical 3×3 grid

the DFT for each POM in the corresponding redox state, two different bits are encoded when considering two distinct V_T shifts of the flash cell.

Several important observations can be made from the data presented in Fig. 6. Firstly, with increasing of the oxidation state the voltage threshold shifts to higher gate voltages. This is due to the fact that the charge inside of the floating gate increases. As a result, the influence of the floating gate on the current flow is less pronounced and requires a higher gate voltage in order to turn the transistor ON. Secondly, the ON-current ($V_G = 0.9V$) is almost constant for all devices. On a contrary to the ON-current, the OFF-current ($V_G = 0.0V$) shows significant decrease with increasing of the redox state of the molecule. Lastly, the subthreshold slope for all devices is identical, which shows the same level of degradation.

5 Conclusions

In this paper we have presented comprehensive hierarchal and numerical simulations of evaluating the performance of the molecular based flash cells. Our results have shown the device performance in terms of the programming window and current-voltage characteristics. We have also demonstrated that our computational framework provides not only qualitative but also quantitative guidelines for design and optimisation of the molecular based flash cells. Overall, the results of our analysis highlight the important considerations relevant to the molecular based flash cell technology.

References

Kim, Y.S., et al.: New scale limitations of the floating gate cells in NAND flash memories. In: IEEE International Reliability Physics Symposium (RPS), pp. 599–603 (2010)

Park, M., et al.: Direct field effect of neighboring cell transistor on cell-to-cell interference of NAND Flash cell arrays. IEEE Electron Device Lett. **30**(2), 174–177 (2009)

Amoroso, S.M., et al.: Impact of statistical variability and 3D electrostatics on post-cycling anomalous charge loss in nanoscale flash memories. In: IEEE International Reliability Physics Symposium (RPS) pp. 3.B.4.1–3.B.4.6 (2013)

Lu, C.Y.: Future prospects of NAND flash memory technology the evolution from floating gate to charge trapping to 3D Stacking. J. Nanosci. Nanotechnol. **12**(10), 7604–7618 (2012)

Ma, C.H., et al.: Novel random telegraph signal method to study program/erase charge lateral spread and retention loss in a SONOS flash memory. IEEE Trans. Electron Devices (TED) **58**(3), 623–630 (2011)

Amoroso, S.M., Maconi, A., Mauri, A., Campagnoli, C.M.: 3D Monte Carlo simulation of the programming dynamics and their statistical variability in nanoscale charge-trap memories. IEDM Tech Digest, pp. 22.6.1–22.6.4 (2010)

Compagnoni, C.M., Ielmini, D., Spinelli, A.S., Lacaita, A.L.: Optimization of threshold voltage window under tunneling program/erase in nanocrystal memories. Trans. Electron Devices (TED) **52**(11), 2473–2479 (2005)

Shaw, J., Hou, T.H., Raza, H., Kan, E.C.: Statistical metrology of metal nanocrystal memories with 3-D finite-element analysis. Trans. Electron Devices (TED) **56**(8), 1729–1736 (2009)

Dimitrakis, P., et al.: Quantum dots for memory applications. Phys. Status Solidi A **210**(8), 1490–1504 (2013)

Pro, T., Buckley, J., Huang, K., Calborean, A., Gely, M., Delapierre, G.: Investigation of hybrid molecular/silicon memories with redox-active molecules acting as storage media. IEEE Trans. Nanatechnol. **8**(2), 204–213 (2009)

Musumeci, C., Rosnes, M., Giannazzo, F., Symes, M., Cronin, L., Pignataro, B.: Smart high-k nanodielectrics using solid supported polyoxometalate-rich nanostructures. Nano **5**(12), 9992–9999 (2011)

Zhu, H., et al.: Non-volatile memories with self-assemble ferrocene charge trapping layer. App. Phys. Lett. **103**, 053102 (2013)

Paydavosi, S., et al.: High-density charge storage on molecular thin films - candidate materials for high storage capacity memory cells. IEEE IEDM, vol. 11-543, pp. 24-4-1 (2011)

Fay, N., et al.: Structural, electrochemical, and spectroscopic charac-terization of a redox pair of sulfite-based polyoxotungstates: α-$[W_{18}O_{54}(SO_3)_2]^{4-}$ and $\alpha[W_{18}O_{54}(SO_3)_2]^{5-}$. Inorg. Chem. **46**, 3502 (2007)

Shaw, J., et al.: Integration of self-assembled redox molecules in flash memories. IEEE Trans. Electron Devices **58**(3), 826 (2011)

Vilá-Nadal, L., et al.: Towards polyoxometalate-cluster-based nano-electronics. Chem. Eur. J. **19**(49), 16502–16511 (2013)

Georgiev, V.P., et al.: Optimisation and evaluation of variability in the programming window of a flash cell with molecular metal-oxide storage. IEEE Trans. Electron Devices (2014, in press). doi:10.1109/TED.2014.2315520

GARAND. http://www.GoldStandardSimulations.com

Numerical Simulations and Back Analysis in Civil and Mechanical Engineering

Parameter Identification of a Rate Dependent Constitutive Model for Rock Salt

Kavan Khaledi[1], Elham Mahmoudi[1], Maria Datcheva[2(✉)], and Tom Schanz[1]

[1] Chair for Foundation Engineering, Rock and Soil Mechanics, Faculty of Civil and Environmental Engineering, Ruhr-Universität Bochum, Bochum, Germany
[2] Institute of Mechanics, Bulgarian Academy of Sciences, Sofia, Bulgaria
atcheva@imbm.bas.bg

Abstract. The tendency to shift from fossil and nuclear energy sources to renewable energy carriers in Germany leads to the necessity to develop effective energy storage systems. Nowadays, caverns excavated in rock salt formations are recognized as the appropriate places for underground storage of energy in the form of compressed air, hydrogen and natural gas. Accurate design of these underground cavities requires suitable numerical simulations employing proper constitutive models to describe the material behavior of rock salt under various geological conditions. In this paper, a rate dependent model is selected to describe the mechanical response of the rock salt around the cavern. This model is implemented in the finite element code CODE-BRIGHT, then its application in numerical modeling of salt caverns is illustrated. Finally, inverse analysis of the synthetic data is performed to identify the material parameters of the selected model. The applied inverse analysis algorithm employs metamodeling technique in order to reduce the computation time of the parameter identification procedure.

Keywords: Salt cavern · Rate dependent constitutive model · Inverse analysis · Metamodel

1 Introduction

The low permeability and adequate thermal and mechanical properties of rock salt have made it a suitable choice for the underground storage of compressed air, natural gas, CO_2, and H_2. Accurate design of the underground openings in the rock salt formations will be possible if a proper constitutive law is used to describe the material behavior of salt. Numerous investigations have been carried out during the past couple of decades in order to find a good description for the mechanical behavior of rock salt (e.g. [1–4]). In this paper, a rate dependent model developed by Heusermann in [5] is implemented in the finite element code CODE-BRIGHT to simulate the time dependent behavior of rock salt around the underground cavities. Code–Bright(COupled DEformation BRIne, Gas and Heat Transport) is a program that allows for thermo-hydro-mechanical analysis

I. Dimov et al. (Eds.): NMA 2014, LNCS 8962, pp. 207–216, 2015.
DOI: 10.1007/978-3-319-15585-2_23

in geological media. It consists of a finite element program developed at the Department of the Geotechnical Engineering and Geosciences of the Technical University of Catalonia (UPC). In the numerical section, a typical salt cavern is modeled and inverse analysis of synthetic data is performed to identify the material parameters of the selected constitutive model. The inverse analysis method employed in this paper combines genetic algorithm with metamodeling technique to find the optimum set of the material parameters.

2 Mechanical Behavior of Rock Salt

The Lubby2 model is used to describe the time dependent response of the rock salt around the cavern under quasistatic geological loading [5]. This model considers the strain rate as a sum of two parts, i.e. elastic strain rate $\dot{\varepsilon}^{e}_{ij}$, visco-elastic strain rate $\dot{\varepsilon}^{ve}_{ij}$.

$$\dot{\varepsilon}_{ij} = \dot{\varepsilon}^{e}_{ij} + \dot{\varepsilon}^{ve}_{ij} \tag{1}$$

Figure 1 shows the sketch of the employed rheological model. The material characteristic of the dashpots and springs in this model are stress dependent. The visco-elastic strain rate in this model is divided into two parts: (1) transient part (ε^{tr}) (2) steady–state part(ε^{ss}). The following equations define the visco-elastic strain rate:

$$\begin{cases} \dot{\varepsilon}^{ve}_{ij} = \dot{\varepsilon}^{tr}_{ij} + \dot{\varepsilon}^{ss}_{ij} \\ \dot{\varepsilon}^{tr}_{ij} = \dfrac{3}{2}\dfrac{1}{\eta_k \exp(k_2 q)}\left(1 - \dfrac{\varepsilon^{tr}}{\varepsilon^{tr}_{\infty}}\right) S_{ij} \\ \dot{\varepsilon}^{ss}_{ij} = \dfrac{3}{2}\dfrac{1}{\eta_m \exp(mq)} S_{ij} \\ \varepsilon^{tr}_{\infty} = \dfrac{q}{G_k \exp(k_1 q)} \end{cases} \tag{2}$$

where $\mathbf{S}$ is the deviatoric part of stress tensor. Parameter $\varepsilon^{tr}_{\infty}$ is the value of equivalent strain ε^{tr} at which the transient creep will end. k_1, k_2, and m are material parameters; η_k and η_m are Kelvin and Maxwell viscosity parameters and G_k represents the Kelvin module.

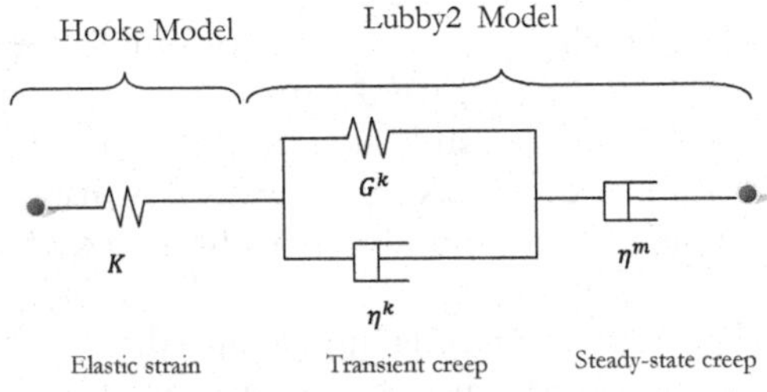

Fig. 1. The schematic sketch of the selected constitutive model

3 Parameter Identification Algorithm

In general, the material parameters of the rock salt around the cavern are determined through the inverse analysis of experimental measurements. To accomplish this, the values of the constitutive parameters should be adjusted in the finite element model used to simulate the experiment until the difference between the calculated results and the recorded measurements is minimized. The main goal of inverse analysis is to identify an optimum set of parameters for which the predicted responses at observation points are closest to the measurements. Mathematically, the identified parameters should minimize the following objective function:

$$f(\mathbf{x}) = \frac{\|\mathbf{u}^c(\mathbf{x}) - \mathbf{u}^m\|}{\|\mathbf{u}^m\|} \tag{3}$$

where $\mathbf{u}^m$ is the vector of measurements and $\mathbf{u}^c$ is the vector of corresponding computed value obtained from the numerical simulation. The minimum of the objective function 3 can be found effectively through evolutionary algorithms like GA or PSO (see [6–9]). In this paper, the genetic algorithm is chosen for solving the optimization problem. Genetic algorithms are inspired by Darwin's evolution theory. The algorithm is started with the initial set of parameter vectors called initial population. The initial population is randomly generated. Some of the population members (individuals) are selected and used to form a new population by applying crossover and mutation functions. The whole process is done with the scope that the new population will be better than the old one. Selection of parameter vectors is done according to their objective function (called fitness function), where, the more suitable they are, the more chances they have to be selected and reproduced. This procedure is repeated until some criteria (for example number of generations or improvement of the best solution) are satisfied.

If the objective function is highly non-linear with a large number of input variables, a large number of evaluations of the objective function may be needed before the best set of parameters is identified. This high computation cost makes the algorithm of inverse analysis inefficient. Therefore, a practical solution is to replace the original finite element model by a simpler model that approximate the response of the original model with high accuracy. The approximated model which mimics the behavior of the original model is called *metamodel* or *surrogate model*. Therefore, computing the value of $\mathbf{u}^c$ directly from the metamodel enables reducing the computation time for solving the optimization problem. The flow chart shown in Fig. 2 describes the parameter identification procedure using the genetic algorithm combined with the metamodel.

3.1 Metamodeling Technique

The main goal of metamodeling is to approximate the unknown function $\mathbf{u}$ which describes the solution of an engineering problem. The only available information is the input and output data in the form of some scattered samples like $(\mathbf{x}, \boldsymbol{u}(\mathbf{x}))$

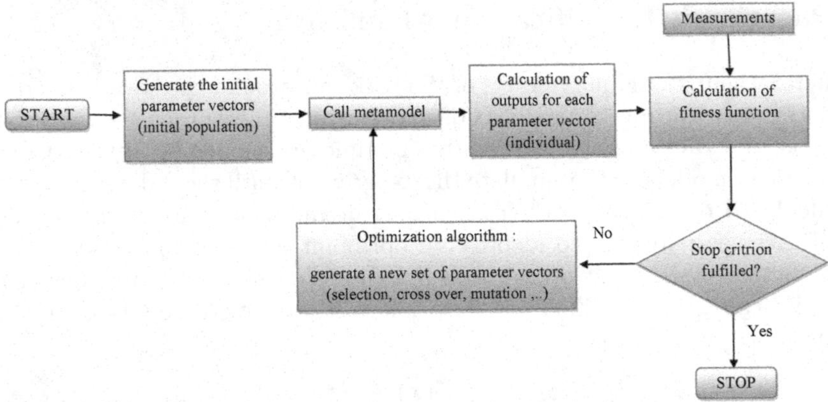

Fig. 2. Flow chart of inverse analysis algorithm using metamodel

obtained from physical or computational experiments. $\mathbf{x}$ is a vector of s parameters and $\boldsymbol{u}(\mathbf{x})$ is a vector quantity which gives the function value at m observation points. In order to construct a metamodel, two main components are required: (1) *the input parameter matrix* ($\mathbf{X}$) which includes the s parameters of n_p sample points (2) *the matrix of system responses or snapshot matrix* ($\mathbf{U}$) in which the n_p function values of m observation points are recorded. Therefore, $\mathbf{X}$ and $\mathbf{U}$ matrices are of size $s \times n_p$ and $m \times n_p$ respectively. Depending on the structure of $\mathbf{X}$ and $\mathbf{U}$, several techniques for approximating $\mathbf{u}$ may be applicable. In this paper, Proper Orthogonal Decomposition (POD) combined with Radial Basis Functions (RBF) proposed by Buljak in [10] is used to construct a reliable metamodel. The algorithm consists of two main parts: (1) proper orthogonal decomposition of the snapshot matrix; and (2) interpolation using radial basis functions. The basic idea of POD method is to present the snapshot matrix $\mathbf{U}$ as:

$$[\mathbf{U}]_{m\times n_p} = [\boldsymbol{\Phi}]_{m\times n_p}[\mathbf{A}]_{n_p\times n_p}, \tag{4}$$

here, $\mathbf{A}$ is the *amplitude matrix* and $\boldsymbol{\Phi}$ includes the *proper orthogonal basis vectors*. The POD basis vectors $\boldsymbol{\Phi}$ can be obtained by finding the normalized eigenvectors and eigenvalues of the symmetric matrix $\mathbf{D} = \mathbf{U}^T\mathbf{U}$ (see [10,11]). Since the matrix $\boldsymbol{\Phi}$ fulfills the orthogonality condition i.e. $\boldsymbol{\Phi}^T = \boldsymbol{\Phi}^{-1}$, the amplitude matrix is calculated as follows:

$$[\mathbf{A}]_{n_p\times n_p} = \left[\boldsymbol{\Phi}^T\right]_{n_p\times m}[\mathbf{U}]_{m\times n_p}. \tag{5}$$

The size of matrix $\boldsymbol{\Phi}$ can be reduced if the basis vectors corresponding to small eigenvalues are omitted. To accomplish this, first the basis vectors are sorted in a descending order according to the magnitude of their eigenvalues. Then, the first k columns of matrix $\boldsymbol{\Phi}$ are taken and the rest are removed ($k \leq n_p$). In this way, the reduced basis vectors $\overline{\boldsymbol{\Phi}}^T$ can be obtained. Subsequently, the reduced amplitude matrix $\overline{\mathbf{A}}$ is calculated as follows:

$$\left[\overline{\mathbf{A}}\right]_{k\times n_p} = \left[\overline{\boldsymbol{\Phi}}^T\right]_{k\times m} [\mathbf{U}]_{m\times n_p} . \tag{6}$$

The second step is to use a linear combination of radially symmetric functions (RBF) in order to approximate the reduced amplitude matrix $\overline{\mathbf{A}}$. Having n_p sample points in the s dimensional space, each component of reduced amplitude matrix $\overline{\mathbf{A}}$ is computed by radial functions as follows:

$$\overline{a}_l^j = \sum_{i=1}^{n_p} b_l^i g_i(\mathbf{x}^j) \quad j = 1, \cdots, n_p \quad l = 1, \cdots, k, \tag{7}$$

where b_l^i are unknown coefficients and $g_i(\mathbf{x}^j)$ gives the value of the radial function g with the center point $\mathbf{x}^i$ at the sample point $\mathbf{x}^j$. In this paper, *inverse multiquadratic* function is applied which has the form:

$$g_i(\mathbf{x}) = \left(\left\|\mathbf{x} - \mathbf{x}^i\right\|^2 + c^2\right)^{-0.5}, \tag{8}$$

where parameter c is a predefined constant which controls the smoothness of the radial basis function. It is computationally of advantage to select this value within the $[0 - 1]$ range. Equation (7) provides $k \times n_p$ linear equations with $k \times n_p$ unknowns. This system of equations is solved to find the unknown coefficients.

$$\left[\overline{\mathbf{A}}\right]_{k\times n_p} = [\mathbf{B}]_{k\times n_p} [\mathbf{G}]_{n_p\times n_p} \quad \Longrightarrow [\mathbf{B}]_{k\times n_p} = \left[\overline{\mathbf{A}}\right]_{k\times n_p} [\mathbf{G}]^{-1}_{n_p\times n_p}, \tag{9}$$

here, matrix $\mathbf{G}$ gathers the values of radial functions at the sample points and matrix $\mathbf{B}$ includes the unknown coefficients. Finally, the equation below is used to find the function value at the observation point m for an arbitrary input point $\mathbf{x}$:

$$\left[\tilde{\boldsymbol{u}}(\mathbf{x})\right]_{m\times 1} = \left[\overline{\boldsymbol{\Phi}}\right]_{m\times k} [\mathbf{B}]_{k\times n_p} \left[\boldsymbol{g}_i(\mathbf{x})\right]_{n_p\times 1} \quad i = 1, \cdots, n_p. \tag{10}$$

4 Numerical Example

A typical salt cavern with a simplified geometry has been modeled using GID software. GID is used as the pre-processor and post-processor of the Code–Bright finite element solver. Because of symmetry, only one half of the cavern has been simulated. The axisymmetrical model with a height of 800 m and a width of 300 m is shown in Fig. 3. The cavern itself has a diameter of 37.5 m and a height of 233 m. On the upper model boundary a load of 10 MPa is applied which represents the overburden load at the top surface. The vertical displacement at the model bottom is restrained. The density of compact rock salt is assumed to be $\rho = 2000$ kg/m^3 and the numerical simulation is done at constant ambient temperature $T = 298$ K. Other material parameters of rock salt are shown in

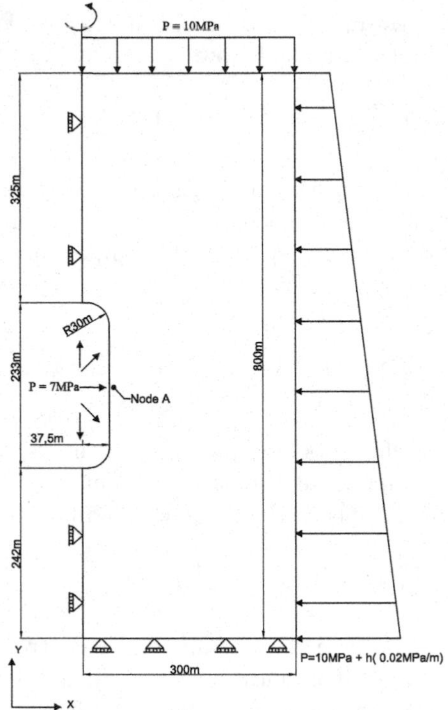

Fig. 3. Geometry and boundary condition of the salt cavern model

Table 1. Material parameters for rock salt

Elasticity		Lubby2 model					
E (MPa)	ν	k_1(1/MPa)	k_2(1/MPa)	m(1/MPa)	η_k(MPa.d)	η_m(MPa.d)	G_k(MPa)
25000	0.3	-0.191	-0.168	0.247	[4.6e4 - 1.1e5]	[5.8e6 - 2.9e7]	[3e5 - 6e5]

Table 1. For simplicity, it is assumed that the cavern is instantaneously excavated at time t = 0. In situ stress state before excavation is assumed to be hydrostatic which means that the initial stresses are equal in all directions. Therefore, the boundary condition at the outer surface of the model is simulated by applying distributed lateral edge loading which is equal to hydrostatic stress in the rock formation. Afterward, due to the difference between the cavern internal pressure and initial stresses in rock formation, elastic stress redistribution occurs and thereafter creep deformation initiates.

4.1 Metamodel Construction

The output data at the observation points (snapshots) can be any physical quantity like pressure, strain, temperature, displacement etc. In this numerical example, the horizontal displacement at the cavern's wall is the quantity that is read and recorded as the output (see Node A in Fig. 3). The numerical simulation is carried out for 100 days. That means, in each solver run, 100 output values are read and recorded. On the other hand, a set of three parameters (η_k, η_m, G_k) is needed to model the visco-elastic behavior of the rock salt according to the Lubby2 model. Therefore, the constructed metamodel for this cavern example will have 3 inputs and 100 outputs. The following steps have been conducted to establish the POD-RBF metamodel for this example:

1. 90 sample points are created inside the input parameter domain. The lower and upper bounds of each parameter have been provided in Table 1. The size of input parameter matrix for this example is 3 × 90. The sample generation has been performed using latin hypercube method.
2. The finite element model is run for each parameter set and the horizontal displacement of node A is stored in the snapshot matrix within the 100 days. This matrix has 100 rows and 90 columns.
3. The input parameter matrix is normalized between 0 and 1 in order to avoid the potential scaling errors due to the disparate magnitudes of input parameters.
4. Having the input parameter and snapshot matrices the POD-RBF metamodel is constructed according to Sect. 3.1.

Before proceeding to the next step, the accuracy of the constructed metamodel is to be evaluated. Therefore, 20 test points have been generated randomly inside the design domain. Then, the exact output value $\mathbf{u}$ (obtained from CODE-BRIGHT model) and the approximate value $\tilde{\mathbf{u}}$ (generated by metamodel) are computed for the test points and compared by the following standard accuracy measure NRMSE.

$$\text{NRMSE} = \left\{ \left(\sum_{i=1}^{20} \sum_{j=1}^{100} (u_j^i - \tilde{u}_j^i)^2 \right) / \left(\sum_{i=1}^{20} \sum_{j=1}^{100} (u_j^i)^2 \right) \right\}^{(1/2)}, \tag{11}$$

The obtained NRMSE for this case is equal to 0.0043 which demonstrates the accuracy of the constructed metamodel inside the selected design domain. The required time for one single evaluation of the FE cavern example by CODE-BRIGHT is 40 min. Thus, it takes about 60 h to create 90 sample points and their corresponding snapshots. However, once the metamodel is created, the computation time decreases drastically. The time needed to obtain results from the metamodel is about one second which is much less than the computation time of the original model.

4.2 Results and Discussion

The objective here is to obtain the material parameters of Lubby2 model by inverse analysis of synthetic data for a salt cavern. The word "synthetic" is used

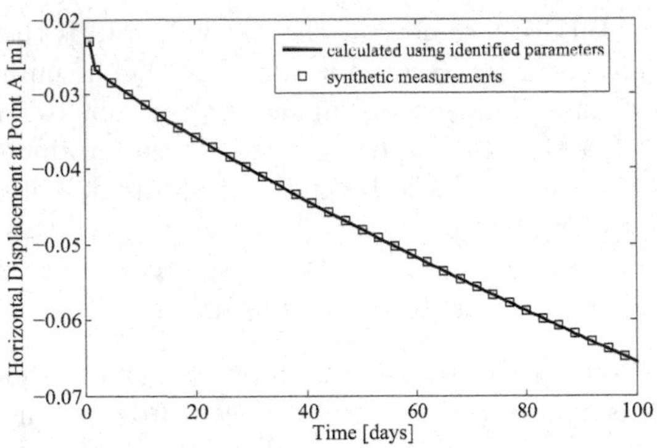

Fig. 4. Obtained results by CODE-BRIGHT using the pre-defined parameters and the identified values

here because the observation data are obtained from numerical simulations and not from field measurements. The horizontal displacement at the observation point within 100 days is first calculated by the FE solver using a set of predefined parameter values of Lubby2 model. Then, the original model is replaced by the POD-RBF metamodel constructed in the previous section. Subsequently, the parameter back calculation is performed according to the flowchart shown in Fig. 2. One verification test has been carried out to find three parameters of the Lubby2 model based on the cavern example. The pre-defined parameters are shown in Table 2. The MATLAB global optimization toolbox, version 2012b, is used for performing the optimization. For the 2D cavern model studied here, an average of 40 min is required on a standard PC for a single evaluation of the objective function. As shown in Table 3, the optimal values of Lubby2 parameters have been found after 3000 evaluations of the objective function. These results could have been obtained after 84 days if the original FE model was employed, while with the aid of the metamodeling, the total time needed for parameter identification reduced to 60 h. The identified parameter values are shown in Table 2. As it can be seen, they are very close to the pre-defined values. To visualize the accuracy of the identified parameters, they have been inserted into the FE model and the responses at the observation points have been compared with the original responses. Figure 4 demonstrates the accuracy of the identified parameter values.

Table 2. Pre-defined parameter set and the identified values by inverse analysis

Pre-defined parameters			Identified parameters		
η_k (MPa.d)	η_m (MPa.d)	G_k (MPa)	η_k (MPa.d)	η_m (MPa.d)	G_k (MPa)
8.9e4	7.89e6	5.97e5	9e4	7.87e6	5.94e5

Table 3. GA parameters and computation time for the test case

Cross over function	Two points
Population type	Double vector
Total evaluations	3000
Best fitness value	0.007
Computation time	FEM solver: 84 days, Metamodel:60 h

5 Conclusion

Inverse analysis of measurements has been carried out for a typical rock salt cavern to identify the material parameters of a visco-elastic model. To accomplish this, the error between the synthetic measurements and the calculated data has been minimized by a genetic algorithm combined with the metamodeling technique. The obtained results show that with the aid of accurate and efficient metamodeling method such as the combination POD-RBF, it is possible to obtain the solution of the optimiuation problem with a very small error in a significantly shorter time. In this way, solving computationally expensive problems such as parameter identification becomes possible to tackle if the original model is replaced by a reliable and robust metamodel.

Acknowledgement. This work was performed in the frame of the project ANGUS+ funded by the Federal Ministry of Education and Research (BMBF) under grant no. 03EK3022C. The authors are grateful for their support.

References

1. Cristescu, N.: Elastic viscoplastic constitutive equations for rock. Int. J. Rock Mech. Min. Sci. Geomech. **24**, 271–281 (1987)
2. Günther, R., Salzer, K.: A model for rock salt, describing transient, stationary, and accelerated creep and dilatancy. In: 6th Conference on The Mechanical Behavior of Salt- SALTMECH6, Hannover, Germany, 22–25 May (2007)
3. Hampel, A., Schulze, O.: The composite dilatancy model: a constitutive model for the mechanical behavior of rock salt. In: 6th Conference on The Mechanical Behavior of Salt- SALTMECH6, Hannover, Germany, 22–25 May (2007)
4. Minkley, M., Muehlbauer, J.: Constitutive models to describe the mechanical behavior of salt rocks and the imbedded weakness planes. In: 6th Conference on The Mechanical Behavior of Salt- SALTMECH6, Hannover, Germany, 22–25 May (2007)
5. Heusermann, S., Rolfs, O., Schmidt, U.: Nonlinear finite element analysis of solution mined storage caverns in rock salt using the LUBBY2 constitutive model. Comput. Struct. **81**, 629–638 (2003)
6. Meier, J., Rudolph, S., Schanz, T.: Effective algorithm for parameter back calculation-geotechnical applications. Bautechnik **86**, 86–97 (2009)

7. Meier, J., Moser, M., Datcheva, M., Schanz, T.: Numerical modeling and inverse parameter estimation of the large-scale mass movement Gradenbach in Carinthia (Austria). Acta Geotech. **8**, 355–371 (2013)
8. Knabe, T., Schweiger, F.H., Schanz, T.: Calibration of constitutive parameters by inverse analysis for a geotechnical boundary problem. Can. Geotech. J. **49**, 170–183 (2012)
9. Levasseur, S., Malecot, Y., Boulon, M., Flavigny, E.: Soil parameter identification using a genetic algorithm. Int. J. Numer. Anal. Met. **39**, 189–213 (2008)
10. Buljak, V.: Proper orthogonal decomposition and radial basis functions algorithm for diagnostic procedure based on inverse analysis. FME Trans. **38**, 129–136 (2010)
11. Bolzon, G., Buljak, V.: An effective computational tool for parametric studies and identification problems in materials mechanics. Comput. Mech. **48**, 657–687 (2011)

Constitutive Parameter Adjustment for Mechanized Tunneling with Reference to Sub-system Effects

Chenyang Zhao[1(✉)], Arash Alimardani Lavasan[1], Thomas Barciaga[1], Raoul Hölter[1], Maria Datcheva[2], and Tom Schanz[1]

[1] Chair of Foundation Engineering, Soil and Rock Mechanics, Ruhr-Universität Bochum, Gebäude IC 5/115, Universitätssträe 150, 44801 Bochum, Germany
chenyang.zhao@rub.de
[2] Institute of Mechanics, Bulgarian Academy of Sciences, Acad. G. Bonchev St., bl. 4, 1113 Sofia, Bulgaria

Abstract. In this research, the effect of sub-system on model response for mechanized tunneling process has been taken into consideration. The main aim of this study is to modify the constitutive parameters in a way that the best agreement between numerical results and measurements is obtained. The sub-system includes supporting pressure at the face of the TBM, contraction along the TBM-shield and grouting pressure in the annular gap. The commercially available finite element code, PLAXIS is adopted to simulate the construction process. The soil behavior during the excavation is numerically reproduced by utilizing Hardening Soil model with small strain stiffness (HSsmall). The constitutive parameters are obtained via sensitivity and back analyses while they have been calibrated based on the real measurement of Western Scheldt tunnel in the Netherlands. Both local and global sensitivity analyses are used to distinguish which parameters are most influencing the soil deformation. Thereafter, the model validation is accomplished by applying different scenarios for face pressure distributions with respect to the slope of the tunnel. In addition, the effect of contraction factor is modified individually or coupled with the variation of grouting pressure. Evaluating the influence of the sub-system is conducted to assess its effects on the model responses and to seek the possibility to decrease the disagreement between the calculated displacement and real measured data.

Keywords: Mechanized tunneling · Numerical simulation · Sensitivity analysis · Meta-modeling · Back analysis · Sub-system

1 Introduction

In order to overcome the plight that limited space can be used for public transportation in urban area, shield supported tunneling has been widely applied.

I. Dimov et al. (Eds.): NMA 2014, LNCS 8962, pp. 217–225, 2015.
DOI: 10.1007/978-3-319-15585-2_24

Numerical simulation as an efficient and useful tool can be conducted to predict the soil deformation before and during the tunnel construction.

This paper mainly focuses on the effects of sub-system on numerical model response. The sub-system includes the face pressure in front of Tunnel Boring Machine (TBM), contraction along the TBM-shield and grouting pressure at the tail of TBM [1]. To avoid the collapse of soil at the excavation face of TBM, face pressure is applied to maintain the balance against with the earth pressure. Conicity shape of TBM means the cross sectional area at the tail is smaller than the front of TBM. It makes the excavation process efficient. Contraction factor is applied to simulate the volume loss due to overcut zone, it increases from the front towards the tail of TBM and keeps constant along the lining segments. Grouting pressure is injected at the tail of TBM to fill the gap between the lining segments and surrounding soils, which aims to decrease the surface settlement.

The Western Scheldt tunnel is located under the Scheldt river in the Netherlands and it is constructed by slurry shield TBM. The tunnel has a length of 6.6 Km and the diameter is 11.33 m. The thickness of each lining segment is 0.45 m and its length is 2.00 m. The total length of TBM is 10.95 m and there is some additional length for the cutting head. The excavation domain consists of several clay and sand layers. The mechanical properties of soil layers are summarized in [2]. Water level is about 1.5 m below the ground surface during tunnel construction.

2 Methodology

2.1 Numerical Simulation of Mechanized Tunneling

Mechanized excavation of Western Scheldt tunnel is simulated via commercially available finite element code $PLAXIS$. To reproduce the soil behavior during tunnel excavation, Hardening soil model with small strain stiffness (HSsmall) is implemented [3,4]. The initial soil constitutive parameters are given in Table 1. Due to the absence of in situ investigation, some parameters are assumed by authors according to the type of soil and other existing parameters.

A total length of 88 m tunnel excavation is simulated in this paper, and the tunnel has an inclination of 4.3 %. The TBM-shield and the lining segments are modeled as circular plate elements with linear elastic model. Young's modulus of lining segment and TBM-shield is 22 MPa and 210 MPa, respectively. Poisson ratio of lining segment and TBM-shield is 0.1 and 0.3, respectively.

Based on some trial analyses, the final mesh discretization and boundary condition are selected in a way that the model response is independent to them. The 3D FE-model has dimensions of 150 m long in X-axis direction, 100 m wide in Y-axis direction and 71 m deep in Z-axis direction (See Fig. 1). These dimensions only represent half of the model due to the symmetry condition. Furthermore, a discretized mesh with a total number of 26,538 10-node tetrahedral elements is adopted.

Table 1. Soil constitutive parameters for HSsmall model

Parameter	Soil layers							Unit
	Dike	K1	Z1	BK1	BK2	GZ2	K2	
φ	20	22	34	28	28	34	40	[°]
ψ	0	0	4	0	0	4	0	[°]
c	5	5	6.4	20	20	11.4	40	[kN/m^2]
E_{50}^{ref}	11 000	24 000	35 000	25 000	30 000	30 000	50 000	[kN/m^2]
E_{oed}^{ref}	11 000	24 000	35 000	25 000	30 000	30 000	50 000	[kN/m^2]
E_{ur}^{ref}	30 000	60 000	80 000	60 000	100 000	90 000	180 000	[kN/m^2]
G_0^{ref}	40 000	150 000	140 000	65 000	100 000	110 000	150 000	[kN/m^2]
$\gamma_{0.7}$	0.0002	0.0002	0.0002	0.0002	0.0002	0.0002	0.00015	[-]
m	0.7	0.7	0.5	0.7	0.7	0.5	0.7	[-]
γ_{unsat}	19	18	18	18	17	17	17	[kN/m^3]
γ_{sat}	20	20	19	21	19.3	20.2	20	[kN/m^3]
K_0^{nc}	0.66	0.63	0.44	0.53	0.53	0.40	0.36	[-]
OCR	1.0	1.0	1.0	2.7	2.8	2.5	3.0	[-]

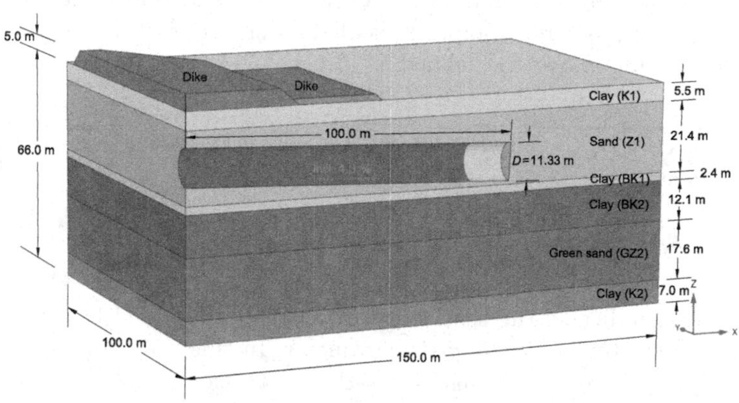

Fig. 1. 3D model geometry

According to the construction reality, the face pressure increases with the advancement of the TBM due to changing the embedment depth. In initial prediction, the face pressure distribution keeps constant for all the excavation stages and the value linearly increases from 137 kN/m^2 at tunnel's crown to 250 kN/m^2 at tunnel's bottom. To simulate the volume loss caused by overcut and conicity of TBM, contraction factor is applied to the plate elements which represent the TBM and lining segments. It increases linearly from 1.4 % at the front of TBM towards 3.8 % at the tail of TBM. Since in reality, the measured surface settlement is quite large and the value of applied grouting pressure is uncertain, the grouting pressure is not considered in the initial prediction.

The consequential excavation process is modeled by staged calculation. The TBM is simulated as 12 m long plate elements. In each excavation, the TBM advances 2.0 m which is the length of one lining segment. The soil elements in front of TBM is deactivated and the face pressure is activated. Additionally, the contraction factor is activated when TBM-shield material is assigned to the plate elements. The installation of lining segments are modeled by assigning lining segment material to the plate elements at the tail of TBM.

2.2 Sensitivity and Back Analyses

Sensitivity analysis is an important and efficient tool to estimate the key parameters for geotechnical applications. There are two main groups of sensitivity analyses, Local Sensitivity Analysis (LSA) and Global Sensitivity Analysis (GSA). For LSA, the model response with respect to the input parameters is evaluated at a given local point and based on the calculation of derivatives. Therefore, the information provided by LSA highly depends on the given local point and the step size used in approximation of derivatives. The result may be not reliable for non-linear models. While GSA explores the whole space of input parameters which makes the result independent of the model nature. In this paper, Variance-Based (VB) method of GSA is applied to evaluate the uncertainty of input parameters. Composite scaled sensitivity index CSS_j and total effect sensitivity index S_{Ti} are defined as [5,9]:

$$CSS_j = \sqrt{\frac{1}{m}\sum_{i=1}^{m}(SS_{i,j})^2}, SS_{i,j} = \left(\frac{\Delta y_i}{\Delta x_j}\right)x_j = \left(\frac{y_i\left(x_j + \Delta x_j\right) - y_i\left(x_j\right)}{\Delta x_j}\right)x_j \quad (1)$$

$$S_i = \frac{\mathbf{y_A}^T\mathbf{y_{Ci}} - n\left(\bar{\mathbf{y}}_\mathbf{A}\right)^2}{\mathbf{y_A}^T\mathbf{y_A} - n\left(\bar{\mathbf{y}}_\mathbf{A}\right)^2}, S_{Ti} = \frac{\left(\mathbf{y_B} - \mathbf{y_{Ci}}\right)^T\left(\mathbf{y_B} - \mathbf{y_{Ci}}\right)}{2\mathbf{y_B}^T\mathbf{y_B} - 2n\left(\bar{\mathbf{y}}_\mathbf{B}\right)^2} \quad (2)$$

Equation (1) indicates the sensitivity information provided by i-th observation points for the estimation of j-th parameter. In this research, $\Delta x_j = 0.1x_j$. $y_i(x_j)$ is scalar of model response for i-th observation point calculated with corresponding input scalar of j-th parameter x_j. $m = 8$ is the number of observation points. In Eq. (2), **A** and **B** are two independent (n, k) matrices and **Ci**, whose columns are copied from matrix **B** except the i-th column copied from its corresponding column in **A**. $\mathbf{y_A}$, $\mathbf{y_B}$, and $\mathbf{y_{Ci}}$ are vectors of model responses calculated with corresponding input vector of matrices **A**, **B**, and **Ci**, respectively. $\bar{\mathbf{y}}_\mathbf{A}$ and $\bar{\mathbf{y}}_\mathbf{B}$ are the mean value of model response calculated with all the input vectors of $\mathbf{y_A}$ and $\mathbf{y_B}$.

Back analysis has been widely used in engineering problems [6,7]. It is employed to identify the unknown parameters with field measurements. In this paper, Partial Swarm Optimization (PSO) algorithm [8] is implemented in back analysis to find the best optimized values of selected parameters.

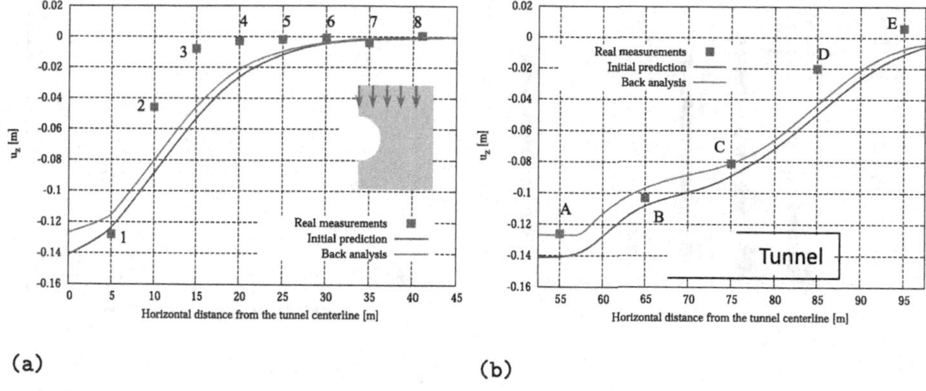

Fig. 2. Numerical prediction of (a) transverse surface settlement (b) longitudinal surface settlement

3 Results

Figure 2 shows the surface settlements when the initially guessed parameters are assigned. It can be found that the affected zone calculated by FE-model is wider than the real measured data in both transverse and longitudinal directions. For improvement, both local and global sensitivity analyses are applied to estimate the key parameters and reduce the degrees of system freedom. Results of LSA and GSA are given in Fig. 3. It is obvious that parameters of sand layer (Z1) play the most important role in soil deformation due to the fact that tunnel is excavated in Z1 layer.

According to the result of GSA, sensitivity of parameter changes with the variation of observation points. Displacements of points above the tunnel are most sensitivity to the friction angle, this is because of the dominating plastic deformation. While for observation points far away from the tunnel, E_{ur}^{ref} and G_0^{ref} generate increasing importance, which is due to the gradually increasing elastic deformation. Since ground settlements at observation points 1–3 are most sensitive to φ, E_{oed}^{ref} and E_{ur}^{ref} of Z1 and K1 layers, they are selected as the key parameters which need to be modified by back analysis. Surface settlements calculated with modified soil parameters are showed in Fig. 2.

In order to further improve the results, effects of sub-systems on model response are studied. Different scenarios are described in Table 2. Figure 4 describes the influence of face pressure. Scenario 1 uses the same pressure distribution described in former simulation. Considering the slope of tunnel, depth dependent face pressure is applied in scenario 2 to study the effect of varying face pressure on model response. Since in reality, face pressure keeps at a low level in the first several excavations before increasing to a high level, scenario 3 is applied to simulate the reality. The result shows high face pressure decreases the surface settlement in longitudinal direction. It means depth dependent face pressure increases the face stability when the earth pressure and water pressure

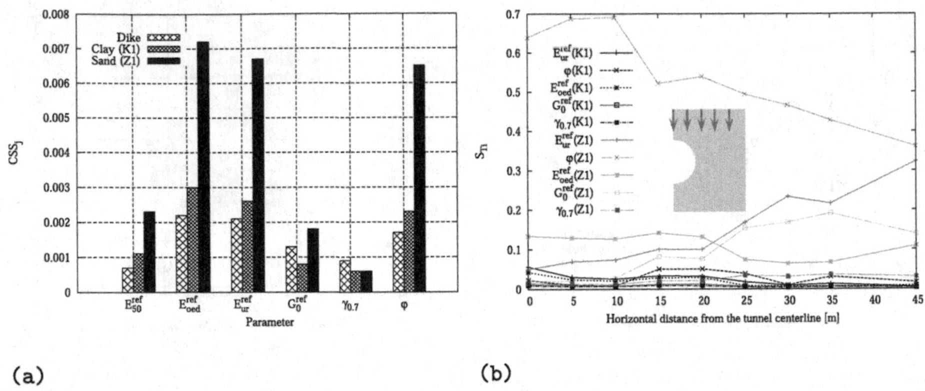

Fig. 3. Results of (a) LSA (b) GSA

increase with the advancement of TBM. Overall, depth dependent face pressure provides surface settlement profiles which match the real measurement better.

Table 2. Different scenarios to study the sub-system effects

No. of scenario	Description of sub-system		
	Face pressure	Contraction factor	Grouting pressure
1	Constant	1.4 % to 3.8 %	Not applied
2	Depth dependent	1.4 % to 3.8 %	Not applied
3	Depth dependent	1.4 % to 3.8 %	Not applied
4	Constant	1.26 % to 3.42 %	Not applied
5	Constant	1.54 % to 4.18 %	Not applied
6	Constant	1.54 % to 4.18 %	75 kPa (constant)
7	Constant	1.54 % to 4.18 %	150 kPa (constant)

Figure 5 shows the effects of contraction factor on model response. The value of contraction factor is decreased and increased 10 % respectively in Scenario 4 and Scenario 5. It is obvious that contraction factor has important effect on surface settlements in both transverse and longitudinal directions. This is due to the fact that surface settlement is mainly caused by the volume loss of soil during mechanized excavation.

In the above simulations, only face pressure and contraction factor are applied to the numerical model. Based on Scenario 5, grouting pressure is applied together with the increased contraction factor to seek possibility to decrease the disagreement between the numerical result and real measurements. The results are given in Fig. 6. It is clear that surface settlement profiles are highly affected by the grouting

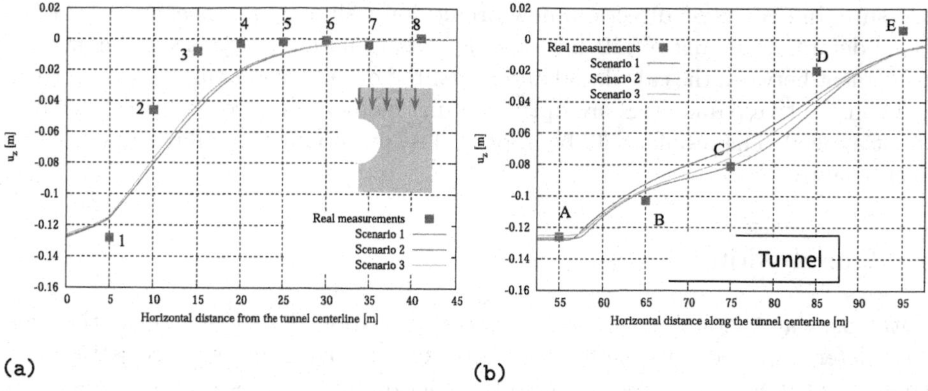

Fig. 4. Effect of face pressure on (a) transverse surface settlement (b) longitudinal surface settlement

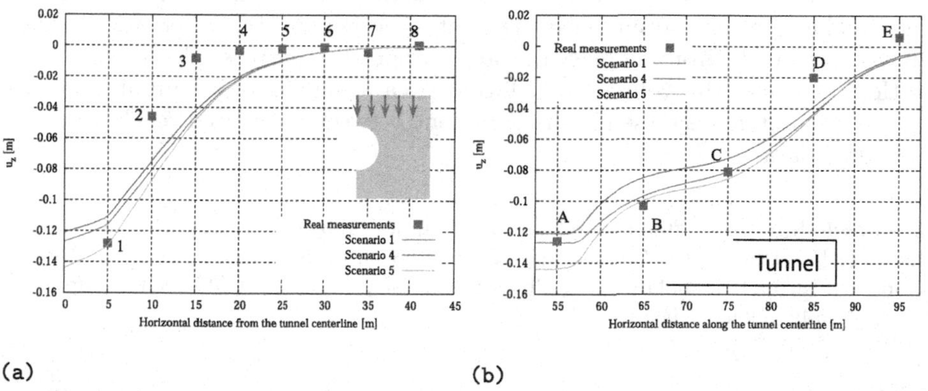

Fig. 5. Effect of contraction factor on (a) transverse surface settlement (b) longitudinal surface settlement

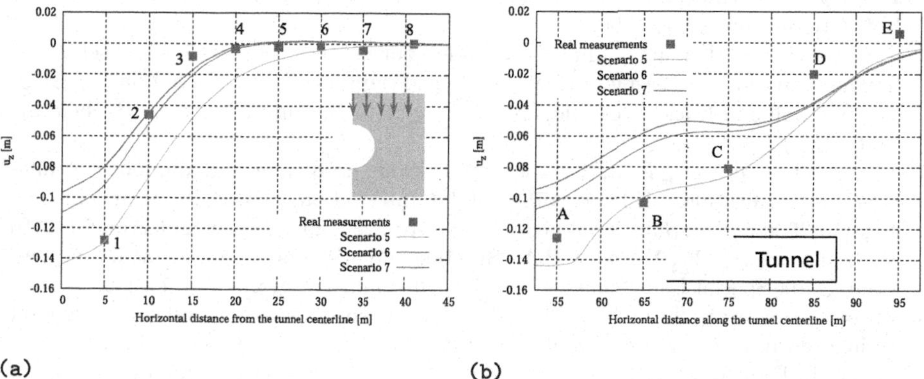

Fig. 6. Effect of grouting pressure on (a) transverse surface settlement (b) longitudinal surface settlement

pressure. In transverse direction, new prediction well matches measured data for small deformation area. While for large deformation area, there is significant disagreement between the calculated and measured data. The possible reason is that soil constitutive parameters are optimized in the model where grouting pressure is not applied. The result would be improved by modifying the soil parameters via back analysis.

4 Conclusions

Both local and global sensitivity analyses are applied to distinguish the key parameter which governs the model response. It is found that surface settlement above the tunnel is most sensitive to the friction angle and stiffness of soil.

Depth dependent face pressure performs better in predicting the soil deformation when tunnel has an inclination. Surface settlement mainly comes from the volume loss of tunnel excavation, contraction factor influences both transverse and longitudinal ground displacement, especially for the observation points above the tunnel. Grouting pressure can be applied to decrease the large surface settlement caused by volume loss during excavation. Modified input parameters of sub-system decrease the disagreement between calculated result and real measured data.

Acknowledgments. This research has been supported by the German Research Foundation (DFG) through the Collaborative Research Center (SFB 837). The first author is sponsored through a scholarship by China Scholarships Council (CSC). These supports are gratefully acknowledged.

References

1. Bezuijen, A., Talmon, A.M.: Processes around a TBM. In: Proceedings of the 6th International Symposium on Geotechnical Aspects of Underground Construction in Soft Ground, pp. 10–12 (2008)
2. Brodesser, M.: Adäquates Simulationsmodell zur numerischen Analyse maschineller Tunnelvortriebe am Beispiel des Westerscheldetunnels. Chair of Foundation Engineering, Soil and Rock Mechanics, Ruhr University Bochum, Germany. Bachelorarbeit (2012)
3. Schanz, T., Vermeer, P.A., Bonnier, P.G.: The hardening soil model: Formulation and verification. In: Proceedings of 1st International PLAXIS Symposium on Beyond 2000 in Computational Geotechnics, pp. 281–296. Taylor and Franci (1999)
4. Benz, T., Schwab, R., Vermeer, P.A.: Small-strain stiffness in geotechnical analyses, Bautechnik Special Issue 2009 - Geotechnical Engineering, pp. 16–27 (2009)
5. Miro, S., Hartmann, D., Schanz, T.: Global sensitivity analysis for subsoil parameter estimation in mechanized tunneling. Comput. Geotech. **56**, 80–88 (2014)
6. Meier, J., Datcheva, M., Schanz, T.: Identification of obstacles ahead of tunnel face applying inverse approach. In: Proceedings of ECCOMAS Thematic Conference on Computational Methods in Tunneling, pp. 673–680, Bochum, Germany (2009)

7. Zarev, V., Datcheva, M., Schanz, T., Dimov, I.: Soil-model parameter identification via back analysis for numerical simulation of shield tunneling. In: Proceedings of 3rd International Conference on Computational Methods in Tunnelling and Subsurface Engineering, pp. 345–356. Bochum, Germany (2013)
8. Kennedy, J., Eberhart, R.C.: Particle swarm optimization. Proc. IEEE Int. Conf. Neural Netw. **4**, 1942–1948 (1995)
9. Zhao, C., Lavasan, A.A., Schanz, T.: Sensitivity analysis of the model response in mechanized tunnelling simulation - A case study assessment. In: Proceedings of 4th International Conference on Engineering Optimization, 2014, Lisbon, Portugal (2014)

Modeling of Textiles as Nets of One-Dimensional Hyperelastic Strings with Friction Controlled by Capstan Equation

Vladimir Shiryaev[1,2](✉) and Julia Orlik[1]

[1] Fraunhofer ITWM, Fraunhofer-Platz 1, 67663 Kaiserslautern, Germany
{vladimir.shiryaev,julia.orlik}@itwm.fraunhofer.de
http://www.itwm.fraunhofer.de/sys/shiryaev.html,
http://www.itwm.fraunhofer.de/sys/orlik.html

[2] Technical University of Kaiserslautern, Gottlieb-Daimler-Straße 47, 67663 Kaiserslautern, Germany

Abstract. This paper deals with the computational modeling of the in-plane stretch behavior of knitted textiles. Yarns in textiles are modeled as one-dimensional hyperelastic strings with frictional contact. The model is the limiting case of the three-dimensional contact model, as diameters of the yarns' cross-sections tend to zero. The model is analyzed theoretically and solved by the finite element method with one-dimensional hyperelastic truss elements, with an extension to frictional point-to-point contact. Numerical results for in-plane loading experiments obtained by this approach are discussed and compared with results of real measurements.

Keywords: Hyperelastic strings · Textile modeling · Coulomb friction · Capstan equation

1 Introduction

Due to the difference in size between thickness of yarns, dimensions of knitting patterns, and macroscopic size of textile products, textiles are generally multi-scale structures. This scale difference causes numerical difficulties for direct numerical treatment. Therefore, various techniques are required to handle such problems.

Our aim in this work is to develop a new model for textiles, where yarns' and whole textiles' bending behavior is not important. We have textile design assistance in mind, therefore the model must meet the following requirements: the model should be able to handle large strains, large displacements, and Coulomb friction model; the model must be able to reflect different knitting patterns and must not require construction of complicated meshes; the model must admit an implementation capable to run in time of order of several minutes for meshes modeling textiles of size of order of several centimeters on modern desktop machines; the model must allow arbitrary physically reasonable force-stretch curves of the constituent fibers. We work with a simplified geometrical model

I. Dimov et al. (Eds.): NMA 2014, LNCS 8962, pp. 226–233, 2015.
DOI: 10.1007/978-3-319-15585-2_25

to meet the first three requirements. Textiles are represented by graphs, where chains of edges represent fibers and some of the nodes represent contact spots. A detailed description is provided in Sect. 2.

To satisfy the last requirement, we employ a special 1D hyperelasticity model. It is described in Sect. 2. It is similar to the model presented in [1,12]. We use its formulation for arbitrary force-stretch curves. Under "physically reasonable" force-stretch curves we understand monotone and piecewise differentiable curves. Since these properties are usually observed in measurements, monotone polynomial interpolants of the measured curves can be plugged directly in our model with no additional parameter fitting.

Our friction model is based on the Capstan equation, also known as Euler-Eytelwein formula. We derive the particular form suitable for our model from Coulomb friction model. The Capstan equation and its extensions are well known in textile industry and other branches of technology. It is widely used for measurements of frictional properties of fibers, see [3,5].

We conclude Sect. 2 with the mathematical problem statement for the whole model. We use the nonlinear evolution equations formulation, prove the corresponding convexity properties of the model and then use its equivalence to the energetic solutions concept to justify our numerical algorithm. Evolution equations are used for various models with rate-independent dissipation, see [8,9]. Application of Capstan equation with the reformulated 1D hyperelastic model to simulation of textiles is novel. A brief description of the numerical algorithm concludes Sect. 2.

Finally, numerical examples are presented in Sect. 4.

2 Problem Statement

2.1 Description of Textile Geometry Model

Fabrics are approximated by weighted graphs similar to the one in Fig. 1. Denote such a graph by Γ. Fibers are approximated by chains of edges of Γ. The contact points between the fibers are a subset of the nodes of Γ.

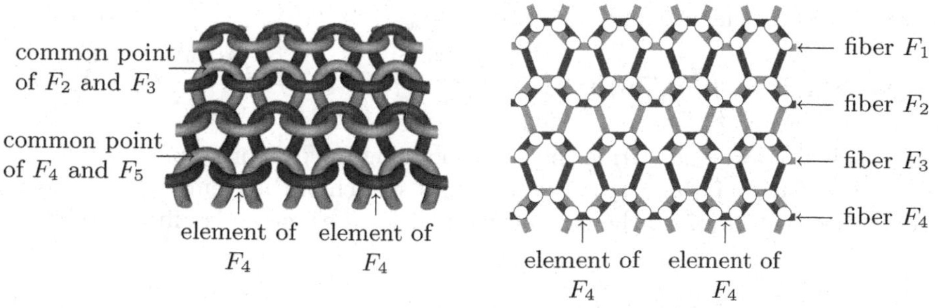

Fig. 1. Knitted fabric and its 1D graph model

Let us introduce rigorous notation. The textile is a collection of fibers F_i, while each fiber F_i consists of elements e_i^j, where e_i^j is the j-th element of the i-th fiber. Fibers are disjoint sets. Each element e_i^j is defined by a pair of nodes $(n_{i,j}^l, n_{i,j}^r)$, and a set of parameters: an undeformed length L_i^j, an initial undeformed length $\mathcal{L}_i^j$, a current length $l_i^j = |\boldsymbol{x}(n_{i,j}^r) - \boldsymbol{x}(n_{i,j}^l)|$ (the symbol $\boldsymbol{x}$ is introduced below), and material properties described in Sect. 2.2. All nodes of Γ form a set N. For each node $n \in N$ a reference position $\boldsymbol{X}(n)$ in $\mathbb{R}^3$ is defined. Denote the vector of all undeformed lengths L_i^j by $\mathbf{L}$. E is the set of all elements e_i^j. The set of common points between two different fibers F_i and F_j is denoted by $N_c^{i,j}$. This is actually the set of contact points between F_i and F_j. It is required that $N_c^{i,j} \subseteq N$ for all i and j. A union of contact nodes is denoted by $S_C = \cup_{i,j} N_c^{i,j}$. The set of contact nodes of F_i is N_i^c.

For each node n define the displacement field $\mathbf{u}(n) = \boldsymbol{x}(n) - \boldsymbol{X}(n)$, where $\boldsymbol{x}(n)$ is the position of the node in the current configuration. For each point of an element e_i^j the displacement field is interpolated by an affine function between the corresponding nodes $n_{i,j}^l$ and $n_{i,j}^r$.

2.2 Description of Hyperelasticity Model

For the modeling of each single element a hyperelastic material is considered, see [2,13]. In one-dimensional case the elasticity model is defined by an elastic energy density function $W(\nabla \mathbf{u})$. Let x_1 be the longitudinal coordinate of the element in the reference configuration.

Assumption 1. *Let $\tilde{f}(\varepsilon)$ be a force-strain curve of an element, then*

1. *$\tilde{f}(x)$ is strictly monotone for $x > 0$,*
2. *$\tilde{f}(x) = 0$ for $x \leq 0$,*
3. *$\tilde{f}(x)$ is continuous and piecewise C^1.*

We use the following form for the density:

$$W(\nabla \mathbf{u}) = \frac{1}{A} \int_0^{\varepsilon(\nabla \mathbf{u})} \tilde{f}(\bar{\varepsilon})\, d\bar{\varepsilon},\ \varepsilon(\nabla \mathbf{u}) = \left\{ \left[1 + \frac{\partial u_1}{\partial x_1} \right]^2 + \left[\frac{\partial u_2}{\partial x_1} \right]^2 + \left[\frac{\partial u_3}{\partial x_1} \right]^2 \right\}^{\frac{1}{2}} - 1.$$

In this work the displacement field in elements is affine and the total strain energy U of an element e is thus given by

$$U(\nabla \mathbf{u}, L) = \int_e W(\nabla \mathbf{u})\, dx_1 = L \int_0^{\varepsilon(\nabla \mathbf{u})} \tilde{f}(\bar{\varepsilon})\, d\bar{\varepsilon} = L \int_1^{\lambda(\nabla \mathbf{u})} f(\bar{\lambda})\, d\bar{\lambda},$$

where $f(\lambda(\nabla \mathbf{u})) = \tilde{f}(\varepsilon(\nabla \mathbf{u}))$ is the corresponding force to principal stretch relationship, $\lambda(\nabla \mathbf{u}) = 1 + \varepsilon(\nabla \mathbf{u})$ is the principal stretch of the element, and L is its undeformed length. Since the displacement field in elements is affine, we have

$$U(\mathbf{u}, L) = L \int_0^{\frac{l(\mathbf{u})}{L} - 1} \tilde{f}(\bar{\varepsilon})\, d\bar{\varepsilon} = L \int_1^{\frac{l(\mathbf{u})}{L}} f(\bar{\lambda})\, d\bar{\lambda}. \tag{1}$$

Note that if the element is compressed, then its elastic energy is zero.

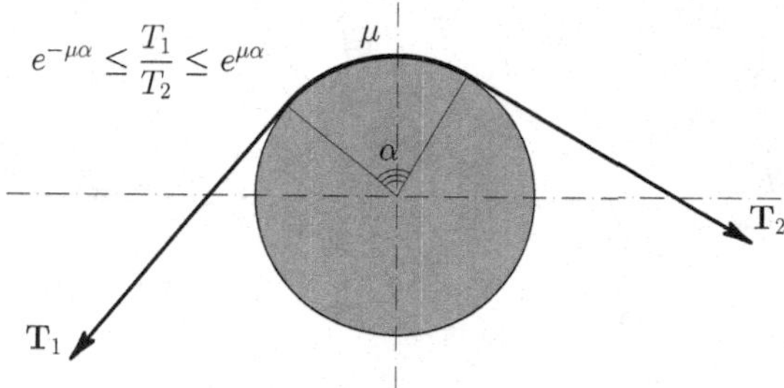

Fig. 2. The Capstan equation

2.3 Description of Friction Model

In case of contact between an inextensible fiber and a rigid cylindrical surface the friction stick or slip condition is given by the Euler-Eytelwein formula, also known as the Capstan equation or the belt friction equation [3–5]. The Euler-Eytelwein stability condition is presented in Fig. 2 and has the following form:

$$\begin{aligned} e^{-\mu\alpha} < \frac{T_1}{T_2} < e^{\mu\alpha} &\Rightarrow \dot{s} = 0, \text{ stick phase,} \\ e^{-\mu\alpha} = \frac{T_1}{T_2} \text{ or } \frac{T_1}{T_2} = e^{\mu\alpha} &\Rightarrow \exists\, \kappa > 0 \text{ s. t. } \dot{s} = -\kappa[T], \text{ slip phase,} \end{aligned} \tag{2}$$

where α defines the total angle, swept by the fiber, and $\dot{s}$ is the distance, which the fiber slides in the tangential direction to the contact interface. The total work of friction forces is given by

$$j_{\text{capstan}}(\dot{s}) = \mu \min(T_1, T_2)(e^{\mu\alpha} - 1)\,|\dot{s}|\,.$$

This result is extrapolated for pairs of fibers in contact, where α is computed from the angle between the direction vectors of the elements that are adjacent to the contact node. In the case of extensible fiber the following expression should be used:

$$j_{\text{Fric}} = \mu\,|\dot{s}| \min(T_1, T_2) \int_0^{\alpha} f^{-1}\left(\min(T_1, T_2) e^{\mu\xi}\right) e^{\mu\xi}\, d\xi. \tag{3}$$

Slip Variables and Undeformed Lengths. Redistribution of undeformed lengths of adjacent elements in fibers is characterized by slip variables. Consider a sample fiber F in Fig. 3.

Assume that F consists of $j+1$ elements $\{e^0, e^1, \ldots, e^j\}$. Then during the loading process their undeformed lengths $L^0, L^1, \ldots, L^j$ change in such a way that (2) is satisfied.

Consider two adjacent elements e^k and e^{k+1}. Let the undeformed fiber length increment s^{k+1}, i.e. the material redistribution parameter or slip variable, move from element e^k to element e^{k+1}. Then we observe, that after this redistribution

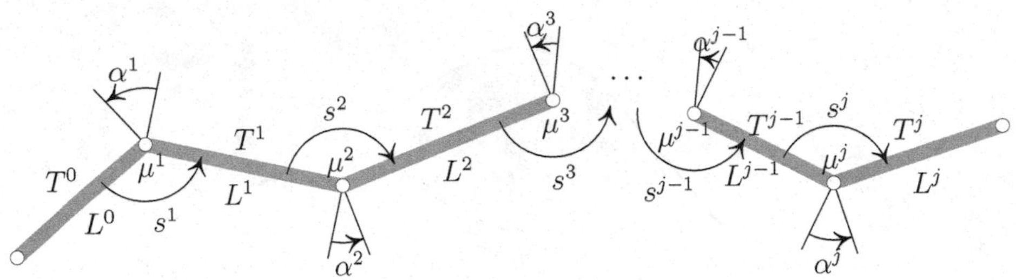

Fig. 3. Slip variables and undeformed lengths of the sample fiber F.

we have $L^k = \mathcal{L}^k - s^{k+1} + s^k$. Obviously, the latter relation between L^k and $\mathcal{L}^k$ automatically ensures that the length conservation equation $\sum_k L^k = \sum_k \mathcal{L}^k$ holds. It is also required that $L^i \geq \varepsilon_{\text{len}}$, where ε_{len} is some small positive constant.

2.4 Description of Aggregate Model

Let us introduce notation $\mathbf{s}$ and $\dot{\mathbf{s}}$ for vectors of all slip variables s_i^j and their derivatives with respect to time. The total elastic energy U_{tot} of the mesh is the sum of the energies of all its elements (1):

$$U_{\text{tot}}(\mathbf{u}, \mathbf{s}) = \sum_{e \in E} U_e(\mathbf{u}, \mathbf{s}),$$

where U_e is defined according to (1). Introduce the regularization term R and the regularized total elastic energy $U_{\text{tot}}^{\text{reg}}$:

$$\text{R}(\mathbf{u}, \mathbf{s}) = \varepsilon_r(\langle \mathbf{u}, \mathbf{u}\rangle + \langle \mathbf{s}, \mathbf{s}\rangle), \quad U_{\text{tot}}^{\text{reg}}(\mathbf{u}, \mathbf{s}) = \text{R}(\mathbf{u}, \mathbf{s}) + U_{\text{tot}}(\mathbf{u}, \mathbf{s}),$$

where $\varepsilon_r > 0$ and the notation $\langle \boldsymbol{u}, \boldsymbol{v}\rangle$ denotes the standard inner product.

The energy dissipated by friction can be computed as the sum of energies, dissipated on each particular fiber:

$$\jmath_{\text{tot}}(\mathbf{u}, \mathbf{s}, \dot{\mathbf{u}}, \dot{\mathbf{s}}) = \sum_{F_i \in E} \jmath_{\text{Fric}}^{F_i}(\mathbf{u}, \mathbf{s}, \dot{\mathbf{u}}, \dot{\mathbf{s}}),$$

where $\jmath_{\text{Fric}}^{F_i}$ is defined according to (3) as a sum of works of friction forces in all contact nodes of fiber F_i.

Since the stretching process is path-dependent, the additional parametrization with the variable t is used. The stretching process is modeled by time-dependent Dirichlet conditions.

The governing principle is a doubly nonlinear evolution equation as stated in [7]: find vector-functions of time $\mathbf{u} \in W^{1,1}([0;T], V_{\mathbf{u}})$ and $\mathbf{s} \in W^{1,1}([0;T], V_{\mathbf{s}})$ such that

$$0 \in \partial_{\mathbf{u},\mathbf{s}} U_{\text{tot}}(\mathbf{u}, \mathbf{s}) + \partial_{\dot{\mathbf{u}},\dot{\mathbf{s}}} \jmath_{\text{tot}}(\mathbf{u}, \mathbf{s}, \dot{\mathbf{u}}, \dot{\mathbf{s}}), \text{ for all time instants } t,$$
$$\mathbf{s}(t) \in \boldsymbol{S}_{\text{adm}}, \ \mathbf{u}(t)\big|_{\partial\Omega_D} = \mathbf{D}(\mathbf{x}, t), \ \forall t \in [0;T],$$

where $V_{\mathbf{u}}$ and $V_{\mathbf{s}}$ are the corresponding finite-dimensional spaces. The notation $\partial_{a,b}$ denotes the subdifferential (see [11]) with respect to variables a and b. Further the following more convenient form will be used: find vector-functions of time $\mathbf{u} \in W^{1,1}([0;T], V_{\mathbf{u}}^{\mathrm{D}})$ and $\mathbf{s} \in W^{1,1}([0;T], V_{\mathbf{s}})$ such that

$$\begin{aligned} &0 \in \partial_{\mathbf{u},\mathbf{s}} U_{\mathrm{tot}}^{\mathrm{D}}(t, \mathbf{u}, \mathbf{s}) + \partial_{\dot{\mathbf{u}},\dot{\mathbf{s}}} j_{\mathrm{tot}}^{\mathrm{D}}(t, \mathbf{u}, \mathbf{s}, \dot{\mathbf{u}}, \dot{\mathbf{s}}), \\ &\mathbf{s}(t) \in \boldsymbol{S}_{\mathrm{adm}}, \end{aligned} \quad \text{for all time instants } t, \tag{4}$$

where $U_{\mathrm{tot}}^{\mathrm{D}}$, $U_{\mathrm{tot}}^{\mathrm{Dreg}}$, and $j_{\mathrm{tot}}^{\mathrm{D}}$ are basically U_{tot}, $U_{\mathrm{tot}}^{\mathrm{reg}}$ and j_{tot} with the Dirichlet conditions plugged in, and $V_{\mathbf{u}}^{\mathrm{D}}$ is the corresponding finite-dimensional space.

3 Properties of the Model and Numerical Algorithm

Lemma 1. *The term $U_{\mathrm{tot}}^{\mathrm{D}}(t, \mathbf{u}, \mathbf{s})$ has positively-semidefinite Hessian matrix with respect to $\mathbf{u}$ and $\mathbf{s}$ on the admissible set $\{\mathbf{s} \colon \mathbf{s} \in \boldsymbol{S}_{\mathrm{adm}}\}$ for all $t \in [0;T]$.*

Lemma 2. *The regularized elastic energy term $U_{\mathrm{tot}}^{\mathrm{Dreg}}(t, \mathbf{u}, \mathbf{s})$ is strictly convex with respect to variables $(\mathbf{u}, \mathbf{s})$ on the admissible set $\{\mathbf{s} \colon \mathbf{s} \in \boldsymbol{S}_{\mathrm{adm}}\}$. The strict convexity is uniform with respect to time with coefficient ε_r.*

Lemma 3. *The frictional energy term $j_{\mathrm{tot}}^{\mathrm{D}}(t, \mathbf{u}, \mathbf{s}, \dot{\mathbf{u}}, \dot{\mathbf{s}})$ is convex with respect to variables $(\dot{\mathbf{u}}, \dot{\mathbf{s}})$ for all $t \in [0;T]$.*

Following [7] and [10], consider the energetic formulation of the problem: find vector-functions of time $\mathbf{u} \in W^{1,1}([0;T], V_{\mathbf{u}}^{\mathrm{D}})$ and $\mathbf{s} \in W^{1,1}([0;T], V_{\mathbf{s}})$ such that

$$U_{\mathrm{tot}}^{\mathrm{D}}(t, \mathbf{u}, \mathbf{s}) \le U_{\mathrm{tot}}^{\mathrm{D}}(t, \hat{\mathbf{u}}, \hat{\mathbf{s}}) + j_{\mathrm{tot}}(t, \mathbf{u}, \mathbf{s}, \hat{\mathbf{u}} - \mathbf{u}, \hat{\mathbf{s}} - \mathbf{s}) \qquad \forall\, \hat{\mathbf{u}} \in V_{\mathbf{u}}^{\mathrm{D}},\ \forall \hat{\mathbf{s}} \in V_{\mathbf{s}} \cap \boldsymbol{S}_{\mathrm{adm}},\ \forall t \in [0, \mathrm{T}], \tag{S}$$

$$U_{\mathrm{tot}}^{\mathrm{D}}(t, \mathbf{u}(t), \mathbf{s}(t)) + \int_0^t j_{\mathrm{tot}}^{\mathrm{D}}(t, \mathbf{u}(\tau), \mathbf{s}(\tau), \dot{\mathbf{u}}(\tau), \dot{\mathbf{s}}(\tau))\, d\tau = \int_0^t \mathrm{P}_{\mathrm{ext}}(t, \mathbf{u}(\tau), \mathbf{s}(\tau))\, d\tau, \tag{E}$$

where the last integral term represents the work of the external forces (caused by the boundary conditions). The connection between statements (S)–(E) and (4) is given by Proposition 2.7 of [7]. The statements are equivalent under proper conditions, which are satisfied in our examples (we do not present this material here due to the lack of space).

For a partition $\{t_\tau^0 = 0 < t_\tau^1 < \ldots < t_\tau^N = \mathrm{T}\}$, $\tau = \max_{j=1,\ldots,N} \{t_\tau^j - t_\tau^{j-1}\}$, consider

Problem 1. Given $(\mathbf{u}_\tau^0, \mathbf{s}_\tau^0) = (\mathbf{u}_0, \mathbf{s}_0)$, find $(\mathbf{u}_\tau^k, \mathbf{s}_\tau^k)$, $k = 1, \ldots, N$ such that

$$(\mathbf{u}_\tau^k, \mathbf{s}_\tau^k) \in \operatorname*{argmin}_{\mathbf{u} \in V_{\mathbf{u}}^{\mathrm{D}}, \mathbf{s} \in \boldsymbol{S}_{\mathrm{adm}}} \left(U_{\mathrm{tot}}^{\mathrm{Dreg}}(t, \mathbf{u}, \mathbf{s}) + j_{\mathrm{tot}}^{\mathrm{D}}(t, \mathbf{u}_\tau^{k-1}, \mathbf{s}_\tau^{k-1}, \mathbf{u} - \mathbf{u}_\tau^{k-1}, \mathbf{s} - \mathbf{s}_\tau^{k-1}) \right).$$

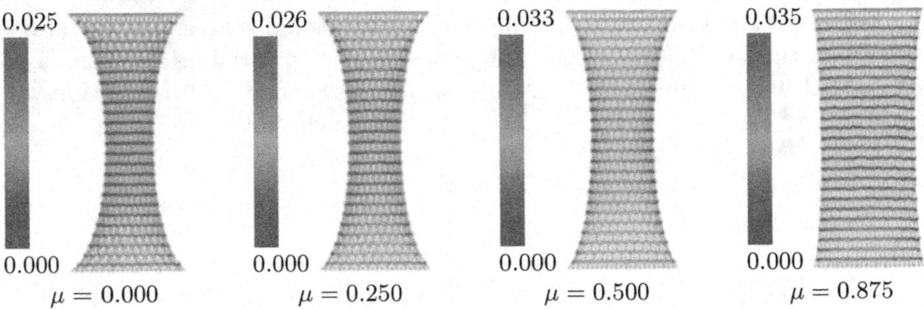

Fig. 4. Tensional force plot of the cutouts for various friction coefficients.

Theorem 1. *Problem 1 has a unique solution and is strongly convex with respect to* $(\mathbf{u}, \mathbf{s})$ *for all admissible* $(t, \mathbf{u}_\tau^{k-1}, \mathbf{s}_\tau^{k-1})$*. The solutions of problem 1 satisfy condition* (S) *for* $U_{\text{tot}}^{\text{Dreg}}$.

The theorem is a corollary of Lemma 4.4 and Corollary 4.5 of [7].

Observe that Problem 1 can be solved numerically. This is the foundation of our numerical strategy. We apply standard regularization technique of the friction term for numeric calculations (see [6]). This renders our problem finite-dimensional and smooth, and standard numerical optimization techniques are applicable. Note that an application of the finite element method with hyperelastic truss elements for our model would yield the same system of equations for each fixed time instant.

4 Numerical Examples

Let us first study the influence of the friction coefficient on the effective behavior of textiles. The results are presented in Fig. 4.

The initially square fabric cutouts are stretched up to 80 % deformation. Geometrical properties of the cutouts are identical, but the friction coefficients differ. As expected, the fabric shows higher contraction for smaller values of the friction coefficient.

We proceed with an investigation of influence of the friction coefficient on the total force applied to the cutouts to reach some fixed deformation.

The results are presented in Fig. 5. The curve for $\mu = 0$ is almost indistinguishable from the curve for $\mu = 0.125$. The higher the friction coefficient, the higher the total applied force for a fixed deformation. This conforms with theoretical expectations.

In the same figure a comparison of measured and computed force for a square cutout of a technical textile is presented. The operating range of the textile measured is between 50 % and 150 %. The figure shows that the model gives a good approximation of the force behavior of the textile.

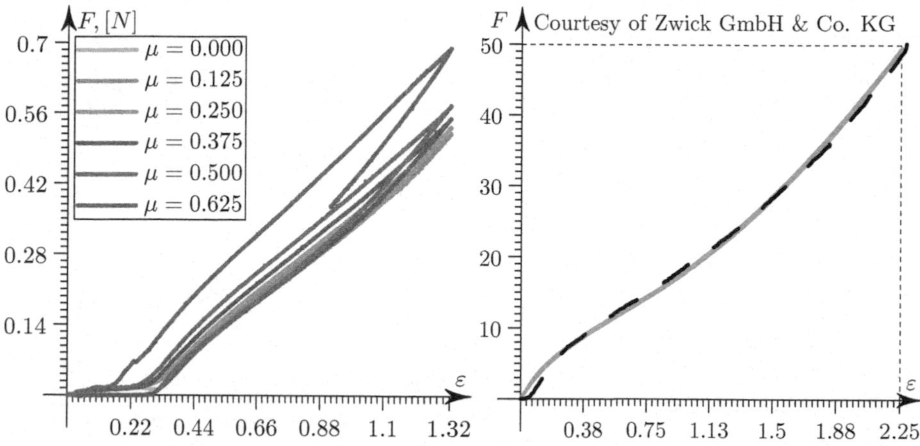

Fig. 5. Hysteresis (on the left) and comparison of computed (green) and measured (dashed) forces for a real fabric sample (on the right).

References

1. Acerbi, E., Buttazzo, G., Percivale, D.: A variational definition of the strain energy for an elastic string. J. Elast. **25**, 137–148 (1991). http://dx.doi.org/10.1007/BF00042462
2. Ciarlet, P.: Mathematical Elasticity: Three-Dimensional Elasticity. Studies in Mathematics and Its Applications. North-Holland, Amsterdam (1993)
3. Gralén, N., Olofsson, B.: Measurement of friction between single fibers. Text. Res. J. **17**(9), 488–496 (1947)
4. Gupta, P.K.: Simple method for measuring the friction coefficient of thin fibers. J. Am. Ceram. Soc. **74**(7), 1692–1694 (1991)
5. Johnson, K.: Contact Mechanics. Cambridge University Press, Cambridge (1987)
6. Kikuchi, N., Oden, J.: Contact Problems in Elasticity: A Study of Variational Inequalities and Finite Element Methods. SIAM Studies in Applied Mathematics. Society for Industrial and Applied Mathematics, Philadelphia (1987)
7. Mielke, A., Rossi, R.: Existence and uniqueness results for general rate-independent hysteresis problems. Math. Models Methods Appl. Sci. **17**(01), 81–123 (2007)
8. Mielke, A., Roubíček, T.: A rate-independent model for inelastic behavior of shape-memory alloys. Multiscale Model. Simul. **1**(4), 571–597 (2003)
9. Mielke, A., Roubíček, T.: Rate-independent damage processes in nonlinear elasticity. Math. Models Methods Appl. Sci. **16**(2), 177–209 (2006). http://www.worldscientific.com/doi/abs/10.1142/S021820250600111X
10. Mielke, A., Theil, F.: On rate-independent hysteresis models. NoDEA, Nonlinear Differ. Equ. Appl. **11**(2), 151–189 (2004)
11. Rockafellar, R.: Convex Analysis. Princeton University Press, Princeton (1997)
12. Trabucho, L., Viaño, J.: Mathematical modelling of rods. In: Ciarlet, P., Lions, J. (eds.) Handbook of Numerical Analysis, vol. 4, pp. 487–974. Elsevier Science (1996)
13. Wriggers, P.: Nonlinear Finite Element Methods. Springer, Heidelberg (2008)

Contributed Papers

Numerical Simulation of Drop Coalescence in the Presence of Inter-Phase Mass Transfer

Ivan Bazhlekov(✉) and Daniela Vasileva

Institute of Mathematics and Informatics, Bulgarian Academy of Sciences, Acad. G. Bonchev Str., Bl. 8, 1113 Sofia, Bulgaria
{i.bazhlekov,vasileva}@math.bas.bg

Abstract. A numerical method for simulation of the deformation and drainage of an axisymmetric film between colliding drops in the presence of inter-phase solute transfer at small capillary and Reynolds numbers and small solute concentration variations is presented. The drops are considered to approach each other under a given interaction force. The hydrodynamic part of the mathematical model is based on the lubrication equations in the gap between the drops and the Stokes equations in the drops, coupled with velocity and stress boundary conditions at the interfaces. Both drop and film solute concentrations, related via mass flux balance across the interfaces, are governed by convection-diffusion equations. These equations for the solute concentration in the drops and the film are solved simultaneously by a semi-implicit finite difference method. Tests and comparisons are performed to show the accuracy and stability of the presented numerical method.

1 Introduction

Together with drop breakup, drop coalescence plays a decisive role in the dynamics of liquid dispersion, which are important in many industrial and natural processes. Among both sub-processes (breakup and coalescence) the latter, involving the interaction of two drops is much more difficult to investigate. This is also due to the presence of a liquid film between the drops. The situation becomes even more complex when surface active species or solutes are present on the interfaces, or/and in the liquid phases. A non-uniform solute or surfactant concentration in the vicinity of the interfaces leads to a gradient of the interfacial tension, which in turn leads to additional tangential stress on the interfaces (Marangoni effect). In the presence of surfactants it is shown (see [1–3]) that the Marangoni stress is always directed against the film drainage and in this way suppresses the coalescence. In the case considered here the inter-phase mass transfer of a solute could either enhance or delay the film drainage [4]. It was shown experimentally [5] and numerically [6] that when the mass transfer of solute is from the dispersed towards the continuous phase the coalescence is faster. In the case of transfer in the opposite direction, from the continuous phase to the dispersed phase, the coalescence is retarded. The present study can be considered as an extension of the work [6]. The present paper considers the

I. Dimov et al. (Eds.): NMA 2014, LNCS 8962, pp. 237–245, 2015.
DOI: 10.1007/978-3-319-15585-2_26

case of mobile film drainage (the flow in the film consists of plug and parabolic parts), while Saboni et al. [6] consider partially-mobile film drainage (only the plug part of the flow in the film). The other extension is that here the flow in the drops is modeled by the Stokes equations, while in [6] the radial velocity in the dispersed phase is approximated by the velocity at the interface.

2 Mathematical Formulation

Hydrodynamic model, approximations. Two drops of the same Newtonian liquid interacting along the line of their centers under a constant force in another immiscible Newtonian fluid are considered in the presence of solute soluble in the film and in the drop (dispersed) phase, see Fig. 1. The drops are considered to approach each other at specified velocity $V(t)$, which is adjusted during the drainage process to maintain a constant interaction force. The same procedure can, however, be used for time-dependent approach velocities, including force-time relationships representative of actual drop collisions. The model is simplified by a number of approximations, which are valid in the limit of gentle collisions (film radius a is much smaller than drop radii R_i) and which have been discussed in [1]. The governing equations are the same for unequal drops

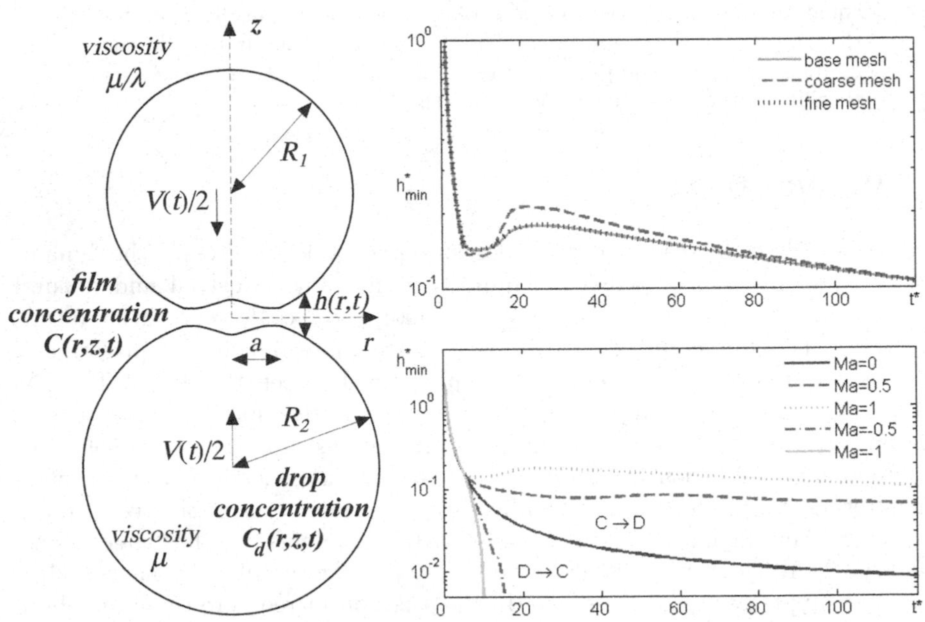

Fig. 1. Schematic sketch of the problem

Fig. 2. Evolution of the minimum film thickness h^*_{min} for different meshes at $Ma = 1$ (top) and for different values of Ma (bottom) and at $\lambda = 1$, $Pe = 250$, $Pe_d = 25000$.

and equal drops when formulated in terms of the equivalent radius R_{eq} (see [1]): $R_{eq}^{-1} = (R_1^{-1}+R_2^{-1})/2$. The hydrodynamic part of the model (based on the lubrication approximation of the Stokes equations in the film and Stokes equations in the drops) is the same as in [2] (see Eqs. (2–10)).

Solute transport model. The convection-diffusion equations govern the solute distribution in the drops and in the film. For the solute transport model we use the one proposed in [6]:

Transport equation in each phase. For constant bulk properties, the solute concentrations $C(r,z)$ in the film and $C_d(r,z_d)$ in the drops are governed by the convection-diffusion equations:

$$\frac{\partial C}{\partial t} + u_r\frac{\partial C}{\partial r} + u_z\frac{\partial C}{\partial z} = D\left(\frac{\partial^2 C}{\partial z^2} + \frac{1}{r}\frac{\partial}{\partial r}\left(r\frac{\partial C}{\partial r}\right)\right),$$

$$\frac{\partial C_d}{\partial t} + (u_r)_d\frac{\partial C_d}{\partial r} + (u_z)_d\frac{\partial C_d}{\partial z_d} = D_d\left(\frac{\partial^2 C_d}{\partial z_d^2} + \frac{1}{r}\frac{\partial}{\partial r}\left(r\frac{\partial C_d}{\partial r}\right)\right),$$

where $0 < r < r_l$, $0 < z < h(r)/2$, $0 < z_d < z_\infty$. Here D and D_d are diffusion coefficients and (u_r, u_z) and $(u_r, u_z)_d$ are the velocities in the both phases.

Interface conditions (for details about parameters see [6]). The first condition assumes quasi-equilibrium solute partition

$$\frac{\mathrm{d}C_d}{\mathrm{d}C} = K = \text{const} \quad \text{or} \quad C_d = K(C+c) \quad (c\text{: a const}).$$

The second condition is that of equality of mass fluxes normal to the interface

$$\rho_d D_d' \frac{\partial C_d}{\partial z_d} = \rho D' \frac{\partial C}{\partial z}, \quad \text{where} \quad D' = \frac{D}{1-C_0}, \quad D_d' = \frac{D_d}{1-K(C_0+c)}.$$

3 Transformed Equations

A simplification of the governing equations is possible via a transformation of the variables that renders them dimensionless and reduces the number of parameters.

Transformation and dimensionless parameters. The transformation of the hydrodynamic variables is (see also [3]):

$$t^* = \frac{t\sigma_s a'}{R_{eq}\mu};\ r^* = \frac{r}{R_{eq}a'};\ z^* = \frac{z}{R_{eq}a'^2};\ z_d^* = \frac{z_d}{R_{eq}a'};\ u_r^* = \frac{u_r\mu}{\sigma_s a'^2};\ (u_r^*)_d = \frac{(u_r)_d\mu}{\sigma_s a'^2};$$

$$u_z^* = \frac{u_z\mu}{\sigma_s a'^3};\ (u_z^*)_d = \frac{(u_z)_d\mu}{\sigma_s a'^2};\ h^* = \frac{h}{R_{eq}a'^2};\ p^* = \frac{pR_{eq}}{\sigma_s};\tau_d^* = \frac{\tau_d R_{eq}}{\sigma_s a'};\ p_d^* = \frac{pR_{eq}}{\sigma_s a'};$$

where a' is the dimensionless radius of the film, $a' = a/R_{eq}$. The dimensional film radius a is given by the condition of the constant interaction force. In the small deformation limit (gentle collisions), considered here, the parameter a' is small ($a' \ll 1$). Note that the dispersed-phase variables z_d, $(u_z)_d$ and p_d are transformed differently from their continuous-phase counterparts.

The solute concentrations are transformed by (see also [6]):

$$C' = C + c, \quad C'_d = \frac{C_d}{K}, \quad C^* = \frac{C' - C'_\infty}{\Delta C}, \quad C^*_d = \frac{C'_d - C'_\infty}{\Delta C},$$

where $\Delta C = (C'_d)_\infty - C'_\infty$. Then the parameters of the problem are reduced to:

$$\lambda^* = \lambda a'; \; P = K\frac{\rho_d D'_d \sqrt{D}}{\rho D' \sqrt{D_d}}; \; Ma = \frac{\Delta C}{\sigma_s a'^2}\frac{\mathrm{d}\sigma}{\mathrm{d}C}; \; Pe_d = \frac{\sigma_s R_{eq} a'^3}{D_d \mu}; \; Pe = \frac{\sigma_s R_{eq} a'^5}{D\mu},$$

the viscosity ratio λ^*; the transformed partition coefficient P; the Marangoni number Ma, Péclet numbers: in the drops, Pe_d, and in the film, Pe.

Continuous phase. In the film we use the lubrication approximation of the Stokes equations (see [1], Eq. (22)):

$$\frac{\partial h^*}{\partial t^*} = -\frac{1}{r^*}\frac{\partial (r^* h^* u^*_u)}{\partial r^*} + \frac{1}{r^*}\frac{\lambda^*}{12}\frac{\partial}{\partial r^*}\left(h^{*3} r^* \frac{\partial p^*}{\partial r^*}\right), \tag{1}$$

where h^* is the film thickness, p^* is the pressure in the film. The radial component of velocity in the film u^*_r consists of the sum of an uniform and a parabolic part:

$$u^*_r = u^*_u + \frac{\lambda^*}{2}\frac{\partial p^*}{\partial r^*}\left(z^{*2} - \left(\frac{h^*}{2}\right)^2\right).$$

The uniform part u^*_u of velocity in the film is equal to the radial component of the drop velocity $(u^*_r)_d$ on the interface ($z_d = 0$) and u^*_z, the z-component of velocity in the film is:

$$u^*_z = -\frac{1}{r^*}\frac{\partial (r^* u^*_u z^*)}{\partial r^*} - \frac{\lambda^*}{2r^*}\frac{\partial}{\partial r^*}\left[r^* \frac{\partial p^*}{\partial r^*}\left(\frac{z^{*3}}{3} - \frac{h^{*2} z^*}{4}\right)\right].$$

Solute transport in the film is described by:

$$\frac{\partial C^*}{\partial t^*} + u^*_r \frac{\partial C^*}{\partial r^*} + u^*_z \frac{\partial C^*}{\partial z^*} = \frac{1}{Pe}\left(\frac{\partial^2 C^*}{\partial z^{*2}} + \frac{a'^2}{r^*}\frac{\partial}{\partial r^*}\left(r^* \frac{\partial C^*}{\partial r^*}\right)\right). \tag{2}$$

As $a'^2 \ll 1$, the last term in (2) will be further ignored.

Dispersed phase. The flow in the drops is governed by Stokes equations:

$$-\nabla^* p^*_d + \nabla^{*2} \mathbf{u}_d{}^* = \mathbf{0}, \qquad \nabla^* \cdot \mathbf{u}_d{}^* = 0, \tag{3}$$

where p^*_d is the pressure and $\mathbf{u}_d{}^*$ velocity in the drops.

Solute concentration C^*_d in the drops satisfies:

$$\frac{\partial C^*_d}{\partial t^*} + (u^*_r)_d \frac{\partial C^*_d}{\partial r^*} + (u^*_z)_d \frac{\partial C^*_d}{\partial z^*_d} = \frac{1}{Pe_d}\left(\frac{1}{r^*}\frac{\partial}{\partial r^*}\left(r^* \frac{\partial C^*_d}{\partial r^*}\right) + \frac{\partial^2 C^*_d}{\partial z^{*2}_d}\right). \tag{4}$$

Interface. The tangential stress exerted on the interface is given by:

$$\tau_d^* + \frac{h^*}{2}\frac{\partial p^*}{\partial r^*} + Ma\frac{\partial C^*}{\partial r^*} = 0. \tag{5}$$

The jump in the normal stress (see Eq. (8) of [2]) in dimensionless form can be approximated with an error $O(a'^2)$ as:

$$p^* = 2 - \frac{1}{2}\left(\frac{\partial^2 h^*}{\partial r^{*2}} + \frac{1}{r^*}\frac{\partial h^*}{\partial r^*}\right). \tag{6}$$

The concentrations on the interface are connected via:

$$C_d^* = C^*, \quad \frac{\partial C_d^*}{\partial z_d^*} = \frac{1}{P}\sqrt{\frac{Pe_d}{Pe}}\frac{\partial C^*}{\partial z^*}. \tag{7}$$

Initial conditions. For the film thickness – corresponds to undeformed drops ($p = 0$) and is given by:

$$h^*(r^*, t^* = 0) = h_{ini}^* + r^{*2}.$$

The initial concentrations are $C^* = 0$ in the film, $C_d^* = 1$ in the drops and $C_0^* = P/(1 + P)$ on the interface. Near the interface the concentrations are smoothed as in [6], Eq. (23*).

Boundary conditions. The outer boundary conditions are a prescribed pressure and a condition for the approach velocity $V^*(t^*)$ at sufficiently large $r^* = r_l^*$:

$$p^*(r_l^*) = 0, \qquad \left(\frac{\partial h^*}{\partial t^*}\right)_{r_l^*} = V^*(t^*), \qquad \int_0^{r_l^*} p^* r^* \, dr^* = 1, \tag{8}$$

where $V^*(t^*)$ is adjusted in order to the above integral condition to be satisfied. The last integral is a measure of the interaction force, which is assumed constant (after rescaling becomes 1).

Boundary conditions of symmetry at $r^* = 0$, $z^* = 0$ and uniform surfactant distribution at large $r^* = r_l^*$ and $z_d^* = z_\infty^*$ are respectively:

$$\left(\frac{\partial C^*}{\partial r}\right)_{r^*=0,r_l^*} = \left(\frac{\partial C_d^*}{\partial r}\right)_{r^*=0,r_l^*} = \left(\frac{\partial C^*}{\partial z^*}\right)_{z^*=0} = \left(\frac{\partial C_d^*}{\partial z_d^*}\right)_{z_d^*=z_\infty^*} = 0.$$

4 Numerical Method

The solution scheme for the mathematical model is the following. Starting from a given $h^*(r^*, t^*)$ and C^*, then p^* is calculated from (6) and τ_d^* from (5), providing a boundary condition for the Stokes equations (3). The solution of these equations in the drop then furnishes u_u^*. Now having u_u^* and p^* the film thickness at the next time step is obtained from (1). The surfactant concentrations C^*, C_d^* are obtained simultaneously at the next time step via Eqs. (2), (7), (4).

Thus the whole process can be repeated. The prescribed interaction force in (8) is satisfied using the same approach as in [1].

Equations (3), governing the flow in the drops, are solved by a boundary integral method, approximating the interface as flat. The velocity in the drops is given by (see [3,7,8])

$$(u_r^*)_d(r^*, z_d^*) = \int_0^{r_l^*} \phi_1(r^*, r', z_d^*)\tau_d(r')\, dr', \quad (u_z^*)_d(r^*, z_d^*) = \int_0^{r_l^*} \phi_3(r^*, r', z_d^*)\tau_d(r')\, dr',$$

$$\phi_1(r^*, r', z_d^*) = \frac{r'}{4\pi} \int_0^{2\pi} \left(\frac{2\cos\theta}{Q(r^*, r', z_d^*, \theta)^{1/2}} - \frac{(z_d^{*2}\cos\theta + r^* r' \sin^2\theta)}{Q(r^*, r', z_d^*, \theta)^{3/2}} \right) d\theta \quad (9)$$

$$\phi_3(r^*, r', z_d^*) = \frac{r'}{4\pi} \int_0^{2\pi} \frac{(r^*\cos\theta - r') z_d^* r'\, d\theta}{Q(r^*, r', z_d^*, \theta)^{3/2}}, \quad Q = r^{*2} + r'^2 - 2r^* r' \cos\theta + z_d^{*2}.$$

Special attention is paid to the singularity in formula (9), which appears at $r^* = r'$ and $z_d^* = 0$. It can be shown that the above solution for the velocity on the interface (at $z_d^* = 0$) is exactly the one given by (39–40) of [2].

Equation (1), governing the evolution of the film thickness h^*, is a nonlinear, fourth-order, stiff partial differential equation with respect to h^*. To solve it an Euler explicit scheme with adaptive time step (of order 10^{-5}) and second order approximation for the spatial derivatives on non-uniform mesh is used. The solution procedure is described in details in [1–3].

For discretization in the z_d^* direction in the drops non-uniform meshes are used: small steps ($\Delta z_d^* \approx 0.01$) close to the interface $z_d^* \ll 1$ and relatively large steps ($\Delta z_d^* \approx 1$) at large z_d^*. Similarly for the discretization in the r^* direction the steps also increase by a geometrical-progression law and thus the mesh is locally almost uniform. The mesh in the z^* direction in the film is also non-uniform. Additionally, the transformation $\eta = 2z^*/h^*(r^*, z^*)$ is applied in order to account for the curvilinear form of the interface. A comparison between the results for the minimal film thickness h_{min}^* obtained using three different meshes is shown in Fig. 2 (top). It is seen that the base mesh, as described above, gives almost identical results with that using the twice finer mesh (fine mesh, as indicated in the figure). The figure also indicates that the twice coarser mesh is not sufficient with respect to the accuracy of the results.

A new element here is the simultaneous solution of the convection-diffusion equations in the drops and in the film. Second order finite-difference approximation in both r^* and z^* directions is used. As the gradients of the surfactant concentration are expected to be higher in the z^* than in the r^* direction, a hybrid (explicit/implicit) method is developed for time integration of the convection-diffusion equations. It consists of explicit time integration in the r^* direction and implicit in the z^* direction. In such a scheme, N five-diagonal systems have to be solved (N is the number of nodes in the r^* direction), instead of one large system. Two time integration schemes are used – first order implicit and second

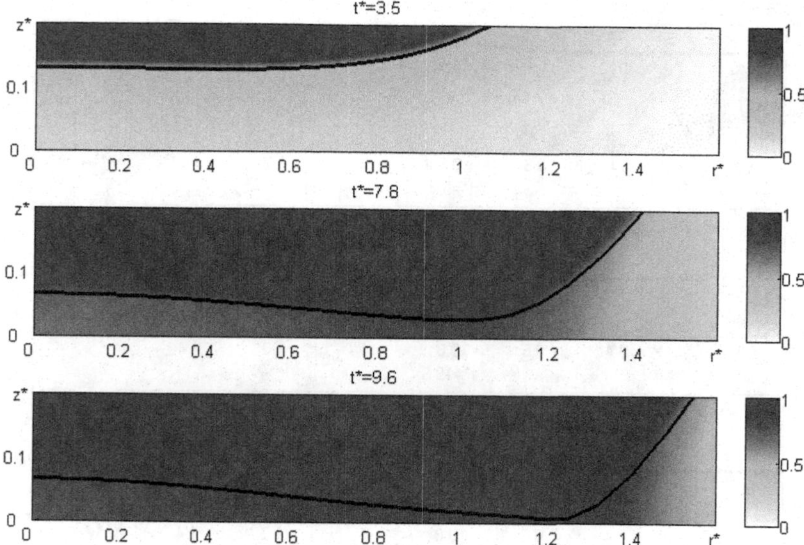

Fig. 3. The solute distributions C'_d in the drop and C' in the film at three time instances for $Ma = -1$; $D \to C$; $\lambda^* = 1$; $Pe = 250$ and $Pe_d = 25000$.

order Crank-Nicolson. The comparisons show that both schemes give identical results with respect to the accuracy and stability. The reason for this is that the time steps are of order 10^{-5}, as described above.

5 Results and Discussion

One of the most important characteristics of the film drainage regarding the drop coalescence is the minimal thickness of the film [1]. Figure 2 (bottom) shows the evolution of the minimal film thickness h^*_{min}. The behavior of h^*_{min} is very close to that obtained in [6] (see their Fig. 10) and is similar to the experimental results of [5]. In the case of mass transfer from the continuous (film) towards disperse (drop) phase ($C \to D$) the film drainage is delayed, while in the case of mass transfer in the opposite direction ($D \to C$) the film drainage is promoted.

For better understanding of the Marangoni effect due to the mass transfer on the drainage rate of the film in Figs. 3 and 4 the solute distributions are presented at several time instances. The Marangoni stress becomes significant when the thickness of the concentration boundary layer in the continuous phase becomes comparable with the half film thickness. Thus at the beginning (till $t^* \approx 4$) the film drainage is not effected by the mass transfer, see Fig. 2 (bottom). The boundary layers corresponding to both interfaces meet in the region where the film thickness is minimal. In the case of $D \to C$ transfer (see Fig. 3) the solute concentration at the interface in this region is higher. In this way the Marangoni stress, directed opposite to the gradient of the concentration on the interface,

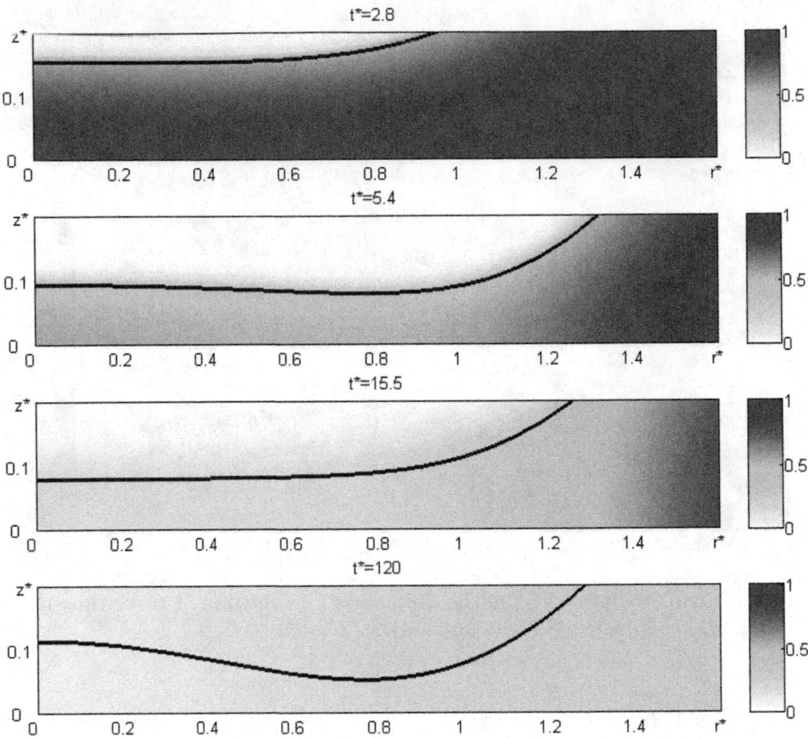

Fig. 4. The solute distributions C' and C'_d at four time instances for $Ma = 1$; $C \to D$; $\lambda^* = 1$; $Pe = 250$ and $Pe_d = 25000$. Here the initial conditions are $C' = 1$ and $C'_d = 0$.

accelerates the local film drainage. In the other case of $C \to D$ transfer (see Fig. 4) the Marangoni stress is directed towards the region of the minimal film thickness, delaying significantly the film drainage. In this case it also leads to disappearance of the dimple at time around $t^* = 16$.

6 Conclusions

A numerical method is presented for simulation of drainage of films between interacting drops in the presence of inter-phase mass transfer. The performed tests, comparisons and numerical experiments indicate that it is capable to simulate drainage of films with thickness of the order or below the critical film thickness, at which drops are expected to coalesce. The results are in good agreement with existing experimental and numerical results and the method will be used for a more extensive investigation of the effect of the parameters on the drop coalescence. An extension of the mathematical model and the numerical method in the case of mass transfer of surfactants, where the surfactants are also present on the interfaces, will be developed further.

Acknowledgment. The second author has been supported by Grant DDVU02/71 from the Bulgarian National Science Fund.

References

1. Chesters, A., Bazhlekov, I.: Effect of insoluble surfactants on drainage and rupture of a film between drops interacting under a constant force. J. Colloid Interface Sci. **230**, 229–243 (2000)
2. Bazhlekov, I.: Numerical simulation of drop coalescence in the presence of film soluble surfactant. AIP Conf. Proc. **1487**, 351–359 (2012)
3. Bazhlekov, I., Vasileva, D.: Numerical simulation of drop coalescence in the presence of drop soluble surfactant. AIP Conf. Proc. **1561**, 333–346 (2013)
4. Chan, D., Klaseboer, E., Manika, R.: Film drainage and coalescence between deformable drops and bubbles. Soft Matter **7**, 2235–2264 (2011)
5. Ban, T., Kawaizumi, F., Nii, S., Takahashi, K.: Study of drop coalescence behavior for liquid-liquid extraction operation. Chem. Eng. Sci. **55**, 5385–5391 (2000)
6. Saboni, A., Gourdon, C., Chesters, A.: The influence of inter-phase mass transfer on the drainage of partially-mobile liquid films between drops undergoing a constant interaction force. Chem. Eng. Sci. **54**, 461–473 (1999)
7. Ladyzhenskaya, O.: The Mathematical Theory of Viscous Incompressible Flow. Mathematics and Its Applications, vol. 2. Gordon and Breach Science Publishers, New York (1969)
8. Jansons, K., Lister, J.: The general solution of Stokes flow in a half space as an integral of the velocity on the boundary. Phys. Fluids **31**, 1321–1323 (1988)

Wavelet Compression of Spline Coefficients

Jostein Bratlie(✉), Rune Dalmo, and Børre Bang

R&D Group in Mathematical and Geometrical Modeling,
Numerical Simulations, Programming and Visualization,
Narvik University College,
PO Box 385, 8505 Narvik, Norway
{jbr,rda,bb}@hin.no
www.hin.no/Simulations

Abstract. Based on a concept for thresholding of wavelet coefficients, which was addressed in [8] and further explored in [6,7], a method for balancing between non-threshold- and threshold shrinking of wavelet coefficients has emerged. Generalized expo-rational B-splines (GERBS) is a blending type spline construction where local functions at each knot are blended together by C^k-smooth basis functions. Global data fitting can be achieved with GERBS by fitting local functions to the data. One property of the GERBS construction is an intrinsic partitioning of the global data. Compression of the global data set can be achieved by applying the shrinking strategy to the GERBS local functions. In this initial study we investigate how this affects the resulting GERBS geometry.

Keywords: Wavelet compression · Spline coefficients · B-splines · GERBS

1 Introduction

The discrete wavelet transform (DWT) [4] is commonly used in signal processing. Among its most typical applications we find signal coding, as a preconditioning for de-noising or data compression, by manipulating the vector of wavelet coefficients. This process is known as wavelet shrinkage [9,10].

Several methods for wavelet shrinkage applicable to functions belonging to a general class of Besov spaces was proposed in [8]. Later, in [6,7], a couple of them was further explored utilizing Sobolev-type embedding withing the Besov-space scale. The main result was an adaptive strategy for balancing between non-threshold shrinking and hard thresholding by considering a signal's smoothness measure.

Within computer-aided geometric design (CAGD) smooth geometric objects, such as curves and surfaces, are usually represented using some kind of splines. Classic B-splines [2] or non-uniform rational B-splines (NURBS) [12] are typically used to represent parametric objects as control points which are blended together using Bernstein polynomials [1] associated with a knot vector as basis functions. Lots of effort has been put into research areas related to data reduction, compression and smoothing with B-splines in previous works. We mention

I. Dimov et al. (Eds.): NMA 2014, LNCS 8962, pp. 246–253, 2015.
DOI: 10.1007/978-3-319-15585-2_27

here the knot removal technique, presented by Lycke and Mørken in [14] and with a different approach by Eck and Hadenfeld in [11], and the shape-preserving knot removal method by Schumaker and Stanley [15].

A more recent family of splines is the so-called generalized expo-rational B-splines [5], GERBS, where local *functions* at each knot are blended together by sufficiently smooth basis functions. Splines in general are smooth evaluable representations where the underlying data, or coefficients, in a way can be considered as discrete. This is not necessarily true in the case of GERBS since the coefficients are functions, however, the type of local functions we consider here satisfy this criterion. On the other hand, we can view the local functions as a natural partitioning of the global function. One approach to perform the DWT on a spline is by sampling, or discretizing, the global spline at some resolution. The inverse transform would then produce a discrete signal which would not be evaluable. Contrary to that, in this paper, we consider wavelet compression of the underlying discrete data and investigate how it affects the global spline.

In the following sections we provide brief descriptions of the wavelet transform, B-splines, and GERBS. Then we describe the type of wavelets and wavelet shrinkage we consider and how it is applied to spline coefficients. Finally we give some concluding remarks where we discuss our findings and suggest topics for future work.

2 The Wavelet Transform

The wavelet transform [4] is a technique to represent any arbitrary function f as wavelets, generated by scaling and translation from one single mother function ψ:

$$\psi_{a,b}(t) = |a|^{-1/2}\psi\left(\frac{t-b}{a}\right), \tag{1}$$

where a and b are constants defining scaling and translation, respectively. It is required that the mother function has mean zero:

$$\int \psi(t)dt = 0, \tag{2}$$

which typically implies at least one oscillation of $\psi(t)$ across the t-axis. Following from the scaling of a single function, compared with the mother function, low frequency wavelets ($a > 1$) are wider in the t-direction, whereas high frequency wavelets ($a < 1$) are narrower.

For application within signal analysis, the parameters a and b in Eq. (1) are usually restricted through discretization. A scaling step ($a_0 > 1$) and a translation step ($b_0 \neq 0$) are fixed, leading to the wavelets for $j, k \in \mathbb{Z}$:

$$\psi_{jk}(t) = a_0^{-j/2}\psi(a_0^{-j}t - kb_0). \tag{3}$$

The discrete wavelet transform (DWT), T, associated with the discrete wavelets in Eq. (3), maps functions f to sequences indexed by $\mathbb{Z}^2$:

$$(Tf)_{jk} = \langle \psi_{jk}, f \rangle = a_0^{-j/2} \int \psi(a_o^{-j}t - kb_0) f(t) dt. \tag{4}$$

Following the principle of decomposition, f can be reconstructed from its wavelet coefficients $\beta_{jk} = \langle \psi_{jk}, f \rangle$:

$$f = \sum_{j,k} \beta_{jk} \psi_{jk}(t). \tag{5}$$

3 Splines

A spline is a piecewise polynomial that is differentiable up to a prescribed order. The different parts are joined together at specified "joints" known as knots. There exists many types of splines and the B-spline is one of the most commonly used.

3.1 B-Splines

A spline $\ell(t)$ of degree d can be written as an affine combination of control points $\mathbf{c} = \{c_k\}_{k=1}^n$:

$$\ell(t) = \sum_k c_k B_{k,d}(t), \tag{6}$$

where the B-splines $B_{k,d}(t)$ associated with a knot vector $\mathbf{t} = \{t_j\}_{j=1}^{n+d+1}$ are defined recursively as follows.

$$B_{k,1}(t) = \begin{cases} 1 & \text{if } t_k \leq u < t_{k+1}, \\ 0 & \text{otherwise,} \end{cases} \tag{7}$$

and

$$B_{k,d}(t) = \frac{t - t_k}{t_{k+d} - t_k} B_{k,d-1}(t) + \frac{t_{k+d+1} - t}{t_{k+d+1} - t_{k+1}} B_{k+1,d-1}(t). \tag{8}$$

The control points $\mathbf{c}$ are typically embedded in Euclidean space, e.g. $\mathbb{R}^2$ or $\mathbb{R}^3$, hence, $\ell(t)$ is a parametric curve.

3.2 The GERBS Blending Construction

The parametric GERBS construction for curves is defined as

$$c(t) = \sum_{i=1}^{n} \ell_i(t) G_i(t), \tag{9}$$

where $\ell_i(t)$, $i = 1, \ldots, n$ are local curves and $G_i(t)$, $i = 1, \ldots, n$ are the GERBS basis functions defined in the next section.

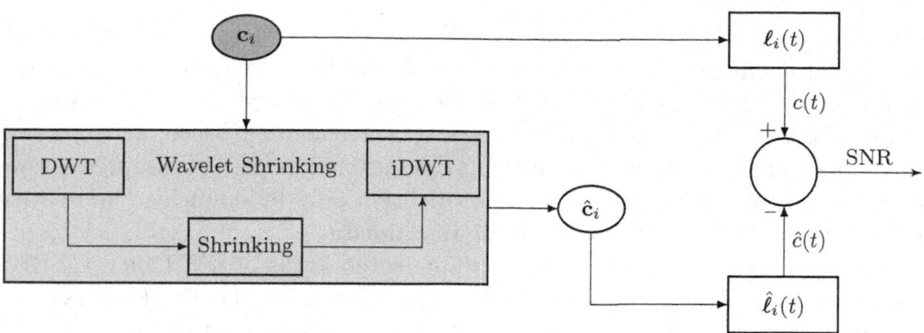

Fig. 1. Discrete vectors of control points $\mathbf{c}_i$ are compressed by wavelet shrinkage and reconstructed into $\hat{\mathbf{c}}_i$. These control points are used by the uncompressed and compressed versions of the B-spline local curves $\ell_i(t)$ and $\hat{\ell}_i(t)$ for the uncompressed and compressed versions of the GERBS curve, $c(t)$ and $\hat{c}(t)$, respectively.

3.3 GERBS-Type Basis Functions

Consider a strictly increasing knot vector $\boldsymbol{t} = \{t_k\}_{k=0}^{n+1}$, $t_0 < t_1 < \cdots < t_{n+1}$, $n \in \mathbb{N}$. The definition of the j-th GERBS basis function is defined in [5] as follows.

$$G_j(t) = \begin{cases} F_j(t), & \text{if} \quad t \in (t_{j-1}, t_j], \\ 1 - F_{j+1}(t), & \text{if} \quad t \in (t_j, t_{j+1}), \\ 0, & \text{if} \quad t \in (-\infty, t_{j-1}] \cup [t_{j+1}, +\infty), \end{cases} \tag{10}$$

$j = 1, \ldots, n$,

where $\{F_i\}_{i=1}^{n+1}$ is a system of cumulative distribution functions such that for F_i, $i = 1, \ldots, n$,

1. the right-hand limit $F_i(t_{i-1}+) = F_i(t_{i-1}) = 0$,
2. the left-hand limit $F_i(t_i-) = F_i(t_i) = 1$,
3. $F_i(t) = 0$ for $t \in (-\infty, t_{i-1}]$,
4. $F_i(t) = 1$ for $t \in [t_i, +\infty)$, and $F(t)$ is monotonously increasing, possibly discontinuous, but left-continuous for $t \in [t_{i-1}, t_i]$.

The GERBS basis function shall be of standard ERBS type, as defined in [13], throughout this paper.

4 Compressing Spline Coefficients

Using the notation from [6] to represent a signal as discrete orthonormal wavelets,

$$f(x) = \sum_{k \in \mathbb{Z}^d} \alpha_{0k} \phi_{0k}^{[0]}(x) + \sum_{j=0}^{\infty} \sum_{k \in \mathbb{Z}^d} \sum_{l=1}^{2^d-1} \beta_{jk}^{[l]} \psi_{jk}^{[l]}(x), \quad a.e. \ \ x \in \mathbb{R}^d, \tag{11}$$

where $\alpha_{0k} = \left\langle \phi_{0k}^{[0]}, f \right\rangle = \int_{\mathbb{R}^d} \phi_{0k}^{[0]}(x) f(x) dx$ and $\beta_{jk}^{[l]} = \left\langle \psi_{jk}^{[l]}, f \right\rangle$ are the scaling and wavelet coefficients, respectively, curve fitting by wavelet shrinkage is performed here by shrinking the wavelet coefficients β_{jk} towards zero in the wavelet domain. For this we use the Lorentz-type hard thresholding, based on decreasing re-arrangement of the wavelet coefficients, as outlined in [8]. By compression we mean, in this case, with respect to quantification only by counting the relative number of wavelet coefficients which are discarded.

The experiment is performed by applying seven levels of DWT on a GERBS curve, having eight cubic B-splines with 128 two-dimensional control points each, as local curves. Then only two scaling coefficients α remain together with 126 wavelet coefficients β. The control polygons for the B-splines are generated from sampling of a square pulse signal and have a large number of inflection points. The points are distributed non-uniformly in both dimensions by varying the amplitude and frequency of the square pulse for each sample.

The individual GERBS local curves are of different shape. We consider the discrete data as height curves and apply the bi-orthogonal B.3.9 [3] and the symlet S.20 wavelets, together with the orthonormal Daubechies D.1 (Haar) wavelet [4] for reference, to one dimension of the vector of control points $(\mathbf{c})_{k=1}^{n}$ where $n = 128$. Plots of one B-spline control polygon and the corresponding cubic B-spline are shown together with examples of their respective compressed versions and error graphs in Fig. 2.

Discrete vectors of control points $\mathbf{c}_i$ are compressed by wavelet shrinkage and reconstructed into $\hat{\mathbf{c}}_i$. These control points are used by the uncompressed and compressed versions of the B-spline local curves $\ell_i(t)$ and $\hat{\ell}_i(t)$ for the uncompressed and compressed versions of the GERBS curve, $c(t)$ and $\hat{c}(t)$, respectively. Then we measure the difference between $c(t)$ and $\hat{c}(t)$ on 1024 uniform samples of each. This process is outlined in Fig. 1.

5 Results

Figure 3 shows the performance for shrinkage applied to the considered test spline. The horizontal axis displays the compression rate while the vertical axis shows the Signal to Noise Ratio (SNR) measured in dB, defined as

$$\text{SNR} = 10 \log_{10} \left(\frac{\| c(t) \|_2^2}{\| c(t) - \hat{c}(t) \|_2^2} \right), \tag{12}$$

where $c(t)$ is the original GERBS curve, $\hat{c}(t)$ denotes the GERBS curve whose local curves are obtained from compressed (shrunk) control points and $\| \cdot \|_2^2$ stands for the square of the L_2 norm. Compression is measured in terms of how many of the wavelet coefficients which are set to zero relative to the size of the signal. The scaling coefficients α_{0k} in Eq. (11) remain untouched.

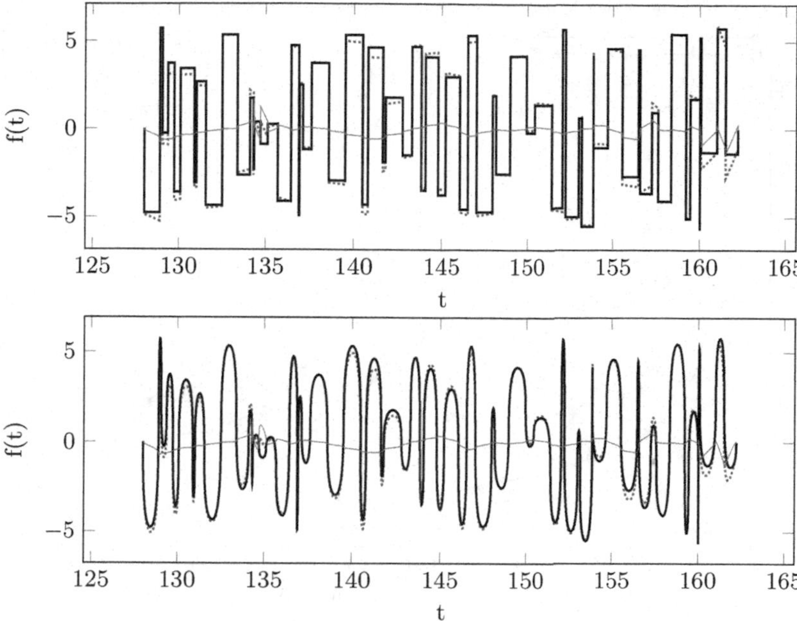

Fig. 2. The "square-pulse" control polygon shown in the top of the figure produces the cubic B-spline in the bottom figure. The uncompressed data are plotted with thick solid lines while the dotted lines show how reconstructed data with approx. 80 % compression applied using the Symlet S.20 wavelet deviates from the original. The thin line shows the difference between the two.

6 Concluding Remarks

Compression of GERBS is achieved by thresholding wavelet shrinkage applied to discrete coefficients of B-spline type local curves. The compression rates are quite high in the case considered here. This is due to the use of long wavelet filters applied to relatively short vectors of control points.

The method could easily be applied in parallel to different partitions of the discrete signal. This is relevant for the intrinsic partitioning constituted by the GERBS local functions.

The compression method presented in this paper is applicable to control polygons of essentially any shape. We note that knot removal may not be necessary for GERBS due to their minimal support property and that the local curves may contain much more information than the point-type coefficients of other types of splines. The control polygons for the B-spline local curves are, in this case, of such character that application of known knot removal methods will not provide satisfying data reduction. However, a preceding knot removal step is relevant for more "smooth" control polygons.

The DWT is applied to one dimension of the vector of control points. A natural extension, which is important for applications, could be to perform

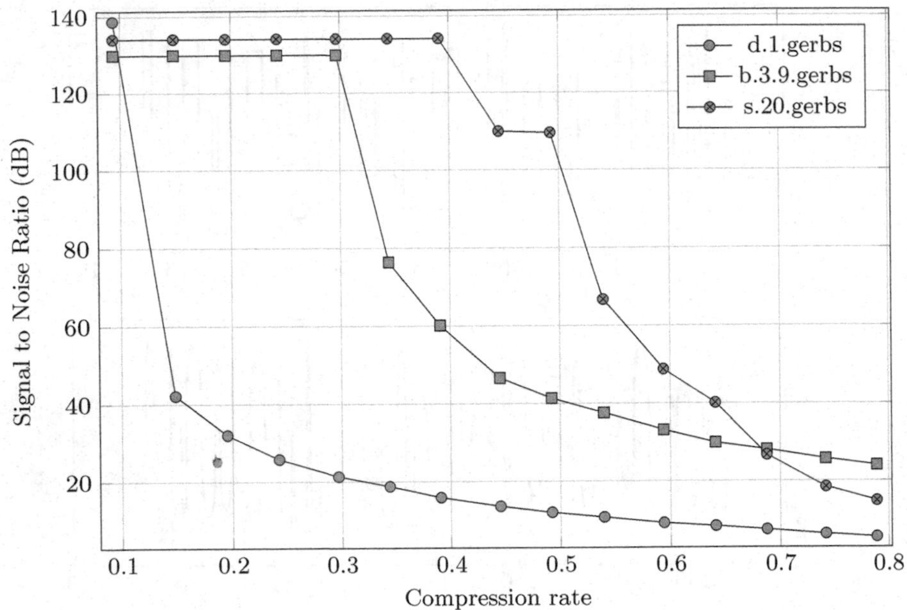

Fig. 3. Performance on a GERBS curve of hard thresholding wavelet shrinkage applied to control polygons of B-spline type local curves. The horizontal axis indicates compression rate, measured by counting the relative number of discarded wavelet coefficients, while the vertical axis shows the SNR measured in dB. Plots for three types of wavelets; bi-orthogonal 3.9, symlet 20 and Haar, are shown.

the DWT on all dimensions of the space where the control points are embedded. Another natural extension would be to apply the considered method to tensor product surface- or volume splines.

References

1. Bernstein, S.: Démonstration du théorème de weierstrass fondée sur le calcul des probabilités. Comm. Soc. Math. Kharkov **13**, 1–2 (1913)
2. de Boor, C.: Splines as linear combinations of b-splines. A survey (1976)
3. Cohen, A., Daubechies, I., Feauveau, J.C.: Biorthogonal bases of compactly supported wavelets. Commun. Pure Appl. Math. **XLV**, 485–560 (1992)
4. Daubechies, I.: Orthonormal bases of compactly supported wavelets. Commun. Pure Appl. Math. **XLI**, 909–966 (1988)
5. Dechevsky, L.T., Bang, B., Lakså, A.: Generalized expo-rational b-splines. Int. J. Pure Appl. Math. **57**(6), 833–872 (2009)
6. Dechevsky, L.T., Grip, N., Gundersen, J.: A new generation of wavelet shrinkage: adaptive strategies based on composition of Lorentz-type thresholding and Besov-type non-threshold shrinkage. In: Truchetet, F., Laligant, O. (eds.) Wavelet Applications in Industrial Processing V. Proceedings of SPIE,. Boston, MA, USA, vol. 6763, pp. 1–14 (2007)

7. Dechevsky, L.T., Gundersen, J., Grip, N.: Wavelet compression, data fitting and approximation based on adaptive composition of Lorentz-type thresholding and Besov-type non-threshold shrinkage. In: Lirkov, I., Margenov, S., Waśniewski, J. (eds.) LSSC 2009. LNCS, vol. 5910, pp. 738–746. Springer, Heidelberg (2010)
8. Dechevsky, L.T., Ramsay, J.O., Penev, S.I.: Penalized wavelet estimation with besov regularity constraints. Math. Balkanica (N.S.) **13**(3–4), 257–376 (1999)
9. Donoho, D.L., Johnstone, I.M.: Ideal spatial adaptation by wavelet shrinkage. Biometrika **8**(3), 425–455 (1994)
10. Donoho, D.L., Johnstone, I.M., Kerkyacharian, G., Picard, D.: Wavelet shrinkage: asymptopia? J. Roy. Stat. Soc. Ser. B **57**(2), 301–369 (1995)
11. Eck, M., Hadenfeld, J.: Knot removal for b-spline curves. Comput. Aided Geom. Des. **12**(3), 259–282 (1994)
12. Farin, G.: Curves and Surfaces for CAGD: A Practical Guide, 5th edn. Academic Press, New York (2002)
13. Lakså, A., Bang, B., Dechevsky, L.T.: Exploring expo-rational b-splines for curves and surfaces. In: Dæhlen, M., Mørken, K., Schumaker, L. (eds.) Mathematical Methods for Curves and Surfaces, pp. 253–262. Nashboro Press, Brentwood (2005)
14. Lyche, T., Mørken, K.: Knot removal for parametric b-spline curves and surfaces. Comput. Aided Geom. Des. **4**(3), 217–230 (1987)
15. Schumaker, L.L., Stanley, S.S.: Shape-preserving knot removal. Comput. Aided Geom. Des. **13**(9), 851–872 (1996)

Target Localization by UWB Signals

Ján Buša(✉)

Department of Mathematics and Theoretical Informatics, FEE&I, Technical University in Košice, Nemcovej 32, 040 01 Košice, Slovakia
Jan.Busa@tuke.sk

Abstract. The high bandwidth of ultra wideband (UWB) radars results in a high spatial resolution, typically a few cm. Thanks to good penetration through materials UWB radars can be very helpful, e.g., also in such situations: through-wall tracking of human beings during security operations, through-rubble localization of motionless persons following an emergency, e.g., earthquake or explosion, through-snow detection of people after an avalanche or through-dress security screening at airports for the detection of non-metal objects etc.

An algorithm for the localization of a point target behind a wall based on the information about times of a signal arrival (TOA) to the receivers will be presented. The 3-dimensional case is considered. We suppose that the permittivity of the considered wall is known. The introduced method may be used for known wall width, and also for the wall width determination.

The determination of the through wall TOA for given point targets, based on Snell's law, has been considered before by other authors. We solve the inverse problem using the Newton method for the minimization of the least squares objective function.

Keywords: Computational geometry · UWB radar · Snell's law · Localization of point target behind a wall · Newton's method

1 Introduction

The object localization belongs to the basic tasks solved within wireless sensor networks (WSN). Direct calculation method (DC), conventional least-squares method (LS), weighted least-squares method (WLS), together with iterative Taylor series method (TS) originally proposed for object localization using time of arrival (TOA) or time difference of arrival (TDOA) measurements were studied, e.g., in [1,4,5,8].

The capability of ultra-wideband (UWB) radar to provide surveillance through a wall is studied and considered in many papers. Author of [2] discussed a difference between using the Snell's law and some simplified method for calculating TOA. Simulator using the finite-difference time-domain method for approximate solution of time-dependent Maxwell's equations is considered in [3]. Interactions with the structure such as current excitation, scattering, multiple scattering, penetration and diffraction are taken into account. Different aspects of the problem

I. Dimov et al. (Eds.): NMA 2014, LNCS 8962, pp. 254–261, 2015.
DOI: 10.1007/978-3-319-15585-2_28

and their practical engineering solutions are considered in the papers [6,7,9–12], where also additional references could be found.

The presented work deals with the inverse problem when the TOA are given, and the position of the point target behind the concrete wall has to be determined. We suppose that the TOA correspond to the fastest paths from the point through the wall to the antennas according to Snell's law (see, e.g., [2]). To determine the position (x, y, z) we minimize the distance between calculated and measured vector of TOA, so we may consider the method to be a Least Squares Method. For minimization the Newton method with approximate Hesse matrices is used, because it is impossible to write formulas for TOA. If more TOA are available, it is possible to estimate also the concrete wall width. Problem of wall parameter estimation based on different principles is considered in [9]. The TOA determination itself is a self-contained technical problem, and we will not be concerned with it.

2 Problem Formulation

Let us consider a *transmitting antenna* placed at the point $T = (0, 0, 0)$, and *receiving antennas* placed in the plane $y = 0$ at the points $R_i = (x_i; 0; z_i)$, $i = 1$, $2, \ldots, N_R$. We suppose that a parallel to the plane $y = 0$ concrete wall of the width w is placed between y_1 and $y_1 + w$, $y_1 \geq 0$. Let us suppose that the *point target* is placed at $P = (x_P; y_P; z_P)$ behind the wall, so $y_P > y_1 + w$.

Let $t(A, B)$ be the time of a wave propagation between two points A and B placed on the different sides of the wall – we suppose that it is the time of the wave propagation along the fastest path between the points A and B, i.e., the time corresponding to the Snell's law of the wave propagation. Then the *Times of Arrival* (TOAs) *for the point* P are defined by[1]:

$$\text{TOA}_i(P) = t(T, P) + t(P, R_i), \qquad i = 1, 2, \ldots, N_R. \tag{1}$$

Problem 1. Let us suppose that N_R times T_i corresponding to the TOAs for receivers at points R_i for the same point $P(x_P; y_P; z_P)$ are given. Find the point $P = (x_P; y_P; z_P)$ such that

$$\text{TOA}_i(P) = T_i, \qquad \forall i = 1, 2, \ldots, N_R. \tag{2}$$

Problem 2. Solve the Problem 1 in the case when the wall width w is unknown, and find the width w, too.

3 Method Description

We will solve Problem 1 minimizing the sum of differences squares:

$$F(P) = \sum_{i=1}^{N_R} [\text{TOA}_i(P) - T_i]^2 \longrightarrow \min_{\substack{P \\ y_P > y_1 + w}} . \tag{3}$$

[1] We may use more precise notation $\text{TOA}_i(P, w)$ to emphasize the dependence on the wall width w.

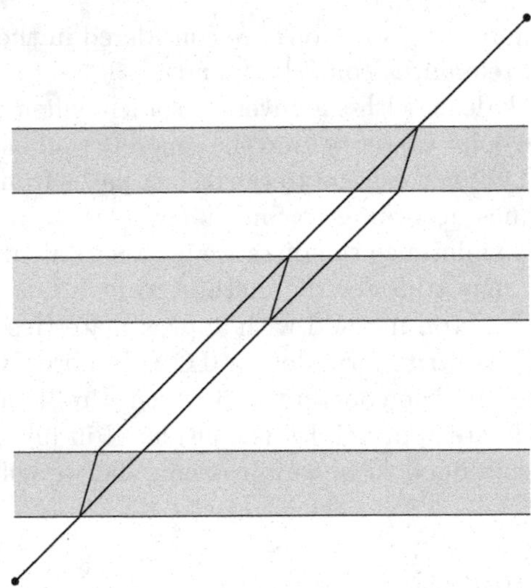

Fig. 1. Wave propagation time doesn't depend on the wall position

The Problem 2 we will solve in the similar way minimizing

$$F(P,w) = \sum_{i=1}^{N_R} [\mathrm{TOA}_i(P,w) - T_i]^2 \longrightarrow \min_{\substack{w,\,P \\ w>0,\ y_P > y_1 + w}} . \tag{4}$$

3.1 Newton's Method with Approximate Hesse Matrix and Gradient

For the solution of Problems 1 and 2 represented by problems (3) and (4) we use the Newton method. Starting from a point $X^{[0]}$, at each iteration a system of linear algebraic equations is solved:

$$X^{[k+1]} = X^{[k]} - [H(X^{[k]})]^{-1} \cdot \nabla F(X^{[k]}), \qquad k = 0, 1, \ldots \tag{5}$$

Both, the gradient $\nabla F(X^{[k]})$ and the Hesse matrix $H(X^{[k]})$, are calculated numerically using the central finite difference approximations of the second order for derivatives with the step $h = 2 \times 10^{-5}$. Columns of the Hesse matrix are calculated using central differences of gradient, and afterwards the Hesse matrix is symmetrized. Instead of the inverse, the pseudoinverse Hesse matrix is used.

For the Problem 2 we first solve the Problem 1 for some initial value of the wall width w_{init}, and on the second stage we are looking for better values with enlarged size of the vector X, i.e., for $X = (x; y; z; w)$.

3.2 TOA Calculation

Three layer Air-Concrete-Air problem of a wave propagation is indeed only two layer Air-Concrete problem (see [6], p. 102). It is evident from Fig. 1, where it

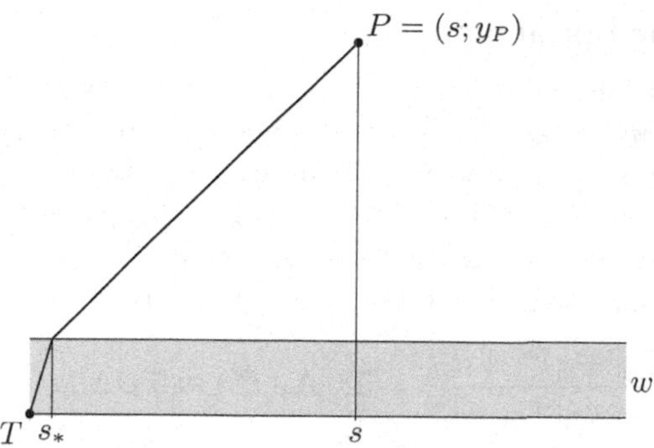

Fig. 2. Wave propagation calculation

is shown that all "rays" in air resp. concrete have to be parallel, respectively, to satisfy the Snell's law.

To compute the TOA_i value for a given point $P = (x_P; y_P; z_P)$ we have according to Eq. (1) to calculate two values: $t(T, P)$ resp. $t(P, R_i)$ for transmitting antenna at the point T (at the origin) and corresponding receiving antenna placed at the point R_i, respectively.

We will discuss only the case of $t(T, P)$ calculation, for $t(P, R_i)$ we first shift points P and R_i to new points $P - R_i$ and $(0; 0; 0)$, and then we use the algorithm for $t(T, P - R_i)$. To be sure that the point $P - R_i$ is not within the wall, we will place one side of the wall onto the plane $y = 0$ (see Fig. 2).

First we construct a plane α containing both points T and P orthogonal to the plane $y = 0$. It is easy to show that the wave propagation "ray" lies in the plane α. Figure 2 shows the α plane section of the space. The distance of the projection $P_0 = (x_P; 0; z_P)$ onto the plane $y = 0$ is equal $s = \sqrt{x_P^2 + z_P^2}$.

Choosing the appropriate value s_* we have to minimize the function

$$f(s_*) = \frac{\sqrt{s_*^2 + w^2}}{c_w} + \frac{\sqrt{(s - s_*)^2 + (y_P - w)^2}}{c_a}, \tag{6}$$

where c_a and c_w are the air and wall wave propagation velocities, respectively.

After differentiation we arrive at Snell's law in the form:

$$\frac{s_*}{c_w \cdot \sqrt{s_*^2 + w^2}} = \frac{s - s_*}{c_a \cdot \sqrt{(s - s_*)^2 + (y_P - w)^2}}. \tag{7}$$

From Eq. (7) we get the algebraic equation

$$\begin{aligned} &\left[c_a^2 - c_w^2\right] \cdot s_*^4 - 2s\left[c_a^2 - c_w^2\right] \cdot s_*^3 \qquad (8) \\ +&\left[c_a^2 y_P (y_P - 2w) + (c_a^2 - c_w^2)(s^2 + w^2)\right] \cdot s_*^2 + 2c_w^2 \cdot s \cdot w^2 \cdot s_* - c_w^2 \cdot w^2 \cdot s^2 = 0. \end{aligned}$$

Solving Eq. (8), and choosing real s_* satisfying Eq. (7) we after the substitution get finally

$$t(T, P) = f(s_*). \tag{9}$$

3.3 Choice of the Initial Point $X^{[0]}$

To find a good guess for the point target position we may use a simplified "wave propagation" assuming that the signal propagates through the wall always perpendicularly [11]. If we place one side of the wall in the plane $y = y_P$, this approach leads us to the shifted point $P' = (x_P; y_P - w; z_P)$ (if we place the wall in the plane $y = 0$ we may shift transmitting antenna $T' = (0; w; 0)$, and receivers $R_i' = (x_i; w; z_i)$). Then the TOA for the i-th receiver is

$$\frac{\|T - P'\| + \|P' - R_i\|}{c_a} = \mathrm{TOA}_i(P') \approx \mathrm{TOA}_i(P) - \frac{2w}{c_w}. \tag{10}$$

The points P' with the same $\mathrm{TOA}_i(P')$-value lie on the circular ellipsoid. Further let us consider two pairs of receivers (placed on the x-axis, resp. z-axis) at points

$$R_1 = (x_1; 0; 0), \quad R_2 = (x_2; 0; 0), \quad R_3 = (0; 0; z_3), \quad R_4 = (0; 0; z_4),$$

with $x_1 > 0$, $x_2 < 0$, $z_3 > 0$, $z_4 < 0$.

We have to find the intersection point of 4 spheroids, which corresponds to the intersection point of two half-circles in 3D:

$$k_x : \quad (x_P; r_x \cdot \cos\varphi; r_x \cdot \sin\varphi), \quad \varphi \in [-\pi/2; \pi/2], \quad r_x > 0, \tag{11}$$

$$k_z : \quad (r_z \cdot \sin\psi; r_z \cdot \cos\psi; z_P), \quad \psi \in [-\pi/2; \pi/2], \quad r_z > 0. \tag{12}$$

For the first circle we get:

$$x_P = \frac{x_1^2 \cdot \mathrm{TOA}_2 - x_2^2 \cdot \mathrm{TOA}_1 + c_a^2\,\mathrm{TOA}_1\,\mathrm{TOA}_2\,(\mathrm{TOA}_2 - \mathrm{TOA}_1)}{2(x_1 \cdot \mathrm{TOA}_2 - x_2 \cdot \mathrm{TOA}_1)}, \tag{13}$$
$$r_x^2 = \frac{\left(x_1^2 - c_a^2\,\mathrm{TOA}_1^2\right)\left(x_2^2 - c_a^2\,\mathrm{TOA}_2^2\right)\left((x_1 - x_2)^2 - c_a^2\,(\mathrm{TOA}_1 - \mathrm{TOA}_2)^2\right)}{4\,c_a^2\,(x_1 \cdot \mathrm{TOA}_2 - x_2 \cdot \mathrm{TOA}_1)^2}.$$

Here $\mathrm{TOA}_i = \mathrm{TOA}_i(P')$, $i = 1, 2$. Similar formulas we get for z_P and r_z changing x to z, index 1 to index 3, and index 2 to index 4 in Eq. (13).

If there exists the intersection point P' that

$$r_x^2 = y_P^2 + z_P^2, \quad r_z^2 = y_P^2 + x_P^2 \quad \Longrightarrow \quad r_x^2 + x_P^2 = x_P^2 + y_P^2 + z_P^2 = r_z^2 + z_P^2,$$

and $P' = (x_P; \sqrt{z_P^2 - r_x^2}; z_P)$. However, for the shifted point P' it is better to use the central point for points defined by formulas (2) and (15) given below, which solve the problem of minimal distance of two half-circles (11) and (12):

1. For $r_x r_z \le |x_P||z_P|$ the distance between two half-circles is minimal for
$$P_x = \big(x_P;\ 0;\ r_x \cdot \mathrm{sign}(z_P)\big), \qquad P_z = \big(r_z \cdot \mathrm{sign}(x_P);\ 0;\ z_P\big). \tag{14}$$
2. For $r_x r_z > |x_P||z_P|$ (including cases $x_P = 0$ or/and $z_P = 0$) the distance between two half-circles is minimal for
$$P_x = \left(x_P;\ \frac{\Delta}{\rho_z};\ z_P \cdot \frac{\rho_x}{\rho_z}\right), \qquad P_z = \left(x_P \cdot \frac{\rho_z}{\rho_x};\ \frac{\Delta}{\rho_x};\ z_P\right), \tag{15}$$
where $\rho_x = \sqrt{r_x^2 + x_P^2}$, $\rho_z = \sqrt{r_z^2 + z_P^2}$, and $\Delta = \sqrt{r_x^2 r_z^2 - x_P^2 z_P^2}$ (see [13]).

4 Simulation Results

Let us consider an example with the point target at $P = (1; 0.5; -5)$ (units are meters). The point target is placed behind the reinforced concrete wall of the width $w = 0.4$ m. The relative permittivity $\varepsilon_w = 7.7$, and the corresponding wave propagation velocity is $c_w \doteq 0.10804$ m/ns, while the propagation velocity in air is $c_a \doteq 0.29975$ m/ns for $\varepsilon_a = 1.00026$. Velocities are calculated by formula $c_r = c/\sqrt{\varepsilon_r \cdot \mu_r}$, where c is the speed of the light, and relative permeability $\mu_r = 1$.

First we calculate corresponding values of TOA for given set of receivers.

```
>>> toa_generation_for_point
Give the wall width > 0 [m]: 0.4

 Material                   Relative Permittivity
==============================================
1 ice                        1.31
...
7 concrete                   5.89
8 reinforced concrete        7.7
9 stone                     10.17
===========================
 Choose wall kind [1-9]: 8
ca=0.29975, cw=0.10804 m/ns.
Receivers:
 -0.40000  0.00000  0.00000
  0.40000  0.00000  0.00000
  0.00000  0.00000  0.40000
  0.00000  0.00000 -0.40000
Give a destination point as vector [meters]:  [1 0.5 -5]
Times [nanoseconds - ns]:
41.24644    40.72468    42.24544    39.62926
```

Now we may try to localize the point target corresponding to given TOA vector:

```
>>> point_by_TOA
Give the wall width > 0 [m]:  0.4
...
Choose wall kind [1-9]:  8
Initial position of the target: 0.98544376    0.49992254    -4.9268018
Initial maximal TOA difference = 0.49784.
After 5 Newton iterations:
P=[0.9999999992    0.5000023513    -4.999999955].
Final maximal TOA difference after stage 1 = 2.4385e-08.
We try to determine more precise wall width!
After 2 Newton iterations:
P=[1.000013961    0.4999732585    -5.000070355].
Width=0.3999723071.
Final maximal TOA difference after stage 2 = 3.8794e-07.
Initial width corresponds better to measured TOA!
```

Using initial wall width value $w \ll 0.4\,\mathrm{m}$, we get:

```
Give the wall width > 0 [m]:  0.01
Initial position of the target: 1.1965945    0.15292128    -5.9880917
After 9 Newton iterations:
P=[1.196726914    0.09413554561    -5.991082667].
Final maximal TOA difference after stage 1 = 0.004219.
After 14 Newton iterations:
P=[1.000013961     0.4999732575    -5.000070357].
Width=0.3999723061.
Final maximal TOA difference after stage 2 = 3.8796e-07.
Determined width corresponds better to measured TOA!
```

Using initial wall width value $w \gg 0.4\,\mathrm{m}$, we get:

```
Give the wall width > 0 [m]:  2
Initial position of the target: 0.10713063            2    -0.54528336
After 8 Newton iterations:
P=[0.1973788749              2    -0.9179265285].
Final maximal TOA difference after stage 1 = 0.13174.
After 43 Newton iterations:
P=[1.000014457     0.2999704209    -5.000072857].
Width=0.3999713226.
Final maximal TOA difference after stage 2 = 4.0087e-07.
Determined width corresponds better to measured TOA!
```

Using initial wall width value $w = 0.4\,\mathrm{m}$ together with incorrect wall medium we get:

```
Choose wall kind [1-9]:  7
ca=0.29971, cw=0.12353 m/ns.
After 8 Newton iterations:
P=[1.029385325     0.4960514064    -5.148152235].
Final maximal TOA difference after stage 1 = 0.00074223.
After 6 Newton iterations:
P=[1.000009137      0.567036007     -5.00004632].
Width=0.4681998329.
Final maximal TOA difference after stage 2 = 3.9208e-07.
Determined width corresponds better to measured TOA!
```

5 Conclusion

Due to space limitation it is not possible to describe program and it features in more details. Especially, the precision of the position localization for non-precise or rounded TOA has to be studied.

We solved here only specific mathematical problem which, we hope, could be used in engineering practice. The determination of TOA itself, e.g., is a difficult technical problem, and there is very much work ahead.

As follows from the described, it is possible to use the method not only for point target localization, but also for specification of the wall width. Very good TOA correspondence has been achieved even for incorrect wall material assignment, the point target position is precise enough, however the method recognized different wall width (better corresponding to the higher speed within the wall).

Very high number of Newton's iterations in some cases is presumably related to the inexact (numerical) determination of gradient and Hesse matrix.

Acknowledgement. This work was supported by the Slovak Research and Development Agency under contract No. APVV-0404-12.

References

1. Foy, W.H.: Position-location solutions by Taylor-series estimation. IEEE Trans. Aerosp. Electron. Syst. **12**(2), 187–194 (1976)
2. Tanaka, R.: Report on SAR imaging. Internal report, 30 p. (2003)
3. Gauthier, S., Chamma, W.: Surveillance through concrete walls. Sensors, and command, control, communications, and intelligence (C3I) technologies for homeland security and homeland defense III. In: Carapezza, E.M. (ed.) Proceedings of SPIE, vol. 5403, pp. 597–608 (2004). doi:10.1117/12.533691
4. Cheung, K.W., So, H.C., Ma, W.-K., Chan, Y.T.: Least squares algorithms for time-of-arrival-based mobile location. IEEE Trans. Signal Process. **52**(4), 1121–1128 (2004)
5. Yu, K.: 3-D localization error analysis in wireless networks. IEEE Trans. Wirel. Commun. **6**(10), 3473–3481 (2007)
6. Aftanas, M., Rovňáková, J., Drutarovský, M., Kocur, D.: Efficient method of TOA estimation for through wall imaging by UWB radar. In: Proceedings of the 2008 IEEE International Conference on Ultra-Wideband (ICUWB 2008), vol. 2, pp. 101–104 (2008)
7. Aftanas, M., Zaikov, E., Drutarovský, M., Sachs, J.: Throughwall imaging of the objects scanned by M-sequence UWB radar system. In: Proceedings of the 18th International Conference Radioelektronika 2008, IEEE Catalog Number: CFP0885B, pp. 1–4 (2008). doi:10.1109/RADIOELEK.2008.4542687
8. Švecová, M., Kocur, D., Zetik, R.: Object localization using round trip propagation time measurements. In: Proceedings of the 18th International Conference Radioelektronika 2008, IEEE Catalog Number: CFP0885B, pp. 41–44 (2008)
9. Aftanas, M., Sachs, J., Drutarovský, M., Kocur, D.: Effcient and fast method of wall parameter estimation by using UWB radar system. Frequenz **63**(11–12), 231–235 (2009). ISSN 0016-1136
10. Kocur, D., Rovňáková, J., Švecová, M.: Through wall tracking of moving targets by M-sequence UWB radar. In: Rudas, I.J., Fodor, J., Kacprzyk, J. (eds.) Towards Intelligent Engineering and Information Technology. SCI, vol. 243, pp. 349–364. Springer, Heidelberg (2009)
11. Rovňáková, J., Kocur, D.: Compensation of wall effect for through wall tracking of moving targets. Radioengineering **18**(2), 189–195 (2009)
12. Rovňáková, J., Kocur, D.: TOA estimation and data association for through-wall tracking of moving targets. EURASIP J. Wirel. Commun. Netw. **2010**, 1–11 (2010). doi:10.1155/2010/420767. Article ID 420767
13. Buša, J., Kažimír, P., Kocur, D., Plavka, J.: Distance of 3D Half-Circles Appearing by UWB Signal Processing (in preparation)

Performance of a Wavelet Shrinking Method

Rune Dalmo(✉), Jostein Bratlie, and Børre Bang

R&D Group in Mathematical and Geometrical Modeling,
Numerical Simulations, Programming and Visualization,
Narvik University College, PO Box 385, 8505 Narvik, Norway
{rune.dalmo,jostein.bratlie,borre.bang}@hin.no
http://www.hin.no/Simulations

Abstract. A concept for shrinking of wavelet coefficients has been presented and explored in a series of articles [2–4]. The theory and experiments so far suggest a strategy where the shrinking adapts to local smoothness properties of the original signal. From this strategy we employ partitioning of the global signal and local shrinking under smoothness constraints. Furthermore, we benchmark shrinking of local partitions' wavelet coefficients utilizing a selection of wavelet basis functions. Then we present and benchmark an adaptive partition-based shrinking strategy where the best performing shrinkage is applied to individual partitions, one at a time. Finally, we compare the local and global benchmark results.

Keywords: Wavelet shrinking · Performance · Orthogonal wavelets

1 Introduction

Shrinking of wavelet coefficients was first introduced by Donoho and Johnstone [5,6] and has been an active area of research since then. Wavelet shrinkage are most notably applied to perform signal de-noising and within the quantification step of data compression.

Several strategies for thresholding- and non-thresholding type wavelet shrinkage of signals that belong to the general scale of Besov spaces were addressed in [4]. Later, in [2,3], adaptive strategies based on composition of Lorentz-type thresholding and Besov-type non-threshold shrinkage, suitable for spatially inhomogeneous signals which exhibit both smooth regions and regions with (isolated) singularities, were introduced and explored.

Motivated by some typical characteristics of curves and surfaces in computer aided geometric design (CAGD), notably that they can have smooth parts, singularities and varying smoothness measures, and that they can be piece-wise polynomials, we are interested in developing partition-based adaptive strategies for wavelet shrinkage.

In the following sections we describe the wavelet transform, coefficient shrinkage, compression, the test data we use and how we apply wavelet compression. Finally we give our concluding remarks where we comment on the results and suggest some topics for future work.

I. Dimov et al. (Eds.): NMA 2014, LNCS 8962, pp. 262–270, 2015.
DOI: 10.1007/978-3-319-15585-2_29

2 Curve Fitting by Wavelet Shrinkage

The wavelet transform [1] is a technique to represent any arbitrary function f as wavelets, generated by scaling and translations from one single mother function ψ:

$$\psi_{a,b}(t) = |a|^{-1/2}\psi\left(\frac{t-b}{a}\right), \quad (1)$$

where a and b are constants defining scaling and translation, respectively. It is required that the mother function has mean zero:

$$\int \psi(t)dt = 0, \quad (2)$$

which typically implies at least one oscillation of $\psi(t)$ across the t-axis. Following from the dilations of a single function, compared with the mother function, low frequency wavelets ($a > 1$) are wider in the t-direction, whereas high frequency wavelets ($a < 1$) are narrower.

For application within signal analysis, the parameters a and b in Eq. (1) are usually restricted through discretization. A dilation step ($a_0 > 1$) and a translation step ($b_0 \neq 0$) are fixed, leading to the wavelets for $j, k \in \mathbb{Z}$:

$$\psi_{jk}(t) = a_0^{-j/2}\psi(a_0^{-j}t - kb_0). \quad (3)$$

The discrete wavelet transform (DWT), T, associated with the discrete wavelets in Eq. (3), maps functions f to sequences indexed by $\mathbb{Z}^2$:

$$(Tf)_{jk} = \langle\psi_{jk}, f\rangle = a_0^{-j/2}\int \psi(a_o^{-j}t - kb_0)f(t)dt. \quad (4)$$

Following the principle of decomposition, f can be reconstructed from its wavelet coefficients $\beta_{jk} = \langle\psi_{jk}, f\rangle$:

$$f = \sum_{j,k}\beta_{jk}\psi_{jk}(t). \quad (5)$$

We address estimating f in the following non-parametric regression problem, as outlined in [2], by using orthonormal wavelets:

$$Y_i = f(X_i) + \epsilon_i, \quad i = 1, 2, \ldots, n, \quad (6)$$

where X_i are independent random variables uniformly distributed on $[0,1]^n$. We assume n independent identically distributed observations $Z_i, i = 1, 2, \ldots, n$, with unknown density $f(x)$, $x \in \mathbb{R}^n$, and errors $E\epsilon_1 = 0$, $E\epsilon_1^2 = \delta^2$.

As proposed in [2], let $B^s_{pq}(\mathbb{R}^n)$ be the Besov space with metric indices p, q and smoothness index s. For $f \in B^s_{pq}$, $0 < p \leq \infty$, $0 < q \leq \infty$, $n(\frac{1}{p} - 1)_+ < s < r$,

$$f(x) = \sum_{k\in\mathbb{Z}^d}\alpha_{0k}\phi^{[0]}_{0k}(x) + \sum_{j=0}^{\infty}\sum_{k\in\mathbb{Z}^d}\sum_{l=1}^{2^d-1}\beta^{[l]}_{jk}\psi^{[l]}_{jk}(x), \quad a.e. \quad x \in \mathbb{R}^d \quad (7)$$

holds, where $\alpha_{0k} = \langle \phi_{0k}^{[0]}, f \rangle$ and $\beta_{jk}[l] = \langle \psi_{jk}^{[l]}, f \rangle$. The empirical wavelet estimator $\hat{f}(x)$ is defined via:

$$\hat{f}(x) = \sum_{k \in \mathbb{Z}^d} \hat{\alpha}_{0k} \phi_{0k}^{[0]}(x) + \sum_{j=0}^{\infty} \sum_{k \in \mathbb{Z}^d} \sum_{l=1}^{2^d - 1} \hat{\beta}_{jk}^{[l]} \psi_{jk}^{[l]}(x), \quad a.e. \quad x \in \mathbb{R}^d, \tag{8}$$

where in this case of non-parametric regression as defined in Eq. (6):

$$\hat{\alpha}_{j_0 k} = \frac{1}{n} \sum_{i=1}^{n} \phi_{j_0 k}^{[0]}(X_i) Y_i, \quad \hat{\beta}_{jk}^{[l]} = \frac{1}{n} \sum_{i=1}^{n} \psi_{jk}^{[l]}(X_i) Y_i. \tag{9}$$

We note here that the estimator $\hat{f}$ can be obtained simply by replacing the coefficients in Eq. (7) by their empirical version, however, this procedure is not as fast as the DWT.

2.1 Coefficient Selection

Coefficient shrinkage can be obtained through the DWT in the following way:

1. Wavelet transform of the input data
2. Manipulation of the empirical wavelet coefficients
3. Inverse wavelet transform of the modified coefficients

The second step is where the shrinking occurs by adjusting the empirical wavelet coefficients towards zero. This manipulation usually depends on a classification of the coefficients where the goal is to obtain noise reduction without loosing too much information about the signal itself. One such classification is the binary case where a coefficient is either noisy and unimportant or relatively noise-free and important. Some sort of threshold on a measure of regularity, or criterion, is required in order to distinguish between such classes. For this purpose we will utilize the general Lorentz thresholding which was introduced in [4] and further explored in [2,3]. Utilizing the *Sobolev-type* embedding within the Besov-space scale: $B_{\eta\eta}^{\sigma} \hookrightarrow B_{pp}^{s}$ if $\sigma - \frac{1}{\eta} = s - \frac{1}{p} =: \tau \in \mathbb{R}$ and $0 < p \leq \eta < \infty$, the method is in brief, for compactly supported f and ψ and assuming that $j_0 = 0$ for any sample size n, as follows.

1. Consider all $(j,k) : \text{supp}(\psi_{jk}) \cap \text{supp}(f) \neq \emptyset$. Denote the set of all such (j,k) by $I(f,\psi)$.
2. Consider the decreasing rearrangement $\{b_\nu \ \nu = 1, \ldots, M\}$ of the finite set $\{2^{j(\tau+1/2)}\}|\hat{\beta}_{jk}| : (j,k) \in I(f,\psi)$. The wavelet estimator f_v^* is defined by

$$f_v^*(x) = \sum_k \hat{\alpha}_{0k} \phi_{0k}(x) + \sum_{\nu=1}^{[v^{-\frac{\eta p}{\eta - p}}]} \hat{\beta}_{j_\nu k_\nu} \psi_{j_\nu k_\nu}(x), \quad x \in \mathbb{R}, \tag{10}$$

where v is a smoothing factor.

3. Ensure uniqueness of f_v^* if the sequence $\{b_\nu\}$ is not strictly decreasing by removing redundant terms that are equal to the limit $b_{\left[v^{-\frac{\eta p}{\eta-p}}\right]}$.

The method outlined above is, according to [3], a far-going generalization of the concept of Lorentz-curve thresholding based on computability of the Peetre K-functional between Lebesgue spaces, in terms of non-increasing rearrangement of a measurable function, and isometricity of Besov spaces to vector-valued sequence spaces of Lebesques type. The significance of every $|\hat{\beta}_{jk}|$ is being assessed with respect to its level j so that the most significant features appear first and less significant details emerge only for sufficiently small ν. The criterion for significance of the coefficients is the regularity assumption expressed in the value of τ. Throughout this paper we shall fix τ to the boundary value $\tau = -\frac{1}{2}$ which corresponds to the critical regularity $\epsilon = -2(\eta - p)(\tau + \frac{1}{2}) = 0$.

2.2 Wavelet Compression

Compressing a wavelet-transformed signal is essentially a two-step process:

1. Quantify the wavelet coefficients
2. Code-word assignment for the quantified coefficients

Errors are introduced when wavelet coefficients are manipulated, eg. through shrinkage. We note that in order to achieve loss-less compression, that step has to be omitted.

The wavelet transformed and possibly quantified signal can be "packed" using error-free compression of the coefficients β, for example by applying Huffman code [7] or run-length encoding (RLE).

We investigate compression in this case with respect to quantification only by counting the relative number of coefficients which are discarded.

3 Wavelet Shrinkage Applied to a Partitioned Signal

In this preliminary experiment we benchmark the wavelet shrinking method, described in Sect. 2.1, on a synthetic test function $F(x) : x \in [0, 1]$ with four predetermined partitions which are re-parameterized to meet the intervals $[0, \frac{1}{4})$, $[\frac{1}{4}, \frac{1}{2})$, $[\frac{1}{2}, \frac{3}{4})$ and $[\frac{3}{4}, 1]$ of $F(x)$, respectively. The partitions are defined by the following "local" functions:

I The "λ-tear":

$$f_1(x) = x_+^\lambda \exp\left(-\tfrac{x^2}{1-x^2}\right), \quad \lambda > 0, \quad x \in [-0.2, 1], \tag{11}$$

where $x_+ = \max(x, 0)$ and we choose $\lambda = 0.25$.

II Double chirp:

$$f_2(x) = \sqrt{x} \exp\left(-\tfrac{x^2}{1-x^2}\right) \sin\left(64\pi x(1-x)\right), \quad x \in [0, 1]. \tag{12}$$

III Sinusoidal density, for $x \in [-3, 2]$:

$$f_3(x) = \begin{cases} \frac{1}{2}|\sin x| & \text{for} x \in [-2\pi/3, \pi/3], \\ 0 & \text{elsewhere.} \end{cases} \tag{13}$$

IV Triangle wave:

$$f_4(x) = \left|2\left(x - \left\lfloor x + \tfrac{1}{2}\right\rfloor\right)\right|, \quad x \in [0, 1]. \tag{14}$$

Each partition is sampled into 1024 uniformly distributed samples in our benchmark tests. 10 levels of DWT are applied such that only two scaling coefficients α are present together with 1022 wavelet coefficients β. We consider the following selection of wavelets:

1. Orthogonal Daubechies: d_1, d_2, d_4, d_8, d_{12}, d_{16}, d_{20}
2. Bi-orthogonal: $b_{1.1}$, $b_{1.3}$, $b_{1.5}$, $b_{2.2}$, $b_{2.4}$, $b_{2.6}$, $b_{2.8}$, $b_{3.1}$, $b_{3.3}$, $b_{3.5}$, $b_{3.7}$, $b_{3.9}$, $b_{4.4}$, $b_{5.5}$, $b_{6.8}$
3. Coiflets: c_1, c_2, c_3, c_4, c_5
4. Symlets: s_2, s_3, s_4, s_6, s_8, s_{10}, s_{12}, s_{14}, s_{16}, s_{18}, s_{20}
5. The discrete Meyer filter

and measure the Signal to Noise Ratio (SNR) in dB, defined as

$$\text{SNR} = 10 \log_{10}\left(\frac{\| F \|_2^2}{\| F - \hat{F} \|_2^2}\right), \tag{15}$$

where F is the original signal, $\hat{F}$ denotes the compressed (shrunk) signal and $\| \cdot \|_2^2$ stands for the square of the L_2 norm. Compression is measured in terms of how many of the wavelet coefficients β which are set to zero relative to the size of the signal. The scaling coefficients α_{0k} in Eq. (8) are not affected by the shrinking procedure.

It was noted in [2] that wavelets with relatively large support tend to oscillate near singularities. This, combined with standard wavelet theory, leads us to the following conjectures:

Conjecture 1. *The best performing wavelet, while shrinking according to some specified criteria of measure, for different kind of signals, are not the same.*

Conjecture 2. *The wavelet shrinking performance for a signal possessing varying smoothness or shape properties can increase if the signal is partitioned and shrunk using the best wavelet for each partition.*

Based on Conjectures 1 and 2 we propose the following method to compress and uncompress the global partitioned signal:

1. Select for each partition the wavelet which performs best according to some criterion, such as
   a. SNR threshold value, or
   b. performs best at high compression.

2. For each individual partition, perform DWT and apply coefficient shrinkage according to
   a. fixed SNR, or
   b. fixed compression ratio.
3. Reconstruct the individual partitions and use them to compose the global signal.

4 Results

Table 1 shows the "best" wavelets for the four individual partitions as well as the global composite function. The criteria used in the benchmark tests include measuring compression rates, where we select the wavelet providing the highest compression while maintaining SNR of 120 dB, 100 dB, 80 dB, and 60 dB, respectively. In addition, we include the wavelets providing the best SNR at approximately 99 % compression.

Table 1. The best performing wavelets according to selected criteria on the individual partitions and the global signal. The first four criteria are high compression rate while maintaining SNR of 120 dB, 100 dB, 80 dB, and 60 dB. The last criterion is fixing the compression rate to 99 % while maintaining high SNR. For each function, values for compression rates are shown in percent and SNR is shown in dB.

Criterion	Partition								Global function	
	I		**II**		**III**		**IV**			
120dB	b.5.5	93 %	s.18	87 %	b.3.3	93 %	d.2	96 %	s.12	85 %
100dB	b.3.3	95 %	s.20	90 %	b.3.1	94 %	d.2	96.5 %	s.10	88 %
80dB	b.3.1	97 %	s.18	93 %	b.3.1	95 %	b.3.1	97.5 %	b.6.8	91 %
60dB	b.3.1	98 %	s.12	95 %	b.2.2	97 %	b.2.2	98.5 %	b.6.8	94 %
99 %	b.3.1	45 dB	s.12	21 dB	b.2.8	28 dB	b.2.2	55 dB	s.16	22 dB

Figure 1 shows the performance on the global function of the best wavelets, as presented in Table 1, together with the performance of the adaptive strategy applied for fixed compression ratio. The horizontal axis displays the compression rate while the vertical axis shows the SNR measured in dB.

5 Concluding Remarks

As expected in Conjecture 1, since the four partitions are of different nature, they have different "best performing" wavelets. The smooth Double chirp function benefits from symlet type wavelets with relatively long support. Relatively short bi-orthogonal wavelets perform better on the Delta tear and the Sinusoidal density functions since they have one and two singularities, respectively, but are

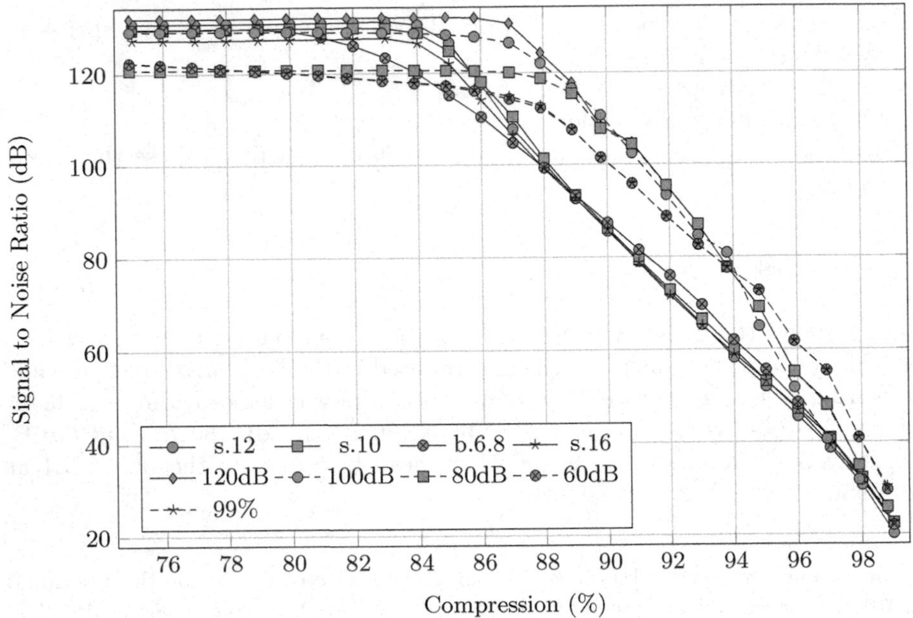

Fig. 1. Performance charts for the best performing wavelets and the adaptive method, for selected criteria as shown in Table 1, on the global composite test function F are shown. The Symlets s.12 and s.10 are those which provide highest compression ratio while maintaining SNR of 120 dB and 100 dB, respectively, while the bi-orthogonal wavelet b.6.8 is best at 80 dB and 60 dB. The Symlet s.16 generates best SNR at 99 % compression. Charts for the adaptive method for fixed compression ratio based on selecting the best wavelets for each partition according to the same criteria are shown as well.

smooth otherwise. Very short filters seem to suit the Triangle wave function well, which is no surprise, because it is linear and has one singularity. When shrinking the global function without invoking the adaptive strategy, fairly long wavelet filters provide the best results.

We conclude that the experiments presented in this paper support both Conjectures 1 and 2. The performance of different wavelets is depending on the signal's smoothness and singularity properties. Thus, for signals with varying smoothness properties, the partitioning-based adaptive approach can provide better coefficient shrinking performance than using one wavelet type on the whole signal.

The adaptive method provides increased compression rates when compared to the non-adaptive approach. Furthermore, it provides a significant increase in SNR for fixed compression rates. When applied to the test function, even for 99 % compression, the SNR is increased by approximately 5 dB.

The method is suitable for signals with varying smoothness properties, such as parametric representations of curves and surfaces.

Wavelet transform and shrinking of individual partitions are candidates for parallel computation since the partitions do not depend on each other.

As an anecdote, we note what is known as *Rose's criterion* [8]; that the SNR needs to be better than around 5 for the human eye to reliably identify an object.

5.1 Future Work

First of all we suggest using the findings presented in this article to construct an adaptive method. It would then be interesting to apply strategies for partitioning of the global signal. Local feature detection, such as identifying singularities or extreme values of functions, could be considered for this purpose.

For partitions containing isolated singularities, one possible improvement can be to invoke Besov type non-thresholding shrinkage as outlined in [2]. According to [4], this tends to produce better fitting of signals near singularities under the penalty of under-smoothing smooth regions. However, such under-smoothing could be compensated for in the partitioning process by selecting relatively small partitions near singularities.

The individual parts of the global signal could be classified by some smoothness measure, which could be seen in connection with the value of the parameter τ in Eq. (10). Lorentz type thresholding is performed here using a fixed value of $\tau = -\frac{1}{2}$ which is appropriate in cases when the signal's smoothness properties are unknown. We note that the method could be improved by considering the qualitative differences between strategies for "less regular" functions ($\tau < -\frac{1}{2}$) and "more regular" functions ($\tau > \frac{1}{2}$). Furthermore, this classification could also be considered to determine the best type of wavelet for each partition, possibly based on correlation.

References

1. Daubechies, I.: Orthonormal bases of compactly supported wavelets. Commun. Pure Appl. Math. **XLI**, 909–966 (1988)
2. Dechevsky, L.T., Grip, N., Gundersen, J.: A new generation of wavelet shrinkage: adaptive strategies based on composition of Lorentz-type thresholding and Besov-type non-threshold shrinkage. In: Truchetet, F., Laligant, O. (eds.) Wavelet Applications in Industrial Processing V. Proceedings of SPIE, Boston, MA, USA, vol. 6763, pp. 1–14 (2007)
3. Dechevsky, L.T., Gundersen, J., Grip, N.: Wavelet compression, data fitting and approximation based on adaptive composition of Lorentz-type Thresholding and Besov-type non-threshold shrinkage. In: Lirkov, I., Margenov, S., Waśniewski, J. (eds.) LSSC 2009. LNCS, vol. 5910, pp. 738–746. Springer, Heidelberg (2010)
4. Dechevsky, L.T., Ramsay, J.O., Penev, S.I.: Penalized wavelet estimation with Besov regularity constraints. Mathematica Balkanica (N. S.) **13**(3–4), 257–376 (1999)
5. Donoho, D.L., Johnstone, I.M.: Ideal spatial adaptation by wavelet shrinkage. Biometrika **8**(3), 425–455 (1994)
6. Donoho, D.L., Johnstone, I.M., Kerkyacharian, G., Picard, D.: Wavelet shrinkage: asymptopia? J. Roy. Stat. Soc. Ser. B **57**(2), 301–369 (1995)

7. Huffman, D.A.: A method for the construction of minimum-redundancy codes. In: Proceedings of the I.R.E., vol. 40, pp. 1098–1110 (1952)
8. Rose, A.: The sensitivity performance of the human eye on an absolute scale. J. Opt. Soc. Am. **38**(2), 196–208 (1948)

Two-Grid Decoupled Method for a Black-Scholes Increased Market Volatility Model

Miglena N. Koleva(✉) and Lubin G. Vulkov

Faculty of Natural Science and Education, University of Ruse,
8 Studentska Street, 7017 Ruse, Bulgaria
{mkoleva,lvalkov}@uni-ruse.bg

Abstract. In this paper we consider a pricing model that predicts increased implied volatility with minimal assumptions beyond those of the Black-Scholes theory. It is described by systems of nonlinear Black-Scholes equations. We propose a two-grid algorithm that consists of two steps: solving the coupled Partial Differential Equations (PDEs) problem on a coarse grid and then solving a number of decoupled sub-problems on a fine mesh by using the coarse grid solution to linearise each PDE of the system. Numerical experiments illustrate the efficiency of the method and validate the related theoretical analysis.

1 Introduction

The modern mathematical modeling in finance starts with the linear parabolic equation of Black-Scholes, see e.g. [12], which was derived under several non-realistic assumptions. Various (non-linear) modifications of this equation have been introduced in order to reflect adequately the market processes [3]. An important question then arises - to construct qualitative and effective methods for solving such problems.

In this work we consider a class of non-linear pricing models, derived in [10], that account for the feedback effect from the Black-Scoles dynamic hedging strategies on the price of the asset. For clarity, in this section we will outline some of the results and model formulation given in [10]. The authors consider the case where the program traders create the aggregate demand function $\phi(x,t)$ as a result of hedging strategies for n different derivative securities with expiration dates T_i ($T_1 \leq T_2 \leq \cdots \leq T_n = T$) and pay-off function $h_i(x)$, $i = 1, 2, \ldots, n$. They assume that the demand function of the reference traders is of appropriate form, such that to ensure the consistency with classical Black-Scholes equation, and derive the following system of n strongly coupled non-linear partial differential equations for the price of the i-th option $c_i(x,\tau)$ expiring at time T_i:

$$\frac{\partial c_i}{\partial \tau} + \frac{1}{2}V^2 x^2 \frac{\partial^2 c_i}{\partial x^2} + r\left(x\frac{\partial c_i}{\partial x} - c_i\right) = 0, \quad \tau \leq T_i, \quad x \in \mathbb{R}^+ \tag{1}$$
$$c_i(x, T_i) = h_i(x); \quad c_i(x,\tau) = 0, \quad \tau > T_i,$$

I. Dimov et al. (Eds.): NMA 2014, LNCS 8962, pp. 271–278, 2015.
DOI: 10.1007/978-3-319-15585-2_30

with volatility function $V(x,\tau,\widetilde{c})$ given by

$$V(x,\tau,\widetilde{c}) = \frac{(1 - S_0^{-1}\frac{\partial \widetilde{c}}{\partial x})\sigma}{1 - S_0^{-1}\frac{\partial \widetilde{c}}{\partial x} - S_0^{-1}x\frac{\partial^2 \widetilde{c}}{\partial x^2}} \quad \text{for } \widetilde{c}(x,\tau) = \sum_{i=1}^{m} \xi_i c_i(x,\tau),$$

where ξ_i is the insuring units for i-th option so that $\phi(x,\tau) = \sum_{i=1}^{m} \xi_i \frac{\partial c_i}{\partial x}$, σ is the volatility constant, r is the interest rate and S_0 is the asset with constant supply, $h_i(x) = \max(0, x - E_i)$ in the case of European Call option for strike prices E_i at the expiration data T_i. At each time interval $[T_{i-s}, T_i]$, $i = 1,\dots,n$, $0 < s < i$, $T_0 = 0$ we have to solve a system of $m = n - i + 1$ non-linear PDEs, corresponding to the m number of options prices c_i with expiration time $\geq T_i$. For example, if we have 5 options with exercise prises $E_1 < E_2 = E_3 < E_4 < E_5$ and $T_1 < T_2 = T_3 = T_4 < T_5 = T$, in time interval $[T_2, T_5]$ $(i = 5)$ we will solve 1 equation, corresponding to the option with exercise prise E_5, in $[T_1, T_2]$ $(i = 2)$ we solve a system of 4 non-linear PDEs, corresponding to options with exercise prises $E_2 = E_3 < E_4 < E_5$ and finally in $[T_0, T_1]$ $(i = 1)$ we solve a system of 5 equations, corresponding to options with exercise prises $E_1 < E_2 = E_3 < E_4 < E_5$, see Fig. 1 (left drawing).

In the case of uniform distribution $\xi_1 = \cdots = \xi_m = \xi$, the ratio ρ of the number of options being hedged to the total number of units of the asset in supply is $\rho = m\xi/S_0$ [10].

The existence, uniqueness and qualitative behavior in time are open questions. The scalar case $(n = 1)$ of the system (1) was studied for optimal systems, symmetry reduction and exact solutions in [1].

In this work we develop efficient numerical methods for solving the model problem (1). Accelerating two-grid algorithms, based on the decoupling procedure for solving the system of non-linear equations, are presented.

Many numerical methods for solving non-linear Black-Scholes equations can be found in the literature. In a series of papers R. Company and L. Jodar with their co-authors develop explicit methods for a large class of non-linear models, see e.g. [2], while P. Heider in [4] discuss implicit numerical scheme. Positive flux limited schemes are constructed in [7,8].

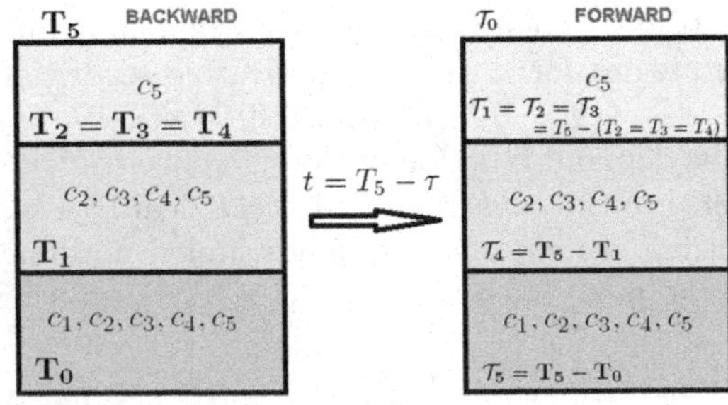

Fig. 1. Number of options at each time interval before and after time inversion

The remaining part of the paper is organized as follows. The basic numerical construction is described in the next section. On this base, two-grid decoupling algorithms are proposed in Sect. 3. Some examples discussed in Sect. 4 illustrate the effectiveness of the algorithms.

2 The Numerical Method

For convenience, as is usual for Black-Scholes models, we invert the time setting $t = T_n - \tau$, denote by $\mathcal{T}_i = T_n - T_{n-i}$, see Fig. 1 and consider the uniform distribution. Thus the model (1) transforms to the following *forward problem*, where boundary conditions corresponding to European call option are incorporated

$$\frac{\partial c_i}{\partial t} - \frac{1}{2}V^2 x^2 \frac{\partial^2 c_i}{\partial x^2} - r\left(x\frac{\partial c_i}{\partial x} - c_i\right) = 0, \quad 0 < t < T, \quad x \in \mathbb{R}^+,$$
$$V(x,t,\widetilde{c}) = \frac{\left[1-(\rho/m)\frac{\partial \widetilde{c}}{\partial x}\right]\sigma}{1-(\rho/m)\frac{\partial \widetilde{c}}{\partial x} - (\rho/m)x\frac{\partial^2 \widetilde{c}}{\partial x^2}}, \tag{2}$$
$$c_i(x,t) = 0, \quad t < \mathcal{T}_{n-i}, \quad n = 1,\ldots,n-1, \quad x \in \mathbb{R}^+, \tag{3}$$
$$c_i(x,t) = x - E_i e^{-rt}, \quad x \to \infty, \qquad c_i(0,t) = 0, \quad t < \mathcal{T}_i, \tag{4}$$

The problem (2)–(4) will be solved numerically on a truncated, large enough computational interval $[0, L]$. We consider uniform meshes in space and time

$$\omega_h = \{x_j = jh, \ j = 0,\ldots,N, \ h = L/N\},$$
$$\omega_\tau = \{t_k = k\Delta t, \ k = 0,\ldots,M, \ \Delta t = T/M\}$$

and denote the numerical solution of (2)–(4) at point (x_j, t_k) by C_j^k. Next, we define the following finite difference operators [9] on the mesh $\omega_h \times \omega_\tau$

$$C^k_{x,j} = \frac{C^k_{j+1} - C^k_j}{h}, \quad C^k_{\overline{x},j} = \frac{C^k_j - C^k_{j-1}}{h}, \quad C^k_{t,j} = \frac{C^{k+1}_j - C^k_j}{\Delta t}.$$

Consider the case of *one option* (scalar case) C with exercise price E. Thus we approximate (2)–(4) by the following implicit-explicit ($V_j^* = V_j^k$) or a fully implicit ($V_j^* = V_j^{k+1}$) difference scheme

$$C^k_{t,j} - \frac{1}{2}(V_j^*)^2 x_j^2 C^{k+1}_{\overline{x}x,i} - r\left(x_j C^{k+1}_{x,j} - C^{k+1}_j\right) = 0,$$
$$V_j^k = \frac{[1-\rho C^k_{x,j}]\sigma}{1-\rho C^k_{x,j} - \rho x_j C^k_{\overline{x}x,j}}, \quad j = 0,\ldots,N, \quad 0 < t^k < T, \tag{5}$$
$$C(0,t_{k+1}) = 0, \quad C(L,t_{k+1}) = L - Ee^{-rt_{k+1}}, \quad 0 < t^k < T, \tag{6}$$
$$C(x_j,0) = \max(0, x_j - E), \quad j = 0,\ldots,N. \tag{7}$$

In *multi-option* case in the interval $[\mathcal{T}_{i-1}, \mathcal{T}_{i+s}]$, $i = 1,\ldots,n$, $0 \le s \le n-i$, instead of solving a system of m non-linear PDEs, the numerical approximation of options C_i ($i = 1,\ldots,m$) can be computed by the following two stages:

1 stage. Noticing that all options in the time layer $[T_{i-1}, T_{i+s}]$ have one and the same volatility term V, we sum up all equations for C_i to obtain one non-linear equation for $\widetilde{C} = \sum_{i=1}^{m} C_i$. The corresponding implicit-explicit approximation is:

$$\widetilde{C}^k_{t,j} - \frac{1}{2}(V^k_j)^2 x_j^2 \widetilde{C}^{k+1}_{\overline{x}x,i} - r\left(x_j \widetilde{C}^{k+1}_{x,j} - \widetilde{C}^{k+1}_j\right) = 0,$$
$$V^k_j = \frac{[1-(\rho/m)\widetilde{C}^k_{x,j}]\sigma}{1-(\rho/m)\widetilde{C}^k_{x,j} - (\rho/m)x_j\widetilde{C}^k_{\overline{x}x,j}}, \quad j = 0,\dots,N, \quad T_{i-1} < t^k < T_{i+s}, \tag{8}$$

$$\widetilde{C}(0, t_{k+1}) = 0, \quad \widetilde{C}(L, t_{k+1}) = iL - \widetilde{E}e^{-rt_{k+1}}, \quad T_{i-1} < t^k < T_{i+s}, \tag{9}$$

$$\widetilde{C}(x_j, T_i) := \widetilde{C}(x_j, T_i) + \sum_{i=1}^{m^*} \max(0, x_j - E_i), \quad j = 0,\dots,N, \tag{10}$$

where m^* is the number of options with maturity data T_{i-1}.

2 stage. Each option C_i, $i = 1,\dots,m$ in $[T_{i-1}, T_{i+s}]$, we find from the corresponding linear problem (volatility term V^{k+1} is known from stage 1) for C_i:

$$(C_i)^k_{t,j} - \frac{1}{2}(V^{k+1}_j)^2 x_j^2 (C_i)^{k+1}_{\overline{x}x,i} - r\left(x_j (C_i)^{k+1}_{x,j} - C^{k+1}_i\right) = 0, \; j = 0,\dots,N, \tag{11}$$
$$C_i(0, t_{k+1}) = 0, \quad C_i(L, t_{k+1}) = L - E_i e^{-rt_{k+1}}, \tag{12}$$
$$C_i(x_j, T_i) = \max(0, x_j - E_i), \quad j = 0,\dots,N. \tag{13}$$

All discrete schemes (5)–(7), (8)–(10) and (11)–(13) can be written in the following equivalent vector form:

$$\alpha^*_j U^{k+1}_{j-1} + \beta^*_j U^{k+1}_j + \gamma^*_j U^{k+1}_{j+1} = \frac{1}{\Delta t} U^k_i, \quad j = 1,\dots,N-1 \tag{14}$$
$$U^{k+1}_0 = 0, \quad U^{k+1}_N = g(t_{k+1}), \quad \text{where} \tag{15}$$

$$\alpha^*_j = -\frac{x_j^2}{2h^2}(V^*_j)^2, \quad \beta^*_j = \frac{1}{\Delta t} + \frac{x_j^2}{h^2}(V^*_j)^2 + \frac{rx_j}{h} + r, \quad \gamma^*_j = -\frac{x_j^2}{2h^2}(V^*_j)^2 - \frac{rx_j}{h},$$
$$U = \begin{cases} C, & \text{for (5)–(7)}, \\ \widetilde{C}, & \text{for (8)–(10)} \\ C_i, & \text{for (11)–(13)} \end{cases}, \quad g(t_{k+1}) = \begin{cases} C(L, t_{k+1}), & \text{see (6)}, \\ \widetilde{C}(L, t_{k+1}), & \text{see (9)} \\ C_i(L, t_{k+1}), & \text{see (12)} \end{cases},$$

and $V^* = \{V^k, V^{k+1}\}$. Next, the scheme (14) can be written in more general matrix form $A^* U^{k+1} = F^k$, where α^*, β^*, γ^* are situated on off-diagonal and main diagonals of A^* and $F^k = [0, \frac{1}{\Delta t}U^k_1, \dots, \frac{1}{\Delta t}U^k_i, \dots, \frac{1}{\Delta t}U^k_{N-1}, g(t_{k+1})]^T$.

Theorem 1. *For any $k = 0, 1, \dots, M$, the matrix A^* of the system (14) is an M-matrix.*

Proof. Note that $\alpha_j^* < 0$, $\beta_j^* > 0$, $\gamma_j^* < 0$ and $\beta_j^* \geq |\alpha_j^*| + |\gamma_j^*| + 1/\Delta t$. Moreover A^* is irreducible matrix and therefore by [11] follows that A^* is an M-matrix.

3 Two-Grid Decoupling Algorithms

Our aim is to construct a fast and accurate numerical method for solving the model problem (2)–(4), implementing the two-grid technique [5,6].

Let us define two uniform meshes in space (just as ω_h in Sect. 2): *coarse mesh* ω_H and *fine mesh* ω_h, $H \gg h$ and denote the numerical solution, computed on the mesh ω_H (ω_h) by C^H (C^h).

Time interval with one option. At each time level t_k, $k = 1, 2, \dots, M$
Step 1. Solve (5)–(7) on the coarse mesh ω_H, where $V^* = V^k$ to obtain C^H;
Step 2. Solve (5)–(7) on the fine mesh ω_h, where $V^* = V^H$ to obtain C^h;

Time interval with multi option. At each time level t_k, $k = 1, 2, \dots, M$
Step 1. Solve (8)–(10) on the coarse mesh ω_H to obtain $\widetilde{C}^H$;
Step 2. For each option C_i, $i = 1, \dots, m$ solve (11)–(13) on the fine mesh ω_h, where $V^{k+1} := V^H$ (i.e. computed from $\widetilde{C}^H$) to obtain C_i^h;

Note that the problems (11)–(13) for C_i at Step 2 can be solved simultaneously, because they are independent of each other.

Numerical experiments with $h = H^{1+\alpha}$, $\alpha > 0$ show that the optimal accuracy on coarse/fine space mesh is achieved at $\alpha = 1$.

For data transfer from coarse to fine and from fine to coarse mesh we apply a cubic spline interpolation.

Using (14) and Theorem 1 one can prove the following assertion.

Theorem 2. *The numerical solution, computed by* Step 1. - Step 2. *is stable in maximal discrete norm and non-negative at each* Step *and each lime level.*

4 Numerical Examples

In this section we test the accuracy and convergence rate of the presented numerical method for problems (2)–(4). Model parameters are $r = 0.04$, $\sigma = 0.4$ [10].

In [10], the authors observe that in scalar case, because of the unboundness of the second derivative of the terminal pay-off function, the denominator of the the volatility term $V(x, \tau)$ becomes zero at maturity time T. Thus the equation (1) becomes meaningless. To prevent this situation a regularization parameter $\varepsilon \sim \mathcal{O}(\rho^2)$ is involved and the problem is solved up to time $T - \varepsilon$ instead of T and for a terminal (initial after time inversion) condition is chosen $c_i(x, T - \varepsilon) = C_{BS}(x, T - \varepsilon; E_i)$, where $C_{BS}(x, \tau; E_i)$ is the solution of linear Black-Scholes equation in the case of European call option with exercise price E_i.

We compute the order of convergence in maximal discrete norm by the following formula:

$$CR_\infty = \log \frac{E_\infty^{N_1}/E_\infty^{N_2}}{\log(N_2/N_1)}, \qquad E_\infty^N = \max_{0 \leq j \leq N} |E_j^N|, \tag{16}$$

where E_j^N is the difference between the numerical solutions at point (x_j, T_i) on mesh with N grid nodes in space and exact solution at the same point. If the exact solution is not available, for exact solution we use the numerical solution, computed on the very fine mesh. Because the meshes may not be embedded, a cubic spline interpolation is used in order to compare the solutions.

Let us consider the case of three options with different maturity times $T_1 = 0.25$, $T_2 = 0.5$, $T_3 = 0.75$ and different exercise prices $E_1 = 4$, $E_2 = 5$, $E_3 = 6$. For the test examples we set $\rho = 0.05$, $\varepsilon = 0.003$ [10] and $\rho = 0.01$ (without regularization), $h = H^2$, $\tau = H$ (for computations only by Step 1) and $\tau = H^2$ (for computations by Step 2), $L = 10$.

We verify the order of convergence, using (16). For the case $\rho = 0.05$ we use as exact solution the numerical solution on very fine mesh (500 coarse and 2500 fine grid nodes in space for two-grid procedure), while for $\rho = 0.01$ we add appropriate residual term in the right hand side of (2), such that $C_{BS}(x, \tau; E_i)$ to be the exact solution of each problem, corresponding to the option C_i.

On Figs. 2, 3, and 4 we plot graphics in log-scale of E_∞^N versus N (the number of coarse grid nodes) for option value C_3, computed with one mesh (Step 1) or two meshes (Step 2) at $t = T_2 = 0.25$ (Fig. 2); numerical option values C_2, C_3 at $t = T_1 = 0.5$ (Fig. 3) and numerical option values C_1, C_2, C_3 at $t = T = 0.75$ (Fig. 4). Comparison lines whose absolute value of the slope is equal to the expected CR are also plotted. The left graphics correspond to $\rho = 0.05$, while the right ones are for $\rho = 0.01$. It is clear that the order of convergence in space is close to 1 for Step 1 and close to 2 for Step 2 with respect to the coarse space mesh, i.e. $\mathcal{O}(\triangle t + H^2 + h)$.

On Fig. 5 we plot evolution graphics of the solutions C_1, C_2, C_3 in regions in which they are available, coming back to the original time.

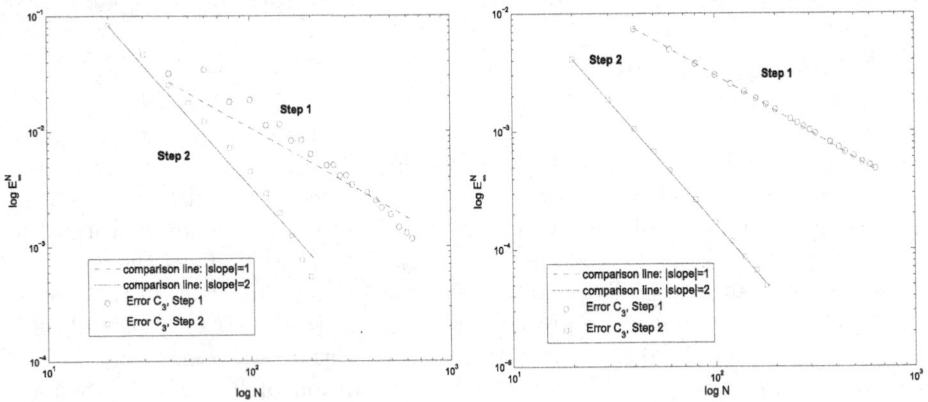

Fig. 2. Convergence rate of the numerical solutions C_3, $t = 0.25$, $\rho = 0.05$, $\varepsilon = 0.003$ (*left*); $\rho = 0.01$, $\varepsilon = 0$ (*right*)

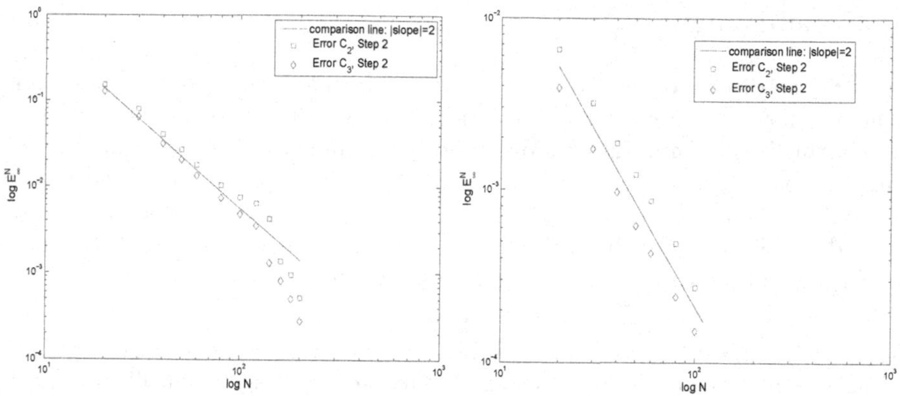

Fig. 3. Convergence rate of the numerical solutions C_2, C_3, $t = 0.5$, $\rho = 0.05$, $\varepsilon = 0.003$ (*left*); $\rho = 0.01$, $\varepsilon = 0$ (*right*)

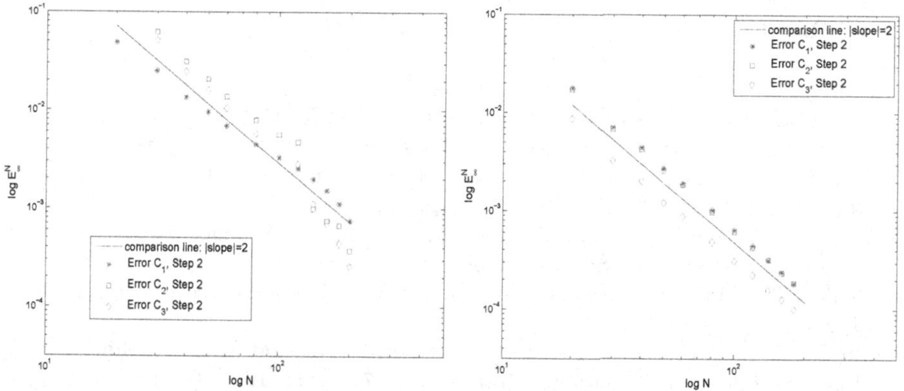

Fig. 4. Convergence rate of the numerical solutions C_1, C_2, C_3, $t = 0.75$, $\rho = 0.05$, $\varepsilon = 0.003$ (*left*); $\rho = 0.01$, $\varepsilon = 0$ (*right*)

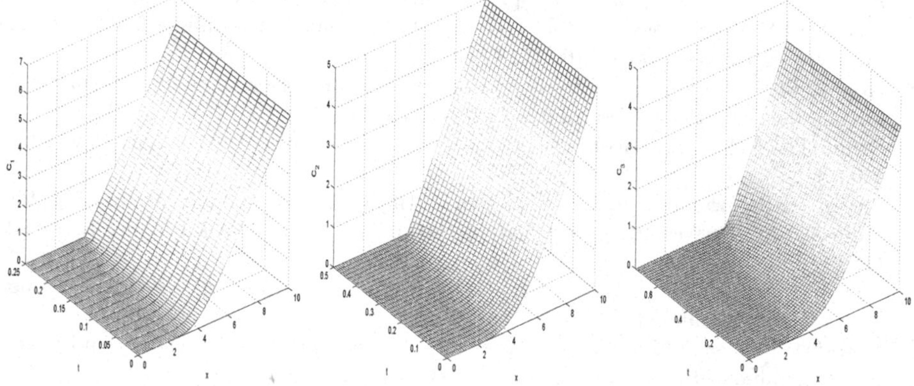

Fig. 5. Evolution graphics of the numerical solutions C_1 (*left*), C_2 (*center*), C_3 (*right*), $N = 81$, $\tau = h$, $h = H^2$, $t = 0.75$, $\rho = 0.05$, Step 2

5 Conclusions

Through the discussion of the results it was concluded that the proposed technique produces an approximate solution that is always stable. In order to remedy this large computational overhead, we implement the two-grid method. This method increases the accuracy as well as the efficiency. Both the solvers have difficulty converging during the first few time steps, because of non-smooth initial data. So, we plan to investigate some adaptive time stepping techniques. We also intend to study the convergence of the two-grid method.

Acknowledgement. This research was supported by the European Commission under Grant Agreement number 304617 (FP7 Marie Curie Action Project Multi-ITN STRIKE - Novel Methods in Computational Finance) and Bulgarian National Fund of Science under Project DID 02/37-2009.

References

1. Bordag, L.A.: Pricing options in illiquid markets: optimal systems, symmetry reductions and exact solutions. Lobachevskii J. Math. **31**(2), 90–99 (2010)
2. Company, R., Jódar, L., Fakharany, M., Casabán, M.-C.: Removing the correlation term in option pricing heston model: numerical analysis and computing. Abstr. Appl. Anal. 2013, Article ID 246724, 11 pp. (2013)
3. Ehrhardt, M. (ed.): Nonlinear Models in Mathematical Finance: Research Trends in Option Pricing. Nova Science Publishers, New York (2009)
4. Heider, P.: Numerical methods for non-linear Black-Scholes equations. Appl. Math. Finance **17**(1), 59–81 (2010)
5. Jin, J., Shu, S., Xu, J.: A two-grid discretization method for decoupling systems of partial differential equations. Math. Comp. **75**, 1617–1626 (2006)
6. Jovanovic, B., Koleva, M.N., Vulkov, L.G.: Convergence of a FEM and two-grid algorithms for elliptic problems on disjoint domains. J. Comp. Appl. Math. **236**(3), 364–374 (2011)
7. Koleva, M.N., Vulkov, L.G.: On splitting-based numerical methods for nonlinear models of European options. Int. J. Comp. Math. (Published online: 27 Mar 2014, in press). doi:10.1080/00207160.2014.884713
8. Koleva, M.N., Vulkov, L.G.: A second-order positivity preserving numerical method for Gamma equation. Appl. Math. Comp. **220**, 722–734 (2013)
9. Samarskii, A.A.: The Theory of Difference Schemes. Marcel Dekker Inc., New York (2001)
10. Sircar, K.R., Papanicolaou, G.: General Black-Scholes models accounting for increased market volatility from hedging strategies. Appl. Math. Finance **5**, 45–82 (1998)
11. Varga, R.S.: Matrix Iterative Analysis. Springer, Heidelberg (2000). (Second Revised and Expanded Edition)
12. Wilmott, P.: Crash Modeling (Chapter 27). In: Derivatives: The Theory and Practice of Financial Engineering, pp. 383–393. Whiley, Chichester (1998)

The Effect of a Postprocessing Procedure to Upper Bounds of the Eigenvalues

A.B. Andreev[1] and M.R. Racheva[2(✉)]

[1] Institute of Information and Communication Technologies, BAS, Sofia, Bulgaria
[2] Technical University of Gabrovo, Gabrovo, Bulgaria
milena@tugab.bg

Abstract. This paper presents a postprocessing technique applied to second- and fourth-order eigenvalue problems. It has been proved that this approach always ensures asymptotically upper bounds for corresponding eigenvalues. The main goal could be formulated as follows: if nonconforming finite elements are used giving lower bounds of eigenvalues, then the presented algorithm is a simple approach for obtaining two-sided bounds of eigenvalues; if conforming finite elements are used by origin, the postprocessing algorithm gives improved approximations of the eigenvalues, which remain asymptotically greater than the exact ones.

Some different aspects of the method applicability are also discussed. Finally, computer based implementations are presented.

1 Introduction

The aim of this paper is to propose and analyze an a-posteriori procedure for the finite element approximations of some second- and fourth-order eigenvalue problems. This method gives a simple way to obtain an approximation from above without solving the eigenvalue problem by conforming finite elements (see [1]). On the other hand, the adaptive procedures based on a-posteriori error estimates which accelerate the order of the FE convergence have gained an enormous importance. Several approaches have been considered in order to construct a method for second- and fourth-order elliptic problems (see [2–4] and the references therein).

Let Ω be a bounded polygonal domain in $\mathbf{R}^2$ with a boundary $\partial\Omega$. Let also $H^s(\Omega)$ be the usual s-th order Sobolev space on Ω with a norm $\|\cdot\|_{s,\Omega}$ and a seminorm $|\cdot|_{s,\Omega}$ and $(\cdot,\cdot)$ denote the $L_2(\Omega)$-inner product.

Consider the following model eigenvalue problems:

$$\begin{aligned} -\Delta^m u = \lambda u \quad \text{in } \Omega, \quad m = 1;2, \\ u = 0 \quad \text{on } \partial\Omega. \end{aligned} \tag{1}$$

The variational elliptic eigenvalue problems associated with (1) are: find number $\lambda \in \mathbf{R}$ and function $u \in H_0^m(\Omega)$, $m = 1;2$ such that

I. Dimov et al. (Eds.): NMA 2014, LNCS 8962, pp. 279–286, 2015.
DOI: 10.1007/978-3-319-15585-2_31

$$a(u,v) = \lambda(u,v), \quad \forall\, v \in V \equiv H_0^m(\Omega), \; m = 1;2, \qquad (2)$$
$$\|u\|_{0,\Omega} = 1,$$

where

$$a(u,v) = \int_\Omega \nabla u \cdot \nabla v \, dx\, dy \quad \forall\, u,v \in V$$

or

$$a(u,v) = \int_\Omega \Delta u . \Delta v \, dx\, dy \quad \forall\, u,v \in V,$$

for second- or fourth-order problem, respectively.

Obviously, the bilinear forms $a(\cdot,\cdot)$ are symmetric, continuous on $H^m(\Omega)$ and coercive on $H_0^m(\Omega)$, $m = 1;2$. It is well known that the solution of (2) in both cases is given by a sequence of pairs $(\lambda_j, u_j, j = 1,2,\ldots,)$, with positive eigenvalues $0 < \lambda_1 \le \lambda_2 \le \ldots \to +\infty$ (see e.g. [1]).

The corresponding eigenfunctions u_j can be chosen to be orthonormal in $L_2(\Omega)$ and they constitute a Hilbert basis for V.

2 Finite Element Method

Let τ_h be a triangulation of Ω which satisfies the usual regularity condition (see [5]), i.e. there exists a constant $\sigma > 0$ such that $h_K/\rho_K \le \sigma$, where h_K is the diameter of the element (triangle or rectangle) $K \in \tau_h$ and ρ_K being the diameter of the largest circle contained in K. Then we denote $h = \max_{K\in\tau_h} h_K$.

In our considerations we also include the case when nonconforming finite elements are used. Then let us define mesh-dependent bilinear form

$$a_h(u,v) = \sum_{K\in\tau_h} a_K(u,v), \quad u,v \in V,$$

where

$$a_K(u,v) = \int_K \nabla u \cdot \nabla v \, dx\, dy$$

or

$$a_K(u,v) = \int_K \Delta u \Delta v \, dx\, dy$$

for second- or fourth-order problem, respectively. In case of conforming FEM, obviously $a(\cdot,\cdot)$ and $a_h(\cdot,\cdot)$ coincide.

Defining a piecewise polynomial space V_h, the approximation of the problem (2) is: find $\lambda_h \in \mathbf{R}$ and $u_h \in V_h$, $u_h \neq 0$ such that

$$a_h(u_h,v_h) = \lambda_h(u_h,v_h), \quad \forall\, v_h \in V_h. \qquad (3)$$

Later on, we will specify the finite element discussing especially the nonconforming case of finite element method giving lower bounds of eigenvalues, i.e. when $\lambda_h \leq \lambda$.

Let u_h be the solution of (3). Then we consider the following elliptic problem:

$$a(\widetilde{w}_h, \widetilde{v}_h) = (u_h, \widetilde{v}_h), \quad \forall \widetilde{v}_h \in \widetilde{V}_h, \tag{4}$$

where the FEM is conforming, so that $\widetilde{V}_h \subset V$.

We introduce the number

$$\widetilde{\lambda}_h = \frac{1}{(u_h, \widetilde{w}_h)},$$

where u_h and $\widetilde{w}_h$ are solutions of (3) and (4), respectively. The number $\widetilde{\lambda}_h$ approximates λ. Furthermore, in [6] the authors determine the conditions under which $\widetilde{\lambda}_h$ is superclose to λ.

Let us consider the function

$$\widetilde{u}_h = \widetilde{\lambda}_h \widetilde{w}_h,$$

where $\widetilde{w}_h$ is the solution of (4). This function approximates the exact eigenfunction (see [7]).

3 Main Results

In this section, we will prove that the additional solution of (4) gives eigenvalue approximation from above. First, we propose a simple method to obtain approximate eigenvalue closer to the exact one up to a multiplicative constant.

For that purpose, let us introduce the number $\overline{\lambda}_h = \mathcal{R}(\widetilde{u}_h)$, where $\mathcal{R}$ is the Rayleigh quotient.

Theorem 1. *For the first (essential) eigenvalue λ_1 we have*

$$\lambda_1 \leq \overline{\lambda}_{1,h} \leq \widetilde{\lambda}_{1,h}. \tag{5}$$

Moreover, $\overline{\lambda}_{1,h}$ and $\widetilde{\lambda}_{1,h}$ approximate the exact eigenvalue by one and the same order of convergence.

Proof. It is easy to see that

$$(\widetilde{u}_h, u_h) = \widetilde{\lambda}_h (\widetilde{w}_h, u_h) = \widetilde{\lambda}_h . \frac{1}{\widetilde{\lambda}_h} = 1.$$

On the other hand

$$(\widetilde{u}_h, \widetilde{u}_h) = (\widetilde{u}_h - u_h, \widetilde{u}_h - u_h) + 2(\widetilde{u}_h, u_h) - (u_h, u_h).$$

Using that u_h is normalized, i.e. $\|u_h\|_{0,\Omega} = 1$, it follows that

$$(\widetilde{u}_h, \widetilde{u}_h) = \|\widetilde{u}_h - u_h\|_{0,\Omega}^2 + 1,$$

and thus

$$\|\widetilde{u}_h\|_{0,\Omega}^2 = \|\widetilde{u}_h - u_h\|_{0,\Omega}^2 + 1 = \varepsilon(h) + 1 \geq 1. \tag{6}$$

Let λ_1 be the first exact eigenvalue and $\widetilde{u}_{1,h}$ be the approximate eigenfunction of u_1 by (4). Using that $\widetilde{u}_{1,h} \in \widetilde{V}_h \subset V$, we easily get

$$\lambda_1 = \min_{\substack{v \in V \\ v \neq 0}} \mathcal{R}(v) \leq \mathcal{R}(\widetilde{u}_{1,h}) = \overline{\lambda}_{1,h}. \tag{7}$$

Moreover, from (6), for any $\overline{\lambda}_h$ and $\widetilde{\lambda}_h$ it follows that

$$\overline{\lambda}_h = \mathcal{R}(\widetilde{u}_h) = \frac{a(\widetilde{u}_h, \widetilde{u}_h)}{(\widetilde{u}_h, \widetilde{u}_h)} = \frac{\widetilde{\lambda}_h^2 a(\widetilde{w}_h, \widetilde{w}_h)}{(\widetilde{u}_h, \widetilde{u}_h)}$$

$$= \frac{\widetilde{\lambda}_h^2 (u_h, \widetilde{w}_h)}{(\widetilde{u}_h, \widetilde{u}_h)} = \frac{\widetilde{\lambda}_h^2 \frac{1}{\widetilde{\lambda}_h}}{(\widetilde{u}_h, \widetilde{u}_h)} = \frac{\widetilde{\lambda}_h}{\varepsilon(h) + 1} \leq \widetilde{\lambda}_h,$$

which, together with (7) proves (5).

Next, we show that the two differences $\lambda - \widetilde{\lambda}_h$ and $\lambda - \overline{\lambda}_h$ have one and the same order of convergence. Consider the equalities:

$$a(\widetilde{u}_h - u, \widetilde{u}_h - u) - \lambda(\widetilde{u}_h - u, \widetilde{u}_h - u) = a(\widetilde{u}_h, \widetilde{u}_h) - 2a(\widetilde{u}_h, u) + a(u, u)$$

$$-\lambda(\widetilde{u}_h, \widetilde{u}_h) + 2\lambda(\widetilde{u}_h, u) - \lambda(u, u) = a(\widetilde{u}_h, \widetilde{u}_h) - \lambda(\widetilde{u}_h, \widetilde{u}_h).$$

In the last equality we use the fact that $\widetilde{V}_h \subset V$ and that u is a solution of (2).

Adopting the notation $\sqrt{a(v, v)} = \|v\|_{a,\Omega}$ for any $v \in V$, we get

$$\overline{\lambda} - \lambda = \mathcal{R}(\widetilde{u}_h) - \lambda = \frac{a(\widetilde{u}_h, \widetilde{u}_h)}{(\widetilde{u}_h, \widetilde{u}_h)} - \lambda$$

$$= \frac{\|\widetilde{u}_h - u\|_{a,\Omega}^2 - \lambda\|\widetilde{u}_h - u\|_{0,\Omega}^2}{\|\widetilde{u}_h\|_{0,\Omega}^2}.$$

Consequently

$$\overline{\lambda}_h - \lambda = \mathcal{O}\left(\|\widetilde{u}_h - u\|_{a,\Omega}^2\right),$$

but this is the same order of convergence for $\widetilde{\lambda}_h - \lambda$ (see, e.g. [4,6,7]).

Remark 1. One could be able to introduce some other approximate eigenfunctions, for example

$$\overline{u}_h = \overline{\lambda}_h \widetilde{w}_h, \quad \text{or } \widehat{u}_h = \lambda_h \widetilde{w}_h.$$

Then the proposed postprocessing technique also accelerates the convergence of eigenpairs. Nevertheless, the order of error estimates is the same for the different cases. Let us emphasize that

$$\mathcal{R}(\widehat{u}_h) = \mathcal{R}(\overline{u}_h) = \mathcal{R}(\widetilde{u}_h).$$

Remark 2. It is obvious to expect that $\overline{\lambda}_{k,h}$ is closer to λ_k than $\widetilde{\lambda}_{k,h}$ for $k = 1, 2, 3, \ldots$ (see the last section of the paper).

Next, an original approach for obtaining approximation from above of eigenvalues is presented.

Consider the following eigenvalue problem applying conforming FEM: find $\widetilde{\Lambda}_h \in \mathbf{R}$ and $\widetilde{U}_h \in \widetilde{V}_h$, $\widetilde{U}_h \neq 0$, such that

$$a(\widetilde{U}_h, \widetilde{v}_h) = \widetilde{\Lambda}_h(\widetilde{U}_h, \widetilde{v}_h), \quad \forall \widetilde{v}_h \in \widetilde{V}_h. \tag{8}$$

We suppose that the solution $(\widetilde{\Lambda}_h, \widetilde{U}_h)$ is available. It is well-known [1] that $\lambda \leq \widetilde{\Lambda}_h$, where λ is the corresponding exact eigenvalue.

Theorem 2. *If the partition τ_h of Ω is uniform, then for h sufficiently small:*

$$\widetilde{\Lambda}_h \leq \widetilde{\lambda}_h.$$

Proof. First, it could be noted that

$$a(\widetilde{u}_h, \widetilde{u}_h) = \widetilde{\lambda}_h a(\widetilde{w}_h, \widetilde{u}_h) = \widetilde{\lambda}_h(u_h, \widetilde{u}_h) = \widetilde{\lambda}_h.$$

Then

$$a(\widetilde{u}_h - \widetilde{U}_h, \widetilde{u}_h - \widetilde{U}_h) - \widetilde{\Lambda}_h(\widetilde{u}_h - \widetilde{U}_h, \widetilde{u}_h - \widetilde{U}_h)$$

$$= a(\widetilde{u}_h, \widetilde{u}_h) - 2a(\widetilde{u}_h, \widetilde{U}_h) + a(\widetilde{U}_h, \widetilde{U}_h)$$

$$-\widetilde{\Lambda}_h(\widetilde{u}_h, \widetilde{u}_h) + 2\widetilde{\Lambda}_h(\widetilde{u}_h, \widetilde{U}_h) - \widetilde{\Lambda}_h(\widetilde{U}_h, \widetilde{U}_h)$$

$$= \widetilde{\lambda}_h - 2\widetilde{\Lambda}_h(\widetilde{u}_h, \widetilde{U}_h) + \widetilde{\Lambda}_h - \widetilde{\Lambda}_h(\widetilde{u}_h, \widetilde{u}_h) + 2\widetilde{\Lambda}_h(\widetilde{u}_h, \widetilde{U}_h) - \widetilde{\Lambda}_h$$

$$= \widetilde{\lambda}_h - \widetilde{\Lambda}_h(\widetilde{u}_h, \widetilde{u}_h).$$

From these equalities and (6), it follows

$$\|\widetilde{u}_h - \widetilde{U}_h\|^2_{a,\Omega} - \widetilde{\Lambda}_h\|\widetilde{u}_h - \widetilde{U}_h\|^2_{0,\Omega} = \widetilde{\lambda}_h - \widetilde{\Lambda}_h\|\widetilde{u}_h\|^2_{0,\Omega}$$

$$= \widetilde{\lambda}_h - \widetilde{\Lambda}_h \left(\|\widetilde{u}_h - u_h\|^2_{0,\Omega} + 1 \right)$$

$$= (\widetilde{\lambda}_h - \widetilde{\Lambda}_h) - \widetilde{\Lambda}_h \|\widetilde{u}_h - u_h\|^2_{0,\Omega}.$$

Finally

$$\widetilde{\lambda}_h - \widetilde{\Lambda}_h = \|\widetilde{u}_h - \widetilde{U}_h\|^2_{a,\Omega} - \widetilde{\Lambda}_h \|\widetilde{u}_h - \widetilde{U}_h\|^2_{0,\Omega} + \widetilde{\Lambda}_h \|\widetilde{u}_h - u_h\|^2_{0,\Omega}. \tag{9}$$

Using the uniformity of partition τ_h we denote $h = \sqrt{h_x^2 + h_y^2}$, where h_x and h_y are the side lengths in x- and y-direction, respectively of any rectangle or right triangle $K \in \tau_h$.

Consider the first two terms in the right-hand side of (9). The function

$$q_h = \widetilde{u}_h - \widetilde{U}_h$$

is a piecewise polynomial function defined on Ω. So, the restriction of q_h on K is a polynomial of degree N.

Let $\widehat{\varphi}_i(\widehat{x}, \widehat{y})$, $i = 1, \dots, N$ be the basic functions determined on the reference finite element $\widehat{K}$, $i = 1, \dots, N$, where $N = (n+1)^2$ or $N = \dfrac{(n+1)(n+2)}{2}$ for rectangular or triangular elements, respectively.

Then for any $K \in \tau_h$ the corresponding functions are $\varphi_i\left(\dfrac{x}{h_x}, \dfrac{y}{h_y}\right)$, $i = 1, \dots, n$.

Obviously,

$$q_{h|K} = \sum_{i=1}^{n} \alpha_i \varphi_{i|K}$$

with coefficients α_i, $i = 1, \dots, n$.

Denote by D^m any partial derivative of order m, where $m = 1$ or $m = 2$. Then, denoting

$$I_0(h) = \int_K q_h^2 \, dx \, dy = \sum_{i=1}^{n} \alpha_i \int_K \varphi_i^2 \, dx \, dy,$$

$$I_m(h) = \int_K (D^m q_h)^2 \, dx \, dy = \sum_{i=1}^{n} \alpha_i \int_K (D^m \varphi_i)^2 \, dx \, dy,$$

it is obvious that for sufficiently small h:

$$I_m(h) \geq I_0(h).$$

Hence $\|q_h\|^2_{a,\Omega} \geq \|q_h\|^2_{0,\Omega}$ and from (9) we have

$$\widetilde{\lambda}_h \geq \widetilde{\Lambda}_h.$$

In conclusion, the postprocessing algorithm gives approximation of eigenvalues from above.

4 Numerical Results

The example is devoted to the eigenvalue problem:

$$-\Delta u = \lambda u \quad \text{in } \Omega,$$

$$u = 0 \quad \text{on } \partial\Omega,$$

where Ω is the square $(0, \pi) \times (0, \pi)$.

For this problem the exact eigenvalues are $\lambda_j = s_1^2 + s_2^2$, $s_{1/2} = 1, 2, 3, \ldots$.

The domain Ω is uniformly divided into $2n^2$ isosceles triangles and thus the mesh parameter is $h = \pi/n$, $n = 4, 8, 12, 16, 20$.

First, the numerical solving of the model problem is implemented by means of nonconforming Crouzeix-Raviart (C-R) finite elements. It is well-known that this type of elements gives asymptotically lower bounds of eigenvalues (see [8] and [9] in case of nonconvex and convex domain, respectively). Postprocessing technique is implemented using conforming linear triangular elements.

In Table 1 the approximations $\lambda_{i,h}$, $i = 1, 2, 3, 4$ of the first four eigenvalues i.e. $\lambda_1 = 2$, $\lambda_2 = 5$, $\lambda_3 = 5$, and $\lambda_4 = 8$ as well as the approximations $\widetilde{\lambda}_{i,h}$, $i = 1, 2, 3, 4$ obtained as a result of the postprocessing are presented. It is seen that the sequence $\{\lambda_{i,h}\}$ is increasing, but the sequence $\left\{\widetilde{\lambda}_{i,h}\right\}$ decreases. The comparison with the exact eigenvalues confirms the result of Theorem 2.

In the next Table 2 the approximations $\widetilde{\lambda}_{i,h}$ are compared with the corresponding values of $\overline{\lambda}_{i,h}$ obtained by means of a-posteriori procedure, too (see Theorem 1). As it is mentioned in Remark 2, $\overline{\lambda}_{i,h}$ is closer to the exact eigenvalue λ_i than $\widetilde{\lambda}_{i,h}$. However, at the same time $\overline{\lambda}_{i,h}$ does not accelerate the convergence to λ_i, compared to $\widetilde{\lambda}_{i,h}$.

Table 1. Eigenvalues computed by means of C-R nonconforming FEs ($\lambda_{i,h}$) and approximations after a-posteriori procedure implementation using linear conforming FEs ($\widetilde{\lambda}_{i,h}$)

n		1	2	3	4
4	$\lambda_{i,h}$	1.965475477	4.546032933	4.546036508	7.430949878
4	$\widetilde{\lambda}_{i,h}$	2.013510627	5.284680595	5.284687356	8.803039536
8	$\lambda_{i,h}$	1.991417651	4.888133308	4.888134617	7.868940522
8	$\widetilde{\lambda}_{i,h}$	2.000890695	5.018169460	5.018211807	8.058654758
12	$\lambda_{i,h}$	1.996189356	4.950404205	4.950405336	7.944600203
12	$\widetilde{\lambda}_{i,h}$	2.000178007	5.003636654	5.003646365	8.014729358
16	$\lambda_{i,h}$	1.997857237	4.972126030	4.972127107	7.971004421
16	$\widetilde{\lambda}_{i,h}$	2.000056563	5.001156922	5.001160437	8.006904816
20	$\lambda_{i,h}$	1.998628845	4.982167613	4.982168667	7.983211324
20	$\widetilde{\lambda}_{i,h}$	2.000023215	5.000475144	5.000476849	8.004683748

Table 2. Comparison of the approximations $\widetilde{\lambda}_{i,h}$ and $\overline{\lambda}_{i,h}$ obtained after a-posteriori procedure implementation using linear conforming FEs

n		1	2	3	4
4	$\overline{\lambda}_{i,h}$	2.012111021	5.224680589	5.244686971	8.478031503
4	$\widetilde{\lambda}_{i,h}$	2.013510627	5.284680595	5.284687356	8.803039536
8	$\overline{\lambda}_{i,h}$	2.000690705	5.0054211807	5.012170457	8.024860755
8	$\widetilde{\lambda}_{i,h}$	2.000890695	5.018169460	5.018211807	8.058654758
12	$\overline{\lambda}_{i,h}$	2.000134909	5.001985964	5.003029649	8.006469725
12	$\widetilde{\lambda}_{i,h}$	2.000178007	5.003636654	5.003646365	8.014729358
16	$\overline{\lambda}_{i,h}$	2.000030491	5.000559501	5.00097222	8.003007807
16	$\widetilde{\lambda}_{i,h}$	2.000056563	5.001156922	5.001160437	8.006904816
20	$\overline{\lambda}_{i,h}$	2.000016717	5.000247046	5.000392201	8.002846348
20	$\widetilde{\lambda}_{i,h}$	2.000023215	5.000475144	5.000476849	8.004683748

Finally, we have to emphasize that in spite of the fact that the considered problem has multiple eigenvalues, the results of Theorems 1 and 2 remain valid.

Acknowledgement. This work is partially supported by the Bulgarian NSF grant DFNI-I 01/5.

References

1. Babuska, I., Osborn, J.: Eigenvalue problems. In: Ciarlet, P.G., Lions, J.L. (eds.) Handbook of Numerical Analysis, vol. II, pp. 641–787. North-Holland, Amsterdam (1991)
2. Ainsworth, M., Oden, J.T.: A Posteriori Error Estimation in Finite Element Analysis. Wiley Interscience, New York (2000)
3. Verfürth, R.: A Review of a-posteriori Error Estimation and Adaptive Mesh-refinement Techniques. Wiley & Teubner, Chichester (1996)
4. Andreev, A.B., Lazarov, R.D., Racheva, M.R.: Postprocessing and higher order convergence of mixed finite element approximations of biharmonic eigenvalue problems. JCAM **182**(2), 333–349 (2005)
5. Brenner, S., Scott, L.R.: The Mathematical Theory for Finite Element Methods. Springer, New York (1994)
6. Racheva, M.R., Andreev, A.B.: Superconvergence postprocessing for eigenvalues. Comp. Meth. Appl. Math. **2**(2), 171–185 (2002)
7. Andreev, A.B., Racheva, M.R.: Superconvergence FE postprocessing for eigenfunctions. Comp. Rend. Acad. Bulg. Sci. **55**(2), 17–22 (2002)
8. Armentano, M.G., Duran, R.G.: Asymptotic lower bounds for eigenvalues by nonconforming finite element methods. Electron. Trans. Numer. Anal. **17**, 93–101 (2004)
9. Andreev, A.B., Racheva, M.R.: Lower bounds for eigenvalues by nonconforming FEM on convex domain. AIP Conf. Proc. vol. 1301, pp. 361–369 (2010)

On a Type of Nonconforming Morley Rectangular Finite Element

A.B. Andreev[1] and M.R. Racheva[2(✉)]

[1] Institute of Information and Communication Technologies, BAS, Sofia, Bulgaria
[2] Technical University of Gabrovo, Gabrovo, Bulgaria
milena@tugab.bg

Abstract. In the recent years, the constriction, analysis and application of nonconforming finite elements have been an active research area. So, for fourth-order elliptic problems conforming finite element methods (FEMs) require C^1−continuity, which usually leads to complicated implementation [1]. This drawback could be surmounted by using nonconforming methods. These FEMs have been widely applied in computational engineering and structural mechanics.

This paper deals with rectangular variants of the Morley finite elements [2]. Beside Adini nonconforming finite element, they can be used for plates with sides parallel to the coordinate axes, such as rectangular plates.

The applicability of different types of Morley rectangles applied for fourth-order problems is also discussed. Numerical implementation and results applied to plate bending problem illustrate the presented investigation.

1 Introduction

Let $\Omega \subset \mathbf{R}^2$ be a rectangular domain. We suppose that the regular meshes τ_h of Ω are such that any two rectangles from τ_h share at most a vertex or an edge.

With a partition τ_h we associate a finite dimensional space of Morley rectangles (Fig. 1). So, any τ_h consists of rectangles with edges parallel to the coordinate axes and $K \in \tau_h$ is a rectangle with vertices a_j and edges l_j, $j = 1, 2, 3, 4$ (see e.g. [2–4]).

We choose the following set of degrees of freedom (v is a test function, see [2]):

$$v(a_j) \quad \text{and} \quad \int_{l_j} \frac{\partial v}{\partial \nu}\, dl, \quad j = 1, 2, 3, 4, \tag{1}$$

where $\dfrac{\partial}{\partial \nu}$ means outer normal derivative.

Let $\mathcal{P}_k$ denote the set of polynomials of degree less than or equal to k in two variables. There are three variants for the polynomial space corresponding to the Morley rectangular finite elements, reported in the literature:

I. Dimov et al. (Eds.): NMA 2014, LNCS 8962, pp. 287–294, 2015.
DOI: 10.1007/978-3-319-15585-2_32

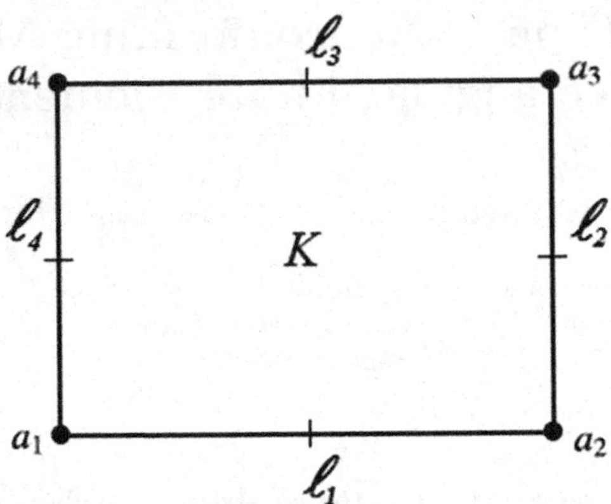

Fig. 1. Morley rectangular finite element

- $Q^{(1)} = \mathcal{P}_2 + \text{span}\{x^3, y^3\}$ [2];
- $Q^{(2)} = \mathcal{P}_2 + \text{span}\{x^3 - 3xy^2, y^3 - 3yx^2\}$ [5,6];
- $Q^{(3)} = \mathcal{P}_2 + \text{span}\{x(1-x)(1-2x), y(1-y)(1-2y)\}$ [7].

Obviously $\mathcal{P}_2 \subset Q^{(i)} \subset \mathcal{P}_3,\ i = 1, 2, 3.$

2 Main Results

Consider the polynomial spaces $Q^{(1)}$ and $Q^{(3)}$ related to the first and third type of Morley rectangular finite element, respectively.

Theorem 1. *If for any function $v \in Q^{(s)}$, then $v \in Q^{(4-s)}$, $s = 1; 3$, i.e. the first and the third polynomial sets are identical.*

Proof. Let v be any function belonging to the polynomial set $Q^{(1)}$ with coefficients $\alpha(\alpha_1, \alpha_2, \ldots, \alpha_8)$, i.e.

$$v = \alpha_1 + \alpha_2 x + \alpha_3 y + \alpha_4 x^2 + \alpha_5 y^2 + \alpha_6 xy + \alpha_7 x^3 + \alpha_8 y^3.$$

We shall show that there exist numbers $\beta(\beta_1, \beta_2, \ldots, \beta_8)$ such that

$$v = \beta_1 + \beta_2 x + \beta_3 y + \beta_4 x^2 + \beta_5 y^2 + \beta_6 xy + \beta_7 x(1-x)(1-2x) + \beta_8 y(1-y)(1-2y)$$

and this representation is unique, consequently $v \in Q^{(3)}$.

This statement is equivalent to the following system:

$$\left| \begin{array}{l} \alpha_1 = \beta_1 \\ \alpha_2 = \beta_2 + \beta_7 \\ \alpha_3 = \beta_3 + \beta_8 \\ \alpha_4 = \beta_4 - 3\beta_7 \\ \alpha_5 = \beta_5 - 3\beta_8 \\ \alpha_6 = \beta_6 \\ \alpha_7 = 2\beta_7 \\ \alpha_8 = 2\beta_8, \end{array} \right.$$

i.e. $\alpha = M\beta$ with a matrix M,

$$M = \begin{pmatrix} 1 & 0 & 0 & 0 & 0 & 0 & 0 & 0 \\ 0 & 1 & 0 & 0 & 0 & 0 & 1 & 0 \\ 0 & 0 & 1 & 0 & 0 & 0 & 0 & 1 \\ 0 & 0 & 0 & 1 & 0 & 0 & -3 & 0 \\ 0 & 0 & 0 & 0 & 1 & 0 & 0 & -3 \\ 0 & 0 & 0 & 0 & 0 & 1 & 0 & 0 \\ 0 & 0 & 0 & 0 & 0 & 0 & 2 & 0 \\ 0 & 0 & 0 & 0 & 0 & 0 & 0 & 2 \end{pmatrix},$$

and the relations above show that if $v \in Q^{(3)}$, then $v \in Q^{(1)}$. The matrix is not degenerated because of $\det M = 4$. So that, there exists M^{-1} and if $v \in Q^{(1)}$ then $v \in Q^{(3)}$.

Let $\widehat{K}$ be the reference element (unit square).

On the base of this theorem we can present the basic functions corresponding to the polynomial set $Q^{(1)}$ (and $Q^{(3)}$):

$$\begin{aligned}
\widehat{\varphi}_1(x,y) &= 1 - \frac{x}{2} - \frac{y}{2} - \frac{3x^2}{2} - \frac{3y^2}{2} + xy + x^3 + y^3;\\
\widehat{\varphi}_2(x,y) &= \frac{x}{2} + \frac{y}{2} + \frac{3x^2}{2} - \frac{3y^2}{2} - xy - x^3 + y^3;\\
\widehat{\varphi}_3(x,y) &= -\frac{x}{2} - \frac{y}{2} + \frac{3x^2}{2} + \frac{3y^2}{2} + xy - x^3 - y^3;\\
\widehat{\varphi}_4(x,y) &= \frac{x}{2} + \frac{y}{2} - \frac{3x^2}{2} + \frac{3y^2}{2} - xy + x^3 - y^3; \qquad (2)\\
\widehat{\varphi}_5(x,y) &= y - 2y^2 + y^3;\\
\widehat{\varphi}_6(x,y) &= -x^2 + x^3;\\
\widehat{\varphi}_7(x,y) &= -y^2 + y^3;\\
\widehat{\varphi}_8(x,y) &= x - 2x^2 + x^3.
\end{aligned}$$

Now, for any $K \in \tau_h$ we introduce the midpoints c_i of l_i, $i = 1,2,3,4$ (see Fig. 1)

$$c_i = \frac{a_i + a_{i+1}}{2}, \quad i = 1,2,3; c_4 = \frac{a_1 + a_4}{2}.$$

By analogy of $K \in \tau_h$, for the reference element $\widehat{K}$ we will use the denotations $\widehat{a}_j, \widehat{c}_j, \widehat{l}_j$, $j = 1,2,3,4$ for its vertices, midpoints and edges, respectively.

Theorem 2. *For any polynomial $v \in Q^{(1)}$ the set of degrees of freedom (1) coincides with the following set:*

$$v(a_j) \quad and \quad \frac{\partial v}{\partial \nu}(c_j), \ \ j = 1, 2, 3, 4.$$

Proof. Using (2), for any function $\widehat{v}(x, y) \in Q^{(1)} = \mathcal{P}_2 + span\{x^3, y^3\}$, defined on $\widehat{K} = [0, 1]^2$ we have that

$$\widehat{v}(x, y) = \sum_{j=1}^{4} \widehat{v}(\widehat{a}_j)\ \widehat{\varphi}_j(x, y) + \sum_{j=1}^{4} \int_{\widehat{l}_j} \frac{\partial \widehat{v}}{\partial \nu}\, d\widehat{l}\ \widehat{\varphi}_{j+4}(x, y).$$

By means of direct calculations we easily get that

$$\int_{\widehat{l}_j} \frac{\partial \widehat{v}}{\partial y}\, dx = \frac{\partial \widehat{v}}{\partial y}(\widehat{c}_j), \ \ j = 1; 3,$$

$$\int_{\widehat{l}_j} \frac{\partial \widehat{v}}{\partial x}\, dy = \frac{\partial \widehat{v}}{\partial x}(\widehat{c}_j), \ \ j = 2; 4,$$

or

$$\int_{\widehat{l}_j} \frac{\partial \widehat{v}}{\partial \nu}\, d\widehat{l} = \frac{\partial \widehat{v}}{\partial \nu}(\widehat{c}_j), \ \ j = 1, 2, 3, 4.$$

Thus, for any $K \in \tau_h$

$$\frac{\partial v}{\partial \nu}(c_j) = \frac{1}{\int_{l_j} dl} \int_{l_j} \frac{\partial v}{\partial \nu}\, dl =, \ \ j = 1, 2, 3, 4.$$

Remark 1. During the last proof, the fact that the sides of the element $K \in \tau_h$ are parallel to the coordinate axes is essential. As a result, the normal derivatives of any function $v \in Q^{(1)}$ on the edges of K are linear functions which attain their mean value at the midside points of the edges. But in reality, this parallel line condition is not restrictive, because the convergence results are valid in this case only (see [8]).

Remark 2. Taking into account Remark 1 it is clear that the result of Theorem 2 is not true for Morley rectangle related to the polynomial space $Q^{(2)} = \mathcal{P}_2 + span\{x^3 - 3xy^2, y^3 - 3x^2y\}$, which is easy to verify directly.

3 Numerical Aspects

The aim of this section is to illustrate the use of Morley rectangular elements for a fourth-order problem numerically solving.

Let V and H be Hilbert spaces with functions defined on the rectangular domain $\Omega \subset \mathbf{R}^2$, where $V \subset H$ with a compact embedding.

Let also $a(\cdot,\cdot)$ be a symmetric, $V-$elliptic and continuous bilinear form on $V \times V$, and $(\cdot,\cdot)$ be a bilinear form on $H \times H$, which is continuous, symmetric and positive definite.

The weak form of eigenvalue problems of the self-adjoint fourth-order elliptic differential operator is: Find a number $\lambda \in \mathbf{R}$ and a function $u \in V$, $\|u\|_{0,\Omega} = 1$, such that

$$a(u,v) = \lambda(u,v), \forall v \in V, \tag{3}$$

where $(\cdot,\cdot)$ is the usual L_2-inner product:

$$(u,v) = \int_\Omega uv\, dx.$$

We consider the plate vibration problem, i.e. the eigenvalue problem (3) with $V = H_0^2(\Omega)$, $H = L_2(\Omega)$, where $H_0^2(\Omega) = \{v \in H^2(\Omega) : \; v_{|\partial\Omega} = \partial_\nu v_{|\partial\Omega} = 0\}$, (see [10], p. 660) and

$$a(u,v) = \int_\Omega (\sigma \Delta u \Delta v$$
$$+(1-\sigma)(2\partial_{xy}u\partial_{xy}v + \partial_{xx}u\partial_{xx}v + \partial_{yy}u\partial_{yy}v))\, dx\, dy, \tag{4}$$

where $\sigma \in [0, 0.5)$ is the Poisson ratio. Clearly, the bilinear form $a(u,v)$ is symmetric and it is also continuous and $H_0^2(\Omega)$-elliptic [1]. The problem (3), (4) has an infinite number of eigenvalues λ_j, all being strictly positive, having finite multiplicity and showing no finite accumulation point (see, e.g. [10]) and arranged as $0 < \lambda_1 \le \lambda_2 \le \ldots \to \infty$.

With V_h, $V_h \subset H$, $V_h \not\subset V$ we denote a nonconforming finite dimensional space.

The nonconforming finite element approximation of (3), (4) states: Find a number $\lambda_h \in \mathbf{R}$ and a function $u_h \in V_h$, $\|u_h\|_{0,\Omega} = 1$, such that

$$a_h(u_h, v_h) = \lambda_h(u_h, v_h), \;\forall v_h \in V_h, \tag{5}$$

where $a_h(\cdot,\cdot)$ is mesh-dependent bilinear form defined by

$$a_h(u,v) = \sum_{K\in\tau_h} a_K(u,v),$$

and a_K denotes restriction of a on $K \in \tau_h$.

Our computer implementation is based on a comparison between results, obtained using Morley rectangular elements in the case of polynomial space $Q^{(1)}$ and nonconforming Adini elements.

It is well-known that Adini element approximates the eigenvalues from below. This fact is proved by Yang in [11] in case of uniform mesh (for the special case of biharmonic operator, i.e. when $\sigma = 0$, see, e.g. [8]). On this base it is illustrated that the considered Morley rectangle give lower bounds for the exact eigenvalues.

Both Adini and Morley rectangular elements give one and the same order of convergence (see, for example [2,9]). Namely, let $u \in H^4(\Omega)$ be the exact

Table 1. Approximations of first three eigenvalues for plate bending problem when $\sigma = 0.2$

n	FE	$\lambda_{1,h}$	$\lambda_{2,h}$	$\lambda_{3,h}$
4	Adini	1167.392908	4866.116932	4926.193944
4	Morley Rect.	1057.618801	4398.948592	4398.948594
8	Adini	1246.188992	5122.267661	5186.867398
8	Morley Rect.	1216.857059	4985.492194	4985.492195
12	Adini	1270.220003	5233.337835	5293.217308
12	Morley Rect.	1258.219231	5189.140988	5189.140989
16	Adini	1280.793015	5291.424872	5333.232331
16	Morley Rect.	1273.858039	5271.335251	5271.345251
20	Adini	1285.101025	5317.351594	5351.895566
20	Morley Rect.	1281.316382	5311.544991	5311.544991

Table 2. Approximations of first three eigenvalues for plate bending problem when $\sigma = 0.4$

n	FE	$\lambda_{1,h}$	$\lambda_{2,h}$	$\lambda_{3,h}$
4	Adini	1148.142969	4779.924216	4855.627159
4	Morley Rect.	1037.119084	4306.333945	4306.333946
8	Adini	1237.628351	5076.056998	5152.807114
8	Morley Rect	1209.582611	4948.137661	4948.117662
12	Adini	1265.659500	5204.554917	5277.286588
12	Morley Rect	1254.749011	5170.495699	5170.495700
16	Adini	1278.114091	5272.637524	5324.170234
16	Morley Rect	1271.856070	5260.390425	5260.390425
20	Adini	1283.234730	5303.551518	5345.987604
20	Morley Rect	1280.019922	5304.398164	5304.398164

eigenfunction and let u_h be the corresponding approximate solution obtained by (5), then

$$\|u - u_h\|_{2,h,\Omega} \leq Ch(|u|_{3,\Omega} + h|u|_{4,\Omega}),$$

where $\|\cdot\|_{2,h,\Omega}$ is the second-order mesh-dependent Sobolev norm.

Also (obviously $\|\cdot\|_{0,h,\Omega} = \|\cdot\|_{0,\Omega}$)

$$\|u - u_h\|_{0,\Omega} \leq Ch^2(|u|_{3,\Omega} + h|u|_{4,\Omega}).$$

In this case the essential H^2-norm determines the eigenvalue estimates, i.e.

$$|\lambda - \lambda_h| = \mathcal{O}(h^2).$$

Note that for Adini element applied to the uniform mesh, there is an improved accuracy result [9]:

$$\|u - u_h\|_{2,h,\Omega} \leq Ch^2|u|_{4,\Omega}. \tag{6}$$

Let Ω be the unit square. We solve numerically the plate bending problem (5) for $\sigma = 0.2; 0.4$, respectively.

The domain is uniformly divided into n^2 rectangles, where $n = 4; 8; 12; 16; 20$, respectively, so that it should be mentioned here that for Adini element the estimate (6) is valid.

In Tables 1 and 2 we give results for the approximations of first three eigenvalues. The results for any eigenvalue form an increasing sequence when the mesh parameter $h = \sqrt{2}/n$ decreases. Our numerical results show that Morley rectangles give eigenvalues less than these obtained by Adini element. According to (6) in case of uniform mesh Adini element approximates more accurately any eigenvalues λ_j than Morley rectangle. Thus one may conclude that the numerical test is a confirmation of the fact that Morley rectangles give approximation of the exact eigenvalues from below (see [12]).

Acknowledgement. This work is partially supported by the Bulgarian NSF grant DFNI-I 01/5.

References

1. Ciarlet, P.G.: Basic error estimates for elliptic problems. In: Ciarlet, P.G., Lions, J.L. (eds.) Handbook of Numerical Analysis. Finite Element Methods (Part 1), vol. 2, pp. 21–343. Elsevier Science Publishers, North-Holland (1991)
2. Zhang, H., Wang, M.: The Mathematical Theory of Finite Elements. Science Press, Beijing (1991)
3. Wang, M., Xu, J.: The Morley element for fourth order elliptic equations in any dimensions. Numer. Math. **103**(1), 155–169 (2006)
4. Wang, M., Shi, Z.-C., Xu, J.: Some n-rectangle nonconforming finite elements for fourth order elliptic equations. J. Comput. Math. **25**(4), 408–420 (2007)
5. Wang, L., Xie, X.: Uniformly stable rectangular elements for fourth order elliptic singular perturbation problems. Numer. Methods Partial Differ. Eq. **29**(3), 721–737 (2013)
6. Andreev, A.B., Racheva, M.R.: Nonconforming rectangular Morley finite elements. In: Dimov, I., Faragó, I., Vulkov, L. (eds.) NAA 2012. LNCS, vol. 8236, pp. 158–165. Springer, Heidelberg (2013)
7. Nicaise, S.: A posteriori error estimations of some cell-centered finite volume methods. SIAM J. Numer. Anal. **43**(04), 1481–1503 (2005)
8. Lin, Q., Lin, J.F.: Finite Element Methods: Accuracy and Improvement. Science Press, Beijing (2006)
9. Lascaux, P., Lesaint, P.: Some nonconforming finite elements for the plate bending problem. ESAIM: Math. Model. Numer. Anal.-Modelisation Mathematique et Analyse Numerique **9**(R1), 9–53 (1975)
10. Babuška, I., Osborn, J.: Eigenvalue problems. In: Lions, J.-L., Ciarlet, P.G. (eds.) Handbook of Numerical Analysis. Finite Element Methods (Part 1), vol. II, pp. 641–787. North-Holland, Amsterdam (1991)

11. Yang, Y.D.: A posteriori error estimates in Adini finite element for eigenvalue problems. J. Comput. Math. **18**, 413–418 (2000)
12. Lin, Q., Xie, H.: The asymptotic lower bounds of eigenvalue problems by nonconforming finite element methods. Math. Pract. Theory **42**(11), 219–226 (2012)

A Numerical Study of the Upper Bound of the Throughput of a Crossbar Switch Utilizing MiMa-Algorithm

Tasho Tashev(✉) and Vladimir Monov

Institute of Information and Communication Technologies, Bulgarian Academy of Sciences, Acad. G. Bonchev, Bl.2, 1113 Sofia, Bulgaria
{ttashev,vmonov}@iit.bas.bg
http://www.iict.bas.bg

Abstract. In the present paper we propose a family of patterns for hotspot load traffic simulating. The results from computer simulations of the throughput of a crossbar packet switch with these patterns are presented. The necessary computations have been performed on the grid-cluster of IICT-BAS. Our simulations utilize the MiMa-algorithm for non-conflict schedule, specified by the apparatus of Generalized Nets. A numerical procedure for computation of the upper bound of the throughput is utilized. It is shown that the throughput of the MiMa-algorithm with the suggested family of patterns tend to 100 %.

Keywords: Numerical methods · Generalized nets · Switch node · Modeling

1 Introduction

Crossbar switch node is a device which maximizes the speed of data transfer using parallel existing flows between the nodes of a communication network. In the ideal case the switch sends packets with a speed corresponding to the speed with which nodes produce these packets, without delay and without losses [6]. This is obtained by means of a non-conflict commutation schedule calculated by the control block of the switch node.

From a mathematical point of view the calculation of such a schedule is NP-complete [5]. The existing solutions partly solve the problem, using different formalisms [3]. Constantly increasing volumes of the information traffic requires new more effective algorithms, which have to be checked for efficiency. The efficiency of the switch performance is firstly evaluated by the throughput (THR) provided by the node. The next important characteristic is the average time for waiting (average cell delay), before the packet is sent for commutation.

At the stages of design of switches, it is firstly assessed the THR of algorithms for non-conflict schedule. For a given algorithm, its THR will depend on the type of incoming traffic. The incoming traffic in real conditions is greatly variable. In order to evaluate the properties of the suggested algorithms, they should be

I. Dimov et al. (Eds.): NMA 2014, LNCS 8962, pp. 295–303, 2015.
DOI: 10.1007/978-3-319-15585-2_33

compared by using strictly defined properties of the incoming traffic [3]. For a chosen traffic model, THR of a switch depends on the load intensity ρ of its input lines.

For a chosen algorithm, traffic model and load intensity ρ of the input lines, THR depends on the dimension of its commutation field $n \times n$ (n input lines, n output lines) and the dimension of the input buffer i. In our computer simulations of THR, we shall denote this dependence by a function f i.e.:

$$0 \leq THR(n,i) = f(n,i) \leq 1, \text{where } n = 2,3,\dots \; i = 1,2,\dots$$

Here, THR with value 1 corresponds to 100 % - normalized throughput with respect to the maximum throughput of the output lines of the switch.

During the simulations as well as in analytic investigations we shall look for an answer of the questions:

$$\lim_{\substack{i \to \infty, \\ n = const}} f(n,i) = ?, \qquad \lim_{\substack{i \to \infty, \\ n \to \infty}} f(n,i) = ?$$

where $i \to \infty$ means infinitely large input buffer and $n \to \infty$ means infinitely large commutation field.

In the present paper, a numerical procedure for computation of the upper bound of the THR [10] is utilized, which allows calculation of the first limit mentioned above. If it exists then the solution is unique. In this procedure we use the results from a computer simulation of the THR performed on the grid-structure BG01-IPP of the Institute of information and communication technologies IICT-BAS. Our modeling of the THR utilizes our MiMa-algorithm [9] and a family of patterns for hotspot load traffic [4] with $\rho = 100\,\%$ load intensity of each input (i.i.d. Bernoulli). The obtained results give an upper bound of the THR for $n \in [3, 100]$ which enables us to estimate the limit of the THR for $n \to \infty$. This estimate is obtained to be 1 (100 % THR).

2 Computation of the Upper Bound of Throughput

We shall perform simulations for a specific algorithm for non-conflict schedule, a model for incoming traffic and a load intensity. We choose the interval for values of n and i, where i will denote the size of the input buffer. As a result, we will have a set of curves for selected values of $n \in [n1, n2]$, and $i \in [1, 1000]$. Typical curves obtained in our previous work [11] are shown in Fig. 1 for the throughput of PIM-algorithm [1] with hotspot load traffic [4].

Let us chose values for i :

$$i = 1, m_1, m_2, m_3, ..., m_p, \text{ where } 1 = m_0 < m_1 < m_2 < m_3 < \cdots < m_p \tag{1}$$

We shall perform $p + 1$ simulations in order to obtain $p + 1$ curves for THR. The obtained curves will be denoted as follows:

$$f_1(n,i) = f(n, m_0),\; f_2(n,i) = f(n, m_1),\; \dots, f_{p+1}(n,i) = f(n, m_p) \tag{2}$$

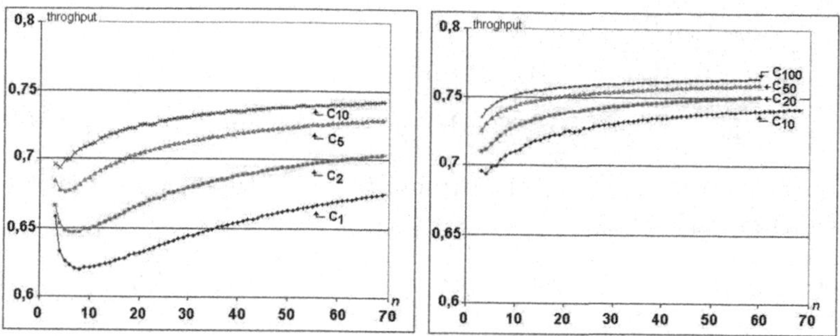

Fig. 1. Throughput for $Chao_1, \ldots, Chao_{100}$ hotspot traffic with PIM-algorithm

Denote the difference between two successive curves f_j and f_{j+1} by res_j:

$$\begin{aligned} res_1(n,i) &= f_2(n,i) - f_1(n,i) = f(n,m_1) - f(n,m_0) \\ res_2(n,i) &= f_3(n,i) - f_2(n,i) = f(n,m_2) - f(n,m_1) \\ &\ldots \\ res_p(n,i) &= f_{p+1}(n,i) - f_p(n,i) = f(n,m_p) - f(n,m_{p-1}) \end{aligned} \tag{3}$$

Denote the ratio of the values of two curves res_j and res_{j+1} through δ_j:

$$\begin{aligned} \delta_1(n,i) &= \frac{res_2(n,i)}{res_1(n,i)} = \frac{f(n,m_2) - f(n,m_1)}{f(n,m_1) - f(n,m_0)} \\ \delta_2(n,i) &= \frac{res_3(n,i)}{res_2(n,i)} = \frac{f(n,m_3) - f(n,m_2)}{f(n,m_2) - f(n,m_1)} \\ &\ldots \\ \delta_{p-1}(n,i) &= \frac{res_p(n,i)}{res_{p-1}(n,i)} = \frac{f(n,m_p) - f(n,m_{p-1})}{f(n,m_{p-1}) - f(n,m_{p-2})} \end{aligned} \tag{4}$$

Simulation data allow us to calculate $\delta_1, \delta_2, \ldots, \delta_{p-1}$. If we can find a dependency $\delta_{j+1} = \phi(\delta_j)$ for $\delta_1, \delta_2, \ldots, \delta_{p-1}$ in the case $j \to \infty$, then we can determine the expected upper bound.

From the last formula we obtain:

$$f(n,m_p) = f(n,m_{p-1}) + \delta_{p-1}(n,i).(f(n,m_{p-1}) - f(n,m_{p-2}))$$

or

$$f_{p+1}(n,i) = f(n,m_{p-1}) + \delta_{p-1}(n,i).(f(n,m_{p-1}) - f(n,m_{p-2}))$$

and for a known dependency $\delta_{j+1} = \phi(\delta_j)$, we can write

$$f_{p+2}(n,i) = f(n,m_{p-1}) + [1 + \phi(\delta_{p-1}(n,i))].\delta_{p-1}(n,i).(f(n,m_{p-1}) - f(n,m_{p-2}))$$

$$\ldots$$

$$f_{p+q}(n,i) = f(n,m_{p-1}) + [1 + \phi(\delta_{p-1}(n,i)) + \phi(\delta_{p-1}(n,i)).\phi(\delta_p(n,i)) + \cdots +$$

$$\phi(\delta_{p-1}(n,i)).\phi(\delta_p(n,i))....\phi(\delta_{p+q-3}(n,i))].$$
$$\delta_{p-1}(n,i).(f(n,m_{p-1}) - f(n,m_{p-2})) \tag{5}$$

When $q \to \infty$ then $f_{(p+q\to\infty)}(n,i)$ is the necessary bound $\lim_{\substack{i \to \infty, \\ n = const}} f(n,i)$.

If there is an upper bound of the throughput of a switch node, it is clear that the dependency $\delta_{j+1} = \phi(\delta_j)$ exists. Then the sum

$$[1 + \phi(\delta_{p-1}(n,i)) + \cdots + \phi(\delta_{p-1}(n,i)).\phi(\delta_p(n,i))....\phi(\delta_{p+q-3}(n,i))]$$

for $q \to \infty$ is convergent and has a boundary.

3 Existence of the Dependence $\delta_{j+1} = \phi(\delta_j)$

We have found a relation $\delta_{j+1} = \phi(\delta_j)$ for our model [11] of PIM-algorithm [1] (specified by means of Generalized nets [2]) with Chao-model for "hotspot" load traffic, for which we defined the family of patterns $Chao_i$ for traffic matrices [7]. For a simulation with this family of patterns (shown below - traffic matrix T^1 for model $Chao_1$ (6), traffic matrix T^i for $Chao_i$ (7)), we have chosen the sequences for i : $i = 1, m^1, m^2, m^3, ..., m^p, ...$

$$T^1_{(2\times2)} = \begin{bmatrix} 1 & 1 \\ 1 & 1 \end{bmatrix} \; T^1_{(3\times3)} = \begin{bmatrix} 2 & 1 & 1 \\ 1 & 2 & 1 \\ 1 & 1 & 2 \end{bmatrix} \; \cdots \; T^1_{(k\times k)} = \begin{bmatrix} (k-1) & \cdots & 1 \\ \vdots & \ddots & \vdots \\ 1 & \cdots & (k-1) \end{bmatrix} \tag{6}$$

$$T^i_{(2\times2)} = \begin{bmatrix} i & i \\ i & i \end{bmatrix} \; T^i_{(3\times3)} = \begin{bmatrix} 2i & i & i \\ i & 2i & i \\ i & i & 2i \end{bmatrix} \; \cdots \; T^i_{(k\times k)} = \begin{bmatrix} (k-1)i & \cdots & i \\ \vdots & \ddots & \vdots \\ i & \cdots & (k-1)i \end{bmatrix}. \tag{7}$$

In this case the dependence $\delta_{j+1} = \phi(\delta_j)$ is a constant, i.e. $\delta_{j+1} = \delta_j = m^{-1/2}$ with an accuracy depending on the error of simulations. Thus, $\delta_j(n,i) = const$ when $i \in [1,\infty)$, $n \in [n1, n2]$, $m = const$, $m \in [2,3,4,\ldots)$ $(i=1, m^1, \ldots, m^p, \ldots)$, with an accuracy within the error of simulations [10].

Here, we will test the validity of this assertion for a different algorithm by simulations with $m = 2$. The utilized algorithm will be our MiMa-algorithm [9], working with the same model of load traffic (Chao-model). The algorithm MiMa can be described formally by the means of Generalized Nets (GN). The model is developed for switch node with n inputs and n outputs. Its graphic form is shown on Fig. 2 [9].

The model has possibilities to provide information about the number of switching in crossbar matrix, as well as about the average number of packets transmitted by one switch. Analysis of the model proves receiving a non-conflict schedule. Computational complexity of the solution is $(O(n^3))$ where n is the dimension of matrix T. Numerical modeling should provide us with the answer to the question: do we have a better solution with this algorithm or not in comparison with existing ones (for example PIM)?

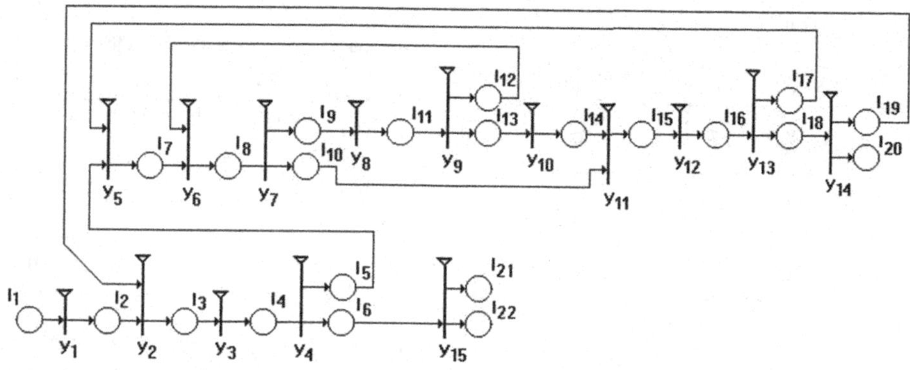

Fig. 2. GN-model for MiMa-algorithm

The transition from a GN-model to executive program is performed as in [8] using the program package VFort provided free of charge by P. Vabishchevich, Institute of Applied Mathematics, RAS [12]. The source code has been compiled by means of the grid-structure BG01-IPP of the Institute of information and communication technologies - Bulgarian Academy of Sciences (www.grid.bas.bg). The resulting code is executed in the grid-structure locally. The operation system is Scientific Linux release 6.5 (Carbon), kernel $2.6.32-431.20.3.e16.\times 86\_64$. We used the following grid-resources: up to 16 CPU (2 blades), 32 threads, 2 GB RAM. The main restriction is the time for execution ($\leq$72 h).

4 Numerical Procedure for Calculation of the Upper Bound of Throughput

The numerical procedure for computation of the upper bound of the THR which allows calculation of the first limit mentioned above is described in [10]. If the limit exists then the solution is unique.

We choose value $m = 2$ which is the minimal value in its definition area $m \in [2, 3, 4, \dots)$. When $m = 2$, then $i = 1, 2, 4, 8, 16, 32, 64, \dots, 2^p, \dots$. The initial estimate of the required number of curves for THR is at least 4 (from Pattern $Chao_1$). In our example, we have nine curves (patterns). In the figures below, $Chao_i$ is denoted as Ci for $i = 1, 2, \dots$ We get results for $C1$, $C2$, $C4$, $C8$, $C16$, $C32$, $C64$, $C128$, $C256$ which are shown in Fig. 3.

The dimension n varies from 3×3 to 100×100 and n simulations (runs) for each size $(n \times n)$ of pattern $Chao_i$ are executed. To achieve this goal we propose a modification of family of patterns $Chao_i$, as it is shown below: for $n = 3$ we have three traffic matrices T^1 (see (8) for model $Chao_1$), for $n = k$ we have k traffic matrices T^i (see (9) for $Chao_i$). The resulting throughput is the average for n runs for each size $n \times n$.

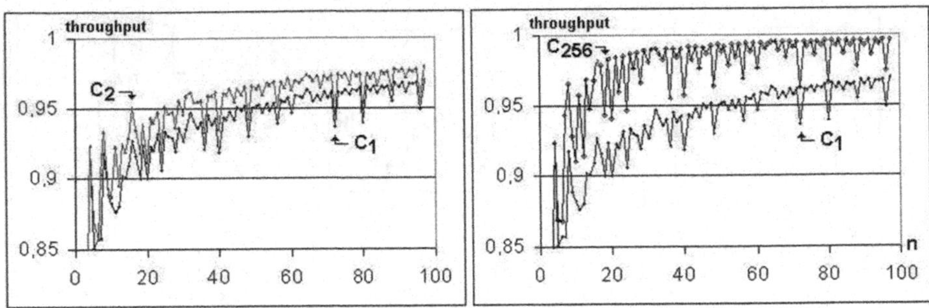

Fig. 3. Throughput for $Chao_1, \ldots, Chao_{256}$

$$T^1_{(3\times3)} = \begin{bmatrix} 2 & 1 & 1 \\ 1 & 2 & 1 \\ 1 & 1 & 2 \end{bmatrix} \Rightarrow \begin{bmatrix} 2 & 1 & 1 \\ 1 & 2 & 1 \\ 1 & 1 & 2 \end{bmatrix} \begin{bmatrix} 1 & 2 & 1 \\ 1 & 1 & 2 \\ 2 & 1 & 1 \end{bmatrix} \begin{bmatrix} 1 & 1 & 2 \\ 2 & 1 & 1 \\ 1 & 2 & 1 \end{bmatrix} \tag{8}$$

$$T^i_{(k\times k)} \Rightarrow \begin{bmatrix} (k-1)i & i & \cdots & i \\ i & (k-1)i & \cdots & i \\ \vdots & & \ddots & \vdots \\ i & \cdots & i & (k-1)i \end{bmatrix} \cdots \begin{bmatrix} i & i & \cdots & (k-1)i \\ (k-1)i & i & \cdots & i \\ \vdots & & \ddots & \vdots \\ i & \cdots & (k-1)i & i \end{bmatrix}. \tag{9}$$

Then we calculate the difference between throughput for neighboring patterns according to (3). The obtained curves for the differences are shown in Fig. 4. Then we calculate the convergence parameter δ_j which is the ratio of the differences according to (4) and the obtained curves are shown in Fig. 5. The values of δ_j tend to $(1,5)^{-1}$.

From our simulations in the case $m = 2$, we have drawn the following conclusion:
Confirmed: The dependence $\delta_{j+1} = \phi(\delta_j)$ is a constant, i.e. $\delta_{j+1} = \delta_j = 2^{-1/2}$ with an accuracy depending on the error of simulations for the MiMa algorithm.

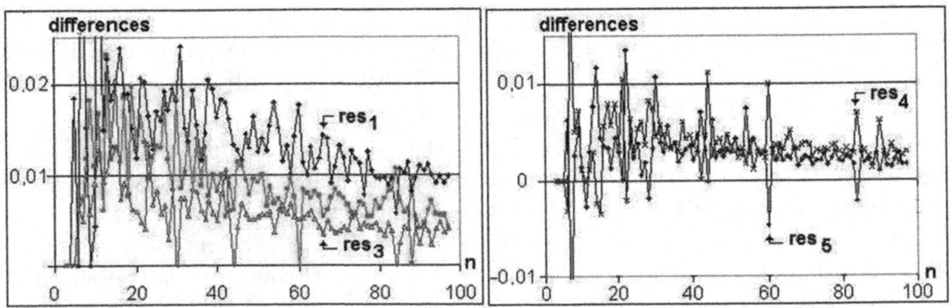

Fig. 4. Differences between throughput

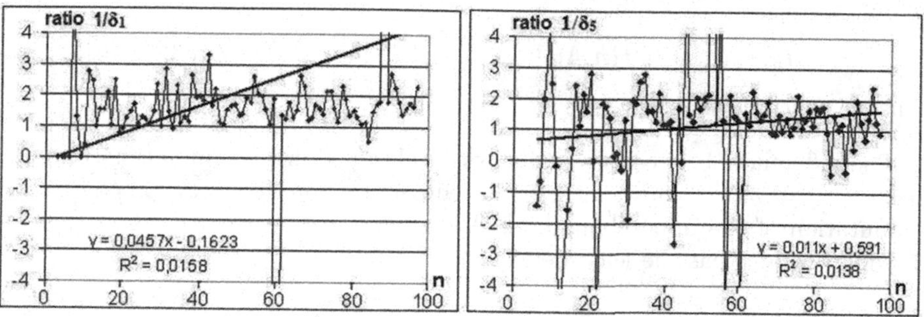

Fig. 5. Ratio $1/\delta_1$, $1/\delta_5$ between differences

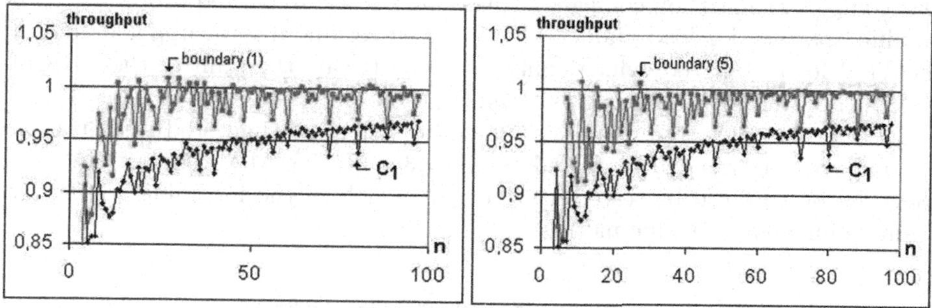

Fig. 6. Upper boundary of throughput

As a consequence, the upper boundary in case $m = const = 2$ can be calculated according to (5) as:

$$f_{p+1}(n,i) = f(n,m^{p-1}) + \delta(m).(f(n,m^{p-1}) - f(n,m^{p-2}))$$
$$f_{p+2}(n,i) = f(n,m^{p-1}) + (\delta(m) + \delta^2(m)).(f(n,m^{p-1}) - f(n,m^{p-2}))$$
$$\dots$$
$$\begin{aligned} f_{p\to\infty}(n,i) &= f(n,m^{p-1}) + [\delta(m) + \delta^2(m) + \dots + \delta^p(m) + \dots](f(n,m^{p-1}) \\ &\quad - f(n,m^{p-2})) \\ &= f(n,m^{p-1}) + [m^{-1/2} + (m^{-1/2})^2 + \dots + (m^{-1/2})^p + \dots] \\ &\quad (f(n,m^{p-1}) - f(n,m^{p-2})) \\ &= f(n,m^{p-1}) + [(m^{1/2} - 1)^{-1}].(f(n,m^{p-1}) - f(n,m^{p-2})). \end{aligned}$$

In this simulation ($m = 2$) we calculate the boundary by

$$f_{p\to\infty}(n,i) = f(n,64) + [(2^{1/2} - 1)^{-1}].(f(n,64) - f(n,32))$$

This result is obtained for δ_5 which has the least deviation from $m^{-1/2}$. The result is shown in Fig. 6 (right). For comparison in Fig. 6 (left) we have shown a boundary which is calculated for δ_1 :

$$f_{p\to\infty}(n,i) = f(n,4) + [(2^{1/2} - 1)^{-1}].(f(n,4) - f(n,2))$$

Thus we conclude that $\lim_{\substack{i \to \infty, \\ n \to \infty}} f(n,i) = 1$.

The differences between the values of δ_j obtained in the simulations and the value $\delta(m) = m^{-1/2}$ are a measure of the simulation accuracy. Therefore for computation of the upper bound we chose these two successive curves f_j and f_{j+1} for which δ_j has the least deviation from $m^{-1/2}$.

5 Conclusion

Our computer simulation confirms applicability of the suggested procedure with modified pattern for load traffic. The obtained results give an upper bound of the THR for $n \in [3, 100]$ which enables us to estimate the limit of the THR of MiMa-algorithm for $n \to \infty$. This estimate is obtained to be 100 %.

In a future study, the numerical procedure with the suggested modification of family of patterns will be tested for $m = 3, 4, 5$ using MiMa-algorithm. This modification can also be tested using other models of the incoming traffic, for example unbalanced traffic models.

Acknowledgments. The research work reported in the paper is partly supported by the project AComIn "Advanced Computing for Innovation", grant 316087, funded by the FP7 Capacity Programme (Research Potential of Convergence Regions).

References

1. Anderson, T., Owicki, S., Saxe, J., Thacker, C.: High speed switch scheduling for local area networks. ACM Trans. Comput. Syst. **11**(4), 319–352 (1993)
2. Atanassov, K.: Generalized Nets and System Theory. Prof. M. Drinov AcademicPublishing House, Sofia (1997)
3. Chao, H., Lui, B.: High Performance Switches and Routers. Wiley, New York (2007)
4. Yu, C.-L., Chang, C.-S., Lee, D.-S.: CR switch: a load-balanced switch with contention and reservation. IEEE/ACM Trans. Netw. **17**(5), 1659–1671 (2007)
5. Chen, T., Mavor, J., Denyer, P., Renshaw, D.: Traffic routing algorithm for serial superchip system customisation. IEE Proc. **137**(1), 65–73 (1990)
6. Kang, K., Park, K., Sha, L., Wang, Q.: Design of a crossbar VOQ real-time switch with clock-driven scheduling for a guaranteed delay bound. Real-Time Syst. **49**(1), 117–135 (2013)
7. Tashev, T.: Modelling throughput crossbar switch node with nonuniform load traffic. In: Proceedings of the International Conference "DCCN 2011", 26–28 October 2011, pp. 96–102. Moscow, R&D Company, Moscow, Russia (2011) (in Russian)
8. Tashev, T.: MiMa algorithm throughput modelling for crossbar switch with hotspot load traffic. In: Proceedings of the International Conference "DCCN 2013", 7–10 October 2013, Moscow, Russia, Moscow, JSC "TECHNOSPHERA", pp. 257–264 (2013) (in Russian)

9. Tashev, T., Atanasova, T.: Computer simulation of MIMA algorithm for input buffered crossbar switch. Int. J. Inf. Technol. Knowl. **5**(2), 183–189 (2011)
10. Tashev, T., Bakanov, A., Tasheva, R.: Determination of the value of convergence parameter in a procedure of calculating the upper boundary of throughput for packet switch. In: Proceedings of International Conference on ROBOTICS, AUTOMATION AND MECHATRONICS 2013 RAM: 8–10 October 2013. Prof. M. Drinov Academic Publishing House, Sofia, pp. 34–37 (2013)
11. Tashev, T., Monov, V.: Modeling of the hotspot load traffic for crossbar switch node by means of generalized nets. In: Proceedings of 6th IEEE International Conference Intelligent Systems (IS), Sofia, Bulgaria, pp. 187–191, 6–8 September 2012
12. Vabishchevich, P.: VFort. http://www.nomoz.org/site/629615/vfort.html Last checked 16 September 2014

Extremal Scattered Data Interpolation in $\mathbb{R}^3$ Using Triangular Bézier Surfaces

Krassimira Vlachkova(✉)

Faculty of Mathematics and Informatics, Sofia University, "St. Kliment Ohridski"
Blvd. James Bourchier 5, 1164 Sofia, Bulgaria
krassivl@fmi.uni-sofia.bg

Abstract. We consider the problem of extremal scattered data interpolation in $\mathbb{R}^3$. Using our previous work on minimum L_2-norm interpolation curve networks, we construct a bivariate interpolant F with the following properties:

(i) F is G^1-continuous,
(ii) F consists of triangular Bézier surfaces,
(iii) each Bézier surface satisfies the tetra-harmonic equation $\Delta^4 F = 0$. Hence F is an extremum to the corresponding energy functional.

We also discuss the case of convex scattered data in $\mathbb{R}^3$.

1 Introduction

Scattered data interpolation is a fundamental problem in approximation theory and finds applications in various areas including geology, meteorology, cartography, medicine, computer graphics, geometric modeling, etc. Different methods for solving this problem were applied and reported, excellent surveys can be found in [4–7].

The problem can be formulated as follows: Given *scattered data* $(x_i, y_i, z_i) \in \mathbb{R}^3$, $i = 1, \ldots, N$, that is points $V_i = (x_i, y_i)$ are different and non-collinear, find a bivariate function F defined in a certain domain D containing points V_i, such that F possesses continuous partial derivatives up to a given order and $F(x_i, y_i) = z_i$. One of the possible approaches to solve the problem is due to Nielson [8]. The method consists of the following three steps:

Step 1. Triangulation. Construct a triangulation T of V_i, $i = 1, \ldots N$.

Step 2. Minimum norm network (MNN). The interpolant F and its first order partial derivatives are defined on the edges of T so as to satisfy an extremal property. The MNN is a cubic curve network, i. e. on every edge of T it is a cubic polynomial.

Step 3. Interpolation surface. The obtained network is extended to F by an appropriate *blending method.* The interpolant F is a rational function on every triangle of T.

I. Dimov et al. (Eds.): NMA 2014, LNCS 8962, pp. 304–311, 2015.
DOI: 10.1007/978-3-319-15585-2_34

In [1] Andersson et al. pay special attention to the second step of the above method - the construction of the MNN. Using a different approach, the authors give a new proof of Nielson's result. Their approach allows to consider and handle the case where the data are convex and we seek a convex interpolant. Andersson et al. formulate the corresponding extremal constrained interpolation problem of finding a MNN that is convex along the edges of the triangulation. The extremal network is characterized as a solution of a nonlinear system of equations. The authors propose a Newton-type algorithm for solving this type of systems. The validity and convergence of the algorithm were studied further in [11].

In this paper we focus on Step 3 of the discussed approach. Since the MNN is a polynomial curve network it is natural to require that the interpolant F also is a polynomial on every triangle of T. Although the MNN is C^1-continuous at the vertices of T, it is preferable and more appropriate to require G^1-continuity for the interpolant instead of C^1-continuity since the latter is parametrization dependent. Two surfaces with a common boundary curve are called *G^1-continuous* if they have a continuously varying tangent plane along that boundary curve.

Let D be the union of all triangles in T. For simplicity we assume that D contains no holes. For given data and the corresponding MNN we construct an interpolation surface $F(u, v)$ defined on D with the following properties:

(i) F consists of triangular Bézier surfaces (patches) defined on each triangle of T;
(ii) F is G^1-continuous;
(iii) F satisfies the tetra-harmonic equation $\Delta^4 \mathbf{x} = 0$ a.e. for $(u, v) \in D$, where $\Delta = \frac{\partial^2}{\partial u^2} + \frac{\partial^2}{\partial v^2}$ is the Laplace operator. Hence F is a solution of the extremal problem

$$\min_F \int_D \|\Delta^4 F\|_2 du dv \tag{1}$$

i.e. F is an extremum to the corresponding energy functional.

We also consider the constrained interpolation problem. In this case, despite that the MNN is edge convex, in general it is not globally convex. Therefore a convex interpolation surface may not exist. We propose the following approach. We modify if necessary the edge convex MNN to obtain an edge convex polynomial curve network with the same tangent planes at the vertices of T. Then we construct a G^1-continuous interpolation surface $\widehat{F}(u, v)$ still satisfying (iii).

The paper is organized as follows: In Sect. 2 we introduce the notation and present some related results from [1]. In Sect. 3 we investigate the G^1-continuity conditions for adjacent Bézier patches and prove that they correctly apply to our problem. The construction of surface F is considered in Sect. 4. In the final Sect. 5 we briefly discuss the constrained interpolation problem.

2 Preliminaries

Let $N \geq 3$ be an integer and (x_i, y_i, z_i), $i = 1, \ldots, N$ be given scattered data. Points $V_i := (x_i, y_i)$ are the projection points of the data onto the plane Oxy.

A *triangulation* T of points V_i is a collection of non-overlapping, non-degenerate closed triangles in Oxy such that the set of the vertices of the triangles coincides with the set of points V_i. For a given triangulation T there is a unique continuous function $L : D \to \mathbb{R}^1$ that is linear inside each of the triangles of T and interpolates the data. Scattered data in D are *convex* if there exists a triangulation T of V_i such that the corresponding function L is convex. The data are *strictly convex* if they are convex and the gradient of L has a jump discontinuity across each edge inside D.

The set of the edges of the triangles in T is denoted by E. If there is an edge between V_i and V_j in E, it will be referred to by e_{ij} or simply by e if no ambiguity arises. A *curve network* is a collection of real-valued univariate functions $\{f_e\}_{e\in E}$ defined on the edges in E. With any real-valued bivariate function F defined on D we naturally associate the curve network defined as the restriction of F on the edges in E, i.e. for $e = e_{ij} \in E$,

$$f_e(t) := F\left(\left(1-\frac{t}{\|e\|}\right)x_i + \frac{t}{\|e\|}x_j,\ \left(1-\frac{t}{\|e\|}\right)y_i + \frac{t}{\|e\|}y_j\right), \tag{2}$$

$$\text{where } 0 \le t \le \|e\|, \text{ and } \|e\| = \sqrt{(x_i - x_j)^2 + (y_i - y_j)^2}.$$

Furthermore, according to the context F will denote either a real-valued bivariate function or a curve network defined by (2). We introduce the following class of functions defined on D

$$\mathcal{F} := \{F(x,y) \mid F(x_i,y_i) = z_i,\ i = 1,\dots,N,\ \partial F/\partial x, \partial F/\partial y \in C(D),\\ f_e' \in AC_{[0,\|e\|]}, f_e'' \in L^2_{[0,\|e\|]}, e \in E\}$$

and the corresponding classes of *smooth interpolation curve networks*

$$\mathcal{C}(E) := \{F_{|E} = \{f_e\}_{e\in E} \mid F(x,y) \in \mathcal{F},\ e \in E\}$$

and *smooth interpolation edge convex curve networks*

$$\widehat{\mathcal{C}}(E) := \{F_{|E} = \{f_e\}_{e\in E} \mid F(x,y) \in \mathcal{F},\ f_e'' \ge 0,\ e \in E\}.$$

For $F \in \{\mathcal{C}(E), \widehat{\mathcal{C}}(E)\}$ we denote the curve network of second derivatives of F by $F'' := \{f_e''\}_{e\in E}$. The L_2-norm of F'' is defined by

$$\|F''\|_{L_2(T)} := \|F''\| = \left(\sum_{e\in E}\int_0^{\|e\|} |f_e''(t)|^2 dt\right)^{1/2}.$$

We consider the following two extremal problems.

$$(\mathbf{P}) \quad \textit{Find } F^* \in \mathcal{C}(E) \textit{ such that } \|F^{*\prime\prime}\| = \inf_{F\in\mathcal{C}(E)} \|F''\|,$$

$$(\widehat{\mathbf{P}}) \quad \textit{Find } \widehat{F}^* \in \widehat{\mathcal{C}}(E) \textit{ such that } \|\widehat{F}^{*\prime\prime}\| = \inf_{F\in\widehat{\mathcal{C}}(E)} \|F''\|.$$

In [1,8] it has been shown that $(\mathbf{P})$ and $(\widehat{\mathbf{P}})$ for strictly convex data have unique solutions.

3 The G^1-Continuity Conditions

3.1 Control Points that Are Next to a Boundary Curve

Let C_1 and C_2 be cubic triangular Bézier patches with a common boundary which is cubic polynomial $q(t)$. Let $q(t) = \sum_{i=0}^{3} \mathbf{q}_i B_i^3(t)$ where $\mathbf{q}_i$, $i = 0, \ldots, 3$ are the control points of $q(t)$, and $B_i^n(t)$ are the Bernstein polynomials of degree n, $n \in \mathbb{N}$, defined for $0 \le t \le 1$ as follows:

$$B_i^n(t) := \binom{n}{i} t^i (1-t)^{n-i},$$

$$\binom{n}{i} = \begin{cases} \frac{n!}{i!(n-i)!} & \text{if } 0 \le i \le n, \\ 0 & \text{otherwise.} \end{cases}$$

Let $\mathbf{p}_i$ and $\mathbf{r}_i$, $i = 0, \ldots, 3$ are next to the boundary control points of C_1 and C_2, respectively. Let us degree elevate $q(t)$ to quartic polynomial and denote the degree elevated control points by $\hat{\mathbf{q}}_i$, $i = 0, \ldots, 4$, where $\hat{\mathbf{q}}_0 \equiv \mathbf{q}_0$ and $\hat{\mathbf{q}}_4 \equiv \mathbf{q}_3$. Then $q(t) = \sum_{i=0}^{4} \hat{\mathbf{q}}_i B_i^4(t)$ where

$$\hat{\mathbf{q}}_i = \frac{i}{4}\mathbf{q}_{i-1} + \left(1 - \frac{i}{4}\right)\mathbf{q}_i, \; i = 0, \ldots, 4. \tag{3}$$

Farin [3] proposed the following sufficient conditions for G^1-continuity between C_1 and C_2.

$$\frac{i}{4} d_{i,4} + \left(1 - \frac{i}{4}\right) d_{i,0} = 0, \; i = 0, \ldots, 4, \text{ where} \tag{4}$$

$$\begin{aligned} d_{i,0} &= \alpha_0 \mathbf{p}_i + (1-\alpha_0)\mathbf{r}_i - (\beta_0 \hat{\mathbf{q}}_i + (1-\beta_0)\hat{\mathbf{q}}_{i+1}), \\ d_{i,4} &= \alpha_1 \mathbf{p}_{i-1} + (1-\alpha_1)\mathbf{r}_{i-1} - (\beta_1 \hat{\mathbf{q}}_{i-1} + (1-\beta_1)\hat{\mathbf{q}}_i), \end{aligned}$$

and $0 < \alpha_i < 1$, $i = 0, 1$. Next we shall prove that system (4) always has a solution. From (4) for $i = 0$ and $i = 4$ we obtain

$$d_{0,0} = 0 \Rightarrow \alpha_0 \mathbf{p}_0 + (1-\alpha_0)\mathbf{r}_0 = \beta_0 \hat{\mathbf{q}}_0 + (1-\beta_0)\hat{\mathbf{q}}_1, \tag{5}$$

$$d_{4,4} = 0 \Rightarrow \alpha_1 \mathbf{p}_3 + (1-\alpha_1)\mathbf{r}_3 = \beta_1 \hat{\mathbf{q}}_3 + (1-\beta_1)\hat{\mathbf{q}}_4 \tag{6}$$

The points $\hat{\mathbf{q}}_0$, $\hat{\mathbf{q}}_1$, $\mathbf{p}_0$, and $\mathbf{r}_0$ are coplanar since they lie on the tangent plane at $\hat{\mathbf{q}}_0$, see Fig. 2(a). Hence α_0 and β_0 are uniquely determined from (5) by the intersection point of the diagonals of the planar quadrilateral $\hat{\mathbf{q}}_0 \mathbf{r}_0 \hat{\mathbf{q}}_1 \mathbf{p}_0$. Note that the quadrilateral could be non-convex and in this case either $\beta_0 > 1$, or $\beta_0 < 0$. Analogously, α_1 and β_1 are uniquely determined by (6). Therefore system (4) has three equations and four unknowns $\mathbf{p}_1, \mathbf{r}_1, \mathbf{p}_2, \mathbf{r}_2$ as follows.

$$\left| \begin{aligned} &\alpha_0 \mathbf{p}_1 + (1-\alpha_0)\mathbf{r}_1 && = c_1 \\ &\alpha_1 \mathbf{p}_1 + (1-\alpha_1)\mathbf{r}_1 + \alpha_0 \mathbf{p}_2 + (1-\alpha_0)\mathbf{r}_2 && = c_2 \\ &\qquad\qquad\qquad\qquad \alpha_1 \mathbf{p}_2 + (1-\alpha_1)\mathbf{r}_2 && = c_3 \end{aligned} \right. , \tag{7}$$

where

$$\begin{aligned} c_1 &:= \beta_0\hat{\mathbf{q}}_1 + (1-\beta_0)\hat{\mathbf{q}}_2 - \tfrac{1}{3}(\alpha_1\mathbf{p}_0 + (1-\alpha_1)\mathbf{r}_0 - \beta_1\hat{\mathbf{q}}_0 - (1-\beta_1)\hat{\mathbf{q}}_1),\\ c_2 &:= \beta_0\hat{\mathbf{q}}_2 + (1-\beta_0)\hat{\mathbf{q}}_3 + \beta_1\hat{\mathbf{q}}_1 + (1-\beta_1)\hat{\mathbf{q}}_2, \\ c_3 &:= \beta_1\hat{\mathbf{q}}_2 + (1-\beta_1)\hat{\mathbf{q}}_3 - \tfrac{1}{3}(\alpha_0\mathbf{p}_3 + (1-\alpha_0)\mathbf{r}_3 - \beta_0\hat{\mathbf{q}}_3 - (1-\beta_0)\hat{\mathbf{q}}_4). \end{aligned} \tag{8}$$

We shall prove the following

Lemma 1. *System* (7) *always has a solution.*

Proof. If $\alpha_0 \neq \alpha_1$ then the rank of matrix M of system (7) is 3 and the system always has a solution. If $\alpha_0 = \alpha_1$ we have

$$0 = c_1 - c_2 + c_3 = \frac{1}{3}(\beta_1 - \beta_0)\sum_{i=0}^{4}(-1)^i\binom{4}{i}\hat{\mathbf{q}}_i. \tag{9}$$

Thus, rank(M) $= 2$ and the system is compatible if and only if the right-hand side of (9) is zero. This holds obviously for $\beta_0 = \beta_1$. If $\beta_0 \neq \beta_1$ we use (3) and obtain consecutively

$$\begin{aligned} \sum_{i=0}^{4}(-1)^i\binom{4}{i}\hat{\mathbf{q}}_i &= \sum_{i=1}^{4}(-1)^i\binom{4}{i}\frac{i}{4}\mathbf{q}_{i-1} + \sum_{i=0}^{3}(-1)^i\binom{4}{i}\frac{4-i}{4}\mathbf{q}_i \\ &= \sum_{i=1}^{4}(-1)^i\binom{3}{i-1}\mathbf{q}_{i-1} + \sum_{i=0}^{3}(-1)^i\binom{3}{i}\mathbf{q}_i \\ &= \sum_{i=0}^{3}(-1)^{i+1}\binom{3}{i}\mathbf{q}_i + \sum_{i=0}^{3}(-1)^i\binom{3}{i}\mathbf{q}_i = 0. \end{aligned}$$

□

3.2 The Vertex Enclosure Problem

Let $\mathbf{q}_0$ be an inner vertex in T with $\deg \mathbf{q}_0 = n$ where the *degree* is the number of the edges incident to $\mathbf{q}_0$. For $k = 1, \ldots, n$ let Q_k be the quartic Bézier patches with common vertex $\mathbf{q}_0$; $q^k(t) = \sum_{i=0}^{4}\hat{\mathbf{q}}_i^k B_i^4(t)$ be the degree elevated cubic curves of the MNN emanating from $\mathbf{q}_0$ with the corresponding α_i^k, β_i^k, $i = 0, 1$; and $\mathbf{t}_k$ be next to $\mathbf{q}_0$ inner control point of Q_k, see Fig. 1 for $n = 4$. We apply (5) to Q_k and obtain the following linear system for the unknowns $\mathbf{t}_k$,

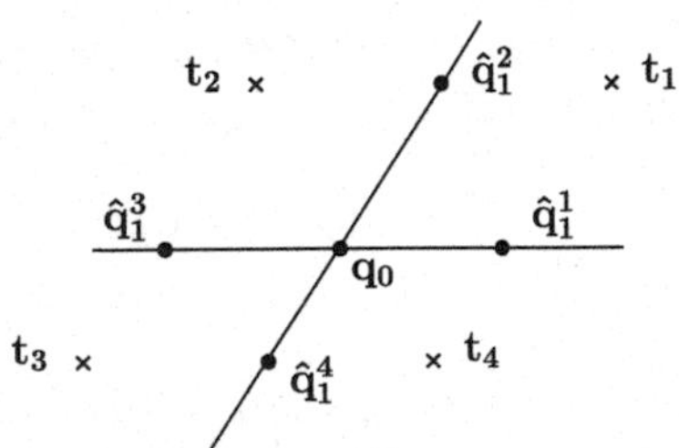

Fig. 1. The vertex enclosure problem: points $\mathbf{t}_i$, $i = 1, \ldots, 4$ must satisfy a linear system of equations

$$\begin{pmatrix} 1-\alpha_0^2 & \alpha_0^2 & \ldots & 0 & 0 \\ 0 & 1-\alpha_0^3 & \alpha_0^3 & \ldots & 0 \\ \vdots & & & & \\ 0 & 0 & \ldots & 1-\alpha_0^n & \alpha_0^n \\ \alpha_0^1 & 0 & \ldots & 0 & 1-\alpha_0^1 \end{pmatrix} \begin{pmatrix} \mathbf{t}_1 \\ \mathbf{t}_2 \\ \vdots \\ \mathbf{t}_{n-1} \\ \mathbf{t}_n \end{pmatrix} = \begin{pmatrix} \mathbf{s}_1 \\ \mathbf{s}_2 \\ \vdots \\ \mathbf{s}_{n-1} \\ \mathbf{s}_n, \end{pmatrix}, \tag{10}$$

where

$$\begin{aligned}
\mathrm{s}_i &= \beta_0^{i+1}\hat{\mathbf{q}}_1^{i+1} + (1-\beta_0^{i+1})\hat{\mathbf{q}}_2^{i+1} - \tfrac{1}{3}(\alpha_1^{i+1}\hat{\mathbf{q}}_1^{i+2} + (1-\alpha_1^{i+1})\hat{\mathbf{q}}_1^{i} \\
&\quad -\beta_1^{i+1}\hat{\mathbf{q}}_0 - (1-\beta_1^{i+1})\hat{\mathbf{q}}_1^{i+1}),\ i=1,\dots,n-2, \\
\mathrm{s}_{n-1} &= \beta_0^{n}\hat{\mathbf{q}}_1^{n} + (1-\beta_0^{n})\hat{\mathbf{q}}_2^{n} - \tfrac{1}{3}(\alpha_1^{n}\hat{\mathbf{q}}_1^{1} + (1-\alpha_1^{n})\hat{\mathbf{q}}_1^{n-1} - \beta_1^{n}\hat{\mathbf{q}}_0 - (1-\beta_1^{n})\hat{\mathbf{q}}_1^{n}), \\
\mathrm{s}_{n} &= \beta_0^{1}\hat{\mathbf{q}}_1^{1} + (1-\beta_0^{1})\hat{\mathbf{q}}_2^{1} - \tfrac{1}{3}(\alpha_1^{1}\hat{\mathbf{q}}_1^{2} + (1-\alpha_1^{1})\hat{\mathbf{q}}_1^{n} - \beta_1^{1}\hat{\mathbf{q}}_0 - (1-\beta_1^{1})\hat{\mathbf{q}}_1^{1}).
\end{aligned}$$

The determinant of (10) is

$$\mathrm{Det} = (-1)^{n+1}\alpha_0^1\alpha_0^2\dots\alpha_0^n + (1-\alpha_0^1)(1-\alpha_0^2)\dots(1-\alpha_0^n).$$

It can be verified that $\dfrac{(1-\alpha_0^1)(1-\alpha_0^2)\dots(1-\alpha_0^n)}{\alpha_0^1\alpha_0^2\dots\alpha_0^n} = 1$, and therefore, we have $\mathrm{Det} = \begin{cases} 2\alpha_0^1\alpha_0^2\dots\alpha_0^n, & n \text{ odd} \\ 0, & n \text{ even} \end{cases}$. The latter implies

Lemma 2. *The rank of the matrix of system (10) is* $\begin{cases} n, & n \textit{ odd}, \\ n-1, & n \textit{ even}. \end{cases}$

Therefore if n is odd then system (10) always has a solution, and if n is even then (10) could be incompatible and may not have a solution. The existence of a solution to system (10) is known as the *vertex enclosure problem*, see [10].

4 Construction of the Bézier Patches

In this section we show how to construct successfully G^1-continuous Bézier patches in the presence of even degree vertices. We apply procedure called *splitting* similar to the one proposed by Clough and Tocher, see [2,9]. Let T^1 denote the set of triangles in T that have an inner vertex of even degree. We *split* all triangles in T^1. Let $\tau \in T^1$. We partition τ into three new sub-triangles with a common vertex in τ, see Fig. 2(b). This new vertex with appropriate

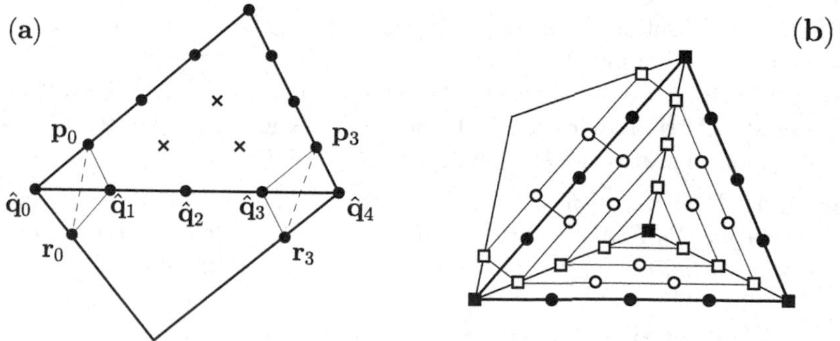

Fig. 2. Construction of the G^1-continuous Bézier patches: (a) without splitting; (b) splitting the patch into three sub-patches

z-value is added to the data. In [10] it is shown that splitting leads to admissible data. Further, computing the new vertex in τ is done through computation of control points into three sub-triangles obtaining in this way the three G^1-continuous Bézier sub-patches. Algorithm 1 below takes a triangle τ in T^1 and degree-elevated quartic boundary control points of the corresponding patch and computes the control points of the three G^1-continuous Bézier sub-patches.

Input: Degree elevated quartic boundary control points ■,● of a Bézier patch
Output: Control points of three G^1 – continuous interpolating sub-patches
Step 1. Find the first layer of inner control points that are next to the boundary:
1.1 Points □ are centers of the three triangles with vertices ●■●.
1.2 Then points ○ divide segments □□ into three equal parts.
Step 2. Find the second layer of inner control points:
2.1 Points □ are centers of the three small triangles with vertices ○□○ from the first layer.
2.2 Then points ○ are midpoints of segments □□.
Step 3. Find the third layer of inner control points: Three points □ are centers of the small triangles with vertices ○□○ from the second layer.
Step 4. Find the last inner control point ■ as the center of the triangle with vertices □ from the third layer.

Algorithm 1. Splitting - Fig. 2(b)

For a triangle in $T \setminus T^1$ (see Fig. 2(a)) we have $\alpha_0 = \alpha_1$ and $\beta_0 = \beta_1$ since the projections of the quadrilaterals $\hat{\mathbf{q}}_0\mathbf{r}_0\hat{\mathbf{q}}_1\mathbf{p}_0$ and $\hat{\mathbf{q}}_3\mathbf{r}_3\hat{\mathbf{q}}_4\mathbf{p}_3$ onto the plane Oxy are congruent. We compute the three inner control points marked by $\times$, from the corresponding three systems (10) for each of the triangle vertices. Two of the equations in systems (10) are the same as in system (7) for the G^1-continuity conditions. The third equation in (7) is

$$(\alpha_1 - \alpha_0)(\mathbf{r}_1 - \mathbf{p}_1 - \mathbf{r}_2 + \mathbf{p}_2) = \frac{1}{3}(\beta_1 - \beta_0)\sum_{i=0}^{4}(-1)^i\binom{4}{i}\hat{\mathbf{q}}_i.$$

It is automatically satisfied since $\alpha_0 = \alpha_1$ and the right-hand side is zero according to the proof of Lemma 1.

Using Algorithm 1 we construct G^1-continuous surface $F(u,v)$ defined on D which consists of triangular quartic Bézier patches and interpolates the MNN. The next theorem states the extremal properties of F.

Theorem 1. *$F(u,v)$ satisfies the tetra-harmonic equation $\Delta^4\mathbf{x} = 0$ for $(u,v) \in D \setminus E$. Consequently F is a solution to the extremal problem (1) and hence F is an extremum to the energy functional $\Phi(\mathbf{x}) = 1/2\int_D \|\Delta^4\mathbf{x}\|^2 dudv$.*

5 The Constrained Extremal Problem

Let the given data be strictly convex. In this case $\widehat{F}^*$ on every edge is either a convex cubic polynomial or a convex cubic spline with one knot, see [1]. If $\hat{f}_e^*$

is a polynomial we do not modify it. If $\hat{f}_e^*$ is a spline, we slightly modify it to obtain a convex cubic curve with the same tangents at the ends. Then, using the results from Sects. 2 and 3 we construct G^1-continuous surface $\widehat{F}$ defined on D which consists of triangular quartic Bézier patches, interpolates the modified edge convex MNN, and still satisfies Theorem 1. The main difficulty in this case is in the algorithm for splitting since the projections of the control points onto the corresponding edge are not equally spaced. The details will be presented in the full version.

Acknowledgments. This work was partially supported by the Bulgarian National Science Fund under Grant No. DFNI-T01/0001.

References

1. Andersson, L.-E., Elfving, T., Iliev, G., Vlachkova, K.: Interpolation of convex scattered data in $\mathbb{R}^3$ based upon an edge convex minimum norm network. J. Approx. Theory **80**(3), 299–320 (1995)
2. Farin, G.: A modified Clough-Tocher interpolant. Comput. Aided Geom. Des. **2**(4), 19–27 (1985)
3. Farin, G.: Curves and Surfaces for CAGD: A Practical Guide, 5th edn. Morgan-Kaufmann, San Francisco (2002)
4. Foley, T.A., Hagen, H.: Advances in scattered data interpolation. Surv. Math. Ind. **4**, 71–84 (1994)
5. Franke, R., Nielson, G.M.: Scattered data interpolation and applications: a tutorial and survey. In: Hagen, H., Roller, D. (eds.) Geometric Modeling, pp. 131–160. Springer, Berlin (1991)
6. Lodha, S.K., Franke, K.: Scattered data techniques for surfaces. In: Hagen, H., Nielson, G.M., Post, F. (eds.) Proceedings of Dagstuhl Conference on Scientific Visualization, pp. 182–222. IEEE Computer Society Press, Washington (1997)
7. Mann, S., Loop, C., Lounsbery, M., Meyers, D., Painter, J., DeRose, T., Sloan, K.: A survey of parametric scattered data fitting using triangular interpolants. In: Hagen, H. (ed.) Curve and Surface Design, pp. 145–172. SIAM, Philadelphia (1992)
8. Nielson, G.M.: A method for interpolating scattered data based upon a minimum norm network. Math. Comput. **40**(161), 253–271 (1983)
9. Percell, P.: On cubic and quartic Clough-Tocher finite elements. SIAM J. Numer. Anal. **13**(1), 100–103 (1976)
10. Peters, J.: Smooth interpolation of a mesh of curves. Constr. Approx. **7**(1), 221–246 (1991)
11. Vlachkova, K.: A Newton-type algorithm for solving an extremal constrained interpolation problem. Num. Linear Algebra Appl. **7**(3), 133–146 (2000)

Author Index

Printed in the United States
By Bookmasters